understanding new media

Augmented Knowledge & Culture

KIM H. VELTMAN

UNIVERSITY OF
CALGARY
PRESS

We acknowledge the financial support of the Government of
Canada through the Book Publishing Industry Development
Program (BPIDP). We acknowledge the support of the Canada
Council for the Arts and the Alberta Foundation for the Arts for
our publishing program.

  Canada Council
for the Arts   Conseil des Arts
du Canada

Library and Archives Canada Cataloguing in Publication:

Veltman, Kim H
    Understanding new media : augmented knowledge and culture
/ Kim H. Veltman.

Includes bibliographical references and index.
ISBN 1-55238-154-4

    1. Computers and civilization. 2. Digital communications
Social aspects.
I. Title.

P94.6.V44 2005   303.48'33   C2005-905624-X

Cover design by Mieka West.
Page design & typesetting by Elizabeth Gusnoski.

Printed and bound in Canada by Houghton Boston.

Consider for a moment ... how unevenly technology has impacted the various fields of knowledge in the twentieth century.... The sciences are utterly dependent on advanced technologies.... But what of the humanities? During this same time what has happened to them? ... The scholar of literature or history works exactly as his predecessors did a hundred years before.... Because no new technology assists them. No one has ever developed a new technology for the benefit of historians – until now.

– Michael Crichton, *Timeline*.[1]

To the Student Team at the McLuhan Program (1990–96), who taught me to see how the present can transform our past to help the future:

Raad Abdulateef, Hameed Amirzada, Brendan Balson, Allan Brolley, Sam Cauchi, Wen Yen Chan, **Jordan Christensen**, Paul Chvostek, Darren, Du Dang, Eric Dobbs, Olivier DuCourneau, David Faria, Hugh Finnigan, Sean Graham, Eitan Grinspun, Tony Hu, Ivan Huterer, **Rakesh Jethwa**, Jon, Michael Karczmarek, Rani Talut Kharbutli, Ming Lim, John MacDonald, **Andrew McCutcheon,** Eric Mang, Mark, Sascha Matzkin, Jeremy Meaghan-Cargill, Hasan Murtaza, Hormoz Nabili, Gijs Nijholt, Perseus Missirlis, Effi Ofer, Björn Ottenheim, Darwin Ouyang, William Patterson, Colin Peart, **David Pritchard**, Sanjeev, David Seale, **Jonathan Shekter**, Ronodev Shinha, Steve Singer, Daniel Skutelsky, Greg Stuart, Mark Swierszcz, Darius Tse, Avenindra Utukuri, Marc Verspaandonk, Daniel Woo, Jimmy Woo, and Jeff Zakrzewski.

000056859

contents

preface

In 1994, the Canadian futurist, Frank Ogden, published *The Last Book You Will Ever Read*. One is reminded about Mark Twain's remark: "Reports of my death are greatly exaggerated." Books will remain because they are extremely efficient ways of communicating organized knowledge and information on a given subject. At the same time, as McLuhan and others have made us very aware, books also have severe limitations. They are static and present knowledge in a linear way. To speak of the future of inter-networked communications and a shift from Information Communication Technologies (ICT) to Universal Convergence Technologies (UCT) only in book form would be both paradoxical and a lesson in frustration. For this reason, the book version is accompanied by a CD-ROM which explores four new versions:

1) *Electronic*: This is essentially the same as the printed book but more readily searchable.
2) *Hyper-Linked*: This highlights a number of key concepts as hyperlinks and links them with bibliographical references.
3) *Hyper-Illustrated*: This provides a far greater number of illustrations than would be economically feasible in a printed edition.
4) *Omni-Linked*: This provides a new approach whereby every word in the book is hyperlinked. Hence this may not be the last book you read but will be the first omni-linked book that you use.

In future there will also be a fifth version.

5) *Dynamically-Linked*: This will offer automatic updates to quickly changing statistics by linking directly with key Internet sites.

An Internet version and a CD ROM version are the work of Alexander and Vasily Churanov (Smolensk, Maastricht). The Internet version, which assumes an ADSL connection, is freely available online at http://www.sumscorp.com/new_media. htm. For those with slower connections, this site also contains information about the CD-ROM, which is available at a reduced price for those who have purchased the book.

We are very conscious that this is an initial experiment rather than a final product. In this initial version the printed book is organized traditionally such that it can be read in isolation as a stand-alone product. In future, we foresee that the content of the printed book will decrease. It will have less details and statistics. It will focus on basic concepts and claims. Examples in the form of current projects, illustrations in terms of recent results and the latest research will be relegated to electronic versions. Like Robert Darnton (Princeton), we believe that the electronic book will act as a supplement to and not as a substitute for the printed book. Technologically, our notion of augmented books means that printed books may in future a) be read in tandem with e-books and b) be with portable, mobile devices acting as links to virtual memory institutions. Ideally such links will be in the context of a Distributed European Electronic Resource (DEER) that combines virtual reference rooms, virtual repositories, and virtual agoras (figure 14).

Philosophically, our approach has parallels with, but is not identical to, Darnton's vision of electronic books with pyramidal layers.[2] Darnton sees the layers of electronic versions primarily in terms of access to different approaches (theoretical, pedagogical, critical). We see the electronic versions as access methods to different layers of knowledge (figure 16), such that the contribution of an individual book will become linked with personal knowledge, collaborative knowledge and with the cumulative, enduring knowledge of memory institutions. In our view, creating links between and across kinds of knowledge and ways of knowing is the challenge of future scholarship.

introduction

The Internet is growing quickly. An estimated 1.4 billion gigabytes of information were produced in 1999.[1] In July 2000, Cyveillance claimed that 7 million new pages are added each day and that the Internet had surpassed 2.1 billion pages.[2] Companies such as Intelliseek and BrightPlanet say this is only the surface web and speak of a deep web with more than 550 billion online documents,[3] which includes all the databases and intranet materials not available through simple web pages. In 2000, it was claimed that only about 1 billion of these pages had been catalogued by standard search engines. By January 2004, Google had indexed over 2 billion pages. That number doubled in February 2004 and, as of 1 April 2004, there were 4,285,199,774 indexed pages. By November 2004, this number had increased to 8,058,044,651 pages. In 2000 there were no indexed images.[4] In April 2004 there were 880,000,000 indexed images.

The number of users is growing quickly.[5] When the Internet began (1968 in Britain, 1969 in the United States), it was an experimental method linking a few scientists. By 1989 there were 100,000 hosts. In 1990, Tim Berners-Lee and Robert Cailliau (CERN) introduced the hypertext transfer protocol (http) that began the World Wide Web (WWW). By 1992, the number of hosts had increased to 1 million. The advent of browsers, beginning with Mosaic in 1993 (then Netscape), transformed the Internet from a platform for geeks to a new tool for the world. In 1995 there were approximately 5 million users. In the autumn of 1995 Microsoft Explorer came out.[6] By 1996 there were 50 million users. By 2000, there were 211 million. The so-called dot.com bust did not change this trend. By December 2004, there were 812 million users.[7] By the end of December 2005, there were 1,018,057,389 users, according to World Internet Usage Statistics. Estimates claim that the (fixed line) Internet will rise to 1,460 million by 2007.[8] In Denmark there are predictions that by 2008, 100 per cent of the population will have personal computers and cell phones.[9]

The languages of the Internet are also changing quickly.[10] In 1995, most users were in the United States and the Internet was over 90 per cent English. By June 2000,[11] English had dropped to 51 per cent[12] and was now one of thirty-two major languages on the Internet.[13] In 2004 English accounted for 35.8 per cent, Chinese was the second language of the Internet at 14.1 per cent and Asian language sites outnumbered those of North America.[14] Some predict that Chinese will be the primary language of the Internet within three to five years.

In 2000, there were 300 million cellular phones worldwide. In 2002 the number of mobile phones exceeded the number of fixed phones.[15] In April 2004, there were 1.32 billion global mobile users.[16] In November 2004, there were 1.52 billion global mobile users with 300 million in China alone. Cellular phones are becoming Internet enabled and will soon outnumber Internet connections by computer.[17] This is introducing new forms of communication. In 2002, users sent 366 billion short texts as Short Message Services (SMS). It also means that if we add the regular Internet and mobile Internet users together there were already well over one billion Internet users in 2004 and that this number is likely to increase to about 2.5 billion by 2007.

While it is still the case today that over three billion persons on our planet have never yet made a telephone call, or seen a television, enormous, recent advances in technology mean that the Internet Society's slogan of Internet for everyone can literally become a reality in the next generations.[18]

While the United States is already planning an interplanetary Internet linking Earth with Mars and other planets by 2008,[19] the full consequences of the Internet for Planet Earth are relatively unexplored. To be sure, many speak of the computer revolution as if it were something that had already happened, as if it began with Vannevar Bush's article (1945),[20] with the founding of the ARPANET (1969), or with the establishment of the World Wide Web (1989). Meanwhile, others speak of the computer revolution as if it were something which is nearing completion,[21] as if it consisted mainly in the use of personal computers and resulted primarily in the production of Word files, Power Point presentations, and CD-ROMs. As always there are some who claim that the Internet is mainly hype or even unimportant.[22]

Our approach differs from the above in three ways. First, we believe that the revolution underway today needs to be seen as part of a larger control revolution, which has been underway for well over a century. Here we follow the important work of scholars such as James Beniger and Armand Mattelart. Second, the revolution now underway has scarcely begun. The mass media may speak of Internet speed as days, months or years, but the full changes will take at least a century to reveal deeper implications of the so-called revolution. Third, the revolution in new media, which most persons assume is only about computers and the Internet, is not really about computers as such: it is about a reorganization of all knowledge. Mattelart has explored some aspects of this problem showing that the rise of universal communication systems is linked with the rise of universal claims to knowledge.[23] We go further to suggest that the systemic approach of computing is permeating every dimension of society.

We begin by examining the technology itself. An opening chapter traces developments in size and speed; examines basic changes in the functions of computers from devices to calculate and write, their expansion to include multi-media and inter-media, becoming methods to interact with, to augment and delegate knowledge. As a result, computers are increasingly multi-purpose, multi-functional devices, serving as a telephone, fax machine, camera, video conferencing unit, and as personal digital assistants. Some predict that they will soon become instruments for synthetic reason, intelligent machines, even spiritual machines.

A second chapter examines some consequences of wireless communication: mobility through cellular phones, which will permit us to operate devices from anywhere at anytime. A third chapter explores developments in miniaturization. In the past decades, computers have kept shrinking from a desktop, to a portable, a laptop, and more recently to handheld devices. Wearable computing is becoming a reality. At present, there are initiatives on at least four fronts to reduce the size of computers to the nano-level of billionths of a metre.

Within the next two decades the computer will become invisible. Herein lies a first paradox. Computers are about making things visible. They help us to visualize processes, concepts and many things, which we cannot see. Yet, as they develop, computers are becoming part of the furniture, disappearing into the woodwork. When the technology is mature, our chief means of rendering things visible will be invisible.

The next three chapters consider the material implications of computers; exploring how these innovations are re-structuring the physical world. As computers disappear into their environments, they are changing 1) the means and meanings of production, 2) the roles of transactions and services, and 3) the institutions where they are housed. This includes obvious consequences of computers for e-business and e-commerce. Again there is a paradox: the implications of computers for the material world entail a new emphasis on virtuality. This entails much more than a simple substitution of the real by the virtual. It involves many new interplays between real and virtual.

Chapters seven to nine explore the organizational implications of networked computers, which have little to do with the physical machines and entail instead their underlying, logical principles. These principles, which have become closely linked with systems theory, are having profound effects on our theories of organization and knowledge management, focussing our attention so much on process, that we are in danger of losing sight of the importance of content. Chapter nine explores possible implications thereof for learning. These represent unexpected side effects of the new media which, as Marshall McLuhan has taught us, are often as important as the media themselves, all the more so because they are often unnoticed.

Chapters ten to twelve examine the intellectual implications of computers for networked content; showing how they are changing our approaches to knowledge itself, in terms of personal, collaborative, and enduring knowledge. The final three chapters of the book explore some of the immaterial, philosophical, and spiritual implications of networked computers. Although the book as a whole focusses on what is possible and particularly on the positive potentials of networked computing, chapter thirteen examines some of the challenges and dangers involved. These include a need for interoperability of content; the dangers of privatization of knowledge; dangers which are linked with re-definitions of real versus virtual; truth versus viewpoints; inner versus outer; public versus private, and the need for a new public good.

Chapter fourteen turns to the challenge of synthesis. To claim that the Internet is solely about e-commerce is to limit attention only to a material dimension. The rise of the open source movement; the emergence of virtual communities are but two expressions of spiritual dimensions in the context of computers. In the long term, intellectual and spiritual implications are more important than technological, material, and organizational consequences. Only an integration of all these dimensions will unleash the full potentials of networked computers. The concluding chapter claims that networked computers challenge us to re-define all our fundamental concepts, what it means to know, even what it is to be human.

One of the underlying themes of this book is that there are a number of competing goals and visions for these new media. Potentially, these goals and visions are as myriad as the number of users. In fact, while goals and visions are abundant, ability to make them happen requires great political power, incredible economic investments and/or profound spiritual visions, which can unite the efforts of hundreds of millions and potentially billions of individual users.

On the political front we discern three main goals. One focusses primarily on profit, a second includes human dimensions, and a third seeks a more systematic integration of persons and technology. We shall suggest how these very different goals lead to three quite different visions. One seeks an information highway (United States). A second seeks an information society (Europe). A third aims at a knowledge society (Japan). On a strictly economic front is a fourth goal, which seeks to develop profit on a global basis. Authors such as David Korten have described some of these dangers.[24] Finally, there is an emerging international vision that recognizes the importance of working together and sharing in order to achieve something better.

These visions affect the whole of society. They affect the production and distribution of goods, interactions of persons in the organizational worlds of business and government, education and training, and ultimately ideals of knowledge and truth. These visions are competing, yet need not exclude each other. Indeed this book combines aspects of all four visions in order to arrive at a new synthesis. We need somehow a combination of the American profit motive, the European historical and multicultural social motive, and the Japanese quest for a new kind of knowledge, which combines ancient samurai concepts such as *kaizen* with the latest technological advances.

Any attempt to sketch major trends risks becoming of caricature.[25] The United States is a collection of over 290 million individuals. Its history of civil war reminds us that a single vision has never completely dominated the country. Today, the

United States is certainly many things. The same country, which has developed Echelon, the international spy initiative, which is watching all of us, has also seen the development of the Electronic Frontier Foundation. The country of proprietary software and hardware solutions has developed the European open source idea into a movement.

The same country that sometimes acts as if computers and the Internet were mainly a U.S. phenomenon has permitted the development of the Internet Society as a global organization. The same country that sometimes acts as if it can ignore standards (because it assumes that its own practice will define that of the world) has played a role in the development of global standards through bodies such as the International Standards Organization (ISO) and the International Tele-communications Union (ITU). And at the same time the United States has made Silicon Valley into a world symbol for new electronic media.

The same is true in Europe and Japan. The European Union, which is one of the leaders of world science through organizations such as CERN (Organisation Européenne de Recherche Nucléaire), is also a combination of many cottage industries and age-old traditions. Within Europe there are significant differences between countries such as Britain, France, Germany, Italy, etc. The same Japan, that leads the world in some combinations of knowledge theory, robots, and aspects of computers (e.g., display screens) also has very complex traditional strands.

To reflect all these complexities at every turn would lead far beyond the confines of a book. Characteristics such as the profit motive, particularly evident in America, are also evident in Europe, Japan, and around the world. Hence, our characterizations of the United States, Europe, and Japan will function as three personae in a complex play, knowing that they represent aspects of their peoples without pretending to be them.

By the same token, we are very aware that there are many other visions. Canada is not the same as the United States. In Asia, there are other significant voices such as China, India, Malaysia and Korea. One must not forget the role of Africa and South America and other countries such as Australia. While their importance is duly acknowledged, to survey all possible currents and developments throughout the world is beyond the scope of this book.

Essentially we see five major consequences of networked computers. A first is technological; they lead to invisibility. A second is material; they lead to virtuality. A third consequence is organizational; they lead to systemicity. A fourth is intellectual; they can lead to a new contextuality. Finally, at a philosophical level we suggest that they could lead to a new spirituality. Each of the four visions has its own take on these issues. Can their seeming contradictions be united into a larger vision? This book offers a possible answer, or at least the outlines of a new approach. It also points to emerging areas for new research.

The title is a conscious homage to the late Marshall McLuhan's *Understanding Media* (1964, reprint, 1994).[26] Since then there have been a series of books on *Understanding*

New Media: Compaine (1984)[27] emphasized electronic distribution of information; Whitehouse (1986)[28] focussed on mass media; Fidler (1997)[29] examined their effects on journalism; Monaco (1999)[30] offered a dictionary; Grusin and Bolter (2000)[31] have emphasized remediation. Where McLuhan focussed on books, radio, and television as extensions of man, we explore new media as extensions of the human spirit, how they can augment our knowledge, culture, and spiritual horizons.

The field of new media poses particular problems. Abbreviations, jargon, and statistics are annoying but unavoidable. Therefore they are used as sparingly as possible. Those interested in new media want to get to the point without distractions. They find footnotes and references irritating. Therefore, the text is written such that it can be read independently and there are footnotes for those who wish to pursue some of the myriad strands in this complex field. Books for further reading are listed separately by themes (Appendix 8).

Revolutions have curious spinoffs. There are the actual developments and then their meanings: interpretations, considerations of consequences, implications, musings, moral, ethical, philosophical, and religious. Inevitably these go in two opposite and often opposing directions. On the one hand, some inevitably see such developments as a starting point for their own utopias. Meanwhile, others inevitably see the same developments as the beginning of new dystopias, scenarios of doom and gloom, prologues for the end of days.

We tend to the former of these two extremes. We try to give a lay of the land, to introduce a whole range of emerging fields including mechatronics, holonics, molectronics, biocommunication, neuromorphic engineering, and bio-mimetics. We try to see the possible good in what is evolving. We try also to point to genuine challenges, hurdles, and problems along the way. We try not to moralize on everything that could go wrong with the Internet, with global corporations, nano-technology, bio-technology, the human genome, or electronic warfare.

Aside from the inherent dangers of trying to predict the future,[32] the reasons for our optimistic approach are simple. First and foremost, those who see the dangers of computing are producing shelves of books on these themes. The problems they discuss are very real and very important, and we shall cite them, especially in the appendix for further reading.

At a deeper level, almost everyone is afraid of computers in some way. I remember a very distinguished lady in Los Angeles in the 1980s who went to computer courses and spent an entire lesson learning not to be afraid to turn the machine on and off. Many of us are afraid that computers will not function, that the work we do on them could be lost, that they could corrupt our children and ourselves and so on. We fear what we could do with them and what they could do to us. We fear what we might find with them and what we might not find with them.

It often takes children to remind us that there is nothing to be afraid of at all. Children turn computers on and off the way older persons flick a light switch. This was the case with me. My uncle had worked on computers in a bank in Rotterdam in the 1930s. I dreamed about them in 1961 and started writing on the subject in the late 1970s. Even so it was teenagers and students in the early 1990s who helped me experience how computers can be a source of hope rather than fear. In a spiritual sense this book is a testament to what they taught me: a story of new hope, a story of how computers can lead to dynamic and augmented knowledge and culture and can lead ultimately to the theological virtues.

acknowledgments

This book was initially to be a paper for INET 2000. I began writing, soon found that I had written ninety-two pages, and felt as if I were scarcely past the introduction. Theoretically that was far too long for a paper, but the committee generously accepted it anyway as the longest contribution to INET in the first year of the new millennium. So my first thanks go that committee, which included Steve Cisler, Jean-Claude Guedon, David Lassner, and George Sadowsky. I thank them especially because they encouraged me to develop what at the time was still rather half-baked, which, as my mentor Kenneth Keele always pointed out, is the first step to being fully cooked.

A series of lectures in the academic year 1999–2000 further helped this process. A keynote on *Virtuality in Europe* helped to draft what became chapters six to nine. A paper in the cultural track of WWW9 helped formulate ideas, which form the basis of chapters 12 and 14. I am grateful to Professor Butterfield of the Academia Europeae, and Professor Alfredo Ronchi of the MEDICI Framework, respectively, for these incentives. Invitations by the European Commission to speak on Internet governance issues at Autrans, Brussels, and Namur helped clarify ideas, which have been developed in chapters 13 to 15. In this context, I am grateful for the encouragement of Richard Delmas and Christopher Wilkinson.

A pretext for taking the time to write a full-scale book was provided by the short-lived International Institute on Infonomics (III, Heerlen) with which the Maastricht McLuhan Institute (MMI) was closely linked. I am grateful to Professor Luc Soete, the director of III and my own directors, Ir. Anneke Eurelings, and Hans Koolmees, for their continual encouragement.

The physical book was written in a year. The metaphysical ideas behind this book go back almost forty years.[1] First, thanks go to my parents and my relatives, especially Gerrit and Gina Adema, Mother Superior, Sister Ancilla Veltman, and Sister Dr. Maria Laeta Veltman. Second, thanks go to my teachers notably: at York University (Professors Brayton Polka, Theodore Allan Heinrich, and Dean Sidney Eisen), at the University of Toronto (Professor Stillman Drake, Father Leonard Boyle, Professor Natalie Zemon Davis), at the Warburg Institute (Professors A.I. Sabra, Sir Ernst Gombrich, Charles Schmitt, B.A.R. Carter), at Oxford (Dr. Alistair Crombie).

---

1 †Indicates friends and colleagues who are now deceased.

Third, thanks go to the individuals who supported my post-doctoral research, namely, at the Wellcome Institute (Dr. Kenneth Keele and Dr. Noel Poynter); at the Herzog August Bibliothek (Dr. Sabine Solf, Professor Paul Raabe, Professor Walter Killy, Professors Wolfgang Paul, Dr. Heinrich Pfeiffer, Dr. Thomas Berberich); and at the Getty Institute (Professors Kurt Forster, Françoise Forster Hahn, Dr. Herb Hymans).

The ideas have grown out of many years of discussions with a circle of friends, including Dr. Rolf Gerling, Ing. Udo Jauernig, Father John Orme Mills, O.P., Professor André Corboz, Eric Dobbs, Rakesh Jethwa, Professor Sergio Sismondo, and more recently, Dr Eric McLuhan and Hans Koolmees. Jaap van Till stimulated new ideas, which helped to crystallize chapter 11. I am grateful to Eddy Odijk (Philips) and John Gage (Sun) for discussions of new technologies. For specific news items re: technological developments I am grateful to Dr. Anne Tyrie (and, since June 2002, Tony Florio), editor of the CITO-Link Line; to Jeffrey Harrow, editor of The Rapidly Changing Face of Computing, and Michel Bauwens (Belgacom) editor of Digital Revolution Alert.

Over the past decades, friends like Professor André Corboz have sent thousands of clippings. He has been matched only by my colleagues a) Drs. Johan van de Walle, who has constantly sent e-mail references, suggested books, and insights, and b) my doctoral student, Nik Baerten, who made constructive suggestions and helped with some illustrations. I am deeply grateful to each of them. Mr. Jo Beerens has kindly helped with scanning in materials.

A number of persons have generously read the text in various stages of unfinishedness and offered many useful comments and suggestions: my colleagues at MMI: Nik Baerten, John Beckers, Dr. Geert de Haan, Dr. Charles van den Heuvel, and Johan van de Walle; Professor Jun Murai (Keio University); Dr. Kamiuchi (Hitachi) and Dr. Eddy Odijk (Philips); Eelco Bruinsma (Cheperu); Dr. Jonathan Collins (Milton Keynes); Professor M. P. Satija (India). I am deeply grateful also to Dr. Ingetraut Dahlberg (Bad König), who has long been a source of inspiration.

Hundreds of persons all over the world, friends, colleagues, and acquaintances, have generously provided me with information through e-mails, letters, notes, telephone calls, and chats at conferences. A small sample of these include: Madhu Acharya (Kathmandu), Jan Amkreutz (Montana), Professor Fréderic Andres (Tokyo), Professors Eugenio†,[1] Giuseppina and Francesco Battisti, Professor Benedetto Benedetti (Pisa), Heiner Benking (Berlin), Graham Bibby (now Paris), Rector Jacques Berleur (Namur), (former Dean) Professor Wiebe Bijker (Maastricht), Professoressa Francesca Bocchi, Father Leonard Boyle† (Prefect, Vatican Library), Dr. Nadezhda and Misha Brakker (Moscow), Professor Gerhard Budin (Vienna), Vint Cerf (ISOC), Rector Arturo Colorado y Castellary (Segovia), Dr. Gisela Comes (Wolfenbüttel), Bruce Damer and Galen Brandt (San Francisco), Professoressa Marisa and Ing. Antonio Dalai-Emiliani (Rome), Roland and Audrey Davies (Farnham), Professor Derrick de Kerckhove (Toronto), Dr. François Deneuil (Paris), (former President of

Universiteit Maastricht) Karl Dittrich, Douglas Engelbart (Fremont), David Fabish (Ottawa), Dr. Andreas Göppelt (Ulm), Professor Bruno Helly (Lyon), Dr. James Hemsley (EVA, VASARI), Gerry Jayasuriya† (IIC, London), Dr. Anthony Judge (Brussels), Dr. Matthias Kasemann (DESY), Andrey Kotov (Smolensk); Professor Chris Llewellyn Smith (Director, CERN), Linda Kempster (Sarasota), Dr. Riemer Knoop (Amsterdam), Traugott Koch (Lund), Martin Lee (Didcot), Dr. André and Laura Loechel (Paris), Dr. Andre Meyer (Philips, now TNO), Dr. R. Niall D. Martin (Edinburgh), Dr. Paul Miller (UKOLN), Gilles Mousseau (Hummingbird), Mag. Franz Nahrada (Vienna), Dr. Ted Nelson (Oxford), Dr. Ronald Ng (Singapore), Peter Peiker (Bad Homburg), Jon Postel† (ISOC), Professor Jacques Poulain (Paris), Dr. Alan Radley (Kreospheres), Rafael Raddi (San Paolo), Jonathan Robin (Paris), Professor Alfredo Ronchi (Milan), Professor Massimo Scolari (Venice), Dr. Tengku Azzman Mohammed Sharifadeen (Kuala Lumpur), Alexander Siegel (Bonn), Dean Paul Tummers, Patricia Young (CHIN, Ottawa), Dr. David Williams (CERN), Professor Nancy Williamson (Toronto), Dr. Christof Wolters (Berlin), Dr. Chris Zielinsky (Geneva).

In Canada, there is a team of supporters. They include: Bob Baser (Industry Canada), the Hon. Jon Gerrard (then Secretary of State for Science and Technology), Dr. Richard Gerrard (Toronto Historical Board), Professor Ian Hacking, Peter Homulos (founder of CHIN), Michael Kupka (Toronto), Eric Livermore (Nortel), Rachel McAfee (Pixel), Stuart McLeod (Bell), Gary McGregor (Greenfield), Ian McCallum, Keith Medley (Toronto), Larry Moore (OLA), and Harry Rogers (PRECARN).

At the G7 level with respect to Multimedia Access to World Cultural Heritage (Pilot project 4), I thank Ministro Anna Blefari Schneider and Lucia Fiori (Rome) and colleagues in both the Canadian Department of Heritage and Industry Canada. At the European Commission, I am grateful for the help and encouragement of Peter Johnson, and particularly Mario Verdese, with whom I worked closely on the Memorandum of Understanding for Multimedia Access to European Cultural Heritage and the MEDICI Framework.

In addition to those who have helped in a technical sense, a number of friends have given their moral support to the vision underlying this book: William Balasingam, Elizabeth Flavelle and David Windeyer, Phyllis Glasson, General Sir Ian Gourlay, Professor Barbara Keyser†, Ian Stuart, Professor Deirdre Vincent, and Marianne Winder†. There are my close friends Dr. Jonathan Collins, John Gordon, Ing. Udo Jauernig, and Mary Lynn Hanley.

Technically, the project began at the Getty Center for the History of Art and Humanities (Santa Monica) with the help of Dr. Richard Dolen, and input by Coley Grundmann (1986–87), and was continued by Alan Brolley (1987–89) and Paul Chvostek (1989–90). For the next six years, as acknowledged in the dedication, a remarkable team of mainly high school students had a profound impact on the vision. The key figures were initially Jonathan Shekter, and subsequently Andrew

McCutcheon, David Pritchard, Jordan Christensen and Rakesh Jethwa. The latter became the only students in the world to represent their country, Canada, at the G7 Ministerial Conference and Exhibition (Brussels, February 1995), the World Summit (Halifax, June 1995) and the G7 Information Society and Developing Countries (ISAD) Conference and Exhibition (Midrand, May 1996). From 1996-2000, the Toronto team has been led by John McDonald and Greg Stuart. These were the vanguard of a much larger team, whose members are duly acknowledged on the Institute's web site. I am grateful also to the members of the SUMS advisory board: John Bell, Elizabeth Lambden, John MacDonald, Larry Moore, and John Volpe.

The book was to have been published in Germany but the translator died unexpectedly at thirty-four and that project was abandoned. In September, 2003, at the Digital Resources in the Humanities Conference (Cheltenham), Dr. Frits Pannekoek (Calgary) suggested that the University of Calgary Press might be interested. I am very grateful to him and to Walter Hildebrandt, Director of University of Calgary Press, and his staff for their patience in making the manuscript into a published book. Particular thanks go to John King who spent many hundreds of hours patiently transforming a Word document into a real book. I thank Alexander Zakharevich for producing the figures. I am very grateful to the twins, Vasily and Alexander Churanov (Smolensk) who produced the internet and CD-ROM versions.

Finally, there are very special thanks to nine special ladies who have encouraged me over the decades: Professoressa Giuseppina Battisti (Rome), Lady Vera Dawe† (London), Lady Margaret Delacourt Smith (London), Professoressa Anna Dell'Agata (Rome and Pineto), Frau Christel Gerhard (Wolfenbüttel), Corinne McLuhan (Toronto), Dr. Sabine Solf (Wolfenbüttel), Shelley Vaughan Wiliams (London), Dr. Maria-Luise Zarnitz (Hannover, now Tübingen). Especially these gave me hope when it seemed rather scarce. They were my personal muses.

PART I

technological
consequences:
INVISIBILITY

1

computers

> The average ... worker with a $799
> Pentium-chip laptop computer has more
> computing power at his fingertips than
> was contained in all the computers in
> the entire world during World War II.
> One hundred years ago, all of the greatest
> mathematicians in the world together did
> not have the problem-solving resources of
> today's fourth grader with a $19.95 Texas
> Instruments pocket calculator.
> — Cato Institute, *Policy Analysis*,
> December, 1999

1. Introduction

In North America and Europe computers are almost every-where. There are some books on their history[1] and many books on their use and implications.[2] There are also so many hyped claims and so many acronyms concerning computers that it is useful to begin with some basic facts about size, capacity, processing speed, and transmission speed. We shall then examine briefly how the function of computers has changed radically over the past century and particu-larly during the past decades, before considering debates re: centralized and personal computers and the paradox that a computer is not a machine.

TABLE 1A Basic terms and measures of the metric system[17]

$$
\begin{array}{rcl}
1 \text{ Kilometre} & = & 10^{3} \\
1 \text{ Hectometre} & = & 10^{2} \\
1 \text{ Metre} & = & 10^{1} \\
1 \text{ Centimetre} & = & 10^{-2} \\
1 \text{ Millimetre} & = & 10^{-3} \\
1 \text{ Micrometre or micron} & = & 10^{-6} \\
1 \text{ Nanometre} & = & 10^{-9} \\
1 \text{ Ångström} & = & 10^{-10} \\
1 \text{ Picometre} & = & 10^{-12} \\
1 \text{ Femtometre} & = & 10^{-15} \\
1 \text{ Zeptometre} & = & 10^{-21} \\
1 \text{ Yoctometre} & = & 10^{-24}
\end{array}
$$

TABLE 1B Basic terms of Internet sizes: bytes and their multiples[18]

$$
\begin{array}{rcl}
\text{Yotta-byte} & = & 10^{24} \\
\text{Zetta-byte} & = & 10^{21} \\
\text{Exa-byte} & = & 10^{18} \\
\text{Peta-byte} & = & 10^{15} \\
\text{Tera-byte} & = & 10^{12} \\
\text{Giga-byte} & = & 10^{9} \\
\text{Mega-byte} & = & 10^{6} \\
\text{Kilo-byte} & = & 10^{3} \\
\text{Hecto-byte} & = & 10^{2} \\
\text{Deka-byte} & = & 10^{1} \\
\text{Byte} & = & 1
\end{array}
$$

2. Size

The old phrase about all shapes and sizes applies to computers. A nineteenth-century computer from Manchester, now in the Science Museum (London), covers the space of a living room. The English Colossus computer (early 1940s) and the ENIAC[3] computer (1945) were hundreds of cubic metres and required a very large room. The world's largest computer in 1999 and the latest IBM supercomputers are still hundreds of cubic metres in size. A Cray computer with a storage capacity of multiple terabytes is normally about ten cubic metres. An SGI[4] machine capable of high-level graphics is typically a little smaller than a cubic metre.

Personal computers are usually much smaller than a cubic metre. Handheld computers are often as small as twenty centimetres. As will be shown, there are at least four thrusts underway to produce computational devices only a few microns in size to produce exabytes of data (Table 1a, b). Within thirty years most computers will be invisible.

TABLE 1C New technologies and their storage capacity per cubic inch;[19]

DIGITAL AMOUNT	STORAGE TECHNOLOGY
375 megabytes	Magnetic hard disk
100 megabytes	Holograms 1992
100 gigabytes	Holographic 2007
50 terabytes	10 micron ion etching
190 terabytes	3 micron ion etching

TABLE 1D Comparisons between computer storage, CD-ROMs, miles of paper, and trees.

DIGITAL AMOUNT	CD-ROMS	PAPER: MILES HIGH	TREES
1 Megabyte	0.0016		0.0423
1 Gigabyte	1.6		42.3
32 Gigabytes	41	1	1,354
1 Terabyte	1,600	31	42,500
1 Petabyte	1,600,000	31,600	42,500,000
1 Exabyte	1,600,000,000	31,600,000	42,500,000,000
12 Exabytes	19, 200,000,000	392,000,000	524,000,000,000

3. Capacity

The capacity of computers is also growing. In 1984, a home computer typically had ten megabytes of storage space. In 2005, a home computer often has hundreds of gigabytes[5] of storage space.[6] The areal density of data storage on disks continues to grow at a pace of 50 to 60 per cent a year.[7]

Linda Kempster, an expert in high-level storage makes these developments come alive simply by adding some more familiar terms of reference. A gigabyte (1,000 megabytes) is about 1.6 CD-ROMs.[8] Hence a terabyte is equal to 1,600 CD-ROMs; a petabyte is equal to 1,600,000 CD-ROMs, and an exabyte is equal to 1,600,000,000 CD-ROMs. She also gives the corresponding amounts in miles of paper (Table 1d). Another useful measure she gives is in terms of filing cabinets. One filing cabinet is roughly the equivalent of 499 megabytes. Hence a petabyte is roughly equal to 50 million filing cabinets or 11,666 football fields of file cabinets. Her estimate of the data that was scanned by 1996 was 900 petabytes, which amounts to the equivalent of 28,569,600 million football fields of file cabinets. In 2000, that number rose to 12,000 petabytes (12 exabytes) or the equivalent of 571,392,000 million football fields of file cabinets.[9] The future is said to lie in 3D Volume Atomic Holographic Optical Data Storage.[10] We are told that a ten terabyte removable disk will someday cost $45.[11]

Such enormous amounts might seem excessive until we realize that full motion video generates 555 megabytes per minute in uncompressed form.[12] Higher-quality motion video in uncompressed form requires one gigabyte per minute, and the eighty-three minutes of the film Snow White digitized in full colour amount to fifteen terabytes of space. At a professional level it is sobering to realize that in 2000, Judith Storck at the Library of Congress did forty terabytes of backup daily. A considerable part of the Library of Congress's database consists merely of titles of books rather than their full contents. Exceptions are special projects such as the American Memory initiative. In 2002 the Library of Congress began scanning a sixth copy of the Gutenberg Bible at 767 megabytes per page.[13] This amounts to ½ terabyte for a single book.

In future, as the full contents of libraries, museums, and archives become available, the capacities required will expand dramatically.[14] A new technology in Japan, called VZoom, is being used with scenes scanned in at three gigabytes for a single image. By 2003 new technologies made such images accessible by Internet. At the Centre de Recherche et Restauration des Musées de France (C2RMF), linked with the Louvre, paintings are being scanned in at thirty gigabytes per painting. If all the 120,000 images in the Louvre were scanned in at this resolution, this would amount to thirty-six petabytes. At present the C2RMF collection is a modest 5+ terabytes.

In science, the quantities involved are even larger. At the Institute for the Fundamental Study of Matter (FOM, Amsterdam), regular experiments often generate six hundred megabytes of data on a regular day. The Astronomical Observatory at Concepcion, Chile, produces 224 gigabytes of data each day. At CERN (the Organisation Européenne de Recherche Nucléaire), high-level experiments can generate a petabyte of information per minute. Their new Large Hadron Collider (LHC) will entail 1 billion collisions of protons per second. One megabyte is required to record each collision, which means that 1 petabyte of storage space per second is required, although ultimately only a hundred of these collisions per second may prove of lasting interest. Using traditional methods this would require 1.6 million CD-ROMs annually, amounting to a pile that is three kilometres high.[15] CERN estimates that its storage needs will increase from 40 to 740 petabytes from 2004 to 2007.[16] In medicine the latest high-level medical scans range from 4.5 terabytes to 4.5 petabytes.

4. Processing Speed

Personal computers in the early 1980s had a processing speed of 30 then 60 megahertz. That speed gradually increased to reach 1,000 megahertz or 1 gigahertz in the year 2000. With the advent of Extreme Ultra Violet (EUV) chip technology this is predicted to increase to 10 gigahertz by 2006.[20] Throughout the 1990s the performance of mini-supercomputers such as the SGI (Silicon Graphics Incorporated) "Infinity Engine" were typically in terms of Millions of Instructions Per Second

(MIPs). There are predictions that we shall have Trillions of Instructions per Second (TIPS) on ordinary desktops by the end of this decade.[21] The average Pentium III desktop system today has more computational power than the combined power of all of the computers that existed in 1950.

Meanwhile supercomputers already have processing speeds well beyond 1 trillion instructions per second (or 1 teraflop per second in jargon). The fastest supercomputer in the world in 1999, Intel's ASCI Red, used 9,632 Pentium Pro processors each with a capacity of 200 megahertz.[22] In June 2000, IBM tested ASCI White, which will be leased to the Lawrence Livermore National Laboratory (LLNL) in Livermore, California. ASCI White has 8,192 CPUs and 12.3 trillion calculations per second.[23] This is approximately "30,000 times faster than a powerful PC and 1,000 times more powerful than IBM's own Big Blue"[24] supercomputer. On August 20, 2000, Compaq announced that it will be providing the U.S. Department of Energy with the "world's fastest and most powerful supercomputer, a 30+ TeraOPS system code-named 'Q'.... This computing behemoth (filling five basketball courts) will contain near 12,000 EV68 Alpha chips running at 1.25 GHz or beyond. They will be housed in 375 AlphaServers running Tru64 UNIX, and will have access to 600 terabytes of storage."[25]

In 2000, this was part of a larger plan to create a computer with 100 trillion instructions per second by 2004 as a first step towards 1,000 trillion instructions per second sometime in the future.[26] By June 2001, both Compaq and IBM announced that they would build bio-supercomputers with 1,000 trillion instructions per second by 2004.[27] Precisely how fast things will develop is a matter of debate. The military vision of the Accelerated Strategic Computing Initiative (ASCI)[28] to be used for Problem Solving Environments (PSE) is very dramatic. Meanwhile, Denning and Metcalfe's (1998) civilian vision gives a more conservative estimate for the future of computation. Such rhetoric about who has the biggest computer is sometimes reminiscent of discussions in men's locker rooms or about the fish that got away. What is claimed is not always matched by reality. In November 2003, the world's fastest computer was Japanese at (Rmax) 35 teraflops,[29] with peaks of 40 teraflops. The top U.S. computer was 13 teraflops with peaks of 20 teraflops.

In 1999, a survey of the top five hundred computers[30] revealed that, of the top twenty, thirteen were in the United States, three were in Japan, two in Germany, and two in the United Kingdom. A new Hitachi machine at the Leibniz Rechenzentrum in Munich, which was planned to have 2 teraflops by 2002, became the seventh[31] most powerful worldwide in 2000. But things change very quickly. In November 2003 it was number 64 on the list of top 500 computers. Even in the ranking of the top twenty there have been dramatic changes during the past decade (Table 2). While the United States clearly still has many of the most powerful computers, these are used for military purposes or closely related topics such as computational fluid dynamics (CFD), theoretical physics; computational chemistry/biology; plasma physics, weather forecasting, and climate modelling.

TABLE 2   The number of top 20 supercomputers per country for the decade 1993–2004. The fastest computer was in Japan.

COUNTRY	1993	1999	2003	2004
Japan	2	3	2	3
United States	16	13	15	14
Canada	1	0	0	0
United Kingdom	1	3	1	2
France	0	2	0	0
Germany	0	0	1	0
China	0	0	1	1

In 1999, the top Japanese computers were devoted to academic research (at positions 5 and 15) and company research (position 17). Britain, had three of the top twenty computers. Two of these (positions 11 and 13) were used to study weather. (Perhaps the Avengers film was not just about science fiction). The third British computer was used for research (position 14). By November 2003, position 14 had been taken by China. In June 2004 China held positions 10, 26, and 42. In Germany, the top computers were used to study weather (position 9) and for research (position 20). Meanwhile, the new Munich computer is dedicated to science in a broader sense. In other words, computers may be a global phenomenon, but the uses to which they are put vary considerably. This relates to our underlying theme that there are at least three major visions for computers in the future: an information highway (America); an information society (Europe), and a knowledge society (Japan).

Futurists such as Denning and Metcalf predict that within the next fifty years processing speed will increase up to the level of exabytes[32] per second.[33] Some believe that this time scale is conservative and that we may reach such remarkable computational speeds much sooner. For instance, another claim for the next three years of computing is provided by the Accelerated Strategic Computing Initiative (ASCI) coordinated by Sandia Labs in the United States. By the year 2003, they foresee devices with a computing speed of 10^{14} flops, memory of 50 terabytes, archival storage of 130 petabytes, parallel input/output (I/O) of 5,000 gigabytes per second and network speeds of 130 gigabytes per second. It is, of course, important to recognize that the military have other resources at their disposal than have civilians.

The largest machines are presently about 8,000 square feet in size. For instance, ASCI White "takes up two basketball courts worth of floor space and weighs 106 tons."[34] Hence, in the realm of supercomputing, computers show no signs of disappearing. But they are definitely getting smaller. In 2000, it was estimated that IBM's Blue Gene computer, employing all the latest developments in miniaturization would be less than 2,000 square feet.[35] By 2001, this was revised to the size of two refrigerators.[36]

5. Transmission Speed

In the early 1980s, transmission by modem was at 200 baud (c. 200 bits/second), then 800 and soon 2,000 baud. In the past eighteen years these capacities have changed dramatically. Basic transmission now ranges from modems at 56,000 bits (56 kilobits) to Asynchronous Digital Subscriber Lines (ADSL) at 1.5 megabytes. At the commercial level business connections at 2 gigabits/second are now available. The military is working at 20–40 gigabits/second. Researchers at the Hitachi labs are working on optical responses at the level of femtoseconds (10^{-15} seconds) with a view to terabit throughput by 2010.[37] At the experimental level speeds of up to 7 terabits per second have already been demonstrated.[38]

In November 1999, Bell Labs announced that they would have a ten-terabit router by July 2000 and that within a decade they would have transmission at the petabyte level, i.e., a quadrillion bytes/second.[39] Scientists at Bell Labs have sent 160 gigabits by optical fibre using only one wavelength or colour of light. If all the 1,022 different colours of light in each of the 864 fibres of a single cable were used one could theoretically convey 141 petabits/second.[40]

We need to remember, of course, that there are great differences between what is theoretically possible, what is demonstrated in a research laboratory, what is available to the military, what is used in experimental networks, and what is available on a daily basis in the home. Europe's GEANT which is the leading global network at this time is typically working in 1–10 gigabit range and plans to reach 70 gigabits in the next five years. Even so, others at the experimental level announced that 16 terabits/second would be delivered to some homes in 2001.[41] Companies such as Alloptic[42] are pioneers in this field.

6. Functions

As the size, capacity, processing speed and transmission speed of computers have increased, so too have their functions changed dramatically. Although we speak of computers as if they were a single object, they are, in fact, a series of devices to perform a number of functions: 1) calculate; 2) write, 3) visualize, 4) create multi-media, 5) enable multi-sensory study, 6) permit inter-media, 7) interact, 8) augment, 9) delegate information/knowledge and 10) simulate synthetic reason.

Calculate

From the 1870s to the 1940s early computers were glorified calculators, which typically took up an entire room. As their name suggests, computers were designed to compute. Although Vannevar Bush (1945) introduced the idea that computers could be used to access enduring knowledge, a main incentive for developing computers such as the ENIAC was simply to do number crunching with respect to the trajectories of shells fired from large guns. Ironically, this ability to do ever-greater amounts of number crunching remains one of the chief functions of supercomputers.

Write

Second, computers help us to write. With the advent of the Personal Computer (PC), computers were supposed to bring a revolution in personal expression and to improve greatly the horizons of inter-personal communication among humans. In practice, computers became objects on desks designed for word processing, charts, and the like. Secretaries were to be replaced by machines. Under the rhetoric that everyone could now be an author, executives and scholars alike were supposed to write their own letters. For many, computers became synonymous with e-mail and word-processing software. For others, computers were a means of creating personal organizers,[43] Personal Information Managers (PIMs),[44] Personal Digital Assistants (PDAs),[45] or Personal Intelligent Assistants (PIAs).[46]

Draw, Visualize

Third, computers became tools for visualizing.[47] They are helping us to see new dimensions of the physical world, both in terms of the visible world, and the invisible world with respect to natural processes: both with respect to the incredibly small (nano-level) and the incredibly large (outer space). They have also led us to visualize abstract phenomena such as concepts and economic processes, as well as possible worlds, creative worlds (see Appendix 1), and even destruction of worlds. The U.S. military is said to use the world's largest supercomputers to visualize atomic explosions.

Multimedia

A fourth function of computers is their capacity to deal with multiple media. The advent of sound and speakers in the mid-1980s meant that presentations invariably started with a few stirring chords of music. The advent of video[48] on the computer often led to the insertion of moving images to highlight the technology rather than the content. By the mid-1990s, after almost a decade of technology-driven presentations, those at the vanguard began to speak disparagingly of the M word. By 2000, multimedia had become part of a larger phenomenon called Information and Communication Technologies (ICT). Multimedia also became linked in turn with three further functions: multi-sensory, inter-media, and inter-action.

Multi-sensory

Computers have done much more than extend vision and sound. They have become multi-sensory devices. The idea of machines as mechanical extensions of man goes back to Karl Marx (1867),[49] and was developed by Ernst Kapp who spoke of "organ projection"[50] and spoke of the not yet understood machinery that resulted as the "unconscious."[51] This idea was pursued by Sigmund Freud (1929), who noted: "With every tool, man is perfecting his own organs, whether motor or sensory, or is removing limits to their functioning."[52] This idea was taken much further by Marshall McLuhan (1964), who spoke of technologies as extensions of man.[53] In the past, those technologies were invariably extensions of physical aspects of the human condition. Through a mechanical "extension" of our arms, bulldozers allowed us to push more than we could ever do with our bare hands. Similarly cranes allowed us to lift more. Telephones are extensions of our ears and voice; televisions are extensions of our eyes and ears.

The Internet began as an extension of our writing capacities: asynchronously through e-mail and synchronously through chat-rooms, MultiUser Domains (MUDs), MultiUser Domains Object Oriented (MOOs), and the like. Through web-telephone and web-TV we have digital extensions of our ears and eyes. Through web cameras on the Internet we can see news halfway around the world without having to go there, and in some cases can actively control the camera to see what we choose. Computers and the Internet are extending to all of the senses (Table 3).

Although sensors were first developed in the nineteenth century, the advent of microprocessors has led to new links between measurement and networked communication. As a result sensors are recording events in the oceans, on earth, and in space. This includes sensors in fish, animals, and birds.

Sight: Sight is the most developed of these digital senses. As noted elsewhere (Appendix 1), computers have helped to extend the realms of the visible far beyond the limits of everyday vision. This is leading to new fields such as scientific visualization and information visualization with hundreds of projects around the world.[54]

Stereoscopic displays in cockpits were introduced at Wright Patterson Airforce Base by Tom Furness III as early as 1966. Work on this theme continues around the world at centres such as the University of Hull. A series of other display methods are also emerging. These range from small screens in portable cell phones such as Nokia or Kyocera and responsive workbenches by the GMD[55] to auto-stereoscopic devices[56] and to 360-degree panels such as that used by NASA at Mountainview.[57]

Sound: Speakers were one of the earliest characteristics of early multimedia computers. This was typically a passive functionality limited to playing music or a short voice clip. In the past decade there have been enormous developments in voice over IP[58] and in the field of speech recognition which have led both to new voice-activated navigation systems and direct dictation. A recent product in the audio field is SpeechBot which: "listens to Web-resident audio programming, converts the sound into a textual transcript, and then indexes those words so that you can type in queries and receive 'hits' – not to pages of text – but to the very section of audio that interests you within a long program." [59]

A research project[60] at the Fraunhofer Gesellschaft in Germany provides a virtual scene of different players in a quartet and permits their being repositioned in visual space with corresponding adjustments to the sounds in acoustic space.[61] As we shall see (chapter 5.6 below), MP3 is also having an impact. Meanwhile, at the global level there are still debates about basic standards.[62]

Touch: Tactile: Force Feedback has been developed in the context of virtual reality. At the non-military level the Teletact (1991)[63] project of Jim Helicon and

TABLE 3 Five senses, their physical organs, and their digital counterparts, which helps explain why computers are now called communication devices

SENSE	ORGAN	TECHNOLOGICAL EQUIVALENT
Sight	Eyes	Cameras
Hearing	Ears	Microphone, Speaker
Touch	Fingers	Force Feedback Glove
Smell	Nose	Digiscent, Neural Nose
Taste	Tongue	Trisenx
Synaesthesia	All Organs Together	Neural Implants

Robert Stone was a pioneering effort. The University of North Carolina at Chapel Hill was one of the pioneers of force feedback at the microscopic level.[64] MIT[65] has a Tangible Media Group[66] under Professor Hiroshi Ishii, which works on Tangible Bits.[67] In Japan, Professor Michitaka Hirose at the Hirose Lab[68] of the Department of Mechano-Informatics is working on haptic displays. Professor Hiroo Iwata at the University of Tsukuba[69] is working on force display, on haptization, the haptic representation of scientific data; and a surgical simulator with force feedback as well as autonomous virtual objects and cooperative work.

Related to the above is the emerging field of gesture technology which could be seen as touch at a distance. MIT, for instance, is working on a Gesture and Narrative Language.[70] Mark Lucente, in the Dreamspace project, working with MIT and IBM, has demonstrated how one can move virtual objects on a screen at a distance using only gestures in a process called Natural Interactivity.[71] NASA is working on using human muscle-nerve signals linked to a computer to control objects,[72] which is leading to a new process called sub-vocal speech.[73] In insects, remote control is already being used to send cockroaches on rescue missions into disaster zones after an earthquake. Companies such as Dimension Technologies Inc. are developing auto-stereoscopic displays which provide three-dimensional images without the need for special glasses.[74] There is considerable work on interactive, immersive,[75] and three-dimensional television,[76] which are all related to the wireless revolution.

Smell: In the autumn of 1999, *Wired*[77] reported on the new company Digiscent,[78] which is making smells available on line. Meanwhile, a group led by France Telecom have provided the first sniffs on the Internet.[79] Behind the scenes are other developments which are potentially much more dramatic. The Pacific Northwestern Labs of the U.S. Department of Energy are developing an electronic, neural nose,[80] the environmental applications of which include: identification of toxic wastes, analysis of fuel mixtures, detection of oil leaks, monitoring of air quality, and testing ground water for odours. This means that robots could in future enter a room, a mine, or some other uncertain place in order to determine whether poisonous gases are present.[81] It also means that a personal robot of the future might sniff their master and provide them with a deodorant or perfume appropriate for the occasion.

Taste: An American company, Trisenx, in Savannah, Georgia, has developed: "a new technology that makes it possible to bring the taste of objects which are represented on the net by graphic images. Special software and a special device, resembling a Jet printer, brings up a special substance on a sticky golden piece of paper."[82] Developments at the microscopic level suggest that soon direct stimulation of the sensory cortex via neuronal implants will make it possible to evoke any or all of the senses at will. Meanwhile, there is work on sensory transducers,[83] which allow us to translate experiences from one sense to another. Magnetic Resonance Imaging (MRI) is an elementary example where sound scans are translated into visible images. A next stage would be glasses that translate such sounds into real-time images. As a result, some now call computers communication devices (cf. Table 4). In the past years there has also been increasing attention to how the Internet can be accessible to help persons with one or more senses that are lacking. Pioneering efforts in this context were made by the Trace Centre (Wisconsin). The W3 Consortium's Web Accessibility Initiative (WAI) plays a central role in this context.[84] Companies such as IBM[85] and groups such as the International Visual Theatre (IVT)[86] are also active. A European Union project called WISDOM is working on automatic translation of regular spoken language into sign language for the deaf.[87] Gurus such as Donald Norman have listed many of the shortcomings of current technology. Innovations include a trend towards user-modelling and user-adapted interaction,[88] namely, person–machine interfaces; intelligent help systems; intelligent tutoring systems, and natural language dialogues. This is leading towards adaptive learning environments.[89] Scholars such as Coutaz and Carbonell have drawn attention to the importance of multi-modality.[90] My student, Nik Baerten, is studying the role of organic metaphors for future interfaces and interaction.[91] Michel Riguidel at the Ecole Nationale Supérieure des Communications speaks of a "rhizomorphic architecture of cyberspheres."[92]

Intermedia

Computers have a sixth function. They act as inter-media devices linking printers, fax machines, microphones, speakers (sound), monitors, cameras (visual), etc. This intermediary function increases the range of recording and publishing in different media. A recent example is the use of mobile phones to control televisions and record programs at a distance.[93] The early sales representatives focussed on one detail in this process, namely, the transition from analog bits of paper to digital bytes and thus believed that the personal computer heralded a paperless office. This overlooked the real significance of digital versions. Digital versions can be translated potentially into any of the other media from print to oral sound or potentially even manuscript or cuneiform (Table 4): which is why offices continue to have secretaries and paper.

TABLE 4   Examples of types of communication as indicators of levels of discourse

UNI-MEDIA	*Unrecorded Verbal*		
	Aural	Conversation	Private
		Speech	Public
	Recorded Visual	Letter	Private, Public
		Manuscript	Private, Public
		Painting, etc.	Private, Public
		Book	Private, Public
		Newsletter	Private, Public
		Photography	Private, Public
		Silent Film	Public
		Periodical	Public
		Newspaper	Public
	Recorded Audio-Verbal	Tape Recorder	Private, Public
		Radio	Public
BI-MEDIA	*Recorded Audio-Visual*	Video	Private, Public
		Television	Public
		Film	Public
MULTI-MEDIA	*Omni-Sensory*	Computers	Private, Public
INTER-MEDIA	*Bridging Omni-Sensory*	Computers	Private, Public

The changes lie in new input (e.g., voice dictation) and output devices (e.g., 3-D printers, stereo-lithography machines[94] and the new field of micro-lithography).[95] Some optimists believe that automatic translation will also soon become part of this process.[96]

The list above (Table 4) reveals a fundamental difference between earlier advances in communication and the electronic revolution. In a tribal culture, authority was based in the chief's oral words. The scope of his knowledge was limited to his tribe. Knowledge about outside tribes was frequently seen as a threat. When the Greeks moved from oral to written culture, the new medium claimed to replace the earlier one in terms of validity. Of course, conversation continued,[97] but the written word came to have greater authority. Written knowledge from other states now theoretically had to be taken into account. The shift from oral to written, to manuscript, and later, printed knowledge, entailed an increasing universalization in the scope of knowledge. For the past two millennia it seemed that each innovation meant abandoning one medium and replacing it with another. There is also a trend from private to public. We are moving to a world where as some say "information wants to be free." Indeed an extreme interpretation assumes a gradual erosion of the private sphere such that everything will be public.

Computers embrace rather than replace earlier methods a) by integrating them into a single system and b) by providing tools where one means of communication

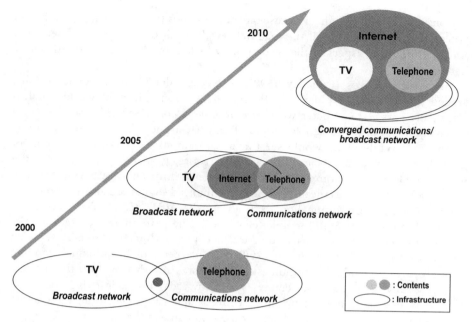

Figure 1 Japanese scenario for convergence of Internet, broadband, and telecommunications networks according to Hiroshi Fujiwara, Internet General Research Centre (2000).

can be translated into another. Hence we can listen to a speech as if it were being given "live" by Thucydides in ancient Greece. We can consult a manuscript record thereof, thus allowing us to record and publish information and knowledge from every level of discourse.

Electronic devices are making us aware of the narrowness of earlier media, be it speech in the manner of a medieval monk, or consulting the latest critical edition in book form in a modern library. We can now study the recorded evidence with the aid of hypertext and hyperpicture (or hypericonic) functions linking words with dictionaries, maps, architecture, sculpture, and art by recording and publishing mechanisms.[98]

In Ancient Greece, the advent of the alphabet opened a world of communication to those who were literate but at the same time excluded all those who were illiterate. In the Renaissance, the introduction of printing greatly expanded the realms of inclusion and at the same time increased the exclusion of those who remained illiterate. If conversions from one input/output (I/O) medium to another are combined with the translations between senses outlined above, the enormous potentials of the Internet digital revolution become clear. Since it is now possible to have text read out as oral communication and conversely, this means that illiterate persons, and even those unable to use one of the senses (sight, hearing, speech) can potentially have access to all the materials available through literacy. Herein, lies another important aspect of the revolution, which many have not yet sufficiently understood.

Speaking at Davos (February 1998), Nobuyuki Idei, then President of Sony, argued that electronics today is still divided into four different worlds: audio-visual, the personal computer world, the mobile telephone world, and the world of set-top boxes in the cable television industry. He argued that all four need to be combined.[99] While many would see this as overambitious, a Dataquest report of June 2000 reported that 44 million persons are already surfing the Internet while watching television.[100] Companies such as Intel and Philips have strategies for such integration. Intel, for instance is working on Enhanced Digital Broadcast, Immersive Entertainment, Sports Immersion, and new Media Appliances.[101] There are plans for visual radio by 2005 and mobile television in the years thereafter. Meanwhile, it is useful to consider a scenario by Hiroshi Fujiwara (Internet General Research Centre, Japan) who claims that by 2005 the Internet will be on equal standing with broadcasting and telecommunications networks and that by 2010 the Internet will have fully absorbed these (Figure 1). Already today this is bringing enormous changes whereby telephone companies are investing in cable, television, and satellite companies as well as Internet, whereby cable companies are acquiring phone capabilities and indeed almost every imaginable combination is being explored.[102]

Scenarios from Siemens help to bring home the enormity of the changes that are underway. A scenario of technologies in 2002 shows a core with three separate networks for 1) telephone, 2) Internet, and 3) cable television (CATV) distribution. A Siemens scenario for the year 2015 makes essentially the same point as the Japanese prediction. The distinct networks will be become one as we move from separate Information Communication Technologies to Universal Convergent Technologies: from ICT to UCT.

Researchers connected with the Defense Advanced Research Projects Agency (DARPA) speak of a progression from the ARPA-net through the Internet leading to an Interspace. Meanwhile, a Next Generation Internet (NGI) Initiative led by organizations such as NASA is working on convergence between terrestrial Internet standards and space Internet standards in order to create an InterPlanetary Internet Architecture (IPN).[103] Whereas the terrestrial Internet relies highly on optical fibre, the interplanetary Internet will rely on radio frequency or laser, and, whereas the terrestrial backbone relies on the Internet Protocol (IP) for the network layer, the interplanetary backbone will entail bundle routing.

Interact

Closely related to the role of computers in inter-media (linking between media) is a seventh function, whereby they interact with multiple devices such as embedded devices. Very subtly, multi-media and multi-sensory computers are extending the principle of machine to machine communication. The coupling of computers through the Internet implies that this principle of control at a distance can be extended globally. Connectivity thus became a buzzword. Initially, this meant that computers became a new kind of timer: to adjust the lights of a home, regulate the temperature, and activate other devices such as printers, faxes, radios, or televisions. But this was only a first step in the direction of intelligent objects (chapter 5.14–16 below). As Robin Milner, who led computer science at Cambridge, put it: "networking allows computer science (theory of calculation) to grow into informatics (theory of interaction)." [104] A Forrester report of May 2001 predicted that the Internet as we now know it will die and soon be replaced by a more interactive, pervasive medium.[105] Meanwhile, others such as Willy Zwaenepoel predict that as we move from an information web to a service web interactive will be replaced by programmatic.

Augment

An eighth function of computers entails their ability to augment reality. While some argued that Artificial Intelligence (AI) was a cure for everything, pioneers such as Fred Brooks (UNC, Chapel Hill), suggested that the world needs Intelligence Augmentation: IA instead of AI. Of course, this idea of using devices to augment abilities is not new. In the seventeenth century, it inspired the invention of the telescope to extend our vision towards the infinitely far and the microscope to see the infinitely small. New in the past decades is the idea that augmentation can apply to interfaces and objects as well as persons. New also is the idea of superimposing lines, figures, charts and other information onto images in both physical and the virtual worlds. Whereas early virtual reality scenarios assumed that they would replace the real world, augmented reality combines the real and virtual in new ways (cf. chapter 14).

Delegate

The advent of machine-machine communication also gave computers a ninth function. They can delegate tasks. An agent (possibly in the form of an avatar – an electronic representative ranging from a comic book figure to a full simulation of ourselves) can substitute for a user and perform a number of tasks in their absence. The functions of a traditional butler are thus subsumed by an electronic equivalent. A fundamental difference of the electronic avatar is that its activities are not limited to the spatial confines of a house. Given its electronic nature it can readily perform one task in the home and then perform other tasks in different locations thousands of miles away in ways that would be unthinkable for even the most exemplary butler. A company called Artificial-Life.com is producing avatars of different cultures for business purposes.[106]

Moreover, such avatars, can be linked into multi-agent systems, whereby a complex series of tasks can be coordinated. This potentially extends enormously the role of owner and butler alike, but also raises new questions of responsibility and identity.

If these electronic extensions of myself buy books, which my profile suggests that I should like, am I responsible for paying the bills even if I have not made that decision? Indeed, who am I if my avatar butler and its related multi-agent systems are constantly doing things in my name and on my behalf, often without consulting directly with me? These are questions to which we shall return (chapters 6, 13).

Synthetic Reason

In the eyes of some futurists, even the above visions are very conservative. Manual de Landa, for instance, in his *Virtual Environments and the Emergence of Synthetic Reason* depicts much more dramatic developments:

> The term "intentionality" is the technical term used by philosophers to describe the relation between a believer and the states of affairs his beliefs are about. That is, an important feature of the mental states of human beings and other animals (their beliefs and desires) is that they are about phenomena that lie outside their minds. The top-down, symbolic approach to Artificial Intelligence sacrifices this connection by limiting its modeling efforts to relations between symbols. In other words, in the analytical approach only the syntactic or formal relations between symbols matter (with the exception of an "internal semantics" involving reference to memory addresses and the like). Hence, these designs must later try to reconnect the cognitive device to the world where it must function, and it is here that the main bottleneck lies (unless the "world" in question is a severely restricted domain of the real world, such as the domain of chess). Not so in the synthetic approach:

> The connectionist approach to modeling cognition thus offers a promise in explaining the aboutness or intentionality of mental states. Representational states, especially those of hidden units, constitute the system's own learned response to inputs. Since they constitute the system's adaptation to the input, there is a clear respect in which they would be about objects or events in the environment if the system were connected, via sensory-motor organs, to that environment. The fact that these representations are also sensitive to context, both external and internal to the system, enhances the plausibility of this claim that the representations are representations of particular states[107]

Not everyone would agree. Charles Jonscher, in his recent book on *The Evolution of Wired Life* has, for instance, warned about the inherent shortcomings of computers: "The fundamental limitation of digital processing will cast its shadow over every computer-based solution. That is that the teaching idea ... must first be reduced to the yes-no logic of the AND, OR and NOT guts which are at the core of every computer."[108] Also entirely lacking in de Landa's view of synthetic reason, are cultural and historical dimensions of knowledge, which are a central concern of the present book. We shall raise questions about this overly optimistic and in our view rather naïve prediction of the potentials of computers later (chapters 13–15).

7. Combinations or Multiplicity

Hand in hand with this enormous growth in the functions of computers is an ambivalence as to how computers should evolve. On the one hand, there is a vision of a single machine which combines all the above functions. This machine is sometimes called a transputer. Some call this the Swiss Army Knife Syndrome. This trend is also evident in the realm of smart phones. David Wood (Symbian) sees smart phones as increasingly creating new links between functions such as alarm-clock, book, blackberry, calculator, camcorder, camera, diary, dictionary, game console, keys, music player, newspaper, Personal Digital Assistant (PDA), radio, tickets, to do list, voucher, wallet and watch. On the other hand, there is a tendency to create new devices for each new functionality, as seen in the multiplicity of gadgets surrounding personal telephones, personal assistants, and communication devices. For instance, Charles Davies (Psion) foresees a continual diversification of instruments ranging from desktop, laptop, palmtop, through communicator, smartphone, feature phone, to mobile phone, and fixed phone. A third movement, supported by the World Wide Web consortium calls for device-independent computing, whereby one is not dependent on any given gadget for any given functionality.[109]

8. Centralized or Personal

The earliest computers were centralized, i.e., they were the centre of activity and had attached to them a number of dumb terminals, which served as passive access points to the central machine. In this model, all the intelligence of the system was in a single place. This gave the systems operator access to everything. Individual users, on the other hand, found that they had a) access to only their bit of the whole and b) no privacy. Side effects of the centralized computer were that the systems operators (sys ops) could act as if they were God or Big Brother. Some link this with the end-to-end principle in network design.[110]

The so-called personal computer brought with it the assumption that one could have a basic set of tools on one's own computer. Some link this with the rise of the stupid network and peer-to-peer communication.[111] From a user's viewpoint, this was immensely important because a) they now had complete control of their little microcosm, and b) they had privacy therein. A side effect thereof was that some became rich selling many individual copies of software.

As the burdens of updating software increased, persons searched for alternatives. Would it not be convenient, thought some, if one could simply download these software updates as they became available and allow "the system" to do all the work of adjusting the local machine environment? Might it not also be more speedy and efficient, thought others, if one could store various individual files in very large databases running on supercomputers?

Large corporations and governments have a natural attraction to such a centralized model. It provides them with a means of verifying who entered their systems and precisely what was done there. Hence, one of the reasons why portals have become such a buzzword in industry. As with all gateways, however, advantages more often accrue to the gatekeepers than to users of the gate. This helps to explain why "portals" is also becoming a politically laden term. According to a report by Forrester Research (17 May 2001), the Internet as it now is will soon be replaced by an X Internet which is net-centred, with executable applications which will increase to more than 10 billion Internet devices by 2010 and which will allow corporate buyers to navigate: "a virtual marketplace with a Doom-like user interface — buyers could simply shoot the deals they want.… Users will get real-time, interactive experiences over the Net through disposable code — programs you use once and throw away — downloaded to their PCs and handheld devices."[112]

Some argue that there is a natural tension between the corporate approach, which wants intelligence at the centre and a personal approach which wants intelligence at the end. They see the quest for end-to-end (e to e) control as a key strategy of large corporations. Some predict that Internet Protocol version 6 (Ipv6) will play a major role in the future of end-to-end.[113] Also linked with these debates are trends towards so-called active networks.[114]

As noted earlier, there are fundamental differences between large, impersonal supercomputers and small, personal computers. Supercomputers will necessarily have numerous centralized functions and will remain large, immoveable objects. Personal computers will become ever-more mobile and invisible. Some speak in this context of the disappearing computer. It is to be hoped that this disappearance will be limited to its visibility as a physical object, and not to its functionality as a potentially autonomous microcosm. Otherwise, one set of the aspirations that led Steve Jobs to create his alternative freedom will go lost. At another level, supercomputers and personal computers are becoming interconnected through computational grids.

9. Not a Machine

We have dwelt at some length on these ten functions of computers to make it clear that the term "computer" is elusive. One could say that "computer" is actually a kind of metonymy, a part for the whole: we say "computer" and we mean a whole range of devices including a Central Processing Unit (CPU), Operating System (OS), printers, speakers, CD-ROMs, recording devices, and the Internet. Robert Cailliau, one of the co-founders of the World Wide Web Consortium puts it more provocatively: the computer is not a machine.[115] Aside from a fan and an occasional whirring disk drive, computers have no moving parts. Even if we insisted that a single computer is somehow practically a machine, the Internet revolution is about connectivity and not machines. Otherwise, there would not be a paradox that hardware capabilities often become software and conversely. Hence, the rise of virtual machines and emulators.[116]

Things that change the world are usually more than an isolated machine or a single invention. They bring about systemic changes in society. Here there are interesting parallels with printing. The printing press is a machine but the printing revolution was much more than a machine. The invention of printing around the year 805 in Korea was important.[117] But it was not until Gutenberg in the 1440s had the idea of using that invention for spreading knowledge that something systemic changed. With Gutenberg's approach, printing became one aspect of a new way of organizing knowledge, a new way of communicating theory and practice. Gutenberg went broke. It took over a century and a half for the full vision which changed the world to manifest itself.

The invention of the computer has been compared to the invention of printing. This is both misleading and true. It is misleading because a computer is not really a machine in the manner of a printing press. It is true because both the printing revolution and the computer revolution entail systemic changes in society. Computers are closely connected with at least four other technological trends: 1) mobility; 2) miniaturization; 3) Global Information Systems (GIS) or Global Positioning Systems (GPS), and 4) agents (cf. chapters 2–3).

The first of these, mobility, is intimately connected with the wireless revolution that began over a century ago with the advent of the telegraph, telephone, and subsequently the radio. Mobility implies that a) we shall soon be able to access equipment literally in anything, anytime, anywhere and partly as a consequence thereof, b) most of the neat distinctions between different kinds of devices will disappear. The second trend, miniaturization will reduce computing and many other operations to the nano-level, which means that the processes will become invisible.

The third development, whereby GIS (initially Geographical Information Systems) and GPS are combined through Universal Mobile Telecommunications Services (UMTS) implies that most of our day-to-day distinctions between broadcast media (radio and television) and other media need to be reassessed. The fourth development, agents, means that many routine tasks can increasingly be relegated to software. This will affect all areas of life, including those in memory institutions (librarians, museum conservators, archivists) and scholars. Related to these large trends are also more specific technological developments such as optical character recognition (OCR). This means that digital versions of Xerox machines are emerging, that we scan anything we wish. In 2004 the first fax machines that were also scanners appeared. This also means, as we shall see (chapter 12), that hypertext takes on a new meaning.

Most persons expected that systemic changes of connected computers would take the form of a killer-application that invariably removes or replaces all competition.[118] Perhaps something more subtle is happening. These systemic changes are inspiring us to use what we already have in new ways. Hence, it is useful to begin with a brief survey of these new technologies, which at first sight have no connection with one another. This will lead to a review of material and organizational consequences before focussing on the intellectual and spiritual implications of computers which are the key themes of this book.

Douglas Engelbart, inventor of the mouse and a pioneer of the Internet, claimed that collaborative efforts with computers could lead to new, augmented knowledge. We shall claim that the frontiers of computing lie in integrating three kinds of knowledge: personal, collaborative, and enduring knowledge. Herein lie new frontiers for augmented books, knowledge, and culture as well as possibilities for a new synthesis of knowledge and understanding. The computer revolution seemed to be mainly about new technological developments. The Inter-net-worked computer revolution is as much about software as hardware. Indeed as we shall show, it is changing our definitions of everyday objects and their relation to subjects. And beyond this world of objects, it has even more implications for the realms of the intellect and spirit.

2
mobility

The future masters of technology will have to
be lighthearted and intelligent. The machine
easily masters the grim and the dumb.
— Marshall McLuhan, 1969

1. Introduction

Mobile communications are not quite as young as they seem.
Alexander Graham Bell invented the photophone, which
transmits speech by light rays in 1880.[1] Marconi's initial
experiments in wireless communication go back to the years
1894–95, resulting in a patent the next year (1896).[2] The first
mobile radio in the United States was introduced by the Detroit
Michigan Police Department in 1921. The first public mobile
telephone system was introduced in St. Louis, Missouri, in
1945. The concept of cellular phones was introduced in
1947 and in 1953 AT&T proposed a broadband, mobile
telephone system.[3] Even so, it was not until the invention of

the microprocessor in 1971 that personal computers and cellular phones became possible. The first analog cellular phone system was introduced in Japan in 1979 followed by Scandinavia in 1981. Europe established a Global System for Mobile Telecommunications (GSM)[4] between 1982 and 1987.

Mobile and wireless computing is all the rage. In 2000, the DoCoMo phenomenon in Japan saw the sale of 50,000 new cell phones per day. Worldwide, in 2000, it was estimated that at least 200,000 cell phones were being sold daily.[5] By 2004 there were 1.52 billion mobile users worldwide[6] with an estimated 630 million units sold that year alone.[7] At the same time the amount of fibre optic cable continues to grow. In 1998, according to KMI, 46 million fibre kilometres were installed around the world. In 1999, it was 63 million kilometres. In 2000 it is estimated that 90 million new kilometres were installed.[8] The revolution of the Internet is a combination of wired and wireless connections.[9]

2. Ubiquity

In everyday life, mobile communications were initially limited to using mobile (cellular) telephones. The enormous advantages of being able to reach persons almost anywhere has led to an amazing growth in their use. The first thirty years brought 300 million users. Underlying the mobile revolution is a larger vision of ubiquitous computing[10] introduced by Mark Weiser at Xerox Park. In this vision, computing is not just about a gadget on a desk but potentially involves miniature gadgets spread everywhere in our work and home environment: a vision for which he decided wireless communications were necessary. This process has already begun and is becoming associated with the term "embedded computing."[11] In 1997, there were one thousand times more microprocessors than regular computers.[12] Connected with such developments is the rise of nomadic computing in the military, developed by pioneers such as Leonard Kleinrock.[13] Some now refer to pervasive computing and to global computing.

3. Microprocessors and Miniaturization

The rapid development of microprocessors since 1971 has brought computers to the desktop, then to portables, to the laptop, the notebook, notepad, smartpad,[14] tablet PC[15] and more recently to handheld devices such as the Palm Pilot[16] and the Treo.[17] Among these new handheld devices is the electronic book.[18] Books are heavy. Important books such as the *Bible* often weigh ten pounds or more. The complete *Oxford English Dictionary* in twenty-six volumes is so heavy that no ordinary individual can carry all of it around. The Compact Edition of the *Oxford English Dictionary* with 4,116 pages in two volumes is portable but at the expense of the making the print so small that a magnifying glass is needed for the experience. Electronic versions as electronic books will be portable. As of March 2004 e-ink and electronically sensitive paper are a reality.[19]

The process of miniaturization is continuing. Today's smallest transistors measure about 180 nanometres. In November 1999, Lucent's Bell Labs announced "the world's smallest" transistor gates measuring "just 50 nanometers, which is about 2,000 times smaller than a human hair.... Future refinements should shrink transistor gates to less than 30 nanometers."[20] In the summer of 2001 Hitachi introduced the Mew chip, less than half a millimetre in size and small enough to fit into a dollar bill.[21] Within two decades we are told that an object the size of a fly will be sufficient space for a computer that is 100 million times more powerful than a contemporary Pentium computer.[22] Technically speaking this means that the electronic equivalent of millions of books can potentially be carried around easily. Wearable computing, a trendy phantasy even five years ago, will probably become an everyday reality within a decade, thanks partly to developments in new fields called molecular electronics or molectronics,[23] mechatronics and holonics (chapter 4.9).[24]

In 1998, a number of new consortia (WAP, HAVI)[25] moved discussions of wireless technologies from futuristic scenarios into the front line. This has had two basic consequences. First, there are new prospects of interoperability among a whole range of electronic devices and appliances beginning in the home and soon spreading elsewhere especially after the introduction of Universal Mobile Telecommunications Services (UMTS) originally slated for 2002, and then delayed until 2005.[26] This will link mobile phones and computers via satellite anywhere at anytime. Meanwhile, a new invention in June 2001 promises to speed up radio data 100 times.[27]

4. Convergence and Multi-functionality

Convergence is a buzzword which refers to many things. At a basic level, there is convergence between the worlds of telephony,[28] television, film,[29] and Internet (Figure 1). Traditionally, technological devices were typically linked with a specific function. A telephone, for example, was for making telephone calls. A camera was for making photographs. A fax machine was for faxes and a computer was for e-mail or word processing. Through convergence, this traditional notion of devices with a specific function is fast disappearing. Hence, the two years from 1998 to 2000 brought a number new mobile devices, which perform all of these functions in a single instrument. Some of these instruments have grown out of hand-held Personal Digital Assistants (PDAs).[30] A number of these devices resemble telephones with miniature screen displays. Perhaps the most striking examples are those of Nokia,[31] a company which is consciously working towards what they term "personal in-formation bubbles."[32] For instance, their "7710 model features a touch screen, pen input, a digital camera, an Internet browser, a radio, video playback and streaming and recording capabilities."[33] In October 2004, Intel introduced a new technology called Spot Codes, which allows mobile telephones to communicate directly with public information kiosks.[34] In November 2004, Nokia and Philips introduced a Near Field Communication (NFC) chip that allows passengers to pay their bus fares using their handsets, a principle that will soon be extended to pay for tickets at the cinema and elsewhere. Other important players in the field include Sony-Ericsson,[35] Kenwood,[36] Motorola[37] and Kyocera. IBM has a concept phone called JPC 2K that has continuous speech recognition, paper-like interfaces,[38] visual programming, digital cellular speech synthesis, personalized news, intelligent agents, video, TV, or conferencing.[39]

Qualcomm has a telephone which incorporates Palm Pilot functionality directly.[40] Telenor has smartphones with high speed Internet access.[41] A number of such devices are already available.[42] Sony has Net-MDs (Mini-Discs).[43] Some players believe that there may well also be a new wave of divergence of devices. There will however be one crucial difference. Such future telephones, PDAs and other instruments will increasingly become systems of devices with new levels of connectivity and interoperability.

Meanwhile, companies such as Telecom Italia are exploring the idea of virtual interfaces. In this approach, an electronic notepad-like device has a simple screen that can be reconfigured to resemble the interface for a telephone, a fax machine, a computer terminal, etc. Hence, interfaces are reconfigurable and a change of interface permits a new functionality. As a result of these developments, within five years, access to the Internet, which today is still largely dependent on a fixed connection, will be possible in many ways at any time from anywhere on Earth. The linking of phones and computers to an orbiting satellite will no longer be limited to the equivalents of James Bond. It will become an everyday affair.

The price of such devices also continues to decrease. Personal computers, which used to cost a few thousands, now cost a few hundreds of dollars.[44] In the spring of 2004, India produced a Linux-based[45] Simputer (Simple Computer) for around $200.[46] A variant of the Palm Pilot called the Handspring Visor sells for less.[47] Once embedded into everyday devices such as telephones, it is quite feasible that simplified versions of computers could be made available for as little as $25. Robert X. Cringely predicts a $15 computer within five years.[48] Persons at the frontiers of the field[49] assure us that the actual cost could well sink to less than $10. More radical claims speak of future computers for $1.[50] If so, the Internet Society's motto of "Internet for all," will become more than rhetoric. Universal accessibility, now thinkable only in the most advanced countries, can potentially help the entire six billion persons of our planet.

Convergence is also underway at a larger scale. At present there are three main networks: 1) a broadcast network (of television and radio); 2) a communications network (of telephones), and 3) the Internet. As noted earlier the Japanese predict that the Internet will be the framework for all three by 2010 (Figure 1).[51] Linked with these phenomena of convergence, new technologies, which began as independent inventions, are coming together. These include Optical Character Recognition (OCR), new treatments of space through Geographical Information Systems (GIS), Global Positioning Systems (GPS), and agents.

At another level convergence is bringing new partnerships. For instance, the Swedish Telecom Telia has a new company called Scanova for business to consumer transactions which includes some 1,600 advertising-related companies, 171 television and radio operators, 320 producers of film and video, and 45 distributors. These will form a Scandinavian Media Exchange (SMX) with a value chain that entails gathering, encoding, Media Asset Management (MAM), Collaboration, Broadband Distribution and Broadband Operation.

5. Optical Character Recognition

The quest to turn printed documents into digital form was outlined clearly in Buckminster Fuller's *Education Automation* (1962), where he proposed a universally accessible digital library that would enable anyone, anywhere, to study, learn, and grow. He believed that this intellectual freedom of the masses would bring humanity's best ideas to reality. This vision led authors such as Tony McKinley to explore Optical Character Recognition (OCR) devices.[52] Throughout the 1980s and early 1990s, OCR devices were fairly accurate but invariably not fully reliable. In the past few years their accuracy has improved greatly. Raj Reddy at Carnegie Mellon envisaged the idea of a new universal library.[53]

One of the unexpected consequences of such advances has been the arrival of electronic pens for scanning materials as one reads, such as the C-Pen[54] and Quicklink Hexaglot.[55] The reader simply runs the pen over a passage in the way that some persons run a marker over an interesting passage and the "pen" scanner immediately uploads it. This passage can subsequently be transferred to one's computer via a wireless connection. In future, such transmission from mobile to fixed devices can readily be automated. In short, scanning small or even larger passages, making excerpts, is no longer a problem: Nor is making annotations. Where a medieval scribe would have made marginalia, the modern world will have its electronic equivalents such as the W3C's Annotea.[56]

A second unexpected consequence of such advances has been the advent of new technologies such as the Quicktionary.[57] Using this device, which resembles a fat pen with a small viewing screen, a user can touch any word, which is then scanned by the device and a definition for this term is immediately provided. A present limitation of the Quicktionary is that the number of terms is limited to the internal memory of the pen-like device, which was around 285,000 definitions in 1998. By 2004, the Quicktionary or super pen had up to 430,000 definitions, was available in twenty languages, had variants that read words aloud and could be used to scan in a thousand pages of text.

A combination of the innovations outlined above introduces much more dramatic possibilities. Given wireless connections, a pen-like device can scan in a word, which is conveyed to an electronic book, notepad, or tablet.[58] As the term enters the electronic book the user is offered options concerning different levels of knowledge (items one to five in Figure 16, below). Let us say the user chooses definitions. They are then offered a choice of standard dictionaries such as the *Oxford*

TABLE 5 Alternative modes of communication based on four different interplays of space and time adapted from Mitchell (1999).[80] The crosses indicate how personal contact and cost decrease as one goes from synchronous, local to asynchronous, remote.

SPACE		TIME		
Local	1	Synchronous Transportation Coordination Personal ++++ Cost ++++	2	Asynchronous Transportation No Coordination Personal +++ Cost +++
Remote	3	Synchronous No Transportation Coordination Personal ++ Cost ++	4	Asynchronous No Transportation No Coordination Personal + Cost +

English and *Webster's*. Their choice of dictionary is then coupled with the word identified through the pen scanner and relayed via the Internet to a Virtual Reference Room and the corresponding definition is then sent back to the user's electronic book, notepad, or a Personal Intelligent Assistant (e.g., PIA by Philips). Whereas the Quicktionary was limited a) by the memory of the pen device, and b) by screen space to providing a single word or very short definition, our vision provides as full a definition as desired. This same principle applies to all kinds of reference works including encyclopaedias,[59] book catalogues, and specialized bibliographies.

This can be complemented by a series of elementary add-ons. With voice recognition software,[60] users will have an alternative of making their choices voice-activated, which is frequently an obvious convenience.[61] In the everyday workplace this means that medical doctors can already receive, fill, and ship orders filed via handheld prescription pads.[62] With augmented reality doctors can have statistics concerning a patient superimposed on an image of the patient during an operation.[63]

Every Word Hypertext

There are applications for e-paper with paper-thin screens. For instance, Ericsson is working on a new kind of intelligent paper coupled with geographical information systems.[64] Procter and Gamble are said to have plans to produce free toilet paper with banner ads.[65] The ETH in Zurich is also working on e-paper.[66] Jeffrey Harrow in a discussion of e-paper in his electronic bulletin on *The Rapidly Changing Face of Computing*, drew attention to a new approach to hypertext by Gurunet,[67] whereby every word can become a hypertext link.[68] In 2002, this still seemed almost like science fiction. Now the CD accompanying this book heralds new versions of omni-linked books.

Electronic Books

The past decade has seen a number of prototype electronic books (e-books)[69] which keep changing names as they change companies. These include the NewsPAD,[70] the SoftBook System[71] and RocketBook[72] supported by Barnes & Noble and Bertelsmann, now e-book-Gemstar.com; Dedicated Reader,[73] Cyberglass,[74] Adobe eBook Reader[75] and Microsoft e-Book reader.[76] A number of these experiments have ended almost as quickly as they began. Research at MIT has led to an e-ink Inc.[77] Closely related to this are a number of projects to create e-newspapers.[78]

6. Space

Geographical Information Systems (GIS) have been developing steadily since the 1970s. They allow a precise linking between maps and enormous amounts of other information, which can be arranged in layers. Hence there can be one layer indicating where electrical lines exist. A second layer can trace the position of all the sewers. A third can show the position of all the railway lines on a map. A city such as Toronto has over sixty such layers in its Geographical Information System (GIS). In the last decade there has been an increasing trend to link this information with Facilities Management Systems (FMS), such that one can also trace where all the telephones, computer terminals, printers, and fax machines are in the offices of a skyscraper. Such innovations introduce new interface challenges in moving from two-dimensional to three-dimensional information spaces – a field where the augmented reality work of pioneers such as Steve Feiner is particularly interesting.[79]

In parallel with the rise of GIS has been a development of Global Positioning Systems (GPS). These were initially developed in the military and continue to be developed in this context, where they are said to have achieved an accuracy within less than a centimetre. Civilian versions are much less accurate but can readily determine one's position anywhere on Earth, via a satellite link, to within about ten metres. In cases where there are clearly defined roads and landmarks, this accuracy can be increased to within a few feet.

Hence the recent rise of navigation aids in automobiles which show us how to reach a destination via a map. If all this sounds futuristic, a combination of cell phone, Personal Digital Assistant, and Global Positioning System (GPS) is already commercially available.[81] As we shall note below, a combination of GIS and GPS has considerable consequences for our interests.

7. Space and Time

Some claim that the Internet is destroying the barriers of space and time. This is misleading as one discovers when one tries doing collaborative work with persons on different continents. Even so, there are important ways in which the Internet is changing our relations to and with both space and time. McLuhan made similar claims regarding the invention of printing. Matellart (1994) has shown similar claims have been made for earlier technologies such as the telegraph, telephone, radio, and television.

William Mitchell, in his fascinating book, *E-topia*, outlined four fundamental relations of space and time and noted that these corresponded roughly to four major periods of history:

1) Pre-literate man was limited to local space and synchronous time: communication was only possible with those with whom one was in direct contact, with minor exceptions of those who used smoke signals.

2) Once literacy entered the scene and it was possible to leave messages, then local asynchronous communication was possible.

3) The advent of tele-communications made remote synchronous communication possible through telephones.

4) The advent of voice-mail, computers and e-mail made possible remote asynchronous communication.

Mitchell was primarily interested in the architectural consequences of these four stages, each of which he claimed was successively less costly and less personal (Table 5). There is, however, an historical dimension that Mitchell overlooks. Synchronous meetings in local space and time may be the most expensive form of communication today. In a primitive society, however, where the other three alternatives were not available, persons did not think of synchronous communication in terms of costs. One would not think of charging one's neighbour for a chat. It is only in complex societies, where we seldom know our neighbours, that meetings become an economic process. So the new technologies have not only introduced new alternatives; they have led us to treat as commodities and transactions what we once thought of as everyday experiences.

The latest mobile developments make further havoc of Mitchell's very logical evolution. Teenagers in Helsinki are using mobiles to send asynchronous messages to their friends in order to make a rendezvous in local, synchronous time. Travelling business persons increasingly use mobile phones from a remote synchronous or asynchronous situation to inform their partners about their arrival back into the local, synchronous scene.

Indeed the new mobility is bringing about transformations in what seemed to be fundamental oppositions between those who are nomadic and settled. In the past, the nomad had the advantage of new experiences through travel and the disadvantage of having no collections, almost no materials to which they permanently had access. By contrast, settled persons in cities and towns had the advantage of their own collections and access to the collections of the place where they lived, but the disadvantage of not having new experiences through constant travel. The new mobility permits everyone to explore new combinations of settled and nomadic life, while still having access to collections at home and elsewhere continually.

Precisely where this will lead is a matter of conjecture. In April 2001, Ken Henderson offered a visionary scenario whereby the advent of computers as implants led 90 per cent of the population to return to a rural environment by the year 2055.[82] Others would claim that the trend to move towards urban environments is an irreversible dimension of an ever-more technological world.

8. Agents

The introduction of object-oriented programming set out from a notion that individual bits of code could be treated as objects, and thus be made reusable. The idea of encapsulation led to the notion of inheritance. The amount of code potentially contained within such an object soon grew to include simple characteristics, instructions, routines, and the like.[83] From this emerged the idea that individual agents, each linked with specific instructions, could perform simple routines autonomously. From a systems engineering view, the notion of objects, led to components and then agents. These approaches from Artificial Intelligence (AI), combined with principles of Distributed Systems (DS) evolved into a more complex vision of Multi-Agent Systems (MAS), and subsequently agent societies, whereby hundreds, thousands, or even hundreds of billions of agents co-operate amongst themselves to perform tasks, which are cumulatively much more complex.

These developments are potentially of the greatest significance for all realms including memory institutions (museums, libraries, and archives). Such institutions typically have great numbers of catalogues. The Vatican Library, for instance, had over eighty catalogues for its secret archive alone. As a result, every time a person wished to search for a new title they had to consult eighty books. If all the catalogues are in electronic form, agents can potentially collate all these names and titles such that a future user will need only to consult a single list in searching for a title.[84] More wide-ranging uses for agents will be considered below.

New Convergence

Convergence has been underway for a long time. Radio and television, which were once quite separate, are now dealt with under the umbrella of the International Telecommunications Union. High Definition Television (HDTV) has been a serious subject since 1972. Digital Television has been a topic since the early 1990s.[85] In the past five years, discussions of digital telephony and television have become almost synonymous with developments in Internet telephony and television.

Already in the 1980s major international publishers (Reed, now Reed-Elsevier, Thompson and Murdoch) were concerned with access to the entire communication cycle including satellites, book and newspaper publishing, and broadcasting (both terrestrial television and cable). The 1990s saw a gradual shift from Information Technologies (IT) to include Information and Communication Technologies (ICT).

As the images on both (high-resolution) computer monitors and High Definition Television (HDTV) screens became more defined, set top boxes blurred the distinctions between their functionality.

In a sense there were only a handful of major players on the global stage in 2000, namely, AOL Time Warner; Bertelsmann, News Corp, Viacom, Vivendi Universal, now GE-NBC, and Walt Disney Company,[86] and that number is decreasing. The merger of America Online (AOL) and Time Warner was no coincidence. Nor was Vivendi's acquisition of Universal or NBC's (i.e., General Electric's) acquisition of Vivendi-Universal in May 2004. The plans of Sony to acquire MGM, which became a reality in 2004 and the attempts of Comcast to buy Disney in 2004 are other examples of this trend. In June 2004 there were rumours that there could be a new merger of TimeWarner/CNN/CBS/Via-com to rival General Electric/NBC/Universal and Disney/ABC/Miramax.

The new convergence is pointing to a day when effectively all communications devices can communicate with one another, as every object potentially becomes "intelligent" and there will be ambient intelligence. Once we understand how this new convergence is also linked with a process of miniaturization, we shall understand why the technological consequences of networked computers are leading to invisibility.

3
miniaturization

By the year 2099: Even among those human
intelligences still using carbon-based neurons,
there is ubiquitous use of neural implant
technology, which provides enormous augmentation of human perceptual and cognitive
abilities. Humans who do not use such implants are unable to meaningfully participate
in dialogues with those who do.[1]
— Ray Kurzweil,
The Age of Spiritual Machines (1999)

1. Scale

By way of introduction, it is useful to get some further
bearings in terms of relative sizes at the miniature scale.
Most of us in Europe and Canada are familiar with the
upper limits of the metric system. We are used to dealing in centimetres, metres, and kilometres. A centimetre
is approximately the width of a pen. A millimetre is approximately the width of the lead in a pencil. Most of us
have heard of micrometres or microns (10^{-6}) and nanometres
(10^{-9}). Table 1 shows some smaller sizes. A human hair is
roughly 100,000 nanometres. Current work at the frontiers
of computers is happening roughly at the range of 25 to

50 nanometres, namely, 2,000–4,000 times smaller than a human hair. An angstrom (10^{-10}) is the approximate size of a few atoms strung together.

In May 2004, "a microscopic biped with legs just 10 nanometers long and fashioned from fragments of DNA" took its first steps.[2] The most advanced research is now attempting serious work at the level of 1 nanometre, 1/100,000 the size of a human hair or 1 billionth of a metre. Interventions at the levels of atoms are also occurring ever since researchers at IBM wrote the company name in individual atoms using electron tunnel microscopy. A project with Professor Kenneth Lacrosse at the University of Illinois reports that they are "working with chemists now who are designing molecules that, when attached, will act like transistors that can switch at 100 trillion times a second."[3]

2. Nanocomputing

As was mentioned earlier, developments in miniaturization are leading to the rapidly growing new fields of Micro-Electro-Mechanical Systems (MEMS)[4] and molecular electronics or molectronics. An article in Wired drew attention to the work of Jim Tour (Purdue University and Moletronics Electronics Company, MEC); of Ari Aviram (IBM, Watson) and related projects at Hewlett Packard and Mitre.[5] Joe Strout, in the Metalab at the University of North Carolina, provides an excellent survey of developments in this context, namely, protein-based, molecular, nano-, optical-, and quantum-computers.[6] The Mitre Corporation provides a more systematic overview in terms of four basic directions in nanotechnology, namely, i) electronic, ii) biochemical or organic; iii) mechanical, and iv) quantum.[7]

Electronic

In the early 1970s, two scientists, Ari Aviram and Mark Ratner, envisaged electronic circuit elements made from single molecules and described in detail how they might function. This led to a new field of molecular electronics, or molectronics, also called molecular-scale electronics.[8]

Quantum-dot Cellular Automata (QCA): Linked with these efforts of molectronics[9] is the quest for quantum dot cellular automata. A project at Notre Dame University, led by Dr. Marya Lieberman, has as its goal the production of a "logic device less than 50 nm on a side, with associated input and output structures."[10] What makes this project remarkable is that high-level computation could potentially occur without the electricity necessary in today's computers. This would remove the one remaining stumbling block in contemporary portable and mobile devices: the need for batteries.

Molecular Computing: The latest development, which does not yet have an official name, is dealing with computing at the level of single molecules. In December 1999, Professor Mark Reed (Yale) demonstrated a memory element the size of a single molecule, using a "self assembly" method.[11] Meanwhile, a California firm has developed a Chiropticene switch at the level of a single molecule, deriving its different states from spatial mirror images.[12]

Biochemical, DNA, or Organic

In August 2000, researchers at the Canadian National Research Centre used atoms and molecules to create "a self-assembling nanoscale wiring system by adding organic matter to silicon devices.... [T]his is the first hint of how we can go about building in a very controlled way nanostructures on surfaces."[13]

Protein-Based Computers: Strout has noted that bacteriorhodopsin,[14] a light-sensitive bacterial protein, has recently been applied to optical data storage and computing. Cubes of material can theoretically store nearly 100 trillion bits per cubic centimetre (compared to about 100 million bits per $cm^{\wedge 2}$ in two-dimensional media). This data can be read, written, and acted on in a highly parallel manner.[15] A new company, Engeneos, is developing "Engineered Genomic Operating Systems to enable the design and construction of programmable Biomolecular Machines employing natural and artificial building blocks" for commercial applications including biosensors, chemical synthesis and processing, bio-electronic devices and materials, nanotechnology, functional genomics, and drug discovery.[16]

Recent work is imitating the conditions of Boolean logic. In May 2001, for instance, Michael Simpson and his team at the Oak Ridge National Laboratory "modified the bacteria *Pseudomonas putida* to produce biological and or gates."[17]

DNA Computers: In addition to the above, there are also considerable efforts in the context of DNA computers.[18] Researchers are accessing data stored in life's instruction set by using strands of DNA to mimic the operations of microprocessor circuitry. At Stanford University, for example, graduate student, Daniel Shoemaker, is working on a gene chip developed by Affymetrix, a biotechnology firm based in Santa Clara, California. This chip: "can tell scientists which of thousands of genes are 'switched on' – or present in a cell – at any given time. From this information, researchers can understand how a cell, and subsequently an entire organism, changes when a gene is turned on."[19] This provides a new tool to diagnose illnesses.

Meanwhile, at the University of Rochester, New York, Animesh Ray,[20] a biologist working with computer scientist Mitsunori Ogihara, is building on the work of mathematician Leonard Adleman, who built the first DNA computer. Ray and his colleagues "have used a strand of DNA in a drop of water to successfully duplicate the binary logic operations of microcomputer chips." This rudimentary device uses nucleotides to perform functions typically handled by transistors in a silicon processor. They hope that this will result in a DNA computer, "a machine designed to perform the most complex computations."[21] DNA computing is rapidly becoming an important field[22] with centres in Harvard, Jerusalem, Leiden, and Japan.

Professor Richard Lipton (Georgia Tech and Telcordia), who invented a coding procedure for translating DNA base pairs into strings of ones and zeros, identifies three major incentives for DNA computation: 1) to compute more quickly (in moving from digital to digital); 2) to construct new objects (in moving from digital information to objects) and 3) in performing conversions (in moving from objects to digital).[23]

Cellular Neural Networks (CNN): Meanwhile, scientists such as Leon O. Chua (Berkeley) are working on cellular neural networks (CNN) with respect to applications in real-time image processing and neuromorphic modelling. This has led to a recently tested CNN Universal Chip, "a supercomputer on a chip with a potential capability of executing more than one tera [i.e., 1 trillion] instructions per second."[24] There is related work in France with scientists such as Patrick Thiran,[25] and others elsewhere.[26]

Mechanical and Optical

Strout draws attention to two further developments. One, based on the ideas of Eric Drexler,[27] entails mechanical computers at the molecular level with "a switch density of roughly 15 trillion switches per cubic centimeter in a CPU with a 1 GHz clock speed, processing about a billion instructions per second (1000 MIPS)." A second is "to build optical equivalents of transistors, the basic component of computers.... [T]he chief advantage is that such a computer can pass signals through each other without interference, allowing for much higher component density."[28]

Quantum Computers

Paul Benioff, of the Argonne National Laboratory, first applied quantum theory to computers in 1980[29] and David Deutsch of Oxford proposed quantum parallel computers in 1985.[30] That same year, the Nobel laureate physicist Richard Feynman also proposed a quantum computer.[31] Quantum computers are a futuristic dream that is coming ever closer to reality. For instance, in March 2001, scientists at Los Alamos Labs demonstrated a prototype with seven atoms. The significance of this seemingly small number has been noted by Jeffrey Harrow. Since each atom can do two calculations simultaneously, 2 atoms can do 4 calculations; 3 atoms can do 8; 4 atoms can do 16; 10 atoms can 1,024, and 40 atoms can do ten trillion calculations (a teraflop) simultaneously.[32] On 1 February, 2005, researchers at Hewlett Packard (HP) announced a breakthrough in the form of a "functioning 'crossbar latch'—an electronic switch that can flip a binary 0 to a 1 and vice versa, and preserve the output of that computation for use in subsequent ones—without using the electronic transistors that form the building blocks of today's computers."[33] Some claim that this breakthrough could replace the use of transistors.

Quantum Mirage: On 2 February 2000, researchers from IBM (Almaden) announced a new technique quantum mirage,[34] which may allow for transfer of information through nanoscale circuits without the use of wires. They call it "mirage" because they project information about one atom to another spot where there is no atom.

3. Nano-technology

The same bacteriorhodopsin that is being used in the context of protein-based computers outlined above is being explored with respect to intelligent materials. As Professor Felix Hong explained in a recent paper: "by allowing sensor/processor/ actuator capabilities to be packaged into a single molecule or a supramolecular cluster, avenues are open in the design of integrated information processing systems with massively parallel distributed processing capabilities."[35]

Such developments are the subject of a fascinating book by Dr. Michael Gross, *Travels to the Nanoworld: Miniature Machinery in Nature and Technology*.[36] What emerges from such descriptions is that fields such as biology and computing, which were completely separate fifty years ago, are becoming ever-more intimately interdependent. For example, British Telecom is working on brain-chip implants partly because "the workings of the human central nervous system can teach chip makers a thing or two about network efficiency."[37]

If all this sounds too close to the speculation of science fiction, it is sobering to recall that the University of North Carolina has developed a nano-manipulator which deals with objects of 1 micron [i.e., 10^{-6} or 0.000001 metre] on one side. Meanwhile, Pennsylvania State University has an Electronic Materials and Processing Research Laboratory, which is in turn part of a National Nanofabrication Users Network (Nanonet or NNUN)[38] that includes Cornell, Stanford, Howard University, and the University of California at Santa Barbara. In the past few years there have been increasing links between nanotechnology and medicine through the human genome project (cf. chapter 13).[39] A project at Berkeley called "smart dust" is concerned with autonomous sensing and communication in a cubic millimetre.[40] In March 2004, Mind Game demonstrated the use of brainwaves for video games.[41] There is now a Foresight Institute with a goal: "to guide emerging technologies to improve the human condition. Foresight focuses its efforts upon nanotechnology, the coming ability to build materials and products with atomic precision, and upon systems that will enhance knowledge exchange and critical discussion, thus improving public and private policy decisions."[42]

4. Interfaces

All these developments will have profound effects on the future of interfaces, a field which is being developed by the Special Interest Group for Computer Human Interface (SIG CHI) of the Association of Computing Machinery (ACM), by the Advanced Visual Interfaces (AVI) Group and by a series of projects on Intelligent Information Interfaces (I^3 or I cube) sponsored by the European Commission. Many of us are aware of a trend away from graphical user interfaces (GUIs) to tangible user interfaces (TUIs) as explored by Professor Hiroshi Ishii at the Things that Think Lab at MIT or perceptual user interfaces (PUIs) as championed by Matthew Turk (UCSB). Companies such as Vision Control Systems[43] are exploring the potentials of eye-tracking. A number of other adaptive interfaces for (dis-)abilities (access) are

TABLE 6   Sizes of structures in the nervous system based on Posner (1989).[65]

0.001mm	10^{-6}	SYNAPSES	tip of a connection between neurons
0.1 mm	10^{-4}	NEURONS	brain cell
1 mm	10^{-3}	LOCAL CIRCUITS	small networks of cells
10 mm	10^{-2}	MAPS	spatially organized topographic maps
100 mm	10^{-1}	SYSTEMS	e.g., the visual system
1,000 mm	10^{1}	CENTRAL NERVOUS SYSTEM	including spinal cord

being explored at the Trace Center (Madison, Wisconsin),[44] and the International Center for Disability Resources on the Internet (ICDRI)[45] and are being integrated within the vision of the W3 Consortium. There are also alternative human web interaction systems,[46] such as those of Solutions Matrix,[47] or Reality Fusion,[48] which involve interacting on screen with one's body using video cameras.

Speech recognition and voice activated interfaces are becoming ever-more popular.[49] Lucent and HP are working on Elemedia.[50] Nortel is working on CallPilot, a unified messaging system featuring speech recognition, which will integrate with a variety of e-mail systems and Private Branch eXchanges (PBXs). Mitre has a project led by David House.[51] Among the ESPRIT Long Term Projects 2000, there is Speech Recognition Algorithms for Connectionist Hybrids (SPRACH)[52] led by Dr. Hervé Bourlard.

Speech and gesture combined are the theme of Natural Interactivity in IBM's Visualization Space.[53] Gesture recognition is being explored by Jakub Segen,[54] in the Perseus[55] project. Ever since CHI 95[56] there have been an increasing number of individuals[57] and tools[58] in this area. There is also work on gesture and movement[59] as well as on gesture and sound.[60] There is work on communication by gaze interaction.[61] These developments make the data gloves and suits of early virtual reality look rather primitive.

Meanwhile, a number of projects are exploring direct brain control. In Germany, the main work is being done at the Nordstadt Krankenhaus in Hanover,[62] the Fraunhofer Institut für Biomedizinische Technik (IBMT) in St. Ingbert and the Naturwissenschaftlich-Medizinisches Institut (NMI) at the University of Tübingen (Reutlingen campus). In Japan, Hidenori Onishi[63] of Technos and the Himeji Institute of Technology has a Mind Control Tool Operating System (MCTOS). The Joint Research Centre (JRC) the European Commission is working on adaptive brain interfaces.[64]

In the United States, Masahiro Kahata in New York has developed an Interactive Brainwave Visual Analyser (IBVA).[66] Dr. Grant McMillan,[67] director of the Alternative Control Technology Laboratory at Wright Patterson Airforce Base is exploring navigation using brain waves, namely, Alpha, Beta, Theta, Delta, and Mu, for mental (hands-off) control of flight simulators and has noted that "All control is brain-actuated control, as far as we know. All we're doing is measuring the output at a different point." He predicts that within thirty years pilots will operate their control sticks simply by manipulating their brain activity.[68] In 2004 the frontiers of the field such as the Donoghue Lab allow monkeys with implants to control robotic arms and patients with a braingate interface to control computer cursors with their thoughts. A conservative estimate of those implications was recently offered by Bell Labs:

> Software-driven intelligent networks and wireless technology will enable people to be reached wherever they are and will give the consumer the power to choose if a message will be an e-mail, voice mail or video clip.... By 2025 you'll be wired into a global communications network through devices as small as a lapel pin.... The small metaphones on your lapel will be able to read Web sites and e-mail to you. What's more ... that global network will be more like a "communications skin" capable of sensing everything from weather patterns to how much milk is in your refrigerator.... The "skin" will include millions of electronic measuring devices — thermostats, pressure gauges, pollution detectors, cameras, micro-phones — all monitoring cities, roadways, and the environment.[69]

5. Animal Robots and Implants

Some of the earliest work on implants in dogs goes back to H. S. Levert (1829). In the twentieth century, robots were often clunky equivalents of earlier Frankenstein monsters. We begin to appreciate how dramatic are the implications of these trends towards miniaturization with nanotechnology when we realize that there are now robots that look like ordinary butterflies. The natural and mechanical worlds are no longer distinguishable to the untrained eye.

Meanwhile, in the animal world, computers are getting under the skin. The sea otters in Monterey Bay in California all have a tiny microchip and their IDs are catalogued in a computer database: "The chip, a powerless device the size of a grain of rice, is injected under the animal's skin with a special syringe. Each chip is programmed with a distinctive ID number that can be read using a scanner. The number is linked to a database containing information about each animal.... The goal is to microchip all animals."[70]

More complex chips are also being developed. Mike Maher (1995), then at the Pine Lab on Living Neural Networks at the California Institute of Technology (Caltech), was working on technology: "to chronically interface neurons with electronics, to help determine how biological neural networks operate." They do this by putting "immature neurons into small wells etched into a silicon substrate. Each well has an electrode attached to external electronics, to record the activity of the neuron and to provide a means of stimulation."[71]

6. Human Implants

The author of the article on animal implants cited earlier claims that "within the next decade, human implants are almost certain to become available, too."[72] Not many of us are aware of how much work is being done in this field.[73] By way of orientation it is again useful to remind ourselves of the scale involved, as outlined by Posner, in his *Foundations of Cognitive Science* (Table 6). The sizes in the nervous system are relatively large when compared to those at the frontiers of nanotechnology considered above. Nonetheless, as Professor Strout has pointed out, there are approximately 100,000 (10^5) neurons and 1,000,000,000 (10^9) synapses per cubic millimetre and "a typical brain cell receives inputs from thousands of other cells, and the influence of each connection is 1–5% of threshold – that is, only 1–5% of what the cell needs to respond."[74]

Gazzaniga's *New Cognitive Neurosciences*[75] gives an excellent survey of the field. Some idea of the enormous activity in this field is provided by the Neuroscience Virtual Library maintained by Cornell University.[76] There are important centres for cognitive neuroscience[77] at Duke University and Dartmouth College.[78] There is a Society for Neuroscience[79] and a Cognitive Neuroscience Society.[80] There is an Organization for Human Brain Mapping (OHBM)[81] and a Website of Recent Neuroscience (WREN).[82] There is an important database for neurosciences on the Internet (neuroguide.com) with mirror sites in Freiburg,[83] Glasgow, and Pittsburgh.

The Program in Computation and Neural Systems (CNS) at Caltech,[84] is particularly active in this area, with research in areas such as computational biology, computer graphics, developmental neurobiology, neuromorphic engineering, information coding and network dynamics in brain local circuits, learning systems, living neural networks, molecular neurobiology, molecular neuroscience, neuroethology, neurophysiology of vision, and optical information processing. An additional reason for this intense activity is due to a new field called "neuromorphic engineering," which seeks:

> … to understand how the brain computes so effectively, using six orders of magnitude less energy than human-engineered computers.… On the scientific side, electronic VLSI [Very Large Scale System Integration], based on the structure and function of the nervous system, are built to test hypotheses about how the brain works, and are analyzed to understand the tradeoffs involved in the brain's design. Since these tradeoffs arise from physical limitations, they can only be understood in the context of real physical models; the abstract models used in computer simulations shed no light on these issues.… On the engineering side, our understanding of these tradeoffs is used to synthesize more effective and energy-efficient computer designs for performing bio-morphic tasks, such as dynamic prediction and self-organization, real-time sensory-motor control, adaptive sensing and multimodal associative learning.[85]

The Living Neural Networks Lab at Caltech mentioned above, led by Professor Jerome Pine, has "developed a number of new technologies for studying neural systems. Examples include an x-ray microscope for living cells, multi-electrode cell culture chambers, fiber-optic photodiode arrays and high-speed CCD cameras for imaging of neural activity, and silicon probes for long-term interfacing of neural tissue with external electronics."[86] This lab has also developed a neurochip implanted into a fetal rat. This research entails very detailed study of different receptors and the insertion of synthetic neurons into living tissue. Also at Caltech is the Human Brain Project,[87] which includes the GEneral NEural SImulation System (GENESIS) project.[88]

This research is heading directly toward a new reality-simulation loop (cf. chapter 4.6), with one fundamental difference, that this involves living beings. Related is the work of Dr. Dick Normann (Richard Normann) and Dr. Christopher Gallen[89] on future brain implants in human beings, which was the subject of a film by the BBC: *Future Fantastic*. There is serious work on controlling computers with neural signals.[90] These problems are being studied at the Human Systems Information Analysis Center[91] and are related to the emerging fields of bio-communications and bio-cybernetics through scientists like Richard L. McKinley[92] They have also inspired more speculative books such as William Ickes' *Empathic Accuracy*.[93] Sensationist ideas of cyborgs have been popularized by individuals such as Kevin Warwick.[94]

While sceptics emphasize the magnitude of the practical hurdles that need to be overcome for brain implants to become a reality and continue to discuss this topic as if it were merely science fiction, it is important to note that there is a growing community which views human implants as a very real possibility. For instance, Professor Melody Moore (Georgia Tech State) outlined emerging possibilities at a conference on assistive technologies (November 2000). She described a: "neurotrophic electrode, which is about the size of the head of a ballpoint pen, and is designed to be directly inserted into a brain so it can interface with neurons. It's connected to a tiny amplifier and transmitter, which are inserted closer to the surface of the skin, just under the scalp. Also present is a small power source that allows wireless transmission of the signals to a nearby computer."[95]

Meanwhile, Peter Cochrane, who was the head of research at British Telecom, sees the merging of machine and organism as merely an extension of the evolutionary process. He initiated work on a Soul Catcher that "seeks to develop a computer that can be implanted in the brain to complement human memory and computational skills" and enable gathering of "data transmitted by wireless networking."[96]

It is not surprising that the military is also exploring the implications of such technologies for wartime situations. Manuel De Landa discusses the military's developments in such implant technologies under "wetware" in his book *War in the Age of the Intelligent Machine*.[97] The U.S. Airforce also has a vision for the year 2025, which was outlined in a report on *Information Operations: A New War-Fighting Capability* (1996).[98]

TABLE 7 Technology areas versus cyber-situation components in the U.S. Airforce 2025 report.

TECHNOLOGY AREAS

Cyber Situation Component	Collection Platform	Communications Infrastructure	Computing Power	Intelligent Software	Human Systems & Biotechnology
All Source Information Collectors	x	x	x	x	
Archival Databases	x	x			
Information Integration Centre (IIC)		x	x	x	x
Implanted Microscopic Chip		x	x	x	x
Lethal & Non-Lethal Weapons		x	x		

The authors explore a Cyber situation resulting from a nexus of five basic technologies: 1) collection platform, 2) communications infrastructure, 3) computing power, 4) intelligent software, and 5) human systems and biotechnology (Table 7). This is convergence at a higher level.[99]

The report gives reasons why an implanted microscopic chip is preferable to other methods such as specially configured rooms, helmets, or sunglasses, which could be employed to interface the user with an Information Integration Centre. The authors claim that such chips would a) eliminate biased inputs from one person to another; b) eliminate need for a mental picture based on another's biases; and c) be able to query for further information and receive in-time answers. It would be complemented by a decision support tool in transmitter and receiver to filter, sort, and prioritize information, which prompts a user concerning significant events for monitoring and action.

While acknowledging that the chip raises some ethical and public relations questions, the authors note that the public already uses mechanical hearts and other organs. By 2025, it is possible that there will be nerve chips that allow amputees to control artificial limbs and eye chips that allow the blind to see. The authors conclude that the military "will freely accept the chip because it is a tool to control technology and not as a tool to control the human [sic!]."[100]

Slightly more low key but very upbeat, nonetheless, is an another visionary document for the year 2020 in the realm of manufacturing: "Advances in the control of processes and microstructures at submicron scales and the analysis and unlocking of the chemical and biological secrets of nature will have an overwhelming effect on the future understanding of processes and chemical makeup. This will lead to new and exciting ways to manufacture, clone, grow, and fabricate a vast array of products."[101]

7. Brain Control

While the above scenarios represent control in cases of survival in war, others are exploring the implications of such chips in peacetime situations. There is talk of an *IBM 2020 Neural Chip Implant*. Experiments with live prisoners are said to have occurred in 1994 and contracts are said to have been signed with the U.S. government for widespread adoption of the technology in 2020. Patents for related technologies have been filed.[102] Such research can also be guided by good intentions. For example, Dr. Michael Persinger, a psychologist and neuroscientist at Laurentian University (Ontario), has been working on a brain entertainment device and has discovered that:

> … when he aims for the amygdala, his subjects experience sexual arousal. When he focuses the solenoids on the right hemisphere of their temporal lobes, they sense on the left side of their body a negative presence — an alien or a devil, say. When he switches to left hemisphere, his subjects sense a benevolent force: an angel or a god.
>
> Focused on the hippocampus, the personal electromagnetic relaxation device will produce the sort of opiate effects that Ecstasy does today. So far, subjects report no adverse side effects. However, "if you interfere with the opiate pattern, people get very irritated," Persinger says. In fact, "they'll actually cuss you out."[103]

The area of mind control is, of course, nothing new. It is a theme in Huxley's *Brave New World/Revisited* and recent movies such as *Visitor* and *Control Factor*. It is a well-established field linked with the professional study of propaganda, dis-information, psycho-logical and psycho-tronic warfare.[104] Those interested in this subject are referred to the Mind Control Forum.[105] Some of the emerging possibilities make discussions of Big Brother look rather primitive. There is, for instance, a new mind control technology known as a "Frequency Fence" which "is a bio-neurological, electromagnetic induced form of mind control which will block your higher sensory abilities."

By 2006 we are told that there will be holographic inserts whereby "three-dimensional reality can be artificially manufactured and inserted right over your present reality scene in a seamless fashion so you will be unable to determine where organic reality ends, and manipulated, artificial reality begins."[106] This throws a new light on so-called science fiction in Schwarzenegger films such as *Total Recall*.

As is often the case with subjects of central importance to humanity, some of the items on such sites entail opinions from individuals at the fringes of rational discourse. Others are very serious indeed. For our purposes we shall cite two further examples.

8. Human Uploads and Downloads

In 1963, Robert White at the Cleveland Medical Hospital successfully transplanted a living head from one ape to another.[107] Joe Strout,[108] a scientist at the Salk Institute, has a web site on Mind Uploading "dedicated to the putative future process of copying one's mind from the natural substrate of the brain into an artificial one, manufactured by humans," specifically addressing "the science behind the science fiction!" The site opens with some introductory facts concerning neuroscience and then outlines four basic mind uploading procedures: 1) microtome, 2) nanoreplacement, 3) Moravec, and 4) nondestructive procedures, which include: gamma-ray holography, X-ray holography, MRI (Magnetic Resonance Imaging), biphoton interferometry, and correlation mapping. The relative merits of these alternatives are discussed.

This leads to an important section on philosophy which addresses the questions: What is life? What is a person? and "personal identity: the central issue."[109] The site distinguishes between virtual reality and artificial reality,[110] discusses artificial bodies,[111] acknowledges that this raises "a host of policy issues," and thus proposes a policy for artificial realities.[112] This leads to sections on brain enhancements, deletions from the brain, memory alterations, and mind-probing technologies.[113]

Lest one be tempted to dismiss the above as the opinions of an eccentric out of touch with real science, it is sobering to compare them with the ideas of one of the fathers of the human genome projects, the Nobel Prize-winning chemist Kary Mullis, who speaks about "our evolutionary right to invent ourselves."[114] Films such as *Freejack* (1992) have explored these possibilities very vividly.

9. Transhumanism

All this is leading to new fields such as bionics,[115] ideas of increasing the individual (the idea of superman at a new level)[116] and transhumanism, which rejects "the assumption that the 'human condition' is at root a constant."[117] Where this could lead is outlined by Nick Bostrom,[118] now at the Department of Philosophy in Oxford. While admitting that some of the possibilities are "quite extreme and sound like science-fiction," Bostrom considers ten rather dramatic scenarios: 1) super-intelligent machines, 2) lifelong emotional well-being through re-calibration of the pleasure-centres, 3) personality pills, 4) space colonization, 5) molecular nanotechnology, 6) vastly extended life spans, 7) extinction of intelligent life,[119] 8) the interconnected world (a new level of Internet), 9) uploading of our consciousness into a virtual reality, and 10) reanimation of cryogenically suspended patients.[120] All this sounds like something from an Austin Powers film. Indeed, when I first encountered the above claims there was a temptation to dismiss them as the musings of a proverbial "mad professor." Since then I have learned that there is a World Transhumanist Association (WTA), the home page of which reads like a new utopian manifesto:

> Transhumanism advocates the use of technology to overcome our biological limitations and transform the human condition. At the present time or in the near future, human capabilities will be extended through such means as genetic engineering, memory-enhancing drugs, collaborative information-filtering, smart agents, intelligence amplification, wearable computers, and the Internet. In the slightly longer term, the accelerating pace of technological development opens up such revolutionary prospects as superhuman artificial intelligence and molecular nanotechnology. The consequences of these developments may include: the abolition of disease; the elimination of aging; the enrichment of our reward-centers so we enjoy a wider diversity of emotions, exhilarating peak experiences and life-long well-being; and perhaps the gradual replacement of human bodies with synthetic enhancements. Or by contrast, it could mean that intelligent life goes extinct, maybe as the result of an accidental or deliberate misuse of powerful weapons technologies such as self-replicating nanomachine viruses. These are extreme possibilities. Yet they are taken seriously by an increasing number of scientists and scientifically-literate philosophers.[121]

There are local groups in Britain, Germany, the Netherlands, Sweden, and the United States.[122] There is a *Journal of Transhumanism*, there are conferences, mailing lists, newsgroups, and newsletters. All this is still futuristic. Meanwhile, in the very near future, Alan Ganek (IBM), predicts the advent of designer drugs, whereby a doctor takes: "a drop of blood and using biochips it analyses you, your genetic makeup, medical history; then a drug is manufactured on the spot, unique to you, for your situation, age and weight."[123] Monash University in Australia has a project *DesignDrug@Home* now renamed the Virtual Laboratory.[124] For 2010, the Starlab (now defunct) predicted "customized medicine based on our individual genetic makeup. Genes will be used as a form of identification."[125]

10. Implications

Five thousand years ago, the advent of cuneiform writing brought a revolution because knowledge could be recorded on stone tablets. This extended human memory, but left it hardly portable. The advent of parchment meant that one could carry a few bundles of knowledge. Books meant that one could carry a handful of tomes. The advent of CD-ROMs meant that one could carry thousands of volumes, while being able to access only a few at a time. A new technique at Keele University allows 3.4 terabits of memory within the surface area of a credit card. This means that one can theoretically include all the contents of the British Library on a single chip.[126] The advent of nano-computing such as DNA means that a single gram of DNA can contain the contents of 1 trillion CD-ROMs.[127] For the first time in history a person will be able carry all the knowledge of the great libraries, museums, and archives on their person and thus have access to any bit of knowledge, anywhere, at any time. Nano-computing gives a new sense to the old song: "I've got the whole world in my hands." Ironically, we have spent the past half-century focussing on networks to gain access to repositories of knowledge, only to find ourselves discovering ways to store knowledge without networks. The future role of networks may lie mainly in updating our personal repositories and in sharing our knowledge.

Some thirty-five years ago when Robert Ettinger, the founder of cryogenics began writing on this theme, the possibilities seemed largely, some thought exclusively, in the realm of science fiction. The film *Fantastic Voyage* (1966),[128] which described a trip through the bloodstream of a human being, seemed a brilliant example of science fiction at the time. Given the trends in miniaturization, this could become reality within two decades. Ray Kurzweil, in a keynote at Siggraph 2000, claimed that: "progress will eventually allow machines to reach the human level of intelligence, with 20 billion billion-operation/second performance available for $1,000 in 2020. That will let people send nanobots – tiny micro-electromechanical systems – through the bloodstream to reach nerve endings, where they will switch off physical signals and switch on 'virtual environment' signals so that humans can inhabit worlds limited only by their imaginations."[129]

Meanwhile, the September 2000 edition of *Wired* described a project already underway to construct a machine that navigates through the bloodstream. In Israel a "video pill" is being developed, which will allow photos from inside the digestive system.[130] In November 2000, a team at Cornell University demonstrated a microscopic helicopter, with a size of 80 billionths of a metre, which could one day serve as a nano-nurse.[131] This is significant because it marks the first biomolecular motor and as such blurs the distinction between mechanical objects and living organisms.[132]

One of the unexpected spinoffs of developments in quantum computing is the concept of quantum teleportation, namely "the feat of making an object or person disintegrate in one place while a perfect replica appears somewhere else."[133] In 1993, "an international group of six scientists, including IBM Fellow Charles H. Bennett, confirmed the intuitions of the majority of science fiction writers by showing that perfect teleportation is indeed possible in principle, but only if the original is destroyed."[134] This means that the teleportation part of the so-called science fiction of Michael Crichton's *Timeline* (2000)[135] is potentially true. In this context, it is fascinating that Timothy Leary, often remembered for his experiments with the use of psychedelic drugs in the 1960s, also founded Foutique (1983), which developed computer programs:

... designed to empower individuals to digitize their thought-images and create new realities on the other side of their screens.... Mind Mirror allows the performer to digitize (scope) any thought, compare it with other thoughts, and compare thoughts with others, and to engage in simulation of various roles.... Head Coach ... allows 'performers' to decipher their own thoughts and translate them into digital code for clear communication to others. Head Coach allows performers to build up digital representations of their minds. Important concepts become mental files that can be continually revised and, when desired, shared with others.[136]

Leary's company also developed an electronic version of *Neuromancer*, which was subsequently developed by Interplay,[137] a company with numerous such games. Hence, long before visions of mind-jacking in *Strange Days* (1995) and dramatic visions of global mind control by use of thought waves,[138] or the embedded chips discussed in this chapter, Timothy Leary was working towards wireless communication of thoughts between individuals. From all this emerges a first consequence of networked computers, namely invisibility.

Hereby, classical distinctions between an organic world of nature and the mechanical world of man-made machines are also disappearing. The two realms are becoming part of a single emerging frontier, which is reflected in a family of new terms. A generation ago we had engineering, robotics, communications, and cybernetics. Today we have bio-engineering, bio-robotics, bio-communications, and bio-cybernetics. We also have the prefixes "neuro-" and "nano" for the same terms which are appearing together as if they were part of some new combinatorial game: e.g., bio-nano-robotics. Rick Satava (University of Washington, Seattle) sees an increasing interplay of the Biological, Physical and Information domains and speaks of the Biointelligence Age as the successor to the Information Age. Nik Baerten (Maastricht) goes further to claim that organicism is now becoming a basic metaphor to explain advances in the both the living and the mechanical realms. If the Renaissance hailed the rise of the mechanistic world picture, the twenty-first century heralds the rise of an organic world picture that embraces rather than replaces earlier mechanical achievements.

In the past decades, roughly a dozen thinkers have greatly expanded our understanding of these developments (Appendix 8).[139] Some are now searching for a biological basis of spirituality.[140] No one fully understands the implications of such nanotechnology for human communication and for the human condition. Consideration of the ethical and philosophical implications alone could readily lead to numerous volumes. Already in the mid-1980s, futurists (e.g., Drexler) were warning that there are many dangers with these visions. These were taken up anew in an article by Bill Joy just before he left Sun[141] and in books by Jeremy Rifkin on *The Biotech Century*[142] and *The Age of Access* (cf. chapters 13–15, below).

Meanwhile, some would note that the difficulties of building such systems must not be underestimated. Many single technologies exist but putting them all together sensibly remains a major challenge. According to this view, visionaries such as Kurzweil are simply too optimistic in their convictions about what machines can reasonably do. The road to invisible computing is still littered with very visible obstacles. Even so, nanotechnology is transforming the connotations of Blake's phrase of "seeing infinity in a grain of sand."

PART II

material
consequences:
VIRTUALITY

4
production

An envisioning laboratory could simulate
the impact of a new product before it is
actually built.
— John Seely Brown,
HBR on Knowledge Management
(1997, p. 173)[1]

1. Introduction

Superficially the objects of production look the same as fifty
years ago. The cars, lamps, books, and other objects that we
buy today still look so much like their predecessors that most
of us are unaware how the new media are transforming the
nature of production in at least seven ways: 1) production is
becoming distributed, 2) there are networks for all stages of
production, 3) design is on-line, 4) there are new production
and supply chains, 5) virtuality has new meanings, 6) the
nature of work is changing, and 7) agents play new roles.

The growing emphasis on a global infrastructure for
manufacturing and production could make production the

same everywhere, such that cars in the United States are exactly the same as cars in Europe or Asia. Different visions of the world make this unlikely. Should systems be proprietary or open? Can agents replace humans entirely or should they be relegated to an ancillary role? We shall suggest that competing visions offer different answers to such questions: one vision is for an information highway (United States); another for an information society (Europe), and a third for a knowledge society (Japan). Later, we shall show that these competing visions ultimately affect much more than production.

2. Distributed Production

In the past, production was a physical process in a fixed place. Hence, cities such as Wolfsburg (Volkswagen) and Detroit (Ford, General Motors), where steel was readily available through nearby mines and foundries, became famous for their production of automobiles. As cars became more complex, they often needed parts, which were not available locally. Gradually, these parts came from all over the world and became so numerous that the place of production remained little more than an assembly place for parts. A Volkswagen in Wolfsburg is likely to have parts from America, Japan, Korea, and other countries. Hence, parts lists and product catalogues are now available globally. This is transforming patterns of sales and buying (cf. chapter 5).

3. Networks

Within the United States, there are a number of networks devoted specifically to manufacturing. One of the earliest was the National Information Infrastructure (NII), with a subtitle that is often forgotten: for Industry with Special Attention to Manufacturing,[2] which included the Multidisciplinary Analysis and Design Industrial Consortium (MADIC).[3] There is a National Center for Manufacturing Sciences.[4] The U.S. government's Sandia Labs has a project on Integrated Manufacturing.[5]

The manufacturing world has seen important developments towards globalization. There is, for instance, a Global Engineering Network (GEN),[6] initiated by companies such as Siemens, which seeks to coordinate all the basic laws and processes of engineering. Parallel with this, Autodesk has led a consortium called the International Alliance for Interoperability (IAI), concerned with establishing Industry Foundation Classes (see below).[7] Another project aims at Universal Access to Engineering Documents.[8] Competing automotive consortia[9] are combining into a new global consortium called Covisint with co-opetiton (i.e., co-operation plus competition) among leading firms. At the research level there are plans for a Global Terabit Research and Education Network (GTREN).

4. Design

Traditionally, design involved physical models and prototypes. Now, design increasingly entails virtuality[10] and simulation. In the past, a designer or a small team worked secretively on a new model of a car. Now teams of designers, often in different countries, are working together in virtual environments. Since the early 1990s, there have been experiments involving collaborative design.[11] Architecture was once about designing buildings. It is now becoming a process, which includes marketing research, concept design and development, prototype, testing, validating, and planning.

During the 1990s individual projects were evolving in semi-isolation around the world. For instance, the University of Maryland, College Park, was working on a System for Computer-Aided Manufacturability Analysis (IMACS) to: "determine whether or not the design attributes (e.g., shape, dimensions, tolerances, surface finishes) can be achieved. If the design is found to be manufacturable, determine a *manufacturability rating*, to reflect the ease (or difficulty) with which the design can be manufactured."[12]

All this needs to be seen in the context of a larger move towards control at a distance. Speaking of a second industrial revolution at the 1996 CEBIT fair, Michael Rogowski[13] described tele-design as one element in a tele-revolution which includes: tele-construction, tele-system engineering, tele-manufacturing, and tele-service.[14] Since then, there has been a dramatic trend towards a global approach. For example, meetings among members of the U.S. building industry in 1994 led to an alliance as a public organization in September 1995 and to a formal, global organization in May 1996, which was renamed as the International Alliance for Interoperability (IAI) based in Oakton, Virginia: "Its mission is to define, publish and promote specifications for Industry Foundation Classes (IFC) as a basis for project information sharing in the building industry (architecture, engineering, construction, and facilities-management). The information sharing is world-wide, throughout the project life cycle, and across all disciplines and technical applications."[15]

One of the key players in this consortium is Autodesk. Inherent in their Industry Foundation Classes (IFC)[16] is a quest to catalogue key technical characteristics of building blocks of architecture such as windows, doors, etc., defining in each case the characteristics pertinent to a given context, to produce so-called intelligent parts. Hence, if one is building a cottage, the program immediately "knows" the appropriate windows and doors for a cottage. If one is designing a skyscraper, the program automatically "knows" that different windows and doors are required. A challenge lies in linking these generic solutions with specific cultural and historical examples to avoid the dangers of what Barber has called a Mac World effect[17] (cf. chapter 14).

The scope of Industry Foundation Classes goes far beyond architecture. It includes building services, civil engineering, construction management, codes and standards, estimating, facilities management, structural engineering, project management, and cross-domain projects such as referencing external libraries, 2D drawing links and performance attributes of materials. One of the incentives for such a vast enterprise was a report, which claimed that use of new technologies could bring savings of up to 30 per cent for building projects.[18]

Industry Foundation Classes are one important initiative on this front. Uniclass is another. The British BOW and ARROWS project combines both of these methods. Herein, a Building Objects Warehouse (BOW) serves as a virtual warehouse system with required tools and services to allow interaction between a user and Advanced Reusable Reliable Objects Warehouses (ARROWs), as distributed object libraries (databases) created, populated, and maintained by information providers, e.g., manufacturers:

> The BOW system will allow designers, specifiers and facility managers to select building components that are right for their task and to check against manufactured components in order that contractors can buy components which actually fit and perform to specifications.... The concept of intelligent objects is employed as a novel means for storing, using and re-using data and information about products and or components used within the building and construction industry. Intelligent Objects (IOs), know what they are, what their pedigree is, who produced them, what their primary usage/purpose is, what their attributes/ properties are, what they look like, and how they should present themselves in different environments.[19]

To achieve its goal, the BOW and ARROWS project is consciously building not only on the International Alliance for Interoperability (IAI), but also on a European Union project[20] called Computer Models for Building Industry in Europe (COMBINE), which has sections for managers, designers, energy and lighting. It also uses the ISO Standard (ISO 10303) for the Exchange of Product Model Data (STEP).[21] This comprehensive standard describes how to represent and exchange digital product information: "to cover a product's entire life cycle, from design to analysis, manufacture, quality-control testing, inspection and product support functions. In order to do this, STEP must cover geometry, topology, tolerances, re-lationships, attributes, assemblies, configuration and more."[22] The first twenty-nine parts of this standard were presented at the beginning of 2000.[23] STEP, in turn, is but one of four sections under the aegis of the Developers of International Industrial Data Standards (ISO TC184/SC4): product data, manufacturing management data, oil and gas automation systems and a parts library.[24]

Projects such as STEP are changing fundamentally the nature of design and the whole production process. In the past, designers made small-scale physical models before proceeding to full-scale physical versions. Now the preliminary models are virtual. A generation ago one spoke of the four Cs: Computer Aided Design (CAD), Computer Aided Engineering (CAE), Computer Aided Manufacturing (CAM), and Computer Integrated Manufacturing (CIM).[25] Now these are increasingly aspects of a much bigger picture where the examples are from databases all around the world.

There are new production and supply chains linking everything. As we shall see later, this is transforming interactions of virtual and real objects.

At the micro-level, the past decades have seen the rise of Advanced Systems and Integrated Circuits (ASICS). The design thereof typically entailed Libraries of Advanced Systems and Integrated Circuits (ASICS Libraries). With increasing miniaturization companies such as ST Microelectronics (Grenoble) are effectively creating dynamic libraries almost on the fly, including all the constraints dynamically. Thereby design becomes global and closer to being fully customized. One of the intriguing results thereof is that designers are increasingly able to decide during the design process whether to produce a component as material hardware or as immaterial software.[26] Hence, this is a new area where the distinctions between physical and virtual are becoming conflated.

5. Production and Supply Chains

These developments are leading to visions that one can document every step of the production and supply chains, through methods such as Product Lifecycle Management (PLM) and Manufacturing Resource Planning (MRP[27]) systems: "When the manufacturing data has been collected (parts, assemblies, resources) the lead time and cost of every component can be predicted under any manufacturing conditions. As soon as an order is received the workload on the manufacturing organization and the delivery time can be calculated." These MRP systems also allow tracking of customers, suppliers, accounting functions, just in time inventory and inefficiencies in the production line.[28] Such systems have benefited from recent developments in Visual Inventory Control.[29] Closely related are Enterprise Resource Planning (ERP), and Supply Chain Management (SCM) systems:

> Supply-chain management applications execute corporate operations such as managing warehouses, inventory supplies and distribution channels. There are two types of software: execution and planning. Execution applications track the storage and movement of products. They also track the management of materials, information and financial data among suppliers, manufacturers, distributors and customers. Planning applications, also known as optimization software, use advanced algorithms to find the best way to fill an order based on set operation constraints. For example, a planning application can be used to decide how to fill an unexpected large order.[30]

The above definition is from PriceWaterhouseCoopers, which could seem surprising until one recognizes that the financial assessment activities of major brokerage firms (and banks) are increasingly becoming fully intertwined with these new systems that assess the life cycles of employees, processes and products. This explains why PriceWaterhouseCoopers has technology assessment centres and why it co-operates with theoretical competitors such as Ernst and Young in these domains (chapter 5.13).

They are not alone. The Agile Manufacturing Integrators and Implementors, Inc.[31] has recognized how this is extending e-commerce into automated technologies for production, and trading partners for supply chains or Business to Business Material Requirements Planning (B2B–MRP™): "The emerging Internet supply chain software will extend MRP across the supply chain, exploding dependent demands and balancing them against supplies in real-time. The suggested planning actions will be delivered to planners across a network of locations and companies through a simple, browser based interface."[32]

In 2000, Agile Manufacturing was partnered with Logistical Software, which was developing a Supply Chain Action Network™ (SCAN)[33] This promised to link an "equipment manufacturer, a contract electronics manufacturer, a component manufacturer and a component distributor."[34] It promised to extend traditional Enterprise Resource Planning (ERP) systems, from the inputs to the manufacturing process (cf. Bill of Material) to include process and output to result in fast, new products.[35] Not all promises are fulfilled. In 2004, SCAN had disappeared as quickly as it came and there are new promises such as Agile Product Lifecycle Management (Agile PLM).

In 2004, the European Commission supported a Consortium to lead Grid Technology for Product Development and Production Process Design (SIMDAT), "which aims to test and enhance grid technology for product development and production process design as well as to develop federated versions of problem-solving environments by leveraging enhanced Grid services."[36]

The Consortium for Advanced Manufacturing International (CAM-I) has an even larger view of Next Generation Enterprises (NGE): "Lean enterprises will focus on selected markets by exploiting their high value, core competencies. Virtual enterprises (alliances formed dynamically from networks of real companies) will merge core competencies to produce complex products and systems."[37] In this vision, Agile Manufacturing is but one ingredient in a much larger trend. It is not surprising, therefore that the Consortium for Advanced Manufacturing – International (Cam-I), has a project on Autonomous Distributed, Biological, Fractal, and Agile Manufacturing Systems to enhance the enterprise of the future,[38] which in turn is linked with a truly global vision of the Intelligent Manufacturing Systems (IMS) Initiative.

6. Virtuality

Closely connected with this emerging global vision is a new approach to virtuality, i.e., relations between the virtual and the real. The idea of Virtual Reality (VR) goes back to the pioneering work of Sutherland (1967),[39] Furness,[40] and Krueger (1983),[41] but did not gain popularity until a team at NASA including Warren Robinett, Scott Fisher and Stephen Ellis linked the 3-D glasses and the data glove for the first time

(1986) inexpensively using off-the-shelf products. One of the earliest goals of virtual reality was to help visualize things that cannot be seen in everyday life, such as the bonding structures of molecules. It soon became associated with the notion of tele-presence, which initially meant handling objects at a distance. Here the concern was using robots to enter places that might be unfit for human beings. For instance, it was imagined that one might in future have a robot enter a nuclear reactor such as Chernobyl before it reached a breakdown stage and perform key operations at a distance.

In places such as Toronto, the notion of tele-presence became linked with advanced forms of tele-conferencing in the form of collaborative work-spaces. Such notions of tele-operation and tele-collaboration led to the idea that one could also do experiments at a distance. Hence, a scientist in one city without high-powered devices could use the Internet to link with a centre that had the appropriate high-level computers and other instruments. From this emerged the idea of virtual laboratories and collaboratories (cf. chapter 11). Tele-operation also brought with it the possibility of remote monitoring of processes.

In a second stage, virtual reality became linked with simulations. One could use it to visualize, for instance, the development of a major storm or tornado in order better to predict the consequences of natural disasters. One could also use it to simulate all the operations of a complex machine or a combination of machines as in the case of a ship. In the Virtual Environments for Training, for example, this is used to teach persons the workings of a ship's many instrument panels – each of which functions as an independent device through Java programming.

Alan Dix has listed at least four major application areas of virtual reality: 1) to simulate dangerous/expensive situations, including command and control, virtual tourism, practising medical procedures, treatment of phobia; 2) to see hidden real-world features such as the virtual wind tunnel; 3) to visualize complex information; and 4) fun.[42]

Simulation-Reality Feedback Loop

More recently, a third stage has begun to integrate the above developments. Hence, one can now use virtual reality to simulate the workings of a complex set of operations such as those in a nuclear reactor. This simulation establishes the workings of a reactor under ideal conditions. Various discrete processes in this simulation can then be linked with devices that monitor an actual reactor and check for anomalies. If such anomalies are found, the simulation can be used as a basis for correction.

For instance, in 2000, the Industrial Computing Society's Web estimated that $20 billion is lost annually with respect to Abnormal Situation Management (ASM). They believed "that we must move the control system design from a reactive mode to a predictive mode and a long time before an alarm is initiated." To this end, they were developing the AEGIS system to predict events using the latest State Estimation tools. They were also evaluating the Canadian Advanced Process Analysis & Control

System (APACS) and the French FORMENTOR tools.[43] APACS is a tool that uses the ideal conditions in a simulation as the basis for monitoring real conditions and processes in the physical world, anomalies in which are used to adjust the simulation and lead in turn to preventative action.

This approach is also implicit in the Visible Human project which is linked with the validation of a new field of Virtual Endoscopy (VE): "The main difficulty consists in the provision of a 'ground truth' measure. The VHD cryosection data precisely offers the standard against which the image processing effects can be calibrated and judged whereas the very same VHD data forms the basis to produce realistic simulations for testing procedures. The VHD models serve as a relevant framework for medical education, anaesthesiology training, surgery rehearsal and endoscopic simulation."[44]

The Visible Human was limited in that it was based on only three examples of human bodies, namely one man and two women. Other projects such as Virtual Animation of the Kinematics of the Human for Industrial, Educational and Research Purposes (VAKHUM) are working towards templates of the molecular skeletal system involving twenty to a hundred individuals.[45]

This approach is explicit as well in a European project entitled Bridging Reality and Virtuality with a Graspable User Interface (BREVIE), which permits one to change between "operations on real physical objects and their virtual counterparts," and prepare for an "era in which real physical parts have an adequate functional, structural and behavioural description, to build from these components a composite system which again shows the correspondence between the physical and the virtual system." The project aims to demonstrate the advantages and feasibility of this concept through a "construction kit of TWIN-Mechatronic-Objects suitable for vocational training in production automation."[46] The Lab@future project is building on these experiences to create a network of experts in mixed and augmented reality.[47]

A European IST project, DERIVE (Distributed real and virtual learning environment for mechatronics and tele-service) is also exploring this problem.[48] Such projects are part of a larger effort at methods for co-operative mastery of the complexity of design.[49] Yet another example of this emerging simulation reality feedback loop was provided at a lecture by Ian Maxwell (Avantium), who works with clients such as Shell and Glaxo Smith Kline. He described a loop that includes the following four elements: Robotic Library Synthesis, Informatics and Simulation, Microreactor Arrays, and High Speed Performance Analyses. In his approach, atomic models are being linked with 1) kinetic models, 2) process models, and 3) separation models. He foresees the evolution of virtual labs with virtual libraries of knowledge.[50]

This trend can be seen on other fronts also. For instance, at the National Center for Atmospheric Research (NCAR, Boulder), scientists are combining satellite images of an actual storm (Hurricane Herb) in order to generate their simulations thereof.[51] At the Institute for the Fundamental Study of Matter (FOM, Amsterdam),

Professor Frenkel is developing complex simulations of molecular bonding as a basis for creating new experiments using atomic structures in the physical world.

The problems of relating an ideal model with the real world have a long history. They were a central concern of Plato, who opposed objects in an ideal world of ideas with those in the physical world. In Plato's approach the ideal world was the perfect, "real" world, and the physical world represented a copy, often an imperfect, deceptive world of (mere) appearances. In the centuries that followed, philosophers such as Plotinus, tried to bridge the Platonic world of ideas with the physical world through a hierarchy of being whereby one moved from the perfection of the ideal to the imperfection of the physical world. It took centuries before the Christian belief in a physical world created by God brought the physical world to a plain where it could vie with the reality of the ideal. Even so, the manner of linking the two remained more a domain of theoretical debate between philosophers than something that could be addressed in practical terms.

The profound breakthrough of the new technologies outlined above is that there is now a complete loop between an "ideal" simulation and an actual process in the real world. Instead of being an abstract ideal, it serves as a model for the real situation and then uses sensors to monitor this actual situation and to register discrepancies, which can then be adjusted using the ideal conditions of the simulation as a control (Figure 2a). There are interesting parallels between this model and the basic elements of a mechatronic system as described by Professor Kaynak (Figure 2b). As a result of such reciprocal feedback through machine-machine communication, human intervention is theoretically no longer necessary.

Virtual Machines
In the United States, teams of scientists in cosmology, environmental hydrology, molecular biology, and nanomaterials are working on a Virtual Machine Room (VMR).[52] Related to this is work on High Performance Virtual Machines (HPVM): "which leverage the software tools and developed understanding of parallel computation on scalable parallel systems to exploit distributed computing resources."[53] The objective is to create faster machines more easily. Jean-Pierre Antikidis (CNES) has asked whether it might be possible to replace conventional computer installation by their virtual emulation. He has explored this idea in a vision called Hosting of Emulated Applications in a Virtual Environment (HEAVEN).[54]

7. Work
As a result, the nature of work itself is changing. Here, an extreme school has prophesied the end of work.[55] Less apocalyptic alternatives claim that, as we move from direct involvement in physical production to virtual activities, there will be a shift from products to services. Moreover, work of individuals is becoming part of a quest for quality control, Total Quality Control (TQC), as it is called in the United

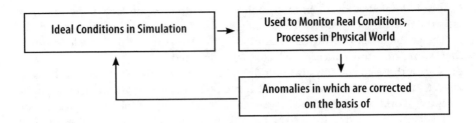

Figure 2a How a simulation can monitor real conditions in the physical world and correct anomalies therein.

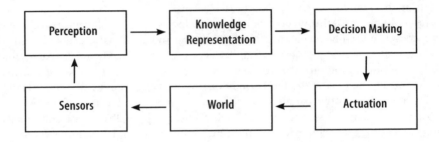

Figure 2b Basic elements of a mechatronic system according to Professor Kaynak (UNESCO chair, Istanbul).

States, which is integrating the entire production cycle. Here the most interesting developments are coming from Japan.[56]

Hand in hand with this automation of the physical production process are new technologies to plan production in all its stages. As we have seen above, there are major efforts in Manufacturing Resource Planning (MRP), Enterprise Resource Planning (ERP), and Supply Chain Management (SCM), which are leading to new production and supply chains and more recently Demand Chain Management (DCM).[57] Linked with these are concepts such as flow manufacturing, just-in-time purchasing, logistics management, materials management, and quick response. Together these are changing the role of work.[58] The military variant of these developments is "kill chains."[59]

Commercial companies such as System Analyse und Programmentwicklung (SAP)[60] began with financial control and supervision systems, which increasingly included workflow products. In 2001 a site listed over fifty such workflow packages.[61]

Less well known are a number of activities at MIT's Center for Coordination Science (CCS),[62] including their Process Handbook[63] (cf. chapter 7.4) or the numerous workflow organizations.[64]

One important part of this trend is towards automation though scenarios where robots and/or agents increasingly replace human activity (chapter 5.15–16). This approach, which has inspired dramatic predictions about the end of work, the death of work, etc., tends to view human workers as inefficient bottlenecks in an otherwise smooth-running set of mechanical processes and falls beyond the scope of this study because it has already been dealt with in detail by Rifkin,[65] Zuboff[66] and others (cf. Appendix 8).

Another school perceives a shift from direct, physical work with real machines to virtual work using virtual reality environments. Here, one of the pioneers is Anthony Steed (University College, London), whose web page on virtual work has articles going back to 1993.[67] Virtual work can entail simulations of reality or entail physical work at a distance through the intermediary of virtual reality environments and thus lead to what we have called a simulation-reality feedback loop (chapter 4.6). Hence, the rise of tele-activities that are one of the leitmotifs of this book: tele-presence, tele-manufacturing, tele-operation (medicine), tele-observation (spies, police), tele-immersion,[68] tele-centres,[69] and even tele-epistemology.[70] Tele-medicine, which was once a buzzword, is now leading to a series of new fields including tele-pathology, tele-dermatology, tele-radiology,[71] tele-ultrasound (cf. tele-invivo[72]), tele-surgery,[73] (e.g., tele-cranio-maxillofacial surgery[74]), as well as neurosurgery[75] and real time micro-tomography online.[76] All this is part of a revolution in collaborative learning, work and knowledge (chapter 11).[77]

Quality Control

Initially it was a quest for quality control that led to new methods of observing workers on the job. This inspired the so-called Taylorization of work, which began with blue-collar workers on the factory floor and gradually made its way to white-collar workers (chapter 7). James Beniger has shown brilliantly how the control revolution, which led to the early stages of automated manufacturing, is also linked with the technological and economic origins of the information society.[78] The quest for control is of particular interest for our story because it reveals how American efforts were improved in Japan.

Japan has a long tradition in the motion and drive control business. Yashkawa Electric, for instance, began manufacturing electric motors in 1915[80] and went on to become a champion of quality control. In the United States, Walter A. Shewhart (1891–1967) was one of the pioneers of quality control in the 1930s.[81] William Edwards Deming, who was active in mathematical statistics, became his assistant.[82] Deming developed his own philosophy of management.[83] In May, 1946, the Union of Japanese Scientists and Engineers (JUSE) was established. JUSE applied the statistical quality control tools developed by Shewhart and Deming in the 1930s and 1940s.

TABLE 8   The seven old tools and seven new tools for quality in Japan.[79]

SEVEN OLD TOOLS	SEVEN NEW TOOLS
Histograms	Relations Diagram
Cause and Effect Diagram	Affinity Diagram (KJ method)
Check sheets	Systematic Diagram (Tree Diagram)
Pareto Diagrams	Matrix Diagram
Graphs	Matrix Data Analysis
Control Charts	Process Decision Program Chart (PDPC)
Scatter Diagrams	Arrow Diagram

In 1951, JUSE established the Deming prize for companies, which achieved distinctive results by carrying out Total Quality Control (TQC).[84] JUSE gradually became known as a Centre of Quality Management in Japan.[85]

Initially these methods were intended as a form of American aid to help in Japanese economic recovery. Through their concept of continuous improvement, the Japanese soon developed them into something new, all the more so because they adapted their philosophical values. The Japanese Samurai traditionally carried seven tools into battle. In the 1960s, Kaoru Ishikawa, the head of JUSE, introduced seven tools, namely: histograms, cause and effect diagram, check sheets, Pareto diagrams, graphs, control charts, and scatter diagrams. These tools were developed as a guide to quality control.[86] In 1966, Yoji Akao, introduced the concept of Quality Function Deployment (QFD), a "method for developing a design quality aimed at satisfying the consumer and then translating the consumer's demand into design targets and major quality assurance points to be used throughout the production phase…. [QFD] is a way to assure the design quality while the product is still in the design stage."[87] QFD reduced design times by one-third.

By 1972, a Consortium for Advanced Manufacturing International (CAM-I) was founded to support member companies in their quest for excellence in today's highly competitive global marketplace.[88] In 1976, the Japanese Society for Quality Control Technique Development, under Nyatanni, after a worldwide search, proposed seven new tools for management and planning quality control (Table 8).[89] Subsequently seven creativity tools were also added, namely, problem definition, brainstorming, brainwriting, creative brainstorming, word and picture association, advanced analogies, and morphological chart.[90]

To improve the implementation of total quality control in Japan, Genichi Taguchi developed Taguchi methods.[91] The seven tools and the Taguchi methods became part of a much larger picture, closely associated with the Japanese term *kaizen*, which is intimately connected with maintenance and innovation[92] "*Kaizen* means improvement. Moreover it means continuing improvement in personal life, home life, social life, and working life. When applied to the workplace *Kaizen* means continuing improvement involving everyone – managers and workers alike…. In its broadest sense, quality is anything that can be improved."[93] *Kaizen* is, in turn, linked with the development of a Japanese business planning method known as *Hoshin Kanri*[94] and a complex guild-like system of corporations called *keiretsu*.[95] A Western interpretation of these ideas places a customer-driven master plan at the centre (Figure 3a).[96] From this principle comes the idea of just-in-time production, which was subsequently made famous through Honda's global local (glocal) approach.[97] Problem solving, cross-functional improvement and planning are then the basis for more detailed approaches (Figure 3b).

By the 1980s this led to surprising results. For instance, the Ford Motor Company sub-contracted production of automobile engines to a company in Japan and subsequently set out to check whether they met the American specifications: "the variation between parts in the Japanese engines was so small that the Ford technician thought at first that his measurement instrument was broken. But the Japanese engines with minimal variation, ran quieter, were more reliable and were asked for by customers. Continuous Improvement had become essential."[99]

In 1985, Yasuhiro Monden published a book on innovations in management with respect to Japanese corporations,[100] and the following year he published a book on the just-in-time approach comparing American and Japanese practices.[101] That same year, the Consortium for Advanced Manufacturing International published a dictionary of supply-chain management terms.[102] In 1986, Taguchi published a book on his methods, and that same year, Maasaki Imai also published a book claiming that *kaizen* was the key to Japan's competitive success.[103] In short, the mid-1980s saw a series of publications, which made these Japanese methods accessible to the West. It is no coincidence that by 1990 just-in-time (online) learning (JITOL) was becoming a buzzword at the frontiers of North American business and education.

In 1993, Deming, now an old man, published a book on the new economics.[104] Ironically, many Americans were unaware that he was an American who had brought to Japan ideas that the Japanese transformed and made their own. By 1994, NASA had a site summarizing the key ideas of the Japanese approach in passages such as the following: "Experiential design optimization is the management led optimization of a design using human experience within a system which contains, hardware, software, people, processes, information, organization, structure, synchronization, function and behavior. Quality function deployment (QFD) as implemented under the philosophy of *kaizen* within the process of total quality control (TQC) is a prime example."[105]

In Japan, these ideas continue on many fronts. For instance, the Manufacturing Information Systems Research Laboratory: "studies factory automation (FA), computer aided design and manufacturing (CAD/CAM), computer integrated manufacturing (CIM), and robotics." The Japanese are conscious that these developments "have been a major driving force to promote Japan into a major industrial country in the world."[106]

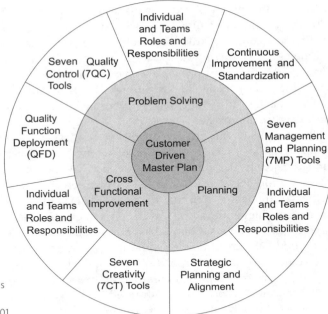

Figure 3a
A western interpretation
by GOAL/QPC of the ideas
entailed in the Japanese
approach to quality in 2001

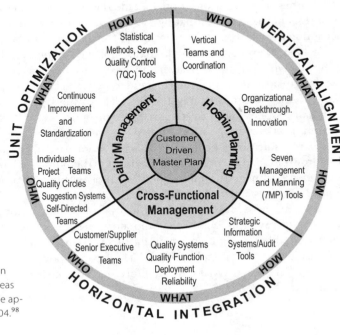

Figure 3b
A western interpretation
by GOAL/QPC of the ideas
entailed in the Japanese approach to quality in 2004.[98]

While the United States may originally have thought of (total) quality control as their domain, this idea has spread throughout the world. In Europe, the International Organization for Standardization (ISO or OSI) was established in 1947. The ISO first published its quality assurance and management standards in 1987 and then republished an updated version in 1994, which are known as the ISO 9000 standards.[107] Since 1988, there has been a European Foundation for Quality Management (EFQM).[108] In 1995, the British Government commissioned an IT Infrastructure Library (ITIL).[109] The European Commission has also been active on this front through a number of projects.[110]

In retrospect, Japan adapted the American principles and surpassed them. This led the United States to copy Japanese principles. The *kaizen* methods were, for instance, taken up by Motorola in their six-sigma methods (cf. chapter 8). A new global concept of quality is thus emerging that transcends the idiosyncrasies of any given company or nation.

8. Agents

The simulation-reality feedback loop (cf. chapter 4.6) introduced a new level of machine-machine communication whereby persons are theoretically no longer necessary in the process and can be replaced by agents. The notion of agents has been traced back to the fields of Distributed Artificial Intelligence (DAI), Distributed Problem Solving (DPS) and Parallel Artificial Intelligence (PAI). Carl Hewitt (1977) proposed "a self-contained, interactive and concurrently-executing object which he termed 'actor'. This object had some encapsulated internal state and could respond to messages from other similar objects."[111] Until about 1990, study of agents focussed on macro issues, theories, architectures, and languages. In the past decade there has been a proliferation in different kinds of agents.[112]

Agents were originally conceived as software. Pfeifer noted the need for situated cognition grounding.[113] They can also be hardware in the form of robots. Humanoid robots, for instance, have been a project at Honda since 1986.[114] The Communicating Autonomous Agents Research Group at the Takase Lab (Tokyo) is doing important work on autonomous agents relating to both humans and robots: "which can communicate with unspecified agents or humans in order to achieve their goals or to satisfy their desires, and making it clear how to design such agents." This entails "integration of software for language/knowledge processing, vision and motion generation."[115]

In the United States, there are tele-presence agents such as the NASA Mars Rover. Agents are playing an increasing role in design and production. The virtual Environments Laboratory at Northeastern University is using agents for autonomous vehicles in a virtual environment simulation.[116] Stanford has both an agent-based engineering group[117] and a next link design agent.[118] In addition, Stanford, Berkeley, and Sandia laboratories are working together on agents.[119] Sandia is working on design agents for features tolerances; a manufacturing agent for material removal, and an inspection agent for inspection path probe points.[120] The Sandia vision is clear:

> Agent architectures are the enabling technology to facilitate the integration of heterogeneous software tools to support an agile manufacturing information infrastructure. Such software includes legacy software, data bases, knowledge bases, commercial CAD/CAM software, and newly developed software in an agile manufacturing environment.... To accomplish the goals of concurrent engineering, CAD tools must be integrated with simulation and modeling software to validate the design prior to manufacturing a part. We are wrapping existing design codes in agent wrappers and developing agent interfaces to CAD packages.[121]

More ambitious is the NIIIP's Consortium: Solution for Manufacturing Execution Systems Adaptable Replicable Technology (SMART). This seeks to enable "integration and interoperability amongst Manufacturing Execution Systems (MES) as well as the full range of Enterprise Information Systems (EIS) within a single enterprise or amongst multiple enterprises."[122]

Agents were originally seen as playing an ancillary role, complementing tasks regularly performed by human beings. In the Japanese approach, agents interact with both live human beings and robots. Implicit in both the Sandia Labs and NIIIP projects is a rather different approach, whereby agents effectively take over most, if not all, of the elements in a manufacturing process. As we shall see, this is not accidental. Underlying these approaches are competing visions of the future.

9. New Fields

We have shown how the means of production and work are changing. As a result the products themselves are also being transformed. In the past, people produced lifeless objects. People were active; objects were passive. Now objects are increasingly acquiring sensors whereby they can react to their environment. Light sensitive street lamps are a simple example. They turn off automatically, without human intervention, in the morning once there is a certain amount of daylight, and they turn on again when night falls or when there is a dark storm. More complex links between simulations with sensors attached to physical objects are changing the nature of both simulations and objects. The scope of such sensors is also increasing enormously. In oceanography there is a project to insert sensors on the entire Juan de Fuca tectonic plate in the Pacific Ocean.[123]

The rise of these so-called intelligent materials (cf. chapter 5) and integrated production are in turn blurring distinctions between living producers and lifeless products. A quest to apply the autonomous aspects of living systems to the realm of mechanical production is leading to a new field of holonics. A parallel quest to link computer science and control systems with electrical and mechanical engineering is leading to the emergence of production chains and another new field called mechatronics. It is leading also to a third new field of agile manufacturing, which in turn is linked with rapid and virtual prototyping.

Holonics

In 1995, Patrick McHugh, Giorgio Merli, and William Wheeler published a book claiming that the holonic enterprise marked the next step beyond Business Process Engineering (BPE).[124] David Korten mentioned holonics as one of the emerging phenomena of the post-corporate world.[125] Since then, holonics[126] has become one of the Intelligent Manufacturing Systems projects. Arthur Koestler first broached the idea of holons[127] (from the Greek word *holos*, meaning *whole*, and the suffix *on* meaning *particle* or *part*), in his book *The Ghost in the Machine*.[128] The Holonic Manufacturing Systems (HMS) consortium aims to translate Koestler's concepts for social organizations and living organisms into appropriate concepts for manufacturing industries, thus giving them "stability in the face of disturbances, adaptability and flexibility in the face of change, and efficient use of available resources."[129] Thus social organization is a model for new technological organization.

As we shall see later (chapter 7), systems thinking from technology is simultaneously a model for many of the new organizational theories in business. At one level, there is a reciprocal influence between social and mechanical organizations. At the same time there is a danger that this becomes a tautological cycle: whereby the systemic aspects of machines are imposed upon social organizations in business to the extent that individual persons are no longer seen to play a unique role. They are reduced, as it were, to cogs in the wheels of a systemic machine. Some strands of autonomous systems, artificial life, complexity, and emergent systems exhibit this limitation.

Holonic Manufacturing Systems (HMS) is now an international consortium with various international partners working on very specific aspects of the problem. In the United States, for instance, the Center for Intelligent Systems of Professor Kawamura at Vanderbilt University is part of the Academic Coalition for Intelligent Manufacturing Systems (A-CIMS) at a national level.[130] At the international level, they are also part of HMS and working specifically on: Production Planning and Scheduling; Flexible Human Integration and Software Architecture for System Integration. Holonic Manufacturing, is in turn, but one of four parts in their approach to intelligent systems, namely: 1) Holonic Manufacturing, 2) Scheduling for Flexible Manufacturing, 3) Virtual Manufacturing Village, and 4) Remote Manufacturing Systems.

According to Dr. Ulieru (University of Calgary)[131] holons have an open architecture, are decentralized and reconfigurable, and have the following characteristics: communication and co-operation; autonomy; self-diagnosis; self-repair, and inter-changeability and can entail different aspects of the manufacturing process. If all this sounds too abstract, it is useful to look at the work of Mitsubishi Heavy

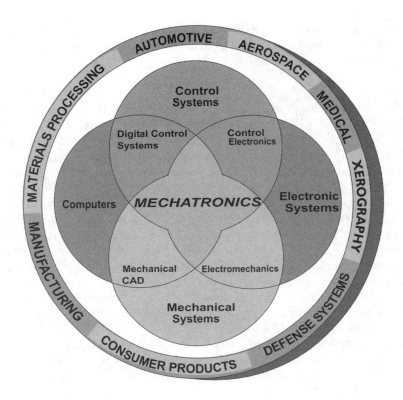

Figure 4   Elements of mechatronics according to the Rensselaer Institute.

Industries Limited in the domain of micromachine technology: "The so-called ho-lonic mechanism 'can develop different functions if identical elements or elements having the same kind [of] functions (holon) are gathered in large numbers and mechanically assembled into a system'.... This new mechanism has tremendous freedom that requires new control methods."[132]

Mechatronics
Another of the emerging fields is *mechatronics*, which is a combination "mecha" of mechanisms and "tronics" of electronics. The term was coined by a senior engineer at the Yaskawa Electric Company in 1969. Trademark rights on the term were granted in 1971 and later given up in the interests of faster development.[133] In 1971, Professor Kajitani also established a mechatronical laboratory at the University of Electro-Communications (Tokyo).[134] Their work focusses on automatic measuring,

control systems, and robotics.[135] On the Internet, the mechatronics home page is now at Linz University where the subject began as a five-year program in 1990 as a combination of computer science, electrical engineering, and mechanical engineering. In 2001 the University of Linz site claimed that there were thirty-five mechatronics labs in Europe, seventeen in the United States, nine in Australia, eight in Asia, and two in Canada.[136] This overlooked seventeen others in Japan[137] and indeed was unaware of the importance of the Japanese contribution to the field. Indeed, it is interesting to note three quite different directions in mechatronics research. In the United States, the emphasis is mainly on technological solutions. At Stanford, for instance, mechatronics is used in the context of a Smart Product Design Laboratory (SPDL). Berkeley's mechatronics program has research in robot design and control; manufacturing process control; human-machine systems; motion control; machine design; computer software for real-time control and diagnostics; mechanical systems modelling, identification, control and computer mechanics.[138]

The precise definitions continue to change almost by the year. In 2001, Johns Hopkins University defined "mechatronics" as "the design of microprocessor-controlled electromechanical systems."[139] The University of Washington (Seattle) saw mechatronics as "the integrated study of the design of systems and products in which computation, mechanization, actuation, sensing, and control are designed together to achieve improved product quality and performance."[140] Rensselaer[141] envisioned mechatronics as a combination of fields with numerous practical applications. To Linz's three fields they add a fourth: control systems[142] (Figure 4). In Europe, there is greater emphasis on the philosophical and systems aspects. Louvain sees mechatronics as a "concurrent-engineering thinking framework in the process of designing complex machines in order to achieve optimal positioning, tracking, dynamic or vibro-acoustic behaviour, etc." and describes how: "This system supports and guides the designer through the range of technological options available, using appropriate tools to perform processing of the design data at the proper level for design abstraction, concept generation, variant design, technology selection and matching, model execution, optimization, simulation and visualization. Work has been initiated for the conceptual design of global topologies of metal-cutting machine tools."[143]

Loughborough University defines mechatronics as "a design philosophy that utilizes a synergistic integration of mechanics, electronics and computer (or information) technology to produce enhanced products, processes or systems."[144] A similar basic definition is given by the UNESCO chair as: "the synergistic integration of mechanical engineering with electronics and intelligent computer control in the design and manufacture of products and processes."[145] A closer look at the diagrams explaining this (Figure 5a, cf. figure 2a) reveals links between machines and the physical world through sensors and actuators, which act as mechanical perception devices and bring us back to the phenomena outlined in the reality-simulation feedback loop. Such links between perception, robotics, and control are also reflected in the research of the Centre for Intelligent Machines (CIM) at McGill University.[146]

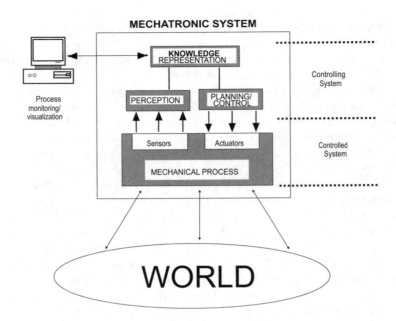

Figure 5a Elements of mechatronics. Courtesy of Professor Kaynak, UNESCO chair of Mechatronics, Istanbul

Figure 5b Tree of new Inter-Related Disciplines according to the Department of Precision Engineering, University of Tokyo

Another way of looking at this feedback loop is to see it as a way towards automated knowledge acquisition. In this context, it is extremely fascinating to learn from Professor Kaynak that there have been further developments in the 1990s that link mechatronics with developments in semiotics (cf. chapter 15).

A third approach is evident in Japan. On the surface, the Japanese and the American approaches are analogous. Both are very interested in technological solutions. But whereas the Americans are interested in concurrent and/or agile manufacturing in general, the Japanese are much more interested in robots.[147] Another difference is the Japanese emphasis on micro-mechatronics. Hence, in 2000, Yashkawa, which introduced the term, was producing the world's smallest servo-actuators,[148] while the Department of Precision Engineering at the University of Tokyo was working on micro-mechatronics cell manipulation. Here, mechatronics and molecular electronics (molectronics) overlap.[149]

A third difference is philosophical. Whereas the American approaches emphasize efficiency as a means solely towards greater economic advantage, the Japanese ask: "What can we do to maintain an affluent society?" In their view: "The key is improving the quality of individual life."[150] Hence, the Department of Precision Engineering (Tokyo) is focussing on three fields beyond the narrow bounds of engineering: 1) environment and manufacturing technologies, 2) medical and welfare technologies, and 3) information and communication technologies (Figure 5b). We shall see below that this is no coincidence.

Agility Manufacturing

The philosophical ideas of kaizen linked with the Japanese concept of seven old and new tools were interpreted as a quest for total quality control in the United States.[151] Some saw it as a part of the post-mass-production enterprise.[152] Others found therein the challenge of concurrent engineering and an inspiration for cost-reduction methods, which led subsequently to visions of the lean – and mean – corporation. From this, in turn, emerged the idea of agile or agility engineering. It is said to have begun in the United States as a "federally-funded, industry-led program to make business competitive" in 1990.[153] Others claim that the concept of agile manufacturing was first proposed in a ground-breaking report from the Iacocca Institute in 1991.[154] A CNN article (1996)[155] acknowledged that these ideas had begun in "Asia and Europe."

Brian Maskell Associates outlines four steps to agile manufacturing: traditional, gaining control (ERPs or MRPs), world class, and agile manufacturing[156] Paul Kidd,[157] who was one of the first to write a book on agile manufacturing and has since created one of the most important web sites on the subject, has drawn attention to two quite different definitions of agility manufacturing. One is a fuzzy, catch-all, meaning that includes concepts such as "strategy driven manufacturing, concurrent engineering, virtual enterprises, just-in-time manufacturing, flexible manufacturing, time compression, and mass customization." It is instructive, in

TABLE 9   Six grand challenges for Manufacturing 2020 in the United States

1	Concurrent manufacturing
2	Integration of Human and Technical Resources
3	Conversion of Information to Knowledge
4	Environmental Compatibility
5	Reconfigurable Enterprises
6	Innovative Processes

this context, that IBM's vision of informatics as 1) massification and personalization, 2) digital services, and 3) new links or strong marriages as they call them between informatics and telecommunications (telematics) and entertainment (infotainment) follow this definition.[158] A second definition of an agile or adaptive enterprise: "is a fast moving, adaptable and robust business. It is capable of rapid adaptation in response to unexpected and unpredicted changes and events, market opportunities, and customer requirements."[159]

Engineers in the United States tended to focus on the first definition, although they soon recognized agile manufacturing as a strategic research area with a view to: "understand and model the processes and organization, to develop supporting technologies and tools, and to implement agile manufacturing and concurrent engineering testbeds." For instance, in 1994, the National Infrastructure for Science and Technology (NIST) initiated a program for Systems Integration for Manufacturing Applications (SIMA).[160] The National Science Foundation initiated a series of Agile Manufacturing Research Institutes (AMRIs). Other projects provided test beds, enabling technologies, protocols, and a forum.[161] It is striking, however, that the American approach quickly took a turn towards purely technological solutions in contrast to the philosophical approach of the Japanese.

The Sandia National Labs developed an Agile Manufacturing Prototyping System (AMPS) and software tools for virtual manufacturing which: "goes beyond current concepts of integrated product and process design by providing models and simulations of production processes to product designers to ensure cost-effective manufacturability."[162] As early as 1996, NIST had produced a Virtual Manufacturing Enterprise demo.[163] Once again, saving money was the focus of this U.S. approach.

10. Competing Visions

In our discussions of mechatronics, agents, and agile manufacturing, we noted that there were significant differences between approaches to production in the United States (which also has an imperialistic international version), Europe, and Japan. We also noted an emerging global vision, which transcends national interests.

United States

One of the guiding principles of the U.S. approach is that systems are proprietary. This is particularly evident in the world of software, where there is a growing gulf between two fundamentally different models, epitomized in the struggles between Microsoft and Linux.[164] Some see this as a struggle between a purely financial and an idealistic model. The Microsoft-Linux debate is the visible tip of a much larger iceberg. On the surface, this larger iceberg entails a contest between proprietary and open systems and entails not only software but the entire production process. At a deeper level, this debate entails differing visions of the future.

Proprietary Systems

The inordinate amount of press devoted to Microsoft can readily lead us to overlook some basic facts. In 1999, Microsoft's annual sales were approaching $20 billion. On the world scale this is relatively small. In 1999, the annual sales of Philips were 31.5 billion euros[165]; those of Siemens were approximately 136 billion.[166] Sales of General Motors were $161 billion in 1998. PDES Inc., which is stimulating the development and implementation of ISO 10303 (STEP) in the United States, includes "20 major industrial companies and government agencies that represent over $500 billion in annual revenue."[167] And even these amounts are modest when compared with the manufacturing revenues of the G7 countries. Hence, there is much at stake.

The U.S. approach is multi-faceted but essentially proprietary and ad hoc in its assumptions. One of its points of departure is the Internet Engineering Task Force (IETF), which assumes that problems can be outlined by a Request For Comment (RFC), which subsequently lead to committees and "working solutions."[168] There is a complex way in which technology projects with economic aims are linked with the military. Hence, the Computer Assisted Technology Transfer (CATT) program, which emphasizes electronic commerce and electronic data exchange, is funded by the Department of Defense (DOD).[169] Although phrases of the 1960s, such as the "military-industrial complex," are no longer in vogue, their underlying principles are still in effect. The U.S. system is very much concerned with American economic gain at the expense of others.[170] This is rendered less apparent through American participation on many international fronts.

The name of an American initiative such as the International Alliance for Interoperability (IAI) sounds as if it is open. Indeed, the IAI claims that their Industry Foundation Classes (IFC) are public and "open." But the use thereof is only open for members: "Software implementation of IFC is proprietary to protect the data and technologies of member companies that compete in the market."[171] A similar mentality becomes evident if one examines more closely the aims of the National Industrial Information Infrastructure Protocols (NIIIP) Consortium in the United States. The consortium has fifteen phase one members, including Digital Equipment (now Compaq), Hughes Defense, IBM, Lockheed Martin, Taligent, and the National Institute for Standards and Technology (NIST).

TABLE 10 Eight enabling technologies required to convert information to knowledge according to the authors of *Visionary Manufacturing Challenges for 2020* [174]

1 Educational Technology
2 Collaboration Technology, Teleconferencing, Telecontrol, Telepresence
3 Natural Language Processing
4 Data and Information Filters and Agents
5 System Security
6 Artificial Intelligence and Decision-Making Systems
7 Automatic Sensors and Actuators for Process and Equipment Control
8 Integrated Modeling and Simulation

The NIIIP Consortium wants to help "America's industrial base to take advantage of recent advances in object information technology (CORBA); product data definition (STEP); and communications networks (INTERNET) to assemble Virtual Enterprises."[172] It is instructive that a private American firm, PDES Inc., ensures the establishment of the STEP standard in the United States,[173] which may help explain why the international basis of the CORBA and STEP projects is not mentioned by the NIIIP.

Technically there is a global system whereby each country has its national standards bodies. Accordingly the United States has an American National Standards Institute (ANSI),[175] which links with the International Standards Organization (ISO). The United States also has a National Institute of Standards and Technology (NIST).[176] This sometimes operates as if there were no need for the International Standards Organization (ISO), the claim being that ISO is too slow and the assumption being that the United States is practically the only one to make standards. Of late, there have been documented cases of the United States trying to boycott and even undermine ISO.[177]

This attitude is not entirely new. In 1995, when Europe sponsored the G7 Conference and Exhibition on the Information Society, the G7 proposed eleven pilot projects from all over the world. The United States paid lip service to participation but at the same time initiated its own Global Information Initiative (GII) test-beds[178] at a national level, focussing on virtual environments[179] in four domains:[180] 1) teraflop class wide area computing, 2) close coupling of immersive virtual environments and supercomputing, 3) advanced applications development resource, and 4) a test bed to identify future research areas.

The dangers of such a debonair attitude are evidenced in the realm of a Global System for Mobile Communications (GSM), on which Europe began working in the early 1980s and which has led to a third generation Universal Mobile Telecommunications System (UMTS). In the United States, GSM is only one of series of alternatives for mobile communication. Hence, in 1999 there were some 6.8 million GSM phones in North America, over 12 million in Eastern Europe, some

58 million in Asia, and over 148 million in Western Europe. By 2001 China was the largest mobile phone market. Mobile telephones are one area where the United States is well behind the rest of the world.

Nonetheless, the American vision of manufacturing design processes and products is very far-reaching, as becomes clear from the projects listed by the National Coordination Office for Computing, Information and Communications.[181] The full breadth of the American agenda emerges from a report on *Visionary Manufacturing Challenges* for 2020,[182] which sees six grand challenges for manufacturing within the next two decades (Table 9). The first of these goals, concurrent manufacturing, can be seen merely as a further step in what Kidd has termed the "fuzzy definition of agility" (cf. §9 above). The second goal is more far-reaching. As enabling technologies, the report foresees "systems models for all manufacturing operations, unified methods and protocols for exchanging information and adaptable, reconfigurable manufacturing processes and systems." It also foresees the conversion of information to knowledge. Here no particular philosophical approach is entailed (cf. chapter 12). Rather, the authors outline enabling technologies to make this happen:

> The two main challenges will be (1) to capture and store data and information "instantaneously" and transform them into useful knowledge and (2) to make this knowledge available to users (human and machine) "instantaneously" wherever and whenever it is needed in a familiar language and form. One of the challenges for future manufacturing will be to reduce the lead-time for new products. Concurrent design and manufacturing will require the real-time transfer of information between designers and manufacturers. The global distribution of manufacturing resources and expanded supply networks will challenge information systems to maintain operating control. The logistics of physically moving material and inventories will also require real-time transaction-based information systems.[183]

While education is acknowledged as the biggest challenge, it is described purely in terms of ability in fast decision-making.[184] According to the authors, education and training will simply "have to change to meet the needs of the workforce.... Computer-based training will become the norm."[185] In Table 10, collaboration technology, tele-conferencing, tele-control, and tele-presence are bundled together. The solution to problems is seen in terms of technological tools independently of language and culture, which is the opposite of the European approach: "A major task will be to create tools independent of language and culture that can be instantly used by anyone, regardless of location or national origin. Tools will have to be developed that allow for effective remote interaction. Collaboration technologies will require models of the dynamics of human interactions that can simulate behaviors, characteristics, and appearances to simulate physical presence."[186]

TABLE 11 Examples of open source software and their role in the Internet.

OPEN SOURCE SOFTWARE	CHARACTERISTICS
Apache	Runs over 50% of the world's web servers
Perl	Engine behind most of the 'live content'
BIND	Software that provides Domain Name Service (DNS)
Sendmail	Most important and widely used e-mail transport software

The quest is to identify stereotypes, which can be used to simulate and ulti-mately replace the complexities of reality.[187] It is very instructive that the second grand challenge (in Table 9), integration of human and technical resources includes technologies for converting information into knowledge. It also includes processes for the development, transfer, and utilization of technology; new educational meth-ods; design methodologies with a broad range of product requirements and new software design methods. In the name of integrating the human, technological solutions dominate the horizon.

If we return for a moment to National Industrial Information Infrastructure Protocols (NIIIP), we learn that ultimately their vision is "to make U.S. industrial companies more globally competitive and efficient through a new form of collab-orative computing that will support the formation of Virtual Enterprises,"[188] which are defined as: 1) temporary consortia of member companies that 2) are constituted for cost effectiveness and product uniqueness and 3) share costs, skills and core competencies "to access global markets with world-class solutions that could not be provided individually."[189]

Technology as an End in Itself

Striking in this vision, however, is the emphasis on technology effectively to the exclusion of human intervention. Whereas European discussions of virtual compa-nies emphasize the importance of building trust among individuals involved in the process, the American system emphasizes speed, efficiency, and profits.[190] Whereas Japanese visions would speak of continuous personal improvement (*kaizen*),[191] the American system ultimately focusses on the importance of impersonal agents,[192] who do the job more cost effectively: as if humans were dispensable in cases where machines are cheaper and faster.

In its extreme versions the American "vision" emphasizes a shift from pro-duction through physical companies to production with companies which are ever-more virtual, where agents play an increasing role such that eventually physi-cal workers are no longer necessary. This trend has its parallels in other areas. In organizations (chapter 7) there is a tendency towards virtual jobs, a euphemism for their abolishment. In education (chapter 9) there is a tendency towards virtual schools and classrooms, in which teachers are also virtual, i.e., no longer necessary. This leads ultimately (chapters 14–15) to a great paradox that America, the land of the free, which sees itself as the unparalleled champion of the individual, becomes committed to a technological virtuality and systemicity whereby individual persons no longer count. In this framework, even CEOs can come and go as mergers and hostile takeovers become the order of the day and the corporate system continues as if nothing happened.

Hence, the frightening thing about the American approach is ultimately not its proprietary assumptions, nor that it favours things American over others. The real problems are that it seeks to impose the unilingual, unicultural model of the United States upon the entire world and ultimately assumes that there are technological fixes rather than human answers. The American information highway is about rushing to get somewhere, without a real home at the end of the journey. As was noted in the Introduction, the United States is many things. The same country that sometimes acts as if it can make its own standards has also played a significant role in the development of global standards through bodies such as the ISO, and ITU. The question remains: which strand of U.S. interests will win the day?

Europe

Whereas the U.S. has increasingly sought to make a business case even for open source under names such as shared source,[193] Europe has taken a different approach of considering the possibility of open source as something that is not only shared freely but also shared for free.[194] The contrast between the proprietary approach of Microsoft and the open system of Linux is symptomatic of something much deeper, not just because Bill Gates is American and Linus Torvalds is European.

In August 1999, the French Ministry of Culture formally announced that it would convert all its operations to the Linux platform. In April 2000, at the *www.intranet2000.net* conference in Paris, representatives of the French government confirmed their plans to convert all activities of the French government to the Linux platform.[195] France is not alone. Germany and Britain are considering it.[196] The Chinese government is moving entirely to open source, although their reasons for doing so are obviously different.

Those at the frontiers of the European Commission's plans for new educational environments suggest that these should use open source. Significant individuals within the World Wide Web Consortium (W3) urge the need for open source, as does Philippe Quéau at UNESCO.[197] Meanwhile, in the United States, the President's Information Technology Advisory Committee (PITAC) also recommended (September 2000) that the federal government encourage the development of "open source" software.[198] A report by Paul Jones surveyed open source developments and claimed that Germany makes the greatest contributions to open-source:

50 percent were people adding just one or two pieces to the growing project. Jones estimates that 250,000 developers worldwide are involved in open-source work, either contributing code, writing documentation, or tracking bugs. Europeans represented 37 percent of contributions; followed by 23 percent from .com addresses; 12 percent from .edu domains; 10 percent from .net; 7 percent from .org; and 11 percent from other sources.[199]

Open source is characteristic of something deeper (cf. chapters 14–15). When Tim Berners-Lee developed HTML, he "gave it away." When the scientists at the Joint Research Centre (JRC) developed the Apache Server, they "gave it away." Theoretically the same happened with the Netscape browser, except that this happened with a very clear business case in mind.[200] Nonetheless, or perhaps as a result, this was one of the events that sparked the open source movement around the world and now includes a number of other products (Table 11).[201]

Open source is symptomatic of something larger. It plays a role in the Milan Declaration on communication and human rights. It entails a quest to share knowledge freely using open standards. Hence, Siemens, which is interested in open source, is also active in the Global Engineering Network (GEN) project, which seeks to catalogue all the basic processes in engineering. This is but one of a number of such German initiatives. There is a Virtual Factory Consortium,[202] which has some similarities with endeavours towards Virtual Enterprises in the United States, yet differs considerably with respect to the detail of approach and in their assumption that the human dimension remains of central importance.[203]

At the end of the last chapter we noted a growing fusion between the mechanical world of machines and the organic world of nature. In the past there were clear distinctions between static (mechanical) products and fluid (organic) processes. Today there are projects that aim at Integrated Product and Process Innovation (IPPI).[204] We have seen that there are American projects that are international. There are analogous projects in most European countries, which set out from very different assumptions. First, they assume that the importance of their original language(s) remain(s) paramount. Second, they accept implicitly the need for global standards that go beyond their own boundaries.

Europeans would agree with U.S. critics that the ISO was, for a time, too slow in adapting to rapidly changing technologies. But, instead of using this as grounds for rejecting the whole process, they have worked with organizations such as the European Telecommunications Standards Institute (ETSI), the European Broadcasting Union (EBU), and the International Telecommunications Union (ITU) in developing fast-track procedures to arrive at new ISO standards. Part of this larger reality is a commitment in Europe to include the individual in any technological innovation. Whereas the United States is fascinated by the technology as if it were an end in itself, as if it were value-free, and as if it could exist without humans, Europe is constantly concerned with the humane dimension of technology, what happens to the individual, what the impacts on society will be. As we shall show later, whereas the United States aims at an information highway, Europe strives for an information and a knowledge society.[205]

Japan

Japan, shares the U.S. fascination with technology, with robots, and the whole field of robots as agents, whereby the boundaries between software agents and physical robots become increasingly blurred. Curiously, however, although they appear to follow through the consequences of technology even more systematically than the United States, the Japanese also have a deep commitment to society, different than in Europe, and yet one where persons are cared for, even though there is less evidence of individualism and more a sense reminiscent of the clan tradition in Northern Europe. There is also a commitment to understanding the technology as part of a larger reality, whereby knowledge of nature, individuals, society, and nature is integrated in a way different than either in the United States or in Europe.

An Emerging Global Vision

As we saw, major corporations are attempting to impose U.S. technology-centred, profit-driven models at the global level. Meanwhile, there is another trend at the global level, in the direction of global sharing and co-operation, e.g., an important initiative of the ISO, the Standard for the Exchange of Product Model Data (STEP), which in turn is part of the Intelligent Manufacturing Systems (IMS) Initiative (cf. §5 above). This was founded in 1995 as an international consortium of some 250 companies and 200 research institutes. The European Commission, which has some 150 projects on integrated manufacturing,[206] is playing an active role in IMS.[207] IMS is concerned with a very big picture, including problems such as International Supply Chain Integration.[208]

The IMS framework is very large. There are fifteen other projects that have been endorsed with a total amount of $250 million.[209] Further projects are under review or being revised.[210] In isolation, mere titles of proposed projects are not a reliable analytical tool. However, seen in the context of real projects now underway in the Intelligent Manufacturing Systems Initiative, they provide a glimpse of the enormous vision that is emerging. The Renaissance was about many new individual inventions. In the seventeenth and early eighteenth centuries, scientists such as Kepler, Galileo, Descartes, and Newton articulated basic laws underlying terrestrial and celestial mechanics. The quest at the dawn of the twenty-first century is of an entirely different order. It is not just about laws of individual objects or even just about systems. It is seeking new relations between mechanical systems, biological systems, and production systems and integrating knowledge at different scales.

11. Conclusions

We have shown that the new media are transforming the nature of production in at least seven ways: 1) production is becoming distributed, 2) with networks for all stages of production, 3) design is on-line, 4) there are new production and supply chains, 5) virtuality has new meanings, 6) the nature of work is changing, and 7) agents play new roles.

We have suggested that there are quite different approaches to these challenges: between imperialistic nationalism and a global vision; between proprietary solutions and open source. At another level, there are differences between technological solutions and those that integrate human values; differences between an information highway (America), an information and knowledge society (Europe) and a knowledge society (Japan). In the next chapters we shall show that these different approaches affect far more than theories of production. They affect approaches to services, to education, and ultimately to knowledge itself. Will the new technologies and the new media help us in what we are or change us into something beyond all recognition? Will robots in their new forms as agents remain mechanical aids in the sense of surrogate butlers? Or will they take on an ever-more essential role in all processes, to such an extent that the necessity of human intervention will be dismissed as passé by others? This is why there is so much at stake in understanding the new media. If we do not understand them, we shall stand under them and be dominated by forces we can no longer control.

5
services

Artificial Intelligence promises many
benefits in a wide range of areas
(medicine, for example). However, it
also constitutes an enormous step in de-
skilling. In effect, more and more people
will lose the opportunity and perhaps the
ability, to think for themselves.
— George Ritzer,
The McDonaldization of Society
(2000, p. 122).

1. Introduction

The material consequences of computers lead to virtuality. We
have seen how they transform many aspects of production
(chapter 4). We shall show that they also bring a shift from
hardware to software; from products to services; a shift from
physical transfers of money to e-commerce.

The precise amount of e-commerce is very difficult to
determine. For example, CIO Communications claimed
that there would be "$21–57 billion in retail sales in 2000,
with business to business sales 2 to 2.5 times larger." It also
claimed that there would be a total of $100 billion in on-line
commerce revenue in 2000.[1] IDC claimed that e-commerce

would expand to $129.2 billion in 2000.[2] Acumen was more optimistic with a projection of $350 billion worldwide for the year 2000.[3] Forrester predicted that e-commerce would increase to $6.8 trillion by 2004.[4] Meanwhile, the Japanese cyber guru, Ken Ichi Ohmae claimed that the world is rapidly moving towards a massive exchange of $10 trillion daily effectively functioning as a Virtual Single Company. He claimed that there is a four-stage evolution in economics from a) Keynesian through b) borderless and c) cyber to d) multiples.

For a time, much was made of electronic ads but these play a relatively small role. Forrester estimates that these accounted for approximately $1 billion in 1998.[5] But here again there is much controversy. Another source claimed that in 2000: "global advertising revenues should top USD7 billion, with the US accounting for 75 percent, or USD5.3 billion of that. Revenues in Europe will be just over USD900 million, while the figure for Asia should be just over USD500 million."[6]

Meanwhile, at INET 2000 it was claimed that in 2000 advertising accounted for $15 billion globally (with 10.5 in the United States, 2.8 in Europe, and 1.25 in Asia).[7] Even so, the real money lies elsewhere in domains such as sales, transactions, licensing, training, maintenance, repair, and consulting. In all these domains, the role of agents looms ever larger, and as in the case of production there is no single model. There are competing American, European, and Japanese (or rather Asian) visions of the future.

2. Sales

In traditional business, the sales department played a central role. Sales personnel stood on the premises. Then they went out as door to door salesmen. At the end of the nineteenth century the idea of mail-order catalogues created a complicated physical loop. A customer read a catalogue and sent an order with a cheque. Upon receipt of the order the company sent the cheque to a bank where it was cashed whereupon the order was processed and an object from a warehouse was sent to the customer. The new media are transforming the nature of sales catalogues. For example, a company called AGENTics has developed UNIClass and uses a virtual catalog which: "is linked by means of … UNIClass to a set of supplier Internet catalogs. To access product information, requisitioners identify their requirements…. A centralized unified product classification residing at the catalog-integration server, UNIClass contains an entry for each product type available in each of the connected suppliers catalogs."[8]

Virtual catalogues are one of the changes brought by the new media.[9] In electronic transactions, the whole process of ordering theoretically becomes much simpler. A person reads an electronic catalogue, orders using an on-line form to make an e-transaction, which is automatically confirmed, whereupon the object is sent from the warehouse. We call this link between tangible persons and objects via intangible transactions a "tangible-intangible loop." It means that ultimately one need not even have warehouses: that one could link orders directly with the production cycle in order to generate products on demand, which potentially spares enormous overhead costs. One corollary is a need to control the complete production and supply chain. Where this is not the case, as with Amazon.com, all is well until a book is out of stock with their suppliers. Then the process is very much longer than one would expect. Some claim that Barnes & Noble, which combines physical stores in this loop is potentially more effective than Amazon.com.

Sales required salesmen. Transactions can occur without salesmen. The good news is potential savings in the cost of salesmen. The bad news is that no one knows precisely what will happen or how to guarantee successful transactions. In 1996, Nicholas Negroponte thought the answer lay in dis-intermediation, a process of cutting out the middleman. Tim Clark disagreed.[10] Don Willmott called dis-intermediation a buzzword from hell.[11] Paul Taylor suggested that a cycle was involved. According to Taylor, first, there was intermediation. Then, the advent of Internet processes brought dis-intermediation. Finally, new players came into the scene and there was re-intermediation. He called this the IDR (Intermediation–Dis-intermediation–Re-intermediation) cycle.[12] Richard Grusin and Jay Bolter speak of "remediation." Thus America posits doing away with intermediaries, and then reintroducing them.

In Europe, by contrast there is an assumption of at least a three-fold system: 1) usage and trades with producers and users, 2) Internet connectivity via telecoms and Internet Service Providers, and 3) intermediaries who add value to the process. There are a series of models. Some foresee an increase in the number of intermediaries.

3. Transactions

One of the new words for sales is "transactions." Sales were traditionally between a business and its customers. Transactions include money transferred in both business to customer (B2C) and business to business (B2B). In the past, each company developed their own supply systems. Now competing firms are working together in combining their supply chains via the Internet. In the spring of 2000, for instance, the automotive industry created a Global Automotive Industry Exchange called e-marketplace. It is said that the supply system of Ford consumes $300 million annually and that the supply system of General Motors consumes $500 million. According to Edupage and the *Financial Times*, these are moving on-line to save time and money, which "could have a new car buyer driving on the asphalt highways only a few days, rather than weeks, after placing their order" and "generating $1 billion in savings during the first 18 months, and as much as $5 billion in savings over five years."[13]

In May 2000, twelve major high-tech firms, including Hewlett Packard (HP) and Compaq[14] agreed to contribute $100 million each to create a new independent company to serve as an Internet exchange. They estimate that a collaborative, integrated approach to procuring supplies from manufacturers will save them between 5 and 7 per cent.[15] They also estimated selling $600 billion in parts and components over the next few years. Interestingly enough HP claims to be among the thirteen "largest industrial companies in the United States and the leader in implementing business to business e-commerce APS (Advanced Planning and Scheduling), SCM (Supply Chain Management) and ERP (Enterprise Resource Planning)."[16] These activities help explain why HP, which is typically considered a computer company, attempted to buy one of the world's leading consultancy firms, KPMG.[17]

In May 2000 also, IBM, in conjunction with other vendors worldwide, announced that they would form E2open.com.[18] One source claimed that the computer and electronics industry were "expected to account for online business-to-business purchases of $593 billion by 2004."[19] Meanwhile, "Forrester Research projects that business-to-business trade will soar to $US1.4 trillion worldwide by 2004".[20] Jupiter Research claimed that computers and telecommunications would "become the biggest online B2B market, with sales soaring past US$1 trillion by 2005."[21] Other leading research firms claimed that the business-to-business market was already $131 billion in 1999 and would reach between $2.7 trillion and $7.3 trillion by 2004.[22] It is striking that many of these predictions were made in 2000 and that updates are now often available only on subscription sites such as e-Marketer.[23]

Another idea of the scale involved is provided by Lockheed Martin, a firm that is known to many as a Missiles and Space Company. The Lockheed Martin, Palo Alto Lab is working with the University of Southern California on Virtual Environments for Training (VET).[24] It also has a division called Lockheed Martin Integrated Business Solutions which described itself in 2001 as "the world's pre-eminent systems engineering and integration company:"[25] They "enabled one of the country's largest residential home lenders to realize its potential for financing over $1 trillion in mortgages" and "delivered a new multi-tiered data warehouse and client/server architecture to one of the nation's largest telecommunications companies, enabling it to maximize network services and decrease the threat of telephone fraud."[26]

Such convergence is also occurring in the banking world. On 6 June 2000, "Switzerland's UBS Warburg and Credit Suisse First Boston; HSBC, the London-based world bank; and four leading international investment banks in the United States (Bank of America, Goldman Sachs, JP Morgan, and Morgan Stanley Dean Witter) announced Fxall.com. Hereby, 'clients of seven of the world's biggest banks are to be offered online access to the global foreign exchange market, the world's largest market with transactions of around $1,400 billion every day.'"[27] This amounts to $511,000 billion annually or US$511 trillion. Granted these are the amounts involved and not the profits but even so it confirms that the transactions field is a large domain.

In the 1980s, the United Nations became involved in Electronic Data Interchange (EDI). This led in 1990 to the establishment of Electronic Data Interchange For Administration, Commerce and Transport (EDIFACT).[28] The past years have seen an important initiative through a joint effort of the United Nations CEFACT and the Organization for the Advancement of Structured Information Standards (OASIS)[29] to produce an ebusiness eXtensible Markup Language (ebXML, cf. Appendix 7).[30]

Aside from these mega-ventures, there were more than 325 sites on e-commerce and e-markets sites listed by @brink.com in 2000.[31] That year, the term "transactions" generated 1,608,110 pages in Altavista and over 500,000 sites in Hotbot, which provides some idea of the immensity of the field. Among the many questions raised by electronic transactions is the precise manner of payment. The most obvious, of course, is simply using a credit card in a secure on-line context to do a traditional debit. However, a number of other models are being explored. These include auctions, micro-payment, invocation-based payment (or superdistribution), open source, and licensing.

4. Auctions

One of the paradoxes of the Internet is that it is constantly re-inventing electronic versions of familiar processes in the physical world. Auctions are a good example. For instance, Bid.com[32] is a Canadian firm founded in 1995 that introduced its on-line auction in the United States in 1996. In addition, to the traditional top bid method (Vickery auction), it also has a Dutch auction wherein the price continues to decrease every few seconds until a bidder comes. Bid.com also has agents in the form of a Search Buddy, which will search for things a week in advance on a given subject and Bid Buddy, which will place a bid on one's behalf within a given amount. This implicitly raises questions relating to identity (cf. chapters 10, 13).

Perhaps the best known of these electronic auction places is *www.ebuy.com*, which has sold 22 million objects. Others include *www.etrade.com* and E-*bay*,[33] which was founded on Labour Day 1995 and had sold over twelve million items by 2001. That year E-bay had twelve basic categories and further search options in terms of themes and regions.[34] By 2004 these basic categories had doubled and there were no less than 275 subcategories for Antiques alone. E-bay is rediscovering the value of library type classification systems.

A glance at the Yahoo Auction site in 2001 revealed that there are over 1.5 million items under their twelve categories.[35] In May 2004, there were seventeen categories but the number of items available had decreased dramatically. For instance, there were 10,548 listed under Antiques and 5,812 items listed under Art. In 2001, the Internet Auction List revealed no less than ninety-four sites under the title of Internet auctions in general and literally hundreds of sites with respect to individual topics. In 2004 this list remained almost unchanged qua the basic headings but the numbers of auctions listed had also decreased dramatically.[36]

Striking about these electronic auctions is how much their themes reflect topics of auctions, bazaars, and flea markets in the physical world. The economic potentials of such electronic auctions were clearly envisaged by Jean-Paul Jacob who headed IBM's Informatics research sector until 2002:

> You can make an instant offer to purchase a "perishable good" such as an airplane seat or a hotel room (see *Priceline.com*). You can also form instantaneous alliances with others around the world to collectively buy large quantities of a product at prices that decrease depending upon the quantity to be purchased (see *Mercata.com*). It is a new world where instantaneous changes in prices are possible, not possible in bricks and mortar stores or catalogs.[37]

5. Micro-Payment

In 1992, Ted Nelson, of Xanadu fame, proposed the idea of micropayment in connection with his idea of transcopyright.[38] This idea was formally introduced by Cyber Cash in April 1997: "The CyberCash wallet and CyberCoin micropayment software will be used to load money from a bank account, which can then be used for payments of 25 cents to US$10."[39] In February 1999, CyberCash had over 2.6 million transactions. By February 2000, they had over 8 million transactions through over 20,000 Internet merchants. Over a million of these transactions were through a single client, H&R Block, the tax forms company.[40]

Although there is still much discussion about security on the Internet, it is interesting to note that the cost of an electronic payment gateway is now at $39.95 per month.[41] MasterCard which is reported to have $857 billion in transactions is said to have had 0.08 per cent fraud in face-to-face situations and 0.005 per cent in Internet situations.[42] Robert Cailliau, a co-inventor of the World Wide Web, expects the W3C to agree on a micropayment system.[43]

6. Licensing

As long as a physical product is changing hands, the economics of the situation is elementary: when *A* sells a product to B, B pays for it at the latest on receiving the product in good order. In the case of immaterial objects such as music, software, and digital products generally, the situation is more problematic. Some cite the ease of making copies as a reason for abandoning entirely the traditions of licensing and the underlying concept of copyright.[44]

Theoretically there are a number of measures that can be taken to protect digital objects. Pages of text, images, or sounds can be given visible and/or invisible digital watermarks. The digital object can be given a time frame such that it can only be played within a given time, say six months from its first use, or only be used a certain number of times (say four viewings of a movie, or ten hearings of a song) and then vanish. This principle is being explored by *www.disappearing.com*, IBM and others.

Music

The case of music is particularly interesting. In 1998, the Internet accounted for 0.4 per cent of all music sales. By 2005, this is predicted to increase to 11 per cent of sales valued at $5 billion.[45] These predictions are complicated by an underground scene which is against copyright and which champions MP3[46] through companies such as Liquid Audio,[47] and non-official sites such as MP3.com – since bought by Vivendi.[48] Companies such as Diamond Multimedia and Samsung are producing MP3 recorders such as the Rio and the Yepp. This scene includes the Internet Underground Music Archive (IUMA) and Napster,[49] which was sued by the Recording Industry Association of America (RIAA)[50] and was closed down and then re-opened as a paying site.[51] Meanwhile, some claim that we should forget about codecs and file formats, because RealNetworks' new Entertainment Center hopes to bring digital music to the masses.[52] There are parallels between the MP3 debates and efforts of Icrave television.[53] To counter these developments, Leonardo Chiariglione, of CSELT (the research arm of Telecom Italia), has been developing the Motion Picture Experts Group (MPEG 4 and 7) standards with four motives: "(a) content providers must be given mechanisms to track the evolution of their content through the delivery chain; (b) service providers must be given the possibility to push content targeted to users' needs; (c) delivery systems providers must be given the possibility to charge the usage of their infrastructure depending on the quality of service requested by the service provider or consumer; (d) consumers must be given the possibility to pull content targeted to their needs."

There are outlines of this approach on the Internet. In early 1999, Chiariglione was also invited to lead a new Secure Digital Music Initiative (SDMI).[54] This began as a group of fifty leading companies in the recording and technology industries and by 2000 had grown to 180 firms, working on two tracks: "The first has already produced a standard, or specification, for portable devices. The longer-term effort is working toward completion of an overall architecture for delivery of digital music in all forms."[55] This is leading to Digital Music Access Technology (DMAT). To test the new system there was an open appeal to try to crack the system. When a Princeton professor was successful in so doing he was promptly ordered not to publish his results and at the beginning of June 2001 went to court with the support of the Electronic Frontier Foundation.[56]

Meanwhile, the International Music Joint Venture (IMJV)[57] was founded by three music copyright organizations: the American Society of Composers, Authors and Publishers (ASCAP, U.S.A.), Buma/Stemra (Netherlands) and the Mechanical-Copyright Protection Society –Performing Right Society (MCPS-PRS, U.K.) Alliance, in order to: "eliminate duplication in, and improve the accuracy of, common databases; reduce costs and improve efficiency, upgrade systems and embrace new technology."[58]

At the same time, major corporations are seeking independent solutions. IBM, for instance has launched the Madison Project, which includes a partnership of the "big five"[59] in the sound industry, Universal, Sony, Time-Warner, EMI, and the Bertelsmann Music Group (BMG), as well as British Telecom and Deutsche Telekom. IBM has also developed an Electronic Media Management System (EMMS), which is accepted by two of the top five, namely, Sony and BMG entertainment.[60] Three of the big five (namely, Warner Music, Sony, and EMI) have also joined with BSkyB to create Music Choice Europe.[61] Meanwhile, AT&T was working with Universal (owned by Seagram) to create A2Bmusic.com which was in turn linked with SDMI.

On 8 December 2000, Vivendi acquired Universal. In April 2001, Yahoo and Duet also announced an alliance to present and market an on-demand music subscription service created by Vivendi Universal Music Group and Sony Music Entertainment.[62] In June 2001, Duet was renamed Pressplay and Vivendi and Sony agreed to distribute this via Microsoft's MSN network.[63] In June 2001, Vivendi also bought MP3.com. Although Napster was sued, the year 2000 saw three fundamental developments.

First, there were no less than fourteen alternatives to Napster between June 1999 and June 2000 (Table 12). By October 2000 this list had expanded to twenty-six as part of 240+ downloads, services, and related information resources.[64] In August 2001 four new file-sharing systems: FastTrack, Audiogalaxy, iMesh, and Gnutella "were used to download 3.05 billion files."[65] In January 2002, the chief clones of Napster were Bearshare, Grokster, Aimster, Limewire, and Audiogalaxy.[66] By July 2002 listen.com had a catalogue for all of the big five with 170,000 songs available for only $10 per month.[67] By 2003, Gnutella and KaZaA were illegal and there were a number of commercial music-sharing sites such as E-Music, Hotvision.de, iTunes Music Store, Liquid.com, Pop File, Weblisten.com.[68] Second, in August 2000, Andy Grove the CEO of Intel announced that Intel would support the Napster initiative. This was important according to Malcolm Maclachlan, media e-commerce analyst at International Data Corp. (IDC).[69]

Third, at the end of October 2000, Bertelsmann announced a new agreement with Napster to sell music on line on a subscription basis.[70] Bertelsmann noted that these plans had been long in the making. Was the noise around Napster an elaborate publicity stunt? In January 2001, edel Music and TVT Records joined the alliance. In April 2001, RealNetworks, AOL Time Warner, Bertelsmann, and EMI Group formed a pact to establish a subscription on-line music service called MusicNet.[71] On 5 June 2001, Napster became "an affiliate of MusicNet, the world's first digital distribution platform for downloading and streaming music."[72] Napster has since been taken over by Roxio Inc. Some characterize the Napster phenomenon as part of a shift towards peer-to-peer computing. This has led Sun to launch new software such as JXTA.[73]

Michel Bauwens (Belgacom) sees peer-to-peer (p2p) as a technological para-digm, as distribution mechanism, production method, as important in politics, in spirituality, for global knowledge exchange, co-operative societal practices and for manufacturing. Edward Haskell's theory of co-action proposed that there were three basic relationships between individuals: adversarial (win-lose), neutral and synergistic (win-win).[74] Bauwen has suggested that we also need to include a societal dimension whereby synergistic relationships become win-win-win.[75] For this reason he sees peer-to-peer as the potential basis for a new civilization.

On the technological front, the situation continues to change so rapidly that it is difficult to see the wood for the trees. Of the fourteen sites from 2000 listed below (Table 12) at least two have been abandoned and at least two others have become paying sites. On the other hand dozens of new sites have emerged. One site lists over eighty-five file-sharing sites.[76] New alternatives continue to appear. In April 2004, *Wired* claimed that Gnutella was passé and that Justin Frankel's Waste "is where it's at." Meanwhile the rise of paying sites continues to evolve. Since 1997, MusicMatch has sold 50 million copies of its digital music management jukebox. Apple's subscription service, iTunes was joined in May 2004 by Sony's Connect, while Microsoft was working on Janus.

In his weekly *Rapidly Changing Face of Computing* (19 February 2001), Jeffrey Harrow raised another dimension of the Napster discussion entailing variations of rapid prototyping and stereo-lithography, such as digital fabricators (or fabbers).[77] He suggested that the same principles that are being applied to music could be extended to physical objects such as a sculpture, or a particular dinner plate: "you could 'download' its pattern from someone else over the net. Then, as you might do using an MP3 file to create a physical CD in a CD burner, you could create a real dinner plate from the digital file."[78]

Not everyone is so optimistic about these developments. In the enormous debates concerning Napster, some have discerned larger battles: namely, attempts to shift the business model from purchase of goods to licensing of goods. Rosetta books has produced a disappearing book that self destructs after ten hours.[79] Clifford Lynch has suggested that these attempts to redefine the rules for music are part of a larger plan to use music as a model for other media, including books. He notes that this potentially entails grave dangers with respect to freedom:

> License restrictions on the use of content that you might acquire, now under license rather than purchase – might prohibit you from making personal copies, loaning it to another person, or even criticizing it publicly, or only allow you to use the content for a limited period of time. Such license terms – many of which are not enforceable by technical protection systems (one cannot imagine a technical protection system that tries to block the writing of critical essays about a work for example) – may be equally or even more severely at odds with consumer expectations....
>
> In the print world U.S. research libraries have spent a great deal of money and effort to create and maintain specialized research collections of the local literature and culture of foreign nations. Technological controls to enforce national boundaries and content policies or regional markets may well put an end to such activities, or at least make them much more difficult and costly.[80]

TABLE 12 Fourteen alternatives to Napster in 2000[82]

1	IMESH.COM	Site that allows people to exchange various files directly from their desktops without setting up web sites or uploading files to a server.
2	GNUTELLA	Open-source, fully distributed search and download system for media and archive files.
3	CUTEMX	Site that offers software for searching and downloading any type of file on a network.
4	SCOUR EXCHANGE	Central server through which requests flow, allowing movie-trading on line.
5	FREENET	Peer-to-peer, decentralized network designed to distribute information efficiently and without censorship.
6	NAPIGATOR	A way for people to run their own Napster servers after the company is forced to shut down.
7	FILEFURY	Software that allows people to share files of any type and search other computers.
8	HOTLINE	Site that enables live chat, conferencing, messaging, data warehousing, and file transfer and viewing.
9	JUNGLE MONKEY	Distributed file-sharing program created as a research project at the University of Michigan.
10	SPINFRENZY.COM	Site that offers MP3 files available for other music and video lovers connections.
11	WRAPSTER V1.0	File sharing software for the Napster community that can be used to share content other than music, including movies.
12	FILEPOOL	Offers to allow users to share files in any format.
13	POINTERA	Sells itself as a "legitimate" way for people to share files.
14	RAPSTER	Brazilian alternative to Napster

Jeremy Rifkin has pointed to similar dangers in his *Age of Access*. In the past, he argues, we purchased things directly. In the future, we shall merely licence things from major corporations who give us access on a limited time basis to things we formerly purchased. In Rifkin's scenario the concept of ownership will soon become obsolete. While very provocative, there is a serious flaw in their reasoning. The rhetoric that ownership would become obsolete is really an attempt to remove ownership from the realm of consumers and individuals. For the scenario to work, (major) corporations would have to expropriate total and enduring ownership over their products. However, these products are very frequently produced by creative individuals outside these corporations.

In the past, persons wrote books, music, scripts for films, etc., and then entered agreements with publishers, production houses, and other companies to ensure that their work was successfully produced and distributed. These agreements were typically for limited editions under specific spatial (for given countries) and temporal (for a given period) constraints. If publishers and production houses now lay claim to complete ownership over materials that are not originally theirs[81] and for which they merely play an intermediary role, then there is every reason to believe that both the producing authors and their paying consumer audiences will find a solution closer to creators' and users' needs. From all this emerges a paradoxical picture. An opposition between America as interested in paid proprietary software and Europe concerned with free open source is too simplistic. America produces Napsters and the like which assume no direct financial gain, whereas it is Europe that is trying through MPEG and other initiatives to find realistic means of payment. At another level, however, the American quest towards an access economy, where goods and services are accessed rather than bought reintroduces a dimension of greed that is foreign to Europe. Ironically the same America that makes so much noise about owning rights especially to films has just sold one of its largest collections (MGM) to Sony in Japan. Hollywood may yet find itself paying royalties to Japan for their earlier products.

7. Copyright

Closely connected with the above is the realm of copyright. Here there are fundamentally different traditions. In French law, copyright, or rather the author's rights are seen as an inalienable part of a person. In Anglo-Saxon law, this notion is much weaker. Meanwhile, in the American variant, copyright is assumed to be something that can be acquired from others in the way that one can buy things. In this tradition intellectual property is not unlike physical property. It goes to the highest bidder.

As long as books, music, art, and other non-physical products were published in a single country, one was faced only with the copyright laws of the country in question. The advent of the Internet changes this fundamentally because now anything on a web site can potentially be accessed anywhere in the world. To meet these challenges, a number of bodies are working at a new international solution. These efforts are being headed by the World Intellectual Property Office (WIPO, Geneva). At the European level, besides MPEG, there are a number of initiatives headed by the European Commission such as IMPRIMATUR and more recently INDECS. There is also an Intellectual Property Institute (London).[83] On the assumption that these problems will be resolved, the major corporations have visions of a whole range of digital services that can be offered on-line, including personalized news through a pointcast network (chapter 10) and digital libraries.[84] It is assumed further that intelligent agents will play an important role in this process.

Some of the copyright debates are paradoxical. In the United States, for instance, the major film companies have taken action against individual web sites of fans. In 2004, such actions have spread to the United Kingdom. Meanwhile one Hollywood studio is making their own fan site such that one can, in future, have fans on demand.[85]

8. Open Source

In the previous chapter we discussed the rise of open source, which was started by Linus Torvalds, of Linux fame. A similar idea of sharing freely was one of the guiding principles underlying the Internet when it was founded in 1969 (cf. chapters 14–15). When Richard Stallman started his career at MIT in 1971, he worked in a group that used free software exclusively.[86]

Gradually, however, the United States transformed this idea. In 1977, for instance, Bruce Perens developed the Debian free software.[87] As the authors of the Debian "free software" note, there are seventeen definitions of "free." "Only one of them is 'at no cost'. The rest refer to liberty and lack of constraint. When we speak of Free Software, we mean freedom not price."[88] There were other groups such as the Free Standards Group[89] and the Free BSD.[90] In 1983, Richard Stallman began the GNU (Gnu's Not Unix) Initiative wherein free pertained not to price but to three specific freedoms: "First, the freedom to copy the program and give it away to your friends and co-workers; second, the freedom to change the program as you wish, by having full access to source code; third, the freedom to distribute an improved version and thus help build the community." He adds a proviso that those who redistribute GNU software "may charge a fee for the physical act of transferring a copy," or simply give them away.[91]

In 1991, Linus Torvalds developed the Linux operating system in Europe. In 1996 the Free Software Foundation (FSF)[92] became a tax-exempt charity to raise funds for work on the GNU Project.[93] The origins of a business model for open source can be traced back to Apple's approach to the Darwin. The immediate inspiration was the announcement to make the source code for Netscape browser available free of charge on 22 January 1998. This led to a brainstorming session in Palo Alto on 3 February 1998, which coined the term "open source" and led in the following week to Linus Torvalds giving his support with respect to Linux and to the launching of http://www.opensource.org.[94] It is often overlooked that on the same day Netscape announced the launching of "a host of enhanced products and services that leverage its free client software to make it easy for enterprise and individual customers to adopt Netscape solutions."[95] In this approach giving away was part of a larger business case very much concerned with money and markets.

The Debian model became a basis for the open source initiative in the United States[96] and led to the development of a clearly articulated business case,[97] which includes paradoxical steps such as giving away the software product, but selling "distribution, branding, and after-sale service." Eric Raymond has traced the history of these developments in an important book: *The Cathedral and the Bazaar*[98] (cf. chapters 14–15).

One U.S. version of the open source project is now called the Visual Basic Open Source Project and is working on open source development of ActiveX controls, Dynamic Link Libraries (DLLs), software and source code, all free and in the public domain. Their explanation of why people co-operate was "gestalt," which they defined as: "'the whole is greater than the sum of its parts'. With over 900 email members (as of 18 June 2000) and 35,000 unique visitors to VBXML each month (growing at approximately 30–50% per month, depending on the month), VBXML is the top Windows XML developers resource."[99]

9. Free Software

Meanwhile, companies are exploring more radical solutions by giving away their products, such that sales disappear entirely on some fronts. The Netscape browser is a simple case in point. Sun's Java code is a more complex example. Giving away free computers, free Internet use or free cell phones are more complex examples again. The old adage about there never being a free lunch is still true. Companies give something away because it furthers other interests in a larger chain, and the cost is inevitably bundled at a less evident part of the chain. If telcos give away cell phones, then those costs will be absorbed in the price of calls. Or they may be absorbed indirectly, which is another reason why training, consulting, maintenance, repair, and agents are becoming ever-more important.

The X Consortium's X Window System (version X11) offers free software. But then there are popular workstations and PC graphics boards for which non-free versions are the only ones that work. In such ways, the United States makes a business out of the open source idea. Even so, the year 2000 saw a radical shift in this field. The GNU Network Object Model Environment (GNOME)[100] Foundation: "is offering a set of software standards for a common software environment in which to create a viable but free alternative to Microsoft's Windows operating system, a unified desktop user interface, and a set of productivity programs (also free) to compete against Microsoft's Office suite. Sun has decided to adopt the Gnome desktop system for its Solaris operating system."[101]

If this initiative is successful then open source offers a serious alternative for all desktop software in the near future. In August 2000, Forrester Research forecasted that by 2004 "all traditional software vendors will need to change their proprietary business models to open-source ones, or drastically lower the price of enterprise application licenses."[102] In 2004 proprietary software was still very much in evidence, although the importance of open source continues to grow.

10. Invocation-Based Payment

In the realm of software, a variant on this idea, called superdistribution, has been developed in Japan by Dr. Ryoichi Mori (Tsukuba University): "Superdistribution is an approach to distributing software in which software is made available freely and without restriction but is protected from modifications and modes of usage not authorized by its vendor."[103] This idea was taken up in the United States by Dr. Brad Cox, in his book, *Superdistribution*, where he prefers to call the process "invocation-based payment." Hence the user pays no large fees up front and only pays for the software if they decide to use it on a regular basis. In October 2000, Mark Benioff, formerly of Oracle, began a new startup company Salesforce.com to implement this idea in the realm of Customer Relationship Management (CRM) software.[104]

Related to the above is the development of Application Service Providers (ASPs). Companies are often daunted by the costs of creating and maintaining an IT infrastructure (hardware and software), knowing how to choose the right specialized staff, and how to make such facilities available in networks linking offices and sites in multiple locations. ASPs promise to solve such problems by effectively renting companies what they claim is the necessary technology and staff on the basis of a monthly subscription. More recently there are Application Infrastructure Providers (AIPs).[105] As noted earlier, and as Jeremy Rifkin has discussed in his *Age of Access*, this is part of a larger trend whereby companies no longer try to sell products but to lease them through subscriptions such that ownership remains with the producer and all that the buyer has is access for a limited period.

While the sale or licensing of physical and digital products will almost certainly remain an important aspect of business, the largest corporations are focussing on what happens before and after a product has been sold. This includes identifying and legitimizing, training, consulting, maintenance, repair, and increasingly, agents.

11. Identifying and Legitimizing

In personal transactions, problems of identification are minimal. We see the buyer. They give their money and they receive the product. Traditionally, whenever larger sums were involved, banks entered the picture. Banks interviewed the buyers and sellers in order to establish that they could fulfill their promises. Banks identified and legitimized the partners before the transaction was made.

In on-line transactions, problems of identity and legitimation are much greater. How do I know that the person is giving their true name? Even if I can identify the computer from which they are working, how do I know that this computer is legitimately linked with the person and is not simply a front from which they are working? The first decade of the Internet brought a large number of interim solutions. As a result users are faced with the burden of constantly re-identifying themselves (entering different passwords each time) and legitimizing themselves under different rules each time. It would be enormously helpful to users if this plethora of different rules could be reduced.

In this context, pioneering work has been done in the realm of adult (sexual) sites. Until recently there were thousands of sites each with its own identification and subscription rules. Since 1999, there has been a dramatic increase in umbrella organizations, which make a business of ensuring a user's age and identification. Using such a subscription gives one access to a whole series of sites using a single ID and password without having to sign in differently each time. In 2000, this principle began to spread to mainstream activities on the Internet. The first edition of ASPnews report (July 2000) identified the significance of centrally stored profile information: "In an Internet-centric computing model, directory services act as a central store of information about the location, identity and access profiles of users, content and computing resources. Directory store operators ... effectively become the banking institutions of the Internet economy."[106]

Not surprisingly this is one of the new frontiers. In March 2001, Microsoft unveiled a new strategy called Hailstorm,[107] whereby its attempt to become the equivalent of a banker is linked with a larger plan to work closely with key Application Service Providers (ASPs) such as Usinternetworking, ManagedOps.com, Qwest Communications, and their European equivalents, NetStore and Equant. In the process of identifying and legitimizing others, Microsoft is trying to move from a software company to a service provider. Companies such as IBM have been pursuing such a strategy on a number of levels for some time.

On the surface, Hailstorm promised user-centric XML services to manage and protect user information and to provide it consistently, personalized "from any application device, service and network."[108] In the process, however, each user was expected to reveal "my profile," which included their address, favourite web sites, location, wallet, calendar, and contacts. This raised important privacy issues. By 2004 Microsoft had abandoned Hailstorm and was pursuing Paparazzi as its latest effort in the direction of SPOT (Smart Personal Object Technology).[109]

In May 2001, Microsoft also introduced the idea of an electronic or e-wallet, which plans to replace traditional credit card payment on the Internet with a Passport system, which links the individual's purchase with their e-mail and other personal information, ostensibly for purposes of verification and stores this in Microsoft's database. AOL complained that this is unfair but introduced a similar technology.[110] By 2004, eWallet version 4 was released for Microsoft Smartphones.[111]

12. Training

In the case of major software packages such as Alias-Wavefront, Catia, AutoDesk, Bentley or database systems such as Oracle, the cost of the package is only the beginning. Training persons how to use the software typically costs more than the original package. Searchlight, for instance, claims that "extended costs (system administration, software, upgrades) can outweigh the initial hardware investment by a ratio of seven-to-one."[112] They also cite a report claiming that it costs "$10,000 to develop just one hour of computer-based training."[113]

IBM has been active in this field. In August 1998, IBM Global Services launched a new Training Management Services (TMS) with 1,500 full-time professionals. TMS provides "not only training content through classroom settings and computer- and Internet-based methods, but also services such as skills assessment and training enrollment and administration."[114] On 30 May 2000, IBM and Rational submitted the "Unified Process Model (UPM) as an industry standard to the Object Management Group. This model which uses Unified Modelling Language 'enables the interchange of process know-how between organizations, and the creation of tools for process authoring, process customization and process improvement.'"[115]

In 1998, IBM's reported annual revenue was $81.7 billion, while IBM Global Services had a reported revenue of $26 billion. Hence, approximately 31 per cent of IBM's activities are now in services. These are divided into three large categories: business innovation services; integrated technology services, and strategic outsourcing services.[116] The business innovation services alone include trust and e-commerce services, web application development, procurement services, e-business strategy and design, knowledge management, custom systems integration, enterprise resource planning, supply chain management, business intelligence, customer relationship management, and skills transformation services for e-business. IBM's e-business consulting services has a special Content Management Solutions organization with: "consulting and systems integration services related to creating, managing and delivering content over the Web ... across the entire project life cycle, from front-end process reengineering through requirements definition, product selection, systems integration, delivery, installation, training, production, conversion of existing documents and post-acceptance support."

IBM is not alone in this trend towards services. Ed learning systems, Inc., founded in 1993, was a privately held learning solutions provider "focused on customers who use the Internet to deliver and provide business solutions." On 9 June 2000, Sun Microsystems acquired Ed learning and its affiliate, e-tech, as part of its strategy to "increase support, through quality training, for the high availability needs of its dot-com customers."[117]

Increasingly there are new universities specifically aimed at training. For instance there is a Rational University for professional education and product training.[118] On 14 June 2000, an IBM affiliate, NetObjects, Inc., a leading provider of e-business solutions and services, announced NetObjects University: "an innovative 'dot.com' approach toward classroom instruction, geared toward helping businesses to maximize their investment in Web technologies."[119] The National Computer Systems, Inc. (NCS) has Virtual University Enterprises (VUE) with a network of more than 2,000 testing centres in over 110 countries dealing with both testing and training.[120] SRI Consulting has a Learning on Demand (LoD) system directed at business intelligence. In this vision e-learning might well stand for economic learning.[121]

13. Consulting

Some cynics would say that consultants are merely former employees without a regular job and without the security of a pension. There is serious evidence that major corporations are trying to undermine the concept of regular jobs and to replace them with part-time consultancy positions, which can be terminated at any time (cf. chapter 6.4). To make these trends more attractive, they are often cloaked in attractive names. Hence, "freelance" has become "e-lance," although there is evidence that self-employment is decreasing in the new economy.[122]

Whole branches of activities are reconfiguring themselves through mergers and alliances. Five years ago there were four areas: 1) large consultancy firms (e.g., Price Waterhouse, Ernst and Young); 2) computer companies (e.g., IBM, HP, and Hitachi); 3) Enterprise Resource Planning (ERP) companies (e.g., Peoplesoft, SAP, Baan, J.D. Edwards, and since 1999, Oracle) and 4) business to business pioneers (notably Commerce One, founded 1997, from Distrivision, 1994[123] and Ariba). These four areas are becoming inextricably interconnected.

A first fundamental step was a series of mergers between consultancy firms and computer firms, which has led to a radical decline in the number of players. For instance, IBM Global Services has acquired Lotus, Rational Software, and Informix. Price-Waterhouse and Coopers and Lybrand, once four independent companies, joined into one and have also become part of IBM. A.T. Kearney, founded in 1925, had a history of helping business leaders gain and sustain competitive advantage. In 1995, Kearney joined EDS to become the world's second largest high value management consulting firm.[124] MCI Systemhouse,[125] once owned by MCI WorldCom, is also now part of EDS. Along with management consulting, EDS now specializes in e.solutions, business process management, and information solutions.[126] Klynveld, Peat, Marwick, and Goerdeler are now a single company KPMG. Cap Gemini, Sogeti and Ernst and Young (which in turn had acquired Clarkson and Gordon) are now one company. Not surprisingly these mammoth consultancy firms now have divisions for almost every sector of the economy. As a result over forty five large companies have become thirteen major corporations (Table 13).[127]

Traditional hardware firms are now focussing ever more on training and consultancy services. The examples of Hewlett Packard's Enterprise Resource Planning Services (ERP) and IBM's Global Services have already been mentioned. Another example is the General Electric Center for Financial Learning which is an: "on-line educational resource intended to offer information and planning tools on personal finance and investments, where you can take on-line courses, explore the world of personal finance, and attend moderated discussions led by a financial advisor."[128]

Beginning in November 1999, there were two further developments: 1) new alliances and mergers between a) Enterprise Resource Planning (ERP) companies, b) Business to Business (B2B) companies, c) consultancy companies, and d) computer companies; 2) new links between these companies and specific industry sectors. These alliances and mergers have spread to a whole range of key industries (Table 14).[129] Not all the attempts are successful. Within a year the IBM, i2, Siebel alliance stopped. So too had the alliance between Commerce One and SAP to create on-line marketplaces.[130] By October 2001 Sun Microsystems and vendors Arbortext, Boeing, Commerce One, SAP, and others founded a Universal Business Language (UBL) committee, which led to a draft in May 2004. Approved by OASIS, this provides "a description language for XML based purchase orders, invoices and shipping orders."[131] UBL is part of a larger business framework covered by ebxml (ISO 15000). Through these developments computer companies, consulting firms, Business to

TABLE 13 The big picture: mergers of accounting, consultancy[136] and software firms in the past decade[137]

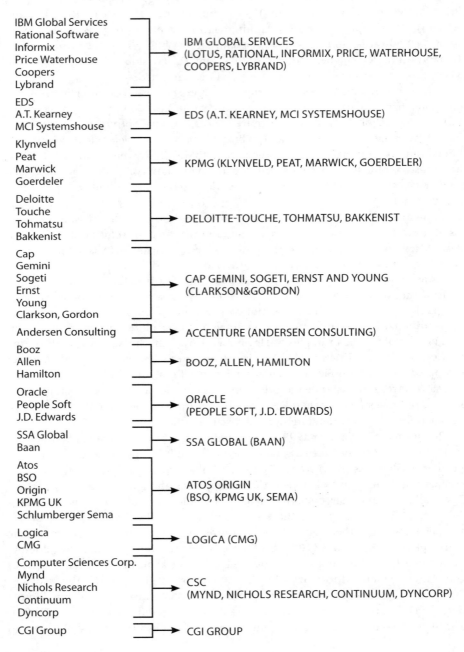

IBM Global Services
Rational Software
Informix
Price Waterhouse
Coopers
Lybrand

→ IBM GLOBAL SERVICES
(LOTUS, RATIONAL, INFORMIX, PRICE, WATERHOUSE, COOPERS, LYBRAND)

EDS
A.T. Kearney
MCI Systemshouse

→ EDS (A.T. KEARNEY, MCI SYSTEMSHOUSE)

Klynveld
Peat
Marwick
Goerdeler

→ KPMG (KLYNVELD, PEAT, MARWICK, GOERDELER)

Deloitte
Touche
Tohmatsu
Bakkenist

→ DELOITTE-TOUCHE, TOHMATSU, BAKKENIST

Cap
Gemini
Sogeti
Ernst
Young
Clarkson, Gordon

→ CAP GEMINI, SOGETI, ERNST AND YOUNG
(CLARKSON&GORDON)

Andersen Consulting

→ ACCENTURE (ANDERSEN CONSULTING)

Booz
Allen
Hamilton

→ BOOZ, ALLEN, HAMILTON

Oracle
People Soft
J.D. Edwards

→ ORACLE
(PEOPLE SOFT, J.D. EDWARDS)

SSA Global
Baan

→ SSA GLOBAL (BAAN)

Atos
BSO
Origin
KPMG UK
Schlumberger Sema

→ ATOS ORIGIN
(BSO, KPMG UK, SEMA)

Logica
CMG

→ LOGICA (CMG)

Computer Sciences Corp.
Mynd
Nichols Research
Continuum
Dyncorp

→ CSC
(MYND, NICHOLS RESEARCH, CONTINUUM, DYNCORP)

CGI Group

→ CGI GROUP

Business (B2B) and ERP firms are becoming linked in ever new ways.[132] Here, RosettaNet with its Partner Interface Processes (PIPs) is making a contribution.[133]

Enterprise Resource Planning (ERP) companies such as Oracle, PeopleSoft, and J. D. Edwards had been affected by developments in Customer Relationship Management (CRM), Supply Chain Management (SCM), and Procurement Management (PM) software. Sales Force Automation (SFA)[134] is another buzzword in this field. In April 2000, Oracle announced a new integration of ERP and CRM. Implicit herein is a new vision of e-business as unifying all "business processing – from marketing, sales, and procurement – to manufacturing, supply chain, and service – to financial operations, project management, and human resources – to business intelligence systems."[135]

These trends help explain why computer software companies are trying to buy consulting companies, e.g., Micosoft-SAP and Oracle-PeopleSoft. From all this, a complete integration of products, raw materials, parts, and service is emerging. Unlike some developments that are specifically American, European, or Japanese, these developments are global. In a keynote at WWW10 (May 2001), John Chen, CEO and President of Sybase discerned two main approaches: 1) making everything the same in a single system, 2) attempting to make existing, diverse programs work together. While the first solution entails simplified management and easier upgrading cycles, he claimed that it is considerably more expensive than the second solution, namely, $8.9 million, as opposed to $5.4 million at the enterprise level.

14. Maintenance

In the past, each new version of software required buying a new package almost as cumbersome as the original version. Increasingly these updated versions are available on-line. Some envisage that all software will soon be on-line. A more radical view is that such updates will happen automatically. Agents will recognize that a new update is available, determine that it is covered in an existing contract, and install the new version without even needing to disturb the user. By 2004 this has begun to happen.

At the frontiers, persons are concerned with downloading much more than simple software. For instance, the textile industry in Japan and Europe is digitizing all the major textile patterns with a view to producing new patterns on-line. It is already the case that "Bernina, Pfaff, and Singer all have developed product lines that connect to the Internet (via a PC) so you can download patterns and embroidery."[139]

These new methods of maintenance take many forms. The Bauhaus University (Weimar) uses augmented reality for revitalization of buildings.[140] Siemens has Zylinderkonstruktion (CyliCon), which uses augmented reality to create 3-D additions or modifications to existing industrial pipelines.[141] The Fraunhofer Society (Darmstadt) is using augmented reality for mechanical maintenance and repair.[142] The Center for Engineering Systems and Advanced Research (CESAR, Oak Ridge National Laboratory) is developing cooperating autonomous robots for industrial/household maintenance and other purposes.[143] The U.S. government's Sandia Labs

TABLE 14 The details: Links between specific Business-to-Business (B2B) companies, corporations and industry segments from November 1999 to June 2000.[138]

1999				
2 Nov.	Commerce One	GM	Trade Xchange	Auto
2 Nov.	Oracle	Ford	AutoXchange	Auto
15 Dec.	Commerce One, PeopleSoft	Guess	Apparelbuy.com	Clothes
2000				
19 Jan.	Ariba	Chevron	Petrocosm	Oil and gas
13 Jan.	Commerce One	Shell	GlobalOneTrading	Oil and gas
18 Jan.	Ariba	Dupont	Omnexus	Chemical
19 Jan.	SAP	Statoil	SAP for Oil & Gas	Oil and gas
25 Feb.	Commerce One, Oracle	GM, Ford, Daimler	Covisint	Auto
29 Feb.	Commerce One	Sears, Carrefour	GlobalnetXchange	Retail
2 Mar.	Commerce One	Ispat	Metique	Metals
14 Mar.	Ariba	Cargill	Novopoint	Food, beverage
28 Mar.	Commerce One, Microsoft	Boeing, Lockheed	Exostar	Aerospace, defence
1 May	HP	AMD, Hitachi....	Ehitex, Converge	Technology
2 May	Ariba	Sabre	Sabre-marketplace	Travel, hospitality
1 Jun.	Commerce One	Carolina Power	Pantellos	Energy and utility
6 Jun.	Ariba, Andersen	B2Build	B2Build	Construction
7 Jun.	Ariba, IBM, i2	Hitachi, IBM	E2open.com	Computer, telco
20 Jun.	Ariba	BASF, Dow	Omnexus.com	Plastics injection
20 Jun.	Ariba, EDS, CoNext	Textron	Plano	Indirect goods
21 Jun.	IBM, i2, Siebel	Dassault	IBM PLM electronics	Product lifecycle

have a project on Predictive Maintenance.[144] General Electric and Cisco Systems are collaborating: "to wire up industrial plants so that managers can monitor what's happening on the factory floor via a Web site.... GE Cisco Industrial Networks will offer products and services ranging from simple assessment and troubleshooting of existing networks, to design, installation and maintenance of an entire system."[145]

A glimpse of things to come is in a list of projects of the Micro Machine Centre (MMC, Tokyo) and includes: "an experimental system for internal tube inspection, in which a wireless micromachine moves through the interior of a tube under its own power and transmits information relating to blockage and other situations encountered within the tube."[146]

15. Repair

In the past, when a punctured tire was flat, it had to be taken for repair. When a machine or a device broke down, one took it to a garage or a repair shop. There is a trend towards self-healing materials and so-called intelligent materials which "know" when they are no longer working. There is a fashion to speak of self-everything (i.e. self-managing, self-monitoring, self-healing, self-repairing etc.). In Sweden there is work on Intelligent Speed Adaption (ISA) systems.[147] Yrjö Nuevo at Nokia speaks of intelligent products.[148] Stewart Brand speaks of how buildings learn.[149] NASA has an intelligent mechanisms group linked with its Mars Explorer.[150] We are on the way to self-monitoring machines, which are a first step towards self-healing mechanisms.

Self-Healing

In 1961, William J. Buehler, a researcher at the Naval Ordnance Laboratory in White Oak, Maryland, accidentally discovered an alloy with the property of shape memory, i.e., one could bend the object and it would go back to its original shape. This shape memory alloy was named Nickel Titanium Naval Ordnance Laboratory (NITINOL).[151] At Northwestern University, "the shape memory alloys of special interest are those that are potentially of the 'self healing' type which are useful in damage tolerant structures."[152] They are not alone. At the University of California at Los Angeles (UCLA) there is an Active Materials Lab which studies shape memory alloys.[153] At MIT, there is an Active Materials and Structures Lab.[154] Researchers at the University of Akron are studying self-healing surfaces.[155] Discussions of such self-healing materials go back to the early 1990s.[156] Professor Amon (Belfast) notes that in the case of spacecraft: "the entire fabric of the vessel will be a 'genius' material woven with microsensors and microeffectors. ME [Micro-Electronics] opens the possibilities of materials that can grow subsystems, heal damage and that are homeostatic like living systems."[157]

Such materials are already being built. There is a product called Snokote, the self-healing, corrosion-control composition of which "was specifically designed for use in environments where rust and corrosion are problematic. Snokote penetrates into the surface to form a barrier against moisture and other corrosive elements."[158] In 1998, Los Alamos (Albuquerque, New Mexico) and North Hand Protection (Charleston, South Carolina) won a prize for real-time, puncture detecting, self-healing materials: "When an object pierces the materials, bringing the two gooey layers in contact with each other, an electrical circuit is completed, sounding an alarm that can be either audio, visual, or displayed on a computer. Their plastic gooey properties also allow them to close over punctures and small tears."[159]

The product, called Instalarm, allows instant detection of punctures or other breaches of personal protective equipment, such as gloves, bodysuits, biohazard suits and boots, or containment vessels, such as hazardous waste drums, chemical drums, and radiation sources.[160] The CONstruction MATerials and Systems (CONMAT) program is very much interested in such self-monitoring/self-healing materials and envisions: "constructed facilities that can monitor their 'health' and report that information to maintenance personnel" and "structures that could 'heal' damage by using smart materials in the structure."[161] Needless to say this points to future cost savings. CONMAT is part of a larger picture entailing four inter-related fields: 1) micro-structural engineering, 2) multi-phase materials, 3) micro-manufacturing, and 4) self-monitoring/self-healing materials.

On 15 February 2001, Scott White and a team of researchers at the University of Illinois at Urbana Champaign (UIUC) announced that they had developed a new material "capable of healing itself in much the same fashion as a biological organism."[162] Here again the boundaries between lifeless objects and living human beings are becoming blurred. A representative from the U.S. Air Force which helped fund the project has noted that the new material would be "particularly useful for applications for which repair is either impossible or impractical, such as electronic circuit boards or other components of deep-space probes or implanted medical devices."[163]

As might be expected the military is very active in these domains. In the United States, for instance, there is discussion of "self-monitoring and self-healing materials to permit in-flight battle damage repair."[164]

> While remote diagnoses and sensing of maintenance problems will be possible, neural nets and parallel processing will allow systems to reconfigure themselves around defective areas, becoming "self-repairing" parts.... The self-repairing part has the ability to detect degradation in performance and repair itself by eliminating the failed component from use or rerouting its circuits around the defective area. This concept will operate as a standby redundancy system, whereby the spare components or circuits are operated only when required to keep the part functioning. The maintenance strategy used will be that of non-maintained redundancy. As such, the repair is only commenced when the part completely fails. It will be more cost-effective to build this self-repair capability into the parts, even with its redundant circuitry, rather than removing, repairing, and replacing parts in a cyclic pattern over the useful life of the part.[165]

While this solution is interesting, it entails building into the system twice the number of components needed to operate a device at a given moment. While fully understandable as a solution for certain military needs, and also for special situations such as a space voyage, it is hardly a feasible proposition for everyday life where a lack of raw materials looms as a problem, especially as the Internet becomes global.

In the life sciences, medicine has seen a trend from a reactive treatment of existing diseases, to a pro-active preventative medicine, whereby one removes the causes before the disease even appears. Similarly, companies such as Origin are working towards pro-active systems management: software agents try to detect and fix problems before they become evident to human users and thus save money on subsequent repairs.

Intelligent Materials

Self-healing materials are part of a larger trend towards intelligent or smart materials, which emerged as a field in the mid-1990s.[166] We discussed earlier how architectural design software is adding "intelligence" to doors and windows such that a computer image of a door in a skyscraper "knows" the characteristics of its subsequent physical equivalent. Intelligence in this sense is now increasingly being extended to objects in the physical world. Objects are no longer lifeless things. They can react to changes in their environment. Light-sensored flush toilets are an everyday example. As soon as we leave the washroom the toilet flushes automatically. In some trains they now also rinse the seat automatically. Alarms that go off when we get too close to a painting or a locked car are other elementary examples.

The members of the Universal Plug and Play Forum want to extend this concept to smart objects and intelligent appliances in the home.[167] So do others such as the Home Audio Visual Information (HAVI) consortium which include Philips. Low-level artificial intelligence systems "currently monitor military systems, optimize the water level in dishwashers, control the actions of simulated pets, and help predict natural disasters."[168] Professor Jun Murai (Keio University) has identified 133 items in an automobile that can be traced via sensors. He foresees all automobiles having their own Internet addresses such that these functions can be monitored remotely. He suggests that individual Internet addresses will spread to other appliances such as cellular phones, digital video cameras, digital cameras, and microwaves.[169] Keiji Tachikawa, the former President of DoCoMo, foresees Internet-enabled mobile devices, not just in automobiles, but also in bicycles, motorcycles, and even pets, namely, 20 million cats and dogs by 2010.[170] Jean Paul Jacob, one of IBM's visionaries links this with the rise of invisible computing in the next thirty years: "computing resources (embedded chips) will be present in hundreds of billions of devices making computing ubiquitous and pervasive and invisible. Your cellular phone will give you access to the Web, your refrigerator will call the repair shop when it is in need of repair or adjustment."[171]

A Japanese start-up company, V Sync Technology, has already developed an intellifridge, which combines Internet access and a refrigerator in the same appliance.[172] Ericsson has Screenfridge. Electrolux, Sun, Nokia, and Whirlpool have recently announced something similar.[173] The Schwarzenegger film, The Sixth Day (2000), shows such an intelligent fridge in action. Bill Gates is working on e-Home software.[174]

In January 2001, the city of Barcelona introduced 18,000 microprocessors into garbage cans so that they could inform garbage collectors when they were full, when they were last emptied and when they need to be repainted.[175] As Beniger has shown, this idea of embedded chips is linked with control theory and has a long history. What is different in these new developments is the enormous scale of the process. With "hundreds of billions of devices" one arrives at quantitative advances that bring qualitative changes. Object are no longer objects: "they become self-aware."

If products are "self-aware," they can do more than simply react to the presence of human beings. According to Professors Mange and Tomasini such products can theoretically self-repair and self-replicate, following a "unified approach to bio-inspiration based on the so-called POE model: phylogeny (evolution of species), ontogeny (development of individual organisms), and epigenesis (life-time learning)."[176] Under the heading of "robodyne cybernetics," Joe Michael (Open University) has taken this idea of self-repair much further with fractal, shape-changing robots,[177] which as he notes have considerable consequences for defence technologies.[178] Linking robots with agents is introducing radically new possibilities. In 2000, Alexander Straub (Oxford), then still a graduate student, envisaged: "ladders that alert us when they are overburdened and may soon collapse under the strain; buildings and bridges that reinforce themselves during earthquakes and seal cracks of their own accord. Like living beings, these systems would alter their structure, account for damage, effect repairs and retire."[179]

The Center for Intelligent Material Systems and Structures (CIMSS, Virginia Polytechnic) is concerned with related problems: "Examples of these mechatronic structures include buildings, bridges and roadways that can sense and control damage, aircraft that can actively monitor structural integrity, and automotive components that use active materials to reduce vibrations and enhance performance."[180]

There are already reports of computers that improve themselves without human intervention.[181] The Intelligent Materials and Structures Laboratory (Michigan State University) is working "on a diverse range of actuators and sensors embedded in fibrous composite materials to mimic the behaviour of naturally occurring materials."[182] Meanwhile, this quest for intelligent materials is leading to new fields such as biomimetics, which is a technological variant on the tradition of "art imitates nature." There is a Biomimetics Company[183] and a Centre for Biomimetics (Reading). As Beuckers and van Hinte have noted:

> The ultimate smart structure would design itself. Imagine a bridge, which accretes material as vehicles move over it and it is blown by the wind. It detects the areas where it is overstretched (taking into account a suitable safety factor) and adds material until the deformation falls back within a prescribed limit. We have the technology to detect the overload, but lack the means to add material automatically. We are part-way there with Carolyn Dry's self-repairing concrete structures, in which fractures cause reinforcing material to be released from embedded brittle containers and added to the structure. The ideal would be for the material to be added from an external source so that the structure was not compromised by having to contain its own salvation, necessarily reducing its load-bearing ability. Combine this with adaptive prestressing and the ability to remove material from areas which are underloaded, and we have a truly adaptive

architecture. This approach would result in lighter and safer structures, since stress concentrations would never occur, and the safety factor could be reduced as the structure reached its design optimum – registered as a reduction in the rate of internal re-organisation. The paradigm is our own skeleton.[184]

In Europe, Philips is working on the concept of ambient intelligence,[185] which combines notions of ubiquitous computing, nano-technology and intelligent objects. Today there are separate devices for television, stereo equipment, and computers, etc. The vision of ambient intelligence effectively makes the devices invisible as they become embedded systems within the everyday context of our homes. Hence, a window will in future serve also as a television screen, a computer monitor, and a projection surface for our favourite land- and sea-scapes. Like computers the intelligent ambience of tomorrow will be invisible. Objects with extraordinary capabilities may well look like completely ordinary objects. This is leading to situated and autonomic communications with new paradigms for self-organizing networking systems ranging from sensor networks to virtual networks of humans.[186] It is also leading to new research on presence – the sense of being there – and interaction in mixed reality environments.[187]

16. Agents

Transactions, maintenance, and repair are increasingly being relegated to agents. As one enthusiastic visionary at Bell Lab's Lucent put it: "the Internet will be transformed from a cache of data to a smarter 'HiQNet' in which personal cyberclones will anticipate humans' information requirements."[188]

A stimulus-response model of the behaviourist school leads to an assumption that systems can anticipate human information requirements. If I look at A, then the system assumes that I will want more of A, which may or may not be true. A simple example: I move to a new town and begin looking at houses. The system infers that I am interested in houses. This is true until I have bought one. Thereafter I may never be interested in this problem again unless I get a larger family, the family living at home becomes smaller, or I move again.

A slightly less obvious example. I am writing an article on topic B and search for material. When I am finished I may well have no interest in such materials, yet the agent keeps sending materials. I am an expert so the agent chooses expert-level articles. But precisely because of this, I may also want to see so-called non-expert materials. Or my car is about to break down. The agent plans to repair it, but I have decided that it is time to scrap it and hence do not want it repaired. Another scenario: the automobile has its own agents. Just as organizations have a tendency to self-perpetuate, automobiles may develop their own strategies for survival. If I want to have a new car, does this mean I have to get into arguments with my old car? If I insist on getting a new car, do I have to "kill" my old car agents? The technologists assure us that all this can be customized. But is there not a danger that we spend a large amount of time just establishing what we do not want? Speaking of the semantic web, one technologist recently promised that it would allow you to "solve problems you never knew you had." But what if we didn't want more problems. These are dangers of over-personalization (cf. chapters 10, 13).

17. Play

The extensions of technology that lead to new dimensions of maintenance, self-healing, and self-repair lead also to new forms of play. As Johan Huizinga demonstrated in Homo Ludens, play has a long history and can often be very serious. Michael Schrage in Serious Play is rediscovering this. Scenarios, simulations, and prototypes are becoming ever-more important for at least four reasons.

First, they render visible our ideas in such a way that others can understand them more clearly. Instead of asking abstractly: Do you see what I mean? we can explicitly ask: You see what I mean: what do you think about it? In the past, a verbal scenario was a point of departure for diverging opinions. Now a visual scenario or simulation becomes a starting point for consensus-building.

Second, they allow us to practice difficult operations virtually before experiencing the consequences of the real. A medical doctor can make mistakes on a virtual body, which would kill a real one. If practice makes perfect then it is better to practice virtually, before being perfect with the real.

Third, they enable us to make virtual models and mockups of buildings and environments prior to building costly physical objects. These virtual models are less expensive than scale models of the past.

Fourth, virtual models or simulations can be done very quickly and altered easily. Where scale models often took many months, virtual models can appear in draft form in days. This changes the whole planning and decision-making process. In the past, to speak of a decision being cast in stone was often literally true. Today, our play may be very serious with respect to its goals. At the same time, it can be much more light-hearted such that a change of course will not usually mean months or years of revisions. Hence, there is a lot more "proto" in our prototypes.

The historical and cultural dimensions of play affect our treatment of the past, present, and future. Traditionally there were fairy tales, which consciously blurred the boundaries between the real and the imaginary. As such they could become cautionary tales for real life. Fairy tales invariably began with phrases such as: "Once upon a time," to remind us that they were in the realm of playful story rather than grim reality. Else hearing about granny wolves who eat unsuspecting grandchildren would have been more a cause for sleepless nights than ideal bedtime reading.

The new media are transforming the old stories into new challenges for animation. Walt Disney began by transforming fairy tales into animated films and then into actual places one could visit in Fantasyland. As such he built the first theme park and began what Pine and Gilmore call the experience economy. Others have followed. In 1912, Sir Arthur Conan Doyle wrote The Lost World about prehistoric creatures on a forgotten island. This inspired Spielberg's film *Jurassic Park*, its sequel, *The Lost World*, *Jurassic Park III*, an actual theme park at Universal Studios and a Warner Brothers television series.

In addition to fairy tales, the past had legends, fables, courtly tales, tales of quest and adventure, where a lone figure, Arthur, Lancelot, or Parsifal sets out against all odds in their quest to slay dragons, save the world, and find the Holy Grail. In the Latin West, such heroes were knights. In Japan, such heroes were samurai. Parallel with this, there was always an ironic and half-satirical form. In the past this was Don Quixote. In our time this is Monty Python.

In the new media, such quests have many forms. Some, such as *Myst* and *Riven*, are quiet, near-philosophical meanderings through mythic spaces on CD-ROMs, DVDs, and now on-line. Some have become the stuff of near epic films such as *Willow*. Many have become the realm of video games.[189] Films such as *AI* (July 2001) are linked with games and commentaries before their premiere.[190] These frequently began as landscapes with rough cartoon-like figures. They have become ever-more realistic, interactive, including multiple players in on-line games.[191] In Sweden, experiments are underway with 1,500 players linked on-line in a single game. In April 2002 there were an estimated 150 million on-line gamers worldwide with 1.5 million playing at any given time. IBM has introduced Butterfly.net – a grid architecture that will enable over one million players to be linked simultaneously.[192] Some games link players in imaginary battles within a real landscape.[193] Other games such as *Fire Department* 2[194] combine entertainment and training simulations. *Bioforce*, a new product by Madcatz.com combines virtual reality in video games with the reality of physical electrical shocks. A German game called *Painstation* communicates "sensations such as heat, punches and electroshocks of varying duration."[195] A company called Virtual Showcases has reconstructed a virtual Turkish chess player, which combines a physical chessboard with virtual chess pieces to create a new kind of augmented reality experience. In 2004, a new European IST project, IPerG began to explore showcases for a series of novel game genres including: crossmedia, socially adaptable games, massively multi-player reaching out, enhanced reality live role-playing, city as theatre, trans-reality gaming, and telling stories from pervasive games.[196] One of the leaders of this project, the Interactive Institute, also has a project on Ubiquitous Gaming.

Parents worry about the violence of these games, yet often think nothing of watching the same kind of violence in a war movie, forgetting that their children are actually doing a virtual gymnastics to keep themselves fit for the eternal epic quest that lies in us all. This quest kills lives virtually and upholds the noble in times of so-called peace. In times of war it saves real societies.

While America is very active, Japan leads the world in this realm. Japan is also digitizing all the scenes from Kurosawa's films in order that one can interact with them, walk through their streets, and enter into the lives of the players.[197] America speaks of interactivity but is so focussed on the challenges of action and activity that the "inter-" often fades. The Germans have introduced the world's first interactive crime movies.[198]

In Europe, there is as always a fascination with historical events. A CD-ROM of Versailles allows us to enter into the glamour of the enlightenment court and participate in a whodunit. There are now two CD-ROMs and a film with whodunits in the Louvre. Infobyte, which was one of the pioneers in recreating the spaces of churches such as San Francesco (Assisi) and St. Peter's Basilica (Vatican) in virtual reality, has introduced a novel idea of using these spaces as a starting point for a new interactive game called the *Holy Grail*:

> The main idea is to connect already built virtual monumental and artistic environments (such as Giotto's frescoes, Saint Peter's Basilica, the Nefertari Tomb, etc.), via appropriate passing environments modelled and implemented for this purpose, in order to form a virtual artistic universe made up of all these interconnecting worlds.
>
> There are two classical roles; the goody and baddy. The former, who holds the Grail, has to find the Temple, whilst the latter has to oppose this search. In order to facilitate this search the environment is covered with clues which have to be found and interpreted so that they can lead to the final goal.
>
> This virtual environment was installed in the Guggenheim-Soho room for virtual reality. Each game involves the participation of two players and a crowd of spectators in front of them. The two players each wear a head mounted display and have the commands to move freely within the universe. Each player is only able to see the portion of world in front of him and meets others only if they are both in the same environment at the same time. The spectators are however able to see the entire universe. Each session lasts about 15–20 minutes. Since the universe is open to many interconnectable worlds it gives the possibility, within the hardware limits, to add (or substitute) new worlds in time so that the universe can grow and evolve.[199]

In their reconstructions of San Francesco (Assisi) and Stanze (Vatican), Infobyte has recreated not only the space wherein the frescoes exist but also the space within the frescoes. This opens up new areas of study for art history. In the context of the game outlined above one can imagine future cultural studies, which would include new combinations of a classic text such as Dante's *Commedia* and then walking through the described spaces using reconstructions of famous paintings. This would give the phrases: "Go to hell" and "go to paradise" an entirely new meaning. Similar journeys could be imagined using other classics such as *Shanahmah* or the *Tale of Gengi*.

De pinxi, a Belgian company specializing in virtual reality, has made an archaeological reconstruction of Mexico City in the fifteenth century, a three-dimensional virtual visit of a Tuscan Villa, a voyage through a painting dating from the eighteenth century, an interactive immersion in Kegopolis (the city of the future), and an interactive group experience where all the public interact called

Sauza 2000.[200] Together with researchers at Laval University, they are engaged in a European Commission IST project (MUVI) whereby they are combining elements from fifty paintings by the nineteenth-century French painter, Rousseau, to create an imaginary space based on his work.

A second dimension entails the present. Here again immersive cinemas such as IMAX, Omnimax, IMAX 3-D, and theme parks put us into the hot seat of a race car driver. Or they take us on forms of virtual tourism to places we love to see but would not usually dare to go in real life such as the top of Everest or the edge of an active volcano. All this sounds very novel. Historically, of course, a similar enthusiasm began over two hundred years ago, using remarkably similar themes, with the rise of panoramas and dioramas. Already in medieval times, camera obscuras had supplied more primitive special effects.

With respect to the present, video games[201] again play an important role, as do computerized role-playing games. These are sometimes in the present, sometimes in the past or the future, and sometimes move seamlessly through various epochs. Walt Disney's genius was that he covered all three phases of time: Fantasyland (past); Frontierland and Adventureland (present), and Tomorrowland (future). The four together became Disneyland. Subsequently the Epcot Center was devoted specifically to the future. On the surface, these Disney worlds cater to individuals. At an another level, they control experiences, depersonalize them, and threaten the very idea of truly "personal" experiences linked with tacit knowledge (cf. chapter 9).

Japan has its copy of Disneyland but also has its own versions of theme parks. These focus on simulations of real events, earthquakes, tsunamis, volcanoes, and storms. In contrast to the American themes, the Japanese focus on nature and on the dangers it poses. This contrast is also evidenced on a regular airline flight. Aboard an American airline the descriptions of emergencies are in animations, whereas the rest of the time there are usually regular videos and movies. On Japan Airlines the basic warnings about smoking, drinking, etc., are in animated cartoons and highly exaggerated, but the instructions on how to leave a plane in case of emergency use footage with live persons. The Mechatronic Lab at University of Electro-Communications (Tokyo) has as their motto: "The amusive ability is the academic ability" (*Gaku-ryoku, Gaku-ryoku*), which is considerably subtler than edu-tainment.[202]

Yet another dimension of play entails the future in the form of science fiction. Throughout this book we cite fiction as one of the dimensions of the possible because there are curious ways in which science fiction and reality overlap. The latest James Bond movie, *The World is not Enough*, is about two competing oil lines in the Middle East. Such a competition exists in real life.[203] HAL, the computer in *2001: A Space Odyssey*, could become a reality. In the 1990s, Arnold Schwarzenegger became famous for his *Terminator* movies, playing the part of a robot-humanoid. Such bionic specimens are now possible. *The Fifth Element* shows a Robo-Roach. The University of Tsukuba has produced one. In Michael Crichton's *TimeLine*, the protagonists do teleportation. As we have seen, this has been shown to be possible in theory, although the scenario of "Beam me up, Scotty" definitely is still a long way off. Meanwhile, Sony's latest games allow us to go back to the past in virtual form.[204] In James Redfield's "fictional" *Secret of Shambala*, the dangers of implanted neurochips are clearly stated.

In the 1890s, the neo-Kantians called artists the "researchers of science." Some sixty years later, Marshall McLuhan called artists the "early warning systems of the future." Writers such as Jules Verne or Isaac Asimov have given us many glimpses into what would one day come about. It is no surprise therefore that many at the forefront of computers, including Bill Joy, Eric Raymond, and Marc Andreessen, are also science fiction fans. At the same time, fortunately, there is no necessary correlation between science fiction and science. Orwell's *1984* did not become 1984 or conversely. There is freedom and there are choices.

In all this there have been interesting developments in terms of control, management, and planning. More than a half-century ago companies began to focus on production (activity) control (1948). Four decades later, this extended to Statistical Production Control (SPC, 1988). A quest for synthesis began. Efforts at Computer Aided Design (CAD), Computer Aided Engineering (CAE) and Computer Aided Manufacturing (CAM) led to Computer Integrated Manufacturing (CIM).

A concern with inventory management (1953) spread to production management (1986), capacity management (1989), and more recently Supply Chain Management (SCM, 1998[205]) and Customer Relation Management (CRM, 2000[206]). In the 1970s there was planning in terms of Material Requirements Planning (1973) and production planning (1974). This led to Manufacturing Resource Planning (MRP, 1986) and Advanced Planning and Scheduling (1996), and Enterprise Resource Planning (ERP, 1999). As Callaway (2000)[207] has noted, ERP has become a new umbrella term that embraces e-commerce, Advanced Planning and Scheduling (APS), Internet-based procurement, Business Intelligence (BI), and Customer Relationship Management (CRM).[208]

It is both fascinating and confusing, however, to note how every major firm combines these elements in their own way. In 2000, e-marketplace and e-procurement were major buzzwords. In 2004, Commerce One described these as only a stage in "composite process management," while e2open spoke of an "intelligent supply network," and "multi-company process management." By 2004, Ariba had Spend Management Solutions. By 2004, Oracle's E-Business suite claimed to "Order, Plan, Procure, Make, Logistics, Maintain, Service, HR, Finance, Projects, Intelligence, Develop, Market, Sell."[209] Meanwhile, consultants such as Richard Bourke emphasized a new trend toward "Collaborative Product Commerce."[210] One begins to wonder how billion dollar corporations can adjust so quickly in a field where buzzwords and even entire models can change in the course of a couple of years.

Even so, a fundamental shift of the past five years is that these efforts towards automation in control, production, management, and planning, which were hitherto isolated efforts, are being linked within a single framework through the Internet. Even researchers see their role as playful. Describing the role of a nano-manipulator,

University of North Carolina professor Sean Washburn claims: "The nanoManipulator reduces physical chemistry into a game of tinker toys. If I want to push a molecule around to see what happens, I just reach out and push it. We play with these things the way children play. I'll say, 'I wonder what'll happen if I do this?' Then I'll just reach out and do it."[211] In all this, the traditional oppositions between work and play are disappearing. We play at many different levels at work, and during our so-called play time we work ourselves into new pastimes. In the past we would work out a plan. Increasingly we play out a scenario.

18. Conclusions

The Internet began as a means of enhancing human-human communication. It is becoming also a means of increasing machine-machine communication. This is due partly to a paradox. As connectivity increases the potentials of direct communication, there is a parallel trend to create ever-more agents, acting as intermediaries, whereby there is ever less direct communication among humans. In the world of business there were traditionally sales persons who were intermediaries between products and clients. The Internet is changing this in several ways and posing new problems on at least five fronts.

First, on the surface there is a trend from production to services. Hence, IBM which was once a producer of hardware is now a producer of software and services. But is it that simple? The hardware of IBM was not machines to produce things but "business machines," a hardware version of service. Is then the real shift from hardware to software? If so, why is IBM moving to open source for its software and why is it joining the trend of many other companies to translate non-material software into hardware chips? If the trend is towards services, why were companies that have long been specialized in services such as Baan on the verge of bankruptcy in 2000 and why have firms such as SAP often "produced" solutions that do not work?[212]

Second, there is a trend to reduce such human interactions of sales to mechanical transactions whereby, as the saying goes, a product or a customer is but a click away.[213]

Third, while there is ever-more discussion of the core competencies of companies, it is increasingly difficult to understand where these truly lie.[214]

Fourth, we are told that Supply Chain Management (SCM) will create enormous efficiencies of scale and save billions. In practice, however, small companies often do not wish to or cannot invest in the necessary software.[215] Moreover, the new systems often present so much information and so many new options that most companies are not equipped to know how to deal with the information. Some critics thus predict a decline in SCM.[216]

Fifth, partly because of such paradoxes, there is an increasing uncertainty as to who owns what or, more precisely, which bits of ownership are worth owning and protecting. Traditional companies continue to emphasize Intellectual Property Rights (IPR) and assume that they will continue their control as long as they have enough copyrights and patents. But when the money lies not so much in the product as in services, does this mean that only serviceable products remain viable?

An extreme school argues that the key to future business lies in giving away the product and making a business around helping the customer to use, maintain, and even develop the product. An even more extreme school argues that the future lies in making the customer the product (cf. chapter 11). This begins with a so-called experience economy in theme parks and culminates in making a business of transforming the person physically through fitness, psychologically through so-called "self-help," and ultimately spiritually through pseudo-religions where one improves in direct proportion to how much one invests. This could lead to a world where, as Oscar Wilde used to say, people "know the price of everything and the value of nothing." In any case it suggests that the virtuality introduced by computers is something much more profound than the obvious paradox that when non-machines make our machines, they render the machines themselves irrelevant.

Examples such as the Napster phenomenon suggest that, notwithstanding all the legal barricades to defend old structures, something is happening that cannot be captured by simple prohibitions. The material is leading to the virtual. As we shall see presently, the virtual requires the intellectual and the intellectual cannot thrive without the spiritual. Long ago there was a distinction between the spirit and the law, and the spirit ultimately triumphed. Computers are showing us that the situation is still virtually the same.

6
institutions

Physical facilities will shrink by at least
25 percent in the coming years as firms
make the transition to electronic commerce and to a network approach to
organizational activity.
— Jeremy Rifkin,
The Age of Access
(2000, p. 32)[1]

1. Introduction

The material consequences of computers lie in virtuality. This
affects production (chapter 4), entails a shift from production
to services (chapter 5), and is also transforming institutions
in at least five ways. 1) When the concept of intelligence is
extended to rooms and environments, elements such as windows acquire multiple functions. 2) Through (wireless and
wired) connectivity, the physical space of a room can be
linked with the spaces of other physical (video conferencing)
or other virtual rooms. 3) Connectivity brings new sharing
of information and knowledge with others. What was once
accessible only via a physical school, government building, or

TABLE 15 Traditional professions and potential replacements according to Ken Ichi Ohmae

TRADITIONAL PROFESSION	POTENTIAL REPLACEMENT
Family lawyer	e-law
Accountants	Quicken
Dealers & buyers	Trade exchange
Travel agents	e-tickets
Teachers	Distance learning
Doctors	Tele-medicine
Bureaucrats	Electronic government

other public institution is now potentially accessible to persons all over the world. 4) Partly because of this, the bricks and mortar of buildings are in some cases replaced by virtual institutions. 5) The new media imbue existing structures with new meaning.

Ken Ichi Ohmae, the Japanese cyber guru, claims that the new media threaten the extinction of professions (Table 15). In his view, e-economy is at odds with nation states. He warns that cyber crimes are soaring and that, as the digital divide widens, anti-globalization will destabilize society. This was before the protests in Genoa and even before those in Seattle. His solution is a shift from technology to e-culture, which entails an e-legal-framework, e-trade-agreement, e-infrastructure, and e-education/retooling. Just as computers need to be re-booted occasionally, he believes that individuals and society need to bootup anew.[2]

As on other fronts, conceptions of virtual institutions vary considerably. In the United States, there is sometimes a rhetoric that the virtual can replace the physical entirely. In Europe, there is a notion that the virtual should always complement physical contact. In Japan, there is a greater emphasis on the virtual but at the same time a commitment to include implicit and tacit dimensions. We shall explore these developments with respect to the home, office, government, schools, and memory institutions before reconsidering definitions of virtuality.

2. Home

United States

The new media, which were initially limited to specialized machines, are increasingly becoming part of everyday objects such as cars, toys, and telephones (chapter 5). The trend towards ubiquitous computing means that the new media are spreading everywhere, to rooms, and the entire environment. Through the insertion of sensors, intelligent objects, rooms, homes,[3] housing,[4] and environments can respond actively to persons and other changes. At MIT a team led by Michael Coen is working on a prototype intelligent room with 125,000 feet of cable, twelve cameras, and numerous computers which: "will get to know your habits.... For example, if you watch a program every night and then don't show up one night, the computer will know to record it. Or if you fall asleep while you're watching, the computer will know to turn off the speakers and record the rest of the show."[5] Such interaction is further explored in Ted Selker's Context-Aware Computing Lab at MIT, which has a talking couch:

> With sensors under its cushions, the couch greets new arrivals and may encourage them to relax if they sit leaning forward for too long.... What if you're carrying a wireless, Net-connected personal digital assistant (PDA) and the couch sees you have an appointment coming up in a half-hour? The couch might check your schedule and offer to remind you when it's time for you to leave.
>
> It might also recognize that it's time for your favorite show and turn it on before you get a chance to reach for the remote. Been working out extra hard? The couch might someday sense you've lost a pound or two recently and compliment you for the efforts or offer to order a celebratory pizza.[6]

The assumption that one can know persons by observing their external actions has its philosophical roots in pragmatism and behavioural psychology (chapter 7) and has deeper consequences for culture (chapters 14–15). One of the aims of the MIT researchers is that computers will "make choices depending on the person's tendencies." This requires extracting "perceptual and causal knowledge of the activity in the environment by using the sensory information from the scene."[7] In simple terms, this implies ever-more cameras so that a person's every movement can be traced. The good news is that these can also be used for home surveillance.[8] The bad news is that this potentially removes almost every remnant of privacy (cf. chapter 13).

Such intelligence in terms of responsive rooms is only a first step. The team at MIT is working on new kinds of interactivity between persons in a room and those seen elsewhere via a television or a computer. One goal, for instance, is to create Hyper Soap [Opera], whereby a user can be watching a soap opera, be attracted by the clothes, jewels or other accessories of one of the performers, and then be able to order these items immediately.[9] Bill Gates has similar ideas. A second prototype at MIT being developed for the home is a Virtual Circus: "for collaborative storytelling, visual communication from remote locations, or game playing. The participant's image is subjected to all graphics transformations that can apply to graphical objects, including scaling."[10]

This can be used simultaneously by a number of users. Another project[11] will create "spaces to share common alternate realities," wherein users are represented "locally and remotely, by avatars: sometimes human, sometimes realistic video, often not."[12] This is leading to Artificial Life companies,[13] which are removing clear distinctions between real life and the fictive realities of the screen. In America, the subject-object distinction between passive (mechanical) objects and living subjects is disappearing or at least is being challenged.

Europe

In Europe, distinctions between the real world and the ludic worlds of games and entertainment are theoretically much sharper, although this becomes less clear at the time of football finals. Companies such as Philips are also developing interactive television[14] applications with respect to sports such that a viewer can focus on a given player and learn more about them. In 2000, Philips and other companies invested in the development of so-called personal television (TiVo).[15] This is only a first step. In the short term, Philips foresee the use of flat-panel displays. In the longer term, they foresee windows (and potentially whole walls) that can be transformed into projection screens at the flip of a switch, sometimes functioning as traditional windows, sometimes offering views of favourite places, sometimes serving as computer monitors, leading to ambient intelligence. According to Xerox PARC, by 2010 "plazas, town squares, and other public spaces will be reinvented to include interactive digital-art installations."[16]

This notion of intelligence is planned equally for other rooms such as kitchens.[17] As mentioned earlier, Japan has intellifridges (cf. chapter 5.15 above). In the United States technophiles envisage refrigerators that will know what food is missing and alert their users or, better still, do the ordering themselves. Or refrigerators that will know when they need repair and call the repair shop on their own. Or, in a Nortel scenario, refrigerators that will, on the basis of the food present, offer advice for choosing and potentially help in preparing possible dinner recipes.

The house of the future, we are told, will also have intelligent washrooms, whereby one's weight and medical condition (temperature, blood pressure, heart rate) will potentially be linked to on-line medical records. This is wonderfully useful if security is assured. In a nightmare scenario drug companies would monitor one's health and constantly bombard potential patients with advertisements for drugs seemingly appropriate to their situation. Sixty years ago the house of the future was cluttered with fancy appliances. Thirty years ago the house of the future featured novel energy sources such as solar heating. Today's house of the future looks much emptier. Each appliance and every item has invisible computers.[18] In Japan there is software to design one's own kitchen personally. In Japan, there are also trends towards smart houses.[19]

There are trends towards virtual animals and fish.[20] One of the more interesting developments is a quest to create virtual pets.[21] Waseda University is working on a virtual dog.[22] Sony has a Robot dog, AIBO,[23] which can express six emotions: happiness, sadness, fear, dislike, surprise, and anger using sound and melodies (AIBO's "tonal language"), body language, and light (shining from the eyes and the tail).[24] A new version of AIBO, in conjunction with a PC running "AIBO Messenger" software, "will announce when new mail is available, and then read the messages (and selected Web pages) aloud."[25] The latest version is cheaper and has training capabilities. Over half of all the robots in the world are in Japan.

The Japanese firm Takara has developed a new canine communicator gadget that "claims to be able to translate barks, growls and whines into common human emotions such as frustration, menace, hunger, joy and sorrow."[26] Meanwhile, Amazon.com has an electronic Kitty. Omron has produced a pet cat robot called Tama:

> ... that can sense touch, motion and voice to understand human behavior and respond appropriately. Eight separate tactile sensors and three motion sensors enable Tama to sense touch and body position, so she knows when she's being cuddled in someone's arms or hung upside down by her tail. She also has four auditory sensors that enable her to hear, to tell what direction sound is coming from, and to distinguish her owner's voice from the voices of other people. Based on all of the sensor input data she collects, Tama can generate one of six emotions in response (anger, surprise, satisfaction, anxiety, dislike, and fear), and display actions associated with them. Through her built-in self-learning ability, her responses gradually change over time.[27]

Virtual Communities

In England, the term "virtual community" is being used for web sites of counties such as Cambridgeshire, Durham, or Lincolnshire.[28] This usage is also found in the United States.[29] Howard Rheingold, in his pioneering book *The Virtual Community* (1993),[30] was interested in something deeper. Rheingold used his personal experiences with the Whole Earth Link Line (WELL) as a point of departure. He tells a fascinating anecdote, which finally convinced his wife of the usefulness of the Web. One day his child had an accident. His wife called a doctor. Rheingold used the Internet to contact on-line friends who were able to provide helpful advice before a doctor was able to get to the child. In one of his web sites, Rheingold points to fifteen virtual communities around the world.[31]

While isolated individuals, such as Frank Weinreich, claim that the whole idea of virtual communities is wrong,[32] there is ever-more attention to the concept. UCLA has a Center for the Study of Online Community. There are numerous sites on virtual communities.[33] Cliff Figallo, in a book on *Hosting Web Communities*,[34] claims that they have three characteristics: 1) focus, through a central subject or theme, 2) cohesion, through member to member relationships, and 3) interactivity, through member to member communication. He also claims that these lead to three kinds of (virtual) institutions: a shrine, a theatre, and a café. The practice of such approaches was discussed at ConferNet 99 Community Discovered.

Three examples at INET 2000 confirm the variety of applications. For instance, the Smithsonian Museum is using the idea of virtuality to give voices to members of different communities. LEAD, an international leadership organization, is using such virtual contexts to keep their members in touch with one another.[35] Meanwhile, Etsuko Inoue, in a small Japanese village has formed *Yokakusa Koga*, which provides Internet classes, guides to local commerce, reports of visits to Okinawa, latest results concerning the election of a mayor, and human interest stories about the threatened nest of a bird in a tree using webcam technologies.[36] Such examples confirm that virtuality is about something much more profound than a simple substitution of real objects by virtual equivalents. They can imbue the physical world with new meaning and make us aware of aspects therein which we had not noticed earlier. They can help us to see everyday reality in new ways. Evolution is embracing not replacing.

3. Business

The same technology, which is bringing smart rooms to the home, is leading to smart rooms at work, with one crucial distinction. On the home front, the smart room remains part of where one lives: sleeping on virtual beds with physical bodies would pose difficulties. In the case of offices, rooms can be virtual and thus save on the rental costs of physical office space. Hence, in the United States, there are virtual offices, which are run from private homes where persons (often mothers) function as tele-secretaries.[37]

At MIT, researchers are working on smart desks[38] with a view to collaborative tele-work (cf. chapter 11). In their view: "Smart Rooms act like invisible butlers. They have cameras, microphones, and other sensors, and use these inputs to interpret what people are doing in order to help them."[39] The good news is that our every movement can be used to help the task at hand. The bad news is that we are constantly being observed.

One of the liberating effects of laptops is an ability to work outside one's office. In positive terms this means that one's office can be anywhere. One also risks never being away from one's work. At the moment there is not always a power line in one's plane or train. This is changing. Some airlines have introduced wired connections for their business-class passengers. Meanwhile visionaries are already describing new scenarios, whereby we will have a ubiquitous office:

> This device consists of a small Palm-size pocket computer into which you plug an earpiece and goggles. The goggles provide an image of a 21-inch monitor that sits in front of you at a variable distance (you choose programmatically). You also have a virtual keyboard and mouse, which you can position as though they too were actually sitting on a desk in front of you.

What's going on here is that the computer is using retinal tracking to tell what you are looking at. You are given a virtual desktop set, and when you reach out to touch or grab anything on the set, the computer sees what you are doing and adjusts things in real time as though you were, say, moving a mouse or typing.... You'll have full-time access to the screen, the Internet, and the keyboard as you walk around or sit in meetings. If you want to take notes or type, you can position the virtual keyboard (which only you can see) and bang away silently on the table as the retinal tracking sees what keys you are hitting (even peripherally) and types for you.[40]

McLuhan would find this an excellent example of looking to the future through a rear-view mirror: envisaging earlier technologies as the basis for the future. All this is fine and well when an office is virtual. But what if one wants to meet a customer? Some large hotels offer spaces for just this purpose and charge accordingly. To an extent, call centres also perform these functions. Even so an approach to business without personal interaction and hence without the need for physical buildings is much more likely to find acceptance in the United States than in Europe or Japan.

4. Corporations

Developments in new media through visualization, combined with corporate Intranets mean that managers can now have access to vital company information at a distance. A manager can theoretically have access to more material from their desktop than if they were actually on the shop floor. The past years have seen a great surge of new literature on virtual teams[41] and organizations.[42] Fukuyama and Shulsky have related the virtual corporation to army organization.[43] Igbaria and Tan have discussed the virtual workplace.[44] Virtual corporations should, however, be seen as part of much larger trends towards tele-work,[45] towards networked organizations,[46] and towards virtual communities,[47] a topic on which there are now books[48] and conferences[49] (cf. chapter 11).

The United States has a more radical vision of such virtual corporations, as reflected in new web sites for executives such as firmbuilder.com, which identify twelve disciplines of outsourcing.[50] While Europe and Asia prefer to keep their expertise in house, Americans such as Michael Corbett and Associates have identified two stages in the development of (radical) outsourcing. In a first stage, one maintains one's earlier structure while introducing innovations. In a second stage, one restructures: "the company into a virtual information and process backbone to which internal and external areas of functional excellence, as well as customers, are connected."[51] This second phase supposedly takes from one to two years.

Some describe this process of outsourcing as a trend towards jobs on the fly. Others, such as Charles Derber in *Corporation Nation*, link the rise of virtual corporations and virtual workers: "Nike has contracted out all employment in its core line of business. The virtual company is a jobless company. As such it is practicing job genocide, a strategy for cutting costs and ending long term corporate obligations to employees by getting rid of jobs as we know them." Derber notes that jobs are being replaced by "projects " and "fields of work."[52] He cites one executive who insists: "Employers have an obligation to provide opportunity for self-improvement: employees have to take charge of their own careers."[53] Similar rhetoric is being used in education where students are being told to take charge of their own learning.[54] Trends towards the virtual in this sense mean eliminating jobs and teachers. In the guise of efficiency, this could undermine the very infrastructure that is needed.

Banks

Traditional service institutions such as banks are offering more and more of their services through Automatic Teller Machines (ATMs) and directly on-line. Compubank, which is rated as the number one bank on-line by Smart Money, offers a whole range of services. At the business level this includes domestic wire transfers, direct transfers, bill payment, visa cheque cards, and click miles. This is leading to a new field called digital financial media.

For personal accounts this includes basic and interest chequing; savings; money market funds; and certificates of deposit.[55] In 2000, it was estimated that 8.8 million U.S. families used the Internet for banking.[56] Software companies such as Hamilton and Sullivan were already providing virtual banks which had loan, bookkeeping, and reporting functions on the wall as hotspots.[57] Since then, Hamilton and Sullivan have been taken over, their virtual web site has disappeared and become virtual in a new sense.

What is striking about such virtual spaces is their generic appearance, with nothing of the individuality that once characterized bank buildings.[58] In some estimates, the need for physical bank buildings will disappear entirely within the next thirty years. With respect to everyday transactions, this is a plausible scenario. It is difficult, however, to imagine how personal and business loans, which require assessing whether one can trust a potential customer, is amenable to this kind of automation.

Law

On-line legal databases have been in progress for over a decade. There are virtual law libraries,[59] virtual law schools,[60] and virtual law offices.[61] More recently there have been more dramatic steps towards a virtualization of the legal system. In the United States, KPMG in conjunction with the Pennsylvania State Police have been working on a Justice Network (Jnet) "a virtual single system for recording, updating and sharing criminal justice information."[62] In Germany, there is a national project, Juris.[63] In Britain, there are efforts to create an on-line Offenders Assessment System (OASYS).[64] At the Harvard Law School, there is the Berkman Center for Internet and Society.[65]

As in other areas, there is a tendency in the legal profession to assume that the challenge of the Internet lies mainly in translating analog physical documents into their digital, virtual equivalents. In the long term this is likely to be seen as a side-issue. More significant are questions of boundaries and jurisdiction. For while some enthusiasts insist that the Internet is removing all boundaries through its virtual spaces, for the legal field, the Internet introduces many new problems of boundaries, which also affect governments.

For instance, if images on a server in Los Angeles offend a person in Kabul, Riad, or Singapore, whose laws apply? Those of the United States, Saudi Arabia, or Singapore? If the server is on a ship that sails the world such questions are compounded. Fortunately, this is an area to which legal experts and scholars are devoting increasing attention (cf. Appendix 8).

5. Government

The idea of making government services accessible on-line is not new. In Canada, for example, politicians such as Dalton Camp were discussing the possibility of on-line voting in the late 1960s. In 1995, government was one of the eleven G7 pilot projects. In the meantime most governments have begun putting some materials on-line.

Virtual Government

Precisely what should be included in such sites is a matter for discussion. When the United States first opened its virtual government site on 10 February 1997, they proposed that on-line services include: "allowing college students to apply for and get answers to loan requests, and to receive funds in online transfers; providing police with instant access to fingerprints and criminal records; letting potential home buyers check for environmental problems in areas where they are thinking of moving."[66] In the spring of 2000, then vice president Al Gore outlined a revised vision under the title of e-government:

> Together we will transform America's collection of ramshackle bureaucracies into an 'e-government' that works for you.... Gore proposed that all the federal agencies be required to put their services online by 2003 so people could in-stantly obtain a bevy of federal data – ranging from the purity of drinking water to the quality of a nursing home to the amount of a pending Social Security check.... Imagine if a child in the poor neighborhood could have access to the richest educational materials and most illustrious museums.[67]

Not everyone is so optimistic. Mark Poster has noted that: "The local geography of cyberspace follows the lines and contours of American racism, sexism and classism. An entire world lives outside those lines and they have been redlined out of cyberspace.... The political geography of cyberspace effectively mirrors the prevailing patterns of global resource distribution."[68]

In 2000, a glance at the list of on-line web sites for various government departments in the United States revealed that energy and the military had 126 sites.[69] In addition the individual sections of the military (i.e., army, navy, etc.) had a further 187 web sites,[70] which together made 313 sites. All the other departments together had 201 sites, with only one for education and none for culture. By contrast, the main list of the European Union had one entry point for each of its seventeen policy areas.[71] In Japan, there was also a nearly even distribution, although there were six sites for trade.[72]

Japan also has public corporations for every major area of government[73] in contrast to the United States where corporations are now considered private. Companies such as Litton have developed e-government software, which includes the following: information dissemination (i.e., computer-aided dispatch, mobile data communications, message switching, and productivity services) and transaction processing.[74] Companies such as IBM and the major consultancy firms are also active in this domain, through bodies such as Development Gateway.[75] Companies such as Cisco would have us believe that the challenges of government and those of business are essentially the same in that both are concerned with satisfying customers. This overlooks certain realities: e.g., businesses are designed to make profits, and governments have a number of tasks that entail the public good and have nothing to do with profit.

Traditionally governments had their own printing presses to publish their materials. This established a fixed official record, which could readily be consulted at a later date. As these materials are made available in on-line sites, there is a tendency to update them constantly, thus producing multiple versions. In the case of official documents, which version is then the document? Here our standards and methods are still in terms of print media and have not yet caught up with the reality of the new media. The world of virtual documents needs a methodology for versioning, analogous to the concept of different editions in the print world. Needed is a new concept of dynamic knowledge. Possible are new kinds of dynamic documents and books with self-revising dimensions (cf. chapters 12, 14–15).

While no one knows precisely what will happen to government at all levels, there is a wide range of scenarios. At the local level, especially in Europe, there are hopes that the new media offer new possibilities for cyber-democracy.[76] In this context, the city of Bologna was an early example. This was also one of the first virtual cities. In France, the rise of the Internet is becoming closely linked with local authorities (collectivités locales) through bodies such as the Association des villes numériques.[77]

At the national level, there are extreme views in the United States that describe the decline of the public sphere in terms such as the end of politics, arguing that corporate power will soon overtake all the functions of government.[78] Others see the rise of information democracy.[79] More balanced views note that the rise of virtual states raise basic questions about the boundaries of the nation state.[80] For instance, if a company has its headquarters in the United States, are its actions in Europe or Asia subject to the laws of these other countries? Corporations such as America

Online (AOL) insist that they are subject only to the laws of the United States while operating internationally. Such examples make governance of cyberspace[81] a very volatile issue as the organizers of the Internet Consortium on Assigned Names and Numbers (ICANN) have discovered (cf. chapter 13).[82]

Each new medium gives the illusion of greater accessibility but also increases the number of barriers to the very persons one is trying to reach. The advent of the postal service did not bring an end to meetings with politicians and civil servants, nor did the advent of the telephone. Nor is the rise of government services in virtual form likely to replace the traditions of a physical government. For instance, Malaysia is the first country in the world with a coherent approach for access to all its government services on-line in electronic form. As it does so, it is also building an entirely new city, Putrajaya, to house their government of the twenty-first century. In this case, the new media are replacing the present physical institutions with new physical institutions better suited to the challenges of electronic communications. China too is exploring e-government seriously.[83]

Virtual States

Some see virtual states as a realm for political expression and action not always possible in the physical world. Special interest groups, minorities, and separatist groups frequently have web sites to make themselves seen where they cannot usually be heard. For instance, Catalonia has been attempting to create a virtual state.[84]

Virtual Cities

Meanwhile, there is a trend to reconstruct modern cities in virtual space.[85] The reconstructions of Paris by Canal+ and France Telecom and Virtual Helsinki[86] are among the most elaborate of these. MIT has a project for scanning physical cities and making their images accessible (cf. Appendix 1).[87] In 2004 the U.S. military announced plans to create a 1:1 digital model of the entire earth.[88]

6. Schools

The emerging notions of virtual schools and virtual universities have grown out of a tradition of distance education in the form of correspondence courses, dating back to 1890 in the United States. By the 1920s, courses were offered nationally via radio. In 1926, the Distance Education and Training Council was founded.[89] In the 1950s, Pennsylvania State University offered such courses through an on-campus interactive television network.[90] In 1963, the Canadian Association for Distance Education (CADE) was founded.[91] In 1969, the Open University was founded in England.[92] In 2000 if one looked for distance education under a site such as global education, one found a great number of sites in the United States (124), a good number in Japan (77), and a small number in Europe (England 14, Netherlands 2, and France 1).[93]

TABLE 16 Key features of the NetSchools approach[102]

Curriculum browser

Curriculum search

On-line lesson plan archiving

Curriculum reporting

On-line Communication Tools

Web-based e-mail for every teacher and
administrator, address book

Community calendars: personal, class,
school, district

Discussion group tool for school/district
use, teacher chat and forums

On-line Content

As in the case of homes and offices, there is a trend towards smart classrooms. Often, however, smart classrooms are merely multimedia lecture halls or electronic classrooms. At Northwestern University: "Smart classrooms are equipped with ceiling projectors, sound systems, computers, VCRs, laserdisc players, slide projectors, and/or overhead visualizers."[94]

Schools On-line

Schools are eager to have their own Internet presence as part of their identity. Children often work together as junior web-masters in order to create electronic equivalents of school newspapers, magazines, and yearbooks. Children also communicate with others of their age in schools elsewhere in the world. The Canadian Schoolnet became part of a global vision in 1995 when it joined G7 pilot project three on education "Standards Alignment and Assessment Tools" and thus became linked with the European Schoolnet and similar initiatives around the world.[95]

Virtual Schools

Making children computer literate and giving them access to the Internet is part of a much larger agenda leading to virtual schools.[96] George Lucas' Educational Foundation[97] is a positive example. So too is the Schools Online Project.[98] MIT's Center for Innovative Learning Technologies is active in this domain.[99] Net Schools offers a "complete" technological solution to the classroom (Table 16). Their on-line content is considerable. In 2000, the NetSchools Library had "over 200,000 pre-selected volumes, including books, periodicals, encyclopedias, thesauruses, dictionaries, atlases, maps, and correlated lesson plans by grade level and subject." There is a NetSchools Bookshelf with a dictionary and encyclopedia, content developed by NetSchools teachers, on-line tutorials, articles, reviews, and interviews, as well as useful links.[100] WebCT claims to be an e-learning market leader. Between

1999 and 2000 they had 5 million student accounts in more than 123,000 courses at over 110 institutions in forty-eight countries.[101]

In traditional schools it was relatively easy to determine the orientation of a school: whether it was conservative, progressive, etc. With on-line schools this is much more difficult. Their knowledge packages pose dangers because they are implicitly closed universes: packaging can obscure or even deliberately hide the sources of knowledge, such that students remain unaware how a package represents a particular version of the facts, events, etc., without revealing the philosophical or political motivations underlying these choices. Virtual schools thus introduce new needs to determine the orientation, quality, and levels of knowledge; to distinguish between local, regional, and international knowledge (cf. chapters 13–15).

While much is made of California's Silicon Valley with respect to computers and Internet development, student access to such technology in California ranks a low forty-five out of the fifty states.[103] In 2000, there were exciting reports that Pete Wilson of the California Government raised $100 million for Digital High California. It is not always explained that schools have to match such funds from the government with donations from business.

Striking is the extent to which industry is engaged in the virtual learning discussions. The CEO of 3-Com is the President of the Advisory Council of the virtual university called Western Governors University. In the Digital High project, Oracle has donated $10 million (i.e., 10%). In return, however, Oracle is pushing its Network Computer (NC) and the Oracle Learning Architecture as inexpensive learning tools.[104] Meanwhile, the head of Cisco claims that the stage is now set for "e-learning" to be the next big wave in Internet-based applications.[105] Cisco has a Networking Academy.[106]

Sun has an Educational Portal and School Time Alliance Program "to cost effectively and securely deliver curriculum, administrative content, digital libraries and communications tools to Kindergarten to grade 12 (K–12) institutions worldwide."[107] The business network, Brint.com[108] has a section on education and research. Elsewhere in the United States large corporations are making "donations" to education in return for advertising time during classes. The National Lambda Rail project is a private consortium that owns its own Internet pipelines. The good news is that it provides 10 gigabit connections to members who can afford to pay. The bad news is that poorer constituencies are again on the wrong side of the (Lambda) tracks. Meanwhile, The U.S. Department of Commerce has a vision for a classroom of 2020 from Kindergarten to postgraduate (K–20), where a student will move among molecules, interact with virtual dinosaurs, and visit the Parthenon before lunch. In this vision, virtual classrooms will have holograms, interaction, and perhaps avatars in immersive environments.[109] Alas there is not much discussion of how one creates low-tech critical skills for viewing such high-tech simulations and reconstructions.

Virtual Universities

Virtual universities[110] are emerging at a number of levels, internationally, through bodies such as UNESCO[111] nationally through bodies such as the American Distance Education Consortium (ADEC)[112] and the Canadian Association of Distance Education (CADE),[113] and through individual sites.[114] Canada had a TeleLearning Network of Centres of Excellence (TeleLearning·NCE) with seven themes: 1) Learning Models, 2) Socio-economic Models, 3) Systems Models, 4) K–12 Education, 5) Post-secondary Education, 6) Workplace and Continuing Education, and 7) Educating the Educators (now called Professional Development).[115] This network also had a Virtual University Research Project[116] that included a customizable campus, collaborative design, course design support, personalization, multilingual support, and security. One of the users of the Canadian Virtual University software is the University of Aalborg, where this is linked with a Virtual Learning Environment (VIRT) – including HyperNews, GMD's Basic Support for Collaborative Work, a Calendar system[117] – and WebCT.

As in the case of "virtual schools," the meaning of "virtual universities" varies considerably.[118] In some cases it is associated with a list of on-line courses available at different institutions. The University of New Brunswick at Fredericton, for instance, has a Telecampus,[119] which lists 17,000 courses. The Virtual University in Santa Maria, California, began in 1981 with touch-tone telephone and has had 500,000 students thus far.[120] At Michigan State University, "virtual university" is "used to refer to courses and instructional programs offered through the Internet and other technologically enhanced media."[121] At the Virtual University (VU), which links Millersville University, Shippensburg University, and West Chester University (Pennsylvania): "Course materials can be accessed from work or home on a schedule that suits students' busy schedules. By carefully planning faculty-student interaction, the Virtual University aims to give those who choose internet classes the same advantages as those students who choose on-campus classes."[122]

In 2000, institutions such as Kennedy Western University believed that classrooms remain the best solution for young adults and that virtual courses by correspondence are suited to professionals who are working fulltime. They claimed that distance learning simply "lacks the sense of community and social interaction which can be achieved by sharing the same environmental spaces and experiences." By 2004, these reservations were gone: "By leveraging the power of the Internet, Kennedy-Western has refined the academic process and opened up countless opportunities to adult learners," and they used Jones e-Global Library.[123] Meanwhile, the founders of The World Virtual University Project (TheU, 1996)[124] believe that Virtual Worlds technology can become "a tool for enabling completely new and innovative teaching methods."[125] Detlef Skaley and Udo Ziender (GMD) are doing interesting work on Virtual Physics and Astronomy.[126]

Donald A Norman, one of the pioneers of Human Computer Interface studies, and one of the original founders of Unext.com,[127] an Internet education company for business professionals, also agrees that live situations in real classrooms are preferable to distance learning scenarios of virtual universities but argues that virtual universities are increasingly important for persons who cannot afford the time needed for live encounters. When asked who such persons are, he tells us that these are likely to be persons in countries such as Brazil or China. Implicit here are assumptions about a fundamental digital divide where some persons will have the time for live education and, moreover, the resources to make a for-profit business out of giving the rest of the world a virtual education. While this may be an excellent proposition for short-term profit, it is not a healthy long-term solution for equilibrium on the world stage. We need a global vision for real and virtual education.

As in the case of virtual schools, there is much evidence of direct business interest and intervention. The California Virtual University,[128] for instance, receives about $75,000 each, from sponsors such as Oracle, Sun Microsystems, Cisco Systems, Pacific Bell, and International Thomson Publishing.[129] Recently, the California State University scrapped plans for a ten-year, money-making partnership with four high-tech giants, including Microsoft. The deal would have financed a $300 million technological and telecommunications retrofit for the CSU's twenty-three campuses by the year 2000, but it was fraught with controversy and halted after financial negotiations collapsed.[130] In 2004, there was again something new, the Digital California Network.

In the realm of Master of Business Administration (MBAs), video conferencing was assumed to be an obvious tool. Yet the Richard Ivey School of Business (London, Ontario), with campuses around the world, abandoned this approach because of the cost of keeping the equipment up to date. The Wharton school has had similar experiences. Nonetheless, new alliances in this field continue such as a partnership between Queen's University (Kingston) and Cornell University (Ithaca).[131] In a strictly profit-oriented approach to education, courses that are cheaper and more popular (i.e., sell more) will be more attractive than those that are more expensive and less popular. This can lead to an emphasis on cheap, popular courses to the exclusion of others. As a result the diversity and variation of courses declines. Content diversity is as essential as cultural- and bio-diversity.

Europe: The Clyde Virtual University (CVU), founded in 1995, claims to be Europe's first virtual university. CVU links four universities and a school of art using: "custom-built tools and materials such as virtual reality educational worlds, online assessment and automated marking, desktop video conferencing, text-based discussion forums and a state of the art virtual library in a unique infrastructure for the provision of education over the Internet."[132]

The European Commission has sponsored experiments in classrooms for interactive teaching and learning.[133] In addition to work on virtual education in general (UC Dublin), a number of different models were explored: an automated easy-to-use interactive learning station (Nancy); an individual learner

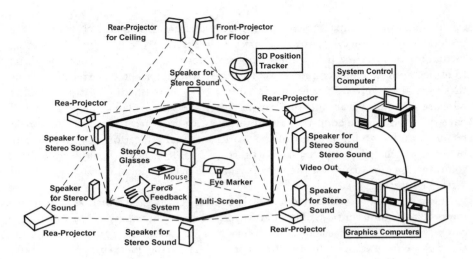

Figure 6 Tele-Existence Environment for Learning eXploration (TEEeX) at the National Institute for Multimedia Education

workstation (Helsinki University of Technology); a (traditional) candid classroom (Politecnico di Milano) and a mobile group to group facility (Katholieke Universiteit, Louvain).[134]

Japan: According to the former Web 66 site,[135] in 2000, there were at least 63 elementary and 128 secondary schools with their own web sites in Japan. Even so the National Institute for Multimedia Education (NIME) organized an international symposium (1999) on Roadblocks to the Information Highway with three panels: 1) lack of technology support for faculty and staff in educational institutions; 2) institutional changes necessary to implement IT, and 3) ways of involving teachers at all educational levels in using and communicating IT technology to students.

It is noteworthy that the Japanese attribute the prolonged economic slump throughout the nineties to Japan's "slowness in adapting to information technology."[136] NIME has developed a Satellite Communication System (SCS), which, by the end of 1998, had stations at 139 connected sites in 116 institutions. NIME has also been working on TEELeX (Tele-Existence Environment for Learning exploration, which they described in 2000 (Figure 6):

> The virtual environment system TEELeX can give us immersive experiences of the three-dimensional (3D) environment, and this is applicable to an open and flexible learning. We develop educational applications such as effective 3D materials, dynamic learning materials, and learning evaluation tools. Collaborative lectures

would be possible, using the virtual environment as an interface through various networks. We then investigate the effect of 3D images at the psychological and physiological view so that one can get safety in the 3D virtual environment.[137]

NIME has also developed a Support System for Distance Spatial Workspace Collaboration: "Spatial data transmitted from the instructor site is displayed as the CG [Computer Graphics] model of the workspace and operation of the instructor is aligned to the reference frame of the operator. Therefore the operator can watch the workspace and operation of the instructor without aligning his or her reference frame. Automatic alignment by the system reduces cognitive load of the operator so that the operation is facilitated."[138]

The Communications Science Section of the same institute has also been working on educational television programs using a virtual studio.[139] These are but isolated examples to give some glimpse of Japan's activities with respect to developments in virtual education. Striking is the fact that, although the technology is used to enhance distance education, there is little discussion of replacing teachers with technology. Here Japan is closer to the European than to the American approach.

Africa: An African Virtual University (AVU), linked with the World Bank, was launched in a pilot phase in 1997. Since then it has provided: "over 2,500 hours of interactive instruction in English and in French. More than 12,000 students have completed semester-long courses in engineering and in the sciences and over 2,500 professionals have attended executive and professional management seminars."[140] In 2001, AVU entered into partnership with ADVTECH Skills Group, the African distributor for Skillsoft's products, to launch comprehensive packages for e-learning.

South America: In South America, there were over a hundred distance education institutions in 2004.[141] A telematics site drew attention to three centres in Argentina and one each in Bolivia, Brazil, Columbia and Costa Rica respectively.[142] The Inter-American Distance Education Consortium (CREAD) linked some 85 institutions in Central and South America with the United States, Canada and Europe.[143]

Virtual Military Learning: The military is one of the chief protagonists of virtual reality and virtual environments in distance education, as becomes clear from a report on *Professional Military Education in 2020*:[144]

> We cannot overemphasize the importance of and the many advantages of using virtual reality and other interactive technology in education. First and foremost, interactive technology takes advantage of the strengths of experiential learning. It also provides flexibility. Well-constructed, interactive technology lessons allow for tailoring lessons to the individual, the individual's learning style, schedule, and the job at hand. It s also timely. Updated information can easily be dropped into the lesson and, if using a direct mode of delivery, is instantly available without waiting to deplete last year's printing. And finally, it is very student-centered. It can be self-paced and take advantage of the student's existing knowledge-teaching in

the gaps. It can also provide personalized immediate feedback for everything the
student does or asks....[145]

One can as easily imagine a virtual high school, technical school, or university, which provides access to information and expertise that is anywhere in the
world. Even difficult concepts, skills, and attitudes might be taught using vivid,
three-dimensional and tactile representations of real world objects and issues.
This kind of learning environment could be embedded in the work environment
(even a non-virtual one) much as today's new performance support systems
provide on-line training and reference on the assembly line. The worker need
not leave his or her workplace to be trained; organizations need not establish and
support fixed training facilities and travel costs can be reduced. Learning done in
direct context with work is likely to be more efficient and effective....[146]

The military has already laid the foundation for the virtual reality world of the
future. For example, Navy, Marine, and Army hospitals worldwide already use an
interactive video, text, sound, and graphics system for training medical personnel
in preventive medicine and the treatment of combat trauma in combat zones.[147]

It is not surprising therefore to learn that the Armstrong Lab is exploring Human
Sensory Feedback (HSF) for Telepresence,[148] or that DARPA had a project on
Intelligent Collaboration and Visualization Community (1997–99),[149] with four
interrelated goals: 1) develop collaboration middleware, 2) tools for sharing
meaning, 3) tools for sharing views, and 4) prototype and evaluate collaborative
applications (cf. chapter 11). In 2001, the U.S. Army awarded a contract of over
$500 million to Price WaterhouseCoopers (PWC) for new educational software, the
largest contract of its kind in history. Some say this was the reason why IBM bought
PWC shortly afterwards.

Hospitals: As with education, where it is often difficult to have schools in remote places, in health care it is not feasible to have hospitals in isolated locations.
The idea of medical assistance at a distance has thus become increasingly attractive.
Hence, just as distance education has emerged, so too has tele-medicine become an
important new field. In the United States, the Nebraska Psychiatry Institute was a
pioneer. The field grew in the 1960s in connection with NASA's activities in space.[150]
During the 1970s there was considerable funding for projects that ended when
funding stopped.

Since 1993, tele-medicine has been used in a number of crisis spots around the
world.[151] Since 1995, reduced costs and better technology have led to an explosion
in this field. The military have been very active. The U.S. Navy began their Virtual
Naval Hospital[152] in October 1996. The army, navy, and air force have a weekly
telemed-(icine) bulletin.[153] In the United Kingdom there have been tele-medicine
and tele-care projects since 1992.[154] The American Telemedicine Association was
founded in 1993.[155] There is a Telemedicine Information Exchange (TIE).[156] Europe
has a Trans European Networks Telemedicine (TEN-Telemed) Program.[157]

The primary thrust of tele-medicine is not to replace hospitals but rather to provide persons in remote places with access to expert information in larger centres. The first active surgical robot was used on a live patient in March 1991 at Shaftesbury Hospital (London).[158] Tele-surgery is an emerging field.[159] Related developments such as tele-radiology reflect a larger trend towards collaborative work (chapter 11).

A side-effect of tele-medicine is an increasing interest in gadgets to follow the conditions of (potential) patients in everyday life. This has led, for instance, to dog tags with immunization information, devices for blood tests without needles, and reflected red and infra-red wave lengths to give oxygen saturation in the blood.[160] Such devices may soon be inserted in the body: "Using nanosensor technology, miniscule instruments that temporarily attach themselves within the body, clinical data could be streamed in real time to independent reviewers and/or companies' medical teams."[161] Here again loom questions of privacy (cf. chapter 13).

A second trend has been to provide practitioners and patients with on-line information about medicine. For instance, in 1992, the University of Iowa began The Virtual Hospital, a digital health sciences library to make "the Internet a useful medical reference and health promotion tool for health care providers and patients. The Virtual Hospital digital library contains hundreds of books and brochures for health care providers and patients."[162] There are popular sites such as Drkoop.com.

As a result, members of the public increasingly seek medical knowledge on their own, with a view to "do it yourself" treatments. This has advantages. Through better awareness of the problems, there are a) less fears of doctors and hospitals, and b) more informed hospital treatments. There are also disadvantages: a) patients may think they know better than a doctor what needs to be done; b) patients may try unproved remedies from unauthorized sources: the traditional problem of quack doctors in electronic form. Meanwhile, pioneers such as Greg Mogel (UCLA) speak of digital medicine with a vision of integrating acquisition, storage, display, and sharing of medical data.[163] In the military there is talk of virtual soldiers whereby holographic equivalents allow doctors to keep track of hopefully live soldiers in the field.

7. Memory Institutions

The implications of the new media on memory institutions such as libraries, museums, and archives are complex. Many assume that one merely needs to translate the analog documents into digital form, in which case a massive scanning project would solve the problem. Much more is required, including a reorganization of content, which can lead to augmented knowledge and culture (chapters 12, 14–15). At this stage we shall simply outline what is entailed.

Libraries and Archives

The convergence of new media is leading to a digitization of all reference works. A next step will be to link these in order to move seamlessly between classification systems, dictionaries, encyclopaedias, bibliographies, abstracts, and reviews. This will lead to more fundamental changes, whereby the contents of reference works are transformed using systematic levels of knowledge.[164]

Many assume that the advent of electronic books will quickly replace physical books and render obsolete the notion of libraries. As we have already suggested, this is unlikely. There are at least three reasons. First, the role of libraries, archives (and museums) as repositories of human memory will remain a basic need. Even so there are unexpected developments. In a world where people are ever-more mobile, there is a new phenomenon of *bookcrossing*, whereby, instead of collecting books, persons give away their books for free and then follow their continued travels via the Internet.[165]

Second, as Michael Ester (of the Getty AHIP program) has demonstrated, the eye sees 3,500 lines/inch when reading from a book and only 2,000 lines/inch when reading from a computer screen. This is because direct light from computer monitors affects the rods and cones in the eye in a very different way than reflected light from the page of a book. Hence, we see a third more when reading a traditional printed book than when viewing a computer monitor or an electronic book. This makes electronic books excellent for quick reference, but means that books are better suited when it comes to close reading. Some would disagree.[166]

Third, the new technologies point to augmented books, whereby the contents of printed books are linked via wireless connections to various reference works. In this scenario, there is a symbiosis between the best aspects of printed books and the new potentials of electronic media (cf. chapter 14).

As miniaturization advances, an increasing number of standard reference works can simply be downloaded onto an electronic book or Personal Intelligent Assistant (PIA). Such works can thus come under an annual subscription scheme or be part of basic services to a citizen in the way that use of public libraries has traditionally been a free right in the past. Meanwhile, less frequently used works can be accessed via an Internet connection through on-line virtual reference rooms. Libraries can thus continue to perform an important role as repositories of our collective memory. At the same time, digital versions of their contents will provide us with new insights into their vast collections.

Museums

Memory institutions typically display three-dimensional objects such as vases and books. These are usually in display cases, often against a wall. As a result we can usually see one side and not the other and certainly not the base. If this vase were photographed from all sides with a camera, a museum visitor could look at the original and see the rest of the object using a handheld screen or glasses. The virtual object thus complements the physical object rather than competing with it.

This complementary function of the virtual can be extended. The handheld screen or glasses can show the original context(s) of museum objects, which typically come from churches, palaces, monuments, archaeological sites, etc. Standing in front of a museum display, it is almost impossible to appreciate this original context. Virtual museums[167] can thus provide a history of where the object was situated: i.e., a three-dimensional version of the Getty Provenance Index. As a result we can see where the painting hangs today along with all the places it hung previously in other galleries, including where it was initially commissioned. We can also see a given painting in the context of others by that artist and/or their contemporaries. As a result a given painting evokes a much richer set of connotations.

The glasses can also provide a history of restorations. In the case of a painting, the same approach can allow viewers to look beneath the surface of the painting using infrared refectography, X-rays, and other methods. This applies equally in the case of palimpsests in books or in the case of parchments that have been burned or carbonized. For conservators the glasses can provide detailed views at a microscopic level. Electronic media thus allow viewers to see things invisible to the naked eye.[168]

In the case of rare books on display, the book is inevitably open on a given page. The book would soon be ruined if passers-by continually flipped through the real pages. However, viewers can do this flipping of pages virtually on a nearby screen. The British Library has demonstrated this principle using books such as the *Diamond Sutra* (the world's oldest extant printed book, 868) and Leonardo da Vinci's *Codex Arundel*. Ian Witten (New Zealand) is creating an open-source version of turning the pages for developing countries. Alternatively, visitors could do this directly with the original, using special virtual reality glasses, which simulated the turning of the pages. In either case, visitors see more and the book does not suffer.

In present-day museums, objects typically have a small explanatory caption. Sometimes there is no caption at all. Sometimes the caption is in a language we do not understand. Frequently the caption is too superficial or it goes into more detail than we need. In future, handheld devices or glasses can provide customized captions, simple for children, more advanced for adults, and with much greater detail for experts. The same object remains visible, but the electronic tools surrounding it help reveal more about the object and its context. Projects such as HIPS and COMRIS point in this direction.[169] The Consortium for the Interchange of Museum Information (CIMI), disbanded in December 2003, had a Handscape project to explore the potentials of wireless tools in museums.[170] The intellectual consequence of new media is contextualization (chapters 12–15).

Intelligent museum objects can reveal aspects of themselves not readily visible from their position in a display. A scenario: A personal digital assistant (PDA) is linked through the Internet with a much larger array of materials in a virtual reference room. I am standing in front of a copy of Brueghel's *Winter Landscape* in the Bonnefanten Museum (Maastricht). My notepad computer is equipped with a camera that recognizes the painting via pattern recognition, the title, or simply via the equivalent of a bar code. This information is taken up by a (low-level) agent, which

TABLE 17 Twelve roles for virtual museums.[174]

1	Orientate visitors to find paintings
2	Stimulate looking more attentively at originals
3	Contextualize paintings and cultural objects/processes
4	Visualize techniques used (perspective, chiaroscuro, pentimenti, etc.)
5	Provide virtual restorations and reconstructions of paintings and sites
6	Include other sensorial effects such as sound, touch, or even smell
7	Raise awareness of other works in storage
8	Bring together objects in a fictive space of an imaginary museum
9	Provide a virtual history of exhibitions
10	Provide a history of the museum
11	Show collections in distant sites
12	Show sites not open to the public

notes that this is a copy of a more famous original now in the Kunsthistorisches Museum (Vienna). The software agent then offers me a possibility of seeing various other copies and versions of the same painting.

Implicit in this approach of intelligent museum objects is the notion that every cultural object receives its unique identifier, which goes further than a traditional ISBN number in the book world, to identify a single object. This number with its links to descriptors can serve as the equivalent of a passport for cultural objects, which can be used in the case of stolen objects or illicit tracking in cultural policy.[171] This idea of augmented culture becomes all the more essential when we look at works outside of our own heritage. In a global village we are all neighbours, but we are also constantly ignorant of dimensions of our neighbours' many cultures (cf. chapter 14).

All this has direct implications for tourism. While preparing to visit Florence, I can "have a chat" with my Personal Intelligent Assistant (PIA). The assistant determines which museums and churches are open when I am there, tells me what exhibitions will be on at that time, provides information about past[172] and future exhibitions, and offers itineraries. If I am a specialist, the assistant can provide more detailed itineraries linked with the painters or themes that concern me at the time. The assistant thus serves as an electronic Baedecker for tourists.

Such innovations are equally significant for museum professionals and other specialists. Traditionally, curators were connoisseurs who studied the surfaces of paintings, whereas conservators studied the layers underneath. Often these acted as if they were dealing with completely different objects. In fact, a conservator's detailed knowledge of layers beneath the surface can provide vital clues for the attributions of connoisseurs. Whereas the traditional visitor saw only the surface painting in visible light, future visitors could also see the same picture in Ultra Violet Fluorescence, InfraRed photography in pseudo-colours, in InfraRed Reflectography and X-Radiography.[173] The new media can thus bring new interactions between conservators and curators, which will ultimately further enrich the viewing experience of visitors.

Electronic versions of libraries can produce new print versions of a quality equal and sometimes superior to the original. Digital images of museum objects can also serve to print new images for postcards or illustrations in books. Digital libraries can serve as substitutes for the original. While virtual museums cannot serve as substitutes in the same way, they serve at least twelve valuable functions (Table 17).

8. Conclusions

The material consequence of the new media is virtuality. This is transforming production (chapter 4), services (chapter 5), and the institutions where they occur (chapter 6). Virtuality is something much more profound than a simple substitution of physical objects by electronic simulacra.[175] In many cases the original physical objects remain but are linked with persons, objects, and images, imbuing them with new meaning.

135

The Oxford English Dictionary defines "virtuality" as: "1. The possession of force or power (Caxton, 1483); 2. Essential nature or being, apart from external form or embodiment (Sir Thomas Browne, 1649) and 3. A virtual as opposed to an actual thing: a potentiality." Sir Thomas Brown (Pseud. Ep., 1649) used "virtuality" in a way analogous to Aristotle's concept of *entelechy* and thus combined elements of two and three when he claimed: "In one graine of corne there lyeth dormant the virtuality, of many other, and from thence proceed an hundred eares."[176]

This meaning derived from the medieval Latin term *virtualitas* and was linked with the Latin term *virtualis* (i.e., virtual). This medieval notion of the virtual serves as a starting point for Pierre Levy's discussions in *Becoming Virtual. Reality in the Digital Age*.[177] Levy's book has chapters on the virtualization of the body, text, economy, intelligence qua subject and object, as well as an ontological *trivium* and *quadrivium*.[178] He identifies virtualization as a particular kind of transformation linked to final causes and eternity and ultimately sees the virtual as a process that includes the potential, the real, and the actual.

A quite different approach is taken by Milgram, Takemura, Utsumi, and Kishino (1994),[179] who use a combination of three factors to define a reality–virtuality continuum that applies to augmented reality, namely, 1) Reproduction Fidelity (RF), 2) Extent of World Knowledge (EWK), and 3) Extent of Presence Metaphor (EPM).[180] This approach was pursued by Drascic and Milgram (1996, our Figure 7).[181]

A third approach to virtuality in the realm of organizations is offered in a perceptive paper by Gristock (1998),[182] who relates it to grids of space, time, and

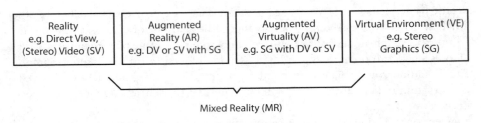

| Reality
e.g. Direct View,
(Stereo) Video (SV) | Augmented
Reality (AR)
e.g. DV or SV with SG | Augmented
Virtuality (AV)
e.g. SG with DV or SV | Virtual Environment (VE)
e.g. Stereo
Graphics (SG) |

Mixed Reality (MR)

Figure 7 Simplified version of the reality–virtuality continuum according to Drascic and Milgram (1996)

organization. Indeed, virtuality has a wide range of meanings. Some simply refer to their presence on the web as their virtuality.[183] The Cultural Studies section of the University of Vienna opposes models (virtuality) and ongoing activity (reality).[184] A project in Helsinki links virtuality and digital nomadism.[185] The difference between virtuality and cyberspace has been explored by Wooley.[186] A number of scholars have explored the implications of virtuality for public space, the concern being that public space will be commercialized.[187] They have also explored its potentials for expression of virtual space via interfaces with direct links to the senses[188] and its connections to a number of disciplines including: biosciences,[189] literary theory,[190] political theory,[191] and political economy.[192]

Virtuality is also connected with new methods of work (cf. chapter 11). In the short term, these methods are leading to global networks of knowledge in individual fields and new interplays among different fields. In the long term, virtuality promises to be much more than a new gateway to reality. Virtuality is extending our senses in ways far beyond those considered by Freud and McLuhan. It relates to scientific visualization: it is expanding the horizons of the visible, invisible, possible, and creative worlds. It is affecting a wide range of fields including astronomy, military planning, industrial design, nano-technology, film,[193] video, crime reconstruction, stock markets, and weather prediction (Appendix 1). Even the possibility of being paid to deal with virtual objects, which never existed physically, has been considered.[194]

A future study should place these developments within a larger historical framework. Virtuality in the sense of making something as a model or simulation for something to be constructed physically goes back to antiquity. During the Renaissance, the building of physical scale models as a preparation for a full-scale, real building became standard practice among architects such as Brunelleschi, Leonardo, and Michelangelo. Virtuality in the new sense replaces the physical scale model, with an electronic surrogate, which can be worked on by hundreds or even thousands of designers around the world linked by a network. Moreover, given stereo-lithography, such virtual models can be rendered physical at any time, at any place (as long as one has a stereo-lithographic printer).

Dynamic simulations such as flight simulators are said to go back to the 1930s. Controlling objects at a distance is known to almost everyone in the developed world through the everyday use of remote control instruments for television. The origins of such control systems are linked with the development of V1 and V2 rockets in the 1940s. The advent of Sputnik in 1957 introduced a new meaning to remote control. Soon, rockets, satellites, and even space stations could be manoeuvred from thousands, and later hundreds of millions, of miles away. Most of these early experiences entailed very simple operations, turning an engine or some other machine on or off, changing direction or adjusting basic inputs such as temperature, pressure, etc. The developments of the past decades are fundamentally different for at least six reasons:

First, they entail much more complex tasks. Medical operations can now be performed at a distance. Using simulations, a doctor can practice before the actual operation.

Second, these tasks draw on different databases as in the MICE project, where description and structure databases are combined to generate reconstruction scenes of molecules "on the fly" (cf. chapter 11).

Third, through a simulation-reality feedback loop, a simulation is connected to real machines or factories through a series of sensors, which inform the model of anomalies. The model then adjusts inputs into the physical machine or process. Simulation and reality are thus linked in a new way, enabling machine-machine communication potentially without human intervention.

Fourth, there is a question of scale. Models and simulators of the past entailed an artist's or architect's impression of an object or a building. Today's virtuality involves fully detailed simulations of a complex factory or even whole cities (Appendix 1).

Fifth, there is a far greater range of scales. In the past, physical scale models were primarily about future, full-scale, physical objects and constructions. The new simulations of virtuality extend from the nano-scale (10^{-15}) to macro scales of thousands of light years (10^{24}).

Sixth, the ever-greater ability to document physical reality from the smallest particle to the largest galaxies of outer space has brought an increasing fascination with the creative implications of these worlds. Bodyscapes, space, and science fiction are becoming new categories of art. The quest for new patterns of science thus points to new experiences in art. The discovery of reality through virtuality is leading to discoveries of new creative realities.

These advances in virtuality are part of a larger revolution. There are predictions that within twenty years computers will use DNA to store information: that one gram of DNA used for computing will have a storage capacity equal to 1 trillion

CD-ROMs. This means that the entire contents of the world's great memory institutions could be carried in one's pocket. It would technically be possible for every human being to have access to all knowledge that was ever recorded. Indeed, we are entering a world where almost everything is possible. To appreciate this better, we need to go beyond technological and material consequences and explore the organizational, intellectual, and philosophical consequences of the new media in a networked context.

PART III

organizational
consequences:
SYSTEMICITY

7

organizations

> The single greatest challenge facing managers in the developed countries of the world is to raise the productivity of knowledge and service workers. This challenge … will ultimately determine the competitive performance of companies. Even more important, it will determine the very fabric of society and the quality of life of every industrialized nation.
> — Peter Drucker,
> *Post-Capitalist Society*
> (1997, p. 69).

1. Introduction

The technological and material consequences of computers are invisibility and virtuality, respectively (chapters 1–6). The organizational consequences of computers entail systemicity. We shall focus on three aspects: changes in approach to organizations as a whole (chapter 7); developments with respect to knowledge management in organizations (chapter 8), and how this affects our theories of learning (chapter 9).

A recent survey, based on experts at leading U.S. business schools, identified the ten most influential authors on business in the twentieth century (Table 18). Frederick W. Taylor (1911)[1] was concerned with optimizing persons' effectiveness

TABLE 18 Ten greatest authors on management of the twentieth century according to Worthing Brighton Press[6]

1911	Frederick Winslow Taylor	*The Principles of Scientific Management*
1919	Henry L. Gantt	*Organizing for Work*
1933	Elton Mayo	*The Human Problems of an Industrial Civilization*
1938	Chester Irving Barnard	*The Functions of the Executive*
1946	Peter Ferdinand Drucker	*Concept of the Corporation*
1954	Abraham Harold Maslow	*Motivation and Personality*
1959	Frederick Herzberg et al.	*The Motivation to Work*
1961	Rensis Likert	*New Patterns of Management*
1964	Chris Argyris	*Integrating the Individual and the Organization*
1973	Henry Mintzberg	*The Nature of Managerial Work*

in the work process. Gantt (1919),[2] through his charts, shifted the emphasis to effective work systems.[3] Mayo (1933)[4] sought to identify the stumbling blocks, which lowered team performance and discovered the importance of social factors through the so-called Hawthorne effect: that persons work harder when attention is being given to them and have a sense that they are special. Barnard (1938)[5] attempted a synthesis between Taylor's scientific management and Mayo's human relations theory of management and also turned to executives to define the structure and flow of power.

Peter Ferdinand Drucker (b. 1909) is particularly interesting. Having written *The End of Economic Man* in 1939,[7] just before World War II, he wrote *The Concept of the Corporation* in 1946[8] and then made a comeback in 1969 with *The Age of Discontinuity*[9] and a study in Japanese on *Industrial Management*. He has since written some fifteen books in this field and is credited with having introduced the notion of a corporate society. One of his latest books is about managing oneself,[10] a single person rather than a whole organization. Appropriately, the business hype now speaks of marketing to groups of one (see chapter 9).

Whereas authors in the first half of the twentieth century focussed on getting the best out of existing facilities, those in the latter half explored how psychological dimensions of work could improve the status quo. Maslow (1954)[11] studied the role of motivation, Herzberg (1959)[12] the role of culture. Likert (1961)[13] and Argyris (1964)[14] returned to the role of leaders in this process. Mintzberg (1973)[15] considered anew the managerial process.

If we look at these individuals, and in each case the initial classic text that made them famous, we discover that two began writing in the first quarter of the twentieth century, three in the second quarter, five in the third quarter, and none in the last quarter. That five of the above authors produced their first classic work before 1950, five between 1950 and 1975, and none in the last three decades, is deceptive. First, the authors remained active long after their first publication and indeed some are still active today. Second, the list is exclusively about American authors and does not mention Americans who worked abroad, such as William Deming, or non-Americans such as Ikujiro Nonaka,[16] or Don Tapscott.

There are further anomalies in this list. Although Drucker and Argyris mention *corporation* and *organization* in their title, American authors focus on the management of individuals in organizations rather than on the organizations themselves. Two major approaches to management have emerged from these American thinkers: so-called scientific management (Taylor)[17] and a human relations theory of management (Mayo).[18] An attempt at synthesis between these two main approaches (e.g., Argyris[19]) is sometimes called "revisionism."[20] The European view is considerably more complex. It is instructive to note, for instance, that a standard Dutch textbook on management identifies no less than twelve schools.[21]

Study of organizations as such has come through the field of sociology. In the early twentieth century, the German sociologist Max Weber became fascinated by the rise of bureaucracies in the West, which he saw as a trend towards rationalization in terms of four factors: 1) efficiency, 2) predictability, 3) calculability, and 4) technologies that control people. Weber's analysis is the starting point of a fascinating study by George Ritzer concerning *The McDonaldization of Society* (2000).[22]

Related to Weber's fourth factor is something more subtle. The new technologies do more than simply control people and processes. They entail assumptions about the nature of rationality, which are systemic in nature and are changing the structures and organizations themselves. To understand these assumptions, we need to look briefly at a) pragmatism and b) some developments in computer theory. These are linked with c) systems theory, which emphasizes structures rather than individuals, d) action theory, and e) action science. These assumptions relate to theories of organizational culture, organizational learning, visualization, and virtualization. Again, the United States, Europe, and Japan have their own approaches to these developments.

2. Pragmatism

William James, in *Pragmatism* (1907), "argued that if an idea works, it is true; insofar as it makes a difference to life in terms of cash value, it is meaningful."[23] John Dewey went further and argued that only external actions matter. For Descartes man is because he thinks. For Dewey persons are because they do. This externalization of the inner world helps to explain the rise of behaviorist psychology in America. If persons what they do, or how they respond, then stimulus-response becomes the solution to problems. If organizations are like individuals, then the good news is that all one needs to do is find the stimulus in order to know the response. The bad news is that individuals and organizations are constantly responding to some external stimulus. It means that they are essentially passive, or to use a more politically correct term, they use adaptive learning.

The stimulus-response theory is pervasive in much of twentieth-century economics. Someone does something and then "the market responds." The market does something and the organization responds, etc. In this view, we are all problem solvers, i.e., responding passively to problems that have been imposed upon us from outside. Hence, when Alfred Marshall states that "Knowledge is our most powerful engine of production," he means knowledge of economic capital. Implicitly he means that we must respond to external trends of the market. In this framework, organizations are inevitably passively responding to a given direction rather than actively proposing a new direction. And because this given direction too often becomes visible only at the last moment, there is a constant tendency to make last-minute emergency responses rather than working within a long-term framework.

3. Computer Theory

In the United States, the pragmatic school of philosophy led to a behaviourist school of psychology with a stimulus-response model of reality. In computer science this was translated into input-output systems. At Carnegie Mellon University, Newell and Simon took this further to produce condition-action production systems. Herbert Simon's computer theory gave the illusion of a programmatic reality to the stimulus-response approach of behaviourist psychology based on this pragmatic philosophy. Simon saw organizations as information-processing machines.[24] In order to produce a scientific model of problem solving, he built a computer model of human thought processes. His books *Administrative Behaviour* (1947) and *Organizations* (1958) linked logical human, problem solving with a) machines, b) organizations, and implicitly c) learning.

In the 1980s, the work of Newell, Simon and Margolis[25] made explicit connections between cognitive science, problem solving, and learning (cf. chapters 14–15, below). This work also helped to make thought in artificial intelligence as models for logical thought: "After the initial statement of the law, definition or principle that will solve the problem, the solutions attached here proceed in a logical, step-by-step manner with successive steps being guided by cues derived from the current state of the solution. This is similar to computer methods that apply artificial intelligence to problem solving."[26] In light of this, one recent commentator claims that it is alarming how "contemporary organization in presenting physics subject matter and using that knowledge in problem solving is in about the same state that computer programming was 30 years ago."[27] Robert Sternberg, the IBM Professor of Psychology and Education at Yale University, has helped spread this approach to the educational field.[28]

4. Systems Theory

Such links between theories of the mind, computer science, and organizations were further developed at the Rand Corporation and the Sloan School of Management (MIT).[29] In addition to economic analyses and management manuals, the Sloan School has publications on cognition and social behaviour,[30] the bureaucratization of the world,[31] information technology,[32] computers and the learning process in higher education,[33] learning organizations,[34] the knowledge-based economy,[35] and e-lance, the electronic form of freelance.[36]

The Sloan School endorsed *Control through Communication: The Rise of System in American Management* by Joanne Yates (1993) and her book on the role of information technology in organizational transformation (2000).[37] Indeed, the Sloan School of Management at MIT has played a particular role in the rise of systems theory with respect to business, specifically through the Systems Dynamics Group, the Center for Organizational Learning and Center for Co-ordination Science.

The Systems Dynamics Group at MIT's Sloan School was founded in 1956 by Jay W. Forrester, the inventor of "random-access, coincident-current magnetic storage, which became the standard memory device for digital computers."[38] Forrester graduated in Mechanical Engineering at MIT (1945), worked for a decade with the military and turned then to societal systems. This led to basic books: *Industrial Dynamics* (1961), *Principles of Systems* (1968), *Urban Dynamics* (1969) and *World Dynamics* (1971).[39]

This work brought him into contact with Eduard Prestel, one of the founders of the Club of Rome and led to his involvement with the important study of that group on the *Limits of Growth* (1971).[40] Accordingly, Forrester's second edition of *World Dynamics* in 1973[41] included a chapter on physical versus social limits. His *Collected Papers* were published in 1975.[42] In the next years he worked with Edward Roberts with whom he published *Managerial Applications of Systems Dynamics* (1978).[43] Since then, Forrester developed the System Dynamics National Model and has been working on System Dynamics in Education.[44]

Peter Senge published *The Fifth Discipline* in 1990.[45] The widespread interest in his book led Senge and his colleagues to found the Center for Organizational Learning (OLC) at MIT's Sloan School of Management in 1991 to study: "concepts (concerned with the art and practice of learning organizations) built on decades of research in system dynamics, action science, group process and the creative processes as well as from practical experience in consulting and leading workshops."[46]

Related to the Sloan School at MIT is the Center for Co-ordination Science (CCS), which has projects in coordination technology,[47] organizational structures, information technology,[48] and coordination theory.[49] One of the chief research activities at CCS is the compilation of a Process Handbook "by collecting, organizing, and analyzing numerous examples of how different groups and companies perform similar functions, and by ... developing new methodologies for representing and codifying these organizational processes."[50] Other research includes the development of a process interchange format[51]; "brokers in electronic commerce market for evaluations and Oval – a 'radically tailorable' environment for supporting group coordination."

A site on systems thinking[52] provides many more links. Meanwhile, the Systems Dynamics Society[53] in Albany reminds us that systems are applied to a wide range of fields including corporate planning and policy design, public management and policy, biological and medical modelling, energy and the environment, theory development in the natural and social sciences, dynamic decision-making, and complex nonlinear dynamics. We shall show that systems theory plays an integrating role in bringing together a number of other seemingly unrelated trends such as action learning, action science, and organizational learning. This is linked to a growing concern with control through companies such as International Control Systems.[54] A consequence of this emphasis on systems is that the impersonal processes of organizations are ultimately deemed more important than the personal dimensions of individuals.

5. Action Learning and Science

The founding father of action learning as a management learning and development strategy was Dr. Reg Revans, who eventually became President Emeritus of International Management Centres (IMC).[55] As a young man in the 1930s while working with a group of scholars at Cambridge: "he found that they would sit down together and ask one another lots of questions. No one person was considered more important than any other and they all had contributions to make, even when they were not experts in a particular field. In this way they teased out workable solutions to their own and one another's problems." Revans was so inspired by this approach that he introduced it at the Coal Board when pit managers had problems. "The technique proved so successful that the managers wrote their own handbook on how to run a coal mine."[56]

As explained by the Centre for Action Learning (CALL),[57] the essence of Revans' insight can be reduced to the formula $L = P + Q$. In this formula, L is Learning, P is programmed learning and Q is questioning learning, namely "what you learn by looking at the way people work in your environment and wondering why they do it that way.[58] "By focusing on the right questions rather than the right answers, Action Learning focuses on what you do not know rather than what you do know. This means that it deals not with puzzles but with problems."[59]

Action learning is thus concerned with turning experience into learning in a four-stage process: 1) having an experience, 2) reviewing the experience, 3) concluding from the experience, and 4) planning the next steps. These stages are linked respectively with the activist, reflector, theorist, and pragmatist learning styles derived from Carl Gustav Jung.[60] This leads to the definition of a management wheel, which entails eight kinds of persons: reporter-advisers, creator-innovators, explorer-promoters, assessor-developers, thruster-organizers, concluder-producers, controller-inspectors, upholder-maintainers.[61] Action learning groups thus become a foundation for "cultural change"[62] and produce "learning to learn courseware."[63] Action learning has gradually become part of a larger phenomenon called "creativity tools," meaning idea-generation methods.[64]

At first sight all of this is wonderfully stimulating. In terms of the business world, where the active life (*vita activa*) dominates, where the emphasis is on action, doing, making, and production, this approach to action learning undoubtedly represents an excellent strategy. But the life of learning, the contemplative life, has traditionally explored an alternative to this purely action-oriented approach.

It is instructive that, in Dutch, "action learning" is translated as "learning while working" (*lerend werken*). The Dutch Action Learning Association (*Vereniging Lerend Ondernemen*) has a number of further references to related techniques.[65] This tendency can also be observed elsewhere. For instance, at Skagit Valley College (Washington), we find Learning Into Action (LIA), an independent project, which allows students to demonstrate skills and abilities while working in "real life" situations, travelling, or completing special activities.[66] When we turn experience into learning, we are learning to do and risk not doing much more. As we shall see (chapter 9), Learning as Doing is a significant new trend especially in the United States.

Closely related to action learning is action research, on which there is a refereed on-line journal. In Britain, Gwilym Jenkins, founder of the first systems department in that country (at Lancaster University) in the mid-1960s, initiated a program of action research. Partly inspired by Optner's concept "that an organization could be taken to be a system with functional subsystems," Jenkins was determined to develop systems for real-world organizations. This led to the work of Peter Checkland and the gradual distinction between soft systems and hard systems.[67] Pioneers in the computing field such as Herbert Simon had assumed that computer code could be reduced to clear-cut problems, as in other areas of engineering, i.e., quantitative statements of user requirements. This had led to hard systems. Checkland's contribution was to insist that there were other less tangible factors that played a role, including culture, informal interactions, and attitudes – which he termed the "Human Activity System." His Soft System Methodology (SSM) was to investigate, understand, and identify problems that were not clearly defined.

Besides action research, there is also action science, resources on which are collected by the Institute of Workplace Research Learning and Development (WoRLD), within the School of Social and Workplace Development (SaWD) at Southern Cross University (Australia), which again has support from the International Management Centres (IMC).[68] Definitions of the subject use terms from computer science and artificial life such as data, iterative process, and emergent process.[69]

6. Organizational Culture

As mentioned earlier, the twentieth century produced two major approaches to management in the United States: 1) scientific management (Taylor) and 2) a human-relations theory of management (Mayo). This second alternative found new

TABLE 19 Basic differences between traditional and organizational learning.

TRADITIONAL LEARNING	ORGANIZATIONAL LEARNING
Heighten individuality	Push individuality into the background
Study individuals	Study issues, problems, achieve products
Understand subject for its own sake	Use subject as step to economic goal
Not for profit	Only for profit
No business case	Only business case
No goal	Goal only
Mind and intellect	Products, anti-intellectual
Hand on tradition	Change
Search for new	Search to exploit what is already known

expression in the 1980s. Pfeffer (1981)[70] viewed organizations as "systems of shared meanings and beliefs" and organizational culture thus became shared beliefs and knowledge. Peters and Waterman (1982)[71] claimed that sharing of values among employees was a key to corporate culture and saw this as the basis for a humanistic approach to management. Schein (1985)[72] took this further, claiming that one needed shared experiences to achieve a shared view. Culture, he claimed, was "a pattern of basic assumptions – invented, discovered, or developed by a given group as it learns to cope with problems of external adaptation and internal integration."[73]

Culture in Schein's sense has nothing to do with culture in the traditional sense. Traditional culture is linked with enduring beliefs and expressions in various media, which lead to a cumulative memory (cf. chapter 14). Schein's culture is neither linked with enduring beliefs nor expressions. This has the advantage that it can theoretically be changed on a whim. As a result, mission statements that define a corporation's goals and thereby its culture become of fundamental significance. Culture is no longer something one has but rather something one needs to learn. This notion of organizational culture thus leads to ideas of organizational learning.

7. Organizational Learning

The term "learning organization" is attributed to Chris Argyris, a prolific author who has continued to publish over the past four decades. His first book was *Integrating the Individual and the Organization* (1964).[74] This led to a case study of renewal in a local newspaper (1974),[75] work on action theory (1985),[76] studies on how to overcome defensiveness in organizations (1985,[77] 1990,[78] 1993[79]), which then led to organizational learning (1994,[80] 1996,[81] 1999[82]). His latest work explores how to make computers more accessible to human beings (1999).[83]

Strongly influenced by John Dewey[84] and Kurt Lewin,[85] Argyris' views of organizational learning, also called "action inquiry" or "action research," are based on action "science," which derives from the organizational development field. There are two types of theories of action: technical theories (autonomous distanced models) and human theories (e.g., interpersonal relationships and effective leadership). The methods of action science appear to give enormous freedom to individual employees. Their purpose is supposedly personal mastery: to define goals and to try to achieve them (unilaterally), to maximize winning and minimize losing, to minimize expressing or generating negative feelings, to be rational and to minimize emotionality.[86]

On closer scrutiny, this is something quite different than the personal mastery required for nirvana. The employee works for a corporation with a mission statement that defines the goal a priori. They are free to define any goal they wish in this context as long as it corresponds with the corporation's mission, is the most profitable possible, and minimizes personal dimensions such as feelings. By contrast, personal mastery is part of a larger vision, which includes mental models, shared vision, team learning, and systems thinking.[87] All this may be an excellent way to coordinate the energies and abilities of employees within a corporation.

The learning of learning organizations is fundamentally different from traditional learning, which eliminates external goals as much as possible in order to deepen the individual. Organizational learning eliminates individuals as much as possible to reach a goal of the corporation. Traditional learning is concerned with study of a subject in order to understand it on its own terms and deals with individuals in their own right. By contrast, organizational learning focusses on issues and problems to be overcome in reaching profitable products and goals. Organizational learning is not concerned with understanding a subject, only concerned with how it can be used to make money. Traditional learning is not for profit. Organizational learning is purely for profit. Without a business case, a subject is not worth learning. Traditional learning leads inward to a study of mind and intellect. Organizational learning leads outward to a mastery of products and in that sense is ultimately anti-intellectual (Table 19).

The term "traditional" means that something is handed-down. Traditional learning implies a continuity with the past. Organizational learning is focussed instead on change and transformation, on the different. At the same time there is a paradoxical way in which traditional learning is more committed to the new than organizational learning. It used to be said of research that if one knew the result before one began, then it was not really research. Organizational learning reverses this position: if one does not know the end result when one begins, then there is no clear goal and it is ultimately unacceptable.

Traditional learning focussed on research in order to discover something new. Organizational "learning" focusses on development in order to exploit what is already known. To be sure, there is a constant rhetoric of new products, but this is more qua using what one has in new ways rather than creating original products. In a paradoxical way, the goal-oriented thrust of organizational learning is so concerned with getting to its end-product that it is subtly and nonetheless fundamentally against truly new things. As a result, organizational learning puts an ever-greater emphasis on system, on process, on planning, on decision support.[88] It is thus no coincidence that one of the starting points for organizational learning is Don Michael's book: *On Learning to Plan — and Planning to Learn* (1973).

Learning Organizations

Peter Senge took the notion of organizational learning and reversed the terms to focus on learning organizations. If organizations have learning disabilities, they need to become a learning organization to go further. This requires at least five disciplines: 1) systems thinking, 2) personal mastery of one's life, 3) externalizing mental models and challenging them, 4) building a shared vision, and 5) facilitating team learning. In Senge's approach, systems thinking is "the discipline that integrates the disciplines, fusing them together into a coherent body of theory and practice."[89] Senge's approach to organizational learning has nothing to do with traditional approaches to learning by individuals. It is about imposing systemic approaches to eliminate individual views such that individuals work systematically and organizations operate as if they were without individuals.

Similarly when Eppel and Conklin speak of *Blending Cultural Transformation and Groupware to Create a Learning Organization*[90] and state that they are using collective intelligence, they are not talking about culture or collective intelligence in a traditional sense. Rather they are describing a new technology for visualizing decisions more effectively. The learning of learning organizations is something fundamentally different from learning in the traditional sense.

From Knowledge Repositories to Core Competencies

The very word "firm" suggests that companies traditionally saw themselves as basically static entities that changed only insofar as their sales grew (or declined). In the past fifty years, as the emphasis has shifted increasingly to change, there has been ever-more attention to elements in companies that can be transformed. The emphasis shifted from what a company was to what it plans to become: from a company's essence to its strategy. Penrose (1959)[91] effectively looked upon firms as a repository of knowledge, albeit mainly in terms of explicit human and material resources. This approach was developed by Nelson and Winter (1977, 1982)[92] and Winter (1988).[93]

As Nonaka (1995)[94] has observed, this led, in the 1990s, to a new resource-based approach to strategy, beginning with the work of Prahalad and Hamel (1990)[95] who defined core competence as "the collective learning in the organization, especially how to coordinate diverse production skills and integrate multiple streams of technologies."[96] Others, such as Teece, Pisano, Shuen (1991)[97], emphasized the importance of problem-finding and problem-solving as keys to learning, adaptation, change, and renewal. Stalk, Evans, Schulman (1992),[98] outlined success as a quick response to changing customer needs. In all this, the focus was on a behavioural mode of passively responding to market forces and so-called customer needs rather than positive actions.

The growing interest in resources and core competencies has led in Europe to the idea of "trees of competencies" (*arbres de connaissances*), which have grown out of the work of Pierre Levy. On the surface these are concerned with identifying the unique capacities of each individual that the Gingo software will valuate: "The principle is simple: each user is asked to define themselves in terms of their competencies and know how. Knowing how to repair a diesel motor, how to speak English fluently, how to count, write, organize a theatre piece, lead a discussion … each of us has particularities, talents which can be useful to one's neighbours."[99] The Gingo software thus leads to a "tree of knowledge" (*arbre des connaissances*) or more specifically a tree of competencies. On closer inspection this approach is more problematic. Individuals enter their own subjective assessment of their competencies, which become part of a tree relating to their group. If the individual moves to another group or company his or her profile and the resulting tree is different. The tree of competencies appears objective, but it is ultimately subjective.

Traditionally universities did research that business later developed. Then there was a time when the approach of the Research ANd Development (RAND) Corporation became Research and Development (R&D) departments in universities. This led to "pre-competitive research." Increasingly universities speak of research but mean development. While universities speak of business partnerships, there are subtle and sometimes not so subtle ways in which the goals of organizational learning are undermining the traditional learning of universities (cf. chapter 9). In the past decade, these ideas of learning organizations have spread rapidly beyond individual companies.[100] Meanwhile, Dave Ulrich of the University of Michigan and Hope Greenfield from Digital Equipment Corporation (DEC, now Compaq), listed ten transitions in moving organizations from a training mentality to one of true learning that brings "organizations to new levels of competitiveness" (Table 20).

8. Visualization

The Taylorization of work (1911)[102] made visible individual aspects of the work process. Gantt (1919)[103] took this a significant step forward with his charts, which are now the basis of most project planning and workflow software. While some of the software entails individual projects, other software extends to Enterprise Resource Planning (ERP). In the past years these methods to visualize work patterns in human activities have been adapted for the visualization of computer operations. Hence in computer processing, a Gantt chart: "depicts the activity of individual processors by a horizontal bar chart in which the color of each bar indicates the busy/overhead/idle status of the corresponding processor as a function of time, again using the traffic-signal color scheme."[104]

TABLE 20 Ten transitions in moving from training to learning according to Dave Ulrich.[101]

1	Move from generic classroom … to tailored competence-based training
2	Change from case studies to action learning
3	Migrate from individual competence to organizational capabilities
4	Shift from individual to team participation
5	Transition from classroom to overall learning
6	Change from competence-based classes to strategy-based courses
7	Move from external to internal presenters
8	Shift from bounded to unbounded training sessions
9	Migrate from company to value chain participation
10	Move from local to global learning models

TABLE 21 Differences between data and intelligence according to Fuld &Co.[110]

DATA	Scattered bits and pieces of knowledge
INFORMATION	A pooling of these bits of knowledge
ANALYSIS	Distilled information
INTELLIGENCE	The implication that will allow you to make a decision

One of the reasons why many of us have not fathomed the immensity of the changes at hand is because the management gurus are using familiar terms in very unfamiliar ways. Hence it is vital to understand the differences between traditional learning and organizational learning, if we are to understand what sounds familiar. When Diane McGinty Weston speaks of integrating learning with everyday work, she does not mean doing night courses while maintaining a job. She means mental modelling, action learning, and the leveraging of learning.[105]

The early workflow charts provided a static overview of various stages in a project or a work process. The past years have seen an increasing trend to visualize such processes dynamically. One of the pioneers in this field was a Toronto-based company, Visible Decisions.[106] This led to new companies such as Asymptote. A dramatic example of their work is Hani Rashid's three-dimensional visualization of the Virtual Trading floor, which allows one to follow fluctuations in the stock market in real-time. As a result, even seemingly abstract concepts such as stock market speculation are becoming visible and accessible electronically. Paradoxically the ever-greater visualization of companies is closely linked with trends towards their virtualization.

9. European Models

As might be expected, Europe has a different approach to organizations.[107] While the rhetoric of American companies is constantly on the role of the individual, their focus is paradoxically on a system where individuals play no decisive role. In Europe there is a reverse paradox. European rhetoric pays more attention to systems than to individuals and yet ultimately individuals play a more central role in corporations.

For instance, at the St. Gall Center for Futures Research,[108] systems science is linked with organizational development, the learning organization, cybernetics, evolution theory, cognitive science, and complexity.[109] In America, knowledge management is mainly about management. In Europe, knowledge management entails theories of knowledge (cf. chapter 8).

10. Japanese Alternatives

Nonaka and Takeuchi (1995)[111] have provided an excellent survey of basic differences between Japanese and Western organizations (Figure 8). They have drawn attention to at least five shortcomings in the western approach as they see it: 1) learning in organizations is seen within the stimulus-response model of behavioural psychology, which leads to 2) a passive, adaptive change process rather than to new knowledge. 3) There is a (rhetorical) emphasis on the individual rather than on how individuals work as teams and groups within an organization. 4) This poses the need for a double-loop approach, and a need for intervention through organizational development programs. 5) There is a challenge, therefore, to create methods for new knowledge.

This requires a dynamic, interactive model, which includes epistemological, ontological, and temporal dimensions. Ultimately, Nonaka wants to link traditions of the theory of knowledge (epistemology), with organizational theory, and a theory of innovation. Herbert Simon sought a "general treatment of the design process" by understanding "how organizations acquire new products, new methods of manufacture and new organizational terms."[112] Nonaka and Takeuchi seek this by understanding "how organizations create new knowledge that makes such creations possible."[113]

11. Conclusions

While the business community in the United States constantly speaks of corporations as organizations and stresses the importance of organizational culture, organizational learning, and learning organizations, their central concern is with the management of individuals in organizations rather than with understanding the organizations themselves. In this context, the past century has seen the rise of two competing approaches to management: the so-called scientific management (Taylor) and a human-relations theory of management that draws on psychology and sociology (Mayo).

Meanwhile, European sociologists such as Max Weber became fascinated by the rise of bureaucracies in the West, which they saw as a trend towards rationalization in terms of four factors: 1) efficiency, 2) predictability, 3) calculability, and 4) technologies that control people (and processes). As technologies that control

Japanese Organization	Western Organization
Group-based	Individual-based
Tacit knowledge-oriented	Explicit knowledge-oriented
Strong on socialization and internalization	Strong on externalization and **combination**
Emphasis on experience	Emphasis on analysis
Dangers of "group think" and "overadaptation to the past success"	Danger of paralysis by analysis
Ambiguous organizational intention	Clear organizational intention
Group autonomy	Individual autohomy
Creative chaos through overlapping tasks	Creative chaos through individual differences
Frequent fluctuation from top management	Less fluctuation from top management
Redundancy of information	Less redundancy of information
Requisite variety through cross-functional teams	Requisite varienty through individual differences

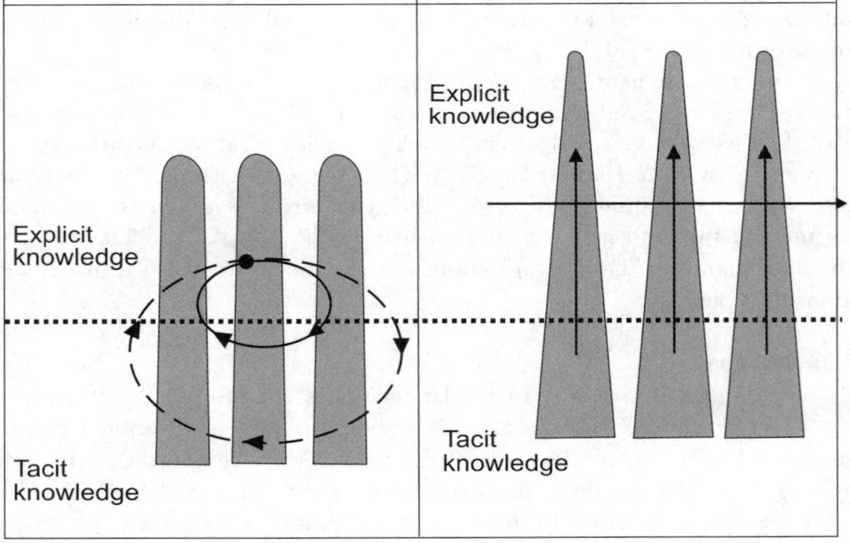

Figure 8 Contrast between Western and Eastern organization according to Nonaka (1995, p. 199).

processes, the new media have unexpected consequences. They are also used to control people. Especially in the United States, where pragmatism rules, there is a trend to focus on external actions and behavioural psychology with its assumptions of stimulus-response as descriptions of reality. Organizations are seen as being ruled by the stimulus-response model of behaviourism. This leads to a passive approach to reality. More insidiously, computer scientists have become cognitive scientists whereby their theories of the human mind have become integrated into computer programs. The externalizing quest of pragmatism thus leads to action science, action learning, organizational learning, and learning organizations as well as American extroverts.

If learning is learning to act and intelligence is ability to make a decision, then knowledge is action, doing things, producing. Hence organizations focus on products. Knowledge management within these organizations seeks to identify processes that make this possible. Thus there are close links between knowledge management and Process Modeling (PM), Business Process Reengineering (BPR),[114] Business Process Redesign (also BPR), Process Innovation (PI),[115] Enterprise Resource Planning (ERP), Enterprise Integration (EI)[116] and Enterprise Application Integration (EAI).[117] Since 2000, EAI is being replaced by Application to Application (A2A) Integration. Even so, we need new study of e-organization, which studies the actual operations of organizations, both with respect to their internal control and functioning, and to their external activities.

We noted that organizational learning is something very different from traditional learning. Knowledge management is also something very different than knowledge organization. Often knowledge management is simply a new term for management and might appropriately be called knowledge of management. In other cases, knowledge management is concerned with identifying and handling the "know how" of personnel rather than their "know what." For instance, Fuld & Co. distinguishes between data, information, analysis, and intelligence but does not have a separate category for knowledge[118] (Table 21, cf. chapters 14–15).

Major corporations are, of course, very much aware of the need to access the knowledge of their researchers. In Germany there is a saying that "If Siemens knew, what Siemens knows … " ("*Wenn Siemens wüsste was Siemens weiss …*"), the implication being that if they did then they would be much more efficient. In America, there is a similar saying: "If only HP knew what HP knows,"[119] Very large corporations such as IBM often have researchers in one lab competing with those in another lab. Often researchers are working in such secrecy on a particular development that they are unaware of solutions already existing within their own company (cf. chapter 13). The development of Intranets has helped this problem only somewhat. Researchers at Nortel are very aware of this problem and are searching for a solution, and yet all this has nothing to do with knowledge management as used by those in business management.

When we turn to consider knowledge management in the business sense (chapter 8), we shall see that there are again at least three political approaches: 1) management (United States); 2) theories of knowledge (Europe), and 3) an integration of new knowledge (Japan).

8
(knowledge) management

Toffler observes that knowledge has gone from being an adjunct of money power and muscle power to being their very essence, and that is why the battle for the control of knowledge and the means of communication is heating up all over the world. He believes that knowledge is the ultimate replacement of other resources.
— Ikujiro Nonaka, H. Takeuchi, *The Knowledge Creating Company* (1994, p. 7)

1. Introduction

In traditional businesses there was a strict hierarchy of (blue-collar) workers, middle management, and executives in top management. Executives typically had visions. Middle management linked these visions with the realities of the work floor and also maintained corporate memory. In larger firms, there was often one corporate librarian for every hundred persons. This ensured that the firm's knowledge was well catalogued and maintained.

In the United States, the rhetoric of a new economy in the 1980s claimed that middle management was an unnecessary luxury, that one could become a "lean and mean" firm if one did away with the middle layer. Unfortunately when middle management disappeared, so too did most of the links concerning the firm's knowledge. The quest to be lean and mean thus created a new need for knowledge management. It is tempting to characterize the developments of the past half-century as a gradual shift from management to knowledge management. In the United States, the emphasis remains on management rather than knowledge. Moreover, while definitions of "knowledge" in this context are many and varied, they usually have very little to do with knowledge organization as used in the scholarly world (cf. chapter 12).

Dr. Fred Kofman (MIT), for instance, claims that: "Learning is the enhancement of, or increase in, knowledge, and knowledge is the capacity for effective action in a domain, where effectiveness is assessed by a community of fellow practitioners."[1] While very attractive, this has no relation to traditions of truth and is more closely related to action learning and the traditions of systems theory discussed in the previous chapter. A related definition is given by Intelligent KM.com: knowledge management is "information in context to make it insightful and relevant for human action."[2] As noted earlier this is the heritage of Dewey's pragmatism.

The Knowledge Management Forum offers a number of further definitions, e.g., that knowledge is a set of models describing various properties and behaviours within a domain[3] and that knowledge management is the collection of processes governing the creation, dissemination, and utilization of knowledge.[4] At the University of Texas, knowledge management is defined as "the systematic process of finding, selecting, organizing, distilling and presenting information in a way that improves an employee's comprehension in a specific area of interest."[5] John T. Maloney claims "Knowledge Management is a discipline using human expertise and information to improve productivity and productivity growth (innovation)."[6] Yet another definition by Denham Grey claims: "Knowledge management is an audit of 'intellectual assets' that highlights unique sources, critical functions and potential bottlenecks which hinder knowledge flows to the point of use. It protects intellectual assets from decay, seeks opportunities to enhance decisions, services and products through adding intelligence, increasing value and providing flexibility."[7]

In the United States, the Total Quality Management (TQM) of the 1960s and 1970s led to a fascination with re-engineering in the 1980s and 1990s. As a result of Business Process Engineering (BPR), the U.S. military claimed to have saved $108 billion during the 1990s.[8] Meanwhile, some claim that the fashion for Business Process Re-engineering (BPR) made worse the need for knowledge management because it was over-optimistic in its conviction that companies could change rapidly. If re-engineering brought a far greater awareness of work processes, it did not always imbue them with knowledge and insight.[9] According to Amidon Rogers, the history of knowledge management goes back to approximately 1987.[10] Intelligent KM (Knowledge Management) identifies four reasons for the rapid growth of knowledge management: 1) downsizing, 2) functional business unit fragmentation [i.e., change], 3) globalization, 4) [new] technology. Cap Gemini Ernst and Young

TABLE 22 Problems of knowledge management according to KM Central.com[29]

Search engines, filtering software, information categorization, agents
Enterprise management
Intranets, extranets, webs and portals
Collaboration, groupware, conferencing, e-mail, messaging
Competitive intelligence
Customer service support
Document/records management, image processing
Data warehousing, data mining
Workflow management
Consultants and systems integrators

identify three further reasons: 5) an increase in "virtual" work among far-flung teams demands explicit knowledge sharing, 6) customers who demand specialized products and services, and 7) shareholders who seek greater value from their investments.[11]

There are numerous institutions devoted to knowledge management.[12] The large management consultancy firms initially built knowledge databases.[13] In the past years, these management consultancy firms have developed quite different approaches to knowledge management. For instance, Arthur Andersen and the American Productivity and Quality Center have produced a Knowledge Management Assessment Tool (KMAT) that entails four steps: to identify the culture of a firm, to measure, to suggest technology, and to give leadership and process.[14] Deloitte-Touche[15] and PricewaterhouseCoopers[16] see knowledge management as a part of intellectual asset management.

KPMG sees knowledge management as one element of a complex consulting package which includes: e-business, e-integration, e-outsourcing, customer management, supply-chain management, knowledge management, world-class finance, and world-class human resources. In 2001, Cap Gemini Ernst and Young had a Knowledge Management (KM) Strategy and Architecture Development, which entailed: Knowledge Portals, Community Enablement, Decision Solutions, Knowledge Web Solutions, Knowledge Shared Services Solutions, and KM Solution Outsourcing.[17] So rapid are developments in the business world that this section is no longer visible in 2004. One of the most inclusive definitions of knowledge management was given by Dorothy Yu (Andersen Consulting, 1999) to include the whole range of regular and tacit knowledge.[18]

2. Chief Information and Knowledge Officers (CIOs and CKOs)

These developments are leading to new professions such as Chief Information Officers (CIOs) and Chief Knowledge Officers (CKOs). It is estimated that companies worldwide are spending $52 billion a year on re-engineering, of which $40 billion goes annually into information technology. Part of the CIO's task is technical planning

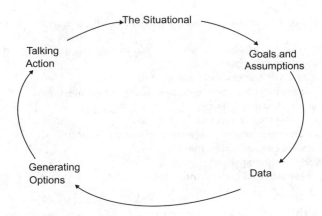

Figure 9a Main stages in action research according to Enderby and Phelan[39]

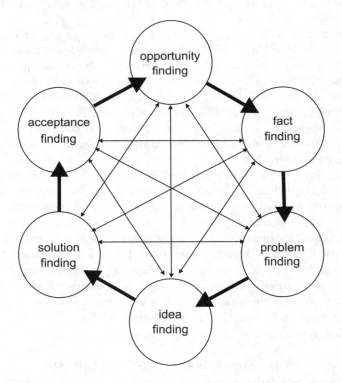

Figure 9b Professor Murli Nagasundaram's summary of Alex Osborne and Sidney Parnes' Creative Problem Solving Technique[40]

and implementation of data processing, as would have been carried out by a Chief Technology Officer (CTO) in the past. Another part of the CIO's position relates to knowledge management in its broader sense. In the past fifteen years there has been a gradual shift towards more attention to strategic planning.[19] Hughes appointed its first CIO (1999), Radhakrishnan, who was "responsible for co-ordination of company wide information technology issues, as well as corporate business systems, information systems policy and standards, information security and disaster recovery, and information systems outsource management."[20]

Since 1997, there has been increasing attention to Chief Knowledge Officers (CKOs).[21] This is partly a new division of labour whereby a CIO implements technology for managing company information, which is gathered, evaluated, assimilated, structured, integrated, and later filtered and distributed for both internal and external uses by the CKO. This new attention to CKOs has also been spurred partly by the rapid growth of intranets.

Knowledge officers sometimes entail "skills previously handled by human resources"; they need to manage intellectual property "to create systems and strategies" to identify valuable information in the company. It can then be tracked and made available when needed. This requires a combination of skills in human dynamics and "advanced computer skills with particular emphasis on computer interfaces and database management and organization."[22] Meanwhile, smaller firms such as the Gigo Corp had a Chief Knowledge Officer who headed a Chief Concept Officer, Chief Thought Officer, Chief Opinion Officer, and Chief Information Officer.[23]

3. American Models

In the United States, the notion of Total Quality Management (TQM) took on a new name as Six Sigma integration. Quality standards had focussed on reducing defects per thousand items (three digits) in production lines. In the early 1980s, Bill Smith, an engineer at Motorola wanted to increase this precision to six digits: i.e. defects per million items of production.[24] This quest became known as Six Sigma and its tools included Pareto [charts], cause and effect diagrams, process maps, statistical analysis, capability analysis, and regression analysis,[25] all of which were very reminiscent of Japanese *kaizen* tools (Figure 3). The six sigma method reduced errors to 3.4 per million. Six sigma was first implemented at Motorola in 1985 and formally launched in 1987. Between 1985 and 1994 it led to quality gains and over $2 billion in bottom-line savings. General Electric is said to have saved $12 billion over five years using this method.[26] In 2001, the Six Sigma Academy described a four-step method with the acronym MAIC (Measure, Analyse, Improve, Control).[27] By 2004 this had been replaced by a "Breakthrough Strategy." Others have identified a seven-phase approach for implementation.[28]

A number of tools for knowledge management are emerging. A Canadian contribution is Livelink,[30] software developed by the same company that originally developed the search mechanisms for the new Oxford English Dictionary. The Rigel

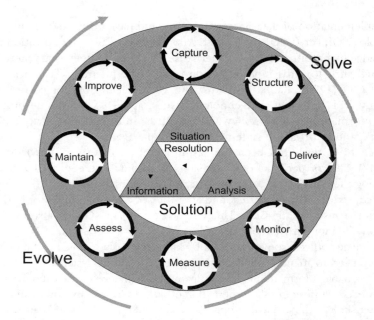

Figure 9c Key elements of Solution Centred Support (SCS) according to the Customer Support Consortium

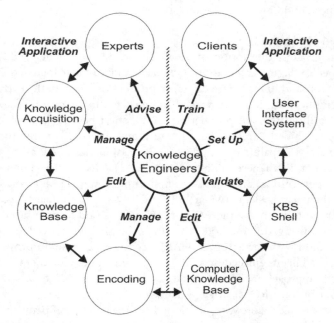

Figure 9d Brian Gaines and Mildred Shaw's Model (Calgary)[41]

Corporation has more traditional tools relating to the paperless office [sic]: namely, legacy data, scanning paper files, integrating electronic media into private and public databases. Rigel's knowledge management entails data storage in terms of automatic backups via secure Internet connections and integrating storage into databases.[31] The Dialog Corporation, now owned by Thomson, has software for knowledge management called Smartlogik which allows one to categorize, map, discover, filter, and share "knowledge."[32] Kanisa (which means "know" in Lingala)[33] develops products that allow corporations to develop new kinds of customer relationships.[34]

In 2001, Autonomy had middleware to link electronic customer relationship management, portals, business-to-business, knowledge management, Enterprise Resource Planning, security, and applications with five functions: 1) aggregate and organize all internal and external information, 2) categorize and tag all documents "based on the actual ideas of each text," 3) insert hypertext links, 4) profile users based on ideas in texts they read and write, and 5) route interesting information. By 2004 this had evolved into an Intelligent Data Operating Layer (IDOL) Server with the following functions: Active Matching, Agents, Alerting & Information Delivery, Automatic Categorization, Automatic Clustering, Automatic Contextual Summarization, Automatic Hyperlinking, Automatic Profiling, Collaboration & Expertise Networks, Dynamic Taxonomy Generation, Intelligent XML Handling, Metadata Handling, Personalization, and Retrieval.[35]

The past years have seen increasing attention to the ingredients and conditions necessary to acquire knowledge. For instance, Davenport and Prusak (1998)[36] identify five modes of knowledge generation: acquisition, dedicated resources, fusion, adaptation, and networks. Meanwhile, Gersting, Gordon and Ives (Andersen Consulting)[37] have studied critical success factors for knowledge management, notably executive commitment, sponsorship, and leadership.

The meaning of knowledge management is also shifting anew. Gersting, and Kaczmarowski, for instance, claim that: "the capture, sharing, and use of insights is key to providing personalized e-Commerce solutions and content."[38] KMCentral. com sees knowledge management as an umbrella concept for a whole range of recent technologies and developments, including data mining (Table 22). At the same time, numerous mergers and partnerships are radically changing approaches in management and financial consulting, and linking hitherto unrelated sectors of society (cf. chapter 5). For instance, companies such as Collaboratory.com are combining Customer Relationship Management (CRM, e.g., Siebel) and Enterprise Resource Planning (ERP, e.g., People Soft, who also do SCM: i.e., Supply Chain Management) with Active directories and lists of employees. They are integrating Project Management, Task Record Keeping, and Competency Management Systems.

In all this, simulation, in the form of playing through scenarios, is becoming ever-more important.[44] A new company called Outsights[45] claims that "a knowledge architecture is needed that will drive operational efficiencies, organizational learning,

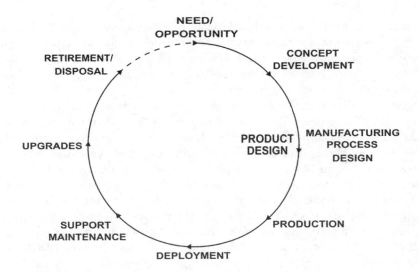

Figure 9e Philip Koopman, Life cycle[42]

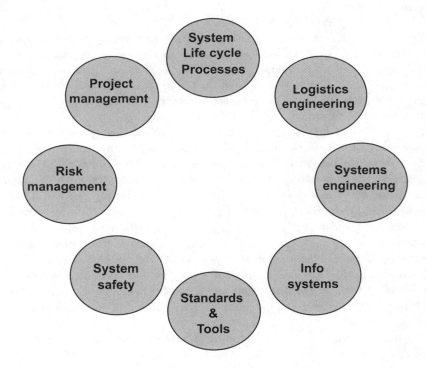

Figure 9f Life cycle as part of another cycle in Syntell[43]

and create a community that includes partners, suppliers, and customers." They seek "e-Services strategies enabled through knowledge."[46] To this end, Outsights established a Customer Support Consortium (CSC), with sixty-five companies in order to develop a "set of principles and practices that enables support organizations to improve service levels to customers, gain operational efficiencies, and increase the support organization's value proposition to their company."[47]

The Consortium developed Solution Centred Support (SCS). In their view, companies are moving from a hero-based system to a collaborative knowledge-based system. This is leading to collaborative knowledge networks.[48] Solution Centred Support begins from: 1) environmental contexts in terms of operational processes (greater efficiency, lower unit costs, reduced time-to-resolution), 2) nature of the workforce (more mobile, less experienced, who want to integrate personal life and have distrust of organizations), and 3) customer market expectations (branding of services, competitive differentiation, improved service/product).

The process requirements and competencies of a company are then analyzed with a view to re-frame, i.e., "to rethink the underlying principles and trends upon which the models of the organization are based." To this end, Solution Centred Support (SCS) identifies three enablers, namely: 1) the workforce (scout, coach), 2) operations (statistician, knowledge facilitator/ mediator), and 3) the market (promoter, evangelist, and liaison). It also examines organizational structures and seeks to define a value-based compensation system.[49] This leads to a combined cycle of solve (capture, structure, deliver) and evolve (monitor, measure, assess, maintain, improve) (Figure 9c). While the particular constellation is new, the trend towards an ever-greater control through analysis of the system is clearly a recurring element. Meanwhile, Sun has recently published a pamphlet: *How to .com Your Business, Road Map from Strategy to Implementation* (2000),[50] as if one could reduce everything to steps in a recipe.

Scholars have long ago noted etymological links between revolution/revolutionary and circular thought. One might add to this nexus an etymological link between cycle and re-cycled. Standing back for a moment, it is interesting to note a similar underlying trend towards circular models in learning circles (cf. Figure 9a,b), those where this cycle is applied to the life of products (Figure 9e) or where this life cycle becomes one part in a larger circular process (Figure 9f).

While interest in Knowledge Based Systems (KBS) is perhaps more developed in Europe (see below), important work in this context is being done by the KBS group at the Beckman Institute (Chicago),[51] which "focuses on the interplay between expert system shell architectures, machine learning, probabilistic reasoning, and immersive expert interfaces."[52] This work is especially concerned with heuristic classification; decision making that has an explicit probabilistic scheduling control level and "statistical regression methods to accurately predict average case learning speed curves."[53]

TABLE 23 Karl-Erik Sveiby's basic distinctions

LEVEL	MANAGEMENT OF INFORMATION **Knowledge = Object**	MANAGEMENT OF PEOPLE **Knowledge = Process**
Organization	Re-engineers	Organization theorists
Individual	AI-specialists	Psychologists

A project at Stanford University (Section on Medical Informatics, School of Medicine) is concerned with reusable KBS in the context of problem-based learning.[54] Such analyses are bringing a philosophical approach to knowledge management. Hence, Bellinger (Outsights) sees knowledge in a spectrum between information and wisdom:[55] "Information relates to description, definition, or perspective (what, who, when, where). Knowledge comprises strategy, practice, method, or approach (how). Wisdom embodies principle, insight, moral, or archetype (why)."[56] In this context knowledge tends to be reduced to a utility and there is a trend towards Service Oriented Knowledge Utility as if the only value of knowledge is the extent to which it is used. This is a long way from the idea of knowledge for its own sake.

Meanwhile, some persons in the United States remain interested in developments elsewhere. The U.S.-Japan Center for Technology Management at Vanderbilt University, founded in 1991, aims "to create a corps of American scientists, engineers, and managers with significant experience in the Japanese industrial and technology management practices."[57] Ikujiro Nonaka,[58] who works both in America and Japan, distinguishes between tacit, explicit, and procedural knowledge. Nonaka also identifies a fourfold process of SECI, i.e., Socialization, Externalization, Combination, and Internalization (Table 28). Socialization, in this context, means tacit to tacit knowledge; Externalization entails tacit to explicit. Combination entails explicit to explicit and Internalization entails explicit to tacit. While Western thinkers had long recognized the distinction between tacit and explicit knowledge, the Japanese contribution was to see this as a cyclical process which could then be broken down into discrete steps.

4. European Models

The importance of personal and tacit knowledge was noted by Michael Polanyi nearly half a century ago (1958).[59] As Karl-Erik Sveiby[60] has noted, one of the important sources for European thinking (which has since been widely adopted in American thinking) comes from the Swedish community of practice in the 1980s, which brought into focus the importance of tacit knowledge in business. Sveiby identifies two tracks: 1) Human Resource Cost Accounting and 2) Intangible Assets, whereby one uses "primarily non-financial indicators to monitor and publicly present their intangible assets."[61] Based on the concept of a knowledge organization

TABLE 24 Knowledge management initiatives according to Karl Erik Sveiby

EXTERNAL STRUCTURE	INTERNAL STRUCTURE	COMPETENCE INITIATIVES
Gain Knowledge from Customers	Build Knowledge Sharing Culture	Create Careers Based on Knowledge Management
Offer Customers Additional Knowledge	Create New Revenues from Existing Knowledge	Create Micro Environments for Tacit Knowledge Transfer
	Capture Individuals' Tacit Knowledge, Store it, Spread it and Re-use it	Learn from Simulations and Pilot Installations
	Measure Knowledge Creating Processes and Intangible Assets	

(1986),[62] this provided a "theoretical framework for public reporting of intangible assets and coined concepts such as 'Structural Capital' and 'Human /Individual Capital'."[63]

Sveiby returned to these ideas in a book on knowledge-based assets in 1997.[64] A series of books made this idea of intellectual capital a buzzword (see Appendix 8). Sveiby[65] identifies two major strands (which he calls "tracks" or "levels") in knowledge management. One entails management of information by computer and/or information scientists involved in construction of information management systems, AI, re-engineering, groupware, etc. "To them Knowledge = Objects that can be identified and handled in information systems."

A second strand entails management of people by philosophers, psychologists, sociologists, or business/management experts, who are primarily involved in assessing, changing, and improving human individual skills and/or behaviour. "To them Knowledge = Processes, a complex set of dynamic skills, know how, etc." (Tables 23–24). Building on the work of Sveiby, Edvinsson worked on the notion of structural capital and subsequently worked with Saint-Onge to define three kinds of intellectual capital: 1) human, 2) structural (or organizational), and 3) customer capital, to which Tapscott et al.[66] have recently added 4) digital capital, "information about money." Sandra McLeod (Echo Research) urges us to include emotional and confidence capital.

A few European companies have championed Sveiby's approach.[67] Elsewhere in Europe we find attempts to identify the precise ingredients of knowledge management and to develop programs to deal with these. For instance, the AIAI (Edinburgh) claims that: "Knowledge management involves the identification and analysis of available and required knowledge assets and knowledge asset related processes, and the subsequent planning and control of actions to develop both the assets and the processes so as to fulfill organizational objectives."[68]

The AIAI also notes that knowledge management in Europe developed out of earlier business management such as Strengths Weaknesses Opportunities Threats

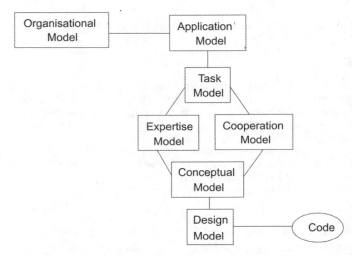

Figure 10a Aspects of the Knowledge Acquisition and Design Support (KADS) approach: Construction of Approximate Models

Level	Relations	Objects	Organisation
Domain	Describes	Concepts, relations, structures	Flat facts
Inference	Applies	Data structures, functions	Data-flow-diagram
Task	Controls	Goals, tasks	Structure chart
Strategy		??	??

Figure 10b Aspects of the KADS approach: Expertise Model

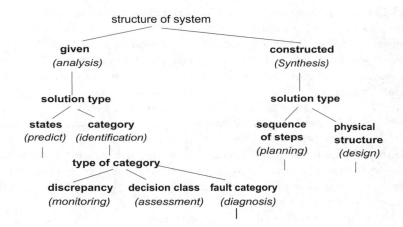

Figure 10c Aspects of the KADS approach: Partial Expertise Model Hierarchy

TABLE 25 Levels of knowledge management according to H. Mandl and G. Reinmann-Rothmeier.[74]

LEVEL	PERSPECTIVE	KNOWLEDGE MANAGEMENT AS
Individual	Psychological	Individual Competence
Group/Organization	Organizational/Theoretical	Organizational Method
Individual	Social Cultural	Societal Challenges

New Information and communication technologies

(SWOT) analysis; Balanced Scorecards[69]; modelling languages such as Process Flow and Object State Description Capture Method (IDEF)[70]; Role Activity Diagrams (RADs)[71]; and the knowledge techniques previously used for the disciplined development of Knowledge-Based Applications.[72] Van der Spek and De Hoog (1995)[73] created a framework for knowledge management with three essential steps: 1) identifying what knowledge assets a company possesses, 2) analyzing how the knowledge can add value, and 3) specifying what actions are necessary to achieve better usability and added value. This has been adopted by the AIAI and others.

European developments in knowledge management need to be seen in a larger context of expert systems and the growth of Knowledge Based Systems (KBS) worldwide. Early steps were made with the introduction of canonical systems (Post, 1942),[75] rules (Newell and Simon, 1972)[76], frames (Minsky, 1975),[77] and tasks and tests (Clancey, 1983).[78] This entailed the idea of situated cognition, and led to the idea of a knowledge level (1982).[79] It was discovered that one could have Expert Systems (ES) without detailed knowledge of data structures (Chandrasekaran, 1986).[80] This led to a gradual distinction between knowledge level A and knowledge level B, and then a series of new tools culminating in 1992 in Knowledge Acquisition and Design Support (KADS).[81]

KADS begins with the construction of approximate models (Figure 10). This leads to creation of an expertise model which defines level, relations, objects, and organization (Figure 10b). The domain level or layer "maps implementation-independent concepts to domain-dependent concepts" (i.e., the analysis of the code). This leads to the construction of a partial KADS expertise models hierarchy (Figure 10c). KADS, which became an ESPRIT project and then a commercial product, was thus a culmination of decades of expert systems research. It combined Knowledge Management (KM) and Knowledge Analysis (KA). Task analysis in systems such as KADS suggested that "above the level of rules and frames in expert systems, there exist meta-level patterns of inference for diagnosis, classification, prediction, causal reasoning, verification, propose-and-revise, etc.," and that "within these meta-level patterns, there exist re-usable mini-inference procedures such as classify, select, generalize, etc."[82] This has led since to Common KADS.[83]

TABLE 26 Building blocks of knowledge management according to Gilbert Probst[90]

Knowledge Goals	Knowledge Assessment
Knowledge Identification	Knowledge Saving
Knowledge Acquisition	Knowledge Use
Knowledge Effects	Knowledge Distribution

New advances came with the advent of Risk Driven Development (Boehm, 1995),[84] Cases with conditions and structures (Rumbaugh, 1994),[85] Critical Success Metrics (CSM, Fox, 1995),[86] and more recently the concept of worlds and ontologies (Appendix 3, Figure 20b). There are interesting parallels between the growing distinctions between levels/worlds in expert systems and frames for ontologies in the realm of human knowledge (cf. chapter 13).[87]

The past decade has brought a number of tools for knowledge capture and knowledge sharing.[88] This has led to the Metapack Software of Systemics that includes eleven tools: a protocol editor, tools for hypertext, laddering, card sorting, matrix manipulation, and repertory grid, editors for rules/induction, control, a Generalized Directive Model (GDM) Workbench, an entity-relationship tool and a dependency editor. Systemics has also produced the POWER-Pack Software and a Common CADS tool called I-KEW (Integrated Knowledge Elicitation Workbench, which addresses a whole range of different knowledge types).[89] At the high level, the trend of knowledge management has been towards a) intelligent knowledge-based systems, which, in large corporations such as Siemens, is increasingly dovetailing with trends towards b) systematic analysis of processes in production, and c) collaborative workspaces linking hundreds or even thousands of computers in different countries.

Psychologists such as Professor Mandl[91] have noted that knowledge management needs to integrate at least three different perspectives: 1) the psychological view of individuals with respect to individual competence, 2) the organizational view of how groups interact, and 3) the social cultural/view of how individuals relate to societal challenges (Table 25). He has also drawn attention to a number of new tools such as Weber and Schumann's Concept Mapping Software Tool (COMASOTO) for the diagnosis of structural knowledge.[92] By contrast, John Chambers at Cisco (Figure 11a) is concerned only with what leads Cisco to greater profits and ignores entirely this societal dimension.[93] At the same time, theoreticians such as Malik (1993),[94] who claim that modern organizations are highly complex systems, which are more effectively seen as organisms than as machines, continue to extol the centrality of individuals over systems.

In smaller firms, consultants often use this emphasis on special individuals in an opportunistic sense. While large firms have systematic financial, accounting, and archival departments, smaller firms often have no fixed procedures for processing of information and/or knowledge. As a result, knowledge organization is

TABLE 27 Categories according to the Israeli Knowledge Management Group

DOCUMENT MANAGEMENT	CONTENT MANAGEMENT	WORKFLOW	COLLABORATIVE WORK MANAGEMENT
Data Mining	On-Line Analytical Processing	Intelligent Content & Context	Searching & Navigation Electronic Messaging
Automated Data Capture	Smart Push	Internet Channel Delivery	Decision Support
Communities of Practice	Business & Competitive Intelligence	Business Process Design	Intellectual Asset Management[100]

frequently reduced to the introduction of a company's equivalent of yellow pages, simple databases and the establishment of an elementary archive. Meanwhile, theoreticians such as Probst have offered a more readily understandable overview of key steps entailed in knowledge management (Table 26).[95] A number of firms are trying to implement such an approach including: AGI Information Management consultants,[96] SEC Consulting,[97] and Knowledge agent.[98]

European countries have a variety of approaches. Sweden has drawn attention to intangible factors. The Netherlands and Germany have developed some of the most effective solutions. The French approach is different again.[99] Other countries have a more pragmatic approach. For instance, the Israeli Knowledge Management Group defines knowledge management as: "the ability to expect the best decisions and actions possible from your people at any time, by providing them with the best information possible from any source." This goal-oriented approach, which is reminiscent of American pragmatism, leads to original combinations of ideas and approaches (Table 27).

5. Japanese Traditions

Knowledge Management in Japan has at least seven characteristics that set it apart from America, Europe, and most other efforts elsewhere. First, there is a tradition of *zaibatsu*, which has become known as *keiretsu*[101] since 1945. This entails something reminiscent of a guild system at an enterprise level, whereby a series of companies join forces at a national and international level. In the West, the virtual corporation and agile engineering were intended to be a reply to this concept, but rather naively assumed that serious ties could be made and disbanded "on the fly," which is effectively the opposite of *keiretsu*, where a traditional group continues to work together.

Second, in Japan, middle managers remain a key to top, continuous innovation. By contrast, when American management gurus witnessed the efficiency of Japanese firms in the 1980s, they believed they had discovered a way to become even more "lean and mean." The United States thus eliminated most of middle-management which effectively set the stage for new needs in knowledge management in the West.

TABLE 28 Four elements of the SECI model

Socialization	tacit to tacit
Externalization	tacit to explicit
Combination	explicit to explicit
Internalization	explicit to tacit

Third, in many fields,[102] Japan has integrated quality into their work more thoroughly than either Europe, or the United States, although the latter constantly speaks of Total Quality Management (TQM, cf. chapter 4). Some experts say that it is no coincidence that Japan leads the field of advanced visual displays. They are attentive to great detail.

Fourth, Japan has a long-standing tradition of tacit knowledge. This entails publishing a certain amount of codified knowledge about a subject, say Zen gardens and then, in the midst of such a text, referring to further steps that need to be consulted orally. As noted earlier, in Japan, tacit knowledge is integrated with explicit knowledge models through four modes of knowledge conversion, known as the SECI model (Table 28). In the West, tacit knowledge is typically opposed to explicit knowledge (Table 29).

Fifth, partly because of this quest to integrate tacit knowledge, the Japanese emphasize the context of knowledge (*ba*), which is roughly equivalent to the English notion of space and can be seen as "a shared space for emerging relationships. It can be a physical, virtual, or mental space. Knowledge, in contrast to information, cannot be separated from the context – it is embedded in *ba*." To support the process of knowledge creation, a foundation in *ba* is required.[103]

The Knowledge Management Society (KMS) of Japan explicitly hopes "that our society will further develop as a 'place for exchange.' KMS has been "organizing consortiums to ensure that the 'collaboration of knowledge' takes root as a cultural tradition among industries in Japan."[104] They see this as the only way of overcoming "the current economic stagnation." Underlying such groups is a quest to involve everyone in the organization. As Hirotaki Takeuchi has noted: "Only then can the organization be viewed as a living organism capable of creating continuous innovation in a self-organizing manner."[105] Western attempts to see businesses as eco-systems can be seen as an attempt to comprehend this dimension of the Japanese approach.

Sixth, in the West, knowledge management and knowledge organization are opposed (cf. chapters 12, 14). In Japan, there is a quest to integrate knowledge management and knowledge organization: "Unlike information, knowledge is about communication and beliefs; it is a function of a particular stance, perspective or intention. In this respect it is as much about ideals as about ideas and that fact fuels innovation. Similarly, unlike information, knowledge is about action; it is always knowledge 'to some end.' The unique information an individual possesses must

TABLE 29 Basic differences between explicit and implicit knowledge from a Western viewpoint

EXPLICIT KNOWLEDGE	IMPLICIT KNOWLEDGE
Codified	Tacit
Information, theories, formulae, procedures	Experience, abilities, attitude
Handbooks, manuals, drawings, schemas	Being able and willing
Transfer by instruction	Sharing through demonstration
Obtainable by study	Copying and imitation
Explicit Knowledge is power	Implicit knowledge can be power

be acted upon for new knowledge to be created. This voluntary action also fuels innovation."

Seventh, in the United States, knowledge management is often reduced to management. In Japan, there is a quest to get beyond the management of existing knowledge and discover ways of creating new knowledge and innovation. Thus, whereas the rhetoric of U.S. companies is to produce ever-clearer goals with narrower deadlines, Japanese companies believe that only by providing greater "slack" can innovators be truly innovative.

6. Global Trends

There are also a number of global organizations for knowledge management. There is a Knowledge Management Consortium (KMC), the International Society of Knowledge Management Professionals (KMCI) in Gaithersburg, Maryland, and a Knowledge Management Think Tank. Recently there was an Intranets for Knowledge Management Conference. There is a Federation for Enterprise Knowledge Development (FEND), which has an Enterprise Knowledge Development (EKD) Agora to discuss EKD in relation to knowledge management, complexity management, business modelling, and feedback handling. There is a WWW Virtual Library on Knowledge Management and a site on Knowledge Management Resources.[106]

7. Conclusions

One of the underlying themes of this book is that there are three major political visions for the future of new media. These entail different approaches to knowledge management. In the United States, where there is no clear distinction between knowledge and information, knowledge management is more about management than about knowledge.

The American quest for managing knowledge is intimately linked with a quest to externalize processes. This explains why scientific and information visualization are becoming so important (Appendix 1). There is a quest to visualize the steps/stages/phases in processes and production; a Taylorization of the whole spectrum of human activity from physical labour to the creative process itself using simulations,

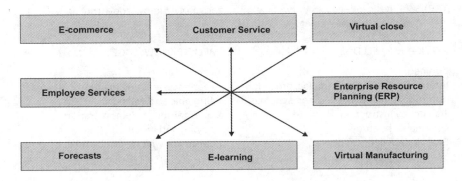

Figure 11a Key elements of new business according to John Chambers (Cisco)

workflows, and enterprise integration. One could argue that Engelbart's concept of augmented knowledge at the Bootstrap Institute is effectively another step in this direction. And as this mastery of processes becomes ever-greater, there is a corresponding emphasis on change, (business) process (re)engineering, and management. Hence, there has been a shift from scientific management of work (Taylor) to knowledge management.

These attempts to visualize processes are closely linked with trends towards: 1) operation at a distance (through tele-operation, and tele-presence, etc.) and 2) virtualization (through virtual communities, virtual corporations, schools and universities). Concurrently, there is an increasing emphasis on learning organizations, on learning applied to entities, companies, and corporations. These quests to master new knowledge owe much to systems theory, chaos theory, complexity,[107] and developments in neural networks, whereby systematic treatments of apparently random forms bring unexpected patterns of order. These further define the American fascination with the management side of knowledge management (cf. chapters 12–14).

In the United States, there is a focus on systems regardless of human consequences. For instance, an increasing emphasis on Customer Relationship Management (CRM) has led to a Customer Support Consortium. Ironically that consortium is proposing Solution Centred Support. Hereby, the customer is given the impression of personalization but is in fact reduced to supporting a solution-centred approach (cf. chapter 10), which can also be seen as a consequence of a problem-based orientation.

In Europe, the fascination with systems is frequently greater but is balanced by a concern that personnel in the system are treated fairly. The European approach is based on a systematic understanding of logical systems underlying knowledge

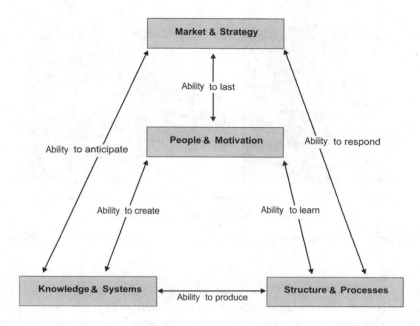

Figure 11b Basic elements of a learning organization according to Tissen et al. (2000)

management. Thanks to the Swedish tradition of practice, there has also been attention to 1) human resource cost accounting,[108] and 2) intangible assets.

In Europe, the study of expert systems and knowledge-based systems remains primarily a domain of computer science largely independent from other traditions of knowledge organization[109] such as philosophy, logic, and library science. In Japan, by contrast there is a quest to integrate knowledge management with knowledge organization in order to achieve a more global understanding of all knowledge. In Japan, tacit knowledge and context are also more important than elsewhere, although these features are now also being studied in the West. Whereas the West continues to see tacit knowledge as somehow opposed to explicit knowledge, Japan is intent on methods that bring these together.

At the global level, mergers of multinationals have taken the ideals of profit making to new levels. Using slogans such as "lean and mean," the emphasis is almost entirely on management and "knowledge" is an empty term. In this context, systemicity dominates and even the notion of a physical corporation is challenged. Everything can theoretically be outsourced as long as one "knows" how best to manage profits.

We outlined how production is becoming virtual (chapter 4), how production is shifting to services (chapter 5), and how these shifts are undermining traditional

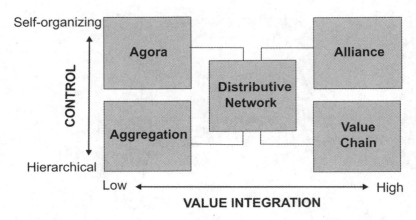

Figure 11c Business web (b-web) typology according to Tapscott, Ticoll and Lowy

notions of bricks and mortar (chapter 6). Having examined developments in organizations (chapter 7) and knowledge management (chapter 8), we can discern that the shift from products to services is part of a spectrum that extends in the direction of management and knowledge. In this view, the shift from material products towards services leads to a virtual organization that has its strength through its networked knowledge, which allows it to be managed more efficiently. In this vision computational grids are a key to scalable virtual organizations.[110]

For instance, John Chambers (CEO, Cisco) sees knowledge as but one factor in change along with creative thinking, emotion, and instinct. In addition to e-commerce and Enterprise Resource Planning (ERP), customer service (or customer care support), and virtual manufacturing, Chambers emphasizes the importance of a virtual close, which provides access to one's accounting books at any time without waiting for the end of quarter statements.[111] He describes this combination as the network effect (figure 11a). He predicts that this network effect will have an impact on many aspects of everyday life including e-learning (from prescriptive to subscriptive), e-living, e-laundry, e-shopping, and e-dentist. The company's success record in the years 2000–03 was less convincing, although it regained popularity as a good investment in 2004.

The Canadians, Tapscott, Ticoll and Lowy,[112] offer a lucid survey of the main trends in the past fifteen years after U.S. industries realized they were losing out to competition from Japan. On the process side, they point to 1) agile manufacturing, 2) total quality, 3) supply-chain management (SCM), and 4) business process engineering (BPR). On the structural (business model) side, they include: 5) the Japanese *keiretsu*, 6) the virtual corporation, 7) outsourcing, 8) business eco-systems, and 9) business webs.

Tapscott et al. distinguish between four kinds of capital: human capital (what people know); customer capital (who you know and who knows and values you); structural capital (how what you know is built into your business values), and digital capital (internetworking). While they theoretically focus on digital capital as a fourth kind of intellectual capital, they are particularly interested in business webs (b-webs), which they define as: "a distinct system of suppliers, distributors, commerce service providers, infrastructure providers and customers that use the Internet for their primary business communications and interactions."[113]

Such webs include Internetworked enterprises, teams and individuals with two main functions: economic control and value integration. Tapscott and his colleagues identify four types of such b-webs: 1) agora (e-bay), 2) aggregation (Webvan), 3) value chain (Cisco), 4) alliance (Linux), all of which are linked by distributive networks, and create a handy typology for these (Figure 11c). In this framework Ciscos's value-chain approach emerges as one of four alternatives in deciding between hierarchical or self-organizing control and between low or high value integration.

While offering an extremely useful summary of some major trends in the United States, this explanation obscures distinctions between the U.S., European, and Japanese approaches noted above. It is instructive, for instance, to contrast Chambers' view of Cisco (Figure 11a), with Tissen's European view (Figure 11b). Chambers uses technology to achieve a completely updated view of the company at any point. Individuals are mentioned implicitly and are included qua employee and customer services, but the emphasis is on services provided by the system. By contrast, for Tissen, people and motivation play a central role.[114]

Ultimately these different emphases on the four kinds of capital help us understand to what degree countries are willing to go in the spectrum from concrete, material production to abstract, virtual or agile manufacturing. In the United States, where networked systems dominate, and where human capital is seen as incidental, the trend is towards (knowledge) management. In Europe and Japan, where human and structural capital play a greater role even when companies move towards management, there is a greater balance through attention to human factors. For instance, Japan's *keiretsus* may appear to be virtual corporations, but they are based on centuries-old bonds of honour, quite the opposite of relationships on the fly.

From all this emerges a much bigger picture than what is typically found in North American management books. The United States, Europe, and Japan have basically different approaches to knowledge management. In addition, at the global level, there is a) an imperialistic extension of the U.S. view and b) an emerging vision of global co-operation. As we shall see in the next chapter, these competing, systematic approaches from the business world are also having an impact on theories of learning.

learning

I think we have a unique opportunity at this conference to begin to improve the understanding of human knowledge around the world. I think we can increase human understanding through the sharing of knowledge and the culture of our different countries. We have access now to the records of many different cultures in the libraries, the archives, the museums, the galleries of our nations and our communities. The opportunities presented for education from the very youngest children to the very oldest of our senior citizens are endless.[1]

– T. C. Bearman,
G7 Ministerial Conference (1995).

1. Learning Trends

We have shown how the business world adapted the tutorial approach of the academic world and transformed it into a management strategy called action science, how they also used systems theory to integrate this into a far more wide-ranging approach, which is subtly inimical to traditional concepts of learning and knowledge (chapter 8).

Thanks to the influence of computer science, in a new guise of cognitive science, and with the help of systems theory, aspects of action learning from the business world are being integrated into the educational world. Traditional teaching and study entailed education, from the Latin *e-ducere*,

TABLE 30 Basic shifts according to the Denver constructivists.

Hypertext	*shifts*	control from author to reader.
Connectionism	*shifts*	control from algorithm to experience.
Postmodern Thought	*shifts*	means from centre to periphery.
Constructivism	*shifts*	agency from teacher to learner.

"to lead out from." Education is becoming learning or, as one company puts it: "the twenty-first century has no room for students, only learners."

In the United States, the buzzwords of the new approach are very revealing. They emphasize "learning to learn,"[2] with ever-less emphasis on teachers. They speak of learning environments, which are often classrooms with technology, rather than teachers. The School of Education at the University of Colorado (Denver) calls learning environments the technology of constructivism.[3] In their view, constructivism shifts "agency from teacher to learner" and is related to three other shifts. First, there is hypertext, which shifts control from the author to the reader. Second, there is connectionism, which shifts control from algorithm to experience. Third, there is post-modern thought, which in their interpretation shifts means from centre to periphery (Table 30).

In the Denver approach, such concepts represent theoretical sources along with instructional design models; semiotics, sociology of knowledge; cognitive science, socio-cultural theories, cybernetics, systems theory, complexity, Internet culture, learning environments, foundational texts, virtual learning communities, and media. In educational circles it has become the fashion to criticize old-fashioned education, forgetting that this too had its serious doses of seminars, tutorials, and one-on-one discussions between teacher and student. Catchy phrases such as "From the sage on the stage to the guide on the side"[4] make light of the conceptual influences from industry and technology underlying this trend. To understand better these influences we shall examine briefly a series of approaches to learning: problem-based learning, process-based, project-based, product-based learning, and learning-environments. We shall show that the American emphasis on action and doing in the business world is having direct effects on the American educational scene at all levels of education.

The new theories of learning are about something very different than learning in the traditional academic sense for at least six reasons. First, the new university is based on the metaphor of a cauldron, wherein "practice and research are thoroughly mixed."[5] Second, the purpose of universities is moving away from creating and applying knowledge to an "ability to solve problems in one or more cultural or community settings."[6] Third, the emphasis on problems "incorporates and mixes nearly all of the central ingredients of a constructivist anchored conception of learning."[7] Fourth, they favour the active and practical almost to the exclusion of the contemplative and are thereby anti-intellectual in the literal sense. Fifth, their rhetorical emphasis on learning environments has a technological agenda. Machines replace live encounters with experienced teachers. Sixth, this is obscured by a parallel rhetoric about the importance of assessment and evaluation, which gives the process a seemingly objective veneer.[8]

In the United States, there is often so much emphasis on the technology and methods, on the form of learning, that content as such is pushed into the background or disappears entirely. This heightens the need for good management, which in turn increases the influence of business models of learning. Technology managers thus become the new elite. As a result, scholarship, in the old sense, disappears ever more in the background or disappears altogether. While this American approach is too often copied with greater enthusiasm than insight, European models, Japanese traditions, and global alternatives bring some reason for optimism.

We saw earlier that the material consequence of networked computers is virtuality. A side effect is a potential undermining of the physical nature of institutions of learning through the advent of virtual learning (chapter 6). In the short term, a fundamental challenge of new content remains. Too often, educational software becomes a form of computer-based training where traditional lists of printed material now appear on a computer screen. Implicit in this approach are two assumptions: 1) that new learning merely requires scanning in analog textbooks and presenting them in digital form; 2) that old testing methods need only to be digitized in order to be much more efficient.

In fact, the new media make possible very different approaches to education. The Internet allows new levels of sharing information. This is leading to new kinds of collaborative knowledge and various telematic methods (chapter 11). It is also leading to augmented books, knowledge, and culture. This calls for a complete reorganization of knowledge, which will change the nature of knowledge itself (cf. chapters 12, 14–15).

Among educational theorists, there is a growing conviction that the workings of the human central nervous system can serve as a model of network efficiency for programmers and chip makers, that human learning can inform machine learning. Here our concern is to show how the converse is also true: namely, that theories of computing are influencing our theories of learning. This story is considerably more complex than a general claim that our theories of artificial intelligence (AI) have an impact on theories of intelligence.

2. Problems to Products

The programming paradigm, which was process-based, has shifted to a product-based approach. The business paradigms of a) rewarding only action and b) working towards product-based-design are invading the classroom. Educational theory is shifting to activity-based, problem-based, process-based, and now product-based learning models. For instance, the School of Education in Denver refers to activity theory as "artifact-mediated object-oriented action."[9]

Problem-based Learning (PBL)

As in the case of action learning and action research, some trace the roots of problem-based learning back to inquiry training, John Dewey, and apprenticeships. The possible use of PBL was discussed in a number of disciplines. As early as 1950, it was discussed in psychology. During the 1960s, it was discussed in education (1960), science (1965), biology, and information science (1968). During the next decade, problem-based learning was considered in neuroscience (1973), agriculture, mathematics, medicine (1974), engineering (1975), and library science (1976). Management and social health followed in 1982.[10]

In the early 1950s, Case Western Reserve University incorporated instructional methods and strategies into a multidisciplinary laboratory. They claim that their approach has become the basis of "curriculum at many secondary, post-secondary, and graduate schools including Harvard Medical School (Savery, 1994).[11] In fact, over 80% of medical schools use the problem based learning methodology to teach students about clinical cases, either real or hypothetical."[12]

Nonetheless, it is generally accepted that the Faculty of Health Sciences at McMaster University (Hamilton, Canada) introduced problem-based learning (PBL) as a tutorial process to promote learner- or student-centred education for lifelong learning and success. The key person behind the McMaster University program was Howard S. Barrows,[13] who set out from the premise that: "A problem can best be thought of as a goal where the correct path to its solution is not known.… In PBL learners are progressively given more and more responsibility for their own education and become increasingly independent of the teacher for their education. PBL produces independent learners who can continue to learn on their own in life and in their chosen careers. The responsibility of the teacher in PBL is to provide the educational materials and guidance that facilitate learning."[14]

To understand better the trend towards problem solving, it is useful to note the influence of four other fields: 1) the military, 2) computer science, 3) cognitive science and artificial intelligence, and 4) mathematics. First, there is the military. The U.S. Armed Forces claim to develop a problem-solving ability,[15] and it is not surprising therefore to find that the army has courses in basic problem solving,[16] military leadership, and problem-solving skills.[17] The implications for education loom when an academic in military science insists that problem-solving is a decision-making progress and not a thought process: "Failure to accept this as a decision making process can only lead to interminable bickering and arguing over the courses of action without making progress toward the ultimate goal of problem resolution through the execution of a feasible and most favorable solution that satisfies as many students as possible."[18]

The purely military consequences thereof are undoubtedly excellent. There is, of course, a recent fashion in business to speak also of management as guerilla warfare, which includes insights into weaponry and attacking when speaking of everyday commerce.[19] Even so, we must be very attentive that education is more than preparing persons for the battlefield. Such military actions are primarily defensive responses to other persons' attacks. Education is ultimately concerned with something more than passive responses. It entails the creation of new visions.

Meanwhile, problem-solving in the context of virtual reality and synthetic environments are an integral part of the military's preparations for the dangers of cyberwar.[20] As Victor Reis, Department of Defense (DOD), director of defence research and engineering, has noted: "synthetic environments represent a technology to let us learn how to use technology better. It's that feedback loop that does it.... Network simulation is a technology that elevates and strengthens the collective problem-solving abilities of ... design teams, manufacturing teams, education teams, training teams, acquisition teams, or war fighting teams."

Second, since the 1960s there has been a connection between computer science and scientific problems. This gained in importance in the late 1980s and has since become connected with a shift from scientific software libraries to problem-solving environments,[21] whereby computers are described as thinkers/doers:

> A PSE [problem-solving environment] is a computer system that provides all the computational facilities needed to solve a target class of problems. These features include advanced solution methods, automatic and semiautomatic selection of solution methods, and ways to easily incorporate novel solution methods. Moreover, PSEs use the language of the target class of problems, so users can run them without specialized knowledge of the underlying computer hardware or software. By exploiting modern technologies such as interactive color graphics, powerful processors, and networks of specialized services, PSEs can track extended problem solving tasks and allow users to review them easily. Overall, they create a framework that is all things to all people: they solve simple or complex problems, support rapid prototyping or detailed analysis, and can be used in introductory education or at the frontiers of science.[22]

Third, as noted earlier, there has been attention to problem-solving in cognitive science and artificial intelligence (chapter 7). The work of Newell, Simon and Margolis,[23] helped to make thought in artificial intelligence as models for logical thought. Since the late 1980s, there has also been a growing interest in metacognition and metacognitive development. This is one of the inspirations for the *learning to learn* movement, wherein problem-solving becomes one of ten educational themes: 1) consciousness, 2) metacognition, 3) learning styles, 4) memory, 5) language, 6) reading, 7) writing, 8) problem-solving, 9) creativity, and 10) the biology of learning.[24] This school, which is closely linked with constructivism, assumes that "knowledge is constructed through mental model activities of the learner through thinking games and exercises such as linking and problem solving" and also describes itself as process-based learning.[25] Some enthusiasts become so enthralled with this process that content is quietly forgotten.

TABLE 31 Role of PBL compared to other approaches according to the Illinois
Mathematics and Science Academy[32]

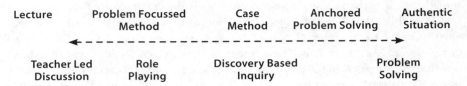

Lecture	Problem Focussed Method		Case Method	Anchored Problem Solving	Authentic Situation
Teacher Led Discussion	Role Playing		Discovery Based Inquiry		Problem Solving

Fourth, there is a tradition of problem-solving in mathematics that goes back to the 1940s.[26] More recently, this tradition, inspired by the examples of computer science and cognitive science cited above, has adopted computers as part of their program. For instance, the National Council of Teachers of Mathematics (NCTM) claims that: "Computers are powerful problem-solving tools. The power to compute rapidly, to graph a relationship instantly, and to systematically change one variable and observe what happens to other related variables can help students become independent doers of mathematics."[27] While this National Council is very explicit that "Computers extend the tools for cognition. Computers do not replace the essential teacher/student relationship," it is easy to see how some might forget this last line in their pursuit of the bottom line.

Meanwhile, Samford University (Birmingham, Alabama) has identified fourteen objectives and outcomes of PBL, namely: 1) problem-solving skills, 2) self-directed learning skills, 3) ability to find and use appropriate resources, 4) critical thinking, 5) measurable knowledge base, 6) performance ability, 7) social and ethical skills, 8) self-sufficient and self-motivated, 9) facility with computer, 10) leadership skills, 11) ability to work on a team, 12) communication skills, 13) proactive thinking, 14) congruence with workplace skills.[28] These are magnificent goals. Would Einstein qualify?[29] While some note the disadvantages of PBL,[30] the trends of seeing the teacher as coach, and the student as problem-solver have encouraged claims that this is brain-compatible learning[31] and slogans such as "learning to learn." The Illinois Mathematics and Science Academy associates problem-solving inquiry along with authentic situations and places it at the opposite end of the spectrum from lectures and teacher-led discussions, as if these were somehow unauthentic (Figure 49).

The PBL school emphasizes electronic learning environments, electronic notebooks, and many technological ingredients not associated with traditional scholarship. A radical version of this problem-based approach prompted F. S. Keller to write an article entitled: "Goodbye Teacher."[34] The visions of Western Governors University and some of the virtual universities are very much in this direction.

TABLE 32 Six-step model for creative problem-solving in the Future Problem Solving Program (FPSP, cf. Figure 9)

1. Identify Challenges in the Future Scene
2. Determine an Underlying Problem
3. Produce Solution Ideas to the Underlying Problem
4. Generate and Select Criteria to Evaluate Solution Ideas
5. Evaluate Solution Ideas to Determine the Better Action Plan
6. Develop an Action Plan.[33]

Creative Problem-Solving

Quite closely related to problem-based learning, but with a wider audience – including non-academics in the creativity field – is the creative problem-solving process. Alex F. Osborn developed this in the 1950s and founded the Creative Problem Solving Institute (CPSI, Buffalo). He was joined by Sidney Parnes[35] in the 1960s, who further developed the method (Figure 9b).[36] Systems thinking is seen as essential for creativity and problem-solving.[37] For instance, the U.S. government's Computer and Information Science and Engineering (CISE) division has, as one of its seven experimental and integrative activities, the creation of collaborative problem-solving tools. In Lexington, Kentucky, Dr E. Paul Torrance has developed the Future Problem Solving Program (FPSP) with a six-step model for creative problem-solving (Table 32).

In the management world, problem-solving is linked with other analytical techniques including: brainstorming, critical path analysis, decision trees, force field analysis, De Bono's PMI (Plus/Minus Interesting), and SWOT (Strengths, Weaknesses, Opportunities and Threats) analysis.[38] At Florida State University, in professional education and training for management and marketing, a systems approach to problem-solving uses a whole range of techniques to identify problems that affect quality, namely: quality improvement teams, flow charts, check sheets, Pareto analysis, cause and effect analysis, how to analyze problems to improve quality, output charts, histograms, scatter diagrams, control charts, X-Bar and R charts, C charts and P charts.[39] We have shown (chapter 4), that many of these concepts also relate directly to production.

Systems thinking is also being developed in Japan. For instance, Hidetoshi Shibata (Tokyo) claims: "Systems thinking is a more scientific Problem Solving approach than the rational thinking approach. We set the system, which causes problems, and analyze them based on systems of functions." His system includes seven elements, namely: purpose, input, output, function, inside cause (solvable cause), outside cause (unsolvable cause), and result. Mr. Shibata also includes nine kinds of thinking: 1) cause and effect, 2) contingent thinking, 3) Toyota's five times WHY,[40] 4) thinking patterns for efficient thinking, 5) hypothesis, 6) conception, 7) structure, 8) convergence and divergence, and 9) time order thinking.[41] Such

TABLE 33 Seven characteristics of exemplary project-based learning according to a California-based Challenge 2000 project.

1 Anchored in core curriculum; multidisciplinary
2 Involves students in sustained effort over time
3 Involves student decision-making
4 Collaborative
5 Has a clear real-world connection
6 Systematic assessment: both along the way and end product
7 Takes advantage of multimedia as a communication tool.[42]

examples confirm that problem-solving has as much to do with the worlds of production and management as with education *per se*.

Project-based Learning

Project-based learning is more typically used in high school settings. A good survey of project-based learning is provided by the Buck Institute of Education (Novato, California).[43] As with action learning, problem-based learning and creative problem-solving, the emphasis is on experiential learning, as is clear if one looks at the California-based Challenge 2000 Multimedia Project with its "characteristics of exemplary project-based learning with multimedia" (Table 33).

Product-based Learning

Through product-based learning (also PBL), universities are reflecting the needs of industry. Professor Larry Leifer, the Director of the Center for Design Research, Industrial Affiliates Program at Stanford University, sees widespread PBL adoption and assessment as "financially feasible for graduate and undergraduate engineering education."[44] In a keynote at a conference in Osaka (1995), Leifer acknowledged the role of Piaget and Vygotsky. He noted that: "Mechatronics is a particularly good medium for introducing PBL because of its deep dependence on interdisciplinary collaboration."[45]

Also at Stanford University, Dr. Renate Fruchter, was the Director of P5BL (Problem-Project-Product-Process-People-Based Learning) in the Department of Civil Engineering.[46] She was specifically concerned with Computer Integrated Faculty Engineering (CIFE) which combines Architecture/Engineering/Construction (AEC) in new ways.[47] Fruchter was even more articulate about the role of industry in product-based learning. Meanwhile, the Architecture, Engineering, Construction (AEC) industry claims that PBL brings at least four advantages.[48] Another interpretation of how problem-based learning, research-based learning, and product-based learning relate is offered by the Professional Development Network (PDN), which claims at least four advantages. Their Net Learning Experience entails five by now familiar points (Table 34). This emphasis on problem-, project-, and product-based learning has three basic consequences: 1) learning environments, which are suspiciously

TABLE 34 Five steps in the net learning experience of the Professional Development Network (PDN).[49]

1. Determine a learning track and complete a performance contract.
2. Explore area of interest by gathering, reflecting, organizing, processing and evaluating information.
3. Apply what you have gained in your learning track.
4. Create a product for others and the professional's portfolio.
5. Share the finished product with fellow PD Netters and others.

reminiscent of problem-solving environments (PSEs) in the computer world; 2) action or learning by doing, and 3) a trend towards teaching machines.

Learning Environments

As noted earlier, learning environments are seen as the technology of the constructivist approach. The University of Denver page on learning technologies alone lists some fifty web sites on the subject.[50] It is not generally known that both constructivism and post-modernism are Western translations of the Russian concept *stronie* or *prostronie*.[51] The constructivist approach has also received stimuli from unexpected quarters such as genetic epistemology.[52] There are sites on constructivism,[53] constructivist learning,[54] and social construction of reality.[55]

There are also at least four competing views on constructivism. A first view claims that learning entails "active construction of a personal, conceptual knowledge base" (Piaget, Jonassen, Novak)[56]. A second sees learning as reflective, building on and developing the learner's existing knowledge (Bruner, Ausubel, Kolb)[57]. A third view claims that learning "benefits from multiple views of a subject area" (Duffy, Beishuizen, Jacobson).[58] A fourth view holds that learning "is facilitated by authentic activity, relevant to the situation in which it will be applied" (Brown, Honebin, Koschmann).[59] Those in problem-based learning (PBL) pay most attention to the third view and some to the fourth view.

3. Action and Learning by Doing

Project-based learning is linked with action, learning by doing, and work-based learning,[60] also called dual-learning, which raises the question whether persons who are working fulltime have adequate time to think. In practical trades, this is perfectly natural. But should education be limited to this? Dr. Roger C. Schank (Northwestern University) believed that schools should do away with multiple-choice tests and lectures and claimed that: "Students learn better through experiential and emotional learning.... Your education starts when you start doing things. Let's create everything in a learn-by-doing environment because that's what works."[61]

Roger Schank, whose team of 170 at Cognitive Arts was supported by Andersen Consulting believed that the same approach could be applied in all areas of learning.

TABLE 35 Dr. Roger Schank's eightfold path for education.[64]

1   Doing, not reviewing
2   Possible answers, not right answers
3   Fun, not discipline
4   Interest groups, not age groups
5   Visible projects, not invisible rejects
6   Hearing and needing, not listening and reading
7   Motivation, not resignation
8   Fun fun fun.

Simulating real-world environments thus became central to the on-line learning courses that they developed for Columbia University and Harvard Business School. Schank is an excellent example of the complex interactions between technology and education.[62] He is very critical of contemporary schools: "Instead of allowing students to learn by doing, we create courses of instruction that tell students about the theory of the task without concentrating on the doing of the task. It's not easy to see how to apply apprenticeship to mass education. So in its place, we lecture."[63] This culminates in his formulation of the eightfold path for education (Table 35).

Roger C. Schank wrote *Virtual Learning* (1999) and *Dynamic Memory Revisited* (1999), in which he shifted "his focus from artificial intelligence to human intelligence." As one reviewer put it, the new book: "contains the theory of learning presented in the original book, extending it to provide principles for teaching."[65] In addition to his concern with case-based reasoning, Dr. Schank addressed problems of non-conscious knowledge (his term for tacit knowledge) and goal-based scenarios for education. As his institute's web site explained, goal-based scenarios (GBS) are: "complex, guided simulations in which the student learns through the active pursuit of motivating goals. The multimedia capabilities of the computer are used to create rich simulations, and to make video clips of experts available to coach the student and answer questions as he or she attempts to achieve the goals of the scenario." These goal-based scenarios create "a realistic computer environment that allows people to practice skills and apply knowledge in simulated worlds." They are, moreover, based on "three key components of our educational philosophy," namely, learning by doing, learning from failure, and learning from stories. Schank led the Learning Environment Design Group at the Institute for the Learning Sciences.

Kristian J. Hammond, who headed the Intelligent Information Laboratory (Info Lab) at the same institute,[66] shared Dr. Schank's interest in Cased Based Reasoning (CBR) and was concerned with "understanding the role of examples and experience in reasoning. In particular, I study how encapsulated experience, or cases, can be used to inform planning, problem solving, and the control of action." His research projects were focussed on intelligent (learning) environments, notably, the Intelligent Classroom, where the classroom "watches" the teacher.[67] Professor

Hammond developed FAQFinder, an automated question-answering system,[68] which is intimately connected with a trend towards personalization (cf. chapter 10). At the Intelligent User Interfaces conference (IUI, 1999), he also gave a keynote: "Anticipating User's Needs: Redeeming Big Brother in the Information Age."[69] The Institute for the Learning Sciences has two other sections: a Qualitative Reasoning Group and an Autonomous Mobile Robots Group. Its larger mission was "to extend the understanding of human learning, to develop computer-based learning environments based on that understanding, and to train the educational software developers of tomorrow in both the theory and practice of creating the next generation of learning environments."[70]

These developments at Northwestern University were fascinating. They seemed to confirm that doing is where the action is. They also brought to light how new technological developments could be closely linked with a given set of intellectual theories. But then there was a change in the economy and the entire institute was closed. Today there is no longer any record of any of these "achievements" on-line. Being too close to the fashions of the day may mean that one is too closely affected by their changes. The quest to become more relevant must not obscure the traditional virtues of permanence, visibility, and access.

Such developments at Northwestern are noteworthy because they reflect tendencies elsewhere. For instance in August 2000, EnterTech, one of the learning technology programs showcased at Human Code's learning summit, simulated "a realistic work environment with virtual coworkers, a supervisor, and human resources." The three-week course was delivered "in conjunction with classroom time over the Internet or using CD-ROMs."[71] Elsewhere, the SciTech Curriculum Facilitator's Guide emphasizes action learning, which they describe as "a process through which participants learn with and from each other, by mutual support, advice and questioning, as they work on real issues or practical problems while carrying real responsibilities in real conditions."[72]

We suggested earlier that this American propensity for action is symptomatic of something much deeper. It is linked with their quest to externalize everything, which explains their emphasis on behaviourism in psychology. In Europe, it is a man's word that counts; in America, it is a person's actions that count, or more precisely their sincere actions. And because sincere action is so closely linked with reality, play becomes either a deadly serious business play or some form of escapism as in Fantasyland, Adventureland, Frontierland, and Tomorrowland. And if entertainment becomes escapism, attempts to bring back the playful dimensions of learning is doomed to an edu-tainment, which amuses more than it edifies. This has many implications (cf. chapters 14–15).

Teaching Machines

The extreme versions of the American educational dream assume a "Goodbye teacher" scenario, in which computers completely replace teachers, just as the extreme versions of the American business dream get rid of middle management and the most extreme versions strive to eliminate fulltime jobs entirely.[73] Meanwhile, there are a number of companies with self-paced learning products.[74] Courseware has, of course, become a field onto itself.[75]

Notwithstanding the rhetoric of replacing education with learning, there is a more subtle trend to replace learning with training. Too often the technology exists for its own sake, i.e., once it arrives, learning is redefined as if it were a case of: Ask not what the new hardware and software can do for you, ask rather: what you can do to (be able to) use the new hardware and software. The U.S. Educational Testing Service Network[76] has sites on computer-based testing. This body recently published a report on the future of large-scale testing: "The same competitive forces driving U.S. industry will compel test makers to (a) satisfy new market needs through continuous innovation, (b) improve productivity, (c) enhance customer service, and (d) address population diversity. In response, large-scale assessment will reinvent itself."[77]

While there are explicit parallels with the jargon of business management, this report, entitled "Reinventing assessment," makes no mention at all of how new media might provide new content that could change the scope and perhaps even the very nature of what needs to be tested and assessed. A similar attitude is evident at the National Center for Research on Evaluation, Standards, and Student Testing (CRESST),[78] where Eva L. Baker recently asked what technology is intended to do and identified four goals for classroom technology: 1) "focus on learning the use of tools to assist in other areas of learning," 2) "to use technology power to address new goals that cannot be met in any other way," 3) "to use technology more efficiently to deliver instructional opportunities that match the background and pace of the learners," and 4) "focus on the management of classrooms by teachers, but for the moment, let us address the evaluation of students' learning."[79]

Here again, there is no mention of how new media can provide access to new realms of content. At the beginning of this book, we cited Michael Crichton, the popular author of thrillers, in terms of twentieth-century innovations in the sciences and humanities. Some educators would go further and claim that teaching is the only profession where the methods of today use exactly the same technologies as the nineteenth century, namely, blackboards and chalk.

Citations such as those above prove that there is good news: classrooms now have many technologies. The bad news, alas, is that the emphasis is on the power and efficiency of the technology, on using machines to manage people. We are assessing how individuals can use gadgets without asking how the gadgets open new worlds of learning. Testing and assessment have a view of individuals that is older than the eighteenth century. It only enters into the twentieth century qua machines and has seen nothing of the potentials of technology to transform the horizons of what, how, where, when, and why we know, which is the promise of the twenty-first century.

4. European Models

Most of the trends found in the United States are found also in Europe. Buzzwords such as problem-based learning, collaborative learning, and electronic learning environments are found on both continents. Stanford University has a Learning Lab. So too do the universities in Maastricht and Stockholm. While there is common ground between the United States and Europe, there are at least four fundamental differences in approaches to education with respect to: 1) multilingualism and multiculturalism, 2) theory, 3) humans and machines, and 4) public education.

Common Ground

EDUCAUSE[80] linked with EDUCOM has a National Learning Infrastructure Initiative (NLII)[81] to produce an Instructional Management System (IMS)[82] "to enable an open architecture for online learning." IMS is co-operating with the European Union concerning an Annotatable Retrieval of Information and Database Navigation Environment (ARIADNE)[83] on development of information content metadata.[84] IMS is actually a global coalition of more than two hundred educational institutions, commercial organizations, and government entities. In 1999, they optimistically announced the release of "the IMS Meta-data Specification," designed to promote the discovery of distributed learning resources on-line.[85] This has some links with the Dublin Core Education group.[86]

IMS is also part of an Advanced Distributed Learning (ADL) project sponsored by the Department of Defense and the White House[87] and the Office of Science and Technology Policy (OSTP).[88] To develop its own course, Europe has an Educational Multimedia Task Force initiative (EMTF),[89] and a Memorandum of Understanding for partnership and standardization in the field of learning technology (MOU Learning).[90] Europe also has another ARIADNE (Alliance for Remote Instructional Authoring and Distribution Networks for Europe) Consortium and a project for Multilevel Annotation, Tools Engineering (MATE)[91]

Multilingualism and Multiculturalism: The United States may pay lip service to Spanish, Indian cultures (how many North American Indian languages are online?) and the Pennsylvania Dutch (i.e., Germans), but in practice U.S. web sites remain almost exclusively in English. By contrast, the official sites of the European Commission were in eleven languages and have now become twenty-five languages, which will increase as the Union expands While small countries such as the Netherlands typically have some of their web sites and educational materials in English, there is a great deal of material available in different languages. Recent statistics (2003) show 29.3 per cent of the Internet in European languages, 26.4 per cent in Asian languages, and the rest in English. In Germany, where culture and education are under the auspices of individual states, there is also considerable regional variation between Lower Saxony in the North and Bavaria in the South.

In France, although there is a centralized Ministère de l'Education, many connections with local groups (*collectivités locales*) assure that these are also becoming

TABLE 36 Stages in Autonomy Oriented Teaching (AOT) according to Roni Aviram.

1   Recognition of meaningful events/activities
2   Recognition of entitlement to
3   Awareness of the will for
4   Search for meaningful event
5   Formation of plans for
6   Implementation of plans
7   Conflicts (back to 5)
8   Frustration (back to 4)

visible on the web. And while culture is not officially, directly within the mandate of the European Commission, linguistic and cultural diversity are very much issues. A new initiative on e-content emphasizes the importance of localization to ensure such diversity.[92] While e-content has become one of the new buzzwords, it is striking how many discussions surrounding this word are about business strategies with little interest in the content per se.

Theory: Europe and the United States have very different approaches to educational theory. The United States emphasizes technology and is strong on systems theory and on theories of constructivism.[93] For instance, the Technology Source has helpful and interesting technology information for educators.[94] Many universities have centres.[95] One very curious development, called Research/Academic Reform (REAR),[96] has a comprehensive vision to replace a philosophy of outcomes with a philosophy of progress, to replace science with good intentions, and to replace precise interventions with global good efforts.

While rhetorically almost as attractive as Dr. Schank's vision of "fun, fun, fun," such a "feel good" approach is unlikely to advance progress of the exact sciences and knowledge generally.[97] An unexpected paradox is that intelligent students are bored by easy tasks and learn best when they face extremely difficult tasks. This explains their fascination with topics such as cryptography and viruses.[98]

While the United States emphasizes problem-based learning, we noted that this method was first implemented in the Faculty of Medicine at McMaster University (Hamilton, Canada). This served as a starting point for the Problem Based Learning (PBL) approach at Maastricht University, which first applied PBL to all its faculties and maintains one of the most important sites on the subject.[99] Meanwhile, the University of Aalborg (Denmark)[100] remains an important site for theories of project-based learning and for the development of ideas concerning a European Doctorate in Science.[101] The European Commission's Ortelius project offers a database on higher education.[102]

The European Commission sponsors a EuRopean Multimedia Educational Software Network (ERMES) and a Multimedia Educational Innovation Network (MENON). All European countries have their own methods and philosophies concerning education and learning. To cite an example from Israel, Professor Roni Aviram (Tel Aviv) has recently developed a new method of Autonomy Oriented Teaching (AOT), with eight levels of meaning (Table 36). This confirms that the American fascination with process has its European equivalents. A radical form of such an approach could raise questions as to whether content is still relevant.

Humans and Machines: In Europe, there is an assumption that the technology can at most be complementary to the efforts of teachers; it should never replace them. A group at Freiburg explicitly called "Learning in Humans and Machines" has a project and a book.[103] A project in Hanover, with the attractive title of "How to Enhance Teaching and Mentoring Productivity,"[104] shows that these environments are not just classrooms with technology. While they have an explicit agenda of sparing mentors (i.e., teachers) "overhead of scheduling face-to-face meetings," which sounds like a euphemism for reducing direct teacher-student relations, there is no question here of eliminating teachers entirely: "most of the communication among the group members can be organized through electronic media. Each group uses a mailing list as a medium for discussion and problem solving within the group (including the mentor)."[105]

Public Education: In the United States, higher education is largely private. In Europe, it is largely public. There are trends for big business to have advertisements during class time in the United States. In Europe, this is not acceptable. In the United States, the creation of proprietary software for the educational market is a big business. In America, education is the next frontier for private enterprise. In the United States, links between EDUCAUSE and new technologies such as Blackboard become more disturbing when it is realized that both have close links with the Carlyle Group, which is closely linked to the present administration and the war in Iraq.

By contrast, in Europe, there is a growing consciousness that education is very definitely part of the public domain, that this is a key to maintaining cultural diversity.[106] This is linked with a growing trend to create multilingual, multicultural, open-source products, which will then be available for the whole of the European Community. Even so, Europe also has organizations such as the European Education Partnership (EEP),[107] concerned with "understanding of the possible business models in an education environment based on new technologies."[108] And, of course, all over the world there is also a considerable market for school textbooks, which are independent of these questions of private versus public education.

5. Japanese Traditions

On the surface, Japan has many parallels with developments in the United States and Europe. For instance, the agenda of the G8 meeting in Yokohama (July 2000), had four sessions which sound very familiar: 1) Educational Challenges in a Changing Society, 2) Lifelong Learning and Distance Learning, 3) Educational Innovation and

ICT, and 4) Promoting International Exchange of Students, Teachers, Researchers and Administrators.[109]

However, there are many differences. A government report (Science Council of Japan) of 1993[110] emphasized the importance of culture in education in ways unknown to the West.[111] Professors such as Takehiko Kariya emphasize the need to prepare students for the future[112] and one has only to look at a recent Comprehensive Proposal for Promoting University Research Aimed at Making Japan a Nation Capable of Original and Profound Contributions to the Fostering of Intellectual Affluence within Global Society to recognize that Japan has a very different approach from the West.[113] They have clear plans for a move towards a global civilization in which Japan makes serious intellectual contributions.

6. Global Learning

Internationally, there is some activity at the United Nations level,[114] particularly with respect to UNESCO, which has a Virtual Training Center.[115] There is a Globewide Network Academy (GNA)[116]; a Global Telecommunication University (GTU), and a Global Telecommunication Training Institute (GTTI).[117]

The World Bank,[118] in conjunction with the Canadian International Development Association (CIDA) and others, organized two conferences on Global Knowledge (GKI, Toronto 1997; GKII, Kuala Lumpur 2000), which have led to a Global Knowledge Partnership (GKP).[119] There are efforts to create a Global Knowledge Activity Information Management System (AIMS)[120] and to "re-engineer the education system to have universal principles with customized parameters, new forms of education, teacher training." The G7 Ministerial Conference and Exhibition (1995) initiated the idea of eleven pilot projects. Although they "lacked funds" to support these, the third project on education was linked with the concepts of Schoolnets such as that developed by Canada. This has advanced greatly. The University of New Brunswick (Fredericton) in conjunction with Schoolnet created a Telecampus[121] with a list of over nine thousand courses. In 2004, the list was no longer maintained, thus pointing to another of the challenges of the new media: the need for continuity and cumulative effects. There is a European Schoolnet (EUN, Aarhus)[122] and there are a considerable number of other schoolnets in other countries[123] and other initiatives.[124] There is a VR Learners Consortium[125] and OnLine Learning News.[126]

Corporations: From the economic viewpoint of global corporations, learning is a place where there are a number of jobs, ergo a new market niche. At the G7 Ministerial Conference in Brussels (1995), Dr. De Benedetti, then president of Olivetti, gave some statistics about new jobs for the year 1993: "200,000 jobs have been created in education in the United States, 300,000 jobs in software-related activities compared with 33,000 jobs in the automobile industry."[127] Multinational corporations see learning and education as a new job opportunity. Hence, the great surge in e-learning projects in corporations.

With the development of enterprise networks, Internet Integration Services Companies and the large management consulting companies increasingly see education as a potential market. For instance, the Global Knowledge Education Integration Co., has annual revenues of over $400 million in education solutions and integration.[128] IBM has a Global Campus[129] with links to the National Technological University and the Open University and is developing Automated Training Systems. There is IMS Global Learning,[130] which focusses on enterprise versions of instructional management systems, also called course management systems, Computer Based Training (CBT) systems, learning servers, and integrated learning systems. There are further global initiatives in Britain,[131] Australia, and elsewhere.[132]

7. New Content

At the same G7 Ministerial Conference, where global business leaders spoke enthusiastically of education as a new (job) market, Dr. T. C. Bearman, a dean from Pittsburgh University, outlined a vision of education that has parallels with our own. It was cited in the header to this chapter and emphasizes the importance of content, which thus far is sadly lacking. To be sure there are numerous pilot projects.[133] In Japan, the situation is somewhat different. At the national level, the Ministry of International Trade and Industry (MITI), made available some $20 million simply for digitizing important cultural objects. The City of Kyoto has a Digital Archives project, which is scanning in materials from museums, libraries, temples, folk festivals, the tea ceremony, and even the films of Kurosawa.

8. Conclusions

Looking back over the extraordinary developments in learning, we can discern seven clear trends. First, there is a tendency for schools and universities to adapt learning models from a) business, b) manufacturing, c) software, and d) the military.[134] Second, educational theorists seek legitimacy for such trends in constructivism. Third, in the past, an education meant learning how to think independently with a view to applying these critical faculties to other disciplines and professions. A student thus became equipped for active participation in the world. The new approach may emphasize action and active learning, but through its emphasis on problem-, project-, and product-based learning, it makes the student a passive responder to problems defined by an external source. The methods that claim to put the student in the centre, reduce the student to being fully dependent on others' problems, others' orders – perhaps an excellent employee in the lower echelons, but not someone with the independence that management claims it seeks.

Both the learning of the learning organization and the trends towards product-based learning and learning by doing entail a response-based passive learning, diametrically opposed to the independence of traditional education with its emphasis on the individual's inner growth. Business and industry legitimately seek graduates who are prepared for the realities of the workplace. Training students to respond only to the immediate needs of the workplace limits their horizons. Economics and production are important realities. But the world is more than a balance sheet and a production list. Learning is also a domain of the soul, the spirit, the imagination.

Fourth, the Internet is introducing a parallel trend towards greater co-operation, with virtual laboratories, collaboratories, and various forms of tele-operation, which bring unprecedented access to new knowledge. This trend, combined with new access to enduring knowledge in digital collections, offers a key for future learning. Fifth, there is a tendency, especially in the United States, to treat technology more for its own sake than as a tool for deeper understanding. Sixth, notwithstanding much rhetoric and many useful pilot projects, there has been almost no systematic work on providing serious content for education from a) memory institutions or b) more recent media such as film and television. Moreover, this content typically copies the limitations of print media and leaves unexplored the possibilities of the new media. Seventh, especially in the United States, the realm of testing and evaluation also continues to base its assumptions on traditional content. The question of how the new tools will transform our treatment of content, and thus the very nature of education, remains unexplored. "Content is king" and "context is king" are well-known epithets, but these seem to be in a different kingdom than the world of learning.

The organizational consequences of networked computers are systemicity with respect to organizations (chapter 7); knowledge management (chapter 8), and learning (chapter 9). This emphasis on system favours process over content. Needed is a vision of how traditional content in new forms combined with new content can vastly enrich our understanding of education and learning. Needed is a new vision of global sharing of such content. This will be goal of the chapters that follow. We shall examine how personal, collaborative, and enduring knowledge might be coordinated. We shall then show that the intellectual and philosophical consequences of new media are contextuality and spirituality, respectively.

PART IV

intellectual
consequences:
CONTEXTUALITY

10
personal
knowledge

Your own government is also developing
methods to keep you in its power. Chips that
you can implant in the body of masses of
troops and in unsuspecting troublemakers.
And that is not all.… We know that when
persons think, a given pattern of brain
waves is transmitted. Every government is
busy with machines, which can register and
identify that sort of brain waves, namely,
angry ones or feelings directed against the
authorities.[1]
— James Redfield,
The Secret of Shambala (1999)

1. Introduction

In parts one and two, we showed that the technological and
material consequences of computers were invisibility and
virtuality, respectively. In part three we showed that the organizational consequences of computers are a new emphasis
on systemicity. In this fourth section, we shall show how the
intellectual consequences of networked computers are a new
kind of contextuality. This entails personal, collaborative,[2]
and enduring knowledge (chapters 9–12), which ultimately
calls for a new synthesis. (chapters 14–15).

In the *Old Testament*, (personal) knowledge was linked with
knowing someone carnally. In the modern world, personal

knowledge has very different meanings including a) explicit meanings relevant only to ourselves and a small circle of friends, and b) implicit, tacit dimensions of communication, which are usually non-verbal. The new media introduce a number of new possibilities with respect to personal expression and at the same time provide technologies for new means of personalization. The new media also bring new dangers regarding unwanted observation, new needs for protection, and further questions concerning inner versus outer and public versus private (chapter 13).

2. Expression

Traditionally personal expression was typically oral or written. The nineteenth century brought the rise of regular postal services, which meant that sending letters became an everyday event. As early as 1870,[3] a U.S. government study noted that the fax could have an impact on postal services, but this innovation took more than a century to become widespread.

The rise of telephones meant that one could share conversations over a distance, with the drawback – or some thought the advantage – that there was no recorded version. The rise of tape recorders in the 1960s meant that spoken messages could be sent by mail and kept for posterity. The 1990s saw the rise of voice mail and voice messages, whereby incoming messages could potentially be recorded and saved. The rise of mobiles is changing dramatically where persons can be reached and is transforming also the nature of communication. Children in Helsinki, for instance, use mobile phones to arrange where their group of friends might meet next.

New methods of expression introduced by the Internet include e-mail, chat groups, list serves, discussion groups, Multi-User Domains (MUDs),[4] Multi-Object-Oriented (MOOs),[5] Multi-User-Shared-Hallucination (MUSHs),[6] Short Messaging Services (SMS), which have been hailed as a new epistolary art,[7] and, more recently, BLOGs. Pioneers such as Bruce Damer speak of personal memespaces.[8] A shortcoming of these methods is that, apart for the system operator, one typically has no access to a record of one's chats and conversations.

The twentieth century saw the rise of numerous methods for archiving personal experience: cameras, video cameras, and digital video cameras. Until recently, these methods were typically proprietary, and it was difficult to translate images from one medium to another. Companies such as Philips and Sony are working on home editing devices, whereby such materials will become readily accessible and will give a whole new dimension to the concept of home movies.[9] Recent developments make it possible to maintain a copy of all telephone calls ever made on one's own telephone. Extreme scenarios, as in the *Truman Show*, foresee recording everything a person ever experiences. By 2004, there was a new threat: that all one's communications might potentially be made available on-line and thus destroy any sense of personal privacy in communication, e.g., Google's proposals to make all e-mails searchable. All this both increases the potentials of archiving personal experience and increases the need for privacy.

Personal Culture

In the realm of culture, the theme of personalization has taken interesting forms. In the United States, there is, for instance a trend towards ever-greater combinations of education and entertainment in the form of edu-tainment, In Europe, by contrast, there is a growing commitment to create personal virtual museums. For instance, Professor Isidro Moreno Sanchez (Madrid) notes that in the sixteenth and seventeenth centuries only princes were able to have their own collections in the form of private museums (called *Kunst-* and *Wunderkammer*). Today, this is potentially open to everyone in digital form. One of the most interesting examples of such a personal museum is Carol L. Gerten-Jackson's Fine Art (CGFA)[10] museum. The Metropolitan Museum in New York has a feature, which allows one to create one's own Met Gallery.[11]

Professor Sanchez foresees the creation of virtual spaces in which individuals make their own collections of art. This would begin as extensions of the idea of bookmarks, whereby persons collect their favourite sites. As a next step, this would entail three-dimensional virtual spaces in which persons collected paintings and sculptures from all over the world. While basic versions of these images would be available free of charge, high-definition images could be bought in the manner that one now buys postcards. Such images could then be swapped among friends in the manner that children now trade their hockey cards, etc.

This idea is gaining ground in the educational field. The Louvre (Paris) has a special section devoted to education, i.e., Louvre.edu. They have created software, that allows children to tour a virtual Louvre, make their own personal subset of this enormous collection, and then create their own exhibitions. The Hermitage (St. Petersburg), which has sixty persons working fulltime in their multimedia education department, is developing various games that children can play using images from their collections. A Spanish project[12] also uses paintings from museums for educational purposes. For instance, a still life with flowers becomes a starting point for botany lessons. Details from paintings are used to develop children's sense of what are real and false objects. The National Museum for Science (Madrid) has a CD-ROM (*El Peque Museo*) that uses virtual spaces to introduce children to basic concepts of physics such as light and heat.

Such developments can be seen as reflections of a larger trend. When collections were private, paintings typically had no descriptions at all. It was assumed that one knew. Indeed, in the case of visitors, it was often an excellent way to test the knowledge of guests to see if they were really aware of different painters, their students, and their schools. In the nineteenth century, with the rise of large public museums, which were primarily storehouses, individual items typically had only a minimal description, which reflected the authoritative statement of the curator. The twentieth century saw an increasing awareness that there were in fact numerous different audiences each requiring their own descriptions.

In the past decade, there were a number of European projects that attempted to provide multiple descriptions for different audiences. One such project (CAMPIELLO) combined the formal knowledge of museum experts with the informal knowledge of local residents. In the United States, paintings became associated with the stories connected with them, their narratives, often very anecdotal in form. In some radical cases, such as the Art Gallery of Ontario (Canada), a pioneering curator, Doug Worts, allowed visitors to provide their own commentaries on paintings. As a result a painting is no longer simply an object with a laconic name-tag: it has a number of descriptions and stories attached to it, which can potentially be accessed on demand.

Companies such as Sony foresee using devices such as their Navicam to create personal viewing histories. Hence, I could record my own commentaries on each painting during a visit to a museum such as the Louvre. On my next visit, the Navicam could remind me of what my thoughts were about the *Mona Lisa* last time and also remind me which other things I might want to see while there. Nokia speaks of personal information bubbles. Philips is concerned with collecting all one's personal experiences in a more systematic form such that all the photos from scrap albums and home movies, etc., can be stored digitally. This is the traditional idea of memory theatres in virtual form, but such that they can be shared with other persons. Just as not every home movie is necessarily memorable, these personal memory collections will vary greatly in quality. What is important from our point of view is that they will introduce new kinds of personal documentation, which will be as important for future biographies as correspondence was in the past.[13]

Tacit Knowledge

In Japan, there has been a long tradition of concern with tacit knowledge. In Europe, this topic has received increasing attention since the 1960s (Appendix 8, chapter 10). We have noted that the Swedish School drew attention to some aspects of this in organizations in the late 1980s (chapter 8.4). Tacit knowledge in a larger sense entails attention to context. One of the fascinating developments during the past years has been the commercialization of this tacit dimension.[14] For instance, Tony Buzan, who was a pioneer in self-actualization in the 1970s, now has software for mind-mapping.[15] Some aspects of these developments are potentially disturbing to the extent that companies now claim that software can capture effectively all aspects of tacit knowledge: "The breakthrough you are seeking is converting personally felt tacit knowledge into organizationally stored (and conveyed) explicit knowledge for everyone to share and use."[16]

The International Federation for Agricultural Development (IFAD, Rome) has drawn attention to the importance of local knowledge and recently organized a panel discussion on this theme.[17] Some call this autochtonous knowledge.[18] The World Bank prefers to call this indigenous knowledge.[19] The World Bank is working with IFAD, the Global Knowledge Partnership and others to make this indigenous knowledge more generally available. Optimists hope that this will provide new sources of income for developing countries.[20] Pessimists fear that this knowledge risks being appropriated by multinational corporations for their own advantage.[21]

In the Middle Ages, scholars made notes, annotations, and commentaries in the margins of manuscripts. With the advent of printed books, such annotations were increasingly relegated to notebooks. We have shown that the new media are introducing new possibilities. A student can now make a series of systematic connections and make these available on-line. Another student can then use these links as the starting point for further connections. Instead of writing notebooks in isolation, students can now share work in arriving at something larger than would be possible if they worked alone.

The 30,000 resources in Professor Tony Beaver's *Noesis*[22] (University of Evansville, Indiana) offer one example of the potentials of this approach. The emergence of the W3 Virtual Library (cf. chapter 11) offers another high-level example of this trend. Implicit in the above are new kinds of collaboration and new kinds of sharing (cf. chapters 14–15). Individuals can sign their contributions, thus gaining recognition of their work, and at the same time contribute to something far beyond the efforts of a single person. Inherent in this approach are many new horizons for education at all levels. Teachers, scholars, and students can work together at all levels to create knowledge packages, which are at once personal and collective. Pilot projects along these lines were explored by SUMSED at the Marshall McLuhan Secondary School in Toronto. Anyone can make links. Not all links are meaningful. Not all links are true. Hence, there need to be electronic equivalents of footnotes and some kind of authentication in order to assure that the links are reliable and not just ad hoc connections (cf. chapter 13).

3. Personalization

Closely linked with these new methods of capturing tacit knowledge is a trend towards personalization, which is also becoming increasingly commercialized through sites such as personalization.com.[23] Personalization is evident on four fronts: 1) sales tools, 2) news and content, 3) experience, and 4) learning.

Sales Tools

The origins of personalization as a sales tool go back to the early 1980s when Charles River Analytics became a pioneer in neural expert systems and learning agent technology. This became the OpenSesame technology.[24] Another company, Neuron Data (founded in 1985), subsequently became Blaze Software. Web personalization software products are generally grouped into two categories, "rules-based," which uses logic statements and "collaborative filtering," which relies on statistical methods to suggest what is appropriate.[25]

In the field of rules-based products, one of the pioneers is the Art Technology Group (ATG, 1993), which has developed dynamo personalization foundation classes.[26] As a result, the system can "selectively capture and summarize data that the business user deems significant. The business reports also summarize correlations between user segments and activity, not just the summary of activity provided by log-analysis reports," known as smart reports.[27] Guest Track[28] (1996) combines one-to-one marketing with web and e-mail personalization. Neuromedia (1996), now Native Minds, has developed vReps (virtual representatives): "automated online personalities that effectively engage and support customers on the Internet in the same way human sales representatives do at leading brick-and-mortar companies."[29] Meanwhile, Broadvision (1997) claims to be the leader in personalized e-business applications, including one-to-one: billing, business commerce, enterprise, financial, publishing, retail commerce, and tools.[30]

With respect to collaborative filtering products, one of the pioneers was Andromedia (formerly Like Minds, 1996), which joined Macromedia (1999). Their products capture, record, and analyze "high-value visitor data in real-time and reports on customer behavior" and subsequently engage "customers with highly accurate product recommendations and personally relevant content that helps them decide what to try and what to buy." Andromedia claims to be the "only integrated solution for performance measurement and personalization."[31] A competitor, Net Perceptions, offers "automatic knowledge organization and modelling."[32] Meanwhile, OpenSesame, mentioned above, has a patent-pending learning agent that builds dynamic profiles of users "nonintrusively – from their browsing behavior." This will be combined with Allaire's technology to further develop the software's "personalization and business intelligence features."[33]

As a result of the above, there has been an enormous surge in software for one-to-one relationships.[34] Even Microsoft's *Backoffice* has a personalization system that "enables Web sites to deliver targeted information and a personalized experience based on their customers' preferences."[35] Mediapps, a recent firm in the area of mass-personalization technologies, contrasts task-based relationships "oriented toward processes and activities" with needs-based relationships, which are "upgradeable and proactive": "By developing personalized relationships with individuals, users feel the company knows them personally. Communications specialists refer to this as 'intimacy marketing,' which reverses the traditional marketing model and replaces product differentiation with customer differentiation."[36]

Mediapps focusses not only on business to business (btb) but also on business to employee (bte). While possibly very persuasive, such techniques have nothing to do with intimacy or personal relations in the traditional sense. Their effectiveness lies in treating potentially everyone, employee and customer alike, as a product that can be psychologically manipulated in the interests of business. When companies such as Backflip offer "a fundamental advance in how consumers capture enduring value in their everyday Web experiences … to help people enjoy, personalize and get the most from the Web,"[37] they are also assuming that we shall give them information about our choices, desires, and friends. When companies such as Coke sell lifestyle more than a beverage, this is part of a much larger picture. (cf. chapters 14–15).

The claims made for software in this field are ever-more dramatic. For instance, Allan.com claims to have personalized e-mail newsletters and targeted e-mail ads. It also claims that it can manage content in database publishing.[38] NetMind (1996) has a patented technology that "lets you track any web page at any level of detail – including images, forms, links and keywords – then alerts you via mobile access (cell phone, PDA, or pager), email or My Page."[39] A new Personalization Consortium advocates proper use of personalization.[40]

Personalized Content and News

In the United States, personalization is a euphemism for mass customization, which in turn is closely connected with the vision of agile manufacturing discussed earlier (chapter 4).[41] Using a rhetoric of creating a customer-centric or customer-driven market, where the "customer is king," personalization is really a new set of tools to use information about customer's habits and tendencies without their permission.

These developments in personalization[42] are particularly evident in the realm of news. For instance, using Hotbot in 2000, the term "personalized news" led to more than 370,300 hits. "Personalized TV" generated fewer than 32,300 hits, including Click TV,[43] NewsHound,[44] and even personalized TV guides.[45] "Personalized contents" led to fewer than 29,000 hits on Hotbot,[46] including personalized web pages such as those of Yahoo[47] or Excite Live.[48] The term "personalized newspapers" generated more than 9,800 hits, including CReAte Your Own Newspaper (CRAYON),[49] Silicon.com, and a personalized Indian newspaper such as Samachar.[50] Such statistics change quickly. On 7 November 2004, Google registered 2,710,000 hits for "personalized news"; 1,670,000 for "personalized TV"; 2,210,000 for "personalized content," and 587,000 hits for "personalized newspapers." No doubt, the great increases were due partly to the enormous growth of the searchable web, and to better search algorithms. Even so, these enormous numbers of hits re: personal amounted to impersonal proportions.

The rationale for such personalized services was stated in 1987 by Stewart Brand. He dismissed traditional newspapers as inefficient because: "only 10% of the news collected is printed in the paper and only 10% of that is read." By contrast, with personalized newspapers, "100% of what the newsroom owns can be accessed, and most of what is selectively sent to the reader, would be read." Customized newspapers create "only one copy of The Daily Me, but it would have a devoted readership."[51]

Tailor-made personalization also brings two dangers. First, it obscures the original sources and thus raises questions concerning the authentic and the manipulated. Second, it undermines our sense of community (chapter 13.7).

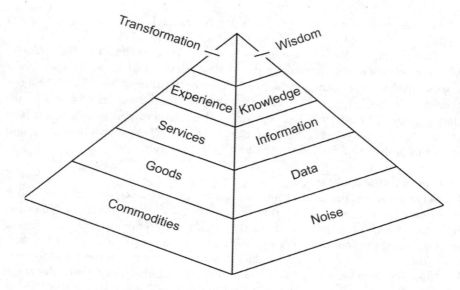

Figure 12 Five stages in the spectrum of noise to wisdom and its links with economics according to Pine and Gilmore.[55]

Experience

Closely related to the above is a trend toward personalization in entertainment. This goes far beyond simple adaptations of newspapers and television programs. There is a new quest to personalize experience,[52] such that rides, theme-parks, and the like will be tailored for the particular inclinations of an individual. A study by the European Commission on "The Future of Content" describes personalized content delivery[53] in the context of multimedia and virtual reality. Andy Hopper (ATT Labs, Cambridge) has noted: "Personalization can encompass the control part of an interface only, or it can include the data as well. It can be extended to live applications, which in effect become 'follow-me' and are never shut down."[54]

In the early 1990s Joseph Pine II wrote about mass personalization.[56] More recently he worked with James Gilmore in writing The Experience Economy.[57] Pine and Gilmore outline five stages of a spectrum from noise to wisdom (Figure 12). They link these stages with economic approaches. The first three of these recall the shift from products to services (chapters 4–5). One has traders who produce commodities, then manufacturers who produce goods, and providers who offer services.

Pine and Gilmore's contribution lies in making explicit two further stages in this process. In phase four, one becomes a stager and sells experiences. In stage five, the business becomes selling transformations. This leads to an economic pyramid. With commodities, the task lies with discovering and extracting things (minerals, etc.). With goods, one develops and makes things. With services, one devises and delivers them. With experiences, one depicts and stages them and finally with transformations, one determines and guides. While phases one to three focus on objects in the material world, phases four and five shift to the experiential world and then to the mental world of persons.

One thus moves in five stages from 1) markets, to 2) users, 3) clients, 4) guests, and 5) where the customer is the product. When the customer becomes product, one is no longer offering material, a product, an operation, or an event, but rather a change in the individual themselves.[58] The book helps to explain a shift from cinemas to the emergence of theme parks such as Disneyland and Universal Studios, where one is not just viewing *Back to the Future* but experiencing it live, totally immersed in the scene, living it. As the authors embark on describing the fifth stage, where the customer becomes the product, they introduce a so-called three-*S* model, of satisfaction, leading to sacrifice, and surprise. Their method works with, plays with, and consciously manipulates these sensations. Business is no longer a physical product but a psychological game with the customer as product.

While the authors do not discuss it, their analysis offers unexpected insight into pseudo-religious sects such as Bhagwan's movement[59] and L. Ron Hubbard's Scientology. Implicitly, the analysis points at darker themes: shades of social engineering,[60] which is linked with eugenics. And in a world where everything is business, where Mammon has won, even the realms of traditional religion, even the quest for insight, inspiration, and God, become new market propositions.

Could one go further than these five stages, ask the authors? They claim that the utmost would be perfection and conclude: "There can be no sixth economic offering because perfecting people comes under the province of God, the Author and Perfecter of our faith."[61] The book is also dedicated: "To the Author and perfecter of our faith." Ironically, a quest for perfectibility of the human being was an Enlightenment idea, which was taken up by the freemasons who also spoke of the Author, the Great Architect of the universe, and other symbols, which were usually far removed from Christian religion. Ultimately Pine and Gilmore offer more insight into profit today than enlightenment tomorrow. Moreover, this profit, which comes at the customer's expense is disturbing, because it confirms that the mass customization that leads to personalization is ultimately very impersonal. It uses persons as products to make a buck. Jeremy Rifkin goes even further: "Assigning life time values (LTVs) to people with the expectation of transforming the totality of their lived experience into commercial fare represents the final stage of capitalist market relations."[62] Even Rifkin does not endorse this extreme statement of the American view. We shall offer an alternative to this complete commercialization of objects and persons (chapters 14–15).

Learning

We have noted (chapter 9) disturbing trends whereby the models of business organization in terms of action learning are applied to schools. Children in school are subjected to advertisements as if they were customers as part of a trend towards personalization in school.[63] Hereby, children and students are treated as one-to-one marketing opportunities which borders on indoctrination and is very different from learning to have a healthy appreciation of business and other realities of the world.

4. Conclusions

At the personal level, the Internet brings many new possibilities with respect to expression. In the name of personalization, many new possibilities are being introduced. These new technologies promise us everything that we could ever desire. There is a concern, however, that these pleasures could be all too much like those on the island that Pinocchio encountered. There is a need for authentication: to decide who is allowed to do observation; for protection and for reflection about the changing role of public and private. This applies both at the micro-level with respect to inner and outer within individual persons, and at the macro-level of the state versus individuals (cf. chapter 13).[64]

11
collaboration

Over the past ten years, the explicit focus in the Augmentation Research Center (ARC) has been upon the effects and possibilities of new knowledge workshop tools based on the technology of computer timesharing and modern communications. Since we consider automating many human operations, what we are after could perhaps be termed "workshop automation." But the very great importance of aspects other than the new tools (i.e., conventions, methods, roles) makes us prefer the "augmentation" term that hopefully can remain "whole-scope." We want to keep tools in proper perspective within the total system that augments native human capacities toward effective action.
– Douglas C. Engelbart, Richard W. Watson, James C. Norton, "The Augmented Knowledge Workshop," *AFIPS Conference Proceedings*, Vol. 42, National Computer Conference, June 4–8, 1973, pp. 9–21.[1]

1. Introduction

Collaboration is as old as civilization itself. Working together and sharing are essential dimensions of civilized life. In Ancient Greece, Plato's Academy was essentially a meeting place for collaboration. In the Middle Ages, monasteries formed a network of collaborating monks linking thinkers all over Europe. During the Renaissance, the palaces and courts of the Medici, the Sforzas, the d'Estes, and the Fuggers played a similar role. In the seventeenth century, with the rise of organized science, new institutions, such as the Académie Royale and the Royal Society, served as focal points for new levels of collaboration among scientists all over Europe and gradually all over the world.

Manufacturing Organization

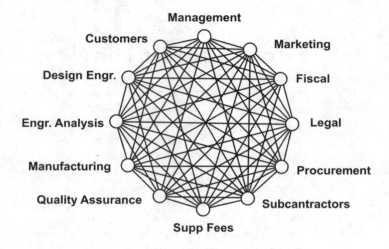

Management
Customers
Marketing
Design Engr.
Fiscal
Engr. Analysis
Legal
Manufacturing
Procurement
Quality Assurance
Subcantractors
Supp Fees

Figure 13a Sketch by Douglas Engelbart showing co-operation between various departments in a manufacturing organization where each functional domain is a candidate for working interchange with all others

Two Aerospace Companies, required to do "Program Teaming"

Mc Donnell Aircraft Go (Mc Air)   Northrop Aircraft Div (NAD)

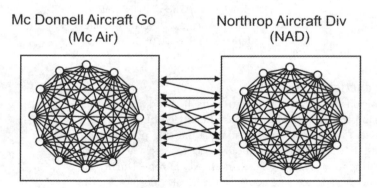

Figure 13b Sketch by Douglas Engelbart showing co-operation between two aircraft companies.[7]

In the 1950s and 1960s, three projects heralded the way for new kinds of collaboration: 1) the Delphi method, 2) the work of Douglas Engelbart on augmented knowledge, and 3) the Internet. Originally developed as a strategic planning technique, the Delphi process demonstrated that: "the averaged opinion of a mass of equally expert (or equally ignorant) observers is quite a bit more reliable a predictor than that of a single random-chosen observer."[2]

The Delphi method uses group discussions, which lead to anonymous lists of suggestions, which serve in turn in helping to achieve a group consensus.[3] It is of particular interest in our story for three reasons. First, it has become one of the major methods used in social policy and public health by bodies such as the World Health Organization.[4] Second, Eric Raymond explicitly cites it as one of the stimuli behind the open-source movement[5] (cf. chapter 14). Third, as Murray Turoff has shown, the Delphi method, in its electronic versions now used on the Internet, is closely connected with Computer Mediated Communication (CMC), Computer Supported Collaborative work (CSCW), and other forms of collaboration.[6]

During the 1960s, when Helmer and Dalkey were working on the Delphi method at Rand, Douglas Engelbart, one of the most original minds of the twentieth century, was developing his own vision of collaboration. His work in this field began in 1945, when he read Vannevar Bush's essay, "As we may think." Engelbart, one of the fathers of the Internet and the inventor of the mouse, foresaw the possibility of hypermedia e-mail and Computer Supported Collaborative Work (CSCW)[8] for large corporations and ultimately for everyone. He foresaw that a company could gain by sharing information among all its departments (Figure 13a). As we have seen in the chapters on production and services, this is what happened through the rise of Enterprise Resource Planning (ERP), etc. In the meantime, the principle of co-operation has gone beyond the individual departments of a company to include both suppliers and customers.

Engelbart also foresaw that major companies could gain from working together. To make his point, he used the example of two aircraft companies (Figure 13b). As we have shown, this has also happened, except that, in cases such as automobiles, the principle has spread to include effectively all the major players in the field in a single global network. Underlying Engelbart's vision was the idea of augmented knowledge, that one could gain much more by sharing than by hoarding. This vision led eventually to the Bootstrap Institute where the philosophical potentials of these ideas continue to be explored.

When the Internet was founded in 1969 as ARPAnet, collaboration was one of its primary goals. Physicists at different research laboratories wanted to share information in the interests of physics and astronomy as well as for defence purposes. This notion spread from the West Coast of the United States, to the East Coast and to other international centres, notably the Centre Européenne de Recherche Nucléaire (CERN). There the efforts of Tim Berners-Lee led to what is now known as the

World Wide Web. The Internet differs from earlier forms in that it allows both synchronous and asynchronous collaboration.

On the surface, it might appear that this spirit of collaboration has gradually faded as the realities of a dominant competitive ethic of the United States lead to an ever-greater emphasis on e-commerce,[9] whereby short-term commercial gain dominates over long-term intellectual advantage. Some have claimed that one now needs to collaborate in order to compete. For instance, Logan and Stokes, describe the evolution of thought as Data-Production-Competition in the 1970s, Information-Solution-Cooperation in the 1980s, and Knowledge-Innovation-Collaboration in the twenty-first century.[10] The Japanese have rightly noted that there is a trend in the United States to use the Internet more as a tool for managing knowledge than as a method for creating new knowledge.

And yet this is again only one trend. The collaborative quest may have moved into the background but it continues to develop. The past decades have seen enormous progress in all realms of tele-activity. There is a Tele-Foundation (Honolulu). The past five years have seen a dramatic rise in the concept of virtual laboratories, whereby complex instruments including microscopes and telescopes can be operated at a distance. Closely connected with this has been the rise of collaboratories, whereby teams of scientists or researchers can work together on-line. This idea is also spreading to business. Behind the scenes the United States is every bit as much intent on using collaboration to develop new products as Michael Schrage explains in *Serious Play*.

The cumulative effect of these developments is a gradual transformation of the entire research process. Fifty years ago, a scientist had to be at one of the great labs such as CERN or Fermi in order to have access to very specialized equipment costing tens or even hundreds of millions of dollars. Similarly scholars in the humanities were dependent on a handful of great libraries. The Internet is connecting these great centres. It is also doing something more. The enormous supercomputers of the great laboratories are being linked with ordinary computers through a new concept of computational grids. A next stage could be an everyman's grid.[11] This also promises new possibilities for virtual libraries, museums, and archives.

Ironically as the Internet spreads beyond the United States to include Europe, Asia, and the rest of the world, the importance of Engelbart's vision increases. The collaborative spirit underlying the Internet points to augmented knowledge and to a new vision of augmented culture. Examples include the rise of shared open content,[12] open theory development,[13] open development,[14] and collaborative encyclopaedias such as Wikipedia.[15] It is also leading to new forms of generative art.[16] For instance, protoquadro is "a synaesthetic audio-visual entity that transforms the space, the perception of the viewers, and the intention of the artist."[17] This is a vast new field that deserves a book in itself.

2. Tele-Activity

The W3 consortium has an ongoing interest in collaboration in the form of Computer Supported Co-operative Work (CSCW).[18] Collaboration is essentially the ability to share work at a distance (Greek tele-). In the past decade there has been a striking increase in activities at a distance. Tele-work has become a major theme within the European Commission. There is also tele-conferencing, tele-collaboration, and tele-presence, all of which support this notion of tele-work.

Tele-Conferencing

Companies such as Picture-Tel have made tele-conferencing generally accessible through the use of simple television screens linked through two phone lines. At conferences such images are typically projected onto large screens on walls, occasionally using ISDN or even ATM connections for added effect as was the case with the Teleport conference linking Toronto and London (1995). At the National Infrastructure for Science and Technology (1997) in Kuala Lumpur, fourteen cities were linked simultaneously by an ATM connection and displayed on three screens of the conference hall. A project by Pavel Curtis takes the idea of tele-conferencing considerably further through the construction of a Virtual Auditorium.[19]

Philippe Galvez (CERN) has developed a Virtual Room Videoconferencing System (VRVS) that links researchers at most of the great high energy physics labs around the world.[20] The U.S. Department of Defense (DOD) has Virtual Briefing Rooms, an idea that has spread (in name, at least) to the home page of the White House. The University of Twente (The Netherlands) has developed Cyberchair software for reviewing conference papers at a distance.[21]

Tele-Collaboration

In the world of education, the notion of Computer Supported Collaborative Work (CSCW) has taken the form of Computer Supported Collaborative Learning (CSCL). Here there is an assumption that young children and students can benefit from collaboration even before they have specialized knowledge. Sharing becomes a virtue in itself even before there is content to be shared. It is striking that mobile instruments play an important role in this vision. For instance, Stanford University's Learning Lab foresees working with collaborative learning tools, interactive spaces, and personal learning strategies and tools. One such example is their Personal Electronic Notebooks with Sharing (PENS).[22] A European Union project is exploring Collaboration Environments and Service Architectures for Researchers (CESAR)[23]

A next stage is to go beyond a simple screen. A new NRC Institute for Computer Integrated Manufacturing (London, Ontario) has a projection screen with a single plate of glass four metres by two metres. The Gesellschaft für Mathematik und Datenverarbeitung (GMD, Sankt Augustin, now Fraunhofer) has a project on Co-operative Work called i-land[24] and a Collaborative Wall as part of their Tele Port project, whereby speakers at a remote location are projected as if they were sitting at the other side of a table. A related development at the National Center for Supercomputer Applications (NCSA, Urbana-Champaign) is modestly called an Infinity Wall.[25]

Collaborative work tools have become very big business. In 1996, Boeing, Ford, Kodak, MacNeal-Schwendler,[26] and Structural Dynamics founded the Technology for Enterprisewide Engineering Consortium.[27] Recently, Boeing has begun licensing its collaborative software.[28] New companies, such as Alibre[29] and Aristasoft,[30] are joining the ranks of more established firms in the field such as SherpaWorks, which produces Enterprisewide Product Data Management,[31] and Nexprise,[32] which is used by Lockheed Martin. The financial aspects thereof were discussed under services (chapter 5). Volvo, is "launching a set of collaborative product development applications for its truck-making operations" and is also using product life-cycle management (PLM) applications developed by Paris-based Dassault Systemes SA and sold by IBM.[33]

Structural Dynamics Research Corp. (SDRC, Cincinnati) has a three-fold strategy for e-business collaboration, namely: tools for 1) product knowledge management (PKM), 2) collaborative product commerce (CPC), and 3) e-design automation. CoCreate Software, a Hewlett-Packard company, makes two- and three-dimensional collaborative design tools. SolidWorks, a manufacturer of 3-D CAD software, now has 3-D Meeting, which enables vendors, manufacturers, and customers to view and share mechanical designs in real time over the Internet. Meanwhile, General Electric Industrial Systems has created Web City, the company's intranet, for collaboration, which is now being applied to more than a hundred plants and twenty design centres globally: "In Web City, projects can be broken down into tasks and tracked. Web City stores updates in virtual folders that other team members can see, and also allows the company to capture best practices and repetitive tasks to apply to new projects."[34]

Tele-presence

Tele-presence was originally a term used by the military for tele-operation: how to operate a robot at a distance in the case of hazardous environments such as a Chernobyl or to repair a submarine far below the ocean surface. Increasingly, tele-presence recreates environments completely by projecting on four walls as well as a floor and/or ceiling. In Europe, this began as a Distributed Interactive Virtual Environment (DIVE). In the United States this began as a Computer Aided Virtual Environment (CAVE). The GII Testbed 7 aimed to achieve remote engineering using Cave to Cave Communications. A series of European projects have explored tele-presence.[35] Ultimately, there is an interest in using such new visualization methods to forecast future developments. For instance, one of the G7 pilot projects addressed the problem of global emergencies in the form of earthquakes and typhoons. There is also a quest to understand global trends in population, energy, insurance, investment and other patterns.

3. Virtual Laboratories

Virtual laboratories range considerably in their scope. For instance, the pressure chamber at the University of Oregon[36] to demonstrate the ideal gas law is simply a simulation of a physical environment as a Java applet. The Microscape Virtual Microscope Lab[37] shows on the web examples of images seen by using a microscope. The Lawrence Livermore Laboratory Virtual Frog project represents a further level of interactivity. Here, students can manipulate reconstructions of a frog, various parts and layers of which are linked with film clips and other materials of a physical frog.

Meanwhile, another level is concerned with so-called remote instrumentation in real time, as is the case with the World-Wide Laboratory (WWL), a joint venture of the Beckman Institute, the Biomedical Magnetic Resonance Lab, and the National Center for Supercomputer Applications (NCSA). WWL has two important educational projects: Chickscope,[38] whereby students can watch the embryo of a chicken through a microscope on-line in real time, and Bugscope,[39] whereby classrooms can control an Environmental Scanning Electron Microscope in the Chicago lab from their schools via the Internet. A recent report describes three kinds of access, namely, for 1) single users, 2) multiple non-co-operating users, and 3) multiple co-operating users.[40]

The Beckman Institute has, moreover, three basic goals with respect to these experiments, namely, to provide: [1] "a set of specifications for developing instrument control servers, ... [2] initial implementations of those servers, [3] ... image processing tools which can be accessed over the internet through a variety of user interfaces." The experiments presently entail four kinds of instruments: Transmission Electron Microscopes (TEM), Magnetic Resonance Imaging (MRI) Systems, Scanning Tunneling Microscopes (STM), and Laser Scanning Confocal Microscopes.[41] Related work, which has been operational since 1997, is being done in the Microsystems Technical Laboratories at MIT: "The Remote Microscope is part of a project to aid in the remote fabrication of integrated circuits. It allows one or more users to remotely view and control a microscope connected to a local or wide area network."[42]

Such remote experiments are a subset of a more comprehensive quest for operation at a distance, which began in the military as the goal of tele-presence. There are striking parallels between this quest and developments in virtual libraries qua traditional libraries. In the past, access to great libraries was limited to those who were privileged to be in a city that could afford a great collection. Similarly, major scientific experiments were only possible in places that could afford to have the latest scientific equipment.

Thanks to virtual libraries and virtual laboratories, such centralized resources can now function in a distributed way[43] and be accessible to a far greater range of users around the world. For example, TNO, in the Netherlands, has recently opened a virtuality laboratorium.[44] In the realm of restoration, a Virtual Laboratory opened at the Foundation for Fundamental Research on Matter (FOM) in Amsterdam in the summer of 2000.[45] Rutgers University uses virtual laboratories to do virtual biology experiments (ViBE).[46] Monash University in Australia has a virtual laboratory to do "Molecular Modelling for Drug Design" on a World Wide Grid.[47]

These developments are enormously significant because the principles can be applied to every kind of instrument. For instance, the Argonne Laboratories have a Futures Lab that is exploring three kinds of virtual reality applications: 1) visualization for atomic and molecular simulations, 2) multi-resolution fluid dynamics, and 3) visualization of databases.[48] The results of such processes and even the processes themselves can be made accessible on-line. The frontiers of this field are represented by organizations such as the Metropolitan Research and Education Network (MREN), which provides access to remote instrumentation in "high energy physics, for example, the key facilities at Fermilab" (e.g., collider detectors, high energy physics computational processors, and astronomy facilities, such as those related to the Sloan Digital Sky Survey project).[49]

The University of Wisconsin-Milwaukee and Lawrence Berkeley National Laboratory have a remote Spectro-Microscopy at the Advanced Light Source. The Advanced Analytical Electron Microscope (AAEM) at the Argonne National Labs has a Tele-presence Microscopy site, which focusses on materials microscopy.[50] The National Center for Microscopy Imaging Research (NCMIR, San Diego) has been working with Japan to develop Trans Pacific Tele-microscopy.[51] The reasons are fourfold: 1) there are too few experts; 2) operators can easily cause disturbances in cases with high resolution; 3) even if one is on location it is not easy to get to the instrument and 4) often the samples can be dangerous as in the case of viral material.

There are virtual labs at the Mauna Kea Observatories and the Subaru Telescope (both) in Hawaii.[52] The Association of Universities for Research in Astronomy (AURA) recently recommended establishing a "National Virtual Observatory (NVO) – a new kind of observatory that enables discovery of new phenomena via exploration of huge (tera- and peta-byte) image and catalog databases using innovative software tools for finding rare and unexpected patterns."[53]

4. Collaboratories

Closely related to the above trend towards remote instrumentation is a further development known as collaboratories. Here, distributed groups of experts work together using combinations of tele-conferencing, collaborative tools, and common repositories of knowledge in the form of complex databases. Thomas Finholt and G. W. Olson (1996), listed collaboratories in atmospheric and space science, biology, chemistry, medicine, and physics.[54]

By 2000 at least eleven other collaboratories had appeared[55] in the fields of education,[56] microscopic digital anatomy, developmental biology, chemistry, crystallography,[57] culture, research on electronic work, team engineering, environmental and molecular sciences, fusion, libraries,[58] management information systems, medicine, physics, space physics, upper atmosphere research, and spectro-microscopy. The Biomedical Informatics Research Network (BIRN) is becoming an important focus for collaboratories.[59] The Electronic Visualization Labs collaboratories range from medical and cosmological to combustion.[60] While these collaboratories are primarily in the United States, they are increasingly becoming an international phenomenon.[61]

The National Center for Microscopy Imaging Research (NCMIR) has a series of collaboratory projects including: parallel tomography,[62] a Microstructure Image-Based Collaboratory (MIBC), Collaboratory for Microscopic Digital Anatomy (CMDA), tele-science project, a 3-D Cell Centered Neuronal Database, and a Database for the Analysis of Neuronal Structure and Function.[63] There is a Space Physics and Aeronomy Research Collaboratory (SPARC) at the University of Michigan.[64] Sandia Labs has a Diesel Combustion Collaboratory.[65] Argonne Labs have a Materials Micro-Characterization Collaboratory (MMC).[66] The University of Michigan has a Medical Collaboratory Testbed.[67] Harvard, Stanford, and Columbia have the Intermed Collaboratory Project.[68] Lawrence Livermore National Laboratory, Princeton Plasma Physics Lab, Oak Ridge National Laboratory, and General Atomics are working together on remote control for fusion. These experimental testbeds in distributed computing include security architectures and even sociological aspects of remote collaboration.[69] In Sweden there is also work on a Collaborative Web with Social Navigation (CoWeb).[70] By November 2004, the Science of Collaboratories Allliance[71] listed some 175 collaboratories worldwide.

217

Emerging from this is a new vision of science where all researchers in a field from all over the world are connected through a single network. For instance, researchers at CERN (Geneva), DESY (Hamburg), and Cal Tech (Pasadena) are working together on a distributed particle physics research network.[72] They are also working on a Virtual room Videoconferencing System for collaboration.[73] Others are developing on-line monitoring and steering of remote black hole simulations.[74]

It is sobering to learn that, notwithstanding enormous advances in technology, the shortcomings of technology qua bandwidth mean that an estimated 99 per cent of all evidence in radio astronomy is still thrown away. Simon Garrington (Jodrell Bank) estimates that we would need 60 gigabit connections to handle the full volume of astronomical data on-line. Plans are underway for collaboratories for real time input from space data to observatories with respect to solar flares and supernova. Plans are also underway for virtual astronomical observatories that would link a number of telescopes across a continent to create a single virtual instrument via the network.

While the earliest collaboratories were strictly in scientific fields, more recent examples include libraries and culture.[75] There is also research into the process, through Thomas Finholt's[76] Collaboratory for Research on Electronic Work (CREW)[77] and the Collaborative Systems Research Group (CSRG).[78] In the Netherlands, there are experiments in an Architectural Linked Immersive Environment (ALIVE).[79] In Japan, there are experiments in digital cinema.[80] In Germany there is a project called Mediazine, which combines television, text, live audio, video, and 3-D computer graphics.[81] These testbeds are also beginning to produce some content such as Virtual Harlem,[82] a Virtual Cookbook (VC), a Video Encyclopedia, reconstructions of cultural sites such as Shared Miletus,[83] produced by the Hellenic Cosmos Cultural Centre (Athens). The National University of Singapore has a Human Anatomy Lecture on demand for teaching purposes.[84] Virtual laboratories and collaboratories are gradually affecting every aspect of work, design, learning, and research.

In the world of digital libraries there was concern that the social dimensions of traditional libraries were being insufficiently represented. To address this, a project at the University of Illinois at Urbana-Champaign is working on an Interspace Collaborative Environment to provide direct support for community, collaboration, and communication.[85]

There are also an increasing number of collective action tools.[86] These tools accomplish something that sounds simple and obvious. They give researchers new access to knowledge in different databases. The brain model interface is an excellent case in point. In the past, scientific literature was stored in libraries. Experiments and experimental data were in laboratories and models were often in other university departments. Through the new interfaces, both scientific literature in libraries and experimental results in laboratories all over the world are accessible at one's own desk. Indeed, given the developments in virtual laboratories outlined earlier, a researcher can theoretically repeat experiments at a distance.

An analogous project at San Diego State College (SDSC) is the Molecular Interactive Collaborative Environment (MICE).[87] Here the innovation lies in integrating information from descriptive and structural databases in order to generate three-dimensional scenes for discussion "on the fly." Implicit here are new problems of knowing about the context of sources, their level of interpretation, and their reliability (chapter 13).

The computational environment at the Stanford 5Plab is also fascinating in this context. It supports Internet Mediated Collaborative Team-Work through Computer Integrated Manufacturing (CIM) and Agent Computer Aided Design (CAD), which links in turn with a Task Network of Activities. We saw earlier (chapter 9.2), how this is leading to Computer Integrated Engineering, Architecture and Construction in education.[88]

An important result of these networks is that they are bringing new interplay among different disciplines. For instance, the nano-manipulator project at the University of North Carolina, Chapel Hill, is part of a consortium of institutions in North America and Europe involving a wide range of disciplines: chemistry, computer-supported collaborative work, distributed systems, education, gene therapy, graphics, information and library science, physics, and psychology. Similarly the STAR TAP consortium has projects in biology, computer and information sciences, education, engineering, geosciences, mathematics, physical sciences (astronomical sciences, chemistry, materials science, physics), polar research, social and behavioural sciences, as well as crosscutting programs.[89] From the above it is clear that the I-grid demonstrations at the Internet 2000 Global Summit (Yokohama) linked with Internet2, STARTAP, CANARIE's CA 3 Net, Holland's Gigaport, Europe's TEN 155 projects, and others are but visible tips of an enormous iceberg.[90]

The EU IST program has a project CYCLADES which is creating an open Collaborative Virtual Archive Environment and another project, COLLATE, which is a Collaboratory for Annotation, Indexing and Retrieval of Digitized Historical Archive Material.[91]

5. Business

Not all collaboration is only about altruistic sharing. In the United States, collaboration is increasingly being seen as yet another business tool. According to Dan Rasmus, "Collaboration is the fundamental starting point for e-business transformation."[92] In California, John T. Maloney, has trademarked www.collaboratory.com. He is working with Lumeria, which is developing a Super Profile Markup Language (SPML). In Maloney's view, the development of the Internet can be characterized as an evolution from file transfer through publish and subscribe transactions and e-business to collaborative environments. Concurrent with this evolution is a gradual move from simple Internet Service Providers (ISPs) to Application Service Providers (ASPs), and finally Full Service Providers (FSPs).

Maloney has drawn attention to a number of software products specifically designed for this purpose, including Web Project, Quick Team's ThoughtStar, InterOffice's Integrated Application Technologies, and Intandem's Intractive. In an earlier chapter, we examined developments in knowledge management and organizational learning. According to Maloney, these, combined with collaboration, lead to collaborative ecosystems (or communities) value networks. New companies such as Flypaper promise software for collaborative commerce.[93] Flypaper has a Teamspace that includes: Team Discussion, Group Scheduling, Document Sharing, Online Conferencing, Issue Tracking, and Team Workflow for buyers, vendors, and partners.[94]

6. Computational Grids

Meanwhile, the sheer quantity of data has continued to increase dramatically in the past decade. As noted in the Introduction, by November 2004, Google alone had indexed over 8 billion pages on the Internet, and the Internet was reported to be growing at a rate of 7 million pages per day.[95] In addition, there are many materials not yet commonly accessible on the Internet. The Radio telescope at Conception produces 224 gigabytes of new information per day. The NASA Earth Observation Satellite (EOS) produces 918 gigabytes of new information per day, i.e., 27.5 terabytes per month and 330 terabytes per year. High Definition Television (HDTV) produces 0.23 gigabytes/second, i.e., 9.8 gigabytes per minute, 588 gigabytes per hour, 14.1 terabytes per day, or 98.7 terabytes per week, and 4.1 petabytes per year. This is for one station. In a five-hundred-channel HDTV universe, the figure would be just over 2 exabytes per year. If this still seems futuristic, in December 1999, Ian Foster et al. of the Argonne National Labs reported: "In the immediate future, we anticipate collecting data at the rate of terabytes per day from many classes of applications, including simulations running on teraflop-class computers and experimental data produced by increasingly more sensitive and accurate instruments."[96] A new project, LOFAR:

> ... is an IT-telescope. The antennas are simple enough but there are a lot of them – 25,000 in the full LOFAR design. To make radio pictures of the sky with adequate sharpness, these antennas are to be arranged in clusters that are spread out over an area of ultimately 350 km in diameter. (In phase 1 that is currently funded 15,000 antenna's and maximum baselines of 100 km will be built). Data transport requirements are in the range of many Tera-bits/sec and the processing power needed is tens of Tera-FLOPS.[97]

To meet such needs there has been a trend towards parallel computing, i.e., using a number of machines within a facility to tackle a problem.[98] In the last decade, this has led to a more dramatic concept of computational grids.[99] "Grids are persistent environments that enable software applications to integrate instruments, displays, computational and information resources that are managed by diverse organizations in widespread locations."[100] As Dongarra and Moore (University of Tennessee) have noted: "The underlying metaphor of a 'grid' refers to distribution networks that developed at the beginning of the twentieth century to deliver electric power to a widely dispersed population. Just as electric power grids were built to dependably provide ubiquitous access to electric power at consistent levels, so computational grids are being built to provide access to computational resources that is equally reliable, ubiquitous, and consistent."[101] These computational or scientific grids are distinct from enterprise grids in business and from the intranet and Internet grids that we associate with everyman's grid.

Some visionaries foresee that the electric power grids themselves will also be transformed in the future. Electricity has traditionally been a one-way transmission from power stations to consumers. In future, consumers could become their own producers and there could be a two-way flow of energy. In other words, the interactive metaphors from the computer world are also transforming our images of what some now call the energy web.[102] A recent development is the National Science Foundation's Distributed Terascale Facility.[103]

The National Laboratory for Applied Network Research (NLANR) has provided an excellent short history of the computational grid, although it manages to overlook other pioneering contributions such as the ATM satellite transmission of T-Vision between Berlin and Osaka (1994) and the G7 demonstrations linking Canada and

Brussels (via Berlin using ATM connections with 27 MB of throughput (February 1995). According to this history, NCSA introduced the idea of running computations across multiple machines (meta-computing) in the 1980s as a first step to distributed computing. Gigabit testbeds began in the early 1990s. The I-WAY demo at SC '95 (SuperComputing 1995) connected dozens of centres and pointed the way to NASA's Information Power grid (1999).[104]

A number of the collaboratories mentioned above serve as first steps towards computational grids.[105] In the field of brain science, Dr. Suzumu Date (Osaka) has demonstrated that one can achieve twenty-two times acceleration with thirty-two processors.[106] In order to make the grid possible, the Argonne National Laboratory is working on the Globus project, which includes research, software to integrate geographically distributed computational and information resources, testbeds (via GUSTO), and applications. In June 2000, Globus was used to tie together computers "to solve the 'nug30' Quadratic Assignment Problem (QAP) that was first posed in 1968. The computational crunching to solve the problem involved over 1,000 computers from eight different institutions scattered around the world."[107] Using a single machine, this problem would have taken 6.9 years. Using the combined force of over a thousand machines, the problem was solved in 6.9 days.

The scope of such projects is expanding dramatically. In 2000, the DARPA meta-computing Gusto Testbed for the Globus Toolkit had twelve sites with two thousand nodes.[108] Globus is planned to have resource brokers.[109] While Globus is the largest of these testbeds at present, Legion (University of Virginia) and Condor (University of Wisconsin–Madison) are related projects, as are Polder (University of Amsterdam) and MOL (University of Paderborn, Germany) in Europe.[110]

NASA is also working on an Information Power Grid, which brings together supercomputing, networked mass storage, and new software tools. An enormous amount of work is being devoted to new software. For instance, the Electronic Visualization Lab (EVL) is working on a series of new tools, including Virtual Mail (V-Mail), Virtual Annotator, a Virtual VCR, a Tele-Immersive Data Explorer (TIDE), Collaborative Information Visualization, Collaborative Image Based Rendering Viewer, Collaborative Volume Visualization Applications and the Biology Workbench, which is "a computational interface and environment that permits anybody with a Web browser to readily use bio-informatics, for research, teaching, or learning."[111]

The National Center for Supercomputing Applications (NCSA) is also producing a number of other integrative tools such as Biology Workbench, Cave5D, Virtual Director, and Emerge – "a new search infrastructure which addresses issues of scale and heterogeneity using a distributed architecture." Oak Ridge National Lab has the (Cumulus) project on remote collaboration, which will allow dynamic attachment/detachment and independent views of information.[112] Los Alamos is working on a Parallel Application WorkSpace (PAWS).[113] Pacific Northwest National Laboratories is working on a Spectroscopists' Notebook.[114] Related to these is Lawrence Berkeley National Laboratory's work on an electronic notebook: "The prototypes will conform

TABLE 37A Statistics in the Search for Extraterrestrial Intelligence (SETI) project on 30 July 2000

	TOTAL	LAST 24 HOURS
Users	2,192,077	2,896
Results received	158,575,548	482621
Total CPU time	346,873.71 years	838.46 years
Floating Point Operations	3.171511e+20	9.652420e+17 (11.17 TeraFlops/sec)
Average CPU time/work unit	19 hr 09 min 43.0 sec	15 hr 13 min 07.6 sec

TABLE 37B Statistics in the Search for Extraterrestrial Intelligence (SETI) project on 24 December 2004.[130]

	TOTAL	LAST 24 HOURS
Users	5,293,194	958
Results received	1,696,685,423	1352044
Total CPU time	2,168,452,945 years	975.308 years
Floating Point Operations	6.201258e+21	5.272972e+18 (61.03 TeraFLOPs/sec)
Average CPU time/work unit	11 hr 11 min 44.6 sec	6 hr 19 min 08.7 sec

to a common notebook architecture and communications mechanism, thus allowing them to interoperate and to share components for input and display of sketches, text, equations, images, graphs, and other data types, as well as tools for authentication and other services."[115]

In the United Kingdom there is an E-Science grid.[116] IBM is helping Oxford to build a British National grid.[117] In Germany there is the UNiform Interface to Computing Resources (UNICORE) project.[118] In Europe, there is a DataGrid for data intensive science.[119] There is a EUROGRID IST project,[120] which has four application-specific work packages, namely, Bio, Meteo, Computer Aided Engineering (CAE), and High Performance Computing (HPC).[121]

By 2005, the new Large Hadron Collider at CERN[122] (costing $1.8 billion) will generate the world's biggest challenge in distributed computing. "Several thousand scientists in 40 countries will be working on the LHC, requiring 100 to 1,000 times more processing and networking power than CERN can handle."[123] This will introduce a new scale of computing needs: "On average 20 particle collisions occur within an LHC detector every time the particle bunches in the beam cross at the centre of the apparatus. This happens 40 million times per second, or every 25 nanoseconds, giving a raw event rate of almost a thousand million per second. This corresponds to a (compressed) data rate of about 40 TeraBytes per second."[124]

Needless to say the LHC will introduce a series of new research and development challenges[125] and new kinds of collaboration that will involve 1,500 to 2,000 researchers from over a hundred different institutes, who will require easy and effective access to the data on the world-wide basis.[126] In 1999, there was a workshop to discuss these challenges. It was concluded that "a concerted action from the EU and the USA should support the establishment of a worldwide distributed computing environment with a few large centres hosting large multi-Petabyte data bases and archives."[127]

At first it seemed that the Globus project offered a natural framework for such a global effort. There was some feeling, however, that the system was too ad hoc. Researchers such as Keith Jeffery (Rutherford Appleton Labs) proposed a British solution. Gradually the notion of an independent European approach to grids emerged as one of the central goals of the seventh Framework Programme (2007–2011).

7. Everyman's Grid

Governments and industry have demonstrated that co-operation through Computer Supported Collaborative Work (CSCW) is effective, particularly in mega-projects such as the design of the Euro-Fighter. When the Hubble Space Telescope broke down, a team of 10,000 scientists worked together to repair it. Indeed, such stories have thus far been limited to a relatively small group of a few thousand scientists working at the frontiers of science. Not many have passwords for the world's supercomputers. But here too there are changes.

We noted that the world's largest computer in 2000, ASCI White, is capable of 12.3 teraflops, i.e., 12.3 trillion calculations per second, which is 30,000 times more powerful than a personal computer. But what if 30,000 personal computers were linked together via parallel computing to create a computational grid for everyman? This would theoretically lead to a machine as powerful as ASCI White. This idea has occurred to others. For instance, in 1999, *The Chronicle of Higher Education* reported how a climatologist at the Rutherford Appleton Laboratory called for volunteers in the hopes of harnessing a million desktop machines for a distributed experiment.[128] Allan received 15,000 replies within two weeks.[129]

Sceptics who object that all this is mainly speculation concerning future possibilities are invited to recall a project that has already been underway for several years. The Search for Extraterrestrial Intelligence (SETI) project began from a very simple standpoint. Radio astronomy is producing too much information to process on a single computer. Why not invite persons to lend the processing power of their PCs when they are not in use? Volunteers were requested and volunteers have been forthcoming. For instance, on 30 July 2000, there were 2,896 new volunteers within twenty-four hours and a total of 2,192,077 persons, who made their computers available on a part-time basis.

Even so this generated 11.17 teraflops per second, which was a little bit slower than the new ASCI White machine but faster than all the other supercomputers of the world in 2000.[131] The corresponding statistics for 2004 revealed that the SETI now produced five times more computing power than the greatest machine in the world in 2000. A related project is the Intel Philanthropic Peer-to-Peer Program,[132] whereby volunteers again make available the spare time of their computers.[133] There is, for instance, an Intel-United Devices Cancer Research project. On 27 April 2000, this had 309,292 members with 426,023 devices, which produced 34,962,038 hours of CPU time. The leukemia project is hoping to have six million volunteers. Since September 2000, Arthur Olson, a scientist at the Scripps Research Institute in La Jolla, California, has been tapping the power of 26,000 computers around the world for free, thanks to a distributed computing service offered by Entropia (San Diego) for a project called FightAIDS@Home.[134] Related projects such as Folderol, Folding@home, and United Devices are devoted to solving complex protein problems.[135] These are first steps towards peer-to-peer computing in the full sense of the term.

One day in 1999, a friend, Jaap van Till, sent me a brief article, "Just Imagine"[136] (Appendix 4). He drew an analogy between 'people networking' and a lens in optics. A lens works in parallel such that one can cover part of the lens, and still see the image, although the image is somewhat lessened in strength. The more people who contribute, the better the resolution of the vision becomes for all who co-operate. Therefore, he suggested transforming the structure of Internet in the direction of a worldwide observatory using methods from optical processing to combine observations from thousands of people focussing their awareness on one thing at a time.

At the time I was unaware of the SETI figures and must admit that I myself was still a sceptic. Indeed, it took me nearly a year to begin to appreciate the enormous implications of Jaap van Till's visionary statement. One can, for instance, do some very rough calculations. The statistics above suggest that the sparetime use of the personal computers of a million volunteers generates approximately 5.5 teraflops (i.e., 11/2). If one had access to all the personal computers used in 2000, namely, 332 million PCs, then would have access to 1,826 teraflops per second. In layman's terms, this is 1,826 trillion or 1.826 quadrillion calculations per second, if one uses the machines only in their spare time.

We noted above that one ASCI White is as powerful as 30,000 PCs. It follows that the 332 million PCs of Internet in 2000 are 11,066.6 times more powerful than the world's most powerful supercomputer today. Say one had access to all these PCs for at least the two weeks when people go on vacation each year. During that time, one would have access to roughly 121,126 trillion calculations per second. According to the predictions of Vint Cerf (INET 2000) by the year 2006, there will be 2.4 billion Internet users,[137] which means multiplying the foregoing figure by seven. We are also told that computers will expand enormously in their capacity within the next twenty years. Pessimists can multiply the foregoing figure by a million. Optimists can multiply it by 100 million.

This book is not meant to become a math exercise, nor does it intend to become a chapter in the *Guinness Book of World Records* with respect to which gadget has the biggest teraflops, etc. The point is very simple: Networked computing in this new sense can create a grid for everyman, a grid which is thousands of times more powerful than the combined power of all the world's supercomputers today. Computer scientists will be quick to remind us that the situation is much more complex than simply putting computers on-line for sharing. In 2004 one of the most important demonstrations of the grid principle at INRIA involved only 294 computers, and there was a project to make it work for 5,000, which was still a long way from billions.[138] What interests us is the principle: It opens up possibilities far beyond word processing, such as tools that can help scientists as well as humanists and historians. We can accomplish something truly challenging such as reorganizing the whole of knowledge.

It is often said, of course, that the humanities do not lend themselves to co-operation. It is true that great monographs are typically still the product of a single individual, the argument being that one mind is needed to synthesize the information and create a coherent line, a single story. In the case of major reference works, the situation is clearly different: the *Oxford English Dictionary*, the *Grove Dictionary of Art* (in 34 volumes) or the *Encyclopaedia Britannica* would have been unthinkable without the co-operation and collaboration of large teams of authors. One could argue that such works are out of fashion. Viewed with the eye of an historian, the idea of universal encyclopaedias was more an eighteenth-century goal. The nineteenth century saw the advent of visionaries such as Otlet and LaFontaine, who wanted to establish a global system for bibliography and a Universal Decimal Classification (UDC) in their Mundaneum.[139] The nineteenth century also developed a wonderful vision of universal classifications and dictionaries (including Thieme-Becker's *Lexicon of Artists*), plus corpora of all the texts in a field such as Max Müller's *Sacred Books of the East* or Eitelberger von Edelberg's *Source Books for Art History*.

The twentieth century continued some of these projects including the *Catalogue of Italian Manuscripts* (which after a century has just reached volume 104), began a few others such as the *Complete Catalogue of Incunabula* (books printed before 1500)[140] or the *Records of Early English Drama* (REED) project, but for the most part became increasingly sceptical with respect to monumental projects. Another explanation is that it produced some 200 million hours of radio and television but was so taken up in the excitement that it did not get around to cataloguing these properly. Some would say that the twentieth century was simply too distracted or even too lazy. To be sure, the tumult of the two world wars, and the even greater tumult of the electronic revolution, provided legitimate explanations or excuses. But now after a century of distractions, after surviving the Y2K fears, perhaps the time has come to explore what computers can really do to help us. In a sense it has already begun.

8. Virtual Libraries

The spirit of open co-operation, which inspired the Internet and later the World Wide Web, has also led to the development of a WWW Virtual Library with fourteen major categories, including education (Table 38). There have been experiments to link these original categories with those of the Library of Congress Classification Scheme.[142] Each of these basic categories is divided and further subdivided to provide access to numerous sites around the world. Each individual topic is maintained by a volunteer expert in their field. Such lists can be linked to a harmonized list that

TABLE 38 Major headings in the WWW Virtual Library.[141]

Agriculture	Information Management
Business and Economics	International Affairs
Computer Science	Law
Communications & Media	Recreation
Education	Regional Studies
Engineering	Science
Humanities	Society

serves as a switching system between multiple classification systems and gives access both to electronic resources existing solely on the web and traditional resources in libraries, museums, and archives.[143] Commercial equivalents of such virtual libraries are also appearing. On 16 November 1999, twelve major scientific and scholarly publishers[144] announced a "market-driven reference-linking initiative to begin in the first quarter of 2000." While the official description of this initiative sounds wonderful indeed,[145] it nonetheless means that only very large libraries able to pay the enormous fees of specialized scientific literature can provide their readers with access to these materials (cf. chapter 13).

There are well-publicized initiatives such as Project Gutenberg, but these are small in scale, involving only a few hundred books.[146] NASA is making thousands and eventually millions of its photographs from space available completely free of cost.[147] There are dramatic projects such as the reconstruction of the Library at Alexandria, but that is about the frontiers of knowledge two millennia ago. The Bibliothèque Nationale is scanning in the full texts of 80,000 books. The Coalition for Networked Information is discussing a project that entails scanning in 10 million texts. On a lesser scale there are hundreds of similar projects throughout the world. Companies such as IBM are engaged in a number of projects at locations such as the Vatican Library, The Luther Library at Wittemberg, and the Catalogo de los Indos in Seville. Lacking thus far are serious attempts on a global level corresponding to earlier visions such as Aby Warburg's *Mnemosyne* or Vannevar Bush's *Memex*.

In the past decade there have been new technologies for scanning materials. We no longer need to copy everything by hand in the manner of the medieval monks. Ironically, however, we face the same challenge that they did: how to copy everything and make commentaries. In the Middle Ages, monks in monasteries patiently set about copying, annotating, and interpreting the whole of recorded civilization. Today's challenge is essentially a digital version of the same. It is too big for a typical project. It is not military, so it will never get the funding that is available for variants of the Star Wars projects. And yet ultimately, what can be more precious than assuring that we have the equivalent of a scrap album for civilization – a key to our collective memory? One idea (Figure 14) is to create a Distributed European Electronic Resource (DEER) as a first step towards a World Online Distributed

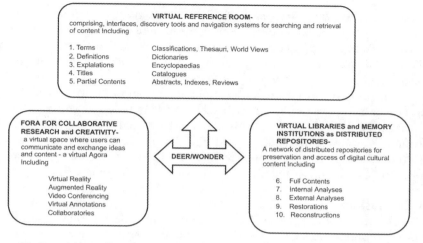

Figure 14 Essential ingredients for a Distributed European Electronic Resource (DEER) as a first step towards a World Online Distributed Resource (WONDER)

Resource (WONDER). This would link distributed repositories (digital libraries), virtual reference rooms, and a virtual agora for collaborative research and creativity. The European Union's quest for Integrated Resource Networks could be seen as an initial step in this direction.

9. Global Databanks and Networks

Meanwhile, there are important initiatives on the part of governments to make accessible public information and to create networks for dissemination of knowledge from scientific fields. At a national level, Canada was, in 1972, the first country to introduce a national network in the cultural area through the Canadian Heritage Information Network (CHIN). Germany was the second country to do so through its Marburg Archive. In 1990, Canada created a Pre-Competitive Advanced Research Network (PRECARN). In Europe, there were some twenty-two networks of centres of excellence in the ESPRIT project alone.[148] In 2000, there were over two hundred European cultural networks, some with minimal, others with considerable, amounts of information as documented by the European project E-Culture Net.[149]

In 1995, the eleven G7 pilot projects marked an attempt to move such efforts to a global level. These included projects on education, libraries, and culture but accomplished less than hoped due to lack of funding. More recently, at the European level, a Memorandum of Understanding for Multimedia Access to Europe's Cultural Heritage and the MEDICI Framework, with its plans for a European Network for Centres of Excellence in Digital Cultural Heritage, outlined a possible vision that has yet to be pursued.[150] The challenge for integration remains.

Essentially we need to use networks to combine a) virtual reference rooms, b) theory from virtual memory institutions in the form of distributed repositories, and c) practice from networked competence centres. This could build on work begun by MEDICI, Cultivate and foreseen by e-Culture Net to create new interoperability of content laboratories and demonstration rooms in the form of virtual agoras (Figure 14). To make this a reality requires a long-term commitment to metadata.[151] In Europe, the European Commission already has a long-term Network of Excellence for Digital Libraries (DELOS).[152] This needs to be extended to include a) memory institutions and b) universities, in order to deal properly with cultural and historical dimensions. Recently, the European Commission's increasing attention to a European Research Area suggests that this vision could become a reality.

10. Conclusions

Collaboration is nothing new and yet the Internet has opened entirely new dimensions to collaboration. This is due partly to the theoretical framework provided by the Delphi method and the ideas of thinkers such as Vannevar Bush and Douglas Engelbart. From the time of Aristotle, action at a distance has been a philosophical problem. The Internet has made action at a distance a reality through tele-activity.[153] There are also collaboratories, whereby whole teams of persons can work together at a distance. These are pointing to a new vision of computational grids whereby regular computers and large numbers of supercomputers will eventually be linked in a seamless network. Some continue to see this in terms of power politics. As one of the U.S. labs put it recently: "The intellectual challenge presented by environmental stewardship is at least as great as that presented by the Manhattan Project in the 1940s and the space race in the 1960s and 1970s – and so is the potential payoff."[154]

At another level, however, the challenges of computational grids are so great that the United States, Europe, and Japan are already collaborating. As a result, the power of the world's greatest supercomputers will be combined in future. Billions of dollars are being invested in all this. One of the unexpected fringe benefits thereof is a more general infrastructure that can ultimately serve everyone, just as what began as the ARPAnet is now becoming an Internet for everyone.

Ironically, a project without real funding has demonstrated a principle more sensational than any of these international initiatives with billions of dollars. SETI, a volunteer project, confirms that everyday computers, when harnessed together, working only in their spare time, already generate the same orders of teraflops as the world's largest supercomputer. If this principle were extended, one could readily have available computing power far in excess of all the supercomputers of the world. This means that a computational grid for everyman is now possible. If this were combined with the trends towards virtual libraries and integrated with global databanks and networks, miraculous things would be possible. We need a cultural as well as a scientific grid.[155]

12
enduring knowledge

Where is the wisdom we have lost in knowledge? Where is the knowledge we have lost in information?
— T.S. Eliot, *The Rock* (1934).

1. Introduction

Much of personal and collaborative knowledge (chapters 10–11) is about the day-to-day. By contrast, enduring knowledge,[1] or perennial knowledge as it is called in the Far East, concerns what is stored in our memory collections (libraries, museums, and archives). Enduring knowledge covers a great spectrum.[2] It includes facts, the so-called eternal truths, in terms of mathematics, philosophy, and science. It also includes fiction, where truth is not a criterion. Hence, enduring knowledge is frequently seen as part of a spectrum ranging from bytes to wisdom (Table 39).

TABLE 39 Differences between information, knowledge, and wisdom.

UNIT	DEFINITION	GRAMMATICAL EQUIVALENT
Bytes	Random 0s and 1s	Letter
Data	Ordered Bytes	Word
Information	Ordered Data	Phrase
Knowledge	Organized Information	Logical Sentences
Wisdom	Humane Knowledge	Valuable Sentences

While knowledge management is primarily concerned with know-how in organizations, knowledge organization is concerned with the structure of knowledge itself. Individuals have been concerned with knowledge organization ever since the first libraries were established thousands of years ago,[3] and this has led to new professions especially in the past century (Appendix 2), with an attendant danger that the wheel is constantly being re-invented.

Ever since Gutenberg, print media have been our primary method for codifying enduring knowledge. This remains true, although the past century brought radio and television, and the past decades have brought multimedia. Marshall McLuhan made us aware that storing knowledge in a given medium affects our treatment and conception of that knowledge: the container affects the contents. Hence, print led to a greater emphasis on the logic (dialectic) of language than on its structure (grammar) and its effects (rhetoric), whereas the advent of television shifted greater attention to effects.

Print, McLuhan taught us, is linear. A consequence of this insight, which McLuhan did not explore, is that print gives us the equivalent of a static snapshot of knowledge at a given time. To take a simple example: in his time, Linnaeus was the world expert on plants. His print version gave a snapshot of what he knew then. Fifty years later, the list of plants had grown. Such a list continues to change even now as new species continue to be discovered and in some cases are produced. We could observe the same process in the case of all things animal, mineral, and vegetable, and indeed also in the conceptual world. In short, knowledge is dynamic. Printed knowledge only captures static snapshots of this dynamic process.

Theoretically, we could print all the snapshots together, but in practice the limitations of publishing make it unrealistic to do so in any single text. Alternatively, we could set all those static snapshots side by side and then we would be able to trace how changes occur in knowledge, how fields grow, etc. This is exactly what the great libraries of the world try to do. But while such a goal is simple and obvious, no library in the world has managed to get everything in one place. Alexandria claimed to have done so, but it burned. And ultimately even Alexandria specialized in the knowledge of the Middle East, not the world. Completely centralized contents do not work.

The networked computer revolution offers new possibilities with respect to these age-old problems. First, computational grids (chapter 11) suggest how a distributed system can provide access to all knowledge. Indeed, the major library projects of the past decades such as PICA, RLIN, OCLC, GABRIEL, and the major national catalogues can be seen as pilot projects in this direction, even though their emphasis has been on author and title catalogues. A next stage would be to include a complete range of reference materials and full contents. These experiences have brought to light one further prerequisite. Distributed systems can only work if they share metadata.

How much is a matter of discussion. For instance, the Dublin Core believes it can be reduced to fifteen fields. The Dublin Core is standardizing fields: only containers but not contents. Agreeing on field names such that one can integrate the fields for creator, author, painter, and composer is a vital first step.[4] It creates categories for interoperability. But this is not yet interoperability of content. We can both agree on the field creator, but if you put in the name Vinci, Leonardo da, while I write Leonardo da Vinci, unless there is a centralized authority file that establishes that these are the same person, we still cannot share our resources. We also need centralized authority files for names, places, titles, etc.[5]

Electronic documents on computer screens may look like pages of books but do not have their limitations. Hence, all the snapshots of knowledge on plants, which cannot fit into a single book, can fit on a large electronic storage device. If this were then reorganized in database form, alphabetically, chronologically, spatially, linguistically, then we could have dynamic knowledge about plants or, for that matter, on any other subject. As we have seen, there are various projects to scan in the full contents of physical libraries and make them available in digital form. There is increasing excitement about the advantages of these new digital libraries: less wear and tear on the physical book, ability to consult it at a distance without burdening the physical book with the stress of travel. Much more is possible. We see four stages to reach a context that fully exploits the potentials of knowledge in digital form.

In a first stage, the reference rooms of libraries[6] can be seen as the search methods of the collective memory of "mankind." Needed are electronic versions in the form of virtual reference rooms. These will create digital links with existing reference materials in order to gain new access to information in memory institutions. These virtual reference rooms will serve as new kinds of finding aids and will need to be linked to evolving digital libraries in the form of distributed repositories.

In a second stage, there is a challenge of relating such finding aids (in the form of virtual reference rooms) to new methods of textual analysis and to integrate them with Internet efforts such as domain names and the Resource Description Framework (RDF). Here we are fortunate that the last decades have seen a number of developments with respect to systematic markup of the full contents of books

TABLE 40 Basic levels of knowledge in a System for Universal Multi-Media Access (SUMMA).

TYPE OF KNOWLEDGE		LEVELS	EXAMPLES
Reference	1	Names, Concepts, Terms	Classification Systems
(Pointers)	2	Definitions	Dictionaries
	3	Explanations	Encyclopaedias
	4	Titles	Catalogues, Bibliographies
	5	Partial Contents	Abstracts, Indexes
Objects *(Primary Sources)*	6	Full Contents	Books, Paintings, etc.
Interpretations	7	Internal Analyses	Critical Editions
(Secondary Sources)	8	External Analyses	Comparative Studies
	9	Restorations	X-Ray Reflectography
	10	Reconstructions	Virtual Reality

and articles (e.g., SGML, XML, RDF). These allow new methods of textual analysis[7] and are already beginning to find their use in digital libraries.

In a third stage, we need to use the latest principles of knowledge organization to restructure our classification systems, thesauri, and reference works and thus develop new kinds of virtual reference rooms to provide a next generation of finding aids. This will lead, in a fourth stage to new kinds of dynamic knowledge, which take into account historical and cultural implications of knowledge. Implicit herein is a virtual reorganization of knowledge, which will require new methods of abstraction to create new overviews and lead to new concepts of augmented books, knowledge, and culture. The digital revolution thus requires much more than scanning campaigns. It calls for a virtual reorganization of the whole of knowledge. There follows a preliminary sketch of what this entails.

2. Virtual Reference Rooms[8]

In very simple terms, our memory institutions are about three things. First, memory institutions have developed a number of reference works, which serve as pointers to content. Second, they contain the objects of knowledge itself, contents: from dinosaur bones and vases to paintings and drawings, letters and books. In the library world, we call these primary sources. Third, memory institutions link these primary sources (dinosaur bones, etc.) with what we know about them in the form of secondary sources or interpretations. These lead to some further distinctions such that we can reasonably speak of ten levels of knowledge[9] (Table 40, figures 16–17).

Historically, there has been a tendency to put the objects in specialized institutions such as local museums, natural history, ethnological, crafts, science, maritime, musical instruments, war, and other museums and archives. The reference materials and the details of interpretations about the objects have often gone to libraries. While it makes little sense to abandon all our present physical museums, there is a challenge to integrate knowledge from wherever it exists in order to optimize our museums, archives, and libraries in their role as memory institutions. This requires changes in our approach to reference, objects, and interpretations.

The reference rooms of libraries typically contain five kinds of materials: 1) names, concepts, and their terms (classification systems and thesauri), 2) definitions (dictionaries), 3) explanations (encyclopaedias), 4) titles (catalogues, bibliographies), and 5) partial contents (abstracts, reviews, indexes). Digital libraries initially focussed on aspects of level one (namely, author catalogues, sometimes subject catalogues) and level four (in the form of electronic title catalogues). A virtual reference room needs to integrate all five of these levels and relate them to objects (level 6) and interpretations (levels 7–10).

Classifications

As Samurin[10] has shown in his standard history of the field, attempts at structuring knowledge were traditionally discipline-based, often using categories of the seven liberal arts as their point of departure. Under these disciplines, divisions and subdivisions were typically made on an ad hoc basis. Hence, in retrospect, the great library classification systems such as Göttingen, Dewey, and Library of Congress are haphazard from a systematic point of view. Even so, as a first step, there is much to be gained by mapping terms in one system to equivalents and near equivalents in another. This is exactly what major European projects such as TermIT,[11] DESIRE,[12] ERGO,[13] and Renardus[14] have begun to do.[15]

Definitions

A next stage in the process will be to link concepts and their terms in classification systems with definitions in dictionaries. Quicktionaries, new pen-like devices, can recognize any word on a page and find its definition. Quicktionaries assume that the dictionary is on-site. In a next stage, the pen-like device will simply be a wireless device that connects with large-scale, offsite dictionaries and makes their contents available.

In the bigger picture, every term in a classification system will automatically be hyperlinked to appropriate dictionaries. User profiles will instruct agents to determine what is appropriate. For instance, a child will receive a simpler definition. An English university student might get a definition from the *Shorter Oxford*, as a default. If this is insufficient, they will be free to go to the full *Oxford English Dictionary*. Similarly, a French student will get a preliminary definition from Larousse, a German student from Duden, etc. These were problems addressed in a project of the European Commission called IMASS (Maastricht, Pisa, Rome, and Vienna).[16] Philips is also working on a smart walls and ambient intelligence that will help to make the functionalities of a reference room available in the classroom, at home, and eventually everywhere.

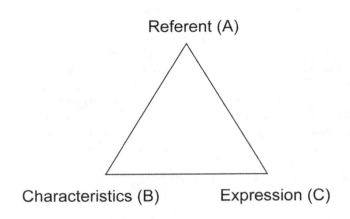

Referent (A)

Characteristics (B)   Expression (C)

Figure 15   Dahlberg's three components in a conceptual triangle

More is required. The pioneers of modern terminology (Wüster) and knowledge organization (e.g., Diemer, Dahlberg) discovered that there is a basic distinction to be made between isolated words in natural language and formal concepts. Dahlberg, for instance, has shown that definitions of concepts entail three elements (Figure 15): *A*, Referent; *B*, Characteristics, and *C*, Expression. Changing relations among these three elements determine the kind of definition. These can be ostensive (when $C = A$), nominal (when $C = B$) or real definitions (when $C = B$ from A).[17]

Hence, when I point to a man and say: "That is a man," I am giving an ostensive definition. This also applies when I point to a picture of a man. A picture may be worth a thousand words, but the picture does not explain itself. It remains the equivalent of an ostensive definition, unless I already know what it represents beforehand. When I describe a man as having a head and two feet, I am providing some characteristics as in a nominal definition. Another person can then describe a man as having two arms and reproductive organs, which includes other character-istics and is also a nominal definition. Both of these nominal definitions are correct but remain incomplete. By contrast, a real definition encompasses all the character-istics of a man, including, a head, two arms, two legs, and reproductive organs.

The extent to which such a real definition is objectively possible differs in the sciences and the humanities. In the sciences, there is a quest to find one real defini-tion independent of time, space, and culture. We expect the real definition of zinc to have the same properties in the United States, Europe, and everywhere else in the world. In the humanities, by contrast, cultural and historical variants are central to such real definitions. For instance, a Japanese real definition of poetry (such as *haiku*) can differ considerably from a French, German, or English real definition of poetry. Even in such cases, however, the quest for a real definition saves us many unnecessary fights. Indeed, a failure to distinguish between these three kinds of definitions was one of the reasons why nominalism led to such fights in the fourteenth century. More recently, this has led to related fights under fancier names such as constructivism, deconstructionism, and post-modernism.

All this has three important implications. First, our existing dictionaries have been constructed without these distinctions between ostensive, nominal, and real. If all existing definitions are re-arranged by these criteria, there will be far less ambiguity. Also needed is a cross-referencing between words in various dictionaries, and ultimately across languages. Here the work of the Electronic Dictionary Research Institute in Japan offers one example of how one might proceed.[18]

Second, the above implies that a concept cannot be understood simply as natural language in the sense of being treated as a word in isolation. Referents have uses that may be written or oral. They may or may not be linked with or based on standard dictionaries (e.g., the *Oxford English Dictionary* in the case of English) and may also have a number of cultural and historical variants. This is often forgotten. Hence when Americans say "Have a nice day," they are surprised by some English reactions because they are unaware that nice can also mean "slothful" and "immoral."

While dictionaries and other reference works are our main methods of determining formal meaning, this cannot exhaust all the possibilities of personal meaning and significance surrounding a word. For example, a dictionary can tell me that Rome is the capital of Italy. An atlas can show me where Rome is. An encyclopaedia can give me much more information about its seven hills, how many inhabitants it has, but all of these combined cannot capture the magic of memories of important experiences there.

Ultimately we need a new organization of knowledge that indicates level of definition, whether the agreement about a term is local, regional, national, or international. At the local level, we need further distinctions between a) terminological meaning (with domain-specific semantics where meanings of contents have been negotiated locally), b) dictionary meaning (formal meaning), c) corpus (written, not formalized), d) oral recorded (archived, not written), and e) oral (not systematically archived).[19]

There is a third, basic consequence of these different kinds of definitions. Knowledge is about organized information: distinguishing between words and concepts, distinguishing between different kinds of definitions, including cultural and historical variants, and especially, organizing knowledge in terms of relations. Without such distinctions, the difference between information and knowledge disappears.[20] Here again there are important differences between American, European, and Japanese approaches (chapter 14).

Encyclopaedias

Major encyclopaedias such as Britannica, Larousse, and Brockhaus are already available on-line. This is an important first step. In the future, every entry in these encyclopaedias can be hyperlinked back through the same term in dictionaries and classification systems, and since these also function as subject catalogues, each entry in an encyclopaedia can be hyperlinked with the full, primary and secondary literature relating to that entry. Eventually, one could go even further and apply the every word hypertext feature mentioned earlier,[21] leading to omni-linked texts.

Titles

The hyperlinks need to be extended from classifications (level one) downwards to include titles (level four). However, titles are more problematic for two reasons. First, there is a tradition of standard titles, short titles, and long titles. In cases such as Tolstoy's *War and Peace*, this brings no unexpected problems. In the seventeenth century, however, full titles were often an entire page long, in which case the corresponding standard title and short title is not always clear and a master file is needed. A second reason involves the various versions of a title in different languages. Hence, Alberti's *Della pittura* is *De pictura* in Latin, *On Painting* in English, *Traktat von der Malerei* in German, and *O Malarstwie* in Polish.

The Library of Congress catalogue lists all titles alphabetically under author. Under this system, one book by Alberti becomes spread out amongst all his other works. A future system will let us choose a title, see how many editions it had, and if desired by language, chronologically or geographically, by place of publication. If one uses the categories already in existence in the MARC (Machine Readable Record Cards) records to their full advantage, this problem can be solved.

Partial Contents

At present, partial contents are mainly of two kinds. One is linked with the book itself in the form of tables of contents and indexes. Another is external to the original in the form of abstracts and reviews. We have separate books to indicate these abstracts and reviews. In future, agents can simply trace all such abstracts and reviews (level 5 in Figure 16) and hyperlink them automatically with levels one to four. Hence, if I come across a title, I can discover immediately what reviews were available, and if I so wish, I can read them using a fixed or a mobile device. Further information on the partial contents of books is frequently found in learned monographs and commentaries in secondary literature with their own indexes usually established under different principles than those in the primary literature. Hence, the virtual reference room must eventually contain hyperlinks to materials not presently situated in physical reference rooms.

Implicit in the above is a new approach to reference materials as a whole. In the past, reference rooms contained a whole range of resources (1–5 as outlined in Figure 16). In a traditional library, I would consult a classification scheme to study related terms and use what I found to check another part of the subject catalogue. Or possibly, I might check the definition of a subject term and then go back to the subject catalogue. In a virtual reference room, all of these individual levels are linked, and I can thus go from any of the levels to re-enter my search mode.

In a traditional library, each time I wished to consult a new source, I had to open some other book, often with its own idiosyncratic methods of organization. Given a virtual reference room where all these works are linked through common authority lists, which reflect historical and cultural dimensions of knowledge, I can go from a term to a definition, an explanation, a list of authors, titles, to partial contents (abstracts and reviews), to full text without leaving my desktop or notepad. At a very practical level initial steps have already been taken in the direction of virtual reference rooms.[22] Hence, electronic media will transform physical reference rooms into virtual reference rooms and thus change the way we point to contents.

New Approach to Standards

All this is transforming our approach to standards. The nineteenth century developed an ideal of standards, the notion of authority files, and made it seem that the challenge was to persuade everyone to use the official spelling of a name. The good news was that everyone who followed this approach could exchange information efficiently. The bad news was that this approach excluded everyone else and blocked access to all variant spellings of the same name.

The twentieth century revealed that in many ways the nineteenth-century ideals were too optimistic: that complete consensus even on the fields of MARC (Machine Readable Card) records was not possible. But surely there were a few fields about which everyone could agree? The Dublin Core efforts revealed that even this limited application of the top-down approach was not universally acceptable. Gradually those in technology realized that the way ahead is not to force everyone to change their practices to fit the technology but rather to adjust the technology to fit persons' different practices.

Standards that bring authority files remain important but need to be complemented by tables that record all the variants of those names. As a result, local, regional, national, and international variants of names of persons and places can be used and one can still arrive at the proper co-reference. Philosophically this is of profound importance because it means that standards no longer threaten (cultural) diversity. Standards plus variants can help diversity to prosper.

The philosophy that combines authority files for names with their variant names can readily be extended to languages. For example, the original language of a text can be the authority file and translations in different languages function as variant names. To take a concrete example: this means that a Hungarian can type in the title "A festészetről" and arrive at a standard name of "De pictura" (On Painting) without needing to know how to spell the title in Latin or in English. Conversely, this means that an English-speaking person can find Hungarian titles without knowing how to spell in that language.

This simple philosophical breakthrough thus has major technological and political consequences. There are over 6,500 languages in the world and no one can be expected to learn them all. Technologically it implies that we can create a semantic web that reflects the diversity of the world's languages and cultures. Politically this means that instead of threatening linguistic and cultural diversity, a global Internet can foster their growth and development. It also means that standards for mapping between various distributed databases become ever-more significant. Politically and technologically this also means that virtual reference rooms are becoming a necessity. The old standards were top-down and imposed by centralized bodies. The new standards are necessarily bottom-up and need to connect local, regional, and national.

3. Content Analysis

Electronic media will also transform our ways of dealing with the objects in our memory institutions, both in terms of their visible contents (cf. chapter 6) and their verbal contents. Besides the fact that on-line digital copies of books can be read anywhere, electronic media have two basic implications for verbal contents. First, they introduce a new stage in the story of separating form and content. Second, they enable new levels of hypertext such as conceptual hypermedia.[23] This approach (also called semantic indexing) uses a "semantic index layer in its model of hypermedia architecture" and typically entails thesaurus-based access to collections.[24] This has led also to the rise of topic maps,[25] which now entail companies such as empolis,[26] InfoLoom,[27] Modeca[28] and Ontopia.[29]

Content and Form

Aristotle distinguished between content (substance) and form (accidents). One of the important developments of the new media has been to separate form and content electronically. One of the great pioneers in this domain was Claude E. Shannon (1916–2001) who worked at Bell Labs (now Lucent) and was later professor at MIT (Cambridge, Mass.). One of Shannon's[30] fundamental goals was to separate "the technical problem of delivering a message from understanding what a message means"[31]: to separate form from content. To this end he introduced the idea of **bi**nary un**its** or bits. By using bits, one could communicate words without worrying about their meanings.

The latest efforts of the W3 Consortium to produce a semantic web extend this quest. In terms of the *trivium*, this amounts to separating the rules for structure (grammar) from the rules for logic (dialectic or meaning) and for style and effects (rhetoric). This applies to objects, words, images, and sounds. In the case of objects, this separation of a basic object from the forms in which it is expressed has led to the development of Industry Foundation Classes (IFC, cf. chapter 4). In the case of words, this separation of content and form goes back before the time of the Internet, when manufacturers faced an unexpected dilemma. In the past, every product was accompanied by an instruction and repair manual. By the 1960s, the repair books for a large jet were so big that, if loaded on board, the jet could not take off. Similarly, those of an aircraft carrier were so enormous that, if placed on deck, the ship would sink. An electronic version thus became a necessity.

There was a problem, moreover, that the basic information in these repair manuals frequently needed to be displayed in alternative forms for users at various professional levels and with different needs. This led to the development of Standard Generalized Markup Language (SGML), which separated content from form in order to reduce the costs of printing different versions for various audiences.[32] In the scholarly world, SGML also led to projects such as the Dictionary of Old English (DOE) and the Records of Early English Drama (REED)[33] and later the Oxford Text Archive and the Text Encoding Initiative (TEI).

In the eyes of the world, the introduction of HyperText Markup Language (HTML), in 1989, marked a revolutionary step forward, because it made the World Wide Web an almost instant reality. From a technical standpoint, it marked a step backwards insofar as this interim solution conflated anew content and form. As a result any change in the form of an HTML document, required re-writing the entire contents of the document. While the earlier SGML remains valid and perfectly suited for repair manuals of aircraft carriers, it is far too complex for everyday use. The World Wide Web (W3) Consortium thus developed XML, (which can be seen as a subset of SGML), better suited to the needs of everyday use, called eXtensible Markup Language (XML). This provides a common denominator for regular content. Specialist users are writing extensions such as Chemical Markup Language (CML), Mathematical Markup Language (MML),[34] International Development Markup Language (IDML),[35] and Genetic Expression Markup Language (GEML).[36] XML deals with content; XSL (eXtensible Style Language)[37] deals with form, i.e., different styles and versions of expression of that content (cf. Appendix 7). One of the dilemmas has been a proliferation of markup languages for a wide range of fields and disciplines, including systems biology, theological, financial products, speech synthesis, and quest markup language (for adventure games).

Images and Sounds

The W3 Consortium has set out to do the same for images, i.e., to separate the basic content of an image from the various versions or styles in which it is expressed. Scaleable Vector Graphics (SVG)[39] will replace various two-dimensional (e.g., TIFF) proprietary solutions with an open standard. SVG will do for images what XML did for words and as such is seen as a next step in the "XMLification" of the web. The X3D Consortium will extend this to three-dimensional software.

Although not yet included within the formal plans of the W3 Consortium, a similar trend is discernible for sounds. There is already a Standardized Music Description Language (SDML). Music software typically allows one to separate content (notes) from the styles in which it is played. An obvious consequence of all this is that the W3 consortium is gradually creating an electronic equivalent of the ancient seven liberal arts, with its trivium (grammar, dialectic, and rhetoric) and quadrivium (geometry, arithmetic, astronomy, and music, Table 41). More important consequences of this separation of content and form concern a new approach to universals and particulars (cf. chapter 14).

TABLE 41 The seven liberal arts and their equivalents in the Internet[38]

Grammar	Structure, Syntax	Extensible Markup Language	XML
Dialectic	Logic, Semantics	Resource Description Framework	RDF
Rhetoric	Effects, Style, Pragmatics	Extensible Style Language	XSL
Geometry	Continuous Quantity	Mathematical Markup Language	MML
Arithmetic	Discrete Quantity	Mathematical Markup Language	MML
Astronomy	Applied Continuous Quantity	Astronomical Markup Language	AML
Music	Applied Discrete Quantity	Standardized Music Description Language	SMDL

Hypertext

Hypertext[40] was one of the ideas that helped to inspire the Internet. It was implicitly described by Vannevar Bush in his pioneering article, "As we may think" (1945)[41] and was developed by Douglas Engelbart,[42] who coined the term "text link," linked the concepts of hypertext and multimedia to create the term "hypermedia" and later "open hyperdocument systems." The term "hypertext"[43] as such was coined by Ted Nelson, who defined it in *Literary Machines* as "non-sequential writing."[44] Nelson also drew attention to what he termed the framing problem of ordinary hypertext and in his Xanadu system accordingly called for a universal hypermedia environment. As to the origins of the concept, Nelson claimed: "The hypertext is a fundamental document of Jewish religion and culture and the Talmudic scholar is one who knows many of its pathways."[45] In Nelson's vision, everything can be linked with everything. On the positive side, this introduces enormous freedom. Indeed, his quest to create tables that can easily be re-configured is a brilliant contribution. On the negative side, this approach can create a complete spaghetti effect qua connections. If everything leads to everything else, one cannot see the big picture or the frameworks for understanding due to the unbelievable complexity of links, which Nelson terms the "intertwingledness" of things.

Particularly attractive in Nelson's vision is the potential for all users effectively to become authors, something that the World Wide Web has effectively made a reality. Attractive as all this seems, it also introduces unexpected problems. A good author must be a good organizer of knowledge. Everyone becoming an author does not yet mean that everyone is necessarily a good organizer of knowledge. In practice, many individuals with no experience of organizing knowledge are now presenting their materials on the web. This is a major reason why web sites and the Internet as a whole pose such problems qua navigation.[46]

Fortunately these problems of a disorganized web are so universally recognized that a number of improvements are being explored. Major publishers are developing Cross-Ref, which is useful but depends on the use of Digital Object Identifiers (DOI),[47] requires membership in Publishers International Linking Association

(PILA),[48] and has links determined by publishers' preferences for which they pay. One limitation of CrossRef is that it is primarily to link titles of articles with full-text copies. A more subtle danger is that this initiative shifts metadata efforts into the private sphere. As John Erickson (HP) recently put it: "Metadata is the life-blood of e-commerce."[49] Metadata is ultimately also our only hope for public access to information across the board and should therefore not be controlled by private interests alone.

The library world has developed SFX.[50] Meanwhile, the W3 Consortium has developed an XML Linking Working Group to design advanced, scalable, and maintainable hyperlinking and addressing functionality for XML.[51] Authors such as Jakob Nielsen and Robert Horn have provided a useful brief history of the Internet with respect to hypertext approaches[52] and have also developed the idea of information mapping.[53] Horn, for instance, outlined a method for navigating through structured hypertrails (i.e., sequences of hypertext trails), which he divided into nine kinds: prerequisite, classification, chronological, geographical, project, structural, decision, definition, and example. This offered a first helpful glimpse of a more systematic approach to the potentially infinite connections.[54]

In Horn's hypertrails, the chronological approach is one of nine alternatives. In our view, the chronological dimension potentially applies to every hypertrail, i.e., maps have a history, structures have a history, definitions have a history, etc.[55] Similarly the geographical dimension can apply to all the hypertrails. Structures in China are frequently different than structures in the United States.[56] It is also useful to identify different levels of hypertrails, i.e., single terms as in classifications; a few terms/words as in definitions, etc. (cf. Figure 16). We shall pursue this theme below under dynamic knowledge after exploring how hypertext affects indexing and interpretations.

Retrospective Indexing

Some books have indexes. Many do not. A more systematic use of hypertext has implications for indexing. A first scenario: I am reading a book on the history of physics, which has no index (as is often the case particularly with French books). I come across the name Galileo and would like to know how often this name occurs in the book. The pen-like object scans the name, conveys it to my notepad, which translates it into a request, checks the on-line version of the book, and relays to my notepad all the occasions within the book where the name of Galileo is cited. This is effectively a first step towards retrospective indexing or indexing on demand. Alternatively, I can use new algorithms to omni-link the book.

A second scenario: From the title of a work, my handheld or desktop computer determines that it is a book about physics. An agent then goes to an authority list of all names and culls a subset of all names of physicists. This list is then used as a master list against which to check every name mentioned in the book. At the end of this exercise, the agent has a subset of this master list, which represents an index of all

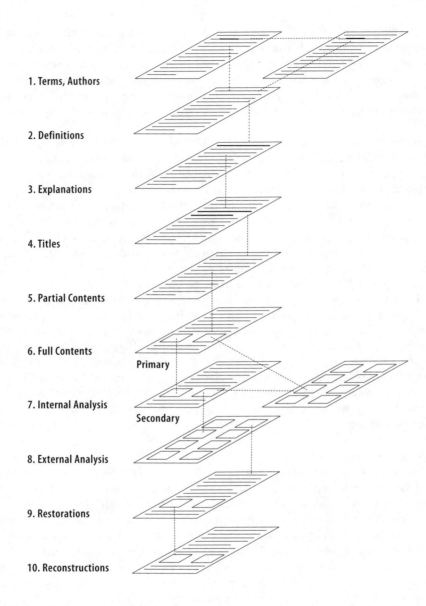

1. Terms, Authors

2. Definitions

3. Explanations

4. Titles

5. Partial Contents

6. Full Contents

Primary

7. Internal Analysis

Secondary

8. External Analysis

9. Restorations

10. Reconstructions

Figure 16 Ten levels of knowledge. Connections between reference levels (a term, a definition, an explanation, a list of authors, titles, partial contents as in abstracts and reviews) and full text, links between primary and secondary literature and different kinds of content, namely, internal analyses, external analyses, restorations, and reconstructions.

the names of physicists within this given book. A similar approach can be applied to subjects, places, etc. In the case of more famous books, which exist in various editions of which some have indexes, agents can then compare their own lists with these existing indexes in order to arrive at more comprehensive indexing.

The professional indexer and library scientist will rightly insist that such techniques are never as profound as the indexing skills of human professionals in the field. On the other hand, in a world with 7 million new pages a day, there are never likely to be enough professional indexers to index retrospectively all the hundreds of millions of existing old books. In such a non-ideal world, limited methods are considerably better than nothing.

A fundamental claim of professional indexers is that simply making a list of all the words in a text may produce a concordance but not a proper index. The radical form of this claim states that even the author of a text is incapable of indexing properly their own work.[57] What is needed, argue these indexers, is a careful analysis of the text to determine the underlying concepts or processes, which are often not directly listed in the text. Say the book is about botany and there is discussion of *papaveraceae*. At other times, there is discussion about poppies. Only an expert indexer who is also familiar with botanical classification will know that poppies belong to the *papaveraceae* family.

Major reference rooms contain our knowledge about classification systems, thesauri, and other methods of ordering subjects and processes. If these are available digitally through a virtual reference room, other possibilities emerge. I identify the term "poppy," which is relayed to the virtual reference room. The word is identified as a botanical term, an appropriate botanical classification is found, and I am shown on my notepad the relation of poppies to the *papaveraceae* family. Or conversely, I am reading about the *papaveraceae* family and wonder what actual plants or flowers belong to this family. By a similar process, the virtual reference room can show me that poppies are an example of this family.

Interpretations

As noted above, the contents of a library are traditionally seen in terms of: 1) primary sources and 2) secondary literature that discusses these texts. In terms of memory institutions, primary sources are the original objects, which can be anything from books and paintings to vases and dinosaurs. Secondary literature contains descriptions and different interpretations about these objects. These interpretations vary considerably and four basic levels suggest themselves: a) internal analyses of the object itself as in the close reading of a text: What does Hamlet mean in act three, scene two?, b) external analyses when an object is compared to related objects: How does Shakespeare's *Hamlet* compare with other literary descriptions of princes feigning madness?, c) restorations, when the object has built into it the interpretation of a restorer, and d) reconstructions, when the object has built into it the interpretations of the persons who reconstructed it. Electronic media have brought

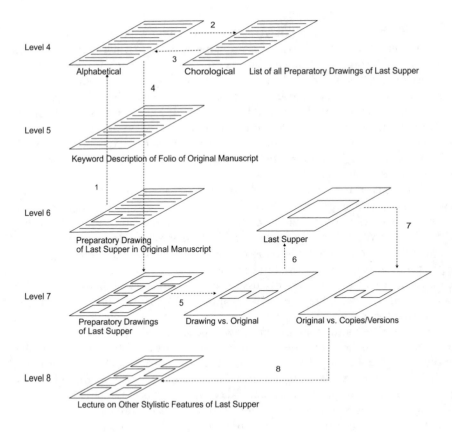

Level 4   2   3
Alphabetical   Chorological   List of all Preparatory Drawings of Last Supper

4

Level 5
Keyword Description of Folio of Original Manuscript

1

Level 6
Preparatory Drawing
of Last Supper in Original Manuscript   Last Supper   7

6

Level 7
Preparatory Drawings   5   Drawing vs. Original   Original vs. Copies/Versions
of Last Supper

8

Level 8
Lecture on Other Stylistic Features of Last Supper

Figure 17 Connections between different levels of reference, contents and interpretation: a folio from a primary text (level 6); titles in alphabetical and chronological lists (level 4); preparatory drawings in a secondary source (level 7), internal analysis (level 7), and external analyses (level 8)

these distinctions into focus. If we link these levels with those discussed earlier, we arrive at ten levels of knowledge (Figure 16). Within these levels there will be further distinctions between publication types (e.g. dissertation, book, journal, magazine, newspaper) and media types (e.g. documentary film, video, television, Internet) to permit further subtlety in searching. At any stage within these levels materials can be searched alphabetically, geographically and chronologically.

In traditional physical libraries, such distinctions between levels of knowledge are impractical qua arranging books on shelves. In digital libraries, a systematic use of agents in connection with hypertext can distinguish between these various levels and, potentially, go much further. Within internal analyses, for instance, some works describe an object in scientific terms ("fact" or non-fiction); others use the object as a basis for their own speculations. Still others use the object as a point of departure for fiction or poetry. Agents using hyperlinks can separate these different kinds of interpretation and link them in turn with the reputation of the author, informing me whether they were a local amateur or an international authority in their field. This is the idea of Tim Berners-Lee, of a semantic web, separating rhyme from reason, applied not only to contemporary knowledge on the web, but extended to the enduring knowledge of memory institutions.

This approach using levels of knowledge can also transform our search engines.[58] If one examines the results of today's major systems such as Google, Altavista, or Hotbot, one sees that they list results indiscriminately: HTML headers (electronic versions of titles, level 4), definitions (level 2), texts (level 6), commentaries (level 7) are all jumbled together. Even if Google or Altavista presented today's findings systematically by levels of knowledge, it would already be a great help. Just think what would happen if they did it properly. The technology is there; we simply need to apply it methodically.

One can readily imagine going much further still. There is already work on authoring interactive stories using virtual identities[59] and cyber-narratives. In the past generation literary critics and increasingly historians have become attentive to different narrative styles. These have been linked to both theories of perspective and to psychological frame theories. As the rules of grammar (structure or syntax), dialectic (logic or semantics), and rhetoric (style and effect) become fully translated in electronic form, it will be possible to group authors who followed a particular literary style (Ciceronian, Dickensian, etc.). It will even become possible to write new histories of literature in terms of relative complexity of viewpoints: whether a historical text or a novel is entirely first person, whether it shifts from first to third, how often, how precisely, and so on (cf. chapter 13).

This will completely change the way we deal with books and with knowledge as a whole. If I am browsing a shelf of books, or a list of titles, I simply ask the contextualizer to decide on the level of a book. In some cases, of course, the con-textualizer can also provide preliminary suggestion lists as personal profiles already do at a much more personal level. The bad news is that this requires a) not just linking existing reference materials but creating new reference structures as a next step leading to a complete virtual reorganization of the contents of our memory institutions. The books can stay where they are, but the reference pointers to them and the contents of the books need to be restructured. Some will say this is actually good news. It means that academics and indeed all of us still have much to do.

4. New Reference Structures

Towards the end of the nineteenth century, Paul Otlet and Henri Lafontaine realized that many of the categories of classification systems were too superficial and that one could make progress if one had more precise categories. They persuaded John

Melvyl Dewey to let them do this. They founded the Mundaneum (Brussels, now moved to Mons) and thus emerged the Universal Decimal Classification (UDC), which subsequently came under the auspices of the International Federation for Information and Documentation (FID, in the Hague). In the course of the twentieth century, it was also realized that classification systems can fruitfully be seen in terms of relations. Indeed, a significant part of what we know is reflected in how precisely we are able to establish systematic relations among things. If one starts from scratch once more, it will be important to integrate relations. At this stage, in the interests of clarity, a small historical excursus is needed.

Categories and Relations

Aristotle distinguished between substance and (nine) accidents. Dahlberg renamed Aristotle's substance as entities and classed Aristotle's nine accidents, quality, etc., under properties, activities, and dimensions.[60] Aristotle included relation as one of his accidents. Dahlberg explored relation more systematically and distinguished four kinds of material relations, namely, abstraction (is a), partition (is a part of, has a), opposition (is not), and functional or syntactic. In terms of the above, relations link substance or matter via activities with properties and dimensions. Herein lie also the basics of grammar.

As Dahlberg noted, material relations of abstraction, partition, and opposition have a long history, with their roots in classical logic where they were called divisio, partitio, and oppositio, respectively. Opposition is as old as disagreement. The abstraction relation is basic for taxonomy in botany and biology. The partition relation plays a fundamental role in medical classification of the human body. While abstraction and partition relations have inspired many persons to new study in the past century, most of these were unaware of the history of the field. As a result, various communities have developed different names for the same concepts, leading to a Babel-like situation.[61] At the risk of sounding pedantic, it is useful to give some examples. Hence an abstraction relation begins with an entity (noun) combined with an intransitive verb (being in the form of is a) and a predicate (namely the entity with which it is being equated). An opposition relation is a negation of the foregoing.

A partition relation begins with an entity (noun) combined with a transitive verb (having in the form of has a) and an object. A functional or syntactic relation begins with an entity (noun) combined with a transitive verb (action, suffering) and an object. Here the predicate includes a verb, object (as well as properties and dimensions).[62] On the surface, this sounds very much like an entity relationship, which uses logic as its point of departure and entails a subject and predicate in the tradition of formal logic. In its simplest form, an entity relationship has only a subject and a predicate. Hence the sentence "Dick has an address" becomes subject: Dick, plus predicate: (has an) address. Because the entity relationship is assumed to be logical, the verbal aspect of the predicate becomes implicit and one is left with two nouns: 1) Dick and 2) address. The same happens in the case of a simple subject–object relationship. The sentence "Dick is a friend" again becomes two nouns 1) Dick, and 2) friend. In the interests of easily constructed databases, this is splendid because it does away with the tiresome reality of the original statements in the form of noun (+verb + adjective) + noun.

With respect to grammar, the solution comes at a considerable price. If one drops the verb on the assumption that it is obvious, then one is only able to represent the completely obvious. In making no distinction between "is a" and "has a," one removes the difference between abstraction relations and partitive relations. In the case above, one loses the ability to distinguish between "Dick is a friend" and "Dick has a friend"[63] (cf. chapter 14). By contrast, Dahlberg's functional or syntactic relation requires a combination of subject (noun) and predicate object (transitive verb plus noun). In this definition, a predicate is a combination of entities, activities, properties, and/or dimensions. In Dahlberg's approach, predication is more than simply making a statement about an entity with respect to some or all of its accidents. In grammatical terms, predication is a combination of noun, verb, and object in order to make a statement or a claim, which is then open to being verified or refuted. Thus, in the first level of Dahlberg's analysis, syntax can answer questions such as "Who did what (Whodunit)?"

A second level of Dahlberg's functional or syntactic analysis further defines the claim in level one by adding details about purpose (Why did they do it?), conditions (How did they do it?), time (When did they do it?), place (Where did they do it?), persons (Who else was involved and affected?) and objects (What else was involved and affected?).[64] Dahlberg's analysis thus leads to a definition of syntax, which involves not just structure, but meaningful structure with real claims.

This approach is different from most of the simple definitions of predicate, semantics, and syntax in the library and the computer world at present and is important because it clarifies some of the underlying reasons why American and European thinkers often talk past each other. The *Oxford English Dictionary*, for instance, notes that predication is "to state or assert (something) of or about the subject of a proposition." It also states that, in logic, to predicate is "said of a subject in a proposition; the second term of a proposition, which is affirmed or denied of the first term by means of the copula, as in, 'this man is my *father*.'" In this definition, predicates are limited to *is* and *is not* statements: to be or not to be. In Aristotle's terms, this is *being*. Following this definition, abstraction relations are predicates. In the language of computer science, predicates are a claim about inheritance: parent–child. In naïve computer science, such inheritance can be about "is a" or "has a," i.e., predicates can be either about abstraction or partition relationships and both are called entity-relationships.[65]

Dahlberg's approach extends predication to all of Aristotle's nine qualities, combines entities and activities with properties and dimensions, and distinguishes clearly between intransitive and transitive verbs. By contrast, simple predication a) reduces it to two qualities (being and having) and b) obscures distinctions between intransitive and transitive verbs. Moreover, this simple predication is typically linked with a particular definition of semantics and syntax. Semantics is taken to mean definition of containers or fields. For example, what does the field *author* mean and to what extent is it equivalent to the field *creator*? In this context, syntax is about the form in which something is expressed, e.g., HTML or XML. In Dahlberg's approach, the discussion is not about the fields but about the contents and their relations. (cf. Appendix 6).

In these seemingly trivial distinctions lies a key to understanding fundamental differences between North American and European approaches. In North America, semantics (and syntax) is assumed to lie in isolated individual categories such as creator or title. In Europe, syntax (and even more so semantics) entails meaningful arrangements of concepts and terms in the form of statements within those fields, which can be tested and refuted.

Isolated words are information. If semantics (meaning) is identified with isolated words, the distinction between information and knowledge disappears or becomes meaningless. Without this distinction, there is no basis for making claims that can be proved right or wrong. In such a world where *is* dominates, one falls back into statements such as "That's the way it is" and the concept of truth is seen as passé. Is this not exactly what is happening in the United States? By contrast, in Europe, knowledge arises out of a meaningful organization of ideas in statements that can be proved right or wrong. In this context, truth matters; the distinction between information and knowledge is essential, and knowledge organization is an important field.

J. M. Perreault[66] has provided a new classification for relations in terms of three basic types, namely, subsumptive, determinative, and ordinal, corresponding to entities, activities, and dimensions, respectively. He defined three basic categories of subsumptive relations.[67] These he subdivided into a number of further categories (cf. Appendix 5). Implicit in this approach is a framework for a reorganization of knowledge. If relations become a basis for our catalogues in libraries, memory institutions, and ultimately for a new Internet-based master catalogue, we shall have something much richer than a tool that tells us where books are on shelves. It will become a new kind of connection-seeing device, a knowledge tool in its own right.

This connection-seeing device, which could also be called a contextualizer, will become all the more powerful if it maintains links with existing classification systems. To take a simple example: The contextualizer treats water as an entity and follows its physical characteristic throughout various scales, from its atomic composition as H_2O, through its microscopic shape, its appearance as a single droplet, as rising steam, cloud, rain, puddle, pond, sea, and ocean. On the other hand, it allows us to look at water, as does Dewey, under the disciplines of geology, biology, engineering, and transport.

The depth to which one makes such connections depends on one's goal: Do we want a simple answer or to do a thoroughgoing research? Accordingly, there will be ten strategies to reflect these different needs: 1) A guided tour; 2) A direct strategy searches for only one word; 3) Personal terms opens the search to a cluster of related terms around that word; 4) Database fields expand the search to include topics used by professionals in a given field; 5) Subject headings expand the search to include the official categories of a memory institution; 6) Classification refines that search by showing how such subjects fit into a standard organization of knowledge; 7) Comparative classifications expand this process to include alternative systems for organizing knowledge; 8) Relations explore the details of a topic in terms of subsumptive, ordinal, and determinative relations; 9) Comparative ontologies extend this analysis diachronically; 10) Creative emergence applies this principle to new knowledge where precise definitions of fields and domains is still in flux.

These strategy levels are reminiscent of the ten levels of knowledge. But whereas the ten levels of knowledge deal with different levels concerning a single term, the ten strategies expand the scope of research from a single term to a whole range of related concepts or disciplines. They also expand the search from a personal approach to one that reflects the views of enduring knowledge as reflected by memory institutions. One thus shifts from personal views to those of the collective memory of mankind. Comparing earlier classification systems allows us to look at objects through earlier categories. In so doing, we move toward a concept of dynamic classification that does away with the seeming oppositions that some see between empiricism, rationalism, historicism, and pragmatism as either/or choices in classification. Dynamic classification is thus a first step towards dynamic knowledge.

5. Dynamic Knowledge

A fundamental shortcoming of most digital reference and digital library projects to date is that they still approach electronic media using the assumptions and limitations of print media. Hence they are concerned with providing digital facsimiles of printed reference materials and books. As a result, they offer us digital forms of the static knowledge imposed by print, rather than offering the potential of dynamic knowledge inherent in electronic media. By way of illustration, some examples are useful.

Individuals (Who?)

Traditional reference rooms provide static knowledge about individuals. In the case of an author, we are given a list of their publications. In the case of a painter, we are given a list of their paintings, their complete works in the form of a *catalogue raisonnée*. Such lists represent a standard contemporary view of what a given author or painter accomplished.

Dynamic knowledge of individuals entails at least three factors: 1) changing historical knowledge about an individual, 2) changing perceptions of an individual, and 3) changing assessments about the authority of literature concerning an individual. First, there is a problem that what is known about the writings or paintings of an individual changes over time. For instance, the list of paintings attributed to Rembrandt was longer in 1945 than after the Rembrandt Commission published its findings. This needs to be integrated into our search strategies such that the question: What did Rembrandt paint? will become time-sensitive. This same principle applies across the board to authors, painters, musicians, architects, engineers, philosophers, etc. In future, such electronic lists need to be dynamic.

Second, there is paradox that persons now famous such as Leonardo were judged very differently throughout the centuries, almost forgotten in some generations, particularly praised and often for different reasons in other generations. Most of our present methods of presenting individuals do not take such aspects into account. Electronic biographies need to be more than our present opinions and include all the earlier standard views.

Third, with a genius such as Leonardo, thousands of persons feel prompted to write something about the man. The number of persons in any generation who have actually read his notebooks has never been more than a handful. The Internet potentially offers us access to everyone who cites Leonardo but has almost no mechanisms in place to distinguish between standard works, generally respected works, and non-authoritative lists. The radical proposal of some to reintroduce censorship is not a reasonable solution. The problem is made the more elusive because the recognized world authority in one decade may well be replaced in another decade.

Needed, therefore, are new kinds of dynamic, weighted bibliographies, which allow us to have subsets on the basis of field-specific acceptance, new ways of expressing and recording electronically the well-established traditions of peer review. (This is totally different from attempts to do simplistic electronic computations of quality). One thus arrives at peer review with an historical dimension in electronic form and yet still has access to a wider range of less-authoritative, or more precisely, less-established by the authorities, sources in a field. In tackling such alternatives between the authority of sources vs. (mere) citations, we can use technologies to return to central questions of how we assess quality and importance. This will transform the emerging field of bibliometrics. To address these challenges, agents combined with hypertext need to be developed. These bibliographies must also be dynamic in another sense, that they include all earlier bibliographies.[68] Thus we can trace not only what is known about Leonardo today but have a means of assessing how much was known at an earlier period.

Objects (What?)

Beyond the initial problem of access to a specific object in a museum, library, archive or to free-standing monuments is a larger challenge of how we can access all related objects that are derived from or have been affected by the object: the copies, replicas, versions, imitations, caricatures, and sometimes pastiches.

Present-day sources typically focus on objects as static entities. The limitations of print frequently lead us to focus on one example as if it were the whole category.

Accordingly, we all know about the Coliseum in Rome, but most of us are unaware of the dozens of coliseums spread throughout the Roman Empire. Using dynamic maps and chronologies, new kinds of cultural maps can be developed that allow us to trace the spatial-temporal spread of major cultural forms such as Greek theatres, Roman coliseums, or Christian Romanesque and Gothic churches. This will allow novel approaches to long-standing problems of central inspiration and regional effects, the interplay between centre and periphery, in some cases between centre and colonies. Such questions pertaining to original and variants (versions, copies, imitations) are central to the challenges faced by bodies such as a European Union, which aims to maintain diversity within a larger unity. At another level, this is a global challenge.

As in the case of individuals, dynamic knowledge requires an integration of temporal and cultural changes. It is not just a question of scanning in the Coliseum as it is today, but being able to trace the history of this building in various media (paintings, drawings, engravings, photographs) in the course of the centuries. This includes various restorations and reconstructions, such that differences between Italian, German, French, and other conservationists and archaeologists are revealed.

Concepts and their Relations (What?)

The challenge of creating dynamic classification systems was broached earlier. Presently we have many different classification systems and thesauri. Theoretical proposals for mapping among these systems exist.[69] We could also use a practical approach for mapping between these systems (cf. §3 above). In the interim, the Universal Decimal Classification (UDC) might be expanded using Perreault's subsumptive, determinative, and ordinal relations (Figure 68 and Appendix 5).[70]

A dynamic system that allows us to switch between classifications in different cultures and historical periods provides new kinds of filters[71] for appreciating subtleties of historical and cultural diversity. The enormous implications for learning range from philosophy (especially epistemology), where we can trace changing relations of concepts dynamically, to the humanities with courses on culture and civilization (a term which again has very different connotations in French, German, and English). Instead of just citing different monuments, works of art, and literature, we shall be able to explore different connections among ideas in different cultural traditions. For example, with respect to metaphysics and religion, Ranganathan's classification (India) is much stronger than western systems such as Dewey, which is to be expected from a country with entire sacred cities in a way unknown to the West.

Historical and Cultural Concepts (What?)

This approach leads to new kinds of knowledge maps that allow us to trace the evolution of concepts both spatially in different countries and temporally in different historical periods. This will lead to dynamic bibliographies. We shall be able to trace how a concept is frequently broached at a conference, developed in articles and books, and gradually evolves into a recognized discipline, which may subsequently recombine with another, e.g., how biology and chemistry lead to bio-chemistry. This approach will provide new insight into problems of standard and model versus variants and versions; of centre versus periphery and the role of continuity in the spread of major forms and styles of expression. Ultimately, it will lead us to reconsider universals and particulars (cf. chapter 14).

Space (Where?)

Current printed maps in atlases are static. Historically, the boundaries of maps change. The Joint Research Centre (JRC) has already developed very impressive three-dimensional maps.[72] In conjunction with the European Space Agency, much work is being done in the area of co-ordinating Geographical Information Systems (GIS) and Global Positioning Systems (GPS).[73] The SANTI project in Spain links satellite images with augmented reality information about landscapes and town-scapes. Spatial metadata can produce dynamically changing atlases and link this with GIS and GPS. This is a prerequisite for visualizing changing political boundaries. Coupled with information concerning cities, events, and other historical data, this will permit much more effective search strategies.

This will lead to a new dynamic cartography. For instance, the map of Poland keeps changing. A Polish city in 1400 might well have been a Russian or a German city in a different century. It also means that the number of places in a country varies enormously over time. If I am searching for all the places in Poland in 1440, the number of places will be much larger than centuries earlier or later when the geographical expanse of Poland was much smaller.[74]

Thus the question: Where is Poland? will adjust with time. Applied globally this will furnish us with more than simple instructions of how to get there. It will make visible persons' misconceptions of geography at various points of history. It will show us how India's maps of India and Pakistan may well be different than Pakistan's maps of the same two countries. A new kind of dynamic cartography needs to link satellite photos of towns with maps and aerial views. Both global co-operation and new software agents are needed.

Time (When?)

Connected with this is a challenge of historical temporal metadata, whereby we have a standard method for correlating the different time scales of various chronological systems and calendars (including Jewish, Chinese, Indian, Gregorian, Islamic, and Julian calendars). Those of the Hebrew faith had their fourth, not second, millennium problem some time ago. Coupled with historical data, this will be a significant step towards studying history from multicultural points of view. If, for instance, I am reading an Arabic or Jewish manuscript and come upon the date 380, the system can provide direct equivalents in other calendars.[75] This entails a transformation of how we store and access information and knowledge, and requires a continual reorganization of knowledge.

6. Reorganization of Knowledge

Initially, new media pose a seemingly straightforward problem: How do we rear-range what we have so far in order to make new sense thereof? To achieve dynamic knowledge requires a long-term commitment to metadata and classification.

We may continue to store physical objects in libraries, museums, and archives but the sources of insight will come through virtual reference rooms and reposito-ries beyond the shelves of those institutions. The systematic links of these electronic repositories could well become more extensive than the original sources, although much smaller physically. They will be metadata banks of authority lists with all the key pointers concerning a given person, object, event, or process, properly reflect-ing their cultural and historical complexities. As noted earlier, these authority lists will also contain all known variants at the local, regional, and national levels.

Such a reorganization of knowledge will transform how we approach knowl-edge, how we study, how we learn. By way of an example, another scenario: I am reading a traditional printed book and encounter the name Leonardo da Vinci. I am aware he was a Renaissance figure but want to know more. My pen-like object scans the name, transmits it to my notepad, and offers a number of options. The default is a basic introductory bibliographical sketch. I choose this. The notepad sends a wireless command via the Internet to the nearest virtual reference room, acquires the relevant bibliographical sketch, and transmits this back to the monitor of my notepad along with a new set of options. Do I want to know more about Leonardo's life, the titles of his paintings, a list of his (primary) publications, a survey of (secondary) literature concerning him, or am I content with this sketch and now want to go back to the book that I was reading? Regular digital books merely offer me traditional contents on a new screen. The contextualizer allows me to read traditional books in a new way, augmenting their value through reference materials available elsewhere. I have the privileges of a reference room in one of the world's great libraries without needing a) to be there or b) to carry any of those heavy reference books.

I want to know more. A master index provides me with a list of all subjects in his manuscripts. These subjects correspond to a standard classification system, such that I can switch to broader or narrower terms. I choose optics and receive a list of all references to optics. I can ask for subsets relating to a given date or period (e.g., 1505–1508), and/or a given place (e.g., Milan). I choose a folio in the *Codex Atlanticus* (Milan). Low-level agents will (have) search(ed) all the secondary literature concerning that folio and subject. This results in a list of all secondary literature relevant to that folio as a whole, to that folio with respect to optics, and to optics elsewhere in the notebooks. Alternatively, I am reading secondary literature and encounter a reference to optics. The system now allows me to go back to that folio in Leonardo's notebooks and, then, for example, back to a list of all other references to optics in Leonardo's writings.

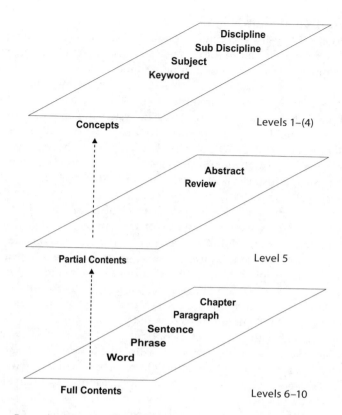

Figure 18a   Examples of three basic levels of granularity in searching for materials

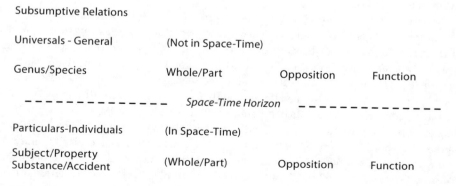

Figure 18b   Universals, particulars and levels of abstraction in light of Perreault's relations

In future, these connections will not be limited to traditional library materials. Lectures given by Leonardo scholars and university professors will be on-line. Agents will search these and create appropriate links. The order in which these are searched will vary. Sometimes it will follow a vertical model (as in Figure 16). At other times, the sequence may be quite different (Figure 17). Say I have a folio from the *Codex Atlanticus* with a preparatory drawing for *The Last Supper*. Agents produce alphabetical, geographical, and chronological lists of all preparatory drawings for *The Last Supper*, link these such that I can view the corresponding images accordingly, i.e., alphabetically, geographically or chronologically, then go to an image of *The Last Supper* in Milan. From there I could go a) to all copies and versions thereof; b) to a lecture which compares all these drawings and originals and/or c) to a lecture which considers other aspects of *The Last Supper*.

The power of this approach is that the sequence is open. Hence, while viewing the lecture in b) above, I can return to the original folio from which the preparatory drawing comes, follow the figure it represents through various versions and copies, or study the history of restoration of the original fresco with respect to that figure. This differs from conventional hypertext in two ways. First, the contextualizer is not just a hyperlink-happy technological device. It sets out from the premise that some links are more equal than others and provides lists to guide us through various choices. The potentially infinite intertwingledness of things is thus reduced to systematic matrices that serve as orientation guides. Second, Americans are typically interested in capturing contemporary knowledge. By contrast, the contextualizer deals with knowledge throughout the ages. It has historical and cultural changes in knowledge as a built-in feature. Hence, whereas Donald Norman can finish off the topic of intelligent reference guides in a page and a half,[76] we require a book to outline something much more comprehensive.

In the interests of simplicity, we have focussed on examples of textual knowledge. Electronic augmented books[77] allow much more. If an original printed book has a verbal description, an engraving, or black/white photograph of the Acropolis, the corresponding augmented book potentially allows us to call up colour photographs, QuickTime Virtual Reality (VR) sequences, movie clips, and even live video feeds. In short, it unleashes the whole range of multimedia on any book we happen to be reading. The bad news is that to get there we have to start all over again in many senses. The good news is we are going somewhere interesting and many are already working in this direction: memory institutions, the Internet Society, and the World Wide Web Consortium (Appendix 7).

7. New Overviews

Searching at different levels of knowledge is typically referred to as "granularity." This has a long history. Searching at the level of titles of books goes back to the earliest-known libraries in the third millennium before Christ. The idea of searching at the level of titles of articles came only at the end of the nineteenth century when

Otlet and Lafontaine founded their Mundaneum. At a manual level, full-text searching began with the introduction of indexes in the latter Middle Ages. Automated full-text searching has only emerged with the advent of more powerful computers in the course of the past decades.

Paradoxically an ability to search at the level of every word has introduced a concurrent need to search at higher levels of abstraction in order still to see the wood for the trees, or more precisely, the word for the paper. Hence, as persons have gone from studying individual titles to indexing some words, to concordances of every word, there has been a parallel trend to study concepts at higher levels of abstraction in order to understand larger patterns. The closer we get to studying the details of every word in the text, the more we need to stand back and see what all this means[78] (Figure 18). A trend from partial contents (level 5) to study of the full contents of books (levels 6–10) thus goes hand in hand with a need to return to study the terms pointing to and describing those books (levels 1–4). This both expands the domains at our disposal and increases the potential accuracy of our searches. These levels can be visualized in three-dimensions.[79] This also poses new problems about what to prestructure and what to structure on demand.

In this context, Perreault's approach to subsumptive relations is particularly useful. This enables us to go from a subject, from material relations, down to its properties or up to whole/part and type/kind relations.[80] Such subsumptive principles lend themselves to integration with scale. With augmented versions of traditional printed books, we can thus use classification systems in virtual reference rooms as an intermediary to show more abstract concepts (through broader terms) or more concrete examples (through narrower terms) of any word that is encountered in any book that we are reading. Here the Resource Description Framework (RDF) is doing important work on classification and thesauri.

Using Perreault's distinctions as a starting point, one can go much further and propose a new approach to the age-old debate concerning universals (Plato) and particulars (Aristotle) by introducing a space-time horizon. Universals are above this horizon, while particulars are below it. For instance, the universal concept of a dog is not linked with a specific time or place. On the other hand, the description of my particular dog, Rover, is linked with a specific time and place. Earlier ages fought about whether knowledge was universal or particular. We can recognize that it is both, and using modern databases it is possible to envision a gradual reorganization of all knowledge such that we are able to use the different relations in going both up and down dynamically evolving hierarchies of concepts, subjects, and objects.

As the term "overviews" suggests, it lends itself also to insights gained from the emerging field of scientific visualization.[81] George Robertson's recent taxonomy confirms that there are a surprisingly small number of basic methods (Table 42).[82] The extent to which each of these is useful (and under what circumstances) is one of the many fields awaiting further study.

TABLE 42 Taxonomy of visualization methods by George Robertson

INDENTATION	CLUSTERING	NODE LINK DIAGRAMS	CONTAINMENT	GEOGRAPHIC
Tree Control	Galaxy of News	2 D Diagrams	Treemaps	Floorplans
Fish eye Theme	Semnet	Pad++	StreetMaps	
	Hot Sauce	Cone Tree		
		Fish Eye Cone Tree		
		Hyperbolic Viewer		
		FSN		
		XML 3D		

There is work on three-dimensional (3-D) interfaces.[83] For example, Alan Radley (Kreospheres, now Spectasia) is developing new methods for visualizing a whole series of objects at once. Such dynamic presentation methods are important for product lines and introduce new possibilities with respect to visualizing links between universals and particulars, as outlined above.

8. Augmented Books

Whereas memory institutions and most members of the web community are still focussing on digital books as surrogates of printed books, we foresee the advent of augmented books. With omni-links, which Harrow calls "every word hypertext," (chapter 2.5), one takes any given term, sends it to an Internet search engine, and finds what corresponding sites are available. Our vision of augmented books uses this potential of omni-links in combination with new media to do much more.

A traditional book makes handily accessible a certain amount of knowledge within its two covers. The rules for organizing this knowledge of authors, subjects, or places frequently vary from one book to another. For instance, one book refers to Eric Blair, another refers to George Orwell, and yet both are referring to the same individual. Electronic library catalogues and digital library projects have brought attention to authority lists qua authors' names, subjects, places, etc., in library catalogues. This tendency towards standardization needs to be extended throughout the entire reference section of libraries such that the names, subjects, and places in classification systems, dictionaries, encyclopaedias, national book catalogues, abstracts, reviews, etc. are all correlated.

The librarian, information scientist, and classification specialist may dismiss this as impossible because of difficulties in correlating terms. How can one be sure, they may ask, that one can know precisely what the equivalent for a given word (caption, descriptor, term) in Dewey should or could be in the Library of Congress or some other classification system?

Fortunately a pragmatic solution is possible. Instead of musing about possible equivalents, we can trace equivalents that practitioners have established. Major books have been classed under most of the major classification schemes at least once. So we could start with a book such as Dürer's *Instruction in Measurement* (*Underweysung der Messung*), examine under what words it is classed in a Dewey library, under what descriptors it is classed in a Library of Congress library, and so on.[84] At the end of this process, we have one title with a series of equivalent words in a number of classification systems. This rather dreary task is sufficiently mechanical that it can quite readily be assigned to low-level agents. After checking many millions of books against several hundreds of classification systems, we will have an empirical list of equivalent terms in the main classification systems. As such, the new technologies provide us with novel ways of looking at the materials classed using old classifications.[85]

This same approach can be extended to the subject lists in national book catalogues and earlier bibliographies. Historical bibliographies such as Draud and Murhard frequently listed books under very different subjects than those to which we are accustomed. Agents using our empirical approach will simply use a given title as a point of departure and collect all the subject names under which it has been listed. Manually this process would be overwhelming. With the help of agents, it is fully feasible. This will result in a new kind of metadata, whereby any book is linked with a set of subject terms found in classification systems, subject catalogues, national book catalogues, and bibliographies, all of which are again correlated to a given date. We can then trace the history of terms with which a book is associated in the course of centuries. This will prepare the way for a history of metadata, which at a later date will also include cultural dimensions such that we can visualize how German classes are different from French or Japanese classes. Ultimately this will link the names and concepts authority files with all the variant names associated with them.

Such augmented books offer many new possibilities. A first scenario: I am reading a book and come across the name Timbuctoo. I have a vague notion it is probably in Africa — or is it one of those unlikely place names in the United States such as Kalamazoo? — and would like to know where it is. I scan the term with my pen-like object or I simply speak the word into my notepad, which then gives me options. Do I wish to see it on a regular map, a terrain map, a political map, a population map, etc.? The notepad then conveys my choice via a wireless connection to the nearest virtual reference room on the Internet and then relays back to my notepad an appropriate map with Timbuctoo highlighted.

A second scenario: I am travelling in Turkey and have with me a Baedecker or some other travel book. I know that I am within a hundred miles of Uzuncaburc, a former Greek city with an impressive temple, but am lost. Using the same basic approach, I am shown where Uzuncaburc is on the map, with the difference that a Global Positioning System now determines the position of my jeep and also shows where this is on the map. An automobile navigation system can then compute how I get from where I am to Uzuncaburc, my destination.

As mentioned earlier, this is different from the basic hypertext idea. While acknowledging that all connections are possible, the contextualizer suggests that if I am reading a book and begin searching for names or places, there is a certain sequence that makes more sense than others: to determine the name of an author before asking what are the titles of that author's publications; to know the titles before choosing the full text of a specific title. This is also different from the recent fashion which claims that concept mapping can be automated and that the patient work of classification systems is now passé.[86] Of course, the complexity of these sequences varies with different users. A child needs a simpler list than a university student. A general practitioner has other medical requirements than a cardiologist who is the world expert on the left aorta of the heart. Middle-level agents can deduce a user's level and adjust choices and interfaces accordingly.

Physical books are likely to remain because we can see more on a printed page than on an electronic screen. Traditional physical books are limited to the contents on the page. Electronic books are ideal if we need reference materials especially in a mobile environment. Augmented (physical) books, when linked via wireless technologies with virtual reference rooms, give us the privileges of a world-level library from anywhere at anytime.[87] They give access to millions of hours of analytical knowledge, which have been sorted and analyzed,[88] guide us through different kinds and levels of knowledge (cf. figures 16–17), and thus connect us with the cumulative memory of mankind. In future, numerous developments are foreseeable. Another scenario: My notepad has context awareness. It is "aware" that my research is focussed on bio-chemistry. It also "knows" which languages I am able to read. Accordingly, through user-modelling, an agent culls the books in print and periodicals to keep me in touch with what is happening.

Assuming a semantic web as envisaged by Tim Berners-Lee,[89] these books and articles have metadata tags identifying which are by major authors in the field, which are by specialists, and so on. Subsets of these lists can therefore be offered on the basis of whether I want just the latest views of authorities in the field or also wish to include alternative views. In all this there is a paradox: the most famous titles are inevitably those that are best known and thus most readily found. Hence, one of the challenges of searching is how to retrieve the unknown, the unexpected, to keep alive that special sensation introduced by the Princes of Serendip.

The reference dimension is only a first step. Our notion of an augmented book is closely linked with the idea of dynamic knowledge. As always there are precedents. In 1968, Alan Kay (then a student at Utah, later Xerox PARC) proposed the creation of a Dyna Book.[90] What he envisioned was a laptop computer close to the new electronic books that are now emerging. The traditional notion of a static printed text is here replaced by a notion of a dynamic text, which can be edited and replaced.

The Scholarly Technology Group (Brown University) has developed their version of a Dyna Book,[91] and there is also a commercial product by Toshiba.

As noted earlier, one of the great innovations of Standardized Graphical Markup Language (SGML) was that it effectively separated form and content (cf. §3 above). This inspired a conference entitled *The Dynamic Text* (Toronto, 1986), which focussed on new editing possibilities introduced by SGML. The advent of HyperText Markup Language (HTML) was both a step forward, in that it was easier to do, and a step backward, in that it conflated anew form and content. This led to Dynamic HyperText Markup Language (DHTML), which allowed one to create "labelled menus, pop-up tool tips, description boxes," and a tool to convert "old arrays by simple cut-and-paste."[92] This has since inspired new commercial products.[93]

For instance, Astound Incorporated has created Dynamite DHTML software, which permits users to "create visually rich, interactive web pages without the need for scripting or programming. And, since these web pages use Dynamic HTML for playback, there is no need to install plug-ins or proprietary controls on the viewer's browser."[94] Giraffics Multimedia has created dynamic texts such as Little Bo Beep, whereby individual words and pictures are linked with music and other multimedia effects.[95] Netscape also refers to dynamic documents by which they mean a push-pull dimension in their browser, which allows a given document such as a stock market quote to be uploaded at regular intervals.[96]

Meanwhile the W3 Consortium is developing the notion of eXtensible HyperText Markup Language (XHTML). They note that "authors need a way to ensure that the content they produce will render as intended on target devices." To address this W3C's solution entails: "1) characterizing browser capabilities; 2) document profiles for authoring content and 3) selecting/transforming content to match."[97] These solutions focus on the editing of future texts. Our notion of augmented books with dynamic knowledge goes further by focussing on the realities of adjusting existing published content at different levels of automation. A very simple example has already been mentioned. I am reading an old text, which discusses a painting. The text gives a rough idea of the painting in the form of a line drawing or engraving. Using a pen-like object, I can call on a virtual reference room to provide modern colour photographs of the painting in question.

This idea can be extended to claims. An historical text states that the population of Paris is 100,000. Using our pen-like object, now equipped with an agent that recognizes the syntax of quantifiable claims (i.e., all quantitative claims about there are *x* inhabitants in Paris, as opposed to qualitative claims such as there are many beautiful women in Paris), the statistic is sent to a virtual reference room and is a) checked against other claims at the time and b) compared with additional statistics for different periods: e.g., Paris in 1850, 1900, 1950, and 2000.

This approach can be extended to the challenge of updating facts in contemporary books. In traditional print media this required producing a revised or an entirely new edition. The twentieth century saw the introduction of ring-binder-type books with loose-leaf pages, which could then be added to or substituted at will. Most of our software today is aimed at being able to change the claims to keep them up to date. Hence if a book in 1995 claims that there are 5 million PCs, we might expect that an agent would update this automatically to c. 200 million in 1999 and 307 million by the end of 2000. A next step, especially applicable in the case of works in electronic form, will introduce an option where every quantitative claim translates itself into a chronological graph such that we can trace how such statistics change over time.

Some statistics are firm. Others are open to debate. An American site may claim that Japan has *x* million PCs. A Japanese site may well claim that the number of PCs is actually *x* + *y*. Ultimately the augmented book should provide us not only with a record of firm statistics which change over time, but also offer us a means of comparing debated statistics. In a traditional printed book, one of the chief functions of footnotes was to offer the source of one's claims in order that a sceptical reader could check the sources themselves. With an augmented, dynamic book, in our sense of the term, this ability of comparative study is enhanced. We are not merely presented with static claims about knowledge but given access to its changes over time and over place, i.e., its historical and cultural dimensions.

Hence, just as the world of manufacturing envisages the advent of intelligent materials that are self-maintaining and self-healing, the world of learning can envisage the advent of intelligent books, which are self-revising and produce new editions automatically. Even today, in the case of important texts, there are translations into a number of languages. If these were linked with on-line databases such as UNESCO's *Corpus Translationum*, then a French person encountering an English text could "automatically" be transferred to a French translation of same. Eventually one could imagine a world where any phrase or claim could have both its literal and its cultural translation, whereby, for instance, one "Thank you" becomes "1,000 *grazie*" in Italian, or whereby, "Not bad" in Scots is recognized as the equivalent of "*splendido*," "*stupendo*" or "*incredibile*" in Italian. Thus augmented books will ultimately increase greatly the scope of any text because they will add to an initial version various other cultural variants that can be consulted at will. Whereas some might complain that this completely erodes the notion of a firm, original text, and claim this leads to utter relativism, we would insist that this introduces a new sense of dignity to the original text, while allowing any number of variants, each of them properly documented.

For the purposes of this book, we have focussed on how the new media can breath new life into existing books by linking them with the collective memory of mankind. In the future, more dramatic combinations are possible. We have noted how mobile phones are now equipped with cameras and other multimedia capabilities. As a result, mobile phones are already being linked with GPS and GIS systems in order to provide new kinds of mobile orientation devices. Further scenarios suggest themselves. I am hiking and find an interesting mushroom but am unsure whether it is safe to eat. In the past, I would have consulted a standard manual or asked an expert, if they were available. In this future scenario, I photograph the plant with the camera of my mobile, send this image to a reference room where image recognition methods identify the species, consult the pertinent information and relay this back to my mobile. In the past, cameras were primarily devices for passively capturing images from the external world. In the future, multimedia mobile devices can increasingly become active knowledge collecting, comparing and even knowledge-increasing devices, e.g., each undocumented new species is automatically sent to key repositories (see Epilogue 1).

9. Conclusions

Our memory institutions (libraries, museums, and archives) are the guardians of enduring knowledge. Most of that enduring knowledge is stored in the form of static knowledge in books. Many of the projects pertaining to digital libraries, digital archives, and virtual museums that are currently underway risk continuing the limitations of static print media in digital form.

Electronic media can overcome these static limitations through dynamic knowledge and the concept of augmented books. This transforms the three basic aspects of memory institutions: their reference sections, the objects themselves, and the interpretations concerning these objects. It introduces the notion of levels of knowledge to offer a more coherent framework for systematic study at different levels of granularity. It also introduces the notion of strategies for knowledge to distinguish between a simple search and long-term research. In electronic versions of libraries, these levels and strategies provide important new approaches to orientation and contextualization within a field of knowledge.

We have outlined four steps in a new approach: 1) to create new finding aids in the form of virtual reference rooms[98] that provide digital links to existing reference materials, 2) to relate these virtual reference rooms to new methods of textual analysis, 3) to restructure existing classification systems, thesauri, and reference works in order to develop new kinds of virtual reference rooms, and 4) to develop a new concept of dynamic knowledge that takes into account historical and cultural implications of knowledge. This will lead to new methods of abstraction and to augmented books and will entail a virtual reorganization of knowledge.

Our vision to reorganize knowledge is thus linked with a curious paradox. As electronic tools allow us to approach every detailed word of the full contents of texts, there is a new need to step back and create new kinds of overviews that allow us to see not only the bits but also the patterns that those bits evoke. As we come closer we need to stand back. There are a number of further challenges standing in the way (chapter 13). If we can overcome these, augmented books can be a first stepping stone towards a more comprehensive vision, which includes augmented knowledge and augmented culture (chapters 14–15). Among the many consequences of these changes is a need to study anew what is meant by e-content.

PART V

philosophical
consequences:
SPIRITUALITY

13
challenges

Fewer than 6% of Internet users reside in
developing countries, which account for
84% of the world's total population.
— *NewsScan Daily*, 24 August 2000

1. Introduction

This book outlines a vision of possibilities introduced by new
media and thus describes a dream for a digital future. Such a digital dream is by no means inevitable. Many challenges, obstacles,
and dangers stand in the way, which could readily transform the
future into a digital nightmare. As noted in the Introduction, a
thorough assessment of these problems is beyond the scope of
this book. Even so, this chapter draws attention to six fundamental challenges, namely: a) rich versus poor, b) computers
versus ecology, c) virtual versus real, d) truth versus viewpoints,
e) observation versus protection, f) public versus private, and
outlines the need for a new public good.

TABLE 43 Resources used to make one 8-inch wafer.[10]

Bulk gases	4,267 cubic feet
Waste water	3,787 gallons
Chemicals	27 pounds
Hazardous gases	29 cubic feet
Hazardous waste	9 pounds
De-ionized water	3,023 gallons

2. Rich versus Poor

The Internet Society's motto of "Internet for everyone" is not matched by reality.[1] Computers may be falling in price, but they remain too expensive for persons in developing countries. Worse, the discrepancies between the developed and the developing countries are increasing: "The income gap between the richest fifth of the world's people and the poorest fifth – measured by average national income per head – increased from 30 to one in 1960 to 74 to one in 1997."[2]

There are organizations such as UNESCO, the World Bank, and the International Monetary Fund, the stated aim of which is to improve this situation. Yet recent studies confirm that, partly because the developing countries often lack public innovation policies, even the amount of R&D in these countries is decreasing,[3] thus making their future even bleaker.

Here the rich countries are not helping as much as they could. Why, for instance, should a telephone call from Chile to America cost ten times more than the same connection the other way round? Or, as Philippe Quéau of UNESCO has pointed out, why should the world be paying the United States $5 billion annually to connect via the United States, when the United States pays nothing for the use of others' information and knowledge, especially when the rest of the world now represents the majority of Internet content?[4] A recent ITU report explores public service applications of the Internet in developing countries.[5]

Statistics of over 800 million computers sound impressive in a country such as the United States with a population approaching 300 million people in 2005.[6] Still, it is but a small amount compared to 6 billion persons worldwide of whom 1.8 billion are living in abject poverty and have never used any new media. Not only is there a lack of technology in such poor countries, there is also a trend to provide them with information that is inadequate. As Jan Pronk, the former Dutch minister of co-operation for development recently noted, the information offered these countries is not infrequently distorted.[7]

3. Computers versus Ecology

As noted earlier, the price of computers continues to decrease, so much so that some optimists predict computers for a single dollar. Others claim that such prices do not acknowledge the hidden costs in terms of detriment to the environment.

Semiconductor manufacturing, for instance, is the worst air polluting industry and also uses several million gallons of water a day. More seriously, the resources used to make one 8-inch wafer are staggering (Table 43). If this rate continued, it would be ecologically disastrous to provide all 6 billion inhabitants of the planet with wafers. The computer revolution would be technologically possible but ecologically impossible. There is every reason to believe, however, that there will be dramatic advances in production, which introduce considerable economies of scale.

Old-fashioned computers had too many wires. The prototype intelligent room with 125,000 feet of cables, discussed earlier (chapter 6.2) confirms that these inconveniences are not yet past. As we have seen, however, there are visions for a mobile future where almost everything is wireless.[8] Most of us assume that because it is invisible it will not hurt. The early users of X-rays and radioactive materials sometimes made the same mistake. But what are the effects of transmitting such enormous amounts of messages, radio and television programs, and potentially great sections of the Internet over wireless connections through the air? Will it literally just go past us or will it affect us?[9] There are some who claim that there is a connection between an 80 per cent increase in brain tumors in 1999 and the enormous rise of mobile phones. Others rightly object that the most mobile nations, the Scandinavians, are not particularly unhealthy. Even so, these are matters of concern and areas for research.

4. Virtual versus Real

Problems of distinguishing between the virtual and the real are not new. Ever since civilization began, magicians and illusionists have played with the boundaries between the physical world and illusionary worlds. Even so, the advent of the new electronic media has brought these problems to a new level. Even a few decades ago, the special effects for a monster such as Frankenstein or Godzilla in an otherwise realistic film were invariably so crude that one could readily distinguish between the two. This is no longer the case.

The Harrier jet in *True Lies* exists only through computer graphics. Many of the figures in *Star Wars* are entirely digital. In the case of films such as *Toy Story*, everything is digital. War games in the military and video games in everyday life are constantly eroding our once-clear distinctions between real and virtual.[11] There are anecdotes of young teenagers walking with their games who, on encountering a friend in trouble, instinctively press the escape button on their computer, rather than helping out directly. Films such as *Forrest Gump* offer examples of deliberate editing of documentary evidence. How shall we, in future, be able to discern which images are straight records and which have been edited?[12]

To illustrate the deeper problems concerning veracity and sources,[13] here is another scenario (Figure 19a): There is a plane crash. Let us posit that there are three eyewitnesses at the event; three on-site reporters who may not have been eyewitnesses. These send their material back to (three) off-site press bureaus. These

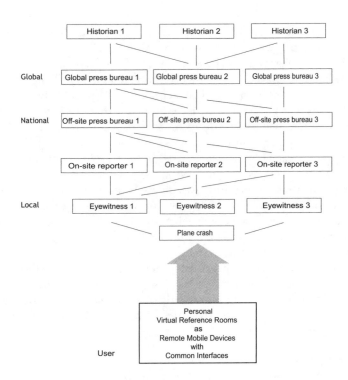

Figure 19a Contemporary event: Different eyewitnesses, reporters, and press bureaus concerning a plane crash

gather information and send them on to (three) global press bureaus. This means, that the "event" has gone through some combination of twelve different sources (3 eyewitnesses, 3 on-site reporters, 3 off-site press bureaus and 3 global press bureaus, ignoring for the moment the fact that the latter institutions typically entail a number of individuals). When we look at the six o'clock news on the evening of the event, however, we are usually presented with one series of images about the event.

It may be the case that all twelve of the intermediaries have been very careful to record their intervention in the process, i.e., the metadata is usually encoded in some way. What is important from our standpoint, however, is that we have no access to that level of the data. There is usually no way of knowing whether we are looking at eyewitness one as filtered through on-site reporter two, etc. More importantly, even if we did know this, there would be no way of gaining access at will to the possibly conflicting report of eyewitness two, on-site reporter three, and so on. There may be much rhetoric about personalization of news, news on demand interactively, and yet we have no way of checking behind the scenes to get a better picture.

Such a level of detail may seem superfluous if the event is as straightforward as a plane crash. But the bombing of the Chinese Embassy during the Kosovo war offers a more complex case. We were given some facts: the embassy was bombed, but were not told how many persons were killed. We were told that the Chinese objected as if they were being unreasonable, and only many weeks later were we told that this had been a failed intervention of the CIA. Until we have useable metadata, which allow us to check references, to compare stories, and to arrive at a more balanced view, we are at the mercy of the persons or powers who are telling the story, often without even being very clear as to who is behind that power. Is that satellite news the personal opinion of the owner himself or might it represent the opinions and views of those who influence them? If we are unable to check such details, we must ultimately abandon our attempts at truth concerning what we see.

There are related problems concerning print media. To continue with the scenario of the plane crash: At a local level, all the details of this event are recorded. We read in the local paper about who was killed, who their families were, how this has affected their neighbours, their colleagues at work, and so on. At the national level, there will be a matter-of-fact report of yet another plane crash. At the global level, the actual event is not likely to be described in detail. Rather, we shall witness a tiny fluctuation in the annual statistics of persons who have died. In historical terms, say the statistics concerning deaths in the course of a century (what the *Annales* School calls the *longue durée*), this fluctuation becomes all but invisible.

This example points to a fundamental problem concerning metadata. Those working at the local, regional, national, and historical levels typically have very different foci of attention, which are frequently reflected in quite different ways of dealing with, recording, and storing facts. The same event that requires many pages at the local level may merely be recorded as a numerical figure at the historical level. Unless there is a careful correlation among these different levels, it is impossible to move seamlessly through these different information sources concerning the same event.

Implicit in the above is an unexpected insight into a much-debated phenomenon. Benjamin Barber, in his *Jihad vs. McWorld*,[14] has drawn attention to the paradox that there is a trend towards globalizations with McDonalds (and Hiltons) everywhere and at the same time a reverse trend towards local and regional concerns as if this were somehow a lapse in an otherwise desirable progress. From the above, it becomes clear why these opposing trends are not a coincidence. Clearly we need a global approach if we are to understand patterns in population, energy, and the crucial ingredients whereby we understand enough of the big picture in order to render sustainable our all-too-fragile planet. But this level, however important, is also largely an abstraction. It reduces the complexity of the everyday into series of graphs and statistics allowing us to see patterns that would not otherwise be evident.

Yet in that complexity are all the facts, all the gory details, that are crucial for the everyday person. Thus trends towards CNN are invariably counterbalanced by trends towards local television, local radio, community programs, and local chat groups on

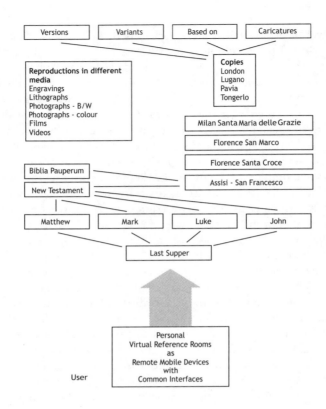

Figure 19b Historical event: The Last Supper recorded in many versions

the Internet. This is not a lapse in progress. It is a necessary measure to ensure that the humane dimension of communication remains intact.

In retrospect, Marshall McLuhan's characterization of this trend as one towards a "global village" is much more accurate than Barber's metaphor because it acknowledges the symbiotic co-existence rather than the dualistic opposition between the two trends. Metaphors aside, unless we have very careful means of tracing events through these different levels of detail, our distinctions between the virtual and the real are undermined. It is all fine and well for films such as *Galaxy Quest* (2000) to make fun of imaginary aliens viewing television serials as if they were historical documents, but this is to forget deeper problems of determining truth and veracity through sources.

The problems concerned with these contemporary events fade in comparison with historical and cultural events, which are the main focus of our concern. It is generally accepted that in the year AD 33 (give or take a year or two, depending on chronology and calendar adjustments), there occurred the most famous dinner party ever: the Last Supper. If we believe the *New Testament*, there were twelve eyewitnesses (the Apostles) of whom four were also the equivalents of on-site reporters (Matthew, Mark, Luke, and John). In today's terms, their reports were syndicated and are better remembered as part of a collection now known as the *New Testament* – a collation of all the reports of the time. Popular versions with less text and more pictures were also produced: known as the *Biblia pauperum* (Figure 19b).

The theme was then taken up by the Franciscans in their fresco cycles. This idea developed in Assisi and in Florence (Santa Croce), where the idea caught on and soon became the rage, so much so that there are over 70 Last Suppers in Florence alone and that the Dominicans soon used this theme in San Marco and elsewhere, including the church of Santa Maria delle Grazie (Milan) where Leonardo da Vinci gave it a new twist. The idea soon spread. Copies appeared on walls as paintings in Pavia, Lugano, Tongerlo, and London. There were multimedia versions in the form of engravings, lithographs, photographs, 3-D models, and eventually even films and videos. In the old tradition that imitation is the sincerest form of flattery, even the competition used the motif, culminating in a version where Marilyn Monroe herself and twelve of her Hollywood colleagues made out of the Last Supper a night on the town.

As a result of these activities in the course of nearly two millennia, there are literally tens of thousands of versions, copies and variants of the most famous dinner in history, which brings us back to the problems of metadata. If I go to one of the standard search engines such as Google Images and type in "Last Supper," I am given 14,000 hits, which is an indiscriminate subset that happens to be on-line, of the tens of thousands of images concerning the event.[15]

There is no way of limiting my search to the text versions of the original reporters, to large wall-sized versions in the scale of Leonardo's original, let alone to distinguish between Franciscan and Dominican versions, authentic copies as opposed to lampoons, caricatures and sacrilegious spoofs. To a great expert, requiring a system to find such details might seem excessive because they know many of these things at a glance. But what of the young teenager living in Hollywood who, as an atheist, has no religious background and sees the version with Marilyn Monroe for the first time? How are they to know that this is a spoof rather than something downloaded from a 1950s equivalent of CNN online? A true search engine will help the young Hollywood teenager and every true searcher.

We noted earlier how object-oriented programming led increasingly to a bundling of instructions concerning a given operation. Applied to cultural objects, this implies that all the knowledge concerning a given subject such as the Last Supper can be bundled together, such that one can trace its development alphabetically, chronologically, and spatially throughout a range of media. Since the Renaissance, we have used media to separate objects: books into libraries, paintings into art galleries, drawings into drawing collections (French: *cabinets de dessein*), engravings into engraving collections (German: *Kupferstichkabinett*), maps into map rooms, etc. We need a reorganization of knowledge whereby a theme such as the Last Supper,

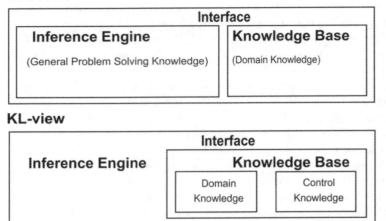

Figure 20a New view of expert systems according to the authors of KAD

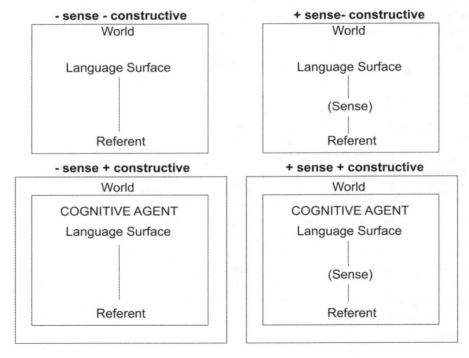

Figure 20b Four basic ontologies according to Roland Hausser (Erlangen-Nürnberg).[16]

which entails most of these individual media will be hyperlinked to all these objects spread out through numerous institutions around the world.

Underlying the difficulties considered above with respect to the Last Supper are deeper problems. We expect our search engines to provide a single, static answer. By contrast, the realities of cultural and historical knowledge entail multiple, dynamic answers with respect to space, time, individuals, objects, concepts, etc. A given text has commentaries and interpretations. We need dynamic metadata.

We need a dynamic knowledge that includes cultural and historical dimensions. We need a system that reflects distinctions between truth and viewpoints. As we shall see in the section that follows, existing ontologies and models of agents offered by those in artificial intelligence and cognitive science are unsatisfactory.

5. Truth versus Viewpoints

In our discussion of enduring knowledge (chapter 12), we distinguished between primary sources and secondary literature, i.e., there is content and there are interpretations. In the nineteenth century, this seemed straightforward. There were objects, and about these objects there were both objective facts and subjective interpretations. By the late nineteenth century, a few individuals such as Nietzsche recognized that the situation was not so straightforward.[17]

To state the problem provocatively, he suggested that any attempt at knowledge was an interpretation, or to use his language, a viewpoint or a perspective. In the twentieth century, perspectivism emerged as a term in philosophy and literature; theories of literary viewpoints emerged, narrative typologies based on viewpoints developed, and even classification experts began to explore how perspective might be integrated into their systems. Many of the -isms of literary critic-ism were a result.

The emerging fields of computer science and artificial intelligence have paid almost no attention to such debates. Early theories of expert systems began with the idea of a knowledge base (with domain knowledge). Like the knowledge of printed books, this was assumed to be static. Any changes that did occur were relegated to an inference engine, which was assigned to deal with general problem-solving knowledge. There was no versioning in these early models. Because knowledge was assumed to be static there seemed no need to include dynamic treatments of time or space, let alone cultural and historical changes. Gradually a new view of expert systems with knowledge levels emerged. The knowledge base was now subdivided into domain knowledge (static part) and control knowledge (dynamic part), with the inference engine running things. But there was still no attention to changes in knowledge (Figure 20a).

In this context, those in computer science and artificial intelligence speak increasingly of ontologies. Roland Hausser,[18] a professor of computer linguistics at Erlangen, has identified four major schools. A first sees language as a surface beneath which there are referents. This, he claims, is the approach of Russell, Carnap, Quine, and Montague. A second school also sees language as a surface, but linked with an underlying referent through a sense. This, he claims, is the approach of Frege.

TABLE 43 Eight types of searching agents in the Story Archive of the ASK system at Northwestern University.

1 The Scientific Agent
2 The History Agent
3 The Economics Agent
4 The Psychology Agent
5 The Dramatic Agent
6 The Logic Agent
7 The Thematic Agent
8 The Description Agent

Alan Newell, a professor at Carnegie Mellon University, inspired, it is said, by the philosopher Franz Brentano, wanted to go further by taking into account the intentionality[19] of the observer. Hence, the notion of language as a surface beneath which there are referents became subsumed to a cognitive agent. Starting in the 1950s, Newell working with his colleague Herbet Simon, a Nobel laureate in economics, developed the idea of a general problem solver in the form of a simulation programme that led to the engineering approach in software programming. Hausser claims that this third approach of Newell and Simon is shared by Terry Winograd, a professor at Stanford, who was a pioneer in natural language programming and Roger Schank, a computer scientist at Northwestern, whose work on Learning we shall discuss below. A fourth approach subsumes the second within the framework of a cognitive agent. This, claims Hausser, is the approach of John R. Anderson, a psychologist at Carnegie Mellon and author of the SLIM Theory of Language. Hausser sees these approaches as four variants of sense and constructivism (Figure 20b). It is worth looking more closely at these ontologies in order to show why they are not up to the challenges of dealing seriously with examples such as the plane crash and the Last Supper mentioned above.

Ontology 1: Language Surface and Referents
In this model, if the language surface is a specific plane crash, one could make each of the twelve sources different referents, i.e., the three eyewitnesses, the three reporters, etc., but there would be no clear method to distinguish between the truth of the situation and false reports. Similarly in the case of a Last Supper, there is no framework for separating the physical event, from either the serious religious symbolism or the frivolous caricatures it generates.

Ontology 2: Language Surface, Sense and Referents
In this model, if the language surface is a specific plane crash, one could make each of the twelve sources different senses of referents, but there would still be no clear method to distinguish between the truth of the situation and false reports. In the case

of a Last Supper, there is again no framework for separating the physical event, from either the serious religious symbolism or the frivolous caricatures it generates.

Ontology 3: World and Cognitive Agent with Language Surface and Referents
In this model, one might try to make the crash the world and then treat each of the twelve sources as agents, but this reduces the world to an accident within the world rather than a world within which accidents happen. Such a decision can assign a truth-value to the world and assign interpretation value to the sources. But there is still no clear method to establish how the world situation is linked to the agents, i.e., we still have no method for determining which are true and which are false reports. In the case of a Last Supper, there is still no framework for separating the physical event from either the serious religious symbolism or the frivolous caricatures it generates (cf. §2 above).

Ontology 4: World, Cognitive Agent with Language Surface, Sense and Referents
This model takes the layers one step further, but it too cannot deal with the interpretative problems of either a plane crash or a Last Supper. The depths of historical interpretation pose many more problems. There is a manuscript text by an author (primary literature). Then there are various transcriptions and translations (critical and non-critical editions). Then there are interpretations based on those transcriptions and translations (secondary literature in the form of internal analyses). There are interpretations discussing this text in the context of other texts on the subject (secondary literature in the form of external analyses). Then there are the interpretations entailed when a book or object is restored or reconstructed.

There is also a changing history of assessment of the significance of a text, an object, or a person. And there is the changing history of assessment of the authors of those assessments. For instance, in one generation, a scholar may be considered the authority on Leonardo, in another generation, access to new sources may change the standing of that scholar within the academic community. Then there are cultural differences. Each nation tends to emphasize its own scientific heroes. A German scientist such as Max Planck may be very famous in Germany, less so in France, and have a much different standing when in books written by historians of physics elsewhere, e.g., the United States, India, or China.

The four ontologies outlined above are incapable of dealing with these complexities. Worse, under the guise of a seeming objectivity, they entail dangers of profound distortions of reality, which cannot be checked, and the risk of losing any sense of truth that can be verified. They threaten the possibility of even establishing criteria for a search for truth. Lest this sound like a gross exaggeration, it is useful to cite a concrete example to illustrate the problems.

At Northwestern University, there was an Institute for Learning Sciences, which was discussed earlier in the context of education (chapter 9). There, Professor Schank, who subscribes to the third ontology (cf. Figure 20b) has been working for over a decade on the ASK systems. This began with a prototype called Ask Tom, which dealt with bank trust consulting and Ask Michael, based on a book by Michael Porter.[20] In 1991, during the Gulf War, the U.S. Transportation Command (TRANSCOM) decided to develop this approach.[21] The system presently foresees the use of eight types of searching agents for the story archive (Table 43). On first reading, the idea is clear and seems very impressive. The agents search for us, they look for either general principles or specific examples, they find interesting stories, and they adapt these to one of two persona.[22]

On closer reflection, this approach entails all the shortcomings mentioned above concerning the four ontologies. How, for instance, can such a scientific agent deal with the validity of different scientific theories historically or reflect the levels of disagreement about certain theories or experiments? In the case of the economics agent: how will it distinguish between micro and macro approaches, between Marxist and capitalist views, between Keynesian economics and what came before or after, etc.? In the case of the psychology agent, how will it convey the different views depending on whether one is a behaviourist or not; whether one follows Jungian or Freudian psychology, whether one is an American looking at Freud, a colleague of Freud in Vienna or London, or a member of another culture such as China or India? In the case of the history agent, there is a choice between the view of Herodotus (general principles persona) and Tacitus (specific examples persona).[23] Once again, this sounds extremely impressive. It is striking, however, that while Professor Schank's description of agents above refers to perspective, it is implicitly always from an American viewpoint. There is nothing in his description to suggest that ASK helps one to understand how the Iraqis felt, what factions there were within the country, and how they interpreted the experiences that were imposed upon them. Iraq is a Muslim country, where 95% of the population belong to the Shi'á sect and 5% belong to the Sunni sect. How can the professor's system help us to learn of differences between Sunni and Shi'ite Iraqis?

The history agent is telling the story only from the viewpoint of the victor, much like U.S. web sites on the Desert Storm war, which offered the following: "The United States suffered 148 killed in action, 458 wounded, 121 killed in nonhostile actions and 11 female combat deaths. In June 1991 the U.S. estimated that more than 100,000 Iraqi soldiers died, 300,000 were wounded, 150,000 deserted, and 60,000 were taken prisoner. Many human rights groups claimed a much higher numbers of Iraqi killed in action."[24] If we doubted the figures, how could we check them? If we wanted to understand the viewpoint of the loser, how could the history agent in its present form do so? How could we learn about other viewpoints concerning the war?[25]

But what of more complex cases? North American and European history books typically speak of the fall of Constantinople. But the same event in 1453 was also the rise of the Ottoman Empire from another point of view. Every presentation tends towards being a selection, a selection that filters the evidence and chooses only the evidence that supports the winning side. Unless we are extremely careful, we shall have very effective agents that provide us with a small sample of the evidence without revealing the criteria of the selection. We like to complain about this danger using examples such as Russia and China, invoking the spectre of censorship in such countries, but the problem exists equally and perhaps more insidiously in countries like the United States where no official censorship is at play.

In some fields, such as law, the scope of different relevant views is necessarily more limited. Pasi Tiitinen is leading an interesting European project called *Eulegis*, which provides three different views on the same corpus of legal material, namely a producer actor view (Who?), a source information view (What?), and a process view (How?).[26] While extremely useful, this is still entirely from a contemporary viewpoint. Needed is an approach that includes cultural and historical differences. The law in Germany applies to all German citizens. But if the German citizen happens to be a forty-five-year-old individual who is a political exile from Turkey where they had spent the first forty years of their life, then it would be helpful for them to be informed of differences between Turkish and German law, just as it would be helpful for a lawyer needing to defend such a plaintiff to understand how or why the so-called crime might be perceived quite differently by the political exile.

Equally important is an historical understanding of subjects. To remain with the example of German law, there were historically so many links between Germanic law and Hebraic law that, when Hitler openly adopted his extreme position in 1937, he was soon forced to close the law school at Göttingen and elsewhere. A deeper appreciation of these historical links throws a rather different light on the complexity of the Hebraic tradition in Germany. Here our concern is not to list all the possible examples but rather to draw attention to a basic shortcoming of Internet materials generally and search engines particularly.

Thanks to the largely positivistic and sometimes blatantly naïve assumptions of those in cognitive science and artificial intelligence, most of our models of information and knowledge depart from a strictly contemporary position, as if everything can be captured by a static field, as if there were no role for different languages, cultural differences, historical changes, alternative interpretations, very different audiences, different corpora, and different canons. In the United States, this trend is closely linked with the dictum on the American dollar bill: E[x] pluribus Unum (From the many, one). At the international level, this trend is called globalization, McDonaldization.

It is important to recognize that the fight for domination over portals is about much more than dividends in technology investments. It is ultimately a political struggle to control viewpoints. For if one can present enough material that persons believe that they have access to the full story, then one can readily hide the bits of the stories that prove embarrassing to the party that is presently in power. So a challenge looms: aside from obvious state secrets, how can we provide access to knowledge in memory institutions such that individuals are free to study and reinterpret the meaning and significance of both primary sources and the existing secondary literature concerning those sources?

Audiences

Closely related to this question of perspectives, viewpoints, and interpretations is the problem of different audiences. The question of audiences is always cited with respect to the need to protect small children from pornographic materials and the need to distinguish between beginners and experts.[27] As we have seen in the discussion of personalization (chapter 10), marketers are now targeting an audience of one.

Such audiences may be attractive for business but may be dangerous for communities. As we shall see below (§7), communities rely on audiences that have a shared heritage of religious beliefs, basic values, and cultural expressions. We shall suggest that there is no contradiction if, within a community, there are at the same time persons who belong to different minorities that are smaller subsets of the original. In short, a same individual can be many different audiences and thus belong simultaneously to a number of different communities.

6. Observation versus Protection

Also related to the phenomenon of personalization (chapter 10) is the idea that everyone is an author. According to the rhetoric, in the past, only a small elite was allowed to publish. Now everyone is able to publish. In practice the situation is more complex. Potentially everyone who has a computer with appropriate software is able to publish. At present this is 800+ million out of 6+ billion. A first step will be to ensure that everyone has access to such networked computers.

While everyone can potentially be an author, not everyone can be at the level of a Shakespeare. Hence, the closer we come to making everyone an author, the more urgent is the need for new methods to distinguish between different levels of quality. We need new tools to identify levels of respect, reputation, and ultimately trust. Is the person I am reading accepted locally, nationally, or internationally? Are they respected by their respective professions or not? How do we create electronic equivalents of peer review?

Authentication

As we create ever-more access to a universe of diverse materials, there are new needs for authentication, which go hand in hand with new arguments for observation. These problems have inspired a range of suggestions and proposed solutions. Even within the W3 Consortium, there are two approaches. For instance, in the vision of Tim Berners-Lee, the W3 is working on the idea of 'web of trust' whereby one will be able to determine the logical truth-value of claims (Appendix 7) and the reliability of products. Meanwhile, Robert Cailliau, a co-founder of the World Wide Web, claims "all Internet users should be licensed so surfers on the information highway are as accountable as drivers on the road."[28] At one end of the spectrum are groups such as Echelon, the international spy organization led by the United States, which claim that everyone and everything should be subject to both authentication and observation.

It is striking to note just how many technologies for tracking[29] and observation are now emerging, including voice recognition, fingerprints, DNA, finger-scans, digital photographs, hand geometry, digital signatures, retinal scans, and social security number identification.[30] This capacity applies to work, home, and potentially anywhere. Tracking devices include inside-in systems (gloves and suits), electromagnetic position and orientation, acoustic position and orientation, mechanical position and orientation, electrostatic position and orientation, video and electro-optical, eye movement tracking, and multi-button and force ball devices.[31] The efforts at a Total Information Awareness (TIA) represent an extreme approach to these challenges.

Using the rhetoric of dangers of identity theft, some are increasingly urging the adoption of these new tracking technologies for authentication. They argue that retinal scans are much more reliable than passwords or identity cards. Ironically, their proposed solution only makes the problem worse. If there is an identity theft with a password or an identity card, these are easily replaced. But if someone has successfully stolen an image of my retinal scan, how do we create an alternative? And what do I do in the meantime while my own identity has been "suspended"?

Work

It has long been assumed that while one is at work one is subject to being supervised. The Taylorization of work began at the blue-collar level and subsequently spread throughout the entire workplace. In recent years, this trend towards observation has increased greatly. Employees at large corporations generally assume that their e-mail is open to scrutiny. More recently, devices for recording every tab on a keyboard mean that an employee's every move can be followed, recorded, and reconstructed. Some companies are reported to be tracking employees' waste in washrooms. Some major companies are reported consciously to be looking for employees' weaknesses so that this can be used to leverage their "performance." In one recent case, the private "I Seek You" (ICQ) discussions of a CEO of a company were made public, which led to the resignation of several executives, threatened the future of the company, and led some to suggest that "privacy may become a thing of the past."[32] Meanwhile, in Europe and specifically in countries such as the Netherlands, there are new laws that require a) that employers inform their employees about monitoring, b) that employers provide reasonable grounds for doing so, and c) that employees must voluntarily give up their right to privacy.

Home

Numerous devices are also entering the home. Some of these are very unobtrusive such as child alarms for child safety[33] or web cameras (webcams), which allow our friends to see us but can inadvertently be used by others to observe us. Some are literally invisible. For example, web "cookies" can a) provide us with a personal greeting or b) act as a counter. In January 1999, a suit was filed against DoubleClick for creating a "sophisticated and highly intrusive means of collecting and cross-referencing private personal information without the knowing consent of users."[34] Such cookies can also be used for criminal purposes: "such as stealing credit card numbers and passwords, or tracking your Internet uses."[35]

Among the many new developments are various attempts of governments to render it legal for them to record one's Internet searching even when there is no clear evidence of criminal activity. Fortunately organizations such as the Electronic Frontier Foundation and newsletters such as Depesche track these on a daily basis. As mentioned above, in Europe there are also laws to protect individuals against excesses in this context.

Everywhere

In the discussion of nano-technology (chapter 3), we noted dangers of chips implanted in prisoners as tracking devices. Some will be tempted to dismiss this as science fiction – all the more so because a film such as The Art of War includes such an implant. Similarly, the latest sequel to Mission Impossible (MI-2) includes an injectable version of a tracking device. Meanwhile, tracking devices for commercial trucks and even some private vehicles are now an everyday matter.[36]

A new development in the realm of emergency numbers called E911 will give emergency service personnel a call, plus "the originating cell phone's telephone number and, more significantly, the location of the cell site that handled the call." This will allow them to locate a phone within a 125-metre radius. James Dempsey, senior staff-counsel at the Center for Democracy and Technology has noted: "With the implementation of E911, … your phone has become an ankle bracelet. Therefore we are urging the standard for government access be increased to a full probable cause standard. [Law enforcement agencies] have to have suspicion to believe that the person they are targeting is engaged in criminal activity."[37] If concern for such matters sounds exaggerated, then it is sobering to recall that, in former communist East Germany, dissidents were given radioactive tracers, sometimes shot from special guns, in order that they could be followed everywhere.[38] Meanwhile, visionaries such as Salman A. Khan predict that, within a decade, the Internet will have personal profiles that go far beyond present-day credit card information:

Now imagine if that information were extended to represent your political views, your spending habits, who you spend your time with – not to mention a complete physical description of you. That would allow for perfect marketing. "You wouldn't mind seeing ads, because they would be ads for things you were [already] thinking about buying and would probably [anticipate and answer] all the questions you have about the product…. Imagine, for example, news that fills in any background information that you don't know, or a science text that is written at exactly your level of understanding. This concept of data representation can be extended even further to active data [or a software-based proxy] that could act on your behalf. In 10 years, you may have agents that roam the Web and perform transactions as you would have performed them yourself. Since these agents would conceivably have your tastes and spending habits, they could conceivably try on and purchase clothing for you."[39]

Many persons may not share Mr. Kahn's optimism that being so closely tracked is desirable. In the George Orwell's book 1984, there were visions of a Big Brother, who could track persons everywhere through cameras even in their homes. In real life, surveillance cameras were traditionally in high security areas. The past two decades have seen an enormous increase in the use of such cameras in banks, malls, most public places, and even along highways and some streets. Persons have rightly noted that there are serious privacy issues when, in certain major cities, it is theoretically possible to follow a person's tracks as they go from building to building.

A puzzling recent phenomenon is where persons are consciously giving up their privacy in order to be seen. In television shows such as Survivor, cameras follow persons everywhere for a number of weeks. The Internet has brought new dimensions to this trend. In 2000, at a public level, there were many web cameras in cities and sites. Virtual Berlin has 129 panoramas of the city on-line.[40] There are twelve web cameras or webcams of Mount Fuji alone.[41] There are over two thousand such live webcams worldwide.[42] In New York there are live webcams in taxis.[43] Webcams, also called vuecams, cover a wide variety of themes, including animals, arts, entertainment, and business. Researchers such as Professor Takeo Kanade (Carnegie Mellon) are taking this general approach much further. Using a principle he calls "virtualized reality," Professor Kanade uses numerous cameras to take photographs from fifty-one positions in a room. He then uses these real photographs in order to make a virtual reality reconstruction of the original room, which can potentially be viewed even from positions where there was no camera in the original.[44] Others speak of real virtuality.[45]

Professor Takade applied this principle to the Superbowl on Sunday 28 January 2001[46] in order to bring live action replays to a new level. Theoretically one can look at any play, even from angles where there was no camera. Using an autonomous helicopter, Professor Kanade applied the same principle to the Haughton Crater on Devon Island, in the Northwest Territories (Canada) in July, 1999.[47] He has noted that the same principle could be extended to entire countries. The potentials for cinema were further explored in The Matrix sequels, where the camera took 122 positions.[48]

The positive side of such developments is that they make possible new worlds of immersive, interactive, experience, including television, through methods such as Interactive Virtual Viewpoint Video (IVVV).[49] For the first time in history, these new visualization techniques allow us literally to see things from all sides. The negative side is that they plunge us into a new set of paradoxes. The same methods can be used to create visually compelling images of things and events that could not happen in the physical world: witness the scenes in Matrix II and III. So the new visualization method is also one that undermines our sense of vision as the basis of veracity: seeing is no longer believing. Moreover, these new images can be edited and altered. This is potentially disturbing because there are as yet no reliable mechanisms to trace which images have been altered. Unless there are new mechanisms to ensure the veracity and authenticity of images to ensure that they have not been tampered with, the problems to which William Mitchell drew attention in The Reconfigured Eye will become much more acute. The Forrest Gump syndrome could become an everyday one, as political and other enemies are falsely placed with dubious company or in compromising positions, or both.

Meanwhile, at a personal level, persons are choosing to have cameras trace their activities at work, at home, and even in their bedrooms. There are now hundreds of college webcams.[50] A few of these are sexually oriented, but what is remarkable is that many involve healthy, "ordinary" young persons who see this as a new form of expression, a new tool for autobiography.[51] Traditionally, one would have seen all this as an invasion of privacy.[52] With these individuals, one senses that privacy is scarcely a serious concept in their lives. Is this a consequence of the Internet or a symptom of something else?

Tele-presence, as it was originally used by the U.S. military, was about being able to control and operate objects at a distance. Telepresence (or tele-science) has become an experience of being there: how much one feels the vicinity of another person through video conferencing or virtual reality. The individuals who are present on the web through their on-line cameras are clearly striving for tele-presence in this new sense, Is this a religious aspiration of trying to achieve the omnipresence traditionally seen as the domain of God alone? Or is the lack of real relationships simply leading persons to a new kind of exhibitionism of everyday life?

Protection

Beneath these promises of personalization (cf. chapter 10) lurk other problems. In the past there was a clear distinction between public and private life, at least in theory. In public, a person was expected to follow all the rules of propriety. In private, a person was free to go to adult movies, watch them in the privacy of one's home or a hotel room or read a magazine of the Playboy variety. What happens if all our actions are recorded, if there is no longer a distinction between our on-line activities as professionals in the office and as private persons at home? Who will have access to that information? Who has the right to know what programs we watch in private? Who will ensure that such potentially incriminating information is not simply used for smear campaigns? Will the government know, our banks, our insurance companies, our employers, or everyone? In which case will there still be a sense of privacy?

One particular area of concern is children. They need some protection from pornographic, violent, and other sites on the Internet. This has led to a series of responses. In the United States, the fascination with technology has led to a number of filters such as Net Nanny, which attempt to block unwanted sites. In Europe, some local regions such as Namur, continue the old traditions of censorship whereby a person visits web sites one by one and judges each one individually, an approach that is doomed to be more exhausting than exhaustive. In Japan, NEC has seven fulltime persons who sift through on-line materials to determine whether they are acceptable for their offerings in education.[53]

In Canada, there are different approaches that are more interesting. At the national level, the government sponsors a Canadian Schoolnet whereby a series of suggested web sites are listed in order to point children in the right direction. In some cases such as the Toronto Separate School Board, children and parents are asked to sign a paper that effectively commits them to a code of honour while using the Internet on the school premises. If a young person does not obey the code, they are disciplined just as they would be if they misbehaved in the past. This has the advantage that children are free to search the entire Internet and the onus is on them to be decent.

Minorities

Such problems are all the more dramatic in the case of various minorities. Rhetorically, the Internet is for everyone. In practice, in 2000 only about 5 per cent of the world's population was connected and, even if we accept the most optimistic predictions of the Vint Cerfs, by 2006 that percentage will still be well under 40 per cent. Thus for the near future the great majority of the world remains excluded.

Even among the small percentage who has access to the Internet, there are other problems of minorities. It is claimed that on the Internet no one knows that you are a dog, or rather a *New Yorker* cartoonist. According to this claim we are anonymous. But if we all have unique IP addresses and unique identifiers for "secure" transactions, then every action and every interaction on the web can be traced. That is why the personalization techniques outlined earlier (chapter 10) work so well. Hence, someone not only knows you are a dog but also what kind and what your habits are. A corollary is that all is comfortable as long as one is an everyday kind of dog recognized by everyone.

Silent and Excluded Views

Rhetorically, the web gives us new opportunities for expression, which could be a euphemism for saying that it is a tool for laying bare all our secrets. In any case, this introduces a corollary that only those who speak are heard. Those who choose to be silent or those who are kept silent effectively do not exist. If the expressed world is reduced to the politically correct world, then the good news is that all is well on the surface. The bad news is that there is nothing left under the surface, there is no longer depth that is recorded, there are no longer dissenting voices.

7. Public versus Private

From a business point of view, personalization is a wonderful new method of "getting closer to the customer" (cf. chapter 10). It amounts to using personal information about individuals in order to sell them more things, frequently building on their weaknesses, and ultimately making a business thereof: whereby the customer becomes product. From an immediate business point of view, personalization is excellent because it brings more sales. But it also undermines serendipity, whereby a reader accidentally notices something of great interest.

Personalization versus Community

From a social point of view, personalization, especially when applied to content, entails more serious dangers. Society is about shared values, which come through common beliefs and shared experiences. During the Middle Ages, in the Latin West these shared values came mainly through Christianity and specifically through shared access to the *Bible*. As scholars have shown, the *Bible*[54] was much more than a source of religion. It was also an inspiration for Dante's *Divine Comedy*, Milton's *Paradise Lost*, and much of Western literature. From the eighteenth century onwards, there emerged an idea of classics, great books, which still exists at universities such as Oxford and Harvard. From this emerged the notion of a canon: a list of basic books that every civilized person was expected to read.

The rise of the nation state in the nineteenth century brought with it the notion of national canons: Chaucer, Shakespeare, Milton, Pope, and Keats were as quintessentially British, as Lessing, Goethe, and Schiller were essentially German. At another level, the rise of national newspapers played a complementary role. The *Times*, *Le Monde*, *La Reppublica* and *Frankfurter Allgemeine Zeitung* became shared experiences and views of the world for the British, French, Italians, and Germans, respectively. This had the added advantage that a person in England wishing to understand the French view had merely to read *Le Monde* or other French newspapers. A profound advantage was that it gave everyone a common ground for discussion. There was always some disaster, scandal, or problem, which was a common point of departure. Persons were always free, of course, to read as much or as little of the news as they chose.

Ironically, just as Europe was defining this canon in the late nineteenth and early twentieth centuries, it was also engaged in discovering that Eurocentrism was no longer a viable concept. Max Müller's monumental *Sacred Books of the East*, made it clear that there were many more sacred texts than the *Talmud*, *Bible*, and *Koran*. Texts such as the *Rig Veda*, *Mahabharata*, *Ramayana*, *Shahnama*, *I Ching*, *Tao Te Ching*, and the *Four Books of Confucius* could not be ignored. This applied equally in the realm of literature where the Chinese *Three Kingdoms* or the Japanese *Tale of Gengi*[55] were clearly at the world level. The advent of the two world wars raised further problems. If the values of the West were so noble, how could something so terrible have occurred? Long before the deconstructionists had begun destroying the canon, the foundations of the traditional canon were already endangered.

If personalization gives everyone their own version of "my paper," the common ground provided by a canon disappears. If one individual reads only politics, another only business, and a third only legal cases, there will no longer be common topics as points of departure for discussion and debate. Similarly, if personalization were to give everyone their own version of "my book," then an Indian child might reasonably read only Hindi authors, an American child might read only American authors and there would no longer be a common heritage of symbols that everyone in a culture is expected to understand. Here again loom dangers of de-contextualization. A first step towards a solution may well be a layered approach.

A challenge for the Internet thus becomes not just to offer individuals things aimed at or chosen by them, but also to provide them with basic local, national, and international texts, art and other expressions in order to develop new shared experiences. This is all the more urgent because the Internet is making us aware that there are universal images such as cosmic eggs and world trees that serve as integrating foundations across and among cultures. Ultimately the Internet should lead to new sharing, in order that our social fabric be reconstituted rather than undermined (cf. chapter 14).

Inner versus Outer

Computers link human users in the physical world with a series of computational worlds often behind a screen. From the 1950s to the 1980s while computing occurred mainly on a two-dimensional surface, the window and mouse metaphors were dominant. We saw earlier (chapter 1) that some see a shift from Graphical User Interfaces (GUIs) to Tangible User Interfaces (TUIs) and Perceptual User Interfaces (PUIs).

We noted also how the rise of mobility and miniaturization (chapters 2–3) are bringing new combinations of gesture technology and voice activation. It is feasible that these new methods will be tailored to an individual. If so what methods will there be to ensure authentication? How will the system cope with competing commands – as when two persons want to watch different programs on the same screen? If we have such means for action at a distance, will the scenarios concerning Tangible User Interfaces be replaced? If they are combined, how will this work?

More radical scenarios include nano-technology, direct brain implants, and wireless control of humans and machines. Possible brain interfaces raise many new questions. Suppose that thoughts can replace the mouse as a means of moving between interfaces. Presumably children will not have the same access and power as adults. So there will be hierarchies of commands. What about two persons at the same level with different plans? How will an interface deal with this?

Such developments challenge us to rethink the entire subject-object distinction, which evolved from the Renaissance. Where does inner end and outer begin? How much of a "person" will become "visible"? These are the old questions of privacy at an entirely different level. It is useful, for instance, to map a spectrum or continuum from the unconscious to the conscious (Table 45). Will the entire spectrum be visible? If so, what point along this continuum in the inner world will trigger action in the external world? Clearly it cannot be the whole spectrum or else everything that passes through our minds would be translated into action and thus remove one of the most central qualities of a human being: the ability not to do everything one is able to do, which is the essence of choice.

TABLE 45 Twelve steps in a spectrum from an unconscious notion to a conscious act.

1	Dream
2	Intuition
3	Suspicion
4	Passing Thought
5	Wild Idea in Passing
6	Thought
7	Contemplate
8	Intend
9	Pre-Meditate
10	Plan
11	Rehearse
12	Act

In the past, if someone was "thinking" of writing a letter, they might well mull it over for a few days: first whether to write or not to write, then what to write. Thereafter, there might well be various rough drafts, which might well end with a decision not to send the letter after all. E-mail has considerably increased the ease with which to create a draft and also increased the tendency to send on impulse before we have considered the possible consequences of what we have just jotted down. Mind-mail and thought-mail will increase these problems.

Thought interfaces raise fundamentally new ethical and legal questions. Traditionally we have made a very clear distinction between a) a healthy, sane, upright individual, who reads about murder in a detective novel or watches a film of the same and b) a criminal who performs a murder. The rise of the Internet has already brought some confusion into this distinction. Persons describing murders of real persons in "fictive" on-line novels have on occasion been charged with being criminal.

Will the mind become like a home: a place that is private in principle and open to searching only under special search warrants? If so, what will constitute the right to enter the complete mind? These problems exist not only in criminal cases but also in everyday life. In the past, I might well have many thoughts about an enemy, a boss, or even a neighbour, which I usually did not "express" as part of being a civilized human being. Will this remain the case? Or will a boss in the future literally be able to see what I mean, think, suspect, etc. If so, will all this be "wireless" from one brain to another? Or will the scenarios from the film, *Minority Report*, become a reality? Or will there be projections in the external world? Will artists and designers project their "ideas" onto boards for collaborative work, collaborative design? Will there be collaborative "creation"?

The viewpoint of an individual historian or author in the humanities has typically made their work a solitary act as opposed to collaborative acts in the sciences and especially in so-called big science projects such as advanced physics. How can interfaces represent viewpoints? How can they render visible differences between conjecture and fact, between different schools of interpretation, between levels of logical coherence, between accepted fact and uncertainty? How can interfaces reflect differences in world views: between the creation of a subject-object distinction in the West and the an aesthetic that seeks to unite subject-object in the East?

Public Good

These questions of inner and outer at the micro-level are reflected as further problems of public and private at the macro level with respect to governments and other political entities. In this larger social sense, there is a rhetoric that claims that governments are no longer relevant, that public initiatives represent undue and unnecessary intervention, and that we should instead rely entirely on private initiatives. This rhetoric is linked with an assumption that economics is the sole paradigm for society (cf. chapter 14).

While the rhetoric of the Internet inevitably champions free speech and at the same time a need to let market forces decide, this belies an assumption that all persons are theoretically equal, which they are not. If the expressed word is limited only to the most intelligent, what about the majority who fall below the Nobel level? If the expressed word is limited to those who can afford it, will not expressions gradually become those of persons who can afford to represent themselves as they would like to be seen, i.e., paid political advertisements, more than expressions of the heart? Underlying these debates are fundamental questions of public versus private interests, and the proper domains of each. What is the role of the individual and what is the role of government? Once again, very different approaches are evident in the United States, Europe, and Japan.

In the United States, there is a rhetoric that there should be as little government as possible. There is a pretence that government should be like business, reacting to needs just in time rather than making long-range plans. Hence totalitarian governments have five-year plans, America strives for government on demand. Critics like Derber, see greater dangers in these trends: "The new privatization movement is an explicit effort to turn public resources, services and functions – for centuries operated by governments – over to corporations."[56]

Rhetorically there are a number of (false) dichotomies: a public government is opposed to private business and private individuals. As a corollary, the regulation of government is opposed to the *laissez-faire* of business. The control of government is seen as being at odds with the freedom of business. However, as Lessig[57] and others have noted, corporations, and the patents which protect them, are technically created by the public functions of government. Without the regulation of government, all *laissez faire* would be meaningless. Moreover, while government may appear to be dwindling in the United States, the hidden arms of government in security (FBI, CIA), military, and space programs, continue to grow.

Paradoxically, the U.S. government continually preaches non-interference in the case of foreign governments and then proceeds to interfere on all fronts when its own interests are at stake. The American government also preaches privatization especially in the realm of telcos, but when foreign companies propose to buy these companies on what is purportedly the open market, the government appears to have no qualms with interfering. The proposed Hollings Bill on cryptography is another example of this interfering non-interference.[58] Proof of freedom and non-interference in the American system is assumed to lie in the press and media. It is they who express freedom and draw attention to all deviations from the path. Or at least that is the theory.

Films such as *The Insider* remind us that this story becomes more complex when the quest for truth brings to light evidence that is uncomfortable for some of the large financial interests. Indeed, more than sometimes it appears that the country that praises e-business above all else has lost all criteria other than money. On the surface, America talks of electronic media as a new means of democratic media, but in practice there is an assumption that the Internet is just another realm of advertising that can be bought. Everything has its price. To be sure, there are projects such as the Government Information Locator Service (GILS), a metadata initiative to make government materials more easily accessible and as we saw earlier (chapter 6) there are initiatives to make government materials available on-line.

In Europe, although there are many versions of government with differing emphases on federal and state models, there is, as a whole, a much greater sense of a public good. In France, particularly, there is a clear belief that public monies from taxpayers must be used for the public good and cannot be used for private ends. Accordingly, there is much more concern in Europe with public information and matters of public concern. While some parts of Europe, and notably Britain, have adopted as practice the American rhetoric for privatization, especially in the realms of railway, telecommunications, and research, there has on the whole been a healthy scepticism about giving up the role of government. Indeed there has been a conviction that government is needed particularly in the realm of infrastructure.

In Japan, government is much more organically part of society. Unlike the United States, where corporations are now seen as almost purely private, Japan continues to have a number of public corporations. In addition, the age-old traditions of the *zaibatsu*,[59] now called *keiretsu*, mean that major companies in Japan remain bound by a code, which reminds one of the ancient European guilds, but works at a national and international level. When the Nissan Corporation, which employs some 300,000 persons, was seen to be headed towards bankruptcy, the Japanese government worked with the French government to ensure a modernization program through a combined effort with Renault. In Japan, government consciously intervenes when the public good is seen to be at stake.

Privatization of Knowledge

In this rhetoric about government being unnecessary lie various dangers, one of which is the privatization of knowledge. This in turn is but one aspect of a larger challenge to redefine the concept of a public good in a global world where actions are no longer defined by the traditional jurisdictions of nation states. Trends towards privatization of knowledge have come from many fronts including small companies, but mainly from publishers and multinational corporations, although recently universities have also become active in this domain.[60]

Small Companies

National and provincial governments as well as cities produce a great amount of public information. Sometimes they work specifically with small companies in order to make this material available in the form of CD-ROMs and web sites, often with a view to cost recovery. Hence, public information, paid for by taxpayers' money, is made available to the public on the condition that they pay for it a second time. In some cases, this is done in the name of government being responsible and cutting expenses.

More insidious are cases where publicly available information is taken, sometimes without asking, and incorporated into a private web site. This is increasingly happening in the case of information about cities in Germany and to a certain extent in France.[61] Fortunately, in France, there is now an *Association des Villes Numériques*, which is helping the local authorities to regain control of their information.

Why, one might ask, would private companies go the trouble of taking public information and making it privately available? Their business case is simple. They link this local public information with information about shops, events, and local industries and then get advertising revenue from these parties. A positive interpretation of this trend would be that small businesses are generating jobs and the public gets free information without having to pay. It may look like a win-win situation, but, in fact, the advertising fees paid by local producers also need to be recovered, which happens by having the public pay higher prices for the same goods. This is a case of re-intermediation at the public expense.

Publishers

Since late medieval times, city-states and cities created city libraries for their citizens. In some university towns (e.g., Bologna, Padua, Heidelberg, Oxford), the university library informally served a public function. Such examples evolved into the concept of public libraries paid for by taxpayers and readily accessible to citizens.[62]

Until recently publishers played an essential role in publishing the works of authors, which were then bought by libraries and thus made available to members of the public who could not afford to have their own collections of books. While this basic pattern has continued, other trends in the past fifty years have undermined this long, positive tradition of publishers.

One problematic area is research. Often a scholar is paid by a university to do research. In the case of specific projects, a scholar then gets public monies in the form of research grants and fellowships. When the work is finished, a publication grant, also often public money, is needed to publish the results. When the book appears, the university libraries and other public institutions need to buy the publication using public money. In all this, the scholar usually sees no remuneration at all. But some publishers find that this provides them with opportunities of using public funds for private profit. One of the latest developments is a new company, Contentville.com, founded by the broadcaster CBS and the publisher Steven Brill, which are charging for dissertations without even asking the authors.[63]

Another problematic area concerns reference materials. There was an enormous rise of universities during the 1960s and 1970s. This was spawned partly by the "baby boom" after the Second World War and also by a new philosophy, which held that potentially everyone has a right to a university education. Publishers realized that there was a new market in providing reference books and classics for these new institutions. This inspired the rise of a reprint industry.

The good news was that new universities now had their own copies of standard reference works. The bad news was that these reprint companies increasingly assumed the copyright of works, which they had merely reprinted. As these materials became increasingly connected with electronic databases through companies such as Dialog, there were new deals between reprint companies and those offering electronic services (e.g., Reed, later Reed-Elsevier). This meant that reference materials, which had begun largely in the public domain, were now in the hands of private companies, themselves subsidiaries of multinational conglomerates.

These reference materials entail two things: 1) names and subjects of reference materials and 2) the actual contents of reference works, i.e., dictionaries, encyclopaedias, etc. If those names and subjects are viewed as proprietary, then the hope of combining them with others to make universally accessible authority lists becomes nearly impossible. This is not to say, of course, that publishers no longer have a role to play, only that with respect to the metadata which they use, qua names, subjects, places, etc., more co-operation with public institutions is needed. Else the concept of universal access becomes infeasible.

Here a basic danger lies in fragmentation of resources. Or to put it positively, there is an ever-greater challenge to arrive at something greater than specialized catalogues. All is well if one is doing work in a field such as chemistry, which has its regular bibliographies in the form of *Chemical Abstracts*, etc. But what happens if one is working in a multidisciplinary context and does not have access to one of the world's great libraries? With the catalogues of great library collections on-line, one can at least search for their titles. But what if one wants to do a more global search? Here projects such as the Gateway to European National Libraries (Gabriel), now called the European Virtual Library[64] and The European Library (TEL) are promising.[65] At the world level, there was a G7 pilot project called "Bibliotheca Universalis," which continues to develop slowly.[66] But the problem of integrating knowledge from distributed collections remains.

Germany is an extreme case in this respect. Because culture is governed at the state level, there has traditionally not been a national library in the manner of

Britain or France. There are now important efforts to link specialized collections from different centuries, sixteenth century (Bayerische Staatsbliothek); seventeenth (Wolfenbüttel), eighteenth (Göttingen), nineteenth (Leipzig), and twentieth century (Frankfurt). Meanwhile, Germany has a number of central libraries in specific fields: medicine (Cologne),[67] agriculture (Bonn),[68] business (Kiel),[69] Social Sciences (Bonn),[70] and technical information (Hanover).[71] For technology there is an international centre (Karlsruhe).[72] These are public bodies that offer free services but do not provide us with a global integrated survey. For medicine, the German Institute for Medical Documentation and Information[73] gives access to a wide range of databases. In technology, an excellent private firm linked with the FIZ-Technik[74] gives access to 60 million items from a hundred databases. This gives a near comprehensive view of the German scene with numerous connections worldwide.

In England, the main British Library catalogue is available free of charge, but their more specialized databases are on a subscription basis. In the absence of a global approach to knowledge, private companies are providing partial solutions in areas where they feel they can make money. NEC, for instance, has CiteSeer,[75] which has 150,000 computer science articles containing over 2 million citations. Dialog has three products Dialog, Profound, "information engineered for knowledge," and Datastar.[76] The Institute for Scientific Information (ISI, Philadelphia) produces Web of Science, Science Citation Index, Social Sciences Citation Index, and Arts and Humanities Citation Index.[77] Then there are private companies such as Aventis, which put together privatized little subsets of reference works.[78]

Publishers are becoming very active in this domain. Swets and Zeitlinger[79] has SwetScan with 14,000 scholarly and research journals and other periodicals. Springer has Link.[80] Elsevier claims to have the world's largest scientific database to desktop, namely, Science@direct web edition.[81] Then there is ultr*Access 2000,[82] which combines Springer's Link, Elsevier, Academic Press, etc. Dow Jones has its own Interactive[83] site. Meanwhile, newspapers such as the New York Times and Financial Times are providing access to their databases. This is being bundled. The Frankfurter Allgemeine Zeitung (FAZ)[84] is now offered by Dialog, Compuserve, Lexus Nexis, and the Financial Times.

Here we have three concerns: 1) Notwithstanding all these developments, we are nowhere close to a comprehensive overview of world knowledge. Ironically, that vision seems more distant now than a century ago when Otlet and LaFontaine were embarking on their dream of the Mundaneum. 2) Lack of a public vision in this domain means that private companies are creating new proprietary software qua databases and search engines, which is likely to make integrated searches across the board more difficult than ever. 3) Finally, the increasing privatization of these initiatives means that only very rich institutions can hope to have continuous access to these dispersed, partial solutions. The RLIN database alone, for instance, costs $50,000 annually without the trimmings.

To be sure, there are also other developments such as the decision of the Max Planck Gesellschaft to make all their e-preprints freely available on-line. Recent initiatives such as the National Electronic Site Licence Initiative (NESLI)[85] and similar developments in Canada also point to reasons for hope in the future, but the problem is far from being solved. Such schemes introduce the idea of public site licences whereby a whole range of institutions have access to materials for which they could not afford a licence on an individual basis.

Industry

A second stumbling block towards this vision comes from an unexpected quarter: industry and business.[86] The business world assures us that a knowledge society is the emerging paradigm for the twenty-first century. One might have expected that business would do everything in their power to facilitate this. To understand why this is not the case, some history is needed. Traditionally there has been a single institution that was responsible for co-ordinating the whole of known knowledge. In the Latin West, from about the fourth to the eleventh century, this task was almost exclusively in the hands of the Catholic Church. The eleventh and twelfth centuries saw the rise of universities, and although certain orders of the church (notably the Franciscans, Dominicans, and later the Jesuits) continued to play a considerable role, as the universities gradually became secularized, they effectively became the central repositories of learning until the nineteenth century. Since then, six major changes have occurred.

First, there has been the rise of polytechnics (in France the *Ecole Polytechnique*) and technical colleges (in Germany the *Technische Hochschule* as at Braunschweig, Berlin, Darmstadt, and Munich and the *Eidgenössische Technische Hochschule* in Switzerland). As a result, technical knowledge came increasingly into the purview of these new institutions. Second, the rise of nation states led to the idea of national libraries. Here Panizzi's vision for the British Museum soon became a model for national libraries in Europe and all around the world. By the end of the nineteenth century, the enormous public support of these national libraries made them the new central repositories of knowledge.

Third, as the idea of the nation state flowered, the notion of national research laboratories became an increasingly natural prospect. One had to do specialized research in order to protect the competitive advantage of one's country. In countries such as Italy, this national research council (*Consiglio Nazionale delle Ricerche*) typically maintained close contact with the great universities (Rome, Bologna, Pisa), but at the same time produced major bodies of knowledge not readily accessible to those within the university. In the United States, these institutes grew into a vast network, often wrapped in secrecy. For instance, the Department of Energy alone has twenty major laboratories, including Ames, Argonne, Lawrence Livermore, Los Alamos, and Sandia.[87] It is significant that the names of these institutions are familiar while their activities are not. Fourth, in other countries such as Britain, another development emerged in the 1960s and 1970s. Under a rhetoric that government must focus on its "core business," there was a trend to privatize their holdings, with a result that major research laboratories were sold, often to private enterprise.

Fifth, the major corporations found it useful to develop their own research labs. These grew steadily in scale. IBM, for instance, has major laboratories such as Watson and Almaden, plus an Advanced Semiconductor Research and Development Center (in East Fishkill, NY),[88] as well as laboratories in Winchester (England), Zürich (Switzerland), and Naples (Italy), etc. Similarly, the Japanese firm NEC has a number of laboratories in Japan, namely, Kawasaki, Osaka, Ohtsu, Sagamihara, and Tsukuba, as well as others in Europe (Bonn, Berlin) and North America (Princeton[89] and San José). Philips has its main laboratory in Eindhoven with others in England (Redhill), France (Limeil-Brévannes), Germany (Aachen), and the United States (Briarcliff Manor). In 1997, Hitachi had 17,000 researchers in thirty-five labs with an annual budget of $4.9 billion. The University of Bologna, one of the oldest universities of the world, and also one of the largest with 103,000 students in 1998, has an annual budget approaching $1 billion of which a large part goes for day-to-day teaching and administration rather than to research.

Sixth, meanwhile, there has been a rise of private universities, often connected with a specific corporation. There are over a thousand corporate universities in the United States alone. Some are larger than most public universities. For instance, the campus of Motorola University has 100,000 students. The new campus of the British Telecom University will have 125,000 students.

These six changes pose a serious threat for any vision of true sharing of knowledge. The medieval aim of the university as representing the universe of studies (universitas studiorum) is mainly wishful thinking today. A study on research funding (1999, Table 46) reveals that strictly speaking universities now represent only about 2 per cent of R&D in the United States. To be sure industry, government, and other bodies also contribute to research at universities. If all these sources are included, universities continue to represent some 15 per cent of overall research. Universities have research centres, but they are no longer the centres of research.

While some universities continue to pursue their quest for the public good, large domains of new knowledge are now in the hands of national institutes that continue to work on their interpretation of the public good. Similarly there are corporate research institutes that are concerned only with the private gains of the companies they represent. Meanwhile, other universities, conscious of these dangers, are now trying to privatize the intellectual property of their professors with a view to retaining at least some stakehold in an ever-more divided vision of the universe.[90]

Some members of that corporate world spend their lives trying to convince us that the traditional distinctions between public and private good are now outdated and that we need to devote all our energies in the direction of private interests. In Britain, there is even support for the creation of a National University of Industry, a title which implies that public and private interests are now one and the same.

Yet they clearly are not. The public interest assumes that we share knowledge in reaching new insight. For this reason, entry to the greatest libraries of the world has always been on the basis of who is most academically qualified, rather than who pays

TABLE 46 Research and Development spending in the United States in billions of dollars (1999).[91]

State & Local Government	$2,950,000,000
Non-Profit	$3,913,000,000
University	$5,838,000,000
Federal	$65,853,000,000
Industry	$169,312,000,000
Total	**$247,866,000,000**

the largest entry fee. Private interest claims that each corporation must hoard as much knowledge as possible through patents, copyright,[92] non-disclosure agreements, and other protection measures to prevent others from having access to this knowledge.

Paradoxically we have a corporate structure that is calling, on the one hand, for us to think internationally and indeed to become global in our outlook. Meanwhile, this same corporate structure is leading to an increasing privatization and segmentation of knowledge that stands in the way of the very global vision that they are preaching. Some businessmen urge that we must develop new (private) business models for the knowledge society and they are right. But something even more important is required. We must also develop new public models for sharing knowledge, else we shall increasingly find that, notwithstanding fashionable trends towards knowledge management, all of us, including private laboratories, are unaware of developments elsewhere and billions will be wasted re-inventing the proverbial wheel.

Human Genome

In 2000, the human genome project contained 9.5×10^9 letters. It acquires 15 megabytes of new information per day, doubles in size every seven months,[93] and is one of the areas where the tensions between public and private interest are most dramatically evident. This project is proceeding on two fronts: 1) public[94] and 2) private, through a company called Celera, which is consciously building on the publicly funded research to develop a private enterprise alternative. Some persons are very concerned that knowledge about human life should not be open to patents.[95] It means, for example, that persons dying of cancer might find their chances of survival depending on how much they are willing or able to pay for a cure.[96]

In their race to be first, Celera have developed what they call a "shotgun sequencing" for the genome. Some are concerned that haste in an area where we do not know the rules could unleash unforeseen dangers.[97] Others are concerned that, once the human genome sequence is complete, employers and insurance companies could use knowledge of one's DNA to determine one's premiums and one's career.[98] The science fiction film *Gattaca* (1997) explored this danger in an extreme version. Olympic sports officials now see a danger of genetic engineering being used to create "designer athletes."[99]

Celera is not alone. In December, 2000, NuTec Sciences (Atlanta) acquired the fastest supercomputer in commercial use, capable of 7.5 trillion instructions per second in connection with the human genome.[100] A host of smaller companies are also involved.[101] There are groups such as the Raelians that support cloning.[102] More significantly, as David Pilling of the *Financial Times* pointed out: "The biggest pharmaceuticals merger of all time was the direct result of the genetic klondike." Glaxo Smith Kline are now spending $4 billion/year on the human genome project.[103] This is leading to new fields such as molecular mining[104] and bioinformatics.[105] Meanwhile, as Jeremy Rifkin has noted: "In the past three years, four of the giants of the petrochemical revolution – Monsanto, Novartis, Dupont and Aventis – have made a decision to shed or sell some or all of their chemical divisions and concentrate almost exclusively on genetic research and genetic-based technologies and products."[106]

Related to this is the field of genetically altered products. In the past, herbal medicine originated because a number of everyday plants are directly beneficial for medical purposes, such as digitalis in the case of heart disease. Some medical companies are now creating genetically altered versions of such natural plants in order that they can patent the results. In a worst case scenario, using natural remedies becomes outlawed. In a world of limited resources, this may be a profitable alternative for some, but it is not in the public's interest, as Rifkin has shown.[107] The theme of cloned texts has already inspired a horror novel.[108]

8. A New Public Good

In the nineteenth century, the nation state became the guardian of the public good. This continued throughout the twentieth century until the last decades, which have seen an increasing rhetoric telling us that government regulation is no longer necessary. This is described as intervention in the sense of meddling. We must return, they say, to a *laissez-faire* approach as originally foreseen by Adam Smith. That the father of capitalism also spoke very clearly about the need to share resources with poorer nations is often omitted by such individuals.

The domain in which these arguments are most vividly discussed is telecommunications. Government regulation, we were assured, is the only stumbling block to progress. For a few years these government bodies earnestly examined whether their role was no longer relevant. In the meantime, they have discovered that their presence is more necessary than ever and that more co-operation is necessary if they are to be effective at the global level.

The limitations of privatization are also evident in other domains. A decade ago, for instance, there were enthusiastic movements towards the partial privatization of railways in Britain and elsewhere in Europe, under the rhetoric that increased competition would lead to lower prices and better service. The actual results have been quite different. In many cases the prices are higher, the service is less, and, much more disturbing, there is increasing evidence that simple greed has compromised traditional safety standards, resulting in disastrous train accidents. Needed is a new study of *e*-society that focuses on the institutions, mechanisms, legal procedures, and human capital that facilitate the workings of a digitized society at the aggregate level.[109]

In its national government, the United States relies on a concept of checks and balances to ensure that the relative powers of the president and Congress are kept in equilibrium. Internationally we need a corresponding set of checks and balances between public and private interests, between the intrinsic, implicit rights of all citizens, and the legitimate, explicit ambitions of global business. For instance, the whole area of Internet governance, which, through ICANN is still dominated by a U.S. viewpoint, needs to reflect adequately the rights of all citizens, including the majority of the world's population, which does not yet have access to Internet, telephones, or television.[110] The Multilingual Internet Names Consortium (MINC) and more recently the efforts of the International Telecommunications Industry (ITU) and the World Summit on the Information Society (WSIS) are addressing some of these issues.[111]

In terms of private interests, we have many global corporations. These corporations are guided in the first instance by a short-term profit motive. The public efforts of individual governments are not enough. We need new spokespersons for the public good to coordinate these efforts: locally, regionally, nationally, and internationally. There are many international organizations working in the direction of such co-operation, often unaware of each others' efforts.[112] We need more attention to ethics in the cyberworld.[113] Multinational organizations such as the European Union and ASEAN can play a significant interim role in bringing us closer to true international co-operation in this sphere. At present, we have only one global organization devoted to the public domain, namely UNESCO, a body whose annual budget, as Philippe Quéau has observed, is equal to seven minutes of the annual budget of the U.S. military.[114]

There was a meeting in Florence (4–7 October 1999), which brought together for the first time leading members from the World Bank, UNESCO, and the realms of culture (including ministers of culture from 40 countries). The President of the World Bank, James Wolfensohn, explained that the bank's interest in culture was ultimately determined by enlightened self-interest. In the past, ignorance of cultural dimensions often led to the failure of considerable investments.[115] Meanwhile, George Sadowsky, one of the pioneers of ISOC has founded a Global Internet Policy Initiative (GIPI).[116]

A similar insight is needed in the realm of knowledge as a whole. Without international sharing, without a global vision of access to both enduring and new knowledge, we cannot make sufficient progress. Persons, universities, memory institutions, companies, corporations, and governments need to work together in building something which is greater than any single body could ever hope to achieve on its own. The once fiercely competitive world of business has recently learned the power of co-operation combined with competition in the form of "co-opetition."[117] An awareness along these lines is required in order to arrive at a new kind of public good at a global level.

14
synthesis

> The fact that digital systems can interpret
> content at some level – can examine it,
> process it, and change it in accordance with
> the instructions of the user – is fundamen-
> tal to their character and their significance.
> It is what makes them able to enhance the
> mental powers of users.
> – Charles Jonscher,
> *The Evolution of Wired Life*
> (1999, p. 95).

1. Introduction

The Internet has introduced an incredible range of developments, which can be summed up in a single word: sharing.
There is sharing for profit and sharing for other reasons.
Sharing for profit is the basis for an exchange economy: for e-
business and e-commerce.[1] We have explored its fundamental
importance for production, services, institutions, organizations, knowledge management, learning (chapters 4–9), and
some aspects of knowledge (chapters 10–11). Sharing for
profit is the basis of all developed countries. The importance
of this dimension is unquestionable.

Extreme versions of the American approach focus exclusively on sharing for profit. Indeed, most discussions of the Internet are solely about this sharing for profit, for it is assumed that this alone is the key to the new economy. In addition to cases where no direct profit is entailed, sharing can readily be for selfish purposes: to attain eternal fame, to gain a place in heaven, etc.

In these final chapters, we shall suggest that, although this kind of sharing explains technological, material, and, partly, organizational consequences of the Internet, there are other dimensions that may be even more important than these ultimately narrow, financial dimensions. The intellectual and philosophical implications of the Internet entail new kinds of communication, imply a reorganization of knowledge, of our inner world as well as our physical world. Herein lie unexplored frontiers.

A second kind of sharing entails giving to help others, a giving that acknowledges implicitly dimensions and powers beyond oneself. It is the opposite of selfishness because it begins from the premise that the worthwhile is something much more than "me." This is the basis of most enduring knowledge that we have in our universities and memory institutions (chapter 12). This kind of sharing also leads to open source[2] and is why we claim that the philosophical implication of new media is spirituality. We shall show that in the Latin West this notion of sharing is closely linked with Christianity and explain why this calls for a re-examination of Raymond's explanation in his *Cathedral and the Bazaar*.

Such sharing implies much more than a simple exchange of information and knowledge to help others. We have shown (chapter 12) that, whereas printing required a static, linear presentation of facts, the new media imply multi-dimensional access, which requires a reorganization of knowledge. This points to a new kind of collective intelligence, requires a new approach to the age-old problem of universals and particulars, and points to dynamic cultural and historical knowledge, which we associate with augmented knowledge and culture.

2. Sharing

The Internet brings enormous new possibilities for sharing without an eye for money, and this is ultimately why it is truly destined to change the world. At the Internet Global Summit 2000, historian of science Jean Claude Guedon reminded us of Robert Merton's work on the origins of the scientific movement in the seventeenth century. What made modern science possible, claimed Merton, was a new kind of communalism. The rise of early modern science was linked with the discovery of the importance of symbolic capital: new networks of academies and societies (chapter 11), new networks of letter writing (hence the notion of a world of letters), and new publication methods in the form of learned journals.[3] The rise of science was thus closely linked with a new level of sharing knowledge.

The ideas of symbolic capital, communalism, and sharing that Merton describes reached a new stage in the seventeenth century, but they were hardly new. Michael Giesecke, in his authoritative study of the history of printing, has shown how the rise of printing in the West in the 1440s and 1450s was closely connected also with a notion of the "common good," a sense of the "public good," which led ultimately to the rise of the nation state as we now know it. Even this notion was not new. "For the public good" (*pro bono publico*) was introduced by the Romans. But the city-states of the thirteenth century, which grew through dukedoms and counties into the nation states of the nineteenth century added a further dimension. They changed a traditional Roman political motto into a Christian spirit of giving and gift culture.[4]

If Gutenberg reinvented the printing press, his real "invention" was something much more profound. Korea invented printing around AD 800 and China had used printing to control and discipline people more effectively. Gutenberg adapted the Christian spirit of gift culture and used printing as a means of sharing ideas. As always, there were unexpected side effects. Hence a Catholic idea helped Protestantism get started by making available the ideas of Martin Luther in print form. The Reformation led to the Counter-Reformation, a spiral of reactions, and modernity. In all this, the "win-win" idea was sharing. To be sure, there are many histories about the period that focus on defensive castles, offensive wars, inquisitions, power, and even torture. But ultimately even the strongest castles were stormed, and ever so slowly there arose an awareness that one got further by sharing knowledge than by trying to hoard it through violence, war, secrecy, or censorship.

By the nineteenth century, the Renaissance idea of city states had led both to nation states and national libraries, museums, and archives, which sought to house in a single building all that was known at the time, with a view to sharing it. This again led to unexpected side-effects. Karl Marx, for instance, spent forty years using the resources of the British Library to write what he thought was a definitive plan to overthrow the system that fed him. Marx preached a new freedom but inspired a new kind of control. The big picture works in mysterious ways, for at about the same time, Kropotkin, came to an interesting discovery: "I began to appreciate the difference between acting on the principle of command and discipline and acting on the principle of common understanding. The former works admirably in a military parade, but is worth nothing where real life is concerned and the aim can be achieved only through the severe effort of many converged wills."[5]

This passage is of particular interest, because it was cited by Gerald Weinberg[6] when he was trying to capture the generosity of hackers (in the original sense) and programmers as a whole. Weinberg spoke of egoless programming.[7] Meanwhile, Kropotkin's passage was cited anew by Eric S. Raymond who has become one of the most articulate spokesmen for the Open Source movement. Raymond proposes that, to lead collaborative projects, hackers [his word for virtuous programmers], "have to learn how to recruit and energize communities of interest in the mode vaguely suggested by Kropotkin's principle of understanding."[8] The Open source movement is related to trends towards an open directory,[9] open data,[10] open theory, open content[11] and open design.[12]

In his analysis of the principles underlying open source, Raymond uses words which, in spirit, are essentially Christian. Raymond speaks of a need for humility,[13] a need to be fair. He urges the need to find "difficult ends that can only be achieved through sustained co-operation."[14] To achieve these ends, he urges the "construction of voluntary communities of interest."[15] Some say hackers do their thing just for the fun of it. Some say hackers are terrorists in disguise. But could one not see hackers as the modern-day equivalents of monks living in distributed (lay) monasteries?

To explain further the principles underlying the open source movement, Raymond distinguishes between exchange cultures and gift cultures.[16] Exchange cultures thrive on scarcity. By contrast, gift cultures "are adaptations not to scarcity but abundance. They arise in populations that do not have significant material scarcity problems with survival goods."[17] In Raymond's mind, cathedrals were "carefully crafted by individual wizards or small bands of mages,"[18] which he associates with the control culture of closed software. As if cathedrals were kept hermetically sealed and only released to the public at the last minute in the manner of shrink-wrapped software. Understandably, Raymond opposes his notion of cathedrals to the spirit of open source.

In fact, the history of cathedrals is rather different. Notwithstanding evidence that there were master masons, who kept some secrets to themselves, cathedrals were mostly built in a spirit of voluntary co-operation. There was no master plan that was secretly smuggled from city to city. Nor was there a specific release time. Some of the most famous cathedrals including Cologne and Ulm took centuries to build. Sometimes the citizens of a town became over-ambitious in their plans and the building collapsed. Whereupon they had to start anew. This was the case at Beauvais. Ultimately, cathedrals were not the work of isolated individuals. They were the voluntary achievements of collaboration and co-operation. They represented the aspirations of a town, a city, and sometimes a whole region. They remain some of the most noble examples of gift culture to date.

The ideas in Raymond's book, the *Cathedral and the Bazaar* are brilliant, but the title is misleading. He wants to distinguish between gift culture and exchange economy. Exchange economy is in the agora, the bazaar, the market, and more recently the stock market. The market may appear open, but ultimately it depends on closure. Hence, business speaks of closing deals and in the end wants to possess money. This does not mean that wealthy merchants are incapable of gift culture. Traditionally this was called philanthropy. Now it often poses as venture capital, especially in Silicon Valley.

But, ironically, it is the cathedral that represents gift culture. In its day, the cathedral was only one expression of something much more profound. Monasteries were another. Ultimately these buildings were unimportant; they were merely material expressions of a spirit of co-operation that was visible for a time. Monasteries without this spirit fell to ruins and many of the cathedrals became more like coffins of the spirit than obvious expressions of the spirit's nobility. Indeed, Clairvaux, one of the starting points of the great Cistercian movement, is now a prison.

What made the cathedrals and monasteries important was the activities they fostered. Before there were libraries and universities, cathedrals and monasteries were places where knowledge was collected, interpreted, taught, and passed on – tradition in the literal sense of the term. Medieval monks and priests developed the techniques of writing and copying in their scriptoria and then co-operated in order to uphold tradition and civilization.

There are contemporary efforts to link traditional ideas of scriptoria with the Internet. The Dominican order has its own Internet committee. In Sri Lanka, the Komale Project is linking local radio and the Internet and is being used by young priests to propagate Buddhist teachings.[19] The Monastery of Christ in the Desert[20] already functions as an electronic monastery. There are electronic resources for theological study.[21] At the same time, the new hacker monks do not belong to orders. Their software tools are the tools for a new kind of scriptorium. At the outset medieval monks were faced with challenges of finding good quills and appropriate writing materials, not unlike the way the new hacker monks are faced with finding bugs and developing electronic tools in hardware and software[22] (cf. chapter 5).

In all this Raymond is very clear about the inspiration of Linus Thorwald and a whole generation of others. Raymond's great contribution as an accidental revolutionary (as he calls himself) has been to make many persons who were working in seeming isolation aware that they are part of a larger picture. One of the purposes of this book is to show that the picture is much larger still.

Within two years of its founding, the open source movement became linked with some of the most important free software. Dr. Jacob Broadman has been leading a Virtual Learning Community, which has been using Linux since 1997. The Sustainable Development Networking Plan (SDNP) has adopted Linux,[23] as has Science for Humanity.[24] The Global Knowledge Initiative, the Canadian International Development Organization (CIDA), and even the World Bank are integrating open source into their visions for the developing world. We noted earlier that Linux is being used by a number of governments.

As Linux spreads,[25] there are ever-more explanations for its success. Economists such as Rishab Ghosh now speak of non-monetary economics. Bernard Lang (INRIA), who heads the French Linux group, pointed out at INET 2000 that Moore's law (about the expanding rate of computer power) and Metcalfe's law (the value of the EDI network is roughly equal to the number of users squared) are not enough. They need to be complemented by: 1) Ferengi's rules of acquisition, 2) the law of self-organization, 3) the law of unlimited effects, 4) the law of large numbers, and 5) the law of zero marginal cost. Herein lie clues, not only for the spread of Linux and open source, but also for fundamental aspects of the Internet.

Sharing characterizes all these phenomena. Related words are "volunteer" or its derivatives, "voluntary," "volunteering," etc. It is instructive that Charles Derber, one of the most articulate critics of the dangers of a *Corporation Nation*, sees voluntary sharing as one of the principle hopes of the future. Derber calls: "families, churches, schools, foundations, volunteer agencies and other community based organizations" the third sector. He notes that in the United States non-profit organizations employ 10 per cent of the workforce and that there are 90 million volunteers. "If it were an economy it would be the seventh largest in the world; it's made up of 1.4 million organizations."[26]

Derber is building on the ideas of Jeremy Rifkin, the author of *The End of Work*. Ironically, those most in tune with the extreme materialistic version of American life are pointing back to a non-materialistic solution: a spiritual solution, not in the sense of waving incense and singing halleluiahs, but in the sense of sharing, doing something for others, for the common good: a gift culture, without any ulterior motive. A recent book by Ray Kurzweil, one of the visionaries in the new technologies, is explicitly entitled: *The Age of Spiritual Machines: When Computers Exceed Human Intelligence.*[27] These thinkers are harbingers of something new.

3. Collective Intelligence

We noted that computers are causing an extension of the senses (chapter 1.6). The new technologies continue this trend and at the same time take it inward. Augmented books are extending our memory and the capacities of our minds. In the past, the amount one knew depended on how much one had learned personally. Now, through augmented books, linked via notepads and wireless connections to virtual reference rooms, all this changes. I can have at my fingertips the cumulative memory of civilization through enduring knowledge as found in our libraries, museums, and archives.[28]

These developments promise a new kind of convergence that goes far beyond technological dimensions. Some authors have written about collective intelligence[29] or connected intelligence.[30] Other authors refer to it as an infinite resource, as a distributed mind, as a global brain,[31] as a global superbrain, or as a global super-organism. They have talked about bringing existing knowledge on-line. Our concern goes further. The connected world of the Internet, with its emerging computational grids, is unleashing almost unimaginable amounts of computing power. This makes possible a shift from static to dynamic knowledge, a new approach to the age-old question of universals and particulars and ultimately a reorganization of knowledge.

4. Universals-Particulars

General versus Unique

The creative arts entail a paradox. While they are based on laws and rules, which are generic and universal, their ultimate expression is personal, unique, and particular. Music, for instance, has clear laws of harmony such that some notes are clearly right and others are wrong. But while most persons may play the notes correctly, only one in a million will perform them in a way that is truly memorable. To some extent, this phenomenon applies to all the arts. Technologists have addressed this twofold nature of creativity with two very different approaches. First, they have created software that fixes objective dimensions in terms of generic solutions.[32] For example, music software, such as *Band in a Box*, allows me to choose a melody, adjust it, and then have it played by a number of different instruments in different styles. Hence, I can begin with a tune that Mozart wrote for a violin and have the software play this tune on a clarinet, a drum, a trombone, or even a jazz saxaphone. Subsequently, the software plays the same piece in a different style such as Eric Clapton. Although immensely impressive, this never generates the unique experience of an unforgettable performance.

Second, technologists have recorded the unique aspects of performance. In music, this has led to the recording industry (in analog vinyl records or videos, and more recently in digital CD-ROMs and Digital Video Discs or DVDs). In theatre, this has led to both audio recordings of great actors, videos, and in rare cases films of their performances. So we have generic software on the one hand and unique recordings on the other hand. These need to be integrated. Similarly, in the case of writing, technology has produced a) excellent generic software to do word processing and b) ways of scanning unique examples of great literature,[33] manuscripts of Dante's *Commedia* or the *Tale of Gengi*; editions of Shakespeare and original texts of Proust.

Objects

This is related to a more general problem. There is a challenge to link generic software with examples of unique expressions. To take a concrete example: In our study of production (chapter 4), we learned that, in architecture and construction, firms such as AutoDesk have created a consortium to deal with Industry Foundation Classes. We saw how this leads to a concept of "intelligent doors," such that the software provides a basic shape, which automatically adjusts itself to the context at hand. This saves architects and designers the trouble of calculating the parameters of every single door, window, and other architectural unit. It also brings an inherent danger. If applied mindlessly, this leads to stereotyped architecture whereby all doors and windows become alike, whereby buildings in one country are effectively copies of those in other countries, a world-wide homogenization – which Barber has called the "MacWorld effect."[34]

This software for the construction of "intelligent" doors provides generic solutions. It will produce millions of safe doors efficiently but no unique doors. The richness of the architectural tradition lies precisely therein that the doors and windows of Michelangelo are different than those of le Corbusier or Richard Meier. Fortunately, our memory institutions have been collecting evidence about all the unique doors: the doors to the Baptistery of Florence, in St. Zeno in Verona, the Cathedral at Hildesheim, and so on. If these traditions are combined, we could have a new integration of universals and particulars.

Theoretically it is possible to go much further. One could add historical knowledge of individual doors. In the case of an historic home or building of the

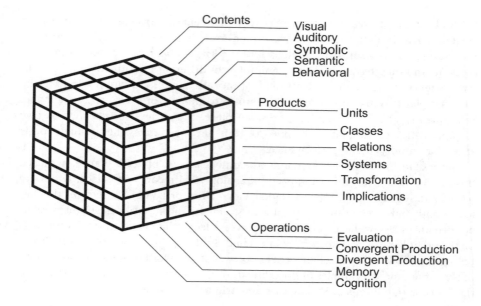

Figure 21 J. P. Guilford's Structure of Intellect (1967).[37]

fourteenth century, this information can be extended to provide the entire history of restorations that the building has undergone. This can serve both as a basis for conservation and as a source of inspiration for new creativity. In cases where historical buildings are destroyed, such electronic memories can serve as a new type of insurance against disaster. Including cultural and historical dimensions in the concept of Industry Foundation Classes (IFCs) is also a key to cultural diversity, which civilization requires as deeply as bio-diversity in order to survive. In the medieval period, architects developed a combination of wood and stucco in architecture, which became known as Elizabethan architecture in England and *Fachwerk* in Germany. Each city used the same "standard," but each city also produced its own unique versions. Such diversity is needed today.

Another way of looking at this is that we have two kinds of knowledge. We have detailed catalogues of individual items and we have schemas for classifying these items. Elsewhere we discussed the botanical example of poppies being a member of the *papaveraceae* family. With a contextualizer, I could be reading about or be standing in front of a poppy and ask for its family. Or to take a cultural scenario: I am reading about or standing in front of a Greek vase. The contextualizer shows me the class to which this belongs and thus allows me to look for others in that class or to look through different classes. An integration of universals and particulars is thus another step in the direction of contextualization.

Integration of Generic Software and Unique Examples

The unique examples from the content industries can greatly enrich the generic examples of the software industry.[35] Hence, music software can provide general instructions about how to play a piece of music such as the *Cello Sonatas* by Beethoven and then how Pablo Casals, Mstislav Rostropovich, and André Navarra have their unique interpretations thereof. Similarly, a multimedia edition of Shakespeare can provide, not only the generic text of *Hamlet*, but also individual interpretations by Sir Laurence Olivier or Kenneth Branagh.[36]

Such combinations of generic software with unique examples can open new markets and unleash new creativity for users. Suppose that the worst fears of the RIAA and the large music firms come true and that peer-to-peer music sharing triumphs to the extent that anyone is able to download their favourite tunes. In the case of literature, this has already happened. It is possible to download the whole of Shakespeare or even the whole *Bible*. Does this mean that Shakespeare and the *Bible* are no longer being sold as books? Of course not. Such printed editions remain economically viable because their critical notes and ease of use make them more attractive than an electronic text in isolation. For the moment, snuggling up in bed with a book is more attractive than trying to snuggle up to bits and bytes. Hence, a challenge for the music industry and the creative industries in general is to create add-ons and qualitative superiority that make paid "originals" more attractive than free, pirate editions. Thus free sharing need not threaten the market economy. It provides a new stimulus for it to produce worthwhile new products.

What interests us is how these developments point to a new integration of science and art. Science focusses on universal, generic rules and laws. Art focusses on particulars, the exceptions, the unique. Building industry standards for doors are necessary. Art historical examples of unique doors are inspiring. If we link these bodies of information, we shall come closer to a global information (and knowledge) ecology[38] sought by the European Commission and others. Integrating universals and particulars also takes us towards augmented knowledge and culture and a step closer to a new synthesis.

5. Augmented Knowledge

In Douglas Engelbart's vision (Figure 13), augmented knowledge arises from sharing while working together collaboratively. This vision, which forms the basis for his Bootstrap Institute, bears interesting parallels to Frederick Brooks' insistence on the need for IA versus AI: Intelligence Augmentation as opposed to Artificial Intelligence.[39] The Internet has introduced other potentials for augmented knowledge. While the United States focusses on managing contemporary knowledge, Europe sees the potentials of the Internet for access to enduring knowledge[40] and Japan has drawn attention to its potentials for creating new knowledge. We need to combine these three approaches to enduring (European), contemporary (American), and new knowledge (Japan) in order to arrive at new levels of insight for the whole of humanity.

TABLE 47A Two challenges: a) an integration of memory institutions, broadcast media and unstable media. Cf. model of the DEER (Figure 14)

ENDURING KNOWLEDGE (COLLECTIVE MEMORY INSTITUTIONS)

Libraries	Museums	Archives	Broadcast Media	Unstable Media
Books	Paintings	Documents	Film	Internet
Manuscripts	Drawings	Letters	Television	Multimedia
	Sculptures	Protocols	Video	Interactive TV
				Interactive Video
				Kinetic Art
				Performance Art

Virtual Reference Rooms

Distributed Repositories   **Virtual Agoras**

Thinkers concerned with the systematization of intellect, such as Guilford, have intuitively sought to link units, classes, relations, systems (concepts relating to understanding enduring knowledge) with products and operations (concepts relating to managing contemporary knowledge, Figure 21).

Two levels of integration are necessary: 1) We need to integrate the enduring knowledge of memory institutions with broadcast media and unstable media[41] (Table 47a). Unstable media include the emerging field of Internet art.[42] 2) An integration of this enduring knowledge with collaborative and personal knowledge will further this quest (Table 47b). When linked via Virtual Reference Rooms, Distributed Repositories, and Virtual Agora, this takes us back to the vision of a DEER (Figure 14) and gradually a World Online Distributed Electronic Resource (WONDER).

Much more is involved here than simply linking old, contemporary, and new knowledge. We need to combine the logical rigour of the innovations in knowledge organization by the champions of enduring knowledge in memory institutions with the dynamic methods being developed by those using new knowledge in the worlds of science, technology, business, and finance. We need to link our quests to identify knowledge of the moment with our quest to classify knowledge that is lasting – the so-called eternal truths. We need also to recognize that the notion of knowledge as power (to do and to make) is a peculiarity of the Anglo-Saxon tradition, that knowledge in French is linked with taste (*savoir*), as is wisdom in Italian (*sapienza*), that knowledge in Sanskrit is linked with life and parturition, that knowledge in Hebrew is linked with carnal knowledge (which is effectively a prelude to the Sanskrit). We need to reflect the different kinds of knowledge of other languages, such as the differences between *savoir* and *connaissance* in French. We have structures for knowledge. We need structures that help us understand different ways of knowing. In Canada and Australia, there is increasing awareness that the aboriginal persons who were there before the colonial settlers arrived also had their

TABLE 47B Two challenges: b) an integration of enduring, collaborative and personal knowledge

COLLABORATIVE KNOWLEDGE   PERSONAL KNOWLEDGE

Tacit Knowledge
Knowledge as Power to Do
Knowledge as Creation
Knowledge as Life

Virtual Reference Rooms

Distributed Repositories   Virtual Agoras

own valuable ways of knowing. Such augmented knowledge will bring further steps towards a reorganization of knowledge.[43]

Augmented knowledge in this richer sense is a key to our future. This entails the challenge of creating filters for cultural and historical dimensions – with views from all continents, cultures, and languages.[44] These then need to be fine-tuned such that they can reflect accurately the diversity of individual countries, provinces, cities, and ultimately individuals. This may seem overwhelming. But then if we are prepared to tackle information from the whole of outer space, the inhabitants of earth should be able to manage and gain new insights from their own knowledge.

In Wendy MacKay's[45] definition, augmented reality has three domains, namely, augmenting the user, the environment, or the object (Table 48). As a means of augmenting the user, there are obvious possibilities with respect to glasses. Some such applications are already in use. Others are predicted. For instance, Antii Ellonen at the Helsinki Institute of Arts and Design imagines a consumeter, which allows a user to look at products, to discern which are good for a diet, which are potentially troublesome for allergies, which are ripe, which are not. Visionaries such as Odd-Wiking Ralff assume that by 2020 there will be a global wireless infrastructure that allows much more than simple mobile communications. Persons and objects will be imbued with various levels of knowledge.

Augmented reality glasses will allow us to look at an environment from different viewpoints such as general or implicit information, or with a view to fun or love.[47] According to an article in *PC Magazine* (September, 2000), such gadgets will be available by 2010: "you recognize someone standing in line. You can't recall who she is, so you discreetly click a button on your wristwatch to call up a display embedded in your glasses. A tiny LCD projects a menu into your right eye. Using your watch, you select Identify from the menu. The camera in your glasses snaps a picture of the mystery woman and wirelessly transmits it to the credit-card-size computer in your jacket pocket. The machine identifies the person"[48]

TABLE 48 Three forms of augmented reality according to Wendy Mackay (Xerox)[46]

AUGMENTATION APPLIED TO	PROJECT
User	Charade
	Karma
Environment	Digital Desk
	Smart Desk
	Ubiquitous Computing
	Active Badges
Object	Lego Logo
	Digital Ink

This may sound like science fiction, but IBM, building on the work of Steve Feiner (Columbia University), has already created the first prototypes for such devices. Brown University uses augmented books in medical operations. Sony has also created a Navicam, which permits the superimposition of text on a scene through augmented reality. IBM's device shows a typically Western conception of the constellations superimposed upon the night sky. In the future, one would wish to go further and allow viewers to see the differences between Chinese, Indian, Arabic, and other constellations. Augmented culture thus helps us to see through different persons' eyes.

This approach to augmented reality has enormous potentials for tourism. For instance, I am standing in front of the ruins of a Greek temple and would like to see how it appeared when it was still intact. An European Commission Information Society Technologies (EC IST) project called ARCHEOGUIDE worked on a prototype.[49] This is being further developed to include various display devices, including mobile phones and PDAs. It is possible to imagine webcams positioned around major archaeological ruins and linked with such reconstructions such that they can be consulted either on site via mobile devices or at a distance via the Internet. Ericsson was working on augmented reality glasses with GPS features that would coordinate one's view of real buildings in the old town of Stockholm with information about those buildings. A deep map virtual tourist guide for Heidelberg at Bruchsal University has similar aims.[50] As we have suggested earlier, cameras in our mobile phones could perform the same functions. The revolution is not about glasses or cameras: it is about a new interplay between inner worlds of knowledge and the outer physical and man-made world.

Augmented culture is taking these trends considerably further. Buildings have a history, the various stages of which are often difficult or nearly impossible to imagine. Santa Sophia in Istanbul is now a museum. Previously, it was a Muslim Mosque, and before that it was one of the leading Christian churches. Augmented reality glasses and similar devices could show us the different phases. Tourism would become not only a question of visiting a place as it is today but also a voyage of tracing how places have changed over time. In complex cases, this will include a series of competing interpretations.

Augmented books are an example of augmented objects. A universal application of augmented knowledge would involve all three domains. It would be a world where every object could not only be self-describing, as in the vision of Tim Berners-Lee, but in which every object has its own history, hence its own bibliography and thus alternative stories about itself. If each object is intelligent, it is aware of its own state and can be self-repairing or self-healing. Similarly each environment can have access to descriptions of its own condition and also become self-monitoring and self-restoring. If a pond has too much algae, it activates a robot to give it proper doses of chlorine, pH, and so on. As machine-to-machine communication and agent technologies mature they will bring interplays among environments, objects, and users; new interactions between physical objects and virtual information and knowledge. The notion of special institutions for knowledge will have a different meaning than in the past. Not only will all the world be a stage, all the world will be a knowing, knowledge stage.

Where are the limits to this approach? How much intelligence will we delegate to machines, robots, and agents? At what point are we no longer in control? Here we have questions rather than answers. Needed somehow is a balance between the possible and that which furthers society in a deeper sense. In this context, it is very interesting to compare the vision of Tengku Mohammed Azzman Shariffadeen, which has helped to inspire the Multimedia SuperCorridor (MMC) in Malaysia. He is concerned that new technologies should improve quality of life.[51] While accepting the need for material and quantitative measures (such as GDP), he notes that human fulfillment goes beyond materialistic needs and ultimately involves spiritual values: the right thing to do, more than doing things right. Where Americans typically see a tension between public and private, Tengku Azzman sees a threefold symbiosis between the private, which creates value; the public, which maintains law and order; and community interest, which sustains quality of life. The role of good governance is to integrate these three realms.[52]

Tengku Azzman distinguishes between modern knowledge and perennial (which we call "enduring") knowledge. In his larger vision, there is a threefold challenge. First, there must be access to this perennial or codified knowledge. Second, the infostructure must bring empowerment through tacit knowledge. Third, governance must ensure that quality of life includes not just the material but also intellectual and spiritual dimensions of persons. This is a considerably richer view (Table 49) than a strictly profit-driven model. Where countries such as the United States preach a rhetorical need for the state to retreat from moral questions, Malaysia, and indeed most of Asia, is very much concerned with these dimensions.[53] Tengku Azzman very rightly emphasizes both the intellectual and spiritual qualities of life, which can result

TABLE 49 An informational framework for improving quality of life according to Tengku Mohammed Azzman Shariffadeen.

DOCUMENTED & ACCESSIBLE INFORMATION	SOCIAL ORDER & INFRASTRUCTURE	POTENTIAL FOR DEVELOPMENT
Access	**Empowerment**	**Governance**
Information & Codified Knowledge	Tacit Knowledge Learning & Skills Development Institutional Framework	Quality of Life Material Intellectual Spiritual

from the electronic revolution. One dimension of the spiritual lies in the realm of augmented culture, which is of particular concern to us.

6. Augmented Culture

Augmented cultural objects were discussed earlier: using technology to see a vase from all sides, to add captions at different levels of complexity, in different languages, etc. (chapter 6). Augmented culture is much more because it assures cultural diversity, which is the spiritual equivalent of bio-diversity at the physical level. At an almost banal level, this means recognizing that when a French person says "Liège," a Dutch person says "Luik" and a German says "Lüttich," they are speaking about the same physical city, even though their understanding of its historical role might vary considerably. It means being aware that a book or cultural object, which a French person classes in one way, will probably be classed quite differently by an Italian, a Russian, an Indian, a Chinese, or an Australian. These differences extend to all human activity, especially in the field of interpretation. Philosophers tell us that people have different worldviews (cf. German *Weltanschauung*). Augmented culture needs to make such differences visible.

A simple scenario: I am looking at the Roman forum with a view of the back of the Campidoglio. It is a field of ruins. Augmented culture allows me to see various views throughout the ages, to see how the scene changed from the Renaissance to our day. More significantly, it also allows me to see different reconstructions of the same scene: how a French conception of how the forum was in the days of its glory varies enormously from a German or Italian conception.

Narratives (How? Why?)

A next stage entails a better understanding of narratives. If I am reading a physical copy of the *Bible* and encounter an unfamiliar name, the concept of augmented books outlined earlier can provide me with basic information about the person and also about the stories with which they are associated. A continent such as Europe is defined by a relatively small number of major narratives deriving from two traditions: 1) Judaeo-Christian (the *Bible*, Lives of the Saints) and 2) Greco-Roman (Homer,

Virgil, Ovid). We belong to the same culture if we know the same narratives, if we have the same stories in common.[54]

Paradoxically, those who have the same stories inevitably develop very different ways of telling those stories. The media differ. For instance, in Italy, the lives of the saints most frequently become the great fresco cycles on the walls of churches. In France and the Netherlands, the lives of the saints are more frequently treated in illuminated manuscripts. In Germany, they frequently appear in complex altarpieces. Not only do the media vary but also the ways of telling stories. The *Life of Christ* in Spain is very different than in the Balkans or within the Orthodox tradition in Russia. Even so, the commonality of themes means that Europeans can feel an affinity towards a Russian Orthodox church because they recognize the same stories. If they knew the stories from other traditions, they could feel commonality also with tales from the *Mahabharata* in Indian temples, Buddhist stories in Chinese temples, and so on.

In these transformations of the familiar lie important lessons about the keys to diversity. The most diverse narratives are precisely about the most familiar stories. Uniqueness cannot simply be generated by trying to be different, by rejecting others and removing them through ethnic cleansing. Uniqueness comes through sharing common stories, which inspire fundamental values (e.g., the ten commandments), and then expressing them differently.

To visualize and make visible the complexities of these historical diversities of expression is our best hope for understanding the challenges of future diversity. Inherent in such questions lie the seeds for understanding changing definitions of our world, processes rather than static definitions: dynamic, augmented, culture. The term "culture" is linked with the word "cult" – that which binds us. It is linked with "religion" (from *religio*: to bind) and other fundamental aspects of our identity such as food and language. In the United States, some see culture as what we do together (faith, family, associations). In Europe, culture is seen more in terms of the expressions that result from what we believe in and do together.

New Models of Culture

For a long time, the great civilizations defined cultures in terms of themselves.[55] China created a Sinocentric view of the world, which ignored everything beyond the Great Wall. Europe created a Eurocentric view. The Arabic world created its own.[56] We need new models of culture that do not impose the preferences of one group on others. To have real understanding among persons in an era of global communications, we need a more comprehensive approach. How can we give due recognition to the inherent dignity of all persons and yet recognize properly the outstanding achievements of some without falling into simplistic models of cultural imperialism? Some initial ideas follow.

A generation ago, the efforts of UNESCO made us aware that in addition to the important role of tangible culture in the form of the built environment (temples, churches, monuments, etc.), intangible culture also plays a significant role. UNESCO's definition

TABLE 50 Seven goals and seventeen means as ingredients for a new approach to culture.

GOAL OF CULTURE	MEANS
1 Connecting	1 Mythology
	2 Religion
	3 Philosophy
	4 Literature
2 Ordering	5 Art
	6 Mathematics
	7 Doing
	8 Making
	9 Building
3 Imitating	10 Direct Expressing
	11 Representing
4 Matching	12 Expressing in Different Media via Written
5 Mixing	13 Translating among Media
6 Exploring	14 Transforming among Media
7 Spreading	15 Publishing with Tolerance
	16 Sharing
	17 Helping

of intangible culture was primarily in the context of cultural products, especially in pre-literate or non-literate cultures, e.g., language, customs, food, music, and dance. We need a wider definition of intangible culture. At one level, there is intangible culture in the form of mythology, religion, philosophy, and (epic) literature. This generates a whole range of expressions in terms of both tangible and intangible culture. If culture is defined as the cumulative, collective memory of a group of persons, then the range and complexity of these expressions becomes a measure of the richness and greatness of a culture. This richness is partly a function of literacy for the simple reason that oral traditions impose limits on the amount of collective memories that can remembered by a group no matter how learned and clever the shamans and priests. Herein lies a basis for high and low culture independent of all discussions of imperialism and colonialism. Oral cultures have myths and beliefs that are literally memorable (cf. 1–2 in Table 50). Pre-literate cultures have stories. Literate cultures have stories plus cumulative interpretations and commentaries. Literate cultures also have philosophy and literature that generate more complex cosmologies and stories (cf. 3–4 in same). These stories are not only more complex in themselves but also have a cumulative complexity that comes from citing previous literary sources. Hence, Milton and Dante are more complex because they cite the *Bible* and many classical writings.

Oral cultures typically produce some forms of intangible culture a) in the form of organic or geometrical patterns (cf. 5–6 in same), b) in the form of doing (eating, drinking, customs, cf. 7), and c) in terms of expressing themselves directly (language, speech, cf. 10). Until ways and means are found of recording these expressions, oral cultures remain in constant danger of extinction. Oral cultures typically also produce some forms of tangible culture in terms of making (pottery, ornament, cf. 8) and building (cf. 9). Again, unless ways and means are found to conserve and preserve these products, they too remain in constant danger of extinction.

The shift from oral to written culture is thus much more fundamental than a simple translation exercise from one medium to another.[57] Once myths and beliefs are recorded, they can be developed into ever-more complex cosmologies and stories, which can have their own national, regional, and local variants. These cosmologies and stories can also generate an ever-greater spectrum of expressions ranging from the static arts (the so-called fine arts of painting and sculpture, often favoured in the West) to the performance arts (e.g., theatre, dance, and music, often favoured in the East, cf. Table 51).

In print culture, it is not only the range of expressions but also the complexity of interplay between expressions in different media (cf. 12–13) that plays a fundamental role: how, for instance, the Buddha can appear as a manuscript illustration, as a mandala painting, as a tiny hand-held sculpture, as a life-sized sculpture, or as an enormous statue as in Yokohama or Hong Kong. In more advanced cases, this process of translating from one medium to another is complemented by a process of transformation as one explores new possibilities (cf. 14). There are also new efforts at building and representing (cf. 9 and 11). Hence, print cultures foster the complexity and range of expressions in both tangible and intangible culture (cf. 7–14).

Cultural ideas (myths, beliefs) and cultural products are not the only criteria for the sustainability, richness, and quality of a culture. Anyone can produce images of their myths and beliefs, but such expressions are not always kind, benevolent, or tolerant. In the eighth century, Tibet had a cruel set of beliefs that caused much suffering. As a result the Tibetan King, Trisong Detsen, decided to invite the Buddhist monks, Santarakshita and Padmasambhava, in order to establish Buddhism as the official religion of the country. One of the reasons why the great religions of the world have had such an influence is because their central tenets have expressed greater tolerance (cf. 15) than minor sects. Indeed radical, intolerant branches are typically disowned by the mainstream in all the great religions.

The test of a mythology, religion, or belief system is not only in its ability to tolerate others, but also in its capacity to share with others. Cultures that have an isolationist policy may have a certain inherent value and coherence in themselves, but if they are not willing to be open to others and share their expressions with others, this limits their value beyond the narrow limits of their original parameters. Hence another test of a serious culture is the extent that it remains intact when placed in the context of another culture (cf. 16). Cultures that ignore this criterion will find themselves endangered in a world of global villages. Ultimately it is not only openness to other persons and other cultures but a commitment to help others. Everyone helps their friends. Not everyone helps others. The Christian story of the good Samaritan, although hardly followed by every Christian, is a universally appealing story because it points to helping a stranger and not just a friend. Thus

TABLE 51 Advanced culture: when a text inspires expressions in other media[60]

		STATIC FINE ARTS				DYNAMIC PERFORMANCE		
		Mosaics	Illustrations	Paintings	Sculptures	Theatre	Puppets	Music
India	*Mahabharata*		x	x	x	x	x	x
	Ramayana		x	x	x	x	x	x
	Buddhist Texts		x	x	x	x	x	x
Israël	*Bible*	x	x	x	x	x		x
Greece	*Iliad*	x	x	x	x			
	Odyssey	x	x	x	x			
Rome	*Aeneid*	x	x	x	x			
China	*3 Kingdoms*		x	x	x	x		
Japan	Tale of Genji		x	x	x	x	x	
Italy	*Commedia*		x	x	x	x		
Persia	*Shanahmah*		x	x	x			

a further criterion for a sustainable culture is the extent to which it reaches out beyond itself to help others (cf. 17).

These different means of expression are linked with a small number of goals of culture and art,[58] which evolve from a pre-literate to a literate context. In pre-literate cultures an initial goal is typically in the form of 1) connecting a physical person or group with a metaphysical, magical world beyond. A second goal in pre-literate cultures, sometimes linked with the first, entails 2) ordering the world (i.e., bringing a sense of order to the world) in the form of regular patterns, often as organic or geometric forms.[59] The shift from oral to written culture typically brings a new goal of 3) imitation (mimesis). Hereby one compares a number of different examples and creates ideal combinations from these examples as in the famous story of Greek sculptors who combined the faces of beautiful ladies to create an ideal face of a goddess. The shift from written to print culture brought further goals of 4) matching in the sense of copying, 5) mixing in the sense of combining realistic and imaginary features, 6) exploring as in more recent modern art, in the sense of transforming images entirely to the point that no necessary link with physical reality remains, and 7) spreading in the sense of making publicly known, which includes marketing and sponsoring.

Taken together, these seven goals and seventeen criteria can be seen as ingredients for a new model of culture. They form neither a simple hierarchy nor any simple form of linear progress. The goals of connecting and ordering have consequences for expressing, making, representing, and building, but how they do so varies from one culture to another. High cultures tend to require ingredients 15 to 17. To be sure, there have been significant cultures that were cruel and unkind. Even so, almost without exception, they were replaced by cultures that were more kind. Being open did more than expand the boundaries of influence of cultures. Typically it made their original expressions richer. Buddhism became much richer by spreading to Tibet, China, Japan, Southeast Asia, and around the world. Christianity became richer as it spread beyond the Holy Land to address Europe and eventually the world. Islam became much richer in its expressions when it spread first to Europe and later to Asia and around the world.

Once writing exists then one's beliefs can be spread beyond one's local area. Hence all the great religions of the world have written texts. One measure of advanced culture/civilization[61] is the extent to which these written beliefs inspire physical expressions of spirituality. These may be places of worship, e.g., cathedrals in Christianity, temples in Buddhism, or mosques in Islam. Indeed these account for some of the most remarkable monuments, including Angkor Wat (the largest planned city), Pagan, Machu Pichu, Borobodur, Isfahan, and the Vatican. In a sense these are physical, visual commentaries on the sacred texts. These written beliefs also inspire a range of artistic expressions. In the West, there is a focus on the (static) fine arts (painting, sculpture). In the East, there is a greater emphasis on expression through the (dynamic) performance arts (theatre, puppets, music, dance; cf. Table 51). This seeming opposition between static Western culture and dynamic Eastern culture may itself have been aggravated by the advent of printing, and, as we shall suggest at the very end of this book, the new media offer new means of transcending these differences.

As cultures advance, there is usually a secularization of beliefs. When Homer wrote the *Iliad*, it was closely linked to the fundamental beliefs of the Greeks. In the course of the centuries, it was increasingly seen as literature. In the West, however, something else also happened. Aside from periodic bouts of iconoclasm, stemming largely from the Judaic tradition, there was a fascination with visualizing texts. As written beliefs became expressed in an ever-greater number of media, they fostered an increasing aesthetic distance between a believer and what is believed.

This process took nearly three thousand years from around 1000 BC to about AD 1800. First the statue was a god, then it represented a god ,and very gradually it represented a god playfully. The Greeks believed in Hermes. The Romans represented Hermes as Mercury. By the eighteenth century, Boucher could paint Mercury as ,a man with wings tied to his feet with ribbons. Noble gods and goddesses of Antiquity became the instruments of play and satire in the eighteenth century, by Jove (cf. Table 52). This sense of aesthetic distance entails some of the most fascinating and elusive aspects of advanced culture. Hence the Puritans tried to ban Shakespeare's "plays." Eighteenth-century authors and playwrights such as Voltaire found that they had to situate their plays in Persia in order to make criticisms about the home front.

To this day, totalitarian states have difficulty in accepting subtle distinctions between artistic expression and simple criticism of a regime. And yet this ability at not taking oneself too seriously, in having aesthetic distance, a sense of irony, remains

TABLE 52 Links between art and levels of abstraction.

DATE	PROCESS	TERM
–1000	statue equals god	equivalence
1000–200 BC	statue represents god	substitution
AD 200–300	statue, painting represents man as if god	euhemerism
300–1200	statue, painting represents *a* but means *b*	symbolism
1200–1450	painting represents *a* and means *a*	literal
	O.T. and means N.T.	allegorical
	Christ's actions in relation to man	moral
	Christ's actions in relation to Eternity	anagogical
1450–1560	painting represents *a* in guise of *a1*	(allegorical)
1650–1800	painting represents *a* in playful guise of *a1*	(caricature)

one of our most profound measures of an urbane figure of culture, the difference between a civilized person and a primitive brute. Memory institutions help to preserve these wonderful expressions of high culture. Ironically, in the West, they have also contributed greatly both to our sense of aesthetic distance and distance from our own beliefs. A devout Christian will kneel before an altar in a church but is unlikely to do so in a museum. Museums decontextualize objects from their original locations.

Herein lies one of the paradoxes and also one of the dilemmas of western culture. While objects are fully in their original context, a believer often concentrates so much on the religious functions of the object that they do not notice its aesthetic aspects. Once a totem stands in the Rockefeller wing of the Metropolitan Museum of Art, a viewer sees these aesthetic aspects clearly but has difficulty in believing or even understanding its original function. Put in radical terms: religious objects often only become art once their religious dimensions no longer function entirely. This is why culture is more than art. It must bind persons at the original moment of expression and continue to bind them when that initial impulse has weakened. Without this continuity, the individuality expressed by that culture is absorbed into another.

In the West, culture tends to separate one from nature. One goes to great centres such as Berlin, London, or Paris to see culture. The East has a very different approach. In Japan, for instance, there is a national gallery in Tokyo. But for the most part, the great artistic expressions are still in their original contexts in religious centres such as Kyoto, Nara, Kamakura, Nikko, etc. They have not been decontextualized in the way of objects in a museum. Moreover, as one contemplates the statues in these Zen, Shinto, and other temples, one discovers that the temples, especially through their gardens, were very consciously built to unify us with nature. The West creates aesthetic distance. The East removes it. The temple is not an object imposed on the natural world. It is built organically as part of the natural world. It is very consciously built of wood, in order that parts of it can be rebuilt regularly, so that the building skills will remain alive and continuity is assured.

TABLE 53 Seven levels of culture.

1	Urban	Cities	Beijing, Cairo, Istanbul, London, Paris
2	Regional	Provinces	Basque, Limburg
3	National	Traditional Countries	Scotland, France
4	National	Recent Countries	Especially Africa
5	Multicultural	Large Countries and Units	Canada, Russia, United States, Europe
6	International	Major Literature, Art	Shakespeare, Tolstoy, Leonardo
7	International	Major Religions	Buddhism, Hebraism, Christianity, Islam

Here also, contextualization has its roles. The summer gardens of the Imperial Palace in Kyoto were inspired directly by scenes from the *Tale of Gengi*. For those of us who are unaccustomed to seeing literature in botanical form and for whom the passages of Gengi are not uppermost in our minds, augmented culture will help. Zen Buddhist statues are based on Chinese Buddhist models, which themselves are based on originals in India, with influences from Nepal, Tibet, and elsewhere. A first stage in contextualization is to make clear those roots.

In the past, most of us only learned the texts of our own culture. In the West, one began with the *Bible* and some of the classics, Homer, Virgil, etc. One tended to specialize in the literature of one's country (cf. chapter 13).[62] In the nineteenth century, when cultural tourism became something more than the grand tour for a chosen few, *Baedecker* and the *Guide Michelin*, became essential aids in the experience. In a global context, we need much more. We can never hope to know all the myriad myths, legends, fables, and stories, all the symbols, patterns, and ornaments and their significance, just as we cannot hope to learn all the 6,500 languages of the world fluently. Here again a contextualizer is needed, which provides us with cultural and historical variations. In a global society, we should be familiar with literature regionally, nationally, and internationally. To achieve this we could readily spend our whole lives just reading all the sacred texts and all the great literature. Most of us have the distractions of jobs, family, etc. So augmented culture, which helps us to find our way, especially in other cultures, becomes a necessity rather than a luxury.

The frontiers of the new technologies are exploring the potentials of immersive interactive narratives and interactive comics using the concept of transfiction. An European Commission IST project called art.live is experimenting with display walls that show images from comics. Using the principles of blue screen technology, a camera takes an image of a live person and inserts them into the display of the comic, which they can then in turn manipulate.[63] This is leading to new forms of trans-fiction and new experiments in visualizing imaginary (so-called dark) cities: Urbicande, Blossfeldtstad, Calvani, Alaxis, Xhystos, Pahry, Brüsel, Mylos, and the green lake. Siemens is developing wireless virtual reality gaming consoles.[64] Intel is experimenting with interactive on-line immersive games. If the predictions of fibre-optic connections directly to the home become a reality, it is fully possible

TABLE 54 The challenge of correlating facts, events, and stories from towns, cities, regions, national capitals, international capitals, and so-called global centres.

RANGE	AREA	SCOPE OF INTERPRETATION
Local	Rural Village, Town	Fact
Urban	City	Event
Regional	Province	Story
National	National Capital	History
International	International Capital	History of Culture or Empire
Global	Global Centres	World History and World View

to foresee entering immersively into videos, films, and other narratives, perhaps sometimes as an observing avatar to see how individuals in different cultures see, experience, and live their narratives differently.

Augmented culture in this new sense will need to distinguish between at least seven different levels, ranging from local to international (Table 53). Cities with long histories such as Beijing or Cairo have their own local culture through experiences shared only within that city. Peoples in regions, such as the Basques in Catalonia or the Québécois in Canada, have their own cultural expressions through shared experiences in a language that separates them from other parts of the country in which they live. National cultures vary greatly depending on whether they have evolved over the centuries, as in the case of Scotland, or whether they entail very recent nations which may not reflect the boundaries of a given tribe or people (as in parts of Africa). Very large countries such as Canada and Russia entail multicultural dimensions, which are a class unto themselves.[65] At the international level, major religions form the most common context for shared experiences.

Finally, there is a corpus of world cultural heritage of major literature, art, and other expressions, to which UNESCO is drawing our attention, which belongs to us all.[66] These include natural wonders such as Uluru (Ayers Rock) in Australia, the Victoria Falls between Zimbabwe and Zambia in Africa, and Mount Everest in Nepal. They also include a small number of basic symbols such as cosmic eggs and world trees, trees of life, which link the cosmological worlds of myths, legends, and religion with both the changing cycles of the physical world and the enduring cycles of astronomy. It is this list on which we must build: of things we have in common, of experiences all humans can share as part of our collective imagination. For these can serve as bridges between the different levels and forms of culture in helping us arrive at new maps of culture, which allow us to see larger patterns in expressions within the global village.

In the past, there was an assumption that culture was something monolithic: that one's culture defined one's person and one's being. A key insight is that one and the same person can potentially operate in terms of all these different levels of culture without contradiction. I can participate in the local culture of more than one city (e.g., Toronto, London, Maastricht), be proud of my regional roots[67] (e.g., Frisia), follow a particular religion (e.g., Christianity), participate in national cultures (e.g., Canada, Netherlands), and still be very enthusiastic about aspects of international culture. In the past such awareness was open only to some merchants and international diplomats. Today it is open to an increasing number of spirits.

In the future more and more of us need to learn these multiple dimensions of awareness. Herein lies a new key to tolerance. Inherent in this idea of one individual being multiple audiences, belonging to multiple communities, is a new approach to the ways in which we organize our historical records of cultural heritage. In the past, it was assumed that a given fact or event was static. In future, we need to relate viewpoints of a given city, region, and country with international viewpoints. It is not a question of opposing local, regional, and a national approaches, but rather of co-ordinating their different views in order to compare their different interpretations (Table 54). If we stand back to see the big picture, we realize that it is much more than a simple co-or-dination of enduring, collaborative, and personal knowledge as outlined above (Table 47ab). In a sense, each village, city, province, and country has its own take on this great spectrum. If we want a connected world that reflects this complexity, we need much, much more than one standard "take" on reality.

Inherent also is a new approach to the much-debated problem of different corpora and different canons. Instead of fighting about the borderline cases, we should recognize the value of such lists as charters for identities of communities. Part of feeling English is the common experience of having read Shakespeare and Milton or recognizing a line from Keats and Pope. If we accept that each individual can have multiple identities, the danger of being hemmed in by a single list of a given canon disappears and we discover that we can enjoy the benefits of multiple corpora, pluriform canons.[68]

Such an approach recognizes the importance of national centres and the same time properly brings to light the role of regional realities, the so-called prov-inces, the peripheries, which mysteriously are every bit as important as the great metropoli. Regional realities, precisely in their insistence on being different, in the complexities of their local details, their so-called local colour, contain a key to understanding the ecology of cultural diversity, which is crucial for our future.

Our political structures need to be aligned with these needs. Needed are new levels of co-ordination whereby knowledge and efforts at the urban (local), re-gional, and national levels are integrated with multicultural structures such as the European Union and international efforts at the level of UNESCO. If we are to have global citizens, we need political structures to integrate various levels of their activities. So the new media lead to a reorganization of knowledge, which implies a reorganization of society.

Some continue to see globalization only as a danger, especially in economic terms: as inevitably linked with homogenization and the undermining of diversity. It is true that the expansion of the Roman Empire into Africa and Asia Minor led to an imposition of Roman customs and building forms such as theatres, coliseums, and hippodromes onto these regions. At the same, it also greatly expanded the range of Roman customs and architecture. Rome would not have become the eternal city had it not adapted numerous other influences. Three of the twenty-one catacombs of Rome are Hebraic.

Looking back one sees that the great moments in world history were precisely those when cultures opened themselves to international influences. Greece became great when it looked beyond itself and came under the influence of its colonies in Spain, France, Sicily, Italy, Turkey, Syria, etc. When Justinian closed Plato's Academy in AD 529, seven of its leading scholars made their way to Gundishapur in Tajikistan. Arabic culture rose to new heights when the ruler at Gundishapur welcomed these scholars and decided to have translations made of the greatest writings from the Greco-Roman world. The Gothic period emerged once Abbot Suger and Peter the Venerable started a major translation campaign beginning with Arabic works such as the *Koran*.

Florence transformed itself from a provincial town to one of the towering examples of the Renaissance by bringing in Greek scholars and collecting texts in Arabic, Chaldaean, and many foreign languages. The French Renaissance began by importing Italians such Primaticcio, Serlio, and Leonardo da Vinci. The greatness of Japan lies in its adapting traditions from India, China, Korea, and the West and at same time producing something unique. China is better remembered for the times when it was open to other cultures, when it adapted Buddhism from India, or adopted printing from Korea, than when it tried to keep other influences out by great walls. Cultures become richer and more diverse as they become more open.

The richest cultures are not static. They change with time, gradually transforming their local repertoire, often in combination with motifs from other cultures. The Romanesque churches of Northern Germany adopted lions from Italy for their entrances, which were, in turn, based on lions from the Middle East. The church of San Marco in Venice integrated Byzantine, Greek, Roman, and local motifs. The architects in Palermo at the time of Frederick II created a synthesis of Byzantine, Norman, Arabic, Jewish, and Christian motifs. The architects in Toledo and at Las Huelgas near Burgos created their own synthesis of Jewish, Arabic, and Christian motifs.[69] A comprehensive corpus of variants in local heritage will lead to much more than a glorification of local eccentricities and provincialism. It can prove an inspiration to multiculturalism in its deepest sense. It can include basic building methods, styles, ornament, and decoration and serve as a key to future diversity.[70] This takes us back to the challenge of linking universals and particulars at a new level.

The challenge is to take the myriad alternative examples not as proof that there is nothing new under the sun, that everything has been done, but rather as challenges for something new. Therein lies the secret and hope of culture. This is why we need something much more than long, static lists of cultural objects. We need a contextualizer; we need a reorganization of knowledge, which leads to a re-combination of elements to create new expressions and new knowledge. We need dynamic, augmented knowledge and culture.

15
conclusions

Art is a service, not a product. Created beauty
is a relationship, and a relationship with the
Holy at that. Reducing such work to 'content'
is like praying in swear words.... Cyberspace
is unreal estate. Relationships are its geology.
— John Perry Barlow, *Wired*,
October 2000, p. 242.

1. Introduction

In the previous chapter we noted that sharing is one of the central
themes of this book. We claimed that there was a need to combine sharing for profit and sharing for other purposes. Sharing
for financial gain focusses on material consequences. Sharing for
other purposes expands the scope of new media to intellectual
and philosophical implications of contextuality and spirituality
and extends even to play. What emerges from this is something
profound. There are basic choices. There is freedom. This will
lead to a brief excursus on the ingredients for the spiritual before
turning to a review of the consequences of the new media and
suggestions for ingredients needed for an open future.

2. Play

Even play is affected by the three different visions outlined in this book. In America, play becomes external behaviour. "It is not how much or what they know, it's what they do with their knowledge," claims Schrage in his book on *Serious Play*. In business, this leads to rapid prototyping and rapid marketing, often publicizing products before they are even built. By contrast, in Europe one typically works for years on something and only makes it public after all the bugs have been removed. In Japan, this sense of perfectionism is even greater still. International corporations with offices in all three countries discover that this can lead to complex situations. A product that the home office in Germany and their Japanese colleagues perceive as still in the first stages of development is suddenly made public by the American branch.

Even after a product is on the market in Europe or Japan, it is frequently adopted quietly by experts with little publicity. The CATIA software, which was developed in France and Germany, is an excellent case in point. In the early 1990s, it was being used by leading architectural firms in Europe. It was used also to reconstruct the famous Frauenkirche in Dresden in virtual reality, which was shown at the 1994 CEBIT conference in Hanover. Then it was adopted by Chrysler and Boeing for their design teams. In *Serious Play*, Schrage highlights the importance of the CATIA software in America but forgets to mention its origins.

Returning to the lighter side of play, when Walt Disney wrote instructions to his chief animator in 1928, he urged: "Please try to make all action definite and pointed and don't be afraid to exaggerate things plenty."[1] Hence the American quest to externalize everything into behaviour and action, which we noted in their business, learning, and work, extends also to animation and entertainment. The fascination with computers and theatre by authors such as Laurel, Pine, and Gilmore is symptomatic of something pervasive.

Paradoxically this pervasive quality is more superficial than in Europe or Japan because it assumes that what one acts is all one is. Acting is where the action is. What you see is what you get (WYSIWYG) was an interface problem, but it reflects also Americans' problem of interfacing with Europeans, Japanese, and people from many other countries. In America acting with action is sincerity. In Europe, sincere action is the opposite of acting. Acting is when there is a discrepancy between what one thinks and how one acts. What you do, what you say, and what you get are not necessarily related. This is all, of course, at the level of stereotypes such as French cooks, Italian lovers, and German mechanics.

Americans often perceive this as European snobbishness and insincerity. It need not mean any of those things. It does mean, however, that a European or a Japanese person has a very active inner world, and simply doing things with that person does not mean one knows them. To know a European deeply is to enter into the vast horizons of their inner worlds, their worldviews (*Weltanschauungen*, a word that English lacks), their dreams, and their quests. Americans think that all you have to do is see and you know. There is nothing below the surface, unless one is dealing with spies, etc.

"Normal" American people are "straightforward." That is why Europeans often perceive Americans as being too close to the norm, with no "corners and sides" (*Ecken und Kanten*, another German expression without an English equivalent), without what Americans would call eccentricities, which would make them potential friends for Europeans. It is instructive that the English word "caricature" comes from the French word "caractère." In America, a good character is the opposite of a caricature. In Europe, such oppositions are too easy.

This American approach, which externalizes everything in work and play, has at least three consequences. 1) As we saw earlier, it tends to reduce the personal to a very limited sphere of action. 2) Related to this is a paradox that Americans tend to conflate public and private. If everything is visible action, then what is unseen by others does not count. So one's private things tend to become public or to be so personal that they cannot be shared. Sharing *Private Lives* in the playful sense of Noël Coward is alien to this view. One is either a public figure or a recluse like Howard Hughes. 3) Because acting is sincere action in everyday life, playing with everyday life is as questionable as acting in the European sense. Hence the only realm for play is in escapism.

Fantasyland, Frontierland, Adventureland, and Tomorrowland are more than the sections of Disneyland: they offer a cartography of where play has its outlets. At work there is serious play in Schrage's sense, but to relax, to really play, the American must escape from the realities of everyday life, "get away from it all," watch television, go to a movie, or, better still, go to a theme park.

If entertainment is escapism, is the American quest to make edu-tainment the basis of learning a wise one? By contrast, a European goes to a café. They enter the life of their village, city, or town. Learning is not an escape: it is an adventure of discovering one's own language, culture, and history.[2]

This leads to a comparative scenario: to relax the American goes to a theme park, the European goes to an historical city such as Florence. Both are looking for surprise. In an American theme park, surprise is the recognition of the familiar. When we enter the rides *Back to Future*, or *ET*, it is assumed that we have seen the film. In a visit to Florence, the surprise lies in the discovery of the unfamiliar. Yes, we may have seen a picture of Michelangelo's *David* or even photos of Botticelli's paintings, but most of us are completely surprised. The statues are bigger than they look in the art books. Some of the paintings look smaller. So the American theme park offers us the expected and predictable. The town of Florence offers us the unexpected and the unpredictable.

The theme park is a closed model. It is proprietary in every sense. Florence is an open model. It is an open source. The theme park has gates and, once we pay the admission, the transaction is finished. Florence has open gates, we pay no admission, but the transaction has only just begun. Because it is a closed model, the theme park is very defined. Seeing it once is often enough. It invites an attitude of "been there, done that," and phrases such as "it's a great place to visit, but I wouldn't want to live there." Because it is an open model, Florence is different. When Americans say that they have done Florence, they reveal more about their limitations than their insight.

There are of course threats to erode this distinction, dangers that cities such as Florence become the equivalents of theme parks. It is striking, for instance, how the inner city is ever-more dominated by brand name shops: Boss, Dior, Gucci, and Nike. Disturbing also is a trend where entry to churches is frequently a paid event like a ride and no longer a religious experience. Even Florence faces the danger of becoming a global village in the McWorld sense, and this is a threat for which new solutions must be sought.

Fortunately, Florence has over forty museums that are open at very irregular times so that it would take two months just to see everything once, and by that time one would just be learning how to look at things seriously. Thus Florence is undoable and those who try doing so risk finding it is their undoing. It is worse than addiction to drugs. Once you come you have to come back, as do millions of tourists every year. Meanwhile there are also new dangers looming in Italy.[3]

The American perception of Italians, partly inherited via the English, is that Italians are utterly charming and a little disorganized with a tendency to be lazy. What this overlooks is that Italian tourism is the country's most important source of income and, although it is has just over 1 per cent of the world's population, it is a G7 country, one of the seven most wealthy countries in the world. For persons who are supposed to be lazy, that is rather good. It is interesting to note, moreover, that in all of the G7 countries, the travel and tourism industry is the top employer.[4]

The above comparative scenario also leads to another insight. If we buy the American hype of thinkers such as Pine and Gilmore, then we may be heading to an experience economy. As they point out, this assures us with money earned on the customer today. But in the process the customer is reduced to a product, who is won by playing psychological games. Hollywood films such as *The Game* (1997), revealed that such experiences can be other than comforting. To prevent this there is recourse to what makes the customer feel good and all the restrictions of political correctness. Now there are even politically correct bedtime stories.[5]

By contrast, in Florence there is another kind of experience economy, which depends on cultural and historical dimensions. Florence is an experience where the customer is not the product. There are no psychological games. The experience is real, but you only discover as much as you are prepared to learn. This is another kind of game, another way to play. Florence is an archetypal example of something found in thousands of European towns. It integrates play into everyday society. Play is a slice of life and not a piece of cake in an artificial park. Do you want to escape to the theme park or do you prefer to live in Florence? Florence represents why Europe (and Japan) want more than an information highway.

3. Choices

We have suggested that there are at least three competing political visions, namely: 1) an American vision of an information highway, 2) a European vision of an information or a knowledge society,[6] and 3) a Japanese vision of a knowledge society.

Information Highway

In our discussion of different modes of production above (chapter 4), we noted that the United States consistently tends towards technological solutions where economic considerations rule supreme. The United States has the world's most impressive strategies on the implications during work time. It also emphasizes the commercial aspects of the information highway as if the daily hours at work were all there was to life. By contrast, Europe and Japan are equally interested in the implications of computers for our play (leisure time) and our dreams (rest time). Hence, America's solutions often seem superficial when compared to the social and knowledge-based dimensions present in Europe and Japan. There are deeper reasons for this.

One of the basic premises in American computer science is the notion of entity relationships. These entity relationships serve as an underlying principle of many database structures in the United States. Objects are linked by inheritance using a parent-child relation(ship). This relationship is considered so obvious that it requires no explanation. As we have shown (chapter 12), this has the advantage of being simple. It has the disadvantage of being too primitive to distinguish clearly between abstract (*is a*) and partitive (*has a*) relations.

This has more fundamental consequences. In our earlier discussion, we noted that grammatical statements minimally involve a noun, a verb, and an object in order to make a claim. Entity relationships implicitly make claims about being and having. Entity relationships are about entities but hardly about properties, activities, and dimensions with the full scale of Aristotle's accidents. Without the full range of entities, properties, activities, and dimensions in their various combinations, there can be no statements in the sense of more complex claims that can be defended or refuted. On the positive side, if one only uses obvious entity relationships, then the need to resolve ambiguity disappears and, to put it polemically, the quest for truth becomes superfluous.

If entities are the only "meaningful" relationships in our life, then there is no need to fuss about organizing knowledge. This has the attractive side that we can do away with tedious classification, indexing, and other time-consuming distractions. This has a surprising corollary, however, that the distinction between knowledge and information disappears. It is instructive, for instance, that the National Institute for Science and Technology (NIST) has five layers of software architecture in its model, namely, business, information, applications, data, technology, without any mention of knowledge.[7]

In the United States, those who believe that information is the same as knowledge, rightly strive for an information society. And those who spend their lives fitting into the clarity of that vision successfully avoid many ambiguities found elsewhere. There is a danger, of course, that some of those ambiguous others may perceive Americans as simplistic. The real problems of America run deeper and have to do with the role of the individual versus society. In Europe (and in Asia) one assumes that the primary sources of ordering are at the societal level. Hence, classification systems play a considerable role. Viewed from the outside, it often appears that Europeans and Asians are under the yoke of impersonal systems.

In Europe, the primary sources of meaning are at a societal level. Hence, dictionaries play an important role in the definitions of words. These vary with level of complexity. Hence, there are standard dictionaries, professional dictionaries, dialect dictionaries, and slang dictionaries. These definitions change with time. Hence there are historical dictionaries, and modern dictionaries have an etymological section. In the United States, these historical dimensions are no longer considered important. Hence, the (American) *Webster's Dictionary* abandoned its etymological sections in the 1970s.

It would be wrong to conclude from the above that Europe is impersonal and without viewpoints. As we have seen (chapter 13), Europeans have been writing about viewpoint theories for centuries, and they have developed the most complex theories concerning viewpoints thus far. Even Perreault includes point of view as one of his relations. But these interpretations exist under the official categories of classification systems and thesauri. The deconstructionists of Paris have no doubts about the existence of meanings beneath the surface of language. Nor is there much doubt that persons in Europe lack a personal dimension of meaning, let alone personalities and eccentrics.

In the United States, there is a far greater desire to codify individual viewpoints within major classification systems. Already within the Dewey Decimal Classification, there was some room for individual viewpoints. In the past decades, scholars[8] have sought to go much further and include viewpoints, often their personal viewpoints, within the system itself. If everyone were to do this, of course, the system would collapse because the assumption underlying any major collection is that it will not be affected by every passing whimsy of individuals and remain relatively robust over time.

In this context, it is instructive to return to Hausser's competing ontologies, outlined above (Figure 20b). The third of these by Newell and Simon included the intentionality of the observer. At first sight, this seems like an excellent idea. Subsuming this within a cognitive agent means that each agent can have his or her own intentionality. It also means that each agent is potentially solipsistic because there is no guarantee that there is a clearly defined common link between these different intentionalities. Newell's solution exteriorizes inner, personal meaning in the form of an agent and offers a seeming solution to the problem of intentionality. However, it offers no means of relating this personal meaning to a societal meaning as reflected in dictionaries and other reference works. Nor does this model assume a serious role for personal change, cultural difference, or historical development.

To understand the origin of these problems, it is useful to trace what happened to the *trivium* in the United States. The *trivium*, as noted earlier, was the study of language in terms of its structure (grammar), logic (dialectic), and its effects (rhetoric, Table 41). Rhetoric was traditionally about a whole range of effects: how to be convincing, wooing, persuading, dissuading, suggesting, encouraging, etc., and how to use a variety of styles. In the late nineteenth century, Peirce saw semiotics as the basis of everything and thus redefined the *trivium* as syntax, semantics, and pragmatics, respectively. In this view, syntax deals with signs, semantics deals with interpretants, and: "Pragmatics is the study that relates signs to the agents who use them to refer to things in the world and to communicate their intentions about those things to other agents who may have similar or different intentions concerning the same or different things."[9]

Pragmatics, is closely related to pragmatism, a basis of Dewey's philosophy, which as we noted (chapter 7), was a point of departure for action theory and many twentieth-century developments in organizational theory. Pragmatics reduces the complexity and distracting elements of rhetoric to a clear, useful goal. It also seeks to bridge inner intentions with persons in the external world. These inner intentions might potentially be subjective, but by subsuming them to pragmatics, communication is effectively transformed into useful action and useful behaviour. One of the greatest of all behaviourists, Talcott Parsons, spent much of his life trying to work *Towards a General Theory of Action*.

This approach has several corollaries. First, only action counts, or more precisely, only pragmatic action counts. It follows that theories, reflections, and other ponderings, which do not result in direct action, do not count. Second, the model deals only with individual actions. There are as many actions as there are individual cognitive agents. But there is nothing in the model to deal with a framework for society, the aims of a society or even the actions of society. To state the case polemically, the American approach models individual actions while ignoring those of society. Hence the country that conflates information and knowledge is ultimately unable to envisage an information society.

Ironically, the American preoccupation with action, with doing, means that the process of getting there becomes more important than the result. The goal becomes an information highway, rather than what lies at the end of the road.[10] While Europeans may playfully joke that getting there is half the fun, they never doubt the value of arriving and enjoying the goal at the journey's end.

There is a further consequence that is even more ironical. As we have shown, the organizational consequence of computers is systemicity (chapters 7–9). If one includes society and government in one's model, this can counterbalance the influences of a system. But if one's model includes only individuals, and one treats corporations as if they were individual entities, ultimately human individuals become subsumed as insignificant cogs in a system that ignores both individuals and government. Hence, the country most famous for its individualism creates a system where corporations and the military render insignificant the real power of those individuals, notwithstanding the noble protests of Electronic Frontier Foundations and many an articulate author. The country that publishes business books on *Pursuit of Excellence* also has famous figures, such as Donald Norman, who offers the following portraits of academia and industry: "It is more important to be clever than to be correct, better to be profound than practical. In the pecking order of the university, those who are most abstract and irrelevant are on top, those most practical and useful are at the bottom. The high-technology industry rushes to do this, to do that, The race is to swift and to the clever, not to the best."[11]

What emerges from this is a complex reality. For many outsiders, Silicon Valley represents the epitome of the American ideal. To learn that there are sixty to seventy new millionaires per day in the San Francisco Bay area sounds like a report from Shangri-La. What we are usually not told is that the poverty level in this area now includes all those with wages of $50,000/year or less. As a result, up to 40 per cent of the population who are working full time, sometimes with double jobs, are unable to think of buying a house. So there may be about sixty-five new millionaires a day. That makes 23,725 lucky persons annually, but what of the millions of others? And this is within one of the wealthiest sections of the United States. What of all the others in the third world? This is why the so-called American solution remains problematic.

Information or Knowledge Society

Europe is often confused about its real goals. Often it sees the superficial successes of America as a goal to be imitated. Hence, although it has developed its own theories of knowledge, Europe continues to be fascinated by the lure of an automatic solution where "with friends like statistics, who needs linguistics?"[12] Hence, the same Europe that has developed the International Society for Knowledge Organization is tempted to follow the United States in equating knowledge with information.

If one looks, for instance, at Professor Kaynak's links between semiotics and mechatronics, one recognizes much that seems American. Peirce distinguished between syntax, semantics, and pragmatics. So too does Kaynak, whose ideas on this topic come from the Russian Professor Meystel (Drexel). In Kaynak's system, however, syntax is the sign, semantics the interpretant, and pragmatics is the object. Syntax is linked with perception, semantics with behaviour generation and pragmatics with the world. Between perception and behaviour is knowledge. Between knowledge and the world are sensors and actuation. This is not just a simple equation of knowledge and information.

While Europe often refers to an information society,[13] there is also frequent mention of a knowledge society. Europe has produced not only the knowledge models of Descartes, Leibniz, Hume, Kant, and Hegel. It has created theories of knowledge acquisition (Erkenntnistheorie). These theories of knowledge are much more than logical postulates about ideas. In the tradition of Plato and Aristotle, European theories of knowledge have always been theories of society. Sometimes, as in the case of Marx, one might convincingly argue that they got their theory more than slightly wrong, but society always remained an essential part of the equation.

Herein lies a fundamental contrast with the United States. In America, the government can (often rhetorically) proclaim that government no longer has a role to play, while at the same time continuing to decide very succinctly about which corporations are favoured and which patents are upheld. In Europe, there is a continuing recognition that governments are necessary to protect the public good, to give some direction to the enormous powers of multinational corporations, and to guarantee the continued role of individuals in a world where systemic forces threaten their continued validity. In short, Europe is unwavering in its desire to have something that affects the whole of society, not just the action of a highway rushing somewhere, but of a cohesive society once one has finished rushing. As a result, while Europe may waver whether it wants information or knowledge, it is clear in wanting society as the second part of that equation.

Knowledge Society

In Japan, there is a more coherent aim to create a knowledge society. There is a quest to integrate knowledge of nature, individuals, society, and organizations. This is leading to an integration of diverse fields such as knowledge engineering, systems science, economics, biology, philosophy, and organization science. For instance, at the Japan Advanced Institute of Science and Technology (Hokuriku), there is a School of Social Knowledge Science with a Department of Organizational Dynamics, which: "studies Knowledge that exists in [an] organization and the process in which it is created, transferred, transformed and upgraded without resorting to a specific methodology."

The section on organizational dynamics is led by Professor Ikujiro Nonaka[14] (cf. chapter 7). His department is one of nine sections in the School of Social Knowledge Science, which is linked in turn with a further ten departments in the School of Knowledge System Science. Six of these nineteen sections are laboratories jointly operated by other institutions.[15] In addition to Knowledge Science, there are schools of Information Science and Materials Science, as well as four centres on Research and Investigation of Advanced Science and Technology, Knowledge Science, Information Science, and New Materials, respectively.[16] With respect to knowledge, there is a section on Knowledge System Science, Knowledge Creating Methodology, Knowledge-Based Systems, Knowledge Structure, Genetic Knowledge Systems, and Molecular Knowledge Systems.

In our discussion of institutions (chapter 6), we noted how concepts such as complexity are bringing together a number of scientific fields in the United States. We also noted how emerging fields such as infonomics are bringing together a range of traditional fields in both the arts and sciences in Europe. By contrast, the Japanese experience is bringing together a whole range of evolving fields. For instance, their section on knowledge creating methodology is studying "hierarchical conceptual modeling for problem solving" including Eastern and Western approaches. Their section on knowledge-based systems is doing research on the theory and design methodology of evolving knowledge systems. "We are particularly interested in two collateral but complementary systems: networked information systems and human brain neural networks, which are studied from an analytical and synthetical point of view."[17]

In this approach information science and neuroscience are being combined to arrive at new models of knowledge. There is a section on knowledge structure and another on genetic knowledge systems, which includes "gene knowledge for evolutionary systems, emergent systems and complex systems in the field of knowledge modeling, emotion processing and computational molecular biology." A section on molecular knowledge systems studies "fundamental principles in order to create molecule knowledge systems through which essential knowledge is discovered."[18]

Yet another section does complex systems analysis, investigating "principles and methods for estimating and controlling large-scale and/or complex systems, which may exhibit chaotic or fractal behavior." These are then applied to "environmental problems in social systems and evolution and development in biological and cognitive systems."[19] Together these various departments are trying to understand the organizing structures of nature and society at the macro-, micro-, and nano-level and to see how these affect individuals, organizations, and the structure of knowledge. Instead of an information highway or information society, Japan is aiming at a knowledge society.

Global Information Highway
In addition to these political visions of America, Europe, and Japan, there is a fourth vision, purely driven by economics. It borrows much from the American profit-driven model, and at the same time acts as if it were above the ordinary laws. This is the danger that of which David Korten warned in his book, When Corporations Rule the World.[20] Charles Derber pursued these ideas in Corporation Nation.[21] He noted that this vision aims to establish a Multilateral Law of Investment (MAI), which has as its purpose:

> ... to ensure that capital can flow freely around the world with the same protections and rights in every country ... "National treatment" is mandated for all foreign companies, meaning they must be awarded the same or better treatment than local firms. National or community regulations requiring the hiring of local workers would be outlawed, and the ability of countries to regulate the flow of foreign currency would be effectively decimated. Corporations that felt that any country's environmental or labor laws limited their rightful profits could sue governments for expropriation ... and receive monetary compensation.[22]

Such lawsuits are already underway. In 2000, America OnLine (AOL) announced that it did not intend to be subjected to local laws in its global activities. In the spring of 2000, U.S. media companies sued a Canadian company for broadcasting materials that were legal by Canadian law but were perceived to be inconvenient to the American companies concerned. Lawrence Lessig in his keynote address to the WWW9 Conference in Amsterdam noted that there would be quite an uproar if Canada or any other foreign country suggested they could tell U.S. companies what they were allowed to broadcast on their home soil.

In essence, there is a relatively small group of corporations working on all five continents with a well-established global network. It has been claimed that these corporations have international bodies to secure their interests, namely, the World Trade Organization (WTO), the International Monetary Fund (IMF), and the World Bank. There are no equivalents at a governmental level. Yes, there is the UN and UNESCO, for which the richest country in the world is way behind in paying its modest dues. There are a few international bodies such as the International Standards Organization (ISO) and the International Telecommunications Union (ITU). One welcome development of the past years has been an increasing co-operation between traditional bodies such as ISO, ITU, and new bodies such as IETF.

America is fond of speaking of checks and balances. We are, however, in a world where global activities are a reality for business, but not for government. Business is writing the cheques without the balances of a coherent vision of public interest, of the public good. Perhaps, even more disturbing, we find the leaders responsible for the public good too often merely turning to business and asking them to lead the revolution. In February of 1995, there was a G7 ministerial conference on the global information society. This included a roundtable of business leaders with forty-six official participants. Forty-four were heads of global corporations. Two were academics. Jacques Delors, of the European Commission, in his introduction, told them: "You are at the centre of the development of the information society: market evolution, all the initiatives that you and other companies have taken, launching new products for example, creating new forms of agreement.... Then we will talk about the role of public authorities, what you want them to do."[23]

There were very good things said at that meeting and at the conference as a whole. It was one of the first international meetings where members of the European Commission spoke very consciously of a global information society. There was due mention of the public. There was expressed concern about protecting privacy and personal data. There was considerable mention of users. But there were no users.

The man who is credited with having coined the phrase "information highway" was also there. Mr. Al Gore, began his speech by getting the date of the invention of printing wrong by 600 years. He went on to claim that: "The Clinton administration is committed to the goal of connecting every classroom, every library, every hospital and every clinic to the national and global information infrastructures by the end of this decade." That was in 1995. Since then there have been many political changes, but the vision of connecting every classroom has not happened.

Also in 1995, there was a meeting near San Francisco to discuss the future of the world in the next twenty years. Mikhail Gorbachev was there. Five hundred of the leading persons in finance and politics were there. They concluded that, within twenty years, only 20 per cent of the population would need to be employed in the sense of the old exchange economy. What should one do with the remaining 80 per cent? Their answer was "titty-tainment," a combination of the old tradition of bread and circuses plus the worst that Hollywood represents. Is this really where we want to go?

4. Freedom

Amidst the enormous hype of the mass media, it is important to stand back and look at the very big picture. An approach to global history in the manner of a Toynbee, a Spengler, or a McNeill is now pooh-poohed in most respectable, academic circles. At the same time, it is all the fashion to divide the whole of history into a few neat periods, such as paleolithic, neolithic, industrial revolution, and noolithic (Levy); or agrarian, industrial, service, and experience economy (Pine and Gilmore).

The thrust of such generalizations is that the industrial revolution and industrial economy were a phase that was replaced by the next period in the way that neolithic replaced paleolithic. This is too simplistic. The industrial revolution introduced a new level of machines. Those machines have not gone away. Yes, faster and more efficient machines are being built. Smaller machines are being built. Ever more of those machines are being operated by robots, or by software agents via computers.[24]

Kurzweil has shown that computational power has been increasing dramatically for nearly a century, i.e., for at least seventy years before there was an Internet. Beniger has argued the origins of the information society lie in a control revolution that has been in progress since the nineteenth century. According to Beniger, there are four levels of development: life, culture, bureaucracy, and finally technology. His highest level is a "techno-bureaucratic information society."[25] In our view culture is not just a level one goes past.

From a larger viewpoint we can see that the *Mechanization of the World Picture*[26] outlined by Dijksterhuis is a phenomenon that is in some ways being speeded up rather than replaced by the new technologies. Hence the revolution in new media as typified by computers and the Internet is part of a much bigger phenomenon that has been underway for centuries. The fact that networked computers are part of a much longer historical evolution leads to a further insight. The fears about losing jobs a) due to automation during the industrial revolutions and b) due to automation during the computer revolution are part of a single process. The bad news, say many, is that there are ever-fewer jobs. Some of course predict the end of work entirely.

In the highly industrialized parts of the world, an ever-smaller percentage of persons is required to work on production of food and other materials for survival. A long tradition of pessimists from Malthus through Marx feared that production would not be sufficient. This is not the problem. Each year thousands of tons of good food are destroyed consciously while, elsewhere in the world, alas, many die of hunger. The problem is not production but distribution.

In the language of Eric S. Raymond, an ever-smaller number of persons is needed to maintain the bare necessities of exchange economy. Seen in positive terms, this means that an ever-greater percentage of the population is now free to practice gift culture. Even among those who are working, the number of hours is theoretically falling. A century ago many farm labourers typically worked fifty or even sixty hours per week. Today many regular jobs are down to thirty-five hours per week.

The question is what do we do with all that free time? Do we simply look at this as time to spend in both senses of the word? a) to spend time, "amusing ourselves to death," as Postman would say, b) to spend money in shopping malls, consuming things we did not know we wanted, and not finding things we wanted? Or do we use these potentials for gift culture, to make this a better world? To use Raymond's title in revised form, the question is: will we use the privileges of a gift culture to haggle in bazaars, or will we use it to share in building grand, new things together: to build new cathedrals, physical and metaphysical?

Those who object that this approach lacks a clear business case are invited to consider three scenarios. First, there is (gift economy) Saint Francis, who asks his (exchange economy) father[27] about the prospects of creating a new order of beggars. He wants to create a new monastery, eventually thousands of them, and even universities such as Oxford, without any real investors. All he has is a small group of well-intentioned "believers." Would his father have invested in such a proposal? Would any venture capitalist, even an adventure capitalist, ever invest in such a scheme without a business plan, with no collateral, and only some vague, good vibesy stuff about giving? And yet Saint Francis created one of the great orders of history.

Second imaginary scenario: imagine Gutenberg going in front of the corporate board to explain his idea. Yes, ladies and gentlemen, I have come to the conclusion that manuscripts are inefficient and that it would be a good thing to have them all printed. Do you have an investor? Gutenberg was one up on Saint Francis. He had at least one investor. Are you sure it will work? No. What if you go bankrupt? Actually he did go bankrupt. Well then. Who would have thought this was a way to start one of the most important innovations of the Renaissance?

Third imaginary scenario: imagine the Vatican being run by a corporate committee rather than by a pope. Imagine the great architects, Peruzzi, Sangallo, Michelangelo, and later Bernini, going before the board to describe their plans to build the largest single building in the world (at that time). Why such a large scale? Well, the largest cathedral at this time is in Seville and surely it would not be fitting that the headquarters be smaller than a provincial site? Well, I don't know: aren't we supposed to be de-centralized and distributed? Incidentally, haven't you heard of downsizing? Maybe we should make a scale model a fifth the size and see if it works.

More importantly what materials are you using? Only the most precious possible, marbles from the East and the West, inlays from Byzantium, gold from here, silver from there. How will that increase quarterly sales except for the persons who are selling us the stuff? Surely we can do without the trimmings. Maybe we could get someone to paint it to look like marble. That would save a good deal. And then you want a Sistine Chapel for the pope? What's wrong with you? If he's got the biggest church around why does he need an extra church? And you want that decorated by that expensive painter, Michelangelo, as well? And in addition you want this enormous library? Is that part of our core business? And then you want a painting gallery, and a sculpture section? Have you heard of megalomania? This is clearly a blatant case. And why should we build a completely new building anyway? We already have the mortar without the clicks. Why don't we just settle for some good old renovation?

The history of the rebuilding of Saint Peter's basilica and the Vatican complex is of special interest. Around 1450, Pope Nicholas V decided that the best thing would be to create a new basilica. There were distractions so it was not until 1506 that Pope Julius II commissioned Bramante to knock down the old building and start afresh. In 1546 the basilica remained unfinished. Pope Paul III Farnese gave the commission to Michelangelo. It is often forgotten that Michelangelo did so free of charge on the condition that he could have a free hand in all the decisions. And so it was that the greatest architect of the time spent the last fifteen years of his life on the greatest building on earth at the time without payment. No business model has ever produced something as splendid before or since.

From a business viewpoint, these three projects were hopeless cases from the start. They were indefensible. They had no clear business plan, they had nothing to prove that they would be profitable. And yet, in a curious way, they are almost certainly three of the most important events of the last millennium. They were profound contributions to culture in a larger sense and, in Eric Raymond's language, they were masterpieces of gift culture. In fact, one was the greatest of all cathedrals to demonstrate that there is something much more inspiring than a bazaar.

From a narrow business viewpoint, there would never have been cathedrals or any other of those wasteful artsy monuments. From a narrow business view, Italy would never have created the inestimable cultural treasures that now make it a highlight for tourism and assure its place as one of the richest countries of the world. Paradoxically a commitment to gift culture inspires cultural creativity, which leads to new exchange culture. Exclusive attention to exchange culture constrains creativity and limits future markets. This makes it all the more vital that we remember that there is freedom. There are choices.

A Fifth Vision

Peter Senge outlined a fifth discipline. We suggest a fifth vision, which builds on some of the best international trends. The great corporations are busily building ever-more complex software to do transactions and make more money. This is excellent because it fuels the exchange economy whereby less and less of us have to do hard physical labour and whereby all of us have more time for a gift economy.

If we assume that the predictions about future employment are correct, what would happen if those 80 per cent all refused to be entertained to death and joined Eric Raymond's gift culture? Some will say that this is unrealistic. Traditionally there was a tendency to dismiss persons who were interested solely in money as being too materialistic, the assumption being that there were nobler courses in life. On the surface, this has changed. In a recent American film, *Jerry Maguire* (1996), the protagonist came out with a phrase that has become a kind of slogan: Show me the money!

Perhaps we need a new phrase: Show me something more than money. Ask not what the exchange economy is doing for you; ask what you are doing for the gift economy, for gift culture. The news on television and in the papers is always about disasters, about what is wrong, about suffering and death. But what about hope? What are we doing to increase the three cardinal virtues of faith, hope, and charity? Why are we all not using our spare time to work on what is possible?

We are witnessing what happens when everyman gets involved with the Internet: we can share all kinds of ordinary things. What would happen if we worked together to create extraordinary things? After getting what it takes to survive from our e-bazaars and virtual souks,[28] maybe we could do some useful things: like writing open source code,[29] like augmented books, knowledge, and culture, like working together on a vision for a more hopeful future. In Greek times the place of worship was a temple. When culture was revived after the fall of Rome, the temples had a different name and a very different shape. The cathedrals of tomorrow will again have different shapes and different names. The expressions change, the underlying spirit of sharing remains.

We need a new combination of the best of the American enterprising spirit, the best of European experience in terms of knowledge and society, and the best of the Japanese tradition with respect to doing things excellently. We need a new integration of approaches, which will do much more than create electronic versions of our static knowledge. We need dynamic knowledge, complete with its cultural and historical dimensions. We need augmented knowledge and culture.

5. Consequences

At one level, the consequences of the new media can be summed up in a word: sharing. Networked media (chapters 1–3) introduce many new ways of sharing for financial gain (chapters 4–11) and many horizons for sharing for other purposes (chapters 12–14). At another level, we have suggested that new media have five consequences. First, the technological consequence is that computers will become invisible: so small that we can theoretically carry images of all the contents of the world's memory institutions in our pockets. As usual, there are some prophets who say this will happen within ten years. And as usual there are sceptics who warn us that it could take a hundred years or prove to be impossible. There are always sceptics, but as we have seen, there is enough serious evidence to believe that it will happen. If computers are invisible, in the way that wireless connections are already invisible, then we can get on with using them. Fifty years ago, technology was an enormous hurdle. Today it is not.

Second, the material consequence of computers is virtuality: a possibility of creating virtual equivalents for everything in the physical world. In rare cases they will replace the physical original. In many cases they will not. Governments will remain, just as they did when it became possible to send them letters rather than going there in person. The difference will be that e-mail usually does not have to worry about angry dogs, snowstorms, and other hindrances faced by post persons because e-mail is post person in a new sense. Virtuality is also affecting both production and services. Here again, there is an extreme view that non-secret-agents with secret software will soon replace modern humans and thus be truly postmodern. A more likely and certainly a more humane alternative is that humans will continue to be in the workplace although they will do virtually no work, using their ever-more abundant spare time to develop economical gifts, gift economy, gifts without economy, gift culture, a culture of gifts.

Third, the organizational consequence of computers is systemicity. In this respect, as scholars such as Beniger (1986)[30] and Matellart (1994)[31] have shown, computers are part of larger trends that are intimately connected with the Industrial Revolution. Systemicity implies systems that control and manage physically and virtually. We suggested potential dangers of over applying this idea in the case of organizations, knowledge management, and particularly with respect to education.

Fourth, the intellectual consequence of computers is contextuality. This immediately brings to mind the concept of hypertext, but hypertext is merely the freedom to link, which anyone can do. Contextuality (in order to rhyme with other -ity's) is more elusive because the links have to be meaningful. We outlined how such links can lead to dynamic knowledge, augmented books, augmented knowledge, and augmented culture. This is the one frontier where there is no major funding. Indeed it seems to have all the characteristics that prove that it is a hopeless investment: like starting a Franciscan order, building the world's greatest cathedral, or using printing to change the course of the West. Sometimes a hopeless investment can still bring hope, if there be enough hope to go beyond that original hopeful stage.

Fifth, the philosophical consequence of computers is spirituality. Pundits will point out that computers are objects and objects have nothing to do philosophy, which is a club, nay a world, open only to -sophy's lovers, unless, of course, they take seriously Kurzweil's *Age of Spiritual Machines*. Kurzweil is a technologist and talks more about the machines and less about spiritual. We try the converse. Sharing is spiritual because it takes us beyond ourselves. It connects us without egos rather than merely extending our own. To rephrase Raymond, spiritual is better than egoless because you can develop one and still not lose the other. If McLuhan was interested in media as the extensions of man, we are interested in new media in their role as extensions of the spirit.

Linked with these five consequences are five paradoxes: 1) our chief means for visualizing the world is invisible; 2) the next step in the domination of matter is the immaterial domain of the virtual; 3) physical and social organizations are linked with systems. Completely predictable systems are closed else we cannot define them. Yet we need open systems (an oxymoron in itself) else organizations cannot change and grow. But if they are open we cannot know them. Hence the only reasonable control is to give up command societies and strive for Kropotkin's common understanding. In this kind of common lies the uncommon. 4) Traditionally scholars have tried to nail down static facts. With dynamic knowledge it is not what you nail down but rather how you link it to the rest. It is connections beyond Burke. Knowing is not what you know but placing it in a much larger world than you knew. 5) If sharing is spiritual and computers help, perhaps the road beyond wisdom towards sainthood begins simply by asking: Do you see the connection? And then living it.

6. Spirit

When I was young I was deeply puzzled by a paradox. Looking back to the Middle Ages in the West, I saw a world in which Christianity dominated society. This belief in a power beyond inspired thousands of monasteries, hundreds of cathedrals, and the beginnings of universities. It inspired persons to devote their life to learning, patiently copying manuscripts that kept alive the knowledge and wisdom of Antiquity, creating a corpus that later made possible the Renaissance and our modern world. Hallam reminds us that by the fifteenth century all this had changed: "Poggio Bracciolini, who stands, perhaps at the head of the restorers of learning in the earlier part of the fifteenth century, discovered in the monastery of St. Gall, among dirt and rubbish, in a dungeon scarcely fit for condemned criminals, as he describes it, an entire copy of Quintilian and Valerius Flaccus. That was in 1414".[32]

Hence in a period that we associate with Brunelleschi, Alberti, and the first flowering of the Italian Renaissance, the monasteries were not what they used to be and some of the frontiers of learning had shifted to the secular world. Even so, until the mid-nineteenth century, it was assumed that everyone who went to Oxford would take religious vows.

Today the monasteries are largely in ruins or deserted. Churches are poorly attended. Universities are not what they used to be. Few see them as temples of truth and wisdom. Many see them simply as passports to a higher paying job. So the paradox that faced me was simply this: what happened to all those good intentions, all that good will, all that inspiration that once built the most inspiring buildings then known to man? The easy answer would be that they all sold out and that, instead of building monasteries and cathedrals, they now build banks and corporation offices. In the case of the Petronas Towers in Kuala Lumpur, which are reminiscent of the spires on a Gothic cathedral, this explanation is almost convincing. But most office buildings are not inspiring. So what happened to the quest for inspiring structures, the creative side of the edifice complex?

Michel Laclotte (Louvre) believes that in a hundred years we shall look back on the great museums of the last decades as a contemporary attempt to express the wonder of the cathedrals. Looking at the great new monuments such as Moshe Safdie's National Gallery in Ottawa, Richard Meier's Getty Museum in Los Angeles, Frank Gehry's Guggenheim Museum Bilbao, or Andrew Pei's additions to the Louvre in Paris, it might seem that he was right. In the Diocesan Museum in Cologne, the director is consciously combining traditional religious art with modern art in a new museum that builds on the remains of a former church.

Is art therefore the new religion?[33] Or have we moved so many of the sources of our belief into buildings that they cry out for near sacred walls? If so there is still a profound difference between the cathedrals of then and the would-be cathedrals of now. The original cathedrals were built by the people and for the people. They were community projects in the same way that barn-raising is in America: except a little slower and definitely a bit more impressive. The would-be cathedrals are by the world's most brilliant architects, working in large teams, yes, and yet with very little contact with the public for whom the galleries are intended. If this was the kind of cathedrals Raymond meant, his title would beg less revision. For these so-called cathedrals are partly bazaars.

If Betty Crocker wanted a quick recipe for culture from our analysis in the previous chapter, she might well proceed as follows: 1) take belief or faith, mix with hope and love and shake till firm; 2) distill the fluid belief into written form and distribute freely; 3) use texts to make multimedia versions of various kinds; 4) cover with a firm layer sprinkled with inspiration; 5) bake till the spires are firm.

Even Betty Crocker knows, of course, that culture is something more than a piece of cake or even a whole pie. And yet the frivolous analogy is nutritious because it points to one of the deeper puzzles about culture. The great moments of culture are when all these ingredients fit together as if they were a single confection. The ingredients are always there. There is always some belief (and its accompanying dis- form). There are always texts, there is always art of various kinds, as there is always architecture. A generation ago, the hippies and the hackers[34] were struggling to identify a new belief. The Monkees wrote songs about: now I'm a believer. They preached love not war and they had hope in a better world. They had the three cardinal virtues, but in their own language "it wasn't quite together."

Raymond's accidental, revolutionary idea is to put this new belief into recorded words, but working from an enormous disadvantage. The myth that everything is about money means that he spends great effort trying to justify in economic terms something that is ultimately beyond and much more interesting than the economy.[35] He translates the new belief into language that economists can understand. Perhaps he needs to write some further versions for lawyers, medics, politicians, etc. Raymond, in this parable, is of course emblematic of the whole open-source movement as epitomized by Linus Thorwald and represented by many thousands of quiet believers all over the world. Raymond is clear that more than programming is involved. He talks about homesteading the noösphere and contends: "work that extends the noösphere is better than work that duplicates an existing piece of functional territory."[36] If he would dig deeper, perhaps he would go beyond the agrarian metaphors.

To come back to the question: what happened to all that wonderful energy that was there in the Latin West? The ingredients are all still there. There are efforts to link new beliefs with texts and expressions. And while that is still in the making, in the absence of a coherent new vision, our greatest architects are linking their creations to house the best expressions of older beliefs in memory institutions. A great contribution of these efforts is that they have made us aware that we have memory institutions. We have recognized anew that the memorable is all that is memorable. Material progress is fine but in the end spirit matters.

The great moments of civilization as we saw earlier come when cultures are open to other cultures, when they recognize that it is only by sharing that they can grow, grow richer in experience, and become something more than they were. The twentieth century tried a number of alternatives: imperialism, communism, isolationism, world war, student revolution, hippies, gurus, and new age. Having tried almost everything else, perhaps we are ready for another great moment of civilization.

7. An Open Future

In general terms, the potentials of the new media lie in understanding better the five paradoxical consequences we have outlined: invisibility, virtuality, systemicity, contextuality, and spirituality. More specifically, we see five keys to unleashing the full potentials of new media and the Internet. A first lies in changing the slogan of the Internet Society into reality: If the Internet is for everyone, then everyone should be using the Internet and not just everyone in a country, which is 4 per cent of the world's population.

Second, the emerging field of tacit and personal knowledge can give a recorded voice to many whose voices were all-too-fleetingly oral in the past. Indeed, persons challenged in one or more senses can potentially use others in the new visions of universal access. Providing access to all senses to everything now available in other media is a second key to unleashing the full potentials of new media.

Third, Douglas Engelbart, in his vision of the Internet, foresaw augmented knowledge with respect to collaboration in contemporary knowledge. Three kinds of knowledge are becoming intertwined: personal, collaborative, and enduring knowledge. Through mobile, wireless networks or Mobile Virtual Network Operators (MVNO),[37] this personal knowledge of MOOS, MUDS, Chat rooms, and e-mail can be linked with collaborative knowledge of collaboratories and integrated with the enduring or perennial knowledge of the great libraries, museums, and archives. A combination of these visions is needed:

using systematic access to enduring knowledge plus collaborative methods with contemporary knowledge to arrive at new knowledge that builds on both the past and the present knowledge. This implies linking distributed repositories, virtual reference rooms, and virtual agoras for collaborative research and creativity to create a DEER (Figure 14). This is a third key.

Fourth, a systematic use of hypertext introduces the possibility of augmented books, whereby traditional books are enhanced in their power to convey knowledge through new electronic links with virtual reference rooms. Augmented books lead to augmented minds. Traditionally, the amount of knowledge a book could convey was a simple combination of the book's content plus the reader's prior knowledge. The new technologies greatly enhance this by calling on the collective memory of mankind via virtual reference rooms. These vast repositories, once the instruments of a few thousand scholars with access to a few great historical libraries, can now be made available to everyone.

Making virtual reference rooms accessible leads to much more than a mere translation from printed knowledge to electronic knowledge. Because they entail new indexing and systematic hypertextual cross-referencing, augmented books in combination with virtual reference rooms offer many new potentials with respect to reference, study of the objects themselves, and of the interpretations of those objects. They imply a virtual reorganization of libraries and ultimately a reorganization of the whole of knowledge. Thus connected computers, in combination with a series of interconnected new technologies, and new access to knowledge in memory institutions, point in turn to new kinds of dynamic knowledge, which reflect cultural, linguistic, and historical diversity. Cultural diversity is as vital for the mind as bio-diversity is for the environment. Hence this may ultimately be our only serious hope against a MacWorld, where everything is the same everywhere, where there is no incentive for tourism and where there is nothing to learn from others because everyone is the same.[38]

Augmented books, dynamic knowledge, and augmented knowledge together can lead to augmented culture, which make us aware of synchronicity, help us to understand the riches of civilization on a global scale, and provide us with a constant well for new insight and discovery. It can lead to a synthesis of knowledge, which may serve as the twenty-first century's version of Aquinas's *Summas*, a next step in eternal learning. For such a synthesis of culture, we need to think in terms of decades or even hundred-year plans. We need long-term research on multilingual, multicultural metadata and interoperability.[39] We need to look at these problems in new ways. Implicit here is a shift from a top-down imposition of standards in the form of exclusive authority lists to inclusive authority lists that are bottom-up and include local, regional, and national variants. This is a fourth key for unleashing the full potentials of the Internet.

Fifth, we need to address the major challenges standing in the way of this vision (cf. chapter 13). The most obvious challenge would seem to be that this vision has no real funding. But then the U.S. Army spends $51 billion annually on new software and has not made anywhere near the same progress that open source has made. The European Union gives 1 billion euros in subsidies to the tobacco industry whose products kill

100,000 persons annually in Germany alone. We need to rethink our priorities. So we need to extend the concept of open source to culture and education.[40] They are keys to public identity, the keys to the future of society.

If the Internet is truly for everyone, everyone should be engaged in making it a valuable expression of cultures at all levels, in all languages. This is the fifth key to unleashing the full potentials of the Internet: to have everyone working together in recuperating their culture, copying, annotating, interpreting culture. Even if we are out of work in the exchange economy, there will always be much to do in the gift economy. What is lacking in pay is made up for by insight, inspiration, and ultimately also more hope. If you believe, you can start now. To begin, all you need to do is flick a switch. Culture needs all the help it can get.

From all this emerges a very different view of the Internet revolution. The mass media are constantly telling us about the technological, material, and organizational consequences of the Internet. So they focus on new machines, processes, transactions, on the trend from the physical to the virtual. They focus on the laws of the Internet, not on its spirit. They touch on aspects of invisibility, virtuality, and systemicity. In our view, all this is effectively but a context for the real revolution of the new media, which centres on intellectual and philosophical consequences, which entails a new approach to content, and its continual reorganization. Herein lie the potentials of augmented knowledge and culture. Herein lie the deeper consequences of the Internet: contextuality and spirituality.

In 1997, I was at a conference in Vienna. A young man, about twenty-three, had just read about the Gorbachev conference cited earlier. He began his question with a statement: I am one of the 80 per cent, who will be unemployed in the future. What can be done? He was lacking in hope and in near despair; yet he was healthy, full of life, clearly one of the privileged of the world, compared to the billions who live on a few dollars or less per day. He saw only that there was no place for him in the traditional command structure of the exchange economy. He did not see that his health and obvious native abilities made him perfectly able to help others. I wanted to tell him: Ask not what the exchange economy is doing for you; ask what are you doing for the gift economy, for gift culture.

The way the audience reacted to his question made it clear he was expressing what they felt also. There were a lot of persons at that conference almost desperately looking for hope. Since then, I have discovered almost on a daily basis how many persons are looking for hope as well as faith and love. The theological virtues cannot be bought or even bargained with. But if we give them we shall receive and the world will be a better place. There is truly much for which to be both thankful and hopeful. This book is hopefully a contribution to those virtues. If so, it will be a virtual book in a deeper sense.

EPILOGUE 1:

THE ADVENT OF NEW PLAYERS AND CHANGES SINCE 2000

We have focussed on three major approaches to the Internet and ICT revolution, namely the visions of the United States, Europe, and Japan. The past five years have witnessed four significant developments: 1) the arrival of China and India as players[1] on the world scene; 2) emerging infrastructures; 3) new levels of convergence; and 4) massive content.

1. China and India

In August 2001 China became the largest market in the world for mobile telephony.[2] In 2004, China had 300+ million cellphone users, while the United States had 171 million. It was predicted that by the end of 2005, China will have twice as many cellphones as the United States. Already in 2004 China was the largest mobile phone producer in the world with over 500 million units between 1999 and 2003, including US$20 billion in exports. China is very active in next generation Internet. On 7 December 2004, a trial on the Chinese Education and Research Network (CERNET2) between Beijing and Tianjin "achieved a speed of 40 gigabits per second, the highest in the world in real applications."[3] In 2005, China will spend ¥250 billion on software.[4]

In 1997, there were some 150,000 Internet users in China. By December 1999, there were 7 million users. By May 2005, there were 100 million Internet users, representing 11.8 per cent of all users, making Chinese the second largest language on-line (Table 55). There are predictions that within five years Chinese will be the most widely used language on the Internet.

In a country where Mao Tse Tung (Zedong) and Zhou Enlai stated in the 1970s that it was still too early to assess the significance of the French Revolution (1789), any attempt to assess the enormous changes that are underway is certainly premature. China is a very complex example. On the one hand, there are periodic attempts to impose levels of censorship whereby all connections to AOL or even

TABLE 55 The growth of the Internet in China according to NUA.com in 2002 [5]

MONTH	YEAR	MILLIONS	%
December	2007	300 (projected)	
December	2005	130 (projected)	
June	2004	87	
March	2004	79.5	10.7
September	2002	68.4	10.8
July	2002	45.8	3.58
May	2002	37.55	2.92
January	2002	33.7	2.65
July	2001	26.5	2.08
December	2000	22.5	1.78
July	2000	16.9	1.34
June	2000	12.3	0.97
January	2000	8.9	0.71
December	1999	7	0.56
June	1999	4	0.26
December	1998	1.5	0.1
July	1998	1.175	0.08
January	1998	.5	0.004
August	1997	.15	–

Google are temporarily blocked, and whereby use of Internet is prohibited to children under sixteen.

On the other hand, there are thousands of Internet cafés in Beijing alone. Students at Beijing's universities use Internet on a daily basis. The hotel at Tsinghua University has better Internet connections than the Marriott Hotel in Arlington overlooking the Pentagon. The Chinese are working closely with Western firms to develop the frontiers of ITC. Siemens has 30,000 employees in China. The Chinese Academy of Sciences is involved in high-level Geographical Information Systems (GIS). There are many experiments with IP version 6 and, given its lead position in mobile telephony, China is one of the leading users of this latest technology.

A generation ago, during the Cultural Revolution, it frequently seemed as if China had entered another version of the age-old battle of the ancients versus the moderns. It seemed as if there were a great wall between the old (I Ching, Taoism, Confucianism, Buddhism) and the new (Mao). Then it seemed as if Mao was out. By 2002, it was striking to see how the old monuments (Forbidden City, Altar of Heaven, and Summer Palace) and the old temples were being restored, while at the same time the modern city/country continued to rise.

There is a virtual reality reconstruction of the entire city of Beijing which is being used to prepare for the Olympics in 2008, and at the same time there are projects to depict Chinese athletic traditions that began millennia before the Olympic games. This new recognition of complementarity between old and new is visible also on the Internet. China is a leading proponent of Unicode and has used this to scan in the Chinese classics (800 million characters) and the Emperor's library (some 300 million characters) such that they can be read in eight major dialects. There is a project to scan in the full text of 500,000 Chinese books. Representatives of the Ministry of Culture are enthusiastic that their cultural treasures should become visible to the world and that these materials can be used for education.

The sheer quantity of these initiatives is impressive in itself. Equally impressive and perhaps even more significant is that these new cultural products consciously strive to have a look and feel that is Chinese. Even the English versions of CDs convey the subtlety of Chinese atmosphere, in poetry, song, opera, shadow theatre, and other arts. There is a quest to express philosophies, such as Taoism, using the new media. In China, interface is more than an entry point into their content: interface is a means of entering into their worldviews. For some this is linked with a commitment to open source, which is much more radical than in the West. In China, the commitment to free code, free access, and shared access is almost a political statement.

The Chinese linking of technology with worldviews through interfaces represents a significant new step. There are many cultural products in European languages, American, or Japanese, and yet we are far from having electronic products that are European, American, or Japanese in their look and feel. American cultural products implicitly strive to be universal as if there were nothing else. European and Japanese products often strive to do the same. The advent of China as a fourth player thus represents much more than the addition of hundreds of millions of new users. Potentially it marks a whole new approach, whereby technology gives access not only to information, knowledge, and/or wisdom, but also to different worldviews through different interfaces, an approach, as we have seen, towards which Europe is moving. China as one of the world's oldest civilizations is thus much more than "the new kid on the block." China offers us a new way of looking at the role of technology: not only as a vessel for "what" we know, but also "how" we express it. Being able to represent different ways of knowing is becoming a fundamental challenge. At the same time, large open questions remain. Will China create an Internet largely in Chinese only, or will it seek to share its great traditions and contents in the other great languages?

There is evidence that the latter may be happening. On 8 December 2004, the Lenovo company from China bought IBM's personal computing division for $1.25 billion. On 12 April 2005, China and India made a strategic alliance to reshape the world order.[6] There are rumours that China plans to take over computer hardware

345

and that India will focus on software. Buying IBM's computer division is one piece in a much bigger puzzle. In May 2005, Lenovo opened new offices in India.

Meanwhile, enormous changes are underway in India. In 1994, about 1 per cent of the population in India had access to telephones. In 2005, 7 per cent of the population have telephones[7] and there are now more mobile phones than fixed phone lines. There are over 1.5 million new mobile subscribers every month in India. In filmmaking, Bollywood is now larger than Hollywood. Similar changes are evident in the computer realm. India has become a key player in the outsourcing of computer code. Some estimates suggest that India now writes up to 80 per cent of all software code in the world. We noted earlier that India has been active in creating the first computer designed for illiterate persons: the Simputer (Simple Computer) for under $200. In the meantime, a new company, Novatium, is working on a $75–$100 computer and aims to reach a further 1 billion persons. China and India together have a population of 2.3 billion. Analysts at Harvard have predicted that India might rise above China.[8] What is important is that these two countries, which were effectively invisible in the new media field a decade ago, are now central players in new global developments.

2. Infrastructure

The infrastructure of the Internet continues to evolve and change. On 14 June 2005, in Luxembourg, Minister Viviane Reding formally opened the new version of GEANT network, which switched from using electrons to photons. As a result, capacities of over 300 gigabits are now possible for the high level research community.

In the opening chapter we noted that traditionally there has been a tension between two visions of how networked computers should operate: one, sometimes called end-to-end, favouring centralized control (with large mainframes connected to dumb terminals) and the other, typically called personal computing, favouring the autonomy of individual workstations. During the 1990s, it was usually assumed that the best way to solve the latter approach was through a client/server architecture, i.e., personal computer (acting as a client) linked with a mainframe (acting as a server).

The past five years have seen a shift in this paradigm. At the frontiers of science, the need for new computing power is increasing far more rapidly than our ability to build individual supercomputers. In terms of hardware, this has led to new clusters of smaller (personal) computers. Charles Catlett of the Global Grid Forum has described the developments in software and infrastructure in terms of two emerging models. One is Peer to Peer (P2P) or Client/Client. Hereby, a personal computer continues to serve as a client and links to another computer, which also acts as a client. The other alternative is Server/Server or Grid, whereby a (personal) computer acts as a server and links to another computer, which also acts as a server.[9]

On the surface, this means there are now three options: 1) client/server, 2) client/client and 3) server/server. Some believe that the new alternatives could replace the earlier client/server model. At one level, this means that the challenges of parallel computing and distributed computing,[10] which were the domain of mainframes and supercomputers, are now extending to the desktop and increasingly to hand-held devices. At the same time, the client/client (P2P) versus server/server (grid)[11] alternative also implies a return to the old centralized/personal debate, but now in a much larger context – at least in the eyes of the big corporations.[12]

Since 2000, there has been a steady shift away from computers to computing. Sun and Oracle speak of both Network Computing (2004) and now Utility Computing (2005). Sun has a Vice President of Utility Computing. Cisco Systems lists Grid/Utility Computing. IBM's new CEO, Samuel Palmisano, speaks of Pervasive Computing, On-Demand Computing, and Grid Computing, almost as if they were synonyms, and this is true in the sense that all these visions entail a return to the end-to-end model, where big corporations create the middle-ware and control the networks. Hence, it is no coincidence that IBM should sell its personal computer division to Lenovo in China, while continuing to dominate the world's supercomputers (51.8 per cent).[13] The old paradigm of a monolithic mainframe controlling a dumb terminal risks being replaced by a new paradigm, where a handful of companies have distributed mainframes controlling a new generation of almost dumb terminals, posing as thin clients, network computers and other attractive names. Pessimists would say that this trend may be linked with another shift: a trend towards the closing of open.

In 2000, when this book was written, there was a trend in the United States whereby free software was free in the sense of freedom, but not free in the sense of being available at no cost. We noted that there were similar problems with the word open: that many things which claimed to be open, were open only to subscribers who paid a fee. Since 2000, this trend has become more dramatic.

The Search for Extraterrestrial Intelligence (SETI) project is a striking case in point. It began as a brilliant example of a collaborative project in the spirit of the open source movement. In 2005, the good news is that SETI@home is now one of a half dozen such projects.[14] All these projects are now also part of BOINC (Berkeley Open Infrastructure for Network Computing), "software platform for distributed computing using volunteered computer resources." This sounds splendid, but the bad news is that one now needs to use the (closed) software of BOINC – which is linked with Comcast – and the notion of free sharing comes via the filter of corporate interests. The Open Access Initiative (OAI) and the Creative Commons are also in line with this trend. One of the more disturbing repercussions of September 11, 2001, the now-infamous 9/11, has been the creation of new mechanisms to preclude sharing as an everyday experience.[15]

As always there are other sides to the story. There are exciting developments in terms of a Hyperlearning[16] project, linked with a Hyperjournal project, that allows automatic citation indexes through dynamic contextualization.[17] This re-introduces a vision of more systematic treatment and access to scholarly material. Meanwhile,

Leonardo Chiariglione, formerly a researcher at Telecom Italia's CSELT lab (Turin), and one of the central players in the Moving Pictures Expert Group (MPEG), has written an impassioned article[18] on how the top down approach of the telecoms and large corporations is not working, how the ambitious TINA (Telecommunications Infrastructure Network Architecture) failed and how the past 35 years of efforts in imaging and multimedia standards (e.g. MPEG 4, 7, 21) have remained largely ineffective. To counter this he has embarked on a Digital Media Project.[19]

While the top-down, corporate giants speak of pervasive and network computing, others are speaking of continuous computing, which is grassroots and bottom up:

> ... the emergence of the Web as a platform for personal publishing and so-cial software. The examples are as diverse as informational sites such as blogs, craigslist, and Wikipedia.... and services such as Gmail, LinkedIn, Flickr, and Delicious. All of these are examples of what software developers and Internet pundits have begun to call "Web 2.0"...: more like a collection of programs that talk to one another into a collection of pages that still look like documents but are actually interfaces to full-fledged computing platforms. These Web-based services are proliferating so fast because they can be built using shared, stand-ardized programming tools and languages developed, for the most part, by the open-source-software community.[20]

Three examples will suffice to make our point. First, there is Wikipedia, with 1.8 million articles written by 51,000 contributors in 109 languages, which has grown into the largest collaborative literary work in history[21] within the past five years. A second example is weblogs (blogs). Some persons clearly use them simply for fun or distraction. In terms of traditional categories, some see blogs as conversations or chat rooms with a history function or e-mails on a specific topic within a commu-nity of authors; as new kinds of online diaries, minutes of meetings and lab notes – the beginnings of a virtual agora.

But much more is involved. Jonathan Schwartz, the CEO of SUN, has a personal blog for the company as does John Gage (formerly chief scientist, SUN). Grady Booch, one of the leading software developers of the world, now has a blog for his Handbook of Software in addition to a website. It is claimed that there are now over 4 million blogs and 12,000 new blogs every day.[22] To be sure no one has read them all, let alone digested their meaning and significance. Even so once they are indexed, blogs offer a formidable example of emerging new personal and col-laborative knowledge. The phenomenon of blogs is linked with RSS, which began as something complex, Rich Site Summary (1999) and evolved into Really Simple Syndication. RSS provides short descriptions of web content together with links to the full versions of the content. This is transforming the weblog (blog or blogger community) and leading to new expressions such as podcasting and MP3 blogs. At the University of Prince Edward Island, Mark Hemphill[23] is creating weblogs for all the students on campus, which is leading to new notions of community interaction. In Japan, an i-Pocket project has explored how seniors in Japan might use broadband and has looked at the creation of shared digital scrapbooks.[24]

Today, actual projects at the frontiers of research in this area sound like science fiction. These include mobile blogging; remote control cameras in synthetic environments, web-based cell phone controllers; an augmented inter-display workplace; tele-presence with multiple viewpoints both physically and conceptually, called "augmented viewpoints," such that persons, for instance, can "experience a remote location through the viewpoint of another person with different cultural interests, insights, and opinions."[25]

These projects are first applications of a Wearable Environmental Media platform (WEM), which will allow persons "to browse a spatially correspondent multimedia information database about a specific location as it changes over time, post location-specific information, or access interpretive annotations posted by other domain experts." The long-term goals include virtual field trips, ecological literacy, environmental perception, context visualization and the capacity to "enhance visualization of natural processes, cycles, and systems by connecting them to actual locations in the physical world." This in turn "will result in a worldwide layer of site-specific information that Bell Labs has called a 'Communication Skin.'"[26] As McLuhan said, the future is already here, but it's unevenly distributed.

A third example of social-software applications entails Voice-over-Internet-Protocol (VoIP) networks. VoIP is estimated to reach 40 billion minutes in 2005 with an annual growth of 30 per cent.[27] Vonage, which is subscription based, is said to have had 400 million users at the end of 2004.[28] Meanwhile, Skype, which began in 2002 and is free, is reported as having 144,000 new users per day (February 2005).[29] By July 2005, there were 133 million users worldwide.[30] Sensationalists who insist that this spells the death of dinosaur-like telecoms forget that Bell Labs (AT&T) and Lucent Labs have been working for over two decades on the technology that makes VoIP possible. The telecoms, energy companies and the computer companies clearly have enormous vested interests, whereby they will continue to pursue their top-down approach.

Their partial success is bringing unexpected developments: fixed telephone users (c. 1.3 billion); mobile telephone users (c. 1.4 billion) and internet users (c. 1 billion) are becoming interconnected. A grass roots and bottom-up movement from the owners of over 3.7 billion devices represents more than a wakeup call for any marketing guru. Ultimately such tensions between the top-down (corporations) and bottom-up (users) represent one of the central arguments for democracy in a deeper sense.

New media are about much more than the limited visions of executives and predicted sales from marketing departments: they are about innovations that are truly useful to all users. The computer salesmen have told us a story of the Internet as one of the win –win stories of all time, where the latest machines do everything

349

we want and then some. They do not tell us that computers have managed to make accessible less than 1 per cent of the radio, television, film, and other new media of the twentieth century; that there has been an ever-greater gulf between what we produce and that to which we have ready access.[31] The grassroots efforts of billions of users combined with new convergence and a trend towards mass contents means that this may be about to change.

3. Convergence

In 2000, we also pointed to a larger shift from Information and Communication Technologies (ICT) to Universal Communication Technologies (UCT). In the past five years this trend has acquired new names. In Canada, for instance, this awareness of convergence has set out from a premise of developing foresight in developing research strategies (2002),[32] which led to workshops[33] and a report on "Biosystemics Synthesis" (2003): "The convergence of nanotechnology, ecological science, biotechnology information technology and cognitive science and their prospective impacts on materials science the management of public systems for bio-health, eco and food system integrity and disease mitigation."[34]

In December 2001, the US National Science Foundation and the Department of Commerce held a workshop where it was concluded that "The convergence of nanoscience, biotechnology, information technology and cognitive science ('NBIC') offers immense opportunities for the improvement of human abilities, social outcomes, the nation's productivity and its quality of life; it also represents a major new frontier in research and development."[35] In 2002, Mihael C. Roco and William Sims Bainbridge produced an important report for the National Science Foundation (NSF):

> The phrase 'convergent technologies' refers to the synergistic combination of four major 'NBIC' (nano, bio, info, cogno) provinces of science and technology each of which is currently progressing at a rapid rate: (a) nanoscience and nanotechnology; (b) biotechnology and biomedicine including genetic engineering; (c) information technology including advanced computing and communications; (d) cognitive science including cognitive neuroscience.[36]

In the United States, the abbreviation NBIC (nano, bio, info, cogno) found almost immediate acceptance. By 2003, there was an NBIC conference. There is an NBIC 2004 and it seems that this will become an annual event. A lecture by Philip Bond, the Undersecretary of Commerce for Technology, United States Department of Commerce, revealed that part of the US incentive for NBIC was fear of being overtaken technologically and economically by Japan and Europe with respect to nanotechnology.[37]

Japan[38] and China[39] have both been tracking these developments closely. In Europe, largely as a reaction to the American NBIC report, the Foresight Unit of the European Union organized a High Level Expert Group (HLEG) of 35 experts, chaired by an historian,[40] and commissioned reports including: "Converging Technologies – Shaping the Future of European Societies," edited by a philosopher.[41] The report was aware of criticisms from other fronts. Christopher Coenen et al. summarized the five major points of the report:

> 1) The report ... adds socio, anthro, philo, geo, eco, urbo, orbo, macro and micro to the four "big Os" in NBIC convergence and proposes a distinctively European concept for convergence, which it calls CTEKS, standing for Converging Technologies for the European Knowledge Society ... to advance the so-called Lisbon agenda.

> 2) The group developed its own definition of converging technologies: "Converging technologies are enabling technologies and knowledge systems that enable each other in the pursuit of a common goal" (p. 14) ... the HLEG argues for a special role for the social sciences and humanities, including cognitive science in this category rather than in a group with the NBI part of convergence. It also refrains from hastily taking sides in the emergent new round of debate over free will versus (neuro)determinism.

> 3) HLEG stresses the importance of specific societal needs that must be identified in order to take advantage of and preserve Europe's cultural diversity and to create economic opportunity. Social sciences and humanities should provide orientation where CT could disrupt traditional ways of life, serve as intermediaries between political actors, CT researchers and society, and help to assess risks....

> 4) The HLEG favors an approach to CT that prioritizes "engineering for the mind" as opposed to "engineering of the mind"....

> 5) The report includes a set of recommendations for European policy concerning CTEKS, including quite ambitious endeavours, such as an initiative to widen circles of convergence (WiCC), starting with the creation of a coordinating office....

Hence, once again, we have a contrast between a) an American quest for an information superhighway, that emphasizes doing/performance, and b) an European aim to achieve a more humane life and thus considers Converging Technologies for the European Knowledge Society (CTEKs). These are the same problems that we have outlined throughout this book. Two things have changed. First, the dimensions of the revolution are becoming clear. In the American vision, as noted earlier, the new challenges have been compared to a new Manhattan Project.[42] A European might ask whether we might not rather have a new Gutenberg project. In any case, convergence in telecommunications and new media are now part of a much larger phenomenon. The second thing that has changed is that this awareness has now entered political levels at the highest level. NBIC is part of the luncheon addresses of the US Undersecretary of State for Commerce.

4. Massive Content

An era of massive new content is also beginning. At the frontiers of science, for the first time in history it is becoming possible to link measurement of phenomena with databanks for their interpretation in real time. The Large Hadron Collider at CERN and the quest for an e-VLBI (Electronic Very Long Baseline Interferometry) in radio astronomy are two examples. In the cultural domain, the great libraries and museums are also systematically making their collections available on-line. For instance, the site of the Réunion des Musées de France has an enormous number of paintings and drawings, including sketches by Leonardo not discussed by standard literature even a decade ago. A new world of sharing is opening.

There have also been unexpected developments. Throughout the book we have drawn attention to some of the large scale visions and projects to create digital libraries, which include scanning in the full texts of books and other documents. On 14 December 2004 a single announcement set in motion a series of events that has completely transformed the topic of online content. Google stated the full scale of their mission: "to organize the world's information." Google announced that they were working with the "University of Michigan, Harvard University, Stanford University, The New York Public Library, and Oxford University to scan all or portions of their collections and make those texts searchable on Google."[43] These plans, which entail over sixteen million texts in full text will require at least ten years to be achieved.[44] A spectre of paid access to the Internet now looms.[45]

The Google announcement had great repercussions. Jean-Noël Jeanneney, Director of the Bibliothèque Nationale de France (BNF), saw a danger in what he called the "omnigooglisation"[46] of knowledge, which tended to bias Anglo-Saxon sources and approaches. In early March 2005, he urged "European governments to join forces and set up a digitization plan that would be a European response to Google Print."[47] By 17 March 2005 President Chirac had given the go-ahead for a French project.[48] By 22 April 2005, nineteen National Libraries had signed an agreement that they were willing in principle to work together.[49] On 28 April 2005, six European countries sent an open letter to the European Commission and the Luxembourg Presidency of the Council asking for a European digital library. Inspired by the French president Jacques Chirac, the presidents or prime ministers of Poland, Germany, Italy, Spain and Hungary have signed the letter. On 3 May 2005, the "European Commission responded with an announcement that it will boost its policy of preserving and exploiting Europe's written and audiovisual heritage and stated that would issue a communication by July 2005 outlining the stakes involved and identifying the obstacles to using written and audiovisual archives in the European Union. The communication would be accompanied by a proposal for a Recommendation aimed at enlisting all the public players concerned and facilitating public-private partnerships in the task of digitising the European heritage."[50]

As preliminary steps, the efforts of the G7 pilot project, Bibliotheca Universalis, the Gateway to European National Libraries (GABRIEL), and the EC project The European Library (TEL)[51] are being co-ordinated within the Bibliothèque Nationale de France (BNF). EU Commissioner's Viviane Reding's i2010 vision is supporting these trends.[52] The vision of a European Digital Library has now become one of three flagship projects for the next five years.[53] The plans thus far foresee a massive project that entails scanning four billion pages of text. The great open question remains whether these materials collected with the aid of public monies will be made available freely for the use of all citizens. If they are made readily accessible then the way will be open for a new universal access to our collective memory on a scale that dwarfs all previous efforts.

Meanwhile, Eric Schmidt, the CEO of Google, noted casually in an interview (1 July 2005), that by a current estimate "it will take 300 years to organize all the world's information."[54] It is noteworthy that Schmidt speaks only of information and not of knowledge. Perhaps Google (US) will tackle information. Perhaps Europe and Asia will tackle (formal) knowledge; perhaps Japan will focus on tacit knowledge and perhaps Australia, Canada, South America, and Africa will tackle indigenous, traditional knowledge. In any case, the phenomenon of new media and the Internet, which many still see as the latest gadget of the day or trend of the month, has entered into a time-scale of centuries. In this light, it is fitting and humbling to recall that in 1934, eleven years before Vannevar Bush wrote his famous article, Paul Otlet, one of the founders of modern bibliography, had a vision of electronic access to all human knowledge:

> ... a technology will be created acting at a distance and combining radio, X-rays, cinema and microscopic photography. Everything in the universe, and everything of man, would be registered at a distance as it was produced. In this way a moving image of the world will be established, a true mirror of his memory. From a distance, everyone will be able to read text, enlarged and limited to the desired subject, projected on an individual screen. In this way, everyone from his armchair will be able to contemplate creation, as a whole or in certain of its parts."[55]

The competing visions of the Internet that we have outlined remind us that there is no techno-determinism. The new technologies are not value-free, but these values depend on our inputs and our goals. If we use the new media unwisely, we risk the dark scenarios that authors of science fiction have painted. Or we can use the new media to gain ever-new insights, to augment ourselves, knowledge, culture, and the world in which we live.

EPILOGUE 2:

MCLUHAN IN THE ELECTRONIC AGE

Marshall McLuhan's intellectual journey began in Canada during the 1930s in the field of English literature. His further studies at Cambridge began with a focus on the sixteenth and seventeenth centuries. The topic of his doctoral dissertation was Thomas Nashe. This plunged him into a study of the trivium: grammar, dialectic, and rhetoric, which, along with the quadrivium (of geometry, arithmetic, astronomy and music), comprised the seven liberal arts (and sciences).

One of his important personal discoveries was that grammar, dialectic, and rhetoric had a complex history of their own. At one level, grammar dealt with the structure of language, dialectic with the logic of language, and rhetoric with the effects of language. At another level, grammar was much more than simple structure. It represented an integrating strand in the Western tradition, aiming at synthesis, linking across disciplines, focussing on patterns, including interpretation, phenomenology, etymology, and exegesis. By contrast, dialectic was also more than logic. It represented the quest to test evidence, to find proofs of an argument, the analytical strand in the West, whereby one specialized in specific disciplines and hence dissected and fragmented knowledge. His dissertation was an attempt to trace the complex history of the trivium from Antiquity through the seventeenth century and to show how this helped one to explain developments in English literature.

Three intellectual strands help us to understand McLuhan's development as a thinker. First, at Cambridge, McLuhan was influenced by key figures in the new criticism movement, who emphasized the importance of close reading and structuralism, namely, I. A. Richards, William Empson, and F. R. Leavis. McLuhan was particularly influenced by I. A. Richards, who had studied psychoanalysis, and who, through the ideas of F. C. Bartlett, came to regard structure as percepts.[1] This was a source for McLuhan's distinctions between words and structures, concepts and percepts, and figure and ground.

Second, when McLuhan returned to North America, he became increasingly interested in different aspects of structuralism: Ferdinand de Saussure in linguistics, Siegfried

TABLE 56 Examples of McLuhan's contrast between hot and cool media.

	HOT	COOL
Characteristics	Linear-Sequential	Simultaneous-Spatial
	One way	Two-way communication
	Detachment	Engagement
	Visual	Auditory, Tactile
	Logic	Structure
	Analytical	Integrating
	Specialist	Non-Specialist
	Left Brain	Right Brain
Examples	Print	Speech
	Lecture	Seminar
	Radio	Telephone
	Photographs	Cartoons
	Movies	Television
	Painting	Sculpture

Giedion in art and architecture, Claude Lévi-Strauss in anthropology, Sigmund Freud in psychology, and Max Planck in physics.[2] Structuralism and structure heightened his awareness of ground, background, context, and environment.

Third, in Toronto, there was an interest in the effects of language and literacy through individuals who have subsequently been called members of the Toronto School of Communications.[3] Here, a key figure was the economist, Harold Innis, who wrote on the history of the railway and explored the idea of technology as extensions of man and studied "the roles of communications media in the rise and fall of civilizations." In *Empire and Communications* (1950), Innis acknowledged a number of sources for this work, namely, Kroeber, Mead, Marx, Mosca, Pareto, Sorokin, Spengler, Toynbee, and Veblen. In the classics department, Eric Havelock, who had also begun his studies in Cambridge, wrote *Preface to Plato* (1963), which studied the consequences of literacy on Greek culture.[4] Through this informal circle, Cambridge scholars such as Jack Goody became linked with the Toronto discussions.

When he first returned to North America in 1939, McLuhan was struck by the ways in which American males were becoming increasingly dominated by women, as personified by the comic strip figures of Dagwood and Blondie. To understand these trends, McLuhan planned to write a "guide to chaos," which became *The Mechanical Bride: The Folklore of Industrial Man* (1951) and led to further attempts at creating a Baedecker for modern man. These studies took him well beyond the bounds of traditional English literature into the realms of advertising, comics, radio, television, and film.

McLuhan himself was anything but a simple techno-optimist. He relied on his son to operate his record player. Like Marx, Kapp and Freud, he was fascinated by the potentials of technology as extensions of man. By the time he wrote *The Gutenberg Galaxy* (1962), he was aware how such advances were a double-edged sword.

According to McLuhan, Gutenberg's introduction of the printing press brought important advantages but also imposed a static, linear-sequential framework on the organization of knowledge.

In McLuhan's analysis, the effects of printing were effectively the opposite to those of television. Printing increased a sense of individualism and personal privacy and led to the nation state. Television, by contrast, entailed a loss of individualism, an undermining of privacy and ultimately of the nation state. He predicted that it would lead to a new emphasis on groups, communes, anonymous corporate identities, and a new kind of tribalism, which he sought to convey by his phrase "global village." According to this analysis, the parallel rise of television and of hippie culture was not a coincidence.

Whereas print culture led to a linear-sequential organization of knowledge, television led to a simultaneous-spatial organization of knowledge. McLuhan saw in this contrast an underlying pattern. He discerned a distinction between "hot media" where information was, as it were, pre-packaged, with a high degree of organized material, and "cold media," which required a greater amount of effort on the part of the user, where the beholder's share was greater. Thus a lecture belongs to hot media because the lecturer theoretically does all the active work. By contrast, a seminar belongs to cool media, because here the seminar leader and student alike are engaged in the process. Hot media are one-way communication and lead to detachment. Cool media are two-way communication and lead to engagement. All this led to a series of stimulating oppositions (Table 56), which McLuhan set out to test through a series of informal tests.[5] Cool hippies understood the distinctions. Many hot-shots did not. Traditional scholars were sceptical because they could not see how these distinctions reflected the complexities of the historical evidence.

Evidence in favour of McLuhan's claims came from three unlikely quarters.[6] First, Herbert E. Krugman, the manager of corporate public opinion research at General Electric, found (1965)[7] that viewers of television had a lower number of spontaneous thoughts than others. This seemed to confirm that television led to a loss of individualism, just as McLuhan predicted and pointed to a direct connection between media and different ways of thinking. Second, Steven R. Harnad suggested that McLuhan's distinction between the linear, sequential mode of hot media and the simultaneous-spatial mode of cool media might have a neuro-physiological basis in the distinctions between the left and right hemispheres of the brain.[8] This helps us to understand why right-brain/left-brain distinctions fascinated McLuhan in the later years of his life, long before this had become all the fashion among new age enthusiasts.

A third source of evidence came only in the mid-1980s after McLuhan's death. As noted earlier, Michael Ester, then director of the Getty Art History Information Program (AHIP), compared the perception of quality in printed images with those on computer screens. He found that we see one third more when light is reflected (in a hot medium) than when light is projected directly (in a cool medium), which explains why corrections are more difficult on a screen than when using a printout.

This unexpected parallel between McLuhan's observations concerning television screens and Ester's study of computer screens implied that the loss of individualism, which McLuhan associated with television, might be accelerated in the age of computers where persons often spend many hours in front of a monitor. If so, perhaps it is no coincidence that there are ever-more frequent discussions concerning the death of privacy, the end of the individual and at the same time an increasing emphasis on fitting into a corporate or institutional "culture," which discourages, excludes, or even precludes individualism. To old-fashioned individualists accustomed to print culture, the narcissistic fascination with the web which destroys privacy may seem puzzling. To those who have grown up with new media, it may well seem that post-modern is post-privacy.

McLuhan's specific analysis of print culture in The Gutenberg Galaxy (1962) led to a more wide-ranging analysis in Understanding Media: The Extensions of Man (1964). Here he contrasted print and electronic media in terms of a series of oppositions. Lewis Lapham, in his introduction to a new edition of Understanding Media (1994) added a parallel set of oppositions between citizen and nomad.[9]

In his analyses of media, McLuhan noted how new media adopt the methods of earlier media. Hence early printed books adopted the layout of manuscripts. By implication new media are implicitly burdened by the limitations of their predecessors. This is one of the dilemmas of the present book and was in large part also McLuhan's dilemma. He spent much of his life attempting to convey in print form his analyses of the limitations of print.[10]

He claimed that media work in pairs such that one contains the other. This implied that each new medium contains the previous medium as its content. Hence, the telegraph contains printing, which contains writing, which contains speech, which contains thought. More important than the (visible) content of the old medium is the (invisible) environment of the new medium, whence his insistence on the 'medium is the message.' McLuhan planned to devote a book specifically to this theme. In the course of the proofs a typo had entered the title. He chose not to correct it. Hence the appearance of The Medium is the Massage (1967). That same year, he underwent an enormous operation for a brain tumour. In a sense the man whose first major book launched him onto the world stage in 1962 had a full-fledged career of only five years. Officially he recovered. The next year saw the publication of War and Peace in the Global Village (1968). His son and friends helped in the publication of further ideas such as: City as Classroom (1977). In 1979, there was a massive stroke. On New Year's Eve 1980, he passed away.

In his early work, McLuhan focussed mainly on the positive potentials of media as extensions of the senses. McLuhan gradually became convinced that each new medium brought 1) extension, 2) reversal, 3) retrieval, and 4) obsolescence. This led to his idea of tetrads.[11] Eric McLuhan, who had worked with his father in his youth, faithfully continued and published these ideas as the four Laws of Media (1988) after his father died. This book was also the most thorough explanation of different kinds of space. At first sight, the distinctions presented as oppositions (Table 57) seem simple. McLuhan claims that pre-literate man lived in an acoustic space, which was replaced by a visual space when the alphabet and literacy were introduced, that printing heightened this trend towards visual space, and that the advent of electric media brought a return to acoustic space.

On closer inspection McLuhan's claims are much more complex. Visual space is not just something that we see with our eyes. Rather: "Visual space is the only form of space that is purely mental: it has no basis in experience because it is formed of abstract figures minus any ground and because it is entirely the side effect of a technology [the alphabet]"[12] He claims that "each of man's artefacts is in fact a kind of word, a metaphor that translates experience from one form into another."[13] This linking of everything with words is not surprising for a professor of English literature, but it has profound implications for how he interprets Greek and subsequent history. His discussions are primarily about the implications of this mental visual space on the verbal space of words. Hence, he ultimately overlooks fundamental distinctions between words and pictures established by Ivins,[14] Gombrich,[15] Hanfmann,[16] and others.

In the first half of the twentieth century, historians of philosophy, science, optics, and even historians of art such as Panofsky had pointed to a disjunction between Euclid's curvilinear theories of vision and his linear axioms of geometry. In the German neo-Kantian tradition, Cassirer and Panofsky assumed that 1) worldviews, 2) geometrical systems, 3) theories of vision, and 4) methods of representation were linked. Panofsky went further to claim that Euclid's theory of vision, based on visual angles rather than planes, explained why the Greeks developed a series of vanishing points in what he called "fishbone perspective" (Fischgrätenperspektive). He also claimed that linear perspective only became possible during the Renaissance when a theory of infinity had evolved.[17]

In McLuhan's polar approach in terms of opposites, distinctions between Euclidean geometry and Euclidean visual theory disappear. In this approach, distinctions between 1) philosophical worldviews, 2) abstract, mental, "visual space" of geometrical systems, 3) experiential visual space, and 4) represented visual space as in inverted or linear perspective are also conflated. So too are possible distinctions between Greek and Renaissance methods of representation. Indeed we are asked to believe that there are effectively only three historical phases: pre-literate until sometime between the seventh and the fifth century B.C., literate until the late nineteenth century, and then electric in the twentieth century, which supposedly returned to the pre-literate state.[18]

McLuhan emphasizes the rise of cubism supposedly brought by the advent of electric media. As Cavell (2002)[19] has rightly pointed out, this can be related to trends towards anti-ocularism, as discussed by Martin Jay.[20] But the rise of electric media equally brought an enormous amount of new attention to linear perspective. If the twentieth century brought numerous books on spherical, cylindrical, and other alternative types of perspective, it also brought many more publications on

TABLE 57 McLuhan's opposition of pre-literate and literate cultures.

PRE-LITERATE/ELECTRIC	LITERATE
Acoustic Space	Visual Space
Multisensory	(Mental) Visual
Known	Seen
Percept	Concept
Outer	Inner
Concrete	Abstract
Figure/Ground	Figure
Spherical	Linear
Multiple Viewpoints	Single Viewpoint, Vanishing Point
Discontinuous	Continuous
Non-Homogeneous	Homogeneous
Resonant	Irreducible (Uniform) Bits
Dynamic	Static
Logos	Dialectic (Logic), Grammar, Rhetoric
Synthetic	Analytic
Public	Private
Audience, Group	Individual
Aphoristic Poetry	Logic, Containment
Modifying	Unmodified/Unmodifying Container
Formal Cause	Efficient Cause

linear perspective than the whole of the fifteenth, sixteenth, seventeenth, and eighteenth centuries combined, not least because of its central importance for modern architecture, computer graphics, film, television, video, and computer games.[21]

As we have noted earlier, the twentieth century also brought the combination of a number of individual viewpoints (122, in the case of sequels to *The Matrix*) to arrive at combined images which are convincingly visual but no longer have any direct basis in our visual experience in the physical world. As a result, age-old equations made between optical veridity and veracity, between observation as a cornerstone for experiment and an inductive path to scientific truth, are potentially undermined. McLuhan's polar approach leads him into either/or scenarios in his tetrads, which land him in precisely the kind of containment and limitation about which he complains in the analytical tradition of the logicians. His method predicts that extension necessarily brings reversal, retrieval, and obsolescence. His method does not account for how the twentieth century could both continue linear perspective and develop a number of alternatives.

Meanwhile, in *Laws of Media* (1988),[22] Marshall and Eric McLuhan made another surprising claim that the Shannon-Weaver model of communication (which underlies computers) focused on efficient cause, perpetuated the left-brain linear bias introduced by printing, and was the "basis of all contemporary Western theories of media and communication."[23] This effectively linked the technologies of the electric age back to the linear tradition of print. The following year saw the appearance of another posthumous book by Marshall McLuhan and Bruce R. Powers, *The Global Village. Transformations in World Life and Media in the 21st Century* (1989)[24], which repeated these claims about Shannon-Weaver's model of communication.

Richard Lanhan, in his foreword to a second edition of *Understanding Media* (1994)[25] noted that McLuhan's insights about electric media (radio, television) were almost more prophetic when applied to the new electronic media (computers and the Internet). The new edition of *War and Peace in the Global Village* (1997) echoed this: "It has taken us three decades to see how much the book guides our understanding of how electronic media – such as the Internet – alter us."[26]

The good news was that all this seemed to give McLuhan's insights of the 1950s and 1960s an amazing new relevance for the rise of networked computers in the 1990s. From an analytical point of view, however, this was extremely problematic. On the one hand, the McLuhans (father and son) argued that the electric age implied a return to the acoustic space of pre-literate man. To claim that the Shannon-Weaver mode perpetuated the linear, analytic mode, which typified literate man and especially print culture, implied that the Shannon-Weaver mode theoretically cancelled out the return to acoustic space, which was supposedly the key advance of the electric age.

In terms of computers and our analysis in chapter one, the Shannon-Weaver mode of communication is central to computers with respect to calculation and writing but tells us little about their role in visualization, multi-media, multi-sensory, inter-media, interaction, augmentation, delegating information/knowledge (via agents), or with respect to synthetic reason. To insist that computers and new media are extending one technology and sense, while they reverse, retrieve, and render obsolete earlier ones, risks overlooking deeper dimensions of the revolution.

Computers linked by Internet are not opposed to or replacing telephones, television, film, or video in any simplistic sense. They are creating a new framework whereby all of these technologies can be seamlessly translated from one into the other. For this reason even the umbrella term "Information and Communication Technologies" (ICT) needs to be replaced by a more encompassing term such as "Universal Convergence Technologies" (UCT).[27] Standing back, if one were merely analytical, one could argue that many of the details of McLuhan's claims are open to debate.[28]

Even so he was very right in making us much more aware of the role of media in defining and communicating knowledge. We need to remember that McLuhan was trying to draw attention to synthetic approaches rather than analytical details: to the poetic spirit rather than the letter of the law. As we have noted (chapter 1.6.5), the idea of media and language as extensions of man was not new. Even so, it was McLuhan who argued that this could be used to look more systematically on how they affect knowledge and culture. Terence Gordon, in his official biography of McLuhan, has rightly drawn attention to ten important insights about media. (Table 58).

The complex effects of McLuhan's work are beyond the scope of our study.[30] It is important to recognize, however, that there has been a fundamental shift in scholarship over the past century. In the first half of the twentieth century, the neo-Kantians, the positivists, and the neo-positivists assumed that there were necessary

TABLE 58 Ten insights of McLuhan according to Terence Gordon.[29]

1	Extend our bodies and our minds
2	Work in pairs such that one contains the other
3	Working in pairs has only two exceptions, namely, thought & light
4	Are agents of change in how we interact with the world
5	Do not replace each other: they complement each other
6	Are both hot and cold
7	Have both extending and numbing effects
8	Acceleration leads to reversals whereby explosion becomes implosion
9	Change sense ratios in which psychological factors play a role
10	Change our notions of ourselves

connections between thought (worldviews, theories of space), sight (theories of vision), expression (theories of representation, perspective, etc.), and action (technology, politics). It seemed as if there were teleological, technological determinism. In retrospect, we know that the situation is more complex.

McLuhan used humour, wit, irony, puns, and poetic and other licence to show the limitations of such closed systems. Academia took a more sombre route. In the second half of the twentieth century, philosophers, social scientists, representatives of various contructivist schools, and members of the de-, re- and post- communities (de-constructivism, re-constructivism, post-structuralism, post-modernism, post-normalism, etc.) made their careers in pointing to the dangers of such equations. This was an important corrective. But instead of examining afresh the complexities of such relations, all too often the new schools descended merely into debates about the value of various positions, which amounted to the equivalent of throwing out the baby with the bathwater.

As we have noted, a key insight at the outset of the twenty-first century is that connections between thought, sight, expression, and action cannot be reduced to a single law or formula. These connections have cultural and historical dimensions: they typically have different answers at the local, regional, national, international, and global levels. The challenge for research has shifted from trying to claim that one is dominant or supreme to exploring new methods for seriously comparing their differences and fostering their diversity.

If we read McLuhan narrowly as someone who claimed that the advent of alphabet, printing, television, or another medium had a single, necessary effect, then we are reading McLuhan as a child of his time and need to recognize that his claims are too narrow and contain too much bravura. On the other hand, if we read McLuhan as an individual fascinated with the challenge of how one keeps alive the poetic and the creative spirit, as someone concerned with integrating synthesis rather than fragmented analysis, if one recalls that he saw his work as probes rather than edicts, then his work offers a continuing stimulus for further work. The importance of McLuhan lies not in his answers but rather in the direction of his questions.

Were McLuhan still alive, he would probably acknowledge that his distinctions between hot and cool need further development in light of the new electronic media.

McLuhan used "cool" to describe how television was more participatory than radio or print – more engaging and less detached. Yet television remains a broadcast medium. It is formal, staged, and often artificial in terms of the way its programs are prepared. If television is cool, then the new media with digital cameras, digital video cameras, and web cameras are super-cool. Where traditional cool television highlighted explicit actions, super-cool webcams capture tacit scenes. Where television aimed at the byte-sized message, webcams aim at the bit-sized medium. Television rhetorically set out to capture knowledge of enduring value, worthy of memory institutions, and frequently descended into the level of soap (operas). Webcams are capturing new dimensions of personal and collaborative knowledge and are challenging us to create new spaces within enduring knowledge (Table 59).

One might expect that the rigid, formality of traditional television and the spontaneous, informality of the digital videos and webcams were necessarily headed for a collision course, for a new chapter in the quarrel between the ancients and the moderns. Paradoxically something very different is happening. Television is adopting the methods of its potential enemy, as if they were its own. The situation comedy (sit com) of the 1950s gave way in the 1990s to programs such as *Friends*. *Stranded* was one of the early interactive games (1989–). More recently, programs such as *Stranded*, *Big Brother*, and *Temptation Island* are recording everyday life as if they were using webcams. "Reality" television is becoming an independent genre. Films such as *Forrest Gump* (1994) and *The Truman Story* (1998) explore this trend. The gradual erosion of clear distinctions between games, films, and television is evident on many fronts from *Pokemon* through *Tomb Raider* and *Final Fantasy*.[31]

It is too early to know where these new developments will end or to understand in a deeper sense what they mean and imply. Clearly there is much more than a simple process of a new medium using the previous medium as its content. The new webcams are not adopting the methods of old television. Old television is adopting the "methods" of new webcams. There are new inter-plays between film, television, games, and everyday life, and yet no one is speaking of abandoning these categories. These interplays may be early demonstrations of networked computers as translation devices between different senses and different media (Table 3), brought about by the convergence of telephony, television, and Internet after 2010 (Figure 1), and the shift from ICT to UCT. If so, attempts to extend McLuhan's oppositions between hot and cold into distinctions such as cool and super-cool do not take us significantly further. And while it may be fashionable to see television and computers as being in opposition, the new convergence requires new approaches and whole new sets of terms.[32] This is especially true as telephone companies begin to offer digital television at the same time as they are linking televisions and computers.

McLuhan devoted his life to studying print, radio, and television in the context of the history of literacy. His admirers and critics alike continued this approach. They treated electronic media as if they were extensions of what came before, as if computers simply heightened problems posed by books. It became fashionable to speak of a Digital Divide as another dimension of the haves and have nots in much the same way as one had spoken of the divide between the literate and the illiterate.

TABLE 59 Distinctions between Cool and Super-Cool.

	COOL	SUPER-COOL
Characteristics	Formal	Informal
	Staged	Spontaneous
	Artificial	Everyday Life
	Explicit	Tacit
	Enduring	Personal, Collaborative Knowledge
	Broadcast	Narrowcast
	Unicast	Multicast
Examples	Television	Video Camera, Webcam
	Camera	Digital Camera
	Telephone	Video-Phone

Appropriately enough, a conference on the Global Village (Bangalore, October 1998) introduced a new avenue for discussion. Here the idea of a Simple, Inexpensive, Multi-lingual comPUTER (SIMPUTER) was introduced: "It has a special role in the third world because it ensures that illiteracy is no longer a barrier to handling a computer. The key to bridging the digital divide is to have shared devices that permit truly simple and natural user interfaces based on sight, touch and audio."[33] In the spring of 2004, the Simputer was a reality.

We have claimed that computers are translation devices between different senses and different media (Table 3) and that this has two profound consequences. First, it means that an illiterate persons can record their experiences, their indigenous knowledge, and can share this with persons anywhere on Earth. Second, it means that the collective memory of mankind in memory institutions, which was available only to a literate minority, is potentially available to literate and illiterate alike.[34] McLuhan's worries that the new media were undermining concepts of the individual and the nation state led him to his notion of the "global village" and, not surprisingly, he has been seen as an opponent of globalization and as a father of the anti-global movement.[35] If the above consequences are true, then new media offer unexpected answers to the fears of globalization.

In this context, the term "digital divide" is an unfortunate buzzword and a misnomer. New electronic media potentially introduce a digital bridge whereby the divide between literacy and illiteracy can be spanned. By combining traditional authority files with variant names, the new media foster development of multilingual, multicultural expressions at the local, regional, and national levels, where sharing can truly be global at the same time. This is a momentous new horizon, which helps us to understand why McLuhan's approach will continue to be important in the electronic age, especially in a world where augmented knowledge and culture are possible.

We saw how nineteenth and early twentieth century thinkers (Marx, Kapp, Freud, Buckminster Fuller) explored the idea of mechanical objects as extensions of man. Other early twentieth century thinkers (H.G. Wells, Teilhard de Chardin) explored how ideas and beliefs were extensions of man and could lead to a global brain and nöosphere. McLuhan's genius was the intuitive recognition that media were also extensions of man

TABLE 59.1 Relations between different media, senses, and modes of recording, representation and communication.

MEDIUM	PHYSI-CAL	VISION	TOUCH	SMELL	TASTE	RECORD SCAN	REPRE-SENT (PRINT)	COMMU-NICATE NEAR	COMMU-NICATE DISTANCE
Oral	x	-	-	-	-	-	-	x	-
Written		x	-	-	-	-	~	-	Indirect
Mechanical	x	-	-	-	-	x	~	x	Fixed Tele-
Electric	x	x	-	-	-	-	x	x	Fixed Tele-+
Electro-Magnetic	x	x	-	-	-	x	x	x	Fixed Tele-++
Electronic	x	x	-	-	-	x	x	x	Fixed Mini, Micro
Digital	x	x	x	x	x	x	x	x	Mobile Cyber, Multi
Nano	x	x	x	-	-	x	x	x	Mobile Hyper
Bio, Neuro	x	x	x	x	x	x	x	x	Mobile Aug.
Converged	x	x	x	x	x	x	x	x	Mobile Aug. +

and that these were a key to understanding bridges between the physical (mechanical) and the spiritual. McLuhan's interest in the big picture led him to emphasize major differences between the modes of Antiquity, the Renaissance, and the modern world. Accordingly he focused on Oral, Mechanical (Print), and Electric (Radio, Television). This led him to his crucial insights about electric extensions: the tele- idea taken to its tele-ological limit.

In retrospect, the categories Oral, Mechanical, and Electric are part of a much bigger picture. The revolution of new media in the past century has been the introduction of Electro-Magnetic, Electronic, Digital, Nano, Bio and Neuro and now Converged Media (Table 59.1). There was a great difference between electric telegraphs and telephones, which required fixed cables, and electro-magnetic telegraphs and telephones, which were wireless – a first step towards the mobile revolution. These were not inventions that replaced earlier media. They were additive and cumulative, as we see from their original names, e.g., electric telegraph, electro-mechanical telephone, electro-mechanical digital computing machines, electro-photography (i.e., photocopying). One of the original names of Morse code was the electric alphabet: Mr. Morse can hardly have believed that his electric alphabet would replace the earlier one. Rather, his invention clearly made the traditional alphabet accessible in conditions – instantly at a distance – beyond the limitations of an oral or a written alphabet. Evolution is embracing, not replacing. Electronic media changed the scale of objects and introduced the trend towards miniaturization in the Micro era that has accelerated with the Nano era. Digital extended the range of senses (including synesthesia and sensory transduction) and in combination with the previous advancements introduced a mobile dimension.

This has led to convergence in which it is useful to distinguish between at least three stages or generations. Convergence (generation) 1 was concerned with linking separate media: multi-media and inter-media. Convergence 2 was concerned with extending this through networks which, with the shift from Micro to Nano, increasingly became mobile networks – hence the emergence of ubiquitous and nomadic computing. Convergence 3 links digital with Nano, Bio and Neuro. Some call this biosystemics synthesis (Canada); NBIC (US), CTEK (Europe). We suggest it marks a shift from ICT (Information Communication Technologies) to UCT (Universal Convergence Technologies). In the computer industry this is leading to new buzzwords such as experience computing, natural computing, autonomic computing, bio-inspired, organic, evolvable, evolutionary computing, and synthetic reason computing.

These technological developments of the past century have seen a subtle but fundamental shift in the prefixes used to describe products, activities, disciplines, and ideas. Initially, the focus was on the dimension of distance through the Greek prefix: tele-graph; tele-phone; tele-vision, tele-fax and tele-learning, which culminated in international and global: global village, global learning, global society and global brain. The electronic phase brought an emphasis on size: not "size matters," but "lack of size matters": mini-computer; micro-chip; micro-processor; micro-computer and now the same at the nano-level. Not surprisingly, the digital phase focused on ideas of added (e.g., value-added), annotation, and especially increase. First, things were super: super-markets, super-computers, super-highways. Then they became cyber: cyber-profs; cyber-cafes and cyber-space. Then they became multi: multi-processor, multi-media; multi-user; multi-coordinate, multi-agent; and they became hyper: hyper-text, hyper-journal, hyper-net, hyper-learning. As we move towards convergence (generation) 3, 'augmented' is becoming the prefix of the times: augmented reality; augmented animals; augmented environments; augmented cognition and even augmented knowledge and culture.

At one level such prefixes have their roots in the super-latives and hyper-boles of marketing departments and the advertising industry. At another level, they reflect two fundamental shifts in the meaning of communication in the course of the past century. First, from the advent of literacy in the first two millennia B.C. until the nineteenth century, challenges of recording, representing and communicating (e.g., reproduction) were separate problems and varied with each medium. Even the application of one reproduction medium, such as printing, to different expression media such as text, woodcut, engraving, and lithograph led to separate professions. Convergence in this larger sense saw conflation of these separate tasks. So the author is now also a secretary, and increasingly "liberated" or burdened with other specialized tasks and professions: e.g., editing and layout. In the emerging digital design and production factories, the same product life cycle management applies to print media, film, television, video, and music.

A second, parallel shift has been less obvious. In the past, a medium entailed a given sense (e.g., sight, hearing) and also functioned in a given level of reality. For instance, a book was visual and it entailed a publication in the physical sphere. To be sure, a book could affect other dimensions than the physical, especially if it was fiction, science fiction, or some other tale of the imagination. Today, there are still books, but there are also electronic books, talking books, game versions and movie versions of books that affect a series of levels of reality.

The early enthusiasts of electronic media often saw hypertext as a form of annotation, as an electronic version of the medieval passion for commentaries (scholia, and glossa). This extended to annotation of photographs, video, film (cf. the field of non-linear editing) websites, and distributed environments. Hypertext typically annotated artificial environments with text, a trend that evolved with early artificial reality. Markup languages are a formal manifestation of the quest for annotation. Many have assumed that to transform the World Wide Web into a semantic web merely requires a (self-referential) network of markup and (uniform) resource identifiers that link an internal corpus, with no need to go beyond itself. The creators of topic maps, in a quest for semantic portability, are also creating networks of markup that are disconnected from the physical world.

Meanwhile, augmented reality is taking the process of annotation further and in a different connection. Where the W3 is creating a web of URLs, URNs and URIs separate from the physical world, augmented reality is creating annotations that bridge and link different scales, different worlds, and different realities. Sometimes this entails annotating images from the physical world. This annotation can take place at the whole range of scale from shots in space (1: 1,000,000) to life size, micro and nano-levels (1,000,000: 1). The scenes can be physical places, but they can equally be intellectual, emotional, or spiritual maps. A future geography of cyberspace will take us on journeys that link the physical zooming (popularized by NASA and Google Earth) with parallel zooming among levels of concepts, levels of fiction, and dreams, levels of the mind, levels of belief; even levels of initiation. This is fundamental and has at least four important consequences.

First in very practical terms, it suggests that the way forward lies neither in limiting ourselves to links assumed to be true (W3), nor in focusing only on personal associations (topic maps), but rather in linking objects, words, and concepts to the full range of their historical usages. The contents of etymological dictionaries are not simply for special interests or particular problems: they need to become part of our regular systems. Similarly, definitions in local, regional, and national dictionaries are not a luxury. They are a key to any real attempt at a semantic web. Ultimately, while truth remains an elusive, eternal ideal, it is not enough in isolation for everyday life; we need levels of truth, levels of certainty, belief, hypothesis, conjecture, and even intuition. These need to be integrated within our systems: not just a web of what is assumed to be 100 per cent true, but rather a web that helps us to see degrees and levels to which things and ideas are believed or accepted as true – and why.

Second, it means that search engines need to go beyond mere occurrences. On 14 January 2006, a search in Google produced 229 million hits for peace, 475 million hits for war, and 1.67 billion hits for government. In terms of hits these are success rates so superlative that any attempt to master them is doomed to be unsuccessful. It is true that Google distinguishes between news and its general site; that it is developing scholarly and other levels. But we need much more. A first step is in applying the distinctions from memory institutions between books, periodicals, and other media. A next step will be to introduce different levels of reality. If I am searching for a particular dog in New York, the universal characteristics of dogs as a species are of no interest, and conversely, we need systems that help us distinguish between Rover down the street (a canine version of the white or yellow pages) and general knowledge about dogs; between specific dogs with dog tags and the dogs of stories, games, films and dreams. We need levels of reality: physical, intellectual emotional, spiritual.

Third, it suggests that there is a much larger story that entails both discrete (words and numbers) and continuous (texts and shapes): sciences as well as arts. As a scholar of English literature, McLuhan, building on the insights of Havelock and Innis, was fascinated at how the advent of literacy led first to distinctions between the structure, logic, and effects of language; then to the rise of the trivium of grammar, dialectic, and rhetoric, and eventually to a focus on and privileging of logic over grammar and rhetoric. Since then, the work of Denise Schmandt-Besserat has pointed to a larger picture, whereby the rise of literacy was also linked to distinctions between the alphabet and numbers, i.e., the rise of literacy is linked with a deeper distinction between the arts (trivium) and the sciences (quadrivium). McLuhan traced a history within the trivium of tendencies to dissect and analyze (dialectic in the sense of logic) versus attempts to integrate and synthesize (grammar and rhetoric). There is a parallel history in the sciences of tensions between discrete (arithmetic) and continuous (geometry) approaches, between analysis and synthesis, which still manifests itself today in tensions between raster and vector. The quest for a balance between the analytic and synthetic, which concerned McLuhan in the arts, applies equally to the sciences.

Fourth, this points to the need for a new history of media and communications that goes far beyond existing efforts. McLuhan's categories of oral, written, printed, and electric are useful. But they need to be complemented by mechanical, electro-mechanical, electronic, digital, nano, bio, neuro, and Universal Convergence Technologies (UCT or whatever we might wish to call the new convergence of the third generation). Instead of assuming that each advance replaced the former, we need to explore the extent to which the new forms complemented the former modes. If print had simply replaced manuscript culture, the Corvini, which are some of the most beautiful manuscripts of all time, would never have been produced.

As an English scholar, McLuhan was ultimately concerned with keeping alive and fostering the creative spirit of the literary and especially the poetic. His work in the arts warned of the dangers of focusing too strongly on the linear limits of analytic logic; he pointed to the need for looking beyond the letter of the law to its spirit. He intuitively understood that the shift from mechanical to electric played an important role in this process. This intuitive analysis of the electric was ultimately not a prophetic understanding of the electronic, nano, bio, neuro, and UCT. McLuhan reminded us that the study of dangers in the past was a key to understanding the present. Today, understanding new media requires that in order to understand the present we need to continue looking to the past in order to assess and sense new directions that will emerge in the future. McLuhan warned of the dangers of looking at the future in a rear view mirror. Ironically, this reflective mirror is also a key to understanding his role as a prophet.

APPENDIX 1:

SCIENTIFIC VISUALIZATION

Visible World

In 1878, Jules Marey, one of the pioneers in the development of motion pictures, published his classic book, *The Graphic Method in the Experimental Sciences*,[1] in which he argued that science faced two obstacles: the deficiencies of the senses in discovering truths and the insufficiencies of language in expressing and transmitting those truths that have been acquired. His graphic method aimed to overcome these obstacles by rendering visible otherwise unseen aspects of the physical world.

Ninety years later, when Ivan Sutherland (1968) wrote one of the first articles on virtual reality, he was very articulate about the role of the new medium in visualizing things that had not been seen before.[2] In the past decades, this theme has excited ever-greater interest[3] and has led to the field of scientific visualization. Here we shall outline how it is affecting almost all aspects of the visible and invisible world.

In medicine, projects such as the Visible Embryo[4] and the Visible Human[5] project are providing us with new levels of visualization concerning the entire human body. A human body is frozen, cut into thousands of thin slices, each of which is then photographed and stored digitally. These photographs of a real human can thus serve to correct proposed models. They also lead to new physical models.[6] Thus careful, detailed recording of the physical world, leads to more accurate simulations thereof, which in turn lead to new discoveries about the physical world. A project at the Chihara Lab is exploring a virtual piano player in real time.[7] Virtuality leads to a discovery or rather a re-discovery of reality.

The study of the physical is also leading to new creative variations. For instance, at the Max Planck Institut für biologische Kybernetik (Tübingen), Volker Blanz and Professor Vetter produced a morphable model for 3-D synthesis of faces (Siggraph 99). Using this technique they can take a two-dimensional image of a face such as

Leonardo's *Mona Lisa* and reproduce this in three-dimensional form such that it can then be viewed from different angles.[8] A simple example of such creative visualization is to note how the work of the late Maurits Escher[9] is leading to new Internet examples.[10]

More impressive is a new trend to reproduce famous actors in virtual form as synthespians. For instance, the Miralab (Geneva) did pioneering work on a Virtual Marilyn Monroe.[11] This has led to a the idea of creating virtual celebrities using figures such as Sammy Davis Jr., James Cagney, Marlene Dietrich, Vincent Price, George Burns, W.C. Fields, and Groucho Marx, analyzing video clips of their movements "to create realistic animated 3D likenesses of them for commercials, television, film, and Web sites."[12] On 22 February 2001, Ray Kurzweil demonstrated Ramona, which he claimed to be "the world's first live virtual performing and musical recording artist,"[13] although such experiments by Softimage and Alias in Toronto go back to the early 1990s. The films, *Final Fantasy* (July 2001) and *Thru the Moebius Strip* (now planned for 2005)[14] also explore such virtual effects.[15]

In engineering, CAD models, which were initially applied to individual objects in the workplace, are now being applied to entire factories. A project at the University of Manchester entails a factory with over forty person-years to create a virtual reality version.[16] The Virtual Environments for Training (VET) project involves a reconstruction of the complete interior of a ship where the function of every dial is represented as a working java applet.[17] Visualization is also used in teaching mathematics.[18]

In architecture, companies such as Infobyte have made a virtual reality reconstruction of the church of San Francesco in Assisi, which is being used to repair the original subsequent to its being damaged by an earthquake.[19] In Japan, Infobyte's reconstruction of Saint Peter's Basilica is being projected in a former planetarium called a Virtuarium.[20]

CAD models, which were once limited to individual buildings, are now being extended to entire cities. Bentley Systems, for instance, is creating a virtual Philadelphia,[21] which, in fact, only covers a central portion of the city. Canal+ is creating a reconstruction of Paris, which is presently still limited to portions of the city such as the Eiffel Tower, the Louvre, and the Place des Vosges, but is so detailed that one can see the numbers on individual houses along a street. France Telecom has a similar reconstruction that allows one to enter shops and do tele-shopping. Slightly less detailed, but at least as interesting conceptually, is Virtual Helsinki. This lets us roam virtual streets and will in future allow us to listen to sermons of ministers, lectures of professors, and debates of politicians on-line.[22] Many such virtual cities are appearing at various levels of complexity.[23] These portals to cities can be linked with national portals. For instance, there is a Virtual Portugal,[24] which gives access at a country-wide level.

This development is emerging in parallel with a trend to install webcams in ever-more public and private places (chapter 13.6). A new level of recording the physical world in real time is thus linked with a commitment to reconstruct that same physical world in virtual form. Ultimately this introduces the possibility of new simulation feedback loops in the realm of everyday life. The man on the street was proverbially the random person one interviewed. In the new century, this can take on altogether new meanings.

Parallel to this rise of virtual cities, often linked with physical locations via webcams, is a trend to create historical reconstructions of these physical cities and places. The past decades have seen hundreds of virtual versions of such historical sites and cities, the topic of a fascinating book by Maurizio Forte.[25] Cities such as Rome are perhaps the best known in this context. Some of these are also being put on-line as in the case of La Rochelle, where one can walk through the central part of the old town.[26]

More recently there is a quest to add a dynamic dimension to such reconstructions. Here, the Nuovo Museo Elettronico (NUME) project of the University of Bologna in conjunction with CINECA is perhaps the most important project to date.[27] It provides a dynamic version of the central section of the city of Bologna from the year 1000 to the present. The three-dimensional reconstruction is linked with evidence from manuscripts and other historical documents. Objects that were originally part of monuments in the city and are now dispersed in museums are linked to each other. Linked with this are other projects of the city of Bologna and CINECA devoted to creating an electronic museum of the Certosa of Bologna.[28]

CINECA[29] is also engaged in another project concerning the reconstruction of Pompeii, Herculaneum, and other Roman settlements near Naples. In this case, archaeological evidence is linked with detailed topographical and geological maps and a range of historical evidence. The quest is much more than a simple reconstruction of buildings as they once were.[30] The enormously detailed models are intended to serve as simulations of life in Antiquity against which historical and economic theories can be seriously studied: Sim City goes historical.

An important project, SANTI, visible at the supercomputing centre of the Complutensian University (Madrid) has a reconstruction in virtual reality of the whole of North-Eastern Spain based on satellite images. This geographical fly-through is connected with reconstructions of historical cities such as Santiago da Compostella such that one can go from an aerial view, zoom in, walk through the streets, and then enter individual churches and buildings. This project points the way to a new comprehensive treatment of landscapes, which is complementary to the important historical treatments in the NUME project. There is a Mobile Visualization (MoVi) Project (Fraunhofer, Rostock), headed by Dr. Thomas Kirste.[31] Some of the leading software in this field is produced by Advanced Visual Systems, including their MUSE technologies.[32]

Projects such as SANTI reconstruct not only sacred sites but also the pilgrimage routes used to get there. The development of virtual routes is becoming a genre

TABLE 60 Parallels between International Standards Organization layers, functions, and Brad Cox's different layers of granularity in hardware and software.

ISO LAYER	HARDWARE	SOFTWARE
Network	Gate	Gate
	Block	Task
Transport		
Technical Service	Chip	Chip
	Card	Card
	Appliance	Process

in itself. Perhaps the most important example is UNESCO's work on Virtual Silk Roads.[33]

Invisible World: Natural Processes

Institutes such as the UK Meteorological Office (Bracknell), the Navy Oceanographic Office (Bay Saint Louis), the Deutscher Wetterdienst (Offenbach), and the National Center for Atmospheric Research (NCAR)[34] use virtual reconstructions to study possible developments of heat in air and water (the El Niño effect), gases in the air, clouds, wind currents, storms, tornadoes, and other extreme weather conditions. While some aspects of these phenomena may be visible to the human eye, the simulations allow us to see the processes in a much more comprehensive manner. In the case of storms, for instance, NCAR uses satellite images of real storms and compares these with model reconstructions of such a storm. Once again the evidence of physical reality is being used to modify virtual models in order that they have greater predictive qualities in the future (cf. the simulation-feedback loop in Figure 2 above). The Chesapeake Bay project explored environmental issues pertaining to underwater pollution normally invisible to the human eye.

Invisible World: Nano-Level

In the past decades, new links between electron microscopes, force feedback haptic devices or nano-manipulators, and visualization have led to new fields of imagery. The Hitachi Viewseum[35] and IBM, which was a pioneer by being the first to write IBM in molecules, have on-line galleries of such images.[36] Nano-photography is essential for the evolution of nano-simulation as a field. Again the visualization of hitherto invisible aspects is leading to new fields such as nano-technology and molecular electronics (or molectronics), which are the subject of chapter three above.

Invisible World: Outer Space

Ever since the invention of the telescope, instruments have been opening up the horizons of planets, stars, and galaxies beyond the sight of the unaided eye. The Hubble telescope has greatly expanded the range of images now available to us.[37]

New methods of visualization are also being developed to make available the results of such visual explorations of the sun, the solar system, and outer space. For instance, a project at the Haydn Planetarium, called Digital Galaxy, uses Silicon Graphics machines (with seven pipes) to project images such as those from the Hubble Spacecraft onto the ceiling of a planetarium.

Invisible World: Concepts

Computers are helping us to visualize many hitherto intangible concepts, including the realm of software. In order to distinguish different functionalities in the tele-communications world, the International Standards Organization, established three kinds of layers (entailing seven network layers). More recently, Brad Cox has made a plea for visualizing five different layers of computer hardware and software (Table 60), demonstrating how the major programming languages (Lisp, Smalltalk, C, C++, and Objective C) can be understood better using this approach.[38] In short, virtuality is being used to render visible dimensions of code that were hitherto invisible. The efforts of Dr. Steven Eick at Bell Labs to visualize patterns in software code mark another step in this direction.[39]

Invisible World: Economic Processes

The use of graphs is a well-known practice in economics. In the 1960s, economists began exploring the potentials of three-dimensional graphs to visualize economic trends. More recently, with respect to investments, Visible Decisions[40] rendered such trends visible first in three-dimensional graphs and then with an added real-time dimension. Asymptote's three-dimensional real-time rendering of the New York Stock Exchange is one of the most dramatic developments in this context:

> The Exchange has chosen the world's most powerful visualization supercomputers to generate a completely interactive virtual representation of its trading floor. By consolidating the data streams from the various floor trading systems into one three-dimensional system, a visual display is created that allows users to intuitively understand complex business transactions instantaneously, as well as see system problems at a glance.[41]

Possible Worlds

The virtual reconstruction of entire landscapes has become of ever-greater interest to the military, which now uses such images of the real world in order to develop realistic battle and other emergency scenarios.[42] In this context, war games are deadly serious.[43] In a first stage, such simulations involved a demonstration at a local site, not very different from the way generals traditionally had models or at least maps of battlefields at their disposal. At a second stage, these simulated models became networked such that players in different centres could play the same game:

like playing networked Doom with real scenarios. A third stage is integrating such networked scenarios with physical locations. For instance, the Terravision project at SRI,[44] linked with the Army's supercomputer in Minneapolis, provides persons on the battlefield access to satellite and other aerial images of the situation. This real-time information can be used to modify scenarios on the home front. Virtuality thus leads to the discovery of reality, and reality leads to corrections in the reality of the moment.

In design, the software of companies such as Alias Wavefront is being used for a whole gamut of products ranging from simple cosmetics and furniture to interiors of airplanes and the design of automobiles, trucks, and boats. The design of cars, tractors, and aircraft, once the domain of secretive teams within a single company, is now increasingly the domain of collaborative teams linked with global databases of engineering and design elements.

In Europe, visualization plays an increasing role in design linked with rapid and virtual prototyping. Here the High Performance Computing Center in Stuttgart (HLRS) plays an important role.[45] An excellent survey of these developments was recently given by Dr. Ulrich Lang (HLRS) at the First European High Performance Graphics System and Applications Conference (CINECA, Bologna, 16–17 October 2000).

In film, visualization in the form of special effects has become common-place.[46] *True Lies* introduced a virtual Harrier jet into a cityscape. *Disclosure* created virtual information spaces that bore an uncanny resemblance to St. Peter's Basilica. The film *What Dreams May Come* (1998) offered a visualization of the protagonist's heaven and hell and a library reminiscent of Hubert Robert's architectural phantasies.[47] *Toy Story* was an entirely virtual world. In Manchester, virtual reality was used to reconstruct the scene of a crime: said to be the first time that a reconstruction was used as evidence in a court of law.[48]

Creative Worlds

While many see virtuality as a means of making new scientific links with the physical world, some interpret virtuality as a blurring between the real and the virtual.[49] Artist Michel Moers goes further and links virtuality with playful, creative, illusion: "These simplified shapes often become archetypes that are more than true-to-nature, more colourful, more joyful and, more especially, easier to live with – all they have to do is to appear on the scene and pretend!"[50]

The musicians Martin Kornberger and Volker Kuhn, who created the music CD *Virtuality* in 1992, are more explicit in linking this blurring function with the creative process. Kornberger, for instance, notes that: "Virtuality – signifies the crossing of the borderlines between man, machine and nature. By means of computer technology it is possible now to scan reality and form new virtual ones – at least in music." His colleague Kuhn puts it slightly differently: ""Virtuality – this expresses in some way a longing for illusionary worlds of beauty and power beyond human restrictions. But the closer one gets to them, the more unreal and empty they seem. At last nothing remains but the loneliness of our inner space."[51]

One of the prolific areas of development in this context is the realm of virtual reality worlds being created by artists.[52] In the literary field, novelists such as John Barth have reflected on the meaning of virtuality with respect to culture.[53] One of the most complex experiments in this context is a project on Electronic Arenas for Culture, Performance, Art and Entertainment (eERENA),[54] which includes a vision system, visual content, audio content, user representation, content/story, physical space, virtual storybook of an electronic arena, and a mixed-reality theatre. Information from all of these layers interacts with live players on a stage.

Meanwhile, at Manchester University, Professor Adrian West, one of the pioneers of large-scale virtual reality programs, has become fascinated with the potentials of virtual worlds to convey alternative worlds:

> Cages is a demonstration of the deva world hierarchy, and the idea of environments that impose behaviours on their contents. This is akin to specifying the properties of time, space and physical laws for a particular universe. The complexities of such laws are limited by the computational resources available to impose them. Any object placed within such an environment has these laws and behaviours imposed upon it. We believe this approach will make it significantly easier to create a range of complex virtual environments.[55]

Computer software such as Windows showed the world from one particular viewpoint within a single frame of reference. Professor West's software allows one to change perceptual worlds, e.g., to look as an individual in a room at a fish in a fish tank, then look as a fish in the fish tank at an individual in a room beyond the tank, and then as an individual standing outside the room looking at the individual and the fish. Not only are the viewpoints different, but each of these spaces can have their own laws of physics. For instance, the first individual can be in a room subject to the normal laws of gravity, the fish in virtual water can be subject to different rules, and the person outside could be in a space not subject to ordinary gravity.

Simulation

The trends towards globalization of production are closely connected with developments in simulation and design. Lockheed Martin, also active in collaborative software and virtual environments for training, is developing simulation-based design.[56] The dVISE[57] company has Interactive Product Simulation (IPS) and digital mockups. At the Synthetic Environment Lab (SEL),[58] simulation is a theme along with data analysis, data fusion, manufacturing, and medical modelling. There is a Computer Simulation Council.

Simulation is increasingly important in architecture. The Getty Trust and UCLA have an Urban Simulation Team,[59] which has produced a model of the Roman

Forum. There is an Environmental Simulation Center at the New School of Social Research (New York). The National Center for Supercomputing Applications (NCSA) has work on climate simulations.

The Beckman Institute (Chicago) has a Materials and Process Simulation Center (MSC) with simulations of real material systems. Mississippi State University[60] has an Engineering Research Center for Computational Field Simulation (ERC). The Mechanical Engineering Department at Iowa State University has simulation-based training for manufacturing workers.[61] The University of Pennsylvania's Center for Human Modeling and Simulation[62] has a Multi-Robot Simulation Environment (MRS).

As might be expected, the military is very active in the realm of simulations. There is a Defense Modeling and Simulation Office (DMSO).[63] The Army High Performance Computing Research Center (AHPCRC)[64] has Advanced Flow Simulation and Modeling. The University of Central Florida has an Institute for Simulation and Training (IST) with a Dynamic Environments Group and projects such as[65] Polyshop, Toy Scouts, and Virtopia, as well as Telerobotics, Teleoperation, and Telepresence Research.[66] The University of Southern California uses the University of Chicago's Immersadesk – a monitor in the form of a workbench[67] – for military simulations of the Kuwait desert. The Lucie Naval Lab (Stony Brook) has produced a concurrency workbench, an iterative rapid prototyping process and a distributed iterative simulation. The U.S. Army Research Office recently organized a Workshop on Multi-Agent Systems and Agent Based Simulation (MABS).[68]

NASA and Northeastern University (Boston) have a Virtual Environments Laboratory,[69] with a virtual environments based driving simulation and a numerical aerodynamic simulation division (NAS).[70] The University of Iowa (Iowa City) at its Center for Computer Aided Design (CCAD)[71] also has a Driving Simulation.

Simulation is also entering the software domain. The Mathematics and Computer Science Division of the U.S. Army Research Office is working on Software and Knowledge Based Systems (SKBS),[72] including modelling and simulation. Lucent Technologies/Bell Labs is working on visual simulation discovery. There are, of course, simulation games such SimCity and the SIMS, which allow one "to create, direct, and manage the lives of SimCity's residents by satisfying their needs (hunger, comfort, hygiene, bladder, energy, fun, social, and room) through interaction with other Sims or objects."[73] Players can "teleport" their virtual families to other users on the Sims.com site and interact with peer groups in such scenarios as raising children, adding rooms to their homes and socializing.[74] There is also a dark side to these developments.[75] Meanwhile, Inflorescence Inc.[76] (Portland) works with the Behavior Engine Company, which has software for compositional simulation: "for creating simulations or temporal models from reusable components. The Behavior Engine's encapsulated units of process information are known as 'Simlet®s'," which are used for "complex simulations, training materials and technical documentation."

Medical simulation is an emerging field. The National Cancer Center (Tokyo)[77] is working on surgical simulation, medical virtual reality, and virtual medical communication. The University of Hull has a biomedical model of the human knee joint and haptic feedback for surgical simulation. The University of Manchester has radiation therapy planning in 3-D. There are considerable efforts to simulate the human brain. The Pittsburgh Supercomputing Center,[78] which is linked with Carnegie Mellon University and Westinghouse, has Advanced Methods for Neuroimaging Data Analysis, a project on the Brain in Action[79] and Parallel Simulation of Large Scale Neuronal Models.

At the atomic level, simulation plays a vital role. IBM Almaden's[80] Visualization Lab is working on molecular dynamic simulations. IBM's new Blue Gene supercomputer, one thousand times more powerful than the chess-playing Deep Blue: its sole purpose is to derive protein folds from DNA sequences and conversely. Whereas the human genome project is providing a list of the genetic instructions that make us what we are, Blue Gene will begin to tell us how those instructions work.[81]

The Institute for Operations Research and Management Sciences (INFORMS) has a College on Simulation,[82] to which Scott Ameduri refers as a simulation organization along with Agile Manufacturing Homepage, W3 Virtual Library on Computer Based Simulations, and the newsgroup comp.simulation.[83] Simulation was once for an isolated object/process. The new quest is to simulate all processes in integrated form.

Simulation is also of increasing importance in Europe. INRIA (Paris, etc.) has as its fourth research theme simulation and optimization of complex systems.[84] Trinity College (Dublin) has a Distributed Virtual Environment Simulation. The University of Manchester is working on simulation of buildings. There is a Federation of European Simulation Societies (EUROSIM) since 1989.[85]

In the United States, there is talk of a new simulation millennium in which the boundaries of simulation for science and entertainment will blur such that manufacturing, movie making, education, and web will all work together.[86] In Europe, by contrast, there is a trend towards more detailed and perhaps more fundamental understanding in specific fields. For instance, a German consortium including Audi, Daimler Chrysler, Bosch, Mannesmann, Siemens, Porsche, and Volkswagen have formed an Association for Standardization of Automation and Measuring Systems (ASAM).[87]

APPENDIX 2:

NEW FIELDS RELATING TO
KNOWLEDGE ORGANIZATION

In Antiquity, knowledge organization was part of philosophy. The past two centuries have seen the emergence of a number of new fields relating to different aspects of knowledge organization. The eighteenth century, for instance, saw the rise of 1) taxonomy. The nineteenth century brought the rise of 2) library studies, which has led to library science, and 3) bibliography, which led to developments in 4) classification. The twentieth century has seen the rise of 5) terminology, 6) information science, 7) knowledge organization, 8) automated classification, and 9) ontology. The past decades have seen the rise of further fields with an integrating trend, including 10) complexity, 11) knowledge media, 12) informatics, 13) infonortics, and 14) infonomics.

1. Taxonomy
Ever since Linnaeus, taxonomy has been an important branch of knowledge in the life sciences. In biology, there is now an International Union for Biological Sciences (IUBS) with a Taxonomic Database Working Group (TDWG) and an International Working Group on Taxonomic Databases.[1] Also active in this context are the International Council of Scientific Unions (ICSU) and the Committee on Data for Science and Technology (CODATA).[2] In botany, there is an Integrated Taxonomic Information System (ITIS).[3] In zoology, there is a taxonomy and systematics group at Glasgow.[4] There are taxonomical databases.[5] The Internet has a Taxonomic Resources and Expertise Directory,[6] a significant list of phylogenetics societies and organizations,[7] and also Personal Taxonomies.[8] There is an Expert Centre for Taxonomic Identification (ETI, University of Amsterdam)[9] and there is a Consortium of European Taxonomic Associations (CETA).

2. Library Studies and Library Science
In the Middle Ages and the Renaissance, librarians learned their skills through an apprenticeship method. This continued until the nineteenth century. One of the

early schools was in Liverpool (1861): School of Science established (in Public Library and Museum).[10]

In the United States, the first library science program in the Midwest began in the fall of 1893 with Katherine Sharp and May Bennett as the sole instructors. In the fall of 1897, the Illinois State Library School opened in Urbana.[11] The University of Wisconsin-Madison School of Library and Information Studies had its beginnings in a series of summer sessions that ran from 1895 to 1905.[12]

In Canada, McGill was the first university to offer regular courses in librarianship. Following a series of summer courses (1904–27), the School of Library Science began in 1927–28 and was renamed the Graduate School of Library and Information Studies in 1985. In Toronto, the Library School began within the Ontario College of Education (1928), became the Faculty of Library Science (1972); Library and Information Studies (1982), and then the Faculty of Information Studies (FIS, 1994).[13]

At the Royal School of Librarianship in Copenhagen, there is a Centre for Informetric Studies.[15] In France, the Ecole nationale supérieure des bibliothécaires (1963) became the Ecole nationale supérieure des sciences de l'information et des bibliothèques (1992).[16] At the world level, there is an International Federation of Library Associations (IFLA, The Hague).

3. Classification

With the exception of Italy, where classification[17] grew out of an earlier statistics society (1939), the major national[18] classification societies today were not founded until the last quarter of the twentieth century, i.e., 1977–94 (Table 61). The Classification Society of North America (CSNA) was founded in 1984. There is an International Study Conference on Classification Research (ISCCR).[19] The International Federation of Classification Societies (IFCS)[20] was founded in 1985. Their conference, IFCS 2000 (Namur) includes a variety of topics, methods, kinds of data analysis, and application to a wide number of disciplines (Table 62). A number of major classification systems, thesauri, and controlled vocabularies are available on-line.[21] A striking example is the Visual Thesaurus.[22]

4. Information Science

Many of the library schools at universities in the United States have been transformed into Schools of Library and Information Science. At Drexel University, for instance, there was a school of Library Science (1892). This became the Graduate School of Library Science (1954), the School of Library and Information Science (1978), and the College of Information Science and Technology (1995).[23]

At the University of North Carolina, Chapel Hill, the names are reversed in the School of Information and Library Science.[25] Rutgers University has a School of Communication, Information and Library Studies (SCILS).[26] The University of California, Berkeley, has a School of Information Management and Systems (founded in 1998).[27] The University of Southern California (Los Angeles) has an

TABLE 61 National Classification Societies.[14]

COUNTRY	NAME		FOUNDED
Britain	(British) Classification Society	BCS	1964
France	Société Francophone de Classification	SFC	1977
Germany	Gesellschaft für Klassifikation	GfK	1977
Italy	Società Italiana di Statistica	SIS	1939
Japan	Japanese Classification Society	JCS	1983
Netherlands	Vereniging voor Ordinatie en Classificatie	VOC	1989
Poland	Sekcja Klasyfikacji i Analizy Danych	SKAD	1989
Portugal	Associaçao Portuguesa de Classificaçao	CLAD	1994

Information Science Institute (ISI)[28] with over two hundred researchers. There is a U.S. National Commission on Libraries and Information Science[29] and an Association for Library and Information Science Education (ALISE).[30] In the United States there is also a Society for Information Management (SIM, Chicago).[31] There is a Danish Information Applications Group (DIAG). At their best, these schools are combining library studies with the latest technological advances.

5. Bibliography

In the 1890s, Paul Otlet and LaFontaine set out to create a world bibliography of periodical literature, which led to the foundation of the Mundaneum[32] (originally located in Brussels, but now in Mons). To master this material, they built upon the foundations of the Dewey system to produce a Universal Decimal Classification (UDC). This system later moved to the Hague, where it was under the auspices of the International Federation for Information and Documentation (FID).[33] The FID became responsible for dealing with established terms. Evolving terms became the domain of the Union Internationale des Associations (UIA, Brussels).[34]

6. Terminology

Meanwhile, in Vienna, Eugen Wüster explored the principles of systematic ordering of terms, which led to the establishment of the International Standards Organization, Technical Committee 37 on Terminology (ISO TC 37).[35] In the course of the past decade, this has become part of the Global Group, which now includes four other institutions: the International Network for Terminology (TermNet),[36] the International Information Centre for Terminology (Infoterm), Gesellschaft für Terminologie und Wissenstransfer (GTW),[37] and the International Institute for Terminology and Research (IITF). These organizations, led by ISO TC 37, became responsible for the principles underlying terminology. In addition there are now a number of regional terminology projects such as Nordterm Net.[38] There is a Nordic Terminological Reference Format (NTRF), and there are a number of terminology web sites[39]

TABLE 62 Applications of Classification according to the International Federation of Classification Societies.[24]

Archaeology	Finance
Biology	Image Analysis
Chemistry	Industry
Cognition	Medicine
Communication	Quality Control
Consumer Science	Sensory Analysis
Credit Scoring	Social Sciences
Environmental Science	Textual Analysis

7. Automated Classification

"With Friends like Statistics who needs Linguistics?"[40] This title of an article published in 1995 is indicative of one strand from the realm of artificial intelligence, which assumes that traditional methods of linguistic analysis will soon be completely obsolete. There is a considerable literature on automatic classification,[41] and an enormous amount of research in this field. Xerox PARC, for instance, has work on Quantitative Content Analysis Area (QCA), Automatic Hypertext Indexing, Question Answering and Automatic Thesaurus Term Generation.

There are thesauri-building and editing tools[42] Major systems such as the Library of Congress Classification[43] and the Dewey Decimal Classification (DDC, i.e., as Electronic Dewey[44]) are in electronic form. The Online Computer Library Center (OCLC), which owns the Dewey system, is experimenting with automatic generation of relations. Other important projects in this context include the Automated Categorization of Internet Resources (ARISTOTLE),[45] the AutoClass Project,[46] and Automatic Text Classification by Mortimer Technology.[47]

8. Knowledge Organization

The International Society for Knowledge Organization (ISKO),[48] founded by Dr. Ingetraut Dahlberg in 1980, when the German Society of Classification chose a narrower statistical route, is dedicated to the development of the field. There is also a German branch of ISKO.[49]

9. Ontology

Ontology claims to be one of the newest fields and does not yet have specific institutes to its name. In the eyes of some, ontology is simply a new word for classification. In Germany, the Institut für Angewandte Informatik und Formale Beschreibungsverfahren (AIFB, Karlsruhe[50]) has developed an Ontobroker. They also use the ACM Classification for a bibliography of computer science.[51] The Knowledge Representation and Reasoning Group (KRR, Trento[52]) is working on Formal Ontology. This is part of a larger mandate, which includes: Knowledge Representation and Reasoning in Artificial Intelligence,

Description Logics, Computational Logics, Natural Language Formal Semantics, Conceptual Modeling, and Flexible Access to Information. Closely related to ontologies are Description Logics (DL)[53] and Meta-Logics.[54] The University of Amsterdam has a developed Ontobroker and an Ontology Inference Layer (OIL), which is being liked with DARPA Agent Markup Language (DAML +OIL) in the context of the W3 Consortium's work on the semantic web. There are also other Ontology Services such as Resource Description Framework Schemas (RDFS), Simple HTML Ontology Extensions (SHOE), and On2Broker. There is a quest to complement the efforts towards a semantic web with those of a semantic grid.[55] For the moment these efforts are focussed on creating paid web services for the business community and might more accurately be called efforts at a services or transactions web.

Recently there are the Association for Computational Linguistics Special Interest Group on Semantics (ACL SIGSEM);[56]and the Association for Information Systems Special Interest Group on Semantic Web and Information Systems (AIS SIGSEMIS),[57] and projects such as TIES (Trainable Information Extraction for the Semantic Web).[58] There is work on a number of fronts by the Digital Enterprise Research Group (DERI).[59] They are leaing a Software Development Kit (SDK) Cluster[60] to integrate efforts of two projects: Semantically Enabled Knowledge Technologies (SEKT)[61]; Data, Information, and Process Integration with Semantic Web Services (DIP)[62] and a Network of Excellence, Knowledge Web (KW) [63] in the Sixth Framework Programme. Knowledge Web is working toward a Virtual Institute for Semantic Web Education (VISWE). The SDK Cluster is also co-ordinating the Web Services Modeling Ontology (WSMO), the Web Services Modeling Language (WSML) and Web Services Execution Environment (WSMX).[64] Meanwhile, there is a trend towards algorithms to search for meaning automatically[65]and to create Self Organising Maps (SOM)[66] to visualize contextual relations.

10. Complexity

In our earlier discussion of Organizations (chapter 7), we discussed the importance of systems theory and organization theory, which grew out of the study of cybernetics,[67] and noted the particular role played by MIT's Center for Coordination Science (CCS).[68] Since the 1990s, there have been conferences on Computer Aided Systems Technology.[69] The past decades have seen the rise of new fields such as neural networks. Yahoo lists at least twenty-four neural networks institutes.[70] There is a European "Network of Excellence" in Neural Networks (NeuroNet).[71] There is a Neural Network World (Zeist),[72] and there are Neural Networks Resources.[73]Neural networks are frequently associated with chaos theory[74] and complex systems. Here the Santa Fe Institute[75] has been one of the pioneers. In the past years, these fields have become part of larger cluster under the heading of complexity (Table 63). Complexity is becoming a new umbrella under which to combine a number of recent advances in science and technology. Sorin Solomon has founded a Network of Excellence on Complex Systems.[76]

TABLE 63 Topics related to complexity[77]

Artificial Life	Fractals
Bio-complexity	Learning Systems
Cellular Automata	L[ife] Systems
Chaos	Neural Networks
Connectivity	Non-Linear Dynamics
Criticality	Parallel Computation
Economics	Percolation
Engineering	Self-Organization
Evolution	

11. Knowledge Media

In the humanities, there is no single umbrella for clustering related fields. Even so, there are a few candidates, notably knowledge media, informatics, and infonomics. In Britain, the Open University (Milton Keynes) has a Knowledge Media Institute (KMI)[78] with a Bayesian Knowledge Discovery Project[79] and a Digital Document Discourse Environment (D3E).[80] In Switzerland, there is a Net Academy on Knowledge Media[81] (St. Gallen) which has an important bibliography.[82] In Finland, the Center for Knowledge and Innovation Research (CKIR, Helsinki) has a Knowledge Media Laboratory. In Canada, there is a Knowledge Science Institute (KSI, Calgary).[83] More recent arrivals, such as the Knowledge Media Design Institute (KMDI, Toronto)[84] are clearly inspired by these earlier examples. France has an important new Institut des sciences du document numérique (ISDN),[85] which explores similar themes.

12. Informatics

One of the emerging new disciplines is informatics. This term is sometimes used as a synonym for information science as a branch of computer science. There is Medical Informatics and Health Informatics. In Norway, the SINTEF Group combines Telecom and Informatics.[86] A number of other uses are emerging. For instance, the Informatics Computer Institute (Philippines), founded in 1983, focuses on Information Technology (IT), business training, and education.[87] In Athens, an Institute of Informatics and Telecommunications (IIT)[88] was founded in 1987. An Institute of Mathematics and Informatics (Vilnius) has been publishing papers on mathematical simulation and optimization, recognition and control, programming theory and systems, and automation systems and elements since 1990 in its journal *Informatica*.[89] The Informatics Institute (Skopje)[90] has a Division for the Mathematical Foundation of Informatics.

In New York, The Graphics Research Laboratory, founded by Jack Powers in 1982, became the International Informatics Institute (IN3.ORG) in 1998. It "performs research, education and consulting on global electronic commerce and infrastructure issues."[91] Meanwhile, Informatics International is "a world-wide corporation dedicated to providing superior services in the integrated technologies of Geoinformatics: consisting of Remote Sensing, Geographic Information Systems (GIS), Global Positioning Systems (GPS) and related space systems."[92] At the University of Twente, there was a Centre for Telematics and Informatics, which is now the Centre for Telematics and Information Technology (CTIT).[93] There is an Institute of Neuro-Informatics (Zurich).[94] Perhaps the most active of all is the Japanese National Institute of Informatics (NII) in Tokyo.

13. Infonortics

Harry Collier, an English pioneer in the electronic information industry has founded a company called Infonortics,[95] which organized a significant conference on Search engines and beyond.[96]

14. Infonomics

In 1994, Mark Heyer founded an Institute for Infonomic Research to study the "relationship between people and information." As such, it is effectively a means of optimizing personnel in organizations.[97] Infonomics.net[98] has been publishing a *Revista de Infonomia* on information in organizations since 1995. By contrast, the International Institute on Infonomics (III, Heerlen)[99], founded in 1999, and formally opened on 11 January 2001, served as the umbrella institute for both the Maastricht Economic Research Institute on Innovation and Technology (MERIT)[100] and the Maastricht McLuhan Institute (MMI).[101] The III united work from a large range of fields, including economics, philosophy, history, education, knowledge management, and knowledge organization. The III acted as an umbrella for some one hundred researchers under five sections:

1) e-basics studies the basic concepts of information and communication and the society built around them. E-basics focuses on fundamental changes in digitized society, prompted by the interaction between individuals and networks, information systems, and the Internet.

2) e-behaviour studies individuals, and more generally human and software agents – including intelligent web agents – as they engage in the essential social, economic, cultural, and political interactions to form all sorts of communities. e-behaviour also investigates emerging characteristics and types of behaviour of these actors, who function in a world dominated by rapidly changing information and communication modes.

3) e-organization concerns the actual operations of organizations, both with respect to their internal control and functioning, and to their external activities.

4) e-society focuses on the institutions, mechanisms, legal procedures, and human capital that facilitate the workings of a digitized society at the aggregate level.

5) e-content applies all these branches of study to a varying set of sectors in society.

In 2002, before it had even acquired its own permanent premises, lack of funding led to the III being abandoned as a vision. In 2004, a small remnant continues as the European Centre for Digital Culture (EC/DC). The University of Maastricht also chose to close the Maastricht McLuhan Institute (MMI) for the same reasons: lack of finance. Ideas and visions are not always enough.

APPENDIX 3:

NEW FIELDS RELATING TO
EXPERT AND INTELLIGENT SYSTEMS (1942 - 2002)

TABLE 64 Summary of expert systems, 1942–2002[1]

Canonical Systems		Post	1942
Rules (Structured)	Physical Based System	Newell, Simon	1972
Frames		Minsky	1975
" "		Brachman	1983
Tasks			
Test	Situated Cognition	Clancey	1983
	Knowledge Management	Compton	1990
		Edwards	1995
	Knowledge Based Systems Validation	Menzies	1995
In Between the Rules			
	XCON	McDermott	1981
	R1 Implicit Made Explicit (RIME)	Van de Brug	1986
	MOLE	Kahn	1985
	MYCIN	Shortliffe	1974
	Reverse Engineering of MYCIN	Clancey	1985
Above the Level of Rules & Frames			
	Expert Systems (ES) without detailed knowledge of data structures	Chandrasekaran	1986
Knowledge Level		Newell	1982
	SOAR Rule Based language	Laird, Roosenbloom	1983
	Problem Space Computational Model		1989
		Newell	1993
Knowledge Level B	Generic Tasks	Chandrasekaran	1983, 1986
	Model Construction Operators	Clancey	1992
	Components of Expertise	Steels	1990
	Spark/ Burn/Firefighter	Marques	1992
	Protégé	Eriksson	1995
	KADS (Knowledge Acquisition and Design Support)	Wielinga	1992
		Tansley	1993
Risk Driven Development Cases (Conditions, Structures)		Boehm	1995
Critical Success Metrics (CSM) Worlds		Fox	1995

387

TABLE 65 History of programming languages, according to Simon Brooke (Weft).[2]

LISP	John McCarthy	Stanford	1959
BCPL	Martin Richards	Cambridge	1969
C	Thompson & Ritchie	Bell Labs	1972
Smalltalk	Goldberg, Kay et al	Xerox PARC	1973
Oak	James Gosling	Sun	1995
Java	James Gosling et al.	Sun	1995
Java Database Connectivity (JDBC)		Sun	1996

APPENDIX 4:

JUST IMAGINE,
BY JAPP VAN TILL

Very effective recent examples of "co-operation by networking" are PCs that process parts of the huge amounts of received signals for the Search for Extraterrestrial Intelligence (SETI) while the owner of the PC does not use it; the bazaars of the "Open Source" and LINUX movement, the project to crack an encrypted text by a huge amount of computers in many centres and not to forget the standardization process of the ISOC-IETF, a.k.a. "the Internet Engineering Method"!

Apart from altruism, obvious fun and the benefits of working solutions and results, we can ask: "Why do people join such networked co-operative efforts and contribute time and knowledge?" My answers are: they want to connect, they want to *learn* and they want to get a better and more confirmed vision on things themselves in return to their contribution.

In order to come to that networking conclusion, it is important first to have a better idea about how individuals learn, think, and associate (link) ideas. My guess is that we do that by way of image-processing. I was very impressed by the different views, viewpoints, and impressions you[1] showed at INET '99 from different sources of the Forum Romanum city area. If you see the famous film showing the sequence of self-image paintings of Rembrandt or the sequence of paintings of Monet, the bridge at Giverny, or the sequence of the works of Mondriaan, it is striking that our brain can perform two very useful functions: (a) we can combine and link the trajectory sequence or the various 'shots' from different angles into a cohesive larger whole, and quite opposite in scale, (b) we can extract a kind of shared fingerprint from all the images which lets us later directly recognize a painting of the same artist. You only have to see a fragment of a painting by Herring or Picasso to know who made it. Conclusion is that our brain can build scale-less fractals from huge amounts of similar information and use this pattern either above (to learn) or below (to associate and search) the scale of documents or images that we can see. What may be the mechanism that does that function in the human brain? I propose the following Van Till's Theorem:

The human brain processes information (and knowledge) in parallel in the form of images. The previous mental maps and expectations (M) can be combined and confirmed with perceived images of Reality (R) by a process similar to "Super-Resolution" (optical image Fourier Transform) and by fractal symmetrical folding and unfolding like the Walsh-Hadamard Transform.

Super-resolution is a technique that was developed to enhance radar images by combining the information from fuzzy pictures scattered with noise. The idea is that the echo of a target plane is smeared all over the picture and can be extracted back, thus improving the resolving power of the radar system. The now-unclassified technique works by extrapolating the Fourier Transform spectrum of the image(s) and then inverse the transform. The price we have to pay is that only a part of a (sequence of) picture(s) can be super-resolved at the same time, like the sharp area we focus on when we look. More recently, the technique is used to super-resolve images from a trajectory of fly-by pictures from spacecraft and from multiple pictures of the Mars surface. In fact, it was possible to generate sub-pixel resolution composite images from multiple nearly aligned images (see http://www.arc.nasa.gov/ic/projects/bayes-group/index.html) from the Nasa-Ames Bayesian Model-Based Learning Group). A medical application of this technique is the calculation of a 3-D image of a body from multiple X-Ray/Echo/NMR photos taken from different directions and perspectives. This now takes a supercomputer to do. My conjecture is that our brain does such many-layered combinations and focussed awareness all the time! The blurry images of our two watery eyeballs are combined (super-resolved) by our brain into sharp 3D vision. The brain therefore works like an optical processing system similar to optical lenses.

This brings me back to networked co-operation through the Internet. In my vision I see thousands of people interconnected like an array of eyes like in an insect's eye or like an networked array of small dishes of a radio telescope. The resolving power of the total telescope depends not on the size of the dishes but most of all on the distance of the most far apart (different angle of perspective!) observing dishes whatever their size.

The images that are constructed and super-resolved in this way are better than any the observers could make themselves, and together we can construct "visions" that were never possible to see before. So is the incentive (virtuous circle) to join teams and networked co-operation. Knowledge does become better and more valuable when compared and shared. The mechanism of super-resolution can be built into the Internet as well.

Information spreads rapidly and is echoed and woven into many forms all around us. Echos of all that ever happened anywhere are present in fractions and fragments of our universe. I invite you to help transform the Internet into a worldwide Observatorium, a system of knowledge lenses to extract and exchange wonderful diverse manyfold information, knowledge, imagination, art, culture, and wisdom. We can, by interconnection and networking, build the eyes and brain of Gaia. Together we can make her wake up and become conscious. Just imagine!!

APPENDIX 5:

J. M. PERREAULT'S RELATIONS [1]

TABLE 66 J.M. Perreault's relations and their sub-categories.

SUBSUMPTIVE RELATIONS

Type/Kind
Principle/Manifestation
Genus/Species
Species/Organization

Whole/Part
Organism/Organ
Composite/Conclusions
Matrix/Particles

Subject/Property
Substance/Accident
Possessor/Possession
Accompanance

DETERMINATIVE RELATIONS

Active
Productive
Causing
Originating/Source

Limitative
Restrictive
Orienting, Establishing
Frame of Reference, Point of View
　　Destructive

Injuring
Suppressing, Eliminating
Curing

Interactive
Concordant
Differing
Contrary
Produced
Limited
Destroyed

TABLE 66 J.M. Perreault's relations and their sub-categories (cont.).

ORDINAL RELATIONS

Conditional State	Attitude
	Energy
Comparative Degree	Size
	Duration
	Identical
	Similar, Analogous
	Dissimilar
Positional	Figurative
	Spatial
	Temporal
	Toward
	At
	Any

APPENDIX 6:

SYNTAX, SEMANTICS, AND GRAMMAR

Grammarians distinguish between syntax and semantics, terms which have become confusing through different uses by various communities. Traditionally, the study of language consisted of three parts (trivium), namely, grammar (structure); dialectic (logic), and rhetoric (effects). This was complemented by four scientific parts (quadrivium), namely, geometry, arithmetic, music, and astronomy. Together these made up the seven liberal arts.[1] The last decade has seen the beginnings of electronic equivalents for each of the liberal arts (Table 41).

In the trivium, grammar provided the structure of language or its syntax. Dialectics provided the logic underlying that structure and implicitly its meaning or semantics. Semantics is a modern term. According to the Oxford English Dictionary, "semantics" was first defined by Martineau (1887)[2] as: "that branch of philology which deals with the meanings of words, sense development and the like."[3] Bloomfield (1895)[4] defined semantics as "relating to signification or meaning."[5] A first book in English on the subject was published by Michel Bréal (1900).[6]

With the rise of linguistics, a distinction arose between syntax (i.e., structure) and semantics (i.e., meaning). In the twentieth century, computer science redefined these terms. Computer syntax deals with format, i.e., the spelling of language components and the rules controlling how components are combined.[7] Computer semantics deals with the "meaning" of an instruction.[8] In a slightly different formulation, syntax "specifies the domain of all legal programs" and semantics "specifies the behaviour of all legal programs." In this approach, computer syntax is the computer language or code, and computer semantics relates to the actions, which the code sets in motion. Note how this formulation reduces meaning to action. The Dublin Core group has their own definition of these terms. For instance, Stuart Weibel has made the following distinctions:

TABLE 67 IBM's vision of a business solution given by Robert Sutor at WWW10 (Hong Kong, May 2001).

Service Negotiation	TPA/??
Publishing and Discovery	UDDI
Workflow	WSFL/XLANG/??
Service Disciplines	UDDI, WSDL/WSCL
Transactions/Reliability	??
Message Protocol	SOAP/XML
Transport	HTTP, FTP, SMTP, MQ
Network	Internet/Intranet

Semantic Interoperability	Content Description Standard (DC, AACC2, TEI, FGDC)
Structural	" " RDF (a data model for specifying semantic schemas)
Syntactic	" " XML (a markup idiom for structured data on the web).[9]

At EVA Moscow, 2000, Carl Lagoze made the following distinctions:

Semantics meaning of elements
Structure human readable, machine parseable
Syntax grammars to convey semantics and structure.

While Tim Berners-Lee and the W3 Consortium clearly see XML and RDF as fully complementary, some interpreters perceive a tension between 1) an academic framework favouring RDF and 2) commercial contexts favouring a) XML, b) Universal Description Discovery and Integration of Business for the Web (UDDI),[10] c) Web Services Description Language (WSDL), d) XML plus EDI (eXtensible Markup Language and Electronic Data Interchange)[11] and e) Simple Object Access Protocol (SOAP).[12] Amit Sheth, who holds this view, has a fourfold hierarchy of system, syntax, structure, and semantics.[13] He is also involved in Infoharness and Infoquilt projects, which emphasize semantic interoperability.[14] Meanwhile, IBM emphasizes ebXML, OASIS, and CEFACT. IBM has forums on web services technical and web services business. In a keynote at the WWW10 conference in Hong Kong (May 2001), Robert Sutor outlined a vision where service negotiation might be carried out by a Third Party Administrator (TPA); publishing and discovery by Universal Description Discovery and Integration of Business for the Web (UDDI); workflow probably by Work Services Flow Language (WSFL) and a Microsoft extension of Web Service Definition Language (XLANG); service disciplines by UDDI, WSDL and Web Services Conversation Language (WSCL); message protocol by SOAP and XML and transport by a combination of HyperText Transfer Protocol (HTTP); File Transfer Protocol (FTP) Simple Mail Transfer Protocol (SMTP) and Message Queuing (MQ). (Table 67).[15]

TABLE 68A   Distinctions between semantic and syntactic, according to Moran (1981)[23]

Conceptual Component | Task Level
                         | Semantic Level

Communication Component | Syntactic Level
                            | Interaction Level

Physical Component | Spatial Layout Level
                       | Device Level

	LEXICAL	SYNTACTIC	SEMANTIC	
User	Presentation	Dialogue Gudiance	Application Guidance	Application Direct graphic input

TABLE 68B   Distinctions between semantic and syntactic, according to the Seeheim (Conference) model (1985)[24]

Task Level
Goal Level
Semantic Level
Syntactic Level
Lexical Level
Physical Level

TABLE 68C   Distinctions between semantic and syntactic in Geert de Haan's Extended Task Action Grammar (2000)[25]

Task Level
Semantic Level | User Virtual Machine
                   | Dictionary of Basic Tasks
Syntactic Level | Specification Level
                    | Reference Level
Interaction Level | Lexical Level
                      | Keystroke Level
Spatial Layout Level
Device Level

TABLE 68D   Definitions of syntax and semantics from the viewpoint of a number of disciplines.

SYNTAX	SEMANTICS	DISCIPLINE
Structure	Meaning	Grammar, Philology, Linguistics
Meaningful Structure	Interpretation	Knowledge Organization
Code	Interpretant	Semiotics, Mechatronics
Communication	Conceptual	Human Computer Interaction

Since then, Universal Business Language (UBL) has emerged. So too have a series of experiments with Radio Frequency Identification (RFIDs),[1] which are linking up with Electronic Product Code (EPC) and Universal Product Code (UPC), and a Product Markup Language (PML),[17] all of which raises new questions about privacy as ability to follow objects throughout the entire supply chain improves. There are related experiments with Auto-ID which aims to synchronize material and information flows.

In the larger vision of Tim Berners-Lee, presented at WWW10 (Hong Kong, May 2001),[18] there is no tension between the academic framework and the business framework. Both have as their starting point the semantic web. The academic side begins with process via agents, trust, security, logic, proof, query service, rule/query language, XML encryption, web classification, and XML. The business side entails a) app(lications)2app(lications), which model actual business practices through UDDI and e-business eXtensible Markup Language (ebXML) and b) Inter business activities, which are XML protocol enhanced, such as Reliable Messaging, Rooting, Services, Privacy, Security, Quality of Service, and Binary attachments.

To complicate matters, the Human Computer Interface (HCI) community has its own definitions of these terms. For example, Moran (1981)[19] in his Command Language Grammar distinguished between three components: 1) conceptual, with which he linked the semantic level, 2) communication, with which he linked the syntactic level, and 3) a physical component (Table 68a). Slightly different distinctions between the lexical, syntactic, and the semantic were proposed in the Seeheim (Conference) model (1985).[20] Nielsen (1986)[21] proposed six levels of abstraction in the knowledge of computer users: 1) task, 2) goal, 3) semantic, 4) syntactic, 5) lexical, and 6) physical. More recently, Geert de Haan, in his Extended Task Action Grammar has suggested a refinement.

Others have treated semantics as if it were synonymous with metadata. Bipin C. Desai (Concordia University), for instance, has developed the Cindi system, an "indexing system called semantic header for 'document like' Internet resources. The semantic header contains the meta-information for each 'publicly' accessible resource on the Internet."[22] This use of the word "semantic" is spreading to the developers of the Dublin Core, who now describe their basic categories as "semantic units." More recently, there is a trend to recognize that the fifteen categories of the Dublin Core are simply too limited. This has led to efforts to use the MARC records as an entry point into more complex meaning structures, e.g. the MarcOnt and the related JeromeDL projects.

Part of the debate turns on whether one sees new meaning in terms of concept systems (*Begriffsystem*, e.g., Wüster) or prepositional logic (*Aussagesystem*, e.g., Dahlberg). If one accepts concept systems, then one believes that meaning can be reduced to isolated concepts, terms, and fields. If one accepts prepositional logic, one looks for meaning in the context of claims that can be tested and verified or refuted. The United States has tended to opt for concept systems usually out of

TABLE 69 Kinds of semantic methods, according to Feigenbaum (1989)[26]

REFERENTIAL	Relations of symbols to objects
	Reference
	Intensional
	Denotational
COGNITIVE	Systematic ways subject matter is computationally represented and how reasoning processes are sanctioned
	Truth
	Proof
	Operational
	Reasoning Control
	Interface
SOCIAL	Ways agents use symbol in information
	Action

TABLE 70 Six types of semantic interoperability according to Gerhard Budin, Vienna.

1 Mapping based on conceptual specifications
   (conceptual relations in hierarchies)
2 XML-based approaches
3 SQL-based approaches
4 RDF-based approaches
5 Schema based approaches
6 Description Logic based approaches

pragmatic considerations and often in the absence of an awareness that there was a debate concerning an alternative. Hence, in United States, semantics is typically assumed to lie in individual categories such as creator. In Europe, semantics and in some cases even syntax, arises from the meaningful arrangement of such terms in the form of statements. There is thus a whole range of definitions (Table 68).

Some see an even greater diversity. For instance, Feigenbaum distinguishes between twelve kinds of semantic knowledge (Table 69). A German firm called Readware GMBH (Munich), founded by Hans Heinz Wilcke, claims to achieve semantic classification (*Semantisches Klassifizieren*) automatically.[27] Alexxes Software has developed a Vocabulary Navigator, which claims to be a Conceptual thesaurus and calls synonym sets "semantic domains."[28] Doug Lenat, who favoured Common Sense Knowledge, has developed a notion of concept maps,[29] which has led to a fashion for concept mapping.[30] Meanwhile, Ralf Hauber (Linz) has been working on conceptual bookmarks.[31] Others speak of Concept and Document spaces.[32]

The latest developments of the W3 Consortium's Resource Description Format (RDF) entail four levels, namely:

Morphological: A morpheme is the smallest part of a word that can carry a discrete meaning. Morphological analysis works with words at this level. Typically, a natural-language processor knows how to understand multiple forms of a word: its plural and singular, for example.

Syntactic: At this level, natural-language processors focus on structural information and relationships.

Semantic: Natural-language processors derive an absolute (dictionary definition) meaning from context.

Pragmatic: Natural-language processors derive knowledge from external commonsense information.[33]

This is being linked with a Natural language Processing software called Thought Treasure,[34] developed by Erik T. Mueller (IBM, Watson).

Yet another set of definitions for "syntax" and "semantics" is being explored in the context of the I-MASS Project. "Syntax" is defined (Budin) as the challenge of how to link the elements and thus becomes an issue of markup languages. "Semantics" is defined as the meanings of terms and expressions. Hence semantic interoperability is "the ability of information systems to exchange information on the basis of shared, pre-established, and negotiated meanings of terms and expressions" and is needed in order to make other types of interoperability work (syntactic, cross-cultural, international, etc.).[35] As we have shown, there can be semantic meaning at the local, regional, national, and international levels. A challenge thus lies in bridging these levels and making users aware which alternatives exist in any given case. Budin has identified six methods for semantic interoperability (Table 70). Some of these were explored in I-MASS Project. Meanwhile, some recent work is focussing on emergent semantics.[36]

The preliminary work of the Accès Multilingue au Patrimoine (AMP) consortium suggests that more subtle approaches are needed for semantics in a multilingual context.[37] As we have already suggested, a top-down approach imposing standards through authority files is not the answer. Authority files with variants that reflect differences at the local, regional, national, and international levels offer a model that is bottom-up and introduce the need for reference rooms that map and bridge between distributed repositories.

For centuries, there has been a rhetoric that we can a) hope to find a "lingua franca" and b) translate easily between different languages. We have suggested why both of these quests are illusory. Simple terms, actions and instructions can, of course, be translated. But the real challenge for a semantic web, and indeed all efforts to maximize the potentials of the Internet, is not simply about conveying obvious meanings. The challenge is: how do we recognize the meanings, the different turns of mind, the different approaches, and even different worldviews of our fellow humans? Equations are easy. Learning to respect non-equations, learning to tolerate difference and foster cultural diversity while promoting harmonious communities, is an ongoing long-term challenge. For this we need to study both the underlying symbols that we share and the multiple dimensions whereby we define differences with which we create our identities.

APPENDIX 7:

INTERNATIONAL DEVELOPMENTS

All over the world, individuals have caught glimpses of what is becoming possible. In this context, four organizations deserve particular mention, namely, 1) the International Standards Organization (ISO), 2) the Internet Society (ISOC), 3) the World Wide Web (W3) Consortium, and 4) the Dublin Core. Meanwhile, a series of international initiatives are bringing together key players from memory institutions and industry.

1) International Standards Organization (ISO)
The International Standards Organization (ISO) plays a fundamental role for at least three reasons. First, it sets an international framework for high-level theory. In our context, two Technical Committees (TCs) are crucial. TC 37, mentioned earlier (Appendix 2.6), defines standards for terminology world-wide. TC 46 deals with information and documentation. Subcommittee 9 works on presentation, identification, and description of documents (ISO/TC 46 /SC 9).[1] Meanwhile, ISO/IEC JTC 1/SC 32 has developed a Specification and Standardization of Data Elements (ISO 11179 Parts 1–6).[2] This includes (Part 3) a Metadata Registry Specification,[3] which describes the standardizing and registering of data elements to make data understandable and shareable, especially classification schemes, alternate names, and associations.[4] ISO is also working on a Basic Semantics Register (BSR),[5] which has grown out of an earlier UN project on a Basic Semantic Repository (BSR) linked with EDIFACT.

A second reason why ISO is crucial is because it brings together the global organizations and federations, players who understand why such standards are a necessity, representing the needs of libraries (IFLA), museums (ICOM), music industry (IFPI), etc. Third, ISO links with all the national standards organizations throughout the world, which often adapt aspects of their high-level theory for their own ends. Details of ISO's role will be mentioned below.

2) Internet Society: Domain Names
In a sense, the high-level domain names offer an obvious point of departure for future search strategies. The initial categories such as com, edu, and org were created at a time

when the Internet was almost solely a U.S. phenomenon and there was no need for it to include a country name. As we have seen, this is changing rapidly. In a world where the United States represents approximately 4 per cent of global population, a day will come when it makes eminent sense for the U.S. minority to retain its visibility through its own country name. The European desire to have an eu extension is leading to a gradual identification by continent as well as by country. In time, the com and org without a country suffix might be reserved exclusively for the relatively small number of organizations that literally operate on all five continents.

Initially there was a great race, on the part of companies especially, to have domain names that reflect their companies directly. This is completely understandable. It allows me to type "www.ibm.com" without even needing to think what the address of that company might be. In the case of International Business Machines, most of us have a good idea of what they are about.

Many smaller companies, however, often have exciting names such as Aventis, Excalibur, or Stratix, which reveal nothing about what they do. In such cases it makes sense to continue the direct address approach as in "www.aventis.com" and combine this with a series of subject headings that describe what the company is about, e.g., telecommunications, computer switches, or fibre optics. In cases where the activities of a company, organization, or individual can be summarized in a single subject, this term can be included in the domain name part of the URL (i.e., the http part of the address). In cases where multiple subject headings are needed, supplementary terms could be relegated to the metadata section of the HTML header.

These subjects should be part of a controlled authority list. This can be classed according to principles of terminology indicated earlier and mapped to existing classification systems in memory institutions. Thus, the same instrument that helps us find new materials on the Internet is coordinated with searches for materials in memory institutions.

Again a scenario: I have a reference to company X. It is active in mechatronics, but I have no idea what that is. The contextualizer goes to a virtual reference room and obtains a good dictionary definition. Now I can judge more accurately whether the description on the company's web site is sound or merely hype. With such links between domain names, subjects, and classification systems, search engines will be much more efficient because they provide context concerning the subject searched, whether, for instance, we want Salem, the German school founded by Kurt Hahn; the cigarette, the U.S. city, or the biblical town.[6]

3) World Wide Web: Resource Description Framework (RDF)

In 1987, Ramanathan V. Guha began working as a student, part-time at Cycorp, where he remained for seven years. In 1995, Guha, then at Apple, wrote the Meta Content Framework (MCF) and Project X, a browser plug-in that Apple turned into a web navigation system called HotSauce. In 1997, Guha went to Netscape, met consultant Tim Bray, who was working on XML, and decided to turn MCF into an XML application. This was one of the sources for the Resource Description Framework (RDF). In June, 1998, Tim Bray wrote an article on RDF and Metadata[7] in which he outlined an hypothetical Grand Organizing Directorate (at www.GOD.org).

Meanwhile, by July 1997 Ralph Swick and Eric Miller gave a lecture on RDF in the context of W3C[8] This led to an RDF Model and Syntax Specification Working Draft (2 October 1997).[9] "RDF is designed to provide an infrastructure to support metadata across a variety of web-based activities."[10]

Tim Berners-Lee outlined his vision of a global reasoning web at WWW7 (Brisbane, 1998), a theme which he developed at WWW8 (Toronto, 1999), where he spoke of a semantic web.[11] The web, he noted, began as a method for individuals to communicate with each other. It is rapidly becoming also an instrument whereby machines can "communicate" with each other without human intervention. This requires separating rhyme from reason: separating those aspects that are subjective expressions of individuals (poetry, theatre, literature) from objective logical claims (logical principles, mathematical formulae, scientific laws, etc.). His vision of a semantic web sets out from the premise that all logical claims can be tested by first-order predicate logic. How can this be achieved?[12] Everyone putting things on the web is invited to identify the truth standard of their materials. Those making false claims are then subject to legal challenges. Those who avoid stating their status are by their omission implicitly suggesting that their claims are not as transparent as they would have us believe.

The vision of a semantic web is based on a Resource Description Framework (RDF), which is a format, evolving into a language for metadata in order to describe or express anything. In this vision, the Standard Generalized Markup Language (SGML) of the 1960s is being complemented by a simpler Extensible Markup Language (XML),[14] which has statements consisting of a noun, verb, and object, as in traditional grammar. The statement is linked with a logic formula, which can be quantified, negated, or linked by a conjunction. The noun, verb, and object are linked with a Universal Resource Indicator (URI, Figure 22). The Resource Description Framework (RDF) is a noble goal, which will decrease the gap between approaches in linguistics and computer science noted elsewhere (Appendix 2).

The larger picture of RDF also includes Scalable Vector Graphics (SVG), eXtensible Style Language (XSL), and Extended Links (X Links). Readers are referred to the W3 Consortium's extensive web site for more details.[15] Essentially, RDF addresses the challenge of how we deal with existing knowledge as it is put on the web. It also offers a better strategy for finding things by aiming to make each header self-describing in terms of its contents and its quality.

In terms of our threefold distinction between reference, contents, and interpretation, the Resource Description Framework (RDF) presently focusses on reference, and especially on resource finding. At the same time, XML and XSL provide new methods for dealing with content. RDF is closely linked with the Dublin Core initiative and so there is already a basis for links with memory institutions.

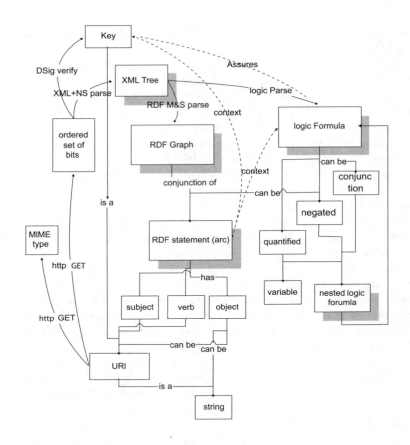

Figure 22 Road map for the Semantic Web by Tim Berners-Lee.[13]

4) Dublin Core

Through the Dublin Core, RDF is working with digital libraries projects. The Dublin Core supported by the OnLine Computer Centre (OCLC) has the great advantage that it is linked with over 26,000 member libraries in the world. In 1994, the Dublin Core set out to define "a simple set of tags for ordinary people to describe their Web pages," a minimal number of categories for description of new materials on the web by persons without the time or the discipline of professional librarians who rely on traditional fields such as those in MARC, etc. This led to fifteen basic fields in noun form (Table 71).

In 1997, it was decided that the Dublin Core needed "formal expression in a Resource Description Framework." Since then, the Dublin Core has become part of a series of levels of metadata (Table 81).[16] It serves as a broker to be a resource finding

TABLE 71 The fifteen basic fields of the Dublin Core in noun form are part of the resource finding aids.

Creator	Title	Subject
Contributor	Date	Description
Publisher	Type	Format
Coverage	Rights	Relation
Source	Language	Identifier

aid in the manner of a searchlight. The Open Archives Initiative (OAI, founded in 1999)[17] has been working closely with the Dublin Core. It offers a simpler and less sophisticated entry to databases than the Z39.50 protocol.

In the context of the Resource Description Framework (RDF), the fifteen basic nouns of Dublin Core are complemented by simple relations (namely abstraction and partition relations) through verbs (i.e., *is a* and *has a*). This leads to a simplified form of language, which Thomas Baker appropriately calls a pidgin language. When the terms syntax, semantics, and grammar are applied to this simplified language, something else is meant than what Dahlberg or classical grammarians would mean by language. In terms of Perreault's relations (Appendix 5), the Dublin Core addresses only the most elementary aspects of subsumptive relations (namely aspects of abstraction and partition) without attention to determinative or ordinal relations. In terms of our levels of knowledge approach (Figure 16), even in its extended form, the Dublin Core focusses on level 1 and 4 with potential links to levels 5 and 6.

Through the European Commission's Schemas project,[18] this broker can be linked with a variety of subject headings and classification schemes, to different kinds of resource descriptions (e.g., catalogue and database fields), and ultimately to content description (SGML, XML, etc.). The Schemas project focusses on links between levels 5 and 6.

Through the ABC[19] project, the scope of the basic Dublin Core nouns is extended further to include some event-based descriptions, some first approaches to space and time, i.e., some aspects of ordinal relations in Perreault's approach. This permits basic description of who performed a concert of a given piece of music by a certain composer. The preliminary classes allow one to go further (Table 72). Even so, the RDF-Dublin Core still 1) deals almost exclusively with contemporary catalogues with effectively no attention to historical or cultural dimensions of the field, and 2) focusses on translating static knowledge into electronic form, i.e., thus retaining the limitations of print media in digital form. ABC thus also focuses on levels 4 and 5.

Ontologies have become a major research field, e.g., SCHEMAS,[20] an Esprit project called Information and Knowledge Fusion (IKF),[21] IBROW (an Intelligent Brokering Service for Knowledge-Component Reuse on the World-Wide Web),[22]

TABLE 72 Preliminary class hierarchies in the ABC project.

Resource
Creation
Concept
Expression
Manifestation
Item
Property
Attribute
Relation
Event
Contribution
Agent
Role
Context
Time
Place
Non-Event-based Relation
Reference and Contextual Relation
Structural Relation

TABLE 73 Basic layers in the Semantic Web in tabular form.

Services	DAML-S		
Trust			
Proof			
Logic	DAML-L		
Ontology Vocabulary	DAML+	OIL	Tractable Inference
Semantics	RDF +	RDF Schema	Implicit Statements
Syntax	XML +	Name Spaces (NS) +	XML Schema
Basis	Unicode +	URI	

the Advanced Knowledge Technologies (AKT) Consortium,[23] and the European Network of Excellence in Human Language Technologies (ELSNET).[24] Some of these projects are particularly focussed on business, e.g., Multilingual Knowledge Based European Electronic Market place (MKBEEM),[25] Corporate Memory Management through Agents (CoMMA).[26]

Compatible with the RDF Schemas project are two initiatives for the interchange of ontologies, namely, Ontology Interface Layer (OIL) and eXtensible Ontology Language, which are part of Onto-Knowledge Web (or Onto Web) led by Dieter Fensel (now DERI, Galway).[27] OIL is working together with an American project, DARPA Agent Modelling Language (DAML),[28] which together have become another important layer in the model of a semantic web.

Parallel with these are initiatives regarding terminology interchange, notably: ISO 12200, Terminology Markup Framework (TMF), and Standards-based Access service to multilingual Lexicons and Terminologies (SALT), which entails an XML-based lex/term-data interchange format combining MARTIF and OLIF, called XLT (hence SALT-XLT).[29] A recent project, Contemporary Culture Virtual Archives in XML (COVAX), aims at distributed cross-domain search based on XML metadata.[30]

Converging Initiatives

In addition to the above institutions, a number of initiatives have led towards a new convergence. The vision of the eleven G7 pilot projects (1995) pointed a way towards a global approach. At the European level, the European Commission's Memorandum of Understanding (MoU) for Multimedia Access to Europe's Cultural Heritage sig-nalled a coherent approach to memory institutions, linking the efforts of libraries, museums, and archives. This approach became a part of the formal plans underlying the 5th Framework. A recent Digital Heritage Support Actions Concertation Event organized by DG Information Society, Cultural Heritage Applications unit (Vienna, June 2001),[31] provided a good survey of a number of these projects.

Within this context, there have also been many preliminary steps towards integration: the MEDICI Framework,[32] and the EXPLOIT[33] and CULTIVATE[34] programs. Organizations such as the Consortium for the Interchange of Museum Information (CIMI), the Istituto Centrale per il Catologo e la Documentazione (ICCD, Italy), the Réunion des Musées Nationaux (RMN, France), European Museum Information Institute (EMII, Britain), and the former Deutsche Bibliothek (Germany) have all played a role. As noted earlier, the efforts of the Council of Europe at the European level and ICOM and UNESCO at the world level are increasingly significant in this context.[35] From all this emerges a new vision of different layers of metadata which link: a) transfer protocols, b) resource numbering, c) rights management, d) re-source finding aids, e) resource finding tools, f) resource description, g) content description, h) style description and i) other senses.

a) Transfer Protocols

In the 1980s, the United Nations became involved in Electronic Data Interchange (EDI). This led in 1990 to the establishment of Electronic Data Interchange For Administration, Commerce and Transport (EDIFACT).[36] The EDI/EDIFACT are both description and transfer protocols and are extremely rich, but are generally seen as too complex to use in their entirety. As a result, companies in various sectors often adapt subsets for their own purposes. There is also a trend to look to XML as an alternative to EDIFACT. The past years have seen an important initiative through a joint effort of the United Nations Centre for Trade Facilitation and Electronic Business (UN/CEFACT) and the Organization for the Advancement of Structured Information Standards (OASIS)[37] to produce an ebusiness eXtensible Markup Language (ebXML).[38]

ebXML[39] is but one of a number of business-oriented alternatives, which include Commerce eXtensible Markup Language (cXML),[40] eXtensible business Reporting Language (XBRL),[41] eCommerce (eCo) of Commerce Net,[42] the BizTAlk Framework

TABLE 74 Five basic international standards from memory institutions.

International Standard Book Number	(ISBN)[48]
International Standard Serial Number	(ISSN)[49]
International Standard Music Number	(ISMN)[50]
International Standard Recording Code	(ISRC)[51]
International Standard Technical Report Number	(ISRN)[52]

TABLE 75 Six claims to uniqueness by the ISRC

1	reliable, international identification system
2	tool for the purpose of rights administration
3	useful identification tool in the electronic distribution of music
4	compatible with standards developed in the field of consumer electronics
5	Readable by hardware already used in the recording industry
6	cost-effective without requiring special investment in equipment or technologies.[54]

Specification of Biz/Talk,[43] the Partner Interface Processes (PIPs) of Rosetta Net,[44] the Open Buying on the Internet (OBI)[45] of Openbuy, and Universal Description Discovery and Integration (UDDI) of Business for the Web.[46] Important in this context is an MoU between ISO, IEC, ITU, and UN/ECE on electronic business. Within the Internet, the best-known protocols are the HyperText Transfer Protocol (http) and the File Transfer Protocol (ftp). In the library world and increasingly the museum world (thanks to the CIMI initiative), the Z.39.50 protocol linked with the Bath Profile has become the standard method. Meanwhile, the industry has developed its own protocols. For instance, the Digital Media Communication System (DCMS), which was developed as an European Commission project, MUSE, in the ESPRIT program, set out to define a basic product envelope for physical objects.[47]

b) Resource Numbering

A first stage in identifying objects is to give them a unique number such that they can be found. Here the International Federation of Library Associations (IFLA) has played a central role by offering Functional Requirements for Bibliographic Records (FRBR)[53] and lists five basic international standards (Table 74). The ISRC, which is administered by an agency within the International Federation of Phonographic Industry (IFPI), is more than a numbering scheme. It identifies individual sound recordings (such as make up the music tracks on CDs) automatically to identify them for royalty payments and makes six claims to uniqueness (Table 75).

Meanwhile, the American National Standards Institute (ANSI/NISO) has created its own variant of an ISSN called ANSI/NISO Z39.56-1996 or Serial Item and Contribution Identifier (SICI).[55] This "has recently been significantly revised to make it more suitable

TABLE 76 Three new standards of the ISO.[62]

ISTC	International Standard Textual Work Code provides a way for textual works to be uniquely distinguished from one another within computer applications and for the purposes of administering rights to such works.
ISWC	International Standard Musical Work Code identifies the musical composition itself, rather than the printed or recorded expression of the work
ISAN	International Standard Audiovisual Number identifies individual audiovisual works such as film or television programs in a similar fashion to the ISRC.

for use at the contribution level in EDI [Electronic Data Interchange], EToCS [Electronic Tables of Contents for Serials] and as a component of Internet developments (URN)."[56]

ANSI/NISO has produced an adaptation of this serials identifier for the book world, called Book Item and Component Identifier (BICI):[57] "The code can be used to identify a part, a chapter or a section within a chapter, or any other text component, such as an introduction, foreword, afterword, bibliography, index, etc. It can also identify an entry or article in a directory, encyclopedia or similar work which is not structured into chapters; an illustration, map, figure, table or other piece of non-textual content which is physically part of the item, or an enclosure which is supplied with but is not physically part of the item."[58] In terms of the levels of knowledge, SICI and BICI thus involve not just level 1 (terms) but also level 5 (partial contents).

In the commercial world, the Publisher Item Identifier (PII) was developed by an informal group of Scientific and Technical Information publishers "as an identifier for internal use and exchange between consortia partners. It was closely modelled on the Elsevier Standard Serial Document Identifier and the ADONIS number, both of which it has now replaced." The American Universal Parcel Code (UPC), together with the European Article Numbering (EAN), form the basis for Bar Code 1. With respect to publishing, the EAN is based on ISBN and ISSN numbering system. An initiative from the publishing industry, the Digital Object Identifier (DOI) is "both an identifier and a routing system" and is attempting to position itself as the integrator of all these initiatives.

c) Rights Management:

The Internet has introduced two further developments: 1) the advent of purely digital materials introduces the need for description principles for this new category; 2) the existence of materials in an on-line environment potentially accessible by persons everywhere raises many questions of copyright and rights management. In this context, the ISO is working on three new standards (Table 76).

TABLE 77 Three basic kinds of Internet domain names.[70]

URL	Uniform Resource Locators
URN	Uniform Resource Name
URI	Uniform or Universal Resource Identifiers

Building on the work of ISO, the International Confederation of Societies of Authors and Composers (Confédération Internationale des Sociétés d'Auteurs et de Compositeurs, CISAC) is working on a Common Information System (CIS).[59] This will integrate 1) ISO ISWC, 2) ISO ISAN, and 3) a Works Information Database (WID) and 4) will extend their Compositeur, Auteur, Editeur number (CAE)[60] and rename it Interested Party (IP) number, which will be stored in a Global and Interested Parties Database. CISAC and the Association of International Collective Management of Audiovisual Works (Association de Gestion Internationale Collective des Oeuvres Audiovisuelles, AGICOA)[61] are working on ISAN.

These standards are still in progress. Meanwhile, the Society of Motion Picture and Television Engineers (SMPTE) have produced a Unique Media Identifier (UMID) and are working on a Universal Program Identifier (UPID), which will go beyond ISAN.

The publishing industry, basing its work on EDI/EDIFACT, and working with the American Association of Publishers (AAP) via Editeur has produced an EDItEUR Product Information Communication Standards (EPICS) data dictionary: "to define the content of a set of data elements which can be used potentially in a variety of carrier formats for the communication of book trade product information between computer systems." Editeur and partners have taken a subset of EPICS to create an Online Information eXchange (ONIX) International, which: "is the international standard for representing and communicating book industry product information in electronic form, incorporating the core content which has been specified in national initiatives such as BIC Basic and AAP's ONIX Version 1."

A second major initiative, Publishing Requirements for Industry Standard Metadata (PRISM), began as a report submitted by Zach Coffin (KPMG Consulting).[63] PRISM is now supported by an alliance, which includes Adobe, Getty Images, and Time. PRISM: "defines an XML metadata vocabulary for syndicating, aggregating, post-processing and multi-purposing magazine, news, catalogue, book, and mainstream journal content. PRISM provides a framework for the interchange and preservation of content and metadata, a collection of elements to describe that content, and a set of controlled vocabularies listing the values for those elements."[64] PRISM is a metadata vocabulary which focusses on describing content, how it may be reused, and its relationship to other resources. The International Press Telecommunications Council (IPTC) is responsible for two related initiatives: a) "News Markup Language (NewsML) an emerging standard aimed at the transmission of news stories and the automation of newswire services" and b) "News Industry Text Format (NITF) provides a DTD designed to mark up news stories."

A related initiative by Adobe, Sun, News Internet services was submitted as a W3C note as the Information and Content Exchange [ICE] protocol.[65] This protocol manages and automates syndication relationships, data transfer, and results analysis. PRISM complements the ICE protocol by providing an industry-standard vocabulary to automate content reuse and syndication processes.

A project at Xerox PARC to develop Digital Property Rights Language (DPRL)[66] led to eXtensible Rights Markup Language (XrML), now being developed by ContentGuard, Inc. and "specifies the behavior of trusted digital rights management systems and repositories. PRISM describes the terms and conditions under which people may reuse content, but does not discuss the behavior of trusted repositories or specify how an application sets out to *enforce these rights and permissions*. The treatment of derivative use rights in PRISM is complementary but separate from the rights and uses that are specified in XrML."[67]

This project also has links with the publisher Thomson International.[68] ContentGuard is in turn part of another organization called Reciprocal Digital Clearing Service,[69] which includes other digital services such as Microsoft, InterTrust, Adobe, Preview Systems, and IBM.

Parallel with these primarily North American developments is a European cluster, Interoperability of Data in E-Commerce Systems (INDECS),[71] which has grown out of the European Commission IMPRIMATUR Project. This group favours the Digital Object Identifier of the International Digital Object Identifier Foundation (IDF)[72] and sees this as a potential unifying solution.

In the music field, one of the most significant developments with respect to rights is the Secure Digital Music Initiative (SDMI),[73] which is headed by the Telecom Italia Lab (formerly CSELT) and involves some 180 companies. There is also interesting work at Linz on metadata for enterprise-wide security administration.[74]

While it is heartening to see the development of more robust rights management systems, it is striking that these are being developed almost exclusively by the private sector. Accordingly, the rights of corporations and companies are being ever-more vigorously defended. It would be even more heartening to find new technologies that defend the rights of authors and creators directly and uphold the concept of a public good.

d) Resource Finding Aids

Closely related to the above attempts at numbering are other attempts to develop resource finding aids. Within the context of the Internet, the most obvious of these entail domain names, as discussed above (cf. §2 above). These are of three kinds (Table 77). The development of URLs, URNs and URIs has officially advanced in the context of the IETF and W3Consortium. Meanwhile, organizations such as the American Corporation for National Research Initiatives (CNRI) have developed a Handle system, which "is a comprehensive system for assigning, managing, and resolving persistent identifiers, known as 'handles,' for digital objects and other resources on the Internet. Handles can be used as Uniform Resource Names (URNs)."[75] Another important tool in the Internet context is the metadata provided within HTML headers.[76] A third is provided through the Dublin Core fields.

e) Resource Finding Tools

Traditionally libraries have created metadata tools such as subject headings and classification systems. These can be both general subject headings such as the Library of Congress Subject Headings (LCSH) or specialized headings such as the MEdical Subject Headings (MESH). There are also many classification systems including Library of Congress (LC), Dewey Decimal Classification (DDC), Universal Decimal Classification (UDC), Bliss, Ranganathan, Göttingen, Riders, etc. Samurin[77] has provided the standard reference work in this field.

Commercial equivalents are also appearing such as the Book Industry Communication Standard Subject Categories (BISC).[78] The International Press Telecommunications Council (IPTC) and the Newspaper Association of America (NAA) have produced an Information Interchange Model (IIM) that describes subject codes for a news system in the form of a Subject Reference System.[79] An important development of the past decade is that these subject headings as well as classification systems are increasingly being coupled as intermediate stages in the search process. This has the advantage of allowing us to broaden and narrow our search parameters more systematically.

f) Resource Description

Long before the advent of the Internet, memory institutions (libraries, museums, and archives) also developed metadata in the form of catalogue entries.

Libraries: The best known of the library catalogue schemes is the Machine Readable Cataloguing (MARC) with UNIMARC and its various national variants such as US MARC, CANMARC, and AUSMARC. There are adaptations such as PICA. A German equivalent of MARC is Maschinelles Austauschformat für Bibliotheken (MAB). There are specialized schemes for serials, such as the Niedersächsischer Zeitschriften Nachweis (NZN). An important attempt to align the major systems has been made by Bernhard Eversberg.[80] IFLA has been working on a Universal Bibliographic Control and International MARC Core Programme (UBCIM).[81]

The Library of Congress (LC) has been active and distinguishes between descriptive, administrative, and structural metadata.[82] The LC also distinguishes levels of metadata: 1) set, 2) aggregate, 3) primary object, 4) secondary object, and 5) terminal object. As mentioned earlier, OCLC has headed the Dublin Core initiative. Meanwhile, the Research Libraries Group has been active in trying to bridge materials from various memory institutions, especially through their Cultural Materials project.[83]

Museums: Traditionally many museums have developed their own ad hoc cataloguing rules. Internationally there are a few important developments. The most important of these is the Documentation Group of the International Committee for Documentation

International Council of Museums (Comité Internationale pour la Documentation de l'Art, ICOM-CIDOC),[84] which produced Guidelines for Museum Object Information (GMOI), which has evolved into a Conceptual Reference Model (CRM).[85] This has been submitted to ISO TC 46. This is of fundamental importance not least because it builds on a series of European projects relating to museums, including the French projects, Remote Access to Museum Archives (RAMA),[86] Remote access to European cultural heritage information (AQUARELLE),[87] and now MESMUSES.[88] In the context of Africa, ICOM through AFRICOM has produced an important *Manuel des Normes.*[89] There are also commercial firms.[90]

The French Ministry of Culture has made available a number of important databases on art and archaeology, including *Joconde* and *Mérimée.*[91] France has also developed an *Inventaire général des monuments et richesses artistiques de la France*[92] and a *Méthode d'inventaire informatique des objets: beaux arts et arts décoratifs.* They have worked together with the Canadian Heritage Information Network (CHIN) to create an important catalogue of religious objects.[93] They were also instrumental in an important database of art called Network of Art Research Computer Image SystemS in Europe (NARCISSE)[94] as part of an European Commission (EC) project. Another EC project is focussed on collections in London (de Witt) and the Hague (RKD), namely, the Visual Arts Network for the Exchange of Cultural Knowledge (VAN EYCK) project.[95] The Getty Trust, through its Art Information Task Force (AITF) has produced Categories for the Description of Works of Art (CDWA).[96] It has also produced an important set of mappings between systems, which they call "crosswalks" (see Mapping Tools, below).

There are a number of other important reference points for museum collections, such as CHIN's databases,[97] the Museum Documentation Association (MDA), which has produced Spectrum[98] and is involved in TERM IT.[99] There is also the Marburg Archive's MIDAS.[100] Russia has developed a Unified Passport for Museum Objects and a format for Internet objects, Russia Internet: Minimum Information Categories for Museum Objects (RIMICMO).[101] The Italian Company SCALA has its own art categories for its catalogue.[102] In the United States, the National Initiative for Networked Cultural Heritage (NINCH) has been developing an International Database of Digital Humanities Projects.[103] IFLA/ UNESCO have done a Survey on Digitization and Preservation (1999).[104]

Archives: In the archival field, the most important norms are: a) the General International Standard Archival Description (ISAD(G),[105] and b) International Standard Archival Authority Records (ISAAR) with its headings for Corporate Bodies, Persons, Families (CPF).[106] In the United States, the Encoded Archival Description Document Type Definition (EAD DTD)[107] is the most important method at present.

Education: Yet another set of players comes from the realm of education. In the United States, the IEEE has formed a Learning Technology Standards Committee (LTSC, namely, IEEE P1484.12), which has developed a Learning Object Model (LOM)[108] that is becoming linked with the military's Shareable Content Object Reference Model (SCORM).[109] The IEEE is part of a much larger initiative called the Instructional Management Systems (IMS) project, with academic, industry,

TABLE 78 Four initiatives towards multimedia convergence.[122]

1	CEN Metadata for Multimedia Information Framework	CEN MMIF
2	IEC ITA Open Platform for Initiative for Multimedia Access	OPIMA
3	ISO/IEC 14496-6 Delivery Multimedia Integration Framework	DMIF
4	ITU SG 16 Framework for Multimedia Standardization	Medicomm 2004

TABLE 79 Eleven content applications of the MPEG 21 standard.[128]

1	Creation
2	Production
3	Distribution
4	Consumption and usage
5	Representation
6	Identification and protection
7	Intellectual property management and protection
8	Financial management
9	User privacy
10	Terminals and network resource abstraction
11	Event reporting.

and government members led by Educom. IMS is working on a Content Packaging Information Model Base Document (CPIMBD).[110] IMS, in conjunction with the Advanced Distributed Learning Co-Lab, is developing a Sharable Courseware Object Reference Model (SCORM).[111] The IMS is also adapting the Computer-Managed Instruction (CMI) of the Aviation Industry Computer-Based Training Committee (AICC) into a standard for education.

While extremely attractive, the IMS initiatives entail two significant dangers. First, they create modules where the emphasis is more on the management of information than on the quality of the content.[112] Second, the IMS reflects a trend whereby the major corporations see e-learning as merely another realm for profit. For instance, it uses commercial tools developed by Sun and Microsoft.[113] This is in direct contrast to a strand within the European Commission that assumes that all educational software should be open source and thus not dependent on purely economic interests.

g) Content Description
Verbal Text: At the level of content description, the standard method for access to verbal texts has been Standard Generalized Markup Language (SGML), which separated form and content. In the book world, this led to the Text Encoding Initiative (TEI),[114] which is linked to a number of implementations, notably the Electronic Text Center in Virginia,[115] the Oxford Text Archive,[116] and a group (CRIBECU) at the Scuola Normale (Pisa),[117] which focusses on applications to historical texts using TRESYS (Text Retrieval System).

Since SGML was too complex for easy use, the W3C has developed eXtensible Markup Language (XML),[118] which serves as a basis for a number of domain-specific

TABLE 80 Four kinds of mappings initiated by the Getty Trust[139]

Dublin Core	to	EAD
USMARC	to	EAD
ISAD (G)	to	EAD
EAD	to	ISAD (G)

applications, including Mathematical Markup Language (MML), Astronomical Markup Language (AML), and Chemical Markup Language (CML). Meanwhile, the news industry has produced News Industry Text Format (NITF).

Visual Still Pictures: In the realm of still pictures, the western standard has been defined by the Joint Picture Expert Group (JPEG), which is leading to JPEG 2000.[119] In Japan, there is an important alternative called Vector Format for Zooming (VFZ or Vzoom),[120] developed by Nissha Co. At the level of two-dimensional (2D) images, the W3C is working on Scalable Vector Graphics (SVG). At the level of three-dimensional images (3D), there has been Virtual Reality Modelling Language (VRML), which has led to a Web3D Consortium that proposes to develop X3D as a standard.[121]

413

Visual Motion Pictures: In the realm of motion pictures, there have been two major sources of standards, the Society for Motion Picture and Television Engineers (SMPTE) in the United States and the Motion Picture Expert Group (MPEG) in Europe. MPEG 4 defined new compression methods. MPEG 7 defined new metadata methods.[123]

Multimedia: With respect to multimedia, there was originally another group: Multimedia Coded Representation of Multimedia and Hypermedia Information (MHEG).[124] There was also Hypermedia/Time-based Structuring Language (HyTime, i.e., ISO/IEC 10744).[125] This led to Standard Music Description Language (SMDL), which provides an architecture for the representation of musical information. Partly because of the dynamism of the MPEG group, the motion picture group has expanded its vision to propose a possible integration of all multimedia formats through a new initiative known as MPEG 21.[126] This is formally linked with the International Standards Organization (ISO/IEC JTC1/SC29/WG11, Coding of Moving Pictures and Audio)[127] but reflects a much larger convergence because there have, for instance, been at least four other important initiatives (Table 78). Meanwhile, the MPEG 21 vision also includes many aspects of content (Table 79).

h. Style Description
As mentioned earlier (chapter 12.3 and 12.8), the methodological breakthrough of SGML was to separate content and form. In the extensible subset, content is covered by XML and form is covered by eXtensible Style language (XSL).

i. Other Senses
Traditionally, multimedia has been limited to vision and sound. In the past decade, there has been increasing attention to touch through force feedback methods.[129]

TABLE 81 Levels of metadata, ranging from resource finding, resource description, and content and style description.[140]

PROBLEM	BODY	SOLUTIONS
a. Transfer Protocols	UN	EDI/EDIFACT
	IETF	HTTP, FTP
	ANSI/NISO	Z.39.50
b. Resource Numbering	IFLA	ISBN, ISSN, ISMN, ISRC, ISRN
	ISO	ISAN, ISWC, ISTC
	ANSI/NISO	SICI (Z.39.56), BICI
	Commercial	PII, UPC, EAN, DOI, INDECS
	Computer	UUID
c. Rights Management	CISAC	CIS (I)SAN, ISWC, WID, CAE=IP
	Publishers	ONIX, EPICS
	SMPTE	UMID, UPID
	UN	CEFACT
	OASIS	ebXML
	Xerox	ContentGuard, XrML (was DPRL)
	KPMG	PRISM
	CSELT	SDMI
d. Resource Finding Aids	IETF	URL, URN, URI, HTML Header
	OCLC	Dublin Core
e. Resource Finding Tools		
General Subject Headings	Library of Congress, etc.	LCSH, BISC, IIM
Domain Specific Subject Headings	Nat'l Library of Medicine	MESH
Classifications	LC, OCLC	LC, Dewey
f. Resource Description	Libraries	MARC
	Museums	CIDOC
	Archives	ISAD (G), EAD
	Education	LOM, SCORM,
g. Content Description		
Verbal General	SGML	SGML, XML, TMF
Verbal Domain Specific		MML, AML, CML, NITF
Visual Still Pictures	JPEG	JPEG 2000, VZoom
Visual 2D	W3	SVG
Visual 3D		X3D
Visual Motion Pictures	MPEG, SMPTE	MPEG 7, SMPTE
Audio Visual	MHEG	MHEG, HyTimeSL, SDML
Multimedia	W3, MPEG	SMIL, MPEG 21
Style Description	W3	XSL
i. Other Senses		Force Feedback
Touch		
Smell		e.g., Digiscent
Taste		e.g., Trisenx

The year 2000 saw the advent of initial examples of on-line smell (FranceTelecom and Digiscent) as well as taste (e.g., Trisenx). As yet, there is no clear vision as to how these might be integrated within multimedia and become part of either our memory institutions or our recorded experience in general.

j. Mapping Tools

If one looks at these efforts as a whole, it is striking that 1) most initiatives have focussed on a single level, as if the other levels did not exist; 2) in terms of levels of knowledge, the work focusses on level one, with some attention to levels four, five, and six. A number of recent initiatives have begun to address this challenge. These are variously called mapping, bridging or, more recently (in American English), crosswalk tools.

Both OCLC and the Library of Congress are working at mapping between DDC and LC and DDC classifications. The important work of Traugott Koch in projects such as Nordic Metadata, DESIRE I and II and more recently RENARDUS has served to map between various classification schemes (level e in Table 81).[130] A mapping or crosswalk has been created to link Online Information eXchange (ONIX) with UNIMARC in order "to lay the ground work for exchange of bibliographic and product data between the library community and the book industry."[131]

Major publishers are developing Cross-Ref. This depends on the use of Digital Object Identifiers (DOI),[132] requires membership in Publishers International Linking Association (PILA),[133] and has links determined by publishers' preferences, for which they pay. Limitations of CrossRef are a) that it primarily links titles of articles with full-text copies and b) subtly shifts metadata efforts into the private sphere. John Erickson (HP) recently claimed that "Metadata is the life-blood of e-commerce."[134] Metadata is ultimately our only hope for public access to information across the board and should therefore not be controlled by private interests alone. Sfx (Ghent University Library) represents a public-domain effort in the same direction as CrossRef.

In the United States, the Getty Trust has produced a useful set of mappings among major American resource description methods, notably: CDWA, VRA, USMARC, Dublin Core, Object ID, FDA Guide, CIMI, and EAD. They have also created four kinds of mappings (Table 80). The XML Metadata Interchange[135] combines features of the W3C's XML with Unified Modeling Language (UML)[136] and Meta Object Facility (MOF),[137] both developed by the OMG.[138]

Standing back, it is possible to discern a fundamental shift in method over the past half-century. In the mid-twentieth century, there was a vision that a single program could achieve everything. This led to solutions such as SGML and EDI/EDIFACT. Both were universal in their scope but so complex that their use was restricted to a handful of experts. This reflected a more general assumption that high-level programming was something for an elite. The new generation of programming sets forth from a very different vision. The XML subset of SGML is compatible with the original vision but is simple enough that it can be used by a great number of others. In this framework, field-specific complexities are dealt with through specialized add-ons such as MML, CML, etc. Or thus the theory. In practice there has been such a proliferation of new markup languages that there is still only as handful of experts able to see the wood for the trees, or more precisely, to see the words for the markup.

It is also possible to discern some very positive trends. As we have noted, there is an increasing interaction (and convergence) between those in the computer world (IETF, W3C), the telecommunications world (ITU, ISO), the business world (e.g., UN EDI/EDIFACT), and various communities within memory institutions and the content world at large (book and music publishing, news, television, etc.). Within the content world, there is increasing interaction among those in different sectors such that those in the phonographic industry are increasingly aware of library, museum, archival, and educational standards.

This again has led to a basic shift in approach. The same mentality that led to SGML and EDI/EDIFACT led to quests for a single cataloguing standard, as if one method would solve everything. The past decades have shown that a single list for description is simply unrealistic. The challenge thus lies in finding bridges between the immense variety of entries via a few common entry points. In retrospect, this may prove to be the fundamental contribution of the Dublin Core. A new challenge lies in creating authority files such that not only the fields but also the names within those fields are standardized and linked with their variants.

The increasing attention by the commercial sector in the realms of education and culture has some obvious benefits, in that it offers the possibility of using standards from private industry for culture and education in the public sector. It also brings inherent dangers. The private sector only publishes information/knowledge that is visibly profitable. Great public institutions function on a completely different principle. Sections of great library and museum collections are often ignored for decades and sometimes for centuries, and yet they inspire new knowledge by having their materials available in the long term.

The standardization[141] and converging trends of the past decades are doing a great deal to integrate many aspects within the levels outlined above but have not provided a systematic linking between the levels. Such linking as exists is still largely in terms of static knowledge. Our concern in this book lies a) in integrating local, regional, national, and international knowledge, and b) in extending this vision by exploring the potentials of dynamic knowledge in order to integrate existing knowledge on the Web (personal, collaborative knowledge in unstable media) with the enormous amounts of enduring knowledge in memory institutions (libraries, museums, and archives) in order to inspire new knowledge in the future.

APPENDIX 8:

FURTHER READING

Further reading follows the plan of the book. Following some background and introductory material, there is literature covering subjects discussed in each of the fifteen chapters. Aside from a few web sites and key articles, this literature focuses on printed books, which are presented under subject headings in chronological order. Corresponding alphabetical author and title lists are available on the CD-ROM. For those who own the book, these multivalent lists are also accessible on the web site. For the moment, newspaper and journal articles are relegated mainly to the footnotes.

Background

Basic Context
Innis, Harold, *The Bias of Communications*, Toronto: University of Toronto Press, 1951.

Havelock, Eric, *Preface to Plato*, Cambridge, MA: Belknap Press, Harvard University Press, 1963.

McLuhan, Marshall, *The Gutenberg Galaxy: The Making of Typographic Man*, Toronto: University of Toronto Press, 1962.

Franklin, Ursula, *The Real World of Technology*, Montreal: CBC Enterprises, 1990. (CBC Massey Lecture Series).

Hauser, Mark D., *The Evolution of Communication*, Cambridge, MA: MIT Press, 1997.

Barck, Karlheinz, ed., and Harold A. Innis, *Kreuzwege der Kommunikation*, Vienna: Springer, 1997.

Understanding (New) Media
McLuhan, Marshall, *Report on Project in Understanding New Media*, Washington: U.S. Office of Education, 1960.

McLuhan, Marshall, *Understanding Media: The Extensions of Man*, New York: McGraw-Hill, 1964, 1965, 1987. Also Grand Rapids: Abacus, 1973. Also London, New York: Routledge, 2001.
Italian edition: *Gli strumenti del comunicare*, traduzione di Ettore Capriolo Milan: Il saggiatore, 1967, 1968, 1971, 1974, 1976, 1977, 1979, 1981, 1986, 1993, 1995, 1997, 1999, 2002. According to ICCU under McLuhan. See: http://opac.sbn.it/cgi-bin/IccuForm.pl?form=WebFrame.
French edition: *Pour comprendre les média: Les prolongements technologiques de l'homme*, Paris: Seuil, 1968, 2nd ed.: 1977. Also: Montreal: Hurtubise HMH, 1968. Reissued in a new edition (Bibliothèque Québécoise, #36) in 1993.

German edition: *Die magischen Kanäle: Understanding Media*, Munich: Egon TB, 1982, 1985, 1996.

New English edition: ed. Lewis H. Lapham, Cambridge, MA: MIT Press, 1994.

Spanish edition: *Comprender los medios de comunicación: Las extensiones del ser humano*, traducción de Patrick Ducher, Barcelona: Paidós Ibérica, 1996.

Dutch edition, *Media Begrijpen*, Amsterdam: Uitgeverij Nieuwezijds, 2002.

New critical edition by Terence Gordon: Gingko Press: Corte Madera, CA, 2003. (Gingko Press is republishing all of McLuhan's major works.)

See: http://www.gingkopress.com/_cata/_mclu/_pubsch.htm.

Compaine, Benjamin, ed., *Understanding New Media: Trends and Issues in Electronic Distribution of Information*, Cambridge, MA: Ballinger, 1984.

Whitehouse, George E., *Understanding the New Technologies of the Mass Media*, Englewood Cliffs, NJ: Prentice Hall, 1986.

Winston, Brian, *Misunderstanding Media*, Cambridge, MA: Harvard University Press, 1986.

Cotton, Bob, and Richard Oliver, *Understanding Hypermedia: From Multimedia to Virtual Reality*, London: Phaidon, 1993.

Fidler, Roger, *Mediamorphosis: Understanding New Media* (*Journalism and Communication for a New Century*), Thousand Oaks, CA: Pine Forge Press, 1997.

Pavlik, John Vernon, *New Media Technology: Cultural and Commercial Perspectives*, Boston: Allyn and Bacon, 1997 (Allyn and Bacon Series in Mass Communication).

Grusin, Richard, and Jay David Bolter, *Remediation: Understanding New Media*, Cambridge, MA: MIT Press, 2000.

Lunenfeld, Peter, ed., *The Digital Dialectic: New Essays on New Media*, Cambridge, MA: MIT Press, 2000. (Leonardo Books). (Cf. a course at Brown University by Professor Darrell West called Understanding Mass Media. See: http://gen.com/course/umm_summary.php)

Basic Reference Books

Monaco, James, *The Dictionary of New Media*, New York: Harbor Electronic Publishing, 1971. New ed.: 1999.

Latham, Roy, *The Dictionary of Computer Graphics Technology and Applications*, New York: Springer, 1991.

Held, Gilbert, *Dictionary of Communications Technology*, Chichester: John Wiley & Sons, 1995.

Hansen, Brad, *The Dictionary of Multimedia Terms and Acronyms*, London: Fitzroy Dearborn, 1997.

Renouard, Horst E. von, *Fachwörterbuch Elektronische Medien und Dienste: Dictionary of Electronic Media and Services*, Berlin: Springer, 1997.

Hoepelman, Jakob, R. Mayer, and J. Wagner, *Elsevier's Dictionary of Information Technology: in English, German, and French*, New York: Elsevier, 1997.

Packer, Randall, and Ken Jordan, eds., *Multimedia: From Wagner to Virtual Reality*, New York: W.W. Norton, 2001.

Lister, Martin, Jon Dovey, Seth Giddings, Iain Grant, and Kieran Kelly (eds.), *New Media: A Critical Introduction*, London: Routledge, 2002.

Introduction

General Books

Beniger, James R., *The Control Revolution. Technological and Economic Origins of the Information Society*, Cambridge, MA: Harvard University Press, 1986.

Webster, Frank, *Theories of the Information Society*, London: Routledge, 1993. 2nd ed. 2003 (The International Library of Sociology).

Scholars such as Castells have provided a masterful survey in the Networked Society.

Castells, Manuel, The Information Age: Economy Society and Culture. Vol. 1: Rise of the Network Society, Malden, MA: Blackwell, 1996; vol. 2: The Power of Identity; vol. 3: End of Millennium, 1998.

Armand Matellart has given a historical context for the role of computers. His importance lies in showing connections between the rise of global media networks and the rise of global claims for knowledge. Among his books:

Matellart, Armand, Mapping World Communication, War, Progress, Culture. Minneapolis: University of Minneapolis Press, 1994.
Matellart, Armand, The Invention of Communication, Minneapolis: University of Minneapolis Press, 1996.
Matellart, Armand, Networking the World, 1794–2000, Minneapolis: University of Minnesota Press, 2000.
Webster, Frank, The Information Society Reader, London: Routledge, 2004.

An excellent introduction from an architect's viewpoint:

Mitchell, William, City of Bits, Cambridge, MA: MIT Press, 1997.
Mitchell, William, E-Topia, Cambridge, MA: MIT Press, 1999.

Among these, the gurus of the field, affectionately known as digerati, have been telling us about the computer revolution for years. See: http://www.edge.org/digerati/.

Negroponte, Nicholas, Being Digital, New York: Knopf, 1995.
Dertouzos, Michael, What Will Be, How the New World of Information will Change our Lives, San Francisco: Harper Edge, 1997.
Dyson, Esther, Release 2.0: A Design for Living in the Digital Age, New York: Broadway Books, 1997.
Jonscher, Charles, The Evolution of Wired Life: From the Alphabet to the Soul-Catcher Chip-How Information Technologies Change Our World, New York: John Wiley & Sons, 1999.
Béra, Michel, and Eric Mechloulan, La Machine Internet, Paris: Odile Jacob, 1999.
Balle, Francis, Médias et sociétés, Paris: Monchrestien, 1999. 9e éd.
Kurzweil, Ray, The Age of Spiritual Machines: When Computer Exceed Human Intelligence, New York: Penguin, 2000.
Jochum, Uwe, Kritik der neuen Medien, Munich: Fink, 2003.

Meanwhile from the business side:

Gates, Bill, The Road Ahead, New York: Penguin, 1996.
Gates, Bill, Business @ the Speed of Thought: Succeeding in the Digital Economy, New York: Warner Books, 1999.

For a critical view of these futurist discussions:

Armytage, W.H.G., Yesterday's Tomorrows: A Historical Survey of Future Societies, London: Routledge & K. Paul, 1968.

Pohl, Frederik, *Yesterday's Tomorrows: Favorite Stories from Forty Years as a Science, Fiction Editor*, New York: Berkeley, 1982.

Wright, Bruce Lanier, *Yesterday's Tomorrows: The Golden Age of Science Fiction Movie Posters, 1950–1964*, Dallas, TX: Taylor Pub. Co., 1993.

Corn, Joseph J., and Brian Horrigan; edited by Katherine Chambers, *Yesterday's Tomorrows: Past Visions of the American Future*, Baltimore: Johns Hopkins University Press, 1996.

Wilde, Rein de, *De Voorspellers: Een kritiek op de toekomstindustrie*, Amsterdam: De Balie, 2000.

Mass Communications and Broadcast Media

In general, those in broadcast media underestimate the impact of Internet:

Bagdikian, Ben, *The Media Monopoly*, Boston: Beacon Press, 1983. (This concerns the growing monopolies in a pre-Internet context but is still important background reading.)

Shiers, George, and May Shiers (compilers); Diana Menkes (ed.), *Early Television: A Bibliographic Guide to 1940 (Science/Reference)*, New York: Garland, 1996.

Gerbner, George, Hamid Mowlana, and Herbert I. Schiller, eds., *Invisible Crises. What Conglomerate Control of Media Means for America and the World*, Boulder, CO: Westview Press, 1996.

Reeves, Byron, Clifford Nass, *The Media Equation: How People Treat Computers, Television and the New Media Like Real People and Places*, Cambridge: Cambridge University Press, 1996.

Litman, Barry, *The Motion Picture Mega Boom*, Boston: Allyn and Bacon, 1998.

Douglas, James Walker, and Douglas Ferguson, *The Broadcast Television Industry*, Boston: Allyn and Bacon, 1998.

Parson, Patrick R., and Robert M. Frieden, *The Cable and Television Industries*, Boston: Allyn and Bacon, 1998.

Dominick, Joseph R., Barry L. Sherman, and Fritz Messere, *Broadcasting, Cable, the Internet and Beyond: An Introduction to Modern Electronic Media*, New York: McGraw-Hill Higher Education, 1999.

Sterling, Christopher, and George Shiers, *History of Telecommunications Technology*, Lanham, MD: Scarecrow Press, 2000.

Gilder, George, *Telecosm: How Infinite Bandwidth Will Revolutionize Our World*, New York: Free Press, 2000.

Severin, Werner J., and James W. Tankard, *Communication Theories: Origins, Methods and Uses in the Mass Media*, Upper Saddle River, NJ: Pearson, 5th ed., 2000.

O'Leary, Seamus, *Understanding Digital Terrestrial Broadcasting*, Norwood, MA: Artech House, 2000.

Vivian, John, *The Media of Mass Communication 2003 Update*, Upper Saddle River, NJ: Pearson Allyn & Bacon; 6th ed. 2002 [sic].

Pavlik, John and McIntosh, Shawn, *Converging Media: An Introduction to Mass Communication*, Upper Saddle River, NJ: Allyn and Bacon, 2003

McChesney, Robert W., *The Problem of the Media: U.S. Communication Politics in the Twenty-First Century*, New York: Monthly Review Press, 2004.

Digital Telephony

Bellamy, John C., *Digital Telephony*, 1991. 3rd ed. New York: John Wiley & Sons, 2000 (Wiley Series in Telecommunications and Signal Processing).

Walters, Robert, *Computer Telephony Integration*, Norwood, MA: Artech House, 1999 (Artech House Telecommunications Library).

Internet Telephony

Muller, Nathan J., *IP Convergence: The Next Revolution in Telecommunications*, Norwood, MA: Artech House, 1999.

Yarberry, William A., *Computer Telephony Integration*, Boca Raton: CRC Press, 1999.

Bayer, Michael, *Computer Telephony Demystified*, New York: McGraw-Hill Professional, 2000.

McKnight, Lee W., William Lehr, and David D. Clark, eds., *Internet Telephony*, Cambridge, MA: MIT Press, 2001, 2001.

Collins, Daniel, *Carrier Grade Voice Over IP*, New York: McGraw-Hill Professional, 2002. 2nd ed.

Ohrtman, Frank, *Softswitch: Architecture for VoIP (Professional Telecom)*, New York: McGraw-Hill Professional, 2002.

Digital Television: North America

See: http://www.technologyage.com/books.shtml

Friedman, Jeffrey, ed., *Television Continuum 1967 to 2017*, SMPTE Television Conference, Detroit: Society of Motion Picture and Television Engineers, 1991.

Morse, Margaret, *Virtualities: Television, Media Art and Cyberculture*, Bloomington: Indiana University Press, 1998.

O'Driscoll, Gerard, *The Essential Guide to Digital Set-Top Boxes and Interactive TV*, Upper Saddle River, NJ: Prentice Hall, 1999.

Silbergleid, Michael, and Mark J. Pescatore, *The Guide to Digital Television*, Tonbridge: Miller Freeman PSN, 1999, 2nd ed.

Whitaker, Jerry, *DTV: The Revolution in Digital Video*, New York: McGraw-Hill Text, 1999.

Forrester, Chris, *Business of Digital Television*, Woburn, MA: Focal Press, 2000.

Massel, Mark, *Digital Television, DVB-T COFDM and ATSC 8-VSB*, New York: Digitaltvbooks.com, 2000.

Robin, Michael, and Michel Poulin, *Digital Television Fundamentals: Design and Installation of Video and Audio Systems*, New York: McGraw-Hill Text, 2000.

Poynton, Charles, *Digital Video and HDTV Algorithms and Interfaces*, San Francisco: Morgan Kaufmann, 2003.

Digital Television: Europe

CDG Eurostudy, *Digital Terrestrial Television in Europe*, Victoria, BC: Trafford, 1998.

Dambacher, Paul, *Digital Terrestrial Television Broadcasting: Designs, Systems and Operation*, Berlin: Springer, 1998.

Bustamante, Enrique, and Jose Maria Alvarez Monzoncillo, eds., *Presente y Futuro de la Television Digital*, Madrid: Edita Edipo, 1999.

Reimers, Ulrich, ed., *Digital Video Broadcasting: The International Standard for Digital HDTV*, Berlin: Springer, 2000.

Digital Television: Japan

Japan: Cable and Satellite Strategy, Torrance: Baskerville Communications, 2000.

Cf.: http://www.teleport.com/~samc/hdtv/).

Nakamura, Kiyoshi, and Koichiro Agata, *Convergence of Telecommunications and Broadcasting in Japan, United Kingdom and Germany: Technological Change, Public Policy and Market Structure*, London: Curzon Press, 2001 (Waseda/Curzon International Series, 1).

Internet Television

Owen, Bruce M., *The Internet Challenge to Television*, Cambridge, MA: Harvard University Press, 1999.

Dominick, Joseph R., Barry L. Sherman, and Fritz Messere, *Broadcasting, Cable, the Internet and Beyond: An Introduction to Modern Electronic Media*, New York: McGraw-Hill Higher Education, 2000.

Internet Video and E-Video

Alesso, H. Peter, *e-Video: Producing Internet Video as Broadband Technologies Converge* (with CD-ROM), Reading, MA: Addison-Wesley, 2000.

Digital Video

Poynton, Charles A., *Technical Introduction to Digital Video*, New York: John Wiley & Sons, 1996.

Watkinson, John, *The Art of Digital Video*, Woburn, MA: Focal Press, 2000.

High Definition Television

Krivocheev, Mark I., and S.N. Baron, eds., *The First Twenty Years of HDTV, 1972–1992*, White Plains, NY: Society of Motion Picture and Television Engineers, 1993. Limited 1st ed.

Dupagne, Michel, Peter B. Seel, and Scott D. Elliott, *High-Definition Television: A Global Perspective*, Ames: Iowa State University Press, 1997.

Persson, Conrad, *Guide to HDTV Systems*, Indianapolis: Howard W. SAMS and Co., 1999.

Poynton, Charles A., *Digital Video and HDTV: Pixels, Pictures, and Perception*, New York: John Wiley & Sons, 2001. 2nd ed.

High Definition Television: Europe

Simmering, Klaus, *HDTV-High Definition Television: technische, ökonomische und programmliche Aspekte einer neuen Fernsehtechnik*, Bochum: N. Brockmeyer, 1986 [i.e., 1989].

Bischoff, Jürgen, *Die politische Ökonomie von HDTV: Internationale Förderstrategien zur Durchsetzung einer neuen Fernsehtechnologie*, Frankfurt am Main: P. Lang, 1993.

Basic Institutions and Sites

Internet Society (ISOC)	See: www.isoc.org
World Wide Web Consortium (W3)	See: www.w3.org
International Institute of Communications (IIC)	See: http://www.iicom.org/
International Association for Media and Communication Research (IAMCR)	See: http://www.mcs.mq.edu.au/courses/ICP/iamcr/iamcr.htm
International Standards Organization (ISO)	See: http://www.worldyellowpages.com/iso/
International Telecommunications Union (ITU)	See: http://www.itu.int/
World Intellectual Property Organization (WIPO)	See: http://www.wipo.org

A series of further organizations are found at	See: http://www.uia.org
Netzwissenschaft by Dr. Reinhold Grether provides an excellent survey of scholars in new media.	See: http://www.netzwissenschaft.org.
A French equivalent is emerging at:	See: http://www.cyber-institut.org
For a survey list of electronic information	See: http://library.usask.ca/~dworacze/SUB_INT.HTM
For a fundamental survey of media organizations by Caslon analytics:	See: http://www.ketupa.net/index.htm
Danish Bibliography on Media Theory Communication	See: http://www.medieteori.dk/english/database/display_cat.php?id=14

Basic Journals

Netzspannung.org is a magazine for media production and inter-media research. See: http://netzspannung.org/journal/issue0/index_en.html

High Definition Television: Japan

NHK Science and Technical Research Laboratories, Prepared under the auspices of NHK (the Japan Broadcasting Corporation), *High Definition Television: Hi-Vision Technology*; trans. James G. Parker, New York: Van Nostrand Reinhold, 1993.

Hart, Jeffrey A., *The Politics of HDTV in Japan and the United States*, Bloomington, IN: Indiana Center for Global Business, Graduate School of Business, Indiana University, [1993].

Digital Motion Pictures

Barclay, Steven, *The Motion Picture Image: From Film to Digital*, Woburn, MA: Focal Press, 2000.

Wheeler, Paul, *Digital Cinematography*, Oxford: Focal Press, 2001.

McKernan, Brian, *Digital Cinema: The Revolution in Cinematography, Post-Production, and Distribution*, New York: McGraw-Hill/TAB Electronics, 2004.

Convergence

Yoffie, David B., *Competing in the Age of Digital Convergence*, Boston: Harvard Business School, 1997.

Moschella, David C., *Waves of Power: Dynamics of Global Technology Leadership 1964–2010*, New York: Amacom, 1997.

United States. Congress. Senate. Committee on the Judiciary. Subcommittee on Antitrust, Business Rights, and Competition, *Convergence and consolidation in the entertainment and information industries: hearing before the Subcommittee on Antitrust, Business Rights, and Competition of the Committee on the Judiciary, United States Senate, One Hundred Fifth Congress, second session ... July 7, 1998*. Washington: U.S. GPO: For sale by the U.S. GPO, Supt. of Docs., Congressional Sales Office, 1999.

Covell, Andy, *Digital Convergence: How the Merging of Computers, Communications and Multimedia is Transforming Our Lives*, Newport: Aegis, 1999.

Muller, Nathan J., *IP Convergence: The Next Revolution in Telecommunications*, Norwood, MA: Artech House, 1999.

Benavidas Delgado, Juan, David Alameda Garcia, and Elena Fernandez Blanco, *Las convergencias de la communicacion: Problemas y perspectivas investigadoras*, Madrid: Fundacion General de la Universidad Complutense, 2000.

Shepard, Steven, *Telecommunications Convergence: How to Profit from the Convergence of Technologies, Services, and Companies*, New York: McGraw-Hill, 2000.

Llana, Andres, *Convergence of Wireless Technology and Enterprise Networks: Integrating the Internet*, Computer Technology Research Corporation, 2000.

Delgado, J., and G. D. Stamoulis, ed., *Telecommunications and It Convergence Towards Service E-Volution: Towards Service Evolution: 7th International Conference on Intelligence in service*, Berlin: Springer, 2000.

Informa Media, *Convergence in Television and the Internet* (3rd ed.), *Authoritative and Up-to-Date Analysis, Vital Statistics and Essential Forecasts on the Global Convergence Industry*, New York: MarketResearch.com, 2001 (ISBN: B00005UEXF).

User Interfaces

For standard references, see the web site of HCI lab at the University of Maryland, HCIL. See: http://www.cs.umd.edu/hcil/; under publications at the HIT Lab (University of Washington) See: http://www.hitl.washington.edu/ and the ERCIM User Interfaces for all conferences. See: http://www.ui4all.gr/workshop2004/.

Bass, Len, and Joëlle Coutaz, *Developing Software for the User Interface*, Reading, MA: Addison-Wesley, 1991. (Sei Series in Software Engineering).

Shneiderman, Ben, "Advanced Graphic User Interfaces: Elastic and Tightly Coupled Windows," *ACM Computing Surveys (CSUR)*, Vol. 28, Issue 4es, December 1996. Special issue: position statements on strategic directions in computing research, Article No. 144, 1996, ISSN: 0360-0300.

Multimodality

Arbib, Michael A., and Jörg-Peter Ewert, *Visual Structures and Integrated Functions*, Berlin: Springer, 1991.

Multimodal Human-Computer Interaction, Scientific organizer, Noëlle Carbonell; ERCIM coordinators, Giorgio Faconti et al.; organization, INRIA-Lorraine, CRIN-CNRS. Le Chesnay, France: European Research Consortium for Informatics and Mathematics, [1994].

Taylor, Richard N., and Joëlle Coutaz, eds., *Software Engineering and Human-Computer Interaction*, Berlin: Springer, 1995 (ICSE '94 Workshop on SE-HCI: Joint Research Issues, Sorrento, Italy, May 16–17, 1994: Proceedings).

Jeannerod, Marc, *The Cognitive Neuroscience of Action*, Oxford: Blackwell, 1997.

Arbib, Michael A., ed., *The Handbook of Brain Theory and Neural Networks*, Cambridge, MA: MIT Press, 1998.

Granstrom, Bjorn, David House, and Inger Karlsson, eds., *Multimodality in Language and Speech Systems*, Dordrecht: Kluwer, 2002.

Chapter 1. Computers

History of Internet

It is interesting that none of the pioneers of the Internet has written a history of the Internet. There is, of course, Vint Cerf's *Brief History of the Internet*, which is more a lecture than a book. See: http://www.isoc.org/internet-history/brief.html. By contrast the two founders of the World Wide Web both have books:

Berners-Lee, Tim, and Mark Fischetti, *Weaving the Web: The Original Design and Ultimate Destiny of the World Wide Web by its Inventor*, San Francisco: Harpers, 1999.
Cailliau, Robert, and James Gillies, *How the Web Was Born: The Story of the World Wide Web*, New York: Oxford University Press, 2000.

For an interesting account which reminds us that one of the founders of the Internet was French, see:

Guedon, Jean-Claude, *Internet: Le Monde en réseau*, Paris: Gallimard, 1996.

General books on the Internet include:

Salus, Peter H., Foreword by Vinton G. Cerf, *Casting the Net: From the ARPANET to Internet and Beyond*, Reading, MA: Addison-Wesley, 1995.
Kahn, David, *The Codebreakers: The Comprehensive History of Secret Communication from Ancient Times to the Internet*, New York: Scribner's, 1996.
Wolinsky, Art, *The History of the Internet and the World Wide Web*, Springfield, NJ: Enslow Press, 1997.
Campbell-Kelly, Martin, and William Aspray, *Computer: A History of the Information Machine*, New York: Basic Books, 1997 (The Sloan Technology Series).
Hafner, Katie, and Matthew Lyon, *Where Wizards Stay Up Late: The Origins of the Internet*, New York: Touchstone, 1998.
Segaller, Stephen, *Nerds 2.0.1: A Brief History of the Internet*, New York: TV Books, 1999.
Abbate, Jane, *Inventing the Internet (Inside Technology)*, Cambridge, MA: MIT Press, 2000.
Naughton, John, *A Brief History of the Future: Origins of the Internet*, New York: Overlook Press, 2000.
Ceruzzi, Paul E., *A History of Modern Computing*, Cambridge, MA: MIT Press, 2003 (2nd ed.).
Peters, Ian, *e-Book on Internet History*, Brisbane, 2004. See: http http://www.nethistory.info/http.

Books which see the Internet in a larger context include:

Rowland, Wade, *Spirit of the Web: The Age of Information from Telegraph to Internet*, Toronto: Somerville House, 1997.
Winston, Brian, *Media Technology and Society: A History: From the Telegraph to the Internet*, London, New York: Routledge, 1998.
Moschovitis, Christos J. P., Hilary Poole, Tami Schuyler, and Theresa M. Senft, *History of the Internet: A Chronology, 1843 to Present*, Santa Barbara: ABC-Clio, 1999.
Wertheim, Margaret, *The Pearly Gates of Cyberspace: A History of Space from Dante to the Internet*, New York: W.W. Norton, 2000.

An attempt to describe only the business side is:

Reid, Robert H., *Architects of the Web: 1,000 Days That Built the Future of Business*, New York: John Wiley & Sons, 1997.

Hardware

Shiers, George, *Bibliography on the History of Electronics*, Metuchen, NJ: Scarecrow Press, 1972.

Gupta, Amar, *Insights into Personal Computers*. Piscataway, NJ: Institute of Electrical & Electronics Engineers, 1985.

Gupta, Amar, *Multi-Microprocessors*. Piscataway, NJ: Institute of Electrical & Electronics Engineers, 1987.

Gupta, Amar, *Advanced Microprocessors, II*. Piscataway, NJ: Institute of Electrical & Electronics Engineers, 1987.

Yost, Jeffrey R., *Bibliographic Guide to Resources in Scientific Computing, 1945–1975*, Westport, CT: Greenwood, 2002.

Software

For insights into some of the frontiers of software, see the web site of Denis Caromel (INRIA). See: http://www-sop.inria.fr/oasis/caromel.

Bradley, Stephen P., Arnoldo C. Hax, and Thomas L. Magnanti, *Applied Mathematical Programming*. Reading, MA: Addison-Wesley Longman, 1977.

Cortada, James W., *An Annotated Bibliography on the History of Data Processing*, Westport, CT: Greenwood, 1983.

Shu, Nan C., *Visual Programming*, New York: Van Nostrand Reinhold, 1988, 1992.

Cortada, James W., *A Bibliographic Guide to the History of Computing, Computers and the Information Processing Industry*, Westport, CT: Greenwood, 1990. 2nd guide, 1996.

Madnick, Stuart, *Software Project Dynamics: An Integrated Approach*, Englewood Cliffs, NJ: Prentice Hall, 1991.

Tannenbaum, Andrew S., *Modern Operating Systems*, Upper Saddle River, NJ: Prentice Hall, 1992.

Coad, Peter, and Jill Nicola, *Object-Oriented Programming*, Engelwood Cliffs, NJ: Yourdon Press, 1993.

Magnanti, Thomas L., *Network Flows: Theory, Algorithms, and Applications*, Englewood Cliffs, NJ: Prentice Hall, 1993.

Booch, Grady, *Object Oriented Analysis and Design with Applications*, Redwood City: Benjamin Cummings, 1994. 2nd ed.

Tannenbaum, Andrew S., *Distributed Operating Systems*, Upper Saddle River, NJ: Prentice Hall, 1995.

Tannenbaum, Andrew S., *Computer Networks*, Upper Saddle River, NJ: Prentice Hall, 1996. 3rd ed.

Cortada, James W., *A Bibliographic Guide to the History of Computer Applications, 1950–1990*, Westport, CT: Greenwood, 1996.

Gabriel, Richard P., *Patterns of Software: Tales from the Software Community*, New York: Oxford University Press, 1996.

Cox, Brad, *Superdistribution: Objects as Property on the Electronic Frontier*, Reading, MA: Addison-Wesley, 1996.

Picard, Rosalind, *Affective Computing*, Cambridge, MA: MIT Press, 1997, 2000.

Databases

Xu Wu, Tadao Ichikawa, and Nick Cercone, *Knowledge Assisted Database Retrieval Systems*, Singapore: World Scientific, 1994.

Connolly, Thomas, Carolyn Begg, Anne Strachan, *Database Systems*, Wokingham: Addison-Wesley, 1996.

Fortier, Paul J., *Database Systems Handbook*, New York: McGraw-Hill, 1997.

Ioannidis, Yannis, Wolfgang Klas, *Visual Database Systems 4 (VDB4)*, London: Chapman and Hall, 1998.

Elmasri, Ramez, Shamkant B. Navathe, *Fundamentals of Database Systems*, Upper Saddle River, NJ: Pearson Addison-Wesley, 2003 (4th ed.).

Virtual Reality

Krueger, Myron W., *Artificial Reality II*, Reading, MA: Addison-Wesley, 1991.
Benedikt, Michael, *Cyberspace: First Steps*, Cambridge, MA: MIT Press, 1991.
Wexelblatt, Alan, *Virtual Reality: Applications and Explorations*, Boston: Academic Press, 1993.
Mazzoli, Graziella, and Giovanni Boccia Artieri, *L'ambigua frontiera del virtuale*, Milan: FrancoAngeli, 1994.
Burdea, Grigoire, and Philippe Coiffet, *Virtual Reality Technology*, New York: John Wiley & Sons, 1994.
Thalmann, Nadia Magnenat, and Daniel Thalmann, *Virtual Worlds and Multimedia*, Chichester: John Wiley & Sons, 1995.
Heim, Michael, *Virtual Realism*, New York: Oxford University Press, 1998.
Dodsworth, Clark, *Digital Illusion: Entertaining the Future with High Technology*, New York: ACM Press, 1998.
Grau, Olivier, *Geschichte der virtuellen Kunst*, Berlin: Reimer, 2001.
Euroimage ICAV3D 2001: International Conference on Augmented, Virtual Environments and Three Dimensional Imaging, Mykonos, Greece, ed. Venetia Giangourta and Michael G. Strinzis, Thessaloniki: ZITI, 2001.
Riegler, Alexander, Markus F. Peschl, Karl Edlinger, Günther Fleck, and Walter Feigl, eds., *Virtual Reality: Cognitive Foundations, Technological Issues and Philosophical Implications*, Frankfurt: Peter Lang, 2002.
Sherman, William R., Alan B. Craig, *Understanding Virtual Reality: Interface, Application, and Design*, San Francisco: Morgan Kaufmann, 2002.
Packer, Randall, Ken Jordan, and William Gibson, *Multimedia: From Wagner to Virtual Reality*, New York: W.W. Norton, 2002 (expanded ed.).
Bartle, Richard, *Designing Virtual Worlds*, Berkeley: New Riders, 2003.
Ryan, Marie-Laure, Stephen G. Nichols, and Gerald Prince, eds., *Narrative As Virtual Reality: Immersion and Interactivity in Literature and Electronic Media*, Baltimore: Johns Hopkins University Press, 2003 (Parallax: Re-Visions of Culture and Society).

Chapter 2. Mobility

Makimoto, Tsugio, and David Manners, *Digital Nomad*, New York: John Wiley & Sons, 1997.
Nummi, Tommi, Arno Rönkä, and Janne Sariola, *Virtuality and Digital Nomadism*, Helsinki: University of Helsinki, Department of Teacher Education, Yliopistopaino, 1998.
Milojicic, Dejan S., Frederick Douglis, and Richard G. Wheeler, eds., *Mobility: Processes, Computers, and Agents*, Reading, MA: Addison-Wesley, 1999.

Chapter 3. Miniaturization

Nano-technology and Neurobiology

Ettinger, Robert C. W., *The Prospect of Immortality*, Garden City, NY: Doubleday, 1965.
Perry, John, ed., *Personal Identity*, Los Angeles: University of California Press, 1975.
Shepherd, Gordon M., *The Synaptic Organization of the Brain*, New York: Oxford University Press, 1979.
Drexler, K. Eric, *Engines of Creation*, New York: Doubleday, 1986.
Fjermedal, Grant, *The Tomorrow Makers*, Redmond: Tempus Books, 1986.
Hameroff, Stuart R., *Ultimate Computing: Biomolecular Consciousness and Nanotechnology*, Amsterdam: Elsevier Science, 1987.
Grossberg, Stephen, ed., *Neural Networks and Natural Intelligence*, Cambridge, MA: MIT Press, 1988.

Moravec, Hans, *Mind Children*, Cambridge, MA: Harvard University Press, 1988.

Shepherd, Gordon M., *Neurobiology*, New York: Oxford University Press, 1988.

Posner, Michael I., ed., *Foundations of Cognitive Science*, Cambridge, MA: MIT Press, 1989.

Drexler, K. Eric, *Nanosystems*, New York: John Wiley & Sons, 1992.

Kurzweil, Ray, *The Age of Intelligent Machines*, Cambridge, MA: MIT Press, 1992.

Gardner, Daniel, *The Neurobiology of Neural Networks*, Cambridge, MA: MIT Press, 1993.

Halperin, James, *The First Immortal*, New York: Del Rey, 1998 (Fiction).

Hayles, N. Katherine, *How We Became Posthuman*, Chicago: University of Chicago Press, 1999.

Nicholson, Kelly Richard, *The Prospect of Immortality*, Cranbrook, BC: Homeward Bound, 1999.

Groß, Michael, *Travels to the Nanoworld: Miniature Machinery in Nature and Technology*, New York: Plenum, 1999.

Timp, Gregory, ed., *Nanotechnology*, Berlin: Springer, 1999.

Rietman, Edward A., *Molecular Engineering of Nanosystems*, New York: Springer, 2000.

Scherge, Matthias, and Stanislav N. Gorb, *Biological Micro- and Nanotribology Nature's Solutions*, New York: Springer, 2001.

Wilson, Michael, Kamali Kannangara, Geoff Smith, Michelle Simmons, and Carol Crane, eds., *Nanotechnology: Basic Science and Emerging Technologies*, CRC Press, 2002.

Poole, Charles P., and Frank J. Owens, *Introduction to Nanotechnology*, New York: Wiley-Interscience, 2003.

Nanotechnology: Europe

Hirst, Peter, et al., *Making it in Miniature: Nanotechnology, UK Science and its Applications*, [London]: Parliamentary Office of Science and Technology, [c1996].

Nanotechnology: Japan

Fujimasa, Iwao, *Micromachines: A New Era in Mechanical Engineering*, Oxford: Oxford University Press, 1996.

DNA Computing

Lipton, Richard J., and Eric B. Baum, ed., *DNA Based Computers: Proceedings of a Dimacs Workshop, April 4, 1995, Princeton University*, Providence: American Mathematical Society, 1996.

Paun, Gheorghe, Grzegorz Rozenberg, Arto Salomaa, and W. Brauer, eds., *DNA Computing: New Computing Paradigms*, Heidelberg: Springer, 1998 (Texts in Theoretical Computer Science).

Hagiya, Masami, Azuma Ohuchi, and Ji-Tao E. G. Wang, eds., *DNA Computing: 8th International Workshop on DNA Based Computers, Dna8, Sapporo, Japan, June 10–13, 2002: Revised Papers* (Lecture Notes in Computer Science, 2568).

Chen, Junghuei, J.H. Reif, eds., *DNA Computing: 9th International Workshop on DNA Based Computers, Dna9: Madison, WI, June 1–3, 2003: Revised Papers* (Lecture Notes in Computer Science).

Quantum Computing

In the past years, there have been a number of books on the subject:

Williams, Colin P., and Scott H. Clearwater, *Explorations in Quantum Computing*, New York: Springer, 1997.

Lo, Hoi-Kwong, Tim Spiller, and Sandu Popescu, *Introduction to Quantum Computation and Information*, River Edge, NJ: World Scientific, 1998.

Gramss, Tino (ed.), and M. Gross, M. Mitchell, and T. Pellizzari (contributors), *Non-Standard Computation: Molecular Computation – Cellular Automata – Evolutionary Algorithms – Quantum Computers*, New York: John Wiley & Sons, 1998.

Williams, Colin P., and Scott H. Clearwater, *Ultimate Zero and One: Computing at the Quantum Frontier*, New York: Copernicus Books, 1999.

Brooks, Michael, ed., *Quantum Computing and Communications*, New York: Springer, 1999.

Milburn, Gerard J., Paul Davies, *The Feynman Processor: Quantum Entanglement and the Computing Revolution*, Boulder, CO: Perseus, 1999. (Helix Books Series).

Brown, Julian, *Minds, Machines and the Multiverse: The Quest for the Quantum Computer*, New York: Simon & Schuster, 2000.

Bouwmeester, Dik, Artur K. Ekert, Anton Zeilinger, eds. *The Physics of Quantum Information: Quantum Cryptography, Quantum Teleportation, Quantum Computation*, New York: Springer, 2000.

Hirvensalo, Mika, *Quantum Computing*, Berlin: Springer, 2004.

Biotechnology

Lappe, Marc, and Britt Bailey, *Against the Grain: Biotechnology and the Corporate Takeover of Your Food*, Milford, CT: LPC, 1998.

Barnum, Susan R., and Carol M. Barnum, *Biotechnology: An Introduction*, London: Wadsworth, 1998.

Rifkin, Jeremy, *The Biotech Century*, New York: Penguin/Putnam, 1999.

Palsson, Bernhard, Jeffrey A. Hubbell, Robert Plonsey, and Joseph D. Bronzino, eds., *Tissue Engineering*, CRC Press, 2003 (Principles and Applications in Engineering).

Slater, Adrian, Nigel W. Scott, Mark R. Fowler, *Plant Biotechnology: The Genetic Manipulation of Plants*, New York: Oxford University Press, 2003.

Chapter 4. Production

Design, Virtual Prototyping and e-Design

Ulrich, Karl T., and Steven D. Eppinger. *Product Design and Development*, New York: McGraw-Hill, 1995.

Rix, J., S. Haas, J. Teixeira, *Virtual Prototyping — Virtual Environments and the Product Design Process*, Dordrecht: Kluwer, 1995.

Virtual Prototyping, Computer-Modeling, and Computer Simulation, Warrendale, PA: Society of Automotive Engineers, Inc., 1998.

Beckmann, John, ed., *The Virtual Dimension: Architecture, Representation and Crash Culture*, New York: Princeton Architectural Press, 1998.

Anders, Peter, *Envisioning Cyberspace: Designing 3D Electronic Spaces*, New York: McGraw-Hill, 1999.

Maher, Mary Lou, Simeon J. Simoff, and Anna Cicognani, *Understanding Virtual Design Studios*, Berlin: Springer, 2001 (Computer Supported Cooperative Work).

Computer Simulation

Schrage, William, *Serious Play, How the World's Best Companies Simulate to Innovate*, Boston: Harvard Business School, 1999.

Engquist, B., L. Johnsson, M. Hammill, and F. Short, eds., *Simulation and Visualization on the Grid*, Berlin: Springer, 2000.

Laguna, Manuel, and José Luis González Velarde, ed., *Computing Tools for Modeling, Optimization, and Simulation: Interfaces in Computer Science and Operations Research*, Boston: Kluwer, 2000.

Nørgaard, M. et al., *Neural Networks for Modelling and Control of Dynamic Systems: A Practitioner's Handbook*, Berlin: Springer, 2000.

Fogel, David B., *Evolutionary Computation: Toward a New Philosophy of Machine Intelligence*, New York: IEEE Press, 2000, 2nd ed.

Fujimoto, Richard M., *Parallel and Distribution Simulation Systems*, New York: John Wiley & Sons, 2000.

Stilman, Boris, *Linguistic Geometry: From Search to Construction*, Boston: Kluwer, 2000.

Haas, S., J. Rix, and J. Teixeira, eds., *Virtual Prototyping*, Dordrecht: Kluwer Print on Demand, 2002.

Work and Virtual Work

Zuboff, Shoshana, *In the Age of the Smart Machine: The Future of Work and Power*, New York: Basic Books, 1988.

Rifkin, Jeremy, and Robert L. Heilbroner, *The End of Work: The Decline of the Global Labor Force and the Dawn of the Post-Market Era*, Boston: J. P. Tarcher, 1996.

Grantham, Charles E., *The Future of Work: The Promise of the New Digital Work Society (CommerceNet)*, New York: McGraw-Hill Professional, 1999.

Hildreth, Paul M., *Going Virtual: Distributed Communities of Practice*, Hershey, PA: Idea Group, 2004.

Godar, Susan H., and Sharmila Pixy Ferris, eds., *Virtual and Collaborative Teams: Process, Technologies, and Practice*, Hershey, PA: Idea Group, 2004.

Huws, Ursula, and Colin Leys, *The Making of a Cybertariat: Virtual Work in a Real World*, New York: Monthly Review Press, 2004.

Process (Re-)Engineering

Takamatsu, T., *Process Systems Engineering*, Oxford: Pergamon Press, 1983.

Roberts, Lon, *Process Reengineering: The Key to Achieving Breakthrough Success*, Milwaukee: American Society for Quality, 1994.

Vollmann, Thomas E., Thomas E. Vollman, William Lee Berry, and David C. Whybark, *Manufacturing Planning and Control Systems*, New York: McGraw-Hill, 1998: "Central themes are master planning, material requirements planning, inventory management, capacity management, production activity control, and just-in-time."

Kruchten, Philippe, *The Rational Unified Process, An Introduction*, Reading, MA: Addison-Wesley, 2000 (The Addison-Wesley Object Technology Series).

Business Process (Re-)Engineering

Coulson-Thomas, Colin, ed. *Business Process Engineering: Myth and Reality*, London: Kogan Page, 1994.

Hammer, Michael, *Beyond Reengineering: How the Process-Centered Organization Is Changing Our Work and Our Lives*, New York: Harper Business, 1996.

Rockefeller, Benjamin W., *Using Sap R/3 Fi: Beyond Business Process Reengineering*, New York: John Wiley & Sons, 1998.

Ansari, Shahid, *Business Process Reengineering*, New York: McGraw-Hill, 2000 (Modular Series).

Miller, Landon C. G., *Business Process Re-engineering: A Management Handbook*, Eden Prairie: Vertical Systems, 2003 (Ver. 3).

Automated Production

Lamming, Mik, and William Newman, *Interactive System Design*, Reading, MA: Addison-Wesley, 1995. See: http://www.rxrc.xerox.com/public/isd/us-overheads.htm.

Foston, Arthur L., Carolena L. Smith, and Tony Au, *Fundamentals of Computer Integrated Manufacturing*, Upper Saddle River, NJ: Prentice Hall, 1997.

Tzafestas, Spyros G., ed., *Computer-Assisted Management and Control of Manufacturing Systems*, Heidelberg: Springer, 1997 (Advanced Manufacturing).

Chang, Tien-Chien, Richard A. Wysk, and Hsu-Pin Wang, *Computer-Aided Manufacturing*, Upper Saddle River, NJ: Prentice Hall, 1997. 2nd ed. (Prentice Hall International Series in Industrial and Systems Engineering).

Hannam, Roger, *Computer Integrated Manufacturing: From Concepts to Realisation*, Reading, MA: Addison-Wesley, 1998.

Information Control in Manufacturing 1998: (Incom '98): Advances in Industrial Engineering. A proceedings volume from the 9th Ifac Symposium on Information Control in Manufacturing (1998 Nancy), Pergamon, 1998.

Usher, John M., Uptal Roy, and H. R. Parsaei, eds., *Integrated Product and Process Development: Methods, Tools, and Technologies*, New York: John Wiley & Sons, 1998 (Wiley Series in Engineering Design and Automation).

Vajpayee, S. Kant, *Principles of Computer Integrated Manufacturing*, Upper Saddle River, NJ: Prentice Hall, 1998.

Ashayeri, Jalal, and William Sullivan, *Flexible Automation and Intelligent Manufacturing*, Proceedings of the Ninth International Faim Conference, Center for Economic Research, New York: Begell House, 1999.

Brandimarte, Paolo, and A. Villa, ed., *Modeling Manufacturing Systems: From Aggregate Planning to Real-Time Control*, Heidelberg: Springer, 1999.

Sen, A., A.I. Sivakuma, and R. Gay, eds., *Computer Integrated Manufacturing*, Heidelberg: Springer, 1999.

Computer Integrated Manufacturing Systems (CIM)

Harrington, Joseph, *Computer Integrated Manufacturing*, New York: Industrial Press [1974, c1973].

Computer Integrated Manufacturing Systems, San Jose, CA (4340 Stevens Creek Blvd., Suite 275, San Jose 95129): Creative Strategies International, 1982.

Evans, David, ed., *CIM: Mechanical Aspects*, Oxford: Pergamon Infotech, 1988.

Weiss, Peter A., *Die Kompetenz von Systemanbietern: Ein neuer Ansatz im Marketing für Systemtechnologien*, Berlin: E. Schmidt, 1992.

Rolstadås, Asbjørn, and Bjørn Andersen, eds., *Enterprise Modeling: Improving Global Industrial Competitiveness*, Boston: Kluwer, 2000.

Shaw, Michael J., ed., *Information-based Manufacturing: Technology, Strategy, and Industrial Applications*, Boston: Kluwer, 2000.

Groover, Mikell P., *Automation, Production Systems, and Computer-Integrated Manufacturing*, Upper Saddle River, NJ: Prentice Hall, 2000.

Kusiak, Andrew, *Computational Intelligence in Design and Manufacturing*, New York: John Wiley & Sons, 2000.

Rehg, James A., and Henry W. Kraebber, *Computer-Integrated Manufacturing*, Upper Saddle River, NJ: Prentice Hall, 2001. 2nd ed.

Quality Control and Total Quality Management (TQM): Japan

Taguchi, Genichi, *Introduction to Quality Engineering: Designing Quality into Products and Processes*, Asian Productivity Organization, available in the United States from Dearborn, MI: American Supplier Institute, 1986.

Mizuno, S., ed., *Management for Quality Improvement: The 7 New QC Tools*, Cambridge, MA: Productivity Press, 1988.

King, B., *Hoshin Planning: The Development Approach*, GOAL/QPC, Methuen, MA, 1989.

Akao, Yoji, ed., *Quality Function Deployment*, Cambridge, MA: Productivity Press, 1990.

Akao, Yoji, ed., *Hoshin Kanri: Policy Deployment for Successful TQM*, Cambridge, MA: Productivity Press, 1991.

Mizuno, S., and Yoji Akao, ed., *QFD: The Customer-Driven Approach to Quality Planning and Development*, Tokyo: Asian Productivity Organization, available from White Plains, NY: Quality Resources, 1994.

Kaizen
Imai, Masaaki, *Kaizen: The Key to Japan's Competitive Success*, New York: McGraw-Hill, 1986.

Keiretsu
Miyashita, Kenichi, and David Russell, Preface, *Keiretsu: Inside the Hidden Japanese Conglomerates*, New York: McGraw-Hill, 1995.

Quality Control and Total Quality Control (TQM): North America and Europe
Partly because the Japanese books listed above were not published in English until the 1980s the idea of customer satisfaction as an integral element in the equation did not become popular in Europe and America until the 1990s through books such as:

Peters, Thomas, and Robert H. Waterman, *In Search of Excellence: Lessons from America's Best-Run Companies*, New York: Warner Books, 1988.
Eureka, W. E., and N. E. Ryan, *The Process-Driven Business: Managerial Perspectives on Policy Management*, Dearborn, MI: ASI Press, 1990.
Gustafsson, Anders, *QFD and Conjoint Analysis: The Key to Customer Oriented Products*, Linköping: Linköping University, 1993. (Linköping Studies in Science and Technology Thesis No. 393).
Sheridan, B. M., *Policy Deployment: The TQM Approach to Long Range Planning*, Milwaukee, WI: ASQC Quality Press, 1993.
Barnard, W., and T. F. Wallace, *The Innovation Edge: Creating Breakthroughs Using the Voice of the Customer*, Essex Junction VT: Oliver Wight, 1994.
Bagozzi, R. P., ed., *Principles of Marketing Research*, Cambridge, MA: Blackwell Business, 1994; R. P. Bagozzi, ed., *Advanced Methods of Marketing Research*, Cambridge, MA: Blackwell Business, 1994.
Mair, Andrew, *Honda's Global Local Corporation*, New York: St. Martin's Press, 1994.
Colletti, J., *A Field Guide to Focused Planning: Hoshin Kanri – American Style*, East Granby, CT: The Woodledge Group, 1995.

Six Sigma
Pyzdek, Thomas, *The Six Sigma Handbook*, New York: McGraw-Hill Professional, 2000.
Pande, Peter S., Robert P. Neuma, and Roland R. Cavanagh, *The Six Sigma Way: How GE, Motorola, and Other Top Companies are Honing Their Performance*, New York: McGraw-Hill, 2000.
Breyfogle, Forrest W., III, *Implementing Six Sigma: Smarter Solutions Using Statistical Methods*, Hoboken: John Wiley & Sons, 2003, 2nd ed.

Production (Activity) Control
Bethel, Lawrence L., et al., *Production Control*, New York: McGraw-Hill, 1948. 2nd ed.
Aerojet-General Corporation, *The Production Planning and Control Handbook; Industrial Engineering*, Azusa, CA, 1961.
Auburn University, *Simulation of a Production Control System*, Detroit, Management Information Services [1970?].
Plossl, George W., *Manufacturing Control: The Last Frontier for Profits*, Reston, VA: Reston Publ. [1973].
Production Activity Control Reprints, Falls Church, VA: American Production and Inventory Control Society, 1989, c1988. Rev. ed.
Wilhelm, Stefan, *Hierarchische Produktionssteuerung vernetzter Produktions-segmente*, Frankfurt am Main: P. Lang, 1996.

Fleming, Quentin W., and Joel M. Koppelman, *Earned Value Project Management*, Newton Square, PA: Project Management Institute, 2000. 2nd ed.

Grimble, Michael J., *Industrial Control Systems Design*, Chichester, [England]; New York: John Wiley & Sons, 2000.

Just in Time Systems

Japan Management Association, ed., trans. David J. Lu, *Kanban Just-in-Time at Toyota: Management Begins at the Workplace*, Stamford, CT: Productivity Press, 1986.

Malek, Marita, *KANBAN – Gesteuerte Fertigung: Simulative Analyse und Strukturierung eines mehrstufigen Produktionssystems*, Frankfurt am Main: P. Lang, 1988.

O'Grady, P. J., *Putting the Just-in-Time Philosophy into Practice*, New York: Nichols, 1988.

Schniederjans, Marc J., and John R. Olson, *Advanced Topics in Just-in-Time Management*, Westport, CT: Quorum Books, 1999.

Delbridge, Rick, *Life on the Line in Contemporary Manufacturing: The Workplace Experience of Lean Production and the 'Japanese' Model*, Oxford: Oxford University Press, 2000.

Statistical Process Control (SPC)

Clements, Richard R., *Statistical Process Control and Beyond*, Melbourne, FL: Krieger, 1988.

Amsden, Davida M., Robert T. Amsden, and Howard E. Butler, *SPC Simplified for Services*, Portland: Productivity Press, 1991.

Pitt, Hy, *SPC for the Rest of Us*, Springfield: K. W. Tunnell, 1999.

Tennant, Geoff, *Six Sigma: Spc and Tqm in Manufacturing and Services*, Aldershot: Gower, 2000.

Inventory Management

Whitin, Thomson M., *The Theory of Inventory Management*, Princeton: Princeton University Press, 1953.

Silver, Edward A., David F. Pyke, and Rein Peterson, *Inventory Management and Production Planning and Scheduling*, New York: John Wiley & Sons, 1998. 3rd ed.

Zipkin, Paul Herbert, *Foundations of Inventory Management*, New York: McGraw-Hill, 2000.

Toomey, John W., *Inventory Management: Principles, Concepts and Techniques*, Boston: Kluwer, 2000.

Production Management

Prabhu, V., *Production Management and Control*, New York: McGraw-Hill, 1986.

Russell, Roberta S., and Bernard W. Taylor, *Production and Operations Management*, Upper Saddle River, NJ: Prentice Hall, 1995.

Capacity Management

Blackstone, John H., Jr., *Capacity Management*, Cincinnati: South-Western, 1989.

Correll, James G., and Norris W. Edson, *Gaining Control: Capacity Management and Scheduling*, New York: John Wiley & Sons, 1998. 2nd ed.

McNair, Carol Jean, and Richard G. J. Vangermeersch, *Total Capacity Management: Optimizing at the Operational, Tactical, and Strategic Levels*, Boca Raton: CRC Press, 1998.

Supply Chain Management (SCM)

Handfield, Robert B., and Ernest L. Nichols, Jr., *Introduction to Supply Chain Management*, Upper Saddle River, NJ: Prentice Hall, 1998.

Szuprowicz, Bohdan O., *Supply Chain Management for E-Business Infrastructures*, Charleston: Computer Technology Research Corporation, 2000.

Tompkins, James A., *No Boundaries: Moving Beyond Supply Chain Management*, Tompkins Press, 2000.

Fuller, Richard, and David E. Mulcahy, *Global Supply Chain Logistics*, New York: McGraw-Hill, 2000 (Professional Engineering).

Hugos, Michael H., *Essentials of Supply Chain Management*, Hoboken: John Wiley & Sons, 2002.

Chopra, Sunil, and Peter Meindl, *Supply Chain Management*, Upper Saddle River, NJ: Prentice Hall, 2002 (2nd ed.).

Stadtler, Hartmut, and Christoph Kilger, eds., *Supply Chain Management and Advanced Planning*, Heidelberg: Springer, 2003.

Customer Relation Management (CRM), Customer Experience Management (CEM)

Swift, Ronald S., *Accelerating Customer Relationships: Using CRM and Relationship Technologies*, Upper Saddle River, NJ: Prentice Hall, 2000.

Brown, Stanley A., *Customer Relationship Management: Linking People, Process, and Technology*, New York: John Wiley & Sons, 2000.

Newell, Frederick, *Loyalty.com: Customer Relationship Management in the New Era of Internet Marketing*, New York: McGraw-Hill, 2000.

Schmitt, Bernd H., *Customer Experience Management: A Revolutionary Approach to Connecting with Your Customers*, Hoboken: John Wiley & Sons, 2003.

Production Planning

Menthonnex, Jean, *Planification de production et informatique de l'analyse des fonctions du secteur production á la description d'un modèle booléen de planification*, Bern: Herbert Lang, 1974.

Winter, Robert, *Mehrstufige Produktionsplanung in Abstraktionshierarchien auf der Basis relationaler Informationsstrukturen*, Berlin: Springer, 1991.

Minty, Gordon, *Production Planning and Controlling: A Problem-Based Approach*, Tinley Park: Goodheart-Willcox, 1998.

Material Requirements Planning (MRP)

Material Requirements Planning, Washington, DC (2600 Virginia Ave., N.W., Washington 20037): American Production and Inventory Control Society, [1973].

Orlicky, Joseph, *Material Requirements Planning; The New Way of Life in Production and Inventory Management*, New York: McGraw-Hill, [1975].

Material Requirements Planning, Falls Church, VA (500 West Annandale Rd., Falls Church 22046–4274): American Production and Inventory Control Society, [1982].

Lunn, Terry, Susan A. Neff, and Terry Lynn, *MRP: Integrating Material Requirements Planning and Modern Business*, Homewood, IL: Irwin, 1992 (Business One Irwin/Apics Series in Production Management).

Plossl, George W., *Orlicky's Material Requirements Planning*, New York: McGraw-Hill, 1994.

Arnold, J. R. Tony, and Stephen N. Chapman, *Introduction to Materials Management*, Upper Saddle River, NJ: Prentice Hall, 2000 (4th ed.).

Organizational Planning

Emery, James C., *Organizational Planning and Control Systems; Theory and Technology*, [New York]: Macmillan [1969].

Manufacturing (Resource) Planning (MRP)

Cross, Kelvin F., *Manufacturing Planning: Key to Improving Industrial Productivity*, New York: Marcel Dekker, 1986.

Vollmann, Thomas E., William L. Berry, and D. Clay Whybark, *Manufacturing Planning and Control Systems*, 3rd ed. Kansas City: CRC Press, 1994 (The Business One Irwin/Apics Series in Production Management).

Ptak, Carol A., *MRP and Beyond: A Toolbox for Integrating People and Systems*, Toronto: Irwin, 1996.

Drexl, Andreas, and Alf Kimms, eds., *Beyond Manufacturing Resource Planning (Mrp II): Advanced Models and Methods for Production Planning*, New York: Springer, 1998.

Sheikh, Khalid, *Manufacturing Resource Planning (MRP II) with Introduction to ERP, SCM, and CRM*, New York: McGraw-Hill, 2002.

Advanced Planning and Scheduling (APS)

Narasimhan, Seetharama L., Dennis W. McLeavey, Seethrarama L. Narasimhan, Dennis W. McLeavy, and Peter J. Billington, *Production Planning and Inventory Control*. Upper Saddle River, NJ: Prentice Hall, 1994.

Tate, Austin, ed., *Advanced Planning Technology: Technological Achievements of the ARPA/Rome Laboratory Planning Initiative*, Menlo Park, CA: AAAI Press, 1996.

Günther, Hans-Otto, and Paul van Beek, *Advanced Planning and Scheduling Solutions in Process Industry*, Heidelberg: Springer, 2003 (Gor-Publications).

Business Intelligence (BI)

March, James G., *The Pursuit of Organizational Intelligence*, Oxford: Blackwell, 1999.

Liautaud, Bernard, and Mark Hammond, *E-Business Intelligence: Turning Information into Knowledge into Profit*, New York: McGraw-Hill, 2000.

Vitt, Elizabeth, Michael Luckevich, and Stacia Misner, *Business Intelligence*, Redmond: Microsoft Press, 2002.

Biere, Mike, *Business Intelligence for the Enterprise*, Upper Saddle River, NJ: Prentice Hall, 2003.

Internet Based Procurement (IBP) and e-purchasing

Giunipero, Larry C., and Chris Sawchuk, *e-Purchasingplus*, East Troy, WI: JPC Enterprises, 2000.

Oz, Effy, *Foundations of E-Commerce*, Upper Saddle River, NJ: Prentice Hall, 2001.

Antonette, Gerald, Chris Sawchuk, and Larry C. Giunipero, *ePurchasingPlus*, Goshen: JGC Enterprises, 2002, 2nd ed.

Enterprise Resource Planning (ERP)

Shtub, Avraham, *Enterprise Resource Planning (ERP): The Dynamics of Operations Management*, Dordrecht: Kluwer, 1999.

Callaway, Erin, *CTR Report: ERP – The Next Generation: ERP Is Web Enabled for E-business*, Charleston: Computer Technology Research Corporation, 2000.

Norris, Grant, John Dunleavy, James R. Hurley, John D. Balls, and Kenneth M. Hartley, *E-Business and ERP: Transforming the Enterprise*, New York: John Wiley & Sons, 2000.

Sutton, Steve G., and Vickie Arnold, *Enterprise Resource Planning Systems*, Toronto: International Thomson, 2001.

Shanks, Graeme, Peter B. Seddon, and Leslie P. Willcocks, eds., *Second-Wave Enterprise Resource Planning Systems: Implementing for Effectiveness*, Cambridge: Cambridge University Press, 2003.

Agile Manufacturing and Virtual Enterprise (cf. Virtual Organization)

Kidd, Paul T., *Agile Manufacturing: Forging New Frontiers*, Reading, MA: Addison-Wesley, 1994.

Kidd, Paul T., and Waldemar Karwowski, *Advances in Agile Manufacturing: Integrating Technologies, Organization and People*, Amsterdam: IOS Press, 1994 (Volume 4 in Advances in Design and Manufacturing).

Dimancescu, Dan, and Kemp Dwenger, *World-Class New Product Development: Benchmarking Best Practices of Agile Manufacturers*, New York: Amacom, 1995.

Montgomery, Joseph C., and Lawrence O. Levine, eds., *The Transition to Agile Manufacturing: Staying Flexible for Competitive Advantage*, Milwaukee: The American Society for Quality, 1996.

Amos, Jeffrey, *Transformation to Agility: Manufacturing in the Marketplace of Unanticipated Change*, New York: Garland, 1998 (Transnational Business and Corporate Culture).

Goranson, H. T., *The Agile Virtual Enterprise: Cases, Metrics, Tools*, Westport, CT: Quorum Books, 1999.

Guran, S. Lee, *Intelligent Control, Flexible and Agile Assembly in Manufacturing Systems*, Singapore: World Scientific Publishers, 2001 (Series on Stability, Vibration and Control of Structures).

Paolucci, Massimo, and Roberto Sacile, *Agent-Based Manufacturing and Control Systems: New Agile Manufacturing Solutions for Achieving Peak Performance*, Boca Raton: St. Lucie Press, 2004.

Mechatronics

McLean, Mick, ed., *Mechatronics: Developments in Japan and Europe*, Westport, CT: Quorum Books, 1983.

HMT Limited, *Mechatronics and Machine Tools*, New York: McGraw-Hill, 1999.

Kaynak, Okyay, Sabri Tosunoglu, and Marcelo Ang Jr., eds., *Recent Advances in Mechatronics*, Berlin: Springer, 1999.

Billingsley, John, ed., *Mechatronics and Machine Vision*, Baldock, Hertfordshire, England; Philadephia, PA: Research Studies Press, 2000.

Necsulescu, Dan S., *Mechatronics*, Upper Saddle River, NJ: Prentice Hall, 2002.

Bolton, W., *Mechatronics: Electronic Control Systems in Mechanical and Electrical Engineering*, Upper Saddle River, NJ: Prentice Hall, 2002 (3rd ed.).

Chapter 5. Services

Global Economy

Ball, George W., *Global Companies: The Political Economy of World Business*, Englewood Cliffs, NJ: Prentice Hall, [1975].

Helleiner, G.K., *The New Global Economy and the Developing Countries: Essays in International Economics and Development*, Brookfield, VT: Edward Elgar, 1990.

Carnoy, Martin, et al., *The New Global Economy in the Information Age: Reflections on our Changing World*, University Park, PA: Pennsylvania State University Press, 1993.

Veseth, Michael, *Selling Globalization: The Myth of the Global Economy*, Boulder: Lynne Rienner, 1998.

Henderson, Hazel, *Beyond Globalization: Shaping a Sustainable Global Economy*, West Hartford, CT: Kumarian Press, 1999.

Anderson, Sarah, John Cavanagh, Thea Lee, and Barbara Ehrenreich, *Field Guide to the Global Economy*, New York: New Press, 2000.

Bales, Kevin, *Disposable People: New Slavery in the Global Economy*, Los Angeles: University of California Press, 2000.

Dicken, Peter, *Global Shift: Transforming the World Economy*, New York: Guilford Press, 2000.

Rumer, Boris, ed., *Central Asia and the New Global Economy*, Armonk: M.E. Sharpe, 2000.

Weaver, Frederick Stirton, and Ron Chilcote, *Latin America in the World Economy: Mercantile Colonialism to Global Capitalism*, Boulder, CO: Westview Press, 2000.

Koelble, Thomas A., *The Global Economy and Democracy in South Africa*, Piscataway, NJ: Rutgers University Press, 2000.

Mshomba, Richard E., *Africa in the Global Economy*, Boulder, CO: Lynne Rienner, 2000.

Beenhakker, Henri L., *The Global Economy and International Financing*, Westport, CT: Quorum Books, 2000.

OECD, *The Future of the Global Economy: Towards a Long Boom?* Paris: OECD, 2000.

Andersson, Ake E., and David E. Andersson, *Gateways to the Global Economy*, Cheltenham: Edward Elgar, 2001.

Gilpin, Robert, *Global Political Economy: Understanding the International Economic Order*, Princeton: Princeton University Press, 2001.

Information Economy

Porat, Marc Uri, *The Information Economy*, Stanford, CA: Program in Information Technology and Telecommunications, Center for Interdisciplinary Research, Stanford University, 1976.

The Information Economy: Its Implications for Canada's Industrial Strategy: Proceedings of a Conference held at Erindale College, University of Toronto, May 30-June 1, 1984, ed., Calvin C. Gotlieb, Ottawa: Royal Society of Canada, [1985].

Network Advisory Committee. Meeting (1984 Nov. 14–16: Library of Congress) *The Information Economy in the U.S.: Its Effect on Libraries and Library Networks: Proceedings of the Library of Congress Network Advisory Committee Meeting, November 14–16, 1984*. Washington: Network Development and MARC Standards Office, Library of Congress, 1985.

Graf, David, Olive D. Church, and Thomas B. Duff, *Business in an Information Economy*, Glencoe/McGraw-Hill, 1989.

Osberg, Lars, Edward N. Wolff, and William J. Baumol, *The Information Economy: The Implications of Unbalanced Growth*, Halifax, NS: Institute for Research on Public Policy, 1989.

Radding, Alan, *Knowledge Management: Succeeding in the Information-Based Global Economy*, Charleston: Computer Technology Research Corporation, 1998.

Knowledge Economy

Eliasson, Gunnar, Stefan Folster, Thomas Lindberg, and Tomas Pousette, *The Knowledge Based Information Economy*, Philadelphia: Coronet Books, 1990.

The Knowledge Based Information Economy The Knowledge Based Information Economy Bottom of Form 1.

Winslow, Charles D., James Brian Quinn, William L. Bramer, *Future Work: Putting Knowledge to Work in the Knowledge Economy*, New York: Free Press, 1994.

Neef, Dale, ed., *The Knowledge Economy*, London: Butterworth-Heinemann, 1997.

Neef, Dale, *A Little Knowledge Is a Dangerous Thing: Understanding Our Global Knowledge Economy*, London: Butterworth-Heinemann, 1997.

Cortada, James W., ed., *Rise of the Knowledge Worker*, London: Butterworth-Heinemann, 1998 (Resources for the Knowledge-Based Economy).

Thurow, Lester C., *The Wealth Pyramid: New Rules for a Knowledge Based Economy*, New York: Harper Business, 1999.

Cross, Rob, and Sam Israelit, *Strategic Learning in a Knowledge Economy: Individual, Collective and Organizational Learning Process*, Woburn: Butterworth, 2000.

Lesser, Eric L., Michael A. Fontaine, and Jason A. Slusher, *Knowledge and Communities*, London: Butterworth-Heinemann, 2000 (Resources for the Knowledge-Based Economy).

Thurow, Lester C., *Building Wealth: The New Rules for Individuals, Companies, and Nations in a Knowledge-Based Economy*, New York: Harper Business, 2000.

Dunning, John H., ed., *Regions, Globalization, and Knowledge-Based Economy*, New York: Oxford University Press, 2000.
Burton-Jones, Alan, *Knowledge Capitalism: Business, Work, and Learning in the New Economy*, New York: Oxford University Press, 2000.
Doz, Yves L., Jose Santos, and Peter Williamson, *From Global to Metanational: How Companies Win in the Knowledge Economy*, Boston: Harvard University Press, 2003.
Alderman, F. Lee, and Chuck Barritt, *Creating a Reusable Learning Objects Strategy: Leveraging Information and Learning in a Knowledge Economy*, San Francisco: Jossey-Bass/Pfeiffer, 2004.

Internet, Digital and Network Economy

Hammond, Ray, *Digital Business: Surviving and thriving in an On-Line World*, London: Hodder & Stoughton, 1996.
Hagel, John III, and Arthur G. Armstrong, *Net Gain: Expanding Markets through Virtual Communities*, Boston: Harvard Business School Press, 1997.
Meyer, Christopher, and Stan Davis, *Blur: The Speed of Change in the Connected Economy*, New York: Perseus, 1998.
Shapiro, Carl, and Hal R. Varian, *Information Rules: A Strategic Guide to the Network Economy*, Boston: Harvard Business School, 1999.
Tiggelaar, Ben, *Internet strategie: concurrentievoordeel in de digitale economie: theorie en praktijk*, Amsterdam: Addison-Wesley Longman Nederland BV, c1999.
Tapscott, Don, *Creating Value in the Network Economy*, Boston: Harvard Business School, 1999.
Deneuil, François, *Internet et les sept piliers du XXIe siecle*, Paris: Connaissance Partagée, 1999.
Deal, Terrence E., and Allan A. Kennedy, *The New Corporate Cultures: Revitalizing the Workplace after Downsizing, Mergers and Reengineering*, Reading, MA: Perseus, 1999.
Ohmae, Kenichi, *The Invisible Continent: Four Strategic Imperatives of the New Economy*, New York: Harper Business, 2000.
Pottruck, David S., and Terry Pearce, *Clicks and Mortar*, San Francisco: Jossey-Bass, 2000.
Tapscott, Don, David Ticoll, and Alex Lowy, *Digital Capital: Harnessing the Power of Business Webs*, Boston: Harvard Business School Press, 2000.
Brynjolfsson, Erik, and Brian Kahin, eds., *Understanding the Digital Economy*, Cambridge, MA: MIT Press, 2000.
Wiseman, Alan E., *The Internet Economy: Access, Taxes, and Market Structure*, Washington: Brookings Institution Press, 2000.
McKeown, Patrick G., *Information Technology and the Networked Economy*, New York: Harcourt, 2001.
Kogut, Brice, *The Global Internet Economy*, Cambridge, MA: MIT Press, 2003.
"China Internet Economy, 2002–2007" [DOWNLOAD: PDF], IDC, 2003 (ISBN: B000167JJS).

e-business

Deise, Martin V., Conrad Nowikow, Patrick King, Amy Wright, and PriceWaterhouse-Coopers, *Executive's Guide to E-Business: From Tactics to Strategy*, New York: John Wiley & Sons, 2000.
Kalakota, Ravi, Marcia Robinson, and Don Tapscott, *E-Business: Roadmap for Success*, Reading, MA: Addison-Wesley, 1999 (Addison-Wesley Information, Technology Series).
Means, Grady, and David M. Schneider, eds., *MetaCapitalism: The e-Business Revolution and the Design of 21st-Century Companies and Markets*, New York: John Wiley & Sons, 2000.
Menasce, Daniel A., and Virgilio A. F. Almeida, *Scaling for E-Business: Technologies, Models, Performance, and Capacity Planning*, Upper Saddle River, NJ: Prentice Hall, 2000.
Rajput, Wasim, *E-Commerce Systems Architecture and Applications*, Norwood, MA: Artech House, 2000.
Chinoy, Hussain, Tyna Hull, and Robi Sen, *XML for EDI: Making E-Commerce a Reality*, San Francisco: Morgan Kauffmann, 2000.

e-commerce

Cashin, Jerry, *E-Commerce Success: Building a Global Business Architecture*, Charleston: Computer Technology Research Corporation, 1999.

Korper, Steffano, Juanita Ellis, and Jerry D. Gibson, *The E-Commerce Book: Building the E-Empire*, San Diego: Academic Press, 1999.

Fellenstein, Craig, and Ron Wood. *Exploring E-Commerce, Global E-Business and E-Society*, Upper Saddle River, NJ: Prentice Hall, 1999.

Fingar, Peter, Harsha Kumar, and Tarun Sharma, *Enterprise E-Commerce*, Tampa: Meghan Kiffer Press, 2000.

For a serious list of e-commerce and e-business books, see: http://home1.gte.net/pfingar/bookecommerce.htm. For articles, see the e-commerce Research Room: http://webmarketingtoday.com/research/intro.htm

e-enterprise

Hoque, Faisal, *E-Enterprise: Business Models, Architecture and Components*, New York: Cambridge University Press, 2000 (Breakthroughs in Application Development).

O'Brien, James A., *Management Information Systems: Managing Information Technology in the E-Business Enterprise*, New York: McGraw-Hill, 2003. 6th ed.

e-marketing

Strauss, Judy, and Raymond Frost, *E-Marketing*, Upper Saddle River, NJ: Prentice Hall, 2000. 3rd ed., 2002.

Rapp, Stan, and Chuck Martin, *Max-E-Marketing in the Net Future: The Seven Imperatives for Outsmarting the Competition for Internet-Age Supremacy*, New York: McGraw-Hill, 2000.

Fiore, Frank, *e-Marketing Strategies*, Indianapolis: QUE, 2000.

Cox, Barbara, and William Koelzer, *Internet Marketing*, Upper Saddle River, NJ: Prentice Hall, 2003.

e-customer

Siegel, David, *Futurize Your Enterprise: Business Strategy in the Age of the E-customer*, New York: John Wiley & Sons, 1999.

Windham, Laurie, and Ken Orton, *The Soul of the New Consumer: The Attitudes, Behavior, and Preferences of E-Customers*, New York: Allworth Press, 2000.

Intellectual Property Rights (IPR)

Bettig, Ronald V., and Herbert I. Schiller, eds., *Copyrighting Culture: The Political Economy of Intellectual Property*, Boulder: Westview Press, 1997 (Critical Studies in Communication and in the Cultural Industries).

Samuelson, Pamela, and Peter Neumann, eds. *Intellectual Property in the Age of Universal Access*, New York: ACM Press, 1999.

Maskus, Keith E., and C. Fred Bergsten, *Intellectual Property Rights in the Global Economy*, Washington: Institute for International Economics, 2000.

Correa, Carlos Maria, *Intellectual Property Rights, the WTO and Developing Countries: The Trips Agreement and Policy Options*, London: ZED Books, 2000.

May, Christopher, *A Global Political Economy of Intellectual Property Rights: The New Enclosures?*, London: Routledge, 2000.

Long, Clarisa, ed., *Intellectual Property Rights in Emerging Markets*, Colton, CA: AEI Press, 2000.

Braga, Carlos Alberto Primo, Carsten Fink, and Claudia Paz Sepulveda, *Intellectual Property Rights and Economic Development*, Washington: World Bank, 2000 (World Bank Discussion Papers, 412).

Dutfield, Graham, *Intellectual Property Rights, Trade and Biodiversity*, London: Earthscan, 2002.

Sell, Susan K., *Private Power, Public Law: The Globalization of Intellectual Property Rights*, Cambridge: Cambridge University Press, 2003.

Artificial Intelligence

Barr, Avron, and Edward A. Feigenbaum, ed. *The Handbook of Artificial Intelligence*, Stanford, CA: Heuris Tech Press, 1981. (1989).

Winston, Patrick Henry, *Artificial Intelligence*, Boston: Addison-Wesley, 1992 (3rd ed.).

Russell, Stuart J., and Peter Norvig, *Artificial Intelligence: A Modern Approach*, Upper Saddle River, NJ: Prentice Hall, 2002, 2nd ed.

Agents and Avatars

Bradshaw, Jeffrey M., ed., *Software Agents*, Menlo Park, CA: AAAI Press; Cambridge, MA: MIT Press, 1997.

Damer, Bruce, *Avatars! Exploring and Building Virtual Worlds on the Internet*, San Francisco: Peachpit Press, 1998.

Caglayan, Alper, and Colin Harrison, *Agent Sourcebook*, New York: John Wiley & Sons, 1998.

Brenner, Walter, Rüdiger Zarnekow, and Hartmut Wittig, *Intelligente Softwareagenten: Grundlagen und Anwendungen*, Berlin: Springer, 1998.

Jennings, Nicholas R., and Michael J. Wooldridge, *Agent Technology: Foundations, Applications and Markets*, Berlin: Springer, 1998.

Dautenhahn, Kerstin, *Human Cognition and Social Agent Technology*, Amsterdam: John Benjamins Research, 1999.

Ferber, Jacques, *Multi-Agent Systems: An Introduction to Distributed Artificial Intelligence*, Harlow: Addison-Wesley, 1999.

Klusch, Matthias (ed.), *Intelligent Information Agents: Agent-Based Information Discovery and Management on the Internet*, Berlin: Springer, 1999.

Hayzelden, Alex L.G., and Rachel Bourne, eds., *Agent Technology for Communications Infrastructure*, New York: John Wiley & Sons, 2000.

Padget, Julian A., ed., *Collaboration Between Human and Artificial Societies: Coordination and Agent-Based Distributed Computing*, New York: Springer, 2000.

Cassell, Justine, et al., eds., *Embodied Conversational Agents*, Cambridge, MA: MIT Press, 2000.

Meyer, John-Jules Ch., and Pierre-Yves Schobbens, eds., *Formal Models of Agents: ESPRIT Project ModelAge Final Workshop Selected Papers*, New York: Springer, 2000.

Khosla, Rajiv, Ishwar K. Sethi, and Ernesto Damiani, *Intelligent Multimedia Multi-Agent Systems: A Human-Centered Approach*, Boston: Kluwer, 2000.

Yokoo, Makoto, *Distributed Constraint Satisfaction: Foundations of Cooperation in Multi-Agent Systems*, New York: Springer, 2000.

Subrahmanian, V. S., Piero Bonatti, Jürgen Dix, Thomas Eiter, and Fatma Ozcan, *Heterogeneous Agent Systems*, Cambridge, MA: MIT Press, 2000.

Wooldridge, Michael J., *Reasoning About Rational Agents*, Cambridge, MA: MIT Press, 2000 (*Intelligent Robotics and Autonomous Agents*).

Kraus, Sarit, *Strategic Negotiation in Multiagent Environments*, Cambridge, MA: MIT Press, 2001.

Patel, Mukesh, Vasant Honavar, and Karthik Balakrishnan, eds., *Advances in the Evolutionary Synthesis of Intelligent Agents*, Cambridge, MA: MIT Press, 2001.

Shen, Wei-min, D. H. Norrie, and Jean-Paul Barthes, *Multi-Agent Systems for Concurrent Intelligent Design and Manufacturing*, London: Taylor and Francis, 2001.

Luck, Michael, Ronald Ashri, and Mark d'Inverno, *Agent-Based Software Development*, Norwood, MA: Artech House, 2004.

Chapter 6. Institutions

Virtual Architecture

Morgan, Conway Lloyd, and Giuliano Zampi, *Virtual Architecture*, New York: McGraw-Hill, 1995.

Toy, Maggie, ed., *Architects in Cyberspace: Post Revolution Architecture in Eastern Europe*, New York: John Wiley & Sons, 1995 (Architectural Design Profile, No. 118). Cf. Maggie Toy, Neil Spiller, eds., *Architects in Cyberspace II*, New York: John Wiley & Sons, 1999 (Architectural Design Profile, No. 136).

Beckmann, John, ed., *The Virtual Dimension: Architecture, Representation and Crash Culture*, New York: Princeton Architectural Press, 1998.

Harris, Judi, *Virtual Architecture: Designing and Directing Curriculum-Based Telecomputing*, Eugene, OR: International Society for Technology in Education, 1998.

Uddin, Mohammed Saleh, *Digital Architecture: Turn Vision into Virtual Reality with 3D Graphics Hardware, Software, Tips, and Techniques from 50 Top Designers*, New York: McGraw-Hill, 1999.

Galli, Mirko, Claudia Muhlhoff, and Claudia Muhloff, *Virtual Terragni: CAAD in Historical and Critical Research*, Basel: Birkhäuser, 2000.

Kerckhove, Derrick de, *Cyberarchitecture: Wetten van de digitale ruimte*, Hague: Stichting Maatschappij en Onderneming, 2000.

Virtual Classroom and e-classroom

Hiltz, Starr Roxanne, *The Virtual Classroom: Learning Wthout Limits via Computer Networks*, Norwood, N.J: Ablex; Bristol: Intellect, 1994 (Human/Computer Interaction).

Tiffin, John, and Lalita Rajasingham, *In Search of the Virtual Class: Education in an Information Society*, London: Routledge, 1995.

Kuhlthau, Carol Collier, M. Elspeth Goodin, and Mary McNally, eds., *The Virtual School Library: Gateway to the Information Superhighway*, Englewood, CO: Libraries Unlimited, 1996.

Hobbs, Vicki M., and J. Scott Christianson, *Virtual Classrooms: Educational Opportunity through Two-Way Interactive Television*, Lancaster, PA: Technomic Pub., 1997.

Porter, Lynnette R., *Creating the Virtual Classroom: Distance Learning with the Internet*, New York: John Wiley & Sons, 1997.

Maeroff, Gene I., *A Classroom of One: How Online Learning is Changing our Schools and Colleges*, New York: Palgrave Macmillan, 2003.

Virtual Enterprise (See 4: Agile Manufacturing)

Pucciarelli, Joe (Vice President, Business Management of IT, GartnerGroup), Michael Bell (Research Director, Business Management of IT, GartnerGroup), *The Virtual Enterprise: It's Here!*, Stamford, CT: Gartner Group, 1999 (Audio Book).

Kovacs, George L, Peter Bertok, Geza Haidegger, and George L. Kovacs, *Digital Enterprise Challenges*, Ifip Tc5, Wg5.2, Wg5.3, 11th International Prolamat Conference on Digital Enterprise, Dordrecht: Kluwer, 2002.

Virtual Government and e-government

Constantine, Alex, *Virtual Government: CIA Mind Control Operations in America*, Venice, CA: Feral House, 1997.

Bacon, Kevin, Colleen Wesling, Joseph Casey, Jenny Wodinsky, *E-Government: The Blueprint*, New York: John Wiley & Sons, 2000.

Virtual Library and e-library (cf. Digital Libraries)

Systems and Procedures Exchange Center, *The Emerging Virtual Research Library*, Washington: Association of Research Libraries, Office of Management Services, 1992.

Böllmann, Elisabeth, ed., *The Virtual Library: 17th Library System Seminar, Karl-Franzens-Universität Graz, Meerscheinschlössl, 14–16 April 1993* (European Library Automation Group, ELAG), Graz: Univ.-Bibliothek Graz, 1993.

Saunders, Laverna M., ed., *The Virtual Library: Visions and Realities*, Westport, CT: Meckler, 1993 (Computers in Libraries Conference, Washington).

Sloan, Bernard, ed., *Managing the Virtual Library: Issues and Case Studies*, Westport, CT: Meckler, 1993.

The Virtual Library: An SLA Information Kit, Washington: Special Libraries Association, 1994.

Pastine, Maureen, ed., *Collection Development: Access in the Virtual Library*, Binghamton, NY: Haworth Press, 1998.

Saunders, Laverna M., ed., *The Evolving Virtual Library II: Practical and Philosophical Perspectives*, Medford, NJ: Information Today, 1999.

Kemp, Thomas Jay, *The Genealogists Virtual Library: Full-Text Books on the World Wide Web*, Wilmington, DE: Scholarly Resources, 2000.

Hanson, Ardis, and Bruce Lubotsky Levin, *Building a Virtual Library*, Hershey, PA: Idea Group, 2002.

Ronan, Jana Smith, *Chat Reference: A Guide to Live Virtual Reference Services*, Westport, CT: Libraries Unlimited, 2002.

Lipow, Anne Grodzins, and Clifford Lynch, *The Virtual Reference Librarian's Handbook*, Berkeley: Library Solutions Press, 2003.

Kimmel, Stacey E., and Jennifer Heise, *Virtual Reference Services: Issues and Trends*, Binghampton, NY: Haworth Press, 2003 (Monograph Published Simultaneously As Internet Reference Services quarterly, 1/2).

Virtual Museum and e-museum

Castellary, Arturo Colorado, *Hipercultura Visual: El reto hipermedia en el ate y la educacion*, Madrid: Editorial Complutense, 1997.

Thomas, Selma, and Ann Mintz., eds., *The Virtual and the Real: Media in the Museum*, Washington: American Association of Museums, 1999.

Virtual Organization

Grenier, Raymond, and George Metes, *Going Virtual: Moving Your Organization Into the 21st Century*, Upper Saddle River, NJ: Prentice Hall, 1995.

Lipnack, Jessica, and Jeffrey Stamps, *Virtual Teams: Reaching Across Space, Time, and Organizations With Technology*, New York: John Wiley & Sons, 1997.

Henry, Jane E., and Meg Hartzler, *Tools for Virtual Teams: A Team Fitness Companion*, Milwaukee: American Society for Quality, 1997.

Hedberg, Bo, Goran Dahlgren, Jorgen Hansson, and Nils-Goran Olve, *Virtual Organizations and Beyond: Discover Imaginary Systems*, New York: John Wiley & Sons, 1997. (Wiley Series in Practical Strategy).

Fisher, Kimball, Maureen Duncan Fisher, and Mareen Duncan Fisher, *The Distributed Mind: Achieving High Performance through the Collective Intelligence of Knowledge Work Teams*, New York: Amacom, 1997.

Norton, Bob, and Cathy Smith, *Understanding the Virtual Organization*, New York: Barron's Educational Series, 1998. (Barron's Business Success Guide).

Fukuyama, Francis, Abram N. Shulsky, and United States Army, *The 'Virtual Corporation' and Army Organization*, Santa Monica: Rand Corporation, 1997.

Igbaria, Magid, and Margaret Tan, ed., *The Virtual Workplace*, Hershey, PA: Idea Group, 1998. (Series in Information Technology Management).

Jackson, Paul J., and Jos Van Der Wielen, ed., *Teleworking: International Perspectives: From Telecommuting to the Virtual Organisation*, London: Routledge, 1998. (The Management of Technology and Innovation).

Nilles, Jack M., *Managing Telework: Strategies for Managing the Virtual Workforce*, New York: John Wiley & Sons, 1998. (Wiley/Upside Series).

Vogt, Gudrun G., *Nomaden der Arbeitswelt: Virtuelle Unternehmen, Kooperationen auf Zeit*, Zürich: Versus, 1999.

Burn, Janice, Peter Marshall, and Martin Barnett, *e-Business Strategies for Virtual Organizations*, London: Butterworth-Heinemann, 2001.

Fong, Michelle W. L., *E-Collaborations and Virtual Organizations*, Hershey: IRM Press, 2004.

443

Virtual School and e-school

[Meeting of the minds 2.], *The Net Effect: School Library Media Centers and the Internet*, ed. Lyn Hay, James Henri, Lanham, MD: Scarecrow Press, 1999.

Zucker, Andrew, Robert Kozma, Louise Yarnall, and Camille Marder, *The Virtual High School: Teaching Generation V*, New York: Teachers College Press, 2003.

Cavanaugh, Catherine, *Development and Management of Virtual Schools: Issues and Trends*, Hershey, PA: Information Science Publishing, 2003.

Palloff, Rena M., and Keith Pratt, *The Virtual Student: A Profile and Guide to Working with Online Learners*, San Francisco: Jossey-Bass, 2003.

Virtual State

Everard, Jerry, *Virtual States: The Internet and the Boundaries of the Nation-State*, London: Routledge, 2000.

Frissen, P., and Chris Emery, trans., *Politics, Governance and Technology: A Postmodern Narrative on the Virtual State*, Cheltenham: Edward Elgar, 1999 (New Horizons in Public Policy).

Rosecrance, Richard N., *The Rise of the Virtual State: Wealth and Power in the Coming Century*, New York: Basic Books, 2000.

Fountain, Jane E., *Building the Virtual State: Information Technology and Institutional Change*, Washington: Brookings Institution Press, 2001.

Abramson, Mark A., and Therese L. Morin, eds., *E- Government, 2003*, Lanham, MD: Rowman & Littlefield, 2002.

Virtual University and e-university

Van Dusen, Gerald C., *The Virtual Campus: Technology and Reform in Higher Education*, Columbia, MO: Ashe-Eric, 1997 (Ashe-Eric Higher Education Report, Vol. 25, No. 5).

Technology and the Virtual University: Opportunities and Challenges. Hearing of the Committee on Labor and Human Resources, United States Senate, One Hundred Fifth Congress, first session, April 16, 1997.

Foulke-Ffeinberg, F. X., *The Virtual Campus*, Edinburgh: Cui Bono Books, 1998.

Teare, Richard, David Davies, and Eric Sandelands, *The Virtual University: An Action Paradigm and Process for Workplace Learning*, London: Cassell, 1999 (Workplace Learning Series).

Ryan, Steve, Bernard Scott, Howard Freeman, and Daxa Patel, *The Virtual University: The Internet and Resource-Based Learning*, London: Kogan Page, 2000. (The Open and Distance Learning Series).

Virtual U: A University Simulation Available, Bolton, MA: Anker, 2000.

Robins, Kevin, and Frank Webster, *The Virtual University?: Knowledge, Markets, and Management*, New York: Oxford University Press, 2003.

Nistor, Nicolae, Susan English, Steve Wheeler, and Mihai Jalobeanu, eds., *Toward the Virtual University: International Online Perspectives*, Greenwich, CT: Information Age Publishing, 2003 (Perspectives in Instructional Technology and Distance Learning).

Tiffin, John, and Lalita Rajasingham, *The Global Virtual University*, London: Routledge Falmer, 2003.

Virtuality

Morse, Margaret, *Virtualities: Television, Media Art and Cyberculture*, Bloomington: Indiana University Press, 1998.

Horrocks, Christopher, *Marshall McLuhan and Virtuality*, Kallista: Totem Books, 2001.

Sunden, Jenny, *Material Virtualities: Approaching Online Textual Embodiment*, Bern: Peter Lang, 2003 (Digital Formations, V. 13).

Garsten, Christina, and Helena Wulff, *New Technologies at Work: People, Screens and Social Virtuality*, Oxford: Berg, 2003.

Digital Library/Libraries

Cf. The Future of Libraries: Readings. See: http://www.dochzi.com/bibs/future-libs.html.

Infopedia [computer file]: The Ultimate Multimedia Encyclopedia and Reference Library, Spring Valley, NY: Future Vision Multimedia, 1995.

Lesk, Michael, *Practical Digital Libraries: Books, Bytes, and Bucks*, Morgan Kaufmann, San Francisco, 1997 (Morgan Kaufmann Series in Multimedia Information and Systems).

Beschloss, Michael R., *The Digital Libraries in our Future: Perils and Promise*, Washington: Annenberg Washington Program, Communications Policy Studies, Northwestern University, 1996.

ACM Conference on Digital Libraries, *Digital Libraries: The ... ACM Conference on Digital Libraries*, New York: Association for Computing Machinery, 1998. See: http://info.acm.org/pubs/contents/proceedings/series/dl/.

Stern, David, ed., *Digital Libraries: Philosophies, Technical Design Considerations, and Example Scenarios: Pre-Publication Reviews, Commentaries, Evaluations*, New York: Haworth Press, 1999.

Borgman, Christine L., *From Gutenberg to the Global Information Infrastructure: Access to Information in the Networked World*, Cambridge, MA: MIT Press, 2000.

Bhargava, Bharat, *Digital Libraries and Multimedia*, Boston: Kluwer, 2000.

Arms, William Y., *Digital Libraries*, Cambridge, MA: MIT Press, 2000.

Handler, Peter, *E-Text: Strategien und Kompetenzen*, Frankfurt: Peter Lang, 2002.

Chowdhury, G. G., and Sudatta Chowdhury, *Introduction to Digital Libraries*, Library Association Publications, 2002.

Chapter 7. Organizations

Classic Texts: United States

Taylor, Frederick Winslow (1856–1915), *The Principles of Scientific Management*, New York: Harper & Bros., 1911. Reprint: Mineola, NY: Dover, 1997.

Gantt, Henry L., *Organizing for Work*, New York: Harcourt, Brace and Howe, 1919.

Mayo, Elton (1880–1949), *The Human Problems of an Industrial Civilization*, New York: Macmillan, 1933.

Barnard, Chester Irving (1886–1961), *The Functions of the Executive*, Cambridge, MA: Harvard University Press, 1938;

Barnard, Chester Irving , *The Nature of Leadership*, Cambridge, MA: Harvard University Press, 1940.

Drucker, Peter Ferdinand (1909–), *Concept of the Corporation*, New York: John Day, 1946;Drucker, Peter Ferdinand (1909–), *The End of Economic Man: A Study of the New Totalitarianism*. New York: John Day, c.1939. Ibid., *Concept of the Corporation* (1946), New York: John Day, 1946.

Maslow, Abraham Harold, *Motivation and Personality*, New York: Harper, 1954.

Herzberg, Frederick, Bernard Mausner, and Barbara Bloch Snyderman, *The Motivation to Work*, New York: John Wiley & Sons [1959]. 2nd ed. Cf. Frederick Herzberg et al., *Job Attitudes: Review of Research and Opinion*, Pittsburgh: Psychological Service of Pittsburgh, c.1957.

Likert, Rensis, *New Patterns of Management*, New York: McGraw-Hill, 1961.

Argyris, Chris, *Integrating the Individual and the Organization*, New York: John Wiley & Sons, 1964. Reprint: New Brunswick, NJ: Transaction Publishers, Reprint 1990.

Chris Argyris and Action Science. Cf. *Integrating the Individual and the Organization*, New York: John Wiley & Sons, 1964. Reprint: New Brunswick, NJ: Transaction Publishers, Reprint 1990. Ibid., *On Organizations of the Future*, Beverly Hills: Sage, 1973 (Sage Professional Papers in Administrative and Policy Studies 103006). Ibid., *Increasing Leadership Effectiveness*, New York: John Wiley & Sons, 1976 (Wiley Series in Behavior). Ibid., *Behind the Front Page: Organizational Self-Renewal in a Metropolitan Newspaper*, San Francisco: Jossey-Bass, 1974. (Jossey-Bass Behavioral Science Series). Ibid., Donald A. Schön, *Theory in Practice: Increasing Professional Effectiveness*, San Francisco: Jossey-Bass, 1977 (Jossey-Bass Series in Higher Education). Ibid., Robert Putnam, Diana McLain Smith, *Action Science: Concepts, Methods, and Skills for Research and Intervention*, San Francisco: Jossey-Bass, 1985. Ibid., *Strategy, Change, and Defensive Routines*, Boston: Pitman, 1985. Ibid., *Overcoming Organizational Defenses: Facilitating Organizational Learning*, Needham Heights, MA: Allyn & Bacon, 1990. Ibid., Donald A. Schön, *Theory in Practice: Increasing Professional Effectiveness*, San Francisco: Jossey-Bass, 1992. (Jossey-Bass Higher and Adult Education Series). Ibid., *Knowledge for Action: A Guide to Overcoming Barriers to Organizational Change*, San Francisco: Jossey-Bass, 1993. (Jossey-Bass Management). Ibid., *On Organizational Learning*, Cambridge, MA: Blackwell, 1994. Reprint: 1999. Ibid., Donald A. Schön, *Organizational Learning II: Theory, Method and Practice*, Reading, MA: Addison-Wesley, 1996 (Addison-Wesley Series on Organization Development). 2nd ed.

Mintzberg, Henry, *The Nature of Managerial Work*, New York: Harper & Row, 1973.

Classic Texts: Japan

Nonaka, Ikujiro, Hirotaka Takeuchi, and Hiro Takeuchi, *The Knowledge-Creating Company: How Japanese Companies Create the Dynamics of Innovation*, New York: Oxford University Press, 1995.

Influence of Computers on Thought

Simon, Herbert, *Decision-Making and Administrative Organization*, n.p. 1944. 4th ed. New York: Free Press, 1997.

March, James G., and Herbert Simon, *Organizations*, New York: John Wiley & Sons, [1958].

Newell, Allen, and Herbert A. Simon, *Human Problem Solving*, Englewood Cliffs, NJ: Prentice Hall, 1972.

Carroll, John S., *Cognition and Social Behavior*, Hillsdale, NJ: Lawrence Erlbaum Associates, 1976.

Sternberg, Robert, *Beyond IQ*, Cambridge: Cambridge University Press, 1984.

Frieze, I., D. Bar-Tal, and John S. Carroll, eds., *New Approaches to Social Problems: Applications of Attribution Theory*, San Francisco: Jossey-Bass, 1979.

Carroll, John S., *Applied Social Psychology and Organizational Settings*, Hillsdale, NJ: Lawrence Erlbaum Associates, 1990.

Carroll, John S., and Eric J. Johnson, *Decision Research: A Field Guide to Studying Decision Behavior*, Newbury Park: Sage, 1990.

Jacoby, Henry D., *The Bureaucratization of the World*. Berkeley: University of California Press, 1976.

Bailyn, Lotte, and Edgar H. Schein, *Living With Technology: Issues at Mid-Career*. Cambridge, MA: MIT Press, 1980.

Gerstein, Marc S., *The Technology Connection*, Reading, MA: Addison-Wesley Longman, 1987.

Madnick, Stuart, *The Strategic Use of Information Technology* (Executive Bookshelf: Sloan Management Review). New York: Oxford University Press, 1987.

Margolis, Howard, *Patterns, Thinking, and Cognition*, Chicago: University of Chicago Press, 1987.

Gupta, Amar, *Integration of Information Systems: Bridging Heterogeneous Databases*. Piscataway, NJ: Institute of Electrical & Electronics Engineers, 1989.

Newell, Allen, *Unified Theories of Cognition*, Cambridge, MA: Harvard University Press, 1990.

Ahuja, Ravindra K., Thomas L. Magnanti, and James B. Orlin, *Network Flows: Theory, Algorithms, and Applications*. Englewood Cliffs, NJ: Prentice Hall, 1993.

Yates, Joanne, *Control through Communication: The Rise of System in American Management* (Studies in Industry and Society). Baltimore: Johns Hopkins University Press, 1993.

Allen, Thomas J., and Michael S. Scott Morton, eds., *Information Technology and the Corporation of the 1990s: Research Studies*. New York: Oxford University Press, 1995.

Allen, Thomas J., *Managing the Flow of Technology*, Cambridge, MA: MIT Press, 1979.

Bertsimas, Dmitris J, and John N. Tsitsiklis, *Introduction to Linear Optimization*, Belmont, MA: Athena Scientific, 1997 (Athena Scientific Series in Optimization and Neural Computation, 6).

Nadler, David A., Marc S. Gerstein, and Robert B. Shaw, *Organizational Architecture: Designs for Changing Organizations*, San Francisco: Jossey-Bass, 1992.

Morecroft, John D. W., and John D. Sterman, eds., *Modeling for Learning Organizations* (System Dynamics Series), Portland, OR: Productivity Press, 1994.

Yates, Joanne, and John Van Maanen (eds.), *Information Technology and Organizational Transformation: History, Rhetoric and Practice*. Newbury Park, CA: Sage, 1999.

Marcus, Gary F., *The Algebraic Mind: Integrating Connectionism and Cognitive Science*, Cambridge, MA: MIT Press, 2003.

Baum, Eric B., *What Is Thought?*, Cambridge, MA: MIT Press, 2004.

Jay W. Forrester

Forrester, Jay W., *Industrial Dynamics*, Waltham, MA: Pegasus Communications, 1961.

Forrester, Jay W., *Principles of Systems* (2nd ed.). Waltham, MA: Pegasus Communications, 1968.

Forrester, Jay W., *Urban Dynamics*. Waltham, MA: Pegasus Communications, 1969.

Forrester, Jay W., *World Dynamics* (1973; 2nd ed.). Waltham, MA: Pegasus Communications, 1971.

Forrester, Jay W., *Collected Papers of Jay W. Forrester*. Waltham, MA: Pegasus Communications, 1975.

Cf. Roberts, Edward B., *Managerial Applications of Systems Dynamics*, Waltham MA: Pegasus Communications, 1978.

Peter Senge

Senge, Peter M., *The Fifth Discipline: The Art and Practice of the Learning Organization*, New York: Doubleday/ Currency, c1990.

Senge, Peter M., et al., eds., *The Fifth Discipline Fieldbook: Strategies and Tools for Building a Learning Organization*, New York: Currency/Doubleday, 1994.

Chapter 8. Knowledge Management

Knowledge Management: North America

The Delphi Report on Knowledge Management: In Perspective, Boston, MA: Delphi Consulting Group, 1997.

Harvard Business Review on Knowledge Management, Boston: Harvard Business School Press, 1998.

Radding, Alan, Knowledge Management: Succeeding in the Information-Based Global Economy, Charleston: Computer Technology Research Corporation, 1998.

Davenport, Thomas H., and Laurence Prusak, Working Knowledge: How Organizations Manage What They Know, Boston: Harvard Business School Press, 1998.

Neef, Dale, A Little Knowledge Is a Dangerous Thing: Understanding Our Global Knowledge Economy, Oxford: Butterworth-Heinemann, 2000.

Malhotra, Yogesh, Knowledge Management and Business Model Innovation, Hershey, PA: Idea Group, 2000.

Dutrénit, Gabriela, Learning and Knowledge Management in the Firm: From Knowledge Accumulation to Strategic Capabilities, Northampton, MA: Edward Elgar, 2000.

Teece, David J., Managing Intellectual Capital: Organizational, Strategic, and Policy Dimensions, New York: Oxford University Press, 2000.

Denning, Stephen, The Springboard: How Storytelling gnites Action in the Knowledge Era Organization, Boston: Butterworth-Heinemann, 2001.

Gorelick, Carol, Kurt April, and Nick Milton, Performance through Learning: Knowledge Management in Practice, London: Butterworth-Heinemann, 2004.

Koenig, Michael E. D., T. Kanti Srikantaiah, and T. Kanti Srikantaiab, eds., Knowledge Management Lessons Learned: What Works and What Doesn't, Medford, NJ: Information Today, 2004. (Asis Monograph Series).

Knowledge Management: Europe

North, Klaus, Wissensorientierte Unternehmungsführung. Wertschöpfung durch Wissen, Wiesbaden: Gabler, 1998.

Lanciano, Caroline, et al., eds., Les acteurs de l'innovation et l'entreprise: France, Europe, Japon, Paris: L'Harmattan, 1998.

Projektgruppe Wissenschaftliche Beratung (Hrsg.), Organisationslernen durch Wissensmanagement, Frankfurt am Main: P. Lang, 1999.

Reinmann-Rothmeier, Gabi, and Heinz Mandl, Individuelles Wissensmanagement, Strategien für den persönlichen Umgang mit Information und Wissen im Arbeitsplatz, Bern: Hans Huber, 2000.

Mandl, Heinz, and Gabi Reinmann-Rothmeier, Wissensmanagement: Informationszuwachs-Wissensschwund. Die strategische Bedeutung des Wissensmanagements, Munich: R. Oldenbourg, 2000.

Mandl, Heinz, and Jochen Gerstenmaier, Die Kluft zwischen Wissen und Handeln, Göttingen: Hogrefe, 2000.

Bryson, John, et al., eds., Knowledge, Space, Economy, London: Routledge, 2000.

Mertens, Kai, Peter Heisig, and Jens Vorbeck, eds., Knowledge Management: Best Practices in Europe, New York: Springer, 2000.

Harryson, Sigvald J., Managing Know-Who Based Companies: A Multinetworked Approach to Knowledge and Innovation Management, Cheltenham, UK: Edward Elgar, 2000.

Probst, Gilbert Steffen Raub, and Kai Romhardt, Managing Knowledge: Building Blocks for Success, New York: John Wiley & Sons, c2000. English translation of: Wissen Managen, Frankfurt: Frankfurter Allgemeiner Zeitung, 1999.

Roy, Rajkumar (ed.), Industrial Knowledge Management: A Micro-Level Approach, London: Springer, 2001.

Knowledge Management: Japan and Asia

Banerjee, Parthasarathi and Frank-Jürgen Richter, ed., *Intangibles in Competition and Co-operation: Euro-Asian Perspectives*, New York: Palgrave, 2000.

Nonaka, Ikujiro, Toshihiro Nishiguchi, eds., *Knowledge Emergence: Social, Technical, and Evolutionary Dimensions of Knowledge Creation*, New York: Oxford University Press, 2000.

Krogh, Georg von, Kazuo Ichijo, and Ikujiro Nonaka, *Enabling Knowledge Creation: How to Unlock the Mystery of Tacit Knowledge and Release the Power of Innovation*, Oxford: Oxford University Press, 2000.

Information Management

Borgmann, Albert, *Holding On to Reality: The Nature of Information at the Turn of the Millennium*, Chicago: University of Chicago Press, 1999.

Brown, John Seely, and Paul Duguid, *The Social Life of Information*, Boston: Harvard Business School Press, 2000.

Marchand, Donald A., Thomas H. Davenport, and Tim Dickson, *Financial Times Mastering Information Management: Complete MBA Companion in Information Management*, London: Financial Times, 2000.

Systems

Wiener, Norbert, *Cybernetics or Control and Communication in the Animal*, Cambridge, MA: MIT Press, 1948. 2nd ed.: *Cybernetics: or Control of Communication in the Animal and the Machine*, Cambridge, MA: MIT Press, 1965.

Optner, Stanford L, *Systems Analysis for Business and Industrial Problem Solving*, Englewood Cliffs, NJ: Prentice Hall, [1965].

Von Bertalanffy, Ludwig, *General System Theory: Foundations, Development, Applications*, Ann Arbor: Society for General Systems Research, 1960 (Yearbook of the Society for General Systems Research, vol. 5). New ed. New York: George Braziller, 1976.

Liapunov, A.A.,ed., *Systems Theory Research*, Translated from Russian. New York: Consultants Bureau, 1973. Translation of v. 23 Problemy kybernetiky.

Kramer, Nic J. T. A., and Jacob de Smit, *Systems Thinking: Concepts and Notions*, Leiden: Martinus Nijhoff, 1977.

Cummings, Thomas G., ed., *Systems Theory for Organization Development*, Chichester: John Wiley & Sons, 1980.

Checkland, Peter, *Systems Thinking, Systems Practice*, New York: John Wiley & Sons, 1981.

Wright, Robert, *Systems Thinking: A Guide to Managing in a Changing Environment*, Dearborn, MI: Society of Manufacturing Engineers, 1989.

United Kingdom Systems Society Conference on Systems Thinking in Europe (1991: Huddersfield, England), *Systems thinking in Europe*, ed. M.C. Jackson et al., New York: Plenum, 1991.

Anderson, Virginia, and Lauren Johnson, *Systems Thinking Basics: From Concepts to Causal Loops*, Cambridge, MA: Pegasus Communications, 1997.

Laszlo, Ervin, *The Systems View of the World: A Holistic Vision for Our Time*, Mount Waverly: Hampton Press, 1996. (Advances in Systems Theory, Complexity, and the Human Sciences).

O'Connor, Joseph, and Ian McDermott, *The Art of Systems Thinking: Essential Skills for Creativity and Problem Solving*, London: Thorsons, 1997.

Checkland, Peter, *Systems Thinking, Systems Practice: A 30-Year Retrospective*, New York: John Wiley & Sons, 1999.

Haines, Stephen G., *The Systems Thinking Approach to Strategic Planning and Management*, Boca Raton, FL: St. Lucie Press, 2000.

Sweeney, Linda Booth, *Systems Thinking for Kids, Big and Small: Exploring how Systems Work through Favorite Children's Stories*, Waltham, MA: Pegasus Communications, 2001.

Living Systems

Miller, James Grier, *Living Systems*, New York: McGraw-Hill, 1978. Reprint: Niwot, CO: University Press of Colorado, 1995.

Agazarian, Yvonne, and Susan P. Gantt, *Autobiography of a Theory: Developing the Theory of Living Human Systems and its Systems-Centered Practice*, Philadelphia: Jessica Kingsley, 2000.

Langton, Christopher G., and Taksunori Shimohara, *Artificial Life V: Proceedings of the Fifth International Workshop on the Synthesis and Simulation of Living Systems*, Cambridge, MA: MIT Press, 1997 (Complex Adaptive Systems). Cf. Artificial Life VII, 2000.

Expert Systems; cf. Appendix 3.

Gupta, Amar, *Microcomputer-Based Expert Systems*. Piscataway, NJ: Institute of Electrical & Electronics Engineers, 1988.

Gupta, Amar, and Bandreddi Prasad. *Principles of Expert Systems*. Piscataway, NJ: Institute of Electrical & Electronics Engineers, 1988.

Giarratano, Joseph C., *Expert Systems: Principles and Programming*, Florence, KY: Brooks Cole, 1998. 3rd ed.: 2005.

Durkin, John, *Expert Systems, Design and Development*, NewYork: Macmillan, 1999.

Knowledge Based Systems

Buchanan, Bruce, and David Wilkins, *Knowledge Based Systems, Readings in Knowledge Acquisition and Learning*, San Francisco: Morgan Kaufmann, 1993.

Debenham, John, *Knowledge Engineering: Unifying Knowledge Base and Database Design*, Berlin: Springer, 2001 (Artificial Intelligence).

Baader, Franz, Diego Calvanese, Deborah McGuinness, Daniele Nardi, and Peter Patel-Schneider, eds., *The Description Logic Handbook: Theory, Implementation and Applications*, Cambridge: Cambridge University Press, 2003.

Social Systems

Luhmann, Niklas, *Soziale Systeme: Grundriss einer allgemeinen Theorie*, Frankfurt: Suhrkamp, 1984. Translation: *Social Systems*, Stanford: Stanford University Press, 1995.

Outsourcing

Klepper, Robert, and Wendell Jones, eds., *Outsourcing Information Technology Systems and Services*, Upper Saddle River, NJ: Prentice Hall, 1997.

Greaver, Maurice F., *Strategic Outsourcing: A Structured Approach to Outsourcing Decisions and Initiatives*, New York: Amacom, 1999.

Intellectual Capital

Brooking, Annie, *Intellectual Capital: Core Assets for the Third Millennium*, Eagan, MN: International Thomson, 1996.

Edvinsson, Leif, and Michael S. Malone (contributor), *Intellectual Capital: Realizing Your Company's True Value by Finding Its Hidden Brainpower*, New York: Harperbusiness, 1997.

Allee, Verna, *The Knowledge Evolution: Expanding Organizational Intelligence*, Oxford: Butterworth-Heinemann, 1997.

Klein, David A., ed., *The Strategic Management of Intellectual Capital*, Oxford: Butterworth-Heinemann, 1997.

Stewart, Thomas A., *Intellectual Capital: The New Wealth of Organizations*, New York: Currency/Doubleday,

1998.

Gupta, Jatinder N. D., and Sushil K. Sharma, *Creating Knowledge Based Organizations*, Hershey, PA: Idea Group, 2003.

Business Ecosystems

Rothschild, Michael, *Bionomics: Economy As Ecosystem*, New York: Henry Holt, 1995.

Moore, James, *The Death of Competition*, New York: Harper Business, 1996.

Clippinger, John Henry III, ed., *The Biology of Business: Decoding the Natural Laws of Enterprise*, San Francisco: Jossey-Bass, 1999. (The Jossey-Bass Business & Management Series).

Dasgupta, Partha, and Karl-Goran Maler, *Economics of Non-Convet Ecosystems*, Dordrecht: Kluwer, 2004 (Economics of Non-Market Goods and Resources, V. 4).

Chapter 9. Learning

General

Rockart, John F., *Computers and the Learning Process in Higher Education: A Report Prepared for the Carnegie Commission on Higher Education*. New York: McGraw-Hill, 1975.

Spring, Joel H., *Education and the Rise of the Global Economy*, Mahwah, NJ: Lawrence Erlbaum Associates, 1998 (Sociocultural, Political, and Historical Studies in Education).

Gabbard, David A., ed., *Knowledge and Power in the Global Economy: Politics and the Rhetoric of School Reform*, Mahwah, NJ: Lawrence Erlbaum Associates, 2000 (The Sociocultural, Political and Historical Studies in education).

e-learning

Rosenberg, Marc J., *E-Learning: Strategies for Delivering Knowledge in the Digital Age*, New York: McGraw-Hill, 2000.

Katz, Richard N., ed., *The 'E' Is for Everything: E-commerce, E-business, and E-learning in Higher Education*, San Francisco: Jossey-Bass/Pfeiffer, 2000.

Salmon, Gilly, *E-Moderating: The Key to Teaching and Learning Online*, Sterling: Stylus, 2000 (Open and Distance Learning Series).

Clark, Ruth Colvin, and Richard E. Mayer, *e-Learning and the Science of Instruction: Proven Guidelines for Consumers and Designers of Multimedia Learning*, San Francisco: Jossey-Bass/Pfeiffer, 2000.

Problem-Solving: Harold S. Barrows

Barrows, Harold S., and R.M. Tamblyn, *Problem-Based Learning: An Approach to Medical Education*, New York: Springer, 1980.

Barrows, Harold S., *How to Design a Problem-based Curriculum for Pre-clinical Years*. New York: Springer, 1985.

Barrows, Harold S., *The Tutorial Process*. Springfield, IL: Southern Illinois University School of Medicine. Rev. ed. 1992.

Barrows, Harold S., G. S. Pickell, *Developing Clinical Problem-solving Skills: A Guide to More Effective Diagnosis and Treatment*. New York, London: Norton Medical Books, 1991.

Barrows, Harold S., *Practice-Based Learning: Problem-Based Learning Applied to Medical Education*, Springfield, IL: Southern Illinois University School of Medicine, 1994.

Barrows, Harold S., *What Your Tutor May Never Tell You*, Springfield, IL: SIU School of Medicine, 1996.

Problem-Based Learning

Evensen, Dorothy H., and Cindy E. Hmelo, eds., *Problem-Based Learning: A Research Perspective on Learning Interactions*, Mahwah, NJ: Lawrence Erlbaum Associates, 2000.

Stepien, William J., Peter R. Senn, and William C. Stepien, *The Internet and Problem-Based Learning: Developing Solutions through the Web*, Chicago: Zephyr Press, 2001.

Cunningham, William G., and Paula A. Cordeiro, *Educational Leadership: A Problem-Based Approach*, Boston: Pearson Allyn & Bacon, 2002, 2nd ed.

Marquardt, Michael J., *Optimizing the Power of Action Learning: Solving Problems and Building Leaders in Real Time*, Palo Alto: Davies Black, 2004.

Computer-Mediated Communication and Education

Romiszowski, Alexander J., *Computer Mediated Communication: A Selected Bibliography*, Englewood Cliffs, NJ: Educational Technology Publications, 1992.

Barta, Ben Zion, John Eccleston, and Rudolf Hambusch, eds., *Computer Mediated Education of Information Technology Professionals and Advanced End-Users: Proceedings of the IFIP WG3.4 Working Conference on Computer Mediated Education of Information Technology Professionals and Advanced End-Users, Soest, Germany, 12–16 July 1993*. Amsterdam: North-Holland, 1993.

Ken'ichi, Kawasaki, et al., *Media komyunik⁻eshon: j⁻oh⁻o k⁻ory⁻u no shakaigaku*, Shohan, Tokyo: Fujits⁻u Keiei Kensh⁻ujo, 1994. For other publications Cf. his web site. See: http://www.rieti. go.jp/users/kawasaki-kenichi/index_en.html.

Berge, Zane L., and Mauri P. Collins, eds., *Computer Mediated Communication and the Online Classroom: Higher Education*, Creskill, NJ: Hampton Press, 1994.

Walters, Rob, *Computer-Mediated Communications: Multimedia Applications*, Boston: Artech House, 1995.

Herring, Susan C., ed., *Computer-Mediated Communication: Linguistic, Social, and Cross-Cultural Perspectives*, Amsterdam: J. Benjamins, 1996.

Distance Education

Merrill, David M., and David G. Twitchell, ed. *Instructional Design Theory*, Englewood Cliffs, NJ: Educational Technology Publications, 1994.

Bracey, Gerald W., *Transforming America's Schools: An Rx for Getting Past Blame*, Arlington, VA: American Association of School Administrators, 1994.

Bates, Tony, *Technology, Open Learning and Distance Education*, London: Routledge, 1995.

Dills, Charles R., and Alexander J. Romiszowski, *Instructional Development Paradigms*, Englewood Cliffs, NJ: Educational Technology Publications, 1997.

Keegan, D., *Foundations of Distance Education*, London: Routledge, 1996.

McLellan, Hilary, ed., *Situated Learning Perspectives*, Englewood Cliffs, NJ: Educational Technology Publications, 1996.

Roerden, Laura Parker, *Net Lessons: Web-Based Projects for Your Classroom*; [foreword by Bonnie Bracey], Sebastopol, CA: Songline Studios and O'Reilly & Associates, c1997.

Spierts, Michael, *Beroep in Ontwikkeling: Een orientatie op culturelle en maatschappelijke Vorming*, Elsevier: Maarsen, 1999.

Willis, B., *Distance Education, Strategies and Tools for Distance Education*, Englewood Cliffs, NJ: Educational Technology Publications, 1994.

Wilson, Brent G., ed., *Constructivist Learning: Case Studies in Instructional Design*. Englewood Cliffs, NJ: Educational Technology Publications, 1995.

Carmona-Schneider, Juan-J., Renato Di Ruzza, Serge Le Roux, and Marc Vadercammen, eds., *Le travail à distance: Analyses syndicales et enjeux européens*, Paris: De Boeck Université, 1999.

Thorne, Kaye, *Blended Learning: How to Integrate Online & Traditional Learning*, London: Kogan Page, 2004.

Chapter 10. Personal Knowledge

Buzan, Tony, and Barry Buzan, *The Mind Map Book: How to Use Radiant Thinking to Maximize Your Brain's Untapped Potential*, Plume, 1996.

Tacit Knowledge

Here, Marshall McLuhan's work on *Understanding Media* (1964, cf. Introduction, above) played an important role.

Hall, Edward T., *The Hidden Dimension*, New York: Anchor Books, 1967, further developed the discussion.
Polanyi, Michael, *Personal Knowledge: Towards a Post-Critical Philosophy*, Chicago: University of Chicago Press, 1958. New ed.: 1974, provided a deeper philosophical basis for these discussions.
Polanyi, Michael, *The Tacit Dimension*, Magnolia, MA: Peter Smith, 1983, made explicit his ideas concerning implicit knowledge.

In 1985, Robert J. Sternberg (Yale) pointed to the importance of context in his book *Beyond IQ*.

Wagner, Richard K., *Tacit Knowledge in Everyday Intelligent Behaviour*, 1985, Dissertation Abstracts International, 46, 4049B (University Microfilms International).
Wagner, R. K., and Robert J. Sternberg, *Tacit Knowledge Inventory for Managers*, Unpublished research instrument, 1991 (Available from authors). Cf. Marjory R. Kerr, Royal Canadian Mounted Police. *Tacit Knowledge as a Predictor of Managerial Success: A Field Study.* http://cpa.ca/cjbs/kerr.html based on dissertation, Waterloo, 1991.
Sternberg, Robert J., and Joseph A. Horvath (eds.), *Tacit Knowledge in Professional Practice: Researcher and Practitioner Perspectives*, Mahwah, NJ: Lawrence Erlbaum Associates, 1998. See: http://www.yale.edu/pace/teammembers/personalpages/bob.html.
Reber, Arthur S., *Implicit Learning and Tacit Knowledge: An Essay on the Cognitive Unconscious*, New York: Oxford University Press, 1996 (Oxford Psychology Series, 19).
Baumard, Philippe, *Tacit Knowledge in Organizations*, London: Sage, 1999. English trans. of: *Organisations Déconcertées: La gestion stratégique de la connaissance*, Paris: Masson, 1996, provides a more thorough history and analysis of these trends.
Kikoski, Catherine Kano, and John F. Kikoski, *The Inquiring Organization: Tacit Knowledge, Conversation, and Knowledge Creation Skills for 21st-Century Organizations*, New York: Praeger, 2004.

Personalization and Mass Customization

IBM 5260 retail system – personalization – keying personalization answers, IBM General Systems Division, 1981 (Videodisc).
Sabelli, H., and J. Synnestvedt, *Personalization: A New Vision for the Millennium: Three Essays*, [Chicago, IL]: Society for the Advancement of Clinical Philosophy, [1990].
Goldman, Steven L., Kenneth Preiss, and Roger N. Nagel, *Agile Competitors and Virtual Organizations: Strategies for Enriching the Customer*, New York: Van Nostrand Reinhold, 1997.
Oleson, John D., *Pathways to Agility: Mass Customization in Action*, National Association of Manufacturers, Feb. 1998.
Pine, B. Joseph, *Mass Customization: The New Frontier in Business Competition*, Cambridge, MA: Harvard Business School Press, 1993. Reprint: 1999.

Kelly, Sean, *Data Warehousing: The Route to Mass Customization*, New York: John Wiley & Sons, 1996.

Anderson, David M., and B. Joseph Pine, *Agile Product Development for Mass Customizatiom: How to Develop and Deliver Products for Mass Customization, Niche Markets, JIT, Build-To-Order, and Flexible Manufacturing*, New York: McGraw-Hill, 1997.

Allen, Cliff, Deborah Kania, and Beth Yaeckel, *Internet World Guide to One-to-One Web Marketing*, New York: John Wiley & Sons, 1998 (Internet World Series).

Provides a good survey.

Oleson, John D., *Pathways to Agility: Mass Customization in Action*, New York: John Wiley & Sons, 1998.

Pine, B. Joseph, and James H. Gilmore, *The Experience Economy*, Cambridge, MA: Harvard Business School, 1999.

Pine, B. Joseph, *Mass Customization: The New Frontier in Business Competition*, Cambridge, MA: Harvard Business School Press, 1999.

Gilmore, James H., and B. Joseph Pine, *Markets of One: Creating Customer-Unique Value through Mass Customization*, Cambridge, MA: Harvard Business School Press, 2000 (A Harvard Business Review Book).

Ralph, Daniel, and Stephen Searby, *Location and Personalisation: Delivering Online and Mobility Services*, Edison, NJ: IEE Publishing, 2003.

Contextualization

Barrett, Edward, and Marie Redmond, eds. *Contextual Media: Multimedia and Interpretation*, Cambridge, MA: MIT Press, 1997.

Hesselgrave, David J., and Edward Rommen, *Contextualization: Meanings, Methods, and Models*. Foreword by George W. Peters, Pasadena, CA: William Carey Library, 2000.

Chapter 11. Collaboration

Delphi Method

The Delphi method began in the 1950s with Olaf Helmer and Norman Dalkey at the Rand Corporation and gradually became public through a series of reports from 1960 to 1969:

Brown, B., and Olaf Helmer, *Improving the Reliability of Estimates Obtained from a Consensus of Experts*, RAND Corporation, P2986, September 1964.

Dalkey, Norman C., *The Delphi Method: An Experimental Study of Group Opinion*, RAND Corporation, RM-5888-PR, June 1967.

Dalkey, Norman, B. Brown, and S. Cochran, *The Delphi Method, II: Structure of Experiments*, RAND Corporation, RM 5957-PR, June 1969.

Dalkey, Norman, B. Brown, and S. Cochran, *The Delphi Method, III: Use of Self Ratings to Improve Group Estimates*, RAND, RM-6115-PR, 1969. (This file was rendered in PDF from the original document by Barry K. Sanford, University of Louisville, 1999). See: http://www.rand.org/publications/classics/delphi3.pdf.

It was criticized in the 1970s: Sackman, H., *Delphi Critique: Expert Opinion, Forecasting and Group Process*, Lexington, MA: D. C. Heath, 1974. It was defended: Delbeq, A. L., A. H. Van den Ven, and D. H Gustafson, *Group Techniques for Program Planning: A Guide to Nominal Group and Delphi Processes*, Glenview, IL: Scott Foreman and Co., 1975; Linstone, H. A. and M. Turoff, ed., *The Delphi Method Techniques and Applications*, Reading, MA: Addison-Wesley, 1975.

Problem-Solving in Science

Culler, G. J., and B. D. Fried, "An On-Line Computing Center for Scientific Problems", *Proc. IEEE Pacific Computer Conference*, 1963, p. 221.

Chacko, George K., *The Systems Approach to Problem Solving*, Westport, CT: Praeger, 1989.

Ford, Brian, and Francoise Chatelin, *Problem Solving Environments for Scientific Computing*, Amsterdam: North Holland, 1987.

Gaffney, P., and E. N. Houstis, *Programming Environments for High-Level Scientific Problem Solving*, Amsterdam: North Holland, 1992.

Adler, Michael, and Erio Ziglio, *Gazing into the Oracle: the Delphi Method and its Application to Social Policy and Public Health*, London: Jessica Kingsley, 1996.

Lesh, Richard A., and Helen M. Doerr, eds., *Beyond Constructivism: Models and Modeling Perspectives on Mathematics Problem Solving, Learning, and Teaching*, Mahwah, NJ: Lawrence Erlbaum Associates, 2003.

Virtual Teams

Lipnack, Jessica, and Jeffrey Stamps, *Virtual Teams: Reaching Across Space, Time, and Organizations With Technology*, New York: John Wiley & Sons, 1997.

Henry, Jane E., and Meg Hartzler, *Tools for Virtual Teams: A Team Fitness Companion*, Milwaukee: American Society for Quality, 1997.

Kostner, Jaclyn, *BIONIC eTeamwork*, Chicago: Dearborn Trade Publishers, 2001.

Online and Virtual Communities

Johnson, Timothy, *Network Communities: The Computers in Our Lives*, London: Weidenfeld and Nicolson, 1971.

Rheingold, Howard, *The Virtual Community: Homesteading on the Electronic Frontier*, Reading, MA: Addison-Wesley, 1993. Reprint: Cambridge, MA: MIT Press, 2000.

Hiltz, Starr Roxanne, *Online Communities: A Case Study of the Office of the Future*, Bristol: Intellect, 1994 (Human/Computer Interaction).

Hagel, John III, and Arthur G. Armstrong, *Net Gain: Expanding Markets through Virtual Communities*, Boston: Harvard Business School Press, 1997.

Shelton, Karla, and Todd McNeeley, *Virtual Communities Companion*, Albany, NY: Coriolis Group Books, 1997.

Powers, Michael, *How to Program a Virtual Community*, Emeryville, CA: Ziff-Davis Press, 1997.

Young, Margaret Levine, and John R. Levine, *Poor Richard's Building Online Communities: Create a Web Community for Your Business, Club, Association, or Family*, Lakewood, CO: Top Floor, 2000.

Preece, Jenny, *Online Communities: Designing Usability and Supporting Sociability*, New York: John Wiley & Sons, 2000.

Tsagarousianou, Rosa, Damian Tambini, and Cathy Bryan, eds. *Cyberdemocracy, Technology, Cities and Civic Institutions*, London: Routledge, 1998.

Werry, Chris, Miranda Mowbray, and Hewlett-Packard, *Online Communities: Commerce, Community Action, and the Virtual University*, Upper Saddle River, NJ: Prentice Hall, 2000.

Lesser, Eric L., Michael A. Fontaine, and Jason A. Slusher, *Knowledge and Communities*, Boston: Butterworth-Heinemann, 2000.

Griffoen, H.J., and A.J. van Vliet, *Virtual Communities: Een literatuuroverzicht van motivationele aspecten, groepsprocessen en classificatiedimensies*, TNO Technische Menskunde, Soesterberg, Rapportnummer TM-00-0026.

Earnshaw, R., *Frontiers in Human-Centred Computing, Online Communities and Virtual Environment*, Berlin: Springer, 2001.

Levinson, David, and Karen Christensen, eds., *Encyclopedia of Community: From the Village to the Virtual World*, London: Sage, 2003.

Collaboration

Nof, Shimon Y., ed., *Information and Collaboration Models of Integration*, Dordrecht: Kluwer, 1994 (NATO Asi Series. Series E: Applied Sciences, Vol. 259).

Fishbaugh, Mary Susan E., *Models of Collaboration*, Boston: Allyn and Bacon, 1997.

Kruschwitz, Nina, and George Roth, *Inventing Organizations in the 21st Century: producing knowledge through collaboration*, SWP #4064, 21C WP#21, CCS WP #207, March 1999.

Austin, James E., *The Collaboration Challenge: How Nonprofits and Businesses Succeed through Strategic Alliances*, San Francisco: Jossey-Bass, 2000.

Leuf, Bo, and Ward Cunningham, *The Wiki Way: Collaboration and Sharing on the Internet*, Boston: Addison-Wesley, 2001.

Backer, Thomas E., *Evaluating Community Collaborations*, Berlin: Springer, 2003.

Logan, Robert K., and Louis W. Stokes, *Collaborate to Compete: Driving Profitability in the Knowledge Economy*, New York: John Wiley & Sons, 2004.

Collaboratories

National Research Council (U.S.). Committee on a National Collaboratory : *Establishing the User-Developer Partnership, National Collaboratories: Applying Information Technology for Scientific Research*, Washington: National Academy Press, 1993.

Collaboratories: Improving Research Capabilities in Chemical and Biomedical Sciences: Proceedings of a Multi-Site Electronic Workshop, Washington: National Academy Press, 1999.

Collaborative Environments

Greenhalgh, Chris, *Large Scale Collaborative Virtual Environments*, Berlin: Springer, 1999.

Singhal, Sandeep, and Michael Zyda, *Networked Virtual Environments: Design and Implementation*, Reading, MA: Addison-Wesley, 1999.

Qvortrup, Lars (ed.), *Virtual Interaction: Interaction in Virtual Inhabited 3D Worlds*, New York: Springer, 2000.

Capin, Tolga K., Igor S. Pandzic, and Nadi Magnenat-Thalmann, *Avatars in Networked Virtual Environments*, New York: John Wiley & Sons, 1999.

Mulder, J. D., R. Van Liere, and W. Hansmann, eds., *Virtual Environments 2000: Proceedings of the Eurographics Workshop in Amsterdam, the Netherlands, June 1–2, 2000, Eurographics*, Vienna: Springer, 2000 (Eurographics).

Churchill, Elizabeth F., David N. Snowdon, and Alan J. Munro (eds.), *Collaborative Virtual Environments: Digital Places and Spaces for Interaction*, New York: Springer, 2001.

Andriessen, Jerry, Michael Baker, and Dan Suthers, *Arguing to Learn: Confronting Cognitions in Computer-Supported Collaborative Learning Environments*, Dordrecht: Kluwer, 2003 (Computer-Supported Collaborative Learning, 1).

Wasson, Barbara B., Sten Ludvigsen, Ulrich Hoppe, eds., *Designing for Change in Networked Learning Environments: Proceedings of the International Conference on Computer Support for Collaborative Learning 2003*, Dordrecht: Kluwer, 2003 (Computer-Supported Collaborative Learning Series, 2).

Collaborative e-commerce

Collaborative e-Commerce: A Market a Forecast and Strategic Guide, San Francisco: Collaborative Strategies LLC Office, 2000. See:http://collaborate.com/announcements/announce_4.html.

Samtani, Gunjan, Marcus Healey, and Shyam Samtani, B2B Integration: *A Practical Guide to Collaborative E-Commerce*, London: Imperial College Press, 2002.

Computational Grids

Carey, Graham F., *Computational Grids: Generation, Adaptation, and Solution Strategies*, London: Taylor and Francis, 1997 (Series in Computational and Physical Processes in Mechanics and Thermal Science).

Foster, Ian, and Carl Kesselman, eds., *The Grid: Blueprint for a New Computing Infrastructure*, San Francisco: Morgan Kaufmann, 1999.

Grid Computing – GRID 2000: First IEEE/ACM International Workshop, Bangalore, India, December 17, 2000: Proceedings, Rajkumar Buyya, Mark Baker, eds., New York: Springer, 2000.

Berman, Fran, Geoffrey Fox, and Tony Hey, eds., *Grid Computing: Making the Global Infrastructure a Reality*, New York: John Wiley & Sons, 2003.

Abbas, Ahmar, *Grid Computing: A Practical Guide to Technology and Applications*, Rockland: Charles River Media, 2004 (Programming Series).

Tele-Conferencing

Bretz, Rudy, with a contribution by Laurence A. Dougharty, *Two-way TV Teleconferencing for Government, the MRC-TV System*: Prepared for the Metropolitan Regional Council under a Grant to the Council from the National Science Foundation Santa Monica, CA: Rand, 1974.

Future Systems Incorporated, *Teleconferencing: A New Communications Service for the 1980's*, Gaithersburg, MD: Future Systems, 1980.

Tele-Work

Jackson, Paul J., and Jos Van Der Wielen, ed., *Teleworking: International Perspectives: From Telecommuting to the Virtual Organisation*, London: Routledge, 1998. (The Management of Technology and Innovation).

Nilles, Jack M., *Managing Telework: Strategies for Managing the Virtual Workforce*, New York: John Wiley & Sons, 1998. (Wiley/Upside Series).

Carmona Schneider, Juan J., Renato Di Ruzza, Serge Leroux, and Marc Vandercammen, *Le travail à distance: Analyses syndicales et enjeux européens*, Paris: De Boeck & Larcier, 1999.

Tele-Medicine

Berek, B., *Telemedicine on the Move: Health Care Heads Down the Information Highway*, Chicago: American Hospital Association, 1994.

Bashshur, Rashid L., Jay H. Sanders, and Gary W. Shannon, eds., *Telemedicine: Theory and Practice*, Springfield, Charles C. Thomas, 1997.

Viegas, Steven F., and Kim Dunn, eds., *Telemedicine: Practicing in the Information Age*, Philadelphia: Lippincott Williams & Wilkins, 1998.

Darkins, Adam William, and Margaret Ann Cary, *Telemedicine and Telehealth: Principles, Policies, Performance, and Pitfalls*, Berlin: Springer, 2000.

Bauer, Jeffrey C., and Marc A. Ringel, *Telemedicine and the Reinvention of Healthcare*, New York: McGraw-Hill, 2000.

Economou, George-Peter K., and Phil Sotiriades, *Decision Support Systems for Tele-Medicine Applications*, Baldock: Research Studies Press, 2004.

Chapter 12. Enduring Knowledge

Local Knowledge
Brush, Stephen B., and Doreen Stabinsky, eds., *Valuing Local Knowledge: Indigenous People and Intellectual Property Rights*, Washington: Island Press, 1996.

Information
Machlup, Fritz, *The Study of Information*, New York: John Wiley & Sons, 1962.
Gonzalez-Manet, Enrique, *The Hidden War of Information*, Norwood: Ablex, 1989. (Communication and Information Science). English trans. of: *Guerra oculta de la información*.
Gonzalez-Manet, Enrique, and Laurien Alexandre, *Informatics and Society: The New Challenges*, Norwood: Ablex, 1991. (Communication and Information Science).
Brown, John Seely, and Paul Duguid, *The Social Life of Information*, Boston: Harvard Business School Press, 2000.

Knowledge Organization
Those interested in this theme are advised to study *Knowledge Organization*, the journal of the International Society for Knowledge Organization (ISKO).

Dahlberg, Ingetraut, *Grundlagen universaler Wissensordnung*, Pullach bei München: Verlag Dokumentation, 1974.
Samurin, E. J., *Geschichte der bibliothekarisch-bibliographischen Klassifikation*, Munich: Verlag Dokumentation, 1977. 2 vol. Original Russian: *Oerki po istoirii bibliotecno-bibliograficsoj klassifacii*, Moscow, 1955–1958.
Chamis, Alice Yanosko, *Vocabulary Control and Search Strategies in Online Searching*, New York: Greenwood, 1991.
Langridge, W., *Classification: Its Kinds, Elements, Systems and Classifications*, London: Bowker/Saur, 1992.
Fugmann, Robert, *Subject Analysis and Indexing*, Frankfurt: Indeks, 1993.
Jonassen, David H., *Structural Knowledge: Techniques for Representing, Conveying and Acquiring Structural Knowledge*, Hillsdale, NJ: Lawrence Erlbaum Associates, 1993.
Burckhardt, H., ed., *Universal Knowledge Tools and Their Applications*, Toronto: Ryerson Polytechnic University, 1993.
Chan, Lois Mai, *Cataloging and Classifcation*, New York: McGraw-Hill, 1994. 2nd ed.
Gibbons, Michael, Camille Limoges, Helga Nowotny, et al., *The New Production of Knowledge: The Dynamics of Science and Research in Contemporary Societies*, London: Sage, 1994.
Nissan, Ephraim, *From Information to Knowledge: Conceptual and Content Analysis by Computer*, Oxford: Intellect, 1995.
Stefik, Mark, *Introduction to Knowledge Systems*, San Francisco: Morgan Kaufmann, 1995.
Boisot, Max, *Information Space: A Framework for Learning in Organizations, Institutions and Culture*, London: Routledge, 1995.
Iyer, Hemalata, *Classificatory Structure: Concepts, Relations and Representation*, Frankfurt: Indeks, 1995.
Budin, Gerhard, *Wissensorganisation und Terminologie: Die Komplexität und Dynamik wissenschaftlicher Informations- und Kommunikationsprozesse*, Tübingen: Gunter Narr, 1996.
Hjørland, Birger, *Information Seeking and Subject Representation: An Activity-Theoretical Approach to Information Science*, Westport, CT: Greenwood, 1997.

Luckose, Dickson, Harry Delugach, Mary Keeler, Leroy Searle, and John Sowa, *Conceptual Structures: Fulfilling Pierce's Dream*, Berlin: Springer, 1997 (Lecture Notes in Artificial Intelligence 1257).

Worsley, Peter, *Knowledges: Culture, Counterculture, Subculture*, New York: New Press, 1997.

El Hadi, Widad Mustafa, Jacques Maniez, and Steven A. Pollitt, *Structures and Relations in Knowledge Organization: Proceedings 5th International ISKO Conference*, Würzburg: Ergon, 1998.

Veltman, Kim H., *Frontiers in Conceptual Navigation*, Toronto: Ontario Library Association, 1999.

Sandrini, Peter, ed., *TKE '99, Terminology and Knowledge Engineering*, Vienna: Termnet, 1999.

Hunter, Lynette, *Critiques of Knowing: Situated Textualities in Science, Computing and the Arts*, London: Routledge, 1999.

Prax, Jean-Yves, *Le Guide du Knowledge Management*, Paris: Dunod, 2000.

Begthol, Clare, Lynne C. Howarth, and Nancy J. Williamson, eds., *Dynamism and Stability in Knowledge Organization, Proceedings of the Sixth International ISKO Conference*, Würzburg: Ergon, 2000.

Sowa, John F., *Knowledge Representation: Logical, Philosophical and Computational Foundations*, Pacific Grove: Brooks Cole, 2000. Cf. John Sowa, "Ontology, Metadata and Semiotics," Presented at ICCS'2000 in Darmstadt, Germany, on August 14, 2000. Published in B. Ganter & G. W. Mineau, eds., *Conceptual Structures: Logical, Linguistic, and Computational Issues*, Lecture Notes in AI #1867, Springer, Berlin, 2000, pp. 55–81; J.F. Sowa, J.A Zachman, "Extending and formalizing the framework for information systems architecture," *Systems Journal*, vol. 31, no. 3, 1992, pp. 590–616. See: http://www.bestweb.net/~sowa/peirce/ontometa.htm.

Harmsze, Frederique, *A Modular Structure for Scientific Articles in an electronic Environment*, Tilburg, Proefschrift, 2000.

Bean, Carol A., and Rebecca Green, ed., *Relationships in the Organization of Knowledge*, Dordrecht: Kluwer, 2001.

Green, Rebecca, Carol A. Bean, and Sung Hyon Myaeng, eds., *The Semantics of Relationships: An Interdisciplinary Perspective*, Dordrecht: Kluwer, 2002. (These last two books also offer an excellent survey of recent literature.)

Hypertext

Nelson, Ted, *Computer Lib*, South Bend, IN: Published by the author, 1974. 2nd ed.: Redmond: Microsoft Press, 1987.

Nelson, Ted, *Literary Machines*, South Bend, IN: Published by the author, 1981.

Barrett, Edward, *The Society of Text: Hypertext, Hypermedia and the Social Construction of Information*, Cambridge, MA: MIT Press, 1989.

Horn, Robert E., *Mapping Hypertext: Analysis, Linkage and Display of Knowledge for the Next Generation of On-Line Text and Graphics*, Walham, MA: The Lexington Institute, 1989.

Berk, E., and J. Devlin, eds., *Hypertext/Hypermedia Handbook*, New York: McGraw-Hill, 1991.

Bolter, Jay David, *Writing Space: The Computer, Hypertext, and the History of Writing*, Hillsdale, NJ: Lawrence Erlbaum Associates, 1991.

Schnupp, Peter, *Hypertext*, München: Oldenbourg, 1992.

Landow, George P., *Hypertext: The Convergence of Contemporary Critical Theory and Technology*. Baltimore: Johns Hopkins University Press, 1992. New ed.: Hypertext 2.0, 1997.

Landow, George P., *Hypertext Theory*, Baltimore: Johns Hopkins University Press, 1994.

Schreiweis, Uwe, *Hypertext strukturen als Grundlagen für integrierte Wissens-akquisitionssysteme*, Aachen: Shaker, 1994.

Nielsen, Jakob, *Multimedia and Hypertext: The Internet and Beyond*, New York: Academic Press, 1995. German translation: Jacob Nielsen, *Multimedia, Hypertext und Internet: Grundlagen und Praxis des elektronischen Publizierens*, Braunschweig: Vieweg, 1996.

Roberts, Lisa C., *From Knowledge to Narrative: Educators and the Changing Museum*, Washington: Smithsonian Institution Press, 1995.

Jimenes, Jesus Garcia, *La Imagen Narrativa*, Madrid: Editorial Paraninfo, 1995.

Jimenez, Jesus Garcia, *Narrativa Audiovisuel*, Madrid: Ediciones Catedra, 1996.

Richartz, Martin, *Generik und Dynamik in Hypertexten*, Aachen: Shaker, 1996.

Gaggi, Silvio, *From Text to Hypertext*, Philadelphia: University of Pennsylvania Press, 1998.

Purves, Alan C., *The Web of Text and the Web of God: An Essay on the Third Information Transformation*, New York: Guilford Press, 1998.

Snyder, Ilana, and Michael Joyce, eds. *Page to Screen: Taking Literacy into the Electronic Era*, London: Routledge, 1998.

Kolb, Hans-Peter, *Multimedia- Einsatzmöglichkeiten, Marktchancen und gesellschaftliche Implikationen*, Frankfurt: Peter Lang, 1999.

Modiano, Raimonda, Leroy F. Searle, and Peter L. Shillingsburg, *Voice, Text, Hypertext: Emerging Practices in Textual Studies*, Seattle: University of Washington Press, 2004.

McGann, Jerome, *Radiant Textuality: Literature after the World Wide Web*, New York: Palgrave Macmillan, 2004.

Hypertext and the Future of Narrative

Joyce, Michael, *Of Two Minds: Hypertext Pedagogy and Poetics*, University of Michigan Press, 1994.

Murray, Janet H., *Hamlet on the Holodeck: The Future of Narrative in Cyberspace*, Cambridge, MA: MIT Press, 1997.

Aarseth, Espen, *Cybertext: Perspectives on Ergodic Literature*, Baltimore: Johns Hopkins University Press, 1997.

Schank, Roger, *Tell Me a Story*, Evanston: Northwestern University Press, 1990. 3rd printing, 2000.

Ryan, Marie-Laure, *Narrative as Virtual Reality: Immersion and Interactivity in Literature and Electronic Media*, Baltimore: Johns Hopkins University Press, 2001.

Mehler, Alexander, *Textdeutung: Zur produzierender Analyse und Repräsentation struktureller Ahnlichkeiten von Texten*, Frankfurt: Peter Lang, 2002.

Hypermedia

Cotton, Bob, and Richard Oliver, *Understanding Hypermedia: From Multimedia to Virtual Reality*, London: Phaidon, 1993.

Barrett, Edward, ed., *Sociomedia: Multimedia, Hypermedia, and the Social Construction of Knowledge*, Cambridge, MA: MIT Press, 1994.

Deibert, Ronald J., *Parchment, Printing, and Hypermedia*, New York: Columbia University Press, 1997 (New Directions in World Politics).

Vouillamoz, Nuria, *Literatura e hipermedia. La irrupcion de la literatura interactiva: precedentes y critica*, Barcelona: Paidos, 2000. (Paidos Papeles de Comunicacion, 30).

Reich, Siegfried, Manolis M. Tzagarakis, and Paul M. E. De Bra, eds., *Hypermedia: Openness, Structural Awareness, and Adaptivity: International Workshops Ohs-7, Sc-3, and Ah-3, Aarhus, Denmark, August 14–18, 2001: Proceedings*, Berlin: Springer, 2002. (Lecture Notes in Computer Science, 2266).

Syntax and Semantics

Bréal, Michel, *De la grammaire comparée à la sémantique: Textes de Michel Bréal publiés entre 1864 et 1898*. Introduction, commentaires et bibliographie par Piet Desmet et Pierre Swiggers, Leuven: Peeters, 1995.

Bréal, Michel Jules Alfred, *Semantics: Studies in the Science of Meaning*, translated by Mrs Henry Cust from the French: *Essai de sémantique*, London, W. Heinemann, 1900.

Ullmann, Stephen, *Semantics; An Introduction to the Science of Meaning*, New York: Barnes & Noble, [1962].

Grady, Michael, *Syntax and Semantics of the English Verb Phrase*, The Hague: Mouton, 1970.

Ebeling, C. L., *Syntax and Semantics: A Taxonomic Approach*, Leiden: Brill, 1978.

Seuren, Pieter A. M., *Semantic Syntax*, Oxford: Blackwell, 1997.

Stowell, Tim, and Eric Wehrli, *Syntax & Semantics: Syntax & the Lexicon*, San Diego: Academic Press, c1992. Reprint: 1997.

Valin, Robert D. van, and Randy J. Lapolla, *Syntax: Structure, Meaning, and Function*, Cambridge: Cambridge University Press, 1998 (Cambridge Textbooks in Linguistics).

Crain, Stephen, and Rosalind Thornton, *Investigations in Universal Grammar: A Guide to Experiments on the Acquisition of Syntax and Semantics*, Cambridge, MA: MIT Press, 2000 (Language, Speech, and Communication).

Higginbotham, James, ed., *On Syntax and Semantics*, London: Routledge, 2000.

Alexiadou, Artemis, Elena Anagnostopoulou, and Martin Everaert, *The Unaccusativity Puzzle: Explorations of the Syntax-Lexicon Interface*, Oxford: Oxford University Press, 2004 (Oxford Studies in Theoretical Linguistics, 5).

Information Visualization

Tufte, Edward R., *Envisioning Information*, Cheshire, CT (P.O. Box 430, Cheshire 06410): Graphics Press, 1990.

Tufte, Edward R., *The Visual Display of Quantitative Information*, Cheshire CT: Graphics Press, 1992.

Brown, Judith R., Mikael Jern, John Vince, and Rae A. Earnshaw, *Visualization: Using Computer Graphics to Explore Data and Present Information*, New York: John Wiley & Sons, 1995.

Tufte, Edward R., *Visual Explanations: Images and Quantities, Evidence and Narrative*, Cheshire, CT: Graphics Press, 1997.

Chen, Chaomei, *Information Visualisation and Virtual Environments*, London: Springer, 1999.

Card, Stuart K., Jock D. MacKinlay, Ben Shneiderman, eds., *Readings in Information Visualization: Using Vision to Think* San Francisco: Morgan Kaufmann, 1999 (Morgan Kaufmann Series in Interactive Technologies).

1999 IEEE International Conference on Information Visualization: An International Conference on Computer Visualization & Graphics, 14–16 July 1999, London, England: Proceedings. Edited by E. Banissi et al.; Convened by GraphicsLink; Supported by Visualisation & Graphics Research Unit (VGRU), South Bank University et al.

Ware, Colin, *Information Visualization: Perception for Design*, San Francisco: Morgan Kaufmann, 2000 (Morgan Kaufmann Interactive Technologies Series).

Spence, Robert, *Information Visualization*, New York: Addison-Wesley, 2000.

Staley, David J., *Computers, Visualization and History: How New technology will transform our Understanding of the Past*, Armonk: M.E. Sharpe, 2003.

Shneiderman, Ben, and Benjamin B. Bederson, *The Craft of Information Visualization: Readings and Reflections*, San Francisco: Morgan Kaufmann, 2003.

Geroimenko, Vladimir, and Chaomei Chen, *Visualizing the Semantic Web*, Berlin: Springer, 2003.

Complexity

Nicolis, Gregoire, and Ilya Prigogine, *Exploring Complexity*, New York: W.H. Freeman, 1989.

Maruyama, Magoroh, ed., *Context and Complexity: Cultivating Contextual Understanding*, Berlin: Springer, 1992.

Sigal, Ron, and Elaine Weyuker, *Computability, Complexity, and Languages: Fundamentals of Theoretical Computer Science*, Academic Press, 1994.

Evans, Eric, *Domain-Driven Design: Tackling Complexity in the Heart of Software*, Reading, MA: Addison-Wesley, 2003.

Marcus, Gary F., *The Birth of the Mind: How a Tiny Number of Genes Creates the Complexities of Human Thought*, New York: Basic Books, 2003.

Automatic Classification

Cumming, J., and J. Wainwright, *Automatic Classification of Libraries and their Subject Interests* [microform], [London]: ASLIB Research & Development Dept., 1973.

Sparck-Jones, Karen, *Automatic Keyword Classification for Information Retrieval*, London: Butterworths, 1971.

Grefenstette, G., *Explorations in Automatic Thesaurus Discovery*, Boston: Kluwer, 1994.

Klassifikationen für wissenschaftliche Bibliotheken: Analyse, Empfehlungen, Modelle, Berlin: Deutsches Bibliotheks Institut, 1994.

Felsenstein, Joseph, *Inferring Phylogenies*, Sunderland, MA: Sinauer Associates, 2003.

Chapter 13. Challenges

Developing World

Manet, Enrique Gonzalez, *Informatics and Society: The New Challenges*, Norwood: Ablex, 1992.

Reeves, Geoffrey, *Communications and the Third World*, London: Routledge, 1993.

Mander, Jerry, and Edward Goldsmith, eds., *The Case Against the Global Economy: And for a Turn toward the Local*, San Francisco: Siena Club, 1997.

Global-Regional

Bauman, Zygmunt, *Globalization: The Human Consequences*, New York: Columbia University Press, 1998.

Blanton, Robert G., *Defining the New World Order: Economic Regions and the Patterns of Global Cooperation*, New York: Garland, 1998.

Everard, Jerry, *Virtual States: The Internet and the Boundaries of the Nation State*, London: Routledge, 2000.

Chéneau-Loquay, Annie, *Enjeux des technologies de la communication en Afrique*, Paris: Karthala Regards, 2000.

Ebo, Bosah L., *Cyberimperialism?: Global Relations in the New Electronic Frontier*, Westport, CT: Praeger, 2000.

Niemann, Michael, *A Spatial Approach to Regionalism in the Global Economy*, New York: St. Martin's Press, 2000 (International Political Economy Series).

Stiles, Kendall W., ed., *Global Institutions and Local Empowerment: Competing Theoretical Perspectives*, Hounmills: Palgrave, 2000 (International Political Economy Series).

Pulsipher, Lydia M., Alex Pulsipher, Conrad M. Goodwin, and Mischa M. Kudian, *World Regional Geography: Global Patterns, Local Lives*, New York: W.H. Freeman, 2003.

Bradshaw, Michael J., and George W. White, *Contemporary World Regional Geography: Global Connections, Local Voices*, New York: McGraw-Hill, 2004.

Digital Divide

Falling through the Net: Defining the Digital Divide, A Report on the Telecommunications and Information Technology Gap in America, Washington: U.S. Department of Commerce, National Telecommunications and Information Administration, [1999]; Mass Market Paperback, 1999.

Bolt, David B., and Ray A. K. Crawford, *Digital Divide: Computers and Our Children's Future*, New York: TV Books, 2000.

Thomas, Caroline, ed., *Global Governance, Development and Human Security: The Challenge of Poverty and Inequality*, London: Pluto Press, 2000 (Human Security in the Global Economy).

Norris, Pippa, *Digital Divide: Civic Engagement, Information Poverty, and the Internet Worldwide*, Cambridge: Cambridge University Press, 2001.

Servon, Lisa J., *Bridging the Digital Divide: Technology, Community, and Public Policy*, Oxford: Blackwell, 2003.

Warschauer, Mark, *Technology and Social Inclusion: Rethinking the Digital Divide*, Cambridge, MA: MIT Press, 2003.

Edutainment

Postman, Neil, *Amusing Ourselves to Death*, New York: Penguin, 1985.

Postman, Neil, *Technopoly: The Surrender of Culture to Technology*, New York: Vintage Books, 1993.

Mann, William P., *Edutainment comes alive!*, Indianapolis: Sams Pub., 1994.

Dholakia, Ruby Roy, Norbert Mundorf, and Nikhilesh Dholakia, eds., *New Infotainment Technologies in the Home: Demand Side Perspectives*, Mahwah, NJ: Lawrence Erlbaum Associates, 1996.

Hewitt, Ian E., *Edutainment: How to Teach Language With Fun & Games*, McHenry, IL: Delta Systems, 1998.

Media and Democracy

Abramson, Jeffrey B., *The Electronic Commonwealth: The Impact of New Media Technologies on Democratic Politics*, New York: Basic Books, 1988.

Lanham, Richard A., *The Electronic Word: Democracy, Technology and the Arts*, Chicago: University of Chicago Press, 1993.

Abramson, Jeffrey B., *Democratic Designs for Electronic Town Meetings*, Aspen: Aspen Institute, 1994.

McChesney, Robert W., *Corporate Media and the Threat to Democracy*, New York: Seven Stories Press, 1997 (Open Media Pamphlet Series).

Ledbetter, James, *Made Possible by: The Death of Public Broadcasting in the United States*, London: Verso Books, 1998.

Alger, Dean, *Megamedia: How Giant Corporations Dominate Mass Media, Distort Competition, and Endanger Democracy*, Lanham, MD: Rowman & Littlefield, 1998.

Alexander, Cynthia, Leslie A. Pal, eds., James H. May, Ronald J. Deibert, Michael R. Ogden, Dineh M. Davis, Bill Cross, Julie Thorburn, Michael Mehta, Ann Cavoukian, Sue P. Stafford, and Catherine Alexander, *Digital Democracy*, Oxford: Oxford University Press, 1998.

Herman, Edward S. and Robert Waterman McChesney, *The Global Media: The Missionaries of Global Capitalism*, London: Cassell Academic 1998 (Media Studies).

McChesney, Robert W., *Rich Media, Poor Democracy: Communication Politics in Dubious Times*, Champaign: University of Illinois Press, 1999 (The History of Communication).

Wolf, Michael J., *Entertainment Economy: How Mega-Media Forces Are Transforming Our Lives*, New York: Times Books, 1999.

Gutstein, Donald, *E.Con: How the Internet Undermines Democracy*, Toronto: Stoddart, 1999.

Wilhelm, Anthony G., *Democracy in the Digital Age: Challenges to Political Life in Cyberspace*, London: Routledge, 2000.

Ferdinand, Peter, ed., *The Internet, Democracy and Democratization*, London: Frank Cass, 2000. (Democratization Studies).

Browning, Graeme, *Electronic Democracy*, Chicago: Independent Publishers Group, 2001.

Sunstein, Cass R., *Republic.com*, Princeton: Princeton University Press, 2001.

Privacy

Davies, Simon, *Monitor: Extinguishing Privacy on the Information Superhighway*, Sydney: Pan Macmillan, 1996.

Schneier, Bruce, and David Banisar, *The Electronic Privacy Papers: Documents on the Battle for Privacy in the Age of Surveillance*, Chichester: John Wiley & Sons, 1997.

Brin, David, *The Transparent Society: Will Technology Force Us to Choose between Privacy and Freedom*, Reading, MA: Addison-Wesley, 1998.

Garfinkel, Simson, *Database Nation: The Death of Privacy in the 21st Century*, Beijing: O'Reilly, 2000.

Whitaker, Reg, *The End of Privacy: How Total Surveillance Is Becoming a Reality*, New York: New Press, 2000.

Sykes, Charles, *The End of Privacy*, Torrance, CA: Griffin Trade Publishers, 2000.

Etzioni, Amitai, *The Limits of Privacy*, New York: Basic Books, 2000.

Schulzki-Haddouti, Christiane (eds.), *"Vom Ende der Anonymität": Die Globalisierung der Überwachung.* Hannover: Heise, 2002. 2., aktualisierte Auflage. Cf. http://www.schulzki-haddouti.de/

Elmer, Greg, *Profiling Machines: Mapping the Personal Information Economy*, Cambridge, MA: MIT Press, 2004.

Catudal, Jacques N., *Privacy and Rights to the Visual: The Internet Debate*, Lanham, MD: Rowman & Littlefield, 2004. (Philosophy and the Global Context).

Power of Corporations

Barnet, Richard J., and John Cavanagh, *Global Dreams: Imperial Corporations and the New World Order*, New York: Touchstone Books, 1995.

David Korten, *When Corporations Rule the World*, West Hartford, CT: Kumarian Press, 1995.

Hartmann, Thom, *Unequal Protection: The Rise of Corporate Dominance and the Theft of Human Rights*, New York: Rodale Books, 2004.

Kuttner, Robert, *Everything for Sale*, New York: Knopf, 1996, Reprint: 1999.

Martin, Hans Peter, and Harald Schumann, *Die Globalisierungsfälle: Der Angriff auf Demokratie*, Reinbek: Rowohl, 1996. (This book has a more dire interpretation of global corporations and discusses the "tittytainment" idea of Zbigniew Brzezinski.)

Derber, Charles, *Corporation Nation: How Corporations Are Taking Over Our Lives and What We Can Do about It*, New York: St. Martin's Griffin, 1998.

Albarran, Alan B., and Sylvia M. Chan-Olmsted, *Global Media Economics: Commercialization, Concentration and Integration of World Media Markets*, Ames: Iowa State University Press, 1998.

Korten, David C., *The Post Corporate World*, San Francisco: Berrett-Koehler; West Hartford, CT: Kumarian Press, 1999.

Rifkin, Jeremy, *The Age of Access*, New York: Jeremy P. Tarcher/Putnam, 2000, p. 32.

Ritzer, George, *The McDonaldization of Society, New Century Edition: An Investigation into the Changing Character of Contemporary Social Life*, Thousand Oaks, CA: Pine Forge Press, 2000.

Schwartz, Herman M., *States Versus Markets: The Emergence of a Global Economy*, Houndmills: Palgrave, 2000.

Danaher, Kevin, *Democratizing the Global Economy: The Battle Against the World Bank and the IMF*, Monroe, ME: Common Courage Press, 2000.

Stiglitz, Joseph E., *Globalization and Its Discontents*, New York: W.W. Norton, 2003.

Bok, Derek, *Universities in the Marketplace: The Commercialization of Higher Education*, Princeton: Princeton University Press, 2003.

Cyber War

Landa, Manuel de, *War in the Age of Intelligent Machines*, New York: Swerve, 1991.

Ignatieff, Michael, *Virtual War: Kosovo and Beyond*, New York: Metropolitan Books, 2000.

Adamy, David L., *EW 101: A First Course in Electronic Warfare*, Norwood, MA: Artech House, 2000.

Jordan, Tim, and Paul A. Taylor, *Hacktivism and Cyberwars: Rebels With a Cause*, London: Routledge, 2004.

Cyber Law

Bertrand, André, *Droit à la vie privée et droit à l'image*, Paris: Litec, 1998.

Etoy, Piro Nico, ed., *Cyberterrorismo: Come si organizza un rapimento virtuale*, Rome: Castelvecchi, 1998.

Féral-Schuhl, Christiane, *Cyberdroit: Le droit à l'épreuve de l'Internet*, Paris: Dunod, 1999.

Lessig, Lawrence, *Code and Other Laws of Cyberspace*, New York: Basic Books, 1999.
Lawrence Lessig, Stanford. See: http://cyberlaw.stanford.edu/lessig/.
Drucker, Susan J., and Gary Gumpert, *Real Law at Virtual Space: Communication Regulation in Cyberspace*, Mount Waverly: Hampton Press: 1999 (The Hampton Press Communication Series. Communication and Law).
Alexander, Yonah, and Michael S. Swetnam, *Cyber Terrorism and Information Warfare: Threats and Responses*, Ardsley-on-Hudson, NY: Transnational Publishers, 2003.

Governance (cf. Intellectual Property and Cyber Law)

The term "governance" comes from the corporate world, e.g.:

Sutton, Brenda, ed., *The Legitimate Corporation: Essential Readings in Business Ethics and Corporate Governance*, Cambridge, MA: Blackwell Business, 1993.
Kettl, Donald F., *Sharing Power: Public Governance and Private Markets*, Washington: Brookings Institution Press, 1994.
March, James G., and Johan P. Olsen, *Democratic Governance*, New York: Free Press, 1995.
Loader, Brian D., ed., *The Governance of Cyberspace: Politics, Technology and Global Restructuring*, London: Routledge, 1997.
Tsagarousianou, Roza, Damian Tambini, and Cathy Brian, eds. *Cyberdemocracy: Technologies, Cities and Civic Networks*, London: Routledge, 1998.
Muñoz Machad, Santiago, *La regulacion de la red: Poder y Derecho en Internet*, Mexico: Taurus, 2000.
Stefik, Mark, *The Internet Edge: Social, Technical and Legal Challenges for a Networked World*, Cambridge, MA: MIT Press, 2000.
Harvard Business Review on Corporate Governance, Boston: Harvard Business School, 2000 (The Harvard Business Review Paperback Series).
Kettl, Donald F., *The Global Public Management Revolution: A Report on the Transformation of Governance*, Washington: Brookings Institution Press, 2000.
Brookings Institute. See: http://www.brookings.edu.
Llaneza Gonzalez, Paloma, *Internet y comunicaciones digitales: Regimen legal de las tecnologias de la informacion y la comunicaion*, Barcelona: Bosch, 2000.
Girasá, Roy J., *Cyberlaw: National and International Perspectives*, Upper Saddle River, NJ: Prentice Hall, 2001.
Helewitz, Jeffrey A., *Cyberlaw: Legal Principles of Emerging Technologies*, Upper Saddle River, NJ: Prentice Hall, 2001.
Malkia, Matti, Reijo Savolainen, and Ari-Veikko Anttiroiko, *Transformation in Governance: New Directions in Government*, Hershey, PA: Idea Group, 2004.
Mueller, Milton L., *Ruling the Root: Internet Governance and the Taming of Cyberspace*, Cambridge, MA: MIT Press, 2004.
Perri 6, *E-Governance: Styles of Political Judgement in the Informaton Age Polity*, New York: Palgrave Macmillan, 2004.

Public versus Private

Ray, Barbara J., *Public-Private Partnership: A Bibliography*, Monticello, IL: Vance Bibliographies, 1986.
Weintraub, Jeff, Krishan Kumar, eds., *Public and Private in Thought and Practice: Perspectives on a Grand Dichotomy*, Chicago: University of Chicago Press, 1997 (Morality and Society Series).
Sax, Joseph L., *Playing Darts with a Rembrandt: Public and Private Rights in Cultural Treasures*, Ann Arbor: University of Michigan Press, 1999.
Commissariat Général du Plan, *Diffusion des données publiques et révolution numérique*, Paris: La documentation française, 1999.

Boggs, Carl, *The End of Politics: Corporate Power and the Decline of the Public Sphere*, New York: Guilford Press, 2000.

Oliver, Caroline, Mike Conduff, Susan Edsall, and John Carver, *The Policy Governance Fieldbook*, San Francisco: Jossey-Bass, 1999.

Vayrynen, Raimo, ed., *Globalization and Global Governance*, Lanham, MD: Rowman & Littlefield, 1999.

National Research Council, Committee for a Study Promoting Access to Scientific, Technical Data for the Public Interest, *A Question of Balance: Private Rights and Public Interest in Scientific and Technical Databases*, Washington: National Academy Press, 2000.

Saunders, Frances Stonor, *The Cultural Cold War: The CIA and the World of Arts and Letters*, New York: New Press, 2000.

Gwartney, James D., Richard L. Stroup, Russell S. Sobel, and Rusell Sobel, *Economics: Private and Public Choice*, New York: Harcourt, 2000 (Dryden Press Series in Economics), 9th ed.

Kearns, Kevin P., *Private Sector Strategies for Social Sector Success*, San Francisco: Jossey-Bass, 2000.

Osborne, Stephen P., ed. *Public-Private Partnerships: Theory and Practice in International Perspective*, London: Routledge, 2000.

Hay, Colin, and David Marsh, eds., *Demystifying Globalization*, New York: St Martin's Press, 2000 (Globalization and Governance).

Whitfield, Dexter, *Public Services or Corporate Welfare: Rethinking the Nation State in the Global Economy*, London: Pluto Press, 2001.

Chapter 14. Synthesis

Open Source

Raymond, Eric S., *The Cathedral & the Bazaar: Musings on Linux and Open Source by an Accidental Revolutionary*, Cambridge, MA: O'Reilly, 1999.

Rosenberg, Donald K., *Open Source: The Unauthorized White Papers*, Foster City: IDG Books Worldwide, 2000.

Pavlicek, Russell, and Robin Miller, *Embracing Insanity: Open Source Software Development*, Indianapolis: SAMS, 2000.

Moody, Glyn, *Rebel Code: Linux and the Open Source Revolution*, New York: Perseus, 2000.

Zone Market Report, *The New Religion: Linux and Open Source* [DOWNLOAD: PDF], The Sageza Group, November 1, 2000 (ISBN: B00005MCQC).

Koch, Stefan, *Open Source Software Entwicklung: Analyse und Aufwandsschätzung an einem Beispiel*, Frankfurt: Peter Lang, 2002. (Europäische Hochschulschriften. Reihe 5. Volks- und Betriebswissenschaft, Bd. 2831).

Fink, Martin, *The Business and Economics of Linux and Open Source*, Upper Saddle River, NJ: Prentice Hall, 2002.

Spinellis, Diomidis, *Code Reading: The Open Source Perspective*, Boston: Addison-Wesley, 2003.

Weber, Steven, *The Success of Open Source*, Boston: Harvard University Press, 2004.

Museums

Roberts, Lisa C., *From Knowledge to Narrative: Educators and the Changing Museum*, Washington: Smithsonian Institution Press, 1997.

Collective Intelligence

Levy, Pierre, *L'Intelligence collective, pour une anthropologie du cyberspace*, Paris: La Découverte, 1994, 1999. Cf. English Translation: *Collective Intelligence: Mankind's Emerging World in Cyberspace*, Dordrecht: Plenum, 1997. Reprint: New York: Perseus, 2000.

466

Pierre Levy claims that we have created three kinds of spaces in the past (earth, territory and commodities) and that the new technologies and the Internet are introducing a fourth space entailing knowledge and collective intelligence. Cf.the review by Pierre Drouin in *Le Monde*. See: http://www.alapage.com/cgi-bin/1/affiche_livre. cgi?l_isbn=2707126934): "La Terre fut le premier grand espace de significations ouvert par notre espèce, où Homo sapiens invente le langage, la technique et la religion. Un deuxième espace, le Territoire, se construit à partir du néolithique, avec l'agriculture, la ville, l'Etat, l'écriture. Puis naît, au XVIe siècle, l'espace des marchandises. Nous allons vers un nouvel espace, celui «du savoir et de l'intelligence collectifs», qui commandera les espaces antérieurs sans les faire disparaître. Sans doute, le savoir a-t-il toujours été au coeur du fonctionnement social, mais la nouveauté est triple: vitesse d'évolution des connaissances, masse des personnes appelées à les produire et à les apprendre, apparition de nouveaux outils pour rendre l'information «navigable». / Vers une agora virtuelle / Du coup, on peut réinventer le lien social «autour de l'apprentissage réciproque, de la synergie des compétences, de l'imagination et de l'intelligence collective». Pour Pierre Lévy, «l'effet boule de neige» est assuré: après les groupes organiques (familles, clans et tribus) et les groupes organisés (Etats, Eglises, grandes entreprises), des groupes «auto- organisés» réaliseront «l'idéal de la démocratie directe dans les très grandes communautés en situation de mutation et de «déterritorialisation»."

Richard Barbrook notes that Levy's ideas are inspired by Islamic theology, whereby the "collective intelligence" is rather similar to God and that Levy's real interest is in real-time direct democracy. Richard Barbrook in his review of Pierre Levy's *Collective Intelligence* in the *New Scientist*, 13 December 1997. See: http://www.hrc.wmin.ac.uk/hrc/theory/ cyberbollocks/index/t.2.html. Once we all have access to cyberspace, we will be able to determine our own destiny through a real-time direct democracy: the "virtual agora"... According to Levy, cyberspace therefore is the on-line version of a hippie commune.

Others have also dealt with this process:

Stock, Gregory, *Metaman: The Merging of Humans and Machines into a Global Superorganism*, Toronto: Doubleday Canada, 1993.

Smith, John B., *Collective Intelligence in Computer Based Collaboration*, Mahwah, NJ: Lawrence Erlbaum Associates, 1994.

Kerckhove, Derrick de, *Gekoppelde intelligentie: De opkomst van de WEB-maatschappij*, Hoolberg: Stichting Maatschappij en Onderneming, 1996. English trans: *Connected Intelligence, The Arrival of the Web Society*, Toronto: Somerville Books, 1997.

Fisher, Kimball, Maureen Duncan Fisher, and Mareen Duncan Fisher, *The Distributed Mind: Achieving High Performance through the Collective Intelligence of Knowledge Work Teams*, New York: Amacom, 1997.

Dyson, George B., *Darwin Among the Machines: The Evolution of Global Intelligence*, Helix Books, 1998.

Russell, Peter, *The Global Brain* [Video], c. 1992.

See: http://www.peterussell.com/GBvideo.html.

Russell, Peter, *The Global Brain Awakens: Our Next Evolutionary Leap*, Element, February 2000.

Visionaries in the business world, are pursuing similar themes:

Allee, Charles M. Savage, *Fifth Generation Management: Co-Creating through Virtual Enterprising, Dynamic Teaming, and Knowledge Networking*, Oxford: Butterworth-Heinemann, 1996.

Verna, *The Knowledge Evolution: Expanding Organizational Intelligence*, Oxford: Butterworth-Heinemann, 1997.

Creighton, James L., and James W. R. Adams, *Cybermeeting: How to Link People and Technology in Your Organization*, New York: Amacom 1997.

Halal, William E., et al., ed., *The Infinite Resource: Creating and Leading the Knowledge Enterprise*, Jossey-Bass: San Francisco, 1998. (Jossey-Bass Business and Management Series).

Szuba, Tadeusz M., *Computational Collective Intelligence*, New York: John Wiley & Sons, 2001.

On the Internet there are also a series of *Conceptions of the [sic!] Global Superbrain*. See: http://www.rbjones.com/rbjpub/cs/ai014.htm. In other words, something much more than a reorganization of old and new knowledge has begun. Implicitly there is a new convergence between these.

Aesthetics

Holtzman, Steven, *Digital Mosaics, The Aesthetics of Cyberspace*, New York: Touchstone, 1997.

Creativity

Colford, Ian, *Writing in the Electronic Environment: Electronic Text and the Future of Creativity and Knowledge*, Halifax: Dalhousie University, 1996 (Occasional Papers Series Dalhousie University. Sc).

Sefton-Green, Julian, ed., *Young People, Creativity and New Technologies: The Challenge of Digital Arts*, London: Routledge, 1999.

Wands, Bruce, *Digital Creativity: Techniques for Digital Media and the Internet*, New York: John Wiley & Sons, 2001.

Chapter 15. Conclusions

Culture and Anthropology, Ethnology

Benedict, Ruth, *Patterns of Culture*, Boston: Houghton Mifflin, 1934, 1989.

Benedict, Ruth, *The Chrysanthemum and The Sword: Patterns of Japanese Culture*, Boston: Houghton Mifflin, 1946, 1989.

Steward, Julian H., *Theory of Culture Change: The Methodology of Multilinear Evolution*, Urbana: University of Illinois Press, 1955, 1972.

Geertz, Clifford, *The Interpretation of Cultures*, New York: Basic Books, 1973.

Rodney Needham, ed., *Right and Left: Essays on Dual Symbolic Classification*, Chicago: University of Chicago Press, [1973].

Rosman, Abraham, and Paula G. Rubel, *The Tapestry of Culture: An Introduction to Cultural Anthropology*, New York: McGraw-Hill, 1981, 1998.

Gell, Alfred, *Art and Agency: An Anthropological Theory*, Oxford: Clarendon Press, 1998.

Kuper, Adam, *Culture: The Anthropologists' Account*, Cambridge, MA: Harvard University Press, 1999.

Miller, Daniel, and Don Slater, *The Internet: An Ethnographic Approach*, New York: New York University Press, 2000.

Gannon, Martin J., *Understanding Global Cultures: Metaphorical Journeys through 23 Nations* [abridged], London: Sage, 2003.

Brooker, Peter, *A Glossary of Cultural Theory*, London: Edward Arnold, 2003.

Nisbett, Richard, *The Geography of Thought: How Asians and Westerners Think Differently ... and Why*, Northampton, MA: Free Press, 2003.

Traub, Charles H., and Jonathan Rifkin, *In the Realm of the Circuit: Computers, Art and Culture*, Upper Saddle River, NJ: Pearson, Prenctice Hall, 2004.

Culture and Archaeology

Thomas, Julian, *Time, Culture and Identity: An Interpretive Archaeology*, London: Routledge, 1995.

Renfrew, Colin, and Chris Scarre, eds., *Cognition and Material Culture: The Archaeology of Symbolic Storage*, Oakville, CT: David Brown, 1999.

Brodie, Neil, and Kathryn Walker Tubb, eds., *Illicit Antiquities: The Theft of Culture and the Extinction of Archaeology*, London: Routledge, 2002 (One World Archaeology).

Klein, Richard G., *The Dawn of Human Culture*, New York: John Wiley & Sons, 2002.

Culture and Creativity

Abdel-Malek, Anouar, ed., *Intellectual creativity in endogenous culture*, Asian Regional Symposium, Kyoto, Japan November 1978, Tokyo: United Nations University, 1981.

Mitias, Michael, *Creativity in Art, Religion, and Culture*, Amsterdam: Rodopi BV, 1985 (Elementa 42).

Kearney, Richard, *The Wake of Imagination: Ideas of Creativity in Western Culture*, London: Taylor and Francis, 1988.

Dervin, Daniel, *Creativity and Culture: A Psychoanalytic Study of the Creative Process in the Arts, Sciences, and Culture*, Teaneck, NJ: Fairleigh Dickinson University Press, 1990.

Gailey, Christine Ward, and Stanley Diamond, eds. *The Politics of Culture and Creativity: A Critique of Civilization*, University Press of Florida: Gainesville, 1992 (Dialectical Anthropology, Vol. 2).

Lavie, Smadar, Kirin Narayan, and Renato Rosaldo, eds., *Creativity/Anthropology*, Ithaca: Cornell University Press, 1993 (Anthropology of Contemporary Issues).

Holbrook, David, *Creativity and Popular Culture*, Teaneck, NJ: Fairleigh Dickinson University Press, 1994.

Robinson, Gillian, and John Rundell, eds., *Rethinking Imagination: Culture and Creativity*, London: Routledge, 1994.

Bohm, David, and Lee Nichol, *On Creativity*, London: Routledge, 1998.

UNESCO, *World Culture Report, 1998: Culture, Creativity and Markets*, Paris: UNESCO, 1999.

Throsby, David, *Economics and Culture*, Cambridge: Cambridge University Press, 2000.

Myers, Tona Pearce, ed. *The Soul of Creativity: Insights into the Creative Process*, Novato, CA: New World Library, 2001.

Liep, John, *Locating Cultural Creativity*, London: Pluto Press, 2001 (Anthropology, Culture and Society Series).

Wands, Bruce, *Digital Creativity: Techniques for Digital Media and the Internet*, New York: John Wiley & Sons, 2001.

Florida, Richard, *The Rise of the Creative Class: And How It's Transforming Work, Leisure and Community Life*, New York: Basic Books, 2002.

Ulrich, David, *The Widening Stream: The Seven Stages of Creativity*, Hillsboro, OR: Beyond Words, 2002.

Lessig, Lawrence, *Free Culture: How Big Media Uses Technology and the Law to Lock Down Culture and Control Creativity*, London: Penguin, 2004.

Culture and Electronic Media

Druckrey, Timothy, ed., *Electronic Culture, Technology and Visual Representation*, New York: Aperture, 1996.

Lévy, Pierre, *Cyberculture*, Paris: Odile Jacob, 1997.

Culture and Globalism

Iriye, Akira, *Cultural Internationalism and World Order*, Baltimore: Johns Hopkins University Press, 1997.

Tomlinson, John, *Globalization and Culture*, Chicago: University of Chicago Press, 1999.

García Canclini, Néstor, Kathleen Ashley, and Robert L. A. Clark, eds., *Consumers and Citizens: Globalization and Multicultural Conflicts*, Trans. George Yudice, Minneapolis: University of Minnesota Press, 2001.

Storey, John, *Inventing Popular Culture: From Folklore to Globalization*, Oxford: Blackwell, 2003 (Blackwell Manifestos).

Yudice, George, *The Expediency of Culture: Uses of Culture in the Global Era*, Durham, NC: Duke University Press, 2004 (Post-Contemporary Interventions).

Denning, Michael, *Culture in the Age of Three Worlds*, London: Verso, 2004.

Culture and History

Callinicos, Alex, *Theories and Narratives: Reflections on the Philosophy of History*, Durham: Duke University Press, 1995.

Biersack, Aletta, and Lynn Hunt, *The New Cultural History: Essays*, Berkeley: University of California Press, 1989 (Studies on the History of Society and Culture).

Iggers, George G., *Historiography in the Twentieth Century: From Scientific Objectivity to the Postmodern Challenge*, Middletown, CN: Wesleyan University Press, 1997.

Ralph, Philip Lee, Robert E. Lerner, Standish Meacham, Alan T. Wood, Richard W. Hull, and Edward McNall Burns, eds. *World Civilizations: Their History and Their Culture*, New York: W.W. Norton, 1997.

Wilson, Norman J., *History in Crisis? Recent Directions in Historiography*, Upper Saddle River, NJ: Prentice Hall, 1998.

Culture and Language, Linguistics

Sapir, Edward, *Language: An Introduction to the Study of Speech*, San Diego: Harvest, 1921.

Vygotsky, Lev S., *Thought and Language*, Cambridge, MA: MIT Press, 1999. Originally published in Russian, Moscow, 1934.

Vygotsky, Lev S., *Mind in Society: The Development of Higher Psychological Processes*, Cambridge, MA: Harvard University Press, 1978.

Kramsch, Claire J., and H. G. Widdowson, *Language and Culture*, Oxford: Oxford University Press, 1998 (Oxford Introductions to Language Study).

Spolsky, Bernard, and H. G. Widdowson, eds., *Sociolinguistics*, Oxford: Oxford University Press, 1998 (Oxford Introductions to Language Study).

Duranti, Alessandro, *Key Terms in Language and Culture*, Oxford: Blackwell, 2001.

Culture and Materialism

Murphy, Martin F., and Maxine L. Margolis, *Science, Materialism and the Study of Culture*, Gainesville: University Press of Florida, 1995.

Prendergast, Christopher, *Cultural Materialism: On Raymond Williams*, Minneapolis: University of Minnesota Press, 1995.

Culture and Modernism, Postmodernism

Rossi, Ino, *The Logic of Culture: Advances in Structural Theory and Methods*, New York: Bergin & Garvey, 1982.

Harvey, David, *The Condition of Postmodernity: An Enquiry into the Origins of Cultural Change*, Oxford: Blackwell, 1990.

Rosenau, Pauline, *Post-Modernism and the Social Sciences*, Princeton: Princeton University Press, 1991.

Adam, Barbara, and Stuart Allen, ed., *Theorizing Culture: An Interdisciplinary Critique after Postmodernism*, New York: New York University Press, 1995.

McCallum, Dennis, *The Death of Truth: What's Wrong With Multiculturalism, the Rejection of Reason and the New Postmodern Diversity*, Minneapolis: Bethany House, 1995.

Harris, Marvin, *Theories of Culture in Postmodern Times*, Walnut Creek, CA: Altamira Press, 1998.

Swingewood, Alan, *Cultural Theory and the Problem of Modernity*, New York: St. Martin's Press, 1998.

Hegeman, Susa, *Patterns for America, Modernism and the Concept of Culture*, Princeton: Princeton University Press, 1999.

Eagleton, Terry, *After Theory*, New York: Basic Books, 2004.

Culture and Public Policy

Bell, Robert, *The Culture of Policy Deliberations*, Camden: Rutgers University Press, 1985.

Globerman, Steve, *Culture, Governments and Markets: Public Policy and the Culture Industries*, Vancouver: Fraser Institute, 1987.

Boorsma, Peter B., Annemoon van Hemel, and Niki van der Wielen, eds., *Privatization and Culture: Experiences in the Arts, Heritage and the Cultural Industries in Europe*, Dordrecht: Kluwer, 1998.

Sax, Joseph L., *Playing Darts with a Rembrandt: Public and Private Rights in Cultural Treasures*, Ann Arbor: University of Michigan Press, 1999.

Rao, Vijayendra, and Michael Walton, *Culture and Public Action: A Cross-Disciplinary Dialogue on Development Policy*, Palo Alto: Stanford University Press, 2004.

Culture and Politics

Sardar, Ziauddin, and Jerome R. Ravetz, *Cyberfutures, Culture and politics on the Information Superhighway*, London: Pluto Press, 1996.

Rocker, Rudolf, *Nationalism and Culture*, Montreal: Black Rose, 1998.

Wark, McKenzie, *The Virtual Republic: Australia's Culture Wars of the 1990s*, St. Leonards: Allen and Unwin, 1996.

Brook, James, and Iain A. Boal, eds., *Resisting the Virtual Life: The Culture and Politics of Information*, San Francisco: City Lights Books, 1995.

Harrison, Lawrence E., and Samuel P. Huntington, *Culture Matters: How Values Shape Human Progress*, New York: Harper Collins, 2001.

Bradford, Gigi, Michael Gary, Glenn Wallach, and Center for Arts and Culture, eds. *Politics of Culture: Policy Perspectives for Individuals, Institutions, and Communities*, New York: New Press, 2000.

Lee, Richard E., *Life and Times of Cultural Studies: The Politics and Transformation of the Structures of Knowledge*, Durham: Duke University Press, 2003 (Philosophy and Postcoloniality).

Culture and Religion

Tillich, Paul, and Robert C. Kimball, *Theology of Culture*, Oxford: Oxford University Press, 1964.

Noble, David, *The Religion of Technology: The Divinity of Man and the Spirit of Invention*, New York: Penguin, 1999.

Pearson, James L., *Shamanism and the Ancient Mind: A Cognitive Approach to Archaeology*, Lanham, MD: Rowman & Littlefield, 2002 (Archaeology of Religion).

Lewis-Williams, J. David, *A Cosmos In Stone: Interpreting Religion and Society through Rock Art*, Lanham, MD: Rowman & Littlefield, 2002.

Lewis-Williams, J. David, *The Mind in the Cave: Consciousness and the Origins of Art*, London: Thames and Hudson, 2002.

Amkreutz, Jan, *Digital Spirit, Minding the Future*, Bloomington, IN, 2003.

Culture and Sociology

Hall, Edward T., *Beyond Culture*, New York: Doubleday, 1966.

Hofstede, Geert, *Culture's Consequences: International Differences in Work Related Values*, Newbury Park, CA: Sage, 1980, 1984.

Williams, Raymond, *The Sociology of Culture*, Chicago: University of Chicago Press, 1981.

Gross, Jonathan L., and Steve Rayner, *Measuring Culture: A Paradigm for the Analysis of Social Organization*, New York: Columbia University Press, 1985.

Alexander, Jeffrey C., and Steven Seidman, eds., *Culture and Society: Contemporary Debates*, Cambridge: Cambridge University Press, 1990.

Hannerz, Ulf, *Cultural Complexity: Studies in the Social Organization of Meaning*, New York: Columbia University Press, 1992.

Archer, Margaret S., *Culture and Agency: The Place of Culture in Social Theory*, Cambridge: Cambridge University Press, 1996.

Hoofstede, Geert, *Cultures and Organizations: Software of the Mind. Intercultural Cooperation and its Importance for Survival*, New York: McGraw-Hill, 1997.

Swartz, David, *Culture and Power: The Sociology of Pierre Bourdieu*, Chicago: University of Chicago Press, 1997.

Crane, Diana, *The Sociology of Culture: Emerging Theoretical Perspectives*, Oxford: Blackwell, 2002.

471

Culture: General Works

Sahlins, Marshall, *Culture and Practical Reason*, Chicago: University of Chicago Press, 1976.

Wagner, Roy, *The Invention of Culture*, Chicago: University of Chicago Press, 1975, 1981.

Cunningham, Lawrence, and John Reich, *Culture and Values*, Forth Worth: Harcourt Brace, 1982, 1998.

Shweder, Richard A., and Robert A. LeVine, *Culture Theory: Essays on Mind, Self and Emotion*, Cambridge: Cambridge University Press, 1984, 1997.

Bohannan, Paul, *How Culture Works*, New York: Free Press, 1995.

Burnett, Ron, *Cultures of Vision: Images, Media and Imaginary*, Bloomington: Indiana University Press, 1995.

Frow, John, *Cultural Studies and Cultural Value*, Oxford: Clarendon Press, 1995.

Murray, David, *American Cultural Critics*, Exeter: University of Exeter Press, 1995.

Nuckolls, Charles W., *The Cultural Dialectics of Knowledge and Desire*, Madison: University of Wisconsin Press, 1996.

Silverstein, Michael, and Greg Urban, *Natural Histories of Discourse*, Chicago: University of Chicago, 1996.

Sirchia, Tullio, *Le tre culture Umanistica, scientifica, multimediale*, Marsala: Editrice Scolastica Italiana, 1996.

Sperber, Daniel, *Explaining Culture: A Naturalistic Approach*, Oxford: Blackwell, 1996.

Gibian, Peter, *Mass Culture and Everyday Life*, New York: Routledge, 1997.

Mulder, Niels, *Thai Images. The Culture of the Public World*, Chiang Mai: Silkworm Books, 1997.

Balkin, J. M., *Cultural Software: A Theory of Ideology*, New Haven, CT: Yale University Press, 1998.

Bertman, Stephen, *Hyperculture: The Cost of Speed*, Westport, CT: Praeger, 1998.

Mirzoeff, Nicholas, *The Visual Culture Reader*, London: Routledge, 1998.

Schafer, D. Paul, *Culture: Beacon of the Future*, Westport, CT: Praeger, 1998.

Surber, Jere Paul, *Culture and Critique: An Introduction to the Critical Discourses of Cultural Studies*, Boulder: Westview Press, 1998.

Harris, Marvin, *Theories of Culture in Postmodern Times*, Walnut Creek, CA: Altamira Press, 1998.

Bal, Mieke, Jonathan Crewe, and Leo Spitzer, *Acts of Memory: Cultural Recall in the Present*, Hanover: Dartmouth College, 1999.

Bal, Mieke, ed., *The Practice of Cultural Analysis: Exposing Interdisciplinary Interpretation*, Stanford: Stanford University Press, 1999.

Dunbar, Robin, Chris Knight, and Camilla Power, *The Evolution of Culture: An Interdisciplinary View*, New Brunswick: Rutgers University Press, 1999.

Edgar, Andrew, and Peter Sedgwick, *Key Concepts in Cultural Theory*, London: Routledge, 1999.

Glassie, Henry, *Material Culture*, Bloomington: Indiana University Press, 1999.

Fajors, Nique, *Cultural and Economic Revitalization: A Five Step Reference for Overcoming Black Failure*, Chicago: Cultural and Economic Revitalization, 1999.

Rutten, Paul, *De toekomst van de Verbeeldingsmachie: De Culturele Industrie in d eeenentwintigste eeuw*, Amsterdam: Haarlem/Boekmansstichting, 1999.

Tilley, Christopher, *Metaphor and Material Culture*, Oxford: Blackwell, 1999.

Garber, Marjory, *Symptoms of Culture*, New York: Routledge, 2000.

Harris, Marvin, *Cultural Materialism: The Struggle for a Science of Culture*, Updated edition with an introduction by Allan Johnson and Orna Johnson, Lanham, MD: Rowman & Littlefield, 2001.

Harris, Marvin, *The Rise of Anthropological Theory: A History of Theories of Culture*, Lanham, MD: Altamira Press, 2001.

ILLUSTRATIONS

Tables

12. Fourteen alternatives to Napster in 2000.
13. Mergers of accounting, consultancy, and software firms.
14. Links between Business-to-Business (B-2-B), corporations, and industry sectors in 1999–2000.
15. Traditional professions and potential replacements. Courtesy of Ken Ichi Ohmae, Ohmae and Associates Group, Tokyo.
16. Key features of the NetSchools approach. Courtesy of Netwschools.com, now called Pluto Learning
17. Twelve roles for virtual museums.
18. Ten greatest authors on management of the twentieth century. Courtesy of Worthing Brighton Press.
19. Basic differences between traditional and organizational learning.
20. Ten transitions in moving from training to learning. Courtesy of Professor Dave Ulrich, University of Michigan and Hope Greenfield, Digital Equipment Corporation (DEC, now Compaq).
21. Differences between data and intelligence. Courtesy of Fuld &Co.
22. Problems of knowledge management. Courtesy of KM Central.com.
23. Basic distinctions in Knowledge Management. Courtesy of Karl Eric Sveiby.
24. Knowledge management initiatives. Courtesy of Karl Erik Sveiby.
25. Levels of knowledge management. Courtesy of Professor Heinz Mandl, University of Munich (2002).
26. Building blocks of knowledge management. Courtesy of Gilbert Probst, University of Geneva (1999).
27. Knowledge Management Categories. Courtesy of Israeli Knowledge Management Group.
28. Four elements of the SECI model. Courtesy of Professor Ikujiro Nonaka, JAIST.
29. Basic differences between explicit and implicit knowledge from a Western viewpoint.
30. Basic shifts in knowledge. Courtesy of Professor Martin Ryder, School of Education, University of Colorado, Denver.
31. Role of PBL compared to other approaches. Courtesy of Illinois Mathematics and Science Academy.
32. Six-step model for creative problem-solving. Coutesy of Future Problem Solving Program (FPSP).
33. Seven characteristics of exemplary project-based learning. Courtesy of California-based Challenge 2000 project: Project Based Learning with Multimedia.
34. Five steps in the net learning experience. Courtesy of Professional Development Network (PDN).

35. Eightfold path for education. Courtesy of Dr. Roger C. Schank, Learning Environment Design Group, Northwestern University.
36. Stages in Autonomy Oriented Teaching (AOT). Courtesy of Professor Roni Aviram, Tel Aviv.
37. Statistics in the Search for Extraterrestrial Intelligence (SETI) project. Courtesy of SETI project.
38. Major headings in the WWW Virtual Library. Courtesy of World Wide Web Consortium.
39. Differences between information, knowledge, and wisdom.
40. Basic levels of knowledge in a System for Universal Multi-Media Access (SUMMA). Courtesy of SUMS Corporation.
41. The seven liberal arts and their equivalents in the Internet.
42. Taxonomy of visualization methods. Courtesy of George Robertson, Microsoft Research.
43. Resources used to make one 8-inch wafer. Statistics courtesy of John C. Ryan and Alan Durning cited in www.mindjack.com

44. Eight types of searching agents in the Story Archive of the ASK system at Northwestern University.
45. Twelve steps in a spectrum from an unconscious notion to a conscious act.
46. Research and Development spending in the United States (1999).
47. Two challenges: a) an integration of memory institutions, broadcast media, and unstable media; b) an integration of enduring, collaborative, and personal knowledge.
48. Three forms of augmented reality. Courtesy of Dr. Wendy Mackay (Xerox, Paris).
49. Informational framework for improving quality of life. Concepts courtesy of Tengku Dr. Mohammed Azzman Shariffadeen.
50. Seven goals and seventeen means as ingredients for a new approach to culture.
51. Advanced culture: when a text inspires expressions in other media.
52. Links between art and levels of abstraction.
53. Seven levels of culture.
54. Challenge of correlating facts, events and stories from cities, regions, and nationally from the so-called centres.
55. Growth of the Internet in China. Statistics courtesy of NUA and Global Internet Statistics.
56. McLuhan's contrast between hot and cool media. Courtesy of Estate of Marshall McLuhan.
57. McLuhan's opposition of pre-literate and literate cultures. Courtesy of Estate of Marshall McLuhan.
58. Ten insights of McLuhan. Courtesy of Professor Terence Gordon, Dalhousie University.

59. Author's distinctions between "cool" and "super-cool."

59.1 Relations between different media, senses, and modes of recording, representation and communication.

60. Parallels between International Standards Organization layers, functions, and Brad Cox's different layers of granularity in hardware and software.

61. National Classification Societies.

62. Applications of Classification according to the International Federation of Classification Societies (IFCS, 2000).

63. Topics related to complexity.

64. Summary of expert systems, 1942–2002. Based on Professor Timm, University of New South Wales (UNSW), Australia.

65. History of programming languages. Courtesy of Simon Brooke (Weft).

66. Relations and their sub-categories. Courtesy of J.M. Perreault.

67. Vision of a business solution. Courtesy of Robert Sutor (IBM) at WWW10 (Hong Kong, May 2001).

68. Distinctions between semantic and syntactic. Courtesy of a) Moran (1981)[1], b) the Seeheim (Conference) model (1985)[2], c) Dr. Geert de Haan's Extended Task Action Grammar (2000).[3]

69. Kinds of semantic method. Courtesy of Edward Feigenbaum, Knowledge Systems Laboratory, Stanford University (1989).

70. Six types of semantic interoperability. Courtesy of Professor Gerhard Budin, University of Vienna.

71. Fifteen basic fields of the Dublin Core in noun form are part of the resource finding aids. Courtesy of Dublin Core Consortium.

72. Preliminary class hierarchies. Courtesy of ABC project.

73. Basic layers of the Semantic Web in tabular form.

74. Five basic international standards from memory institutions.

75. Six claims to uniqueness by the International Standard Recording Code (ISRC).

76. Three new standards of the International Standards Organization (ISO).

77. Three basic kinds of Internet domain names.

78. Four initiatives towards multimedia convergence.

79. Content applications of the MPEG 21 standard. Courtesy of Motion Picture Experts Group (MPEG).

80. Four kinds of mappings initiated by the Getty Trust.

81. Levels of metadata, ranging from resource finding, resource description, and content and style description.

Figures

R. Gaines and Mildred L. G. Shaw, "Eliciting Knowledge and Transferring it Effectively to a Knowledge-Based System." See: http://ksi.cpsc.ucalgary.ca/articles/KBS/KSS0/.
e) Philip Koopman, Life cycle. Philip Koopman, "Life cycle Considerations," Carnegie Mellon University, 18-849b Dependable Embedded Systems, Spring 1999.
See: http://www.ece.cmu.edu/~koopman/des_s99/life_cycle/.
f) life cycle as part of another cycle in Syntell Co. Life cycles. See: http://www.syntell.se/.

10. a–c) Aspects of KADS approach. Courtesy of Common Knowledge Acquisition and Design Support (KADS).

11. a) Key elements of new business. Courtesy of John Chambers (Cisco); b) Basic elements of a learning organization. Courtesy of René Tissen et al. (2000); c) Business web (b-web) typology. Courtesy of Don Tapscott, David Ticoll, and Alex Lowy (2000).

12. Five stages in the spectrum of noise to wisdom and its links with economics. Courtesy of B. Joseph Pine, James H. Gilmore, and B. Joseph Pine II (1999).

13. Sketches by Douglas Engelbart showing a) co-operation between various departments in a manufacturing organization where each functional domain is a candidate for working interchange with all others, and b) co-operation between two aircraft companies. Courtesy of Douglas Engelbart, Bootstrap Institute.

14. Essential ingredients for a Distributed European Electronic Resource (DEER) as a first step towards a World Online Distributed Resource (WONDER). Courtesy of E-Culture Net and especially Dr. Suzanne Keene and Francesca Monti.

15. Three components in a conceptual triangle. Courtesy of Professor Ingetraut Dahlberg (Bad König).

16. Ten levels of knowledge: Connections between reference levels (a term, a definition, an explanation, a list of authors, titles, partial contents as in abstracts, and reviews) and full text, links between primary and secondary literature and different kinds of content, namely, internal analyses, external analyses, restorations, and reconstructions. Courtesy of SUMS Corporation.

17. Connections between different levels of reference, contents, and interpretation: a folio from a primary text (level 6); alphabetical and chronological lists (level 4); preparatory drawings in a secondary source (level 7), internal analysis (level 7), and external analyses (level 8). Courtesy of SUMS Corporation.

18. a) Examples of three basic levels of granularity in searching for materials. Figure courtesy of Dr. Nik Baerten; b) Universals and Particulars and Levels of abstraction in Light of Perreault's Relations.

19. a) Contemporary event: Different eyewitnesses, reporters, and press bureaus concerning an event such as a plane crash. Figure courtesy of Dr. Nik Baerten; b). Historical event: The Last Supper as an historical event recorded in many versions. Figure courtesy of Dr. Nik Baerten.

20. a) New view of expert systems. Courtesy of authors of KAD; b) Four basic ontologies. Courtesy of Professor Roland Hausser (Erlangen-Nürnberg).

21. Structure of Intellect. Courtesy of J. P. Guilford, *Structure of Intellect* (1967).

22. Road map for the Semantic Web. Courtesy of Tim Berners-Lee, World Wide Web Consortium.

ABBREVIATIONS

AI	Artificial Intelligence
AR	Augmented Reality
BI	Business Intelligence
BT	British Telecom
CA	Canada, Canadian, California
CG	Computer Graphics
CM	Capacity Management
CN	Connecticut
DL	Digital Libraries
DS	Distributed Systems
EC	European Commission
EI	Enterprise Integration
ES	Expert Systems
FA	Factory Automation
HP	Hewlett Packard
IA	Intelligence Augmentation
IP	Internet Protocol; Interested Party
IPv6	Internet Protocol version 6
IT	Information Technology
KA	Knowledge Analysis
KJ	[Method, named for its inventor, Jiro Kawakita (the Japanese put their last names first), allows groups quickly to reach a consensus on priorities of subjective, qualitative data]
KM	Knowledge Management
KW	Knowledge Web
LC	Library of Congress
ME	Micro-Electronics
MQ	Message Queuing
MR	Mixed Reality
NC	Network Computer
NS	Name Spaces
OS	Operating System

OU	Open University
PC	Personal Computer
PD	Personal Development
PI	Process Innovation
PM	Production Management; Procurement Management
RF	Reproduction Fidelity; Radio Frequency
VC	Virtual Cookbook
VE	Virtual Endoscopy
VR	Virtual Reality
VU	Virtual University
A2A	Application to Application [Sometimes written app2app. Cf. B2B,EAI]; Access to Archives; Airline to Airport
AAP	American Association of Publishers
ACL	Association for Computational Linguistics; Access Control List; Asynchronous Connection-Less (link)
ACM	Association of Computing Machinery
ADL	Advanced Distributed Learning
AEC	Architecture/Engineering/Construction
AEI	American Enterprise Institute
AGI	[a German information consultant firm]
AIP	Application Infrastructure Provider
AIS	Association for Information Systems
AKT	Advanced Knowledge Technologies
AMD	Advanced Micro Devices
AML	Astronomical Markup Language
AMP	Accès Multilingue au Patrimoine
AOL	America OnLine
AOT	Autonomy Oriented Teaching
APS	Advanced Planning and Scheduling
ARC	Augmentation Research Center
ASI	Associated Systems Inc.
ASK	[name of software for Learning by Exploring by the Institute for the Learning Sciences]
ASM	Abnormal Situation Management
ASP	Application Service Provider [cf. FSP, ISP]
	ATG Art Technology Group
ATM	Asynchronous Transfer Mode; Automatic Teller Machine
ATT	American Telephone and Telegraph
AVI	Advanced Visual Interfaces
AVU	African Virtual University
B2B	Business to Business
B2C	Business to Customer
BCS	(British) Classification Society

BIC	Book Industry Communication
BMG	Bertelsmann Music Group
BOW	Building Objects Warehouse
BPE	Business Process Engineering
BPR	Business Process Re-engineering; Business Process Redesign
BSD	Berkeley Software Design
BSO	Buro voor Systemontwikkeling [now part of Atos Origin]
BSR	Basic Semantic Repository, [later] Basic Semantics Register
BtE	Business to Employee
CAD	Computer Aided Design
CAE	Computer Aided Engineering; Compositeur, Auteur, Editeur [number]
CAM	Computer Aided Manufacturing
CBR	Case Based Reasoning
CBT	Computer Based Training; Competency Based Training; Component Based Testing; Canon Buffer Transmission; Core Based Tree
CCD	Charged Coupled Device; Closed Circuit Display
CCS	Center for Coordination Science
CDG	Competitive Development Group; Compact Disc + Graphics
CEM	Customer Experience Management
CEN	Comité Européenne de Normalisation
CFD	Computational Fluid Dynamics
CGI	Common Gateway Interface (web scripting facility); Computer-Generated Imagery
CHI	Computer Human Interface (cf. HCI)
CIM	Computer Integrated Manufacturing; Centre for Intelligent Machines
CIO	Chief Information Officer
CIS	Common Information System
CKO	Chief Knowledge Officer
CMC	Computer Mediated Communication
CMG	Computer Measurement Group [now merged with Logica]
CMI	Computer Managed Instruction
CML	Chemical Markup Language
CNN	Cellular Neural Networks; Cable News Network
CNS	[Program in] Computation and Neural Systems
CPC	Collaborative Product Commerce
CPF	Corporate Bodies, Persons, Families
CPU	Central Processing Unit
CRC	[publisher for professional and technical communities]; Cyclic Redundancy Check
CRM	Conceptual Reference Model; Customer Relationship Management

CSC	Customer Support Consortium
CSM	Critical Success Metrics
CTO	Chief Technology Officer
CTR	Click Through Rate
CVU	Clyde Virtual University
DAB	Digital Audio Broadcasting
DAI	Distributed Artificial Intelligence
DCM	Demand Chain Management
DDC	Dewey Decimal Classification
DEC	Digital Equipment Corporation [now Compaq]
DIP	Data, Information, and Process Integration with Semantic Web Services [Project in EU FP6]
DLL	Dynamic Link Library
DNA	DeoxyriboNucleic Acid, usually 2'-deoxy-5'-ribonucleic acid
DNS	Domain Name Service; Domain Name System
DOD	Department of Defense
DOE	Dictionary of Old English
DOI	Digital Object Identifier
DPS	Distributed Problem Solving
DTD	Document Type Definition
DTV	Digital TeleVision
DVB	Digital Video Broadcast
EAD	Encoded Archival Description
EAI	Enterprise Application Integration [This is being replaced by Application to Application Integration]
EAN	European Article Numbering
EBU	European Broadcasting Union
ECE	Economic Commission for Europe [an advisory group of the United Nations on the Protection and Implementation of Intellectual Property Rights for Investment]
EDI	Electronic Data Interchange
EDS	Electronic Data Systems
EEP	European Education Partnership
EFF	Electronic Frontier Foundation
EIS	Enterprise Information Systems
EKD	Enterprise Knowledge Development
EMI	Electrical and Music Industries, Ltd. [one of the major companies in the music business]; Electro-Magnetic Interference; Early Manufacturing Involvement; Extreme Motion Index
EOS	Earth Observation Satellite
EPC	Electronic Product Code
EPM	Extent of Presence Metaphor

ERC	Engineering Research Center for Computational Field Simulation
ERP	Enterprise Resource Planning
ETH	Eidgenössische Technische Hochschule (Swiss Federal Polytechnic)
ETI	Expert Centre for Taxonomic Identification
EUN	European Schoolnet
EUV	Extreme Ultra Violet
EVA	Electronic Imaging & the Visual Arts
EVL	Electronic Visualization Laboratory
EWK	Extent of World Knowledge
FAZ	Frankfurter Allgemeine Zeitung
FBI	Federal Bureau of Investigation
FDA	Food and Drug Administration
FID	Fédération Internationale de Documentation; International Federation for Information and Documentation
FIS	Faculty of Information Studies
FIZ	Fach Informations Zentrum
FMS	Facilities Management Systems
FOM	Fondamentele Onderzoek van Materie; [Foundation for] Fundamental Research on Matter
FSF	Free Software Foundation
FSN	[(pronounced fusion) is a file system navigator in cyberspace]
FSP	Full Service Provider [cf. ASP, ISP]
FTP	File Transfer Protocol
GBS	Goal Based Scenarios [once George Bernard Shaw]
GDM	Generalised Directive Model
GDP	Gross Domestic Product
GEN	Global Engineering Network
GfK	Gesellschaft für Klassifikation
GII	Global Information Infrastructure
GIS	Geographical Information Systems
GKI	Global Knowledge [number] I (Conference in Toronto); [GK II was held in Kuala Lumpur]
GKP	Global Knowledge Partnership
GMD	Gesellschaft für Mathematik und Datenverarbeitung [now Fraunhofer]
GNA	Globewide Network Academy
GNU	GNUs Not Unix
GOD	Grand Organizing Directorate
GPS	Global Positioning System
GSM	Groupe Speciale Mobile, [later] Global System for Mobile Communication
GTU	Global Telecommunication University

485

GTW	Gesellschaft für Terminologie und Wissenstransfer
GUI	Graphical User Interfaces (cf. PUI. TUI)
HAL	[name of the computer in Space Odyssey 2001. If one goes one letter further in each case one arrives at IBM (International Business Machines)]
HBR	Human Behavior Representation
HCI	Human Computer Interface
HIT	Human Interface Technology [Lab]
HMH	[linked with the publisher Hurtubise, Montreal]
HMS	Holonic Manufacturing Systems
HMT	[company conceived by the Government of India in 1949; incorporated in 1953, with the objective of producing a limited range of machine tools, required for building an industrial edifice for the country]
HPC	High Performance Computing
HSF	Human Sensory Feedback
IAI	International Alliance for Interoperability
IBM	International Business Machines
IBP	Internet Based Procurement
ICE	Information and Content Exchange
ICP	Independent Content Provider; Image CoProcessor; Integrated Channel Processor; Intelligent Communication Protocol; Internet Cache Protocol; Internet Content Provider; Internet Control Pack
ICQ	I Seek You
ICT	Information Communication Technology [often in plural]
IDC	International Data Corp
IDF	Object Identifier Foundation
IDG	International Data Group
IDR	Intermediation-Dis-intermediation-Re-intermediation
IEC	International Electrotechnical Commission
IEE	Institution of Electrical Engineers
IFC	Industry Foundation Classes
IIC	Information Integration Centre; International Institute of Communications
IIM	Information Interchange Model
IIT	Informatics & Telecommunications
IKF	Information and Knowledge Fusion
IMC	International Management Centres
IMF	International Monetary Fund
IMS	Instructional Management Systems; Intelligent Manufacturing Systems
INT	International

IN3	International Informatics Institute
IOS	[a publisher of Scientific, Technical and Medical books and journals]
IPN	InterPlanetary Internet Architecture
IPR	Intellectual Property Rights
IPS	Interactive Product Simulation
IRM	Information Resource Management
ISA	Intelligent Speed Adaption
ISI	Information Systems Institute
ISO	International Standards Organization
ISP	Information Service Provider [cf. ASP. FSP]
IST	Information Society Technologies; Institute for Simulation and Training
ITA	Industry Technical Agreement
ITC	International Trade Centre
ITU	International Telecommunications Union
IUI	Intelligent User Interfaces
IVT	International Visual Theatre
JCS	Japanese Classification Society
JGC	[book publisher in Goshen, New York]
JIT	Just in Time
JPC	Japan Productivity Centre
JRC	Joint Research Centre
JTC	Joint Technical Committee
KAD	Knowledge Acquisition and Design
KBS	Knowledge Based Systems
KEW	Knowledge Elicitation Workbench
KHV	Kim Henry Veltman
KMC	Knowledge Management Consortium
KMI	Knowledge Media Institute
KMS	Knowledge Management Society (of Japan)
KRR	Knowledge Representation and Reasoning [Group]
KSI	Knowledge Science Institute
LCD	Liquid Crystal Display
LHC	Large Hadron Collider [being built at CERN]
LIA	Learning Into Action
LLC	Limited Liability Company; Logical Link Control
LoD	Learning on Demand
LOM	Learning Object Model
LPC	[a now bankrupt group of publishers of comics]
LTV	Life Time Value
MAB	Maschinelles Austauschformat für Bibliotheken
MAI	Multilateral Law of Investment

MAM	Media Asset Management
MAS	Multi-Agent Systems; Manufacturing Execution Systems
MBA	Master of Business Administration
MCF	Meta Content Framework
MCI	Microwave Communications, Inc.; Media Control Interface
MDA	Museum Documentation Association
MEC	Molectronics Electronics Company
MES	Manufacturing Execution System, Mobile Entertainment Service
MGM	Metro-Goldwyn-Mayer
MIT	Massachusetts Institute of Technology
MMC	Materials Micro-Characterization Collaboratory; Micro-Machines Centre
MMI	Maastricht McLuhan Institute
MML	Mathematical Markup Language
MOF	Meta Object Facility
MOL	Metacomputing Online Environment [a generic, fault tolerant, and portable architecture for metacomputing environments at the University of Paderborn]
MOU	Memorandum of Understanding
MRC	Media Research Centre; Mesh Router Chip
MRI	Magnetic Resonance Imaging
MRP	Material Requirements Planning; Manufacturing Resource Planning
MRS	Multi-Robot Simulation [Environment]
MSC	Materials and Process Simulation Center
MSN	Microsoft Network
NAA	Newspaper Association of America
NAS	Numerical Aerodynamic Simulation
NCE	Network of Centres of Excellence
NCS	National Computer Systems
NFC	Near Field Communication [chip]
NGE	Next Generation Enterprises
NGI	Next Generation Internet
NHK	Japan Broadcasting Corporation
NII	National Information Infrastructure; National Institute of Informatics
NMI	Naturwissenschaftlich-Medizinisches Institut
NMR	Not Much Resonance
NRC	National Research Council
NUA	[Nua.com was founded in 1996. Nua Internet Surveys was one of the best references for Internet statistics. The company was acquired in June 2001 by the Scope Communications Group, Ireland's leading IT Media Company. As of September 2002 the site has not been updated. Today Global Internet Statistics is one of the best reference sites]

NVO	National Virtual Observatory
NZN	Niedersächsischer Zeitschriften Nachweis
OAI	Open Archives Initiative
OBI	Open Buying on the Internet
OCR	Optical Character Recognition
OIL	Ontology Interface Layer
OLA	Ontario Library Association
OLC	Center for Organizational Learning
OMG	Object Management Group
ORG	Organization
OSI	Open Systems Interconnection; Open Source Initiative; also = ISO
P2P	Peer to Peer
PAI	Parallel Artificial Intelligence
PBL	Problem Based Learning
PBX	Private Branch eXchange
PDA	Personal Digital Assistant
PDF	Portable Document Format
PDN	Professional Development Network
PIA	Personal Intelligent Assistant
PII	Publisher Item Identifier
PIM	Personal Information Manager (cf. PDA, PIA)
PIP	Partner Interface Process [Sponsored by RosettaNet]
PKM	Product Knowledge Management
PLM	Product Lifecycle Management
PMI	Plus/Minus Interesting [Analysis method developed by Edward de Bono]
PML	Product Markup Language
POE	Phylogeny, Ontogeny, Epigenesis
PRS	Performing Right Society. [Collects licence fees for the public performance and broadcast of musical works. Has an Alliance with MCPS].
PSE	Problem Solving Environment
PSN	[Miller Freeman PSN is one of the world's leading publishers of professional audio/video/broadcast production titles]; Packet Switched Network, Packet Switched Node, Private Switched Network
PUI	Perceptual User Interfaces (cf. GUI, TUI)
PWC	Price Waterhouse Coopers
QAP	Quadratic Assignment Problem
QCA	Quantum Dot Cellular Automata; Quantitative Content Analysis Area
QFD	Quality Function Deployment

QPC	Quality Productivity Center (cf. JPC)
RAI	Radio Televisione Italiana
RDF	Resource Description Format
RFC	Request For Comment
RKD	Rijksbureau voor Kunsthistorische Documentatie
RMN	Réunion des Musées Nationaux
ROM	Read Only Memory
SAN	Standard Audiovisual Number (cf. ISAN)
SAP	System Analyse und Programm-entwicklung
SPC	Statistical Production Control
SCM	Supply Chain Management; Software Configuration Management
SCS	Solution Centred Support; Satellite Communication System
SDK	Software Development Kit
SEC	[name of a Danish Consulting firm concerned with Security]
SEL	Synthetic Environment Lab
SFA	Sales Force Automation
SFC	Société Francophone de Classification
SFX	Special Effects. [A generic linking system developed by the University of Ghent: with underlying concepts that can be applied in a wide range of digital libraries]
SGI	Silicon Graphics Incorporated; Silicon Graphics International
SIG	Special Interest Group
SIM	Society for Information Management
SIS	Società Italiana di Statistica
SIU	Southern Illinois University
SLA	Special Libraries Association
SMS	Short Message Services
SMX	Scandinavian Media Exchange
SOM	Self-Organizing Map
SPC	Statistical Production Control
SQL	Structured Query Language
SRI	Stanford Research Institute
SSA	[An American company specializing in extended Enterprise Resource Planning (ERP) that deliver integrated, end-to-end performance from global supply chain to back office]
STM	Scanning Tunneling Microscope
SUB	Staats und Universitäts Bibliothek (Göttingen)
SVG	Scalable Vector Graphics
SWP	Simple Web Printing
TAB	Technical Advisory Board
TAP	Transit Access Point (cf. STAR TAP)
TEI	Text Entering Initiative
TEL	The European Library

TEM	Transmission Electron Microscope
TEN	Trans European Network
TIA	Total Information Awareness
TIE	Telemedicine Information Exchange
TKE	Terminology and Knowledge Engineering
TMF	Terminology Markup Framework
TMS	Training Management Services
TNO	Toegepast Natuurwetenschappelijk Onderzoek (Applied Scientific Research)
TPA	Third Party Administrator; Trade Practices Act
TQC	Total Quality Control
TQM	Total Quality Management
TUI	Tangible User Interface
TVT	TeleVisionTerminal [largest frontline, freestanding record company in the United States]
UBL	Universal Business Language
UBS	United Bank of Switzerland; Unbundled Bitstream Service
UCT	Universal Convergence Technologies
UDC	Universal Decimal Classification
UIA	Union Internationale des Associations
UML	Universal Modeling Language
UNC	University of North Carolina
UNI	[single as in UNI-Media]
UPC	Universal Parcel Code
UPM	Unified Process Model
URI	Uniform Resource Indicator; Universal Resource Indicator
URL	Uniform Resource Locator
URN	Uniform Resource Name
VCR	Video Cassette Recorder
VET	Virtual Environments for Training
VFZ	Vector Format for Zooming
VHD	Visible Human Data Sets
VMR	Virtual Machine Room
VOC	Vereniging voor Ordinatie en Classificatie
VRA	Visual Resources Association
VSB	Vestigial Sideband Modulation
VUE	Virtual University Enterprises
WAI	Web Accessibility Initiative
WAP	Wireless Application Protocol
WHO	World Health Organization
WID	Works Information Database
WTA	World Transhumanist Association
WTO	World Trade Organization

WWL	World-Wide Laboratory
WWW	World Wide Web
XLT	eXtensible Markup Language representation of Lexicons and Terminologies
XML	eXtensibe Markup Language
XSL	eXtensible Stylesheet Language
ZED	[British alternative publisher mainly in political field]
AAAI	American Association for Artificial Intelligence
AAEM	Advanced Analytical Electron Microscope
ADEC	American Distance Education Consortium
ADSL	Asynchronous Digital Subscriber Line
AHIP	Art History Information Program
AIAI	Artificial Intelligence Applications Institute
AIBO	[Robot dog by Sony]
AICC	Aviation Industry Computer-Based Training Committee
AIFB	Angewandte Informatik und Formale Beschreibungs- verfahren
AIMS	[Global Knowledge] Activity Information Management System
AITF	Art Information Task Force
AMPS	Agile Manufacturing Prototyping System
AMRI	Agile Manufacturing Research Institute
ANSI	American National Standards Institute
ARPA	Advanced Research Projects Agency
ASAM	Association for Standardization of Automation and Measuring Systems
ASCI	Accelerated Strategic Computing Initiative; Advanced Simulation and Computing Initiative
ASQC	American Society for Quality Control
ATSC	Advanced Television Systems Committee
AURA	Association of Universities for Research in Astronomy
BCPL	Basic Computer Programming Language
BICI	Book Item and Component Identifier
BIND	[a software that provides a Domain Name Service [DNS)]
BIRN	Biomedical Informatics Research Network
BISC	Book Industry Communication Standard Subject Categories
CAAD	Computer Aided Architectural Design
CADE	Canadian Institute for Distance Education; Computer Aided Document Engineering (Microstar)
CADS	Command, Control and Display Stations; Computer Assisted Display System; Computer Anomaly Detection System; Computer Aided Dispatching System
CALL	Centre for Action Learning
CAM-I	Consortium for Advanced Manufacturing International
CATT	Computer Assisted Technology Transfer

CATV	Community Antenna TeleVision; Cable Television
CAVE	Computer Automatic Virtual Environment
CCAD	Center for Computer Aided Design
CDRM	Content Delivery and Rights Management: Functional Requirements for Identifiers and Descriptors. [ISO Technical Report 21449]
CDWA	Categories for the Description of Works of Art
CERN	Centre Européenne Recherche Nucléaire
CETA	Consortium of European Taxonomic Associations
CGFA	Carol L. Gerten-Jackson's Fine Art
CHIN	Canadian Heritage Information Network
CIDA	Canadian International Development Agency
CIFE	Computer Integrated Faculty Engineering
CIMI	Consortium for Exchange of Museum Standards
CIMS	Coalition for Intelligent Manufacturing Systems
CISE	Computer and Information Science and Engineering
CITO	Communications and Information Technology Ontario
CKIR	Center for Knowledge and Innovation Research
CLAD	Associaçao Portuguesa de Classificaçao
CMDA	Collaboratory for Microscopic Digital Anatomy
CNES	Centre National d'Etudes Spatiales
CNRI	Corporation for National Research Initiatives
CPSI	Creative Problem Solving Institute
CREW	Collaboratory for Research on Electronic Work
CRIN	Centre de Recherche en Informatique de Nancy
CSCL	Computer Supported Collaborative Learning
CSCW	Computer Supported Collaborative Work
CSNA	Classification Society of North America
CSRG	Collaborative Systems Research Group
CSUR	Computing Surveys [publication of Association for Computing Machinery (ACM)]
CTIT	Centre for Telematics and Information Technology
CXML	Commerce eXtensible Markup Language
DAML	DARPA Agent Modelling Language
DCMS	Digital Media Communication System
DEER	Distributed European Electronic Resource
DERI	Digital Enterprise Research Group
DESY	Deutsches Elektronen-Synchrotron (German Synchrotron Research Centre)
DIAG	Danish Information Applications Group
DIVE	Distributed Virtual Interactive Environment
DMAT	Digital Music Access Technology
DMIF	Delivery Multimedia Integration Framework

DMSO	Defense Modeling and Simulation Office
DPRL	Digital Property Rights Language
e to e	end to end
EFQM	European Foundation for Quality Management
ELAG	European Library Automation Group
EMII	European Museum Information Institute
EMMS	Electronic Media Management System
EMTF	Educational Multimedia Task Force
ERGO	European Research Gateways Online
ETOCS	Electronic Tables of Contents for Serials
ETSI	European Telecommunications Standards Institute
FEND	Federation for Enterprise Knowledge Development
FGDC	Federal Geographic Data Committee
FPSP	Future Problem Solving Program
FRBR	Functional Requirements for Bibliographic Records
GEML	Genetic Expression Markup Language
GILS	Government Information Locator Service
GIPI	Global Internet Policy Initiative
GKII	Global Knowledge Innovation Infrastructure
GMBH	Gesellschaft mit beschränkter Haftung
GMOI	Guidelines for Museum Object Information
GOAL	[is a consulting, training, and publishing company, best known for the Memory Jogger pocket guides to quality tools and teams]
GRID	[not an acronym, rather a metaphor that compares distributed computing with the electricity grid. Grid computing is a form of distributed computing that involves coordinating and sharing computing, application, data, storage, or network resources across dynamic and geographically dispersed organizations]
GTTI	Global Telecommunication Training Institute
HAVI	Home Audio Visual Information [Environment]
HDTV	High Definition TeleVision
HIPS	Hyper-Interaction within Physical Space
HLRS	High Performance Computing Center in Stuttgart
HPVM	High Performance Virtual Machines
HSBC	Hong Kong and Shanghai Banking Corporation
HTML	Hyper Text Markup Language
HTTP	Hyper Text Transfer Protocol
IBMT	[Fraunhofer] Institut für Biomedizinische Technik
IBVA	Interactive Brainwave Visual Analyser
ICCD	Istituto Centrale per il Catologo e la Documentazione
ICOM	International Council Of Museums
ICSE	International Conference on Software Engineering
ICSU	International Council of Scientific Unions

IDEF	Interim Data Exchange Format; ICAM DEFinition, where ICAM is an acronym for Integrated Computer Aided Manufacturing. Developed by the U.S. Air Force; Process Flow and Object State Description Capture Method
IDML	International Development Markup Language
IDOL	Intelligent Data Operating Layer
IEEE	Institute of Electrical and Electronics Engineers
IETF	Internet Engineering Task Force
IFAD	International Federation for Agricultural Development
IFCS	International Federation of Classification Societies
IFIP	International Federation of Information Processing
IFLA	International Federation of Library Organizations
IFPI	International Federation of Phonographic Industry
IITF	International Institute for Terminology and Research
I-KEW	Integrated Knowledge Elicitation Workbench
IMAX	[not an abbreviation: name of a company that produces wide angled films and theatres]
IMJV	International Music Joint Venture
INET	[name of the often annual Internet Society conference]
IPPI	Integrated Product and Process Innovation
IPTC	International Press Telecommunications Council
ISAD	Information Society and Developing Countries
ISAD (G)	General International Standard Archival Description
ISAN	International Standard Audiovisual Number
ISBN	International Standard Book Number
ISDN	Institut des sciences du document numérique
ISKO	International Society Knowledge Organization
ISMN	International Standard Music Number
ISOC	Internet SOCiety
ISRC	International Standard Recording Code
ISRN	International Standard Technical Report Number
ISSN	International Standard Serial Number
ISTC	International Standard Textual Work Code
ISWC	International Standard Musical Work Code
ITIL	Information Technology Infrastructure Library
ITIS	Integrated Taxonomic Information System
IUBS	International Union for Biological Sciences
IUMA	Internet Underground Music Archive
IVVV	Interactive Virtual View Video
I-WAY	Information Wide Area Year [context of next generation Internet demonstrations that began with Super Computing 1995 and were continued at subsequent Internet Society conferences]
JDBC	Java Data Base Connectivity

JPEG	Joint Picture Expert Group
JUSE	Union of Japanese Scientists and Engineers
JXTA	JuXTApose
KADS	Knowledge Analysis and Design System
KMAT	Knowledge Management Assessment Tool
KMCI	International Society of Knowledge Management Professionals
KMDI	Knowledge Media Design Institute
KPMG	Klynveld, Peat, Marwick, Goerdeler
LCSH	Library of Congress Subject Headings
LEAD	[an international leadership organization]
LISP	List Processing [one of the first programming languages in 1960]
LLNL	Lawrence Livermore National Laboratory
LTSC	Learning Technology Standards Committee
MABS	Multi-Agent Systems and Agent Based Simulation
MAIC	Measure, Analyse, Improve, Control
MARC	MAchine Readable Cataloging [cf. AUSMARC, USMARC, UNIMARC]
MATE	Multilevel Annotation, Tools Engineering
MCPS	Mechanical-Copyright Protection Society
MEMS	Micro-Electro-Mechanical Systems
MESH	MEdical Subject Headings
MHEG	Multimedia and Hypermedia Expert Group
MIBC	Microstructure Image-Based Collaboratory
MICE	Molecular Interactive Collaborative Environment
MINC	Multilingual Internet Naming Consortium
MIPS	Millions of Instructions Per Second
MITI	Ministry of International Trade and Industry
MMIF	Multi Media Information Framework
MOLE	[name of an expert system for knowledge acquisition]
MOOs	MultiUser Domains Object Oriented
MoVi	Mobile Visualization
MPEG	Motion Picture Expert Group
MREN	Research and Education Network
MUDs	Multiple User Dimension; Multiple User Dungeon; Multiple User Dialogue
MUSE	[name of a software company specializing in data visualization]
MVNO	Mobile Virtual Network Operators
NASA	National Aeronautics and Space Administration
NATO	North Atlantic Treaty Organization
NCAR	National Centre for Atmospheric Research
NCSA	National Centre for Supercomputing Applications
NCTM	National Council of Teachers of Mathematics
NIME	National Centre for Multimedia Education

NISO National Information Standards Organization
NIST National Institute of Standards and Technology: National Infrastructure for Science and Technology
NITF News Industry Text Format
NLII National Learning Infrastructure Initiative
NNUN National Nanofabrication Users Network
NREN National Aeronautics and Space Administration Research and Education Network (cf. MREN)
NTRF Nordic Terminological Reference Format
NUME NUovo Museo Elettronico
OCLC Online Computer Library Center
OECD Organisation for Economic Co-operation and Development
OHBM Organization for Human Brain Mapping
OLIF Open Lexicon Interchange Format
ONIX Online Information eXchange
OSTP Office of Science and Technology Policy
PAWS Parallel Application WorkSpace
PDES [is an international industry/government consortium accelerating the development and implementation of ISO 10303, commonly known as STEP (STandard for the Exchange of Product model data)]
PDPC Process Decision Program Chart
PENS Personal Electronic Notebooks with Sharing
PICA Project on Integrated Catalogue Automation
PILA Publishers International Linking Association
PIPs Partner Interface Processes
RADs Role Activity Diagrams
RAMA Remote Access to Museum Archives
RAND Research ANd Development
RDFS Resource Description Framework Schemas
REAR Research/Academic Reform
REED Records of Early English Drama
RFID Radio Frequency IDentification
RIAA Recording Industry Association of America
RIME R1 Implicit Made Explicit [expert system by Van de Brug]; Relaynet International Message Exchange
RLIN Research Libraries Information Network
SALT Standards-based Access service to multilingual Lexicons and Terminologies
SAMS [Sams Technical Publishing carries on the traditions started by Howard W. Sams in 1946 with the creation of PHOTOFACT®, repair manuals for consumer electronics devices]
SCAN Supply Chain Action Network

497

SDMI	Secure Digital Music Initiative
SDML	Standardized Music Description Language
SDNP	Sustainable Development Networking Plan
SDRC	Structural Dynamics Research Corp
SDSC	San Diego State College
SECI	Socialization, Externalization, Combination, and Internalization
SEKT	Semantically Enabled Knowledge Technologies
SEMA	[Computer Company subsidiary of Schlumberger now part of
SETI	Search for Extra-Terrestrial Intelligence
SGML	Standard Generalized Markup Language
SHOE	Simple Hyper Text Markup Language Ontology Extensions
SICI	Serial Item and Contribution Identifier
SIMA	Systems Integration for Manufacturing Applications
SIMS	[a computer game that simulates a family and a whole community]; Stalker Internet Mail Server; Societal Institute of the Mathematical Sciences; Student Information Management System; Secondary Ion Mass Spectroscopy; Shuttle Imaging Microwave System; Shuttle Inventory Management System
SKAD	Sekcja Klasyfikacji i Analizy Danych
SKBS	Software and Knowledge Based Systems
SLIM	Surface compositional Linear Internal Matching
SMDL	Standard Music Description Language
SMIL	Synchronized Multimedia Integration Language
SMTP	Simple Mail Transfer Protocol
SOAP	Simple Object Access Protocol
SOAR	[a general cognitive architecture for developing systems that exhibit intelligent behavior]
SPDL	Smart Product Design Laboratory
SPML	Super Profile Markup Language
SPOT	Smart Personal Object Technology
STAR	Science Technology and Research (Sometimes as STAR TAP (Transit Access Point)
STEP	**St**andard for the **E**xchange of **P**roduct Model Data
SUMS	System for Universal Media Searching
SWOT	Strengths, Weaknesses, Opportunities, Threats
TDWG	Taxonomic Database Working Group
TheU	The World Virtual University Project
TIDE	Tele-Immersive Data Explorer
TIES	Trainable Information Extraction for the Semantic Web
TIFF	Tagged Image File Format
TIPS	Trillions of Instructions per Second (cf. MIPS); Theory of Inventive Problem Solving

TiVo	[not an acronym: name of hardware produced by Philips, Sony etc.; name of a company that produces software for above: allows one to store television programmes; sometimes called personal television]
TWIN	[as in TWIN-Mechatronic-Objects which combine real world phenomena and virtual world simulations through a Graspable User Interface that enables one to change freely between operations on real physical objects and their virtual counterparts. These Twin-Objects, real and corresponding virtual components, will compose a new kind of complex construction kit which prepares a new era of simulation technology: Real and Virtual Reality]
UCLA	University of California, Los Angeles
UCSB	University of California, Santa Barbara
UDDI	Universal Description Discovery and Integration
UIUC	University of Illinois at Urbana Champaign
UMID	Unique Media Identifier
UMTS	Universal Mobile Telecommunications System
UNIX	[not an abbreviation: software for multi-user systems produced at Bell Labs in 1989]
UNSW	University of New South Wales
UPID	Universal Program Identifier
UUID	Universal Unique IDentifier
VGRU	Visualisation & Graphics Research Unit
ViBE	Virtual Biology Experiments
VIRT	Virtual Learning Environment
VLBI	[Electronic] Very Long Baseline Interferometry
VLSI	Very Large Scale System Integration
VRep	Virtual Representative
VRML	Virtual Reality Modelling Language
VRVS	Virtual Room VideoConferencing System
WELL	Whole Earth Link Line
WIPO	World Intellectual Property Office
WREN	Website of Recent Neuroscience
WSCL	Web Services Conversation Language
WSDL	Web Services Description Language
WSIS	World Summit on the Information Society
WSFL	Web Services Flow Language
WSML	Web Services Modeling Language
WSMO	Web Services Modeling Ontology
WSMX	Web Services Execution Environment
XBRL	eXtensible business Reporting Language
XCON	[software programme by McDermott using Artificial Intelligence to configure VAX computers, to customers' specifications]

XRML eXtensible Rights Markup Language
ZITI [Greek company linked with Information services and Medical Imaging]
A-CIMS Academic Coalition for Intelligent Manufacturing Systems
AEGIS [system developed by Industrial Computing Society to predict events using the latest State Estimation tools]
AFIPS American Federation of Information Processing Societies
ALISE Association for Library and Information Science Education
ALIVE Architecture and authoring tools for prototype for Living Images and new Video Experiments [European Union project renamed Art.Live]
APACS Advanced Process Analysis & Control System
ASCAP American Society of Composers, Authors and Publishers
ASEAN Association of South East Asian Nations
ASICS Advanced Systems and Integrated Circuits
ASLIB Association for Information Management
C2RMF Centre de Recherche et Restauration des Musées de France
CATIA Computer Aided Three-dimensional Interactive Application
CEBIT CEntrum Büro Information Telekommunikation
CESAR Collaboration Environments and Service Architectures for Researchers
CIDOC Comité Internationale pour la Documentation de l'Art
CIMSS Center for Intelligent Material Systems and Structures
CISAC Confédération Internationale des Sociétés d'Auteurs et de Compositeurs
COFDM Coded Orthogonal Frequency Division Multiplexing
CORBA Common Object Request Broker Architecture
COVAX Contemporary Culture Virtual Archives in XML
CSELT Centro Studi e Laboratori Telecomunicazioni
DARPA Defence Advanced Research Projects Agency (also called ARPA)
DELOS [Network of Excellence on Digital Libraries in the European Union]
DHTML Dynamic Hyper Text Markup Language
ebXML ebusiness eXtensible Markup Language
ENIAC Electronic Numerical Integrator and Computer
EPICS EDItEUR Product Information Communication Standards
ERCIM European Research Consortium for Informatics and Mathematics,
ERMES EuRopean Multimedia Educational Software Network
FLOPS Floating Point Operations per Second
GEANT [Pan-European] Gigabit Research and Education Network
GNOME GNU Network Object Model Environment
GTREN Global Terabit Research and Education Network
GUSTO Globus Ubiquitous Supercomputing Testbed Organization

IAMCR	International Association for Media and Communication Research
IBROW	Intelligent Brokering Service for Knowledge-Component Reuse on the World-Wide Web
ICANN	Internet Consortium on Assigned Names and Numbers
ICDRI	International Center for Disability Resources on the Internet
I Cube (I³)	Intelligent Information Interfaces (cf. AVI)
IMACS	System for Computer-Aided Manufacturability Analysis
IMASS	Information MAnagement and interoperability of content for distributed Systems of high volume data rep through multi agent Systems
INRIA	Institut National Recherche Informatisation Automatisée
ISAAR	International Standard Archival Authority Records
ISCCR	International Study Conference on Classification Research
JAIST	Japan Advance Institute for Science And Technology
JITOL	Just in Time (Online) Learning
LINUX	[open source software invented by Linus Torvald]
LOFAR	LOw Frequency Array. [Largest distributed radio-telescope]
MADIC	Multidisciplinary Analysis and Design Industrial Consortium
MCTOS	Mind Control Tool Operating System
MENON	Multimedia Educational Innovation Network
MERIT	Maastricht Economic Research Institute on Innovation and Technology
MIDAS	Marburger Inventarisations-, Dokumentations-und Administrationssystem
MUVII	Multi-User Virtual Interactive Interface
MYCIN	[an expert system developed at Stanford in the 1970s. Its job was to diagnose and recommend treatment for certain blood infections]
NCMIR	National Center for Microscopy Imaging Research
NESLI	National Electronic Site Licence Initiative
NIIIP	National Industrial Information Infrastructure Protocols
NINCH	National Institute Networked Cultural Heritage
NLANR	National Laboratory for Applied Network Research
OASIS	Organization for the Advancement of Structured Information Standards
OASYS	Offenders Assessment System
OPIMA	Open Platform for Initiative for Multimedia Access
PITAC	President's Information Technology Advisory Committee
PRISM	Publishing Requirements for Industry Standard Metadata
SANTI	Sistema Avanzado de navigacion sobre Terrenos Interactivo
SCALA	[Company in Florence with a large photographic collection]
SCILS	School of Communication, Information and Library Studies

SCORM	Shareable Content Object Reference Model
SMART	Solution for Manufacturing Execution Systems Adaptable Replicable Technology
SMPTE	Society of Motion Picture and Television Engineers
SPARC	Space Physics and Aeronomy Research Collaboratory
SUMMA	System for Universal MultiMedia Access
Sys Op	Systems Operator
UBCIM	Universal Bibliographic Control and International MARC [Core Programme]
UKOLN	UK Office for Library and Information Networking
V-Mail	Virtual Mail
VBXML	Visual Basic eXtensible Markup Language
VISWE	Virtual Institute for Semantic Web Education
XHTML	eXtensible Hyper Text Markup Language
XLANG	[Web Services for Business Process Design]
ADONIS	[a document delivery service (1991-1993) which had its own special record number (XID) for articles available in the service]. This has since been replaced by the Publisher Item Identifier (PII).
ADVTECH	[Southern African group in the areas of Recruitment, Education, Skills Development and Human Resource Management linked with the African Virtual University]
AFRICOM	African Branch of the International Council of Museums
AGICOA	Association de Gestion Internationale Collective des Oeuvres Audiovisuelles
AHPCRC	Army High Performance Computing Research Centre
AQUARELLE	Remote access to European cultural heritage information
ARCHEOGUIDE	Archeological Guide [European Union project on augmented reality applied to reconstructions of archaeological sites with ruins of temples]
ARIADNE	Annotatable Retrieval of Information And Database Navigation Environment; Alliance for Remote Instructional Authoring and Distribution Networks for Europe
ARISTOTLE	Automated Categorization of Internet Resources
ARPANET	Advanced Research Projects Agency Network (cf. ARPA, DARPA)
ARROWS	Advanced Reusable Reliable Objects Warehouses
AUSMARC	Australian Machine Readable Cataloging
BREVIE	Bridging Reality and Virtuality with a Graspable User Interface
CAMPIELLO	[European Union Project]: Interacting in collaborative environments to promote and sustain the meeting between inhabitants and tourists
CANMARC	Canadian Machine Readable Cataloguing (cf. MARC, UNIMARC)

CEFACT	Centre for Trade Facilitation and Electronic Business
CINECA	Consorzio Interuniversitario per il Calcolo Automatico dell'Italia Nord Orientale
CODATA	Committee on Data for Science and Technology
COLLATE	Collaboratory for Annotation, Indexing and Retrieval of Digitized Historical Archive Material
COMASOTO	Concept Mapping Software Tool
COMBINE	Computer Models for Building Industry in Europe
CoMMA	Corporate Memory Management through Agents
COMRIS	[European Union project developing an infrastructure to support social processes in dynamic communities, for instance at large conferences]
CONMAT	CONstruction MATerials and Systems
CoWeb	Collaborative Web with Social Navigation
CPIMBD	Content Packaging Information Model Base Document
CRAYON	CReAte Your Own Newspaper
CRESST	[National] Center for Research on Evaluation, Standards, and Student Testing
CRIBECU	Centro di Ricerche Informatiche per i Beni Culturali
CULTIVATE	[Network for Digital Cultural Heritage in Europe consisting of 15 partners that ended in 2003]
CYCLADES	[European Union project to create an open collaborative virtual archive environment]
CyliCon	Zylinderkonstruktion [augmented reality construction software by Siemens]
DERIVE	Distributed real and virtual learning environment for mechatronics and tele-service
DESIRE	Development of a European Service for Information on Research and Education
EDIFACT	Electronic Data Interchange For Administration, Commerce and Transport
EDUCAUSE	[a nonprofit association whose mission is to advance higher education by promoting the intelligent use of information technology]; best known for a conference by the same name.
EDUCOM	Education Communication
ELSNET	European Network of Excellence in Human Language Technologies
ESPRIT	[name of European Union information technologies programme]
EUROGRID	[European Union project to create an Application Testbed for European GRID computing]
EUROSIM	Federation of European Simulation Societies
EXPLOIT	[an accompanying measure to promote the results of European Union library projects]

FORMENTOR	[French simulation software]
GENESIS	GEneral NEural SImulation System
HEAVEN	Hosting of Emulated Applications in a Virtual Environment
IMPRIMATUR	Intellectual Multimedia Property Rights Model and Terminology for Universal Reference
INDECS	Interoperability of Data in E-Commerce Systems
INFORMS	Institute for Operations Research and Management Sciences
KANBAN	[Japanese term that means "signal," is one of the primary tools of a Just In Time (JIT) system, which signals a cycle of replenishment for production and materials and maintains an orderly and efficient flow of materials throughout the entire manufacturing process. It is usually a printed card that contains specific information such as part name, description, quantity, etc.]
MARTIF	Machine-Readable Terminology Interchange Format
MEDICI	Multimedia for EDucation and employment through Integrated Cultural Initiative
MEDICOMM	Framework for Multimedia Standardization
MESMUSES	[Information Society Technologies (IST) project on metadata for culture]
MKBEEM	Multilingual Knowledge Based European Electronic Marketplace
NARCISSE	Network of Art Research Computer Image SystemS in Europe
NITINOL	Nickel Titanium Naval Ordnance Laboratory
Onto-Web	Ontological Knowledge Web
PRECARN	Pre-Competitive Advanced Research Network
RENARDUS	Academic Subject Gateway Service in Europe
RIMICMO	Russia Internet: Minimum Information Categories for Museum Objects
SCHEMAS	[European Union Metadata Project]
SIGSEM	Special Interest Group: Semantic Web [Sponsored by the Association for Computational Linguistics]
SIGSEMIS	Special Interest Group: Semantic Web and Information Systems [Sponsored by Association for Information Systems]
SIMDAT	Grid Technology for Product Development and Production Process Design
SIMPUTER	Simple Computer
SINTEF	Foundation for Scientific and Industrial Research at the Norwegian Institute of Technology
SPRACH	Recognition Algorithms for Connectionist Hybrids
STARTAP	Science, Technology, And Research Transit Access Point
SUMSED	System for Universal Media Searching: Education
TERM-IT	[Feasibility study for the European Union looking into ways of improving the production and dissemination of multilingual thesauri]

TRANSCOM	Transportation Command
TRESYS	Text REtrieval System
UN/CEFACT	United Nations Centre for Trade Facilitation and Electronic Business
UNESCO	United Nations Educational, Scientific, Cultural Organization
UNICORE	UNiform Interface to Computing Resources
UNIMARC	Universal Machine Readable Cataloging
USMARC	United States Machine Readable Cataloging
VAKHUM	Virtual Animation of the Kinematics of the Human for Industrial, Educational and Research Purposes
VAN EYCK	Visual Arts Network for the Exchange of Cultural Knowledge
VASARI	Visual Arts System for Archiving and Retrieval of Images
WISDOM	Wireless Information Services for Deaf People
WONDER	World Networked Digital Electronic Resource
WYSIWYG	What You See is What You Get
X Links	Extended Links

notes

A fundamental problem with the Internet at present is the non-permanence of web sites. In most cases they do not stop existing: they simply move their address. My own experience has been that by noting titles and keywords that lead to that site, one can use Google to arrive at the new site. For this reason, when there is not a specific author and title, references to web sites in the notes are typically preceded by keywords that may help one in cases of changed addresses. In some rare cases, a web site may be correct and does not allow direct access but does allow access via Google. The correctness of all web sites was tested in April, 2004.

In the interests of historians of the web with access to earlier versions, in cases where a web site is no longer working, I have put the site in brackets with the word "formerly." In the interests of saving space in the printed edition, a) these notes and b) a series of further tables are being relegated to the on-line version.

Frontispiece

1   Michael Crichton, *Timeline*, New York: Ballantine, 1999, pp. 141–42.

Preface

1   Robert Darnton has suggested that electronic books might be arranged in layers like a pyramid beginning from a top layer:
    1. concise account of the subject, available perhaps in paperback.
    2. expanded versions of different aspects of the argument, not arranged sequentially as in a narrative, but rather as self-contained units that feed into the topmost story.
    3. documentation, possibly of different kinds, each set off by interpretative essays.
    4. theoretical or historiographical, with selections from previous scholarship and discussions of them.
    5. pedagogic, consisting of suggestions for classroom discussion and a model syllabus
    6. readers' reports, exchanges between the author and the editor, and letters from readers, who could provide a growing corpus of commentary as the book made its way through different groups of readers.
    Robert Darnton, "A Program for Reviving the Monograph," *American Historical Association. Perspectives*, March 1999: http://www.historians.org/perspectives/issues/1999/9903/9903pre.cfm. Robert Darnton, "The New Age of the Book," *New York Review of Books* 46, no. 5, 18 March, 1999: http:

//www.nybooks.com/articles/546. While in basic agreement, our approach is somewhat different. In future we wish to link references to ten levels of knowledge (Table 40). In this approach, Darnton's levels 2 to 5 are covered by our levels 6 to 10. Darnton's level 6 is covered by our level 5: Partial Contents in the form of reviews, synopses, etc. In addition, our levels 1 to 3 allow access to different terms, definitions, and explanations as found in classification systems, dictionaries, and encyclopaedias, respectively.

Introduction

1 AG Automatiseringsgids: http://www.automatiseringsgids.nl/ for 27 October 2000: "Vorig jaar werd er wereldwijd een informatiewolk van 1,5 exabyte, ofwel 1,5 miljard gigabyte, ge-produceerd. Volgens de universiteit komt dat neer op 250 megabyte voor elke mens op deze aardbol."

UNESCO (lecture by Abdelaziz Abid, Amsterdam Maastricht Summer University, 11 July 2001), estimates 1.5 billion gigabytes of which 90 per cent is stored in digital format. Stuart Feldman (IBM) noted at INET 2002 that one hour of the world's disc production amounts to a petabyte and that annually this leads to 10 exobytes of new information. Jeffrey Harrow in *Rapidly Changing Face of Computing* (RCFoC) for 30 October 2000 cites Hal Varian's and Peter Lyman's report, "How Much Information":

http://www.sims.berkeley.edu/how-much-info/index.html to claim that the information created in 1999, assuming it were all digitized is:

Optical storage (music and data CD and DVDs)	83 terabytes
Paper	240 terabytes
Film (still, movies, and medical images)	427 petabytes
Magnetic storage (camcorder tapes, disk drives)	1.693 exabytes

"That's a grand total of 2.1 exabytes of new information produced that year. Yet if that sounds like a lot, Varian and Lyman found that the growth rate of such information is 50 per cent each year! Where does the Internet fit into this? The 'surface Web' (html pages) consists of 2.5 billion documents growing at the rate of 7.3 million pages – per day! Overall, there's 25 to 50 terabytes of html data on the Web."

2 "Sizing the Internet," *Cyveillance White Paper*, 10 July 2000: www.cyveillance.com/web/down-loads/Sizing_the_Internet.pdf;

3 "Web Is Bigger Than We Thought," *San Jose Mercury News*, 28 July 2000: http://www.nua.ie/surveys/?f=VS&art_id=905355941&rel=true; Mark Frauenfelder, "Deep-Net Fishing," *The Industry Standard Magazine*, 18 June 2001: (formerly) http://www.techinformer.com/go.cgi?id=490878. Cf. http://boingboing.net/markf.html; Mike Nelson (IBM) at the INET 2001 Global Summit claimed that in the next nine years there will be a 1-million-fold increase in information. This amounts to the equivalent of 550,000,000,000,000,000 pages.

4 UNESCO in 2001 claimed that individual information (e.g., personal home pages) is now over 2,600 times larger than published information.

5 Robert Hobbes' Zakon, *Hobbes' Internet Timeline v7.0.* on the Internet Society site: http://www.zakon.org/robert/internet/timeline/. Another look at the history of the Internet is given in the present author's "American Visions of the Internet": http://www.sumscorp.com/new_media.htm.

6 Brian Wilson, Internet Explorer (Windows) (Microsoft) = Index DOT Html/Css: http://www.blooberry.com/indexdot/history/ie.htm. For a claim that browsers were invented earlier at Bath, see the modest article: "How we invented the web": http://www.cs.bath.ac.uk/~pjw/media/web.htm.

7   Figures for these latest results differ considerably. E.g., World Internet usage statistics claimed 740 million users for March, 2004 and 812 million on 3 December 2004: www.internetworld-stats.com. Global Internet Statistics claimed 729 million users in March 2004 but in its lists for individual languages cited 287.5 million English and 516.7 non-English, which amounts to 804.2 million users: http://global-reach.biz/globstats/index.php3. Global Internet statistics also predicted 940 million by the end of 2004 but by 30 January 2005 the site had not been updated beyond September 2004.

8   Statistics for mobile commerce by epay.com: http://www.epaynews.com/statistics/mcommstats.html#top.

9   Statistics of household appliances: www.hgo.dk/year2031/ statistik.htm.

10   Much is often made of the time it took to reach 50 million users. For instance, John Chen, CEO and President of Sybase gave one estimate in his keynote at *WWW*10 (May 2001):

    Radio   38
    Television   13
    Cable   10
    Web   5

     It bears noting that in 2000 alone there were over 120 million new Internet connections and that in the first five months of 2001 there were a further 50 million. This is a new scale of development. For an indicator of global differences, see the Information Society Index: http://www.worldpaper.com/2001/jan01/ISI/2001%20Information%20Society%20Ranking.html.

11   In June, 2000, there were an estimated 134 million users in the United States out of 332.7 million worldwide. On 25 November 1999, in an Internet search for the term "computers," Yahoo found 416 categories and 26,891 sites; Lycos found 2,111,279 sites; Hotbot found 2,386,510, and Altavista found "about 10,363,216." Internet is connecting computers almost everywhere. According to *Wired Magazine*, in November 1999, there were an estimated 205 million Internet sites. Five months later, in March, 2000, there were over 300 million sites. In November, 2000, there were 369 million.

12   Global Internet statistics: http://www.glreach.com/globstats/index.php3.

13   Ibid., One ambitious site allows one to translate between 1,482 language pairs: www.tranexp.com/InterTran/FreeTranslation.html.

14   World Internet usage statistics as above. For other predictions: http://www.infoworld.com/articles/hn/xml/01/04/27/010427hnasia.xml.

15   ITU. Key Global Telecom Indicators for the World Telecommunication Service Sector: http://www.itu.int/ITU-D/ict/statistics/at_glance/KeyTelecom99.html.

16   Latest Mobile, GSM, Global, Handset, Base Station, & Regional Cellular Statistics: http://www.cellular.co.za/stats-main.htm. A panel discussion on the future of telecommunications, www.intranet2000.net conference, Paris, Cité des Sciences, 29 March 2000, predicted that there would be 1 billion by the end of 2003. By the end of 2003 there were in fact over 1.3 billion mobile phone users.

17   At INET 2000 (Yokohama), Vint Cerf estimated that by 2006 there will be 900 million PCs, plus 1.6 billion mobile connections, for a total of 2.4 billion Internet users This seemed too optimistic. In March, 2004, Epaynews.com claimed that by 2007 there would be 1,450 million users of which 56.8 per cent would be wireless: www.epaynews.com/statistics/mcommstats.html.

18   From a global view, the United States represents around 4 per cent of the world's population. In 2000, the U.S. population, including those abroad, was 275.1 million, according to "Monthly Estimates of the United States Population: April 1, 1980 to July 1, 1999, with Short-Term Projections to November 1, 2000": http://www.census.gov/population/estimates/nation/intfile1-1.txt. In 2000, the world population was 6 billion, according to David Levine's world population clock: http://www.ibiblio.org/lunarbin/worldpop.

19   There is now an Interplanetary Internet Project: http://www.ipnsig.org/home.htm. This was the subject of a keynote and a half-day tutorial at INET 2001 (Stockholm): http://www.isoc.org/inet2001/CD_proceedings/T90/INETPlenary_files/frame.htm. This is linked with the development of Space Communications Protocol Standards (SCPS): www.scps.org.

20   Vannevar Bush, "As we may think," *Atlantic Monthly*, Boston, July, 1945: http://www.theatlantic.com/unbound/flashbks/computer/bushf.htm. For other visions of the future, see "The Wired Diaries 2000," *Wired*, January, 2000, pp. 69–103.

21   For a suggestion that persons use the Internet and then leave it: Sally Wyatt, "They came, they surfed, they went back to the beach: Why some people stop using the internet," (Prepared for the: *Society for Social Studies of Science Conference*, San Diego, October, 1999). Under the heading: Virtual Society? the social science of electronic technologies: http://virtualsociety.sbs.ox.ac.uk/text/reports/surf.htm.

22   Ulrich Briefs, for instance, claims that the Information society is largely a myth, that it promises rationality, jobs, qualified work, a healthy environment, more freedom for citizens, democracy, and more diversity of media, but does not deliver. Ultimately, he claims, it is unions who are the real losers. Ulrich Briefs, "Mythos Informations-Gesellschaft," *Zeitschrift Marxistische Erneuerung*, Frankfurt, Nr. 41, March, 2000, pp. 81–93. Cf. Peter Glotz, "War das Internet bloss eine Hysterie?" *Tages-Anzeiger*, 27 December 2002, p. 65.

23   Armand Matellart, *Mapping World Communication, War, Progress, Culture*. Minneapolis: University of Minnesota Press, 1994; ibid., *The Invention of Communication*, Minneapolis: University of Minnesota Press, 1996.

24   David Korten, *When Corporations Rule the World*, West Hartford, CT: Kumarian Press, 1995.

25   An article in *Wired* (April, 2001, pp. 162ff.) identified twelve Gigatrends:

1	The Protein Hunters	custom drugs
2	Personal Fabrication on Demand	desktop factories
3	Plague Years	super bugs
4	The Next Wave	open sea satellite company
5	Debugging Democracy	on-line ballots
6	Disposable Corporations	
7	The New Hot Medium Paper	
8	P2P Health Care	
9	Global Marketplace	always on stock exchange
10	Borderless Bureaucracy	
11	Micropower goes Macro	generating own power
12	Turn on the Light	optical networking

The IEEE defined twenty-one Consumer Electronics Technology megatrends in 2000: http://www.cybercom.net/~slipoff/life02.pdf; "The Innovation Economy. New Ideas and Technologies that are Challenging the World," *Business Week*, 11 October 2004, pp. 90–240.

26   A full list of editions is found in Appendix 8.

27   Benjamin Compaine, ed., *Understanding New Media: Trends and Issues in Electronic Distribution of Information*, Cambridge, MA: Ballinger, 1984.

28   George E. Whitehouse, *Understanding the New Technologies of the Mass Media*, Englewood Cliffs, NJ: Prentice Hall, 1986.

29   Roger Fidler, *Mediamorphosis: Understanding New Media* (Journalism and Communication for a New Century), Thousand Oaks, CA: Pine Forge Press, 1997.

30   James Monaco, *The Dictionary of New Media*. New York & Sag Harbor: Harbor Electronic Publishing, 1999, [1971].

31   Richard Grusin and Jay David Bolter, *Remediation: Understanding New Media*, Cambridge, MA: MIT Press.

32   Rein de Wilde, *De Voorspellers: Een kritiek op de toekomstindustrie*, Amsterdam: De Balie, 2000. Cf. Appendix 8.

Acknowledgements

1   This background is described at further length on the web site under SUMS, in an article "How it all began": http://www.sumscorp.com/how_it_began.htm.

Chapter 1: Computers

1   Vint Cerf, "A Brief History of the Internet": http://www.isoc.org/internet/history/cerf.shtml. For other histories: http://www.isoc.org/internet/history/index.shtml.

2   Appendix 8. For a thought-provoking on-line discussion: Dr. Fernando R. Contreras Medina, "Aproximación a una semiótica de la cibercultura": http://www.cica.es/aliens/gittcus/contreras.html. Dr. Contreras gave a lecture "Cybermundo: Nuovas fronteras de infografía," *Culturetec*, Madrid, November, 2000, in which he explored concepts such as simulation, multimediality, simultaneity, interaction, and virtuality. An insightful recent report from the INPG outlines eight impacts on society: new economy, reglementation, exclusion, mediation, communitization, ephemerizing of culture, information, liberty, and education: INPG, "Les nouvelles technologies de l'information et de la communication, 2000": http://www.inpg.fr/INPG/100.

3   ENIAC=Electronic Numerical Integrator and Computer.

4   SGI= Silicon Graphics International.

5   In 2001, Portable memory is a area where there was as yet no clear standard: Kees Kraaijveld, "De strijd op het draagbare geheugen," *De Volkskrant*, 17 May 2001, p. 2E.

6   In April, 2000, IBM introduced a notebook disk drive with 17 billion bits of data per square inch, yielding a notebook with 32 gigabytes (GB) of storage: equivalent to 50 CDs or a mile-high stack of paper. Joe Wilcox, "IBM breaks density record with new hard drives," *Cnet news.com*, 12 April 2000: http://news.cnet.com/news/0-1003-200-1686757.html. Jeffrey Harrow in RFOC on 19 March 2001 cited a quite different statistic: "PC World estimates that a single 40 gigabyte disk drive can hold: the text from a stack of paper 2,000 feet high; or 27 days of CD-quality MP3 songs; or 3 hours of digital video; or 10 DVD movies, in MPEG-2 format": http://www.theharrowgroup.com/.

7   In 2000, one IBM site claimed that disks with storage of 10 gigabytes per square inch were likely to be commercially available in five to seven years. IBM Almaden, "Informatics Project. The future is not what it used to be": http://www.almaden.ibm.com/projects/informatics.shtml. For a discussion on disc capacity, see Jeffrey Harrow, RFOC, 5 February 2001: http://www.theharrowgroup.com/ He claims that in 2000, IBM's Almaden Research Center, using a new method called Atomic Force Microscope (AMF) Probe, "already demonstrated data storage density of 25 gigabytes per square inch, with a data reading rate of one megabyte per second." In 2001, IBM labs were working towards 100 GB/square inch. Reported by Jeffrey Harrow in RFOC, 19 March 2001: http://www.theharrowgroup.com/. In October, 2002, IBM announced technology with 200 GB/square inch: Philip Ball, "Magnet Islands Boost Memory," *Nature*, 11 October 2002: http://www.nature.com/nsu/021007/021007-11.html. A project called Keele (University) High Density announced the 2,300 GB on a CP card-sized device costing as little as a CD-ROM: "Keele High Density Claims 3D Storage Breakthrough." *Computergram International*, 11 August 1999: www.findarticles.com/cf_dls/m0CGN/ 3722/55420686/p1/article.jhtml. Another article on the same project, Gary Evan Jensen, "Data storage density pushes limits," *electronicsproducts.com*, August, 2001, claims: "Solid-state memory capacities of 10.8 Tbytes on a credit-card-sized surface area are said to be possible using the solid-state memory technology": http://www.electronicproducts.com/ShowPage.asp?SECTION=3700&PRIMID=&FileName=a ugOL3.aug2001 In metric terms, storage density is now roughly at 150 MB/square centimetre. Theoretically, the physical limits are c. 15 GB/square centimetre. Charles Jonscher, *The Evolution of Wired Life*, New York: Wiley, 1999, p. 114.

8   At 640 MB per CD-ROM.

9   These is again an area where there are widely divergent claims. Peter Lyman and Hal Varian at Berkeley claim that 2 exabytes of new information are being added every year. Reported by Kathleen Maclay, "Amount of new information doubled in last three years, UC Berkeley study finds," *Media Relations, UC Berkeley News*, 23 October 2003.

10 Michael Thomas has founded the Colossal Storage Inc. to develop this idea: http://colossalstorage.net/.

11 John Newton, "Every file you ever owned on 1 disk," *p2pnet news*, 25 February 2004: http://p2pnet.net/story/842.

12 I.e., 30 frames per second x 640 x 480 pixels/frame x 8 bits per pixel = 555 mb per minute.

13 The Library of Congress copy is discussed in "Gutenberg Bible Goes Digital. High-Tech Photos of Library of Congress Copy Allow Web Scrutiny," *npr.org*, 19 February 2002: http://www.npr.org/programs/atc/features/2002/feb/gutenberg/020219.gutenberg.html.   For the British Library Gutenberg Bible: http://prodigi.bl.uk/gutenbg/background.asp. For the Gutenberg Bible Online Digital Facsimile. Keio University and Cambridge University Copies: http://www.humi.keio.ac.jp/treasures/incunabula/B42/.   Gutenberg   Digital.   Göttingen Gutenberg Bible: http://www.gutenbergdigital.de/gudi/start.htm. Cf. Gutenberg.de, which gives a list of extant copies: http://www.gutenberg.de/english/bibel.htm. Cf. HRC Online Exhibition University of Austin, Texas: http://www.hrc.utexas.edu/exhibitions/permanent/gutenberg/web/pgstns/01.html.

14 At the National Gallery in Washington, for instance, all the 105,000 paintings and drawings have been scanned in at 30 megabytes per image. If these were all stored in a single file, this would require 3,150,000 megabytes, i.e., 3.15 terabytes. The Uffizi in Florence, which is interested in using its scanned images to aid conservators in restoring paintings, is scanning in its collection at 1.4 gigabtyes per square metre. Assuming that the average size of their paintings was one square metre their collection of 1,300 paintings would require 18.2 terabytes. The Marburg Archive, which represents German collections at a national level has over 1,500,000 images. If these were scanned in at the Uffizi level, this would amount to 21 petabytes.

15 I am grateful to Professor Chris Llewellyn Smith, Director of CERN, who provided these statistics in a lecture at the INET 98 Summit (Geneva) on 22 July 1998.

16 Les Robertson, *Rough Sizing Estimates for a Computing Facility for a Large LHC Experiment*, CERN/IT, May, 1999. This was kindly made available to me by Dr. David Williams (CERN). Even if there were only five minutes of experiments a day, this would still yield 1,100 petabytes or 1.1 exabytes a year. Assuming a typical year with 220 working days. To store the raw data would require much greater numbers. There are new companies such as Yotta Yotta devoted to yottabyte storage: http://www.yottayotta.com/index.htm.

17 For a complete list: "Præfixer for potenser af 10": http://www.biosite.dk/leksikon/prefixer.htm.

18 These terms are based on those of the International System of Units (SI) on the site of the NIST (National Institute of Standards) Reference on Constants, Units and Uncertainty: http://physics.nist.gov/cuu/Units/prefixes.html.

19 Linda Kempster, IIT Research Institute, "High Performance Storage – Dream Versus Reality," presented at *THIC Meeting*, Virginia Beach VA, 13 October 1999: (formerly) http://www.thic.org/pdf/Oct99/iitr.lkempster.991013.pdf. Linda Kempster, was a principal at Imerge: http://www.imergeconsult.com/.

20 Douglas F. Gray, "Prototype Machine for EUV Chip Technology Unveiled. Extreme Ultraviolet technology could boost chip speeds by a factor of ten," *IDG News Service*, Wednesday, 11 April 2001: http://www.pcworld.com/news/article/0,aid,47024,00.asp.

21 Jeffrey   Harrow,   *The   Harrow   Technology   Report*   for   22   December   2003:   http://www.TheHarrowGroup.com.

22   ASCI Red: http://www.sandia.gov/ASCI/Red/; Stephen Shankland, "IBM to build fastest su-percomputers," CNET News.com, 18 November 2002: http://news.com.com/2100-1001-966312.html; Stephen Shankland, "IBM plans second Blue Gene supercomputer," CNET News.com, 20 February 2004: http://news.com.com/2100-7337-5162741.html.

23   Stephen Shankland, "IBM exceeds expectations with supercomputer," CNET News.com, 21 September 2000: http://news.com.com/2100-1001-242567.html.

24   Anne Tyrie, CITO Linkline , 6 July 2000: http://www.cito.ca/network/news_linkline.html.

25   Cited by Jeffrey Harrow, RFOC, 4 September 2000: http://www.TheHarrowGroup.com. In January, 2001, Sandia labs announced they were again developing what will be the world's largest computer now with 30 trillion instructions per second.

26   Stephen Shankland and Erich Luening, "Imagine 1,000 trillion ops per second," Special to ZDNet, 19 January 2001: www.beowulf.org/pipermail/beowulf/ 2001-January/011029.html. An overview of such plans is at the Teraflops/Petaflops/HPCC Computing Page: http://www.aeiveos.com/~bradbury/petaflops/.

27   Jennifer Couzin, "Building a Better Bio-Supercomputer," The Industry Standard Magazine, 18 June 2001. Cf. ibid., CNN.com, 12 June 2001: http://www.cnn.com/2001/TECH/ptech/06/12/bio.supercomputer.idg/.

28   Accelerated Strategic Computing Initiative (ASCI): http://www.llnl.gov/asci/sc96fliers/snl/ASCI.html. At Sandia Labs, the same acronym, "ASCI," also stands for Advanced Simulation and Computing program: http://www.sandia.gov/ASCI/.

29   For a complete list of the Top 500 computers: http://www.top500.org.

30   Ibid., under archive.

31   Ibid., under archive. The Leibniz supercomputer will attain 20 teraflops by 2005. Cf. Muzinée Kistenfeger, "Germany's National High Performance Computing Centres Are Planning Upgrades," British Embassy Berlin, Multimedia Issues, R&T Note no. 017.03(M) Date: 17 February 2003: www.britischebotschaft.de/en/embassy/r&t/notes/rt-note03.4017(m)_high_performance_computers.html; cf. http://www.britishembassy.de/en/embassy/r&t/rt-notes-index4000.html.

32   This is probably too conservative. There is already the "Bigbangwidth" company that calls itself the exabit net Optical company: http://www.bigbangwidth.com/.

33   Peter J. Denning and Robert M. Metcalfe, ed., Beyond Calculation: The Next Fifty Years of Computing, Heidelberg: Springer Verlag, 1998.

34   Stephen Shankland, "IBM exceeds expectations with supercomputer," CNET News.com, 21 September 2000: http://news.com.com/2100-1001-242567.html?legacy=cnet .

35   Cf. the description in IBM News, 6 December 1999: "Blue Gene will consist of more than one million processors, each capable of one billion operations per second (1 gigaflop). Thirty-two of these ultra-fast processors will be placed on a single chip (32 gigaflops). A compact two-foot by two-foot board containing 64 of these chips will be capable of 2 teraflops, making it as powerful as the 8,000-square-foot ASCI computers. Eight of these boards will be placed in 6-foot-high racks (16 teraflops), and the final machine (less than 2000 sq. ft.) will consist of 64 racks linked together to achieve the one petaflop performance": http://www.ibm.com/news/1999/12/06.phtml. For the official IBM site on Blue Gene: http://www.research.ibm.com/bluegene/. On 5 November 2004, it was reported that Blue Gene broke the world speed record with 70.72 trillion instructions per second.

36   Oliver Morton, "Gene Machine," Wired, 9.07, July, 2001, pp. 148–59: http://www.wired.com/wired/archive/9.07/blue.html. Peter Martin and Andrew Gowers, "Gates vision of the future: a home operated from the fridge," Financial Times, 9 December 2001, p. 28.

37   The Femtosecond Technology Research Association (FESTA), which started in 1995 and ends in 2004 is planning terabit connectivity by 2010; Asian Technology Information Program (ATIP), "MITI's Femtosecond Technology Program", ATIP97.099, 12 December 1997: http://www.atip.org/public/atip.reports.97/atip97.099r.html. See also: 10th International Workshop on Femtosecond Technology FST 2003, 16–17 July 2003, International Conference Hall, Makuhari Messe, Chiba, JAPAN.

38 In 1998, Bell Labs demonstrated the first terabit/second transmission, i.e., 1 trillion bytes/second. In 1999, Nortel demonstrated a transmission of 80 gigabits/second through a single fibre, 80 of which were then bundled to produce a speed of 6.4 terabits/second. Cf. the ICFA-SCIC Working Group on Monitoring: http://www.slac.stanford.edu/xorg/icfa/scic-netmon/. In 2002, Siemens demonstrated 7 terabits per second. Cf. Arthur F. Pease, Siemens, "Building the Unlimited Expressway": "In fact, we recently demonstrated this and set the world record of transmitting 7 Tbit/s over a single fiber by using 176 channels, each of which carried 40 Gbit/s. Furthermore, we are exploring systems that can operate at 160 to 320 Gbit/s per channel": http://w4.siemens.de/FuI/en/archiv/pof/heft2_02/artikel11/index.html. Companies such as Hyperchip Core IP Systems are working on challenges of petabit routing: http://www.hyperchip.com/indexflash.html.

38 Steven Bonisteel, "Bell Labs predicts a 'Global Communications Skin' by 2025," *Newsbytes.* 12 November 1999: http://www.headmap.org/index/wearable/wemproje.html. Reported by Anne Tyrie, *CITO Link-Line,* 22 November 1999: (formerly) www.findarticles.com/cf_dls/m0HDN/1999_Nov_12/ 57588359/p1/article.jhtml.

40 "Sci/Tech. Optic fibre world records broken," *BBC News,* 14 November 1999: http://news.bbc.co.uk/hi/english/sci/tech/newsid_517000/517733.stm. Cited by Jeffrey Harrow, *The Rapidly Changing Face of Computing,* 6 December 1999. In his report of 21 May 2001, Harrow cited the Gilder Report for May, 2001, claiming that transmission power would be a thousand times faster by 2010: http://www.compaq.com/rcfoc. In 2001 there was an estimate that the maximum capacity of fibre optic lines lay at 100 terabits. Even so, in December, 1999, scientists at Bell Labs sent 160 gigabits by optical fibre using only one wavelength or colour of light. They also used 1,022 different colours of light to send simultaneous signals down a single optic fibre. A single fibre could, therefore, theoretically send 164 terabits/second. Since a single cable contains 864 fibres, a cable could thus potentially convey 141 petabits/second.

41 Veronika Csizi, "Datenflut treibt Glasfaseraktien auf," *Der Tagespiegel,* Nr. 17 212, 25 October 2000, p. 22.

42 Alloptic has merged with VIPSwitch. See: http://www.alloptic.com/index.htm.

43 For the Product called Personal Organizer: http://www.chronosnet.com

44 E.g., All in One Personal Organizer (APO): http://www.cancellieri.org/pmo_index.htm. There is also an All in One Personal Information Manager (APIM), which includes 44 customizable collections (usage domains): http://www.cancellieri.org/apim_index.htm.

45 For personal digital assistant hardware: http://www.pdastreet.com

46 The same acronym is used for Personal Internet Assistants (PIAs): http://www.doc.ic.ac.uk/~yg/projects/Internet/Index.html. In 2000, there were other names such as Personal Digital Work Creators (PDWCs). In 2004, this term is rarely used. The Personal Work Tablets of 2000 have become a new area of TabletPCs: http://www.tabletpctalk.com/ and http://www.thetabletpc.net/.

47 David J. Staley, *Computers, Visualization and History. How New technology will transform our Understanding of the Past,* Armonk, NY: M.E. Sharpe, 2003.

48 These were usually in the form of AVI (Audio Video Interleave) files. John F. McGowan, "AVI Overview": http://www.jmcgowan.com/.

49 Karl Marx, *Das Capital,* Hamburg: Verlag von Otto Meissner, vol. 1, 1867, 1976, p. 285: "An instrument of labour is a thing, or a complex of things, which the worker interposes between himself and the object of his labour and which serves as a conductor, directing his activity onto that object. He makes use of the mechanical, physical and chemical properties of some substances as instruments of his power, and in accordance with his purposes. Leaving out of consideration such ready-made means of subsistence as fruits, in gathering which a man's bodily organs alone serve as the instruments of his labour, the object the worker directly takes possession of is not the object of labour but its instrument. Thus nature becomes one of the organs of his activity, which he annexes to his own bodily organs." This is cited by Paul Taylor, who notes under Mechanical Extensions that Buckminster Fuller also pursued this idea in his

Operating Manual for Spaceship Earth, 1969, p. 101: http://www.nous.org.uk/mech.ext.html; http://www.futurehi.net/docs/OperatingManual.html#1.

50 Ernst Kapp, *Grundlinien einer Philosophie der Technik. Zur Entstehungsgeschichte der Cultur aus neuen Gesichtspunkten*, Braunschweig, 1877.

51 Discussed in Jacqueline C.M. Otten, "Dress Codes: work environments – wearables – protective wear,": http://www.generativeart.com/papersga2003/a29.htm.

52 Sigmund Freud, *Civilization and its Discontents*, trans. James Strachey, New York: W.W. Norton, 1961. The original edition was 1929. This is cited by William J. Mitchell, *E-topia*, Cambridge, MA: MIT Press, 1999, p. 177.

53 Marshall McLuhan, *Understanding Media: The Extensions of Man*, New York: McGraw Hill, 1964. Reprint: Cambridge, MA: MIT Press, 1994. Particularly chapters 8–10.

54 The Massachusetts Institute of Technology (MIT), for instance, has a project on Aero/Astro Scientific Visualization: Visualization Codes organized by Bob Haimes: http://raphael.mit.edu/haimes.html. MIT is also working on a Virtual Environment Technologies for Training Testbed (VETT) in conjunction with U.S. Naval Air Warfare Center Training Systems Division: http://www.ntsc.navy.mil/Programs/Tech/Index.cfm. On MIT Video Streamer see Eddie Elliott, Glorianna Davenport, "Video Streamer," *Proceedings of the CHI '94 Conference Companion on Human Factors in Computing Systems*, 1994, pp. 65–68. 24–28 April 1994: http://ic.media.mit.edu/icSite/icpublications/Conference/VideoStreamer.html. Cf. the web site of Eddie Elliott: http://www.lightmoves.net/eddie/cv.htm. DyPERS: A Dynamic Personal Enhanced Reality System: http://vismod.www.media.mit.edu/vismod/demos/dypers/. The Brown University Computer Graphics Group has work on Geometric Model Extraction for Magnetic Resonance Imaging (MRI) Data, Ultrasound Image Data Use, Image Guided Streamline Placement, and Vector Field Visualization: http://www.cs.brown.edu/research/graphics/. This was formerly called the Graphics and Visualization Center.The vOICe. Soundscapes from The vOICe Seeing with your Ears! Vision Technology for the Totally Blind: http://www.visualprosthesis.com/voice.htm; http://www.visualprosthesis.com/sitemap.htm. New developments with respect to the Computer/ Human Interface (CHI) at the biological level suggest that direct neural implants allowing the blind to see will be available in the near future: Adrian Michaels, "Breakthrough in artificial sight for the blind," *Financial Times*, New York, Monday, 17 January 2000, p. 4. Cf. *Blind World. Medical News* and *Blindness Research*: http://www.home.earthlink.net/~blindworld/.

55 *Responsive Workbench* is a 3-D interactive workspace originally developed by Wolfgang Krueger at GMD (now Fraunhofer): http://www-graphics.stanford.edu/projects/RWB.

56 Dimension Technologies Inc.: http://www.dti3d.com/. A new technique called "actual depth" by Deep Video Imaging gives the impression of depth without special glasses: http://www.deepvideo.com/. Now called Pure Depth. Cf. "Monitors May Soon Go 3D. Deep Video Imaging has developed a display that gives the illusion of depth – without special glasses," *Reuters*, Monday, 14 May 2001. Mark Jones, "3D Monitors Display their Potential. Deep Video Imaging expects to begin selling 3D desktop displays next year, with handheld versions coming later," *InfoWorld.com*, Tuesday, 7 May 2002: http://www.pcworld.com/news/article/0,aid,98543,00.asp.

57 NASA Future Flight Central: http://ffc.arc.nasa.gov/.

58 "La voix sur IP," *Dossiers de l'Atica*, 13 juin 2002: (formerly) http://www.atica.pm.gouv.fr/dossiers/documents/voix_sur_ip.shtml. Christophe Guillemin, "La voix sur IP fait ses premières armes dans les téléboutiques," *ZDNet France*, Mercredi, 4 février 2004: http://www.zdnet.fr/actualites/technologie/0,39020809,39140424,00.htm.

59 In 2004, *SpeechBot* indexes 17,517 hours of content from a number of web sites: http://www.compaq.com/speechbot.

60 There are many such projects. The University of Bath's Interactive Media Technology Research Centre (http://www.bath.ac.uk/bsc/interactive/html/mtrc.htm) was working on a Platform for Animation and Virtual Reality (PAVR), an EU project that ended in 2001: http://www.cs.bath.ac.uk/PAVR/, which includes sound and music, speech, vision, and image processing. Companies such as IMAX have been working on 3-D sound to complement their

Omnimax and 3-D IMAX films. The Thorn EMI, Creative Research Laboratories (CRL, Hayes) are also working on a combination of a High Definition Video Display (HDVD) image and Sensaura artificial head for 3-D sound recording. With respect to content, there is an International Association of Sound and Audiovisual Archives (IASA): http://www.iasa-web.org/. At the Electrotechnical University (LETI) in St. Petersburg, there is a fascinating *Encyclopaedia of Sound*: http://www.eltech.ru/. The United States has a Digital Audio-Visual Preservation Prototyping Project, which is leading to a new National Audio Visual Conservation Center (Virginia) in 2005: cf. Library of Congress Audio-Visual Preservation Prototyping Project: http://www.loc.gov/rr/mopic/avprot/avprhome.html. As part of the Distance Education and Learning (DELTA) program, there is an interactive learning platform on the Internet about the history of music. This has led to a Virtuelle Optische Bank by Udo Zlender, Konstantinos Fostiropoulos und Sepideh Chakaveh: http://www.gmd.de/de/GMD-Spiegel/GMD-Spiegel-1_2_99-html/VOB.html. This is reported under: Devices and methods for tactile/haptic output as part of Esprit Project 8579/MIAMI (Schomaker et al., 1995): http://hwr.nici.kun.nl/~miami/taxonomy/node30.html#teletact.

61 Hartmut Chodura, "An Interactive Environment for Interactive Music Production,": http://www.igd.fhg.de/igd-a9/research/audio/material/icvc99slides.pdf. Stefan Noll and Frank Morbitzer, "Mediazine- A Cooperative Virtual Environment with Television, radio, WWW, Telecommunication, spatial sound and 3D graphics," *Eurocav3D 2001*, Mykonos, 30 May–1 June, Thessaloniki: ZITI, 2001, p. 258.

62 In 2000, the President of the World Digital Audio Broadcasting Forum (WorldDAB): http://www.worlddab.org/) favoured Europe's Eureka 147 system, which was competing with a series of other solutions:
    1) On In band on channel used in the United States:
       http://en.wipipedia.org/wiki/In-band_on-channel
    2) Worldspace: http://www.worldspace.com/about/index.html.
    3) European Space Agency: http://www.esa.int/export/esaCP/index.html.
    4) Inmarsat: http://www.inmarsat.org/.

63 This is reported under: Devices and methods for tactile/haptic output as part of Esprit Project 8579/MIAMI (Schomaker et al., 1995): http://hwr.nici.kun.nl/~miami/taxonomy/node30.html#teletact.

64 Force Feedback Research at UNC: http://www.cs.unc.edu. For an excellent introduction to the field of tactile force feedback, see Grigore Burdea and Philippe Coiffet, *Virtual Reality Technology*, New York: John Wiley & Sons, 1994; Grigore Burdea, *Virtual Reality and Force Feedback*, New York: John Wiley & Sons, 1996. Cf. Margaret Minsky's "Haptics People Places and Things": http://xenia.media.mit.edu/~marg/haptics-pages.html. Margaret Minsky also has a useful "Haptics Bibliography for the 1980s and early 1990s": http://xenia.media.mit.edu/~marg/haptics-bibliography.html.

65 MIT also has a Touch Lab and work on Mechanics Control and Applications: http://touchlab.mit.edu/.

66 Tangible Media Group: http://tangible.media.mit.edu/.

67 Tangible Media Group Projects. Tangible Bits: http://tangible.media.mit.edu/projects/Tangible_Bits/projects.htm. This lab explores concepts such as haptic holography and the Meta-Desk. Cf. Wendy J. Plesniak, Ravikanth S. Pappu, and Stephen A Benton, "Haptic Holography: A Primitive Computational Plastic," *Proceedings of the IEEE*, vol. 91, no. 9, September, 2003: http://web.media.mit.edu/~wjp/pubs/ieee03.pdf. Northwestern University is working on a Haptic Display in connection with the collaborative visualization (CoVis) project: http://www.covis.northwestern.edu/ and http://www.spider.hpc.naby.mil/. There is a Symposium for Haptic Interfaces for Virtual Environment and Teleoperator Systems. E.g., *Haptics 2002*: http://ieeexplore.ieee.org/xpl/RecentCon.jsp?puNumber=7836. Further work on haptic force and tactile feedback is being done by Steven J. Jacobsen, at the University of Utah (Salt Lake City), which began in the context of the Sarcos artificial arm: http://www.sarcos.com/. Other work is by Corde Lane and Jerry Smith at the University of Maryland,

Force and tactile Feedback: http://www.hitl.washington.edu/scivw/EVE/I.C.ForceTactile.html. Companies such as General Electric have important research on haptic devices: "Haptic Volume Visualization and Modeling": http://www.crd.ge.com/~avila/haptics/visualization.html. Cf. Stanford Haptics page: http://robotics.stanford.edu/~ruspini/haptic.html. In Europe, the Scuola Superiore Sant'Anna (Pisa) has a project on PERCeptual RObotics (PERCRO) with haptic interfaces: http://www-percro.sssup.it/. Haptic feedback for surgical simulation is also being studied in the Virtual Environments Graphics and Applications (VEGA) project at the University of Hull, which also has a Biomedical Model of a Human Knee Joint, a Knee Arthroscopy Training System and Physically Based Modelling (PBM). Cf. Simulation and Visualisation Research Group: http://www2.dcs.hull.ac.uk/simmod/index.htm.

68 Hirose and Hirota Lab: http://www.cyber.rcast.u-tokyo.ac.jp/index.html.

69 VR Lab University of Tsukuba: http://intron.kz.tsukuba.ac.jp/vrlab_web/index.html; "Haptic and Interface": http://intron.kz.tsukuba.ac.jp/vrlab_web/research/research_e.html.

70 IBM Research Natural Interactivity and Dreamspace: http://www.research.ibm.com/natural/.

71 Ibid.: http://www.research.ibm.com/natural/dreamspace/index.html.

72 John Bluck, "NASA Scientists Use Hands-Off Approach to Land Passenger Jet," *NASA News*, 1 February 2001: http://www.spaceref.com:16080/news/viewpr.html?pid=3734. Cf. the Neuro Engineering Technical Area at NASA Ames: http://ic-www.arc.nasa.gov/projects/ne.html.

73 Ames Research Center. Sub vocal speech demo: http://amesnews.arc.nasa.gov/releases/2004/subvocal/subvocal.html; John Bluck, "NASA Develops System to Computerize Silent, 'Subvocal Speech'," NASA Ames RELEASE: 04-093, 17 March 2004: www.nasa.gov/home/hqnews/2004/mar/ HQ_04093_subvocal_speech.html.

74 Light Space Technologies, formerly Dimensional Media Associates: http://www.lightspacetech.com/. For a good survey: Stereo 3D Displays: http://www.stereo3d.com. For Philips Research on 3-D Display Technology: http://www.semiconductors.philips.com/technologies/display/index.html. Marc Op de Beeck, André Redert, "Three Dimensional Video for the Home," *Euroimage ICAV 3D Conference*, Mykonos, June, 2001, pp. 188–91. Cf. Dimension Technologies Inc.: http://www.dti3d.com/. There are a number of players in auto-stereoscopy. One of the earliest was the Rainbow Lab under Cambridge Autostereo Display: http://www.cl.cam.ac.uk/Research/Rainbow/projects/asd/brochure.html. For a Survey of 3DTV Work: http://www2.eng.cam.ac.uk/~arlt1/research/third/all3d.html. There is also the Dresden 3-D display now called Real Technologies: http://3d-picture.net/frame.htm. For American work on Three Dimensional Video: Saied Moezzi, Arun Katkere, Don Y. Kuramura, and Ramesh Jain, "An Emerging Medium: Interactive Three Dimensional Digital Video," 1996 *International Conference on Multimedia Computing and Systems (Multimedia '96)*: http://www.computer.org/proceedings/7436abs.htm. The Visual Computing Lab (UCSD) is also working on Multiple perspective interactive video: Arun Katkere, Jennifer Schlenzig, Amarnath Gupta, and Ramesh Jain, "Interactive Video on WWW: Beyond VCR like Interfaces," Fifth International World Wide Web Conference, 6–10 May 1996, Paris, France: (formerly) http://www5conf.inria.fr/fich_html/papers/P58/www5.html#secproto. For American work on 3DTV: http://www.3dmagic.com/. The Kanagawa Institute of Technology and Waseda University Global Info and Telecommunication Institute are working on a Multi-viewpoint 3-D Movie System (Project number JGN-P112526): (formerly) http://jani.tao.go.jp/project_e/pro_kanto_e.html#.

75 For instance, the EU IST project: Personalised, Immersive Sports TV Experience (PISTE): http://piste.intranet.gr/index.asp and on the cordis web site: http://dbs.cordis.lu/fep-cgi/srchidadb?ACTION=D&SESSION=53262004-4-7&DOC=75&TBL=EN_PROJ&RCN=EP_RPG:IST-1999-11172&CALLER=PROJ_IST.

76 Marc Op De Beeck and Andre Redert, "Three Dimensional Video for the Home," *Euroimage ICAV3D 2001*, Thessaloniki: ZITI, 2001, pp. 188–91; P. A. Redert, *Multi-Viewpoint Systems for 3d Visual Communications*, PhD thesis, Delft University of Technology, 2000; Adrian Travis, "3 D Television Looks a Reality," *Enginuity*, no. 1, Summer 1993: http://www-g.eng.cam.ac.uk/enginuity/issue1/article5.html; Keval Pindoria and G. C. Wong Ping Hung, "The Parents the Kids and THE

INTERACTIVE TV!!!!", *Surprise 96 Journal*, vol. 4, London, 1996: http://www.doc.ic.ac.uk/~nd/surprise_96/journal/vol4/khp1/report.html.

77   Charles Platt, "You've got smell," *Wired*, October, 1999, pp. 256–63.

78   The company closed in 2001 due to lack of funding. Cf. "Digiscents shuts doors," *East Bay Business Times*, 12 April 2001: http://www.bizjournals.com/eastbay/stories/2001/04/09/daily32.html. Formerly at: http://www.digiscents.com/; Deepshikha Ghosh, "Indian gets patent for virtual smell technology," *India Abroad News Service*, 14 February 2001: http://www.apnic.net/mailing-lists/s-asia-it/archive/2001/02/msg00043.html.

79   France Telecom patented the idea in 1989: France Telecom R&D, "The Diffusion of Fragrances in a Multimedia Environment,": http://www.rd.francetelecom.com/en/medias/prof_jour_press_web-parfume.htm.

80   PNNL, Neural Network Based Electronic Nose: http://picturethis.pnl.gov/picturet.nsf/All/48FLLX?opendocument. Cf. Cyrano Sciences: http://cyranosciences.com/, now Smiths Group. http://www.smithsdetection.com/Default.asp?bhcp=1. Rosemary Clandos, "Cyranose Makes Sense of NASA Technology; Space research Propels MEMS Development," *Small Times West Coast*, 4 June 2001: http://www.smalltimes.com; Arlene Weintraub, "Killer tests for deadly germs," *Business Week*, 5 November 2001, p. 33. http://www.keepmedia.com/pubs/BusinessWeek/2001/11/05/28359?extID=10026.

81   Cf. Anne Marie Squeo, "Robo-Lobster Joins U.S. Army," *Asian Wall Street Journal*, 14–16 December 2001, p. 6.

82   "Trisenx will make four models of such a device: FirstSENX $398, Mini-SENX (which will be placed in a regular Hard Drive slot), TranSENX $798 for laptops and UltraSENX $1,198 which will have an extended taste library." Cited in Magazine "*Hacker*" #05 /Y2K [i.e., 2000] in Russian. Kindly brought to my attention and translated from the Russian by Misha Brakker: http://www.trisenx.com.

83   Warren Robinett, "Electronic Expansion of Human Perception," *Whole Earth Review*, 1991; ibid., "Synthetic Experience," *Presence*, MIT Press, vol. 1, no. 2. Cf. Peter Werkhoven, Computers as Sensory transducers: carol.wins.uva.nl/~leo/coll/werkhoven.html.

84   World Wide Web Consortium, Web Accessibility Initiative: http://www.w3.org/WAI/. Re: user agent accessibility guidelines: http://www.w3.org/TR/UAAG10/.

85   IBM CISPH (Centre d'Information et de Solutions pour Personnes Handicappées): http://www-5.ibm.com/fr/cisph/.

86   International Visual Theatre, Centre Socio-Culturel des Sourds: http://www.ivt.fr/.

87   EU WISDOM (Wireless Information Services for Deaf People): http://www.beepknowledgesystem.org/ShowCase.asp?CaseTitleID=177&CaseID=480.

88   Don Norman's jnd web site: http://www.jnd.org/.

89   Peter Brusilovsky, Marcus Specht, and Gerhard Weber, "Towards Adaptive Learning Environments," In: F. Huber-Wäschle, H. Schauer, & P. Widmayer (Eds.), *Proceedings of GISI 95*, Zürich, 18-20 September 1995. Berlin, Springer-Verlag, 1995, pp. 322-329. Cf. Peter Brusilovsky's home page: http://www2.sis.pitt.edu/~peterb/.

90   Whereas a medium focusses on where information is transmitted, a modality includes a medium plus its interpretation, which constitutes a meaningful representation. According to Carbonell, these multimodalities can be:

Combined	Alternate	Synergetic
Independent	Exclusive	Concurrent
	Sequential	Parallel

Joëlle Coutaz, Laurence Ginay, Daniel Salber, "Taxonomic Issues for Multimodal and Multimedia Interactive Systems," *ERCIM '94 workshop on Multimedia Mulrimodal User Interfaces*, Nancy, October 1994: iihm.imag.fr/publs/1993/ERCIM93_Taxonomy.pdf .

91 A new theory of panarchy is being developed by the Resilience Alliance: http://resalliance. org/ev_en.php?ID=1094_201&ID2=DO_TOPIC.

92 Michel Riguidel, "Security and Trust for the Grid," *IST Call 5 Preparatory Workshop on Advanced Grid Technologies, Systems and Services, 31 January–1 February 2005, Venue: Hotel Carrefour de l'Europe, Brussels,* Brussels: EU DG INFSO-F2, January 2005.

93 "Opera Combines TV Recording with Smartphones. Mobile IPG allows smart-phone users to control TV recording remotely," *PDAstreet.com News*, 6 April 2004: http://www.pdastreet.com/ articles/2004/4/2004-4-6-Opera-Combines-TV.html.

94 Lou Hirsh, "3D Printers Could Become Industrial Dynamos," *SCI:TECH, Newsfactor*, 9 May 2002, re: MIT Professor Emanuel Sachs: http://www.newsfactor.com/perl/story/17669.html. Rick Overton, "Fax it up Scotty," *Business 2.0*, February 2001 Issue, 6 March 2001: http://www.business2.com/b2/web/articles/0,17863,528700,00.html. An example of this new communication among media is how one can now take traditional phonograph records and translate them into digital form. Cf. "Je Platencollectie Digitaliseren," *De Standaard*, 11 October 2000, p. 4.

95 Annual *SPIE Microlithography Symposium:* http://www.spie.org/web/meetings/calls/ml01/ml01_ home.html. There are a number of new technologies including: Extreme Ultra-Violet (EUV) lithography; electron beam technology (e-beam), ion beam and X-ray. For a discussion of UUV and e-beam; Jeffrey R. Harrow, *RFOC*, 22 January 2001.

96 Maria Theresia Rolland, "Sprache ist der Zugriff auf die Welt," *Feuilleton*, 3 May 2000; Xerox Multilingual Knowledge Management Solutions: (formerly) http://www.mkms.xerox.com/.

97 Walter J. Ong, *Ramus and the Decline of Dialogue*, Cambridge, MA: Harvard University Press, 1958.

98 These again are problems to which Foucault, Derrida, and their deconstructionist offspring have drawn attention anecdotally, intuitively, and usually superficially because, ironically, they have tried to encompass these new levels of discourse using the straightjacketing limitations of a single level of discourse by trying to write all this in traditional scholarly style. Ultimately our new electronic knowledge access tools will need a moveable levels of discourse bar to complement the levels of knowledge bar.

99 This was linked with the session: "Blueprint for Japan 2020" at the *World Economic Forum:* http: //www.weforum.org/site/homepublic.nsf/Content/13C9C78A94F841ACC1256C23003217E9.

100 Cited on the Intel site under Enhanced Digital Broadcast in 2000. This part of the site is no longer available, but Intel has in the meantime invested $200 million in digital homes. "Intel Bets Big on the Digital Home," *Business Week*, 7 January 2004: http://www.businessweek.com/ technology/content/jan2004/tc2004017_7492_tc057.htm. For a different view on the future of television, see UK Department of Trade and Industry, "A New Future for Communications", *DTI-DCMS Communications White Paper*, London, 2001: www.communicationswhitepaper.gov.uk. A decade ago, Bill Gates was preaching that television and computing are totally unrelated markets. In 2003 he was producing software to link the two; Sébastien Penmec, "Le jeu sur console entame une nouvelle ère," *Le Temps*, 8 October 2003, p. 26.

101 E.g., the work of Sean Murphy; Rajeeb Hazra, "Delivering Immersive Soccer Content to Sports Fans," *Intel Developer Update Magazine*, June, 2001: www.intel.com/technology/magazine/research/ it06012.pdf.

102 This is a very complex topic, which is likely to become the subject of a subsequent book. While the United States has tried to convince the world of a dot.com and telecom bust or bubble burst, a sober look at the ITU statistics confirms that the telco sector has steadily grown in the past decade from some 300 billion to over 1 trillion dollars annually.

103 JPL Space Communications Protocol Standards: www.scps.org. Meanwhile. back on earth, there is increasing attention to the use of grids as a means of dealing with emergent complexity. This is leading to a surge in middleware, which some now divide into under-ware, middle-ware, and upper-ware, while others are beginning to speak of the need for a knowledge organization layer. Among the many experiments in this domain is "Planetlab. A Blueprint for Disruptive Technology into the Internet,": http://www.planet-lab.org. This is a private sector initiative.

104   Discussed at a Future and Emerging Technologies (FET) Forum at Twente.

105   Scarlet Pruitt, "Predicting the Death of the Internet: The Web as we know it will give way to a more interactive and pervasive medium, experts say," *IDG News Service*, Friday, 18 May 2001: http://www.pcworld.com/news/article/0,aid,50366,00.asp.

106   Artificial Life, Inc.: http://www.artificial-life.com/. Cf. "Ein Schwätzchen mit Lucy," *Tages-Anzeiger*, 5 February 2001, p. 14.

107   Manuel de Landa, "Virtual Environments and the emergence of Synthetic Reason": http://www.t0.or.at/delanda/delanda.htm. Manuel de Landa cites: William Bechtel and Adele Abrahamsen, *Connectionism and the Mind*, Cambridge, MA: Blackwell, 1991, p. 129.

108   Charles Jonscher, *The Evolution of Wired Life*, New York: John Wiley & Sons, 1999, p. 95.

109   Web accessibility initiative: http://www.w3.org/WAI/.

110   Jerome H. Saltzer, David P. Reed, and David D. Clark, "End-to-end arguments in system design," *ACM Transactions on Computer Systems*, vol. 2, no. 4 (November, 1984), pp. 277–88: http://web.mit.edu/Saltzer/www/publications/endtoend/ANe2ecomment.html. An earlier version appeared in the *Second International Conference on Distributed Computing Systems*, April, 1981, pp. 509–12; Lawrence Lessig, "In the Matter of the AT&T/MediaOne Merger": http://cyber.law.harvard.edu/works/lessig/MB.html; Mark A. Lemley and Lawrence Lessig, "The end of end to end. Preserving the Architecture of the Internet in the Broadband Era,": http://repositories.cdlib.org/blewp/37/

111   This is the position of David Isenberg in: "The rise of the stupid network": http://www.isen.com/ or http://www.hyperorg.com/misc/stupidnet.html; Cf. Tim Denton, *IIC Conference*, St. Petersburg, FL, September, 2000.

112   Forrester, "The Death of the Web Is Inevitable, according to Forrester Research," Cambridge, MA, 17 May 2001: http://www.forrester.com/ER/Press/Release/0,1769,567,00.html.

113   Fondation Internet Nouvelle Génération (FING), 2002, Atelier ES2: „L'Internet du futur sera-t-il un internet?". http://www.3ie.org/nouvelles_technologies/conference/conference_L_internet_du_futur_sera-t-il_un_internet_.htm

114   Computer Society's journal *Computer*, April, 1999.

115   Robert Cailliau, "The World Wide Web Evolution, Regulation and Perspectives as a Medium of Information," *Internationales Symposion, Zukunft der Information*, ORF, Vienna, 4 May 2000.

116   In this context there are the interesting developments qua the virtual machine. Bill Venners, "The lean mean virtual machine," *Java World*, June 1996: http://www.javaworld.com/javaworld/jw-06-1996/jw-06-vm.html; Jon Meyer and Troy Downing, *Java Virtual Machine*, Cambridge, MA: O'Reilly, 1997. Also important in this context is the realm of emulators (e.g., VM Ware, Virtual PC, Fusion, Basilisk II, MAME). Andreas Heer, "Software simuliert Hardware," *Tages-Anzeiger*, 18 September 2000, pp. 67, 69. Re: emulators unlimited site: http://emuunlim.com. Cf. Phil Winterbottom and Rob Pike, Bell Labs, Lucent Technologies, *The Design of the Inferno Virtual machine*: http://plan9.bell-labs.com/cm/cs/who/rob/hotchips.html.

117   Michael Giesecke, *Der Buchdruck in der frühen Neuzeit. Eine historische Fallstudie über die Durchsetzung neuer Informations- und Kommunikations-technologien*, Frankfurt: Suhrkamp, 1991.

118   For visions for the future, cf. "What science will know in 2050," End of the Millennium Special edition, *Scientific American*, December, 1999: www.sciam.com.

Chapter 2: Mobility

1   The Great Idea Finder: Alexander Graham Bell: http://www.ideafinder.com/history/inventors/bell.htm.
Meanwhile, Antonio Meucci (1808-1889) has been recognized as the real inventor of the telephone: http://www.dickran.net/history/meucci_bell.html .

2   Marconi History: http://www.marconi.com/html/about/marconihistory.htm.

3   Waveguide, "A Brief History of Cellular": http://www.wave-guide.org/archives/waveguide_3/cellular-history.html; Mery Bellis, "Selling The Cell Phone. Part 1: History of Cellular Phones,", *About.com*, 8 July 1999 : http://inventors.about.com/library/weekly/aa070899.htm. Part of the series Inventors.

4   How Stuff Works, "What does GSM mean in a cellphone?": http://electronics.howstuffworks.com/question537.htm.

5   Hamadoun Toure (ITU), speaking at the *Global Knowledge Conference* in Kuala Lumpur (March, 2000) claimed that there are 250,000 new mobiles per day.

6   http://www.cellular.co.za/news_2004/sep/090404-gartner_says_mobile_phone_sales.htm.

7   "Nokia plans 40 new models in '05," *The Economic Times:-*http://economictimes.indiatimes.com.

8   "By the Short Fiber," *Interactive Week*, 30 October 2001.

9   Kevin J. Delaney, "A New LAN of Opportunity. Wireless Systems Are Offering an Inexpensive Alternative to Cellular Models," *Wall Street Journal Europe*, 24–25 November 2000, p. 17.

10 Mark Weiser, "Ubiquitous Computing": http://www.ubiq.com/hypertext/weiser/UbiHome.html; http://www.ubiq.com/weiser/.

11 Real Time and Embedded Systems Forum, "The Open Group launches Real-time and Embedded Systems Forum, 3 August 2000,": http://www.opengroup.org/press/3aug00.htm.

12 Cited by William Mitchell in *E-topia*, 1999, p. 40, from the column by Ted Lewis, "Binary Critic," *IEEE Computer*, September, 1997. At the 100th anniversary of the INPG, a representative from CEA/LETI spoke of communicating objects and noted that these were also much more numerous than personal computers:

TECHNOLOGY	MILLIONS
Smart Cards	2,015
Mobile Telephones	280
Laptop PCs	20
Portable Game Consoles	18
Personal Digital Assistants	3–6
Digital Cameras	6.5
Digital Music Players	1.5
Pocket PCs	0.7

13 Leonard Kleinrock, Professor. Inventor of the Internet Technology: http://www.lk.cs.ucla.edu; cf.: Travler. System support for Nomadic Computing: http://fmg-www.cs.ucla.edu/travler98/intro.html. More recently, this has led to the CoSMoS project (Self-Configuring Survivable Multi-Networks for Information Systems Survivability). Leonard Kleinrock, "Nomadic Computing and Communications," White Paper, 1995: http://books.nap.edu/html/whitepapers/ch-40.html; NCO FY 1997 Implementation Plan: http://www.nitrd.gov/pubs/implementation. The IETF is working on: Mobile ad hoc Networks (MANET): http://www.ietf.org/html.charters/manet-charter.html.

14 Seiko Instruments Products: http://www.siibusinessproducts.com/products/index.html.

15 Microsoft, "Q&A: Tablet PC Brings the Simplicity of Pen and Paper to Computing," Las Vegas, 13 November 2000: http://www.microsoft.com/presspass/features/2000/nov00/11-13tabletpc.mspx; *Tages-Anzeiger*, Zürich, 11 November 2002, p. 51.

16 Palm Pilots are, for instance, being linked with Street Finder GPS software, as described in *Wired*, April, 2000, p. 70. Philips has a similar device called Pronto remote: www.philips.com; Charles W. Bailey, *Scholarly Electronic Publishing Bibliography*, Version 52, 12 December 2003: http://info.lib.uh.edu/sepb/sepb.html.

17 Roger Zedi, "Zur Seite, Palm. Der Treo kommt," *Tages-Anzeiger*, 5 March 2002, p. 63. For Sony's Clié N770G: Roger Zedi, "Palms Führungsanspruch," *Tages-Anzeiger*, 4 November 2002, p. 59. In May, 2004, Sony dropped its Clie product. Some see this as part of a new shift whereby mobile phones and personal digital assistants become merged. Hence a greater Sony-Ericsson connection: Seth Jayson, "Sony clie to fade away," *Fool.com*, 2 June 2004: http://www.fool.com/News/mft/2004/mft04060208.htm.

18 Filip Huysegems, "Het Boek dat alle boeken kan zijn," *De Standaard der Letteren*, 31 August 2000, pp. 8–9. There are a number of these electronic book devices. SoftBook Press developed a SoftBook System. This was taken over by Gemstar eBook, RCA, and was called REB 1200 ebook Hardware: http://www.planetebook.com/mainpage.asp?webpageid=15&TBToolID=1108. In June, 2003, Gemstar decided to discontinue its ebookstore. Cf. "Another important ebook announcement," 16 July 2003: http://www.gemstar-ebook.com/cgi-bin/WebObjects/eBookstore.woa/wa/. Nuvo Media produced the RocketBook, which was supported by Barnes and Noble and Bertelsmann. This was replaced by the RCA ebook, as explained on the Rocket/RCA ebook site: http://www.geocities.com/mjposner2000/. Meanwhile, Every Book Inc. produced the Dedicated Reader described by Daniel Munyan: http://www.futureprint.kent.edu/authors/munyanbio.htm. Franklin produced EbookMan: http://www.franklin.com/ebookman/. Microsoft has Pocket PC: http://www.microsoft.com/mobile/pocketpc/default.asp. There was a Glassbook, which was acquired by Adobe, and renamed the Adobe Acrobat eBook Reader 2, in the direction of reference material: Kendra Mayfield, "Adobe's Novel Approach to E-Books," *Wired News*, 29 January 2001: http://www.wirednews.com/news/print/0,1294,41249,00.html: "Adobe and Barnes &Noble.com Team to offer Adobe PDF Based E-Books": http://www.adobe.com/aboutadobe/pressroom/pressreleases/pdfs/200101/20010129survivor.pdf. There is also a Peanut Reader by Pen Computing: http://www.pencomputing.com/palm/Pen32/peanutreader.html. Related to this are new devices such as the Cyberglass developed by Sony, Paris: Chisato Numaoka, "Cyberglass: Vision-Based VRML2 Navigator," *Virtual Worlds*, ed. Jean-Claude Heudin, ed., Berlin: Springer, 1998, pp. 81–87. Related to the electronic book is the electronic newspaper described by Jim Nagel, "Newspad Makes El Periódico Interactive," *Byte*, February, 1997: http://www.byte.com/art/9702/sec17/art2.htm. Acorn Risc Technologies (Cambridge, UK) has developed the NewsPAD: http://www.futureprint.kent.edu/articles/fidler01.htm linked with research at Edinburgh by Alfonso Molina on the NewsPAD: http://www.futureprint.kent.edu/articles/molina01.htm. In addition, there was the idea of On-line Classrooms by Open Book Systems, a company which now focuses on database solutions. Cf.: http://www.e-books.org/.

19 On the e-ink project launched by Philips and now available on a Sony reader as of 24 March 2004: http://www.eink.com/news/releases/pr70.html and Fabrizio Pilato, "Sony LIBRIe – The first ever E-Ink e-Book Reader," *Mobile Mag*, 25 March 2004: http://www.mobilemag.com/content/100/333/C2658/.

20 Leander Kahney, "Lucent's Major Breakthrough,"*Wired News*, 15 November 1999: http://www.wired.com/news/technology/0,1282,32545,00.html.

21 Don Tapscott, "Be Prepared for the 'Hypernet,'" *Tech Informer*, 16 July 2001.Cf. : http://www.techinformer.com/; Caroline Humer, "IBM Molecular Circuit May Mean Tiny Computer Chips," *Excite News*, 26 August 2001; R. Colin Johnson, "Cascading molecules drive IBM's smallest computer," *EE Times*, 25 August 2002: http://www.eetimes.com/story/OEG20021024S0047.

22 Jeffrey R. Harrow, "The Lesson," *The Rapidly Changing Face of Computing*, 1 November 1999: http://www.compaq.com/rcfoc. This relates to the new field of moletronics or molecular electronics described by John Markoff, "Tiniest Circuits Hold Prospect of Explosive Computer Speeds," *New York Times*, 16 July 1999. Some pioneers such as Bill Joy, formerly chief scientist at Sun Microsystems, are more conservative in their estimates and predict that computers will increase 1 million-fold in their power within the next fifty years. Bill Joy, "Why the Future Doesn't Need Us," *Wired*, April, 2000, pp. 238–63.

23 Rick Overton, "Molecular Electronics will Change Everything," *Wired News*, 8.07, July, 2000: http://www.wired.com/wired/archive/8.07/moletronics.html.

24 University of Notre Dame, Molecular Electronics Based on Quantum-Dot Cellular Automata: http://www.nd.edu/~mlieberm/qca.html.

25 One of the most important of these is a consortium of eight leading consumer electronics firms headed by Philips called Home Audio Visual Interoperability (HAVI): http://www.havi.org. Philips has linked with Wi-LAN (Calgary) using IEEE 1394 wireless transmission at 2.4 GHz. (Firewire); Yunko Yoshida, "Philips demos wireless network with Wi-LAN," *EE Times*, 27 August 1999: http://www.eetimes.com/story/OEG19990827S0032. Using a variant of IEEE 802.11, this solution employs Wide-band Orthogonal Frequency Division Multiplexing (W-OFDM) to achieve 46 Mb raw data and 24 Mb in practice. This technology also uses MPEG2. Also very important is the Open Services Gateway Initiative (OSGI), which includes IBM, Sun, Motorola, Lucent, Alacatel, Cable & Wireless, Enron, Ericsson, Network Computer, Nortel, Oracle, Royal Philips Electronics, Sybase, and Toshiba: http://www.osgi.org. Meanwhile, the Home Radio Frequency Working Group (HomeRF) includes Compaq, Ericsson, Hewlett-Packard, IBM, Intel, Microsoft, Motorola, and Philips Consumer Communications. National Semiconductor and Rockwell Semiconductor are among the supporting companies. This employs a frequency-hopping technology. It transmits data at 1.6 Mbit/s between home PCs and peripherals and supports up to four separate voice channels. They are working on a Shared Wireless Access Protocol (SWAP). "Unwiring the Household," *Wired News*, 4 March 1998: http://www.wired.com/news/news/technology/story/10711.html. Competition was announced by Microsoft – 3-Com (11 March 1999) and by MIT – Motorola (15 March 1999). There is also the Home Plug and Play Alliance which provides Common Application Language (CAL); a Home Automation Association, the American Household Appliance Association, and Home Phoneline Networking Alliance (HomePNA). More important is the Wireless Application Protocol Forum (WAP Forum), which has produced the Wireless Application Protocol (WAP): http://www.wapforum.org/. This initiative includes a number of technologies:
Global System for Mobile Communications (GSM 900, 1,800 &1,900 MHz)
Code Division Multiple Access (CDMA IS-95/IS-707)
Time Division Multiple Access (TDMA IS-136)
Program Delivery Control (PDC)
Personal Handyphone System MOU Group (PHS)
Ericsson's Eritel subsidiary's cellular land radio-based packet-switched data communication system (Mobitex)
DataTAC
CDPD
DECT
iDEN (ESMR)
Iridium (TETRA)
http://www.ora.com/reference/dictionary/terms/M/Mobitex.htm. The WAP Forum is in turn linked with ETSI's Mobile Execution Environment (MEXE): http://www.wapforum.org/pressrel/111198_wapnovmem.htm or http://www.oasis-open.org/cover/wap111198.html). The WAP Forum has since consolidated with the Open Mobile Alliance (OMA): http://www.openmobilealliance.org/index.html. For criticism of WAP, see Rohit Khare, "W* Effect Considered Harmful," 4 K Associates, 9 April 1999: www.4K-associates.com/4K-Associates/IEEE-L7-WAP-BIG.html. At a lower speed but also important is the Blue Tooth Consortium, which includes IBM, Toshiba, Ericsson, Nokia, and Puma Technology, entailing a single synchronization protocol to address end-user problems arising from the proliferation of various mobile devices – including smart phones, smart pagers, handheld PCs, and note-books – that need to keep data consistent from one device to another. It targets short-distance links between cell phones and laptops with a 1-Mbit/s network that connects devices up to ten metres apart. The frequency-hopping technology operates in the 2.54-GHz ISM band:

http://www.bluetooth.com/index.asp. Dan Briody and Ephraim Schwartz, "Blue Tooth consortium pushes radio specification," *IDG.Net*, 13 April 1999: http://www.infoworld.com:80/cgi-bin/displayStory.pl?980413.ehbluetooth.htm. Also significant is Wireless Ethernet (IEEE 802.11) incorporated into ISO/IEC 8802-11: 1999, which was designed for wireless transmission of data only. Isochronous information is excluded. The approach uses the 2.4-GHz band and offers a raw data rate of up to 11 Mbits/s. Cf. IEEE 802 Standards List: http://grouper.ieee.org/groups/802/802info.html. W3C Mobile Access Interest Group is working on: Composite Capability Preference Profiles (CC/PP): http://www.w3.org/TR/Note-CCPP. This initiative under Ora Lassila. This includes HTTP Access Headers, Salutation, IETF CONNEG, MIME and P3P. Cf. ora.lassila@research.nokia.com. There was also the Global Mobile Commerce Forum (GMCF) (formerly at http://www.gmcforum.com/got.html), which now seems to have been swallowed by the Open Mobile Alliance mentioned above. Meanwhile, there is a new Mobile Electronic Transactions (MET) Group: http://www.mobiletransaction.org/. Warner Brothers Online has an Infrared Remote Control. Cf. Data General Network Utility Box (NUB): "A Network Hub a Little Closer to Home," *Wired News*, 3 February 1998: http://www.wired.com/news/news/technology/story/10036.html. Meanwhile, a number of initiatives in the direction of integration are coming from the telephone world. Perhaps the most important is the Voice eXtensible Markup Forum (VXML): http://www.vxmlforum.com/industry_talk.html. Formed by AT&T, Lucent Technologies, and Motorola, and 17 other companies, VXML is working on a standard for voice- and phone-enabled Internet access, says David Unger, an AT&T product strategy and development division manager. Cf. Open Settlement Protocol (OSP), whereby Cisco, 3Com Corporation, GRIC Communications, iPass, and TransNexus have teamed up to promote inter-domain authentication, authorization and accounting standards for IP telephony. Cisco IOS Software Release 12.0(4)XH – No. 948: http://www.cisco.com/. Nortel, Microsoft, Intel, and Hewlett-Packard are working on corporate networking equipment that can handle data, voice, and video communications; Home Phone Network Alliance (Home PNA): http://www.homepna.org/; Data General Network Utility Box (NUB) mentioned above. On mobile developments generally: Electronic bibliography of the ITU in: *World Telecommunication Development Report* 1999 – Mobile Cellular: http://www.itu.int/ITU-D/ict/publications/wtdr_99/material/bibliogr.html. Cf. Information Society Communications, Green Papers since 1996: http://europa.eu.int/ISPO/infosoc/telecompolicy/en/comm-en.htm.

At the Multi-National level, there are the activities of former DGXIIIb ACTS Domains:

Mobility, Personal and Wireless Communications

Future Public Land Mobile Telecommunications Systems (FPLMTS now called International Mobile Communications): http://www.itu.ch/imt-2000

Digital Mobile System (DSM)

Global System for Mobile Communications (GSM)

Digital European Cordless Telecommunications (DECT)

Pan European Paging System (ERMES)

Cf. IETF Mobile IP Working Group (RFC 2002): http://www.leapforum.org/published/mobileIpSurvey/split/node2.html; Charles Perkins, Tutorial: "Mobile Networking through Mobile IP,": IEEE Internet Computing, vol.2, n.1: http://portal.acm.org/citation.cfm?id=613224. At the national level there is also: Virtual Environment Dialogue Architecture (VEDA): Andrew Steed, Virtual Research Page: http://www.cs.ucl.ac.uk/staff/A.Steed/research.html. As of 15 April 2004, there is a Mobile Research Forum: http://mrf.ecdc.info/.

To the outsider this may at first simply seem a complete muddle of techno-jargon. It serves however to make a very important point. The industry does not have a simple blueprint for what is happening. There are dozens of competing intiatives./

26 For a discussion of problems with UMTS: Daniel Metzger, "Hoffen auf das mobile Internet," *Tages-Anzeiger*, 10 March 2001, p. 57.

27 David Legard, "Coding breakthrough speeds radio data 100x," *IDG News Service*/Singapore Bureau, 18 June 2001: http://www.cellonics.com/news/p_idg1.htm; http://www.nwfusion.com/Home/dlegard.html.

28 Vineeta Shetty, "Don't get mad get even," *Communications International*, May, 2001, pp. 23–26: (formerly) www.ci-online.net.

29 Roger Zedi, "Heute im Kino, gestern im Netz," *Tages-Anzeiger*, 22 December 2003, p. 29.

30 The Palm Pilot VII is an example. The Palm Pilot became the more significant in the months of October and November, 1999, through deals with Nokia and Sony to share the technology: Piu-Wing Tam, "Price Wars Hit PDAs, But Should You Buy One Now?" *The Wall Street Journal*, Thursday, 6 May 2002, p. D1.

31 Nokia phones: http://www.nokia.com/nokia/0,8764,73,00.html; Felix Wiedler, "Handys machen den Daten Beine," *Tages-Anzeiger*, 30 April 2001, p. 63.

32 Steve Silberman, "Just say Nokia," *Wired*, September, 1999, pp. 137–49, 202: http://www.wired.com/wired/archive/7.09/nokia.html.

33 Dinesh C. Sharma, "Nokia phone adopts handwriting recognition," *CNETAsia*, Wednesday, 3 November 2004: http://asia.cnet.com/news/personaltech/0,39037091,39199782,00.htm.

34 Douglas Heingartner, " Camera phone snapshots connect the dots," *International Herald Tribune*, 9–10 October 2004, p. 20; ibid., "Connecting paper and on-line world by cellphone camera," tjm.org, 7 October 2004: http://www.tjm.org/notes/SpotCodes/; Anil Madhavapeddy, David Scott, Richard Sharp, and Eben Upton, "Using Camera-Phones to Enhance Human–Computer Interaction," *UbiComp (adjunct proceedings)*, September 2004: ubicomp.org/ubicomp2004/adjunct/demos/madhavapeddy.pdf; David Scott, Richard Sharp, Anil Madhavapeddy, Eben Upton, "Using Camera-Enabled Personal Devices to Access Bluetooth Mobile Services," To Appear. *Mobile Computing and Communications Review, ACM*, January 2005; Richard Sharp, Intel: http://cambridgeweb.cambridge.intel-research.net/people/rsharp.

35 Ericsson: http://www.ericsson.com.

36 Kenwood: http://www.kenwood.net.

37 Motorola: http://www.motorola.com/.

38 "Electronic paper turns the page," *Financial Times*, 25 May 2001. Re: a new class of electro-optical material at Edinburgh university. Bell Labs have a competing technology based on micro-contact printing: Barbara Goss Levi, "New Printing Technologies Raise Hopes for Cheap Plastic Electronics" *Physics Today*, Volume 54, November 2000: http://www.physicstoday.com/pt/vol-54/iss-2/p20.html.

39 This was connected with the Informatics project which was closed when Dr Jacob retired in 2002: http://www.almaden.ibm.com/projects/informatics.shtml; "Liebes Christkind bitte bring mir ein Handy," *Tages-Anzeiger*, 5 December 2003, p. 27 for a glimpse of the growing variety in choices.

40 Antonio Krüger (Krueger@cs.uni-SB.De) has founded EYELED which uses the Palm and Metagraphics as the basis for a Mobile Infra-red Based Information and Navigation System. EYELED mobile competence: http://www.eyeled.de/.

41 Valeria Criscione, "Surf without a PC," *Financial Times*, 22 February 2000.

42 Telenor has produced a Smart phone, an ISDN web-based screen telephone: Valeria Criscione, "Surf without a PC," *Financial Times*, 23 March 2000. Casio-Siemens has produced a multi-mobile, which combines a telephone, e-mail, smart messaging service (SMS), Internet, and an address book. "Zukunftsding," *Tages-Anzeiger*, 27 March 2000, p. 71. SingTel Mobile and Ong Company Partners have produced a mobile phone for e-trading. "Easy Trading," *New Straits Times*, 10 March 2000, p. 32. Lucent has new voice activated phones as does DriveThere.com. "Voice Portals to Navigate the Web," *New Straits Times*, 9 March 2000, p. 34. There is increasing optimism about direct machine translation from one language to another. Steve Silberman, "Talking to Strangers," *Wired*, May, 2000, pp. 224–35. *Comdex* (fall) 2000 had a number of new combinations of phones, cameras, etc.

43 Walter Jäggi, "Mit der Mini Disc hat es angefangen," *Tages-Anzeiger*, 26 August 2003, p. 47.

44 In August, 2000, a Compaq Presario was available with large discounts at $247. In 2004, there are machines as low as $170: http://www.dealtime.com/xPP-Workstations – compaq-3365_128_mb_or_less. In October, 2001, a Compaq Pentium with a 810 MB hard drive was available for US$292.

45 sa.internet.com Staff, "Linux-based 'Simputer' Brings Low-Cost Tech to India,'" *Internet News*, 2 July 2001: http://www.internetnews.com/intl-news/article/0,,6_794851,00.html.

46 Simputer: http://www.simputer.org/. For commercial product launched 26 April 2004: http://www.amidasimputer.com/. For press: http://www.simputer.org/simputer/press/.

47 http://www.handspring.com. In April, 2000, a deluxe version cost $249: Felix Wiedler, Andreas Heer, "Neue Palm-Generation," *Tages-Anzeiger*, 10 March 2001, p. 60, describes Palm m500 and m505: http://www.pencomputing.com/palm/Reviews/visor1.html.

48 Robert X. Cringely, "The $15 PC. Computing is about to enter a hardware revolution that will change the world as we know it,"I,*Cringely* ,18 January 2001: http://www.pbs.org/cringely/pulpit/pulpit20010118.html; Robert X. Cringely, May, 2004, "The Little Engine That Could. How Linux is Inadvertently Poised to Remake the Telephone and Internet Markets": "One of the cheapest Linux computers you can buy brand new (not at a garage sale) is the Linksys WRT54G, an 802.11g wireless access point and router that includes a four-port 10/100 Ethernet switch and can be bought for as little as $69.99 according to Froogle." From the *CA Net Newsletter*, 27 May 2004: http://www.canarie.ca/canet4/library/list.html, who say thanks to Samuel K. Lam for this pointer and cite: http://www.pbs.org/cringely/pulpit/pulpit20040527.html. Cf. Rolltronics: http://www.rolltronics.com/.

49 Personal communication in October, 1999, with John Gage, then Chief Scientist, Sun Microsystems.

50 Edward Cone, "Computers Real Cheap," *Wired*, April, 2000, pp. 218–25. Re: the ideas of Jim Willard.

51 *The State of the Japanese Market* 2000, *Digest*, Tokyo: Impress, 2000, p. 59; Michael Marriott, "Merging TV With the Internet," *The New York Times*, 28 September 2000.

52 These devices include Compuscan, Hendrix and Dest, the Kurzweil Intelligent Scanning System and the Calera Compound Document Processor; "From Books to the Web. The On-line OCR Lab,": (formerly) http://onix.com/tonymck/ocrlab.htm.

53 Claude Settele, "Jedes buch, jederzeit, überall," *NZZ am Sonntag*, 12 May 2002, p. 101; Robert H. Thibadeau, „The Universal Library", Robotics Institute, Carnegie Mellon University: http://www.ri.cmu.edu/projects/project_325.html.

54 Go to site and type in C-Pen: www.ehag.ch; Peter Zeehunke, "Digitaler Allesmerker für unterwegs," *Tages-Anzeiger*, 7 February 2000, p. 65. The Anoto pen that is not a scanner: http://www.anoto.com/.

55 Hexaglot: http://www.hexaglot.de; Sylvie Gardel, "Grace à des Suisses, le stylo intelligent augmentera son Q.I.," *Le Courrier*, 18 October 2000 re: a pen at the CSEM in Neuchatel.

56 Annotea Project: http://www.w3.org/2001/Annotea. Closely connected is the rediscovery of writing pads as a communication tool described by Felix Wiedler, "Der wieder endeckte Papierblock," *Tages-Anzeiger*, 22 January 2001, p. 57.

57 http://youscan.ch/.

58 Such tablet PCs are being developed by Compaq, Toshiba, Fujitsu-Siemens, Hitachi, and Samsung. Bert Keely, "Das Comeback der Schiefertafel," *Tages-Anzeiger*, 20 November 2000, p. 67. More dramatic possibilities would involve linking this with so-called magic books and augmented reality techniques as championed by Brett Shelton (HIT Lab, University of Washington) or Mark Billinghurst (HIT Lab NZ): http://www.hitlabnz.org/.

59 Examples of encyclopaedias already on-line include the Britannica and Zedlers Universal Lexikon: http://mdz.bib-bvb.de/digbib/lexika/zedler/. One of the most important amateur sites in the direction of a virtual reference room is at refdesk.com: http://www.refdesk.com/.

60 George A. Chidi Jr., "AT&T Releases 'Realistic' Voice Software. AT&T Corp. says new voice software is "the most human-sounding computer-speech system in the world." *IDG News*

Service, Tuesday, 31 July 2001: http://www.pcworld.com/news/article/0,aid,56604,tk,dn0731 01X,00.asp.

61 There are numerous situations where speech cannot be used or where it is ineffective, e.g., in cases where one is working in a foreign language and unfamiliar with pronunciation patterns.

62 Bryan Walpert, "E-prescribing: nascent industry or uncertain future?" *American College of Physicians-American Society of Internal Medicine*, 2002: http://www.acponline.org/journals/handhelds/ nov02/e-scripts.htm; Louis J. Carpenito, "Taking Prescriptions from the Pad to PDA," *Symantec, Healthcare*, 17 February 2004: http://enterprisesecurity.symantec.com/industry/healthcare/ article.cfm?articleid=3323&EID=0.

63 Michelle Delio, "Doctor's Guide: Its in the Eyes," *Wired News*, 3 April 2001: http:// www.wired.com/news/technology/0,1282,42783,00.html?tw=wn20010403.

64 Steve Silberman, "The Hot New Medium: Paper," *Wired*, April, 2001, pp. 184–91.

65 "New Free Toilet Paper with Banner Ads," *Future Feed Forward*, 13 December 2013 [*sic*. Almost certainly a typo for 2003]: http://futurefeedforward.com/front.php?fid=35.

66 Simone Luchetta, "Bildschirm rollen und einpacken," *Tages-Anzeiger*, 28 April 2003, p. 57.

67 Gurunet: http://www.gurunet.com/.

68 According to Jef Raskin (note 19 February 2001): "The last model of the Canon Cat (1987) and the Swyft portable (of the same year) had every word hyperlinking. They had a dedicated 'hyperlink' key (with the word 'hyperleap' on it!) and you selected any word or phrase and hit the key to find what it linked to." Jeffrey Harrow, *The Rapidly Changing Face of Computing*, 13 September 1999 at: http://www.compaq.com/rcfoc: "For example, imagine if you could do a special 'tap' on a word displayed on your Epaper and immediately be whisked to relevant information about it. 'No big deal,' you're probably thinking, 'that's just another hyperlink, which already drives the Web.' But in this case, I'm talking about tapping on words that have NOT been previously hyperlinked. For example, I just ALT-clicked on the word 'Cambridge' a few paragraphs above (OK, I had to click, but I'm using a PC, not a book of Epaper) and a window popped up telling me that it was settled in 1630, it's first name was New Towne, and it has a population of about 96,000. Where did this come from? Brought to our attention by RCFoC reader Jack Gormley, a new free service on the Web called GuruNetmakes a stab at turning EVERY word on your screen, not just those in a Web browser, into a 'live' link to further information. With their software installed, ALT-clicking on any word quickly evokes a response from their server, which has licensed numerous reference works to provide more focused, deeper insight than you might get from a search engine. I've only just begun to explore GuruNet, and it is in beta, but it's an interesting concept. And hey, while it didn't directly know what to do with 'RCFoC,' when it drew a blank it offered to feed the mystery word to a search engine, which in this case came back with 487 references. Not too bad. Now try that with an Industrial Age paper book – which gives us an idea of why the day might really come when we can't imagine a 'non-active' book."

69 Ebooks.com: http://www.ebooks.com/. IBM has a new notepad linked with a computer. Cf. Felix Wiedler, "Der wieder entdeckte Papierblock," *Tages-Anzeiger*, 22 January 2001, p. 57; Ruth Wilson, "The Evolution of Portable Electronic Books," *Ariadne*, October, 2001: http: //www.ariadne.ac.uk/issue29/wilson/.

70 Jim Nagel, "Newspad makes El Periodico Interactive," *Byte*, February, 1997: http:// www.byte.com/art/9702/sec17/art2.htm.

71 Softbook was taken over by Gemstar eBook: http://www.gemstar-ebook.com/cgi-bin/ WebObjects/eBookstore.woa/wa/.

72 Rocket Book: http://www.rocket-ebook.com/Products/index.html.

73 On 18 June 2003, Gemstar decided it would stop its ebook plans. "A very important ebook announcement,": http://www.literaturcafe.de/bf.htm?/ebook/byeeboo3.shtml.

74 Chisato Numaoka, "Cyberglass: Vision-Based VRML2 Navigator," *Virtual Worlds*, Jean-Claude Heudin, ed., Berlin: Springer Verlag, 1998. Cf. Apple i.book: http://www.informatik.uni-trier. de/~ley/db/conf/vw/vw1998.html; Kevin Bonsor, "How Power Paper will Work," *How Stuff Works*: http://www.howstuffworks.com/power-paper.htm; http://www.powerpaper.com/.

75 The Adobe ebook reader has since been merged with the Adobe Reader: http://www.adobe.com/products/acrobat/readstep2.html.

76 This has been renamed the Microsoft Reader: http://www.microsoft.com/reader/.

77 James Evans, "E Ink demos first active matrix electronic ink display," *IDG News Service*/Boston Bureau, 10 April 2001. E Ink's partners include IBM, Lucent Technologies Inc., Motorola Inc., Royal Philips Electronics NV, and Hearst Corp. E Ink can be reached at http://www.eink.com/. Another company is Gyricon Media: "E-paper moving closer," *BBC News*, 8 September 2001: http://news.bbc.co.uk/hi/english/sci/tech/newsid_1530000/1530678.stm.

78 Paul Kunkel, "News flash," *Wired*, August, 2000, pp. 138–47. The companies include IBM, Lucent, and Xerox in conjunction with 3M and Philips. By 2000, this attracted the AT&T Wireless, Avanco, and Peanut Press, a division of the e-book venture, Netlibrary, to join together with a series of major newspaper publishers including the Wall Street Journal, Time, Havas, Central Newspapers and the Gruppo Espresso. There is also an Open e-book (OEB) Forum: http://www.openebook.org. A development from Sun LOCKSS (Lots of Copies Keeps Stuff Safe) is an open source, JavaTM and Linux-based distributed system, which: "permanently caches copies of on-line content – enough copies to assure access around the world in case publishers fold or no longer support user access. So when an issue of an on-line journal is misplaced or damaged, LOCKSS takes notice and replaces it." (Cf. the official LOCKSS site: http://lockss.stanford.edu/).

79 Steven K. Feiner web site: http://www.cs.columbia.edu/~feiner. Augmented Reality: http://www.se.rit.edu/~jrv/research/ar/.

80 William Mitchell, *E-topia*, Cambridge, MA: MIT Press, 1999, p. 158.

81 Cited from Jeffrey R. Harrow, *The Rapidly Changing Face of Computing*, 18 October 1999: "That's exactly what Benefon has introduced at the recent Telecom 99 show. Brought to our attention by RCFoC reader Sean Wachob, this pocket GSM marvel will always know where it's at, and it will display moving maps so you know, too. It also provides 14.4 kilobits/second Internet access, and it offers 10 days of standby time (although I haven't seen what using the GPS receiver does to battery life),": http://www.benefon.com/.

82 "Curiously, around 2033, the general availability of several machines, most notably the 'molecular computer (molecomp),' the 'portable petabit satellite modem (PPSM),' and the 'binaural optical implant logic (BOIL),' enabled the technological phase called Convergence to come to full fruition. This started a new cultural paradigm shift, where the population in developed countries (which shifted from 90 per cent rural to 90 per cent urban in the Industrial Revolution) began a precipitous move back to 90 per cent rural, now that vocational and cultural and other social gatherings were no longer tied to central physical locations! The world's populations had returned to 90 per cent rural by 2055, in a single generation." Cited by Jeffery Harrow, *The Rapidly Changing Face of Computing*, 9 April 2001: http://www.theharrowgroup.com/.

83 The objects were arranged in classes governed by parent-child relationships defined as inheritance. As programmers introduced further characteristics such as behaviours and autonomy, inheritance became a problem. Active objects provided an interim solution, until one turned to the concept of agents.

84 In terms of multiple libraries, this process is presently being carried out through collation programs in the context of international projects such as the Research Libraries Information Network (RLIN), the Online Computer Library Network (OCLC), the On-Line Public Access Network for Europe (ONE) and the Gateway to European National Libraries (GABRIEL). In future, collation of the combined holdings of these international databanks of library holdings could be performed by agents.

85 See Appendix 8 for standard literature. Even so, it is striking that when it comes to specific issues there is much uncertainty as witnessed by the DTI/DCMS Communications White Paper: *A New Future for Communications*, London, 2001 re: BBC: http://www.communicationswhitepaper.gov.uk.

86 Bruce Crumley and Thomas Sancton, "Master of the Universe," *Time Magazine*, 6 August 2001, pp. 36–43. Recently, there have been doubts about such mergers: Bruce Orwall, "The Message

of Media Mergers: So Far, They Haven't Been Hit," *The Wall Street Journal*, Friday, 10 May 2002, pp. A1, A5.

Chapter 3: Miniaturization

1   Ray Kurzweil, *The Age of Spiritual Machines*, New York: Penguin, 1999, p. 280. A darker view has been given by Bill Joy (SUN) in a paper, "Why the Future doesn't need us," *Wired*, April, 2000: http://www.wired.com/wired/archive/8.04/joy.html.

2   "DNA robot takes its first steps," *New Scientist*, 6 May 2004: http://www.newscientist.com/news/news.jsp?id=ns99994958.

3   R. Colin Johnson, "Molecular substitution produces terahertz switch arrays," *EE Times*, 10 April 2000: http://www.eetimes.com/story/OEG20000410S0057.

4   Andrew Leonard, "As the MEMS Revolution Takes Off: Small is Getting Bigger every day," *Wired*, January, 2000, pp. 162–64www.mdl.sandia.gov/micromachine Go to http://www.mdl.sandia.gov/. Then look under technologies under micromachines. www.microsensors.com; cf.: www.bell-labs.com/org/physicalsciences/projects/mems/mems.html. Michael Roukes, "Nanoelectromechanical systems face the future," *Physics World*, vol. 14, no. 2, February, 2001: http://physicsweb.org/article/world/14/2/8.

5   Rick Overton, "Molecular electronics will change everything," *Wired*, July, 2000, pp. 140–51. More detailed is David Rotman, "Molecular Computing," *Tech Review*, May–June, 2000. Cf. Jason Bryant and Richard Overstreet, Molecular Computing: http://www.nhn.ou.edu/~johnson/Education/Juniorlab/Presentations.

6   Joe Strout, "Mind Uploading Home page": http://www.ibiblio.org/jstrout/uploading/MUHomePage.html.

7   http://www.mitre.org/research/nanotech/futurenano.html. World Wide Nanoelectronics Researchhttp://www.mitre.org/tech/nanotech/worldnano.html best reached via their nanotechnologies home page (http://www.mitre.org/tech/nanotech/) then Introduction and then Proposed technologies.

8   Quantum Nanocomputers: http://www.mitre.org/tech/nanotech/quantum.html.

9   Quantum dot cellular automata home page: http://www.nd.edu/~qcahome/.

10 Marya Lieberman, Surface and Materials Chemistry: http://www.nd.edu/~mlieberm/. "Quantum-dot cellular automata (QCA) are a completely new architecture for computation. Information is transmitted between QCA cells through Coulomb interactions; depending on the arrangement of the cells, bits can be transmitted, inverted, or processed with logic operations (AND, OR). Information processing does not require the flow of current, so QCA has the potential for extremely low power dissipation…. Switching the cell depends not on voltage gating of a current (as transistors do) but on this tunneling process; thus, the device performance is expected to improve the smaller the QCA cells can be made, with the ultimate size limit being molecular QCA cells…. Classical inorganic coordination chemistry is our main tool for the synthetic work…. Both ultra-high vacuum scanning tunneling microscopy and X-ray photoelectron spectroscopy will be employed to characterize model compounds and molecular QCA cells on the surface of silicon wafers." Cf. QCA home page: http://www.nd.edu/~lent/Qcahome.htm.

11 Karen Peart, "Yale Research Team First to Describe Molecular-Sized Memory – Discovery has Implications for Drastically Reducing Cost of Computer Memory," *Yale News Release*, 1 November 1999: http://www.yale.edu/opa/newsr/99-11-02-01.all.html; Walter Frese, "Physiker und Biochemiker ziehen molekulare Fäden," *Max Planck Forschung*, München, 3, 2000, pp. 26–31.

12 California Molecular Electronics Corp. (Calmec): http://www.calmec.com/chiropticene.htm.

13 Charles Mandel, "Getting a Line on Nanochips," *Wired News*, 10 August 2000: http://www.wired.com/news/print/0,1294,37923,00.html.

14 Bacteriorhodopsin Optical Memory: http://www.fourmilab.ch/autofile/www/section2_84_18 .html#SECTION00841800000000000000.

15 R. Birge, "Protein-Based Computers." *Scientific American*, vol. 272, no. 3, March, 1995, pp. 90–95.

16 Engeneos: http://www.engeneos.com/. See http://www.nanovip.com/directory/ Detailed/329.php.

17 Reported by Jeffrey Harrow, *RCFoC*, 11 June 2001: http://www.theharrowgroup.com/.

18 Cf. Olivier Dessibourg, "Des Ordinateurs qui carburent à l'AND," *Le Courrier*, 17 October 2000, p. 16.

19 The story is in Kristi Coale and John Gilles, "The Future of Silicon may be Carbon," *Wired News*, 19 February 1997: http://www.wired.com/news/news/technology/story/2132.html.

20 For further information concerning Animesh Ray's work on Molecular Computation: http: //fano.ics.uci.edu/cites/Author/Animesh-Ray.html.

21 Thomas A. Bass, "Gene Genie," *Wired Magazine*, August, 1995: http://www.thomasbass.com/ work12.htm.

22 Molecular Computing under M. Ogihara at Rochester: http://www.cs.rochester.edu/u/www/ users/faculty/ogihara/research/DNA/dna.html; Gheorghe Paun, Grzegorz Rozenberg, Arto Salomaa, and W. Brauer, eds., *DNA Computing: New Computing Paradigms*, Heidelberg: Springer Verlag, 1998 (Texts in Theoretical Computer Science); Harvey Rubin and David Harlan Wood, ed., *DNA Based Computers III: Dimacs Workshop, June 16–18, 1997*, American Mathematical Society, 1999. (Dimacs Series in Discrete Mathematics and Theoretical Computer Science, vol. 48). The Center for Discrete Mathematics and Theoretical Computer Science (DIMACS) plays a significant role in the study of DNA computing: http://dimacs.rutgers.edu/SpecialYears/1994_1995/; C. S. Calude, John L. Casti, and M. J. Dineen, eds., *Unconventional Models of Computation*, Heidelberg: Springer Verlag, 1999. (Springer Series in Discrete Mathematics and Theoretical Computer Science).

23 Richard Lipton: http://www.cc.gatech.edu/computing/Theory/theory.html.

24 J. Bokor and Leon Chua, CNN Universal Chip, Berkeley Electronics Research Lab, 1997: http: //www.stormingmedia.us/97/9721/A972133.html.

25 Patrick Thiran, *Dynamics and Self-Organisation of Locally Coupled Neural Networks*, Presses Polytechniques et Universitaires Romandes, 1997: http://ppur.epfl.ch/livres/2-88074-351-6.html.

26 T. Roska and J. Vandewalle, eds., *Cellular Neural Networks*, New York: John Wiley & Sons, 1993; Gabriele Manganaro, Paolo Arena, and L. Fortuna, eds., *Cellular Neural Networks*, Heidelberg: Springer Verlag, 1998. (Advanced Microelectronics, vol. 1); Markus Christen, "Neurocomputer: Rechnen wie die Bienen," *Tages-Anzeiger*, 30 June 2000.

27 K. Eric. Drexler, *Nanosystems*, New York: John Wiley & Sons, 1992.

28 Joe Strout, "Hardware for Uploading": http://metalab.unc.edu/jstrout/uploading/ hardware.html. "Certain materials change their optical properties based on the light passing through them; that is, light changes the way they affect light. This allows us to build optical equivalents of transistors, the basic component of computers. In principle, an optical computer might be smaller and faster than an electronic one. But the chief advantage is that such a computer can pass signals through each other without interference, allowing for much higher component density."

29 Paul Benioff, *Journal of Statistical Physics*, vol. 22, 1980, p. 563, and *Journal of Statistical Physics*, vol. 29, 1982, p. 515.

30 David Deutsch, *Proceedings of the Royal Society*, London, Ser. A, vol. 425, 1989, p. 73.

31 Richard Feynman, *International Journal of Theoretical Physics*, vol. 21, 1982, p. 467. For an introduction, see Elmer Smalling III, *A Brief Overview Quantum Computing*, 1999: http://www.connect.net/smalling/ quantum1.htm. "In late 1993, Seth Lloyd described a general design for a quantum computer which could, in principle, actually be built. The computer consists of a cellular automaton-like array composed of quantum dots, nuclear spins, localized electronic states in a polymer, or any other multistate quantum system, which interacts with its neighbours. The units are switched from one state to another by pulses of coherent light, and read in an analogous manner. Lloyd has shown that such a computer could perform both as a parallel digital computer, and as a

quantum computer in which (for example) bits can be placed in a superposition of 0 and 1 states. Technical difficulties in building such a computer include finding systems with long-lived localized quantum states, and delivering accurate pulses of light." C. Arthur, "The Quantum Computer – Too Weird for Einstein," *Computer News Daily, The Independent*, London, 20 April 1998 (formerly at: http://computernewsdaily.com/).

32 Jeffrey Harrow, *The Rapidly Changing Face of Computing*, 9 April 2001. "In the completely counterintuitive world of Quantum Computing, each atom can perform two calculations at the same time. So, a two-atom Quantum Computer can do four simultaneous calculations; three atoms can do eight calculations; four atoms can do sixteen; and so on. By the time you have ten atoms in your Quantum Computer, it can perform 1,024 (that's 2 to the tenth power) simultaneous calculations. Extend that to a Quantum Computer with a mere 40 atoms, and it could perform ten trillion calculations – at the same time! Dump even more atoms into your Quantum Computer, and just about any calculation that demands huge amounts of computing power (such as global weather forecasting and, yes, breaking encryption codes by factoring numbers far too large for traditional computers) might become as trivial as using your pocket calculator to take a square root."

33 Aaron Ricadela, "HP Reports A Nanotech Breakthrough," *Information Week*, 1 February 2005: http://informationweek.com/story/showArticle.jhtml?articleID=59300089.

34 IBM Almaden Research Center, "Quantum mirage may enable atom-scale circuits," 3 February 2000: http://www.almaden.ibm.com/almaden/media/mirage.html.

35 Felix T. Hong, "Bacteriorhodopsin as an Intelligent Material: A Nontechnical Summary," *The Sixth Newsletter of Molecular Electronics and BioComputing. A Journal of a Multi- and Interdisciplinary Society*. This paper was solicited by the American Chemical Society News Service and related to Paper 52, Division of Biochemical Technology, Symposium on Molecular and Biomolecular Electronics, at the 4th Chemical Congress of North America/American Chemical Society 202nd National Meeting and Exposition/ 27th National Meeting of Sociedad Quimica de Mexico, 25–30 August 1991, New York City. See: http://www.vxm.com/21R.58.html. "Richard Needleman at the Department of Biochemistry, Wayne State University, recently developed a new expression system for the purpose of engineering mutants of bacteriorhodopsin. Preliminary results showed that by changing the genetic code of one out of 248 amino acid units, the pigment changes its electrical characteristics and photonic characteristics dramatically. This raises the hope of breeding mutants with the right type of intelligence for the intended design of the molecular device. The development of intelligent materials is in keeping with the goal of miniaturization at the nanometre scale (one nanometre = one billionth of a metre) (nanotechnology). For example, by allowing sensor/processor/ actuator capabilities to be packaged into a single molecule or a supramolecular cluster, avenues are open in the design of integrated information processing systems with massively parallel distributed processing capabilities. Thus, the progress made in the research of intelligent materials will pave the road towards the development of novel information processing systems so as to overcome the much-dreaded 'von Neumann bottleneck' that characterizes conventional computers."

36 Dr Michael Groß, *Travels to the Nanoworld*, New York: Plenum, 1999. Also Appendix 8 under nanotechnology. (Formerly at: http://nmra.ocms.ox.ac.uk/~mgross/nanointr.html). "We are talking about complicated and highly efficient machines, which are only allowed a few millionths of a millimetre in size. Unbelievable? Not at all, for evolution has solved these problems more than a billion years ago. The motor mentioned above exists already – it is a system mainly consisting of the proteins actin and myosin, and is known to power our muscles. The data store, also known as a chromosome (i.e., a very long stretch of DNA wound up in a complicated way), determines our genetic identity. Nature's nanotechnology relies on long, chain-like molecules, fabricated from a small set of building blocks. The whole management of genetic data is based on an alphabet of just four letters. Most functions of a living cell are performed by proteins consisting of only 20 different amino acids. However, this simplicity is rather deceptive, as the combination of these building blocks to a long chain can happen in an

astronomical number of different ways. If we wanted to 'invent' a rather small protein with 100 amino acid residues, we would have the choice between 20100 (i.e., 10130, or a number with 131 digits) possibilities."

37 Rob Fixmer, "Merging of Man and Machine. Challenges Natural Selection. Technology grows toward a global nervous system," *New York Times*. From the *San Francisco Chronicle*, Friday, 14 August 1998. For evidence of implants in monkeys, Sandra Blakeslee, "In pioneering study, monkey think, robot do," *New York Times*, 13 October 2003: http://www.wireheading.com/brainstim/thoughtcontrol.html.

38 National Nanofabrication Users Network: http://www.nnun.org/.

39 Nanotechnology Industries. Medical Links: http://www.nanoindustries.com/

40 Smart Dust: http://robotics.eecs.berkeley.edu:80/~pister/SmartDust/.

41 CBBC Newsround | SCI TECH | "Brain-controlled video game made," Updated 5 March 2004: http://news.bbc.co.uk/cbbcnews/hi/sci_tech/newsid_3525000/3525487.stm.

42 Foresight Institute: http://www.foresight.org/.

43 Vision Control Systems. The National Research Council of Canada is developing Perceptual Interface Technologies, which allow one to use one's nose as a mouse: http://www.cv.iit.nrc.ca/research/Nouse/publication.html and http://perceptual-vision.com/index_e.html.

44 Trace Center: http://trace.wisc.edu.

45 ICDRI (International Center for Disability Resources on the Internet): http://www.icdri.org/.

46 Interaction Design Lab at the UNC School of Library and Information Sciences: http://idl.ils.unc.edu/newidl/index.php?module=pagemaster&PAGE_user_op=view_page&PAGE_id=4&MMN_position=9:9.

47 This is linked with the Global Education Network: http://gen.com. Cf. also two Esprit Preparatory Measures:
22603–C2 : Connected Community (Augmented reality)
Irene McWilliam, Philips Corporate Design, Eindhoven now Director, Royal College of Art (London).
22642: Inhabited Spaces for Community (INSCAPE) Academy, Polity and Economy
Prof. Yngve Sundblad, Royal Institute of Technology
Dept. of Numerical Analysis and Computing Science, Valhallavägen 79, S–100 44 Stockholm
On Inhabited Information Spaces: http://www.nada.kth.se/inscape/.

48 Reality fusion: http://www.realityfusion.com/, now Santa Cruz Networks: http://www.santacruznetworks.com/about_management.html.

49 E.g., IBM or Lernhout and Hauspie, which acquired Dragon Systems, one of the pioneers in the field, and which have now been integrated into Scansoft: http://www.lhsl.com/.

50 Elemedia is now part of a startup called Agora Labs: http://www.agoralabs.com/.

51 David House: http://www.speech.kth.se/~davidh/.

52 SPRACH (Speech Recognition Algroithms for Connectionist Hybrids): http://tcts.fpms.ac.be/asr/project/sprach/technical-annex/sprach.html.

53 Geoffrey Rowan, "Computers that recognize your smile," *Globe and Mail*, Toronto, 24 November 1997, p. B3.

54 Jakub Segen is the founder of Dialog Table: http://dialogtable.com/; Jakub Segen (Bell Labs), "Vision Based Interfaces for Digital Theatre, Music and Virtual Reality,": http://ruccs.rutgers.edu/talks/speaker/VisionTalkDec042000Segen.html.

55 Formerly at http://www.cs.uchicago.edu/~swain/pubs/HTML/CVPR96-Perseus/.

56 Summary of CHI'95 *Gesture at the User Interface* Workshop: http://wex.www.media.mit.edu/people/wex/CHI95-workshop-writeup.html#Maggioni.

57 Machine Gesture and Sign Language Recognition: http://www.cse.unsw.edu.au/~waleed/gsl-rec/#conferences.

58 Gesture Recognition (tools): http://vision.ai.uiuc.edu/mhyang/gesture.html.

59 On gesture and movement see Cyberstar project at Fraunhofer: http://maus.gmd.de/imk_web-pre2000/docs/ww/mars/proj1_4.mhtml; http://www.asel.udel.edu/.

60 Axel Mulder's home page: http://www.cs.sfu.ca/cs/people/ResearchStaff/amulder/ cf. *Models for Sound in Human-Computer and Human-Environment Interaction*. National project funded by MIUR (Cofin 2000): http://www.dei.unipd.it/ricerca/csc/research_groups/cofin2000.html.

61 COGAIN: http://www.cogain.org.

62 Internationale Stiftung Neurobionik, Director: Professor Dr. Madjid Samii: http://www.neurobionik-stiftung.de/intro.html.

63 "Remote Control System uses Brain Waves," CNN *Interactive*, 25 December 1997: http://www.cnn.com/TECH/9712/25/remote.control.ap/; Michael Kesterton, "All in the mind?" *Globe and Mail*, Toronto, 6 January 1998, p. A14. On the Mind Control Operating System (MCTOS): http://members.aol.com/grpals3/page/MCTOS.htm.

64 Adaptive Brain Interfaces (ABI): http://sir.jrc.it/abi/. Yahoo News reported: "Scientists Developing Mind-Controlled Wheelchair," 23 July 2003. For related work by Guger Technologies: www.gtec.at .

65 Michael I. Posner, ed., *Foundations of Cognitive Science*, Cambridge, MA: MIT Press, 1989, p. 305.

66 Frank Beacham, "Mental telepathy makes headway in cyberspace," *Now*, Toronto, 13–19 July 1997, pp. 20–21.

67 Pat McKenna, "Look Ma No Hands", US Airforce, February 1996: http://www.af.mil/news/airman/0296/look.htm.

68 Bennett Daviss, "Brain Powered," *Discover*, May, 1994, p. 60. A conservative estimate of such developments was provided in: "Professional Military Education in 2020," *Airpower Journal*, Summer 1995: http://www.airpower.maxwell.af.mil/airchronicles/apj/pme2020.html#10. There is more recent work at the Donoghue lab: http://donoghue.neuro.brown.edu/publications.php.

69 Steven Bonisteel, "Bell Labs predicts a 'Global Communications Skin' by 2025," *Newsbytes*, 12 November 1999. Reported by Dr. Anne Tyrie in CITO *Link-Line*, 22 November 1999.

70 Michael Mechanic, "Beastly Implants," *Metro Active*, Santa Cruz, 5–11 December 1996: http://www.metroactive.com/papers/cruz/12.05.96/implants-9649.html.

71 Mike Maher's home page: http://www.neuro.gatech.edu/groups/potter/mike.html. Steve Potter, in whose lab Maher worked, has moved his lab to Georgia Tech: http://www.neuro.gatech.edu/groups/potter/potter.html.

72 Michael Mechanic, "Beastly Implants," *Metro Active*, Santa Cruz, 5–11 December 1996: http://www.metroactive.com/papers/cruz/12.05.96/implants-9649.html. For an excellent introduction to work in this field done over the past century: "Telemetry is Coming of Age." Courtesy of Kathy Kasten. Based on: Dean C. Jutter, "Telemetry is Coming of Age," *Engineering in Medicine and Biology Magazine*, March, 1983: http://www.raven1.net/telem1.htm.

73 Christopher Bowe, "Medtronic shows off future of healthcare," *Financial Times*, 8 February 2002, p. 22. A query on implantable device revealed 101 hits on 27 February 2002 and 212,000 on 11 January 2004. An article entitled "Implants," http://www.geocities.com/skews_me/implants.html, provides a brief survey of the early history of this field: "In 1870, two German researchers named [Eduard] Hitzig and [Gustav] Fritsch electrically stimulated the brains of dogs, demonstrating that certain portions of the brain were the centers of motor function. The American Dr. Robert Bartholow, within four years, demonstrated that the same was true of human beings. By the turn of the [twentieth] century in Germany Fedor Krause was able to do a systematic electrical mapping of the human brain, using conscious patients undergoing brain surgery [Morgan, James P., 'The First Reported Case of Electrical Stimulation of the Human Brain,' *Journal of History of Medicine* at http://www3.oup.co.uk/jalsci/scope/; M. Zimmerman, 'Electrical Stimulation of the Human Brain,' *Human Neurobiology*, 1982]. At a more immediate level children in Japan have RFID implants in their schoolbags and there are trends to barcode humans through Applied Digital Solutions in Florida: Helen Brandwell, "May I scan the barcode in your arm please," *Globe and Mail*, 14 October 2004, p. A19.

74 A Brief Sketch of the Brain: http://metalab.unc.edu/jstrout/uploading/brainfacts.html.

75 Michael S. Gazzaniga, *The New Cognitive Neurosciences*, Cambridge, MA: MIT Press, 1999.

76 WWW Virtual Library Neroscience (Bioscience): http://neuro.med.cornell.edu/VL/.

77 Duke University. Center for Cognitive Neuroscience: http://www.mind.duke.edu/.

78 Center for Cognitive Neuroscience (CCN), Dartmouth College: http://ccn.dartmouth.edu/.

79 Society for Neurosciences: http://www.sfn.org/.

80 Cognitive Neuroscience Society: http://www.cogneurosociety.org/.

81 The Organization for Human Brain Mapping: http://www.humanbrainmapping.org/.

82 Website for Recent Neuroscience (WREN): http://www.sfn.org/wren/.

83 Neurosciences on the Internet <Neuroguide.com>: http://ilsebill.biologie.uni-freiburg.de/neuromirror/.

84 Computation and Neural Systems (CNS): http://www.cns.caltech.edu/.

85 Ibid.: http://www.cns.caltech.edu/.

86 Ibid.

87 Human Brain Project: http://www.gg.caltech.edu/hbp/. For Genesis Neural database and Modeler's Workspace: http://www.genesis-sim.org/hbp/.

88 GENESIS: http://www.genesis-sim.org/GENESIS/. What is Genesis?: http://www.genesis-sim.org/GENESIS/whatisit.html "a general purpose simulation platform which was developed to support the simulation of neural systems ranging from complex models of single neurons to simulations of large networks made up of more abstract neuronal components. GENESIS has provided the basis for laboratory courses in neural simulation at both Caltech and the Marine Biological Laboratory in Woods Hole, MA, as well as many other institutions. Most current GENESIS applications involve realistic simulations of biological neural systems. Although the software can also model more abstract networks, other simulators are more suitable for backpropagation and similar connectionist modeling."

89 Future Fantastic: "Sci/Tech. Future Fantastic, Future Frightening." BBC News, 9 November 1999: http://news.bbc.co.uk/1/hi/sci/tech/505022.stm. On Richard Normann's lab: Sight Restoration for Individuals with Profound Blindness: http://www.bioen.utah.edu/cni/projects/blindness.htm. Dr. Christopher Gallen was at the Pennsylvania Neurological Institute, University of Pennsylvania, which had a section on augmentative/alternative communication: (formerly) www.cse.uconn.edu/~eugene/classes/cse282/ Presentations-Fa-03/Cyberware.ppt. For a useful introduction to Cyberware/Brain Implants: (formerly) www.cse.uconn.edu/~eugene/classes/cse282/ Presentations-Fa-03/Cyberware.ppt; "Brain implant devices approved for trials," CNN.com Health, Thursday, 15 April 2004; http://www.lasierra.edu/wwwboard/messages/1879/2299.html?WednesdayApril1420040912pm; Cyberkinetics Inc.: http://www.cyberkineticsinc.com/.

90 Hugh H. Lusted and R. Benjamin Knapp, "Controlling Computers with Neural Signals," Scientific American, October, 1996, pp. 82–87: http://www.absoluterealtime.com/resume/SciAmBioCtl.pdf.

91 Human Systems Information Analysis Center (HSIAC): http://iac.dtic.mil/hsiac/. This used to be Crew Systems Ergonomics Information Analysis Center (CSERIAC); The Human Performance Center Spider on Human Systems Integration (HIS) Resources: http://www.ott.navy.mil/index.cfm?RID=WEB_OT_1000435.

92 Formerly at http://www.al.wpafb.af.mil/cfb/biocomm.htm. Also at Wright Patterson Airforce Base is Dr. Grant McMillan. Cheryl Walsh, in an article on Nonconsensual Brainwave and Personality (http://www.davidicke.net/mindcontrol/research/re073001d.html), cites The Houston Chronicle, "Brainpower," 16 February 1995: Excerpt: "'Brain-actuated control' is under development at the Dayton, Ohio, base to help pilots deal with the increasing amount of information needed to fly modern jets, said Grant McMillan, director of Patterson's biocybernetics lab. Eventually, pilots may be able to control flight using only their minds, he added. With biofeedback, in which changes in the brain are portrayed on screens, volunteers learn how to control the electrical activity created by their thought processes. Scalp monitors pick up the electrical signals, and a computer translates them into mechanical commands." On Dr. John P.

Donoghue: Andrew Pollack, "With Tiny Brain Implants, Just Thinking May Make It So," *New York Times*, 13 April 2004: http://209.157.64.200/focus/f-news/1116428/posts.

93   William Ickes, *Empathic Accuracy*, New York: Guilford Publications, 1997: http://www.guilford.com/sapp/ickes.htm.

94   Kevin Warwick, "Cyborg 1.0," *Wired*, February, 1999, pp. 145–51;
Kevin Warwick's home page: http://www.kevinwarwick.org/.

95   Nicholas Morehead, "Hey Computer Read my Mind," *Wired News*, 15 November 2000: http://www.wired.com/news/business/0,1367,40194,00.html?tw=wn20001115.

96   Margie Wylie, "A new memory chip – for the brain," CNet news, 18 July 1996: http://news.com.com/2100-1001-218102.html?legacy=cnet.

97   Review by Gareth Branwyn, "The Machines Take Over: War in the Age of the Intelligent Machine," *Wired*, Premier Issue 1993, p. 84. For further information on Manuel de Landa: "Virtual Environments and the emergence of synthetic reason,": http://www.t0.or.at/delanda/delanda.htm; "Economics, Computers and the War Machine,": http://www.t0.or.at/delanda/; John Arquilla and David Ronfeldt, "Fighting the Network War," *Wired*, December, 2001, pp. 148–55. Michael Behar, "The New Mobile Infantry: Battle-ready robots are rolling out of the research lab and into harm's way."*Wired*, 10 May 2002: http://www.wired.com/wired/archive/10.05/robots_pr.html. On wetware based on a novel by Rucker see Arthur Kroker, "RU wetware? Television as Cybernetics,"*theory.net*, 22 August 1993: http://www.ctheory.net/text_file.asp?pick=8. *Wetware*, edited by Geert Lovink and Rik Delhaas, Amsterdam: De Balie, 1991: http://www.wetware.suite.dk/wetware.htm. With respect to the military implications of nanotechnology, see the paper of a former graduate student: Mark Avrum Gubrud, "Nanotechnology and International Security," 1997, draft paper for a talk at Fifth Foresight Conference on Molecular Nanotechnology: www.foresight.org/Conferences/MNT05/Papers/Gubrud/index.html.

98   LTC William B. Osborne (USA), Maj Scott A. Bethel, Maj Nolen R. Chew, Maj Philip M. Nostrand, and Maj YuLin G. Whitehead, *Information Operations: A New War-Fighting Capability: A Research Paper Presented to Air Force 2025*, 1996: http://www.fas.org/spp/military/docops/usaf/2025/v3c2/v3c2-1.htm#Contents.

99   Ibid. The Information section cites John L. Petersen, *The Road to 2015: Profiles of the Future*, Corte Madera, CA: Waite Group Press, 1994, p. 63: "The human-computer systems integration is a vital lead-in to the final technology area. Human systems and biotechnology offers the potential to create a seamless flow of information between human and computer. Mastering these technologies will allow users to select information for direct input into their brains.... Some significant progress already has been made in this area by the Stanford University research centre and their development of a nerve chip. It is an electronic interface for individual nerve cells to communicate with a computer. This human-machine linkage will … enhance human capability in many ways. If artificial eyes can convert video to nerve signals, won't it be possible to use the same technique to superimpose computer-generated information in front of one's field of view? The implanted microscopic brain chip performs two functions. First, it links the individual to the IIC [Information Integration Centre], creating a seamless interface between the user and the information resources (in-time collection data and archival databases). In essence, the chip relays the processed information from the IIC to the user. Second, the chip creates a computer-generated mental visualization based upon the user's request. The visualization encompasses the individual and allows the user to place himself into the selected battlespace. Cf. 2025 Concept, No. 200169," *2025 Concepts Database* (Maxwell Air Force Base, Alabama: Air War College/2025, 1996).

100   John L. Petersen, *The Road to 2015*, as in previous note; Adrien Michaels, "Breakthrough in artificial sight for the blind," *Financial Times*, 17 January 2000, p. 4; Steven Kotler, "Vision Quest," *Wired*, September, 2002, pp. 94–101.

101   *Visionary Manufacturing Challenges for 2020*. Grand Challenge 3. Conversion of Information to Knowledge: http://bob.nap.edu/readingroom/books/visionary/ch2.html#gc3.

102 Formerly at: http://www.trufax.org/reports/2020.html. It is interesting to note that two days after consulting this site on 22 November 1999 the material was no longer accessible. It is accessible under: Sightings sent to Rense.com by End of the Line: http://www.rense.com/political/weapons/ibm_impl.htm: "Federal regulations do not yet permit testing of implants on prisoners, but we have entered into contractual agreements with privatized health care professionals and specified correctional personnel to do limited testing of our products. We have also had major successes with privately owned sanitariums with implant technology. We need, however, to expand our testing to research how effective the 2020 neural chip implant performs in those identified as the most aggressive in our society. Limited testing has produced a number of results. In California, several prisoners were identified as members of the security threat group EME, or Mexican Mafia. They were brought to the health services unit at Pelican Bay and tranquilized with advanced sedatives developed by our Cambridge, Massachusetts laboratories. The implant procedure takes 60–90 minutes, depending upon the experience of the technician. We are working on a device which will reduce that time by as much as 60 per cent [30 min]. The results of implants on eight prisoners yielded the following results:

Implants served as surveillance devices to monitor threat group activity.

Implants disabled two subjects during an assault on correctional staff.

Universal side effects in all eight subjects revealed that when the implant was set to 116 Mhz, all subjects became lethargic and slept on an average of 18–22 hours per day.

All subjects refused recreation periods for 14 days during the 166 Mhz test evaluation.

Seven out of eight subjects did not exercise, in the cell or out of the cell, and five out of eight of the subjects refused showers up to three days at a time.

Each subject was monitored for aggressive activity during the test period and the findings are conclusive that seven out of eight subjects exhibited no aggression, even when provoked.

Each subject experienced only minor bleeding from the nose and ears 48 hours after the implant due to initial adjustment.

Each subject had no knowledge of the implant for the test period and each implant was retrieved under the guise of medical treatment."

This site links the projects with:

INTELLI-CONNECTION A Security Division of IBM.

1200 Progress Way

Armonk, New York 11204

LIMITED DISTRIBUTION ONLY

LEVEL 9 COMMUNICATION

2020 NEURAL CHIP IMPLANT

Cf. a copy at Earth OPS Central under the title Technological Implants for Human Control linked with the name David Tilbury, SUN, UK forwards from ISCNI Flash: http://earthops.org/implant.html. It is also on the site of Kathy Kasten, kkasten@pathology.medsch.ucla.edu as: DOCUMENT 1. "The IBM 20/20 Neural Chip Designed for Monitoring Subjects," Date: Mon, 23 Sep 96 21:20:14 −0500: (formerly) http://members.tripod.com/~mdars/KKasten2.htm. An untitled site links to the above: (formerly) http://members.tripod.com/~mdars/1/resistance.html. This site also documents four IBM patents in the field, namely,

IBM Hearing Device: Patent 4877027

IBM Implant Transponder: Patents 5674288; 5626630 and 5526772

The web sites cited no longer work (formerly at:

http://patent.womplex.ibm.com/details?patent_number=4877027

http://patent.womplex.ibm.com/details?patent_number=5674288

http://patent.womplex.ibm.com/details?patent_number=5626630

http://patent.womplex.ibm.com/details?patent_number=5526772).

The U.S. Patent office records the above as follows:

Patent 5,674,288 Knapp et al., 7 October 1997: Implant with transponder marker to Lipo Matrix Inc.: http://patft.uspto.gov/netacgi/nph-Parser?u=/netahtml/srchnum.htm&Sect

1=PTO1&Sect2=HITOFF&p=1&r=1&l=50&f=G&d=PALL&s1=5674288.WKU.&OS=PN/
5674288&RS=PN/5674288.

Patent 5,626,630 Markowitz et al., 6 May 1997, Medical telemetry system using an implanted passive transponder to AEL Industries: http://patft.uspto.gov/netacgi/nph-Parser?u=/netahtml/srchnum.htm&Sect1=PTO1&Sect2=HITOFF&p=1&r=1&l=50&f=G&d=PALL&s1=5626630.WKU.&OS=PN/5626630&RS=PN/5626630.

Patent 5,526,772 Curkendall, 18 June 1996. Electronic identification tagging method for food-producing animals: http://patft.uspto.gov/netacgi/nph-Parser?Sect1=PTO2&Sect2=HITOFF&p=1&u=/netahtml/search-bool.html&r=8&f=G&l=50&col=AND&d=ptxt&s1=5526772&OS=5526772&RS=5526772. Although the U.S. Patent Office site does not officially link these patents with IBM, this detailed documentation from a series of sources suggest that this cannot simply be dismissed as a hoax. The earliest brain implants are said to go back to 1874: http://www.rense.com/general17/imp.htm.

103 Elizabeth Royte, "The Altered State", via Sharon Shea from: *New York Times Magazine*, 29 September 1996, p. 158; Website of Behavioral Neuroscience, Dr. Michael Persinger: http://laurentian.ca/neurosci/_people/Persinger.htm.

104 For a classification of some available technologies, see Eleanor White, P.Eng., "The State of Unclassified and Commercial Technology Capable of Some Electronic Mind Control Effects," 28 June 2001: www.raven1.net/uncom.htm. For a disturbing account of some historical examples, see an article by the former chief medical officer of Finland, Rauni-Leena Luukanen-Kilde, MD, "Microchip Implants, Mind Control, and Cybernetics,": http://www.conspiracyarchive.com/NWO/microchip_implants_mind_control.htm. (Go to basic site, then New World Order, then the article). For an article on total population control, go to the Educate Yourself site: educate-yourself.org/mc/mctotalcontrol12jul02.shtml. This is leading to new fields such as Psychotronics: mediamatrix.puissante.com/0f/b.htm. For work on psychotronic warfare, see Timothy L. Thomas, "The Mind Has No Firewall," *Parameters*, U.S. Army War College Quarterly, Spring, 1998, pp. 84–92: http://carlisle-www.army.mil/usawc/Parameters/98spring/thomas.htm; Robert C. Beck, B.E., D.Sc, "E.L.F. Infested Spaces. Extreme Low Frequency Magnetic Fields and EEG Entrainment. A Psychotronic Warfare Possibility?" *Preliminary Research Report*, September, 1977, edited 10 March 1978: www.elfis.net/elfol8/e8elfeeg1.htm.

105 Mind Control Forum: http://www.mindcontrolforums.com/.

106 Rev. Terry-ana Robinson, MC, "Global Mind Control Slated for Humanity by 2004 – The Next Revolutionary Battle will be Fought within Your Own DNA," *FourWinds10.com*, 21 January 2004: http://www.fourwinds10.com/news/06-health/E-mind-control/2004/06E-01-27-04-global-mind-control-by-2004.html.

107 "Mens verdrongen door technologie," *Spits*, 17 May 2000.

108 Joseph P. Stout, home page, then to Joe's Handy Page: http://www.strout.net/info/personal/.

109 For another approach to these problems, see Jan Amkreutz, *Digital Spirit: Minding the Future*, 1st Books Library, 2003: http://www.digeality.com/.

110 http://metalab.unc.edu/jstrout/uploading/artificialreality.html. "Artificial Reality": "Most people seem to assume that if you've scanned someone's mind into a computer, the natural thing to do is make an environment in the computer for the patient to live in. Though this is sometimes called 'virtual reality,' I prefer to use 'artificial reality' to avoid confusion with the current generation of immersion-interface for us biological (non-uploaded) folks."

111 http://metalab.unc.edu/jstrout/uploading/bodies.html: "Artificial Bodies": "The alternative to artificial reality is to build a mechanical body which carries the brain simulator around, just as our bodies carry around our brains now. The body would need to duplicate the senses and motor functions of a real human body if we want to minimize the patient's adjustment. Artificial bodies would no doubt be crude at first, with numbed senses and clumsy muscles, but if demand is high, technology is sure to improve. Rather than clunky metal robots such as the famous 'C-3P0' of Star Wars fame, artificial bodies will probably be made of smart polymers, ceramics, and other advanced materials. Note that as artificial bodies will probably run on some

sort of fuel cell or nuclear power source, eating will no longer be necessary. However, a properly designed body may still allow for the act of eating, for the pleasure of it. The same goes for other bodily functions (e.g., sex) – if there is demand for it, then artificial (or simulated) bodies will no doubt be capable of it."

112 http://metalab.unc.edu/jstrout/uploading/artifrealpolicy.html: "Policy of Artificial Realities": "Artificial realities present a host of policy issues. First, will citizenship (or even the rights of humans) be granted to those living in a computer simulation, with no physical bodies? It seems obvious that it should, but it will be a big step for governments to take. Another possibility is that the government may actually require some patients to enter an artificial reality under some circumstances. For example, patients who cannot afford the uploading procedure may be uploaded by the government into artificial realities, which will no doubt be cheaper on the large scale than manufactured bodies. Another possibility would be to upload convicted criminals into a 'prison box' – an artificial reality safely insulated from the rest of society. Finally, artificial reality poses a real threat of abuse. A programmer of such a system would have nearly godlike power over its inhabitants, and 'god syndromes' would be a chilling possibility. To prevent the abuse of uploaded people, careful safeguards will have to be put into place."

113 http://metalab.unc.edu/jstrout/uploading/enhancements.html. "Once the brain is in an artificial form, it will be much easier to modify it. Assuming a good understanding of our neural circuitry, a number of enhancements and deletions will be possible. These will strain the definition of 'human.' At a minimum, it is probably best to prohibit modifying other people's brains without their fully informed consent. It may also be worthwhile to restrict certain types of modifications. Some of the changes which have been discussed follow.
Enhancements: Brain enhancements include added or extended senses (e.g., seeing ultraviolet light); increased working memory capacity; mental calculator or database; language modules, which allow you to speak and understand many languages; and telepathy. Some people may want to go further and more fully integrate their minds with computers, changing their very thought processes.
Deletions: Some people may want to remove instincts which are no longer 'needed.' These could include food, sex, anger/violence, fear, and so on. Some may even try to remove all emotion. Although it may (or may not) be true that these no longer serve a logical purpose in an uploaded person, they are certainly an integral part of what we now understand 'humanity' to be.
Memory Alterations: If mechanisms of human memory are well understood, it may be possible to manipulate our memories almost as easily as we manipulate disk files. This includes procedural memory – for example, the ability to drive a car – and episodic memory, such as your skiing trip last December. Memories could be deleted, added, or swapped between persons. (Note that this complicates the personal identity issue even further, but not beyond what fuzzy logic can handle: if I take some of Jane's memories, then I become a little bit Jane, but still mostly me.)....
Mind Probing: A spin-off of memory technology would be a device which can search a person's memories for knowledge related to a specific event. This could be used to establish guilt or innocence of a crime, for example. However, if there are memory-altering techniques as well, then mind probing would no longer be conclusive. Also, mind probing has frequently been treated in discussion as an invasion of privacy – or is it just a sophisticated polygraph test?"

114 Kary Mullis web site: http://www.karymullis.com/.

115 Anders Sandberg. Bionics: http://www.aleph.se/Trans/Individual/Body/bion_page.html. MIT has a bionics lab.

116 Anders Sandberg, The Individual Sphere: http://www.aleph.se/Trans/Individual/index.html.

117 Anders Sandberg. Transhumanist Resources: http://www.aleph.se/Trans/index.html.

118 Nick Bostrom was formerly at the Department of Philosophy at the London School of Economics. Nick Bostrom's page: http://www.hedweb.com/nickb/.

119 http://www.transhumanism.com/transhumanism.htm: "The risks are as enormous as the potential benefits. In addition to dangers that are already recognized (though perhaps

inadequately counteracted?), such as a major military, terrorist or accidental disaster involving nuclear, chemical, viral or bacteriological agents, the new technologies threaten dangers of a different order altogether. Nanotechnology, for example, could pose a terrible threat to our existence if obtained by some terrorist group before adequate defense systems have been developed. It is not even certain that adequate defense is possible. Perhaps in a nanotechnological world offence has a decisive intrinsic advantage over defence. Nor is it farfetched to assume that there are other risks that we haven't yet been able to imagine."

120 Transhumanism: http://www.transhumanism.com/transhumanism.htm.

121 World Transhumanist Association (WTA): http://www.transhumanism.org/resources/faq.html; http://www.transhumanism.com/.

122 http://www.transhumanism.com/groups.htm.

123 "The Money Report: How to Spot and Profit from the Next Big Leaps Forward in Technology," *International Herald Tribune*, 25–26 November 2000, p. 20. IBM is also active in this field; Jennifer Couzin, "IBM Wants to Play Doctor," *The Industry Standard Magazine*, 30 May 2001.

124 Home page of Rajkumar Buyya: http://www.buyya.com/ then under Virtual Laboratory.

125 Amber Ashton, "Tech Predictions from Leading Scientists," CNET, 9 March 2001: http://www.cnet.com/techtrends/0-6014-8-4962347-1.html#; Jere Longman, "Will Athletes Soon be Designed to Win? Olympic Officials Seek to head Off Attempts at Genetic Engineering," *International Herald Tribune*, 12–13 May 2001, pp. 1ff.

126 Laura Rohde, "University puts British Library on a chip," *IDG News Service*/London Bureau, 13 February 2001.

127 Patricia Reaney, "Scientists build tiny computer from DNA," *CBC News*, Friday , 23 November 2001: http://www.cbc.ca/story/news/?/news/2001/11/22/dna_computer011122. Also Access Research Network, ARN Library Files: http://www.arn.org/docs2/news/dnacomputer112001.htm.

128 Yahoo Movies. *Fantastic Voyage* (1966): http://movies.yahoo.com/shop?d=hv&cf=info&id=1800063964.

129 Nicholas Mokhoff, "Graphics gurus eye nuts, bolts of 3-D Web," *EE Times*, 28 July 2000: http://www.eet.com/story/OEG20000728S0006.

130 "Lights, camera, action – inside the intestine with a 'video pill,'" *CNN.com health*, 30 August 2000: http://www.cnn.com/2000/HEALTH/08/30/israel.videopill.ap/.

131 "Nanocopters leave the drawing board," *BBC News Sci/Tech*, Thursday, 23 November 2000: http://news.bbc.co.uk/hi/english/sci/tech/newsid_1037000/1037730.stm.

132 Roger Segelken, "First biomolecular motors with metal propellers are reported by Cornell nanobiotechnologists," *Cornell News*, 23 November 2000: http://www.news.cornell.edu/releases/Nov00/propeller.hrs.html; Associated Press, "Big Patent on a Molecular Scale," *Wired*, 17 July 2001: http://www.wired.com/news/technology/0,1282,45325,00.html?tw=wn20010718.

133 IBM Research, Quantum Teleportation, 1995: http://www.research.ibm.com/quantuminfo/teleportation/. Cf. "Ein Schritt in die Zukunft. Innsbrucker Wissenschaftler liefern einen wichtigen Beitrag zur Verwirklichung der Quantentechnologien," Universität Innsbruck, 1 January 2001: http://www2.uibk.ac.at/service/c115/presse/2001/01-01.html.

134 C.H. Bennett, G. Brassard, C. Crepeau, R. Jozsa, A. Peres, and W. Wootters, "Teleporting an Unknown Quantum State via Dual Classical and EPR Channels," *Physical Review Letters*, vol. 70, 1993, pp. 1895–99; Peter O'Connor, "Scientists Report 'Teleported' Data," *Space.com*, 18 June 2002: http://www.space.com/businesstechnology/technology/australia_teleport_020618.html.

135 Michael Crichton, *Timeline*, New York: Alfred Knopf, 1999. For subsequent developments: "Photons Teleported Six Kilometers," *Technology Research News*, 16 April 2004: http://www.technologyreview.com/articles/rnb_041604.asp.

136 Timothy Leary's Cyber Archives: http://www.leary.com.

137 Interplay: http://www.interplay.com/. [in bankruptcy procedures]

138 There is, for example, a so-called NASA Project Blue Beam (Source: International Free Press in Canada): http://www.geocities.com/Area51/Shadowlands/6583/project144.html.

139 The special role of Eric Drexler in these developments has recently been reviewed in an instructive article by Mark Pesce, "Thinking Small," *The Feed Special Issue*, October, 1999: http://www.hyperreal.org/~mpesce/, then under "Thinking Small".

140 Sharon Begley, "Religion and the Brain," *Newsweek*, 14 May 2001, pp. 44–49.

141 Bill Joy, "Why the future doesn't need us," *Wired*, January, 2000: http://www.wired.com/wired/archive/8.04/joy_pr.html.

142 Jeremy Rifkin, *The Biotech Century*, New York: Penguin/Putnam, 1999.

Chapter 4: Production

1 *Harvard Business Review on Knowledge Management*, Boston: Harvard Business Review, 1997, p. 173.

2 National Information Infrastructure: http://www.ibiblio.org/nii/toc.html.

3 MADIC comprises NASA, the seven U.S. Aerospace companies, Georgia Tech, Rice, and the Northeast Parallel Architectures Center (NPAC), as well as the Affordable Systems Optimization Process (ASOP). MADIC is listed Code Validation Test Cases under CFD Resources at NASA Langley. Computational Fluid Dynamics: *Codes, Developments, and Applications*: http://ad-www.larc.nasa.gov/tsab/cfdlarc/.

4 National Center for Manufacturing Sciences: http://www.ncms.org/index.htm. The Technology for Enterprisewide Engineering Consortium was founded in 1996 by Boeing, Ford, Kodak, MacNeal-Schwendler, and Structural Dynamics Research.

5 Sandia, Integrated Manufacturing: http://www.ca.sandia.gov/casite/NIST/metrology/metrology.html. Companies such as General Electric had a Manufacturing Technology Library and a Computer Aids to Manufacturing Network (ARPA/CAMnet).

6 Now Global Engineering Networking (GEN) Initiative: http://xml.coverpages.org/genInitiative.html.

7 International Alliance for Interoperability: http://cic.cstb.fr/ILC/Html/iai.htm; Alliance Internationale d'Interoperabilité: http://www.iai-france.org/.

8 Rainer Puittinen, Mika Silander, Eero Tervonen, Juho Nikkola, and Ari-Pekka Hameri, "Universal Access to Engineering Documents," *WWW6*, Santa Clara, April 1997 : http://www.ra.ethz.ch/CDstore/www6/Posters/708/univac.html.

9 E.g., the Automotive Network eXchange (ANX) and the TradeXChange. For Covisint: http://www.covisant.com/; Caren D. Potter, "Digital Mock-Up Tools Add Value to Assembling," *CGW Magazine*, November, 1996; Home page now: http://cgw.pennnet.com/home.cfm. There is a vast literature on this field of automated production using computers. A sample is given in Appendix 8.

10 CD-ROM *Actualité du virtuel. Actualizing the Virtual*, Paris: Centre Georges Pompidou, 1996.

11 Here one of the pioneers was Professor John Danahy at the School of Landscape Architecture (University of Toronto), who worked on real-time design projects with the Swiss Federal Polytechnic (ETH, Zurich), the Graduate School of Design (Harvard), and the School of Architecture (Hong Kong). As early as 1995, Toronto and Zurich were sharing design classes on-line using an SGI reality engine. That same year, Maher and Saad in Sydney published on virtual design studios. Mary Lou Maher and Milad Saad, *The Experience of Virtual Design Studios at The University of Sydney*, 1995; Virtual Design Studio: Resources: http://www2.arch.ubc.ca/research/vds/tools.html; Publications: http://www2.arch.ubc.ca/research/vds/publications.html. By 1996, Engeli and Kurmann (ETH) published a virtual reality design environment with intelligent objects and autonomous objects, Sculptor: Maia Engeli, David Kurmann, "A Virtual Reality Design

Environment with Intelligent Objects and Autonomous Agents," *Design and Decision Support Systems, Conference Proceedings*, Spa Belgium, 1996: http://caad.arch.ethz.ch/research/AGENTS/DDSS-paper/. This became linked with the Interactive Design using Intelligent Objects and Models (IDIOM) project: Claudio Lottaz, "IDIOM – Interactive Design using Intelligent Objects and Models,": http://liawww.epfl.ch/Research/idiom.html. Professor Ludger Hovestadt (Zurich) has co-founded Digital Building. Digitales Bauen: "a company which focuses on internet based building documentation, building programming, computer supported individualized building component production, and the integration of building automation, facility management and eCommerce,": http://www.digitales-bauen.de/. In England, Charlton Somerville offers Tele-Design Drafting: http://www.ch-somerville.com/welcome.htm.

12 Satyandra K. Gupta, William C. Regli, and Dana S. Nau, "IMACS, A System for Computer-Aided Manufacturability Analysis," Institute for Systems Research, University of Maryland, January, 1996: (formerly) http://www.cs.umd.edu/projects/cim/imacs/imacs.html.

13 Then president of VDMA.

14 David Blanchard, "CeBIT '96: Dawn of a Second Industrial Revolution," *Intelligent Manufacturing Report*, vol. 2, no. 3, March, 1996: http://www.lionhrtpub.com/IM/IMsubs/IM-3-96/CeBIT.html.

15 International Alliance for Interoperability: http://www.iai-international.org/.

16 This is being co-ordinated by the International Alliance for Interoperability as in previous note.

17 Benjamin R. Barber, *Jihad vs. McWorld*, New York: Times Books, 1995. For another approach to multicultural dimensions: Edouard Legrain, "Politique Européenne de l'Internet et Multiculturalisme," *Autrans '2000*. Atelier Communautés, cultures et langues de l'Internet.

18 International Alliance for Interoperability (IAI): http://www.iai-international.org/iai_international/.

19 BOW & ARROW. Advanced Reusable Reliable Objects Warehouse BRE and Visual Technology: http://cig.bre.co.uk/arrow/OSdemo/devVer/.

20 For more information concerning the EU's role in construction: http://www.otalib.fi/vtt/bases.html and http://www.otalib.fi/vtt/ture/search.html.

21 ISO STEP Tools: http://www.steptools.com/library/standard/.

22 Step Tools, Inc.: http://www.steptools.com/.

23 There are specific application protocols for the each of the following domains: Electro-Technical Plants; Plant Functional Data and Schematic Representation; Plant Spatial Configuration; Electronic Printed Circuit Assembly, Design and Manufacture; Electronics Test, Diagnostics and Re-manufacture; and Printed Circuit Assembly Manufacturing Planning. The list cited was that of 2001. For the full STEP Protocols: http://www.steptools.com/library/standard/.

24 In 2000, the list included:
Industrial automation systems and integration: product data (STEP)
Industrial manufacturing management data   (MANDATE)
Industrial automation systems and integration   (OIL & GAS)
Parts library   (PLIB).
For Product Data Technology using Internet technologies: http://www.pdtnet.org/file/11361.Flyer_Sy02.
For STEP Vision: http://www.tc184-sc4.org/About_TC184-SC4/About_SC4_Organization/; SC4 Exploders: http://www.steptools.com/forums/standards-dev.html. The rapid rise of XML has led some to raise questions about the future of STEP: http://www.steptools.com/library/standard/step_5.html

25 In the United States, attempts at Integrated Computer Aided Manufacturing led to Integrated Definition Language (IDEF) or DOD 1994 Integrated Definition Language no. 5 KIF: "IDEF is a graphical way to document processes. It is a hierarchical, top down modeling process. Each node in a higher level process can be decomposed to another level, down to more levels, low enough to be able describe a process in roughly a short paragraph. But that's a lot of graphs to

manage. Each node of a process sits in the middle of a graph surrounded by at least 4 arrows (One to link/display Input, One to link/display Resources, One to link/display Constraints, One to Link/display output.)" Cf. Enterprise Engineering's IDEF Models and Methods Page. See: http://arri.uta.edu/eif/idefmodels.htm; J. Sarkis and D. Liles, "Using IDEF and QFD to Develop an Organizational Decision Support Methodology for the Strategic Justification of Computer-Integrated Technologies," *Conference Proceedings of the 25th Annual Meeting of the Decision Sciences Institute,* November, 1994.

26 Joseph Borel, "Les objets communicants," *Manifestations du centenaire Colloque ENSIMAG,* Grenoble, 12–13 October 2000 (http://www-ensimag.imag.fr) and personal communication. Also "Composants et systèmes électroniques": http://www.icp.inpg.fr/~bailly/_elesa3/Elesa2_Bilan_JLS.doc; Joseph Borel, article in *International Solid State Circuit Conference (ISSCC),* 1997.

27 In other contexts, "MRP" means "Management Resource Planning."

28 Caliach: Enterprise Resource Planning: http://www.caliach.com/caliach/whatiserp/whatismrp.html.

29 Visual Inventory Control: http://www.dynamiccontrolsoftware.com/.

30 Formerly at: http://www.erp-people.com/.

31 Formerly at: http://www.agilemfg.com/; Agile Manufacturing Benchmarking Consortium: http://www.ambcbenchmarking.org/; Integrated Supply Chain Management Project: http://www.eil.utoronto.ca/iscm-descr.html. MIT's Tangible Bits Lab has a Supply Chain Visualization project called Sensetable: http://tangible.media.mit.edu/projects/sensetable/

32 Quote formerly at: http://www.agilemfg.com/supplychain.htm: "The recent announcement of a consolidated automative trading hub and Rooster.com for agricultural goods demonstrate that the mainstream of B2B [Business to Business] e-Commerce has now moved into the sphere of production goods and trading partners. This is a major advance from the product catalog and auction approach that characterized the early B2B trading hubs. Of the auto-makers, Ford has expressed the most advanced vision, one where automative trading partners would exchange production information in real-time in order to 'take days and dollars out of the supply chain.' Internet supply chains must preserve the best of MRP [Material Requirements Planning] – the concepts of dependent demand and time phased planning. Up until now, the explosion of dependent demand has been limited to a single company business model and generated by slow, batch based Master Production Schedule (MPS) and Material Requirements Planning (MRP) applications."

33 Supply Chain Action Network: (formerly) http://www.supplychainlinks.com. "REA, a semantic model for Internet supply chain collaboration," by Robert Haugen, CTO, Logistical Software LLC, and William E. McCarthy, Arthur Andersen Alumni Professor, Michigan State University: http://jeffsutherland.org/oopsla2000/mccarthy/mccarthy.htm.

34 Formerly at: http://www.supplychainlinks.com/e-slideshowintro.htm. Charles C. Poirier and Michael J. Bauer, *E-Supply Chain, Using the Internet to Revolutionize Your Business,* San Francisco: Berrett Koehler, 2001.

35 This included "planning responsibility, stage and location are also identified." Access to supply-chain routing and process information from the product family level thus allows for fast, new products.

36 Fraunhofer. Pressemitteilung vom 10 September 2004: http://www.scai.fraunhofer.de/587.0.html

37 In 2001, this vision had four elements:

Agile Manufacturing	U.S.A.
Autonomous & Distributed Manufacturing Systems	Japan
Biological Manufacturing Systems	Japan
The Fractal Company	Germany

Since 2001, the scope has evolved. Cf. Next Generation Manufacturing Systems (NGMS) IMS Program: http://ims.kitech.re.kr/bbs/special13.pdf.

38 CAM-I Program Descriptions under NGMS: http://cam-istandards.org/programs.html and http://www.cam-i.org/.

39 Ivan Sutherland, "The Ultimate Display," FIPS (*Federal Information Program Standards*), 1965.

40 Tom Furness III was at the time at the Wright Patterson Airforce Base, where he designed a virtual reality environment for flight simulation. He subsequently founded the Human Interface Technology (HIT) lab at the University of Washington (Seattle). Because the topic was top secret at a military base, he did not publish at the time. He subsequently left the military to found the Human Information Technology Lab.

41 Myron Krueger, *Artificial Reality*, New York: Addison Wesley, 1983; 2nd ed. 1991.

42 Formerly at: http://www.soc.staffs.ac.uk/~cmtajd/teaching/VAV/VR.html; Alan Dix's home page: http://www.comp.lancs.ac.uk/computing/users/dixa/. For examples of frontiers of virtual reality in culture, medicine, and business: IEEE-VRIC 2004, Laval Virtual, 11–12 May 2004, under the patronage of Michel d'Aubert.

43 APACS is a PRECARN initiative. FORMENTOR, which is a French EUREKA program. Re: Advanced Process and Control Systems (APACS) via Precarn: http://www.precarn.ca/preincorp/nationalresearch/phase1/prjKJxmLITFpE_en.html; Bryan M. Kramer and John Mylopoulos, re: APACS: http://www.cs.toronto.edu/~kramer/paper.doc.html#84736.

44 "Visible Human Datasets form basis for "endoscopic virtuality," *Virtual Medical Worlds Monthly*, Rochester, 17 February 1998: http://www.hoise.com/vmw/articles/LV-VM-04-98-6.html#go_to_top.

45 VAKHUM Project: http://www.ulb.ac.be/project/vakhum/.

46 BREVIE: http://www.brevie.uni-bremen.de/.

47 Lab@future: http://www.labfuture.net.

48 DERIVE: http://www.derive.uni-bremen.de.

49 ARTEC: http://www.arteclab.uni-bremen.de/eng/index.php.

50 Ian Maxwell, Avantium, "The Informatics and Simulation Needs Related to High-Speed Experimentation": http://www.atp.nist.gov/atp/conf/speakers/maxwell.htm.

51 NCAR as an Integrator: http://www.ncar.ucar.edu/stratplan/plan.pdf.

52 The Alliance Virtual Machine Room: http://archive.ncsa.uiuc.edu/SCD/Alliance/VMR/.

53 High Performance Virtual Machines: http://www-csag.ucsd.edu/projects/hpvm.html.

54 HEAVEN: : http://europa.eu.int/information_society/istevent/2004/cf/document.cfm?doc_id=722.

55 Jeremy Rifkin, *The End of Work*, New York: Tarcher Putnam, 1995; Shoshana Zuboff. *In the Age of the Smart Machine: The Future of Work and Power*, New York: Basic Books, 1988.

56 Michael A. Cusumano, *The Japanese Automobile Industry: Technology and Management at Nissan and Toyota* (Harvard East Asian Monographs, no. 122), Cambridge, MA: Council on East Asian Studies, Harvard University, 1989; ibid., *Japan's Software Factories: A Challenge to U.S. Management*, New York: Oxford University Press, 1991; ibid., *How the World's Most Powerful Software Company Creates Technology, Shapes Markets, and Manages People*, New York: Free Press, 1995; ibid., *Thinking Beyond Lean: How Multi-Project Management Is Transforming Product Development at Toyota and Other Companies*, New York: Free Press, 1998. Cf. Joel Cutcher-Gershenfeld, *Knowledge-Driven Work: Unexpected Lessons from Japanese and United States Work Practices*, New York: Oxford University Press, 1998. While our account emphasizes American-Japanese relations, there is also a long tradition of links between Germany and Japan, which are beyond the scope of this book: Erich Pauer, ed., *Technologietransfer Deutschland-Japan*, Munich: Iudicium Verlag, 1992. (Monographien aus dem Deutschen Institut der Philipp Franz von Siebold Stiftung, Band 2); Akira Goto and Hiroyuki Odagiri, eds., *Innovation in Japan*, Oxford: Clarendon, 1997. (Japan Business and Economics); Ralph Hewins, *Japans Wundermänner*, Vienna: EconVerlag, 1968. (cf. formerly at: http://mitsloan.mit.edu/facstaff/books.html).

57 SESAMi Collaborates with HAHT Commerce to Deliver Demand Chain E-Commerce in Asia Pacific, Singapore, 5 April 2002: http://www.sesami.com/eng/newsroom/releases/SESAMi-HAHT.html.

58   For a recent article: Lee Pender, "The 5 keys to Supply Chain success," *CIO*, 15 July 2001: http://www.cio.com/archive/071501/keys.html.

59   Gary H. Anthes, "IT Goes to War. The battlefield of the future will be computerized and networked," *Computerworld*, 11 March 2002: www.computerworld.com/networkingtopics/ networking/story/0,10801,68929,00.html.

60   SAP was founded in 1972 by Hasso Plattner and four ex-IBMers: Daniel Metzger, "Schaffe, schaffe, Software baue," *Tages-Anzeiger*, 13 November 2000, pp. 63–64.

61   Formerly at http://www.sisi.demon.co.uk/workflow/products.htm. In 2004, the dmoz open directory project listed 113 companies: http://dmoz.org/Computers/Software/Workflow/ Products/.

62   Center for Coordination Science: http://ccs.mit.edu/.

63   MIT Process Handbook: http://process.mit.edu/.

64   E.g., Workflow Software.com. World Wide Web Workflow now W4 Process Intelligence: http://www.w4global.com/indexen.htm; Workflow Management Coalition (WfMC): http://www.wfmc.org/; Workflow and Re-Engineering International Organization (WARIA): http://www.waria.com/; Enterprise Engineering Clearinghouse and Enterprise Integration Technologies: http://www.cit.gu.edu.au/~bernus/clearinghouse.html; ESI Technologies is developing Enterprise Management Information Systems (EMIS): http://www.esitech.com/. A consortium of Hitachi and nineteen companies have developed a CORBA-based Workflow Management System. Linked with these efforts are new ergonomics standards. Cf. Hitachi Systems Development Laboratory (HSDL): CORBA Workflow Management System: http://www.sdl.hitachi.co.jp/english/topics/t_work/workflow.htm.

65   Jeremy Rifkin, *The End of Work*, New York: Jeremy P. Tharcher, 1996.

66   Shoshana Zuboff, *In the Age of the Smart Machine: The Future of Work and Power*, New York: Basic Books, 1988.

67   Virtual Work Page of Anthony Steed: http://www.cs.ucl.ac.uk/staff/A.Steed/work.html.

68   UNC, Office of the Future: http://www.cs.unc.edu/Research/stc/.

69   Telecentres and Cybercafes: http://www.cpcug.org/user/kjmorris/telecent.html; UNESCO's program on Community Multimedia Centres. ; s.hughes@unesco.org;.

70   Ken Goldberg, *The Robot in the Garden: Telerobotics and Telepistemology in the Age of the Internet*, Cambridge, MA: MIT Press, 2000.

71   This is particularly important in Africa where there is an average of one radiologist for 10 million persons and there are no radiologists at all in fourteen African countries.

72   Teleinvivo: http://www.igd.fhg.de/teleinvivo/.

73   Computer Assisted Surgery, see Robert Sader (Munich), who is engaged in CAFCAS (Computer tomography with artificial elimination and finite element model for cyber navigational assisted surgery), INTERFACE (Clinical centres of excellence), and CAESAR (Centre for Advanced European Studies and Research [Bonn]): http://www.caesar.de/715.0.html.

74   Hans Florian Zeilhofer and Robert Sader, "Application of mixed reality techniques in computerized cranio-maxillofacial surgery," *Eurocav3D 2001*, Mykonos, 30 May–1 June, Thessaloniki: ZITI, 2001, pp. 254–57.

75   Wusheng Chou, Tianmiao Wang, "Computer and Robot Assisted Tele-neurosurgery," *Proceedings of the 2003 IEEE/RSJ Internatonal Conference on Intelligent Robots and systems*, Las Vegas, October 2003: prism.mem.drexel.edu/desai/MRI/Paper18.pdf .

76   "Real-Time Analysis, Visualization, and Steering of Microtomography Experiments at Photon Sources." G. von Laszewski, M. Su, J. A. Insley, I. Foster, J. Bresnahan, C. Kesselman, M. Thiebaux, M. L. Rivers, S. Wang, B. Tieman, and I. McNulty. *Ninth SIAM Conference on Parallel Processing for Scientific Computing*, April, 1999: www.globus.org/documentation/incoming/siamCmt99.pdf.

77   Ulrich Sigor, "Infarkt der Arbeit in der informatisierten Welt," unpublished manuscript, Vienna, 1996.

78   James R. Beniger, *The Control Revolution. Technological and Economic Origins of the Information Society*, Cambridge, MA: Harvard University Press, 1986.

79 In the table above, the abbreviation "KJ" refers to a method, named for its inventor, Jiro Kawakita (the Japanese put their last names first), that allows groups quickly to reach a consensus on priorities of subjective qualitative data. In 2001, Goal QPC Research provided a slightly different list of these, namely:

1. Affinity Diagram

2. Interrelationship Digraph

3. Tree Diagram

4. Matrix Diagram

5. Prioritization Matrices

6. Process Decision Program Chart (PDPC)

7. Activity Network Diagram (formerly at: http://www.goalqpc.com/RESEARCH/7mp.html).

These have now become twenty-two different tools: Activity Network Diagram, Affinity Diagram, Brainstorming, Cause & Effect (*Fishbone*), Check Sheets, Control Charts, Data Points, Flowchart, Force Field Analysis, Histograms, Interrelationship Digraph (ID), Matrix Diagram, Multivoting, Pareto Chart, Prioritization Matrices, Problem Solving Model, Process Capability, Radar Chart, Run Chart, Scatter Diagram, Team Guidelines, Tree Diagram, Process Decision, Program Chart, and Nominal Group Technique (NGT): http://www.goalqpc.com/.

80 Yaskawa Electric Corporation: http://www.yaskawa.com.

81 Walter Andrew Shewhart, *Economic Control of Quality of Manufactured Product*, New York: Van Nostrand, 1931.

82 Walter A. Shewhart, with the editorial assistance of Willliam Edwards Deming, *Statistical Method from the Viewpoint of Quality Control*, Washington: The Graduate School, The Dept. of Agriculture, 1939.

83 Deming's 14 Points:
http://deming.eng.clemson.edu/pub/den/deming_philosophy.htm#points.

84 JUSE: http://www.juse.or.jp/; Robert E. Kemper, *Quality, TQC, TQM: A meta literature study*, Lanham, MD: Scarecrow Press, 1997.

85 JUSE is also: "a member of the sponsor group of the Campaign 'Quality Month' in November in Japan. During recent years, more than 20,000 people including 500 of senior managers from enterprises have been taking part in our Education and Training Courses every year which is one of our main activities." For an overview of TQC principles: http://www.goalqpc.com/.

86 Kaoru Ishikawa, *Guide to Quality Control*, White Plains, NY: Quality Resources, 1982. In the United States, this is called "statistical quality control."

87 Yoji Akao, ed., *Quality Function Deployment*, Cambridge, MA: Productivity Press, 1990; S. Mizuno and Yoji Akao, ed., *QFD: The Customer-Driven Approach to Quality Planning and Development*, Tokyo: Asian Productivity Organization, available from White Plains, NY: Quality Resources, 1994.

88 CAM-I: http://www.cam-i.org/history.html.

89 S. Mizuno, ed., *Management for Quality Improvement: The 7 New QC Tools*, Cambridge, MA: Productivity Press, 1988.

90 GOAL/QPC TQM Wheel: http://www.goalqpc.com/tqmwheel.htm.

91 Genichi Taguchi, *Introduction to Quality Engineering: Designing Quality into Products and Processes*, Asian Productivity Organization, available in the United States from American Supplier Institute (Dearborn, MI), 1986. It is instructive that all of these ideas have been adopted by NASA. Cf. Introduction to Robust Design (Taguchi Method): http://www.isixsigma.com/library/content/c020311a.asp; http://www.quality.org/html/kaizen.html.

92 Kaizen Institute: http://www.kaizen-institute.com/.

93 Masaaki Imai, *Kaizen: The Key to Japan's Competitive Success*, New York: McGraw-Hill, 1986.

94 L. P. Sullivan, "Policy Management through Quality Function Deployment," *Quality Progress*, vol. 21, June 1988, pp. 18–20. For: What is Hoshin Kanri?: http://www.mcts.com/Hoshin-Kanri.htm.

95   Kenichi Miyashita and David Russell, "Preface," *Keiretsu: Inside the Hidden Japanese Conglomerates*, New York: McGraw-Hill, 1995. Cf. Evolution of Keiretsu and their Different Forms: http://www. mgmt.utoronto.ca/~baum/mgt2005/keiretsu.htm.

96   S. Mizuno, ed., *Management for Quality Improvement: The 7 New QC Tools*, Cambridge, MA: Productivity Press, 1988.

97   Andrew Mair, *Honda's Global Local Corporation*, New York: St. Martin's, 1994.

98   Formerly at: http://www.goalqpc.com/RESEARCH/TQMwheel.html; now: http://www.goalqpc.com/tqmwheel.htm#.

99   Formerly at: http://www.goalqpc.com/RESEARCH/probsolv.html. For a similar story, Vedaraman Sriraman, "4. A Primer on the Taguchi System of Quality Engineering," : http://scholar.lib.vt.edu/ejournals/JOTS/Summer-Fall-1996/PDF/9-2-Sriraman-article.pdf

100   Yasuhiro Monden et al., *Innovations in Management: The Japanese Corporation*, Atlanta, GA: Industrial Engineering and Management Press, Institute of Industrial Engineers, 1985.

101   Yasuhiro Monden, *Applying Just in Time: the American-Japanese experience*, Norcross, GA: Industrial Engineering and Management Press, Institute of Industrial Engineers, 1986; Yasuhiro Monden, *Toyota Production System: An Integrated Approach to Just-in-Time*, London: Chapman & Hall, 1994, 2nd ed.

102   CAM-I, *Strategic Supply-Chain Management. Program Materials. Dictionary of Relevant Terms. Communication and Information Reference*, Texas, 1986. Cf. CAM-I Online Library: http://www.cam-i.org/storeindex.cfm.

103   Masaaki Imai, *Kaizen: The Key to Japan's Competitive Success*, New York: McGraw-Hill, 1986.

104   William Edwards Deming, *The New Economics for Industry, Government, Education*, Cambridge, MA: MIT, Center for Advanced Engineering Study, c. 1993.

105   Interestingly enough, in 2003, the original site disappeared and, in 2004, reappeared in simplified form as best practices enabling lean manufacturing excellences: http://www.superfactory.com/Community/BestPractices/Kaizen/default.aspx Formerly at: http://mijuno.larc.nasa.gov/dfc/mdo/edo.html.

106   Part of the Graduate School of Information Systems, at the University of Electro-Communications: http://www.is.uec.ac.jp/eng/u_major.html; http://www.is.uec.ac.jp/eng/index.html.

107   ISO 9000 Introduction: http://connect.ab.ca/~praxiom/intro.htm.
      The ISO Quality Management Systemic Family includes:
      Fundamentals and Vocabulary   ISO 9000:2000
      Product Customer Satisfaction   ISO 9001:2000
      Organizational Efficiency   ISO 9004:2000
      Quality and Environmental MS Auditory   ISO 19011:2001.

108   EFQM home page: http://www.efqm.org/.

109   OGC ITIL (IT Infrastructure Library): http://www.ogc.gov.uk/index.asp?id=2261.

110   Examples of European Projects include:
      RESPECT (Requirements Engineering and Specification in Telematics): http://www.ucc.ie/hfrg/projects/respect/index.html.
      MEGATAQ (Methods and Guidelines for the Assessment of Telematics Application Quality): http://www.ejeisa.com/nectar/megataq/.
      ESPRIT Long Term Projects: (20072), DEVA (Design for Validation): http://www.newcastle.research.ec.org/deva/index.html.
      (20113) MEASURE (Resource Allocation for Multimedia Communication and Processing Based on On-Line Measurement): http://www.cordis.lu/esprit/src/20113.htm.
      Esprit Working Group 21900 on the Development of Proofs (TYPES): http://www.cs.chalmers.se/ComputingScience/Research/Logic/TypesWG/. There is CURE (Centre for Research and Usability Engineering) in Vienna: http://www.cure.at/. There was a Center for Multimedia Quality (Fife) and a MultiMedia House of Quality (Reading): http://csdl.computer.org/comp/proceedings/metrics/1998/9201/00/92010144abs.htm. Cf. QW2000 Paper 8W1, Mr. Adrian Cowderoy (MMHQ), "Technical Quality is Just the Start – The Real Battle is Commercial Quality,": http://www.soft.com/QualWeek/QW2K/Papers/8W1.html.

111 Carl Hewitt, "Viewing Control Structures as Patterns of Passing Messages," *Artificial Intelligence*, vol. 8, no. 3, 1977, pp. 323–64.

112 BT Exact, "Software Agents, An Overview," Especially: "Collaborative Agents. An Overview", Knowledge Engineering Review, Vol. 11, No 3, pp.1-40, Sept 1996: http://www.sce.carleton.ca/netmanage/docs/AgentsOverview/ao.html

113 Rolf Pfeifer, "Cognition – Perspectives from autonomous agents," *Robotics and Autonomous Systems*, vol. 15, 1995, pp. 47–70.

114 HONDA ASIMO: http://world.honda.com/ASIMO/.

115 Formerly at: http://www.taka.is.uec.ac.jp/projects/caarg/index-e.html.

116 Virtual Environments Laboratory, Northeastern University, Boston: http://www.coe.neu.edu/~mourant/velab-projects.html.

117 Agent Based Engineering (ABE) Group: http://www-cdr.stanford.edu/ABE.

118 NEXT-LINK. The Distributed engineering Vision: http://www-cdr.stanford.edu/NextLink/NextLink.html.

119 Novel Manufacturing Facilities and Processes: http://www-cdr.stanford.edu/RVPP/mfg-to-cad.GIF.

120 Sandia National Laboratories, "How We Are Implementing an Agent Architecture to Support Manufacturing": http://www.ca.sandia.gov/~carmen/defs.html.

121 Sandia National Laboratories, "Agent Architectures to Support Manufacturing": http://www.ca.sandia.gov/~carmen/why_agents.html.

122 UCA Net, C. Gilman, M. Aparicio, J. Barry, T. Durniak, H. Lam, and R. Ramnath, "Integration of design and manufacturing in a virtual enterprise using enterprise rules, intelligent agents, STEP, and workflow,": http://web.democenter.it/ucanet/studi/studi_view.php@studio_id=6.php.

123 NEPTUNE Project: www.neptune.washington.edu. This is but one of a number of global projects that include the Victoria Experimental Network under the Sea (VENUS), the Monterey Accelerated Research System (MARS), the Ocean Observatories Initiative (OOI), the Global Ocean Observing System (GOOS); the Integrated Ocean Observing System (IOOS), and the Ocean Research Interactive Observatory Networks (ORION).

124 Patrick McHugh, Giorgio Merli, and William A. Wheeler, *Beyond Business Process Engineering: Towards the Holonic Enterprise*, Chichester: John Wiley, 1995. Post-Mass Production Enterprise Reading List: http://www.cheshirehenbury.com/agility/postreading.html.

125 David C. Korten, *The Post-Corporate World*, New York: Bennett-Koehler, 1999, p. 114.

126 The project is entitled: Holonic Manufacturing Systems: System Components of Autonomous Modules and their Distributed Control.

127 On the History of Holons: http://www.mech.kuleuven.ac.be/pma/project/goa/hms-int/history.html.

128 Arthur Koestler, *The Ghost in the Machine*, London: Hutchinson, 1976. Reprinted: Arkana Books, 1989. Quoted by: Holonic Manufacturing Systems: http://hms.ifw.uni-hannover.de/: "in living organisms and in social organizations entirely self supporting, non-interacting entities did not exist. Every identifiable unit of organization, such as a single cell in an animal or a family unit in a society, comprises more basic units (plasma and nucleus, parents and siblings) while at the same time forming a part of a larger unit of organization (a muscle tissue or a community). A holon … is an identifiable part of a system that has a unique identity, yet is made up of subordinate parts and in turn is part of a larger whole. The strength of holonic organization, or *holarchy*, is that it enables the construction of very complex systems that are nonetheless efficient in the use of resources, highly resilient to disturbances (both internal and external), and adaptable to changes in the environment in which they exist."

129 Ibid.: http://hms.ifw.uni-hannover.de/.

130 Kazuhiko Kawamura home page: http://www.vuse.vanderbilt.edu/~kawamura/.

131 Quote formerly at: http://www.cpsc.ucalgary.ca/~lamsh/SENG/693/mar22_1.html. For more recent developments, see the web site of Dr. Mihaela Ulieru: http://isg.enme.ucalgary.ca/People/Ulieru/Default.htm.

132 Quote formerly at: http://www.iijnet.or.jp/MMC/no.11/MHI.html. Cf. Mtisubishi Heavy Industries: http://www.mhi.co.jp/indexe.html.

133 UNESCO Chair on Mechatronics and Mechatronics Research and Application Center: http://mecha.ee.boun.edu.tr/. According to Yashkawa, the year was 1972: http://www.yaskawa.co.jp/en/products/product_e.html. These rights were abandoned in 1982 in order to assure its free use.

134 Outline of Lab (i.e., Department of Mechanical and Control Engineering [MCE]) at the University of Electro-Communications (UEC): http://www.kajitani.mce.uec.ac.jp/lab/lab_e.html.

135 This includes research into development of an automatic measuring system for gears applying an image processing technology and the development of a musician robot (MUBOT), which plays the cello, violin, and recorder.

136 „Mechatronik", Linz: http://www.mechatronik.uni-linz.ac.at/.

137 Formerly at: http://www.gmd.gr.jp/Lists/Robotics.Subject.in.Japan.html#Mechatronics. Cf. MEMS Research in JAPAN, 1994: (formerly) http://www.arofe.army.mil/Reports/webelec/mems3z.htm.

138 Mechatronics (of Professor Kazerooni, Berkeley): http://me.berkeley.edu/mechatronics.html.

139 Robot and Protein Kinematics Lab, Johns Hopkins University (Description in 2001 formerly at: http://caesar.me.jhu.edu/gregweb/gregc1.html). Since then the definition has shifted: "Mechatronics is the synergistic integration of mechanism, electronics, and computer control to achieve a functional system,": http://custer.me.jhu.edu/course/mechatronics/index.html.

140 (Description in 2001 formerly at: http://rcs.ee.washington.edu/CR/MECH/). In 2004, this definition has also shifted: "Mechatronics in Mechanical Engineering": http://www.me.washington.edu/faculty/mechatronics.pdf.

141 http://www.rpi.edu/dept/mechatronics/.

142 (Description in 2001 formerly at: http://www.tcgsolutions.com/): "Control systems receive information from sensors and send out signals to actuators. These signals often need to be converted to a more useful form, filtered, buffered, modulated or demodulated, amplified, converted to analog or digital signals, etc. In addition, controllers can be implemented using analog components to form lead, lag, or lead-lag controllers." In 2005, a slight variation is found at the mechatronics site as in previous note.

143 Katholieke Universiteit, Leuven, Mechatronics: http://www.mech.kuleuven.ac.be/pma/research/mecha/default_en.phtml. (Quote 2001 formerly at: http://www.mech.kuleuven.ac.be/pma/research/2_5.htm).

144 Loughborough, Mechatronics Research Group: http://www.lboro.ac.uk/research/mechatronics/.

145 UNESCO Chair on Mechatronics and Mechatronics Research and Application Center: http://mecha.ee.boun.edu.tr/.

146 McGill, Centre for Intelligent Machines: http://www.cim.mcgill.ca/.

147 For instance, the Emura Lab, also known as the Mechatronics Design Lab at Tohoku University, has research on biped and quadruped robots; on Autonomous Land Vehicles (ALV) and an Autonomous Guided Vehicle (AGV); a productive type gear-grinding machine; traction drive and car electronics. Mechatronics Design Lab: http://www.ssme.eng.tohoku.ac.jp/Labs/209emura/.

148 Quote formerly at: http://www.yaskawa.co.jp/en/technology/topics/1999.htm.

149 For another example, see the Biomechatronics Lab at MIT: http://www.ai.mit.edu/people/hherr/biomech.html.

150 Department of Precision Engineering: http://www.pe.u-tokyo.ac.jp/e/n_vision.html.

151 For instance, Kaizen", SaferPak, 2004": (formerly) http://www.saferpak.com/kaizen.htm. Other kaizen resources at: http://www.evolvingenterprise.com/Community/BestPractices/Kaizen/default.aspx.

152   For a reading list on this subject, see that of Paul Kidd, Cheshire Henbury, Agility Master, Post Mass Production Enterprise Reading List: http://www.cheshirehenbury.com/agility/postreading.html.

153   Agility International: http://www.knowab.co.uk/an1.

154   Roger Nagel, Rick Dove, *21st Century Manufacturing Enterprise Strategy*, Bethlehem, PA: Iacocca Institute, 1991. 2 vols.

155   Melissa Sander, "Future of manufacturing may go to the 'agile'," CNN, 8 July 1996: http://www.cnn.com/TECH/9607/08/agile.manufacturing/.

156   Four Steps to Agile Manufacturing: http://www.maskell.com/4boxAgile.htm.

157   Appendix 8 under Agile Manfacturing: http://www.iospress.nl/; H.T. Goranson, *The Agile Virtual Enterprise*: Cases, Metrics, Tools, Westport, CT: Quorum Books, 1999.

158   Based on formerly at: http://www.almaden.ibm.com/cs/informatics/mass.html. Now that Jean Paul Jacob has retired and the Informatics division has been closed, it is not clear how coherently this vision will be pursued.

159   Two definitions of Agility: http://www.cheshirehenbury.com/agility/twodefinitions.html. Re definition two: "Such a business is founded on processes and structures that facilitate speed, adaptation and robustness and that deliver a coordinated enterprise that is capable of achieving competitive performance in a highly dynamic and unpredictable business environment that is unsuited to current enterprise practices."

160   NIST Systems Integration for Manufacturing applications (SIMA): http://www.mel.nist.gov/div826/msid/sima/sima.htm.

161   These U.S. initiatives included:
      – Advanced Manufacturing Systems and Networking Testbed (AMSANT)
      – Technologies Enabling Agile Manufacturing (TEAM) Consortium
      – National Industrial Information Infrastructure Protocols (NIIIP) Consortium
      – The Rapid Response Manufacturing (RRM) Project
      – The Agility Forum
      In Canada, there is a Concurrent Engineering and Agile Manufacturing Research Laboratory at the University of Western Ontario: http://hyperserver.engrg.uwo.ca/ceamrl/. This department has a page of links to information: http://hyperserver.engga.uwo.ca/ceamrl/links.htm. Cf. MSL – Projects – An Architecture for Agile Assembly – Some links to agile manufacturing resources: http://www.cs.cmu.edu/afs/cs/project/msl/www/minifactory/links.html.

162   Formerly at: http://www.sandia.gov/isrc/Capabilities/Prototyping/AMPS/amps.html.

163   Environment for Virtual Manufacturing Enterprise Operation Demonstrated: http://www.mel.nist.gov/msid/96whatsn/6-2-96.htm.

164   It is intriguing to note how companies such as IBM are investing heavily in Linux as a part of their business model. Cf. Andreas Heer, "Liebe, Linux und Luftschlösser," *Tages-Anzeiger*, 30 April 2001.

165   Cited from formerly at: http://www.news.philips.com/profile/main.html.

166   Cited from formerly at: http://www.siemens.de/en2/html/index.html.

167   "PDES, Inc. Restructures to Allow More SMEs to Gain Membership Benefits," PDES, 14 March 2000: http://pdesinc.aticorp.org/whatsnew/restructure.html.

168   This ad hoc approach was reflected also in the Carnegie Mellon Design Management Cluster Producer-Consumer Lists.

169   National Industrial Information Infrastructure Protocols and Related Projects: http://www.niiip.org/. "CATT virtual enterprises mentor small and medium manufacturers, provide electronic commerce/electronic data interchange training, generate contracting opportunities, provide reverse engineering and quality verification, and facilitate parts production." (Quote formerly at: http://catt.bus.okstate.edu/catt2/index.html). This has since been replaced by ASSET Aging Systems Sustainment and Enabling Technologies: http://asset.okstate.edu/asset/index.html.

170 There is a trend for the United States to create its own versions of ISO standards. For instance, in the automotive industry, Ford, General Motors, and Daimler Chrysler have adapted the ISO 9000 standard to create QS 9000, which: "was created to combine the various quality requirements of the domestic vehicle manufacturers into a single, uniform standard that is on par with the world-wide ISO 9000 standard. But its basic purpose is to raise the quality benchmark for all automotive parts, be they new parts or replacement parts." Quality Points: http://www.wellsmfgcorp.com/htmlpages/qualitypoints.htm.

171 International Alliance for Interoperability: http://iaiweb.lbl.gov/.

172 National Industrial Information Infrastructure Protocols: http://www.niiip.org/public/home.nsf?Open. It is interesting to note how in the period since 2001 that the goals have focussed on the shipbuilding industry.

173 PDES: http://pdesinc.aticorp.org/.

174 Ibid.

175 American National Standards Institute (ANSI): http://www.ansi.org.

176 National Institute of Standards: http://www.nist.gov/welcome.html.

177 Reported by the head of AFNOR at the *www.intranet2000.net* conference at Cité des Sciences in Paris in March, 2000.

178 Quote formerly at: http://www.iway.org.nic/toc.html. Cf. Global Information Infrastructure: Agenda for Cooperation: http://www.ntia.doc.gov/reports/giiagend.html.

179 "Virtual Environments and Distributed Computing" at *SC'95*; "GII Testbed and HPC Challenge Applications on the I-WAY," *Supercomputing '95*: http://www.ncsa.uiuc.edu/General/Training/SC95/GII.HPCC.html.

180 The full program entailed 10 basic test-beds with 88 projects in a variety of fields:

1. Astronomy
Astrophysics
   Distributing Spacetime: Computing and Visualizing Einstein's Gravitational Waves across the Metacenter
2. Atmospheric Science
   NCAR Climate Simulation Laboratory
   Near real time detection and visualization of clouds
3. Biochemistry, Molecular Biology and Structural Biology
   Cellular Semiotics: Molecular Recognition in Biological Membranes
   Virtual Biomolecular Environment
4. Biological and Medical Imaging
   Virtual Human
5. Chemistry
   QM View and GAMESS: New Insight into Molecular Structure and Reactivity
   Distributed Computing
   Terravision
6. Earth Science
   Chesapeake Bay Virtual Ecosystem Model
   Exploring Coupled Atmosphere: Ocean Models using Vis5D and VisAD
7. Education
Engineering
   High bandwidth Collaborative Simulation Based Design
   Remote engineering using Cave to Cave communications
Geometric Modeling
8. Materials Science
Mathematics
   Quaternion Julia sets in virtual reality
   LATERNA matheMAGICA
Microphysics and Macrophysics

9. Neuroscience
Performance Analysis
  Performance monitoring in interactive virtual environments
Plasma Physics
10. Teleoperation/Telepresence
  Cityspace project
  Visualization
  Animation of Very High Resolution Data.

181 NITRD (National Co-ordination Office for Information Technology Research and Development): http://www.ccic.gov/pubs/index.html; NCO, "Advancing the Frontiers of Information Technology. Manufacturing – Design, Processes, and Products": http://www.ccic.gov/pubs/blue97/mfg/.

182 *Visionary Manufacturing Challenges for 2020*, ed. Committee on Visionary Manufacturing Challenges, Board on Manufacturing and Engineering Design; Commission on Engineering and Technical Systems; National Research Council, Washington: National Academy Press, 1998; "Grand Challenge 3. Conversion of Information to Knowledge": http://bob.nap.edu/readingroom/books/visionary/ch2.html#gc3.

183 Ibid.

184 Ibid.: http://bob.nap.edu/readingroom/books/visionary/ch2.html#gc3: "Perhaps the biggest challenge will be in education. Well trained, educated people will make better and faster decisions based on an unprecedented flow of data, information, and knowledge. Only trained and educated people will be able to separate useful information from useless information."

185 Ibid.

186 Ibid.

187 Ibid.: "Future systems will have to handle huge image bases in a variety of languages where small nuances could make big differences and where even small differences could become catastrophic."

188 NIIIP: http://www.niiip.org/public/home.nsf.

189 Ibid.

190 Mark Roberti, "No Workers, No Offices: The Virtual Company," *The Standard*, 5 March 2001: http://www.findarticles.com/cf_dls/m0HWW/10_4/71711472/p1/article.jhtml.

191 Japan is, of course, a complex country where there is a very high level of companies along with others at quite a different level. For an introduction to these complexities: Karel van Wolferen, *The Enigma of Japanese Power: People and Politics in a Stateless Nation*, New York: Vintage Books, 1990.

192 OMG Agent Platform Special Interest Group: http://www.objs.com/agent/; Grasshopper, A Universal Agent Platform Based on OMG MASIF and FIPA Standards: http://www.cordis.lu/infowin/acts/analysys/products/thematic/agents/ch4/ch4.htm; K. Villinger and C. Burger, "Generic mobile agents for electronic markets," University of Stuttgart, Institute of Parallel and Distributed High-Performance Systems: http://inforge.unil.ch/isdss97/papers/73.htm.

193 This idea was introduced by Microsoft SVP, Craig Mundie, in a speech on 3 May 2001 criticizing Open Source software development and introducing the competing notion of Shared Source; Craig Mundie, "Eerlijk zullen we alles delen," Achtergrond en opinie, *Computable*, 34 jaargang, 25 May 2001, pp. 41–45: http://www.computable.nl/artikels/archief1/d21ra101.htm; Graham Lawton, "The Great Open Source Giveaway," *Alternet.org*, 1 July 2002: http://www.alternet.org/story.html?StoryID=13494.

194 Oekonux project: http://www.oekonux.org/; Alex Schröder, "Open Source baut Brücken," *Tages-Anzeiger*, 8 December 2003, p. 25.

195 ATICA (Agence pour les Technologies de l'Information et de la Communication dans l'Administration) has since prepared a "Guide de choix et d'usage de logiciels libres pour les administrations," December, 2002: http://www.pilotsystems.net/content/technologies/guide_licences_logiciels_libres_administrations.

196 Felix Wiedler, "Der Staat endeckt Open Source," *Tages-Anzeiger*, 25 September 2000, p. 91.

197 Philippe Quéau (now UNESCO, Moscow) argues strongly that knowledge and culture are not commodities and hence that the notion of a knowledge economy is a misnomer (cf. his speech at EVA Moscow, December 2003). A similar idea has been expressed by Robert Kurz in "The Degradation of Culture": http://obeco.planetaclix.pt/rkurz_en30.htm.

198 PITAC Open Source Panel for High End Computing, Susan Graham, 18 May 2000: www.hpcc. gov/pitac/meetings/2000/20000512/oss/oss.pdf.

199 Stuart Glascock, "Germany Leads In Open-Source Development," *Tech Web News*, 1 November 2000: http://www.techweb.com/wire/story/TWB20001101S0016.

200 Paul Windrum, "Back from the brink: Microsoft and the strategic use of standards in the Browser Wars," Conference paper, *European Meeting on Applied Evolutionary Economics*, Grenoble, 7–9 June 1999.

201 Also interesting in this context is the GNU Network Object Model Environment (GNOME, Mexico): http://www.gnome.org/.

202 Home page VFEB (Virtuelle-Fabrik.com): http://eb.virtuelle-fabrik.com/.

203 While Germany contributes to world standards, it is worth noting that the Association of the German Automobile Society (Verein der Deutsche Automobil Gesellschaft) has also created its own national standard, VDA 6.1. Cf. SQS (Schweizerische Vereinigung für Qualitäts- und Management- Systems): http://www.sqs.ch/e/VDA61E.htm. The German Society of Quality (Deutsche Gesellschaft für Qualität) is also concerned with standards.

204 IPPI (Integrated Product and Process Initiative). This is becoming an important theme: e.g. Peter M. Milling and Joachim Stumpfe, "Product and Process Innovation: A Systems Dynamics-Based Analysis of the Interdependencies," in: *Proceedings of the 18 International Conference of the System Dynamics Society: Sustainabilty in the Third Millennium*, ed. Pal Davidsen, David N. Ford, Ali N. Mashayekhi, Bergen, 2000: iswww.bwl.uni-mannheim.de/Forschung/ Publikationen/BergenPMJS.pdf. In the United States, there is work on Unified Process Specification Language: Requirements for Modeling Process in the introduction to which we read: "There are three government funded projects at Raytheon Electronic Systems that all use a model of manufacturing process, namely Integrated Product and Process Initiative (IPPI http://128.2.199.68/Sadeh/ norman_hp_mirror/Publications_pdf/sadeh_koniecpol_norman_199 6_1.pdf), Integrated Process Planning/Production Scheduling (IP3S http://www.ozone.ri.cmu.edu/projects/ip3s/ ip3smain.html), and Shared Integrated Product Process Development (IPPD http://www. goldpractices.com/practices/ippd/index.php; http://www.lboro.ac.uk/departments/mm/re-search/product-realisation/res_int/ipps/ippd1.htm). Inherent to all of these projects is 'the use of a common representation for exchanging process planning and production scheduling information.' [58] IMPPACT (Integrated Modelling of Products and Processes using Advanced Computer Technologies), a project in ESPRIT (European Strategic Programme for Research and Development in Information Technology) attempted to develop and demonstrate a new genera-tion of integrated modelling systems for product design and process planning." [15] While there are documented shortcomings of all of these approaches and methodologies, there is definite progress toward improved formal representations of process to address the growing need: http://www.mel.nist.gov/msidlibrary/doc/schlen96/11.htm; Jack B. Revelle (ed.), *Manufacturing Handbook of Best Practices: An Innovation, Productivity, and Quality Focus*, Saint Lucie Press, 2001.

205 Thinkers such as Huszai and Philippe Quéau (UNESCO, Moscow) warn against a commoditization of knowledge: Villö Huszai, "Das vermeintlich Erhabene der Datenautobahn," *Neue Zürcher Zeitung*, Nr. 285, 7–8 December 2002, p. 87. Quéau goes further to suggest that the whole term Knowledge Economy is in a sense a misnomer because it undermines the traditions whereby knowledge is something to be shared.

206 ESPRIT Integration in Manufacturing. Project Activities: http://www.cordis.lu/esprit/src/iima3. htm.

207 ESPRIT Integration in Manufacturing. The Intelligent Manufacturing Systems Initiative: http:// www.cordis.lu/esprit/src/iima42.htm.

208 Intelligent Manufacturing Systems (IMS): http://www.ims.org/index2.htm. One of the IMS projects is Global CAPE-OPEN (GCO), which aims to deliver "the power of component software and open standard interfaces in Computer-Aided Process Engineering." A second project, Global Engineering and Manufacturing in Enterprise Networks (Globeman 21), is concerned with demonstrating how to: "1) move the Global Manufacturing practices from rigid supply chain structures into globally distributed, dynamic networks of agile and focused enterprises and 2) support Product Life Cycle Management for the benefit of the end users."; Globeman 21: http://ims.toyo-eng.co.jp/Pub/Gm21pub/mission.htm. A third project, Modelling and Simulation Environments for Design, Planning and Operation of Globally Distributed Enterprises (MISSION), has as its prime objectives the creation of tools and processes needed for both extended enterprises and/or virtual enterprise networks: "An integrated modeling and simulation platform will be built to support engineering on the one hand and systems integration on the other. Modeling techniques will develop a consistent interface with distributed engineering works. Object-oriented and agent-based simulation, and the integration of commercial tools, CAD/CAM, design tools and related business practices will be undertaken." Cf. IMS MISSION (Modelling and Simulation Environments for Design, Planning and Operation of Globally Distributed Enterprises): http://www.ims-mission.de. Globeman 21 is headed by the Toyo Engineering Corporation and includes more than twenty partners, including VTT, the University of Toronto, and the Commonwealth Scientific and Industrial Research Organization (CSIRO). More ambitious still is Knowledge Systematization – Configuration Systems for Design and Manufacturing (GNOSIS), led by Mitsubishi Electric Corporation, which: "aims to establish the framework for a new manufacturing paradigm through the utilization of knowledge-intensive strategies covering all stages of product life-cycle, in order to realize new forms of highly competitive manufactured products and processes which are environment-conscious, society-conscious and human-oriented." Also members of IMS are Mitsubishi Materials, Hitachi Sozen, Shimuzu, etc. For Globeman 21 links: http://ims.toyo-eng.co.jp/Pub/Gm21pub/links.htm. Study topics include: soft artefacts, virtual manufacturing, knowledge management, and various enabling and integration technologies. Cf. Knowledge Systematization for Post Mass Production Manufacturing. GNOSIS: http://www.ims.org/projects/project_info/gnosis.html.

209 Sensor Fused Intelligent Monitoring System for Machining (SIMON)
Recycle system for Composite Material Waste; Thermal Elutriation System (TES)
Intelligent Manufacturing of Wood Products Using Color, X-Ray, and Computer Tomography-Based Quality Control (INTELIWD)
Coping with the Complexity of Business Innovation (HARMONY)
Highly Productive and Re-configurable Manufacturing System (HIPARMS)
Human Sensory Factor for Total Product Life Cycle (HUTOP)
Innovative and Intelligent Field Factory (IF7)
Intelligent Composite Products (INCOMPRO)
Rapid Product Development (RPD)
Digital Die Design System (3DS)
Organizational Aspects of Human-Machine Coexisting System (HUMACS)
Metamorphic Material Handling System (MMHS)
Holonic Manufacturing Systems (HMS)
Next Generation Manufacturing Systems (NGMS)
Cited from formerly at: http://www.ims.org/index2.htm.
For the current list: http://www.ims.org/index_projects.html.

210 These include: A dynamic management methodology with modular and integrated methods and tools for knowledge-based, adaptive SMEs (SYMPHONY); Design System for Intelligent Machining Centres and Cells (SIMAC) and Plant Automation Based on Distributed Systems (PABADIS). Other projects include Intelligent Interface for Modeling, Simulation and Optimization for Global Manufacturing (INTERGLOBAL); Virtual Engineering Product Process Integration in a Global Engineering Network (VE); Virtual Integration of Transport Enterprise

(VITE), and Networked Manufacturing Foundations and Technologies (NET-WORKS): http: //www.ims.org/index_projects.html.

Chapter 5: Services

1 CIO Electronic Commerce Projections: http://www.cio.com/WebMaster/strategy/tsld218.htm.

2 "Electronic Commerce. Still waiting for the boom," *red herring.com*, 1 February 1998: http: //www.herring.com/mag/issue51/overview.html.

3 Acumen.

4 "Forrester Projects $6.8 Trillion for 2004": http://www.glreach.com/eng/ed/art/ 2004.ecommerce.html.

5 Randolph Court, "Another Try at Auctioning Ad Leftovers," *Wired News*, 19 February 1998: http: //www.wired.com/news/business/0,1367,10431,00.html.

6 NUA: "Global Online Ad Revenues to Skyrocket," *Jupiter Communications*, 19 June 2000: http: //www.nua.ie/surveys/?f=VS&art_id=905355850&rel=true.

7 NUA: http://www.nua.ie.

8 "AGENTICS Shows off its Real Time Virtual Catalog," *Computergram International*, 7 December 1998: http://www.findarticles.com/cf_dls/m0CGN/1998_Dec_7/53358996/p1/article.jhtml.

9 Ramakrishnan Srikant: http://www.almaden.ibm.com/cs/people/srikant/.

10 Tim Clark, "You Say, 'D-i-s-i-n-t-e-r-m-e-d-i-a-t-i-o-n'; I Say Don't Count on It," *INTER@CTIVE WEEK*, 8 April 1996. Cited in: J. Stephen Downie, "Jumping off the Disintermediation Bandwagon: Reharmonizing LIS Education for the Realities of the 21st Century," : http://www.lis.uiuc.edu/~jdownie/alise99/.

11 Don Willmott, "Disintermediation: The Buzzword from Hell," *PC Magazine Online*, 10 September 1997. Cited by Kirsten Swearingen, "The New News Intermediaries," Internet Access Seminar. 15 December 2000: http://www.sims.berkeley.edu/~kirstens/Final2.doc.

12 Paul Taylor, "Middle men deleted as word spreads," *Financial Times*, 27 October 1998: http: //graffiti.virgin.net/www3.org/disintermediation.htm.

13 *Financial Times*, 8 November 1999.

14 Namely, AMD, Compaq, Gateway, Hewlett-Packard, NEC, Hitachi, Infineon, Quantum, Samsung, SCI Systems, Solectron, and Western Digital.

15 Dan Briody (InfoWorld.com), "Compaq, HP, Others Form Internet Exchange," *PC World*, 9 May 2000. Cf. Dan Briody, "Compaq, HP, others team up on Internet exchange company," *Network World Fusion*, 1 May 2000: http://archive.infoworld.com/articles/pi/xml/00/05/01/ 000501pihpcompaq2.xml.

16 Cited from formerly at: http://www.hp.com/ssg/docs/090017ad804ed6c6.pdf. For HP's take in 2004 on APS and SCM: http://www.hp.com/hps/erp/ep_scm_solutions.html. For HP's take on ERP: http://www.hp.com/hps/erp/.

17 In September 2000.

18 Including Nortel Networks, Motorola, Nokia, Philips, South Korea's LG Electronics, Japan's Hitachi, and five other major telecommunications and electronics firms: "IBM, Tech Giants Plan B-to-B Exchange," *The Standard*, 31 May 2000: http://archive.infoworld.com/articles/hn/xml/ 00/05/31/000531hnibmmarket.xml.

19 Anne Tyrie in *CITO Linkline* for 5 June 2000, who cites as her source: http://www.ft.com/.

20 "E-tailers Rise, Bug-eyed and Taxed", *Australian Financial Review*, 1 August 2000. John S. McLenahen, Net Gains, Industry Week, 17 May 1999: http://www.industryweek.com/CurrentArticles/asp/ articles.asp?ArticleID=542 .

21 "Research Perspective. B2B E-Commerce Predicted to Soar. Unified online supply chains to dominate B2B trading," *Manager Advisor*, 11 October 2000: http://supplychainadvisor.com/ doc/07261

22 Melanie Austria Farmer, "Software firms gear up to run the e-commerce race," *Cnet.com*, 15 March 2000: http://news.cnet.com/news/0-1007-200-1572686.html.

23 http://www.emarketer.com/SearchBrowse.aspx?pathID=448.

24 Virtual Environments for Training (VET): http://www.isi.edu/isd/VET/vet.html.

25 Ed Hess, *Business Solutions*, September, 1998: http://www.businesssolutionsmag.com/Articles/1998_09/980902.htm.

26 Quote formerly at: http://canada.careermosaic.com/cm/lockheed/lmibs1.html.

27 FT.com staff, "Online global forex offered," *FT.com*, July 2000: www.ft.com.

28 UN EDIFACT: http://www.unece.org/trade/untdid/.

29 OASIS: http://www.oasis-open.org/home/index.php.

30 Now called ebXML Business Process: http://www.oasis-open.org/committees/tc_home.php?wg_abbrev=ebxml-bp. For a comment regarding the relative value of EDI and XML, cf. EAN International under EAN/UCC System: http://www.ean-int.org/index800.html.

31 Brint.com: http://www.brint.com/Elecomm.htm.

32 The Brick bid.com: http://www.bid.com.

33 eBay: http://www.ebay.com.

34 E-Bay categories in 2001: http://antiques.ebay.com/_W0QQexpandZ1QQrefidZ20081:

Antiques & Art	Jewellery, Gemstones
Books, Movies & Music	Photo & Electronics
Coins & Stamps	Pottery & Glass
Collectibles	Sports
Computers	Toys, Bean Bag Plush
Dolls, Figures	Everything Else

35 Yahoo Shopping Auctions: http://auctions.yahoo.com/:

Antiques & Collectibles	402,260	Home & Garden	66,757
Arts & Entertainment	360,541	Sports & Recreation	94,001
Business & Office	6,808	Toys & Games	294,223
Clothing & Accessories	148,967	Trading Cards	412,998
Computers	72,285	Travel & Transportation	25,853
Electronics & Cameras	24,468	Other Goods & Services	58,664

Cf. the list for 2004: http://list.auctions.shopping.yahoo.com/20000-category.html?alocale=0us.

36 Internet Auction List in 2001: http://www.internetauctionlist.com/:

Antiques	57	Computers	41	On-line Auctions	94
Art	90	Consumer Electronics	15	Paperweights	3
Associations	34	Domain Names	13	Photos & Postcards	4
Auction Publications	26	Ephemera	8	Pottery	5
Auction Schools	15	Estate	255	Real Estate	338
Auction Software		Farm Equipment	34	Restaurant Equipment'	15
Automobiles		Firearms	17	Rugs	3
Aviation		Flowers	8	Sporting Equipment	20
Bankruptcy		Furniture	10	Stamps	27
Boats	9	Glassware	9	Storage	7
Books		Government	33	Test Equipment	6
Building Materials		Heavy Equipment	152	Tools	6
Business Liquidation		Horse & Livestock	29	Toys	18
Charity		Jewellery & Watches	28	Trading Cards	22
Clothing	5	Memorabilia	47	Travel	17
Coins	23	Militaria	11	Wine & Cigar	12
Collectible Directories	16	Music	19		
Comics	6	Office Equipment	7		

For instance, in May, 2004, there were 19 traditional auctions in Antiques and 83 in Real Estate.

37 Quote formerly at: http://www.almaden.ibm.com/cs/informatics/excerpt.html.

38 Ted Nelson, "Generalized links, Micropayment and Transcopyright," 1996: http://www.almaden.ibm.com/almaden/npuc97/1996/tnelson.htm.

39 Chris Jones, "Digital Newsstands: The E-Ticket of the Net," *Wired News*, 28 April 1997: http://www.wired.com/news/topstories/0,1287,3441,00.html.

40 Cybercash.com has since been acquired by Verisign.

41 Geomerchant.com EZ Payment Gateway: http://www.goemerchant.com/index.cgi?location=gateway. (Cited from formerly at: http://www.goemerchant.com/ezpaygateway.htm.)

42 Reported at the *WWW*10 Developers Day in Hong Kong (May 2001).

43 Stephanie Nebehay, "Web Inventor Backs Licensing," *Reuters*, 27 November 1999, Geneva. Cf. Interesting People Message. Dave Farber on same day: http://www.interesting-people.org/archives/interesting-people/199911/msg00112.html.

44 Bibliography provided by Public Netbase: http://www.t0.or.at/; Electronic Frontier Foundation, "EFF Overview of Broadcast Protection Discussion Group. Industry Plans to Restrict Use of HDTV Broadcasts, Harming Innovation": http://www.eff.org/IP/Video/HDTV/20020117_eff_bpdg_overview.html. For a discussion of problems with American copyright developments, cf. Pamela Samuelson, "Toward a New Politics of Intellectual Property," presented at World Wide Web 2002. Concerning Pamela Samuelson Publications: http://www.sims.berkeley.edu/~pam/papers.html.

45 Quote formerly at: http://www.emarketer.com/estats/112299_music.html.

46 Andreas Heer, "Musik auf beiden Seiten des Gesetzes," *Tages-Anzeiger*, 13 August 2001, p. 47.

47 Now called: Liquid Digital Media: http://www.liquidaudio.com/. There is also Ogg vorbis alt for mp3: http://www.xiph.org/ogg/vorbis/index.html.

48 http://listen.com/ a subsidiary of realnetworks.com.

49 For the viewpoint of an artist, it is interesting to note the claims of singer Courtney Love: "Courtney Love does the Math," *salon.com*, 14 June 2000: http://www.salon.com/tech/feature/2000/06/14/love/index.html. For the viewpoint of an employee of Microsoft, see Peter Biddle, Paul England, Marcus Peinado, and Brian Willman, "The Darknet and the Future of Content Distribution,": http://crypto.stanford.edu/DRM2002/darknet5.doc. This article makes honestly shared information sound questionable via the word "darknet."

50 Alice Rawsthorn, "Big five shudder at digital jukeboxes," *Financial Times*, 13 January 1999. This was appealed and then confirmed: Bert Lanting, "Rechter legt met verbod Napster aan de ketting," *De Volkskrant*, Amsterdam, 13 February 2001, p. 1.

51 Brad King, "Last Rites for Napster," *Wired*, 14 May 2002: http://www.wired.com/news/business/0,1367,52532,00.html.

52 Brad Kind, "Real's Easy Listening," *Wired News*, 22 May 2000: http://www.wired.com/news/technology/0,1282,36405,00.html?tw=wn20000522.

53 Encyclamedia, Military History. The Legal Battlegorund: http://www.law.duke.edu/student/act/Selaw/encyclawmedia/military_history.htm.

54 Secure Digital Music Initiative: www.sdmi.org.

55 Formerly at: http://www.sdmi.org/public_doc/FinalFactSheet.htm. As of 18 May 2001, SDMI is on hold.

56 Declan McCullagh, "Code-Breakers Go to Court," *Wired News*, 6 June 2001: http://www.wired.com/news/mp3/0,1285,44344,00.html; Amy Harmon, "Judge Asked for Ruling on Copyright Group Seeks Release of Computer Code," *New York Times*, 7 June 2001: http://www.centerforthepublicdomain.org/tech.htm.

57 International Music Joint Venture (IMJV): venture by the MCPS-PRS Alliance has been as a founder member of a joint venture to design, build and operate a back office for some of the major international collecting societies known as International Music Joint Venture ("IMJV"). IMJV will undertake data management and processing such as registration of works,

agreement and analysis of music usage information, both for traditional and on-line uses: http://www.bmr.org/html/submissions/submission53.html.

58 Ibid., A project of the European Commission (EC ESPRIT 22226) is working with the International Federation of the Phonograph Industry (IFPI) at Developing Digital Media Management, Signalling and Encryption Systems for the European Music Industry (MUSE). See p. 83 of ftp://ftp.cordis.lu/pub/esprit/docs/projmms.pdf. Another EC project (IMPACT project 4050) is working on Music on Demand – A European Interactive Music Information and Delivery Service (MODE). Cf. SYGNA.

59 Some speak of six major companies: EMI, BMG, Universal, Sony, Virgin, and Warner. Sony and EMI are merging and Vivendi has taken over Universal. There are also five independent labels: F Com, Fairplay, Atmosphreiques, Melodie, and Edel.

60 Electronic Media Management Systems (EMMS): http://www-306.ibm.com/software/data/emms/.

61 Music Choice: http://www.musicchoice.co.uk/.

62 "Yahoo Announces Alliance with Duet Music Subscription Service," The Write News, 6 April 2001: http://www.writenews.com/2001/040601_yahoo_duet.htm.

63 Lori Enos, "Online Music Service Duet Renamed 'Pressplay' Amid Talk of Sony Exit," E-Commerce Times, 6 December 2001: http://www.ecommercetimes.com/perl/story/11174.html.

64 "p2p Pages. Wired's Guide to Global file Sharing," Wired, October, 2000, pp. 242ff.

65 "Napster eclipsed by Newcomers," Wired News Report, 6 September 2001: http://www.wired.com/news/business/0,1367,46596,00.html?tw=wn20010907.

66 Peter van Ammelrooy, "Muzieksites halen het nog niet bij Napster," De Volkskrant, 24 January 2002, p. 2E.

67 Dawn C. Chmielewski, "Record industry changing tune on Internet," Mercury News, 30 June 2002: http://www.siliconvalley.com/mld/siliconvalley/news/3578189.htm. Cf. Jane Weaver, "Listen.com adds Universal music. E-music subscription service is first to have all major labels," MSNBC, 30 June 2002.

68 Matthias Schüssler, "Vorsprung auf die Tauschbörsen," Tages-Anzeiger, 5 May 2003, p. 51.

69 Ashlee Vance, "Intel to support Napster model," IDG News Service/San Francisco Bureau, 9 August 2000. "The power of a company such as Intel moving into the contentious file sharing space could rewrite the relationship between technology companies and media powerhouses.... Looking to the long term, Intel wants to bring legitimacy to the peer-to-peer space.... If (the recording industry) wants to pick a fight, they will be picking on a giant.... The Napster case is profoundly affecting the way in which some people view the future of copyright laws.... There is a seminal shift occurring in the ways that technology companies and the media interact with each other.": http://www.nwfusion.com/news/2000/0809innap.html.

70 Jim Hu and Evan Hansen, "Record label signs deal with Napster," news.com, 31 October 2000: http://news.com.com/2100-1023-247859.html.

71 Lori Enos, "E-Biz Powerhouses Come Together Right Now Over Music," E-Commerce Times, 5 April 2001: http://www.ecommercetimes.com/perl/story/8719.html; Kristi Essick, "Major Labels to License Tunes to RealNetworks," The Standard, 2 April 2001; George A. Chidi Jr., "Real Networks, EMI, AOL, BMG in online music deal," IDG News Service/Boston Bureau, 2 April 2001; Roger Zedl, "Legale Onlinemusik bleibt rar," Tages-Anzeiger, 10 May 2004.

72 Napster is still at www.napster.com; John Borland, "Napster cuts deal with majors," CNET News.com, 5 June 2001. Cf. Arndt Ohler, Oliver Fischer, "Musik vom Band," Financial Times Deutschland, 21 January 2004: http://news.cnet.com/news/0-1005-200-6198507.html?tag=tp_pr.

73 Project JXTA: http://wwws.sun.com/software/jxta/.

74 Edward Haskell, Full Circle. The Moral Force of Unified Science, New York: Gordon and Breach, 1972: http://www.kheper.net/topics/Unified_Science/. Building on these ideas Timothy Wilken has claimed that co-operation, co-action, and co-laboration were connected: http://futurepositive.manilasites.com/2001/03/22; http://futurepositive.synearth.net/

75 Michel Bauwens, "P2P (1): P2P, Synergetics, and Co-Action Models," *Issue* 53, February 2005: http://news.openflows.org/article.pl?sid=02/04/23/1518208;

http://noosphere.cc/peerToPeer.html.

76 Sphinxmontreal.com: http://www.sphinxmontreal.com/downloads/mp3_file_sharing_software.html.

77 Fabbers.com, "What is a fabber?": http://www.ennex.com/fabbers/fabbers.sht.

78 Jeffrey Harrow, *Rapidly Changing Face of Computing*, 19 February 2001: http://www.compaq.com/rcfoc.

79 Lisa M. Bowman, "Disappearing ink: E-book self-destructs," CNET *News.com*, 8 August 2001: http://news.com.com/2100-1023-271303.html?legacy=cnet.

80 Clifford Lynch, "The Battle to define the future of the book in the digital world," *First Monday*, vol. 6, no. 6, 4 June 2001, pp. 23–24: http://www.firstmonday.org/issues/issue6_6/lynch/index.html.

81 One area where major companies have secured "all the rights" is coverage of Olympic games. In 1960, such rights cost $.5 million. For the Athens games, NBC paid $793 million. Independent of the price, one could reasonably ask why any single company should be given monopoly rights to distribute worldwide an event that includes the best athletes from the entire world. Cf. Duncan MacKay, "US starts countdown for sale of the century," *The Guardian*, 6 June 2003, p. 21.

82 John Borland, "Traffic pressures stall Napster alternatives," *Cnet.com*, 27 July 2000: http://news.cnet.com/news/0-1005-200-2364630.html. FOOL ON THE HILL: An Investment Opinion: Rob Landley (TMF Oak) "Intellectual Property Is an Oxymoron,": http://www.fool.com/news/foth/2000/foth000814.htm.
For a more recent list see Life After Napster: http://www.beachbrowser.com/Archives/eVoid/July-2000/Napster-Alternatives.htm.

83 John Adams. E-mail: j.n.adams@sheffield.ac.uk.

84 This was the vision of IBM's Informatics project, which stopped when Dr. Jacob retired in 2002.

85 Matthias Schüssler, "Gefälscht authentisch," *Tages-Anzeiger*, 2 April 2001, p. 55.

86 Overview of the GNU project: http://www.gnu.org/gnu/gnu-history.html.

87 The Debian Free Software Guide: http://www.debian.org/social_contract.html#guidelines.

88 Debian: http://www.debian.org/intro/free.

89 Free Standards Group: http://www.freestandards.org/.

90 NetBSD Project: www.netbsd.org; Free BSD: www.freebsd.org and Open BSD: www.openbsd.org.

91 GNU Project: http://www.gnu.org/gnu/gnu-history.html.

92 Free Software Foundation: http://www.gnu.org/fsf/fsf.html; http://www.gnu.org/home.html#ContactInfo.

93 What is copyleft?: http://www.gnu.org/copyleft/copyleft.html.

94 History of the OSI: http://www.opensource.org/docs/history.html.

95 Netscape Company Press Relations, 22 January 1998: "Netscape announces plans to make next generation Communicator free on the net": http://www.netscape.com/newsref/pr/newsrelease558.html.

96 OSI: http://www.opensource.org/docs/history.html.

97 Open Source Case for Business: http://www.opensource.org/advocacy/case_for_business.html.

98 Eric S. Raymond, *The Cathedral and the Bazaar: Musings on Linux and Open Source by an Accidental Revolutionary*, Cambridge, MA: O'Reilly, 1999.

99 Quote formerly at: http://www.vbxml.com/admin/whoarewe.asp; Visual basic.net: http://www.gotdotnet.com/team/vb/.

100 GNOME: http://www.gnome.org/.

101   John Markoff, "Developers of Linux Software Planning Assault on Microsoft," *New York Times on the Web*, 14 August 2000: http://www.nytimes.com/library/tech/yr/08/biztech/articles/14linux.html.

102   Michelle Delio, "It'll Be an Open-Source World," *Wired News*, 15 August 2000: http://www.wired.com/news/print/0,1294,38240,00.html. Cf. new companies such as Christopher Montgomery's Xiphophorus: http://www.xiph.org/about.html linked with oggvorbis open free radio: http://www.vorbis.com/.

103   Ryoichi Mori and Masaji Kawahara, "Superdistribution: An Overview and the Current Status," *Technical Research Reports of the Institute of Electronics, Information and Communication Engineers*, vol. 89, no. 44, 1989; "What lies ahead," *Byte*, January, 1989, pp. 346–48; "On Superdistribution," *Byte*, September, 1990, p. 346; Quote from: "Superdistribution. The Concept and the Architecture," (http://virtualschool.edu/mon/ElectronicProperty/MoriSuperdist.html). "By eliminating the need of software vendors to protect their products against piracy through copy protection and similar measures, superdistribution promotes unrestricted distribution of software. The super-distribution architecture we have developed provides three principal functions: administrative arrangements for collecting accounting information on software usage and fees for software usage; an accounting process that records and accumulates usage charges, payments, and the allocation of usage charges among different software vendors; and a defense mechanism, utilizing digitally protected modules, that protects the system against interference with its proper operation."

104   Mark   Benioff,   Salesforce.com: http://www.salesforce.com/us/company/board.jsp?name=benioff.

105   Rich Miller, "The ABCs of AIPs," 19 April 2004: http://www.carrierhotels.net/wiredspace/wired0131.shtml. This has since been replaced by Navisite.com, which speaks of three A-Services: Application Management, Application Hosting, and Application Development, as well as Collaborative Application Management: http://www.navisite.com/application-services.cfm. cf. http://www.navisite.com.

106   The report was entitled: *Internet Application Engines* and cited in Phil Wainewright, "Weekly Reviews: All Hail HailStorm?" *ASP News.com*. March, 2001: http://www.aspnews.com/analysis/analyst_cols/article/0,2350,4431_719171,00.html.

107   Clint Boulton, "Is HailStorm Really a Maelstrom?" *Internet News-ASP News*, 20 March 2001: http://www.internetnews.com/asp-news/article/0,,3411_718601,00.html.

108   Chris Jones, keynote at *WWW10*, Hong Kong, 2 May 2001.

109   Peter Coffee, "On Watch for Intelligent Objects," *eWeek. Enterprise New and Reviews*, 25 October 2004: http://www.eweek.com/article2/0,1759,1682298,00.asp.

110   Adam Cohen, "Coming: The E-Wallet Wars," *Time*, 6 August 2001, p. 46.

111   "eWallet version 4 for Microsoft Smartphone released," *MS Mobiles.com*, 20 July 2004: http://www.msmobiles.com/news.php/2833.html.

112   E-books Enterprise wide. Searchlight. "The Digital Divide. Get over it,": (formerly) http://www.ebook-training.com/Corporate.html.

113   According to the Computer-Based Training Report, SB Communications.

114   Now simply called IBM Training Services: http://www.techdata.com/business/ibm/IBM_Files/IBM_Benefits.pdf. Formerly at: http://www.planetit.com/techcenters/docs/enterprise_apps/news/PIT19980830S0027.

115   Software Process Engineering Management. The Unified Process Model (UPM), OMG document number ad 2000-05-05, 12 May 2000: http://www.51cmm.com/SPIN-CS/DataCenter/No013.pdf.

116   IBM Global Services: http://www.ibm.com/services/portfolios/.

117   Sun, "Sun Microsystems Announces Acquisition of Ed Learning Inc.": http://www.sun.com/smi/Press/sunflash/2000-06/sunflash.20000609.1.html.

118   Now called Rational Software Training: http://www.rational.com/university/index.jtmpl. Cf. IBM, Rational University Case Studies: http://www-306.ibm.com/software/success/cssdb.nsf/

softwareL2VW?OpenView&Start=1&Count=1000&ExpandView&RestrictToCategory=softwar
e_RationalUniversity.

119 Net Objects, "Net Objects launches Net Objects University," websitepro, 14 June 2000: http://
www.netobjects.com/company/html/pr14jun00.html.

120 Pearson VUE: http://www.vue.com/.

121 Now SRI Consulting Business Intelligence: http://www.sric-bi.com/ (formerly at: http:
//future.sri.com/LOD/).

122 David Leonhardt, "Shattering the Myth of E-Lancers. U.S. Data a Show a Drop in Self-
Employment," *International Herald Tribune*, 2–3 December 2000, p. 9.

123 Commerce One: http://www.commerceone.com/.

124 EDS and A.T. Kearney: http://www.eds.com/about_eds/about_eds_history_90s.shtml (quote
formerly at: http://www.eds.com/news/news_releases/news_release_template.shtml?rowid=
1450). EDS claims to have founded the Information Technology (IT) services industry in 1967.
It reported revenues of $18.5 billion in 1999.

125 Merger of EDS and MCI Systemhouse: http://www.wlu.ca/~wwwsbe/sbe2000/html/
laurierinstitute_casestudies/abstract/120041-G.html.

126 EDS Services: http://www.eds.com/services_offerings/so_mc.shtml.

127 On the relative finances of these corporations in 1999 as listed below, see their respective web
sites, and cf. Kennedy Information: http://www.kennedyinfo.com/. Not mentioned in the list
are others such as PA Consulting, Fielden-Cegos, and Monitor, which have no readily available
financial statements on the Internet. Non-profit bodies include the International Council of
Management Consulting Institutes (ICMCI). If one turns to the Fortune lists, there is now, in
addition to the Fortune 500 list, a Fortune e50 list of companies. In 2000, this list actually had 60
companies, namely, 19 e-companies, 16 net software and services, 11 net hardware, and 14 net
communications companies. Hence 35 of 60 companies were predominantly concerned with
software and services rather than hardware:

COMPANY	INCOME IN BILLIONS
IBM Global Services	26
EDS	18.5
Price Waterhouse Coopers	17.3
Klynveld Peat Marwick Goerdeler (KPMG)	12.2
Deloitte &Touche Tohmatsu Bakkenist	10.6
Cap Gemini Sogeti + Ernst and Young (4.3+5.5)	9.8
Andersen Consulting	8.3
Computer Sciences Corporation (CSC)	7.6
Booz Allen & Hamilton	1.8
CGI Group	1.6
SEMA	1.4
Logica	1.3
CMG	0.925
Roland Berger	0.680
Diamond Technology Partners	0.136

Of these major consultancy firms, it is striking that Ernst and Young, Deloitte and Touche, and
KPMG are still private companies.

128 GE Center for Financial Learning: http://www.financiallearning.com/ge/home.jsp. Quote
formerly at: http://www.financiallearning.com/): "The Center is not here to sell or promote
specific GE financial products. It is simply meant to educate and inform adults on the financial
matters that are important in their lives." General Electric also has a GE Capital Information

Technology Solutions (GECITS), with 14,000 employees, annual revenues of $6 billion and assets of more than $250 billion. On 5 October 1998, it announced a Global Service Solutions Alliance to deliver Lotus and IBM e-business software solutions. GE Capital Information Technology Solutions is now listed as a European company: http://www.ge.com/europe/images/geeurope.pdf. Sections of this company are being bought by others. E.g., SCH acquires GE Capital IT Solutions Spain: http://www.gecits-eu.com/press_release_20030206.htm. There is also a GE Information Technology Solutions: http://www.gecitsolutions.com/.

129 On 5 August 1997, SAP and Intel joined forces to create Pandesic: Tim Clark, "SAP, Intel team on e-commerce," *cnet News.com*, 5 August 1997: http://news.cnet.com/news/0-1003-200-321108.html?tag=st.ne.ni.rnbot.rn.ni. Pandesic subsequently (6 June 2000) joined Price Waterhouse: Melanie Austria Farmer, "Pandesic turns to Pricewaterhouse for momemtum," *CNET news.com*, 6 June 2000: http://news.cnet.com/news/0-1007-200-2026561.html?tag=st. Siebel Systems, founded by a former Oracle executive (in 1993), grew into one of the leading e-business application providers and has become a leader in Customer Relationship Management (CRM), along with the Prototyping Management Corporation (PMC), which introduced Customer Relationship Systems in 1994: http://www.pmcworldwide.com/. There are also other companies: e.g. Matrix One: http://www.matrixone.com/matrixone/index.html. In 1999, Siebel, which had worked closely with Oracle, became its competitor by linking with Microsoft's SQL Server. Business to business firms such as Commerce One and Ariba have been buying up competitors. In November, 1999, Commerce One bought Commerce Bid.com for $250 million. In November, Ariba acquired Trading Dynamics for $450 million. In June, 2000, Commerce One bought AppNet, an interactive marketing company. In June, Ariba acquired SupplierMarket.com for $580 million in stock and a stock merger agreement with Tradex: "Ariba to Acquire SupplierMarket.com," 27 June 2000: http://www.softwarestrategies.com/Web_First/ss.nsf/ArticleID/NBAS-4LPMFL/. There is also a new partnership between General Electric, Commerce One, IBM, Ariba, and I2 Technologies. Cf. James Christie, "GE and Commerce One form B2B dynamic duo," *Redherring.com*, 25 July 2000; "Ariba to Acquire SupplierMarket.com," 27 June 2000: http://www.softwarestrategies.com/Web_First/ss.nsf/ArticleID/NBAS-4LPMFL/. For instance, on 25 February 2000, competing companies of the auto industry joined together in a new form of co-opetition in a company called Covisint. On 14 September 2000, Visteon, an automotive systems supplier ($19.4 billion revenues in 1999), joined Covisint. Cf. "Big automotive supplier joining carmakers' exchange," *CNET news.com*, 14 September 2000: http://news.cnet.com/news/0-1007-200-2777308.html. In the first half of 2001, Covisint managed some $33 billion: "Covisint Books 'Impressive' Procurement Volume," *Information Week*, 18 July 2001: http://www.informationweek.com/story/IWK20010718S0005. In June 2001, Covisint joined forces with webMethods "to provide application integration services to suppliers that want to use the marketplace to do business with automakers," and to "let companies stitch their existing back-office and ERP systems to applications being provided by Covisint." In: Chuck Moozakis, "Covisint Picks WebMethods For App Integration," *Tech Web*, Tuesday, 26 June 2001: http://www.internetwk.com/story/INW20010626S0003. Underlying these trends is a concept of e-marketplaces. On 14 June 2000, SAP, an ERP company, bought $250 million in Commerce One shares in order jointly to develop e-commerce marketplaces as explained by Melanie Austria Farmer, "SAP chief touts Commerce One deal at trade show," *CNET news.com*, 14 June 2000: http://news.cnet.com/news/0-1007-200-2077583.html?tag=st. For Commerce One, this is leading to new integration of procurement processes and portal capabilities. According to SAP: "Commerce One will provide the marketplace infrastructure that enables companies to establish and operate trading portals, and SAP will provide functionality in the areas of supply chain management, product life-cycle management, customer relationship management and business intelligence." SAP: http://www.sap.com/. On 14 June 2000 also, Ariba, a leading business-to-business (B2B) e-Commerce platform provider, and MatrixOne, a leading provider of Internet business collaboration solutions, announced their "intent to form a strategic alliance to provide B2B marketplaces and exchanges with an

562

integrated, Web-based, many-to-many product development collaboration and eCommerce environment."; Roger Bataillard, "Web Revolutioniert den Handel,"*Tages-Anzeiger*, 4 February 2002, p. 51; "e2open, MatrixOne and Ariba Join Forces to Deliver Design Collaboration and Commerce Services in Electronics Industry's Leading e-Marketplace," 10 January 2001: http://www.ariba. com/company/news.cfm?pressid=447&archive=1. On 21 June 2000, J.D. Edwards made deals with IBM and Sun Microsystems and software makers iPlanet and i2, in order to "help businesses build their own online trading exchanges,"; Melanie Austria Farmer, "J.D. Edwards signs e-commerce pacts with IBM, Sun," CNET *news.com*, 21 June 2000: http://news.cnet.com/news/0-1007-200-2123121.html?tag=st. They made a separate deal with Atlas Metaprise to create e-hub. Cf. "BORN Forms Partnership with Atlas Commerce; Enables B2B Collaboration," 5 December 2000: (formerly) http://www.born.com/about_born/news/news_120500.cfm. J.D. Edwards was subsequently bought by PeopleSoft, which was subsequently bought by Oracle: http://www.peoplesoft.com/corp/en/public_index.jsp. On 26 June 2000, there was an agreement to link Oracle's Customer Relationship Management (CRM) suite and Lucent's billing methods; Jan Stafford, "Oracle, Lucent Bundle CRM, Billing Apps," *Techweb.com*, 29 June 2000: http://www.techweb.com/wire/story/TWB20000629S0006. Such alliances are becoming ever-more wide-ranging. For instance, the consulting firm Cap Gemini Ernst and Young has worked with the ERP company People Soft, since 1991. It is now also partnered with Cisco, IBM, J. D. Edwards, Microsoft, and Oracle. Re: Cap Gemini Ernst and Young, see: http://cgey.com. KPMG is partnered with the same companies as well as Active, Ardent, Baan, Broadvision, FedEx, HP, Manugistics, Pepper and Rogers Group, and SAP. KPMG is now also called Bearing Point: http://www.kpmgconsulting.com.

130 "SAP, Commerce One drop plans for online marketplaces," *ITworld.com*, 16 January 2002: http://www.itworld.com/Tech/2406/IDG020116sapcommerceone/.

131 Clint Boulton, "Universal Biz Language Ready for Web Services," *Internet News.com*, 3 May 2004: http://www.internetnews.com/dev-news/article.php/3348491.

132 In 2000, Oracle tried to take over Baan, which was subsequently acquired by SSA Global Technologies. In 2003, Oracle tried to take over Peoplesoft just as Peoplesoft was attempting and then succeeded in a takeover of J.D. Edwards. In 2004, Oracle was again trying to takeover Peoplesoft and finally succeeded. In October 2003, HP was in takeover discussions with Cap Gemini Ernst and Young.

133 Rossetta Net: http://xml.coverpages.org/rosettaNet.html.

134 iEnterprises Inc.: http://www.ienterprises.com/.

135 Oracle applications: http://www.oracle.com/applications/. For a French example, Cybion. Online Business Intelligence: www.cybion.fr.

136 Price Waterhouse Coopers Global: http://www.pwcglobal.com/.
KPMG: http://www.kpmg.com/.
Deloitte. Global: http://www.deloitte.com.
CapGemini: http://www.capgemini.com/about/results.html.
Ernst and Young: http://www.ey.com/global/gcr.nsf/US/Firm_Overview_-_About_E&Y_-_Ernst_&_Young_LLP.
Andersen Consulting now Accenture: http://www.accenture.com/xd/xd.asp?it=enweb&xd=aboutus\history\hist_ourhistory.xml.
Booz Allen and Hamilton: http://www.bah.com/shared/facts.html.
On 29 January 2004, Schlumberger Sema was acquired by Atos Origin. S.A.: http://www.sema.atosorigin.com/.
Logica: http://www.logicacmg.com/.
CMG, now part of Logica: http://www.logicacmg.com/.
Computer Sciences Corporation (CSC): http://www.csc.com/.
CGI Group: http://www.cgi.com/.
Roland Berger: http://www.rolandberger.com/.

137 Another example, Diamond Technology Partners is now Diamond Cluster International: http://www.diamtech.com/default.asp.

138 Jack Vaughan, John K. Waters, "Showtime for XML," *ADT Mag.com*, 1 January 2000: http://www.adtmag.com/article.asp?id=3719.

Kim Girard, "Oracle, Ford team on Net venture," *CNET news.com*, 2 November 1999.: http://news.cnet.com/news/0-1008-200-1427351.html.

Melanie Austria Farmer, "Melanie Austria Farmer, "Guess builds business-to-business site in style," *CNET news.com*, 15 December 1999: http://news.cnet.com/news/0-1008-200-1497651.html.

Ariba: http://www.ariba.com/corporate/news/news.cfm?pressid=161&archive=1.

Commerce One and Shell to build Global Internet Marketplace for the IT Industry, , January 2000: (formerly): http://www.commerceone.com/news/releases/shell_announce.html. http://www.shell-me.com/english/feb2000/news-world1.htm#worldnews6.

Melanie Austria Farmer, "DuPont signs on for Ariba e-commerce services," *CNET news.com*, 18 January 2000: http://news.cnet.com/news/0-1008-200-1525545.html.

Melanie Austria Farmer, "SAP drills for business in oil industry," *CNET news.com*, 19 January 2000: http://news.cnet.com/news/0-1007-200-1526259.html?tag=st.

David Welch, "E-Marketplace, Covisint," *Business Week Online*, 5 June 2000: http://www.businessweek.com/2000/00_23/b3684044.htm. Meanwhile, Commerce One, Sears, and Carrefour created GlobalnetXchange. Next, "GlobalNetXchange and Tranora Build 'MegaHub'.": http://www.softwarestrategies.com/Web_First/ss.nsf/ArticleID/NBAS-4T2L6Y?OpenDocument&Click; "Cargill, Ariba announce food and beverage open Internet B2B Marketplace" (i.e., Novopoint): http://www.cargill.com/today/releases/00_3_14novopoint.htm; "Boeing, Lockheed Martin, BAE SYSTEMS and Raytheon to Create B2B Exchange for the Aerospace and Defense Industry": http://www.boeing.com/news/releases/2000/news_release_000328a-old.html.

Peter Burrows, "For Computer Makers, an E-Market of their Own," *Business Week Online*, 25 May 2001: http://www.businessweek.com/ebiz/0005/0525ehit.htm. On 18 September 2000, "eHITEX Selects Commerce One to Power E-Marketplace Pilot.": http://www.commerceone.com/news/releases/ehitex.html. Ehitex was soon renamed Converge. "Vendor-CTX Convergence Continues with eHitex Purchase of NECX from VerticalNet." Source: The *AMR Research Alert on Manufacturing* for 29 December 2000: http://www.amrresearch.com; http://www.softwarestrategies.com/Web_First/ss.nsf/ArticleID/DGRD-4SGVC7/. This led to a Logistics Advisory Council. Cf. Petere P. Miner, Professional Dossier, December, 2002: http://www.minerconnection.net/db1/00094/minerconnection.net/_uimages/Dossier.pdf.

Melanie Austria Farmer, "Hotel giants team on Net marketplace," *CNET news.com*, 2 May 2000: http://news.cnet.com/news/0-1007-200-1799920.html?tag=st.

"Entergy Announces new Internet B2B Procurement Exchange": http://www.entergy-arkansas.com/AR/newsroom/newsDetail.asp?ID=3&RC=Ar&List=Region.

"B2Build Teams with Ariba and Arthur Andersen to Offer World-Leading Ecommerce Technology to the Construction Industry.": http://www.ariba.com/company/press_archive.cfm?pressid=299&selectyear=2000&archive=1.

E2open.com: http://www.e2open.com/.

"Omnexus. The Plastics eMarketplace.": http://www.isworld.org/onlineteachingcases/cases/Omnexus.pdf. "All this is part of a larger vision called Leveraged Sourcing Networks (LSN): EDS CoNext plans to create at least 12 LSN groups for giving more than 400 buying companies maximum buying leverage. The groups will be organized by geography, size and/or industry. Global rollout is expected to begin in June, 2000." From: "EDS/Ariba Create New Net Market." (formerly) http://www.advisor.com/Articles.nsf/ID/OA000117.FALLJ65.

Scott Campbell, "Textron To Use Ariba, EDS CoNext Procurement Solution," *Computer Reseller News*, Mountain View, CA, 20 June 2000: http://www.crn.com/sections/BreakingNews/dailyarchives.asp?ArticleID=17673.

564

"IBM Touts Product Life-Cycle Alliance," *Washington Technology*, vol. 15, no. 8, 17 July 2000: http://www.washingtontechnology.com/news/15_8/federal/1558-3.html.

139   Cited by: Dr Anne Tyrie, *CITO Link-line*, 1 November 1999: http://www.cito.ca/.

140   Dirk Donath, Jakob Beetz, Klaus Grether, Ernst Kruiff, Frank Petzold, and Hartmut Seichter, "Cooling Factory, a concrete project to test new architectural applications for augmented reality," *Eurocav3D 2001*, Mykonos 30 May–1 June, Thessaloniki: ZITI, 2001, pp. 85–88.

141   Siemens, "Turbocharged Reality," *Research and Innovation*, vol. 2, 1999: http://w4.siemens.de/FuI/en/archiv/zeitschrift/heft2_99/artikel01/;

142   Formerly at: http://www.ecrc.de/research/uiandv/gsp/ECRCToday/mechrep.html; Didier Stricker: http://www.igd.fhg.de/igd-a4/kontakt.html;. Dirk Asendorff, "Handbuch im Kopf," *Die Zeit*, 23, 29 May 2002, p. 29.

143   CESAR, Oak Ridge: http://www.cesar.ornl.gov/.

144   *Sandia Lab News*, vol. 52, no. 3, 11 February 2000: http://www.sandia.gov/LabNews/LN02-11-00/la00/tech_story.htm.

145   Dr Anne Tyrie, *CITO Linkline*, 14 June 2000: http://www.cito.ca/ cites: http://www.ft.com.

146   Micromachine Centre Tokyo: http://www.mmc.or.jp/e/index.html under National R&D Project. (quote formerly at: http://www.iijnet.or.jp/MMC/what/invest1.htm). It also includes: "an experimental system for exterior inspection of heat exchange tube banks, in which multiple micromachines travel through the narrow spaces between the tubes, couple and uncouple among themselves to match the shape of the object to be inspected, and perform inspections; an experimental system for performing tasks in narrow complex areas, in which a micromachine is inserted through an inspection port to perform interior inspection and repair work; technologies for the enhancement of functional devices; and shared basic technologies." For a list of Micro Machine Centres, see "MEMS in the World": http://mmc.mpe.ntu.edu.sg/linksOthers.asp.

147   Imita company re: Active car Safety: http://www.imita.se/.

148   Neil A. Gershenfeld, *When Things Start to Think*, New York: Owl Books, 2000. Neil Gershenfeld, *Als de dingen gaan denken*, Amsterdam: Prometheus, 2000.

149   Stewart Brand, *How Buildings Learn: What Happens After They're Built*, New York: Penguin, 1995.

150   NASA, (formerly) Intelligent Mechanisms Group.

151   Memory Metal: http://mrsec.wisc.edu/edetc/modules/HighSchool/memory/Memory_Metal.pdf.

152   L. Catherine Brinston, "Characterization and Modeling of Multidimensional SMA Behavior and Coupled Effects of Temperature, Aging Time and Moisture on Polymer Composite Systems." NSF Career Award CMS 9501792, Northwestern University, 1995-1999.

153   Active Materials Laboratory, UCLA: http://aml.seas.ucla.edu/.

154   Active Materials and Structures Lab, MIT.

155   *Workshop on Self-healing Systems: Proceedings of the First Workshop on Self-Healing Systems*, Charleston, SC, New York: ACM Press, 2002. http://www.cs.cmu.edu/~garlan/woss02/.

156   Ivan Amato, 'Animating the Material World,' *Science*, vol. 255, 1992, pp. 284–86. Harry H. Robertshaw, "Control approaches for intelligent material systems – What can we learn from nature?" *Proceedings of the Second International Conference on Intelligent Materials, Williamsburg, Virginia, June, 1994*, Lancaster, PA: Technomic Publishing, 1994, pp. 63–70.

157   Dale M. Amon, "The Impact of Molecular Engineering on Spacecraft Information Systems," Queen's University Belfast Computer Science Department, Belfast. This was an invited paper for the second special issue on space and nanotechnology, *Journal of the British Interplanetary Society*, August, 1994: http://www.islandone.org/MMSG/JBIS1/.

158   Corrosion Solution: http://www.e-cats.com/globalcorrosion/snokote.htm.

159   "Laboratory captures seven R&D 100 awards.": http://www.lanl.gov/worldview/news/releases/archive/99-103.shtml.

160   Ibid: http://www.lanl.gov/worldview/news/releases/archive/99-103.shtml.

161   Conmat, "Brewing Idea for Advanced Construction Materials and Processes Focus Area.": http://www.cerf.org/conmat/atpcon.htm.

162 "Material Is Self-Healing," *NewsMax.com Wires*, Washington (UPI), Thursday, 15 February 2001: http://www.newsmax.com/archives/articles/2001/2/14/183703.shtml.

163 Sid Perkins, "Scientists develop self-healing composites," *Science News*, Week of 17 February 2001, vol. 159, no. 7.; S. R. White et al., "Autonomic healing of polymer composites," *Nature*, vol. 409, 15 February 2001, p. 794; R. P. Wool, "A material fix," *Nature*, vol. 409, 15 February 2001, p. 773.

164 *New World Vistas: Air and Space Power for the 21st Century.* Unpublished drafts, the Human Systems and Biotechnology Volume, the Materials Volume, and the Sensors Volume, 15 December 1995: http://www.fas.org/spp/military/docops/usaf/vistas/vistas.htm; Gary H. Anthes, "IT Goes to War. The battlefield of the future will be computerized and networked," *Computerworld*, 11 March 2002: http://www.computerworld.com/networkingtopics/networking/story/0,10801,68929,00.html.

165 *AirForce 2025*, Chapter 3: http://www.au.af.mil/au/2025/volume2/chap02/v2c2-3.htm.

166 Craig A. Rogers, "Intelligent materials," *Scientific American*, September, 1995, pp. 122–25; the Smart Materials Workshop, Netherlands Design Institute, 1996: (formerly) http://www.designinsite.dk/htmsider/r1303.htm.

167 Universal Plug and Play: http://www.upnp.org/.

168 Quote formerly at: http://singapore.gamecenter.com/Briefs/Guidebook/Fantasy2Fact/ss03.html.

169 Professor Murai described this in an opening panel at INET 2000, Yokohama,17 July 2000, where he referred to SIC 2000, the Automobile Association of Japan and web sites. Cf. KAME Project: www.kame.net and TAHI Project: www.tahi.org.

170 *WWW10* Keynote Speaker Keiji Tachikawa: http://www10.org/keynoters/tachikawa.html.

171 Paul Jacob, Informatics Presentation Excerpt: http://www.almaden.ibm.com/projects/informatics.shtml?pres.

172 *The Weekly Heat*, 17, 4 May 1998: (now password protected).

173 Marcia Stepanek, "As I Was Saying to My Refrigerator," *Business Week*, E.BIZ – WEB SMART 50 – PRODUCTS, 18 September 2000: http://www.businessweek.com/2000/00_38/b3699037.htm.

174 Roger Zedi, "Auf Stippvisite in der Zukunft," *Tages-Anzeiger*, 6 October 2003, p. 33.

175 Rick Perera, "Barcelona plans high-tech trash cans," *CNN.com*, 22 January 2001: http://www.cnn.com/2001/TECH/computing/01/22/high.tech.trash.idg/index.html.

176 Daniel Mange and Marco Tomasini, *Bio-inspired Computing Machines, Toward Novel Computational Architectures*, Lausanne: Presses Polytechniques et Universitaires Romandes, 1998: http://ppur.epfl.ch/livres/2-88074-371-0.html.

177 Formerly at: http://www.stellar.demon.co.uk/control.htm, then Robodyne Cybernetics Ltd., now Fractal Robots: http://www.autopenhosting.org/robots/.

178 Formerly at: http://www.stellar.demon.co.uk/defence.htm. Cf. previous note. It is interesting that the new site no longer refers to defence as an application.

179 Quote formerly at: http://users.ox.ac.uk/~sjoh0543/. He cites Henry Petroski, *To Engineer Is Human: The Role of Failure in Successful Design*, New York: Vintage Books, 1992.

180 Center for Intelligent Materials and Systems: http://www.cimss.vt.edu/. "Examples of smart structures and materials are the integration of piezoceramic materials, shape memory alloys and other electro-mechanically coupled materials into systems that respond to their environment."

181 Paul Gilster, "Computers that improve themselves," *Newsobserver.com*, 9 April 2001: (formerly) http://joshua.zutnet.org:8000/Onderwerpen/evolving-computer/. See: http://news.nanoapex.com/modules.php?name=News&file=article&sid=238

182 Formerly at: http://www.egr.msu.edu/der//labs/imsl.html; "Robot cuts ribbon at research facility – factory of the future," *University of Michigan News Release*, 22 May 1998: http://www.um-ich.edu/~newsinfo/Releases/1998/May98/r052298b.html; Franklin Hoke, "'Smart' Materials Research Expands Beyond Defense Arena," *The Scientist*, vol. 6, no. 9, 27 April 1992. See: http://www.the-scientist.com/yr1992/april/research_920427.html.

183 Biomimetic Products Inc.: (formerly) http://www.biomimetic.com/.

184 A. Beukers and E. van Hinte, *Lightness; the inevitable renaissance of minimum energy structures*, Rotterdam: 010 Publishers. Centre for Biomimetics: http://www.rdg.ac.uk/Biomim/.

185 Philips, "Ambient Intelligence": http://www.research.philips.com/InformationCenter/Global/FArticleSummary.asp?lNodeId=719&channel=719&channelId=N719A2220; Mathilde Sanders, "Een Big Brother-huis vol onzichbare technologie," *De Volkskrant*, 10 January 2002, p. 2E: http://www.extra.research.philips.com/euprojects/ozone/ .

186 FET Proactive Initiative: http://www.cordis.lu/ist/fet/comms.htm.

187 FET Proactive Initiative: http://www.cordis.lu/ist/fet/pr.htm.

188 "What dreams may Come," Bell Labs Lucent: http://www.bell-labs.com/history/future.html.

189 3D Gamestudio is an excellent example of what is now possible with simple home software: http://conitec.net/gallery.htm; Andreas Heer, "Die Spielstation hat begonnen," *Tages-Anzeiger*, 10 December 2001, p. 57, discusses Harry Potter, Anno 1503, Train Simulator, and Wiggles; Matthias Schüssler, "Ein PC-Abenteuer im Eigenbau," *Tages-Anzeiger*, 30 April 2001, p. 65. Using this software, the company Procom GMBH did a complete reconstruction of the town of Quedlinburg, for the Expo 2000 fair: http://conitec.net/a4faq_d.htm; Cf. also Quake, which was one of the first serious interactive games: http://www.idsoftware.com/; Hannes Seifert, "E-content Produktion am Beispiel Digitaler Speile," Neo software Produktions GmbH, 010730: http://www.wko.at/alpbach/bm/dok/seifert.pdf.

190 Adrian Hon, "Editorials: The Hitch-Hiker's Guide to the Game," *Cloudmakers.org*, 14 May 2001: http://www.cloudmakers.org/editorials/adrian1.shtml.

191 Formerly at: http://www.zdnet.com/gamespot/stories/reviews/0,10867,2540035,00.html. Charles Herold, "A Video Game with Cinematic Aspirations," *New York Times*, 28 September 2000, p. D13. Cf. Matthias Schüssler, "Göttliche Schwarzweissmalerei. Black & White ist ein PC Spiel das MassStäbe setzt," *Tages-Anzeiger*, 23 April 2001, p. 57. For links with edutainment, see Andreas Heer, "Unterhaltung mit Lerneffekt," *Tages-Anzeiger*, 28 October 2002, p. 57.

192 Butterfly.net games: http://www.butterfly.net/. now Energent game technologies: http://www.emergentgametech.com/press_1.html.

193 It's alive.com: http://www.itsalive.com/.
Terraplay Company: www.terraplay.com.
Madcatz Company: http://www.madcatz.com.
Vis-Sim.org: http://www.vis-sim.org/news_comm.asp?ref=3775.

194 Developed by Sergei Gorlatch, Münster.

195 Dermot McGrath, "No Pain, no Game," *Wired News*, 7 March 2002: http://wired.com/news/games/0,2101,50875,00.html. For other interesting games:
Tension graphics: http://www.tensiongraphics.se/;
Liquid Graphics: http://www.go-liquid.com/content/main.htm;
Prelusion: http://www.prelusion.com/.
Cf. Roger Zedi, "Trau Bloss keinem," *Tages-Anzeiger*, 16 March 2004, p. 29. For other game developments: Roger Zedi, "Pack den Manga in die Konsole," *Tages-Anzeiger*, 13 October 2003, p. 33.

196 Research in IPerG: http://iperg.sics.se/research.html.

197 Akira Kurosawa Digital Museum: http://www.alloe.jp/alloe3/pro2/kudm_e/.

198 In May 2000, the German television station, ARD, introduced their first interactive murder mystery. Adam Krause, "Per Mausklick auf Täterjagd im Net," *Die Welt am Sontag*, 21 May 2000, p. 55. For an analysis of developments, cf. Interactive TV Today (ITVT): http://www.itvt.com.

199 Quote formerly at: http://www.infobyte.it/catalogo/indexuk.html. Cf.: http://www.infobyte.it/home_text_en.htm. For a recent survey: *Cultura in Gioco. Le nuove frontiere di musei, didattica e indutria culturale nell'era dell'interattivita*, ed. Pietro A. Valentino and L. Maria Rita Delli Quadri, Florence: Giunti, 2004.

200 For the web site of De pinxi: http://www.depinxi.be/.

201 For an analysis of recent developments: Hannes Seifert, "e-Content Produktion am Beispiel digitaler Spiele," *Europäisches Forum*, Alpbach, 30 July 2001: http://www.wko.at/alpbach/bm/dok/seifert.pdf. Seifert developed a fascinating high-level video game called Pirates Online.

202 Professor Kajitani. Outline of Lab: http://www.kajitani.mce.uec.ac.jp/lab/lab_e.html.

203 Hugh Pope, "U.S. Backed Caspian Pipeline Plan Makes progress on Two Issues," *The Wall Street Journal Europe*, 31 March 2000.

204 Everquest Games. Sony: http://www.everquest.com.

205 SCM includes a Logistic chain, Purchases, Logistics and Production.

206 CRM includes Client Relations, Marketing, Commercial, and Distribution.

207 Erin Callaway, *ERP-the Next Generation: ERPs Web Enabled for E-business*, TBA Edition, CTRC Computer Technology, 2000.

208 Further titles listed in Appendix 8.
   John Maloney of collaborative.com relates these fields as follows:

Supply Chain Management	Enterprise Resource	Product Design	Customer Relationship Management	Planning Management
Collaborative Business Intelligence				
Knowledge Management.				

   For yet another approach: GE IT Solutions: http://www.gecitsolutions.com/IT_Offerings.asp now Compucom: http://www.compucom.com/.

209 Oracle. E-Business Suite: http://www.oracle.com/applications/index.html?content.html.

210 Richard W. Bourke, "Collaborative Product Commerce": http://www.pdmic.com/articles/midrange/Sept2000.html.

211 Cited by Jeffrey Harrow, RCFOC, 29 January 2001: http://www.theharrowgroup.com/.

212 The entry into this market by the world's largest management consultancy firms (figure 13) should theoretically have solved everything. Why then do we constantly hear of projects where these enormous firms fail in their analysis and small firms of a few young individuals are called in to rescue the situation? If the globalization of these firms is as successful as their web pages would have us believe, how is it possible that once mighty banks such as J. P. Morgan could find themselves in dire straights in 2000?

213 As we have seen, in addition to obvious credit card transactions, a number of alternative methods are being explored including a) auctions, b) micro-payment, c) licensing, and d) invocation-based payment. Some see open-source as an alternative (cf. chapters 14–15).

214 Traditionally, the core competencies were centred around products that a company produced. However, as the shift from production to services continues, the product becomes subsidiary to training, consulting, maintenance, and repair. If these tasks are also overtaken by agents, what will a company do other than set in motion a train of sequences? In such a world, the Japanese concern with the importance of acquiring new knowledge to create new things becomes compelling. Does this mean a company effectively needs to become a research institute? If so, what is the long-term difference between a company and a university? If the difference lies merely in the fact that universities do research without products, how can this be defended against research plus products of companies? Traditionally, universities did fundamental research, whereas companies did applied research. Yet even fifty years ago, the great research labs of AT&T or IBM, or national laboratories such as Sandia Labs, GMD, or INRIA, were as significant for fundamental research as the universities. And why is that fundamental research under threat on all fronts now?

215 Marc L. Songini, "Users: Fully automated supply chains hard to pull off," *Computer World*, New York, 7 February 2001: http://www.computerworld.com/industrytopics/manufacturing/story/0,10801,57494,00.html.

216 Crista Souza, "Supply Chain Management Can't Avoid Downturn," *Information Week*, 14 March 2001: Also: http://www.my-esm.com/printableArticle.jhtml?articleID=2911409.

Chapter 6: Institutions

1   Jeremy Rifkin, *The Age of Access*, New York: J.P. Tarcher/Putnam, 2000, p. 32.

2   Ken Ichi Ohmae, "Keynote Address," *INET Global Summit*, Yokohama, 21 July 2000. See Ken Ichi Ohmae, *Invisible Continent*, New York: Harper, 2000.

3   Philips Nat Lab is building a physical, intelligent home and PHENOM, perceptive home environments: http://www.research.philips.com/InformationCenter/Global/FArticleDetail. asp?lArticleId=2213&lNodeId=712&channel=712&channelId=N712A2213.

4   "Intelligent Housing already in place in Hammarby Sjöstad," www.isoc.org/ Inet June, 2001, p. 22; Cf. BBI: http://www.bbi.nu/..

5   Michael Coen: http://www.ai.mit.edu/people/mhcoen/mhcoen.html. The Intelligent room is now: "AIRE: Agent Based Intelligent Reactive Environments": http://aire.csail.mit.edu/.

6   Phil Harvey, "Lab Rat: Talking doors and opinionated couches," *Redherring.com*, 27 July 2000: (now subscription only) http://www.redherring.com/insider/2000/0727/tech-labrat072700. html.

7   "Perceiving Human Actions for Smart Rooms and Environments," at Electrotechnical Laboratory, Image Understanding Section, MIT, 19 March 1996: (formerly) http://www-white.media.mit. edu/~irfan/CV/Talks/etl96.html.

8   Formerly at: http://www.x10.com/homepage.htm; Adam L. Penenberg, "The Surveillance Society," *Wired*, December, 2001, pp. 156–60.

9   Jon Dakss, Stefan Agamanolis, Edmond Chalom, and V. Michael Bove, Jr., "Hyper Soap.": http: //www.media.mit.edu/hypersoap/.

10   Ibid., Virtual Circus: "According to the participant's position in the space, his/her images occlude or are occluded by virtual objects in respect to the 3D perspective of the virtual scene."

11   Artificial Life Interactive Video Environment (ALIVE).

12   MIT, Smart Rooms. This also has the reference to Virtual Circus, cited above. : http:// vismod.www.media.mit.edu/vismod/demos/smartroom/.

13   Artificial Life Companies: (formerly) http://www.it.uom.gr/pdp/digitallib/ALife/Al_ comp.htm.

14   Interactive Television at Philips: "TV TALKS BACK Interactive Television Content Powered by Java[tm] Technology.": http://java.sun.com/features/1999/04/javatv.html; DMOZ Open Directory Project: http://dmoz.org/Arts/Television/Interactive/.

15   Welcome to TiVo: http://www.tivo.com/; Stewart Alsop, "I Want My File-Served TV! If you want to watch Gilligan's antics, you'll order an episode from a server in Atlanta and store it at home," *Fortune*, Monday, 24 June 2002: http://www.fortune.com/fortune/alsop/0,15704,370066,00. html; Don Peppers and Martha Rogers, "We Now Return Control of Your Television Set to You. It's Not the Outer Limits, but Something Much More Insidious: TiVo. How will broadcasters fare in the new viewer-controlled world of TV?" *Broadcast.com*, June, 2002: http://www.darwinmag. com/read/060102/broadcast.html.

16   Amber Ashton, "Tech Predictions form Leading Scientists," CNET, 9 March 2001: http: //www.cnet.com/techtrends/0-6014-8-4962347-1.html#; Cf. Xerox PARC, The Reading Wall: http://www.idonline.com/imdr01/readingwall.html.

17   In the United States, "intelligent kitchens" sometimes simply means an especially well-designed kitchen, e.g., Smartrooms Inc.: http://www.smartrooms.com/kitchens/services.htm or Hanssem Intelligent Kitchens. Cf. Concorsi. DBEW International Design Competition – Hanssem Co., Ltd.: http://architettura.supereva.it/concorsi/2002/20020303.htm. Cf. Matthew Konefal Gray, "Infrastructure for an Intelligent Kitchen": http://hive.sourceforge.net/mkgray-thesis/ html/.

18   In America, the term "smart house" is sometimes a salesperson's term for a well-designed house. For a U.S. Smart House Web Survey: http://www.cc.gatech.edu/fce/seminar/fa98-info/ smart_homes.html.

19 For the inHAUS project (Duisburg) and related projects: www.fraunhofer.de/english/publications/ df/df2001/magazine2_2001_30.pdf.

20 For instance, Joseph Muir Kumph has an MIT Robot Pike (Robopike) project: http://www.mit.edu/afs/athena/org/t/towtank/www/pike/; Virtual Pet Links: http://virtualpet.com/vp/links/links.htm. There are also important projects on robot fish in Japan at Mitsubishi Heavy Industries, with a view to manufacturing boats with fins. Peter Hadfield, "Mitsubishi builds robotic fish.": http://www.robotbooks.com/Mitsubishi-robots.htm.

21 Neha Soni, "Artificial Intelligence": http://www.its.caltech.edu/~sciwrite/journal03/soni.html. Cf. From Animals to Animats 5. *Proceedings of the Fifth International Conference on Simulation of Adaptive Behavior, August 17–21, 1998*, Zurich, Switzerland, ed. Rolf Pfeifer, Bruce Blumberg, Jean-Arcady Meyer, and Stewart W. Wilson, *Artificial Life*, vol. 6, no. 3, Summer, 2000.

22 Professor Muraoka, The Pet Project: http://www.muraoka.info.waseda.ac.jp/eng/research/01.html.

23 Sony AIBO, now called ERS-7: http://www.world.sony.com/Electronics/aibo/index.html.

24 Quote formerly at: http://www.aibo-europe.com/en/sneak_preview/index.html; http://www.aibo-europe.com/1_1_3_ers7_1.asp?language=en#sozial.

25 Jeffrey Harrow, "The Rapidly Changing Face of Computing," 21 May 2001.

26 Robert Uhlig, "High-tech gadget helps humans bone up on dog-speak," *News.Telegraph*, 8 August 2001: http://news.telegraph.co.uk/news/main.jhtml?xml=/news/2001/08/08/wdog08.xml.

27 Anne Lavery, "Robo-cat makes purrfect companion," *BBC News*, Tuesday, 22 February 2000. Tim Larimer, "Man's Best Friend: In a land where people make pets of their gadgets, the root looks set to become the companion of the future," *Time Asia*, 1 May 2000: http://www.time.com/time/asia/magazine/2000/0501/japan.bestfriends.html.

28 Formerly at: http://www.virtual-community.com/. Cf. *Second International Conference on Virtual Communities*: http://www.infonortics.com/vc/99programme.html.

29 Virtual Communities: http://www.davidcoon.com/virtual_.htm.

30 Howard Rheingold, *The Virtual Community. Homesteading on the Electronic Frontier*, Reading, MA: Addison Wesley, 1993. This is also available on-line: http://www.rheingold.com/vc/book/ (formerly at: http://www.well.com/user/hlr/vcbook/index.html).

31 Virtual Worlds Resources. Virtual Communities: http://www.well.com/user/hlr/vircom/index.html#places.

32 Frank Weinreich, "Establishing a point of view toward virtual communities," *CMC Magazine*, February, 1997: http://www.december.com/cmc/mag/1997/feb/wein.html: "It has become popular to look upon users of the Internet as members of a global village or a virtual community. This could also be the main meaning of the term Netizen. This article proposes that the idea of virtual communities is wrong. I point out that communities rely on interaction on a face-to-face basis, and that one can't get to know one another when people are limited to mediated contacts."

33 Groupware: Virtual Communities: http://www.insead.fr/CALT/Encyclopedia/ComputerSciences/Groupware/VirtualCommunities/. Storm A. King has written on *Psychology of Virtual Communities*: http://webpages.charter.net/stormking/. The European Consortium for Informatics and Mathematics (ERCIM), through INRIA and FORTH, and in conjunction with the W3 Consortium, is working on a Community Web (C-Web) project. See: http://www.ics.forth.gr/isl/projects/projects_individual.jsp?ProjectID=10. A related project, SAMIE, Conceptual Modelling of Community Webs, aims to design and validate methods and tools for modelling community-webs: http://www.inria.fr/recherche/equipes/samie.en.html. A joint European-U.S. project, CYCLADES is developing an open collaborative e-print virtual archive environment to support virtual scholarly communities: http://www.ics.forth.gr/isl/projects/projects_individual.jsp?ProjectID=1.

34 Cliff Figallo, *Hosting Web Communities*, New York: John Wiley & Sons, 1999.

35 Lead International: www.lead.org and www.leadcat.org.

36 Etsuko Inoue, "Yokakusa Koga: See the world but live in your Hometown," *INET 2000*, Yokohama: www.koga.org/inet2000/i2k.html.

37 Intelligent Office with "Remote Receptionist": http://www.intelligentoffice.com/.

38 MIT, Smart Desk home page: http://vismod.www.media.mit.edu/vismod/demos/smartdesk/.

39 MIT, Smart Rooms: http://vismod.www.media.mit.edu/vismod/demos/smartroom/.

40 John C. Dvorak, "The Invisible Computer," *ZD Net News, Altavista Live*, 2 June 2000.

41 Appendix 8 under Virtual Teams.

42 Ibid. under Virtual Organizations, Chapter 11: Tele-Work.

43 Francis Fukuyama, Abram N. Shulsky, and United States Army, *The 'Virtual Corporation' and Army Organization*, Santa Monica: Rand Corporation, 1997.

44 Magid Igbaria and Margaret Tan, ed., *The Virtual Workplace*, Hershey, PA: Idea Group Publishing, 1998 (Series in Information Technology Management).

45 Appendix 8 under Chapter 11: Tele-Work.

46 John Sviokla, "The Rise of the Networked Corporation," *Diamond Cluster*, Spring, 2004: http://exchange.diamondcluster.com/Info/Network%20Org%20White%20Paper.pdf.

47 For general literature on the psychology of virtual communities: http://webpages.charter.net/stormking/. For virtual communities in the UK: Online Community Builder's Toolkit: http://www.socio.demon.co.uk/vc/toolkit.html. For Educause virtual learning communities: http://www.educause.edu/asp/doclib/subject_docs.asp?Term_ID=510. Re: Brent Wilson: http://carbon.cudenver.edu/~bwilson/. For relations between virtual communities and electronic commerce: "Virtual Communities Inc. Announces Launch of Its First E-Commerce Marketplace Using Intershop's Technology Platform," *Business Wire*, 14 March 2000: http://www.findarticles.com/cf_dls/m0EIN/2000_March_14/60084270/p1/article.jhtml.

48 David Brütsch, *Virtuelle Unternehmen*, Zurich: vdf Hochschulverlag an der ETH, 1999.

49 *First International Conference on Virtual Communities* (Bath, 1998, 1999; London, 2000): http://www.infonortics.com/vc/; VirComm: http://www.vircommonline.com/; Ceilidh: http://lilikoi.com. Louisiana State University has a Center for Virtual Organization and Commerce (CVOC): http://cvoc.bus.lsu.edu/. The Biz Tech Network links virtual corporations and outsourcing: http://www.brint.com under Virtual Corporation. Further information about these developments is available through the Work on Infonortics by the Association for Global Strategic Information under Infonortics: http://www.infonortics.com/infonortics/infodesc.html. The Global Business Network has a scenario bibliography: http://www.gbn.org and a book club: http://www.gbn.org/BookClubDisplayServlet.srv and the Virtual Organizations Research Network (VoNet): http://www.virtual-organization.net/, which has an *Electronic Journal of Organizational Virtualness* (eJov) and which has now has joined forces with VE-Forum.

50 Firmbuilder.com: http://www.corbettassociates.com/firmbuilder/home.asp.

51 Michael F. Corbett & Associates, Ltd., "Outsourcing Release 2.0: Outsourcing's Transformation to an Information and Processing Backbone,": http://www.corbettassociates.com/home/default.asp.

52 Charles Derber, *Corporation Nation: How Corporations are Taking Over Our Lives and What We Can Do about It*. New York: St. Martin's Griffin, 1998, pp. 103, 110.

53 Ibid., p. 110.

54 For instance, the European Education Partnership claims that "Learners must take responsibility for their learning."

55 "CompuBank puts traditional services on the line," *Houston Chronicle Online*, 13 May 2000: http://www.chron.com/cs/CDA/c100story.hts/special/chron100/552081. Telebanc has since merged with the e-trade bank: http://www.etradebank.com/. E-trade has also acquired Clear Station. "E*TRADE Acquires ClearStation," *Internet News*, 29 March 1999: http://www.internetnews.com/fina-news/article/0,,5_88311,00.html. This is part of a larger ploy. For a discussion of e-trade as a digital financial media company, see General Atlantic Partners. "New E*TRADE Financial Web Site Unveiled," 6 February 2002: http://www.prnewswire.com/cgi-bin/stories.pl?ACCT=104&STORY=/www/story/02-06-2002/0001664010&EDATE=

56 *The State of the Japanese Market 2000, Digest*, Tokyo: Impress, 2000, p. 38.
57 Formerly at: http://www.hsltd.com/corporate/virtual_bank.htm. Cf. "Fidelity National Financial Announces the Acquisition of Hamilton & Sullivan, Ltd," 5 May 2003: http://www.investor.fnf.com/Releasedetail.cfm?ReleaseId=108167. Although it is a little-discussed topic, there is evidence that the banks have lost considerable money through their electronic banking techniques: Simone Luchetta, "Onlinebanken sind knackbar," *Tages-Anzeiger*, 17 November 2003, p. 27.
58 Ohio State University has a OSU Virtual Finance Library: http://www.cob.ohio-state.edu/dept/fin/overview.htm.
59 USC Virtual Law Libraries: http://lawweb.usc.edu/library/resources/search.html.
60 "The Virtual Law School?", 18 November 1998: http://personal.law.miami.edu/~froomkin/articles/virtual/.
61 V-Law. Virtual Law Office of Andrew Sargent: http://www.v-law.com/.
62 Jnet (Justice Network): http://www.pajnet.state.pa.us/pajnet/site/default.asp.
63 Juris: www.juris.de.
64 Marc Roche, "L'informatique peut elle suppléer la justice humaine?" *Le Monde*, 26 aout 2000.
65 Berkman Center for Internet and Society: http://cyber.law.harvard.edu/.
66 "Coming soon to a terminal near you: virtual government," *CNN.com*, 10 February 1997: http://www.cnn.com/TECH/9702/10/virtual.government/.
67 "Gore's New Invention: E-Gov't ," *Reuters*, 5 June 2000: http://www.wired.com/news/politics/0,1283,36784,00.html. In October, 2004, the European Commission also published an *e-government Resource Book*; Todd Ramsey, *On Demand Government*, Lewisville, TX: IBM Press, 2004.
68 Cited by Martin Dodge and Rob Kitchin, *Mapping Cyberspace*, London: Routledge, 2001, p. 41. The reference is to Mark Poster, "Cyberdemocracy, Internet and the Public Sphere," in: David Porter, *Internet Culture*, London: Routledge, 1997, pp. 201–18: http://www.humanities.uci.edu/mposter/writings/democ.html.
69 Official U.S. Executive Branch: department, abbreviations and Web Sites: http://www.loc.gov/rr/news/fedgov.html:

DEPARTMENT	ABBREVIATION	WEB SITES (2001)
Energy	DOE	69
Defense	DOD	56
Health and Human Services	HHS	44
Justice	DOJ	32
Transportation	DOT	27
Commerce	DOC	25
Interior	DOI	23
Labor	DOL	18
Agriculture	USDA	17
Treasury	TD	7
State	SD	7
Veteran Affairs	VA	1
Housing and Urban Development	HUD	1
Education	ED	1

70 Military web sites in the Government of the United States:

MILITARY DEPARTMENT	WEB SITES (2001)
Department of the Air Force	41
Department of the Army	101
Department of the Navy	36
United States Marine Corps (USMC)	9

571

572

There are further sites for the Federal Executive Branch (5), Federal Judicial Branch (5), and Federal Legislative Branch (9): http://www.nttc.edu/gov/branches.html. For a more balanced list of U.S. sites: http://www.thrall.org/govsites.htm.

71 Directorates General and Services in the European Commission include: Agriculture, Competition, Economic and Financial Affairs, Education and Culture, Employment and Social Affairs, Energy and Transport, Enterprise, Environment, Fisheries, Health and Consumer Protection, Information Society, Internal Market, Joint Research Centre, Justice and Home Affairs, Regional Policy, Research, Taxation and Customs Union: http://europa.eu.int/comm/dgs_en.htm.

72 Departments of the Government in Japan, abbreviations, and web sites. For a survey of recent developments in e-government, see the Accenture report, *eGovernment Leadership – Realizing the Vision*, 2002: http://www.accenture.com/xd/xd.asp?it=enWeb&xd=industries\government\gove_welcome.xml:

DEPARTMENT	ABBREVIATION	WEB SITES (2001)
International Trade and Industry	MITI	6
Foreign Affairs	MOFA	3
Posts and Telecommunications	MPT	2
Agriculture, Forestry and Fisheries		2
Education, Science, Sports and Culture		2
Finance		1
Construction		1
Health and Welfare		1
Home Affairs		1
Labor		1
Transport		1

73 Japan Information Network (JIN): http://www.jinjapan.org/ (quote formerly at: http://www.jinjapan.org/jd/org/002000000.html#002001000). Japan has public corporations in: land development; finance; international affairs; industry and economy; transportation; broadcasting; natural resources and energy; science and technology; welfare; environment; academia, education and culture; mutual aid and others.

74 Litton Reshapes Information Systems Group: http://outside-prc.prc.com/services/egov.html.

75 Development Gateway: http://www.developmentgateway.org/.

76 Roza Tsagarousianou, Damian Tambini, and Cathy Bryan. *Cyberdemocracy. Technology, Cities and Civic Networks*, London: Routledge, 1998.

77 Arenotech: http://www.arenotech.org/.

78 Carl Boggs, *The End of Politics. Corporate Power and the Decline of the Public Sphere*, New York: Guilford Press, 2000.

79 Grand Rapids Institute for Information Democracy: http://www.griid.org/index.shtml and the Community Media Center: www.grcmc.org.

80 Jerry Everard, *Virtual States: The Internet and the Boundaries of the Nation State*, London: Routledge, 2000.

81 Brian D. Loader, ed., *The Governance of Cyberspace: Politics, Technology and Global Restructuring*, London: Routledge, 1997. Cf. The Institute on Governance, Ottawa, the director of which, Tim Plumptre, has identified some 27 definitions of governance: http://www.iog.ca/.

82 The year 2000 saw, for instance, the rise of a Multilingual Internet Names Consortium (MINC): http://www.minc.org/. Cf. Karl Auerbach and Daniel Metzger, "Icann behindert Fortschritt," *Tages-Anzeiger*, 7 May 2001, pp. 55, 58.

83 Li Lei, "E-Government: Present and Future," *Euro-China Co-operation Forum on the Information Society* 2002, *Proceedings*, Beijing: China Science and Technology Exchange Center, 2002, pp. 36–45.

84 Ana Montserrat and Salvador Achondo, "Catalonia Trying to Establish 'Virtual State'," *Wired News*, 24 April 1997: http://www.wired.com/news/topstories/0,1287,3385,00.html.

85 These new links between real and virtual are also reflected in a recent book: *Conceptual Competition-ETH World. Virtual and Physical Presence*, intro. Gerhard Schmitt, Zurich: ETH, 2001.

86 Virtual Helsinki: http://www.virtualhelsinki.net/english/. On digital cities, see Toru Ishida and Katherine Isbister, eds., *Digital Cities: Experiences, Technologies and Future Perspectives*, Berlin: Springer Verlag, 2000 (Lecture Notes in Computer Science, 1765).

87 MIT City Scanning Project: Fully Automated Model Acquisition in Urban Areas: http://city.lcs.mit.edu//city.html.

88 "US military creates second earth," BBC News, 23 February 2003: http://news.bbc.co.uk/2/hi/technology/3507531.stm. Meanwhile, the Computer Systems Policy Project (CSPP) has produced a self-assessment tool for (networked) communities, which could be read as the information technology companies' vision for society. Living in the Networked World: http://www.cspp.org/networkedworld/flash/home.htm.

89 Distance Education and Training Council: http://www.detc.org/.

90 History of Distance Education: http://www.cde.psu.edu/DE/history.HTML.

91 Canadian Association for Distance Education: http://www.cade-aced.ca/.

92 History of the Open University: http://www3.open.ac.uk/media/factsheets/Information%20about%20The%20Open%20University/History%20of%20the%20Open%20University.pdf.

93 Quote formerly at: http://www.education.co.jp/EDistance.html.

94 Northwestern University. Smart Classrooms: http://www.at.northwestern.edu/ctg/classrooms.Cf.: Technical Resource Group. Smart classrooms: http://www.ualberta.ca/AICT/ITE/smartclass/.

95 For instance, Venezuala and South Africa also have a significant schoolnet: Red Escolar Nacional (REN): www.rena.e12.ve and http://www.school.za/ respectively.

96 There is a rather America-centric list of a Virtual Schoolhouse: http://www.ibiblio.org/cisco/schools/elementary.html. A site on Virtual Schools: http://www.eun.org/eun.org2/eun/en/index_vs.html. Cf. television program. Brad J Cox, one of the proponents of superdistribution, was also engaged in developing a Virtual School.

97 Now called Edutopiaonline: http://www.glef.org/.

98 Schools Online: http://www.schoolsonline.org/.

99 Center for Innovative Learning Technologies: www.cilt.org.

100 Now under Plato Learning. Class.com, in conjunction with the University of Nebraska links over six thousand high schools. AOL has a Learning Network. Pearson PLC has an e-learning project. The Global Schoolhouse company offers collaborative learning. Lightspan.com is now a part of Plato Learning. The University of Maryland is developing storyrooms for children. Story Rooms: Storykits for building room adventures: http://www.umiacs.umd.edu/~allisond/kidteam/storyrooms.html. Northwestern University has produced the ASK system to offer materials from the viewpoint of different on-line disciplines.

101 WebCT: www.webct.com.

102 Netschools.com now called Plato Learning: http://netschools.com.

103 Courtney Macavinta, "Wilson: Fast times at Digital High," CNET news.com, 19 August 1997: http://news.cnet.com/news/0-1003-200-321488.html?tag=.

104 Ibid.: http://news.cnet.com/news/0-1003-200-321488.html?tag=.

105 Mary Lisbeth D'Amico, "Cisco head sees e-learning as next wave," CNN.com, 17 November 1999: http://www.cnn.com/TECH/computing/9911/17/comdex.elearning.idg/.

106 Cisco, "Education in the Internet Economy": (formerly) www.cisco.com/edu, now Funding Guide in the Internet Economy as part of: http://www.cisco.com/warp/public/779/edu/commitment/edu_internet_economy/edu_tech_fund_opp.html.

107 Sun, "Global Education and Research": http://www.sun.com/edu.

108 Brint.com, Research and teaching: http://www.brint.com/Research.htm.

109 *2020 Visions: Transforming Education and Training Through Advanced Technologies*. Particularly: Diana Walczak, "Encompassing Education" : http://www.technology.gov/reports/TechPolicy/2020Visions.pdf.

110 For a lecture on new virtual universities, American Association for Higher Education, 21 March 1999. Set includes 10 tapes: *What is the new role of faculty in virtual universities? Three perspectives (session 12)*: http://www.ryerson.ca/lt/resources/audiovisuals.htm.

111 http://www.unesco.org/.

112 American Distance Education Consortium, Virtual Universities: http://www.adec.edu/virtual.html.

113 Canadian Association of Distance Education: http://www.cade-aced.ca/; http://http://www.links2go.com/cgi-bin/smartsearch/smartsearch.cgi?username=&keywords=virtual+universities).

114 Contact Consortium: Virtual University Projects: http://www.ccon.org/hotlinks/vedu.html#top; Virtual l University Online. See: http://www.vu.org/; INSEAD's Virtual University list: http://www.insead.fr/CALT/Encyclopedia/Education/Advances/VirtualUniversity/; Virtual Universities: http://www.studentbmj.com/back_issues/1101/reviews/440a.html. This theme is also being studied by Professor Dr. Hans Jörg Bullinger, Fraunhoferinstitut für Arbeitswissenschaft und Organisation, Stuttgart.

115 Now called the Telelearning Experience: http://wildcat.iat.sfu.ca/.

116 Formerly at: http://virtual-u.cs.sfu.ca/vuweb/VUenglish/.

117 Now Learning Lab project: Workplace Learning: Virtual Learning Environment: Collaborative Learning in a Workplace Environment : http://www.lld.dk/consortia/workplacelearning/conferences/gitte2.uk/da.

118 There was a Virtual university or universal virtuality conference: (formerly) http://www.kun.nl/virtueel/speakers.html. There was a *Virtual University Journal* and there was a Virtual University Press.

119 Telecampus: http://www.telecampus.com.

120 Virtual University Online: http://www.vu.org/.

121 Michigan State Virtual University: http://www.vu.msu.edu/.

122 Virtual University: (formerly) http://vu.sshe.edu/index.shtml.

123 Kennedy Western University: http://www.kw.edu/about.asp?active=about.

124 TheU Virtual University: http://www.ccon.org/theu/.

125 Ibid.: http://www.ccon.org/theu/index.html.

126 Virtual Physics and Astronomy now under Fraunhofer: http://mats.gmd.de/~skaley/pwc/. Detlef Skaley is now working on Interactive TV: http://imk.gmd.de/sixcms/detail.php?template=person&id=109.

127 Donald Norman: http://www.jnd.org/; http://www.alteich.com/links/norman.htm. He is no longer heading Unext.com: http://www.unext.com/about.htm.

128 Now renamed: California Virtual Campus: http://www.cvc.edu/ (quote formerly at: http://www.california.edu/); Dr. Jay Thompson, California Virtual University. This historic presentation was given at the 11th *Annual DET/CHE (Directors of Educational Technology/California Higher Education)Conference*, Monterey, November, 1996: http://id-www.ucsb.edu/detche/library/distance/calif/calvu.html.

129 Courtney Macavinta, "'Virtual University' gets boost," *CNET news.com*, 29 July 1998: http://news.cnet.com/news/0-1005-200-331714.html?st.ne.fd.mdh.

130 Ibid.: http://news.cnet.com/news/0-1005-200-331714.html?st.ne.fd.mdh.

131 Della Bradshaw, "An attraction based on similarities," *Financial Times*, 21 May 2001, p. 7.

132 "What is CVU?": (formerly) http://cvu.strath.ac.uk/admin/what-is-CVU.html.

133 Blueprint for Interactive Classrooms: Handbook: http://bic.avnet.kuleuven.be/ ; Teaching and Learning: http://www.sheffcol.ac.uk/links/Internet/Teaching_and_Learning/. Practical courses on the potentials of new media are still in short supply; Roger Zedi, "Didaktische Herausforderung," *Tages-Anzeiger*, 25 November 2002, p. 63. Cf. the Hochschule für Kunst und Gestaltung in Zurich, which is developing Learning Environments (*Lernumgebungen*). Cf. also Luzern.

134 http://www.linov.kuleuven.ac.be/BIC. The Open Society Institute, working with the Hypermethod Company, has created a Distance Learning Studio. Open Society. Distance Learning Studio: http://artinfo.ru/eva/EVA2000M/2000/eng/gipermetod/product1.htm.

135 Quote formerly at: http://web66.coled.umn.edu/schools/JP/Tohoku.html.

136 National Institute of Multimedia Education International Symposium (1999): http://www. nime.ac.jp/conf99/atAGlance.html.

137 National Institute of Multimedia Education (NIME) TEELeX: http://www.nime.ac.jp/research/ virtual-e.html. (quoted in 2000 from site http://www.nime.ac.jp/index-e.html).

138 Hitoshi Ohnishi, Kaname Mochizuki, and Keizo Nagaoka, "A Support System for Distance Spatial Workspace Collaboration," Open Learning 1998. National Institute of Multimedia Education, Japan: http://www.nime.ac.jp/MM/OL98/.

139 http://www.nime.ac.jp/index-e.html.

140 African Virtual University: http://www.avu.org/.The topics they learn include such as Strategy and Innovation, Entrepreneurship, Global Competencies, E-commerce, and Y2K.

141 LANIC (Latin American Network Information Center) Distance education: http://lanic.utexas. edu/la/region/distance/; WWW Virtual Library on Education: http://vlib.org/Education. html. In 2000, there was a section on Distance Education. This was transferred to Edutech in Switzerland: (http://agora.unige.ch/tecfa/edutech/welcome_frame.html) and has now been taken over by UNI.XL which focuses on U.S. choices: http://www.unixl.com/dir/university_ and_college/online_degree/.

142 http://www.fae.plym.ac.uk/tele/resources.html#South/.

143 http://www.cread.org/institutional.htm/.

144 "Professional Military Education in 2020," Airpower Journal, Summer, 1995: http://www.airpower. maxwell.af.mil/airchronicles/apj/pme2020.html#10.

145 Ibid.: http://www.airpower.maxwell.af.mil/airchronicles/apj/pme2020.html. "Joseph Henderson of Dartmouth Medical School, looks at virtual reality in more practical ways as he describes virtual workplaces with virtual colleagues whose 'physical counterpart may exist in any of the far-flung problem-solving teams deployed anywhere in the world.' These virtual coworkers will meet and work in virtual hallways, virtual conference rooms, and virtual laboratories."

146 Linda Jacobsen, "Homebrew VR," Wired, Premier Issue, 1993, pp. 84, 125.

147 Joseph V. Henderson, "Virtual Realities as Instructional Technology," Proceedings of SALT Interactive Instruction Delivery Conference, 20–22 February 1991, pp. 121–25.

148 Formerly at: http://www.al.wpafb.mil/cfb/hsf.htm.

149 Intelligent Collaboration and Visualization Community: http://zing.ncsl.nist.gov/nist-icv/.

150 R. L. Bashshur, P.A. Armstrong, and Z. I. Youssef, Telemedicine; Explorations in the use of telecommunications in health care. Springfield: Charles C. Thomas, 1975.

151 These include: Panama, Cuba, Haiti, Ivory Coast, Germany, Bosnia, Macedonia, Croatia, Kuwait, Egypt, and Somalia. Cf. North Atlantic Regional Medical Command. Telemedicine Directorate: http://telemedicine.wramc.amedd.army.mil/.

152 Virtual Naval Hospital Mission Statement: http://www.vnh.org/Misc/MissionStatement.html. Cf. "The Virtual Naval Hospital. Lessons Learned in Creating and Operating a Digital Health Sciences Library for Nomadic Patrons," D -Lib Magazine, vol. 5, no. 5, May 1999, ISSN 1082-9873: http://www.dlib.org/dlib/may99/05dalessandro.html.

153 Telemedicine and Advanced Technology Research Center (TATRC): http://www.tatrc.org/. News formerly at: http://www.tatrc.org/news/sections/corporate/corpnew.html). The latest update of the news archive is 19 December 2001. Victoria Garshnek and Frederick M. Burkle, Jr., "Telemedicine Applied to Disaster Medicine and Humanitarian Response: History and Future," Proceedings of the Thirty-second Annual Hawaii International Conference on System Sciences, New York: Institute of Electrical and Electronics Engineers, 1998.

154 This has now become TEIS (Telemedicine and E-Health Information Service): http://www.teis. nhs.uk/.

155 American Telemedicine Center: http://www.atmeda.org/about/aboutata.htm.

156 Telemedicine Information Exchange: http://tie.telemed.org/.

157 Institute for Space Medicine and Physiology, Institut de Médecine et de Physiologie Spatiales (MEDES), Telemedicine and Tele-Epidemiology: http://www.medes.fr/HomeTelemedicine. html or go first to http://www.medes.fr/home.html..

158 William G. Mitchell, *City of Bits*, Cambridge, MA: MIT Press, 1995, p. 37.

159 Co-Operative Tele-surgery, Mark Ottensmeyer, MIT: http://web.mit.edu/hmsl/www/markott/ cooptelesurg.html.

160 U.Geek, "Response to Smarter Dog Tags," *Geek News*: http://www.ugeek.com/techupdate/ rdogtag.htm.

161 "Web To Help Streamline Drug Companies," *Reuters*, 23 June 2000.

162 Virtual Hospital: http://www.vh.org/index.html.

163 For Greg Mogel's work, www.tatrc.org. See also the National Institute of Health vision of reducing the time from bench to benchmark: http://nihroadmap.nih.gov. Their vision for the operating room of the future includes total immersion virtual reality and digitally enhanced mannequins.

164 For a more detailed discussion concerning these categories, see the author's "A Databank on Perspective: The Concept of Knowledge Packages," *Metodologia della ricerca: orientamenti attuali. Congresso internazionale in onore di Eugenio Battisti*, Milan, 1991, *Arte Lombarda*, Milan, n. 3–4, parte secunda, 1994, pp. 166–70. Sceptics will invariably say that all this is very attractive in theory but completely unrealistic in practice. Scanning in all the texts is already a monumental task in itself. Creating all these links would create as least as much information again and be too much. This seeming plea for efficiency qua space has limited validity. Thanks to a lack of proper indexing, scholars are constantly re-searching material, unaware that the materials have already been studied by numerous others. The existence of comprehensive indexes would thus prevent duplication and at the same time help fight problems of plagiarism. At a practical level, one would invariably begin with standard works and only use basic subject headings. These would gradually be extended to include all subject headings and then be applied in turn to ever-greater ranges of books.

165 Simone Luchetta, "Wenn Bücher eine Reise machen," *Tages-Anzeiger*, 15 December 2003: www.bookcrossing.com.

166 John Feldcamp, CEO of Xlibris, claims that "we should have 1,200 DPI LCD screens by 2008, and 3,600 DPI screens a couple of years later,"; *NewsScan Daily*, 20 October 2000 ("Above The Fold"), "The future is Bright for E-Publishing." Cited in Sportsci.org: http://www.sportsci. org/jour/0003/mt28.html. Meanwhile, in November, 2000, IBM announced a new kind of screen that is 12 times sharper than regular screens and 4.5 times clearer than HDTV: "The unit is capable of displaying 200 pixels per inch and more than 9 million pixels on a 22-inch screen." Cited by Jeffrey Harrow in *RfoC*. Cf. Xlibris: http://www1.xlibris.com/. IBM, working with Intel, has created a 9.2 megapixel display; Douglas F. Gray, IDG, "Moore's Law? Not for Computer Displays," *Information World*, July, 2001, Computer Weekly.com: 6 June, 2001: http:// www.computerweekly.com/Article102764.htm; Also *TheStandard.com*, Tuesday, 5 June 2001. In August, 2001, Sharp announced a new panel that can display 1 billion colours: Kuriko Miyake, "Sharp Puts a Billion Colors on Display. New technology mimics the work of the human eye, allowing LCDs to feature more colors than ever," *IDG News Service*, Thursday, 2 August 2001: http://www.pcworld.com/news/article/0,aid,56946,tk,dn080201X,00.asp; Ed Scannell, "IBM lays claim to industry's clearest computer display," *InfoWorld*, 10 November 2000: http://www. infoworld.com/articles/hn/xml/00/11/10/001110hndisplay.xml.

167 The International Committee on Museums (ICOM) has a Virtual Library and Museums Pages (VLMP). It also includes other indexes or portals. For instance, in Italy, it links with museumland.com, Museionline, and Yahoo! Italia: http://vlmp.museophile.com/. One country not sufficiently reflected in this list is France. For Russia, the ICOM site mentioned 515 museums in 2001. The Russian list on the site now has 549 museums: http://www.icom.org/vlmp/ russia.html. This does not list two concurrent attempts at a national list: Russian Culture Net: www.russianculture.ru. This site refers to some 55,000+ sites which include:

CULTURAL ORGANIZATION	NO. OF SITES
Libraries	52,177
Museums	1,842
Theatres	489
Zoos	19
Parks of Culture	57

Russian Cultural Heritage Network: www.rchn.org.ru. Important individual museums include:

MUSEUM	WEB SITE
Tretyakov, Moscow	http://www.museum.ru/tretyakov/
Leningrad Region Museums	www.oblmuseums.spb.ru
Kunstkammer	www.kunstkamera.ru
State museum tzarskoje Selo	http://www.tzar.ru

At the regional level, the museums in the Novgorod region have linked a thousand cities as objects of tourism itineraries with an interactive tour that allows one to evaluate the itinerary: www.museum.nnov.ru/tourism. For some examples of virtual museum sites, see:

MUSEUM	WEB SITE
Centre d'art Contemporain, Fribourg	www.fri-art.ch
Kunsthaus, Glarus	www.kunsthausglarus.ch
Migros Museum, Zurich	www.migrosmuseum.ch
Kunsthaus, Zurich	www.kunsthaus.ch
Kunst und Austellungshalle der BRD	www.kah-bonn.de
Guggenheim, New York	http://cyberatlas.guggenheim.org
National Gallery, London	www.nationalgallery.org.uk
Centre Pompidou, Paris	www.cnac-gp.fr
Centre pour l'image contemporaine	www.sgg.ch
J. Paul Getty Museum	www.getty.edu/museum/
State Hermitage, Saint Petersburg	www.hermitagemuseum.org
Whitney Museum, New York	http://www.whitney.org/
Boijmans van Beuningen, Rotterdam	http://boijmans.kennisnet.nl/engels/ehome.htm
ICC, Tokyo	www.ntticc.or.jp
Walker Art Center, Minneapolis	www.walkerart.org
DIA Art Foundation, New York	www.diacenter.org
V2, Rotterdam	www.v2.nl
P.A.R.A.S.I.T.E. Museum, Lubljana	www.ljudmila.org/scca/parasite

Cf. Barbara Basting, "Von der Kunst zum Cybershopping," *Tages-Anzeiger*, 30 May 2000, p. 65.

168 For a further discussion of such possibilities, see the author's "Frontiers in Electronic Media," *Interactions Journal of the ACM*, New York, July-August, 1997, pp. 32–64.

169 Notepad computers and Personal Intelligent Assistants (PIAs), described earlier, offer many new possibilities. Some of these are being explored in the context of the Intelligent Information Interfaces (I3, Icubed) program of the EC: http://www.i3net.org/i3projects/. For instance, the Hyper Interaction within Physical Space (HIPS): http://www.cs.ucd.ie/prism/HIPS/info.htm. This is being tested in the Museo Civico of Siena; it allows visitors to listen to information using earphones and to make notes on a Personal Digital Assistant (PDA). In this case, the information used is limited to that contained within the PDA.

170 Alas CIMI stopped on 15 December 2003. The project, Handscape, Mobile Computing in Museums ended on 30 June 2004: http://www.cimi.org/wg/handscape/index.html.

171 Derek Walcott, "Who Owns Culture? Why Now a Conference on Cultural Patrimony?", *National Arts Journalism Program*, Columbia University, April, 1999: http://www.najp.org/publications/conferencereports/011-031%20Thursday.pdf.

172 The Rijksmuseum already has a list of their 1,250 past exhibitions on-line: http://www.rijksmuseum.nl/asp/framuk.asp?name=collectie.

173 Istituto Nazionale di ottica applicata: www.ino.it/~luca/rifle/ rifleesempio_en.html. Cf. especially the work of the company Editech (Florence): http://www.inoa.it/INO/web_vecchio/presentation.htm.

174 One can, for instance, do retrospective virtual colour restoration. Cf. Toshiro Kamiuchi, Nagaharu Hamada, and Nobuo Ikeshoji, "Digital Image System and its Applications," *Hitachi Review*, vol. 46, no. 5, 1997, pp. 215–19. These are normally inappropriate in a physical museum. An example is el teatro Campesino: http://cemaweb.library.ucsb.edu/etc_ser.html. While traditional museums such as the Gemäldegalerie in Berlin frequently have a digital gallery, there are numerous cases where the new virtual museums entail unexpected contents not associated with traditional museums. For instance, there is:

  1) Ars Electronica Future Lab (Linz):
     http://www.aec.at/en.
  2) Net-Art Virtual Space for Art and Communication (Rome): www.netart.it.
  3) Computer Games Museum: http://www.computerspielemuseum.de/.
  4) Viladonga, which combines the museum and the archaeological site on a single web location: www.aaviladonga.es.
  5) Museo de la erotica (Barcelona): http://www.erotica-museum.com/.

Classing these by themes and showing how there are shifts in what is shown and stored provides new insights into the history of taste. This can both help to recall historic, blockbuster exhibitions and to imagine others that we missed. Many of us know the experience only too well. There is an exhibition by Rembrandt, Monet, Van Gogh, or Picasso in a city such as Paris or Washington and we miss it because we just cannot get away during the few weeks that the exhibition is in town. Or even worse, we get there only to find that the exhibition is sold out for the few days that we are there. Sometimes we manage to get a ticket and find that we have fifteen minutes to see a set of paintings because visitors are being hoarded through as if they were cattle. Alternatively, we get in and find that the hoards are so great that we effectively cannot see the painting at all. This even occurs with paintings that are on permanent display such as the *Mona Lisa*. This same principle can be extended forwards, such that we can also see where paintings will travel for special exhibitions in the near future, which is particularly relevant for tourism. As the capacities of high-level virtual reality, one could have a history of a museum such as the Louvre which shows a) how the complex of buildings grow in the course of the centuries, b) how the paintings of the collection were configured differently over the centuries, c) how these changes in a painting and in their frames reflect shifts in the history of taste, and d) in certain cases, even show reconstructions of how paintings have changed in colour over the ages. Very interesting attempts at such retrospective colour conversion have, for instance, been carried out by Hitachi with respect to the famous engravings of Hokusai, such that one can effectively see how the engraving fades with time. Even those of us who are very familiar with European museums often do not have occasion to see the great collections and monuments of Russia, India, China, and Japan. In fact, almost no one is able to see all the great museums. In the case of endangered sites, such as the Caves of Lascaux or the Tomb of Nefertari, such virtual reality reconstructions are a substitute for viewing the original, in the interests of long-term conservation. Initial examples of this approach such as the Micro-Gallery in London focussed on orienting users qua the public rooms.

175 Flavia Sparacino at MIT: http://xenia.media.mit.edu/~flavia/research.html.

176 *Oxford English Dictionary*, Oxford, which cited the Shorter Oxford that includes the meaning of "incorporate" in the sense of "to combine in one body."

177 Translated from the French by Robert Bononno, New York: Plenum, 1998. For another definition, which dwells on the problematic dimensions of virtuality, see Ellis D. Cooper, "Now – A Natural Theory of Subjective Time": "The first important characteristic of virtuality is that apparent behavior of one kind is entirely reducible to what may be a completely different kind of hidden behavior."

178 In the Middle Ages, the trivium consisted of grammar (the structure of language), dialectic (the logic of language), and rhetoric (the effects of language) and the quadrivium consisted of arithmetic, geometry, music, and astronomy. The combination of these made up the seven liberal arts.

179 P. Milgram, H. Takemura, A. Utsumi, and F. Kishino, "Augmented Reality: A Class of Displays on the Reality-Virtuality Continuum," *SPIE vol*. 2351, *Telemanipulator and Telepresence Technologies*, 1994; P. Milgram and R. van der Horst, "Alternating-Field Stereoscopic Displays Using Light-Scattering Liquid Crystal Spectacles," *DISPLAYS: Technology & Applications*, vol. 7, no. 2, 1986, pp. 67–72.

180 Paul Milgram, Haruo Takemura, Akira Utsumi, and Fumio Kishino "Augmented Reality: A Class of Displays on the Reality–Virtuality Continuum," *SPIE*, vol. 2351, *Telemanipulator and Telepresence Technologies*, 1994: http://vered.rose.utoronto.ca/people/paul_dir/SPIE94/SPIE94.full.html.

181 David Drascic and Paul Milgram, "Perceptual issues in Mixed Reality," *SPIE*, vol. 2653: *Stereoscopic Displays and Virtual Reality Systems*, III, ed. Mark T. Bolas, Scott S. Fisher, and John O. Merritt, San Jose, February, 1996, pp. 123–34. The original illustration is figure one on p. 125: http://gypsy.rose.utoronto.ca/people/david_dir/SPIE96/SPIE96.full.html.

182 Jennifer J. Gristock, "Organisational Virtuality: a conceptual framework for communication in shared virtual environments," Paper prepared for the workshop "Presence in Shared Virtual Environments," BT Laboratories, Martlesham Heath, Ipswich, UK, 10–11 June 1998. Cf. ibid., "Communications and Organisational Virtuality.": (formerly) http://virtual-organization.net/news/NL_1.5/nl_1-5usl.pdf.

183 The former web site of Kevin Shane.

184 Cultural Studies and Europe or the Reality of Virtuality: http://www.inst.at/ausstellung/rea_virt_e.htm.

185 Tomi Nummi, Aarno Rönkä, and Janne Sariola, *Virtuality and Digital Nomadism. An Introduction to the LIVE Project*, Helsinki: University of Helsinki, Department of Teacher Education. Media Education Centre. (Media Education Publication, no. 6): http://www.helsinki.fi/~tella/mep6.html. For a discussion of the Icube projects under I3net Abstracts: http://www.i3net.org/ser_pub/annualconf/abstracts/index.html.

186 Benjamin Wooley, 1992. "Virtuality," and "Cyberspace." *Virtual Worlds: A Journey in Hype and Hyperreality*. Cambridge, MA: Blackwell, pp. 57–72 and 121–36. A thoughtful discussion of the meanings of two key terms "virtuality" and "cyberspace."

187 Stefan Münker, in conversation with Edouard Bannwart, "Cyber City," in: "Virtuality versus Reality", *Telepolis*, Munich: http://www.telepolis.de/tp/deutsch/special/sam/6008/4.html.

188 Bruce Gingery, "Flights of Virtuality."

189 Christoph P.E. Zollikofer, Zoologist, Marcia Ponce de Leon, MD Anthropologist, "Virtual Reality and Real Virtuality in the Biosciences.": http://www.ifi.unizh.ch/mml/people/zolli/vr.html.

190 In connection with Walter Benjamin, cf. Julian H. Scaff, "Art & Authenticity in the Age of Digital Reproduction."

191 "Cyberspace, Virtuality and Critical Theory, Political.": http://www.cyberartsweb.org/cpace/.

192 Marcus Breen, "Information Does Not Equal Knowledge: Theorizing the Political Economy of Virtuality," *Journal of Computer Mediated Communication*, vol. 3, no. 3, December, 1997: http://jcmc.indiana.edu/vol3/issue3/breen.html.

193 A recent development is freeware software for film editing. Cf. Matthias Schüssler, "Das günstige Filmschneiderlein," *Tages-Anzeiger*, 22 January 2001, p. 59.

194 Jacques Neirynck, "Le produit virtuel, concept révolutionnaire," *Le temps*, 9 May 2000.

1   Frederick Winslow Taylor, *Scientific Management*, comprising *Shop Management*, *The Principles of Scientific Management* and Testimony Before the Special House Committee, New York: Harper & Row, 1911.

2   H. L. Gantt, *Organizing for Work*. New York: Harcourt, Brace and Howe, 1919.

3   Most of us forget that Gantt charts are over 80 years old.

4   Elton Mayo, *The Human Problems of an Industrial Civilization*, Cambridge, MA: Harvard University Press, 1933. New edition: New York: Viking, 1960.

5   Chester Irving Barnard, *The Functions of the Executive*, Cambridge, MA: Harvard University Press, 1938.

6   Chester Irving Barnard, *The nature of Leadership*, Cambridge, MA: Harvard University Press, 1940. Frederick Herzberg et al., *Job Attitudes: Review of Research and Opinion*, Pittsburgh: Psychological Service of Pittsburgh, c. 1957. For the full references, see Appendix 8. Quote formerly at: http://www.worthingbrighton.com/result.html.

7   Peter Ferdinand Drucker (1909–), *The End of Economic Man: A Study of the New Totalitarianism*. New York: John Day, c. 1939.

8   Peter Ferdinand Drucker, *The Concept of the Corporation*, New York: John Day, 1946.

9   Peter Ferdinand Drucker, *The Age of Discontinuity: Guidelines to Our Changing Society*. Harper & Row, 1969.

10   Peter Ferdinand Drucker, *The Executive in Action*, New York: HarperBusiness, 1996. Cf. ibid., "Managing Knowledge Means Managing Oneself," *Leader to Leader*, 16, Spring, 2000, pp. 8–10: http://leadertoleader.org/leaderbooks/L2L/spring2000/drucker.html.

11   Abraham Maslow, *Motivation and Personality*, New York: Harper and Row, 1954.

12   F. Herzberg, B. Mausner, and B.B. Snyderman, *The Motivation to Work*, New York: John Wiley & Sons, 1959 (2nd ed.).

13   Rensis Likert, *New Patterns of Management*, New York: McGraw Hill, 1961.

14   Chris Argyris, *Integrating the Individual and the Organization*, New York: Wiley, 1964.

15   Henry Mintzberg, *The Nature of Managerial Work*, New York: Harper and Row, 1973.

16   Ikujiro Nonaka, Hirotaka Takeuchi, and Hiro Takeuchi, *The Knowledge-Creating Company: How Japanese Companies Create the Dynamics of Innovation*, New York: Oxford University Press, 1995.

17   This approach was developed by Henri Fayol (1841–1925), *Administration industrielle et générale*, Paris: Dunod, 1941. English Trans.: *General and Industrial Management*, revised by Irwin Gray, New York: Institute of Electrical and Electronics Engineers, 1984. This led to the structural theories of Max Weber, *The Theory of Social and Economic Organisation*, Oxford: Oxford University Press, 1947.

18   Elton Mayo, *The Social Problems of an Industrial Civilization*, Salem, New Hampshire: Ayer, 1945. Subsequently: Boston; Harvard University Press.

19   Chris Argyris, *Integrating the Individual and the Organization*, New York: Wiley, 1964.

20   Others include Likert, Bennis, Jaques, Maslow, McGregor, Herzberg, Blake, Mouton, Fiedler, Reddin, Thosnud, Vroom, Tannebaum, and Bakke. For an excellent survey of this and the other major schools, see D. Keuning and D.J. Eppink, *Management en Organisatie. Theorie en Torpassing*, Leiden: Stenfert Kroese Uitgevers, 1990, particularly pp. 292–300 and 489ff. I am grateful to Hans Koolmees for this reference.

21   D. Keuning and D. J. Eppink, *Management en Organisatie. Theorie en Toepassing*, Houten: Educatieve Partners Nederland, 2000, pp. 595–611 (7th ed.).

22   George Ritzer, *The McDonaldization of Society. An Investigation Into the Changing Character of Contemporary Social Life*, Newbury, CA: Pine Forge Press, 1993, Rev. ed.: 2000.

23   Ikujro Nonaka, *The Knowledge Creating Company*, New York: Oxford University Press, 1995, p. 27.

24   This position is not universally accepted. It has been attacked by Roger Penrose in books such as *The Emperor's New Mind: Concerning Computers, Minds, and the Laws of Physics*, New York: Penguin, 1991. Cf. Gerald Edelman and Giulio Tononi, *How Matter Becomes Imagination*, New York: Basic Books, 2000, who studied the physical workings of the brain and rejected "the characterization of the brain as

a computer."; Mark Wallace, "Knocking Theories of consciousness on the head," *The Weekend FT*, 23 July 2000, p. viii.

25 Howard Margolis, *Patterns, Thinking, and Cognition*, Chicago: University of Chicago Press, 1987; Allen Newell and Herbert A. Simon, *Human Problem Solving*, Englewood Cliffs, NJ: Prentice Hall, 1972; Allen Newell, *Unified Theories of Cognition*, Cambridge, MA: Harvard University Press, 1990.

26 Howard C. McAllister, "Common Sense Problem Solving and Cognitive Research," October, 1994: http://www.hawaii.edu/suremath/cognitive.html.

27 Howard C. McAllister, "Request-Response-Result. Hierarchical Organization of Knowledge and Hierarchical Use of Knowledge for Problem Solving," 1997: http://www.hawaii.edu/suremath/essentialRRR.html.

28 Robert Sternberg, *Beyond IQ*, Cambridge: Cambridge University Press, 1984. He has also played an important role in developing awareness of tacit knowledge.

29 Sloan School of Management. Faculty. Publications: http://mitsloan.mit.edu/faculty/f-publications.php. For an important recent discussion of these parallels between mind and computer software as well as hardware, there was a lecture by Marta Olivetti Belardinelli at a conference: *Information Science and Technology for the Next Century*, Rome: La Sapienza, 2000. Cf. her books, *La costruzione della realtà come problema psicologico*, Torino: Boringhieri, 1974; *Pensiero produttivo e problem solving*, Roma: Bulzoni, 1977.

30 John S. Carroll, *Cognition and Social Behavior*. Hillsdale, NJ: L. Erlbaum Associates, 1976. Also connected with these discussions are recent debates about memes: Petra Janbroers, "De Mens volgens psycholoog Susan Blackmore," *De telegraaf*, 29 May 1999, p. TA5; UK Memes Central and the work of Susan Blackmore: http://www.susanblackmore.co.uk/memetics/index.htm.

31 Henry D. Jacoby, *The Bureaucratization of the World*. Berkeley: University of California Press, 1976.

32 Bradley, Stephen P., Arnoldo C. Hax, and Thomas L. Magnanti. *Applied Mathematical Programming*. Reading, MA: Addison Wesley Longman, 1977.

33 John F. Rockart, *Computers and the Learning Process in Higher Education: A Report Prepared for the Carnegie Commission on Higher Education*. New York: McGraw-Hill, 1975.

34 David A. Nadler, Marc S. Gerstein, and Robert B. Shaw. *Organizational Architecture: Designs for Changing Organizations*, San Francisco: Jossey-Bass, 1992. John D. W. Morecroft and John D. Sterman, eds., *Modeling for Learning Organizations*, Portland, OR: Productivity Press, 1994 (System Dynamics Series).

35 Lester C. Thurow, *Building Wealth: The New Rules for Individuals, Companies, and Nations in a Knowledge-Based Economy*, New York: Harper Business, 1999; ibid., *The Wealth Pyramid: New Rules for a Knowledge Based Economy*, New York: Harper Business, 1999; ibid., *Fortune Favors the Bold: What We Must Do to Build a New and Lasting Global Prosperity*, New York: HarperBusiness, 2003. Cf.: http://mitsloan.mit.edu/faculty/indexflash.php.

36 Katharine Mieszkowski, "The E-Lance Economy. How Web sites are meeting the needs of Free Agent Nation," *Fast Company*, 29, November, 1999, p. 66: http://pf.fastcompany.com/magazine/29/rftf.html.

37 Joanne Yates, *Control Through Communication: The Rise of System in American Management* (Studies in Industry and Society). Baltimore, MD: Johns Hopkins University Press, 1993; Joanne Yates and John Van Maanen (eds.), *Information Technology and Organizational Transformation: History, Rhetoric and Practice*. Newbury Park, CA: Sage, 1999.

38 Inventor Hall of Fame. Jay W. Forrester: http://www.invent.org/hall_of_fame/61.html.

39 Jay W. Forrester, *Industrial Dynamics*, Waltham, MA: Pegasus Communications, 1961; ibid., *Principles of Systems* (2nd ed.). Waltham, MA: Pegasus Communications, 1968; ibid., *Urban Dynamics*. Waltham, MA: Pegasus Communications, 1969; ibid., *World Dynamics* (1973; 2nd ed.). Waltham, MA: Pegasus Communications, 1971. Cf. Ibid., *Collected Papers of Jay W. Forrester*. Waltham, MA: Pegasus Communications, 1975.

40 Donella H. Meadows et al., *The Limits to Growth; a Report for the Club of Rome's Project on the Predicament of Mankind*, New York: Universe Books [1972] (presented as report 1971). Cf. Eduard Prestel, *Jenseits der Grenzen des Wachstums, Bericht an den Club of Rome*, Stuttgart: Deutsche Verlags-Anstalt, 1988.

41 Jay W. Forrester, *World Dynamics*, Waltham, MA: Pegasus Communications, 1973.

42 Jay W. Forrester, *Industrial Dynamics*, Waltham, MA: Pegasus Communications, 1961. Cf. Appendix 8.

43 Edward B. Roberts, *Managerial Applications of Systems Dynamics*, Waltham MA: Pegasus Communications, 1978.

44 MIT Systems Dynamics in Education Project: http://web.mit.edu/sdg/www/educproject.html. An excellent survey of Forrester's life work from a personal viewpoint is provided by: "The Beginning of System Dynamics," *Banquet Talk at the International Meeting of the Systems Dynamics Society*, Stuttgart, 1989: http://web.mit.edu/sdg/www/Papers/D-4165-1.pdf. For a full list of Forrester's publications, see Jay W. Forrester's home page: http://web.mit.edu/sdg/www/JayForrester.html.

45 Peter M. Senge, *The Fifth Discipline: The Art and Practice of the Learning Organization*, New York: Doubleday/Currency, c. 1990; ibid. et al., eds., *The Fifth Discipline Fieldbook: Strategies and Tools for Building a Learning Organization*, New York: Currency/Doubleday, 1994.

46 Nina Kruschwitz and George Roth, *Inventing Organizations in the 21st Century: Producing Knowledge through Collaboration*, SWP #4064, 21C WP#21, CCS WP #207, March, 1999, p. 78: http://ccs.mit.edu/papers/pdf/wp207and031.pdf.

47 Designing and studying innovative computer systems that help people work together in small or large groups (e.g., "groupware," "computer-supported cooperative work," and "electronic markets").

48 Observing, analyzing, and predicting how information technology affects organizational structures and processes and how firms can use information technology to organize themselves more effectively.

49 The concern is with developing and testing theories about how the activities of separate agents can be coordinated. These theories are expected to both draw upon and illuminate the above kinds of coordination.

50 MIT Process Handbook Project: http://ccs.mit.edu/ph/.

51 This is an adaptive business processes language for explicitly representing process interactions.

52 Society for Organizational Learning. Peter Senge, "Systems Thinking": http://www.sol-ne.org/res/kr/systhink.html.

53 System Dynamics Society, "What is System Dynamics?": http://www.albany.edu/cpr/sds/#mission.

54 The International Control Systems site is now linked with NEG Micon Control Systems: http://www.control-systems.com/.

55 This has links with Anbar Management Intelligence. There are numerous companies dealing with action learning such as:
Action Learning Associates, Columbia, MA: http://www.action-learning.com/staff.html and Action Learning Systems Inc., Monrovia, CA: http://www.actionlearningsystems.com/.

56 "If its good enough for Nobel prize winners: A brief guide to Action Learning": http://www.cambridge-online-learning.co.uk/download/action_learning.doc;   International Management Centres: http://www.i-m-c.org/imcass/VUs/IMC/frame.htm (Quote also at: http://www.i-m-c.org/imcass/VUs/IMC/frame.htm).

57 This is linked with the Oxford Distance Learning Research Unit (DLRU) now Office of Distance and Online Learning (DOL): http://www.online.ox.ac.uk/Index.htm.

58 Definition formerly at: http://www.btinternet.com/~m100/call/definition.html; Action learning in Action: http://www.i-m-c.org/imcass/VUs/IMC/frame.htm; Introduction to Action Learning: http://www.world.std.com/%7Elo/96.10/0064.html; Action Learning: http://www.educ.utas.edu.au/users/ilwebb/Research/action_learning.htm.

59 IMC, Action Learning in Action, as in previous note: http://www.i-m-c.org/imcass/VUs/IMC/frame.htm. "It can be defined as a strategy by which people learn with and from each other as they attempt to identify and then implement solutions to their problems or developmental issues. There are three essential features, which must be present for an activity to be legitimately an action learning programme. These are – 1. There must be action in the real world rather than

in some simulation. 2. The activity must be conducted in a way which involves others, especially other participants who are working on the same or quite different projects. 3. The emphasis must be upon learning not just the taking of action and this is what distinguishes action learning from project team membership." Ibid.: http://www.i-m-c.org/imcass/VUs/IMC/frame.htm. At the end of the session you should be able to: "understand the learning cycle and what it means to learning and problem solving generally; understand your own preferred approaches to learning; make best use of your existing learning preferences, building additional strengths and overcoming blockages; formulate action plans and entries for the Learning Log; review your progress on learning to learn." Cf. Reg Revans, *The Origins and Growth of Action Learning*, Lund (Sweden): Studentlitteratur, Bratt Institut für Neues Lernen, Chartwell-Bratt Ltd., 1982: Reg. Revans, *Action Learning*, Bromley: Chartwell-Bratt, 1982. Connected with Revans is: Douglas A. Schön, *The Reflective Practitioner. How Professionals Think In Action*, New York: Basic Books, 1983, the same individual who worked with Chris Argyris and, incidentally, William Mitchell.

60 Four Approaches to Learning through Experience: http://www.i-m-c.org/imcass/VUs/IMC/frame.htm.

61 Ibid.; Team Management Systems Online: http://www.tms.com.au/tms03.html.

62 Ibid.; Carter McNamara, "Changing Culture in Organizations.": http://www.mapnp.org/library/org_perf/culture.htm.

63 Ibid.; A. Mumford, *Effective Learning*, 1995, Institute of Personnel and Development; Bottom of Form 1; Mumford, *Management Development: Strategies for Action*, 1997, Institute of Personnel Management. Bottom of Form 2; G. M. Robinson, *Managing after the Superlatives: Effective Senior Management Development for the 1990s*, 1992, Tudor Business Publishing. S. Inglis, *Making the Most of Action Learning*, 1994, Gower. Cf. C. J. Margerison and D. McCann, *Team Management: Practical New Approaches*, Herndon, VA: Mercury Books, 1995: http://www.tms.com.au/rm2.html.

64 For a very useful survey: Martin (Harry) Leith.com: http://www.martinleith.com/. Compare also the Open Space movement: http://www.openspaceworld.com/.

65 Dutch Action Learning Association (ALA): http://www.actionlearning.nl/. Their section on methods formerly cited the following:

> Beproefde instrumenten
> M. Daenen:
> "Total Quality Management" van het Instituut Nederlandse Kwaliteit.
> O.H.J. Donnenberg:

U-procedure	U-procedure
Dialogue as Method	dialoog als methode
Project-based work	projectmatig werken
Peer-assisted learning	peer assistent learning
Coaching	coaching
Future search	future search

> R.G. Hallegraeff:

| Working with practice assignments | werken met praktijkopdrachten |

> L. Lap:

Pump-visualization techniques	"pomp" visualisatie-technieken
Consultation scenarios	consultatie-scenario's
Quinn-model	Quinn-model
Learning cycle	Leercyclus

> International Foundation of Action Learning (IFAL)
> Action Learning International (ALI)
> Ideas on Learning Organizations
> IMC Common Multinational Academic Board
> The site of Breakthrough Thinking

66 Skagit Valley College, "Learning into Action": http://www.skagit.edu/news.asp_Q_pagenumber_E_338.

67 Peter Checkland, *Systems Thinking, Systems Practice*, Chichester: J. Wiley & Sons. This includes an excellent introductory section: "Soft Systems Methodology: A 30-Year Retrospective".

68 http://www.scu.edu.au/schools/.

69 Bob Dick, *What is action research?*, 1999: http://www.scu.edu.au/schools/gcm/ar/whatisar.html: "Action research can be described as a family of research methodologies which pursue action (or change) and research (or understanding) at the same time. In most of its forms it does this by 'using a cyclic or spiral process which alternates between action and critical reflection.' In later cycles there is a continuous refinement of 'methods, data and interpretation in the light of the understanding developed in the earlier cycles.' It is thus an emergent process which takes shape slowly; it is an iterative process which converges towards a better understanding of what happens. In most of its forms it is also participative (among other reasons, change is usually easier to achieve when those affected by the change are involved) and qualitative."

70 Jeffrey Pfeffer, *Power in Organizations*, Marshfield, MA: Pitman, 1981.

71 Tom Peters and R. Waterman, *In Search of Excellence*, New York: Harper and Row, 1982.

72 Edgar H. Schein, *Organizational Culture and Leadership*, San Francisco: Jossey Bass, 1985.

73 Ibid., p. 9.

74 Chris Argyris, *Integrating the Individual and the Organization*, New York: Wiley, 1964

75 Chris Argyris, *Behind the Front Page; Organizational Self-Renewal in a Metropolitan Newspaper*. San Francisco: Jossey-Bass, 1974.

76 Chris Argyris, *Action Science: Concepts, Methods, and Skills for Research and Intervention*, San Francisco: Jossey-Bass, 1985.

77 Chris Argyris, *Strategy, Change and Defense Routines*. Boston: Pitman, 1985.

78 Chris Argyris, *Overcoming Organizational Defenses: Facilitating Organizational Learning*, Needham, MA: Allyn & Bacon, 1990.

79 Chris Argyris, *Knowledge for Action: A Guide to Overcoming Barriers to Organizational Change*, San Francisco: Jossey-Bass, 1993.

80 Chris Argyris, "Good communication that blocks learning," *Harvard Business Review*, vol. 72, no. 4, 1994, pp. 77–85.

81 Chris Argyris, *Organizational Learning II: Theory, Method, and Practice*, Reading, MA: Addison-Wesley Longman, 1996. (Schon, D.)

82 Chris Argyris, *On Organizational Learning*, Oxford; Malden, MA: Blackwell Business, 1999.

83 Chris Argyris, "The Next Challenge: Implementing Computer & Information Systems." Keynote address, ECIS'99. For an online bibliography: http://www.actionscience.com/argbib.htm.

84 Center for Dewey Studies. Southern Illinois University, Carbondale: http://www.siu.edu/~deweyctr/.

85 Millie V. Jones, "Class Bios of Kurt Lewin": http://wwwhost.cc.utexas.edu/coc/journalism/SOURCE/j363/lewin.html.

86 "'Technical' theories of action are autonomous or distanced models of expert analysis. They include theories in micro-economic analysis, competitive strategy analysis, activity-based accounting, or rigorous quantitative empirical analysis. 'Human' theories of action are theories about interpersonal relationships, effective leadership, administration, group dynamics, or organizational culture." This is but one of the models: Cf. Action Science Network, "What is Action Science?": http://www.actionscience.com/actinq.htm.

87 Sekretariat Professor Graf, Zentrum für Zukunftsforschung: http://www.sgzz.ch/. While many are focussing on the systematic aspects of these developments, professors such as Karl Weick, the Rensis Likert Collegiate Professor of Organizational Behavior and Psychology, University of Michigan, are particularly concerned with organizational sense-making with research on swift trust in temporary systems, learning moments in organizations, and structures for improvization in team leadership. He is also working on collective mind: http://www.bus.umich.edu/FacultyBios/FacultyBio.asp?id=000119782.

584

88   For an interesting study of the topic, see Edwin C. Nevis, Anthony J. DiBella, and Janet M. Gould, "Understanding Organizations as Learning Systems," MIT *Sloan Management Review*, Winter 1995, Vol. 36, No. 2, pp. 73–85 (Reprint 3626). The Organizational Learning Center at the Sloan School of Management closed in July, 1997 (http://learning.mit.edu/res/wp/learning_sys.html).

89   Peter Senge, *The Fifth Discipline*, 1990, New York: Currency Doubleday, 1990, p. 12.

90   Richard C. Eppel (President, I-BUS) and E. Jeffrey Conklin (Principal, Group Decision Support Systems), "Blending Cultural Transformation and Groupware to Creating a Learning Organization": http://www.3m.com/meetingnetwork/readingroom/gdss_blending.html.

91   Edith Penrose, *The Theory of the Growth of the Firm*, 1st ed., Oxford: Basil Blackwell and New York: John Wiley & Sons, 1959; 2nd ed., 1980, Oxford: Blackwell and New York: St. Martin's; Rev. ed., 1995, Oxford: Oxford University Press. Translated into Japanese, French, Spanish, and Italian.

92   R. R. Nelson and S. G. Winter, "Dynamic Competition and Technical Progress," in B. Balassa and R.R. Nelson (eds.), *Economic Progress, Private Values, and Public Policy: Essays in Honor of William Fellner*, Amsterdam: North-Holland, 1977; ibid., *An Evolutionary Theory of Economic Change*, Cambridge, MA, and London: Belknap Press, 1982. Cf. Nelson-Winter Models Revisited: http://www.business.aau.dk/evolution/evolecon/nelwin/Druidmar96/referancer/NWfinalrefa.html.

93   Sidney G. Winter, "On Coase, Competence, and the Corporation", *Journal of Law, Economics and Organization*, vol. 4, no. 1, Spring, 1988, pp. 163–80. Re: Sidney Winter: http://ideas.repec.org/e/pwi51.html .

94   Ikujiro Nonaka et al., *The Knowledge-Creating Company*, New York: Oxford University Press, 1995.

95   C.K. Pralahad and G. Hamel, "The Core Competence of the Corporation," *Harvard Business Review*, May/June, 1990, pp. 79–91.

96   Ibid., p. 82.

97   David Teece, GaryPisano, and Amy Shuen, *Firm Capabilities, Resources and the Concept of Strategy*, Mimeo. Berkeley: University of California, 1991; David J. Teece, Gary Pisano, and Amy Shuen. "Dynamic Capabilities and Strategic Management," *Strategic Management Journal*, vol. 18, 1997, pp. 509–34.

98   G. Stalk, Jr., P. Evans, and L.E. Schulman, "Competing on capabilities: the new rules of corporate strategy." *Harvard Business Review*, vol. 70, no. 2, March–April, 1992, pp. 57–70.

99   "Le principe est simple: il est demandé à chaque utilisateur de se définir selon ses compétences et savoirs. Savoir réparer un moteur diésel, parler anglais couramment, compter, écrire, organiser un spectacle, animer une conférence… chacun de nous posséde des particularités, des talents, qui peuvent étre utiles à ses voisins. Le logiciel Gingo permettra cette valorisation, permettant parfois même à certains de prendre conscience de leurs savoirs. Cette phase de valorisation des savoirs, des compétences, est essentielle." From: "Quand Pousseront les Arbres de Connaissances?" : http://www.nordnet.fr/montevideo/adc.htm.

100   There is a Stanford Learning Organization Web (SLOW): http://www.stanford.edu/group/SLOW/. There was a Society for Organizational Learning (SOL) until July, 1997: http://learning.mit.edu/. There was a European Learning Network. Cf. David Massart and Frans Van Assche MMGPS, "European Schoolnet Metadata Management in the Celebrate European Learning Network," London, 16 December 2003: http://www.dcs.bbk.ac.uk/~kevin/mmgps/pdf/13-massart.pdf. There was a European Network for Organisational Learning Development (ENFOLD), which reconstituted itself in 1999 as a section of the Society for Organisation Learning: http://www.solonline.org/. There is a European Distance and E-Learning Network (EDEN): http://www.eden-online.org/eden.php. There are also very extensive web sites with resources on Organizational Learning: http://www.albany.edu/faculty/pm157/teaching/topics/orglearn.html. Learning Organizations: http://www.albany.edu/sph/Hoff_learning/index.htm; http://www-i5.informatik.rwth-aachen.de/lehrstuhl/staff/klamma/rkl/oms/oms-bibnet.html; http://www.gpsi.com/lo.html; http://www.syre.com/; http://www.actionscience.com/argbib.htm; Learning Organizations in Development (now Change Management Toolbook). Holger Nauheimer: http://www.change-management-toolbook.com/; Policy implications: http://www.brint.com/NII.htm; Organizational Learning and Knowledge Management: (formerly) http://www.brint.com/OrgLrng.htm.

586

101 Reengineering Resource Center: http://www.reengineering.com/articles/may96/clo.htm.

102 Frederick Winslow Taylor, *Scientific Management*, comprising *Shop Management, The Principles of Scientific Management* and Testimony Before the Special House Committee, New York: Harper & Row, 1911.

103 H. L. Gantt, *Organizing for Work*. New York: Harcourt, Brace and Howe, 1919.

104 Quote formerly at: http://www.ncsa.uiuc.edu/Apps/MCS/ParaGraph/manual/node16.html. "Processor number is on the vertical axis and time is on the horizontal axis, which scrolls as necessary as the simulation proceeds. The Gantt chart provides the same basic information as the Utilization Count display, but on an individual processor, rather than aggregate, basis; in fact, the Utilization Count display is simply the Gantt chart with the green sunk to the bottom, the red floated to the top, and the yellow sandwiched between."

105 Diane McGinty Weston, "Redefining the Corporate Information Center Managing information as a core corporate asset," *Report 848*, Menlo Park: SRI Consulting Business Intelligence, 1998: http://www.sric-bi.com/BIP/Bulletin/B268.shtml.

106 Visible Decisions was a leading company. Then: "Visual Insights acquires Visible Decisions, creating the world's leading provider of data visualization based software and services." For Release, Monday, 24 January 2000: http://www.lucent.com/press/0100/000124.cof.html. This is now Advizor Solutions: http://www.advizorsolutions.com/company/executive_overview.asp.

107 Not discussed here is the whole trend to visualization in the communication of knowledge introduced by thinkers such as Otto Neurath: Jeff Bernard, "Picture Language-Visualization-Diagrammatics," 2nd International Interdisciplinary Symposium, Austrian Museum for Society and Economics, 3–5 December 1993: http://www.uni-ak.ac.at/culture/withalm/semiotics/AIS/sem-rep/rep_conf/93-12-03-AT.html.

108 Systems Thinking Practice: St. Gall Centre for Futures Research: http://www.sgzz.ch/index_systemsthinking.php.

109 Complexity Knowledge Map of Sorin Solomon (Hebrew University) and colleagues: http://www.cs.huji.ac.il/~vish/TG/dev/phpAdm/view.php?2.

110 Fuld and Company. Chapter 1. Understanding Intelligence: http://www.fuld.com/chap1.html.

111 Ikujiro Nonaka and Hirotaka Takeuchi, *The Knowledge-Creating Company*, Oxford University Press, 1995.

112 Herbert Simon, "Decision Making and Problem Solving," *Research Briefings 1986: Report of the Research Briefing Panel on Decision Making and Problem Solving*, National Academy of Sciences. Washington: National Academy Press, 1986, p. 16.

113 Nonaka and Takeuchi, *The Knowledge-Creating Company*, Oxford University Press, 1995, p. 50.

114 Data Management Center, Directory of Process Modeling and Business Process Reengineering Resources: http://www.infogoal.com/dmc/dmcprc.htm; Brint.com under Business Process Reengineering (BPR): http://www.brint.com/BPR.htm; BPRC (Business Processes Resource Centre): (formerly) http://bprc.warwick.ac.uk/bp-site.html#SEC4; Business Process Reengineering Online Learning Center: http://www.prosci.com/bpr_rh1.htm; Reengineering Resource Center: http://www.reengineering.com/; Business Process Re-engineering Advisory Group, University of Toronto: http://www.eil.utoronto.ca/tool/BPR.html.

115 Brint.com BPR: http://www.brint.com/BPR.htm.

116 Association for Enterprise Integration: http://www.afei.org/. Brian Newman has outlined basic differences between knowledge management and knowledge engineering: http://www.km-forum.org/kmvske.htm; The Knowledge Management Forum: http://www.km-forum.org. On the production side there are parallel developments in terms of workflow. Accordingly there is a Workflow and Re-engineering International Association (WARIA): http://www.waria.com/. Research in the field is concerned with practical discovery of knowledge management and agents; UMBC Agent Web: http://agents.umbc.edu/.

117 Tom Yager, "The crown prince of EAI," *InfoWorld*, 1 June 2001: http://archive.infoworld.com/articles/tc/xml/01/06/04/010604tcopener.xml.

118 Other thinkers such as Gene Bellinger have a spectrum of data, information, knowledge, and wisdom: Gene Bellinger, "Knowledge Management – Emerging Perspectives," OutSights: http://www.systems-thinking.org/kmgmt/kmgmt.htm.

119 The original statement is attributed to Lew Platt, former CEO of HP. "If HP Only Knew What HP Knows," Thomas H. Davenport, *Perspectives on Innovation*, Issue 1: *Managing Organizational Knowledge*: http://www.askmecorp.com/pdf/apqc-HP.pdf. Cited in: René Tissen, Daniel Andriessen, and Frank Lekanne Deprez, *Creating the 21st Century Company: Knowledge Intensive, People Rich, Value-Based Knowledge Management*, Amsterdam: Longman, 1998, p. 28.

Chapter 8: Knowledge Management

1 Fred Kofman, "Learning Knowledge and Power": http://www.axialent.com/tmp/downloads/the_infra_consc_business/learning_knowledge_Power.pdf (quote formerly at: http://cgey.ey.com/cap/gcr.nsf/US/Overview_-_Knowledge_Based_Businesses_-_Cap_Gemini_Ernst_&_Young).

2 Mark H. Friedman, "Creating a Knowledge Management Vocabulary," *Intelligent Portals*, 2004: (formerly) http://www.intelligentkm.com/feature/06/SideBar2.shtml.

3 From the introduction to Brian (Bo) Newman, "An Open Discussion of Knowledge Management," *Knowledge Management Forum*, West Richland, Washington, 1991: http://www.km-forum.org/what_is.htm.

4 KM (Knowledge Management) Forum Archives, "The Early Days": http://www.km-forum.org/what_is.htm.

5 Knowledge Management Server at the University of Texas at Austin under FAQs: http://www.mccombs.utexas.edu/kman/answers.htm#whatkm'; http://www.knowledge-nurture.com/.

6 Quote formerly at: http://www.collaboratory.com;
   KM Cluster: http://www.kmcluster.com/.

7 KM Forum, "What is Knowledge Management?": http://www.km-forum.org/what_is.htm. Denham Grey also claimed: "Knowledge management complements and enhances other organizational initiatives such as total quality management (TQM), business process re-engineering (BPR) and organizational learning, providing a new and urgent focus to sustain competitive position."

8 Quote formerly at: http://www.c3i.osd.mil/bpr/bprcd/7223c2.htm.

9 Mark H. Friedman, "Barrier bashing successful knowledge management initiatives rely heavily on a balance between people and technology.": http://www.realtimestrategy.com/files/BarrierBashingRTS.pdf.

10 Wellsprings. Hindsight: http://www.entovation.com/images/wellhind.gif. For a French site, see Intelligence-Innovation-Knowledge Management. Knowledge Management. *L'intelligence en réseau*: http://www.i-km.com/.

11 Quote formerly at: http://cgey.ey.com/cap/gcr.nsf/us/Trends_-_Knowledge_Based_Businesses_-_Cap_Gemini_Ernst_&_Young.

12 In addition to the Knowledge Management Forum, there was a Managing the Knowledge of the Organization (MKO) Consortium, which "brings together a community of business leaders, academics, and researchers to develop a greater understanding of how businesses can better use knowledge to create value.": http://www.businessinnovation.ey.com/mko/index.html). There is a Knowledge Management Resource Centre: http://www.kmresource.com/.
   There are consulting firms such as the Delphi Group: http://www.delphigroup.com/index.html.

13 E.g., Andersen Consulting   Knowledge Xchange
   Booz Allen and Hamilton   Knowledge On-Line
   Ernst and Young   Center for business Knowledge
   KPMG Peat Marwick   A Knowledge Manage
   Price Waterhouse   Knowledge View

14 Randy J. Miller, *Knowledge Management Assessment*, Arthur Andersen, 1999; The Knowledge Management Assessment Tool (KMAT): (formerly) http://www.kwork.org/White_Papers/kmat.html.

15 Deloitte Touche, in July, 2000, had the following categories for Intellectual Asset Management:
Valuation of Intellectual Property and In-Process Research and Development
Valuation of Merger and Acquisition Licensing
Contract and Royalty Management
Knowledge Management
Benchmarking and Best Practices
Intellectual Property Management Holding Companies
Intellectual Property Operations Improvement
Intellectual Asset Management Assessment via DIAMOND (Directed Intellectual Asset Management Opportunities and Needs Diagnostic)

16 In this context, PriceWaterhouseCoopers has supported: Wendi R. Burkowitz and Ruth L. Williams, *The Knowledge Management Fieldbook*, Indianapolis: Financial Times Prentice Hall, 1999: For a critique, see T.D. Wilson, "The nonsense of 'knowledge management'," *Information Research*, vol. 8, no. 1, October, 2002: http://informationr.net/ir/8-1/paper144.html#buk99b.

17 Formerly at: http://cgey.ey.com/cap/gcr.nsf/US/Approach_-_Knowledge_Based_Businesses_-_Cap_Gemini_Ernst_&_Young. In addition, Cap Gemini Ernst and Young work with IBM to provide an Application Framework for e-business and Advanced Development Centres. They are partnered with Microsoft for Custom Application Development, Knowledge Management, E-Commerce, Data Warehousing, Enterprise Resource Planning (ERP), Network Security, Manufacturing, Energy, Health Care, and Telecommunications. They are also partnered with J. D. Edwards to provide Customer Relationship Management, Supply Chain Integration and Optimization, Property Management, OneWorld Implementation Support, e-Commerce, Enterprise Real Estate, Engineering and Construction, Homebuilder [software], and ERP Innovation.

18 Dorothy Yu, "On the Knowledge Edge: How Global Companies Are Building Advantage Through New Approaches to the Ways Organizational Knowledge is Created, Captured and Used" (quote formerly at: http://www.pwckm.com/smart_pub.html). "Technologies that support data warehousing, data mining and portals (single, browser-based points of entry to internal and external information), that disseminate knowledge throughout an organization, and that allow for real-time communication across geographic and functional boundaries are considered staples of the knowledge management discipline. Knowledge categories such as best practices, customer requirements, competitive intelligence and transactional history are typically cited as cornerstones of knowledge management content initiatives.… the sharing of tacit knowledge (the highly subjective and hard-to-codify insight, wisdom, and expertise of employees) in informal, personal settings can also have dramatically positive effects. Together, the explicit and the tacit, the complexly technical and simply personal combine to create a holistic approach to knowledge management, an all-encompassing path which enables organizations to get closer to customers, to become more responsive."

19 Korn Ferry report: "Creating the CIO Executive Success Cycle," October, 2001: http://www.kornferry.com/Sources/PDF/PUB_028.pdf; http://www.brint.com/jobs.htm.

20 "Hughes Names New VP and Chief Information Officer," *Business Wire*, 7 July 1999: http://www.findarticles.com/cf_dls/m0EIN/1999_July_7/55097413/p1/article.jhtml. The U.S. government has a CIO who is now part of a Chief Information Officers Council: http://www.cio.gov/index.cfm?function=home. The U.S. Army also has a CIO: http://www.army.mil/ciog6/. It may be no coincidence, therefore, that the post of CIO was initially linked closely with the notion of business intelligence: "The Quest for Corporate Smarts," *CIO Magazine*, 15 September 1994: http://www.cio.com/archive/091594_comp.html. There was a Competitive Information Systems Development, Futures group; Cf. the Society of Competitive

Intelligence Professionals (SKIP): http://www.scip.org/. There is a CIO Knowledge Management Research Center: http://www.cio.com/forums/knowledge/.

21 Philip C. Murray, Editor-in-Chief, *KM Briefs* and *KM Metazine*, "Part 4 of "New language for new leverage: the terminology of knowledge management": http://www.ktic.com/topic6/13_TERM4.HTM

22 Noted by Hal Varian, Dean of the School of Information Management and Systems at the University of California at Berkeley, in: Bob Weinstein, "Chief knowledge officers in big demand," *Chicago Sun Times*, 29 March 1998 (formerly at: http://www.suntimes.com/output/weinstein/29wein.htm).

23 Formerly at: http://www1.ewin.com/ewin/articles/cko.htm.

24 www.ge.com:
    "The central idea behind Six Sigma is that if you can measure how many 'defects' you have in a process, you can systematically figure out how to eliminate them and get as close to 'zero defects' as possible."

25 Six Sigma Integration Inc.: http://www.6sig.com/pages/526155/index.htm (quote formerly at: http://www.6sig.com/projects.htm).

26 American Society for Quality: http://www.asq.org/; http://www.asq.org/learn-about-quality/six-sigma/overview/overview.html.

27 Six Sigma Academy: http://www.6-sigma.com.

28 Advanced Systems Consultants. Six Sigma: http://www.mpcps.com/SIX0.html.
    Phase 1: Executive Strategy
    Phase 2: Performance Indices
    Phase 3: Process Classification
    Phase 4: Resource Designation
    Phase 5: M/PCpS™ Standardization
    Phase 6: Program Review
    Phase 7: Results Fan-out
    See also: Bill Smith, "Six-sigma design," *IEEE Spectrum*, vol. 30, September, 1993, pp. 43–47.

29 In 2005, KM Central is part of the International Center for Applied Studies in Technology (ICASIT): http://www.icasit.org/ (quote formerly at: http://KMcentral.com/products/products.htm).

30 Open Text Corporation: www.opentext.com.

31 Rigel Corporation under: "Experience": Formerly at: http://www.therigelcorp.com .

32 The Bright Station Corporation has a Knowledge Management Solution. When this company was acquired by Dialog in 2000, the software was renamed "WebLogik." : http://www.dialog.com/pressroom/2000/bstation_0400.shtml. In the meantime, it is no longer visible on the Dialog site as a current product.

33 This is an African tribal language that is used for commerce between tribes.

34 Kanisa Inc.: http://www.kanisa.com/. By 2004, the meaning of the term was no longer explained.

35 Autonomy: http://www.autonomy.com/c/content/Products/IDOL/. Formerly at: http://www.autonomy.com/valueproposition.html

36 Thomas H. Davenport and Laurence Prusak, *Working Knowledge: How Organizations Manage What They Know*, Cambridge, MA: Harvard Business School, 1998: http://www.brint.com/km/davenport/cio/know.htm. This site now contains an article by the same authors called "Know What You Know."

37 Adam Gersting, Cindy Gordon, and Bill Ives, "Implementing Knowledge Management: Navigating the Organizational Journey," Andersen Consulting, March, 1999.

38 Adam Gersting, Nancy Lambert, and Jerry Kaczmarowski, "Thought Leadership. Knowledge Management Driving Personalized eCommerce Solutions," Andersen Consulting.

39 J.E. Enderby and D.R. Phelan, "Action Learning as the Foundation of Cultural Change," *The Quality Magazine*, February, 1994. "In the diagram it is clear that action research is depicted as a circular process. This does not mean that it never ends! What it shows is that having carried out a piece of research, collected the data, taken action, etc., there is a changed situation or an improved situation, which might then be the focus of further research, further action, and so on. On some projects, the researchers will probably go round the cycle a couple of times, whilst others will go round it only once."

40 Boise State University, School of Business.CIS/PM Department, *The CPS Process*: http://cispom.boisestate.edu/murli/cps/cps.html. For other creativity tools, see Murli's (Murli Nagasundaram) Creativity page: http://cispom.boisestate.edu/murli/creativity/.

41 Brian R. Gaines and Mildred L. G. Shaw, "Eliciting Knowledge and Transferring it Effectively to a Knowledge-Based System", Knowledge Science Institute, Calgary, 19 September 1995: http://ksi.cpsc.ucalgary.ca/articles/KBS/KSS0/.

42 Philip Koopman, "Life cycle Considerations," Carnegie Mellon University, 18-849b Dependable Embedded Systems, Spring, 1999: http://www.ece.cmu.edu/~koopman/des_s99/life_cycle/.

43 Syntell Co. Life cycles: http://www.syntell.se/.

44 William Schrage and Tom Peters, *Serious Play: How the World's Best Companies Simulate to Innovate*, Cambridge, MA: Harvard Business School, 1999.

45 Outsights is working with companies such as 3Com, Amdahl, Compaq Computers, Ericsson, Lucent Technologies, Microsoft, Novell, Nortel Networks, Oracle, SGI, Teradyne, and Xerox.

46 Gene Bellinger, "Knowledge Management. Emerging Perspectives," 2004: http://www.systems-thinking.org/kmgmt/kmgmt.htm.

47 Outsights: http://www.outsights.com/. By 2004, there was no mention of the Customer Support Consortium. Instead there is now an Industry Influencers Forum.

48 Deloitte Research, Collaborative Knowledge Networks, 2002: http://www.deloitte.com/dtt/research/0,2310,sid%253D6975%2526cid%253D12924,00.html.

49 Outsights: http://www.outsights.com/. (quote formerly at: http://www.outsights.com/brief/org.htm).

50 Dave Douglas and Greg Papadopoulos, "How to dot.com your business," Santa Clara: Sun Microsystems, 2000: (formerly) http://www.sun.com/executives/wht/.

51 Professor David C. Wilkins, Knowledge Based Systems Group, University of Illinois at Urbana-Champaign: http://www-kbs.ai.uiuc.edu/web/kbs/index.htm.

52 Formerly at: http://www-kbs.ai.uiuc.edu/.

53 Ibid.

54 John H. Gennari, Adam R. Stein, and Mark A. Musen, "Reuse For Knowledge-Based Systems and CORBA Components.": http://ksi.cpsc.ucalgary.ca/KAW/KAW96/gennari/.

55 Gene Bellinger, "Knowledge Management – Emerging Perspectives," OutSightse: http://www.systems-thinking.org/kmgmt/kmgmt.htm.

56 Ibid.

57 Vanderbilt University, U.S.-Japan Center. In 2001, Professor Sam Kurokawa moved to Drexel and the Center at Vanderbilt is no longer active in the same way: http://www.lebow.drexel.edu/admin/index.cfm/fuseaction/lebow_admin.faculty_detail/facultyid/33/.

58 Dean of the Graduate School at the Japan Advanced Institute for Science and Technology is also the Xerox Distinguished Professor in Knowledge, Haas School of Business, University of California at Berkeley. Professor Nonaka is also a member of the International Research Advisory Group at the University of Southern California and at Duke University: http://www.duke.edu/web/NOFIA/international_research.htm. Member of the International Editorial Board of the *Journal of Knowledge Management*: http://konstanza.emeraldinsight.com/vl=5374989/cl=89/nw=1/rpsv/journals/jkm/eabinfo.htm.

59 Michael Polanyi, *Personal Knowledge*, London: Routledge, 1958.

60 Karl-Erik Sveiby, "The Swedish Community of Practice," Paper for PEI Conference, Stockholm, 25 October 1996. Cf. the work of Jan Löwstedt, "On the technological imperative: a criticism of

the contingency theory's possibilities of contributing to the development of knowledge on technology and organization," Stockholm, 1984. (Research paper Ekonomiska forskningsinstitutet vid Handelshögskolan i Stockholm – EFI; 6275).

61 Sveiby calls this the Konrad track in reference to the Konrad Group of Swedish knowledge companies who developed the theory.

62 A term that Sveiby claims to have coined in 1986.

63 Karl Erik Sveiby (ed.), *Den nya Årsredovisningen*, av Arbetsgruppen Konrad, Stockholm: Affärsvärlden, Ledarskap, 1988. (English: *The Invisible Balance Sheet*, Workgroup "Konrad"); .Elisabet Annell, Karl Erik Sveiby (eds.= bokens redaktör), *Den osynliga balansräkningen: nyckeltal för redovisning, styrning och värdering av kunskapsföretag / av Arbetsgruppen Konrad*, Stockholm: Affärsvärlden, Ledarskap, 1989. (English: *The New Organizational Wealth: Managing and Measuring Knowledge Based Assets*, San Francisco: Berrett-Koehler, 1997; Knowledge Nurture.com: http://www.knowledge-nurture.com/.

64 Karl-Erik Sveiby, *The New Organizational Wealth: Managing and Measuring Knowledge Based Assets*, San Francisco: Berrett-Koehler, 1997.

65 Karl E. Sveiby, "What is Knowledge Management?"1996: http://www.sveiby.com/articles/ KnowledgeManagement.html.

66 Don Tapscott, David Ticoll, and Alex Lowy, *Digital Capital: Harnessing the Power of Business Webs*, Boston: Harvard Business School Press, 2000.

67 These include Skandia AFS, which is interested in both human and structural capital: www.skandia.com; WM-Data, a computer software and consulting company: http: //www.wmdata.com/wmwebb/Menu3/reports.asp?TId=3&BId=63. Celemi, which produces creative training tools and has developed an intangible assets monitor: http://www.celemi.com/ ; PLS-Consult, a management consulting firm. Cf. Daniele Chauvel, Charles Despres, "The Intellectual Roots of Knowledge Management," European Center for Knowledge Management, Sophia Antiplois, 2002: http://www.knowledgeboard.com/doclibrary/knowledgeboard/ day_1_intellectual_roots.pdf.

68 Artificial Intelligence Applications Institute (AIAI), Knowledge Systems: http://www.aiai.ed.ac. uk/research/knowledgesystems.html .

69 Robert S. Kaplan and David P. Norton, *The Balanced Scorecard: Translating Strategy into Action*, Boston: Harvard Business School, 1996.

70 Richard J. Mayer, T. Cullinane, Paula de Witte, William Knappenberger, B. Perakath, and Sue M. Wells, "Information Integration for Concurrent Engineering (IICE)," Report # AL-TR-1992-0057, Air Force Systems Command, Wright-Patterson Air Force Base, Ohio, 1992.

71 M. Ould, 1993. Cf. ibid., *Business Processes*, J. Wiley, 1995. Cf. Steve Dawkins, "Role Activity Diagrams for safety process definition.": www-users.cs.york.ac.uk/~steve/Published/TN-98-10.pdf.

72 B. Benus, R. de Hoog, and R. van der Spek, "The paint advisor: a communicative expert system," In: G. Schreiber, B. Wielinga, and J. Breuker, editors, *KADS: a principled approach to knowledge-based system development*, London: Academic Press, 1993, pp. 267 - 286; G. Schreiber, H. Akkermans, A. Anjevierden, R. de Hoog, H. Shadbolt, W. van de Welde, and B. Wielinga, *Knowledge engineering and management. The CommonKADS Methodology*, Cambridge, Massachusets: MIT Press, 2000.

73 R. van Der Spek and R. De Hoog, "A Framework for Knowledge Management Methodology," in: *Knowledge Management Methods: Practical Approaches to Managing Knowledge*, Arlington, TX: Schema Press, vol. 3, 1995, pp. 379–98.

74 H. Mandl and G. Reinmann-Rothmeier, "Wissensmanagement in Organisationen – Konzeption, Förderung, Probleme." In: J. König, Ch. Oerthel, and H-J. Puch, eds., *Qualitätsmanagement und Informationstechnologien im Sozialmarkt*, Starnberg: Schulz, 2000, pp. 95–116, particularly p. 99.

75 The article was submitted to the *American Mathematical Journal* in 1941 and rejected. It was discussed in a letter with Weyl in 1942 and published much later. Emil L. Post , "Absolutely unsolvable problems and relatively undecidable propositions -- account of an anticipation," first published in M. Davis, ed., *The Undecidable*, New York: Raven Press, 1965, pp. 340–433; Cf. Emil L. Post, "Formal reductions of the general combinatorial decision problem," *American Journal of Mathematics*,

vol. 65, 1943, pp. 197–215.; M. Davis, ed., *Solvability, Provability, Definability: The Collected Works of Emil L. Post*, Boston-Basel-Berlin: Birkhäuser, 1994.

76 A. Newell, H. Simon, *Human Problem Solving*, Englewood Cliffs, NJ: Prentice-Hall, 1972.

77 Marvin Minsky, *A Framework for Representing Knowledge: The Psychology of Computer Vision*, P. H. Winston (ed.), New York: McGraw-Hill, 1975.

78 William J. Clancey, "The epistemology of a rule-based expert system: A framework for explanation," *Artificial Intelligence*, vol. 20, no. 3, 1983, pp. 215–52.

79 A. Newell, "The Knowledge Level," *Artificial Intelligence*, vol. 18, no. 1, 1982.

80 V. Sembugamoorthy and B. Chandrasekaran, "Functional Representation of Devices and Compilation of Diagnostic Problem Solving Systems." In: *Experience, Memory, and Reasoning*, eds. J. L. Kolodner and C. K. Riesbeck, Mahwah, NJ: Lawrence Erlbaum Associates, 1986, pp. 47–73.

81 KADS-II. ESPRIT Project P5248: http://arti.vub.ac.be/kads/.

82 Formerly at: http://www.cse.unsw.edu.au/~timm/pub/ai95/tut.html.

83 ISLA, "Engineering and Managing Knowledge. Common KADS": http://www.commonkads.uva.nl/.

84 Barry Boehm, "Software Requirements Negotiation and Renegotiation Aids: A Theory-W Based Spiral Approach," *ICSE '95*, Seattle, 23–30 April 1995: http://sunset.usc.edu/TechRpts/Papers/icse.conf.95.ps.

85 James Rumbaugh, "Getting started – Using use cases to capture requirements," *Journal of Object-Oriented Programming*, vol. 7, no. 4, September, 1994, pp. 8–23.

86 W. B. Frakes and C.J. Fox, "Sixteen Questions About Software Reuse," *Communications of the ACM*, vol. 38, no. 6, June, 1995, pp. 75–87.

87 For a survey of Some Ongoing KBS/Ontology Projects and Groups: http://www.cs.utexas.edu/users/mfkb/related.html. Cf. the home page of Enrico Franconi: http://www.inf.unibz.it/~franconi/. For a business view of ontologies, cf. Howard Smith, "The Role of Ontological Engineering in B2B Net Markets," CSC Europe, August 2000: (formerly) http://www.ontology.org/main/papers/csc-ont-eng.html.

88 AIAI: http://www.aiai.ed.ac.uk/

KNOWLEDGE CAPTURE	
PC PACK	integrated tools for requirements and knowledge engineering.
Clementine	Data Mining
Knowledge Discovery Software package	ISL
Intelligent Miner	Data mining tool IBM
Information Discovery System (IDIS) Data mining tool, Information Discovery.	
KNOWLEDGE SHARING	
ART*Enterprise	object-oriented client/server tool with case-based retrieval of both structured and unstructured information Brightware
GrapeVINE –	two versions: Lotus Notes, Netscape users can set up an interest profile that identifies what is useful to them and so filter information.
Knowledger Software: Personal Knowledge Manager (PKM) Personal Development Plan (PDP) both based on Lotus Notes.	
Knowledge Xchange	Knowledge Management System, Lotus Notes based system current users Andersen Consulting professionals.

89   Epistemics. The functions of the eleven tools in the Epistemics PC Pack tool are:
      Protocol Editor
            Mark up transcripts
            Extract key elements
      Hypertext Tool
            Build structured documents
            Annotate any object
      Laddering Tool
            Organize objects in hierarchies
            Support for OODB design
      Card Sort Tool
            Organize concepts
            Support for hierarchical sorting
      Matrix Tool
            Manipulate elements using a spreadsheet-like tool
      Repertory Grid
            Proven acquisition method
            Handles uncertainty
      Rule Editing & Induction
            Create and edit rule sets
            Machine learning produces rule sets from case data
      Control Editor
            Process decomposition tool
      GDM Workbench
            Support for structured KA and KADS method
      Entity-Relationship Tool
            Support for E-R diagrams using captured knowledge
      Dependency editor
            Edit table based and functional dependencies.

90   Gilbert Probst, Steffen Raub, and Kai Romhardt, *Wissen managen. Wie Unternehmen ihre wertvollste Ressource optimal nutzen*, Wiesbaden: Th. Gabler, 1999, p. 58.

91   Heinz Mandl, and Franz Fischer, eds., *Wissen sichtbar machen. Wissensmanagement mit Mapping Techniken*, Göttingen: Hogrefe, 2000. For more literature on Professor Heinz Mandl, see LMU (Lehrstuhl für Empirische Pädagogik und Pädadogische Psychologie): http://lsmandl.emp.paed.uni-muenchen.de.

92   Ibid., chapter 9. S. Weber and M. Schumann: "Das Concept Mapping Software Tool (COMASOTO)"; Christine Erlach, Gabi Reinman-Rothmeier and Heinz Mandl, "Wissensmanagement in der Weiterbildung: ein kooperatives Weiterbildungsangebot von der Universität München und Siemens," *Industrie Management*, vol. 15, no. 6, 1999, pp. 38–42.

93   Companies were traditionally measured largely in terms of their annual revenues. In the past decade, there has been an increasing trend to judge companies in terms of their market capitalization, i.e., their stock price times the number of shares. By this criterion, Cisco is now the most valuable company in the world. Not everyone accepts this model. Experienced stock advisors accept that market capitalization can readily exceed the earnings of a company. They also note that when a company's capitalization is more than one hundred times their annual revenue, as is the case with AOL, Time Warner, Uniphase, and others, some correction is almost certainly on the horizon. For a claim that the Internet is undermining traditional capitalism; John Browning and Spencer Reiss, "Growth is a Commodity," *Wired*, June, 2000, pp. 230ff: http://www.wired.com/wired/archive/8.06/wired_index.html.

94   Fredmund Malik, *Systemisches Management, Evolution, Selbstorganisation Grundprobleme, Funktionsmechanismen und Lösungsansätze für komplexe Systeme*, Bern, Stuttgart: Paul Haupt, 1993: "Dieses Buch richtet sich an jene Führungskräfte, die den grundlegenden Charakter der Organisationen, in denen sie

handeln, besser verstehen wollen. Die Organisationen einer modernen Gesellschaft sind zum grössten Teil hochkomplexe Systeme, die wir nicht – wie weithin üblich – als Maschinen, sondern weit besser in Analogie zu Organismen verstehen können. Sie können weder bis ins Detail verstanden und erklärt, noch gestaltet und gesteuert werden. Sie haben ihre eigenen Gesetzlichkeiten und werden zwar auch durch Ziele, aber vor allem durch Regeln kontrolliert. Aus dem – unvermeidlichen – Verzicht auf die Gestaltung und Steuerung im Detail folgt aber keineswegs eine Reduktion managerieller Möglichkeiten und Fähigkeiten, sondern im Gegenteil eröffnen sich durch die systemgerechte Anwendung von Regeln neue und bessere Möglichkeiten des Managements komplexer Systeme. Erst und nur auf diesem Wege können Evolution, Selbstorganisation und Selbstregulierung genutzt werden, um die Wirksamkeit der Organisationen der modernen Wissens- und Informationsgesellschaft zu verbessern."

95 Gilbert Probst, Steffen Raub, and Kai Romhardt, *Wissen managen. Wie Unternehmen ihre wertvollste Ressource optimal nutzen*, Wiesbaden: Th. Gabler, 1999.

96 AGI Information Management Consultants: www.agi-imc.de.

97 Formerly at: www.secag.de.

98 Knowledge Agent: www.knowledgeAgent.de.

99 "L'entreprise de demain," *Le monde interactif*, 29 March 2000.

100 Formerly at: http://www.geocities.com/~knowledge2000/index.html.

101 "'Keiretsu' A Japanese term describing a loose conglomeration of companies organized around a single bank for their mutual benefit. The companies sometimes, but not always, own equity in each other": http://www.investorwords.com/2691/keiretsu.html.

102 In fields such as atomic energy, Japan's standards of quality are lower than Europe or North America. In banking, Japan also seems to lag.

103 Ikujiro Nonaka and Noboru Konno, "The concept of 'ba': Building a foundation for knowledge creation," *California Management Review*, vol. 40, no. 3, Spring, 1998, pp. 40–54. Cf. Ikujiro Nonaka, Ryoko Toyama, and Noboru Konnu, "SECI, Ba and Leadership; A Unified Model of Dynamic Knowledge Creation," In: D. J. Teece and I. Nonaka, *New Perspectives on Knowledge Based Firm Organization*, New York: Oxford University Press, 2000. Cf. Peter Schütt, "The post-Nonaka Knowledge Management," *Journal of Universal Computer Science*, vol. 9, no. 6.

104 Knowledge Management Society of Japan: http://www.kmsj.org/english/kmsj.htm. As of June, 1999, the Society had 286 individual and 49 corporate members. In 2004, it had almost 700 individual members.

105 Hirotaki Takeuchi, "Beyond Knowledge Management: Lessons from Japan," June, 1998: http://www.sveiby.com/articles/LessonsJapan.htm.

106 Brint, "The Knowledge Management Think Tank": http://www.brint.com/wwwboard/wwwboard.html. There was an Intranets for Knowledge Management Conference, San Francisco, 3–5 November 1999. This became KMWorld & Intranets 2003, 14–16 October 2003, Santa Clara Convention Center, Santa Clara, CA: http://www.kmworld.com/kmw03/; (FEND): http://www.brint.com/km/; Knowledge Management Resources. E.g. CSIRO's Decision Making and Knowledge Management: http://www.csiro.au/index.asp?id=Petroleum%20Re sources_Decisions_Knowledge&type=researchProgram&xml=relatedResearchAreas,resear chProjects. Cf. AIB Centre: http://www.cikm.ul.ie/research/knowmanagement_links.html (cf. Jim Boylan's former site) and a multi-forum for the Business, Technology and Knowledge Management Community.

107 Eric Bonabeau, Marco Dorigo, and Guy Theraulaz, *Swarm Intelligence. From Natural to Artificial Systems*, New York: Oxford University Press, 1999.

108 This has since been taken up in the United States as the fashion for intellectual capital.

109 Deutsche Forschungs Gemeinschaft (DFG) project by Prof. Dr. Wolfgang Coy, Volker Grassmuck, and Prof. Dr. Jörg Pflüger. From the "Order of Knowledge" to the "Knowledge Order of Digital Media": http://waste.informatik.hu-berlin.de/Forschung/Wissensordnung/abstract-e.html.

110 Ian Foster, Carl Kesselman, and Steven Tuecke, "The Anatomy of the Grid: Enabling Scalable Virtual Organizations," *Journal of Supercomputer Applications*, 2001. Cf. Frank Lekanne Deprez and René

Tissen, *Zero Space: Moving Beyond Organizational Limits*, San Francisco: Berrett-Koehler, 2002: http://csdl2.computer.org/comp/proceedings/ccgrid/2001/1010/00/10100006.pdf.

111 John Chambers' vision: Jennifer Caplan, "The Virtual Close", *CFO Asia*, April 2001: http://www.cfoasia.com/archives/200104-13.htm; Steve Konzman, "The Virtual Close at Cisco Systems", August 1999: https://www.restaurant.org/studygroups/mis/Presentations/2001_05_TheVirtualCloseNRA.ppt; Jennifer Caplan, "A Virtual Close: Easy as One, Two, Three?", *CFO.com*, 8 March 2001: http://www.cfo.com/article/1,5309,2213,00.html.

112 Don Tapscott, David Ticoll, and Alex Lowy, *Digital Capital*, Boston: Harvard Business School Press, 2000.

113 Ibid., p. 17.

114 Rene Tissen, Daniel Andriessen, and Frank R. Lopez, *The Knowledge Dividend: Creating High Performance Companies through Value-Based Knowledge*, New York: Financial Times, Prentice Hall, 2000. For a discussion of applications to teaching, see Hans Koolmees, "Het Nieuwe Beroeps en Opleidings-Profiel van de Opleiding IDM," *Jaarmagazine IDM*, Maastricht, July, 2000, pp. 4–7. In their business-web typology, Tapscott and his colleagues suggest that Linux is an alliance with self-organizing control and high-value integration. This is true, but does not begin to explain deeper dimensions of the Linux phenomenon. For instance, how is it that, in spite of all the efforts to create business propositions for Linux in the United States, the open-source movement is becoming ever-more linked with the public sphere, with something that goes beyond simple money market terms? Here, Eric Raymond in his *Cathedral and the Bazaar* and Rishab Ghosh have pointed to possible answers (cf. chapters 14–15). Tapscott et al. duly acknowledge the role of human and structural capital. They do not explain why the idea of customer capital began in Japan, nor why human and structural capital are given greater prominence in Europe and Japan than in the United States; Rishab A. Ghosh, "Cooking pot markets: An economic model for the trade in free goods and services on the Internet," *First Monday*, vol. 3, no. 3, March, 1998: http://www.firstmonday.org/. Cf. Orbiten Research: http://orbiten.org.

Chapter 9: Learning

1 Dr. T. C. Bearman, *G7 Ministerial Conference*, 1995, p. 22.

2 John C. Lilly, *Simulations of God: A Science of Belief*, in preparation, 1972, who speaks of "a new high level computer controlling the structurally lower levels of the nervous system, the lower builtin programs. For the first time learning and its faster adaptation to a rapidly changing environment began to appear. Further, as this new cortex expanded over several millions of years, a critical size of cortex was reached. At this new level of structure, a new capability emerged: learning to learn. When one learns to learn, one is making models, using symbols, analogizing, making metaphors, in short, inventing and using language, mathematics, art, politics, business, etc. At the critical brain (cortex) size, languages and its consequences appear.": http://www.lycaeum.org/books/books/metaprogramming_with_lsd_25/full_text.html. John C. Lilly first explored these ideas in a book by the same title: New York: Simon & Schuster, 1956. There were updates until 1975. He died in 2001; John C. Lilly website: html http://www.johnclilly.com/ html. The idea of learning to learn is also emphasized by Dr. Fred (Alfredo) Kofman and Peter Senge, "Communities of Commitment: The Heart of Learning Organization," in: *Learning Organizations*. Sarita Chawla & John Renesch, (eds.), Portland, OR: Productivity Press, 1995, where he explores his idea of transformational learning.

3 Martin Ryder, University of Colorado at Denver, School of Education, "Theoretical Sources": http://carbon.cudenver.edu/~mryder/itc_data/theory.html.

4 Edwin M. Bridges and Philip Hallinger, *Implementing Problem Based Learning in Leadership Development*, Eugene: ERIC Clearinghouse for Educational Management, 1995, p. 13.

5 The old university created knowledge through research and bridged this with the world of practice as was noted by Joseph Murphy, Foreword to: Edwin M. Bridges, Philip Hallinger, as in

previous note. As Joseph Murphy has pointed out, they implicitly shift the role of universities and higher institutions of learning. Traditional universities functioned with a bridge metaphor.

6   This corresponds to Gardiner's definition of intelligence. See Howard Gardner, *Multiple Intelligences: The Theory in Practice*, New York: Basic Books, p. 7.

7   Joseph Murphy, Foreword to: Edwin M. Bridges, Philip Hallinger, *Implementing Problem Based Learning in Leadership Development*, Eugene: ERIC Clearinghouse for Educational Management, 1995, p. x ff.

8   One of the paradoxes is that as managers without intellectual credentials gain ever-greater power within an academic framework, they tend to hide their potential shortcomings by sending everyone else off to be tested.

9   Martin Ryder, University of Colorado at Denver, School of Education. Theoretical Sources: http://carbon.cudenver.edu/~mryder/itc_data/theory.html. On these links, see also Jonathan Ostwald, *Knowledge Construction in Software Development: The Evolving Artifact Approach*. Doctoral Dissertation, University of Colorado, 1996: (formerly) http://www.cs.colorado.edu/~ostwald/thesis/.

10   This list is based on the titles in Professor Barrows' bibliography and those on the Maastricht PBL site.

Agriculture: A. E. Deleon, *Preparation of Problem Oriented Learning Materials: Experimental Project*: Farmers Functional Literacy Programme (Kisan Saksharta Yojana), 1974. (A joint integrated project of three Central Ministries, viz. Education, Agriculture and Information and Broadcasting in India)

Biology: T. S. Hall, *Source Materials for General and Human Biology*. Final Report, 1968.

Education: H. A. Shoemaker, "The functional context method of Instruction," *Human Resources Research Office IRE Transactions on Education*, vol. 3, no. 2, 1960, pp. 52–57. Alexandria, VA: George Washington University. M.L.J. Abercrombie, *Aims and Techniques of Small Group Teaching*. London: Society for Research in Higher Education, 1970.

R. C. Dwyer et al. "Evaluation of the Effectiveness of a Problem-Based Preschool Compensatory Program." *Journal of Educational Research*, vol. 66 , no. 4, 1972, pp. 153–56.

M.S. Knowles, *Self-directed Learning: A Guide for Learners and Teachers*. New York: Association Press, 1975.

G. Heijnen and A. Geluk, *Probleemgericht tertiair onderwijs*, Groningen. 1976.

Vincent M. Cowog, "Gaming and simulation with particular reference to the case-study: How well do you use the case method?" *Educational Studies*, vol. 2, no. 2, 1976, pp. 111–20.

G. Heathers et al., *Educators' Guide for the Future*, Philadelphia, 444 North Third Street, Research for Better Schools Inc., 1977.

J. R. Savery, and T. M. Duffy, "Problem Based Learning: An Instructional Model and Its Constructivist Framework." *Educational Technology*, vol. 35, no. 5, 1995, pp. 31–38.

Engineering: J. F. Douglas, *Solution of Problems in Fluid Mechanics: A Problem-Based Textbook*. London, Pitman, 1975.

Information Science: B. Kleinmuntz, *The Processing of Clinical Information by Man and Machine*. Pittsburgh: Carnegie-Mellon University, 1968. Especially chapter 4: "The Formal Representation of Human Judgment."

D. J. Werner, "Information Systems for Problem-Oriented, Interdisciplinary Education," *Annual Meeting of the American Society for Information Science* (37th), Atlanta, Georgia, 1974.

Library Science: R. Warncke, *Planning Library Workshops and Institutes*, Chicago: American Library Association, 1976.

Mathematics: J. F. Lucas, "The teaching of heuristic problem-solving strategies in elementary calculus." *Journal for Research in Mathematics Education*, vol. 5, no. 1, 1974, pp. 36–46.

W. Romey, "Transdisciplinary, problem-centred studies," *School Science and Mathematics*, vol. 76, no. 1, 1975, pp. 30–38.

Management: M. MacNamara and W. H. Weekes, "The action learning model of experiential learning for developing managers." *Human Relations*, vol. 35, no. 10, 1982, pp. 879–901.

Medicine: V.R. Neufeld and H. S. Barrows, "The 'McMaster Philosophy': An Approach to Medical Education," *Journal of Medical Education*, vol. 49, no 1, 1974, pp. 1040–1050.

P. G. Bashook., L. J. Sandlow, et al., "Teaching problem-oriented recording: A systematic approach." *Journal of Medical Education*, vol. 50, no. 10, 1975, pp. 959–64.

S. R. Leeder and D. L. Sackett , "The medical undergraduate programme at McMaster University: learning epidemiology and biostatistics in an integrated curriculum." *Medical Journal of Australia*, vol. 2, no. 23, 1976, pp. 875, 878–80.

Echt, R. and S. W. Chan , "A New Problem-Oriented and Student-Centered Curriculum at Michigan State University." *Journal of Medical Education*, vol. 52, no. 8, 1977, pp. 681–83.

J.H.C. Moust, *Werkboek studievaardigheden: probleemgestuurd doornemen van studiemateriaaltudievaardigheden: probleemgestuurd doornemen* , Maastricht, Rijksuniversiteit Limburg, 1979.

Neuroscience: H. G. Levine and P.B. Forman, "A study of retention of knowledge of neurosciences information," *Journal of Medical Education*, vol. 48, no. 9, 1973, pp. 867–69.

Psychology: L. Szekely, "Productive processes in learning and thinking," *Acta Psychologica*, vol. 7, 1950, pp. 388–407. E. R. Hilgard, R.P. Irvine, and J. E. Whipple, "Rote memorization, understanding, and transfer: An extension of Katona's card trick experiments," *Journal of Experimental Psychology*, vol. 46, no. 4, 1953, pp. 288–92. M. R. Westcott and J. H. Ranzoni, "Correlates of intuitive thinking," *Psychological Reports*, vol. 12, no. 2, 1963, pp. 595–613. Y. Anzai and H. A. Simon (1979). "The theory of learning by doing." *Psychological Review*, vol. 86, no. 2, pp.124–40.

Science: T. C. Chamberlain, "The method of multiple working hypotheses," *Science*, vol. 148, no. 5, 1965, pp. 754–59. (Reprinted from *Science*, vol. 15, no. 92, 1890).

Peter B. Medawar, *Introduction and Intuition in Scientific Thought*, London: Methuen, 1969.

Social Health: M. L. De Volder and P. J. Thung, *Implementing a Problem-Based Curriculum: A New Social Health Program at the University of Limburg, the Netherlands.* Maastricht, Rijksuniversiteit Limburg, 1982.

11   J. Savery, "What is problem-based learning?", paper presented at the meeting of the *Professors of Instructional Design and Technology*, Indiana State University, Bloomington, May, 1994.

12   D.T. Vernon and R.L. Blake, "Does problem-based learning work? A meta-analysis of evaluative research,". *Academic Medicine*, vol. 68, no. 7, 1993, pp. 550–63; E.M. Bridges and P. Hallinger, "Problem-based learning in medical and managerial education," paper presented at the *Cognition and School Leadership Conference of the National Center for Educational Leadership and the Ontario Institute for Studies in Education*, Nashville, TN, September, 1991; David Boud and Grahame Feletti, "Changing problem-based learning": Introduction to the second edition. In David Boud and Grahame Feletti, eds., *The Challenge of Problem-Based Learning*, Guildford and King's Lynn: Biddles Ltd., p. 3. "What is PBL?" : http://edweb.sdsu.edu/clrit/learningtree/PBL/WhatisPBL.html.

13   Barrows now directs the Problem Based Learning Initiative in the School of Medical Education at the Southern Illinois University Articles by Howard S. Barrows: http://www.pbli.org/ bibliography/articles.htm. With D. L Mitchell, "An innovative course in undergraduate neuroscience: Experiment in problem-based learning with 'problem boxes'." *British Journal of Medical Education*, vol.9, no. 4, 1975, pp. 223–30. With R.M. Tamblyn, "An Evaluation of Problem-based learning in Small Groups Using a Simulated Patient," *Journal of Medical Education*, vol. 51, 1976, pp. 52–54. With R. M. Tamblyn, "The Portable Patient Problem Pack: A Problem-Based Learning Unit," *Journal of Medical Education*, vol. 52, no. 12, 1977, pp. 1002–4. Books by Harold S. Barrows: http://www.pbli.org/bibliography/books.htm. With R.M. Tamblyn, *Problem-Based Learning: An Approach to Medical Education*. New York: Springer, 1980. *How to Design a Problem-based Curriculum for Pre-clinical Years*. New York: Springer, 1980. *The Tutorial Process*. Springfield, IL: Southern Illinois University School of Medicine. Rev. ed., 1992. With G.C. Pickell, *Developing Clinical Problem-solving Skills: A Guide to More Effective Diagnosis and Treatment*, New York: Norton Medical Books, 1991. *Practice-Based Learning: Problem-Based Learning Applied to Medical Education*, Springfield, IL: Southern Illinois University School of Medicine, 1994. *What Your Tutor May Never Tell You*, Springfield, IL: SIU School of Medicine, 1996.

14   Problem Based Learning Initiative. Problem Based Learning (PBL): http://www.pbli.org/pbl/ pbl.htm or via http://www.pbli.org. A more recent definition by Finkle and Torp claims that: problem-based learning is a curriculum development and instructional system that simultaneously develops both problem-solving strategies and disciplinary knowledge bases and skills by placing students in the active role of problem solvers confronted with an ill-structured problem

597

that mirrors real-world problems. Specific tasks in a problem-based learning environment include:

 – determining whether a problem exists
 – creating an exact statement of the problem
 – identifying information needed to understand the problem
 – identifying resources to be used to gather information
 – generating possible solutions
 – analyzing the solutions
 – presenting the solution, orally and/or in writing.

S. L. Finkle and L.L. Torp, *Introductory Documents*. (Available from the Center for Problem-Based Learning), Aurora, IL: Illinois Math and Science Academy, 1995, p. 1ff.

Other more recent literature includes:

Doug Boud and G. Feletti, *The Challenge of Problem-based Learning*. London: Kogan, 1991: http://www.pbli.org/bibliography/books.htm.

G. R. Norman and H. G. Schmidt, "The psychological basis of problem-based learning: A review of the evidence," *Academic Medicine*, vol. 67, no. 9, September, 1992, pp. 557–65.

J. G. Brooks and M.G. Brooks, *The Case for Constructivist Classrooms*, Alexandria, VA: Association for Supervision and Curriculum Development, 1993.

W. Stepien and S. A. Gallagher, "Problem-Based Learning: As authentic as it gets," *Educational Leadership*, April, 1993, pp. 25–28.

W. J. Stepien, S.A. Gallagher, and D. Workman, "Problem-Based Learning for traditional and interdisciplinary classrooms," *Journal for the Education of the Gifted*, vol. 4, 1993, pp. 338–45.

Timothy Koschmann, A. C. Kelson, P. J. Feltovich, and Howard S. Barrows, "Computer-Supported Problem-Based Learning: A Principled Approach to the Use of Computers in Collaborative Learning," in *CSCL: Theory and Practice of an Emerging Paradigm*, ed. Timothy Koschmann. Mahwah, NJ: Lawrence Erlbaum Associates, 1996: http://www.pbli.org/bibliography/books.htm.

15 Formerly at: http://www.collegeview.com/careers/miltrain.html.

16 Formerly at: http://www.gordon.army.mil/roa/aftb/probsolv.htm.

17 080:094. Military Leadership and Problem-Solving Skills – 2 hrs: (formerly) http://www.uni.edu/pubrel/catalog02-04/080.html#094.

18 Michael Figliuolo, Assistant Professor, Department of Military Science, Duke University (quote formerly at: http://www.chronicle.duke.edu/chronicle/97/10/22/12ProblemSolving.html). Cf. Garry D. Brewer and Martin Shubik (contributor), *The War Game: A Critique of Military Problem Solving*, Cambridge, MA: Harvard University Press, 1979.

19 Jay Conrad Levinson, *Mastering Guerrilla Marketing*, New York: Houghton Mifflin, 1999.

20 See, for instance, John J. Arquilla and David F. Ronfeldt, *Cyberwar and Netwar: New Modes, Old Concepts, of Conflict*: http://www.rand.org/publications/randreview/issues/RRR.fall95.cyber/cyberwar.html; CRS Report for Congress. *Computer Attack and Cyber Terrorism*, October, 2003 (Order Code RL32114): http://www.fas.org/irp/crs/RL32114.pdf.

21 Ron Boisvert and John Rice, "From Scientific Software Libraries to Problem Solving Environments," *IEEE Computer Science and Engineering*, vol. 3, Fall, 1996, pp. 44–53.

22 Stratis Gallopoulos, Elias Houstis, and John Rice, "Computer as Thinker/Doer: Problem-Solving Environments for Computational Science," *IEEE Computational Science and Engineering*, Summer, 1994: http://www-cgi.cs.purdue.edu/cgi-bin/acc/pses.cgi.

23 Howard Margolis, *Patterns, Thinking, and Cognition*, Chicago: University of Chicago Press, 1987; Allen Newell and Herbert A. Simon, *Human Problem Solving*, Englewood Cliffs, NJ: Prentice Hall, 1972; Allen Newell, *Unified Theories of Cognition*, Cambridge, MA: Harvard University Press, 1990.

24 LDRC Projects. Learning to Learn: Thinking and Learning Skills: http://snow.utoronto.ca/Learn2/modules.html.

25 Ibid.: http://snow.utoronto.ca/Learn2/greg/thetour.htm.

26 Gyargy Polya, *How to Solve It*, Princeton: Princeton University Press, 1945.

27 Howard C. McAllister, Suremath site. "21st Century Problem Solving": http://www2.hawaii. edu/suremath/home1.html under teachers or directly: http://www2.hawaii.edu/suremath/ teachers.html; National Council of Teachers of Mathematics (NCTM); http://standards.nctm. org/document/chapter1/index.htm; Request-Response-Result: http://www2.hawaii.edu/sure-math/essentialRRR.html#return: "[Computers and other technologies] free students from tedious computations and allow them to concentrate on problem solving and other important content.... As paper-and-pencil computation becomes less important, the skills and understand-ing required to make proficient use of calculators and computers become more important.... Evolving technology has made it possible extend our problem solving creativity by using elec-tronic helpers. The basic resources available for this purpose are word processors, spread sheets, draw/paint programs, Math processors. These work together for creative problem solving."

28 Interesting in this context is a project led by seven major corporations called Career Space, which identifies skills in various ICTs: http://www.career-space.com.

29 Samford University, Problem Based Learning: http://www.samford.edu/pbl/.

30 San Diego State University, *Distributed Course Delivery for Problem Based Learnng. Online Workshop at SDSU* 13-14 June 1996, "The Learning Tree: Problems to Overcome: Disadvantages of Problem Based Learning": http://edweb.sdsu.edu/clrit/learningtree/PBL/DisPBL.html.

31 "Brain research-based learning theory gives support to problem-based learning, alternative assessment, education reform and habits of mind – to mention four other IN-SITE areas. Our understanding of the brain gives positive hope for all students, substantiates broad as well as specific aims, and gives reasons to forge connections between and among prior and new learnings. Brain Compatible Learning": http://members.tripod.com/~ozpk/brain.html.

32 Illinois Mathematics and Science Academy, "How does PBL compare with other instructional approaches?": http://www2.imsa.edu/programs/pbln/tutorials/intro/intro7.php.

33 Future Problem Solving Program: http://www.fpsp.org/.

34 F. S. Keller, "Good-Bye teacher," *Journal of Applied Behavior Analysis*, vol. 1, no. 1, 1968, pp. 79–89.

35 Sidney J. Parnes, *Visionizing: State-Of-The-Art Processes for Encouraging Innovative Excellence*, Buffalo: Creative Education Foundation, 1992. Sidney Jay and Harold F. Harding, ed., *A Source Book for Creative Thinking*, New York: Scribner, 1962.

36 This is now the Creative Education Foundation: http://www.creativeeducationfoundation.org/ index.shtml and http://www.idbsu.edu/business/murli/creativity/cpsi.html). See also Gerald Nadler and Shozo Hibino, *Breakthrough Thinking: The Seven Principles of Creative Problem Solving. New Paradigm* (1993). Prima Lifestyles; 2nd rev. ed. (31 August 1998): http://cispom.boisestate.edu/murli/ cps/bibliography.html.

37 Appendix 8: Systems Thinking, e.g., Joseph O'Connor and Ian McDermott, *The Art of Systems Thinking: Essential Skills for Creativity and Problem Solving*, London: Thorsons, 1997.

38 Mind Tools: http://www.mindtools.com/page2.html.

39 Quote formerly at: http://www.cpd.fsu.edu/professional-deve/prob-solving.htm.

40 At Toyota, employees are taught to think WHY consecutively five times. This is an adaptation of cause and effect thinking. If employees think WHY and find a cause, they try to ask themselves WHY again. They continue five times. Through these five WHYs, they can break down causes into a very specific level. This five times WHYs approach is very useful to solve problems.

41 Hidetoshi Shibata, Tokyo, 1998, Frontier Consulting, info@mediafrontier.com. "Problem Solving. Definition, terminology and patterns": http://www.mediafrontier.com/z_ly/ problem.htm.

42 San Mateo County Office of Education, "The Challenge 2000 PBL+MM Model": http://pblmm. k12.ca.us/PBLGuide/model.htm.

43 Buck Institute of Learning, "Overview. Project Based learning": http://www.bie.org/pbl/ index.php.

44 A. Mabogunje and Larry. J. Leifer, "Instrumentation and metrics for Collaborative Team-Design. Predicting collaborative team performance."; Larry Leifer's home page:

http://www-cdr.stanford.edu/~leifer/. To this end, he gives a course: ME310 "Team Based Design Development with Corporate Partners": http://me210.stanford.edu. For videos of his experiences see his tape: *A Collaborative Experience in Global Product-Based-Learning*: (formerly) http://corporate.stanford.edu/education/eduvideo.html.

45   Larry Leifer, *Evaluating Product-Based-Learning Education*, Osaka 1995 Conference: http://cdr.stanford.edu/~leifer/publications/Osaka95/Osaka95.html. "Our curriculum technology focus is on Mechatronic systems design-development (smart products). Mechatronics is frequently defined as the integration of real-time software, electronics, and mechanical elements for imbedded systems. In our definition, we include human-computer-interaction and materials selection. Typical products in this domain include: disk drives, camcorders, flexible automation-systems, process-controllers, avionics, engine controls, appliances and smart weapons."

46   Formerly at: http://pbl.stanford.edu/PBL/overview.html.

47   Dr. Renate Fruchter: http://www.stanford.edu/group/CIFE/renate.html; P5BL: http://www.stanford.edu/group/CIFE/renate.html.

48   Ibid, "-exercise the acquired theoretical knowledge and understand the role of the discipline-specific knowledge in a multi-disciplinary, collaborative, practical project-centred environment,
     − recognize the relationships of the engineering enterprise to the social/ economic/political context of engineering practice and the key role of this context in engineering decisions,
     − learn how to take advantage of computational prototyping facilities and emerging information technologies for collaborative work, and
     − participate in multi-disciplinary teams to design and build environmentally-conscious, high quality facilities faster and more economically."

49   Formerly at: http://www.inet-ads.com/ilearn/pdnet/overview.htm.

50   Martin Ryder, "Learning Environments": http://carbon.cudenver.edu/~mryder/itc/le.html.

51   As my colleague Dr. Geert de Haan has rightly pointed out, this does not mean, however, that Russian (learning) psychology, critical psychology, or genetic epistemology is the same as in the West. In: *Construction and Validation of Scientific Theories*. Genève: Fondation Archives Jean Piaget, 1980, pp. 1–7; Jean Piaget, *Genetic Epistemology*, trans. by Eleanor Duckworth, New York: Columbia University Press, 1970. (Woodbridge lectures series, 8), which explores the idea of intertextuality. Piaget's idea of development is also explored by Jason Ravitz, "Evaluating Learning Networks: A special challenge for Web-based Instruction?" In: Badrul Khan (Ed.)., *Web-based Instruction*, Englewood Cliffs, NJ: Educational Technology Publications,1997, pp. 361-368. For another discussion of Russian constructivism, there is the P.L. Duffy Resource Centre on Constructivism: http://library.trinity.wa.edu.au/subjects/art/construct/default.htm.

52   Jean Piaget, "The constructivist approach: recent studies in genetic epistemology," http://www.npac.syr.edu/users/jravitz/IDE_Model_long.html; http://www.npac.syr.edu/users/jravitz/home_backup.html. For an application of the constructivist approach to a quite different field, see Bruno Latour, *Science in Action: How to Follow Scientists and Engineers through Society*. Cambridge: Harvard University Press, 1987.

53   Martin Ryder, "Constructivism" (list): http://www.cudenver.edu/~mryder/itc_data/constructivism.html.

54   George W. Gagnon, Jr., "Constructivist Learning Links," Prairie Rainbow Company: http://www.prainbow.com/cld/.

55   There was a web site on this subject by Brad Cox (now Unext.com, as mentioned above). For a more recent commentary: "Social Construction of Reality," 30 December 2000: http://cscs.umich.edu/~crshalizi/notebooks/social-construction-of-reality.html.

56   Jean Piaget, B. Inhelder, L. Apostel, R. Garcia, G. Cellérier, G. Henriques, E. Ackermann, I. Berthoud, C. Monnier, and A. Wells, *Construction et validation des théories scientifiques*, Genève: Archives Jean Piaget, 1980; D. H. Jonassen, "Objectivism versus constructivism : do we need a new philosophical paradigm?", *Journal of Educational Research*, vol. 39, no. 3, 1991, pp. 5–14; D. Joseph Novak,

"Human constructivism: a unification of psychology and epistemological phenomena in meaning making," *International Journal of Personal Construct Psychology* 6, 1993, pp. 167–93.

57 Jerome Bruner, *The Process of Education*, Cambridge, MA: Harvard University Press, 1960; Jerome Bruner, *Toward a Theory of Instruction*, Cambridge, MA: Harvard University Press, 1966; David Ausubel, *Educational Psychology: A Cognitive View*, New York: Holt, Rinehart & Winston, 1968; D. A. Kolb, *Experiential Learning: Experience as the Source of Learning and Development*, Englewood Cliffs, NJ: Prentice-Hall, 1984.

58 Tom M. Duffy, J. Lowyck, and D.H. Jonassen, eds., *Designing Environments for Constructive Learning*, Berlin: Springer-Verlag, 1993 (NATO ASI Series F: Computer and Systems Sciences, vol. 105); J. J. Beishuizen, "Studying a complex knowledge domain by exploration or explanation," *Journal of Computer Assisted Learning*, vol. 8, no. 2, 1992, pp. 104–17; Michael J. Jacobson and R. J. Spiro, "Hypertext learning environments, cognitive flexibility, and the transfer of complex knowledge: An empirical investigation," *Journal of Educational Computing Research*, vol. 12, no. 5, 1995, pp. 301–33.

59 J.S. Brown, A. Collins, and P. Duguid, "Situated cognition and the culture of learning," *Educational Researcher*, vol. 18, no. 1, 1989, pp. 32–42; P.C. Honebin, T.M. Duffy, and B.J. Fishman, "Constructivism and the design of learning environments: Context and authentic activities for learning," in T.M. Duffy, J. Lowyck, and D.H. Jonassen, *Designing Environments for Constructive Learning*. Berlin: Springer-Verlag, 1993; T.D. Koschmann, A.C. Myers, P.J. Feltovich, and H. S. Barrows. "Using technology to assist in realising effective learning and instruction: A principled approach to the use of computers in collaborative learning," *Journal of the Learning Sciences*, vol. 3, 1994, pp. 227–64. Quote formerly at: http://www.webtutor.co.uk/Learning/Struct.htm.

60 Joseph A. Raelin, *Work-Based Learning: The New Frontier of Management Development*, Upper Saddle River, NJ: Prentice Hall, 2000; Paul A. Kirschner, *The Inevitable Duality of Education: Cooperative Higher Education*, Maastricht: Universiteit Maastricht, 2000.

61 Katie Dean, "Iconoclast Says Show, Don't Tell," *Wired News*, 17 August 2000: http://www.wired.com/news/culture/0,1284,38169,00.html?tw=wn20000817.

62 Dr. Roger Schank, *The Cognitive Computer: On Language, Learning, and Artificial Intelligence*, in collaboration with Peter G. Childers, *Dynamic Memory: A Theory of Learning in Computers and People*, 1982; *Dynamic Memory Revisited*, New York: Cambridge University Press, 1999. Here he "described how computers could learn based upon what was known about how people learn." *Engines for Education*, Mahwah, NJ: Lawrence Erlbaum Associates, 1995. Here he discussed capturing expertise, knowledge brokerage, training without the trainers. *Virtual Learning: A Revolutionary Approach to Building a Highly Skilled Workforce*, New York: McGraw Hill, 1997.

63 Formerly at: http://www.ils.nwu.edu/~e_for_e/nodes/NODE-120-pg.html.

64 Formerly at: http://www.ils.nwu.edu/~e_for_e/nodes/NODE-284-pg.html.

65 Anonymous review, 1999: "Dynamic Memory Revisited": http://uk.cambridge.org/catalogue/catalogue.asp?isbn=0521633982.

66 Kristian J. Hammond, "Reasoning as Remembering: The Theory and Practice of CBR," *AAAI*, 1992, pp. 865–865 [*sic*] . Cf. Kristian J. Hammond: (formerly) http://dent.infolab.nwu.edu/infolab/people/personal.asp?ID=40.

67 Formerly at: http://www.ils.nwu.edu/~franklin/iClassroom/index.html.

68 Formerly at: http://www.infolab.nwu.edu/faqfinder/.

69 www.cis.strath.ac.uk/~andreas.

70 Formerly at: http://www.ils.nwu.edu/. "ILS develops cutting edge educational software for use by learners of all ages in schools, museums, in the workplace, and at home. In addition to the applications intended to be used directly by learners, we develop underlying technology, including reusable educational simulation engines, tools for authoring learning environments, and tools for building large, highly-structured multimedia knowledge bases."

71 Katie Dean, "Virtual Training for Real Jobs," *Wired News*, 22 March 2000: http://www.wired.com/news/culture/0,1284,33897,00.html.

72 (Formerly) http://www.bhtafe.edu.au/scitech/acthtm.HTM. "It is a social process, carried out when a group of learners (the set) cause each other to examine afresh many ideas that they would otherwise have continued to take for granted. Action learning is not simply learning by doing. It uses both the knowledge that can be gained from formal sources such as books, journals, and individual experts, together with the knowledge that is gained through experience, and it subjects both forms of knowledge to critical questioning and reflection."

73 Human Performance Center, "Functional Area Analysis of Intelligent Computer-Assisted Instruction.": http://www.ott.navy.mil/index.cfm?RID=POL_OT_1000018. The University of Illinois at Urbana-Champaign has Cyber Prof.: http://www.howhy.com/home/. University of Memphis, Tennessee has an Automated Tutorial. Professor Merrill (Utah State University) has developed an Electronic Trainer with five modules: 1) Information Containers, 2) Authoring Systems, 3) Models and Widgets, 4) Built in Instructional Strategies, and 5) Adaptive Instructional Strategies: http://www.id2.usu.edu:16080/MDavidMerrill/ (quote formerly at: http://www.coe.usu.edu/coe/id2/).

74 See *Information Week*, 11 August 1997. Examples of Companies with CBT Systems include:
DigitalThink: http://www.digitalthink.com.
Ibid: www.ibid.com.
Keystone Learning: http://www.keystonelearning.com/keystone/.
LearnIT: http://www.learnit.com.
Mastering Computers was purchased by Platinum Technology in 1998 (http://www.platinumed.com/) and their founder Thomas Graunke went on to become CEO of Knowledge Net: http://www.knowledgenet.com/.
Mindworks Professional Education Group: http://www.mindworksaz.com/.
Productivity Group International: http://www.propoint.com.
Quickstart Technologies: http://www.quickstart.com.
Scholars.com (formerly Scholars.com) now leads to http://www.skillsoft.com/.
Systems Engineering Clinic. Cf. something by same name: http://www.is- edu.hcmuns.edu.vn/WebLib/Books/Misc/Tcweb10/Courses/online/sec_9.htm.
Teletutor: http://www.teletutor.com.
Transcender: http://www.transcender.com/company/default.aspx.
Companies with learning systems include:
Data Distilleries: http://www.spss.com/datadistilleries/.
Sentient Machine Research: http://www.nautilus-systems.com/datamine/msg00720.html and Syllogic, now called Perot Systems: http://www.perotsystems.com/netherlands/.

75 A few innovative examples: Dr. Paul Dekker (Amsterdam) and David Beaver (Stanford) have developed "Electronic Course Dynamic Semantics" (ECDS): http://www.coli.uni-sb.de/esslli/Seiten/Beaver%20and%20Dekker.html. Modus Integrated Media Inc. (Toronto) has Virtual Lesson Technology, an authoring Tool to develop interactive lesson modules. The Canadian Nuclear Utilities Services has Operations Advisor Systems (OAS) such as ChemAND and APACS. There are tools for Automated Knowledge Engineering (TAKE). There are also tools for Hypertext, Hypermedia and Learning: http://www.stemnet.nf.ca/. The reader is referred to EZ-Ref.com which lists dozens of courseware companies. EZ-REF Courseware: http://www.ezref.com/. There is an Association for Computer Based Training (TACT). The Association for Computer Based Training, which published TACT became in 2000 the eLearning Network: http://www.elearningnetwork.org/. There were whole lists of List of Organizations and Institutes of Technology for Training.

76 Educational Testing Service: http://www.ets.org/.

77 Randy Elliot Bennett, *A Policy Information Perspective, Reinventing Assessment*: http://www.ets.org/research/pic/bennett.html. "It will serve high-stakes decision-making as well as instructional purposes, become curriculum-embedded and performance-based, occur at a distance, and measure skills newly valued by society. This reinvention will be facilitated by new technologies and by advances in cognitive and measurement science."

78   CRESST. National Center for Research on Evaluation, Standards and Student Teaching: http://cresst96.cse.ucla.edu/index.htm.

79   Quote formerly at: http://www.ed.gov/Technology/TechConf/1999/whitepapers/paper5.html. See also Eva L. Baker's home page: http://www.cse.ucla.edu/CRESST/pages/EVA.htm.

1) "focus on learning the use of tools to assist in other areas of learning-for instance, using search engines, e-mail, databases, spreadsheets and word processing to find, analyze, represent, and produce documents and other products to display learning. This type of learning may be related to standards set for the school or the state's children to meet. The focus is on using technology to meet requirements. The requirements pull the technology to them."

2) "to use technology power to address new goals that cannot be met in any other way. These could involve the designing of complex simulations, or the collaborative interaction on projects with scientists, other experts, and other students across the nation and the globe. In this case, the technology itself pushes users to new goals and new options."

3) "to use technology more efficiently to deliver instructional opportunities that match the background and pace of the learners. Such uses typically involve integrated programs where students are helped to acquire specific knowledge and skills."

4) "focus on the management of classrooms by teachers, but for the moment, let us address the evaluation of students' learning. It is absolutely critical for evaluation to determine the degree of emphasis among the three kinds of goals identified above, to be clear about them, to communicate them to all collaborators, including students, and if revisions occur, to be open about how goals have changed."

80   Educause: http://www.educause.edu.

81   NLII. National Learning Infrastructure Initiative: http://www.educause.edu/nlii/.

82   IMS Global Learning Consortium, Inc.: http://imsproject.org/.

83   ARIADNE: http://www.ariadne.ac.uk.

84   ARIADNE Collaborative Browsing Project: http://www.comp.lancs.ac.uk/computing/research/cseg/projects/ariadne/.

85   IMS is working on a Meta-data Realignment. "This effort is resolving the drift that has occurred between the IMS Meta-data information model and the IEEE LOM standard, which began as a combination of IMS Meta-data and ARIADNE collaboration.": http://www.imsglobal.org/workinprogress.cfm.

86   Formerly at: http://purl.org/dc/groups/education.htm.

87   Formerly at: http://www.ott.navy.mil/1_4/adl/index.htm. Under Advanced Distributed Learning the basic site (http://www.ott.navy.mil/) now points to Advanced Distributed Learning Network (ADLNET) and SCORM. It also lists some 150 sites related to Learning.

88   Meanwhile the Aviation Industry CBT Committee (AICC) has also made a number of recommendations, guidelines, white papers, and technical reports about a common learning environment model: http://www.aicc.org. The Institute of Electrical and Electronics Engineers (IEEE) has a Learning Technology Standards Committee (LTSC) with a Technical Standards for Learning Technology Working Group (P1484.1) also working on an "Architecture and Reference Model" of a learning environment. These are also co-operating with IMS: http://ltsc.ieee.org/.

89   http://www.ecotec.com/mes/.

90   Formerly at: http://www2.echo.lu/emtf/currentnewsemtf.html. Cf. PROMETEUS: http://prometeus.org/ .

91   Institute for Natural Language Processing: http://www.ims.uni-stuttgart.de/.

92   For a recent conference: *e-content plaza*, Utrecht, December 2000: (formerly) www.eContentplaza.nl.

93   Allan Black and Paul Ammon, "A Developmental-Constructivist Approach to Teacher Education," *Journal of Teacher Education*, vol. 43, no. 5, November-December, 1992, pp. 323–35.

94   *Innovate. Journal for Online Education*: http://horizon.unc.edu/TS/.

95   Columbia University, has a Center for New Media, Teaching and Learning (CCNMTL) with a Virtual Reading Room, Electronic Classrooms, and a site on New Media at other universities: http://www.ccnmtl.columbia.edu/.

There are important individuals, e.g.:

Marie Collins: http://www.emoderators.com/mauri.shtml.

Marcy Driscol: http://www.epls.fsu.edu/people/MarcyDriscoll.cfm.

Thomas M. Duffy: http://education.indiana.edu/ist/faculty/duffy.html.

David Jonassen: http://tiger.coe.missouri.edu/~jonassen/.

Penn State College of Education. Bridges.: http://www.ed.psu.edu/news/publications/bridges_spring00.pdf.

M. David Merrill: http://id2.usu.edu/.

For "Who's Who in Instructional Technology": http://hagar.up.ac.za/catts/learner/m1g1/whoindex.html.

There is an Illinois Center for Problem Based Learning: http://www.imsa.edu/team/cpbl/contact.html.

96   Stanley Pogrow, "On Scripting the Classroom," *Education Week on the Web*, 25 September 1996: http://www.edweek.org/ew/vol-16/04pogrow.h16.

97   More serious theories on education are typically found elsewhere. For instance, Canada has a strong record in this context. The Ontario Institute of Education (OISE) has a Canadian Education Research Institute and a Canadian Education and Research Information System (CERIS), now the Canadian Education Association: http://www.cea-ace.ca/home.cfm. There is a Learning Activity Design Case Library (Tom Carey, University of Waterloo): http://watserv1.uwaterloo.ca/~tcarey/main.html. This has links to themes such as: concept mapping, teaching and learning, how to think about how to learn, evaluation, and a knowledge forum: http://watserv1.uwaterloo.ca/~tcarey/links.html. There is also important work at Simon Fraser University, now redirected to http://wildcat.iat.sfu.ca/.

98   It is claimed that 99 per cent of all viruses are created as experiments and are never used for malicious purposes: Clive Thompson and Ryan McGinley, "Auf allen Viren," *Die Weltwoche*, Jahrgang 72, no. 12, 18 March 2004, pp. 56–65. On virus history: http://www.cknow.com/vtutor/vthistory.htm. The origins go back to John von Neumann. In 1949, at the Institute for Advanced Study in Princeton, New Jersey, in a paper titled "Theory and Organization of Complicated Automata," von Neumann proposed that it was theoretically possible for a computer program to replicate. The paper included a model of what is now known as a computer virus. From: Perry Smith, "Computer Viruses": http://www.perryland.com/viruses.shtml; Cf. Bert Schmid, "Wie die Viren zum Computer kamen," *Tages-Anzeiger*, 19 March 2004, p. 25. Cf. The core wars of the 1950s at Bell Labs. Cf. a report in *Le Courrier*, 29 March 2004: "Sondage: près de 40% des internautes ont subi des dommages dus à des virus."

99   Universiteit Maastricht. PBL Site: http://www.unimaas.nl/pbl/; Center for Problem Based Learning and Communications, Samford University (Birmingham, Alabama), which also has a problem-based learning site map: http://www.samford.edu/schools/artsci/comarts/ca101.html; "Classroom of the Future": http://www.cotf.edu/.

100 Aalborg, Project Based Learning: http://iprod.auc.dk/forsk/poly/articles/ref99-11.htm; O. Borch, J. Helbo, M. Knudsen, and O. Rokkjær, "UniFlex A WWW-environment for project-based collaborative learning," *ITHET'03, 4th International Conference on Information Technology Based Higher Education and Training*, Marrakech, July, 2003. ISBN 9954-8352-0-2: http://www.control.auc.dk/preprint/?action=abstract&abstract=4635.

101 Now based in Italy: http://irsps.sci.unich.it/graduate/eudoct.html.

102 ORTELIUS. The database on higher education in Europe.

103 Learning in Humans and Machines (LHM): http://www.psychologie.uni-freiburg.de/esf-lhm/mission.htm; http://www.psychologie.uni-freiburg.de/esf-lhm/1stbook.htm.

104 Peter Fröhlich, Nicola Henze, and Wolfgang Nejdl, *Virtual Institutes and Virtual Classrooms: How to Enhance Teaching and Mentoring Productivity*.

105 Quote formerly at: http://www.kbs.uni-hannover.de/paper/96/html/vision97/node2.html. "In addition to individual mails mailing lists encourage discussion and interaction within the group. The asynchronous communication via mailing lists also enhances the efficiency of

the mentors and spares them the overhead of scheduling face-to-face meetings with all their groups."

106　UNESCO declaration: http://www.unesco.org/culture/laws/html_eng/declar.shtml.

107　European Education Partnership: http://www.eep-edu.org/.

108　European Education Partnership, *Partnerships in Practice*, Brussels, 1999. p. 8.

109　Formerly at: http://www.monbu.go.jp/news-en/00000070/.

110　Quote formerly at: http://www.monbu.go.jp/news-en/00000069/.

111　Japanese Government Policies in Education, Science and Culture. Towards a Culture-Communicating Society, Tokyo, 1993.

112　Takehiko Kariya, *Responsibility for the Future: What Education Can and Cannot Do*, Okayama: Benesse Corporation, vol. 242, no. 6, 1999: (in Japanese). *Gekkan shinken nyusu chugakusei ban*: http://www.childresearch.net/RESOURCE/RESEARCH/2000/TODAY2/TODAY2.HTM.

113　For a more recent statement of the Japanese vision concerning their plans for 2005: "e-Japan Priority Policy Program Index, II. Future Vision in Each Area." See: http://www.kantei.go.jp/foreign/it/network/priority-all/10.html.

114　Links to related sites: (formerly) http://vulab.ias.unu.edu/mvc98/links.htm.

115　Formerly at: http://www.unesco.org/webworld/tunis/tunis97/com_64.html; UNESCO-UNEVOC (International Centre for Technical and Vocational Education and Training): http://portal.unesco.org/education/en/ev.php-URL_ID=5854&URL_DO=DO_TOPIC&URL_SECTION=201.html; VCILT (Virtual Centre for Innovative Learning Technologies): http://vcampus.uom.ac.mu/.

116　Globewide Network Academy (GNA): http://www.gnacademy.org/.

117　Similarly, the International Telecommunications Union (ITU/BDT) founded a Virtual Training Centre (for Distance Learning and now not accessible). Meanwhile, the International Labour Organization (ILO) has an International Training Centre.

118　World Bank Education: http://www1.worldbank.org/education/.

119　Now called the Global Knowledge Partnership: http://www.globalknowledge.org.

120　http://www.bellanet.org/gkaims/.

121　Telecampus Online Directory: http://teleeducation.nb.ca/content/media/byrory/telecampus/index.html.

122　European Schoolnet: http://www.eun.org/.

123　There was also a Global Schools Project (GSP). Germany has Schulen ans Netz and Schule und Museum in Datennetz: http://www.schulen-ans-netz.de/.

124　There is an International Education and Resource Network (I*Earn): http://www.iearn.org/. There is an Alliance for International Co-Operation in Educational and Vocational Training (Tilburg); an International Society for Technology in Education (ISTE): http://www.iste.org/.cf. Federation for Audio-Visual Multimedia in Education (FAME); The Institute of Social Inventions has a Global Ideas Bank: http://www.globalideasbank.org/. The Union Internationale des Associations (Brussels) has a Global List of Human Potential: http://www.uia.org.

125　Patrick Schouller, *Evariste*, 12 February 1997: http://www.evariste.org/mail/autriche.12Feb97.txt .html. Formerly at: http://www.vrlearners.iis.gr/.

126　Kellogg Community College: www.kellogg.cc.mi.us.

127　Ibid., p. 15.

128　Global Knowledge: http://www.globalknowledge.com/.

129　Global Campus: http://www.csulb.edu/~gcampus/.

130　IMS Global Learning Consortium: http://www.imsproject.org/.

131　In Britain, there is Global Learning Online (GLO): http://atschool.eduweb.co.uk/rmext05/glo/.

132　The Global Knowledge Company in Australia offers enterprise services, education services, and knowledge products, which is a branch of the UK company. The company headquarters have since moved to Cary, North Carolina: http://www.globalknowledge.com. In Tasmania, there is a group on Global Learning Communities: http://www.vision.net.au/~globallearning/. A California State University Long Beach project called Global Campus aims: "to share resources through technology, to provide a means for institutions to make their resources available to

605

others worldwide while respecting intellectual property, and to provide high quality materials for instructional development." See: http://www.csulb.edu/~gcampus/info/index.html.

133   For instance, in the United States, the University of Michigan has a Digital Library specifically devoted to education: http://www.si.umich.edu/UMDL/. In the United States, there is an Internet Engineering Curriculum (IEC) Repository, which is freely accessible: http://iec. caida.org; WIDE University School of Internet: www.soi.wide.ad.jp/. In Japan, photographs of eclipses around the world are being collected and made available for students in schools; Live. Eclipse Broadcaster Misato: (formerly) eclipse.obs.misato.wakayama.jp/. In theory, almost all the work on digital libraries and virtual museums around the world is intended at some stage to be useful to education. In practice, very little is as yet available. In Canada, the University of New Brunswick (Fredericton) has an Electronic Text Project. The Canadian Schoolnet has an Online Toolkit for Publication; a Canadian Electronic Scholarly Network (CESN); and an Online Editions of Scholarly Journals (VIRTUOSO). Cf. Canadian Schoolnet: http://www.schoolnet. ca/. In Europe, the Open University (OU: http://www.open.ac.uk/) produced the first on-line course in history (1 March 1999): "You, Your Computer and the Net": http://www3.open. ac.uk/courses/bin/p12.dll?C01T171. The Open University, in addition to work on Computer Based Learning Environments, and Knowledge Based Systems, is involved with a National Grid for Learning, which links in turn with a Scottish Cultural Resources Access Network (SCRAN); OU Research: http://iet.open.ac.uk/research/calrg/research.cfm (cf. formerly at: http://www. psychology.nottingham.ac.uk/research/credit/themes/learning-environments/). Cf. COGS Graduate Research Centre MSc, PGDip in Knowledge Based Systems: http://www.cogs.susx. ac.uk/grad/kbs/; National Grid for Learning: http://www.ngfl.gov.uk/.

134   In so doing, they often overlook the extent to which the goals of business (making money), manufacturing and industry (making products) and the military (defeating enemies) are not necessarily the goals of teachers and students.

Chapter 10   Personal Knowledge

1   Translation by present author from James Redfield, *Het Geheim van Shambala*, Amsterdam: De Boekerij, 2000, p. 218: "Uw eigen regering is ook manieren aan het ontwikkelen om u in haar macht te houden.Chips die je bij troepmachten en nietsvermoedende oproerkraiers in het lichaam kunt implanteeren. En dat is nog niet het enige.... We weten dat er als mensen denken, een bepaald patroon van hersensgven wordt uitgestraald. Elke regering houdt zich al bezig met machines die dat soort hersensgolven kunnen registreren en identificeren, met name boze of tegen de overheid gerichte gevoelens."

2   Nils Röller, "Eine neue Dirskursfgemeinschaft im Netz," *Tages-Anzeiger*, 4 February 2002, p. 45.

3   For a fascinating outline of fax history: http://www.hffax.de/.

4   Pavel Curtis, "Mudding: Social Phenomena in Text-Based Virtual Realities," *Proceedings of the 1992 Conference on the Directions and Implications of Advanced Computing*: http://www.scara.com/~ole/literatur/ mudding.html; Pavel Curtis and David Nichols, "MUDs Grow Up: Social Virtual Reality in the Real World," presented at the *Third International Conference on Cyberspace*, in Austin, Texas, 15 May 1993. Was available via anonymous ftp from: parcftp.xerox.com in pub/MOO/papers/MUDsGrowUp (1993); See also: http://citeseer.nj.nec.com/342124.html.

5   Amy Bruckman, Mitchel Resnick, "Virtual Professional Community: Results from the MediaMOO Project (1993).": http://citeseer.nj.nec.com/bruckman93virtual.html.

6   Janice R. Walker, "Bibliography of Electronically Available Sources: MOOs, MUDs, MUCKs, and MUSHs. An MLA-style adaptation of the bibliography available at telnet purple.crayon.media.m it.edu 8888.": http://www.cas.usf.edu/english/walker/bibliog.html.

7   Gabriel Sigriet, "Le SMS: un nouvel art épistolaire," *Le Temps*, 9 May 2000 p. 6; Philippe Lejeune, "Les cyberdiaristes créent un réseau d'amitiés," *Samedi culturel*, 14 October 2000, p. 7.

8   Bruce Damer, "Global Cyberspace and Personal Memespace." Originally published on KurzweilAI.
    net on 22 February 2001; updated on 27 February 2004. Also published on The Digital Space
    Commons: http://www.kurzweilai.net/meme/frame.html?main=/articles/art0096.html.
    While Damer's account is not entirely accurate qua the history of VR (which began in the 1960s
    [with Tom Furness III, Ivan Sutherland, and Myron Krueger] and not the 1980s), it is a thought-
    ful and stimulating discussion qua avatars and the potentials of personal communication.
9   Bruce Branit and Jeremy Hunt, 405. *The Movie*: www.405themovie.com.
10 CGFA: http://cgfa.sunsite.dk/.
11 Metropolitan Museum of Art: http://www.metmuseum.org/home.asp. At present, this personal
    gallery is potentially limited to 50 paintings and the choice is from among 3,500 on-line images
    from a collection of 2 million pieces.
12 EDUCARED: www.educared.net. For future classrooms: http://transcriptions.english.ucsb.edu/
    archive/project/talks-essays/classroom-of-future-panel.shtml.
13 For ideas of future communications gadgets, see "Nextfest. The Shape of Things to Come,"
    Wired, May, 2004, Especially, Jessie Scanlon, "NextFest Communication: Dream Machines," pp.
    149–55.
14 "Competition Advantage from Tacit Knowledge: Bringing Some Empirical Evidence," Institut
    de Recherche en Gestion. Université de Paris XII in its series Institut de Recherche en Gestion.
    Université de Paris XII, Paris 1996. This French study outlined the implications of tacit
    knowledge for competitive advantage. Cf. Tacit knowledge discussion: http://www.brint.com/
    wwwboard/messages/1728.html. By 1998, the CChemicals conference (Amsterdam) included
    papers on making explicit knowledge of the customer and knowledge of competitors. Formerly
    at: http://www.firstconf.com/km-chems.
15 Tim Kannegieter, who developed a TacitKM company, which has since been bought out. In 2004,
    Tim Kannegieter was General Manager of Knowledge Services, Fonterra, New Zealand. There
    was a Tacit Knowledge Roundtable at the Tacit Knowledge Corporation, Atlantla, Georgia.
16 E.g., Quality Management International (Exton, Pennsylvania): http://www.aworldofquality
    (quote formerly at: http://www.aworldofquality.com/ten.htm). "A system cannot achieve this
    for any organization unless it embraces and includes vigorous learning from each other all of
    the time and connects with the rest of the world. This thinking and the advent of enterprise-
    wide management systems will heavily influence all of our integrated management or teamwork
    systems for the foreseeable future."
17 IFAD, Panel Discussion on Local Knowledge, Second Global Knowledge Conference, Kuala
    Lumpur, 7 March 2000. For examples of such local or indigenous knowledge, see *Spirit of
    Sustainability: An Anthology of Honey Bee Cover Stories*, SRISTI Amedabad, 1998; *Profiles of Innovators from
    Honey Bee*, Ahmedabad: Society for Research and Initiatives for Sustainable Technologies and
    Institutions (SRISTI), 2000. Cf. Communication for a Sustainable Future: (formerly) http://csf.
    colorado.edu and SRISTI: http://sristi.org; International Fund for Agricultural Development
    (IFAD), *Investing in the Rural Poor*, CD-ROM.
18 Paula Donnelly-Roark, "Systèmes de connaissances autochtones en Afrique subsaharienne," *Notes
    CA. Notes sur les connaissances autochtones*, Washington, no. 1, October, 1998, pp. 1–4.
19 Re: the Kampala Declaration on Indigenous Knowledge for Sustainable Development. *Indigenous
    Knowledge and Development Monitor*, The Hague, vol. 8, no. 1, March, 2000, which, according to their
    Chief Knowledge Officer: "is unique to every culture and society … is the basis for local decision
    making in agriculture, health, natural resource management and other activities … is embedded
    in community practices, institutions, relationships, and rituals is part of everyday life, such as
    herbal medicines, acupuncture etc." Nicolas Gorjestani, "Cultural Diversity on the 21st Century:
    The Role of Indigenous Knowledge for Development," Chief Knowledge and Learning Officer
    World Bank, GK 2000, Kuala Lumpur, 7 March 2000.
20 For optimistic trends, see also the Developing Countries Symposium, Internet Global Summit,
    INET 2000, Yokohama, July, 2000.
21 Word Bank Institute is, for instance, working on knowledge products.

22 *Noesis:* Philosophical Research Online (noesis.evansville.edu). In December, 2004, a website http://argos.evansville.edu/ explained: "The plans to re-release Noesis and Hippias in a new, consolidated form have been indefinitely suspended. For more information, please send email to Anthony Beavers at tb2@evansville.edu."

23 There is now a Personalization Consortium: http://www.personalization.org/.

24 Open Sesame was (1999) bought by Allaire. Now: http://www.macromedia.com/v1/handlers/index.cfm?ID=14674.

25 Quote formerly at: http://www.allen.com/pers-vendors.html. Cf.: http://www.allen.com. "Rules-based products use a coding technique similar to traditional software programming by using logic statements to determine what content to include on a particular Web page. For instance, one rule might be, 'If the person plays golf, then include the descriptive text aimed at golfers.'
Collaborative filtering, on the other hand, uses complex statistical techniques to estimate what is appropriate. An example might be, 'If they live near a golf course, there is a 20% chance that they play golf. If they drive an expensive car, there is an additional 20% chance they play golf. If the chance that they play golf is over 30%, then include the descriptive text aimed at golfers.'"

26 These include: "1. A file system-based content management and tag indexing/cataloging subsystem. 2. An open user profile access framework for plugging in external user databases and for connecting with legacy business systems, LDAP servers, and other business-rule-based content targeting engines. This framework allows more effective marketing and provides for more personalized services to the end user. 3. An open framework for plugging in third party algorithm products and recommendation engines [adapters are sold separately]" (quote formerly at: http://www.atg.com/products/dps/);
ATG: http://www.atg.com/.

27 Ibid.: http://www.atg.com/.

28 Guest Track was acquired in 1999 by Sling Shot Media LLC which now appears under the name ListHost Net: http://www.buckasite.com/lh/.

29 Native Minds was acquired on 3 March 2004 by Verity: http://www.verity.com/products/response/new/.

30 Broadvision: http://www.broadvision.com.

31 Macromedia: http://www.macromedia.com/.

32 Net Perceptions: http://www.netperceptions.com/home/.

33 Opensesame was taken over by Allaire which has since merged with Macromedia: http://www.macromedia.com/v1/handlers/index.cfm?ID=14674.

34 Quote formerly at: http://www.accelerating.com/stuff/accelerating1to1report1.pdf.

35 Quote Formerly at: http://www.mps.com.mx/mps/; "The Microsoft Personalization System": http://docs.rinet.ru/MCIS/ch2.htm#TheMicrosoftPersonalizationSystem /.

36 Quote formerly at: http://www.mediapps.com/web/webus.nsf/$$webdocs/NT000009FA.

37 Backflip: http://www.backflip.com/company/out_corp_index.ihtml.

38 http://www.allen.com (quote formerly at: http://www.allen.com/personalization.html).

39 Now under Intellisync: http://www.intellisync.com/.

40 Personalization Consortium: http://www.personalization.org/. Michael Hahsler, at the Vienna Economic University, writes of creating personal profiles which include: 1) time, 2) language – filtering or automatically translating information in languages unknown to the user, 3) rating – i.e., filtering information outside the level or status of the user, and 4) suggestions in the form of a recommender system. Michael Hahsler's home page: http://wwwai.wu-wien.ac.at/~hahsler/. Meanwhile, Blaze Software has outlined four principles that go "Beyond personalization": 1) "true one-to-one interactions based on the needs and preferences of each user," 2) "Business process personalization," 3) "Enterprise consistency," and 4) "Adaptive personality." Blazesoft began as Neuron Data and is now linked with Fair Isaac: http://www.blazesoft.com/company/. They claim:

"1. True one-to-one interactions based on the needs and preferences of each user while providing the opportunity for maximum returns to the enterprise. Examples are interactive dialogs and personalized recommendations based on a user's goals.

2. Business process personalization incorporates a company's way of doing business and treating its customers in every aspect of business operations. Automated policies, practices, and procedures allow the company's personality to shine through in every transaction.

3. Enterprise consistency applies the same business methodologies no matter how, when, or where customers, employees, suppliers, or partners interact with the enterprise.

4. Adaptive personality responds in real time to changing competition, internal business practices, government regulations, and customer behaviors to provide the most appropriate and effective treatment of each customer transaction."

There were sites for personalizing one's entry to the web such as Mydesktop: http://www.mtnsys.com/pages/MyDesktop.htm. Meanwhile, there are trends to gather data from a Web user's PC when the user visits a Web, without the user's consent, known as "cyberwoozling." This is a "combination of cookie and browser-side add-in code." In 2004, "cyberwoozling" was no longer included in the dictionary. Unless it makes a comeback, this term will have had a usage life of around three years. In 2005, it has re-appeared: http://whatis.techtarget.com/definition/0,,sid9_gci211884,00.html.

41 Appendix 8.

42 Joachim Puppele links: http://schulen.hagen.de/GSGE/welcome.html (formerly at: http://schulen.hagen.de/GSGE/ew/L-132.html).

43 Click TV.

44 Newshound @San Jose Mercury News.

45 Formerly at: www.thegist.com.

46 On 10 July 2000.

47 Yahoo: http://my.yahoo.com/.

48 Excite: http://www.excite.com/.

49 CRAYON. Create Your Own Newspaper: http://crayon.net.

50 Samachar: http://www.samachar.com/.

51 Stewart Brand, *The Media Lab: Inventing the Future at MIT*, Cambridge, MA: MIT Press, 1987. Cited in Marie D'Amico, "Personalized Newspapers," *Digital Media*, vol. 5, no. 11, April, 1996: http://lawcrawler.findlaw.com/MAD/persnews.htm .

52 B. Joseph Pine II, James H. Gilmore, *The Experience Economy*, Cambridge, MA: Harvard Business School Press, 1999.

53 Formerly at: http://ie.echo.lu/Report/files/files.htm.

54 Andy Hopper, "Personalisation": http://www-lce.eng.cam.ac.uk/~hopper/Personalisation.html. "This advance has begun with text and data and will be extended to multimedia information streams. Perpetuating applications and rerouting the sessions may be manageable in situations where the terminal devices are similar, but it is much more difficult if the end points vary in complexity, and research is needed in this area. Furthermore, where many different terminal types are available and the personalisation takes advantage of agents, the scalability of applications is a major research issue."; Kenneth R. Wood, Tristan Richardson, Frazer Bennett, Andy Harter, and Andy Hopper, "Global Teleporting with Java: Towards Ubiquitous Personalised Computing," Presented and demonstrated at *Nomadics '96*, San Jose, U.S.A., March, 1996. In 2000, another major research institute, the GMD (now Fraunhofer), had three active projects in the field of information contextualization, namely, Hyper-Interaction within Physical Space (HIPS); Interactive Simulation Models (InterSim) and Learning about the User (LaboUr). HIPS originally began as a European project led by Siena (cf. next note) from which GMD developed an independent and competing project with the same name. In 2004, HIPS and other Fraunhofer projects are classed under "Nomadic Information Systems": http://www.fit.fraunhofer.de/gebiete/nomad-is/index_en.xml?aspect=fieldsprojects .

Originally: Esprit Project 25574 – HIPS Hyper-Interaction within Physical Space: http://www. cordis.lu/esprit/src/25574.htm. A Variant then developed at GMD, now Fraunhofer: http:// www.fit.fraunhofer.de/~oppi/publications/HCI99.NomadicComputing.pdf. On Labour: http://www.iskp.uni-bonn.de/bibliothek/reports/GMD/2000/e-probl/LaboUr.pdf. InterSim: http://www.ercim.org/publication/Ercim_News/enw33/oppermann.html. An Israeli company, Virtual Self, is developing software for context, providing users "with a complete and accurate understanding of information and people to ensure that users stay informed about information they need to maintain their competitive edge." Virtual Self company: http://www. vself.com/.

55 B. Joseph Pine, James H. Gilmore, and B. Joseph Pine II, *The Experience Economy*, Cambridge, MA: Harvard Business School Press, 1999, p. 189.

56 B. Joseph Pine II, *Mass Customization: The New Frontier in Business Competition*, Cambridge, MA: Harvard Business School Press, 1992.

57 Ibid.

58 B. Joseph Pine, James H. Gilmore, and B. Joseph Pine II, *The Experience Economy*, Cambridge, MA: Harvard Business School Press, 1999, p. 194. The authors explain that: "If you charge for the time customers spend with you then you are in the experience business. If you charge for the demonstrated outcome the customer achieves, then and only then are you in the transformation business."

59 Bhagwan Shri Rajneesh (Oshos) Movement: http://www.stelling.nl/simpos/bhagwan_shree_rajneesh_osho.htm.

60 Wendy McElroy, "Human Ignorance and Social Engineering," *The Freeman*, vol. 48, no. 5, May, 1998, pp. 278–82: http://www.zetetics.com/mac/soceng.htm.

61 B. Joseph Pine, James H. Gilmore, and B. Joseph Pine II, *The Experience Economy*, Cambridge, MA: Harvard Business School Press, 1999, p. 206.

62 Jeremy Rifkin, *The Age of Access. The New Culture of Hypercapitalism. Where All of Life is Paid for Experience*, New York: P. Tarcher/Putnam, 2000, p. 111.

63 E.g., School Redesign Network. See: http://www.schoolredesign.com/; Jakob Nielsen's Alertbox for 4 October 1998: "Personalization is Over-Rated.": http://www.useit.com/ alertbox/981004.html; Personalization Strategies: http://www.meansbusiness.com/Sales-and-Marketing-Books/Personalization-Strategies.htm.

64 One fundamental problem is that the world of learning has its own technical definitions of concepts (cf. Knowledge organization in Appendix 8), which are very (and sometimes completely) different from how they are used in the world of business. "Sites Relevant to Ontologies and Knowledge Sharing": http://ksl-web.stanford.edu/kst/ontology-sources.html. Needed is a new study of e-basics, which studies the basic concepts of information and communication and the society built around them: that focusses on fundamental changes in digitized society prompted by the interaction between individuals and networks, information systems and the Internet. Needed also is a study of e-behaviour that examines individuals and, more generally, human and software agents – including intelligent web agents – as they engage in the essential social, economic, cultural, and political interactions to form all sorts of communities. E-behaviour should also investigate emerging characteristics and types of behaviour of these actors in a world of rapidly changing information and communication modes. These needs were meant to have been the goal of the International Institute for Infonomics, which was closed before it had been fully established.

Chapter 11: Collaboration

1 Bootstrap Org: http://www.bootstrap.org/ Specifically: http://www.bootstrap.org/augdocs/ augment-14724.htm (quote formerly at: http://www.bootstrap.org/augment-14724.htm).

2 Eric S. Raymond, *The Cathedral and the Bazaar*, Cambridge, MA: O'Reilly, 1999, pp. 42, 64.

3   For an short description of the method, see Curtis E. Sahakian, *The Delphi Method*, Skokie, IL: The Corporate Partnering Institute, 1997.

4   Michael Adler and Erio Ziglio, *Gazing into the Oracle: The Delphi Method and its Application to Social Policy and Public Health*, London: Jessica Kingsley, 1988.

5   Eric S. Raymond, *The Cathedral and the Bazaar*, Cambridge, MA: O'Reilly, 1999, p. 42.

6   Murray Turoff, Supplementary lectures notes for cis 679, 1998: http://eies.njit.edu/~turoff/coursenotes/CIS679/679add.htm.

7   Quote formerly at: http://www.bootstrap.org/augment-132082.htm.

8   CSCW as envisaged by Engelbart entails highly educated persons sharing their specialized knowledge. Is this effectively the same as Computer Supported Collaborative Learning (CSCL)? Cf. Lorraine Sherry, "CSCL: Computer-Supported Collaborative Learning" [List]: http://carbon.cudenver.edu/~lsherry/cscl/cscl.html. Cf. *Proceedings of the Computer Support for Collaborative Learning (CSCL) 1999 Conference*, Christopher M. Hoadley and Jeremy Roschelle, eds., 12–15 December 1999, Stanford University, Palo Alto, CA: http://www.ciltkn.org/cscl99/.

9   U.S. Government, E-Commerce: http://www.whitehouse.gov/omb/egov/.

10 Robert K. Logan and Louis W. Stokes, *Collaborate to Compete*, New York: J. Wiley, 2004, p. 259. Although Logan lives in Canada, he has adapted the American approach.

11 Andreas Hirstein, "Ein Supercomputer auf jedem Schreibtisch," *NZZ am Sonntag*, 24 November 2002, pp. 90–91.

12 Franco Carlini, "La diffusion intelligente des idées se fait via le Web," *Le Courrier*, 22 August 2003, p. 16. This article discusses the work of Magnus Cadergren on "Open content and value creation," Rick Prelinger's MIT Dspace, and the Open Directory Project. Related to these is another development in the United States, Public Library of Science Biology (PloS Biology) (http://www.plos.org), whereby scholars are asked to pay $1,500 for the publication of an article, which is then given unlimited distribution. Cf. *Nature*, vol. 425, no. 9, October, 2003, p. 554.

13 Open Theory: http://www.opentheory.org and www.globalvillage.at.

14 Open design: http://www.bitscope.com/about/?p=2. There is now also an Open Design Alliance: http://www.opendwg.org/; Open Collaborative Design: http://www.thinkcycle.org/ .

15 Wikipedia: http://www.wikipedia.org/; Andreas Heer, "Grundidee des Webs neu umgesetzt," *Tages-Anzeiger*, 3 March 2003, p. 37.

16 Generative.net: http://www.generative.net/; http://www.philipgalanter.com/.

17 NG# – Protoquadro: http://www.submultimedia.tv/ng/.

18 W3C, "Collaboration, Knowledge Representation and Automatability": http://www.w3.org/Collaboration/Overview.html.

19 Pavel Curtis, "The PlaceWare Platform: Web-based Collaborative Apps Made Simple," *Stanford Computer Systems Laboratory Colloquium*, 12 November 1996: http://www.stanford.edu/class/ee380/9798fall/lect08.html. Now placeware is linked with Microsoft.Live Meeting: http://www.placeware.com.

20 http://www.vrvs.org/.

21 http://borbala.com/cyberchair/.

22 Lecture by Chris Thomsen, Maastricht University, 27 October 1999. These topics were further discussed at a conference on: *Computer Supported Collaborative Learning (CSCL'99) – connecting learning communities globally*, 11–15 December 1999, sponsored by the Stanford Learning Lab at which Douglas Engelbart gave
    one of the keynote lectures: http://sll.stanford.edu/projects/; This has since become the Stanford Center for Innovations in Learning: http://scil.stanford.edu/. Re: PENS: http://www-cdr.stanford.edu/DesignJournal/html/pens.html.

23 CESAR Project: http://www.eto.org.uk/ist-nmw/present/cesar/index.htm.

24 AMBIENTE, i-Land.

612

25 Marek Czernuszenko, Dave Pape, Daniel Sandin, Tom DeFanti, Gregory L. Dawe, and Maxine D. Brown, "The ImmersaDesk and Infinity Wall Projection-Based Virtual Reality Displays," *Computer Graphics*, May, 1997: http://www.evl.uic.edu/pape/CAVE/idesk/paper/.

26 MacNeal Schwendler: http://www.macsch.com/.

27 International Council on Systems Engineering (INCOSE): http://www.incose.org.

28 Formerly at: http://www.idg.net/go.cgi?id=182825.

29 Alibre: http://www.alibre.com/.

30 Formerly: http://www.aristasoft.com/. It has since gone out of business.

31 Sherpa works was acquired by INSO in 1998 and is now part of EDS: http://support.plms-eds.com/docs/sherpa.html.

32 http://www.nexprise.com/.

33 Ephraim Schwartz and Stephen Lawson, "Online Collaboration revolutionizes design process," *InfoWorld Electric*, 8 November 1999: http://www.infoworld.com/cgi-bin/displayStory.pl?99118.hndesign.htm.

34 Paul Kandarian, "All Together Now," *CIO Magazine*, 1 September 2000: http://www.cio.com/archive/090100/together.html. There is a Collaborative Software Resource Clearing-House: http://www2.ics.hawaii.edu/~csrc/csrcDesc.html. The University of Saskatchewan has a site on Dimensions of Collaborative Learning: http://www.cs.usask.ca/grads/vsk719/academic/890/project2/node4.html;http://www.cs.usask.ca/grads/vsk719/academic/890/project2/node3.html. Kenyon College had a site for Computer Supported Collaborative Learning Resources: (formerly) http://mytilus.kenyon.edu/collab/collab.htm. Remote Collaboration Classroom: http://lbis.kenyon.edu/rcc/.There are also conferences on the subject. E.g., *Second European Conference on Computer Supported Co-operative Work; Collaborative Virtual Environments* (CVE), Manchester 17–19 June 1998: http://www.crg.cs.nott.ac.uk/ under events.

35 Telepresence was explored in the ACTS (AC 089) Distributed Video Production (DVP) project. ACTS (AC 017) entailed Collaborative Integrated Communications for Construction (CICC): http://media.it.kth.se/SONAH/Acts/AC017.html. This project envisaged six stages in a cycle of cognition: map, landscape, room, table, theatre, and home. ACTS (AC 082) aimed to Design Implementation and Operation of a Distributed Annotation Environment (DIANE). One of the ACTS-CHAINS was devoted to Distributed Virtual Environments and Telepresence: http://www.esat.kuleuven.ac.be/~konijn/MCM.html. One of the ACTS-DOMAINS focussed on Multimedia Content Manipulation and Management, with a second cluster on 3D/VR and Telepresence Developments through the 3-D Cluster and Telepresence and Distributed Virtual Environments Chain.

36 Ideal Gas Law: http://jersey.uoregon.edu/vlab/Piston/index.html.

37 MicroScape Virtual Laboratory Microscope: http://www.microscopy.com/MicroScape/MicroScape.html.

38 Chickscope: http://chickscope.beckman.uiuc.edu/.

39 Bugscope: http://bugscope.beckman.uiuc.edu/.

40 Technical report 98-010. *Remote Instrumentation for Service, Collaboration and Education, Lessons Learned*: http://www.itg.uiuc.edu/publications/techreports/98-010/remote_instrumentation.htm:
    "[1] Single User: Allows dedicated access to an imaging system by a single user.
    [2] Multiple non-cooperating users: Allows several users to access the system simultaneously. The users are not aware of each other. Commands from the users are queued and the data is returned to the requesting user. This mode is useful in education projects like Chickscope, where several classrooms may be accessing the instrumentation simultaneously.
    [3] Multiple cooperating users: Allows several users to use an instrument collaboratively by using mechanisms for passing instrument control among the users."

41 Laser Scanning Confocal Microscopes: http://www.itg.uiuc.edu/ms/equipment/microscopes/lscm.htm.

42 Manuel Perez, "Java Remote Microscope for Collaborative Inspection of Integrated Circuits," *Thesis, MIT Microsystems Technology Laboratories*, May, 1997 (CAPAM Memo no. 97–5): http://www-

mtl.mit.edu/mtlhome/ under MTL and other related research links under Remote Microscope. "The control takes place through a client application written entirely in Java, allowing it to run on almost any computer platform and even from an ordinary Web browser. The client boasts a user-friendly interface with advanced features, such as the ability to use a VLSI [Very Large Systems Integration] layout as a navigation tool. This project makes it possible to share a microscope facility among multiple research designers. It also increases the amount of collaboration that can take place during the inspection of a wafer. These uses and features make the Remote Microscope a valuable tool in distributed design."

43   Lieming Huang, Matthias Hemmje, and Erich J. Neuhold, "Admire: an adaptive data model for meta-search engines," *Ninth International World Wide Web Conference Proceedings*, Elsevier, 2000, pp. 431–48. Cf. Spider Redgold, "The Web Cube: The Internet Website of a Distributed Website," Poster Proceedings, *Ninth International World Wide Web Conference*, Amsterdam: Foretech Seminars, 2000, p. 110.

44   Virtuality Laboratory: (formerly) http://www.tno.nl/instit/fel/vl/vl.html, now Human Factors Institute: http://www.tno.nl/tno/index.xml.

45   I am grateful to Dr. Gert Eijkel for providing me with this information re: FTIR Imaging Microspectrometry and Data Analysis in the ICES-KIS Virtual Lab. Cf.: WTCW Virtual Lab: http://www.dutchgrid.nl/VLAM-G/.

46   Rajaram Subramanian, Ivan Marsic, "ViBE: Virtual Biology Experiments," *WWW10 Conference Proceedings, The Tenth International World Wide Web Conference, Hong Kong, 1–5 May 2001*, New York: ACM Press, 2001, pp. 316–25.

47   Virtual Laboratory project: http://www.gridbus.org/vlab/. This project was referred to earlier in chapter three.

48   Virtual and Collaborative Environments: http://www-fp.mcs.anl.gov/division/research/vr_summary.htm.

49   This quote was taken from the MREN site in 2000, which has since changed: http://www.mren.org/mren1.htm. "MREN also provides access to the Advanced Photon Source ... as well as to the massively parallel (128 node) high- performance computer.... MREN is also working on projects to link advanced virtual reality environments among member institutions over high performance networks. These VR laboratories, a type of 'holodeck,' are based on CAVE technology.... Other projects involve linking terabyte mass storage facilities to high performance networks. The CATS project (Chicago-Argonne Terabyte System) is configured for 35 Terabyte and is scaleable to 180 TB. One early project used a satellite to establish digital communications to the UIC's NSF [University of Illinois at Chicago's National Science Foundation] Center for Astrophysics Research in Antarctica (CARA) to create the first interactive digital video-conference to the South Pole."

50   Tele-Presence Microscopy Project: http://tpm.amc.anl.gov/.

51   Advanced Networking for Telemicroscopy: http://www.isoc.org/inet2000/cdproceedings/5a/5a_4.htm.

52   Subaru Telescope: http://www.naoj.org.

53   AURA (Association of Universities for Research in Astronomy): http://www.aura-astronomy.org/.

54   For basic Collaboratory Information: http://collaboratory.emsl.pnl.gov/about_us/Resources.html. See also Thomas Finholt and G. M. Olson, "From Laboratories to Collaboratories: A New Organizational Form for Scientific Collaboration," *University of Michigan, Department of Psychology, Working Paper*, 1996 [Copies available from finholt@umich.edu]; Thomas Finholt, "Internet –Based Collaboratories Help Scientists Work Together," *Chronicle of Higher Education*, 12 March 1999, pp. 21–23.

55   See also Jolene Galegher, Robert E. Kraut, and Carmen Egido, ed., *Intellectual Teamwork: Social and Technological Foundations of Cooperative Work*, Mahwah, NJ: L. Erlbaum Associates, 1990.

56   NLANR Advanced Applications Database: http://dast.nlanr.net/Clearinghouse/Query.htm.

57   Reciprocal Net-A Global Shared Database for Crystallography, Indiana University, U.S.A.: http://www.startap.net/igrid98/recipNetCrys98.html; http://www.startap.net/APPLICATIONS/math.html#Chemistry. See: http://www.reciprocalnet.org/,

58   Binghampton University Bartle Library Collaboratory: http://www.cni.org/projects/net-teach/1994/prop13.html.

59   Biomedical Informatics Research Network: http://birn.ncrr.nih.gov/birn/birn_getpage.php?fname=about_birn_bg.html.

60   Teleimmersion: www.evl.uic.edu/cavern.

61   Collaboratory: http://128.226.37.29/subjects/polsci/collab.html.

62   Telescience. Parallel Tomography: https://telescience.ucsd.edu/.

63   Ibid., https://telescience.ucsd.edu.

64   http://www.si.umich.edu/sparc/.

65   Diesel combustions Collaboratory, now absorbed in the Collaboratory for Multi-scale Chemical Science (CMCS): http://cmcs.ca.sandia.gov/.

66   DOE National Collaboratory Program: http://tpm.amc.anl.gov/MMC/.

67   Medical Collaboratory Testbed: http://www.si.umich.edu/medcollab/.

68   http://smi-web.stanford.edu/projects/intermed-web/Old/Overview.html. This ran from 1996 to 1998.

69   Distributed, Collaboratory Experiment Environments (DCEE) Programme: http://www.dl.ac.uk/TCSC/Subjects/Parallel_Algorithms/steer_survey/node48.html.

70   Andreas Dieberger, "Where did all the people go? A collaborative Web space with social navigation information." Poster at WWW9: http://www9.org/final-posters/poster19.html.

71   Science of Collaboratories: http://www.scienceofcollaboratories.org/Resources/colisting.php.

72   Bandwidth Lust. Distributed Particle Physics Analysis using Ultra High Speed TCP on the Grid: http://pcbunn.cacr.caltech.edu/sc2003/BandwidthChallenge2003.htm.

73   VRVS: http://www.vrvs.org/.

74   Remote Black Hole Simulations: http://www.startap.net/startap/igrid2000/onlineMonBlkHole00.html; http://amira.zib.de.

75   For further collaboratory links: http://www.ks.uiuc.edu/Research/collaboratory/etc/related.shtml. European work on virtual environments: http://www.itd.clrc.ac.uk/Activity/ACTIVITY=VVECC.

76   CREW. Director, Thomas Finholt: http://www.crew.umich.edu/Investigators/tfinholt.htm.

77   CREW: http://www.crew.umich.edu/.

78   Publications of the Collaborative Systems Research Group at the University of Michigan: http://www.eecs.umich.edu/~aprakash/csrg_pub.html.

79   ALIVE: http://www.startap.net/startap/igrid2000/aliveArchEnv00.html; Netherlands Architecture Fund http://www.archfonds.nl; CyberCAD Internet distributed interactive collaborative design: http://www.startap.net/startap/igrid2000/cybercad00.html; Global Design and Manufacturing Website: http://cvd.tp.edu.sg/APAN-GDM/.

80   NTT Super High Definition (SHD) Image – SHD Digital Cinema Distribution System: http://www.onlab.ntt.co.jp/en/mn/shd.

81   Cooperative Virtual Environments: http://www.igd.fhg.de/igd-a9/research/cve.

82   Electronic Visualization Lab: http://www.evl.uic.edu/cavern/lara.

83   Foundation of the Hellenic World: http://www.fhw.gr. Dave Page, Josephine Ansley, Sarvia D'Souza, Tom DeFanti, Maria Rousseau, and Athanasius, Gutatzos, "Shared Miletus: Towards a Networked Virtual History Museum," Eurocav3D 2001, Mykonos, 30 May–1 June, Thessaloniki: ZITI, 2001, pp. 85–88.

84   Human Anatomy Lecture-on-Demand at the National University of Singapore: http://www.cdtl.nus.edu.sg/research/anatomy.htm; Integrated Virtual Learning Environment: http://ivle.nus.edu.sg.

85 Robert J. Sandusky, Kevin R. Powell, and Annette C. Feng, "Design for Collaboration in Networked Information Retrieval," *ASIS Midyear 98 Proceedings. Collaboration Across Boundaries: Theories, Strategies and Technology,* 1998, pp. 1–11: www.asis.org/Conferences/MY'98/Sandusky.htm.

86 (formerly) http://www.si.umich.edu/coa/governing/Ackerman-Mark-cv.doc. Regular commercial software includes: Novell GroupWise 5, Oracle Interoffice, Lotus Notes, Attachmate, ICL Teamware, and Microsoft Exchange.

87 Molecular Interactive Collaborative Environment: http://mice.sdsc.edu/.

88 Computer Integrated Architecture, Engineering and Construction: http://www.stanford.edu/group/CIFE/ce222/aec_projects.htm. For a discussion of related themes in an English context on the Design of Virtual Environments with particular reference to VRML: http://www.agocg.ac.uk/train/vrml2rep/part1/guide7.htm.

89 Star Tap Applications: http://www.startap.net/APPLICATIONS/.

90 Internet2.edu: www.icair.org; www.mren.org; www.startap.net/igrid2000.

91 CYCLADES Project: http://www.ercim.org/cyclades/. COLLATE Project: http://www.collate.de/.

92 Dan Rasmus, VP, Giga Information Group, *Leveraging Knowledge Conference*, Orlando, FL, April, 1999. For Giga Information Group Reports: http://www.marketresearch.com/publisher/22.html

93 Flypaper: http://corporate.flypaper.com/.

94 Flypaper: http://www.flypaper.com/0-54.html.

95 Cited by Jeffrey Harrow, RCFoC, 24 July 2000. See the Cyveillance Whitepaper called "Sizing the Internet": www.cyveillance.com/web/ downloads/Sizing_the_Internet.pdf; http://www.cyveillance.com/web/corporate/white_papers.htm.

96 Ian Foster, Joseph Insley, Gregor von Laszewski, Carl Kesselman, and Marcus Thiebaux, "Distance Visualization: Data Exploration on the Grid," *Computer*, vol. 32, no. 12, December, 1999, pp. 36–43: http://csdl.computer.org/comp/mags/co/1999/12/rz036abs.htm. A tutorial at INET 2001 (Stockholm) on Grids and Grid Technologies organized by Ian Foster (Argonne) and presented by Carl Kesselman gave a survey of these developments: http://www.mcs.anl.gov/~foster. There is now a Global Grid Forum: www.gridforum.org. There is also a Grid Physics Network: http://www.griphyn.org/.

97 LOFAR: www.lofar.org/.

98 Ian Foster, *Designing and Building Parallel Programs (Online)*, Reading, MA: Addison Wesley, 1995.

99 "Brainstorming a Net-powered supercomputer," *CNET News.com*, 16 May 2001: http://news.com.com/2100-1001-257734.html?legacy=cnet.

100 http://www.globus.org/.

101 Prof. Jack Dongarra and Dr. Terry Moore, "Computational Grids – The New Paradigm for Computational Science and Engineering," University of Tennessee, Department of Computer Science, Innovative Computing Laboratory, Knoxville, TN 37996-4030: http://deslab.mit.edu/DesignLab/dicpm/position/dongarra.html.

102 Steve Silberman, "The Energy Web," *Wired*, July, 2001, pp. 114–27.

103 Global Energy Grid: http://www.geni.org/energy/issues/overview/english/grid.html.

104 http://dast.nlanr.net/ (quote formerly at: http://www.dast.nlanr.net/articles/gridandglobus/Grids.html#history). "In the late 1980s the term meta-computing was coined by NCSA Director Larry Smarr. Metacomputing initially meant running computations across multiple machines and was the precursor to truly distributed computing. When developed, the Grid became a superset of metacomputing.

In the early 1990s, Gigabit Testbeds started to be available. These testbeds were research-oriented and helped solve the networking problems needed to get high-speed connections from point A to point B. The research focus was on connection and bandwidth, not necessarily on getting applications to run.

By 1995, the Gigbit Testbeds had shown that a high-speed connection could be established and maintained. The next logical step was to generate 'real' applications that could help move the testbed functionality away from networking and toward application development. Those involved realized that some interesting new things could be accomplished if high-speed networking could be used to connect the various resources across the network.

At Supercomputing 95, researchers were solicited to do network computing that involved supercomputers, Immersadesks, high-speed networks, and high-end visualization. The I-WAY demonstration at SC95 connected dozens of centres world-wide via high-speed OC-3 networks in order to run over 60 applications for one week in San Diego. I-WAY was the first demonstration to clearly show there was a whole new kind of application that was suddenly possible, if the resources could be brought together in a coherent network.

A large segment of the research community, including funding agencies, became aware in 1995 of the concept that would eventually become the Grid. Today active programs are working on various elements of Grid development.

… NCSA and the San Diego Supercomputer Center both decided to participate in the NSF's Partnership for Advanced Computational Infrastructure program (1998).

NASA established the Information Power Grid (1999) that linked together Ames, Glenn (formerly Lewis), and Langley facilities. DOE established ASCI DISCOM (Advanced Strategic Computing Initiative, DIStributed COMputing effort) (1999) that tied together three weapons labs and their users. Vice-President Al Gore's office set-up IT^2, which cuts across all federal agencies to push the high-end level of computing capability.

Ian Foster, from Argonne National Labs describes other efforts in this context: "In distance visualization, networks with varying capabilities can connect geographically distributed data sources, image consumers, and the visualization engines that translate data into images. For example, our distance visualization system allows collaborative online reconstruction and analysis of tomographic data from remote X-ray sources and electron microscopes. The Advanced Photon Source at Argonne National Laboratory in Illinois is the world's brightest high-energy X-ray source, and the most powerful electron microscope is located at Osaka University in Japan…. Our online analysis system couples these instruments to supercomputers at Argonne and the Information Sciences Institute at the University of Southern California and to users across the United States. The Department of Energy's ESnet and the National Science Foundation's vBNS provide network access to supercomputers and to remote users, while the Transpac connection through Star Tap enables high-speed access to Osaka."

Ian Foster, Joseph Insley, Gregor von Laszewski, Carl Kesselman, and Marcus Thiebaux, "Distance Visualization: Data Exploration on the Grid," *Computer*, vol. 32, no. 12, December, 1999, pp. 36–43: http://csdl.computer.org/comp/mags/co/1999/12/rz036abs.htm.

105 Graham F. Carey, *Computational Grids: Generation, Adaptation, and Solution Strategies*, London: Taylor & Francis, 1997. Ian Foster and Carl Kesselman, eds., *The Grid: Blueprint for a New Computing Infrastructure*, San Francisco: Morgan Kaufmann, 1998. B. Engquist, *Simulation and Visualization on the Grid*, Stuttgart: Springer Verlag, 1999.

106 Reported at INET 2000, Yokohama, 17 July 2000.

107 Mark Ward, "Powering up the Grid," *BBC News*, 28 June 2000: http://news.bbc.co.uk/hi/english/sci/tech/newsid_806000/806410.stm.

108 DARPA Gusto testbed: http://www-fp.globus.org/research/testbeds.html.

109 Globus Resource Brokers, now Globus Toolkit 4: http://www.globus.org/toolkit/downloads/4.0.1/.

110 Globus Alliance: http://www.globus.org/about/related.html; R.J. Allan, "Parallel Application Software on High Performance Computers. Survey of Computational Grid, Meta-computing and Network Information Tools," Computational Science and Engineering Department, CLRC Daresbury Laboratory, Daresbury, Warrington WA4 4AD, UK, 5 June 2000: http://www.dl.ac.uk/TCSC/Subjects/Parallel_Algorithms/steer_survey/.

111 Biology Workbench: http://workbench.sdsc.edu/.

112 Formerly at: http://netlib.uow.edu.au/utk/people/JackDongarra/SLIDES/japan-199/sld041.htm.

113 Patricia K. Fasel, "Parallel Application Workspace", CCS3 Lab, Los Alamos: http://www.c3.lanl.gov/~pkf/.

114   William R. Wiley Environmental Molecular Sciences Laboratory, "Collaborative Access Teams," 2004: http://www.emsl.pnl.gov/proj/cats.shtml.

115   Department of Energy, "DOE 2000. Electronic Notebook Project," 1999: http://www.epm.ornl.gov/enote/.

116   UK Research Councils E-Science Core Programme: http://www.research-councils.ac.uk/escience/.

117   Ashlee Vance, "IBM signs with Oxford to build Grid," *IDG News Service*/San Francisco Bureau, 2 August 2001.

118   Unicore Forum: www.unicore.org.

119   EU Datagrid: http://eu-datagrid.web.cern.ch/eu-datagrid/.

120   http://www.eurogrid.org.

121   Closely related is the Distributed Applications and Middleware for Industrial Use of European Markets (DAMIEN): http://www.hlrs.de/organization/pds/projects/damien. There is also a Grid Forum Initiative and a Global Grid Forum which links metacomputing projects around the world.

122   Jean Jacques Dactwyler, "Die globale Rechenmaschine," *Tages-Anzeiger*, 18 January 2002, p. 38.

123   Clive Cookson, "Scientists expect £100m to build super-fast internet," *Financial Times*, 3 March 2000, p. 21: http://styx.esrin.esa.it/grid/press/ft.com.03march00.html. For a recent survey, see Richard Martin, "The God Particle and the Grid," *Wired*, April, 2004, pp. 114–17.

124   Kors Bos, François Etienne, Enrique Fernandez, Fabrizio Gagliardi, Hans Hoffmann, Mirco Mazzucato, Robin Middleton, Les Robertson, Federico Ruggieri, and Gyorgy Vesztergombi, *Outline of a Proposal for a Data-intensive Computational GRID Testbed*. Proposal for an outline of a project to be submitted to the EU and the NSF, Version 1.4, 20 March 2000.

      "Most of these collisions are uninteresting *background* events such as collisions with residual gas molecules in the vacuum of the beam pipe. The process of selecting the interesting events for recording and further analysis is called *triggering*."

125   Ibid. "The need to scale computation capacity (hundreds of thousands of SPECint95s, thousands of processors), disk capacity (hundreds of TeraBytes, thousands of hard disks), local network bandwidth (Terabits per second of throughput), and tertiary storage capacity (tens of PetaBytes of automated magnetic tape storage)."

126   Ibid.

127   Ibid. "The processing power should be distributed across these major centres and the other sites. A high performance network interconnect should support easy Web based access to processing capacity and data. Important new scientific results could be achieved by merging large and different databases and archives."

128   Vincent Kiernan, "To Test Climate Model, Scientist Seeks Computers by the Millions," *The Chronicle of Higher Education*, 22 October 1999: http://chronicle.com/. A climatologist at the Rutherford Appleton Laboratory in Chilton, England, is "calling for volunteers to assist him in evaluating the accuracy of computer models of the earth's climate. Myles Allen, head of the Casino-21 project, says by harnessing the power of at least a million computer desktop machines, he could compare the numerous variables included in computer models with actual data on weather patterns from 1950 to 2000. He could then extrapolate from those results predictions for each year from 2000 to 2050."

      In 2005, the EU has a special Unit F2 to deal with Grid Technologies: http://www.cordis.lu/ist/grids/index.htm.

129   Howard Rheingold, "You Got the Power," *Wired*, August, 2000, pp. 176–84.

130   Seti@home: http://setiathome.berkeley.edu/index.php.

131   For a popular account of similar ideas, see Howard Rheingold, "You Got the Power," *Wired*, August, 2000, pp. 176–84.

132   Intel Press Release, 3 April 2001: (formerly) http://www.intel.com/pressroom/archive/releases/20010403corp.htm. For a discussion of the philosophical and politico-social dimensions

of peer-to-peer (P2P), see Miguel Benasayag, philosophe et psychanalyste, "Résister 'malgré tout'," *Périphéries, Gens de Bien*, January 2001: http://www.peripheries.net/g-bensg.htm.

133   "Napstern für einen guten Zweck," *Tages-Anzeiger*, 9 April 2001, p. 63.

134   Jennifer Couzin, "The Power of Many," *The Industry Standard Magazine*, 18 June 2001: http://www.findarticles.com/cf_dls/m0HWW/24_4/75958950/p4/article.jhtml?term.

135   Alan Boyle, "Can we simulate life's machinery?" *MSNBC.com*, 8 September 2000: http://www.mithral.com/pressroom/archive/2000-09-MSNBC.html.

136   Personal communication from Ir. Jaap van Till of Stratix in Amsterdam, 16 July 1999, translated and augmented by him on 3 February 2000 as "Just Imagine." See Appendix 4.

137   In September, 2004, Nokia predicted that there would be 2 billion cell phones by 2006, up from 1.6 billion at the end of 2004: http://news.zdnet.com/2100-1035_22-5485543.html.

138   For some important European initiatives, see TORRENT, MOICAINE, COREGRID, GRIDCOORD, and Grid 5000. A key figure in these developments is Denis Caromel (INRIA, Nice/Sophia Antipolis).

139   History of the UIA: http://www.uia.org/uiaprof/history.htm. Ariejan Korteweg, "Le Mundaneum. Voorloper van internet of stofnest van de verbeelding," *De Volkskrant*, 3 August 2001, p. 17.

140   *Gesamt Katalog der Wiegendrücke* (Rostock).

141   WWW Virtual Library: http://vlib.org/.
Sub-headings of the World Wide Web Virtual Library under:
Education
   Cognitive Science
   Distance Education
   Educational Technology
Languages
   Aboriginal Languages of Australia
Library Resources
Linguistics
   Applied Linguistics

142   There are also projects such as the Internet Archive: http://www.archive.org/index.php.

143   Ingetraut Dahlberg, "Library Catalogs in the Internet: Switching for Future Subject Access," *Advances in Knowledge Organisation*, Frankfurt: Indeks Verlag, vol. 5, 1990, pp.153–64. Interesting in this context is the TAP project: (Formerly at: http://www.alpiri.org/sw002.html); TAP Project, Stanford University: http://tap.stanford.edu/).

144   1) Academic Press, a Harcourt Science and Technology Company
2) American Association for the Advancement of Science (the publisher of *Science*)
3) American Institute of Physics (AIP)
4) Association for Computing Machinery (ACM)
5) Blackwell Science
6) Elsevier Science
7) The Institute of Electrical and Electronics Engineers, Inc. (IEEE)
8) Kluwer Academic Publishers (a Wolters Kluwer Company)
9) Nature
10) Oxford University Press
11) Springer-Verlag
12) John Wiley & Sons, Inc.

145   American Association for the Advancement of Science: http://www.aaas.org/:
"Researchers will be able to move easily from a reference in a journal article to the content of a cited journal article, typically located on a different server and published by a different publisher. At the outset, approximately three million articles across thousands of journals will be linked through this service, and more than half a million more articles will be linked each year thereafter. This will enhance the efficiency of browsing and reading the primary scientific and scholarly literature. Such linking will enable readers to gain access to logically related

articles with one or two clicks – an objective widely accepted among researchers as a natural and necessary part of scientific and scholarly publishing in the digital age.

The reference-linking service will be run from a central facility, which will be managed by an elected Board and will operate in cooperation with the International Digital Object Identifier (DOI) Foundation. It will contain a limited set of metadata, allowing the journal content and links to remain distributed at publishers' sites.

Each publisher will set its own access standards, determining what content is available to the researcher following a link (such as access to the abstract or to the full text of an article, by subscription, document delivery, or pay-per-view, etc.).

The service is being organized as a not-for-profit entity to safeguard the independence of each participating publisher to set their own access standards and conditions. The service, which is based on a prototype developed by Wiley and Academic Press, was developed in cooperation with the International DOI Foundation and builds on work by the Association of American Publishers and the Corporation for National Research Initiatives. It takes advantage of the DOI standard and other World Wide Web standards and Internet technology. By taking a standards-based approach the international initiative is confident that the sophisticated demands of the readers of scientific and scholarly journals for linking of references can be implemented broadly and rapidly.

Representatives of the participating publishers and the International DOI Foundation are in active discussions with other scientific and scholarly primary journal publishers to make this a broad-based, industry-wide initiative. Through the reference-linking service publishers will have an easy, efficient and scalable means to add links to their online journals."

146 Project Gutenberg at HWG (HTML Writers Guild): www.hwg.org/opcenter/gutenberg: Octavo project of Adobe. Kendra Mayfield, "Out of Print, But Into Digital," *Wired*, 3 May 2001: http://www.wirednews.com/news/culture/0,1284,43330,00.html.

147 NASA Earth from space: http://earth.jsc.nasa.gov/sseop/efs/.

148 EU ESPRIT Networks of Excellence:

European ESPRIT Network	Abbreviation
Agent-Based Computing	AgentLink
AI Planning	PLANET
Computational Logic	COMPULOGNET
Computer Vision	ECV NET
Concurrent Engineering	CE-NET
Distributed Computing Systems Architectures	CaberNet
Evolutionary Computation	EVONET
Fuzzy Logic and Uncertainty Modelling in Information Technology	ERUDIT
High-Performance Computing	HPCNET
High-Temperature Electronics	HITEN
Intelligent Control and Integrated Manufacturing Systems	ICIMS
Intelligent Information Interfaces	i3net
Language and Speech	ELSNET
Machine Learning	MLnet
Model-Based and Qualitative Reasoning Systems	MONET
Neural Network	NEURONET

http://www.i3net.org/ser_pub/services/esprit_network_url.html
(formerly at: http://dbs.cordis.lu/cordis-cgi/srchidadb).
CabreNet is actually a series of projects:
BROADCAST-WG:
Basic Research On Advanced Distributed Computing: from Algorithms to SysTems – Working Group.

C3DS: Control and Coordination of Complex Distributed Services
DeVa: Design for Validation

PEGASUSII: Operating System Support for Distributed Multimedia

SQUALE: Security, Safety and Quality Evaluation for Dependable System.

149   E-Culture Net: http://www.eculturenet.org.

150   In the interim, projects such as Cultivate served as stop-gap measures: www.cultivate-int.org.

151   There are, of course, already very useful metadata watch reports.

Forum for Metadata Schema Implementers: www.schemas-forum.org.

D-Lib: www.dlib.org/;

ARIADNE: www.ariadne.ac.uk.

There are useful initiatives such as the Object Management Group: http://www.omg.org/. They have initiated.

a) Meta Object Facility (MOF): http://www.dstc.edu.au/Research/Projects/MOF/MOFAQ.html.

b) Common Warehouse Model (CWM): http://www.omg.org/technology/cwm/.

c) XML Metadata Interchange (XMI): http://www.omg.org/technology/xml/index.htm.

152   DELOS is now a Network of Excellence in FP6: http://www.delos.info/.

153   This is in the form of tele-conferencing, tele-collaboration, and tele-presence. As a result, scientists can now do tele-microscopy, tele-telescopy, and tele- everything else. Tele- is the scientists' answer to the economists' e- word. There are now also virtual laboratories, which are effectively real laboratories operated at a distance.

154   Quote formerly at: http://www.emsl.pnl.gov:2080/using-msl/about_emsl.html?main=history. html. On the History of EMSL: http://www.emsl.pnl.gov/homes/history.shtml.

155   There are challenges of such magnitude ahead that miracles are needed. For instance, thus far there has been so much excitement about the new possibilities of collaborative learning that there has been relatively little attention to the question of what is collaborative knowledge? How does it differ from more traditional modes? How much is collaboration a process leading to new ideas, and to what extent does the actual process itself need to be recorded? How does this relate to enduring knowledge? What new challenges does this pose? How can collaborative knowledge be integrated with personal and enduring knowledge in order to reach a new synthesis? These are the questions that shall concern us in the final chapters.

Chapter 12: Enduring Knowledge

1   Some persons would prefer the term "sustainable knowledge," but this evokes associations with the environment which do not bear on our discussion. Enduring knowledge is not always fashionable, is sometimes neglected, but entails eternal problems that deserve to be reconsidered constantly.

2   There are many definitions of knowledge. Some hold that, while information can be shared, knowledge cannot: "Data is unrefined ore, undifferentiated facts without context. Information is refined ore, organized data but that which we have not yet internalized. Knowledge is information, which we have internalized, information which we have integrated with our own internal frameworks ... therefore personal and pluralistic. Information can be held in common, knowledge cannot." This is claimed by Ron Steven, A. Russell, et al., *Governing in an Information Society*, Ottawa: Institute for Research and Public Policy, 1992. CIDA, cited in: *Sharing Perspectives*, Ottawa: Ministry of Public Works and Government Services, 1997. If this definition were true, then there would be no reason to save the knowledge of memory institutions and there would be no incentive for universities, or companies for that matter, to share knowledge. Indeed, there would effectively be no reason for universities or knowledge-creating companies. "Data, Information, Knowledge and Wisdom,": http://otec.uoregon.edu/data-wisdom.htm; Ramon Barquin, "From Bits to Bytes to Knowledge Management.": http://www.barquin.com/ documents/from_bits_to_bytes.pdf. Journalists, frequently regard knowledge as any information that has been edited for presentation. In this view, knowledge is the sense people make of information and thus knowledge is more easily communicated than information. Philosophers and historians of science typically define (scientific) knowledge in terms of

some criteria for truth or at least predictability. The American philosopher Santayana claimed: "Imagination that is sustained is called knowledge, illusion that is coherent is called truth and will that is systematic is called virtue." George Santayana, quoted in Frances Stonor Saunders, *The Cultural Cold War*, New York: New Press, 1999, p. 282. Another relativist definition of knowledge is: "Knowledge is defined in one place by one set of people and transferred to use in another place by another set of people."

3 The structuring and organization of knowledge is as old as civilization itself. It has been the quest of philosophers, logicians, mathematicians, librarians, and many others. Professor Dahlberg has suggested that, historically, four branches of knowledge produced at least eight types of classifications. From the time of Plato and Aristotle until the eighteenth century, philosophical classification played a decisive role. During this period, apart from the efforts of isolated individuals in libraries, museums, and universities, there were no formal bodies that dealt with knowledge organization. Some of the first systematic work came through botanists such as Linnaeus, which led to the field of taxonomy. Dahlberg has identified four branches of knowledge and eight types of classification:

BRANCH OF KNOWLEDGE	TYPE OF CLASSIFICATION
Presentation	Philosophical
Paedagogical-Didactic	
Application	Encyclopaedic
Word and Linguistic Thesauri	
Transfer	Library-Bibliographical
Documentary-Informological	
Organization	Scholarly, Business and Administrative-Political Information Systems Oriented

New fields gradually followed (Appendix 2). Since the latter nineteenth century, library bibliographical systems, such as those of Dewey and the Library of Congress, have dominated the scene, even if they were frequently very inadequate. The twentieth century has seen the advent of new methods.

This is also true but to a lesser extent in museums and archives.

4 These pragmatic solutions are important because they promise universal access to at least some basic aspects of collections. Nonetheless, a profound danger remains that an ability subsequently to perform deeper queries of sources could disappear. Moreover, such solutions focus entirely on static knowledge, on contemporary knowledge, without attention to cultural or historical changes in knowledge. As noted earlier, new methods are needed that enable access to these complexities of historical and cultural diversity, such that we can develop new kinds of dynamic knowledge maps that are evolutionary. To this end, it has been recommended that the European Commission, in the context of its long-term research program, promote the creation of a new kind of metadata. This could then become a starting point for further collaboration with other countries around the world. Professor John Mackenzie Owen has kindly brought to my attention a "special topic issue" of the *Journal of the American Society for Information Science and Technology* (JASIST), vol. 50, no. 13, 1999, on metadata (more precisely: "integrating multiple overlapping metadata standards," guest editor Zorana Ercegovac). This marks another step in the right direction.

5 An American approach believes that this is not necessary and that one can use probabilistic methods to arrive at effective results. Bruce R. Schatz, "The Interspace: Concept Navigation Across Distributed Communities," *IEEE*, January, 2002: http://www.canis.uiuc.edu/projects/interspace/index.html. Meanwhile, there is work on a Total Information Awareness System, which has been renamed a Terrorist Information System and plans for predictive crime methods. Wilpen Gorr, "Cloudy with a Chance of Theft," *Wired News*, September, 2003: http://www.wired.com/wired/archive/11.09/view.html?pg=1, which sound very much in the direction of Minority Report.

6 This is also true but to a lesser extent in museums and archives.

7 For textual analysis tools such as TACT and HyperPO, see the Text Analysis Portal for Research at the University of Alberta (TAPor): http://tapor.ualberta.ca/Resources/TASoftware/.

8 There are already preliminary examples that go in the direction of our approach, such as My virtual reference desk: www.refdesk.com/mission.html.

9 The advent of printing did far more than simply "translate" handwritten documents into typeset printed texts. It basically adopted the methods and conventions of mediaeval manuscripts.

10 E. I. Samurin, *Geschichte der bibliothekarisch-bibliographischen Klassifikation*, Munich: Verlag Dokumentation, 1977, 2 vols. Dahlberg's *Grundlagen universaler Wissensordnung*, Munich: Verlag Dokumentation, 1974, provides a handy summary thereof. This is a translation from the original Russian published in Moscow.

11 MDA Term-it: http://www.mda.org.uk/info31ti.htm; Common European Research Information Format (CERIF): http://www.cordis.lu/cerif/.

12 DESIRE Information Gateways Handbook: http://www.desire.org/handbook/.

13 European Research Gateways Online (ERGO): http://www.cordis.lu/ergo/.

14 Renardus: http://www.renardus.org/.

15 There is important work on this front by Professors McIlwaine (London) and Williamson (Toronto). Then there are significant initiatives in specific field such as the DECOMATE II project in economics: http://www.bib.uab.es/decomate2.

16 Other projects in this direction include: CHEIRON: http://www.museum.ro/cheiron/cheiron.htm and the Shared Resources on the Network (SHARON) Project led by Alejandro Delgado Gomez (Cartagena): Adelgado@futurenet.es.

17 Some have objected to this approach and the systems linked therewith on the grounds that they are too much imbued by metaphysical and ontological considerations. There is, claim some, no absolute way to determine which connections are necessary as opposed to possible. This does not, however, render less significant the basic distinctions thereby introduced.

18 Introduction to IT Projects (Electronic Dictionary Research: EDR): http://www.gip.jipdec.or.jp/english/project-e/project20-e.html. Of course, this does not mean that one will always use all these possibilities. On a given day, a major scholar never consults all the dictionaries and reference potentials of a British Library. They go there because they know that, if needed, it is there. That principle has now to be extended worldwide.

19 Professor Manfred Thaller, HKI, Köln has been working on pioneering software that will make possible such connections. HKI: http://www.hki.uni-koeln.de/.
A distinction needs to be made between:
1. Containers/ Fields/ Element: Definitions of Fields , 2. Contents within the Containers/Fields/Elements . Distinctions are also needed between different layers of semantic interoperability.

SCOPE	KIND OF MEANING	DESCRIPTION
International	Terminological Meaning	Domain specific semantics where meanings of contents have been negotiated worldwide (ISO)
	Dictionary Meaning	Formal Meaning
National	Terminological Meaning	Domain specific semantics where meanings of contents negotiated countrywide (e.g., NIST)
	Dictionary Meaning	Formal Meaning
	Corpus	Written not formalized
Regional	Terminological Meaning	Domain specific semantics where meanings of contents have been negotiated regionally
	Dictionary Meaning	Formal Meaning
	Corpus	Written not formalized
	Oral Recorded	Archived not written
Local	Terminological Meaning	Domain specific semantics where meanings of contents have been negotiated locally
	Dictionary Meaning	Formal Meaning
	Corpus	Written not formalized
	Oral Recorded	Archived not written
	Oral	Not systematically archived

20 Conference: *Information versus Meaning*, 30 September–1 October 1999, Vienna: http://www.scope.at/live/ederer.html; www.scope.at.

21 Jeffrey Harrow, *The Rapidly Changing Face of Computing*, 13 September 1999.

22 For instance, the Library of Congress had a Collaborative Digital Reference Service project now Global Reference Network (http://www.loc.gov/rr/digiref/). The University of North Texas Libraries currently provides synchronous reference service through Chat software, although they are averaging only four chat questions a week. Online reference Help Desk: http://nt90907.decal.unt.edu/helpdesk/. The University of New Orleans and Louisiana State University have an e-mail instruction (or e-struction) program: http://www.lib.lsu.edu/louis/. Louisiana Libraries are very interested in pursuing synchronous reference. The Virtual Reference Desk web site has a great deal of useful information on electronic information services: http://www.vrd.org/. Connected with this is a Digital Reference (Dig_Ref) discussion list. But this is a very long way from where we need to go.

23 Here some of the pioneering work was done by Jocelyne Nanard and Mark Nanard, "Using structured types to incorporate knowledge in hypertext," *Proceedings of ACM Hypertext '91*, San Antonio, TX, December, 1991, pp. 329–344. Mark E. Frisse and Steven B. Cousins, "Information Retrieval from Hypertext: Update on the Dynamic Medical Handbook," *Proceedings of ACM Hypertext '89*, Pittsburgh, PA, November, 1989, pp. 199–211. This was developed by Douglas Tudhope and Daniel Cunliffe, "Semantically Indexed Hypermedia: Linking Information Disciplines," *ACM Computing Surveys*, vol. 31, no. 4, December 1999: http://www.cs.brown.edu/memex/ACM_HypertextTestbed/papers/6.html; http://www.comp.glam.ac.uk/pages/research/hypermedia/;
Carole Goble (Manchester) et al. on a Conceptual Open Hypermedia Services Environment (COHSE): http://cohse.semanticweb.org/;
Leslie Carr (Southampton): http://www.ecs.soton.ac.uk/~lac/;
Wendy Hall: http://www.ecs.soton.ac.uk/~wh/; Paul H. Lewis, Wendy Hall, Leslie A. Carr, and David De Roure, "The Significance of Linking," *ACM Computing Surveys*, vol. 31, no. 4, December, 1999: http://www.cs.brown.edu/memex/ACM_HypertextTestbed/papers/20.html; Douglas Tudhope and Daniel Cunliffe, "Semantically-Indexed Hypermedia: Linking Information Disciplines," *ACM Computing Surveys*, vol. 31, no. 4, December, 1999: http://www.cs.brown.edu/memex/ACM_HypertextTestbed/papers/6.html; Intelligence, Agents, Multimedia group (IAM): http://www.iam.ecs.soton.ac.uk/; Information Management Group: http://img.cs.man.ac.uk/semweb/cohse.html.

24 Professor Tudhope, Hypermedia Research Unit: http://www.glam.ac.uk/soc/research/hypermedia/index.php.

25 [ISO13250]: Michel Biezunski, Martin Bryan, and Steven R. Newcomb, ed., *ISO/IEC 13250:2000 Topic Maps: Information Technology – Document Description and Markup Languages*, 3 December 1999: http://www.y12.doe.gov/sgml/sc34/document/0129.pdf; Alexander Sigel, "Towards knowledge organization with Topic Maps," *XML Europe 2000*: http://www.gca.org/papers/xmleurope2000/papers/s22-02.html.

26 Empolis. Information Logistics Company: http://www.empolis.co.uk/home/home.asp.

27 Infoloom Inc.: http://www.infoloom.com/.

28 Mondeca Inc.: http://www.mondeca.com/.

29 Ontopia: http://www.ontopia.net/.

30 Claude Elwood Shannon, *The Mathematical Theory of Communication*, Urbana, IL: University of Illinois Press, 1949.

31 "MIT Professor Claude Shannon dies; was founder of digital communications." *MIT News*, 27 February 2001: http://web.mit.edu/newsoffice/nr/2001/shannon.html. James Evans, "Founder of digital communications dies," *IDG News Service*/Boston Bureau, 28 February 2001.

32 With respect to elementary word processing, this is apparent in packages such as Microsoft Word, whereby the process of entering content (by typing) is separated from questions of format such as adding bold, italic, or underlined scripts, centred, left, or right-aligned scripts, etc.

33 One of the pioneers in this was Yuri Rubinsky (1952–1996), the founder of Softquad, whose ideas about metadata helped to inspire the OCLC metadata initiative and specifically the Dublin Core movement: http://www.oasis-open.org/cover/yuriMemColl.html.

34 These include:
Chemical Markup Language (CML)
Handheld Device Markup Language (HDML)
Hardware Description Language (HDL)
Mathematical Markup Language (MML)
Web Interface Description Language (WIDL)
Precision Graphics Markup Language (PGML)
Extensible Hyper Language (EHL).

35 International Development Markup Language (IDML): www.idmlinitiative.org.

36 Kristen Philipkoski, "Genomics Gets a New Code: GEML," *Wired News*, 12 December 2000: http://www.wirednews.com/news/print/0,1294,40621,00.html.

37 In this context, Cascading Style Sheets (CSS) was an interim measure to deal with different versions of a document.

38 A slightly different arrangement is given by Rohit Khare, "XML: The Least You Need to Know.": http://www.ics.uci.edu/~rohit/cscw98/xml/.
Syntax   SGML
Style   CSS/XSL
Structure   HTML
Semantics XML
XML is a subset of Standard Generalized Markup Language (SGML); John Sowa, "Ontology, Metadata, and Semiotics," International Conference on Conceptual Structures, ICCS'2000, 14–18 August 2000, Darmstadt, Germany: http://www.bestweb.net/~sowa/peirce/ontometa.htm. The distinction between syntax, semantics, and pragmatics comes from Peirce, who saw these as the three branches of semiotics: Charles Sanders Peirce, "On the algebra of logic," *American Journal of Mathematics*, vol. 7, 1885, pp. 180–202; *Collected Papers of C. S. Peirce*, ed. C. Hartshorne, P. Weiss, and A. Burks, 8 vols., Cambridge, MA: Harvard University Press, 1931–58. Particularly vol. 2, p. 229.

39 World Wide Web Consortium (W3C): http://www.w3.org.

40 ACM SIG (Special Interest Group) on Hypertext, Hypermedia and the Internet: http://www.sigweb.org/.

41 Vannevar Bush, "As we may think," *Atlantic Monthly*, July, 1945: http://www.theatlantic.com/unbound/flashbks/computer/bushf.htm.

42 http://www.bootstrap.org/. A basic bibliography for Douglas C. Engelbart (hereafter DCE), includes: "A Conceptual Framework for the Augmentation of Man's Intellect," *Vistas in Information Handling*. ed. P. D. Howerton and D.C. Weeks, Washington: Spartan Books, 1963; DCE and William K. English. *"A Research Center for Augmenting Human Intellect." Proceedings AFIPS Conference, 1968 Joint Computer Conference*. 9–11 December 1968, San Francisco. Montvale, NJ: AFIPS Press, 1968; "Coordinated Information Services for a Discipline or Mission-Oriented Community." *Proceedings Second Annual Computer Communications Conference*, 24 January 1973, San Jose, CA; DCE, Richard W. Watson and James C. Norton, "The Augmented Knowledge Workshop," *Proceedings AFIPS Conference, 1973 National Computer Conference and Exposition*, 4–8 June 1973, New York. Montvale, NJ: AFIPS Press, 1973; "Toward Integrated, Evolutionary Office Automation Systems." *Proceedings Joint Engineering Management Conference*, 16–18 October 1978, Denver, CO. "Toward High-Performance Knowledge Workers," *Proceedings AFIPS Office Automation Conference*. 5–7 April 1982, San Francisco, CA; "Authorship Provisions in AUGMENT," *Proceedings COMPCON Conference*, 21 February – 1 March 1984, San Francisco; "Collaborative Support Provisions in AUGMENT," *Proceedings COMPCON Conference*, 21 February – 1 March 1984, San Francisco, CA.; "Workstation History and the Augmented Knowledge Workshop," *Proceedings ACM Conference on the History of Personal Workstations*, 9–10 January 1986, Palo Alto, CA; DCE and Harvey Lehtman, "Working Together," BYTE, December, 1988, pp.

624

245–52. "Knowledge-Domain Interoperability and an Open Hyperdocument System," *Proceedings of the Conference on Computer-Supported Cooperative Work*, Los Angeles, CA, 7–10 October 1980, pp. 143–56. (AUGMENT, 132082). Also republished in E. Berk and J. Devlin, eds., *Hypertext/Hypermedia Handbook*, McGraw-Hill, 1991. Douglas C. Engelbart, "Toward High-Performance Organizations: A Strategic Role for Groupware," *Groupware '92, Proceedings of the groupWare '92 Conference*, San Jose, CA, 3–5 August 1992, Morgan Kaufmann, pp. 77–100.

43   Standard references on the theme of hypertext are given in Appendix 8. e.g. George Landow, *Hypertext: The Convergence of Contemporary Critical Theory and Technology.* Baltimore: Johns Hopkins University Press, 1992. New edition: 1997. This work makes important distinctions between a number of linking materials, pp. 12–14:
- – Lexia to Lexia Unidirectional
- – Lexia to Lexia Bidirectional
- – String (word or phrase) to Lexia
- – String to String
- – One to Many
- – Many to One.

There are also numerous sites on hypertext on the Internet. For a good introduction: http://www.hawaii.edu/itsdocs/net/webintro/. Some history and a basic bibiliography, Hypertext Places: http://cheiron.humanities.mcmaster.ca/~htp/. For a more thorough bibliography focussing on literary hypertext: http://www.eastgate.com/Map.html. On hypertext and hypermedia: http://www.bradley.edu/las/eng/biblio/. On links with cyberspace and critical theory: http://www.cyberartsweb.org/cpace/. On hypertext fiction or Hyperizons http://www.duke.edu/~mshumate/hyperfic.html. On links between hypertext and intertextuality: http://www.cyberartsweb.org/cpace/ht/jhup/intertext.html. On specific links with Derrida: http://www.public.iastate.edu/~honeyl/derrida/hypertext.html; Jacques Derrida,"The Supplement of Copula: Philosophy before Linguistics." *Textual Strategies: Perspectives in Post-Structuralist Criticism*, ed. Josué V. Harari. London: Methuen, 1979, pp. 28–120; Maggie Swan, Andrew Dillon, and Michelle Fuhrmann, "Hypermedia, and Learning, The State of the Art. Extended Bibliography in Progress," Last Updated 7 November 2001: http://variations2.indiana.edu/pdf/HyperBiblio.pdf. For the MIT Hypertext project: http://hypertext.rmit.edu.au/essays/mia/mia_figure_one.html. On the use of hypertext and WWW: http://www.perzept.de/hypertext/Geolog.htm. On connections with ubiquitous computing: http://www.ubiq.com/hypertext/weiser/UbiHome.html. Re: V. Balasubramanian, Graduate School of Management, Rutgers University, Newark, NJ, "State of the Art Review on Hypermedia Issues and Applications.": http://www.isg.sfu.ca/~duchier/misc/hypertext_review/. Concerning hypertext interfaces to library information systems in the EU project HYPERLIB: http://lib.ua.ac.be/docstore.html. For an information science definition of hypertext: "The term hypertext is used to refer to full-text indexing schemes which are more elaborate and, ideally, more useful in creating 'links' or connections between related subjects or terms.… Hypertext allows the user to move from within one section of text to another, related section of text, without having to exit the current document (or section of document) and re-enter a new document. ([Mary Ann] O'Connor, "Markup, SGML, and Hypertext for Full-Text Databases—Part III," p. 130)."

44   Ted Nelson, *Literary Machines*, South Bend, IN: Self-published, 1981, p. 0/2. The subtitle of this work was: "Project Xanadu, an initiative toward an instantaneous electronic literature; the most audacious and specific plan for knowledge, freedom and a better world yet to come out of computerdom; the original (and perhaps the ultimate) Hypertext System."

45   Ibid., p. 1/16. Ted Nelson overlooks that the Torah had more systematic links through its page layout than a mere ad hoc linking via a spaghetti of connections; David Small's *Talmud Project* (MIT Media Lab, Small Design Firm); Tim Guay, "Web Publishing Paradigms," 1995: http://www.faced.ufba.br/~edc708/biblioteca/interatividade/web%20paradigma/Paradigm.html: "The concept has been use in ancient literature, such as the *Talmud*; with its commentary on commentary on the main text, and its annotations, and references to other passages within the Talmud,

625

and outside in the *Torah* and *Tenach*. It is a very biological form of presenting information that models how our minds processes, organizes, and retrieves information. It creates very organic information space, as opposed to the artificial linear format imposed by the print paradigm. Conceptually, hypertext forms associations called links, between chunks of information called nodes. The resulting structure is commonly referred to as a web, hence the name World Wide WEB for the CERN project. These basic characteristics, coupled with hypertext's other characteristics allows the production is extremely rich, flexible documents and metadocuments, especially when combined with multimedia to form the fusion referred to as hypermedia."; N. Streitz, J. Hannemann, J. Lemke, et al., "SEPIA: A Cooperative Hypermedia Authoring Environment," *Proceedings of the ACM Conference on Hypertext*, ECHT '92, Milan, 1992, pp. 11–22.

46 Further contributing to this confusion are conflicting interests. The owners of search engines such as Yahoo and Altavista gain money from advertising which is calculated on the basis of number of hits. The interests of firms such as Altavista thus favour as many detours as possible on the way to finding what we really want. By contrast, a user wants as few distractions as possible in arriving at their goal. Thus, the advertising interests of the search companies are actually preventing use of the most efficient search strategies. Yet another problem is that a number of web sites are designed by marketing experts, who are only interested in the effects of presentation (rhetoric) rather than the structure (grammar) or logic (dialectic) of the materials. As a result, the substance of the sites is masked by its form.

47 Digital Object Identifier (DOI) System: http://www.doi.org/. Other developments include Universal Product Code (UPC): http://www.adams1.com/pub/russadam/upccode.html and European Article Numbering (EAN): http://www.ean-int.org/index800.html. The idea of Digital Object Identifier (DOI) grew partly out of the idea of Bob Kahn (INET, CNRI) to create a Universal Object Identifier (UOI): http://www.cnri.reston.va.us/bios/kahn.html. Re: Link of DOI with UOI: David Sidman (CEO, Content Directions, Inc.), "The Digital Object Identifier (DOI): The Keystone for Digital Rights Management (DRM)," 26 January 2001. Draft submitted to the SIIA Digital Rights Management (DRM) Working Group: http://www.contentdirections. com/materials/SIIA-DOIandDRM-DavidSidman.doc.

48 Cross Ref.: http://www.crossref.org/. "A researcher clicking on a link (the format of which is determined by publisher preference; for example, a CrossRef button, or 'Article' in html) will be connected to a page on the publisher's web site showing a full bibliographical citation of the article, and, in most cases, the abstract as well. The reader can then access the full text article through the appropriate mechanism; subscribers will generally go straight to the text, while others will receive information on access via subscription, document delivery, or pay-per-view. CrossRef costs the researcher nothing; its expenses are covered by nominal charges to the publishers for depositing their metadata, annual membership fees, and fees to publishers of abstracting and indexing databases for accessing CrossRef's bank of DOIs to create links to full text articles." As such, Crossref is a thinly veiled advertising ploy rather than an independent linking method, because it will link titles with those full text examples that are in the publishers' interests rather than being that which may be important for an individual scholar.

49 Definitions of metadata: http://www.doi.org/doi_presentations/dec2000/metadata/sld003.htm.

50 Herbert Van de Sompel, "Reference Linking in a Hybrid Library Environment, Part 1: Frameworks for Linking," *D-Lib Magazine*, vol. 5, no. 4, April, 1999: http://www.dlib.org/dlib/april99/van_de_sompel/04van_de_sompel-pt1.html; http://www.dlib.org/dlib/april99/van_de_sompel/04van_de_sompel-pt2.html; http://www.dlib.org/dlib/october99/van_de_sompel/10van_de_sompel.html;

51 W3 Xlink. See: http://www.w3.org/TR/xlink/#origin-goals. This entails: 1) XML Linking Language (Xlink) provides a framework for creating both basic unidirectional links and more complex linking structures. It allows XML documents to: Assert linking relationships among more than two resources. Associate metadata with a link. Express links that reside in a location separate from the linked resources. 2) XML Pointer Language (XPointer), which "allows for traversals of a document tree and choice of its internal parts based on various properties, such

as element types, attribute values, character content, and relative position: http://www.w3.org/XML/Linking 3) XML Base.

52 Brief history of hypertext according to Robert Horn, *Mapping Hypertext*, Waltham, MA: Lexington Institute Press, 1989, 1996:

DATE	INDIVIDUAL	PROJECT
1945	Vannevar Bush	Invention of concept in "As we may think"
1962–75	Douglas Engelbart	First operational hypertext: Hypermedia
1965	Ted Nelson	Coined term Hypertext
1968	Van Dam and Brown	First university instruction
1972	Zog Group, CMU	Menu interfaces
1976	Negroponte and Bolt	Spatial Dataland
1986	Brown and Guide	Hypertext for PC and Macintosh
1987	Sculley	Vision of the Knowledge Navigator
1987	Atkinson	First Commercial Hypertext "Hit"

53 Ibid.: http://www.eastgate.com/catalog/MappingHypertext.html. Horn identified seven kinds of information types: procedure, process, structure, concept, fact, classification, and principle.

54 Helga Leiprecht, "Der geklonte Text als Gruselorgie," *Tages-Anzeiger*, 9 January 2001, p. 55.

55 For a recent attempt to use hypertext in an on-line presentation of an historical text, see the work of Margo van den Brink: (formerly) http://www.mmi.unimaas.nl/userswww/delim-online/index.htm.

56 Hyun-Suk Kim, "Ein asiatisches Blick auf die westlichen Kulturtheorien: universeller Geltungsanspruch vs. kulturelle Eigenheit," *Theorien über Theorien über Theoiren*, ed. Anke Jobmann, Bernd Spindler, Universität Bielefeld: Institut für Wissenschafts- und Technikforschung, 1999, pp. 62–73 (IWT Paper 24).

57 For an important statement of this position, see Robert Fugmann, *Subject Analysis and Indexing. Theoretical Foundation and Practical Advice*, Frankfurt: Indeks Verlag, 1993 (*Textbooks for Knowledge Organization*, vol. 1).

58 For a preliminary example of this levels approach, Lexibot: www.lexibot.com.

59 M. Greeff and V. Lalioti, "Authoring Interactive Stories Using Virtual Identities," *Euroimage ICAV3D* 2001, Thessaloniki: ZITI, 2001, pp. 97–100.

60 Comparison between Aristotle, Dahlberg and Perreault:

ARISTOTLE	Being-Substance	Accidents		
	Content Substance	Form		
	Concrete Objects	Abstract Principles		
DAHLBERG	Entities	Properties: Quantity, Quality, Relation	Activities: Action (Operation), Suffering (Process), State	Dimensions: Space, Time, Position
PERREAULT	Subsumptive Relations		Determinative Relations	Ordinal Relations

Dahlberg also reshuffled Aristotle's accidents to produce three categories for each heading:

DAHLBERG	Entities	Properties: Quantities, Qualities, Relations	Activities: Operations, Processes, States	Dimensions: Space, Time, Lage (i.e., Position in Dimension)

Dahlberg has been criticized for letting a desire for symmetry affect her re-arrangement of Aristotle's qualities, on the grounds that this symmetry is guided by metaphysical aims rather than logic. In fact, each systematization typically brings some gains and some losses. By subsuming being and having under states, Dahlberg adds some clarity but detracts attention away from the fundamental verbs of being and having.

61 Abstraction and Partition relations and their variant names by different persons and communities.

Divisio	Partitio	Logic
Generic/Abstraction	Partition	Wüster, Dahlberg
Tree structure	Beam Structure	Wüster, Dahlberg
Type/Kind	Whole/Part	Perreault
Hyponomy/hyperonymy	Meronomy	Shreider, Bean
Taxonomy	Partonomy	Tversky, Pribbenow
Generalization	Aggregation	Smith, Mylopoulos
Hierarchical	Hierarchical	Library Science/Info. Science
Broader/Narrower	Broader/Narrower	Library Science/Info. Science
is a/has a	is a part/has a part	Computer Science
(Inheritance: Parent-Child)	(Inheritance: Parent-Child)	Computer Science
Type Instantiation	Type Instantiation	Computer Science

62 Level one of Dahlberg's analysis of functional or syntactic relations:

SUBJECT	PREDICATE		PREDICATE (OBJECT)
Entities	Activities	Properties	Dimensions
Noun	Verb	Noun	
Dick	(is a) friend	(has an) address	
Noun	(intransitive verb + adjective)	noun (transitive verb + adjective) noun	

63 For more details on the American approach, Thomas Baker, "A Grammar of Dublin Core," *D-Lib Magazine*, vol. 6., no. 10, October 2001: http://www.dlib.org/dlib/october00/baker/10baker.html.

64 For a further discussion, see the present author's "Towards a Semantic Web for Culture," *Journal of Digital Information* (*JoDI*), Oxford, vol. 4, no. 4, Article no. 255, 15 March 2004, pp. 1–87. Dahlberg has two other levels. Level three examines the form of the statement (e.g., whether it is a proposal). Level four examines the general context of the statement (e.g., whether it is a book theme). The details of these further levels are beyond the scope of our present discussion.

65 The frontiers of computer science have long since gone beyond these limitations. Unfortunately, important initiatives such as the Dublin Core and W3 Consortium continue to use these limitations.

66 J. Perreault, "Categories and Relators," *International Classification*, Frankfurt, vol. 21, no. 4, 1994, pp. 189–98, especially p. 195. The original list by Professor Nancy Williamson (Faculty of Information Studies, University of Toronto) lists these in a different order under the heading:
1. Whole-part

2. Field of study and object(s) studied

3. Process and agent or instrument of the process

4. Occupation and person in that occupation

5. Action and product of action

6. Action and its patient

7. Concepts and their properties

8. Concepts related to their origins

9. Concepts linked by causal dependence

10. A thing or action and its counter-agent

11. An action and a property associated with it

12. A concept and its opposite.

67   Perreault's basic subsumptive relations. Cf. Appendix 5.

Logical relation	Subsumptive	Type/Kind	Principle/Manifestation\Genus
			Species\Species
			Individuum
		Whole/Part	Organism/Organ
			Composite/Constituent
			Matrix/Particles
		Subject/Property	Substance/Accident
			Possessor/Possession
			Accompanance

68   A concrete example of such a bibliography, which includes all previous examples, is the author's bibliography on perspective available as a demo at: www.sumscorp.com.

69   Ingetraut Dahlberg, *Grundlagen universaler Wissensordnung. Probleme und Möglichkeiten eines universalen Klassifikationssystems de Wissens*, Pullach bei München: Verlag Dokumentation Saur KG, 1974; Nancy Williamson, "An Interdisciplinary World and Discipline Based Classification," *Structures and Relations in Knowledge Organization*, Würzburg: Ergon Verlag, 1998, pp. 116–24. (*Advances in Knowledge Organization*, vol. 6); C. McIlwaine, "Knowledge Classifications, Bibliographic Classifications and the Internet," *Structures and Relations in Knowledge Organization*, Würzburg: Ergon Verlag, 1998, pp. 97–105. (*Advances in Knowledge Organization*, vol. 6).

70   These possibilities are further outlined in the author's "Conceptual Navigation in Multimedia Knowledge Spaces," *TKE-1999, 5th International Congress and Workshops on Terminology and Knowledge Engineering*, Vienna: TermNet, 1999, pp. 1–27.

71   On the EC's present program on content filtering: http://www.cordis.lu/ist/ka3/iaf/call7_1.htm.

72   Institute for Systems, Informatics and Safety.

73   One of the pioneering efforts in this context was the T(erra)-Vision project of Art+Com (Berlin). In the cultural field, perhaps the most impressive work to date is a project at the Universidad Complutense (Madrid) called Sistema Avanzado de navigacion sobre Terrenos Interactivo (SANTI) linked with Professor Luis Hernandez: http://videalab.udc.es/. At the level of everyday users, there are new sites: www.mapquest.com and http://www.globexplorer.com/, which allow one to type in an address and access the corresponding map automatically. The Iimap company provides overlays of aerial views and street maps: http://www.iimap.com/iiInfo.html; www.spaceimaging.com; www.earthbrowser.com. A recent development is Keyhole, which offers a global approach to this theme: http://www.earthviewer.com/.

74   Preliminary work in this direction has been done by Natalia Adrienko, Gennady Adrienko, Alexandr Savinov, and Dietrich Wettschereck, "Descartes and Kepler for Spatial Data Mining." *ERCIM News*, no. 40, January, 2000, pp. 44–45; Natalia Adrienko, Gennady Adrienko, and Peter Gatalsky, "Analytical Visualization of Spatial Temporal Data," ibid., pp. 45–46. The Adrienkos are interested in 3-D Gestalt theory: (formerly) http://allanon.gmd.de/and/.

75 At a theoretical level some first steps in this direction are provided by Alexander Kaiser, *Die Modellierung Zeitbezogener Data*, Frankfurt: Peter Lang, 2000. He discusses integration of time into entity relationships.

76 Donald Norman, *The Invisible Computer*, Cambridge, MA: MIT Press, 1999, pp. 267–68.

77 For a different approach to this theme, see Robert Darnton, "A Program for Reviving the Monograph," March, 1999. Also Robert Darnton, "The new age of the book," *New York Review of Books*, 18 March 1999: http://www.theaha.org/Perspectives/issues/1999/9903/9903PRE.CFM.

78 On this problem of linking different levels of abstraction, futurists such as Heiner Benking intuitively seek to link subjective and objective elements in arriving at a more systematic understanding of the world. Benking foresees using a universal classification system such as the ICC as a means of switching between various classification schemes and moving from levels of abstraction to levels of detailed knowledge. While a clear method of how one moves between various levels of abstraction still needs to be developed, his intuitive sense of the challenges is very stimulating. Heiner Benking, "Understanding and Sharing in a Cognitive Panorama.": http://www.newciv.org/cob/members/benking/benking.html; http://www.ceptualinstitute.com/genre/benking/homepageHB1.htm.

79 3Dsia: http://threedsia.sourceforge.net/about.html#shot. There are a number of such methods that have been discussed at further length in the author's *Frontiers in Conceptual Navigation for Cultural Heritage*, Toronto: Ontario Library Association, 1999. Other new navigation software includes:
Newsmaps: http://www.newsmaps.com/;
Lightstep: http://lsfaq.litestep.org/;
Skins: (formerly) http://ezskins.iboost.com/.

80 In this context, important work is being done by Martin Graham on visualization of structural change across hierarchies: http://www.dcs.napier.ac.uk/~marting/. Martin Graham is a doctoral student of Professor Jessie Kennedy. Fabio Paterno (CNR), is working on Concur Task Trees: http://Giove.cnuce.cnr.it/ctte.html; http://giove.cnuce.cnr.it/concurtasktrees.html; http://www.honda-robots.com/german/html/asimo/frameset2.html.

81 These developments are discussed in the author's book: *Frontiers in Conceptual Navigation for Cultural Heritage*, Toronto: Ontario Library Association, 1999.

82 Cf. an On-line Library of Information Visualization Environments (OLIVE): http://otal.umd.edu/Olive/.

83 There is important work by Ivan Poupyrev: http://www.mic.atr.co.jp/~poup/.

84 On the theme of switching between systems, see Ingetraut Dahlberg, "Library Catalogues on the Internet: Switching for Future Subject Access," *Knowledge Organization and Change*, Frankfurt: Indeks Verlag, 1996, pp. 155–64. (Advances in Knowledge Organization, vol. 5).

85 Applied to the whole range of materials available in reference rooms of the major libraries, agents will thus lead to a new level of metadata, which not only associates persons, subjects, objects, and places with a number of variant names – which can serve as alternative search strategies – but also with an awareness of cultural and historical shifts in those variant names.

86 The Aquabrowser is an excellent case in point. It is extremely impressive because, yes, it generates a number of terms, which are related in some way to a given contemporary term. This can be very useful, assuming of course that I am sufficiently acquainted with the field in question to recognize which terms are highly relevant and which are less so. While very attractive, the Aquabrowser is essentially giving me a snapshot of one possible configuration of contemporary terms. It might claim to be dynamic to the extent that, if the same software is applied to a slightly different sample of books, a different constellation of terms will be generated. It is not, however, dynamic in our sense because it cannot trace changing connections between terms through different languages in different cultures over time. In some situations, Aquabrowser is an ideal tool. If I have a good general knowledge of a domain and want to have a sense of related terms, then the Aquabrowser provides a useful orientation. On the other hand, if I need insight into the historical context of a term, it is of little use. Aquabrowser is a contemporary contextualizer at a

bibliographical level in the sense of finding me further titles in neighbouring fields. It points to books. It cannot augment my understanding of their contents.
Aquabrowser: http://www.medialab.nl/.

87 The scenarios outlined above concerning virtual reference rooms set out from a simple, but elusive assumption, namely, that the names, subjects, places, and chronologies in the various reference works are all standardized such that one can move seamlessly from one list to another.

88 While proponents of broadband connections will welcome such scenarios, systems analysts might warn that such an approach would totally overload the network and render it useless. Again some balance is required. We need to recall that the storage space on a typical local computer has changed from 20 Megabytes to several Gigabytes in the past decade and will expand even more dramatically in the next two decades. A botanist working on a specific domain will simply have the standard reference books of that field on their local system. Subsets of that will be available on notepads as they go into the field. New combinations can also be foreseen. If they are environmentalists, whose work requires their driving around constantly in remote territory, they can have a large memory capacity in their jeep, which is consulted by wireless from their notepad as they walk around without needing to burden the Internet directly as they do their routine work. On the other hand, if they come across something that is new to them, they can use a satellite connection to check whether there be information concerning this finding in central repositories such as Kew Gardens.

89 Tim Berners Lee's lectures at *WWW*7 and *WWW*8: http://www.w3.org/Talks/. For a discussion of some implications of these developments for knowledge organization, see the author's "Conceptual Navigation in Multimedia Knowledge Spaces," TKE '99, *Terminology and Knowledge Engineering*, Vienna: Termnet, 1999, pp. 1–27.

90 Howard Rheingold, *Tools for Thought*, April 2000: http://www.rheingold.com/texts/tft/11.html. Scott Gasch, "Alan Kay," Submitted in partial fulfillment of the requirements of CS 3604, Virginia Tech/Norfolk State University, Fall 1996.: http://ei.cs.vt.edu/~history/GASCH.KAY.HTML#2.

91 Dyna Book: Formerly at: http://www.stg.brown.edu:1084/dynaweb;
Electronic Books and E-publishing: http://www.chartula.com/1852334355_toc.pdf;
Memex and Beyond Website: http://www.cs.brown.edu/memex/archives.html.

92 Web reference: http://www.webreference.com/dhtml/.

93 Macromedia Dreamweaver: http://www.dhtmlzone.com/index.html.

94 Formerly at: http://www.astound.com/info2/dynapress.html; see also: http://webserver.cpg.com/wt/3.3/ .

5 The Pazooter Works: http://megabrands.com/alice/indexx.html.

96 An exploration of Dynamic Documents: http://home.netscape.com/assist/net_sites/pushpull.html.

97 HTML Working Group Roadmap: http://www.w3.org/MarkUp/xhtml-roadmap/.

98 For a preliminary commercial tool that goes in the direction of what interests us: http://www.spss.com/lexiquest/.

Chapter 13: Challenges

1 As Nicolas Gorjestani has pointed out, third-world countries have five times as much access by radio than by ICTs.

2 *Intermedia*, London, vol. 27, no. 5, October, 1999, p. 31. James Wolfensohn, President of the World Bank, speaking in video-conference as a keynote at the Global Knowledge Conference (Kaula Lumpur, March 2000), noted that there are over 3 billion persons living at under $2/day and nearly 2 billion exiting at under $1/day. He foresees that within 5 years Earth Orbiting Satellites can provide a global gateway. "The richest fifth – the population of the OECD countries has 86 percent of the world's GDP (gross domestic product), 82% of world export markets, 68% of

foreign direct investments), 74% of world telephone lines and 91% of Internet users. The bottom fifth, in the poorest countries has about one percent in each sector."

3 Sunil Mani, *Public Innovation Policies and Developing Countries: in a Phase of Economic Liberalisation*, Maastricht: United Nations University, Institute for New Technologies, 1999.

4 Sam Paltridge, "Local Access Pricing and the Global Divide," The Global Policy Issue, *On the Internet*, Reston, VA, Summer, 2000, pp. 12–16.

5 "Public Service Applications of the internet in Developing Countries," Update of sections IV.1 and V of the *Draft report of the focus group on promotion of infrastructure and use of the Internet in Developing Countries*, Question 13/1. ITU-D Study Group 1, *UNESCO Preprint*, April, 2001, pp. 1–86.

6 CIA Factbook: http://www.cia.gov/cia/publications/factbook/.

7 "While technology permits an unending flux of information, commercialization, fed by popularity ratings, limits the field of this information. The news is presented through a distorting lens. It has the appearance of being larger but we see less. In our society of communication, it is becoming almost impossible to furnish veridical information. The world of communications, which produces products with a lucrative goal and the world of information, which searches for truth, are in the course of melting into a single entity. The transfer of cultural values on our information circuits are manipulated by interest groups who put their economic power in the service of commercial ends." Author's translation from: *Le pouvoir de la culture. Conférence intergouvernementale sur les politiques culturelles pour le développement, 4, Stockholm 30 mars–2 avril 1998*, Paris: UNESCO, p. 88: "Alors que la technologie permet la diffusion d'un flux d'information inépuisable, la commercialisation – alimentée par l'audimétrie – limite le champ de cette information. Les nouvelles sont présentées à travers un verre grossissant. Elles ont l'air plus grandes, mais nous en voyons moins. Dans notre société de la communication, il devient presque impossible de fournir une information véridique. Le monde des communications, qui crée des produits dans un but lucratif, et le monde de l'information, qui recherche la vérité, sont en train de se fondre lentement en une entité unique. Le transfert et léchange des valeurs culturelles sur nos circuits d'information sont manipulés par des groupes d'intérêt qui mettent leur pouvoir économique au service des finalités commerciales."

8 Precisely how this wireless future will appear is a matter of great debate. Four disruptive technologies are emerging, namely, smart antennas, mesh networks, ad hoc architectures, and ultra-wideband transmission. Economist Staff, "Wireless Telecoms: Watch This Airspace," *The Economist*, 21 June 2002: http://www.cfo.com/Article?article=7359.

9 Walter Jäggi, "Ein Boom mit Risiken und Nebenwirkungen," *Tages-Anzeiger*, 25 September 2000, p. 97.

10 John C. Ryan and Alan Thein Durning "Chips Ahoy: The hidden toll of computer manufacture and use," cited by: Cate Gable, *Information Technology Meets Global Ecology: Computers and Consciousness*: http://www.mindjack.com/gable/itecology.html.

11 Bill MacKrell, "U.S. Army Introduces 'America's Army'," *PC Game*; "Realistic Game Parallels Authentic Army Missions, Values," *LA Times*, 22 May 2002; Vis-sim.org: http://www.vis-sim.org/news_comm.asp?ref=3775.

12 William Mitchell, *The Reconfigured Eye*, Cambridge, MA: MIT Press, 1994. For another analysis of such films, see Andrew Darley, *Visual Digital Culture: Surface Play and Spectacle in New Media Genres*, London: Routledge, 2000 (Sussex Studies in Culture and Communication).

13 Ibid.

14 Benjamin Barber, *Jihad vs. McWorld*, New York: Times Books, 1995.

15 In fact, it is technically a subset of somewhere between 10% and 30% of that amount which have been successfully found by the leading search engines.

16 Roland Hausser, "The four basic ontologies of semantic interpretation," Universität Erlangen-Nürnberg Abteilung Computerlinguistik (CLUE): http://www.linguistik.uni-erlangen.de/~rrh/papers/ontologies/dublin.html.

17 For a more thorough discussion of this tradition, see the author's *Literature on Perspective*, chapter 5: Applications Metaphorical.

18   Cf. Roland Hausser, *Foundations of Computational Linguistics. Man-Machine Communication in Natural Language.* Berlin: Springer Verlag, 1999.

19   It is interesting that this notion of intentionality is linked by Sowa to Peirce's notion of pragmatics: Lukose, Dickson, Harry Delugach, Mary Keeler, Leroy Searle, and John Sowa, *Conceptual Structures: Fulfilling Pierce's Dream*, Berlin: Springer Verlag, 1997 (Lecture Notes in Artificial Intelligence 1257): "Pragmatics is the study that relates signs to the agents who use them to refer to things in the world and to communicate their intentions about those things to other agents who may have similar or different intentions concerning the same or different things."

20   Roger Schank is now the President of Socratic Arts: http://socraticarts.com/. Formerly at: http://www.ils.nwu.edu/~e_for_e/nodes/NODE-255-pg.html.

21   Formerly at: http://www.ils.nwu.edu/~e_for_e/nodes/NODE-253-pg.html.

22   Formerly at: http://www.ils.nwu.edu/~e_for_e/nodes/NODE-258-pg.html. "These eight agents are responsible for searching for related information for any given story that is discovered in the archives. When set in motion, it is their job to find other stories to tell, and to alert the user to the existence of those stories. Thus, they can be seen as a kind of dynamic index, telling the listener of the story about what else there is to know, given what he has just found out. Each agent can behave in two different ways, looking either for general principles or specific examples. When looking for general principles, agents attempt to find stories that include perspective, theoretical discussions, principles, and lessons. When looking for specific examples, agents attempt to find interesting stories rich in relevant concrete detail. These behaviors seem different enough to users to give each agent two distinct personas. Accordingly, we have given each agent two names, one to reflect each persona."

23   Formerly at: http://www.ils.nwu.edu/~e_for_e/nodes/NODE-260-pg.html. "Herodotus, the general principles persona of the History Agent looks for analogous cases that, although they have nothing to with the current case as far as historical cause, contain lessons that apply to the current case. Thus, after the Story Archive gave us a story about the Gulf War, we might expect it to bring up the Vietnam War, Germany's incorporation of the Sudetenland, and the U.S. invasion of Panama.

Tacitus, is the specific examples persona of the History Agent. It is charged with presenting the context in which this war fits. So, when considering the Gulf War, Tacitus would certainly want to tell us about the Arab-Israeli situation, the Iran-Iraq war, the British domination of the Middle East in the early twentieth century, the Iraqi invasion of Kuwait, etc.

If the History Agent is to be able to do its work, the Story Archive must provide it with appropriate raw material. Taking the example of the Gulf War, the Archive would need to contain information about the event's historical roots directly, and information about the characteristics of the players (large, rich, powerful, aggressor, imperialistic, etc.) in the Gulf War that would enable similarity searches to be made.

The personas of the History Agent pursue these guiding questions:
   – Herodotus: 'When has something like this has happened before?'
   – Tacitus: 'What is the historical background of this story?'"

24   Formerly at: http://www.netwizards.net/~cryan/war.html.

25   In some ways, the first Iraq war is an unfortunate example because many persons may feel that it was justified.

26   EULEGIS: http://www.cs.jyu.fi/~airi/docman.html#eulegis.

27   While this is clearly an issue the following quote bears reflection: "But after more than two years of aggressive effort to collect data, the pro-censorship organization Filtering Facts identified only 196 such incidents. Considering that an estimated 344 million children visit public libraries each year and that nearly three-fourths of these libraries offer some form of public Internet access, this evidence belies the claim that there is a problem of 'epidemic' proportions."; Paul McMasters, "First Amendment Ombudsman Tools' fail as strategies to keep kids away from Net sex at libraries," *Freedom Forum Online*, 18 July 2000: http://www.freedomforum.org/templates/

document.asp?documentID=3022; John Perry Barlow, "Censorship 2000," The Global Policy Issue, *On the Internet*, Reston, VA, Summer, 2000, pp. 30–32, 45–49.

28 Stephanie Nebehay, "Web Coinventor backs Licensing," *Reuters*, 27 November 1999, Geneva: http://www.xent.com/nov99/0209.html.

29 Jennifer Schenker, "The Taxman in the Sky. A Dutch entrepreneur wants to install wireless tracking devices in cars as a way to tax drivers," *Time*, 6 August 2001, p. 47.

30 "Fight the Fingerprint" Web Site!: (formerly) http://www.networkusa.org/fingerprint.shtml. See: http://onin.com/fp/.

31 Human Movement Tracking technology: http://www.cs.sfu.ca/people/ResearchStaff/amulder/personal/vmi/HMTT.add.html.

32 Paul Festa, "ICQ logs spark corporate nightmare," *CNET news.com*, 15 March 2001: http://news.cnet.com/news/0-1005-200-5148422.html;
Digital Future Coalition: http://www.dfc.org/;
Digital Consumer.org: http://www.digitalconsumer.org/;
Audio Home Recording Act: http://www.virtualrecordings.com/ahra.htm.

33 Child Safety with Child Guardian: http://www.browsermall.com/baby_gifts/ChildSafety.htm.

34 Sandeep Junnarkar, "DoubleClick accused of unlawful consumer data use," *CNET News.com*, 28 January 2000: http://news.com.com/2100-1023-236216.html?legacy=cnet.

35 Formerly at: http://www.ebicom.net/~lashona/cookie.html;
Cookie central: http://www.cookiecentral.com/.

36 Teletrac: http://www.teletrac.net/index.asp.

37 Chris Oakes, "'E911' Turns Cell Phones into Tracking Devices," *Wired*, 6 January 1998: http://www.wired.com/news/topstories/0,1287,9502,00.html.

38 "Stasi bestraalde dissidenten," *Volkskrant*, 4 January 2001, p. 5.

39 Roberta Fusaro, "Future so bright. Interview with Salman A. Khan, The Next 10 Years,"1 April 1999.

40 Virtual Berlin: http://userpage.fu-berlin.de/~jenskna/virtual.html.

41 Formerly at: http://www.livewebcam.com/NON-US/j-n.htm.

42 Livewebcam: (formerly) http://www.livewebcam.com/; www.camcentral.com; www.earth-cam.com; www.webcam-center.de.

43 Belmar Beach Camhttp://www.belmarbeachcam.com/nj_web_cams.htm; New York Web Cams. http://www.leonardsworlds.com/states/newyork.htm.

44 Virtualized Reality: http://www.cs.cmu.edu/afs/cs/project/VirtualizedR/www/VirtualizedR.html.

45 Rob Jellinghaus, "Real Virtuality," Unreal Enterprises, 16 August 1995, http://www.unrealities.com/web/reality.htm.

46 "Carnegie Mellon goes to the Superbowl,"January 2001: http://www.ri.cmu.edu/events/sb35/tksuperbowl.html.

47 "Autonomous Helicopter Project. Haughton Crater Mission" Carnegie Mellon University, 1998: http://www.cs.cmu.edu/afs/cs/project/chopper/www/haughton-do.html.

48 Steve Silberman, "Matrix2. Bullet time was just the beginning." *Wired News*, 5 May 2003: http://www.wired.com/wired/archive/11.05/matrix2_pr.html; Joe Morgenstern, "Digital Magic Excites. But Where's the Soul in the Film Sequel?" *Wall Street Journal*, 16–18 May 2003, p. P1.

49 Christoph Fehn, Eddie Cooke, Oliver Schreer, Peter Kauff, "3D Analysis and Image Based Rendering for Immersive TV Applications," *Euroimage ICAV3D 2001*, Thessaloniki: ZITI, 2001, pp. 192–95.

50 For a list of the 100 best Top Student Webcams: http://www.studenthouse.net/topcams/index.htm.

51 Brian Miller the author of one of these sites explains why he created his site as follows: "Boredom. Plus its a cool way to express myself. I like the creating process of it as well actually thinking up a design etc, etc.… Let's see oh yeah plus its cool to tell people that you have your own web site." : http://members.tripod.com/mrion/.

52 Hans Masselink, "De Hele dag in Beeld," *Trouw*, 22 January 2001, p. 11.

53 Personal communication from NEC at INET 2000.

54 See, for instance, Northrop Frye, *The Great Code: The Bible and Literature*, New York: Harcourt Brace, 1983.

55 The *Tale of Gengi* is a part of UNESCO's new Global Heritage Pavilion: http://webworld.unesco.org/genji/en/part_1/1-1.shtml. Hitachi is also doing important work on retrospective virtual restoration of the original manuscripts. See Toshiro Kamiuchi, "DIS (Digital Image System) Applications for Digital Library," *2000 Kyoto International Conference on Digital Libraries: Research and Practice*, pp. 1–6.

56 Charles Derber, *Corporation Nation*. New York: St. Martin's Griffin, 1998, pp. 169–70. "Corporations are buying schools and supplying them with curricula-complete with commercials in the classroom-while governments distribute vouchers to make them viable. Huge parcels of federal land, as well as public airways and satellite bands are being handed over, free or at bargain prices to corporate giants."

57 Lawrence Lessig, *Code and Other Laws of Cyberspace*, New York: Basic Books, 1999.

58 Rebecca Vesely, "New Crypto Bill in Senate," *Wired News*, 17 June 1997: http://www.wired.com/news/topstories/0,1287,4489,00.html.

59 Zaibatsu of Japan: http://www2.sjsu.edu/faculty/watkins/zaibatsu.htm. Hidemasa Morikawa, *Zaibatsu: The Rise and Fall of Family Enterprise Groups in Japan*, Tokyo: University of Tokyo Press, 1992.

60 Thomas Barlow, "Universities and the Faculty for Making Profit," *Financial Times*, 10 June 2001, p. 11.

61 In Germany: www.meinestadt.de and www.allesklar.com.

62 For an eloquent vision of libraries as places for seekers of truth and beauty, see Mikael Böök, "Public Libraries, Portals and Power," *EVA Moscow*, November, 2000.

63 Michael "from the do-as-I-say,-not-as-I-do dept", "95 (thousand)Theses (for sale)" *SlashDot. News for Nerds*, . Monday, 14 August 2000: http://slashdot.org/yro/00/08/14/2019202.shtml.

64 This was listed under GABRIEL, and has now been integrated into the European Library: http://libraries.theeuropeanlibrary.org/libaries_en_xml; Networked Digital Library of Theses and Dissertations (NTLTD): www.ndltd.org.

65 Monika Segbert provided an excellent survey of the European Commission's activities in this realm, including a European Network of Public Libraries: http://www.monikasegbert.com/short_curriculum.htm.

66 Bibliotheca Universalis: http://www.kb.nl/gabriel/bibliotheca-universalis/.

67 Deutsche Zentralbibliothek für Medizin (ZBM, Cologne):): http://www.zbmed.de/info.html.

68 Deutsche Zentralbibliothek für Landbauwissenschaften (ZBL, Bonn): http://www.dainet.de/zbl/zbl.htm.

69 Deutsche Zentralbibliothek für Wirtschaftswissenschaften (ZBW, Kiel): www.uni-kiel.de/ifw//zbw/econis.htm.

70 Informationszentrum Sozialwissenschaften (Bonn): http://www.social-science-gesis.de.

71 Technische Informationsbibliothek (TIB, Hannover): www.tib.uni-hannover.de.

72 Science and Technology International Network STN FachInformationszentrum Karlsruhe.

73 Deutsches Institut für Medizinische Dokumentation und Information (DIMDI): See: www.dimdi.de.

74 FachInformationsZentrum (FIZ-) Tecknik: www.fiz-technik.de.

75 CiteSeer.IST: http://citeseer.ist.psu.edu/.

76 Thomson Dialog: http://www.dialog.com/.

77 Thomson. ISI Web of Knowledge: www.isinet.com.

78 Formerly at: www.rt.aventis.com.it.

79 Swets: www.swets.nl.

80 Springer, Link: http://www.springerlink.com/app/home/main.asp?wasp=cmw75594wp0yxk983k0j .

81 Science Direct: http://www.web-editions.com; Elsevier's Synthetic Methodology Databases and MDL Information Systems: http://www.mdl.com/products/knowledge/crossfire_beilstein/.

82 TLC: http://www.tlcdelivers.com/tlc/default.asp.

83 Factiva: www.factiva.com.

84 Frankfurter Allgemenine Zeitung: www.FAZ.de/archiv.

85 National e-Journals Initiative (NESLI2): www.nesli.ac.uk. Now: http://www.nesli2.ac.uk/

86 Some persons are more pessimistic about these developments. See Appendix 8: Corporations.

87 US Department of Energy: http://www.doe.gov/engine/content.do?BT_CODE=OF_NLTC.

88 IBM Semiconductor research; New York State Governor's Regulatory Room, 10 October 2000: http://www.gorr.state.ny.us/gorr/10_10_00gov_ibm.htm.

89 NEC Research Institute: An Industrial Lab with a Basic Mission: http://www.siam.org/siamnews/12-98/nec.htm.

90 On this problem of the privatization of knowledge, see Seth Shulman, Owning the Future, Boston: Houghton Mifflin, 1999. For a plea to keep universities out of the copyright domain, see Claire Polster, "The University Has No Business in the Intellectual Property Business," CAUT Bulletin ACPPU, Ottawa, September, 1999, p. 36.

91 "Inquiring Minds, Funding Academic R&D," Wired, April, 2000, p. 89. In fact, the total amount of research funding available through universities is much higher due to support from other sectors as indicated below:

Federal	22,306,000,000
University	5,838,000,000
Industry	2,163,000,000
State and Local Government	2,085,000,000
Nonprofit	2,032,000,000
Total in billions	34,424,000,000

92 On a possible licensing structure: IFLANET Licensing principles: http://www.ifla.org/V/ebpb/copy.htm.

93 S. Rasten and L. J. Beeley, "Functional Genomics: Going Forward from the Databases", Current Opinion in: Genetics and Development, vol. 7, 1997, pp. 777–83.

94 An example of public traditions is Professor Steve Brenner, who is working on open-source genetics. Paul Elias, "Computer scientists push to publish code powering genetic research," SFGate.com, San Francisco, 24 November 2001: http://www.sfgate.com/cgi-bin/article.cgi?file=/news/archive/2001/11/24/state1717EST0047.DTL.

95 Josef Straus, "Entscheiden Patente die Schlacht um Gene?," Max Planck Forschung, München, vol. 3, 2000, pp. 64–71; Tom Abate, "Do gene patents wrap research in red tape?," San Francisco Chronicle, 25 March 2002: http://www.sfgate.com/cgi-bin/article.cgi?f=/c/a/2002/03/25/BU97425.DTL.

96 Tom Buerkle, "Historic Moment for Humanity's Blueprint," International Herald Tribune, Bologna, pp. 1, 10. Cf. Brian Alexander, "Biopoly Money," Wired, June, 2000, pp. 279–290; Francis Williams, "Basmati rice patent is piracy, say activists," Financial Times, 22 November 2000, p. 8.

97 "Celera Sequences First Part of the Human Genetic Map," Wall Street Journal Europe, 7 April 2000, p. 4.

98 Neal Head Rapson, "The high price of knowledge," The Times, London, 4 July 2000, p. 15. Cf. Scott Hensley, "The End of the Beginning. Map of Human Genome Marks Start of Race for Profits," The Wall Street Journal, Europe, 27 June 2000, p. 25.

99 Jere Longman, "Will Athletes Soon be Designed to Win?" International Herald Times, 12–13 May 2001, pp. 1, 8. Cf. Rick Weiss, "Efforts to Ban Human Cloning May Not Hold Up, Legal Scholars Warn," International Herald Tribune, 24 May 2001, p. 3.

100 Jennifer Couzin, "Building a Better Bio-Supercomputer," CNN.com, 12 June 2001: http://www.cnn.com/2001/TECH/ptech/06/12/bio.supercomputer.idg/. Cf. ibid., The Industry Standard Magazine, 18 June 2001.

101 Some recent genomics companies.

COMPANY	LOCATION
Celera Genomics Group PE Corp)	Rockville, MD
Cura Gen	New Haven, CT
Double twist	Oakland, CA
Exelxis	San Francisco, CA
Gene Logic	Gaithersburg, MD
Orchid BioSciences	Princeton, NJ
Incyte Genomics	Palo Alto, CA
Genset	Paris, France
Decode	Reykjavik, Iceland
Gemini	Cambridge, UK
Human Genome Sciences	Rockville, MD
Engeneos	Waltham, MA

The development of such companies will be explored in greater detail in the author's *American Visions of Convergence.*

102 The Raelian Message: http://www.rael.org.

103 David Pilling, "Stand by for the Gene Rush," *Financial Times*, 27 June 2000, p. 5.

104 According to Dr. Anne Tyrie, Molecular Mining was co-founded by Dr. Janice Glasgow, with Dr. Fortier, Dr. Weaver, and Dr. Steeg of Queen's University and Larry Hunter of the U.S. National Institute of Health the University of Colorado Health Science Department; University of Waterloo's Dr. Ming Li and Dr. Paul Kearney, who founded Bioinformatics Solutions: http://www.bioinformaticssolutions.com/.

105 E.g., The European Bioinformatics Institute: http://www.ebi.ac.uk/ or the Bioinformatics Group: http://life.anu.edu.au/.

106 Jeremy Rifkin, *The Age of Access*, New York: Jeremy P. Tacher/Putnam, 2000, p. 64. On the dangers of private research hindering progress, see Nicholas Thompson, "May the Source Be With You. Can a band of biologists who share data freely out-innovate corporate researchers?", *The Washington Monthly Online*, July/August 2002: http://www.washingtonmonthly.com/features/2001/0207. thompson.html.

107 On the question of different policies in Europe and America re: biotechnology, see David Vogel, "Ships Passing in the Night: GMOs and the Politics of Risk Regulation in Europe and the United States," Haas School of Business and INSEAD (European Institute of Business Administration). Unpublished paper: http://www.insead.fr/events/gmoworkshop/papers/1_Vogel.pdf. There are much more disturbing developments that can only be signalled here. One is a tendency to link genomics with race, e.g., Matthew Herper, "Race-Based Medicine, Genomics, and You," *Forbes Magazine*, 9 November 2004: http://www.forbes.com/technology/sciences/2004/11/09/cx_mh_1109ntmd.html. Another is a trend for the U.S. government to use public monies to develop both AIDS vaccines and Anthrax antidotes via private companies such as Vaxgen, in which members of the same government have strong private interests via bodies such as the Carlyle group, linked with Halliburton and also with both the destruction and reconstruction of Iraq.

108 Vladimir Sorokin, *Der Himmelblaue Speck*, Cologne: Du Mont Verlag, 2000; Helga Leiprecht, "Der geklonte Text als grosse Gruselorgie," *Tages-Anzeiger*, 9 January 2001, p. 55.

109 One useful initiative in this direction is the Virtual Society? Programme, which was at Brunel and has now moved to Oxford: http://virtualsociety.sbs.ox.ac.uk/.

110 Internet governance is an important new field of study. See Appendix 8. There are a number of organizations concerned with aspects of the problem. The Internet Society has a Task Force on Privacy and Security. There are groups on: Global Information Policy now World Information Technology and Services Alliance: www.witsa.org; Global Business Dialogue: gbde.org; Computer

Systems Policy Project: cspp.org; Privacy: privacyalliance.org. For a recent view that the United States should continue to control the Internet, see Stephen Macklin, "U.N. Internet Takeover," *eTalkinghead*, 26 March 2004: http://www.etalkinghead.com/archives/un-internet-takeover-2004-03-26.html.

111 Multilingual Internet Names Consortium (MINC): http://www.minc.org.

112 For an interesting history of such movements, see Akira Iriye, *Cultural Internationalism and World Order*, Baltimore: Johns Hopkins University Press, 1997. The author sees great value in common understanding derived from sharing cultural experiences. He does not deal sufficiently with the potentials of these international efforts to increase awareness of local cultural expression.

113 Thomas Cooper, "Speed-Up and New technology Ethics: An Acceleration of Effects," *Pacific Telecommunications Review*, Honolulu, 1st Quarter 2000, pp. 11–28. The ISTF has a sub-committee on Cyber Ethics. Richard Burbank (U of Westminster) has written a Manifesto of Cyber Communication.

114 Philippe Quéau, Lecture at Le Club de l'Arche, Paris, 1999.

115 *Culture Counts, Financing Resources and the Economics of Culture in Sustainable Development*, Conference sponsored by the Government of Italy, World Bank, UNESCO, Florence, Fortezza del Basso, October, 1999.

116 Global Internet Policy Initiative: http://www.gipiproject.org.

117 Adam M. Brandenburger, Barry J. Nalebuff, *Co-opetition: 1. A Revolutionary Mindset That Redefines Competition and Cooperation; 2. The Game Theory Strategy That's Changing the Game of Business*, New York: Doubleday, 1996.

Chapter 14: Synthesis

1 Some argue that "e-commerce" is a general term for selling things on-line, whereas "e-business" is about the whole gamut of business relationships.

2 Julian Stallabrass, "Digital Commons," *New Left Review*, vol. 15, May-June, 2002: http://www.newleftreview.net/NLR24907.shtml;
Con Zymaris: conz@cyber.com.au: "Shoulders of Giants – A Paper on the Inevitability of Open Source Dominance," Created: 2 November, Modified: 23 March 2004, Version: 0.7: http://www.cyber.com.au/users/conz/shoulders.html.

3 The Open Archives movement seems to be pointing to an Internet equivalent of learned journals: www.openarchives.org. Important also in this context is the development of pre-print archives; *Nature*, vol. 408, 14 December 2000, p. 757:
"The Max Planck Society (MPS) has created a Centre for Information Management in Garching, near Munich. Its role will be to enable scientists at its 78 laboratories to publish their work in open-access electronic repositories.
When the centre opens next month, its managers will decide whether the MPS should operate its own server, or get involved in similar initiatives elsewhere. These include E-BioSci, a publication server for the life sciences managed by the European Molecular Biology Laboratory, and PubMed Central, a similar project run by the U.S. National Institutes of Health. But the centre's main partner will initially be the Los Alamos National Laboratory in the United States, whose e-print archives are the primary means of electronic communication in areas such as high-energy physics, maths and computer science. Richard Luce, head of Los Alamos' 'Library Without Walls' project – which provides digital library resources – is advising the new centre."
Also: (formerly) http://www.infer.it/pressrelease.html. Related to such pre-print facilities are related initiatives such as: BioOne: A Collaborative Online Publishing Co.: www.bioOne.org; Bioline publication of journals in Developing Countries: http://www.aibs.org/announcements/040330_bioone_bioscience_content.html.

4 Michael Giesecke, *Der Buchdruck in der frühen Neuzeit. Eine historische Fallstudie über die Durchsetzung neuer Informations- und Kommunikations-technologien*, Frankfurt: Suhrkamp, 1991.

5 Peter A. Kropotkin, *Memoirs of a Revolutionist*, Boston and New York: Houghton Mifflin, 1899, Part Third, Section VII: http://dwardmac.pitzer.edu/Anarchist_Archives/kropotkin/memoirs/memoirs3_7.html.

6 Gerald Weinberg, *The Psychology of Computer Programming*, New York: Van Nostrand Reinhold, 1971.

7 Had he known Saint Francis, he might have found the term "selfless programming" more precise.

8 Eric S. Raymond, *The Cathedral and the Bazaar*, Cambridge, MA: O'Reilly, 1999, p. 64.

9 DMOZ Open Directory Project: http://dmoz.org/about.html.

10 Open Data Format Initiative: http://odfi.org/.

11 Berkman Center for Internet and Society: http://cyber.law.harvard.edu/projects/opencontent.html.

12 Collaborative Open Design Systems (CODES) project home page. This project is sponsored by the DARPA Rapid Design Exploration and Optimization (RaDEO) program. The CODES project is located at the Institute for Complex Engineered Systems (ICES) at Carnegie Mellon University: http://codes.edrc.cmu.edu/CODES/contents.html.

13 Eric S. Raymond, *The Cathedral and the Bazaar*, Cambridge, MA: O'Reilly, 1999, pp. 108ff.

14 Ibid., p. 65.

15 Ibid., p. 66.

16 Ibid., pp. 97ff. Interestingly enough, his examples of such gift cultures include the potlatch parties of the Kwakiutl Indians, parties of the wealthy, and persons in show business, and not the generosity of the Christian tradition.

17 Ibid., p. 99.

18 Ibid., p. 29.

19 Formerly at: www.kirana.lk. Re: Buddhist Resources; http://online.sfsu.edu/~rone/Buddhism/Buddhism.htm; AMARC: www.amarc.org.

20 Monastery of Christ in the Desert:
http://www.digitalabiquiu.com/pages/tours/monestary_t.html.

21 St. Tikhon's Orthodox Theological Library. Electronic Resources for Theological Study: http://www.stots.edu/library/links.htm.

22 Eric S. Raymond, *The Cathedral and the Bazaar*, Cambridge, MA: O'Reilly, 1999., p. 150, points to the sites of Metalab and freshmeat.com, p. 150.

23 United Nations Development Programme: www.sdnp.undp.org.

24 IDRC: http://web.idrc.ca/en/ev-1-201-1-DO_TOPIC.html.

25 "Linux schleicht sich in den Alltag," *Tages-Anzeiger*, 28 April 2003, p. 55.

26 Charles Derber, *Corporation Nation*. New York: St. Martin's Griffin, 1998, p. 294. He cites the last chapter of Jeremy Rifkin and Robert L. Heilbroner, *The End of Work: The Decline of the Global Labor Force and the Dawn of the Post-Market Era*, Boston: J. P. Tarcher, 1996.

27 Paperback: New York: Penguin, 2000. Jay W. Richards, *Are We Spiritual Machines? Ray Kurzweil vs The Critics of Strong AI*, Seattle: Discovery Institute Press, 2002.

28 As my colleague, Dr. Riemer Knoop, has rightly pointed out, most of the examples in this book concerning transformations in scholarship are largely at the footnote level, at the level of names, places, bibliographical references, etc. This is because we are focussing on an emerging new infrastructure, which will potentially bring the reference materials of the great libraries into the realm of tools for everyday use. It is too soon to know or even pretend to know what the effects thereof on scholarship will be. We need to reorganize knowledge before we can assess what effects this will have and what new insights will emerge.

29 Pierre Levy, *L'Intelligence collective, pour une anthropologie du cyberspace*, Paris: La Découverte, 1994. Pierre Levy, who has also warned of the dangers of a second flood in information, has at the same time worked with others in developing the idea of trees of knowledge (skills) in the sense of competencies in the book: Michel Authier et Pierre Levy, *Les arbres de connaissances*, Paris: La Découverte, 1993 (Collection Essais), to analyse persons competencies which has taken the form of a company for knowledge management, Trivium: http://www.trivium.fr/; Christophe

d'Iribarne, "Etude de l'Arbre de Connaissances d'un point de vue mathématique; Michel Authier, "Arbres de Connaissances, Controverses, Expériences"; ibid., "Eclaircissement sur quelques fondamentaux des Arbres de Connaissances," *Revue Documents du Cereq*, Numéro 136, juin, 1998 (Numéro spécial).

30 Derrick de Kerckhove, *Connected Intelligence: The Arrival of the Web Society*, Toronto: Somerville House, 1999. Here the author examines hypertextuality mainly in terms of news, books, and museums. His focus is access to existing knowledge rather than transformation of knowledge leading to new insights and new knowledge. Professor de Kerckhove's techno-optimism does not reflect upon the dangers and pitfalls of the new technologies.

31 The idea of a global brain was raised by H.G. Wells, *World Brain*, London: Methuen, 1938; W. Boyd Rayward, "H.G. Wells's Idea of a World Brain: A Critical Re-Assessment," *Journal of the American Society for Information Science*, 1999: http://alexia.lis.uiuc.edu/~wrayward/Wellss_Idea_of_World_Brain.htm.

32 This has its roots in a long tradition of theoretical literature concerning the arts.

33 In addition to complex, professional scanners such as the IBM Brandywine camera, the VASARI scanner, the Canadian NRC laser camera, there are now inexpensive methods using a Mac.

34 George Ritzer, *The McDonaldization of Society, New Century Edition: An Investigation into the Changing Character of Contemporary Social Life*, Thousand Oaks, CA: Pine Forge Press, 2000.

35 The entertainment industry has been trying to recycle its unique products such as films with generic offshoots. In the past, one went to see a film in a cinema. This was then licensed for replays on television, as home videos, then franchised as an array of new products: Pocahontas tee-shirts, model figures, books, comics, and the like. Recently, *Star Wars* has become a new kind of video game, which allows us to use scenes from films as a point of departure for our own purposes. The original film thus serves as a starting point for personal editing and creative play.

36 IBM sponsored a pilot example of such an approach using the *Tempest*.

37 J.P. Guilford, *The Nature of Human Intelligence*, New York: McGraw-Hill, 1967. Structure of Intellect: http://tip.psychology.org/guilford.html.

38 Some also speak of a knowledge ecology: "Knowledge ecology is an interdisciplinary field of management theory and practice, focused on the relational and social/behavioral aspects of knowledge creation and utilization. Its primary study and domain of action is the design and support of self-organizing knowledge ecosystems, providing the infrastructure in which information, ideas, and inspiration can travel freely to cross-fertilize and feed on each other." See: http://www.co-i-l.com/coil/knowledge-garden/kd/index.shtml.

39 University of North Carolina, Chapel Hill.

40 Americans frequently interpret the European trend as a recognition that content is king, but this is too simplistic a characterization. The European emphasis on libraries, museums, and archives is much more than a quest for access to content. It is a search for new ways of accessing our awareness of cultural diversity and differences as new keys to tolerance.

41 There are several projects working in this direction, e.g., an EC Project International Network for the Conservation of Contemporary Art (INCCA); a Digital Performance Archive (Nottingham Trent University): http://socks.ntu.ac.uk/dpa_site/. Important is the work of Harald Kraemer, "A New Methodology for the Documentation of Contemporary Art," *EVA 2000 Scotland Conference*, Fleet: VASARI UK, pp. 5-1–5-5: http://www.transfusionen.de, Interesting work is also being done in Russia by Alexei Isaev and colleagues with respect to contemporary art: http://www.da-da-net.ru/98/j10.htm; http://rhizome.org/thread.rhiz?thread=650&text=1667#1667.

42 Roberto Bosco, Stefano Caldana, "10 Years of Net.art," *ARCO*, no. 31, Spring, 2004, pp. 27–28.

43 Considerably more is needed. Personal and collaborative knowledge environments introduce a profound challenge to maintain proper levels of privacy while establishing methods to integrate their enduring aspects within the repositories of our memory institutions. Part of the problem here is that personal and collaborative knowledge include implicit or tacit knowledge, whereas enduring knowledge is focussed primarily on explicit knowledge. Cf. Michael Polanyi, *The Tacit*

Dimension, London: Routledge & Kegan Paul, 1966. Tacit Knowledge: http://www.cordis.lu/cybercafe/src/greylit.htm#TACIT.

44 R.G.H. Siu, *The Tao of Science: An Essay on Western Knowledge and Eastern Wisdom*, Cambridge, MA: MIT Press, 1957.

45 Keynote at the *Virtual Worlds Conference*, Paris, July, 1998; Wendy Mackay, A-L. Fayard, L. Frobert, and L. Médini, "Reinventing the Familiar: Exploring an Augmented Reality Design Space for Air Traffic Control," in: *Proceedings of ACM CHI '98 Human Factors in Computing Systems*. Los Angeles: ACM/SIGCHI: http://www-ihm.lri.fr/~mackay/publications.html. For another discussion of virtual reality, see Didier Verna and A. Grumbach, "Can we Define Virtual Reality, The MRIC Model," in: *Virtual Worlds*, ed. Jean-Claude Heudin, Berlin: Springer Verlag, 1998, pp. 29–41.

46 Thomas Baudel and Michel Beaudouin-Lafon, "CHARADE: Remote Control of Objects using Free-Hand Gestures," *Communications of the ACM*, vol. 36, no. 7, July, 1993, pp. 28–35.
KARMA: Steve Feiner, Columbia University: http://www1.cs.columbia.edu/graphics/projects/karma/karma.html.
Digital Desk: Pierre Wellner (ATT and Europarc), "Interacting with Paper on the Digital Desk," *Communications of the ACM*, July, 1993, pp. 86–96; Digital Desk: http://www.cc.gatech.edu/fce/seminar/Presentation/Vision/DigDesk.html.
MIT, SmartDesk home page: http://www-white.media.mit.edu/vismod/demos/smartdesk/.
Mark Weiser, "Ubiquitous Computing": http://www.ubiq.com/hypertext/weiser/UbiHome.html.
Olivetti Research Active Badge: http://koo.corpus.cam.ac.uk/projects/badges/.
MIT, Epistemology and Learning Group. Lego Logo: http://lcs.www.media.mit.edu/groups/el/projects/legologo/.
Carnegie Mellon University. Digital Ink: http://www.cs.cmu.edu/~wearable/ink.html.

47 This was part of an I3 workshop organized by Massimo Zancanaro, who also raised interesting questions under the title "Do appliances fear contradiction?"

48 Dylan Tweney, "2010: A PC Odyssey. Where will technology take you next? We peer into the labs and take a thought-provoking look at the next generation of computing," *PC World Magazine*, October, 2000: http://www.pcworld.com/resource/article/0,aid,18059,00.asp. (cf. ibid., *PC Magazine*, September, 2000).

49 Didier Stricker, Patrick Dähne, Frank Schubert, Ioannis T. Christou, Luis Almeida, Renzo Carducci, and Nikos Ioannidis. "Design and Development Issues for ARCHEOGUIDE: An Augmented Reality Based Cultural heritage On -Site Guide," *Euroimage ICAV3D 2001*, Thessaloniki: ZITI, 2001, pp. 1–5: http://archeoguide.intranet.gr/.

50 Deepmap: http://www.eml-development.de/english/Research/Memory/1 (formerly at http://www.eml.villa-bosch.de/english/research/deepmap/deepgis/virtualtourist.html).

51 Tengku Mohd Azzman Shariffadeen, "Addressing the Information Divide: Improving Quality of life," *Global Knowledge Conference*, Kuala Lumpur, 7 March 2000.

52 In practical terms Malaysia has web sites on Business: www.ivest.com.my; Living (formerly at: www.living.net.my); Learning: www.sls.mimos.my.

53 Malaysia is particularly interesting because it includes three major cultures and religions: Malaysian (Islam), Chinese (Buddhism), and Indian (Hinduism).

54 The Council of Europe has an interesting site on European tales and legends: http://www.coe.int/T/E/Cultural_Co-operation/culture/Completed_projects/Legends/.

55 For a wider view of culture not limited to the high culture traditions of literature: Maryann Bird, "Is Culture Just for Humans," *Time*, 6 August 2001; Frans de Waal, *The Ape and the Sushi Master*, New York: Penguin, 2001.

56 Arab Net: http://www.arab.net.

57 As a series of scholars in the footsteps of Havelock, Innis, and McLuhan, such as Ong and Giesecke have explored these problems.

58 For a further discussion of these themes, see the author's "Goals of Culture and Art," Abridged Version of Lecture to the International Institute of Communications, Kuala Lumpur, September,

641

1999. Also on the site of the International Institute of Communications (http://www.iicom. org). Published electronically in TRANS. *Internet-Zeitschrift für Kulturwissenschaften*, Vienna, vol. 1, 1999: http://www.adis.at/arlt/institut/trans/0Nr/veltman1.htm.

59 These goals continue after the advent of literacy. Indeed, in iconoclastic cultures, the sense of ordering can evolve into an extraordinarily complex set of patterns, e.g., organic and geometrical patterns of Islamic culture.

60 The *Koran* did not produce the same array of media, but inspired an extraordinary range of calligraphic, ornamental patterns, and geometric forms.

61 A discussion of all the expressions of culture is beyond the scope of this book and has been the subject of a separate study, *Goals of Culture and Art*, available via the web site: http: //www.sumscorp.com/new_models.htm.

62 There is, of course, much more to culture than the expressions of great religions via sacred texts. Culture includes what was once called primitive art, whereby totems serve to link persons in the physical world magically with a world beyond. Culture includes an ordering of the world through patterns and ornament. Ordering is connected intimately with the craft tradition and appears as ornamental patterns in tapestries, clothing, pottery, and architecture. This is a universal quest among cultures and continues in more subtle forms as they enter literate phases. In Islamic culture, where there is a ban on images, there is a correspondingly greater emphasis on ordering through elaborate geometrical patterns, which often acquire metaphysical connotations. Culture also includes imitating (*mimesis*) and matching. Some art mixes realistic and abstract aspects in a single work as frequently occurs with early modern painters such as Cezanne or Picasso. This mixing may also entail different verbal sources, as when Gauguin combines a visualization of *Christ on the Cross*, a Biblical theme, with autobiographical aspects. More recent art frequently also explores worlds other than the physical, namely, mental worlds (the world of dreams, hallucinations, and imagination), perceptual worlds (attempts to render curved images as they occur on the retina), algorithmic worlds (in computer art) and chance worlds (e.g., Jackson Pollock's attempts at throwing paint).

63 Xavier Marichal, "Immersive Interactive Environments. The art.live consortium, IST project 10942," *Eurocav3D 2001*, Mykonos, 30 May–1 June, Thessaloniki: ZITI, 2001, 259–62: http://www.tele.ucl.ac.be/PEOPLE/MARICHAL/papers/artlive_icav3D.pdf. http://www.tele.ucl.ac.be/PEOPLE/MARICHAL/papers/artlive_laval02.pdf.

64 Daniel Metzger, "Hoffen auf das mobile Internet," *Tages-Anzeiger*, 20 March 2001, p. 57.

65 Potentially this also obtains in large countries such as the United States. However, the U.S. tendencies towards mono-culture as reflected in the motto, *E pluribus unum*, undermines their multiculturalism.

66 UNESCO World Heritage: http://www.unesco.org/whc/nwhc/pages/home/pages/ homepage.htm. UNESCO has four main projects: Heritage Projects and Campaigns (CLT), World Heritage Centres (WHC), Memory of the World Programme (MOW: http://www.unesco.org/ webworld/mdm/en/index_mdm.html [formerly at: http://thoth.bl.uk/ddc/index.html]), and Man and the Biosphere Programme (MAB: http://www.unesco.org/mab/). In addition to these main sites, UNESCO has regional locations such the Almaty office: www.unesco.kz/. They in turn are linked with important projects such as Catalogue of Persian Manuscripts of the National Library of the Czech Republic: http://digit.nkp.cz/persica.html. At the European level the Council of Europe has created a European Heritage Net: http://www.european-heritage.net/ sdx/herein/index.xsp. This site also offers a portal to other heritage sites.

67 This regional dimension also includes a new awareness of different languages. To the outside world, France has always been a country where one speaks French. There are in fact 80 languages spoken in France. Philippe Guedi and Marc Bounjnah, "Régions: Les langues se delient," *France TGV*, Neuilly sur Seine, 2001, pp. 24–30.

68 Such complexities are also absent from all our present notions of user profiles.

69 These combinations were successful because they were guided by culture and taste. Combinations *per se* do not guarantee interesting results. If taste and sensibility are lacking, the

results are merely hybrid versions of kitsch. So the technology must not be seen as an answer in itself. It offers a magnificent tool, which needs to be used in combination with awareness of the uniqueness and value of local traditions. These new possibilities of using technology to expand the vocabulary of cultural expression apply not only to the physical built environment of the man-made world. Potentially, they apply to the whole of knowledge. Thus the reorganization of knowledge.

70   At the *Conference of the International Committee on the History of Art* (CIHA, London, 2000) Robert Derome (Québec) organized a session on Digital Art History Time: http://www.unites.uqam.ca/AHWA/Meetings/2000.CIHA/index.html. His web site gives useful references to methodological problems in the field: http://www.er.uqam.ca/nobel/r14310/.

Chapter 15: Conclusions

1   Bob Thomas, *Walt Disney. An American Original*, New York: Pocket Books, 1976, p. xv.
2   Interestingly enough, a Japanese institute has as its motto: "The amusive ability is the academic ability," which is considerably subtler than edu-tainment. The Mechatronic Lab at University of Electro-Communications, Tokyo has this motto. Outline of Lab: http://www.kajitani.mce.uec.ac.jp/lab/lab_e.html.
3   Prime Minister Berlusconi has created a new company called Patrimonio.spa whereby the cultural heritage of Italians can theoretically be used as collateral for the country's deficit and can ultimately be sold. See: SENATO DELLA REPUBBLICA GRUPPO DEMOCRATICI DI SINISTRA– L'ULIVO, Ufficio Stampa e Comunicazione, *www.senato.it/dsulivo/*, "PATRIMONIO SPA E SALVADEFICIT: LA GRANDE TRUFFA DI TREMONTI E BERLUSCONI. SVELATI TUTTI I TRUCCHI DEL PRESTIGIATORE TREMONTI.": www.senato.it/dsulivo/dossier/patrimonio%20spa.doc; "L'Italia non è in vendita! Patrimonio spa, cartolarizzazione, alienazione…." Istruzioni per l'uso: Scarica tutto l'articolo sul tuo disco fisso: Assemblea dei Circoli di Legambiente, Rispescia, 30 novembre – 1 dicembre 2002: http://www.abruzzonatura.com/Italianoninvendita.asp.
4   Jeremy Rifkin, *The Age of Access*, New York: Jeremy P. Tarcher/Putnam, 2000, p. 146.
5   James Finn Garner, *Politically Correct Bedtime Stories*, New York: Macmillan, 1994.
6   For a discussion of differences between European and American capitalism, see John Palmer, "Review: Will Hutton, *"The World We're In,* New York: Little, Brown, 2002," Red Pepper, July, 2002: http://www.redpepper.org.uk/.
7   Office of the Chief Information Officer, U.S.A: http://cio.doe.gov/iap/backgrdnav.htm.
8   E.g., Professor C. Begthol (Toronto).
9   Sowa (2000) cites Peirce explicitly in his analysis of syntax, semantics, and pragmatics. This confirms that there are parallels between the semiotics of Peirce and more recent theories of knowledge representation. C.W. Morris in his *Foundations of the Theory of Signs, International Encyclopedia of Unified Science*, ed. Otto Neurath, Chicago: University of Chicago Press, vol. 1, no. 2, 1938, organizes *semiotics*, the study of signs, into three areas: *syntax* (the study of the interrelation of the signs), *semantics* (the study of the relation between the signs and the objects to which they apply), and *pragmatics* (the relationship between the sign system and the user): http://whatis.techtarget.com under semantic.
10   The full depth of these differences between the American, European, and Japanese world views could readily become a book in itself. Here, we shall explore briefly but a single further example. In Europe, meaning is something that is acquired largely through shared traditions texts of which we have in common. Meaning is thus the basis of shared values. We have access to the meaning of Christian art through a shared awareness of the *Bible*. Similarly, the meaning of the great symbols of the Greco-Roman world (Apollo, Venus, Mars, Cupid) comes through our shared awareness of Greco-Roman literature and other writings in the classical tradition. Hence, in Europe, digital culture is about the digitization of cultural objects and cultural traditions. In the United States, by contrast, it has been argued that meaning is something that is entirely

personal; it has to do with defining our originality and uniqueness and is thus opposed to value. In this context, digital culture becomes something that has not made links to traditions, the canon, etc. In Europe, meaning is very much linked with a history that evolves and changes over time but is inextricably linked with history. Saint Nicholas (of Bari), who was Bishop of Myra in Turkey is usually linked in some ways with this past, even though versions of the man vary considerably. In America, after September 11, when there was a sense that firemen needed more acknowledgement and recognition, Americans promptly started to make Santa Clauses in the guise of a fireman: a connection that seems incomprehensible in the European tradition. See also: Francisco J. Ricardo, "Field Notes From the Secret War Between Meaning and Value," *Digital Arts and Culture 98*: http://cmc.uib.no/dac98/papers/ricardo.html.

11 Donald Norman, *The Invisible Computer*, Cambridge, MA: MIT Press, 1999, pp. 1–2.

12 Natalia V Loukachevitch, Alla D. Salii, and Boris V. Dobrov, "Thesaurus for Automatic Indexing," TKE 99, Innsbruck, 1999.

13 Cf. IST 2000. *Realising an information Society for All*, Brussels: European Commission, 2000.

14 http://www.jaist.ac.jp/ks/index-e.html.

15 Departments of the School of Social Knowledge Science and Knowledge System Science at the Japan Advanced Institute of Science and Technology (Hokuriku). * Denotes a laboratory operated jointly with other institutions: http://www.jaist.ac.jp/ks/labs/index-e.html:

School of Social Knowledge Science	Knowledge System Science
Organizational Dynamics	Knowledge Creating Methodology
Decision-Making Processes	Knowledge-Based Systems
Social Systems	Knowledge Structure
Creativity Support Systems	Genetic Knowledge Systems
R&D Processes	
Socio-Technical Systems	Complex Systems Analysis
Industrial Policy Systems*	Brain Science*
Corporate Strategy Systems*	Human Interfaces*
Regional Systems*	Intelligent Production Systems*
	Science of Complex Systems

16 Ibid.: http://www.jaist.ac.jp/ks/labs/index-e.html.

17 JAIST, School of Knowledge Science: http://www.jaist.ac.jp/ks/index-e.html.

18 Ibid.

19 Ibid., Formerly at: http://www.jaist.ac.jp/ks/index-e.html#kiso.

20 David Korten, *When Corporations Rule the World*, Bloomfield, CT: Kumarian Press, 1995.

21 Charles Derber, *Corporation Nation*, New York: St. Martin's Griffin, 1998.

22 Ibid., p. 276.

23 *G7 Ministerial Conference on the Global Information Society. Round-table meeting of business leaders. Brussels 25 and 26 February 1995*, Luxembourg: Office for Official Publications of the European Communities, p. 13.

24 For instance, Omron has agents as Java applets that run robots. Cf. vision of knowbotic systems: http://io.khm.de/kr_www/content/bibliography_biography/bio.html.

25 James R. Beniger, *The Control Revolution: Technological and Economic Origins of the Information Society*, Cambridge, Mass: Harvard University Press, 1986, p. 103.

26 E. J. Dijksterhuis, *The Mechanization of the World Picture*, Princeton: Princeton University Press, 1986. Originally in Dutch: *De mechanisering van het wereldbeeld*, Amsterdam, J.M. Meulenhoff, [1950].

27 It is interesting, for a moment, to go back to twelfth century Italy, which saw the rise of international trade and commerce. In Assisi, for instance, a wool merchant who traded with France was one of the richest men of his region. He was a champion of the new exchange economy. Over the centuries, via the agoras, marketplaces, and bazaars, this has led to the modern notions of e-business. Theoretically, Pietro Bernardone might have become a symbol of the new economy. In practice, most persons have forgotten his name, though everyone remembers him as the

father of one most famous sons of all time born in 1182. Pietro was a good father, and assumed that his son would take over the business. Instead, the son rejected the idea of living by business and voted instead to live by giving. He rejected the exchange economy and fostered a gift culture. History remembers him not as Mr. F. Bernardone, Jr., but simply as Saint Francis of Assisi. He has a simple prayer which states: "For it is in giving that one receives."

"O Master, make that I search not so much:
To be consoled as to console
To be understood as to understand
To be loved as to love.
For it is in giving that one receives
In pardoning that one is pardoned and
In dying that one is resuscitated to eternal life."

Saint Francis lived a new level of self-less being. In a sense, he was simply restating an ideal that St. Benedict and other monks had been practising ever since the fourth century. But the formulation by Saint Francis was so powerful that it inspired a whole new order with thousands of monasteries and hundreds of churches and cathedrals all around the world. He inspired a new interest in narrative in art, which led eventually to the development of perspective in the West. A generation later, Fransciscans such as Grosseteste helped to found Oxford University, which, as the late Professor Crombie has shown, was another of the stepping stones that led to early modern science.

28   Virtual Souk: www.elsouk.com.

29   There is important work by Stephan Merten, "Wizards of OS 2," 23 August 2001. "Open Cultures & Free Knowledge." *International Conference at the House of World Cultures*, Berlin, 11–13 October 2001: http://www.noemalab.com/sections/news_detail.asp?offset=380&IDNews=85.

30   James Beniger, *The Control Revolution. Technological and Economic Origins of the Information Society*, Cambridge, MA: Harvard University Press, 1986.

31   Armand Mattelart, *Mapping World Communication. War, Progress, Culture*. Trans. Susan Emanuel and James A. Cohen, Minneapolis: University of Minnesota Press, 1994.

32   Henry Hallam, Willam Smith, *View of the State of Europe during the Middle Ages*, New York: Harper and Brothers, 1891, p. 678.

33   For another discussion on the links between religion and cyberspace, see Manfred Kremser, "Transforming the Transformed: African Derived Religions in Cyberspace," *Hightech and Macamba*, 1999: http://www.goethe.de/br/sap/macumba/kremser_long.htm; ibid., "CyberAnthropology und die neuen Räume des Wissens," *MAGW*, Band 129, 1999: http://www.nhm-wien.ac.at/AG/Mag129/Kremser.html.

34   Although hackers as such are said to have begun in the 1980s, their predecessors the Phreakers were active in the 1970s. On hacker history: http://www.slais.ubc.ca/people/students/student-projects/J_Heaton/phreakers.htm.

35   There is, of course, a long tradition where each profession has its go at explaining everything. Once there were philosophers. In America, there is presently a race between the lawyers and the economists. The economists are quite happy to talk of gift economy and non-monetary economy as long as they can advise on and preferably decide on everything. Meanwhile, the lawyers will not rest their case until they have made a case of everything. And sometimes it seems as if the medical profession thinks it has its own recipe. We need to remember, of course, that already in the Middle Ages law, medicine, and theology were the only higher faculties. At that time economics was more doing than preaching academically. Yet it has always required a combination of these major strands to produce society. And here we encounter one of the most delicate aspects of culture. Culture needs to be based on belief, but belief alone can too readily become religious fanaticism, which is far removed from the tolerance that culture requires and inspires. Culture constantly has to struggle to find languages and expressions, which break the

closed hierarchies of the law, medicine, and ultimately of religion itself, since all of these noble traditions have a hankering towards the principles of command and discipline. Perhaps that is why there are all those titles about art and revolution and why the establishment is so ambivalent towards culture. The products are fine but the producers are an inconvenience.

36 Eric S. Raymond, *The Cathedral and the Bazaar*, Cambridge, MA: O'Reilly, 1999., p. 116.

37 *MVNO: The Next-Generation Mobile Company*, Cambridge, MA: Pyramid Research, 1 April 2001.

38 This is seen all too clearly, for instance, in films like *Babe in the City*, where all the highlights of the world's great cities are clustered in a single metropolis.

39 Because such a long-term approach to metadata will entail very high level and large-scale technologies in areas where industry will reasonably not see immediate gain, it has also been recommended that the underlying technologies be developed by the Joint Research Centre (JRC), probably in conjunction with national research institutes in countries such as Germany (GMD), France (INRIA) and Italy (CNR). Second, given the complexity of the challenge, a modular approach has been suggested.

40 The vision of Dr. Roger Schank links this with the future of home video: "Imagine Road Trip, Dustin, ASK systems, and Movie Reader. Each of these programs could be adapted to help you plan a trip to France. Road Trip could allow you to take a simulated trip around France, seeing for yourself what there is to see there. At any point where you desired more information, you could enter an ASK system. Let's say you were in Champagne and decided it looked pleasant there. You looked around the town of Reims, visited a winery and saw them make champagne and have decided to find out more. You want to see the hotels in the area, ask about the history of how champagne came to be made in this region, and want to understand if aged champagne is worth drinking. A well-constructed ASK system, connected to Reims in Road Trip, makes itself available to you and you easily find your answers. You now ask to talk to the simulated travel agent. You ask questions, and a video talking head supplies the answers. You book the trip by conversing with the simulated agent.

"Now you are thinking that you'll need to know some French to help your trip go smoothly. You use Dustin in a variety of situations, restaurants, hotels, wineries, clothing stores, that you anticipate you will be in. You practice with Dustin until you feel confident. Next, you are ready to watch French movies. You ask the movie expert, who after some discussion with you about your taste and language ability, puts a movie on the screen that has been adapted by Movie Reader to highlight difficult expressions and to explain things when you are confused. Examples of each of these programs already exist, though they are not targeted to taking a trip to France. Making this exercise in trip-planning real is therefore a matter of extending what has already been done. It might be a lot of work, but the path has been laid out.... Eventually, selling knowledge in the guise of access to knowledge on video will become a major new growth area. Knowledge suppliers will have to find out how to charge for their best stories."

Epilogue 1

1 Esther Dyson has been a great proponent of the rising significance of Russia. She claims that: "By 2012 Russia will be referred to as the world leader in software development." *Wired*, May 2002, p. 127. This is unlikely, although Russia has traditionally been one of the pioneers in new media. It was linked with early television and invented the term (1900) three decades before it was theoretically invented in the United States. Russia was at the frontiers of early radio developments and today their satellites for distance education are probably the most advanced in the world. At the same time Russia has an enormous wealth of cultural heritage, which is slowly coming online.

2 Global Reach: http://glreach.com/gbc/cn/chinese.php3. With a Gross Domestic Product (GDP) per capita of only $3,800 in China (http://glreach.com/gbc/cn/chinese.php3), one could be tempted to overlook the importance of these figures. But given a population of 1.261

billion, China had a GDP of 4.8 trillion in 1999 and if one includes Taiwan and Hong Kong this figure rises to 5.35 trillion (CIA factlist: http://www.cia.gov/cia/publications/factbook/geos/ch.html), making it the second largest economy in the world after the United States, which had a GNP 8.083 trillion that same year. These statistics were in marked contrast to Forrester Research's predictions that by 2004 the United States would control 47 per cent of the e-commerce, Japan 13 per cent, and China effectively none. (http://glreach.com/eng/ed/art/2004.ecommerce.php3). By contrast, a report on 23 December 2004, predicted that China's E-commerce industry would reach RMB620 billion (roughly $68 billion) in 2005: http://chinatechnews.com/index.php?action=show&type=news&id=2238.

3   Liu Baijia, "China launches new generation Internet," *China Daily*, 27 December 2004: http://www.chinadaily.com.cn/english/doc/2004-12/27/content_403512.htm.

4   JinPeng Huai, "Grid research in China-perspectives for EU-China collaborations," IST Call 5 Preparatory Workshop on Advanced Grid Technologies, Systems and Services, 31 January -1 February 2005, Venue: Hotel Carrefour de l'Europe, Brussels, Brussels: EU DG INFSO-F2, January 2005.

5   NUA: http://www.nua.ie/surveys/how_many_online/asia.html. The statistic for September 2002,is taken from Global Internet Statistics. The NUA statistics predictions of 2002 have not been updated. Statistics about China are very difficult to verify. World Usage statistics claimed in December 2004, that in June 2004, there were 87 million users. See also: http://www.internetworldstats.com/asia/cn.htm. Global Internet statistics claimed that in September, 2004, there were 110 million users; "3721 Launches 'Cmail,' the World's First Chinese Character Email Service; 'Cmail' Marks a Milestone in China's Internet Development", Sinofilenet Press Release, 8 August 2004: www.sinofile.net/Saiweng/swsite.nsf/ Pr?readform&1721; China Education and Research Network, "China to Rival Japan in Internet Users by 2004," 2000: http://www.edu.cn/20010101/22370.shtml. In July 2005, a new estimate stated that there would be 120 million Internet users in China by December 2005 (which is 150 million less than the earlier prediction). Wireless World Forum, 18 July 2005: http://www.w2forum.com/item/china_forecasts_120_mln_internet_users_y.

6   John Lancaster, India, China Hoping to 'Reshape the World Order' Together, *Washington Post*, 11 April, 2005: http://www.washingtonpost.com/wp-dyn/articles/A43053-2005Apr11.html

7   Ashok Jhunjhunwala, "Towards hundred million Telephones and 25 million Internet connections in India," IIT *Madras*: http://www.tenet.res.in/Papers/100m/100m.html "Mobiles outstrip India landlines", *BBC News*: http://news.bbc.co.uk/2/hi/business/3860185.stm Wikipedia paints a more conservative estimate: http://en.wikipedia.org/wiki/Communications_in_India

8   Martha Lagace, "It's India Above China in New World Order," *Harvard Business School. Working Knowledge*, 28 July 2003: http://hbswk.hbs.edu/item.jhtml?id=3604&t=globalization

9   For a clear technical discussion where one might not expect to find it: Charles E. Catlett, "Online Pornography: Closing the Doors on Pervasive Smut," *Subcommittee on Commerce, Trade, and Consumer Protection*, Washington 2004: http://energycommerce.house.gov/108/Hearings/05062004hearing1264/Catlett1972.htm.This is, of course, but one of many possible definitions of what grid means. The makeshift model of the grid as it exists in research today is very different from the hyped versions being offered in industry today and very different again from the models which are being planned via projects such as SIMDAT.

10 Distributed Computing is said to have been introduced by Lenstra (TU Eindhoven and Bell Labs) and Manasse (Bell Labs, 1988), when they used e-mail to compute online.

11 The situation is in fact considerably more complex. Charles Catlett, as the person who founded and until June 2005 ran the Global Grid Forum, has had one vision of how things should go. Individuals such as Keith Jeffery (Rutherford/Appleton labs) have another vision. IBM and the large corporations have their vision. The European Commission is exploring a number of alternatives. At this stage no one knows precisely which of these or which combination thereof will become the dominant mode.

12 After Sun was founded (1982), it soon became clear that one of their truly big ideas was Network File Sharing (1984), which led to their claims of Enterprise Computing (1994). http://www. sun.com/aboutsun/coinfo/history.html. In October 1995, Larry Ellison (Oracle) spoke of the Network Computer as if it would be an inexpensive PC. Scott McNealy soon introduced the mantra that the "Network is the Computer," although SUN's Network computer (N1) continues to be about the size a refrigerator. In 1996–97, IBM began making public how their idea of mobile computing was leading to a vision of pervasive computing. By 1999, HP's Cool Town offered their version of the pervasive vision.

13 Top 500 Computers: http://www.top500.org/lists/2005/06/charts.php?c=7

14 Climateprediction.net (study of climate change); Einstein@home (search for gravitational signals coming from pulsars); LHC@home (to improve the design of the CERN LHC particle accelerator); Predictor@home (to investigate protein-related diseases) and Cell Computing (re: biomedical research).

15 In the past, it was possible to visit military sites in the United States and receive some idea of their research directions, although there were predictably areas that were classified. Since 9/11, most military labs have done away with their search function. NASA, which used to acknowledge the importance of *kaizen* methods and had one of the best English-language introductions to *kaizen*, no longer refers to this. This is one example of a tendency in the United States to deny the existence of knowledge outside America and goes hand in hand with the increasing difficulty for "foreign" students in doing post-graduate research in the U.S. Many technological journals that were freely available in 2000 are now accessible only on a subscription basis. In 1987, Allan Bloom wrote an influential book on *The Closing of the American Mind* (New York: Simon and Schuster). Since 2000, one could argue that we are witnessing a closing of the American Internet. It is true that on the surface we continue to have enormous amounts of news, especially concerning recent wars. But often that information is highly slanted, ambiguous, and even contradictory. Meanwhile, spam, which was an occasional nuisance in 2000, has now grown to take over 50 to 90 per cent of serious mailboxes to the point that technologies to protect us from unwanted content now loom as an important new field.

16 Hyperlearning project. Paolo d'Ilorio: http://www.item.ens.fr/diorio/

17 Hyperjournal with Dynamic contextualization: http://www.hjournal.org/presentations

18 Leonardo Chiariglione, "Riding the Media Bits." http://www.chiariglione.org/ride/

19 Leonardo Chiarigione, "Digital Media Project,"http://www.chiariglione.org/project/

20 MIT Emerging Technologies Friday Update (07.08.2005): http://wwwnl.technologyreview.com/t?ctl=E1C884:2ED00C7

21 Wade Roush, "Larry Sanger's Knowledge Free- for-All," *MIT Technology Review*, January 2005: http://www.technologyreview.com/articles/05/01/issue/forward30105.asp?trk=nl

22 SocialMedia: http://www.socialmedia.biz/ On Google (14 June 2005) the terms blog NBIC produced 6,740 hits; blog and new media produced 29,200,000 hits while blog and technology produced 39,900,000 hits. This is more than the number of existing blogs but gives some hint of this emerging field.

23 Mark Hemphill: http://www.upei.ca/~mhemphil/home.htm

24 Keitai Blogging: http://www.bloggette.com/bloggette/index.htm
    "The scrapbook was also like a heavily imaged blog or diary. As part of this research we were thinking about the creation of the content – digital camera being an obvious one but they require one to get the pictures onto a computer, create an annotation, and then add them to the scrapbook."

25 WEM Applications: http://www.wem.sfc.keio.ac.jp/wem/

26 WEM: http://www.wem.sfc.keio.ac.jp/wem/

27 VoIP: http://breakingnewsblog.com/voip/archives/category/statistics/

28 Cybertelecom. Statistics VoIP: http://www.cybertelecom.org/data/voip.htm

29 Ben Charny, "Skype creeps under phone giants' radar,"*c/net news.com*, 31 January 2005

http://netscape.com.com/Skype+creeps+under+phone+giants+radar/2100-7352_3-5557950.html

30 From personal experience I can report that a recent call from Australia was as clear as any regular telephone call. Developments such as Vonage and Skype are leading to unexpected combinations. In Toronto the artist Michael Kupka is working with Cameron Pour to create Talking Web Pages for new community projects: http://talkingwebpages ca/cgi-bin/01-cam/search.02a/search-05a.cgi?t1=Inside%20Art%20Expo. Cameron Pour is v riting the software to make this possible.

31 In 1890, there were serious visions of systematic access to all of human knowledge. Today, those visions seem further away and more elusive. We are recording and learning more than ever and face ever-greater challenges in digesting the results.The competing visions of the Internet that we have outlined remind us that there is no techno-determinism. The new technologies are not value-free, but these values depend on our inputs and our goals. If we use the new media unwisely, we risk the dark scenarios that authors of science fiction have painted. Or we can use the new media to gain ever-new insights, to augment ourselves, knowledge, culture, and the world in which we live.

32 Jack Smith, Moya K. Mason, "Learning From Technology Foresight Connections": http://www.moyak.com/researcher/resume/papers/seville.html

33 E.g., http://www.2100.org/Nanos/Canadanrc.pdf

34 Raymond Bouchard, Biosystematics: www.2100.org/Nanos/biosystemics-canada.pdf "Convergence of Technologies for Innovative Disruption," *Issues in Defence Science and Technology*, Issue 16, July 2003. http://www.drdc-rddc.gc.ca/publications/issues/issues16_e.asp

35 NBIC Convergence 2004: http://www.infocastinc.com/nbic/nbichome.htm

36 "Converging Technologies for Improving Human Performance. Nanotechnology, Biotechnology, Information Technology and Cognitive Science": http://www.wtec.org/ConvergingTechnologies/Report/NBIC_report.pdf

37 Phillip J Bond: http://www.technology.gov/Speeches/p_PJB_030207.htm

38 *Japan Nanonet Bulletin*, Issue 33, 9 December, 2004:
http://www.nanonet.go.jp/english/mailmag/2004/033.html

39 NBIC Convergence 2005: http://www.mtconference2004.org/chinanano2005/invited.htm

40 Kristine Bruland (University of Oslo).

41 Alfred Nordmann (rapporteur), HLEG (High Level expert Group), *Foresighting the new technology Wave, Converging Technologies. Shaping the Future of European Societies*, Alfred Nordmann, Rapporteur, [Brussels: European Union], 2004:
http://europa.eu.int/comm/research/conferences/2004/ntw/pdf/final_report_en.pdf. Cf. Christopher Coenen et al.: http://www.itas.fzk.de/tatup/043/coua04a.htm
"Additionally, there were reports from several special interest groups (or working groups of the panel as a whole), position papers from individual members of the HLEG, a collection of state of the art reviews and related papers, and finally a set of comments by invited experts submitted prior to the conference."

41 Quoted from formerly: http://www.emsl.pnl.gov:2080/using-msl/about_emsl.html?main=history.html. Cf. The History of EMSL. http://www.emsl.pnl.gov/homes/history.shtml.

42 Google Print Beta: http://print.google.com/; "Google Checks Out Library Books", *Google Press Center*, 14 December 2004, http://www.google.com/press/pressrel/print_library.html Even within the US there is also opposition to the Google vision. Kimberley A. Kichenuik, "Google Begins Digitalization", *The Harvard Crimson Inc.*, 7 June 2005. http://www.thecrimson.com/article.aspx?ref=507937

43 Anonymous, "European Libraries fight Google-ization", *Deutsche Welle, DW-World., DE*, 27 April 2005, http://www.dw-world.de/dw/article/0,1564,1566717,00.html

44 Many details remain unclear. The stated purpose of the site is to help users find material, not to enable them to read it. Those who want to read are expected to buy. The Google Print

site requires that every user log-in. The given reason is copyright – although they have also explained elsewhere that they are only scanning books not in copyright. One of the unstated reasons for log-ins is to track each user's moves and habits. Ranking within Google is due to popularity. The most popular is at the top of the pop[ular]s. Simplified versions of Einstein's special theory of relativity were and remain much more popular than the original paper. But that does not make popularizing reporters more important than Einstein. This use of popularity as dominant criterion is one of central issues that has raised such concerns elsewhere. Yahoo's announcement of paid subscriptions for deep search on 17 June 2005 is seen by some as a sign of things to come.   http://thebosh.com/archives/2005/06/yahoo_deep_sear.php

45   Anonymous, "French answer to Google library", *BBC News*: http://www.123webguru.com/website_design_news/frenchansw704.html

46   Valerie Khanna, "French cry havoc over Google's library plans", *Library Staff Blog*, University of Pennsylvania, 28 March 2005:   http://www.library.upenn.edu/blos/staffweb/Current_Readings/french_cry_havoc_over_googles_library_plans.html

47   Anonymous, "French To Provide Alternative To Google Library Project", http://www.webrank-info.com/english/seo-news/topic-2267.htm

48   Anonymous, "European Libraries fight Google-ization", *Deutsche Welle, DW-World.*, DE, 27 April 2005, http://www.dw-world.de/dw/article/0,1564,1566717,00.html

49   Anonymous, "Initiative European Libraries to digitise books", *EDRI Gram*, no. 3.9, 4 May 2005 http://www.edri.org/edrigram/number3.9/digilibrary

50   Anonymous, "Over 11m Digital Records Now Available At European Library", *Managing Information Newsletter*, Issue 172, 31 May 2005): http://www.managinginformation.com/news/content_show_full.php?id=3893.

51   Viviane Reding, Member of the European Commission responsible for Information Society and Media, i2010: *Europe Must Seize the Opportunities of the Digital Economy Press Conference on the occasion of the launch of the initiative European Information Society 2010*, Brussels, 1 June 2005: http://europa.eu.int/rapid/pressReleasesAction.do?reference=SPEECH/05/312&format=HTML&aged=0&language=EN&guiLanguage=en;
 http://www.euractiv.com/Article?tcmuri=tcm:29-134976-16&type=News

52   Anonymous, "EU: Launches new European Communications strategy 'i2010'":, *UNI Telecom global Union*, 2 June 2005:   http://www.union-network.org/unitelecom.nsf/0/5e33c14432197c30c125701400269b61?OpenDocument "To close the gap between the information society 'haves and have nots', the Commission will propose: an Action Plan on e-Government for citizen-centred services (2006); three 'quality of life' ICT flagship initiatives (technologies for an ageing society, intelligent vehicles that are smarter, safer and cleaner, and digital libraries making multimedia and multilingual European culture available to all (2007); and actions to overcome the geographic and social 'digital divide', culminating in a European Initiative on e-Inclusion (2008)."

53   Anonymous,"Google's 300-year plan", *SMH.com*, 1 July 2005: http://blogs.smh.com.au/razor/archives/search_engines/001426.html

54   Paul Otlet, *Monde: essaie d'universalisme -- connaissance du monde; sentiment du monde; action organisée et plan du monde*, Brussels, Editions du Mundaneum, 1935): http://www.laetusinpraesens.org/docs/otlethyp.php By 1943, Otlet had sketched how such a machine to imagine the world might look (*machine à penser le monde*).

Epilogue 2

1   At Cambridge he is likely to have first encountered Cornford's influential essay on "The Invention of Space." It is bemusing that Marshall McLuhan who went to Cambridge turned to historical sources for understanding, whereas his contemporary, Northrop Frye, who went to Oxford,

wrote *An Anatomy of Criticism*, which discussed universal structures that did not change historically and culturally.

2   Terence Gordon, *Marshall McLuhan. Escape into Understanding: A Biography*, Toronto: Stoddart, 1997, p. 264.

3   McLuhan Program: http://www.mcluhan.utoronto.ca/.

4   In the history department, Natalie Zemon Davis was interested in the role of visualization in Renaissance culture, drawing attention to the work of William Ivins and McLuhan's student, Walter Ong. David Olson, at the Ontario Institute for Studies in Education (OISE), was concerned with the implications of literacy for education. Later, Brian Stock wrote on *Implications of Literacy*, Princeton: Princeton University Press, 1982, which focused on developments in the twelfth century.

5   He took an ordinary room, divided this into two using a semi-transparent screen onto which he projected an image. He then arranged chairs such that one half of the viewers would see the image projected onto a screen in the manner of a normal cinema, while the viewers in the other part of the room saw the image back-projected through the screen in the manner of a television screen. After the screening, he asked the unsuspecting viewers to compare impressions. McLuhan found that those who saw the film on the front projection screen of traditional cinemas had a more detached experience than those who saw the "same" film on a back-projected television-like screen. By implication, those who see films in the new mini-cinemas with back-projection screens are having different experiences than those watching traditional movie screens.

6   Meanwhile, some critics such as Jonathan Miller were almost overly eager to point out that McLuhan's informal experiments lacked the rigour of careful scientific experiments.

7   Terence Gordon, *Marshall McLuhan. Escape into Understanding A Biography*, Toronto: Stoddart, 1997, p. 215.

8   Ibid., p. 281.

9   If this were true, one would expect that McLuhan's terms with respect to electric culture as opposed to those of print culture would be more copiously represented on the Internet. This does not appear to be the case.

10 McLuhan was trying to draw attention back to grammar (in its older senses) and rhetoric, rather than to dialectic and logic; to structures and patterns as opposed to individual elements; to the integrating rather than the dissecting; the synthetic rather than the analytic; the interdisciplinary rather than the specialist – all aspects that print had undermined.

11 The idea of the tetrads became important in the West with Radulphus Glaber's *Historia sui temporis* (1059): "Temperance (Sophrosyne) and the Canon of the Cardinal Virtues," *Dictionary of the History of Ideas*: http://etext.lib.virginia.edu/cgi-local/DHI/dhi.cgi?id=dv4-49. Interestingly enough, tetrads were an important topic in psychology when McLuhan was a student; L. L. Thurstone, "The Vectors of Mind," Address of the president before the American Psychological Association, Chicago meeting, September, 1933; first published in *Psychological Review*, vol. 41, 1934, pp. 1–32: http://psychclassics.yorku.ca/Thurstone/.

12 Marshall and Eric McLuhan, *Laws of Media*, Toronto: University of Toronto Press, 1988, p. 40.

13 Ibid., p. 3.

14 William Ivins, Jr., *Art and Geometry*, Cambridge, MA: Harvard University Press, 1946; ibid., *Prints and Visual Communication*, Cambridge, MA: Harvard University Press, 1953.

15 Sir E.H. Gombrich, *Art and Illusion*, Princeton: Princeton University Press, 1960, p. 129.

16 George Hanfmann, "Greek Narration," in: *Narration in Ancient Art: A Symposium*, ed. Helene J. Kantor, George Hanfmann et al., *American Journal of Archaeology*, 61, January 1957, p. 74.

17 Cf. the author's "Panofsky's Perspective: A Half Century Later," *Atti del convegno internazionale di studi: la prospettiva rinascimentale, Milan 1977*, ed. Marisa Dalai-Emiliani (Florence: Centro Di, 1980), pp. 565–84. At the turn of the twentieth century, Alois Riegl had distinguished between painting and sculpture in terms of visual versus tactile art. Towards the mid-twentieth century, critics such as William Ivins, building on the ideas of Martin Foss, had described sculpture in terms of tactile sensibility, which they claimed came from a fascination with perfection in Antiquity. This

notes: epilogues

was contrasted with a visual sensibility in painting, which they claimed came from a concept of infinity in the Renaissance. Thus they explained why the Greeks preferred sculpture over painting and why Renaissance artists supposedly preferred painting over sculpture; William Ivins, *Art and Geometry*, Cambridge, MA: Harvard University Press, 1946.; Martin Foss, *The Idea of Perfection in the Western World*, Princeton: Princeton University Press, 1946.

18   While it is true that both Greek art at the end of the pre-literate age and cubism at the beginning of the electric age both have multiple viewpoints, it is difficult to claim that they resemble each other. In McLuhan's analysis, the multi-viewpoint acoustic space of pre-literate man is replaced first by an abstract visual space (a conceptual space) with the advent of the alphabet and by linear perspective (a method of representation) with the advent of print in the Renaissance. But the Renaissance also introduced methods of cylindrical and spherical perspective.

19   Richard Cavell, *McLuhan in Space*, Toronto: University of Toronto Press, 2002, p. 57.

20   Martin Jay, *Downcast Eyes: The Denigration of Vision in Twentieth-Century French Thought*, Berkeley: University of California Press, 1993.

21   For an introduction, see the author's "Developments in Perspective," *Visual Mathematics*, ed. Michele Emmer, Cambridge, MA: MIT Press, 1993, pp. 199–205. For a survey of twentieth-century methods, see "Electronic Media: The Rebirth of Perspective and the Fragmentation of Illusion," in *Electronic Culture: Technology and Visual Representation*, ed. Timothy Druckrey, New York: Aperture, pp. 208–27 and "Percezione, prospettiva e rappresentazione nell'America Settentrionale," in *Specchi americani. La filosofia europea nel nuovo mondo*, ed. Caterina Marrone, G. Coccoli, G. Santese, and F. Ratto, Rome: Castelvecchi, 1994, pp. 287–345. (Contatti 6, III convegno di studi filosofici di San Sepolcro). For a more thorough treatment, see the author's *Sources of Perspective* and *Literature of Perspective* available on-line at: www.sumscorp.com.

22   Marshall McLuhan and Eric McLuhan, *The Laws of Media*, Toronto: University of Toronto Press, 1988.

23   Ibid., especially pp. 86–87.

24   New York: Oxford University Press, 1989.

25   Marshall McLuhan, *Understanding Media*, Cambridge, MA: MIT Press, 1994, 2nd ed.

26   Quote from cover dust jacket. Since then, there has also been a Dutch translation of *Understanding Media* (2002).

27   For an important report on such developments: HLEG (High Level expert Group), Foresighting the new technology Wave, *Converging Technologies. Shaping the Future of European Societies*, Alfred Nordmann, Rapporteur, [Brussels: European Union], 2004: http://europa.eu.int/comm/research/conferences/2004/ntw/pdf/final_report_en.pdf.
The report notes that Convergence Technologies have different names. In the United States, they are referred to as NBIC (Nanotechnology, Biotechnology, Information Technology and Cognitive Science) -convergence for improving human performance. In Canada, they are referred to as Bio-Systemics Synthesis. In Europe, there is talk of Converging Technologies for the European Knowledge Society (CTEKs).

28   It is not fruitful to criticize McLuhan for overlooking developments that happened in the future or to dwell on how McLuhan's tetrads do not help us understand the shift from ICT or UCT.

29   Terence Gordon, *Marshall McLuhan. Escape into Understanding: A Biography*, Toronto: Stoddart, 1997, p. 86.

30   Eric McLuhan also published two introductory works about his father: *Essential McLuhan* and *Who was Marshall McLuhan?* (both 1995) and his father's ideas on religion in *The Medium and the Light* (1999). At the same time, Eric McLuhan has also continued his own research with books such as *The Role of Thunder in Finnigan's Wake* (1997) and *Electric Language* (1998). Eric McLuhan is working on an edition of all of McLuhan's writings. Tragically, the University of Toronto has given no support to Marshall McLuhan's son. Other members of the McLuhan family have also contributed to his legacy. His widow, Corinne McLuhan, in conjunction with his literary agent, Matie Molinaro and William Toye published *Letters of Marshall McLuhan* (1987). His daughter, Stephanie McLuhan with David Staines has published a series of lectures and interviews in a book entitled *Understanding*

Me. The introduction to this book connected Teilhard de Chardin's ideas of the noösphere with McLuhan's global village. The theme of collective intelligence now had Catholic roots. Marshall McLuhan was succeeded by David Olson, who focussed on problems of literacy with special attention to the education of children and organized an important conference that resulted in *Media and Symbols: The Forms of Expression, Communication and Education* (1974). Olson's successor was Derrick de Kerckhove, who was called an apostle of the net and proponent of cyberparadise by Jean Claude Guillebaud (*Le principe d'Humanité*, Paris: Editions du Seuil, 2001, p.163); who imaginatively developed McLuhan's ideas about the effects of the alphabet and literacy among the Greeks and proceeded to associate this with theories about the left and right brain in *Brainframes* (1991). De Kerckhove listed psychological trends in terms of oppositions between television during the 1970s and computers during the 1980s, e.g., mass culture vs. speed culture, broadcasting vs. networking and seduction vs. precision. In 1991, Internet users were less than 1 million and few persons foresaw that the computer would affect 1 billion persons by 2005. De Kerckhove's opposition between television and Internet as a psychological trend rather than a technological advance overlooked the potentials of convergence and made it seem as if the Internet was merely another in a line of new gadgets. These oppositions were repeated in his *The Skin of Culture: Investigating the New Electronic Reality* (1995). Here he also coupled McLuhan's insights about electronic media with the ideas of Pierre Levy (1994) in predicting the rise of a connected intelligence, which became the basis for a further book *Gekoppelde intelligentie* (1996) and which, as we have seen, was also considered by others (chapter 10).

McLuhan's first doctoral student, Donald F. Theall, wrote a book, *The Medium is the Rear View Mirror: Understanding McLuhan* (1971) and more recently *The Virtual Marshall McLuhan* (2001), which focusses on his personal interpretation of McLuhan's ideas in the 1950s and 1960s and pays particular attention to his links with literary theory. An appendix contains valuable insights by Edmund Carpenter, who worked with McLuhan in producing the journal *Explorations* (1953–59). Richard Cavell in *McLuhan in Space: A Cultural Geography* (2002) proposes that McLuhan be read as a spatial theorist. Gary Genosko has written on McLuhan and Baudrillard (1999). Meanwhile, Grosswiler in *Method is the Message* (1998) links McLuhan's communications theory with Marxist dialectics and examines his work in light of Adorno, Benjamin, Raymond Williams, Jean Baudrillard, and Umberto Eco. If he were alive, McLuhan would almost certainly have been amused and bemused by these attempts to reduce his brilliant, playful intuitions into full-fledged theories. In Britain, Jonathan Miller in *McLuhan*, London: Fontana, 1971, ignored McLuhan's larger scholarly context, found it easy to attack him on myriad analytical points, and thereby overlooked almost entirely his quest for a new interdisciplinary approach to contextual knowledge studying patterns and structures. McLuhan preached a study of the invisible medium rather than the visible message. Those who attacked the letters of his words missed the spirit of his ways. In Germany, Michael Giesecke, *Das Buchdruck in der frühen Neuzeit: Eine historische Fallstudie über die Durchsetzung neuer Informations- und Kommunikations-technologien*, Frankfurt: Suhrkamp, 1991, used McLuhan as a starting point for his standard book on the history of printing. As we noted earlier, Giesecke showed that printing began in Korea in the early ninth century; that it was used in China for control by the state, whereas in Germany print was linked with a vision of sharing, for the common good, for a "common weal" or commonwealth. In essence, Giesecke's claims about the implications of printing are the same as our claims about the new media. Their effects depend on the visions of those who use them. Cf. the web site of Michael Giesecke, who is now Professor in Erfurt: http://www.michael-giesecke.de/giesecke/menue/index_h.html.

31　For a discussion of tensions between game and narrative, see Jesper Juul (jj@pobox.com), "A Clash between Game and Narrative," paper presented at the *Digital Arts and Culture* conference in Bergen, November, 1998: http://www.jesperjuul.dk/text/DAC%20Paper%201998.html; A theory of the computer game: http://www.jesperjuul.dk/thesis/4-theoryofthecomputergame. html; Cf. what Russian formalists call the "*sjuzet*": Amaryll Beatrice Chanady, *Magical Realism and the Fantastic: Resolved versus Unresolved Antinomy*, New York and London: Garland Publishing, 1985. Ibid.,

"Magical Realism and the Fantastic," *The Café Irreal:* http://home.sprynet.com/~awhit/tcritica. htm.

32 Marshall McLuhan would have been careful to note that these potentially wonderful developments also have their dangers. He was worried how cool television would lead to an undermining of privacy, of our concept of the individual, of our notion of the nation. Eric McLuhan has been studying shifts in literacy over the past decades. If cool television threatens literacy, will the arrival of new electronic media, which permit communication without literacy, lead to a world where we may still buy books and browse them but no longer find the energy and time to read them? Or is this merely one of the so many dangers brought by the new media? If evolution is embracing not replacing, then there are new horizons; Cf. Umberto Eco, *Come si fa una tesi di laurea*, Milan: Bompiani, 1977.

33 Simputer: http://www.simputer.org/. The context for this remarkable advance has been over a century and a half in the making. At one level, the advent of photography and film in the nineteenth century, and the rise of television, video recorders and tape-recorders in the twentieth century, meant that one could record the actions, gestures, and even the words of illiterate persons. These technologies were, however, so complex that their use required the presence and intervention of literate persons. This provided new jobs for archaeologists, ethnologists, anthropologists, and sociologists but did not bring them much closer to the persons they were supposedly studying. As such, these devices served to record images and sounds across the literacy divide but did nothing to bridge it. Indeed, by providing visible and audible evidence of the differences, they served, ironically, to increase the divide between literacy and illiteracy.

34 A person in a village of Nepal, or indeed anywhere, can potentially use a simputer via a satellite connection such as Worldspace and gain access to materials from the world's great libraries, museums, and archives. If they happen to be illiterate, the material can be read out. If they are deaf, the knowledge can be communicated through sign-language. If they are blind, it can be communicated in Braille or other methods for the sight challenged. Hence, knowledge and communication at a distance are potentially no longer limited to a literate minority.

35 Francesco Malgaroli, "Due secoli di teoria dietro le proteste di oggi. Parla il politologo Mario Pinata. Kant, Thoreau, Morel gli 'antenati' del movimento," *La Reppublica*, 10 July 2001, p. 11.

Appendix 1 : Scientific Visualization

1 E. J. Marey, *La méthode graphique dans les sciences expérimentales*, Paris: G. Masson, 1878.

2 Ivan Sutherland was writing a *History of Computer Graphics*, New York: New Riders Press, 2001. Cf. Terrence Masson, *CG 101: A Computer Graphics Industry Reference*: http://www.visualfx.com/.

3 See, for instance, Alex Pomasanoff, *The Invisible World: Sights Too Fast, Too Slow, Too Far, Too Small for the Naked Eye to See*, London: Secker and Warburg, 1981; Jon Darius, *Beyond Vision*, Oxford: Oxford University Press, 1984; Richard Mark Friedhoff and William Benzon, *The Second Computer Revolution: Visualization*, New York: Harry N. Abrams, 1989.

4 Visible Embryo: http://www.visembryo.com/.

5 Visible Man: http://www.crd.ge.com/esl/cgsp/projects/vm/#thevisibleman; Chris North, Ben Shneiderman, and Catherine Plaisant, "User Controlled Overviews of an Image Library: The Visible Human Explorer.": http://www.nlm.nih.gov/research/visible/vhp_conf/north/vhedemo.htm. Visible Human Viewer: http://www.npac.syr.edu/projects/vishuman/UserGuide.html#main.

6 Anatomy Resources.com.: http://www.anatomy-resources.com/.

7 Chihara Lab. Research Field: http://chihara.aist-nara.ac.jp/public/research/research.html.

8 Volker Blanz: http://www.kyb.tuebingen.mpg.de/bu/people/volker/; http://www.mpi-sb.mpg.de/~blanz/.

9 World of Escher: www.worldofescher.com.

10   Ibid. Gallery: http://www.worldofescher.com/gallery/internet/index.html.

11   Kathy Rae Huffman and Margarete Jahrmann, "Nadia Thalmann, creator of the virtual Marilyn Monroe," *Telepolis*, 25 November 1997: http://www.heise.de/tp/r4/artikel/4/4087/1.html.

12   Alex Gove, "Virtual Celebrity Productions puts the dead to work," *The Red Herring Magazine*, January, 1999. Karen Kaplan, "Old Actors Never Die; They Just Get Digitized," *LA Times*, Monday, 9 August 1999: (formerly) http://www.moves.com/film/vcp/latimes.html; Barnabas Takacs: http://cs.gmu.edu/~wechsler/staffs/barna.html.

13   Kurzweil.Net: http://www.kurzweilai.net/index.html?flash=2 under Ramona. In fact, there were similar demonstrations in the early 1990s by both Softimage (before it was acquired by Microsoft) and Alias in the Toronto SIGGRAPH Chapter.

14   Wendy Jackson Hall, "From Here to Infinity. Visionnaire Jean Giraud takes moviegoers on a Moebius trip," *Wired*, June, 2001, pp. 158–61: http://www.wired.com/wired/archive/9.06/moebius.html.

15   Final Fantasy: http://www.imdb.com/title/tt0173840/; Marco K. Della Casa, "Lucas taking special effects to new realms," *USA Today*, 23–25 February 2001, pp. 1–2; Michael A. Hiltzik and Alex Pham, "Synthetic Actors Guild," *Latimes.com*, Tuesday, 8 May 2001.

16   MAVERIK: http://aig.cs.man.ac.uk/maverik/.

17   Virtual Environments for Training: http://www.isi.edu/isd/VET/vet.html.

18   Igor Nikitin, Introduction to String Theory: http://sim.ol.ru/~nikitin/course/course.html.

19   Infobyte: http://www.infobyte.it/.

20   Barco I-Dome: http://www.barco.com/Edutainment/en/products/product.asp?element=1897

21   Bentley Model City: (formerly) http://www.bentley.com/modelcity/gallery/card.jpg.

22   http://www.virtualhelsinki.net/english/.

23   For instance, Virtual Munich has a general map with a handful of places from which one can access Quick Time panoramic views. Virtual London.com is much more detailed, has maps that allow one to zoom from country level to street level, and has lists of museums, etc., but does not link one to the actual sites of the institutions: http://www.virtual-london.com/. Virtual New York does link their general description of institutions with the original sites, has maps and even has a real-time satellite weather map: http://www.vny.com/.

24   Portugal Virtual: http://www.portugalvirtual.pt/index.html.

25   Maurizio Forte, *Archeologia, percorsi virtuali nelle civilta scomparse*, Milan: Mondadori, 1996.

26   Villes 3D.

27   NUME: http://www.storiaeinformatica.it/newdef/italiano/ndefault.html.

28   VISMAN project: http://www.cineca.it/pubblicazioni/scienza_scalc/ssc2003/cul02.pdf.

29   An important recent conference, which surveyed many of these developments: *High Performance Graphics Systems and, Applications European Workshop. State of the Art and Future Trends*, Palazzo Marescotti, Bologna, 16–17 October 2000, Proceedings, Bologna: CINECA, 2000.

30   *Neapolis. La valorizzazione dei beni culturali e ambientali*, ed. Epifanio Fornari, Rome: L'Erma di Bretschneider, 1994, particularly pp. 23–26, 59–63, 115–16 (Ministero per i beni culturali e ambientali soprintendenza archeologica di Pompei, Monografie, 7).

31   Mobile Visualization. Das MOVI Projekt: http://www.gris.informatik.tu-darmstadt.de/jahrber/JahrBe95/b95_2_3.html.

32   Advanced Visual Systems: www.avs.com.

33   Proceedings of the Nara Symposium for Digital Silk Roads, 10–12 December 2003, Tokyo: NII, 2004.

34   National Center for Atmospheric Research: http://www.scd.ucar.edu/vg/MM5/images.

35   Hitachi. Viewseum: http://www.viewseum.com.

36   IBM Research. STM Image Gallery: http://www.almaden.ibm.com/vis/stm/hexagone.html.

37   For a useful site with excellent images of outer space, see Astronomy Picture of the Day Gallery: http://antwrp.gsfc.nasa.gov/apod/calendar/allyears.html; Kitahara site: http://www.janis.or.jp/users/kitahara/english-index.html.

655

38 Brad Cox, *Superdistribution Objects as Property on the Electronic Frontier*, Wokingham: Addison Wesley, 1996: http://www.virtualschool.edu/mon/TTEF.html. Cf. Brad Cox, "Planning the Software Industrial Revolution," *IEEE Software Magazine*, Special issue: *Software Technologies of the 1990's*, November, 1990: http://virtualschool.edu/cox/pub/.

39 Formerly at: http://www.bell-labs.com/user/eick/. His work was linked with Visible Insights, which has now become Advizor Solutions.

40 Visible Decisions has been taken over by Advizor Solutions: http://www.advizorsolutions.com/.

41 Asymptote: http://www.asymptote.net/#.

42 Evans and Sutherland are among the leading producers for the visualization software used by the military: http://www.es.com/Products/Software/EPX/index.asp.

43 Comanche 4 web site: http://archive.gamespy.com/previews/november01/comanche4/. The magazine *PC Gamer* offers a good survey of current games.

44 SRI Digital Earth. Terravision: http://www.ai.sri.com/TerraVision/.

45 High Performance Computing Center, Stuttgart: http://www.hlrs.de/.

46 In February, 2000, there was a major conference at Stanford on Special Effects: http://prelectur.stanford.edu/lecturers/symposia/effects.html. The *National Association of Broadcasters* (NAB) *Conference*, Las Vegas, continues to be a venue for the frontiers in broadcast media. http://www.nabshow.com/.

47 Formerly at: http://www.whatdreamsmay.com/vers3/whatdreams.htm.

48 Maverik: http://aig.cs.man.ac.uk/maverik/.

49 Brygg Ullmer, "Physicality, Virtuality, and the Switch that Lights," Short paper for Mitch Resnick and Sherry Turkle's, "Thinking about Things," March 1996. Formerly at: http://xenia.media.mit.edu/~ullmer/; Cf. http://www.zib.de/ullmer/#tochi04.

50 Michel Moers: (formerly) http://www.damasquine.be/Pages/Photogra/Moers1.htm.

51 Volker Kuhn, „Virtuality", Lectronic Soundscapes, Music CD, 1992: http://www.memi.com/musiker/changing_images/.

52 Formerly at: http://www.vrml-art.org/cgi/vmsprg?tplt=index.

53 John Barth, "Culture. Virtuality," *Johns Hopkins Magazine Electronic Edition*, Special Issue: "Straws in the Wind", September 1994: http://www.jhu.edu/~jhumag/994web/culture1.html.

54 E-Rena: http://imk.gmd.de/images/mars/files/erena99_D6_2.pdf.

55 DEVA gallery under Cages: http://aig.cs.man.ac.uk/research/deva/deva.php.

56 Formerly at: http://sbdhost.part.com. Now being replaced by Web-Based Design Environment Accelerates Weapon System Design: http://www.ml.afrl.af.mil/stories/mlm-00204.html.

57 Division Group plc: http://www.sgi.com/products/remarketed/onyx2/partners/division.html.

58 Sandia Eigen VR Lab: http://www.cs.sandia.gov/SEL/main.html.

59 Urban Simulation Team: http://www.ust.ucla.edu/ustweb/ust.html.

60 ERC (Engineering Research Centre), Mississippi State University: http://www.erc.msstate.edu/research/projects.html.

61 Formerly at: http://www.public.iastate.edu/~jmvance.

62 Human Modeling and Simulation: http://www.cis.upenn.edu/~hms/home.html.

63 U.S. Defense Modeling and Simulation Office: http://www.dmso.mil.

64 AHPCRC: http://www.arc.umn.edu.

65 Visual Systems Laboratory. Institute for Systems and Training: http://www.vsl.ist.ucf.edu/ and http://www.ist.ucf.edu/.

66 Formerly at: http://www.jebb.com.

67 This is based on a development by the German National Centre for Supercomputing (GMD) now Fraunhofer, Schloss Birlinghoven.

68 MABS: http://www.informatik.uni-trier.de/~ley/db/conf/mabs/.

69 Virtual Environments Laboratory: http://www.coe.neu.edu/~mourant/velab.html.

70 NASA Advanced Supercomputing Division: http://www.nas.nasa.gov/.

71 Center for Computer Aided Design: http://www.ccad.uiowa.edu.

72   Computing and Information Science Division: http://www.aro.army.mil/mcsc/skbs.htm.
73   SimCity4: http://simcity.ea.com/.
74   Nicolas Mokhoff, "Graphics gurus eye nuts, bolts of 3-D Web," *EE Times*, 28 July 2000: http://www.eet.com/story/OEG20000728S0006.
75   Mark Ward, "The dark side of digital utopia," *BBC News*, 27 February 2004: http://news.bbc.co.uk/2/hi/technology/3334923.stm.
76   Formerly at: http://www.besoft.com.
77   National Cancer Center, Tokyo: http://www.ncc.go.jp/.
78   Pittsburgh Supercomputing Center: http://www.psc.edu/.
79   http://www.psc.edu/biomed/. Watching the Brain in Action: http://www.psc.edu/science/goddard.html.
80   IBM Vizualization Lab last updated 1995: http://www.almaden.ibm.com/vis/vis_lab.html.
81   Blue Gene: http://www.research.ibm.com/bluegene/.
        http://en.wikipedia.org/wiki/Blue_Gene.
82   Informs College on Simulation: http://www.informs-cs.org.
83   My Links: http://dora.cwru.edu/saa4/links.html.
84   Institut National de Recherche en Informatique Automatisée (INRIA).
        Augmented Reality Mixing Virtual Objects and the Real World
        Thème 1: Reseaux et systèmes
        Modelisation et évaluation des systèmes informatiques (MEVAL)
        Thème 2: Génie logiciel et calcul symbolique
        Thème 3: Interaction homme-machine, images
        Gestion des connaissances pour l'aide à la conception co-operative (AIR)
        Représentations et langages (AIRELLE)
        Représentation des connaissances (REPCO)
        Systèmes de base de données (RODIN)
        Base de connaissances a données (SHERPA)
        Thème 4: Simulation et optimisation des systèmes complexes.
85   EUROSIM: http://iatms13.iatm.tuwien.ac.at/eurosim/.
86   Winter Simulation Conference: http://www.wintersim.org.
87   ASAM. Association for Standardisation and Automation of Measuring Systems: http://www.asam.de/new/01_asam-ev_01.php.

Appendix 2: New Fields Relating to Knowledge Organization

1   Taxonomic Databases Working Group: http://www.tdwg.org/.
2   CODATA: http://www.codata.org/.
3   Integrated Taxonomic Information System (ITIS): http://www.itis.usda.gov/.
4   Taxonomy and Systematics: (formerly) http://taxonomy.zoology.gla.ac.uk/software/software.html.
5   Internet Directory for Botany: http://public.srce.hr/botanic/cisb/Edoc/flora/subject/botflor.html.
6   NBII Taxonomic Resources and Expertise Directory (TRED): http://tred.cr.usgs.gov/cgi-bin/tred_taxon.cgi.
7   Phylogenetics: http://www.ucmp.berkeley.edu/museum/MPL/PhyloSystematics.html.
8   Information on Taxonomies for Personalized Learning: (formerly) http://www.msms.doe.k12.ms.us/~jcarter/plearntx.html.
9   Expert Center for Taxonomic Identification (ETI): http://wwweti.eti.bio.uva.nl/.
10   History of JMJ: (formerly) http://www.livjm.ac.uk/tbe/history.htm.
11   Graduate School of Library and Information Science: http://alexia.lis.uiuc.edu/gslis/school/index.html.
12   Formative Beginnings 1895–1905: http://slisweb.lis.wisc.edu/~historyproject/form.htm.

13 Organizational Learning and Cognition: http://choo.fis.utoronto.ca/fis/OrgCog/.

14 BCS: Personal Communication.
Société Francophone de Classification (SFC): http://sfc.enst-bretagne.fr/.
Societa Italiana di Statistica (SIS): http://w3.uniroma1.it/sis/index.asp.
Japanese Classification Society: http://wwwsoc.nii.ac.jp/jcs/en/index_e.html.
Vereniging voor Ordinatie en Classificatie (VOC): http://www.voc.ac/html/about.htm ;
SKAD: http://www.us.szc.pl/skad_ang.

15 Centre for Informetric Studies: http://ix.db.dk/cis/CISframes.htm.

16 ENSSIB: (école nationale supérieure des sciences de l'information): http://www.enssib.fr/.

17 We are not concerned at this point with classification in the context of shipping, which is covered
by the International Association of Classification Societies (IACS): http://www.iacs.org.uk/; List
of Classification Societies: http://www.nautisk.com/eng/links/class.htm.

18 IFCS Societies: http://vlado.fmf.uni-lj.si/ifcs/IFCSsocs.htm.

19 E.g., ISSCR '91.

20 IFCS. International Federation of Classification Societies: http://edfu.lis.uiuc.edu/~class/ifcs/.

21 Beyond Bookmarks: http://www.iastate.edu/~CYBERSTACKS/CTW.htm.

22 Visual Thesaurus: http://www.visualthesaurus.com/index.jsp;jsessionid=E461B3781EB7E5F8F
829FAA5DAC582A1.s17?content=%2fhome.jsp.

23 Drexel, CIS: http://www.cis.drexel.edu/.

24 IFCS 2000. 7th Conference of the International Federation of Classification Societies: Data Analysis, Classification, and
Related Methods, 11–14 July 2000, Namur, Belgium.

25 Formerly at: http://ils.unc.edu/.

26 Rutgers, SCILS: http://www.scils.rutgers.edu/.

27 Berkeley, SIMS: http://info.sims.berkeley.edu/.

28 Information Systems Institute: http://www.isi.edu/.

29 U.S. National Commission on Libraries and Information Science: http://www.nclis.gov/.

30 ALISE: http://www.alise.org/.

31 Society for Information Management: http://www.simnet.org/.

32 Mundaneum: http://www.mundaneum.be/.The permanent exposition that was at http://
www.pastel.be/mundaneum/ is not functioning. For a history of the Mundaneum, see W. Boyd
Rayward, The Universe of Information: The Work of Paul Otlet for the Documentation and International Organisation,
The Hague: FID, 1975.

33 International Federation of Documentation: http://www.sims.berkeley.edu/~buckland/fid-
sources.html.

34 Union Internationale des Organisations: http://www.uia.org.

35 ISO TC 37. Language Resource Management: http://tc37sc4.org/doc1/ISO%20TC%2037-
4%20N008%20IAC%20Terms%20of%20Reference.pdf.

36 Termnet: http://www.termnet.at/.

37 Gesellschaft für Terminologie und Wissenstransfer (GTW). Association for Terminology and
Knowledge Transfer: http://gtw-org.uibk.ac.at/ now http://www.id.cbs.dk/~het/gtw/gtw.html.

38 Nordterm-Net: http://www.tsk.fi/nordterm/net/da.html.

39 NTRF: http://www.rtt.org/ntrf/ntrf.htm.

40 G.A. Fink, F. Kunnert, and G. Sagerer, "With Friends like Statistics who needs Linguistics?," KI
Künstliche Intelligence, vol. 5, 1995, pp. 31–35: http://www.techfak.uni-bielefeld.de/ags/ai/publica-
tions/abstracts/Fink1995-WFL.html.

41 Literature on automatic classification includes: Amos O. Olagunju, "Nonparametric methods
for automatic classification of documents and transactions," (abstract) in: CSC '90. Proceedings of
the 1990 ACM Eighteenth Annual Computer Science Conference on Cooperation, 1990, p. 448: http://www.
acm.org/pubs/citations/proceedings/csc/100348/p448-olagunju/; Elmar Nöth, S. Harbeck, H.
Niemann, V. Warnke, and I. Ipsic, "Language Identification in the Context of Automatic Speech
Understanding," International Journal of Computing and Information Technology, vol. 4, March, 1996, pp.
1–8, Speech and Image Understanding, pp.59-68. IEEE Slovenia Section, Ljubljana, Slovenien, 1996:

http://www5.informatik.uni-erlangen.de/literature/English/Sprache/1996.html; *"Automatic Classification of Speech Acts with Semantic Classification Trees and Polygrams,"* ed. M. Mast, E. Nöth, H. Niemann, and E.G. Schukat-Talamazzini, *International Joint Conference on Artificial Intelligence 95, Workshop. New Approaches to Learning for Natural Language Processing"*, Montreal, 1995, pp. 71-78.; Barry Litofsky, "Utility of Automatic Classification Systems for Information Storage and Retrieval," SMART Collection: cisi-1419, 1997; Dmitri Roussinov, "A Scalable Self-organizing Map Algorithm for Textual Classification: A Neural Network Approach to Automatic Thesaurus Generation.": http://ai.bpa.arizona.edu/go/intranet/papers/A_Scalable-98.htm. Gerda Ruge, "Combining Corpus Linguistics and Human Memory Models for Automatic Term Association," Communication and Cognition - Artificial Intelligence, 15 (1-2), 1998, pp. 81-112; Gerda Ruge, "Automatic Detection of Thesaurus Relations for Information Retrieval Applications," in Christian Freksa, Matthias Jantzen, and Rüdiger Valk, eds., *Foundations of Computer Science.* Berlin: Springer Verlag, 1997, pp. 499–506. R. Dolin, D. Agrawal, A. El Abbadi, and J. Pearlman, "Using Automated Classification for Summarizing and Selecting Heterogeneous Information Sources," *D-Lib*, January, 1998: http://www.dlib.org/dlib/january98/dolin/01dolin.html.

42   Willpower Information. Software for building and editing thesauri: http://www.willpower.demon.co.uk/thessoft.htm.

43   Library of Congress Classification: http://www.loc.gov/catdir/cpso/lcco/lcco.html.

44   Dewey Decimal Classification: www-lib.nearnorth.edu.on.ca/dewey/ddc.htm – and for the latest edition: http://www.oclc.org/dewey/

45   Project Aristotle (sm): Automated Categorization of Web Resources: http://www.public.iastate.edu/~CYBERSTACKS/Aristotle.htm.

46   NASA Ames. Autoclass Project: http://ic.arc.nasa.gov/projects/bayes-group/autoclass/.

47   Automatic Text Classification by Mortimer Technology: http://seminars.seyboldreports.com/1996_san_francisco/present/h_kest12/tsld010.htm.

48   International Society of Knowledge Organization: http://is.gseis.ucla.edu/orgs/isko/isko.html; http://www.isko.org; http://www.fhhannover.de/ik/Infoscience/ISKO.html; Centre for Database Access Research, Professor Steve Pollitt: http://www.ariadne.ac.uk/issue4/cedar/. This has a journal: *Knowledge Organization* (Amsterdam). There is also an International Society for Knowledge Organization Conference (ISKO). ISKO 2000 was in Toronto. ISKO 2004 was in London, ISKO 2006 is in Vienna.

49   GESIS. Informationszentrum Sozialwissenschaften: http://www.gesis.org/iz/index.htm.

50   AIFB Ontobroker: http://www.aifb.uni-karlsruhe.de/Projekte/viewProjekt?id_db=3.

51   Collection of Computer Science Bibliographies: http://liinwww.ira.uka.de/bibliography/index.html.

52   This is a research group at IRST. KRR sponsored the *Sixth International Conference on Principles of Knowledge Representation and Reasoning* (KR'98): http://www.kr.org/.

53   Description Logics: http://www.ida.liu.se/labs/iislab/people/patla/DL/index.html.

54   For instance, the Max Planck Institut für Informatik (Saarbrücken) has a Programming Logics Group and a section on Meta-Logics and Logical Frameworks: http://www.mpi-sb.mpg.de/.

55   Semantic Grid Community Portal: http://www.semanticgrid.org/.

56   SIGSEM: http://www.coli.uni-sb.de/~bos/sigsem/about.html.

57   SIGSEMIS: www.sigsemis.org.

58   TIES (Trainable Information Extraction for the Semantic Web): http://www.inf.fu-berlin.de/inst/ag-db/projects/project_ties.html.

59   DERI: http://www.deri.org/ especially under projects.

60   SDK Cluster: http://www.sdk-cluster.org/.

61   SEKT: http://www.sekt-project.com/.

62   DIP: http://dip.semanticweb.org/.

63   Knowledge Web: http://knowledgeweb.semanticweb.org/semanticportal/.

64   WSMO: http://www.wsmo.org/.

65 S. S. Goncharov, V. S. Harizanov, J. F. Knight, and C.F.D. McCoy, "Relatively hyperimmune relations on structures," *Algebra and Logic*, 2004, 43: http://home.gwu.edu/~harizanv/RelativelyHyperimmune.pdf.

66 Timo Honkela, Teemu Leinonen. Kirsti Lonka, Antti Reika, "Self-Organizing Maps and Constructive Learning," *Proceedings of ICEUT '2000*, IFIP, Beijing, 21–25 August 2000, pp. 339-343: http://citeseer.ist.psu.edu/honkela00selforganizing.html.

67 Social Science Gateway (SOSIG): http://sosig.ac.uk/; Principia cynernetica web: http://pespmc1.vub.ac.be/cybsysth.html.

68 Center for Coordination Science: http://ccs.mit.edu/.

69 E.g., *Fourth International Workshop on Computer Aided Systems Technology* (CAST94); *Eurocast* 2005: http://www.iuctc.ulpgc.es/iuctc/spain/eurocast/workshop.html.

70 http://asia.yahoo.com/science/engineering/electrical_engineering/neural_networks/institutes/. This was in June, 2000.

71 Neuronet: http://www.kcl.ac.uk/neuronet/.

72 Neural Network World: (formerly) http://www.lib.cas.cz/knav/journals/eng/Neural_Network_World.htm. http://www.vsppub.com/journals/jn-NeuNetWor.html.

73 University of Parma.

74 Brint.com Complexity: http://www.brint.com/Systems.htm.

75 Santa Fe Institute: http://www.santafe.edu/.

76 Exystence: http://sandi.soc.surrey.ac.uk/cs/modules.php?op=modload&name=News&file=article&sid=19.

77 Formerly at: http://lorenz.mur.csu.edu.au/vl_complex/topics.html.

78 Knowledge Media Institute (KMI): http://kmi.open.ac.uk/.

79 The Bayesian Knowledge Discovery Project: http://www.csi.uottawa.ca/ifip.wg12.2/ramoni.html.

80 Digital Document Discourse Environment: http://d3e.open.ac.uk/index.html.

81 NetAcademy on Knowledge Media: http://www.knowledgemedia.org/.

82 Ibid., Publications.

83 Knowledge Science Institute (KSI): http://ksi.cpsc.ucalgary.ca:80/KSI/.

84 Knowledge Media Design Institute: http://www.kmdi.org/index.htm.

85 Institut des sciences du document numérique (ISDN): http://isdn.enssib.fr.

86 SINTEF. See: http://www.sintef.no/eway/default0.asp?e=0&pid=204.

87 "[It] is the only private training and education organization to be listed on the main board of Stock Exchange of Singapore. Today, Informatics Holdings Ltd. has a current market capitalization of over US$120 million and largest network of over 100 training centres in most of the countries in Asia and Middle East." See: http://www.informatics.edu.ph/main.html now http://www.informatics.edu.sg/index.htm.

88 Demokritos National Centre of Scientific Research: http://www.iit.demokritos.gr/.

89 Institute of Mathematics and Informatics (IMI) under Publishing Activity: http://www.mii.lt/

90 Institute of Informatics, Skopje: http://www.ii.pmf.ukim.edu.mk/.

91 In3org: http://in3.org/.

92 Informatics International Inc.: http://www.informatics.org/. For an interesting case that links these developments with cultural heritage: www.sl-kim.de.

93 CTIT, Twente: http://www.ctit.utwente.nl.

94 Institute of Neuroinformatics: http://www.ini.unizh.ch/.

95 Infonortics: http://www.infonortics.com/infonortics/infodesc.html.

96 Search Engine Meeting: http://www.infonortics.com/searchengines/index.html.

97 Heyertech Inc.: http://www.heyertech.com/html/Publications.html: Infonomics focuses on the interaction between people and information systems and how to maximize the effectiveness of these transactions. Infonomics can be extended to the study of organizational information dynamics as the sum of many personal interactions. It provides the basis for the study of large-scale cultural information phenomena.

98 International Institute of Infonomics: http://www.infonomics.nl/.
99 Formerly at: http://www.infonomics.nl/units/main.html.
100 MERIT: http://www.merit.unimaas.nl/index.php\.
101 MMI. Formerly at: www.mmi.unimaas.nl.

Appendix 3: Expert and Intelligent Systems (1942–2002)

1 References (formerly at: http://www.cse.unsw.edu.au/~timm/pub/slides/kltut/sld151.html).
2 LISt Processing (LISP); Basic Compound Programming Language (BCPL).

Appendix 4: Just Imagine by Jaap van Till

1 Here Professor van Till is referring to a lecture given by Kim Veltman at the annual Internet Society Conference.

Appendix 5: J.M. Perreault's Relations

1 J. Perreault, "Categories and Relators," *International Classification*, Frankfurt, vol. 21, no. 4, 1994, pp. 189–98, especially p. 195.

Appendix 6: Syntx, Semantics and Grammar

1 For a more detailed discussion, see the author's "Towards a Semantic Web for Culture," *Journal of Digital Information*, vol. 4, no. 4, Article no. 255, 15 March 2004. Special issue on New Applications of Knowledge Organization Systems: http://jodi.ecs.soton.ac.uk/Articles/v04/i04/Veltman/ (87 pp.). While the principles of the seven liberal arts can readily be traced back at least as far as Aristotle in the third century B.C., formal recognition of the seven liberal arts into a trivium (grammar, dialectic, and rhetoric) of arts and a quadrivium of sciences (geometry, arithmetic, music, and astronomy) appears in the fourth century A.D. in the work of authors such as Martianus Cappellus. It is interesting to note that the history of the trivium was one of the starting points for the work of Marshall McLuhan in his doctoral thesis at Cambridge University on Nashe.
2 Harriet Martineau, *Athenaeum*, vol. 395, no. 1, 27 September 1884, Cited in the OED under "semantics."
3 Ibid. As the OED notes semantics was closely linked with semasiology: "Philology is now advancing towards a new branch having intimate relations with psychology the so-called semasiology of Abel and others."
4 Maurice Bloomfield, "On Assimilation and Adaptation in Congeneric Classes of Words," *American Journal of Philology* 16, 1895 , pp. 409–34; also cited in the OED.
5 Ibid.
6 Michel Jules Alfred Bréal, *Semantics: Studies in the Science of Meaning*, translated by Mrs. Henry Cust from the French: *Essai de sémantique*, London: W. Heinemann, 1900. Reprinted with a new introduction by Joshua Whatmough, New York: Dover, 1964. Michel Bréal, *Essai de sémantique: science des significations*. Genève: Slatkine Reprints, 1976.
7 Webopedia: Syntax: http://www.pcwebopedia.com/Programming/Programming_Languages/ syntax.html.
8 Ibid., Semantics: http://webopedia.internet.com/TERM/s/semantics.html.
9 Three Levels of Interoperabilty: http://sylvia.harvard.edu/~robin/weibel/sld006.htm.

10 UDDI.org: http://www.uddi.org/.

11 XML EDI: http://www.geocities.com/WallStreet/Floor/5815/.

12 W3C SOAP: http://www.w3.org/TR/SOAP/.

13 Amit P. Sheth's home page: http://lsdis.cs.uga.edu/~amit/.

14 Ibid., Projects: http://lsdis.cs.uga.edu/projects/past/InfoQuilt/.

15 IBM Web services forums: http://www-106.ibm.com/developerworks/forums/dw_wsforums.jsp.

16 At a more immediate level, children in Japan have RFID implants in their schoolbags, and there are trends to barcode humans through Applied Digital Solutions in Florida. Cf. Helen Brandwell, "May I scan the barcode in your arm please," *Globe and Mail*, 14 October 2004, p. A19.

17 Dave Piasecki, "Automated Data Collection (ADC) Basics,": http://www.inventoryops.com/ADC.htm.

18 Formerly at: http://www.w3.org/2001/04/roadmap/sw.svg.

19 T. P. Moran, "The Command Language Grammar: A Representation for the User Interface of Interactive Systems," *Journal of Man-Machine Studies*, vol. 15, no. 1, 1981, pp. 3–50.

20 The Seeheim model of user interfaces was developed at the *Eurographics/IFIPS Workshop on User Interface Management* in Seeheim in November, 1983.

21 Jakob Nielsen, "A virtual protocol model for computer-human interaction," *International Journal of Man-Machine Studies*, vol. 24, 1986, pp. 301–12; Jakob Nielsen, R. L. Mack, K. H. Bergendorff, and N. L. Grischkowsky, "Integrated software in the professional work environment: Evidence from questionnaires and interviews," *Proceedings of the Association for Computing Machinery Conference Human Factors in Computing Systems CHI'86*, Boston, 13–17 April 1986, pp. 162–67.

22 Bipin Desai's home page: http://www.cs.concordia.ca/~bcdesai/.

23 T. P. Moran, "The Command Language Grammar: A Representation for the User Interface of Interactive Systems," *Journal of Man-Machine Studies*, vol. 15, no. 1, 1981, pp. 3–50.

24 Seheim Modell: http://www.cs.cmu.edu/~bam/uicourse/1997spring/lecture07softorg.html

25 Geert de Haan, *ETAG, a Formal Model of Competence Knowledge for User Interface Design*. Doctoral thesis. Department of Mathematics and Computer Science, Free University Amsterdam, October, 2000.

26 Edward A. Feigenbaum in A. Barr and E.A. Feigenbaum, *The Handbook of Artificial Intelligence*, Boston: Addison-Wesley, vol. 1, September, 1989.

27 Readware: http://www.readware.com/.

28 Formerly at: http://www.wordmax.com/synset.htm.

29 http://www.cyc.com/. For a review of AI projects, see "Battle of the Brains," *Wired*, November, 2001, p. 82, which discusses CYC, Generic Artificial Consciousness (GAC), Common Sense and HAL.

30 Brian R. Gaines and Mildred L. G. Shaw, "Concept maps as Hypermedia Components," 1995: http://ksi.cpsc.ucalgary.ca/articles/; Jan Lanzing's home page on Concept Mapping: http://users.edte.utwente.nl/lanzing/cm_home.htm; Graphic Organizers: http://www.graphic.org/concept.html; Concept Mapping: http://www.cotf.edu/ete/pbl2.html..

31 Ralf Hauber: http://www.tk.uni-linz.ac.at/people/.

32 Exploratory Analysis of Concept and Document Spaces with Connectionist Networks: http://proxy3.nj.nec.com/did/53755.

33 Chimezie Thomas-Ogbuji, "The future of natural-language processing: Seeking a practical solution to the limitations of NLP methodologies and software," *Unix Insider*, 29 January 2001: http://www.itworld.com/AppDev/916/UIR001229ontology/.

34 Ibid.

35 Gerhard Budin, "Semantic Interoperability for I-MASS," I-MASS Kickoff meeting, 16 January 2001: http://www.i-massweb.org/.

36 L.M. Rocha and Cliff Joslyn, "Simulations of Evolving Embodied Semiosis: Emergent Semantics in Artificial Environments," *The Proceedings of the 1998 Conference on VirtualWorlds and Simulation 1998*. Landauer C. and K.L. Bellman, eds. The Society for Computer Simulation International, pp.

233–38: http://www.c3.lanl.gov/~rocha/ees_web.html; Workshop: Emergent Semantic and Computational Processes in Distributed Information Systems (DIS), Los Alamos, 1998: http://www.c3.lanl.gov/~joslyn/pcp/workshop98.html.

37 Accès multilingue au Patrimoine (AMP): (http://www.culture.gouv.fr/culture/mrt/numerisation/fr/actualit/documents/amp-newsletter1-en.pdf; http://www.culture.gouv.fr/culture/mrt/numerisation/fr/f_01.htm.

Appendix 7: International Developments

1 ISO TC 46/SC 9. Information and Documentation – Identification and Description: http://www.nlc-bnc.ca/iso/tc46sc9/index.htm.

2 JTC 1/SC 32 Data management and interchange: http://www.iso.ch/iso/en/stdsdevelopment/tc/tclist/TechnicalCommitteeDetailPage.TechnicalCommitteeDetail?COMMID=160; ftp://sdct-sunsrv1.ncsl.nist.gov/x3l8/11179/.

3 For U.S. work on metadata registries: http://dublincore.org/groups/registry/.

4 DoD Metadata Registry and Clearinghouse: http://diides.ncr.disa.mil/mdregHomePage/mdregHome.portal. For a significant American adaptation and modification of these ideas, see Len Gallagher and Lisa Carnahan, "A General Purpose Registry/Repository Information Model," Information Technology Laboratory NIST, 2nd Draft, 23 October 2000; IPTC Metadata for News. Subject Reference System: http://www.iptc.org/NewsCodes/.

5 ISO/TC 154 *"Processes, data elements and documents in commerce, industry and administration"* /WG (Work Group) 1, *"Semantic engine."*: (formerly) http://forum.afnor.fr/afnor/WORK/AFNOR/GPN2/TC154WG1/index.htm.

6 Author's on-line articles on "Domain Names and classification Systems," and "Internet Domain Names and Indexing.": http://www.sumscorp.com/new_media.htm.

7 Tim Bray, "RDF and Metadata," O'Reilly *xml.com*, 9 June 1998: http://www.xml.com/pub/a/98/06/rdf.html.

8 Metadata at W3C: http://www.w3.org/Talks/9707Metadata/.

9 For the best survey of all these developments, see the excellent web site of Dave Beckett: http://www.ilrt.bris.ac.uk/discovery/rdf/resources/.

10 http://home.netscape.com/columns/techvision/innovators_rg.html.

11 Tim Berners-Lee, James Hendler, and Ora Lassila, "The Semantic Web," *Scientific American*, May, 2001: http://www.sciam.com/article.cfm?articleID=00048144-10D2-1C70-84A9809EC588EF21.

12 Henry S. Thompson: http://www.ltg.ed.ac.uk/~ht/; Ora Lassila: http://www.lassila.org/.

13 Tim Berners Lee, "Semantic Web Road Map," September, 1998: http://www.w3.org/DesignIssues/Semantic.html.

14 Mary Fernandez, Wang-Chew Tan, and Dan Suciu, "Silk Route: trading between relations and XML," pp. 723–45: http://www.w3.org/RDF/Interest/.

15 W3C: http://www.w3.org.

16 For a bibliography on metadata standards and interoperability, July, 2002: http://www.oclc.org/research/projects/mswitch/1_bibliography.htm. Cf.: http://staff.library.mun.ca/staff/toolbox/standards.htm; For a good introduction to the Dublin Core approach to metadata, there was a presentation by Dr. Eric Miller on Data standards.

17 Open Archives Initiative: http://www.openarchives.org/.

18 Forum for Metadata Schema Impementers. Schema: http://www.schemas-forum.org/.

19 ABC. A Logical Model for Interoperability: http://www.ilrt.bris.ac.uk/discovery/harmony/docs/abc/abc_draft.html.

20 Forum for Metadata Schema. See: http://www.schemas-forum.org/.

21 EUREKA: http://www3.eureka.be/Home/.

22 Ibrow. An Intelligent Brokering Service for Knowledge-Component Reuse on the World-Wide Web: http://www.swi.psy.uva.nl/projects/ibrow/home.html.

663

23 Advanced Knowledge Technologies: http://www.aktors.org/akt/.

24 ELSNET: http://www.elsnet.org/.

25 MKBEEM. Multilingual Knowledge Based European Electronic Marketplace: http://mkbeem. elibel.tm.fr/.

26 Formerly at: http://www.ii.atos-group.com/sophia/comma/HomePage.htm.

27 Dieter Fensel: http://informatik.uibk.ac.at/users/c70385/.

28 The DARPA Agent Markup Language home page: http://www.daml.org/. Cycorp is also involved in this initiative: http://www.cyc.com//.

29 SALT: http://www.loria.fr/projects/SALT; http://www.ttt.org/salt/.

30 COVAX: http://www.covax.org/.

31 Digital Heritage Support Actions Concertation Event: http://www.cscaustria.at/events/ supportactions3.htm.

32 MEDICI Framework: http://www.medicif.org, which in Italy is linked with Museumland: http: //www.museumland.com/.

33 The EC initiated the EXPLOIT project: http://www.exploit-lib.org/.

34 This led to CULTIVATE: http://www.cultivate-int.org/; www.cscaustria.at/cultivate/docmgmt.

35 ICOM: http://www.icom.orgl.
    UNESCO: www.unesco.org/.

36 UNECE: http://www.unece.org/.

37 OASIS: http://www.oasis-open.org/home/index.php.

38 OASIS, "United Nations CEFACT and OASIS to Deliver ebXML Technical Infrastructure Ahead of Schedule," *OASIS Member News*, 2 December 2000: http://www.oasis-open.org/news/oasis_ news_12_12_00.shtml. For a comment re: the relative value of EDI and XML, see EAN under EAN/UCC System: http://www.ean-int.org/index800.html.

39 Education XML: http://xml.coverpages.org/edXML-AnnounceDiscussion.html.

40 Commerce XML: http://www.cxml.org.

41 eXtensible Business Reporting Language: http://www.xbrl.org/Home/. Related is Extensible Financial Reporting Markup Language (XFRML): http://xml.coverpages.org/xfrmlAnn.html .

42 Eco specification: http://eco.commerce.net/specs/index.cfm.

43 Formerly at: http://schemas.biztalk.org/BizTAlk/gr677h7w.xml).

44 Rosetta Net: http://www.rosettanet.org.

45 www.openbuy.org/obi/specs/eyx.pdf.

46 OASIS UDDI: http://www.uddi.org/specification.html.

47 ESPRIT Project 22226 – MUSE: http://www.cordis.lu/esprit/src/ep22226.htm; Results from the KIRMIT project, http://www.cs.vu.nl/~mcaklein/KIRMIT.

48 010 INTERNATIONAL STANDARD BOOK NUMBER: http://www.ifla.org/VI/3/p1996-1/ uni0.htm#b010.

49 011 INTERNATIONAL STANDARD SERIAL NUMBER (ISSN): http://www.ifla.org/VI/3/p1996- 1/uni0.htm#b011.

50 013 INTERNATIONAL STANDARD MUSIC NUMBER (ISMN): http://www.ifla.org/VI/3/ p1996-1/uni0.htm#b013.

51 016 INTERNATIONAL STANDARD RECORDING CODE (ISRC): http://www.ifla.org/VI/3/ p1996-1/uni0.htm#b016.

52 015 INTERNATIONAL STANDARD TECHNICAL REPORT NUMBER (ISRN): http://www.ifla. org/VI/3/p1996-1/uni0.htm#b015.

53 "Functional Requirements for Bibliographic Records: final report," *IFLA UBCIM publications*, new series, vol. 19. Munich: 1998. ISBN 3-598-11382-X. Cf. Stuart Weibel, "The State of the Dublin Core Metadata Initiative," *D-Lib Magazine*, vol. 5, no. 4, April, 1999 (ISSN 1082-9873): http:// www.dlib.org/dlib/april99/04weibel.html.

54 IFPI: http://www.ifpi.org/.

55 ANSI/NISO Z39.56-1996. Serial Item and Contribution Identifier: http://sunsite.berkeley.edu/ SICI/version2.html.

56 Brian Green and Mark Bide, "Unique Identifiers: a brief introduction", Book Industry Communication and EDItEUR 1996, 1997: http://www.bic.org.uk/uniquid.html. "The main changes are the introduction of a Code Structure Identifier for different uses, a Derivative Part Identifier (DPI) to identify fragments other than articles (e.g., tables of contents, index, abstract) and a Media Format Identifier (MFI) to indicate physical format. The DPI and MFI may be used in all SICI types (CSIs)."; IETF group on URNs: (formerly) http://www.ietf.org/html.charters/ urn-charter.html. But see the recent work of Larry Masinter: http://larry.masinter.net/.

57 Book Industry Communication (BIC): http://www.bic.org.uk.

58 Ibid.: http://www.bic.org.uk/uniquid.html.

59 CISAC: http://www.cisac.org/.

60 Andy Powell, "Unique Identifiers in a Digital World," UKOLN, University of Bath, 8 April 1997: http://www.ariadne.ac.uk/issue8/unique-identifiers/.

61 AGICOA: http://www.agicoa.org/.

62 ISO International Standard Text Code (ISTC): http://www.nlc-bnc.ca/iso/tc46sc9/istc.htm. Former ISO/TC 46/SC 9. Working Group 2. International Standard Musical Work Code (ISWC): http://www.nlc-bnc.ca/iso/tc46sc9/iswc.htm.
    ISO/TC 46/SC 9. Working Group 1. ISAN and V-ISAN: http://www.nlc-bnc.ca/iso/tc46sc9/wg1.htm.
    International Standard Audiovisual Number: http://www.isan.org.
    ISO TC 46/SC 9. Information and Documentation – Identification and Description: http: //www.nlc-bnc.ca/iso/tc46sc9/.

63 MPEG21: http://www.chiariglione.org/mpeg/meetings/trondheim03/trondheim_press.htm;. PRISM: http://www.idealliance.org/prism/.

64 Ibid.

65 W3C. The Information and Content Exchange (ICE) Protocol: http://www.w3.org/TR/NOTE-ice.

66 Digital Property Rights Language (DPRL): http://www.oasis-open.org/cover/dprl.html.

67 Xrml (eXtensible Rights Markup Language): http://www.xrml.org/.

68 Formerly at: http://www.onlineinc.com/news/news99/99news11c.html.

69 Reciprocal: http://www.reciprocal.com/.

70 Related to this is the concept of a Persistent Uniform Resource Locator (PURL): http://purl. oclc.org/. Uniform Resource Names (urn): http://www.ietf.org/html.charters/urn-charter. html. W3C Internationalization: http://www.w3.org/International/O-URL-and-ident.html. Internationalized Uniform Resource Identifiers (IURI). http://www.w3.org/International/2000/03/draft-masinter-url-i18n-05.txt.

71 <Indecs>: http://www.indecs.org/.

72 DOI-EB: http://www.doi.org/ebooks.pdf.

73 Secure Digital Music Initiative (SDMI): http://www.sdmi.org/.

74 Wolfgang Essmayr, "Meta-Data for Enterprise-Wide Security Administration.": http://www. computer.org/proceedings/meta/1999/papers/30/wessmayr.html.

75 CNRI Handle System: http://www.handle.net/introduction.html.

76 Development Processes: http://www.december.com/works/wdg/quickref.html.

77 Evgenij Samurin, *Geschichte der bibliothekarisch-bibliographischen Klassifikation*, München: Verlag Dokumentation, 1977. This is a German translation from the Russian original, Moscow, 1955–58.

78 Bibliographic / Product Information: http://www.bic.org.uk/prodinf.html.

79 IPTC: http://www.iptc.org; GEM Subject Element Controlled Vocabulary: http://raven.ischool. washington.edu/help/about/documentation/gem-controlled-vocabularies/vocabulary-subject.

80 Die Formate-Datenbank: http://www.biblio.tu-bs.de/acwww25/formate/hform.html.

81 IFLA Universal Bibliographic Control and International MARC Core Programme (UBCIM): http://ifla.org/VI/3/p1996-1/ucaf.htm.

82 LC Digital Repository Development. Core Metadata Elements: http://lcweb.loc.gov/standards/metadata.html.

83 Joint RLG and NPO Preservation Conference Guidelines for Digital Imaging: http://www.rlg.org/preserv/joint/day.html.

84 CIDOC Documentation Standards Group: http://www.cidoc.icom.org/wgdoc1.htm.

85 CIDOC Conceptual Reference Model (CRM): http://cidoc.ics.forth.gr/.

86 Exploitation of Research and Development Results in Libraries – Proceeding. Case study RAMA (RACE), D. Delouis: http://www.cordis.lu/libraries/en/rdxproce.html#rama.

87 AQUARELLE: http://www.cordis.lu/ist/98vienna/xaquarelle.htm. In the 5th Framework, there are new projects such as ARTISTE, IMAGEN and VIRARTIS, EASEL, MESMUSES, and PILOT, which are potentially of interest in this context.

88 Mesmuses: http://cweb.inria.fr/Projects/Mesmuses/.

89 ICOM Handbook of Standards: http://www.icom.org/afridoc/.

90 One of the important vendors of museum documentation is Mobydoc: www.mobydoc.fr. In Spain, for instance, Mobydoc works with the Instituto Cesing: http://www.spainsoft.es/CESING/index.htm.

91 Formerly at: http://www.culture.fr/documentation/docum.htm.

92 L'inventaire Général: http://www.culture.fr/culture/inventai/presenta/invent.htm.

93 CHIN. Religious objects: http://www.chin.gc.ca/English/Publications/religious_objects.html; http://www.chin.gc.ca/.

94 NARCISSE: http://www.culture.fr/documentation/lrmf/pres.htm.

95 Van Eyck I: http://www.artsh.tcd.ie/VNECK.htm. Van Eyck II.

96 Getty Categories for Description of Works of Art (CDWA): http://www.getty.edu/research/conducting_research/standards/cdwa/.

97 CHIN: http://www.chin.gc.ca/.

98 MDA Spectrum. See: http://www.mda.org.uk/spectrum.htm.

99 MDA Term-it.

100 Foto Marburg: http://www.fotomarburg.de/index.htm.

101 Cf. E.S. Kuzmina, "Minimum Categoires for Museum Object: Another Attempt at Unification," *EVA '2000 –Moscow*, Moscow: Centre PIC of the Ministry of Culture of the Russian Federation, 2000, pp. 145–46.

102 Scala Archives: http://www.scala.firenze.it/.

103 CNI Projects: http://www-ninch.cni.org/projects/.

104 IFLA/UNESCO Survey: http://www.ifla.org/VI/2/p1/miscel.htm.

105 CIA/ICA: http://palimpsest.stanford.edu/lex/icoh.html.

106 International Council on Archives: http://www.ica.org/.

107 EAD: http://www.loc.gov/ead/.

108 IEEE. WG12 Learning Object Metadata: http://ltsc.ieee.org/wg12/.

109 For further discussion of links between LOM, SCORM, DOI, and Dublin Core, see the author's "American Visions of the Internet," 2005:. http://www.sumscorp.com/new_media.htm.

110 IMS. Content Packaging XML Binding http://www.imsproject.org/content/packaging/cp-bind10.html.

111 ADL (Advanced Distributed Learning) Net: http://www.adlnet.org.

112 Formerly at: http://www.imsproject.org/drtomimplement.html.

113 IMS Tools: http://www.imsglobal.org/TI_bro_WEBrgb.pdf.

114 TEI: http://www.tei-c.org/.

115 The Electronic Text Center Introduction to TEI and Guide to Document Preparation: http://etext.lib.virginia.edu/tei/uvatei.html.

116 Oxford Text Archive: http://ota.ahds.ac.uk/.

117 CRIBECU: http://www.cribecu.sns.it/analisi_testuale/.

118 OASIS: http://www.oasis-open.org/cover/.

119 Japan's Vector Format for Zooming (VFZ) now part of the Celartem company: http://www. celartem.com/en/celartem/histry.asp.

120 NISSHA: http://www.nissha.co.jp/english/index.html. This was presented to ICOM-CC, France, 1999, and is being used via Scala to scan Louvre paintings such as Mona Lisa. Vzoom is now also used by Contents Co. Ltd. See: http://www.contents-jp.com.

121 X3D: http://www.web3d.org/x3d/. Companies such as Adobe have developed interim solutions with the Atmosphere software.

122 CEN/ISSS Metadata Framework: The Metadata Framework of CEN/ISSS distinguishes 4 main applications of metadata. These are resource discovery, asset management, interoperability and manipulation: http://www.schemas-forum.org/stds-framework/first/section4.html. CEN is also playing an important role in the Learning Objects Model (LOM): http://jtc1sc36.org/doc/36N0221.pdf

123 MPEG7: http://vision.ece.ucsb.edu/texture/mpeg7/.
MPEG 7 Project at Columbia University: http://ana.ctr.columbia.edu/mpeg-7/.

124 MHEG: http://www.mheg.org/users/mheg/index.php.

125 HyTime. ISO 10744: 1997-Hypermedia/Time-based Structuring Language (HyTime), 2nd ed.: http://www.oasis-open.org/cover/hytime.html.

126 MPEG: http://www.chiariglione.org/mpeg/. In this context, the BBC is working on P/META.

127 Ibid.

128 MPEG 21: http://www.chiariglione.org/mpeg/standards/mpeg-21/mpeg-21.htm.

129 Stephen Brewster, "The Impact of Haptic Touching Technology on Cultural Applications," EVA 2001 Scotland Conference, Friday, 28 July 2001, p. 28-i-14. I am grateful to James Hemsley for this reference.

130 Linda Hill and Traugott Koch, "Networked Knowledge Organization Systems: Introduction to a Special Issue," *Journal of Digital Information*, vol. 1, no. 8, 3 April 2001. Themes: Information discovery: http://jodi.ecs.soton.ac.uk/. Traugott Koch and Diane Vizine-Goetz, "Automatic Classification and Content Navigation Support for Web Services. DESIRE II Cooperates with OCLC," *Annual Review of OCLC Research*, Dublin, Ohio, 1998.

131 Alan Danskin, "Report on an ONIX UNIMARC crosswalk," The British Library: www.bic.org.uk/reporton.doc.

132 DOI: http://www.doi.org/; Universal Product Code (UPC): http://www.adams1.com/pub/russadam/upccode.html and European Article Numbering (EAN): http://www.ean-int.org/index800.html.

133 CrossRef: http://www.crossref.org/. "A researcher clicking on a link (the format of which is determined by publisher preference; for example, a CrossRef button, or 'Article' in html) will be connected to a page on the publisher's web site showing a full bibliographical citation of the article, and, in most cases, the abstract as well. The reader can then access the full text article through the appropriate mechanism; subscribers will generally go straight to the text, while others will receive information on access via subscription, document delivery, or pay-per-view. CrossRef costs the researcher nothing; its expenses are covered by nominal charges to the publishers for depositing their metadata, annual membership fees, and fees to publishers of abstracting and indexing databases for accessing CrossRef's bank of DOIs to create links to full text articles." As such, CrossRef is a thinly veiled advertising ploy, rather than an independent linking method, because it will link titles with those full-text examples that are in the publishers' interests rather than being what may be important for an individual scholar.

134 Definitions of Metadata: http://www.doi.org/doi_presentations/dec2000/metadata/sld003.htm.

135 Now eXchangeable Faceted Metadata Language: http://xfml.org/.

136 UML: http://www.xml.com/pub/a/2002/08/07/wxs_uml.html.

137 Meta Object facility: http://www.dstc.edu.au/Research/Projects/MOF/.

138 OMG XML XMI Specification: ftp://ftp.omg.org/pub/docs/formal/00-06-01.pdf.

139 http://www.getty.edu/research/conducting_research/standards/intrometadata/index.html.

140 MUSE: DMCS W3 Note: ICE (appendage to http).

"What is a Universal Unique Identifier (UUID)?": http://www.dsps.net/uuid.html.

This includes a number of implementations such as TEI, and text archives in Oxford, Pisa, and Virginia.

HTML and XHTML are not included here because they do not make a clear separation of content and form in the manner of SGML and XML.

Cf. Japan's vector format for zooming.

In this context the BBC is working on P/META. In the early stages of the Internet, there was also gopher.

141 To guide one through the maze of standards, the EC developed a project Diffuse, which is no longer extant.

index of persons and institutions

This list excludes (a) commercial companies which are thanked under Credits and (b) individual colleagues and friends who are thanked in Acknowledgments.

M

X

Y

Z

index of subjects

Terms used assume references to alternatives with prefixes such as cyber-, digital, e-, electronic-.

C